CONNECTIONS

Instructional programs from prekindergarten through grade 12 should enable all students to—

- recognize and use connections among mathematical ideas;
- understand how mathematical ideas interconnect and build on one another to produce a coherent whole;
- recognize and apply mathematics in contexts outside of mathematics.

REPRESENTATION

Instructional programs from prekindergarten through grade 12 should enable all students to—

- create and use representations to organize, record, and communicate mathematical ideas;
- select, apply, and translate among mathematical representations to solve problems;
- use representations to model and interpret physical, social, and mathematical phenomena.

Curriculum Focal Points
for Prekindergarten through Grade 8 Mathematics

PREKINDERGARTEN

Number and Operations: Developing an understanding of whole numbers, including concepts of correspondence, counting, cardinality, and comparison.
Geometry: Identifying shapes and describing spatial relationships.
Measurement: Identifying measurable attributes and comparing objects by using these attributes.

KINDERGARTEN

Number and Operations: Representing, comparing and ordering whole numbers, and joining and separating sets.
Geometry: Describing shapes and space.
Measurement: Ordering objects by measurable attributes.

GRADE 1

Number and Operations and **Algebra:** Developing understandings of addition and subtraction and strategies for basic addition facts and related subtraction facts.
Number and Operations: Developing an understanding of whole number relationships, including grouping in tens and ones.
Geometry: Composing and decomposing geometric shapes.

GRADE 2

Number and Operations: Developing an understanding of the base-ten numeration system and place-value concepts.
Number and Operations and **Algebra:** Developing quick recall of addition facts and related subtraction facts and fluency with multidigit addition and subtraction.
Measurement: Developing an understanding of linear measurement and facility in measuring lengths.

GRADE 3

Number and Operations and **Algebra:** Developing understandings of multiplication and division and strategies for basic multiplication facts and related division facts.
Number and Operations: Developing an understanding of fractions and fraction equivalence.
Geometry: Describing and analyzing properties of two-dimensional shapes.

GRADE 4

Number and Operations and **Algebra:** Developing quick recall of multiplication facts and related division facts and fluency with whole number multiplication.

Number and Operations: Developing an understanding of decimals, including the connections between fractions and decimals.
Measurement: Developing an understanding of area and determining the areas of two-dimensional shapes.

GRADE 5

Number and Operations and **Algebra:** Developing an understanding of and fluency with division of whole numbers.
Number and Operations: Developing an understanding of and fluency with addition and subtraction of fractions and decimals.
Geometry and **Measurement** and **Algebra:** Describing three-dimensional shapes and analyzing their properties, including volume and surface area.

GRADE 6

Number and Operations: Developing an understanding of and fluency with multiplication and division of fractions and decimals.
Number and Operations: Connecting ratio and rate to multiplication and division.
Algebra: Writing, interpreting, and using mathematical expressions and equations.

GRADE 7

Number and Operations and **Algebra** and **Geometry:** Developing an understanding of and applying proportionality, including similarity.
Measurement and **Geometry** and **Algebra:** Developing an understanding of and using formulas to determine surface areas and volumes of three-dimensional shapes.
Number and Operations and **Algebra:** Developing an understanding of operations on all rational numbers and solving linear equations.

GRADE 8

Algebra: Analyzing and representing linear functions and solving linear equations and systems of linear equations.
Geometry and **Measurement:** Analyzing two- and three-dimensional space and figures by using distance and angle.
Data Analysis and **Number and Operations** and **Algebra:** Analyzing and summarizing data sets.

www.wileyplus.com

ALL THE HELP, **RESOURCES**, AND PERSONAL **SUPPORT** YOU AND YOUR STUDENTS NEED!

www.wileyplus.com/resources

2-Minute Tutorials and all of the resources you & your students need to get started.

Student support from an experienced student user.

Collaborate with your colleagues, find a mentor, attend virtual and live events, and view resources.
www.WhereFacultyConnect.com

Pre-loaded, ready-to-use assignments and presentations. Created by subject matter experts.

Technical Support 24/7 FAQs, online chat, and phone support.
www.wileyplus.com/support

Your *WileyPLUS* Account Manager. Personal training and implementation support.

Mathematics
For Elementary Teachers
A CONTEMPORARY APPROACH

NINTH EDITION

Gary L. Musser
Oregon State University

William F. Burger

Blake E. Peterson
Brigham Young University

WILEY

John Wiley & Sons, Inc.

To:

Irene, my wonderful wife of 50 years, Greg, my son, for his many interesting discussions, Maranda, my granddaughter, for willingness to listen and learn, my parents, who have passed away but are always with me, and Mary Burger, Bill Burger's wonderful daughter.

G. L. M

Shauna, my beautiful eternal companion and best friend, for agreeing to share her life with me; Quinn, Joelle, Taren, and Riley, my four children, for making good choices and making me proud.

B. E. P

VICE PRESIDENT & EXECUTIVE PUBLISHER	Laurie Rosatone
PROJECT EDITOR	Jennifer Brady
PRODUCTION MANAGER	Dorothy Sinclair
SENIOR PRODUCTION EDITOR	Valerie A. Vargas
MARKETING MANAGER	Jonathan Cottrell
CREATIVE DIRECTOR	Harry Nolan
PRODUCTION MANAGEMENT SERVICES	mb editorial services
SENIOR ILLUSTRATION EDITOR	Anna Melhorn
SENIOR PHOTO EDITOR	Lisa Gee
MEDIA EDITORS	Melissa Edwards & Laura Abrams
COVER & TEXT DESIGN	Michael Jung
COVER PHOTO	Quinn Peterson; sand dune image © Media Bakery

This book was set in 10/12 Times New Roman by PreMediaGlobal and printed and bound by RRD-JC. The cover was printed by RRD-JC.

This book is printed on acid free paper. ∞

Founded in 1807, John Wiley & Sons, Inc. has been a valued source of knowledge and understanding for more than 200 years, helping people around the world meet their needs and fulfill their aspirations. Our company is built on a foundation of principles that include responsibility to the communities we serve and where we live and work. In 2008, we launched a Corporate Citizenship Initiative, a global effort to address the environmental, social, economic, and ethical challenges we face in our business. Among the issues we are addressing are carbon impact, paper specifications and procurement, ethical conduct within our business and among our vendors, and community and charitable support. For more information, please visit our website: www.wiley.com/go/citizenship.

ISBN-13   978-0-470-53134-1

Printed in the United States of America

10 9 8 7 6 5 4 3 2 1

About the Authors

GARY L. MUSSER is Professor Emeritus from Oregon State University. He earned both his B.S. in Mathematics Education in 1961 and his M.S. in Mathematics in 1963 at the University of Michigan and his Ph.D. in Mathematics (Radical Theory) in 1970 at the University of Miami in Florida. He taught at the junior and senior high, junior college, college, and university levels for more than 30 years. He spent his final 24 years teaching prospective teachers in the Department of Mathematics at Oregon State University. While at OSU, Dr. Musser developed the mathematics component of the elementary teacher program. Soon after Professor William F. Burger joined the OSU Department of Mathematics in a similar capacity, the two of them began to write the first edition of this book. Professor Burger passed away during the preparation of the second edition, and Professor Blake E. Peterson was hired at OSU as his replacement. Professor Peterson joined Professor Musser as a coauthor beginning with the fifth edition.

Professor Musser has published 40 papers in many journals, including the *Pacific Journal of Mathematics, Canadian Journal of Mathematics, The Mathematics Association of America Monthly*, the NCTM's *The Mathematics Teacher*, the NCTM's *The Arithmetic Teacher, School Science and Mathematics, The Oregon Mathematics Teacher*, and *The Computing Teacher*. In addition, he is a coauthor of two other college mathematics books: *College Geometry—A Problem-Solving Approach with Applications* (2008) and *A Mathematical View of Our World* (2007). He also coauthored the K–8 series *Mathematics in Action*. He has given more than 65 invited lectures/workshops at a variety of conferences, including NCTM and MAA conferences, and was awarded 15 federal, state, and local grants to improve the teaching of mathematics.

While Professor Musser was at OSU, he was awarded the university's prestigious College of Science Carter Award for Teaching. He is currently living in sunny Las Vegas, where he continues to write, ponder the mysteries of the stock market, enjoy living with his wife, and his faithful yellow lab, Zoey.

BLAKE E. PETERSON is currently a Professor in the Department of Mathematics Education at Brigham Young University. He was born and raised in Logan, Utah, where he graduated from Logan High School. Before completing his B.A. in secondary mathematics education at Utah State University, he spent two years in Japan as a missionary for The Church of Jesus Christ of Latter Day Saints. After graduation, he took his new wife, Shauna, to southern California, where he taught and coached at Chino High School for two years. In 1988, he began graduate school at Washington State University, where he later completed a M.S. and Ph.D. in pure mathematics.

After completing his Ph.D., Dr. Peterson was hired as a mathematics educator in the Department of Mathematics at Oregon State University in Corvallis, Oregon, where he taught for three years. It was at OSU that he met Gary Musser. He has since moved his wife and four children to Provo, Utah, to assume his position at Brigham Young University where he is currently a full professor. As a professor, his first love is teaching, for which he has received a College Teaching Award in the College of Physical and Mathematical Science.

Dr. Peterson has published papers in *Rocky Mountain Mathematics Journal, The American Mathematical Monthly, The Mathematical Gazette, Mathematics Magazine, The New England Mathematics Journal, The Journal of Mathematics Teacher Education,* and *The Journal for Research in Mathematics Education* as well as chapters in several books. He has also published in NCTM's *Mathematics Teacher*, and *Mathematics Teaching in the Middle School*. After studying mathematics student teachers at a Japanese junior high school, he implemented some elements he observed into the student teaching structure at BYU, which is now his research focus. In addition to teaching, research, and writing, Dr. Peterson has done consulting for the College Board, founded the Utah Association of Mathematics Teacher Educators, has been the chair of the editorial panel for the *Mathematics Teacher*, and is the associate chair of the department of mathematics education at BYU.

Aside from his academic interests, Dr. Peterson enjoys spending time with his family, fulfilling his church responsibilities, playing basketball, mountain biking, water skiing, and working in the yard.

About the Cover

When sand is poured in a pile onto flat ground, the shape of the pile is a cone with a circular base. The apex of the cone is directly above the center of the base. While the shape of the pile is somewhat dependent on the consistency of the sand and how it sticks together, it is also dependent on the sand traveling the shortest possible distance down the pile. Thus the apex is directly above the center of the circular base because the center of a circle has the geometric property of being the same distance from every point on the circle.

So what happens when the sand is poured on a triangular shape where the sand can fall off of the side? If the sand is poured until no more can stay on the triangle, where are the ridges located? Check out the figure with the orange sand on the center of the cover. Similar to the apex of the cone, the ridges need to be along a line that is the same distance from the sides. It so happens that the line that bisects an angle has the geometric property of being the same distance from the two sides of the angle. The triangle at the left is the same shape as the base of the triangular pile of sand on the cover. In it, all three angle bisectors are drawn. Point P is on one of the angle bisectors and is the same distance from the two sides of the angle. The three angle bisectors intersect at a common point, and the apex of the pile of sand on the triangle is directly above that point of intersection.

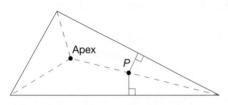

Now consider a pile of sand on a quadrilateral base like the figure with the red sand on the lower left of the cover. We will again assume that the sand is poured until no more can stay on the quadrilateral. The principle of the ridge being along a line that is the same distance from two sides still applies. In this case, however, the four angle bisectors don't intersect in a single point as shown in the figure at the right. The angle bisectors of $\angle A$ and $\angle D$ intersect at point F, and the angle bisectors of $\angle B$ and $\angle C$ intersect at point E. The ridge between points E and F is above the line that is the same distance from side $\overline{AB}$ and side $\overline{CD}$. By extending those two sides to intersect at point G, we can see that the ridge between points E and F lies on the angle bisector of $\angle G$.

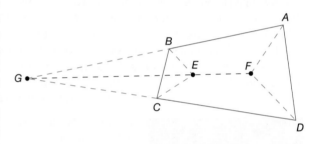

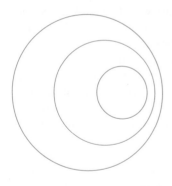

When sand is poured on a circle with a hole in it, the ridge line has an interesting property of being in the shape of an ellipse as shown by the red line in the circle at the left. The figure with the purple sand on the top right of the cover is an example of this.

Each shape has its own unique properties that determine where the ridge lines will lie. The general underlying principle is that the ridges will be along a line that is the same distance from the edges where the sand will fall off. The fact that there are no ridge lines on the ends of the pile of green sand on the oval shape on the top left of the cover would indicate that there are no lines or points that are the same distance from the edges at the end of the oval. The pile of blue sand on the pentagon on the lower right of the cover, however, has distinct ridge lines. See if you can justify the location of those ridge lines.

Next time you see a pile of sand or rocks, take note of the ridge lines and ask yourself: What geometric properties are influencing the location of that ridge?

Special thanks to Troy Jones, a colleague and Saratoga Springs, Utah, high school teacher, for providing the "piles of sand" idea for the cover.

Brief Contents

Contents

Contents of Book Companion Web Site

Resources for Technology Problems
- eManipulatives
- Spreadsheets
- Geometer's Sketchpad

Technology Tutorials
- Spreadsheets
- Geometer's Sketchpad
- Programming in Logo
- Graphing Calculators

Webmodules
- Algebraic Reasoning
- Using Children's Literature
- Introduction to Graph Theory

Additional Resources
- Guide to Problem Solving
- Problems for Writing/Discussion
- Research Articles
- Web Links

Preface

Welcome to the study of the foundations of elementary school mathematics. We hope you will find your studies enlightening, useful, and fun. We salute you for choosing teaching as a profession and hope that your experiences with this book will help prepare you to be the best possible teacher of mathematics that you can be. We have presented this elementary mathematics material from a variety of perspectives so that you will be better equipped to address that broad range of learning styles that you will encounter in your future students. This book also encourages prospective teachers to gain the ability to do the mathematics of elementary school and to understand the underlying concepts so they will be able to assist their students, in turn, to gain a deep understanding of mathematics.

We have also sought to present this material in a manner consistent with the recommendations in (1) *The Mathematical Education of Teachers* prepared by the Conference Board of the Mathematical Sciences, and (2) the National Council of Teachers of Mathematics' *Principles and Standards for School Mathematics* and *Curriculum Focal Points*. In addition, we have received valuable advice from many of our colleagues around the United States through questionnaires, reviews, focus groups, and personal communications. We have taken great care to respect this advice and to ensure that the content of the book has mathematical integrity and is accessible and helpful to the variety of students who will use it. As always, we look forward to hearing from you about your experiences with our text.

GARY L. MUSSER, *glmusser@cox.net*
BLAKE E. PETERSON, *peterson@mathed.byu.edu*

Unique Content Features

Number Systems   The order in which we present the number systems in this book is unique and most relevant to elementary school teachers. The topics are covered to parallel their evolution historically and their development in the elementary/middle school curriculum. Fractions and integers are treated separately as an extension of the whole numbers. Then rational numbers can be treated at a brisk pace as extensions of both fractions (by adjoining their opposites) and integers (by adjoining their appropriate quotients) since students have a mastery of the concepts of reciprocals from fractions (and quotients) and opposites from integers from preceding chapters. Longtime users of this book have commented to us that this *whole numbers-fractions-integers-rationals-reals* approach is clearly superior to the seemingly more efficient sequence of whole numbers-integers-rationals-reals that is more appropriate to use when teaching high school mathematics.

Approach to Geometry   Geometry is organized from the point of view of the five-level van Hiele model of a child's development in geometry. After studying shapes and measurement, geometry is approached more formally through Euclidean congruence and similarity, coordinates, and transformations. The Epilogue provides an eclectic approach by solving geometry problems using a variety of techniques.

Additional Topics

- Topic 1, "Elementary Logic," may be used anywhere in a course.
- Topic 2, "Clock Arithmetic: A Mathematical System," uses the concepts of opposite and reciprocal and hence may be most instructive after Chapter 6, "Fractions," and Chapter 8, "Integers," have been completed. This section also contains an introduction to modular arithmetic.

Underlying Themes

Problem Solving   An extensive collection of problem-solving strategies is developed throughout the book; these strategies can be applied to a generous supply of problems in the exercise/problem sets. The depth of problem-solving coverage can be varied by the number of strategies selected throughout the book and by the problems assigned.

Deductive Reasoning   The use of deduction is promoted throughout the book. The approach is gradual, with later chapters having more multistep problems. In particular, the last sections of Chapters 14, 15, and 16 and the Epilogue offer a rich source of interesting theorems and problems in geometry.

Technology   Various forms of technology are an integral part of society and can enrich the mathematical understanding of students when used appropriately. Thus, calculators and their capabilities (long division with remainders, fraction calculations, and more) are introduced throughout the book within the body of the text.

In addition, the book companion Web site has eManipulatives, spreadsheets, and sketches from Geometer's Sketchpad®. The eManipulatives are electronic versions of the manipulatives commonly used in the elementary classroom, such as the geoboard, base ten blocks, black and red chips, and pattern blocks. The spreadsheets contain dynamic representations of functions, statistics, and probability simulations. The sketches in Geometer's Sketchpad® are dynamic representations of geometric relationships that allow exploration. Exercises and problems that involve eManipulatives, spreadsheets, and Geometer's Sketchpad® sketches have been integrated into the problem sets throughout the text.

Course Options

We recognize that the structure of the mathematics for elementary teachers course will vary depending upon the college or university. Thus, we have organized this text so that it may be adapted to accommodate these differences.

> Basic course: Chapters 1–7
> Basic course with logic: Topic 1, Chapters 1–7
> Basic course with informal geometry: Chapters 1–7, 12
> Basic course with introduction to geometry and measurement: Chapters 1–7, 12, 13

Summary of Changes to the Ninth Edition

- Exercise sets have been revised and enriched, where necessary, to assure that they are closely aligned with and provide complete coverage of the section material. Exercises in Exercise/Problem Sets A and B are arranged in matched pairs, but problems are not. Answers are provided for all Set A exercises/problems. Answers are provided for all Set B exercises/problems in the Instructor Resource Manual.

- Section 2.4 from the Eighth Edition has been moved to be Section 9.3 in this edition to enrich the coverage of algebra.

- Chapter 12 has been substantially revised. Sections 12.1 and 12.2 have been organized to more faithfully represent the first three van Hiele levels. In this way, students will be able to pass through the levels in a more meaningful fashion so that they will get a strong feeling about how their future students will view geometry at various grade levels.
- To further enrich the coverage of algebra, **Algebraic Reasoning** margin notes have been strategically placed throughout the book to help students see how what they are studying is connected to algebra.
- To help students be more active when learning the material, **Check for Understanding** callouts lead students to Part A exercises that are relevant to the subsection they just finished studying.
- **Analyzing Student Thinking** problems have been added to the end of the Part B problems. These problems pose questions that students may face when they teach. Many of the problems that were marked with fountain pen icons at the end of the Exercise/Problem sets have been incorporated into the Analyzing Student Thinking problems in this edition.
- The **Children's Literature** and **Reflection from Research** margin notes have been revised or refreshed.
- Most of the Problems for Writing/Discussion that preceded the Chapter Tests in the Eighth Edition now appear on our Web site.

Pedagogy

The general organization of the book was motivated by the following mathematics learning cube:

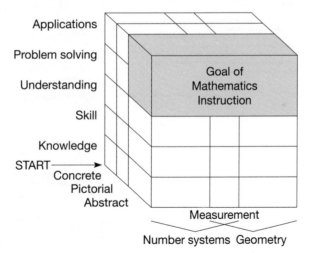

The three dimensions of the cube—cognitive levels, representational levels, and mathematical content—are integrated throughout the textual material as well as in the problem sets and chapter tests. Problem sets are organized into exercises (to support knowledge, skill, and understanding) and problems (to support problem solving and applications).

We have developed new pedagogical features to implement and reinforce the goals discussed above and to address the many challenges in the course.

Summary of Pedagogical Changes to the Ninth Edition

- Student Page Snapshots have been updated.
- Reflection from Research margin notes have been edited and updated.
- Children's Literature references have been edited and updated. Also, there is additional material offered on the Web site on this topic.

Key Features

Problem-Solving Strategies are integrated throughout the book. Six strategies are introduced in Chapter 1. The last strategy in the strategy box at the top of the second page of each chapter after Chapter 1 contains a new strategy.

Mathematical Structure reveals the mathematical ideas of the book. Main Definitions, Theorems, and Properties in each section are highlighted in boxes for quick review.

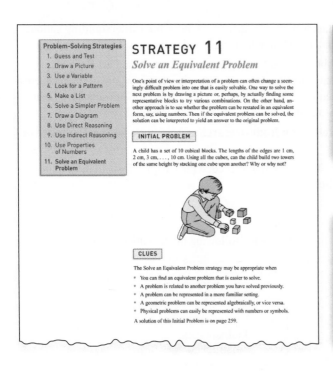

Problem-Solving Strategies
1. Guess and Test
2. Draw a Picture
3. Use a Variable
4. Look for a Pattern
5. Make a List
6. Solve a Simpler Problem
7. Draw a Diagram
8. Use Direct Reasoning
9. Use Indirect Reasoning
10. Use Properties of Numbers
11. Solve an Equivalent Problem

STRATEGY 11
Solve an Equivalent Problem

One's point of view or interpretation of a problem can often change a seemingly difficult problem into one that is easily solvable. One way to solve the next problem is by drawing a picture or, perhaps, by actually finding some representative blocks to try various combinations. On the other hand, another approach is to see whether the problem can be restated in an equivalent form, say, using numbers. Then if the equivalent problem can be solved, the solution can be interpreted to yield an answer to the original problem.

INITIAL PROBLEM

A child has a set of 10 cubical blocks. The lengths of the edges are 1 cm, 2 cm, 3 cm, . . . , 10 cm. Using all the cubes, can the child build two towers of the same height by stacking one cube upon another? Why or why not?

CLUES

The Solve an Equivalent Problem strategy may be appropriate when

* You can find an equivalent problem that is easier to solve.
* A problem is related to another problem you have solved previously.
* A problem can be represented in a more familiar setting.
* A geometric problem can be represented algebraically, or vice versa.
* Physical problems can easily be represented with numbers or symbols.

A solution of this Initial Problem is on page 259.

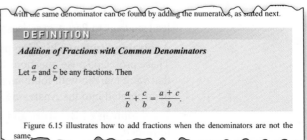

with the same denominator can be found by adding the numerators, as stated next.

DEFINITION

Addition of Fractions with Common Denominators

Let $\frac{a}{b}$ and $\frac{c}{b}$ be any fractions. Then

$$\frac{a}{b} + \frac{c}{b} = \frac{a+c}{b}.$$

Figure 6.15 illustrates how to add fractions when the denominators are not the same.

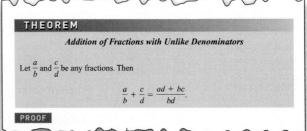

THEOREM

Addition of Fractions with Unlike Denominators

Let $\frac{a}{b}$ and $\frac{c}{d}$ be any fractions. Then

$$\frac{a}{b} + \frac{c}{d} = \frac{ad+bc}{bd}.$$

PROOF

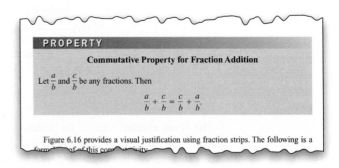

PROPERTY

Commutative Property for Fraction Addition

Let $\frac{a}{b}$ and $\frac{c}{b}$ be any fractions. Then

$$\frac{a}{b} + \frac{c}{b} = \frac{c}{b} + \frac{a}{b}.$$

Figure 6.16 provides a visual justification using fraction strips. The following is a formal proof of this commutativity.

STARTING POINT
Following recess, the 1000 students of Wilson School lined up for the following activity: The first student opened all of the 1000 lockers in the school. The second student closed all lockers with even numbers. The third student "changed" all lockers that were numbered with multiples of 3 by closing those that were open and opening those that were closed. The fourth student changed each locker whose number was a multiple of 4, and so on. After all 1000 students had completed the activity, which lockers were open? Why?

Starting Points are located at the beginning of each section. These Starting Points can be used in a variety of ways. First, they can be used by an instructor at the beginning of class to have students engage in some novel thinking and/or discussion about forthcoming material. Second, they can be used in small groups where students discuss the query presented. Third, they can be used as an advanced organizer homework piece where a class begins with a discussion of what individual students have discovered.

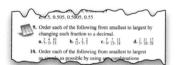

Technology Problems appear in the Exercise/Problem sets throughout the book. These problems rely on and are enriched by the use of technology. The technology used includes activities from the eManipulatives (virtual manipulatives), spreadsheets, Geometer's Sketchpad®, and the TI-34 II calculator. Most of these technological resources can be accessed through the accompanying book companion Web site.

Student Page Snapshots have been updated. Each chapter has a page from an elementary school textbook relevant to the material being studied.

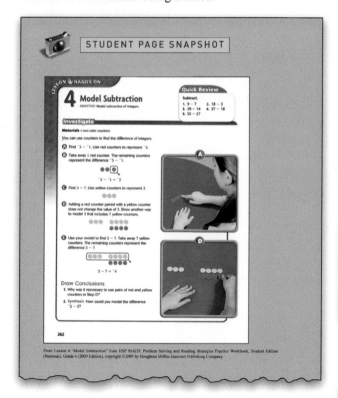

Exercise/Problem Sets are separated into Part A (all answers are provided in the back of the book and all solutions are provided in our supplement *Hints and Solutions for Part A Problems*) and Part B (answers are only provided in the *Instructors Resource Manual*). In addition, exercises and problems are distinguished so that students can learn how they differ.

Analyzing Student Thinking Problems are found at the end of the Exercise/Problem Sets. These problems are questions that elementary students might ask their teachers, and they focus on common misconceptions that are held by students. These problems give future teachers an opportunity to think about the concepts they have learned in the section in the context of teaching.

Analyzing Student Thinking

34. Carlos says that if the ratio of oil to vinegar in a salad dressing is 3 : 4, that means that 75% of the dressing is oil. How should you respond?

35. Scott heard that the ratio of boys to girls in his class next year was going to be 5 : 4. He asks, "Does that mean that

NCTM Standards and Curriculum Focal Points In previous editions the NCTM Standards have been listed at the beginning of the book and then highlighted in margin notes throughout the book. The ninth edition also lists the Curriculum Focal Points from NCTM at the beginning of the book. At the beginning of each chapter, the Curriculum Focal Points that are relevant to that particular chapter are listed again.

Key Concepts from NCTM Curriculum Focal Points

- GRADE 1: Developing an understanding of whole number relationships, including grouping in tens and ones.
- GRADE 2: Developing quick recall of addition facts and related subtraction facts and fluency with multidigit addition and subtraction.
- GRADE 4: Developing quick recall of multiplication facts and related division facts and fluency with whole number multiplication.
- GRADE 5: Developing an understanding of and fluency with division of whole numbers.
- GRADES 4 AND 5: Students select appropriate methods and apply them accurately to estimate products and calculate them mentally, depending on the context and numbers involved.

Problems Relating to the NCTM Standards and Curriculum Focal Points

1. The Focal Points for Grade 3 state "Developing an understanding of and fluency with addition and subtraction of fractions of decimals." Based on the discussions in this section, explain at least one main concept essential to understanding addition and subtraction of fractions.

2. The NCTM Standards state "All students use visual models, benchmarks, and equivalent forms to add and subtract

commonly used fractions and decimals." Explain what is meant by "visual models" when adding and subtracting fractions.

3. The NCTM Standards state "All students should develop and use strategies to estimate computations involving fractions and decimals in situations relevant to students' experience." List and explain some examples of strategies to estimate fraction computations.

Problems from the NCTM Standards and Curriculum Focal Points To further help students understand and be aware of these documents from the National Council of Teachers of Mathematics, new problems have been added at the end of every section. These problems ask students to connect the mathematics being learned from the book with the K–8 mathematics outlined by NCTM.

Reflection from Research Extensive research has been done in the mathematics education community that focuses on the teaching and learning of elementary mathematics. Many important quotations from research are given in the margins to support the content nearby.

Reflection from Research
There is a clear separation of development in young children concerning the cardinal and ordinal aspects of numbers. Despite the fact that they could utilize the same counting skills, the understanding of ordinality by young children lags well behind the understanding of cardinality (Bruce & Threlfall, 2004).

FOCUS ON   *Famous Unsolved Problems*

Number theory provides a rich source of intriguing problems. Interestingly, many problems in number theory are easily understood, but still have never been solved. Most of these problems are statements or conjectures that have never been proven right or wrong. The most famous "unsolved" problem, known as Fermat's Last Theorem, is named after Pierre de Fermat who is pictured below. It states "There are no nonzero whole numbers a, b, c, where $a^n + b^n = c^n$, for n a whole number greater than two."

Fermat left a note in the margin of a book saying that he did not have room to write up a proof of what is now called Fermat's Last Theorem. However, it remained an unsolved problem for over 350 years because mathematicians were unable to prove it. In 1993, Andrew Wiles, an English mathematician on the Princeton faculty, presented a "proof" at a conference at Cambridge University. However, there was a hole in his proof. Happily, Wiles and Richard Taylor produced a valid proof in 1995, which followed from work done by Serre, Mazur, and Ribet beginning in 1985.

The following list contains several such problems that are still unsolved. If you can solve any of them, you will surely become famous, at least among mathematicians.

1. *Goldbach's conjecture. Every even number greater than 4 can be expressed as the sum of two odd primes.* For example, $6 = 3 + 3$, $8 = 3 + 5$, $10 = 5 + 5$, $12 = 5 + 7$, and so on. It is interesting to note that if Goldbach's conjecture is true, then every odd number greater than 7 can be written as the sum of three odd primes.

2. *Twin prime conjecture. There is an infinite number of pairs of primes whose difference is two.* For example, (3, 5), (5, 7), and (11, 13) are such prime pairs. Notice that 3, 5, and 7 are three prime numbers where $5 - 3 = 2$ and $7 - 5 = 2$. It can easily be shown that this is the only such triple of primes.

3. *Odd perfect number conjecture. There is no odd perfect number; that is, there is no odd number that is the sum of its proper factors.* For example, $6 = 1 + 2 + 3$; hence 6 is a perfect number. It has been shown that the even perfect numbers are all of the form $2^{p-1}(2p - 1)$, where $2^p - 1$ is a prime.

4. *Ulam's conjecture. If a nonzero whole number is even, divide it by 2. If a nonzero whole number is odd, multiply it by 3 and add 1. If this process is applied repeatedly to each answer, eventually you will arrive at 1.* For example, the number 7 yields this sequence of numbers: 7, 22, 11, 34, 17, 52, 26, 13, 40, 20, 10, 5, 16, 8, 4, 2, 1. Interestingly, there is a whole number less than 30 that requires at least 100 steps before it arrives at 1. It can be seen that 2^n requires n steps to arrive at 1. Hence one can find numbers with as many steps (finitely many) as one wishes.

Historical vignettes open each chapter and introduce ideas and concepts central to each chapter.

Mathematical Morsels end every section with an interesting historical tidbit. One of our students referred to these as a reward for completing the section.

Check for Understanding: Exercise/Problem __ A #8-13

MATHEMATICAL MORSEL

The University of Oregon football team has developed quite a wardrobe. Most football teams have two different uniforms: one for home games and one for away games. The University of Oregon team will have as many as 384 different uniform combinations from which to choose. Rather than the usual light and dark jerseys, they have 4 different colored jerseys: white, yellow, green, and black. Beyond that, however, they have 4 different colored pants, 4 different colored pairs of socks, 2 different colored pairs of shoes, and 2 different colored helmets with a 3rd one on the way. If all color combinations are allowed, the fundamental counting principle would suggest that they have $4 \times 4 \times 4 \times 2 \times 3 = 384$ possible uniform combinations. Whether a uniform consisting of a green helmet, black jersey, yellow pants, white socks, and black shoes would look stylish is debatable.

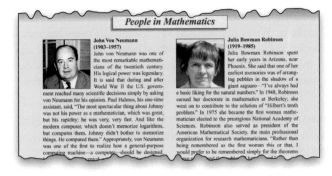

People in Mathematics, a feature near the end of each chapter, highlights many of the giants in mathematics throughout history.

A **Chapter Review** is located at the end of each chapter.

A **Chapter Test** is found at the end of each chapter.

An **Epilogue,** following Chapter 16, provides a rich eclectic approach to geometry.

Logic and Clock Arithmetic are developed in topic sections near the end of the book.

Supplements for Students

Student Activities Manual with Discussion Questions for the Classroom This activity manual is designed to enhance student learning as well as to model effective classroom practices. Since many instructors are working with students to create a personalized journal, this edition of the manual is shrink-wrapped and three-hole punched for easy customization. This supplement is an extensive revision of the *Student Resource Handbook* that was authored by Karen Swenson and Marcia Swanson for the first six editions of this book.

ISBN 978-0470-53136-5

FEATURES INCLUDE
- Hands-On Activities: Activities that help develop initial understandings at the concrete level.
- Discussion Questions for the Classroom: Tasks designed to engage students with mathematical ideas by stimulating communication.
- Mental Math: Short activities to help develop mental math skills.
- Exercises: Additional practice for building skills in concepts.
- Directions in Education: Specially written articles that provide insights into major issues of the day, including the Standards of the National Council of Teachers of Mathematics.
- Solutions: Solutions to all items in the handbook to enhance self-study.
- Two-Dimensional Manipulatives: Cutouts are provided on cardstock.

—Prepared by Lyn Riverstone of Oregon State University

The ETA Cuisenaire® Physical Manipulative Kit A generous assortment of manipulatives (including blocks, tiles, geoboards, and so forth) has been created to accompany the text as well as the *Student Activity Manual*. It is available to be packaged with the text. Please contact your local Wiley representative for ordering information.

ISBN 978-0470-53139-6

State Correlation Guidebooks In an attempt to help preservice teachers prepare for state licensing exams and to inform their future teaching, Wiley has updated seven completely unique state-specific correlation guidebooks. These guidebooks provide a detailed correlation between the textbook and key supplements with state standards for the following states: CA, FL, IL, MI, NY, TX, VA. The guidebooks are available in WileyPLUS. Please contact your local Wiley representative for further information.

Student Hints and Solutions Manual for Part A Problems This manual contains hints and solutions to all of the Part A problems. It can be used to help students develop problem-solving proficiency in a self-study mode. The features include:

- Hints: Give students a start on all Part A problems in the text.
- Additional Hints: A second hint is provided for more challenging problems.
- Complete Solutions to Part A Problems: Carefully written-out solutions are provided to model one correct solution.

—Developed by Lynn Trimpe, Vikki Maurer,
and Roger Maurer of Linn-Benton Community College.
ISBN 978-0470-53135-8

Companion Web site http://www.wiley.com/college/musser
The companion Web site provides a wealth of resources for students.

Resources for Technology Problems
These problems are integrated into the problem sets throughout the book and are denoted by a mouse icon.

- eManipulatives mirror physical manipulatives as well as provide dynamic representations of other mathematical situations. The goal of using the eManipulatives is to engage learners in a way that will lead to a more in-depth understanding of the concepts and to give them experience thinking about the mathematics that underlies the manipulatives.

  —Prepared by Lawrence O. Cannon, E. Robert Heal, and Joel Duffin of Utah State University,
  Richard Wellman of Westminster College, and Ethalinda K. S. Cannon of A415software.com.
  This project is supported by the National Science Foundation.
  ISBN 978-0470-53138-9

- The Geometer's Sketchpad® activities allow students to use the dynamic capabilities of this software to investigate geometric properties and relationships. They are accessible through a Web browser so having the software is not necessary.
- The Spreadsheet activities utilize the iterative properties of spreadsheets and the user-friendly interface to investigate problems ranging from graphs of functions to standard deviation to simulations of rolling dice.

Technology Tutorials
- The Geometer's Sketchpad® tutorial is written for those students who have access to the software and who are interested in investigating problems of their own choosing. The tutorial gives basic instruction on how to use the software and includes some sample problems that will help the students gain a better understanding of the software and the geometry that could be learned by using it.

—Prepared by Armando Martinez-Cruz,
California State University, Fullerton.

- The Spreadsheet Tutorial is written for students who are interested in learning how to use spreadsheets to investigate mathematical problems. The tutorial describes some of the functions of the software and provides exercises for students to investigate mathematics using the software.

  —Prepared by Keith Leatham, Brigham Young University.

Webmodules

- The Algebraic Reasoning Webmodule helps students understand the critical transition from arithmetic to algebra. It also highlights situations when algebra is, or can be, used. Marginal notes are placed in the text at the appropriate locations to direct students to the webmodule.

  —Prepared by Keith Leatham, Brigham Young University.

- The Children's Literature Webmodule provides references to many mathematically related examples of children's books for each chapter. These references are noted in the margins near the mathematics that corresponds to the content of the book. The webmodule also contains ideas about using children's literature in the classroom.

  —Prepared by Joan Cohen Jones, Eastern Michigan University.

- The Introduction to Graph Theory Webmodule has been moved from the Topics to the companion Web site to save space in the book and yet allow professors the flexibility to download it from the Web if they choose to use it.

The companion Web site also includes:

- Links to NCTM Standards
- A Logo and TI-83 graphing calculator tutorial
- Four cumulative tests covering material up to the end of Chapters 4, 9, 12, and 16
- Research Article References: A complete list of references for the research articles that are mentioned in the Reflection from Research margin notes throughout the book

Guide to Problem Solving This valuable resource, available as a webmodule on the companion Web site, contains more than 200 creative problems keyed to the problem solving strategies in the textbook and includes:

- **Opening Problem:** an introductory problem to motivate the need for a strategy.
- **Solution/Discussion/Clues:** A worked-out solution of the opening problem together with a discussion of the strategy and some clues on when to select this strategy.
- **Practice Problems:** A second problem that uses the same strategy together with a worked-out solution and two practice problems.
- **Mixed Strategy Practice:** Four practice problems that can be solved using one or more of the strategies introduced to that point.
- **Additional Practice Problems and Additional Mixed Strategy Problems:** Sections that provide more practice for particular strategies as well as many problems for which students need to identify appropriate strategies.

  —Prepared by Don Miller, who retired as a professor
  of mathematics at St. Cloud State University.

Problems for Writing and Discussion are problems that require an analysis of ideas and are good opportunities to write about the concepts in the book. Most of the Problems for Writing/Discussion that preceded the Chapter Tests in the Eighth Edition now appear on our Web site.

The Geometer's Sketchpad© Developed by Key Curriculum Press, this dynamic geometry construction and exploration tool allows users to create and manipulate precise figures while preserving geometric relationships. This software is only available when packaged with the text. Please contact your local Wiley representative for further details.

ISBN 978-0470-89202-2

WileyPLUS WileyPLUS is a powerful online tool that will help you study more effectively, get immediate feedback when you practice on your own, complete assignments and get help with problem solving, and keep track of how you're doing—all at one easy-to-use Web site.

Resources for the Instructor

Companion Web Site
The companion Web site is available to text adopters and provides a wealth of resources including:

- PowerPoint Slides of more than 190 images that include figures from the text and several generic masters for dot paper, grids, and other formats.
- Instructors also have access to all student Web site features. See above for more details.

Instructor Resource Manual This manual contains chapter-by-chapter discussions of the text material, student "expectations" (objectives) for each chapter, answers for all Part B exercises and problems, and answers for all of the even-numbered problems in the Guide to Problem-Solving.

—Prepared by Lyn Riverstone, Oregon State University
ISBN 978-0470-53147-1

Computerized/Print Test Bank The Computerized/Printed Test Bank includes a collection of over 1,100 open response, multiple-choice, true/false, and free-response questions, nearly 80% of which are algorithmic.

—Prepared by Mark McKibben, Goucher College
Computerized Test Bank ISBN 978-0470-53148-8
Printed Test Bank ISBN 978-0470-53150-1

WileyPLUS WileyPLUS is a powerful online tool that provides instructors with an integrated suite of resources, including an online version of the text, in one easy-to-use Web site. Organized around the essential activities you perform in class, WileyPLUS allows you to create class presentations, assign homework and quizzes for automatic grading, and track student progress. Please visit http://edugen.wiley.com or contact your local Wiley representative for a demonstration and further details.

Acknowledgments

During the development of *Mathematics for Elementary Teachers*, Eighth and Ninth Editions, we benefited from comments, suggestions, and evaluations from many of our colleagues. We would like to acknowledge the contributions made by the following people:

Reviewers for the Ninth Edition

Larry Feldman, *Indiana University of Pennsylvania*
Sarah Greenwald, *Appalachian State University*
Leah Gustin, *Miami University of Ohio, Middleton*
Linda LeFevre, *State University of New York, Oswego*
Bethany Noblitt, *Northern Kentucky University*
Todd Cadwallader Olsker, *California State University, Fullerton*
Cynthia Piez, *University of Idaho*
Tammy Powell-Kopilak, *Dutchess Community College*
Edel Reilly, *Indiana University of Pennsylvania*
Sarah Reznikoff, *Kansas State University*
Mary Beth Rollick, *Kent State University*

Ninth Edition Interviewees

John Baker, *Indiana University of Pennsylvania*
Paulette Ebert, *Northern Kentucky University*
Gina Foletta, *Northern Kentucky University*
Leah Griffith, *Rio Hondo College*
Jane Gringauz, *Minneapolis Community College*
Alexander Kolesnick, *Ventura College*
Gail Laurent, *College of DuPage*
Linda LeFevre, *State University of New York, Oswego*
Carol Lucas, *University of Central Oklahoma*
Melanie Parker, *Clarion University of Pennsylvania*
Shelle Patterson, *Murray State University*
Cynthia Piez, *University of Idaho*
Denise Reboli, *King's College*
Edel Reilly, *Indiana University of Pennsylvania*
Sarah Reznikoff, *Kansas State University*
Nazanin Tootoonchi, *Frostburg State University*

Ninth Edition Focus Group Participants

Kaddour Boukkabar, *California University of Pennsylvania*
Melanie Branca, *Southwestern College*
Tommy Bryan, *Baylor University*
Jose Cruz, *Palo Alto College*
Arlene Dowshen, *Widener University*
Rita Eisele, *Eastern Washington University*
Mario Flores, *University of Texas at San Antonio*
Heather Foes, *Rock Valley College*
Mary Forintos, *Ferris State University*
Marie Franzosa, *Oregon State University*
Sonia Goerdt, *St. Cloud State University*
Ralph Harris, *Fresno Pacific University*
George Jennings, *California State University, Dominguez Hills*
Andy Jones, *Prince George's Community College*

Karla Karstens, *University of Vermont*
Margaret Kidd, *California State University, Fullerton*
Rebecca Metcalf, *Bridgewater State College*
Pamela Miller, *Arizona State University, West*
Jessica Parsell, *Delaware Technical Community College*
Tuyet Pham, *Kent State University*
Mary Beth Rollick, *Kent State University*
Keith Salyer, *Central Washington University*
Sherry Schulz, *College of the Canyons*
Carol Steiner, *Kent State University*
Abolhassan Tagavy, *City College of Chicago*
Rick Vaughan, *Paradise Valley Community College*
Demetria White, *Tougaloo College*
John Woods, *Southwestern Oklahoma State University*

In addition, we would like to acknowledge the contributions made by colleagues from earlier editions.

Reviewers for the Eighth Edition

Seth Armstrong, *Southern Utah University*
Elayne Bowman, *University of Oklahoma*
Anne Brown, *Indiana University, South Bend*
David C. Buck, *Elizabethtown*
Alison Carter, *Montgomery College*
Janet Cater, *California State University, Bakersfield*
Darwyn Cook, *Alfred University*
Christopher Danielson, *Minnesota State University, Mankato*
Linda DeGuire, *California State University, Long Beach*
Cristina Domokos, *California State University, Sacramento*
Scott Fallstrom, *University of Oregon*
Teresa Floyd, *Mississippi College*
Rohitha Goonatilake, *Texas A&M International University*
Margaret Gruenwald, *University of Southern Indiana*
Joan Cohen Jones, *Eastern Michigan University*
Joe Kemble, *Lamar University*
Margaret Kinzel, *Boise State University*
J. Lyn Miller, *Slippery Rock University*
Girija Nair-Hart, *Ohio State University, Newark*
Sandra Nite, *Texas A&M University*
Sally Robinson, *University of Arkansas, Little Rock*
Nancy Schoolcraft, *Indiana University, Bloomington*
Karen E. Spike, *University of North Carolina, Wilmington*
Brian Travers, *Salem State*
Mary Wiest, *Minnesota State University, Mankato*
Mark A. Zuiker, *Minnesota State University, Mankato*

Student Activity Manual Reviewers

Kathleen Almy, *Rock Valley College*
Margaret Gruenwald, *University of Southern Indiana*
Kate Riley, *California Polytechnic State University*
Robyn Sibley, *Montgomery County Public Schools*

State Standards Reviewers

Joanne C. Basta, *Niagara University*
Joyce Bishop, *Eastern Illinois University*
Tom Fox, *University of Houston, Clear Lake*
Joan C. Jones, *Eastern Michigan University*
Kate Riley, *California Polytechnic State University*
Janine Scott, *Sam Houston State University*
Murray Siegel, *Sam Houston State University*
Rebecca Wong, *West Valley College*

Reviewers

Paul Ache, *Kutztown University*
Scott Barnett, *Henry Ford Community College*
Chuck Beals, *Hartnell College*
Peter Braunfeld, *University of Illinois*
Tom Briske, *Georgia State University*
Anne Brown, *Indiana University, South Bend*
Christine Browning, *Western Michigan University*
Tommy Bryan, *Baylor University*
Lucille Bullock, *University of Texas*
Thomas Butts, *University of Texas, Dallas*
Dana S. Craig, *University of Central Oklahoma*
Ann Dinkheller, *Xavier University*
John Dossey, *Illinois State University*
Carol Dyas, *University of Texas, San Antonio*
Donna Erwin, *Salt Lake Community College*
Sheryl Ettlich, *Southern Oregon State College*
Ruhama Even, *Michigan State University*
Iris B. Fetta, *Clemson University*
Marjorie Fitting, *San Jose State University*
Susan Friel, *Math/Science Education Network, University of North Carolina*
Gerald Gannon, *California State University, Fullerton*
Joyce Rodgers Griffin, *Auburn University*
Jerrold W. Grossman, *Oakland University*
Virginia Ellen Hanks, *Western Kentucky University*
John G. Harvey, *University of Wisconsin, Madison*
Patricia L. Hayes, *Utah State University, Uintah Basin Branch Campus*
Alan Hoffer, *University of California, Irvine*
Barnabas Hughes, *California State University, Northridge*
Joan Cohen Jones, *Eastern Michigan University*
Marilyn L. Keir, *University of Utah*
Joe Kennedy, *Miami University*
Dottie King, *Indiana State University*
Richard Kinson, *University of South Alabama*
Margaret Kinzel, *Boise State University*
John Koker, *University of Wisconsin*
David E. Koslakiewicz, *University of Wisconsin, Milwaukee*
Raimundo M. Kovac, *Rhode Island College*
Josephine Lane, *Eastern Kentucky University*
Louise Lataille, *Springfield College*
Roberts S. Matulis, *Millersville University*
Mercedes McGowen, *Harper College*
Flora Alice Metz, *Jackson State Community College*

J. Lyn Miller, *Slippery Rock University*
Barbara Moses, *Bowling Green State University*
Maura Murray, *University of Massachusetts*
Kathy Nickell, *College of DuPage*
Dennis Parker, *The University of the Pacific*
William Regonini, *California State University, Fresno*
James Riley, *Western Michigan University*
Kate Riley, *California Polytechnic State University*
Eric Rowley, *Utah State University*
Peggy Sacher, *University of Delaware*
Janine Scott, *Sam Houston State University*
Lawrence Small, *L.A. Pierce College*
Joe K. Smith, *Northern Kentucky University*
J. Phillip Smith, *Southern Connecticut State University*
Judy Sowder, *San Diego State University*
Larry Sowder, *San Diego State University*
Karen Spike, *University of Northern Carolina, Wilmington*
Debra S. Stokes, *East Carolina University*
Jo Temple, *Texas Tech University*
Lynn Trimpe, *Linn–Benton Community College*
Jeannine G. Vigerust, *New Mexico State University*
Bruce Vogeli, *Columbia University*
Kenneth C. Washinger, *Shippensburg University*
Brad Whitaker, *Point Loma Nazarene University*
John Wilkins, *California State University, Dominguez Hills*

Questionnaire Respondents

Mary Alter, *University of Maryland*
Dr. J. Altinger, *Youngstown State University*
Jamie Whitehead Ashby, *Texarkana College*
Dr. Donald Balka, *Saint Mary's College*
Jim Ballard, *Montana State University*
Jane Baldwin, *Capital University*
Susan Baniak, *Otterbein College*
James Barnard, *Western Oregon State College*
Chuck Beals, *Hartnell College*
Judy Bergman, *University of Houston, Clearlake*
James Bierden, *Rhode Island College*
Neil K. Bishop, *The University of Southern Mississippi, Gulf Coast*
Jonathan Bodrero, *Snow College*
Dianne Bolen, *Northeast Mississippi Community College*
Peter Braunfeld, *University of Illinois*
Harold Brockman, *Capital University*
Judith Brower, *North Idaho College*
Anne E. Brown, *Indiana University, South Bend*
Harmon Brown, *Harding University*
Christine Browning, *Western Michigan University*
Joyce W. Bryant, *St. Martin's College*
R. Elaine Carbone, *Clarion University*
Randall Charles, *San Jose State University*
Deann Christianson, *University of the Pacific*
Lynn Cleary, *University of Maryland*
Judith Colburn, *Lindenwood College*
Sister Marie Condon, *Xavier University*

Lynda Cones, *Rend Lake College*
Sister Judith Costello, *Regis College*
H. Coulson, *California State University*
Dana S. Craig, *University of Central Oklahoma*
Greg Crow, *John Carroll University*
Henry A. Culbreth, *Southern Arkansas University, El Dorado*
Carl Cuneo, *Essex Community College*
Cynthia Davis, *Truckee Meadows Community College*
Gregory Davis, *University of Wisconsin, Green Bay*
Jennifer Davis, *Ulster County Community College*
Dennis De Jong, *Dordt College*
Mary De Young, *Hop College*
Louise Deaton, *Johnson Community College*
Shobha Deshmukh, *College of Saint Benedict/St. John's University*
Sheila Doran, *Xavier University*
Randall L. Drum, *Texas A&M University*
P. R. Dwarka, *Howard University*
Doris Edwards, *Northern State College*
Roger Engle, *Clarion University*
Kathy Ernie, *University of Wisconsin*
Ron Falkenstein, *Mott Community College*
Ann Farrell, *Wright State University*
Francis Fennell, *Western Maryland College*
Joseph Ferrar, *Ohio State University*
Chris Ferris, *University of Akron*
Fay Fester, *The Pennsylvania State University*
Marie Franzosa, *Oregon State University*
Margaret Friar, *Grand Valley State College*
Cathey Funk, *Valencia Community College*
Dr. Amy Gaskins, *Northwest Missouri State University*
Judy Gibbs, *West Virginia University*
Daniel Green, *Olivet Nazarene University*
Anna Mae Greiner, *Eisenhower Middle School*
Julie Guelich, *Normandale Community College*
Ginny Hamilton, *Shawnee State University*
Virginia Hanks, *Western Kentucky University*
Dave Hansmire, *College of the Mainland*
Brother Joseph Harris, C.S.C., *St. Edward's University*
John Harvey, *University of Wisconsin*
Kathy E. Hays, *Anne Arundel Community College*
Patricia Henry, *Weber State College*
Dr. Noal Herbertson, *California State University*
Ina Lee Herer, *Tri-State University*
Linda Hill, *Idaho State University*
Scott H. Hochwald, *University of North Florida*
Susan S. Hollar, *Kalamazoo Valley Community College*
Holly M. Hoover, *Montana State University, Billings*
Wei-Shen Hsia, *University of Alabama*
Sandra Hsieh, *Pasadena City College*
Jo Johnson, *Southwestern College*
Patricia Johnson, *Ohio State University*
Pat Jones, *Methodist College*
Judy Kasabian, *El Camino College*
Vincent Kayes, *Mt. St. Mary College*
Julie Keener, *Central Oregon Community College*

Joe Kennedy, *Miami University*
Susan Key, *Meridien Community College*
Mary Kilbridge, *Augustana College*
Mike Kilgallen, *Lincoln Christian College*
Judith Koenig, *California State University, Dominguez Hills*
Josephine Lane, *Eastern Kentucky University*
Don Larsen, *Buena Vista College*
Louise Lataille, *Westfield State College*
Vernon Leitch, *St. Cloud State University*
Steven C. Leth, *University of Northern Colorado*
Lawrence Levy, *University of Wisconsin*
Robert Lewis, *Linn-Benton Community College*
Lois Linnan, *Clarion University*
Jack Lombard, *Harold Washington College*
Betty Long, *Appalachian State University*
Ann Louis, *College of the Canyons*
C. A. Lubinski, *Illinois State University*
Pamela Lundin, *Lakeland College*
Charles R. Luttrell, *Frederick Community College*
Carl Maneri, *Wright State University*
Nancy Maushak, *William Penn College*
Edith Maxwell, *West Georgia College*
Jeffery T. McLean, *University of St. Thomas*
George F. Mead, *McNeese State University*
Wilbur Mellema, *San Jose City College*
Clarence E. Miller, Jr. *Johns Hopkins University*
Diane Miller, *Middle Tennessee State University*
Ken Monks, *University of Scranton*
Bill Moody, *University of Delaware*
Kent Morris, *Cameron University*
Lisa Morrison, *Western Michigan University*
Barbara Moses, *Bowling Green State University*
Fran Moss, *Nicholls State University*
Mike Mourer, *Johnston Community College*
Katherine Muhs, *St. Norbert College*
Gale Nash, *Western State College of Colorado*
T. Neelor, *California State University*
Jerry Neft, *University of Dayton*
Gary Nelson, *Central Community College, Columbus Campus*
James A. Nickel, *University of Texas, Permian Basin*
Kathy Nickell, *College of DuPage*
Susan Novelli, *Kellogg Community College*
Jon O'Dell, *Richland Community College*
Jane Odell, *Richland College*
Bill W. Oldham, *Harding University*
Jim Paige, *Wayne State College*
Wing Park, *College of Lake County*
Susan Patterson, *Erskine College (retired)*
Shahla Peterman, *University of Missouri*
Gary D. Peterson, *Pacific Lutheran University*
Debra Pharo, *Northwestern Michigan College*
Tammy Powell-Kopilak, *Dutchess Community College*
Christy Preis, *Arkansas State University, Mountain Home*
Robert Preller, *Illinois Central College*
Dr. William Price, *Niagara University*
Kim Prichard, *University of North Carolina*

Stephen Prothero, *Williamette University*
Janice Rech, *University of Nebraska*
Tom Richard, *Bemidji State University*
Jan Rizzuti, *Central Washington University*
Anne D. Roberts, *University of Utah*
David Roland, *University of Mary Hardin–Baylor*
Frances Rosamond, *National University*
Richard Ross, *Southeast Community College*
Albert Roy, *Bristol Community College*
Bill Rudolph, *Iowa State University*
Bernadette Russell, *Plymouth State College*
Lee K. Sanders, *Miami University, Hamilton*
Ann Savonen, *Monroe County Community College*
Rebecca Seaberg, *Bethel College*
Karen Sharp, *Mott Community College*
Marie Sheckels, *Mary Washington College*
Melissa Shepard Loe, *University of St. Thomas*
Joseph Shields, *St. Mary's College, MN*
Lawrence Shirley, *Towson State University*
Keith Shuert, *Oakland Community College*
B. Signer, *St. John's University*
Rick Simon, *Idaho State University*
James Smart, *San Jose State University*
Ron Smit, *University of Portland*
Gayle Smith, *Lane Community College*
Larry Sowder, *San Diego State University*
Raymond E. Spaulding, *Radford University*
William Speer, *University of Nevada, Las Vegas*
Sister Carol Speigel, BVM, *Clarke College*
Karen E. Spike, *University of North Carolina, Wilmington*
Ruth Ann Stefanussen, *University of Utah*
Carol Steiner, *Kent State University*
Debbie Stokes, *East Carolina University*
Ruthi Sturdevant, *Lincoln University, MO*
Viji Sundar, *California State University, Stanislaus*
Ann Sweeney, *College of St. Catherine, MN*
Karen Swenson, *George Fox College*
Carla Tayeh, *Eastern Michigan University*
Janet Thomas, *Garrett Community College*
S. Thomas, *University of Oregon*
Mary Beth Ulrich, *Pikeville College*
Martha Van Cleave, *Linfield College*
Dr. Howard Wachtel, *Bowie State University*
Dr. Mary Wagner-Krankel, *St. Mary's University*
Barbara Walters, *Ashland Community College*
Bill Weber, *Eastern Arizona College*
Joyce Wellington, *Southeastern Community College*
Paula White, *Marshall University*
Heide G. Wiegel, *University of Georgia*
Jane Wilburne, *West Chester University*

Jerry Wilkerson, *Missouri Western State College*
Jack D. Wilkinson, *University of Northern Iowa*
Carole Williams, *Seminole Community College*
Delbert Williams, *University of Mary Hardin–Baylor*
Chris Wise, *University of Southwestern Louisiana*
John L. Wisthoff, *Anne Arundel Community College (retired)*
Lohra Wolden, *Southern Utah University*
Mary Wolfe, *University of Rio Grande*
Vernon E. Wolff, *Moorhead State University*
Maria Zack, *Point Loma Nazarene College*
Stanley L. Zehm, *Heritage College*
Makia Zimmer, *Bethany College*

Focus Group Participants

Mara Alagic, *Wichita State University*
Robin L. Ayers, *Western Kentucky University*
Elaine Carbone, *Clarion University of Pennsylvania*
Janis Cimperman, *St. Cloud State University*
Richard DeCesare, *Southern Connecticut State University*
Maria Diamantis, *Southern Connecticut State University*
Jerrold W. Grossman, *Oakland University*
Richard H. Hudson, *University of South Carolina, Columbia*
Carol Kahle, *Shippensburg University*
Jane Keiser, *Miami University*
Catherine Carroll Kiaie, *Cardinal Stritch University*
Armando M. Martinez-Cruz, *California State University, Fullerton*
Cynthia Y. Naples, *St. Edward's University*
David L. Pagni, *Fullerton University*
Melanie Parker, *Clarion University of Pennsylvania*
Carol Phillips-Bey, *Cleveland State University*

Content Connections Survey Respondents

Marc Campbell, *Daytona Beach Community College*
Porter Coggins, *University of Wisconsin–Stevens Point*
Don Collins, *Western Kentucky University*
Allan Danuff, *Central Florida Community College*
Birdeena Dapples, *Rocky Mountain College*
Nancy Drickey, *Linfield College*
Thea Dunn, *University of Wisconsin–River Falls*
Mark Freitag, *East Stroudsberg University*
Paula Gregg, *University of South Carolina, Aiken*
Brian Karasek, *Arizona Western College*
Chris Kolaczewski, *Ferris University of Akron*
R. Michael Krach, *Towson University*
Randa Lee Kress, *Idaho State University*
Marshall Lassak, *Eastern Illinois University*
Katherine Muhs, *St. Norbert College*
Bethany Noblitt, *Northern Kentucky University*

We would like to acknowledge the following people for their assistance in the preparation of the first eight editions of this book: Ron Bagwell, Jerry Becker, Julie Borden, Sue Borden, Tommy Bryan, Juli Dixon, Christie Gilliland, Dale Green, Kathleen Seagraves Higdon, Hester Lewellen, Roger Maurer, David Metz, Naomi Munton, Tilda Runner, Karen Swenson, Donna Templeton, Lynn Trimpe, Rosemary Troxel, Virginia Usnick, and Kris Warloe. We thank Robyn Silbey for her expert review of several of the features in our seventh edition and Becky Gwilliam for her research contributions to Chapter 10 and the Reflection from Research. We also thank Lyn Riverstone, Vikki Maurer, and Janis Cimperman for their careful checking of the accuracy of the answers.

We also want to acknowledge Marcia Swanson and Karen Swenson for their creation of and contribution to our *Student Resource Handbook* during the first seven editions with a special thanks to Lyn Riverstone for her expert revision of the *Student Activity Manual* for the Eighth and Ninth Editions. Thanks are also due to Don Miller for his *Guide to Problem Solving*, to Lyn Trimpe, Roger Maurer, and Vikki Maurer, for their longtime authorship of our *Student Hints and Solutions Manual*, to Keith Leathem for the Spreadsheet Tutorial and Algebraic Reasoning Web Module, Armando Martinez-Cruz for The Geometer's Sketchpad Tutorial, to Joan Cohen Jones for the Children's Literature Webmodule, and to Lawrence O. Cannon, E. Robert Heal, Joel Duffin, Richard Wellman, and Ethalinda K. S. Cannon for the eManipulatives activities.

We are very grateful to our publisher, Laurie Rosatone, and our editor, Jennifer Brady, for their commitment and super teamwork, to our senior production editor, Valerie A. Vargas, for attending to the details we missed, to Martha Beyerlein, our full-service representative and copyeditor, for lighting the path as we went from manuscript to the final book, and to Melody Englund for creating the index. Other Wiley staff who helped bring this book and its print and media supplements to fruition are: Jonathan Cottrell, Marketing Manager; Melissa Edwards, Media Editor; Ann Berlin, Vice President, Production and Manufacturing; Dorothy Sinclair, Production Services Manager; Kevin Murphy, Senior Designer; Lisa Gee, Photo Researcher, and Laura Abrams, Assistant Media Editor. They have been uniformly wonderful to work with—John Wiley would have been proud of them.

Finally, we welcome comments from colleagues and students. Please feel free to send suggestions to Gary at glmusser@cox.net and Blake at peterson@mathed.byu.edu. Please include both of us in any communications.

G.L.M.
B.E.P.

A Note to Our Students

There are many pedagogical elements in our book that are designed to help you as you learn mathematics. We suggest the following:

1. Begin each chapter by reading the **Focus On** on the first page of the chapter. This will give you a mathematical sense of some of the history that underlies the chapter.

2. Try to work the **Initial Problem** on the second page of the chapter. Since problem solving is so important in mathematics, you will want to increase your proficiency in solving problems so that you can help your students to learn to solve problems. Also notice the **Problem Solving Strategies** box on this second page. This box grows throughout the book as you learn new strategies to help you enhance your problem solving ability.

3. When you finish studying a subsection, work the Set A exercises at the end of the section that are suggested by the **Check for Understanding**. This will help you learn the material in the section in smaller increments, which can be a more effective way to learn. The answers for these exercises are in the back of the book.

4. As you work through each section, take breaks and read through the margin notes: **Reflection from Research**, **NCTM Standards**, and **Algebraic Reasoning**. These should enrich your learning experience. Of course, the **Children's Literature** margin notes should help you begin a list of materials that you can use when you start to teach.

5. Be certain to read the **Mathematical Morsel** at the end of each section. These are interesting stories that will add to your knowledge of mathematics in the world around you.

6. By the time you arrive at the end of Set A exercises, you should have worked the exercises and checked your answers. This practice should have helped you learn the knowledge, skill, and understanding of the material in the section (see our illustrative cube on p. xiii). Next you should attempt to do all of the Set A problems. These may require slightly deeper thinking than did the exercises. Once again, the answers to these problems are in the back of the book. Your teacher may assign some of the Set B exercises and problems. These do not have answers in this book, so you will have to draw on what you have learned from the Set A exercises and problems.

7. Finally, when you reach the end of the chapter, carefully work through the **Chapter Review** and the **Chapter Test**.

Introduction to Problem Solving

| FOCUS ON | *George Pólya—The Father of Modern Problem Solving* |

George Pólya was born in Hungary in 1887. He received his Ph.D. at the University of Budapest. In 1940 he came to Brown University and then joined the faculty at Stanford University in 1942.

In his studies, he became interested in the process of discovery, which led to his famous four-step process for solving problems:

1. Understand the problem.
2. Devise a plan.
3. Carry out the plan.
4. Look back.

Pólya wrote over 250 mathematical papers and three books that promote problem solving. His most famous book, *How to Solve It*, which has been translated into 15 languages, introduced his four-step approach together with heuristics, or strategies, which are helpful in solving problems. Other important works by Pólya are *Mathematical Discovery*, Volumes 1 and 2, and *Mathematics and Plausible Reasoning*, Volumes 1 and 2.

He died in 1985, leaving mathematics with the important legacy of teaching problem solving. His "Ten Commandments for Teachers" are as follows:

1. Be interested in your subject.
2. Know your subject.
3. Try to read the faces of your students; try to see their expectations and difficulties; put yourself in their place.
4. Realize that the best way to learn anything is to discover it by yourself.
5. Give your students not only information, but also know-how, mental attitudes, the habit of methodical work.
6. Let them learn guessing.
7. Let them learn proving.
8. Look out for such features of the problem at hand as may be useful in solving the problems to come—try to disclose the general pattern that lies behind the present concrete situation.
9. Do not give away your whole secret at once—let the students guess before you tell it—let them find out by themselves as much as is feasible.
10. Suggest; do not force information down their throats.

Because problem solving is the main goal of mathematics, this chapter introduces the six strategies listed in the Problem-Solving Strategies box that are helpful in solving problems. Then, at the beginning of each chapter, an initial problem is posed that can be solved by using the strategy introduced in that chapter. As you move through this book, the Problem-Solving Strategies boxes at the beginning of each chapter expand, as should your ability to solve problems.

INITIAL PROBLEM

Place the whole numbers 1 through 9 in the circles in the accompanying triangle so that the sum of the numbers on each side is 17.

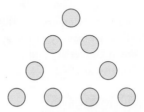

A solution to this Initial Problem is on page 39.

INTRODUCTION

Once, at an informal meeting, a social scientist asked of a mathematics professor, "What's the main goal of teaching mathematics?" The reply was, "Problem solving." In return, the mathematician asked, "What is the main goal of teaching the social sciences?" Once more the answer was "Problem solving." All successful engineers, scientists, social scientists, lawyers, accountants, doctors, business managers, and so on have to be good problem solvers. Although the problems that people encounter may be very diverse, there are common elements and an underlying structure that can help to facilitate problem solving. Because of the universal importance of problem solving, the main professional group in mathematics education, the National Council of Teachers of Mathematics (NCTM), recommended in its 1980 *An Agenda for Action* that "problem solving be the focus of school mathematics in the 1980s." The National Council of Teachers of Mathematics' 1989 *Curriculum and Evaluation Standards for School Mathematics* called for increased attention to the teaching of problem solving in K–8 mathematics. Areas of emphasis include word problems, applications, patterns and relationships, open-ended problems, and problem situations represented verbally, numerically, graphically, geometrically, or symbolically. The NCTM's 2000 *Principles and Standards for School Mathematics* identified problem solving as one of the processes by which all mathematics should be taught.

This chapter introduces a problem-solving process together with six strategies that will aid you in solving problems.

Key Concepts from NCTM Curriculum Focal Points

- **KINDERGARTEN:** Choose, combine, and apply effective strategies for answering quantitative questions.

- **GRADE 1:** Develop an understanding of the meanings of addition and subtraction and strategies to solve such arithmetic problems. Solve problems involving the relative sizes of whole numbers.

- **GRADE 3:** Apply increasingly sophisticated strategies . . . to solve multiplication and division problems.

- **GRADES 4 AND 5:** Select appropriate units, strategies, and tools for solving problems.

- **GRADE 6:** Solve a wide variety of problems involving ratios and rates.

- **GRADE 7:** Use ratio and proportionality to solve a wide variety of percent problems.

1.1 THE PROBLEM-SOLVING PROCESS AND STRATEGIES

STARTING POINT

Use any strategy you know to solve the problem below. As you solve the problem below, pay close attention to the thought processes and steps that you use. Write down these strategies and compare them to a classmate's. Are there any similarities in your approaches to solving the problem below?

Problem: Lin's garden has an area of 78 square yards. The length of the garden is 5 less than three times its width. What are the dimensions of Lin's garden?

Pólya's Four Steps

Children's Literature
www.wiley.com/college/musser
See "Math Curse" by Jon
Sciezke.

In this book we often distinguish between "exercises" and "problems." Unfortunately, the distinction cannot be made precise. To solve an **exercise**, one applies a routine procedure to arrive at an answer. To solve a **problem**, one has to pause, reflect, and perhaps take some original step never taken before to arrive at a solution. This need for some sort of creative step on the solver's part, however minor, is what distinguishes a problem from an exercise. To a young child, finding $3 + 2$ might be a problem, whereas it is a fact for you. For a child in the early grades, the question "How do you divide 96 pencils equally among 16 children?" might pose a problem, but for you it suggests the exercise "find $96 \div 16$." These two examples illustrate how the distinction between an exercise and a problem can vary, since it depends on the state of mind of the person who is to solve it.

Doing exercises is a very valuable aid in learning mathematics. Exercises help you to learn concepts, properties, procedures, and so on, which you can then apply when solving problems. This chapter provides an introduction to the process of problem solving. The techniques that you learn in this chapter should help you to become a better problem solver and should show you how to help others develop their problem-solving skills.

A famous mathematician, George Pólya, devoted much of his teaching to helping students become better problem solvers. His major contribution is what has become known as **Pólya's four-step process** for solving problems.

Reflection from Research
Many children believe that the answer to a word problem can always be found by adding, subtracting, multiplying, or dividing two numbers. Little thought is given to understanding the context of the problem (Verschaffel, De Corte, & Vierstraete, 1999).

Step 1   Understand the Problem

- Do you understand all the words?
- Can you restate the problem in your own words?
- Do you know what is given?
- Do you know what the goal is?
- Is there enough information?
- Is there extraneous information?
- Is this problem similar to another problem you have solved?

Step 2   Devise a Plan

Can one of the following strategies (heuristics) be used? (A **strategy** is defined as an artful means to an end.)

1. Guess and test.	**12.** Work backward.
2. Draw a picture.	**13.** Use cases.
3. Use a variable.	**14.** Solve an equation.
4. Look for a pattern.	**15.** Look for a formula.
5. Make a list.	**16.** Do a simulation.
6. Solve a simpler problem.	**17.** Use a model.
7. Draw a diagram.	**18.** Use dimensional analysis.
8. Use direct reasoning.	**19.** Identify subgoals.
9. Use indirect reasoning.	**20.** Use coordinates.
10. Use properties of numbers.	**21.** Use symmetry.
11. Solve an equivalent problem.	

The first six strategies are discussed in this chapter; the others are introduced in subsequent chapters.

| **Step 3** | Carry Out the Plan |

- Implement the strategy or strategies that you have chosen until the problem is solved or until a new course of action is suggested.
- Give yourself a reasonable amount of time in which to solve the problem. If you are not successful, seek hints from others or put the problem aside for a while. (You may have a flash of insight when you least expect it!)
- Do not be afraid of starting over. Often, a fresh start and a new strategy will lead to success.

| **Step 4** | Look Back |

- Is your solution correct? Does your answer satisfy the statement of the problem?
- Can you see an easier solution?
- Can you see how you can extend your solution to a more general case?

Usually, a problem is stated in words, either orally or written. Then, to solve the problem, one translates the words into an equivalent problem using mathematical symbols, solves this equivalent problem, and then interprets the answer. This process is summarized in Figure 1.1.

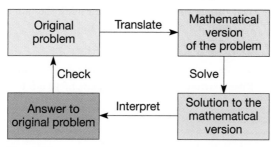

Figure 1.1

Reflection from Research
Researchers suggest that teachers think aloud when solving problems for the first time in front of the class. In so doing, teachers will be modeling successful problem-solving behaviors for their students (Schoenfeld, 1985).

Learning to utilize Pólya's four steps and the diagram in Figure 1.1 are first steps in becoming a good problem solver. In particular, the "Devise a Plan" step is very important. In this chapter and throughout the book, you will learn the strategies listed under the "Devise a Plan" step, which in turn help you decide how to proceed to solve problems. However, selecting an appropriate strategy is critical! As we worked with students who were successful problem solvers, we asked them to share "clues" that they observed in statements of problems that helped them select appropriate strategies. Their clues are listed after each corresponding strategy. Thus, in addition to learning *how* to use the various strategies herein, these clues can help you decide *when* to select an appropriate strategy or combination of strategies. Problem solving is as much an art as it is a science. Therefore, you will find that with experience you will develop a feeling for when to use one strategy over another by recognizing certain clues, perhaps subconsciously. Also, you will find that some problems may be solved in several ways using different strategies.

NCTM Standard
Instructional programs should enable all students to apply and adapt a variety of appropriate strategies to solve problems.

In summary, this initial material on problem solving is a foundation for your success in problem solving. Review this material on Pólya's four steps as well as the strategies and clues as you continue to develop your expertise in solving problems.

Problem-Solving Strategies

The remainder of this chapter is devoted to introducing several problem-solving strategies.

Strategy 1   Guess and Test

Problem

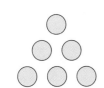

Figure 1.2

Place the digits 1, 2, 3, 4, 5, 6 in the circles in Figure 1.2 so that the sum of the three numbers on each side of the triangle is 12.

We will solve the problem in three ways to illustrate three different approaches to the Guess and Test strategy. As its name suggests, to use the Guess and Test strategy, you guess at a solution and test whether you are correct. If you are incorrect, you refine your guess and test again. This process is repeated until you obtain a solution.

Step 1   Understand the Problem

Each number must be used exactly one time when arranging the numbers in the triangle. The sum of the three numbers on each side must be 12.

First Approach: Random Guess and Test

Step 2   Devise a Plan

Tear off six pieces of paper and mark the numbers 1 through 6 on them and then try combinations until one works.

Step 3   Carry Out the Plan

Arrange the pieces of paper in the shape of an equilateral triangle and check sums. Keep rearranging until three sums of 12 are found.

Second Approach: Systematic Guess and Test

Step 2   Devise a Plan

Rather than randomly moving the numbers around, begin by placing the smallest numbers—namely, 1, 2, 3—in the corners. If that does not work, try increasing the numbers to 1, 2, 4, and so on.

Step 3   Carry Out the Plan

With 1, 2, 3 in the corners, the side sums are too small; similarly with 1, 2, 4. Try 1, 2, 5 and 1, 2, 6. The side sums are still too small. Next try 2, 3, 4, then 2, 3, 5, and so on, until a solution is found. One also could begin with 4, 5, 6 in the corners, then try 3, 4, 5, and so on.

Third Approach: Inferential Guess and Test

Step 2   Devise a Plan

Start by assuming that 1 must be in a corner and explore the consequences.

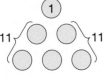

Figure 1.3

Step 3   Carry Out the Plan

If 1 is placed in a corner, we must find two pairs out of the remaining five numbers whose sum is 11 (Figure 1.3). However, out of 2, 3, 4, 5, and 6, only $6 + 5 = 11$. Thus, we conclude that 1 cannot be in a corner. If 2 is in a corner, there must be two pairs left that add to 10 (Figure 1.4). But only $6 + 4 = 10$. Therefore, 2

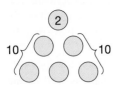

Figure 1.4

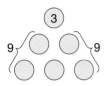

Figure 1.5

Figure 1.6

NCTM Standard

Instructional programs should enable all students to monitor and reflect on the process of mathematical problem solving.

cannot be in a corner. Finally, suppose that 3 is in a corner. Then we must satisfy Figure 1.5. However, only $5 + 4 = 9$ of the remaining numbers. Thus, if there is a solution, 4, 5, and 6 will have to be in the corners (Figure 1.6). By placing 1 between 5 and 6, 2 between 4 and 6, and 3 between 4 and 5, we have a solution.

Step 4   Look Back

Notice how we have solved this problem in three different ways using Guess and Test. Random Guess and Test is often used to get started, but it is easy to lose track of the various trials. Systematic Guess and Test is better because you develop a scheme to ensure that you have tested all possibilities. Generally, Inferential Guess and Test is superior to both of the previous methods because it usually saves time and provides more information regarding possible solutions.

Additional Problems Where the Strategy "Guess and Test" Is Useful

1. In the following **cryptarithm**—that is, a collection of words where the letters represent numbers—*sun* and *fun* represent two three-digit numbers, and *swim* is their four-digit sum. Using all of the digits 0, 1, 2, 3, 6, 7, and 9 in place of the letters where no letter represents two different digits, determine the value of each letter.

$$\begin{array}{r} \text{sun} \\ + \text{ fun} \\ \hline \text{swim} \end{array}$$

Step 1   Understand the Problem

Each of the letters in *sun, fun,* and *swim* must be replaced with the numbers 0, 1, 2, 3, 6, 7, and 9, so that a correct sum results after each letter is replaced with its associated digit. When the letter n is replaced by one of the digits, then $n + n$ must be m or $10 + m$, where the 1 in the 10 is carried to the tens column. Since $1 + 1 = 2$, $3 + 3 = 6$, and $6 + 6 = 12$, there are three possibilities for n, namely, 1, 3, or 6. Now we can try various combinations in an attempt to obtain the correct sum.

Step 2   Devise a Plan

Use Inferential Guess and Test. There are three choices for n. Observe that *sun* and *fun* are three-digit numbers and that *swim* is a four-digit number. Thus we have to carry when we add s and f. Therefore, the value for s in *swim* is 1. This limits the choices of n to 3 or 6.

Step 3   Carry Out the Plan

Since $s = 1$ and $s + f$ leads to a two-digit number, f must be 9. Thus there are two possibilities:

$$\text{(a)}\quad \begin{array}{r} 1\,u\,3 \\ + 9\,u\,3 \\ \hline 1\,w\,i\,6 \end{array} \qquad \text{(b)}\quad \begin{array}{r} 1\,u\,6 \\ + 9\,u\,6 \\ \hline 1\,w\,i\,2 \end{array}$$

In (a), if $u = 0$, 2, or 7, there is no value possible for i among the remaining digits. In (b), if $u = 3$, then $u + u$ plus the carry from $6 + 6$ yields $i = 7$. This leaves $w = 0$ for a solution.

Figure 1.7

Step 4	Look Back

The reasoning used here shows that there is one and only one solution to this problem. When solving problems of this type, one could randomly substitute digits until a solution is found. However, Inferential Guess and Test simplifies the solution process by looking for unique aspects of the problem. Here the natural places to start are $n + n$, $u + u$, and the fact that $s + f$ yields a two-digit number.

2. Use four 4s and some of the symbols $+, \times, -, \div, (\ )$ to give expressions for the whole numbers from 0 through 9: for example, $5 = (4 \times 4 + 4) \div 4$.

3. For each shape in Figure 1.7, make one straight cut so that each of the two pieces of the shape can be rearranged to form a square.

(NOTE: Answers for these problems are given after the Solution of the Initial Problem near the end of this chapter.)

CLUES

The Guess and Test strategy may be appropriate when

- There is a limited number of possible answers to test.
- You want to gain a better understanding of the problem.
- You have a good idea of what the answer is.
- You can systematically try possible answers.
- Your choices have been narrowed down by the use of other strategies.
- There is no other obvious strategy to try.

Review the preceding three problems to see how these clues may have helped you select the Guess and Test strategy to solve these problems.

Strategy 2	Draw a Picture

Often problems involve physical situations. In these situations, drawing a picture can help you better understand the problem so that you can formulate a plan to solve the problem. As you proceed to solve the following "pizza" problem, see whether you can visualize the solution *without* looking at any pictures first. Then work through the given solution using pictures to see how helpful they can be.

Problem

Can you cut a pizza into 11 pieces with four straight cuts?

Step 1	Understand the Problem

Do the pieces have to be the same size and shape?

Step 2	Devise a Plan

An obvious beginning would be to draw a picture showing how a pizza is usually cut and to count the pieces. If we do not get 11, we have to try something else (Figure 1.8). Unfortunately, we get only eight pieces this way.

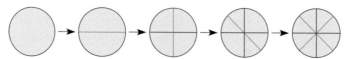

Figure 1.8

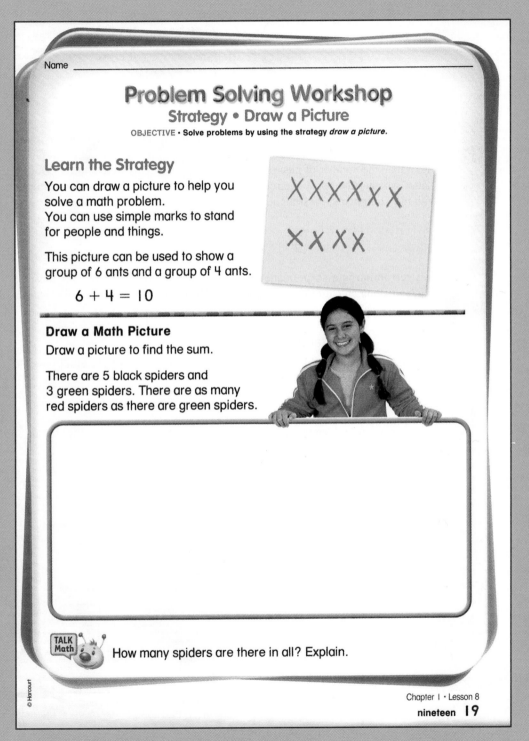

Name _____

Problem Solving Workshop
Strategy • Draw a Picture
OBJECTIVE • **Solve problems by using the strategy** *draw a picture.*

Learn the Strategy

You can draw a picture to help you
solve a math problem.
You can use simple marks to stand
for people and things.

This picture can be used to show a
group of 6 ants and a group of 4 ants.

$$6 + 4 = 10$$

X X X X X X

X X X X

Draw a Math Picture

Draw a picture to find the sum.

There are 5 black spiders and
3 green spiders. There are as many
red spiders as there are green spiders.

TALK
Math   How many spiders are there in all? Explain.

© Harcourt

Chapter 1 • Lesson 8
nineteen **19**

From "Problem Solving Workshop" from HSP MATH, Student Edition (National), Grade 2, copyright © 2009 by Houghton Mifflin Harcourt Publishing Company.

Step 3   Carry Out the Plan

See Figure 1.9

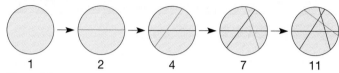

Figure 1.9

Step 4   Look Back

Were you concerned about cutting equal pieces when you started? That is normal. In the context of cutting a pizza, the focus is usually on trying to cut equal pieces rather than the number of pieces. Suppose that circular cuts were allowed. Does it matter whether the pizza is circular or is square? How many pieces can you get with five straight cuts? *n* straight cuts?

Additional Problems Where the Strategy "Draw a Picture" Is Useful

Not a tetromino

A tetromino

Figure 1.10

1. A **tetromino** is a shape made up of four squares where the squares must be joined along an entire side (Figure 1.10). How many different tetromino shapes are possible?

Step 1   Understand the Problem

The solution of this problem is easier if we make a set of pictures of all possible arrangements of four squares of the same size.

Step 2   Devise a Plan

Let's start with the longest and narrowest configuration and work toward the most compact.

Step 3   Carry Out the Plan

Four in a row.

Three in a row with one on top of (or below) the end square. (Note: The upper square can be at either end—these two are considered to be equivalent.)

Three in a row, with one on top of (or below) the center square.

Two in a row, with one above and one below the two.

Two in a row, with two above.

| Step 4 | Look Back |

Many similar problems can be posed using fewer or more squares. The problems become much more complex as the number of squares increases. Also, new problems can be posed using patterns of equilateral triangles.

2. If you have a chain saw with a bar 18 inches long, determine whether a 16-foot log, 8 inches in diameter, can be cut into 4-foot pieces by making only two cuts.

3. It takes 64 cubes to fill a cubical box that has no top. How many cubes are *not* touching a side or the bottom?

CLUES

The Draw a Picture strategy may be appropriate when

- A physical situation is involved.
- Geometric figures or measurements are involved.
- You want to gain a better understanding of the problem.
- A visual representation of the problem is possible.

Review the preceding three problems to see how these clues may have helped you select the Draw a Picture strategy to solve these problems.

NCTM Standard
All students should represent the idea of a variable as an unknown quantity using a letter or a symbol.

| Strategy 3 | Use a Variable |

Observe how letters were used in place of numbers in the previous "sun + fun = swim" cryptarithm. Letters used in place of numbers are called **variables** or **unknowns**. The Use a Variable strategy, which is one of the most useful problem-solving strategies, is used extensively in algebra and in mathematics that involves algebra.

Problem

What is the greatest number that evenly divides the sum of any three consecutive whole numbers?

By trying several examples, you might guess that 3 is the greatest such number. However, it is necessary to use a variable to account for all possible instances of three consecutive numbers.

Reflection from Research
Given the proper experiences, children as young as eight and nine years of age can learn to comfortably use letters to represent unknown values and can operate on representations involving letters and numbers while fully realizing that they did not know the values of the unknowns (Carraher, Schliemann, Brizuela, & Earnest, 2006).

| Step 1 | Understand the Problem |

The whole numbers are 0, 1, 2, 3, . . . , so that consecutive whole numbers differ by 1. Thus an example of three consecutive whole numbers is the triple 3, 4, and 5. The sum of three consecutive whole numbers has a factor of 3 if 3 multiplied by another whole number produces the given sum. In the example of 3, 4, and 5, the sum is 12 and 3×4 equals 12. Thus $3 + 4 + 5$ has a factor of 3.

| Step 2 | Devise a Plan |

Since we can use a variable, say x, to represent any whole number, we can represent every triple of consecutive whole numbers as follows: $x, x + 1, x + 2$. Now we can proceed to see whether the sum has a factor of 3.

Algebraic Reasoning
In algebra, the letter "x" is most commonly used for a variable. However, any letter (even Greek letters, for example) can be used as a variable.

| Step 3 | Carry Out the Plan |

The sum of $x, x + 1$, and $x + 2$ is

$$x + (x + 1) + (x + 2) = 3x + 3 = 3(x + 1).$$

Thus $x + (x + 1) + (x + 2)$ is three times $x + 1$. Therefore, we have shown that the sum of any three consecutive whole numbers has a factor of 3. The case of $x = 0$ shows that 3 is the *greatest* such number.

Step 4   Look Back

Is it also true that the sum of any five consecutive whole numbers has a factor of 5? Or, more generally, will the sum of any n consecutive whole numbers have a factor of n? Can you think of any other generalizations?

Additional Problems Where the Strategy "Use a Variable" Is Useful

1. Find the sum of the first 10, 100, and 500 counting numbers.

Step 1   Understand the Problem

Since counting numbers are the numbers $1, 2, 3, 4, \ldots$, the sum of the first 10 counting numbers would be $1 + 2 + 3 + \ldots + 8 + 9 + 10$. Similarly, the sum of the first 100 counting numbers would be $1 + 2 + 3 + \ldots + 98 + 99 + 100$ and the sum of the first 500 counting numbers would be $1 + 2 + 3 + \ldots + 498 + 499 + 500$.

Step 2   Devise a Plan

Rather than solve three different problems, the "Use a Variable" strategy can be used to find a general method for computing the sum in all three situations. Thus, the sum of the first n counting numbers would be expressed as $1 + 2 + 3 + \ldots + (n - 2) + (n - 1) + n$. The sum of these numbers can be found by noticing that the first number 1 added to the last number n is $n + 1$, which is the same as $(n - 1) + 2$ and $(n - 2) + 3$. Adding up all such pairs can be done by adding up all of the numbers twice.

Reflection from Research
When asked to create their own problems, good problem solvers generated problems that were more mathematically complex than those of less successful problem solvers (Silver & Cai, 1996).

Step 3   Carry Out the Plan

$$
\begin{array}{cccccccc}
1 & + & 2 & + & 3 & + \ldots + (n - 2) + (n - 1) + & n \\
+ & n & + (n-1) & + (n-2) & + \ldots + & 3 & + \quad 2 \quad + \quad 1 \\
\hline
\end{array}
$$

$$(n + 1) + (n + 1) + (n + 1) + \ldots + (n + 1) + (n + 1) + (n + 1)$$

$$= n \cdot (n + 1)$$

Since each number was added twice, the desired sum is obtained by dividing $n \cdot (n + 1)$ by 2 which yields

$$1 + 2 + 3 + \ldots + (n - 2) + (n - 1) + n = \frac{n \cdot (n + 1)}{2}$$

The numbers 10, 100, and 500 can now replace the variable n to find our desired solutions:

$$1 + 2 + 3 + \ldots + 8 + 9 + 10 = \frac{10 \cdot (10 + 1)}{2} = 55$$

$$1 + 2 + 3 + \ldots + 98 + 99 + 100 = \frac{100 \cdot (101)}{2} = 5050$$

$$1 + 2 + 3 + \ldots 498 + 499 + 500 = \frac{500 \cdot 501}{2} = 125{,}250$$

Step 4   Look Back

Since the method for solving this problem is quite unique could it be used to solve other similar looking problems like:

i. $3 + 6 + 9 + \ldots + (3n - 6) + (3n - 3) + 3n$
ii. $21 + 25 + 29 + \ldots + 113 + 117 + 121$

2. Show that the sum of any five consecutive odd whole numbers has a factor of 5.

3. The measure of the largest angle of a triangle is nine times the measure of the smallest angle. The measure of the third angle is equal to the difference of the largest and the smallest. What are the measures of the angles? (Recall that the sum of the measures of the angles in a triangle is $180°$.)

CLUES

The Use a Variable strategy may be appropriate when

- A phrase similar to "for any number" is present or implied.
- A problem suggests an equation.
- A proof or a general solution is required.
- A problem contains phrases such as "consecutive," "even," or "odd" whole numbers.
- There is a large number of cases.
- There is an unknown quantity related to known quantities.
- There is an infinite number of numbers involved.
- You are trying to develop a general formula.

Review the preceding three problems to see how these clues may have helped you select the Use a Variable strategy to solve these problems.

Using Algebra to Solve Problems

To effectively employ the Use a Variable strategy, students need to have a clear understanding of what a variable is and how to write and simplify equations containing variables. This subsection addresses these issues in an elementary introduction to algebra. There will be an expanded treatment of solving equations and inequalities in Chapter 9 after the real number system has been developed.

NCTM Standard
All students should develop an initial conceptual understanding of different uses of variables.

A common way to introduce the use of variables is to find a general formula for a pattern of numbers such as $3, 6, 9, \ldots 3n$. One of the challenges for students is to see the role that each number plays in the expression. For example, the pattern $5, 8, 11, \ldots$ is similar to the previous pattern, but it is more difficult to see that each term is two greater than a multiple of 3 and, thus, can be expressed in general as $3n + 2$. Sometimes it is easier for students to use a variable to generalize a geometric pattern such as the one shown in the following example. This type of example may be used to introduce seventh-grade students to the concept of a variable. Following are four typical student solutions.

Figure 1.11

Example 1.1   Describe at least four different ways to count the dots in Figure 1.11.

SOLUTION The obvious method of solution is to count the dots—there are 16. Another student's method is illustrated in Figure 1.12.

$$4 \times 3 + 4$$
$$4 \times (5 - 2) + 4$$
$\left.\right\} \longrightarrow$

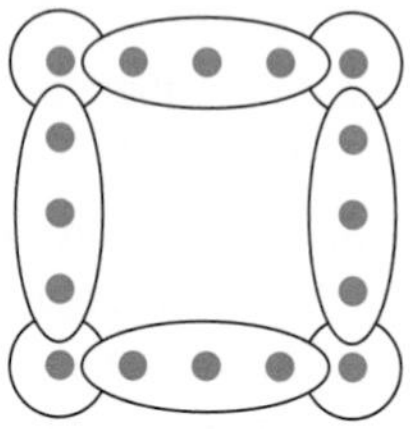

Figure 1.12

The student counts the number of interior dots on each side, 3, and multiplies by the number of sides, 4, and then adds the dots in the corners, 4. This method generates the expression $4 \times 3 + 4 = 16$. A second way to write this expression is $4 \times (5 - 2) + 4 = 16$ since the 3 interior dots can be determined by subtracting the two corners from the 5 dots on a side. Both of these methods are shown in Figure 1.12.

A third method is to count all of the dots on a side, 5, and multiply by the number of sides. Four must then be subtracted because each corner has been counted twice, once for each side it belongs to. This method is illustrated in Figure 1.13 and generates the expression shown.

$$4 \times 5 - 4 = 16 \} \longrightarrow$$

Figure 1.13

Reflection from Research
Sixth-grade students with no formal instruction in algebra are "generally able to solve problems involving specific cases and showed remarkable ability to generalize the problem situations and to write equations using variables. However they rarely used their equations to solve related problems" (Swafford & Langrall, 2000).

In the two previous methods, either corner dots are not counted (so they must be added on) or they are counted twice (so they must be subtracted to avoid double counting). The following fourth method assigns each corner to only one side (Figure 1.14).

$$4 \times 4 = 16$$
$$4 \times (5 - 1) = 16$$
$\left.\right\} \longrightarrow$

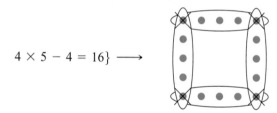

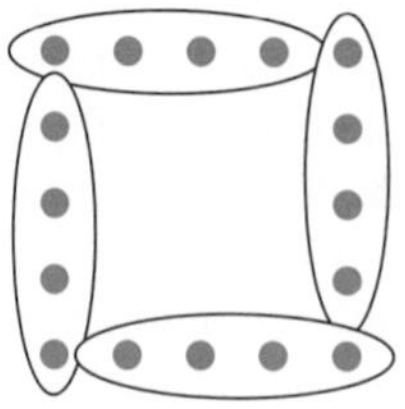

Figure 1.14

Thus, we encircle 4 dots on each side and multiply by the number of sides. This yields the expression $4 \times 4 = 16$. Because the 4 dots on each side come from the 5 total dots on a side minus 1 corner, this expression could also be written as $4 \times (5 - 1) = 16$ (see Figure 1.14). ∎

There are many different methods for counting the dots in the previous example and each method has a geometric interpretation as well as a corresponding arithmetic expression. Could these methods be generalized to 50, 100, 1000 or even n dots on a side? The next example discusses how these generalizations can be viewed as well as displays the generalized solutions of seventh-grade students.

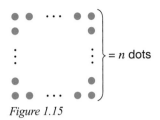

Figure 1.15

Example 1.2   Suppose the square arrangement of dots in Example 1.1 had n dots on each side. Write an algebraic expression that would describe the total number of dots in such a figure (Figure 1.15).

SOLUTION   It is easier to write a general expression for those in Example 1.1 when you understand the origins of the numbers in each expression. In all such cases, there will be 4 corners and 4 sides, so the values that represent corners and sides will stay fixed at 4. On the other hand, in Figure 1.15, any value that was determined based on the number of dots on the side will have to reflect the value of n. Thus, the expressions that represent the total number of dots on a square figure with n dots on a side are generalized as shown next.

$$\left.\begin{array}{l} 4 \times 3 + 4 \\ 4 \times (5 - 2) + 4 \end{array}\right\} \longrightarrow 4(n - 2) + 4$$

$$4 \times 5 - 4 \longrightarrow 4n - 4$$

$$\left.\begin{array}{l} 4 \times 4 \\ 4 \times (5 - 1) \end{array}\right\} \longrightarrow 4(n - 1) \qquad \blacksquare$$

Since each expression on the right represents the total number of dots in Figure 1.15, they are all equal to each other. Using properties of numbers and equations, each equation can be rewritten as the same expression. Learning to simplify expressions and equations with variables is one of the most important processes in mathematics. Traditionally, this topic has represented a substantial portion of an entire course in introductory algebra. An **equation** is a sentence involving numbers, or symbols representing numbers where the verb is *equals* ($=$). There are various types of equations:

$$
\begin{array}{ll}
3 + 4 = 7 & \textit{True equation} \\
3 + 4 = 9 & \textit{False equation} \\
2x + 5x = 7x & \textit{Identity equation} \\
x + 4 = 9 & \textit{Conditional equation}
\end{array}
$$

Algebraic Reasoning
Variable is a central concept in algebra. Students may struggle with the idea that the letter x represents many numbers in $y = 3x + 4$ but only one or two numbers in other situations. For example, the solution of the equation $x^2 = 9$ consists of the numbers 3 and -3 since each of these numbers squared is 9. This means, that the equation is true whenever $x = 3$ or $x = -3$.

A true or false equation needs no explanation, but an identity equation is always true no matter what numerical value is used for x. A conditional equation is an equation that is only true for certain values of x. For example, the equation $x + 4 = 9$ is true when $x = 5$, but false when x is any other value. In this chapter, we will restrict the variables to only whole numbers. For a conditional equation, a value of the variable that makes the equation true is called a **solution**. To **solve an equation** means to find all of the solutions. The following example shows three different ways to solve equations of the form $ax + b = c$.

| Example 1.3 | Suppose the square arrangement of dots in Example 1.2 had 84 total dots (Figure 1.16). How many dots are there on each side? |

Reflection from Research
Even 6-year-olds can solve algebraic equations when they are rewritten as a story problem, logic puzzle, or some other problem with meaning (Femiano, 2003).

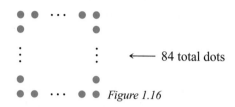

$\longleftarrow$ 84 total dots

Figure 1.16

SOLUTION From Example 1.2, a square with n dots on a side has $4n - 4$ total dots. Thus, we have the equation $4n - 4 = 84$. Three elementary methods that can be used to solve equations such as $4n - 4 = 84$ are *Guess and Test, Cover Up,* and *Work Backward*.

Guess and Test As the name of this method suggests, one guesses values for the variable in the equation $4n - 4 = 84$ and substitutes to see if a true equation results.

Try $n = 10$: $4(10) - 4 = 36 \neq 84$

Try $n = 25$: $4(25) - 4 = 96 \neq 84$

Try $n = 22$: $4(22) - 4 = 84$. Therefore, 22 is the solution of the equation.

Cover Up In this method, we cover up the term with the variable:

$\square - 4 = 84$. To make a true equation, the $\square$ must be 88. Thus $4n = 88$. Since $4 \cdot 22 = 88$, we have $n = 22$.

Work Backward The left side of the equation shows that n is *multiplied* by 4 and then 4 is *subtracted* to obtain 84. Thus, working backward, if we *add* 4 to 84 and *divide* by 4, we reach the value of n. Here $84 + 4 = 88$ and $88 \div 4 = 22$ so $n = 22$ (Figure 1.17). ■

```
      ×4          −4
   ┌──┐        ┌──┐
   │22│        │88│        84
   └──┘        └──┘
      ÷4          +4
```

Figure 1.17

Using variables in equations and manipulating them are what most people see as "algebra." However, algebra is much more than manipulating variables—it includes the reasoning that underlies those manipulations. In fact, many students solve algebra-like problems without equations and don't realize that their reasoning is algebraic. For example, the Work Backward solution in Example 1.3 can all be done without really thinking about the variable n. If one just thinks "four times something minus 4 is 84," he can work backward to find the solution. However, the thinking that is used in the Work Backward method can be mirrored in equations as follows:

$$4n - 4 = 84$$
$$4n = 84 + 4$$
$$4n = 88$$
$$n = 88 \div 4$$
$$n = 22$$

Reflection from Research
We are proposing that the teaching and learning of arithmetic be conceived as part of the foundation of learning algebra, not that algebra be conceived only as an extension of arithmetic procedures (Carpenter, Levi, Berman, & Pligge, 2005).

Because so much algebra can be done with intuitive reasoning, it is important to help students realize when they are reasoning algebraically. One way to better understand the underlying principles of algebraic reasoning is to look at the Algebraic Reasoning Web Module on our Web site: www.wiley.com/college/musser/

Some researchers say that arithmetic is the foundation of learning algebra. Arithmetic typically means computation with different kinds of numbers and the underlying properties that make the computation work. Much of what is discussed in Chapters 2–9 is about arithmetic and thus contains key parts of the foundation of algebra. To help you see algebraic ideas in the arithmetic that we study, there will be places throughout those chapters where these foundational ideas of algebra are called out in an "Algebraic Reasoning" margin note.

We address algebra in more depth when we talk about solving equations, relations, and functions in Chapter 9 and then again in Chapter 15 when algebraic ideas are applied to geometry.

MATHEMATICAL MORSEL

There is a story about Sir Isaac Newton, coinventor of the calculus, who, as a youngster, was sent out to cut a hole in the barn door for the cats to go in and out. With great pride he admitted to cutting two holes, a larger one for the cat and a smaller one for the kittens.

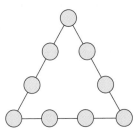

| Section 1.1 | **EXERCISE / PROBLEM SET A** |

1. **a.** If the diagonals of a square are drawn in, how many triangles of all sizes are formed?
   b. Describe how Pólya's four steps were used to solve part a.

2. Scott and Greg were asked to add two whole numbers. Instead, Scott subtracted the two numbers and got 10, and Greg multiplied them and got 651. What was the correct sum?

3. The distance around a standard tennis court is 228 feet. If the length of the court is 6 feet more than twice the width, find the dimensions of the tennis court.

4. A multiple of 11 I be,
   not odd, but even, you see.
       My digits, a pair,
       when multiplied there,
   make a cube and a square
   out of me. Who am I?

5. Show how 9 can be expressed as the sum of two consecutive numbers. Then decide whether every odd number can be expressed as the sum of two consecutive counting numbers. Explain your reasoning.

6. Using the symbols +, −, ×, and ÷, fill in the following three blanks to make a true equation. (A symbol may be used more than once.)

$$6 \underline{} 6 \underline{} 6 \underline{} 6 = 13$$

7. In the accompanying figure (called an **arithmogon**), the number that appears in a square is the sum of the numbers in the circles on each side of it. Determine what numbers belong in the circles.

8. Place 10 stools along four walls of a room so that each of the four walls has the same number of stools.

9. Susan has 10 pockets and 44 dollar bills. She wants to arrange the money so that there are a different number of dollars in each pocket. Can she do it? Explain.

10. Arrange the numbers 2, 3, . . . , 10 in the accompanying triangle so that each side sums to 21.

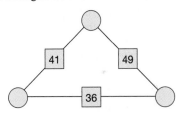

11. Find a set of consecutive counting numbers whose sum is each of the following. Each set may consist of 2, 3, 4, 5, or 6 consecutive integers. Use the spreadsheet activity *Consecutive Integer Sum* on our Web site to assist you.
    a. 84   **b.** 213   **c.** 154

12. Place the digits 1 through 9 so that you can count from 1 to 9 by following the arrows in the diagram.

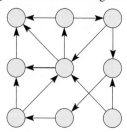

13. Using a 5-minute and an 8-minute hourglass timer, how can you measure 1 minute?

14. Using the numbers 9, 8, 7, 6, 5, and 4 once each, find the following:
 a. The largest possible sum:

 b. The smallest possible (positive) difference:

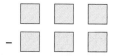

15. Using the numbers 1 through 8, place them in the following eight squares so that no two consecutive numbers are in touching squares (touching includes entire sides or simply one point).

16. Solve this cryptarithm, where each letter represents a digit and no digit represents two different letters:

$$\begin{array}{r} USSR \\ + USA \\ \hline PEACE \end{array}$$

17. On a balance scale, two spools and one thimble balance eight buttons. Also, one spool balances one thimble and one button. How many buttons will balance one spool?

18. Place the numbers 1 through 8 in the circles on the vertices of the accompanying cube so that the difference of any two connecting circles is greater than 1.

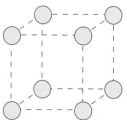

19. Think of a number. Add 10. Multiply by 4. Add 200. Divide by 4. Subtract your original number. Your result should be 60. Why? Show why this would work for any number.

20. The digits 1 through 9 can be used in decreasing order, with + and − signs, to produce 100 as shown: $98 - 76 + 54 + 3 + 21 = 100$. Find two other such combinations that will produce 100.

21. The Indian mathematician Ramanujan observed that the taxi number 1729 was very interesting because it was the smallest counting number that could be expressed as the sum of cubes in two different ways. Find a, b, c, and d such that $a^3 + b^3 = 1729$ and $c^3 + d^3 = 1729$.

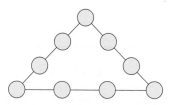

22. Using the Chapter 1 eManipulative activity *Number Puzzles*, Exercise 2 on our Web site, arrange the numbers 1, 2, 3, 4, 5, 6, 7, 8, 9 in the following circles so the sum of the numbers along each line of four is 23.

23. Using the Chapter 1 eManipulative activity *Circle 21* on our Web site, find an arrangement of the numbers 1 through 14 in the 7 circles below so that the sum of the three numbers in each circle is 21.

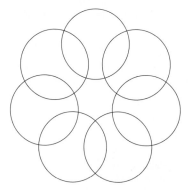

24. The hexagon below has a total of 126 dots and an equal number of dots on each side. How many dots are on each side?

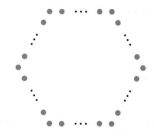

Section 1.1   EXERCISE / PROBLEM SET B

1. Find the largest eight-digit number made up of the digits 1, 1, 2, 2, 3, 3, 4, and 4 such that the 1s are separated by one digit, the 2s by two digits, the 3s by three digits, and the 4s by four digits.

2. Think of a number. Multiply by 5. Add 8. Multiply by 4. Add 9. Multiply by 5. Subtract 105. Divide by 100. Subtract 1. How does your result compare with your original number? Explain.

3. Carol bought some items at a variety store. All the items were the same price, and she bought as many items as the price of each item in cents. (For example, if the items cost 10 cents, she would have bought 10 of them.) Her bill was $2.25. How many items did Carol buy?

4. You can make one square with four toothpicks. Show how you can make two squares with seven toothpicks (breaking toothpicks is not allowed), three squares with 10 toothpicks, and five squares with 12 toothpicks.

5. A textbook is opened and the product of the page numbers of the two facing pages is 6162. What are the numbers of the pages?

6. Place numbers 1 through 19 into the 19 circles below so that any three numbers in a line through the center will give the same sum.

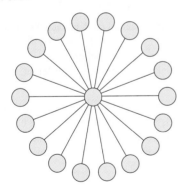

7. Using three of the symbols $+$, $-$, $\times$, and $\div$ *once* each, fill in the following three blanks to make a true equation. (Parentheses are allowed.)
$$6 \_\_\_ 6 \_\_\_ 6 \_\_\_ 6 = 66$$

8. A water main for a street is being laid using a particular kind of pipe that comes in either 18-foot sections or 20-foot sections. The designer has determined that the water main would require 14 fewer sections of 20-foot pipe than if 18-foot sections were used. Find the total length of the water main.

9. Mike said that when he opened his book, the product of the page numbers of the two facing pages was 7007. Without performing any calculations, prove that he was wrong.

10. The Smiths were about to start on an 18,000-mile automobile trip. They had their tires checked and found that each was good for only 12,000 miles. What is the smallest number of spares that they will need to take along with them to make the trip without having to buy a new tire?

11. What is the maximum number of pieces of pizza that can result from 4 straight cuts?

12. Given: Six arrows arranged as follows:

$$\uparrow \uparrow \uparrow \downarrow \downarrow \downarrow$$

Goal: By inverting two *adjacent* arrows at a time, rearrange to the following:

$$\uparrow \downarrow \uparrow \downarrow \uparrow \downarrow$$

Can you find a minimum number of moves?

13. Two friends are shopping together when they encounter a special "3 for 2" shoe sale. If they purchase two pairs of shoes at the regular price, a third pair (of lower or equal value) will be free. Neither friend wants three pairs of shoes, but Pat would like to buy a $56 and a $39 pair while Chris is interested in a $45 pair. If they buy the shoes together to take advantage of the sale, what is the fairest share for each to pay?

14. Find digits A, B, C, and D that solve the following cryptarithm.

$$\begin{array}{r} ABCD \\ \times \quad 4 \\ \hline DCBA \end{array}$$

15. If possible, find an odd number that can be expressed as the sum of four consecutive counting numbers. If impossible, explain why.

16. Five friends were sitting on one side of a table. Gary sat next to Bill. Mike sat next to Tom. Howard sat in the third seat from Bill. Gary sat in the third seat from Mike. Who sat on the other side of Tom?

17. In the following square array on the left, the corner numbers were given and the boldface numbers were found by adding the adjacent corner numbers. Following the same rules, find the corner numbers for the other square array.

6	**19**	13		—	**10**	—
8		**14**		**15**		**11**
2	**3**	1		—	**16**	—

18. Together, a baseball and a football weigh 1.25 pounds, the baseball and a soccer ball weigh 1.35 pounds, and the football and the soccer ball weigh 1.9 pounds. How much does each of the balls weigh?

19. Pick any two consecutive numbers. Add them. Then add 9 to the sum. Divide by 2. Subtract the smaller of the original numbers from the answer. What did you get? Repeat this process with two other consecutive numbers. Make a conjecture (educated guess) about the answer, and prove it.

20. An **additive magic square** has the same sum in each row, column, and diagonal. Find the error in this magic square and correct it.

47	56	34	22	83	7
24	67	44	26	13	75
29	52	3	99	18	48
17	49	89	4	53	37
97	6	3	11	74	28
35	19	46	87	8	54

21. Two points are placed on the same side of a square. A segment is drawn from each of these points to each of the 2 vertices (corners) on the opposite side of the square. How many triangles of all sizes are formed?

22. Using the triangle in Problem 10 in Part A, determine whether you can make similar triangles using the digits 1, 2, . . . , 9, where the side sums are 18, 19, 20, 21, and 22.

23. Using the Chapter 1 eManipulative activity, *Number Puzzles*, Exercise 4 on our Web site, arrange the numbers 1, 2, 3, 4, 5, 6, 7, 8, 9 in the circles below so the sum of the numbers along each line of four is 20.

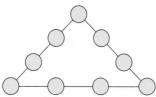

24. Using the Chapter 1 eManipulative activity *Circle 99* on our Web site, find an arrangement of the numbers provided in the 7 circles below so that the sum of the three numbers in each circle is 99.

25. An arrangement of dots forms the perimeter of an equilateral triangle. There are 87 evenly spaced dots on each side including the dots at the vertices. How many dots are there altogether?

26. The equation $\frac{y}{5} + 12 = 23$ can be solved by subtracting 12 from both sides of the equation to yield $\frac{y}{5} + 12 - 12 = 23 - 12$. Similarly, the resulting equation $\frac{y}{5} = 11$ can be solved by multiplying both sides of the equation by 5 to obtain $y = 55$. Explain how this process is related to the Work Backward method described in Example 1.3.

Analyzing Student Thinking

27. When the class was asked to solve the equation $3x - 8 = 27$, Wesley asked if he could use guess and test. How would you respond?

28. Rosemary said that she felt the "Guess and Test" method was a waste of time; she just wanted to get an answer. What could you tell her about the value of using guess and test?

29. Even though you have taught your students how to "draw a picture" to solve a problem, Cecelia asks if she has to draw a picture because she can solve the problems in class without it. How would you respond?

30. When Damian, a second grader, was asked to solve problems like $\square + 3 = 5$, he said that he had seen his older sister working on problems like $x + 3 = 5$ and wondered if these equations were different. How would you respond?

31. After the class had found three consecutive odd numbers whose sum is 99, Byron tried to find three consecutive odd numbers that would add to 96. He said he was struggling to find a solution. How could you help him understand the solution to this problem?

32. Consider the following problem:

    The amount of fencing needed to enclose a rectangular field was 92 yards and the length of the field was 3 times as long as the width. What were the dimensions of the field?

    Vance solved this problem by drawing a picture and using guess and test. Jolie set up an equation with x being the width of the field and solved it. They got the same answer but asked you which method was better. How would you respond?

1. The Focal Points for Grades 4 and 5 state "Select appropriate units, strategies, and tools for solving problems." Find a problem or example in this section that illustrates this statement and explain your reasoning.

2. The NCTM Standards state "All students should describe, extend, and make generalizations about geometric and numeric patterns." Find a problem in this problem set that illustrates this statement and explain your reasoning.

3. The NCTM Standards state "All students should develop an initial conceptual understanding of different uses of variables." Find a problem or example in this section that illustrates this statement and explain your reasoning.

1.2   THREE ADDITIONAL STRATEGIES

STARTING POINT

Solve the problem below using Pólya's four steps and any other strategy. Describe how you used the four steps, focusing on any new insights that you gained as a result of *looking back*. How many rectangles of all shapes and sizes are in the figure at the right?

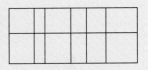

Strategy 4   Look for a Pattern

NCTM Standard
All students should represent, analyze, and generalize a variety of patterns with tables, graphs, words, and, when possible, symbolic rules.

When using the Look for a Pattern strategy, one usually lists several specific instances of a problem and then looks to see whether a pattern emerges that suggests a solution to the entire problem. For example, consider the sums produced by adding consecutive odd numbers starting with 1: 1, $1 + 3 = 4 (= 2 \times 2)$, $1 + 3 + 5 = 9 (= 3 \times 3)$, $1 + 3 + 5 + 7 = 16 (= 4 \times 4)$, $1 + 3 + 5 + 7 + 9 = 25 (= 5 \times 5)$, and so on. Based on the pattern generated by these five examples, one might expect that such a sum will always be a perfect square.

The justification of this pattern is suggested by the following figure.

Algebraic Reasoning
Recognizing and extending patterns is a common practice in algebra. Extending patterns to the most general case is a natural place to discuss variables.

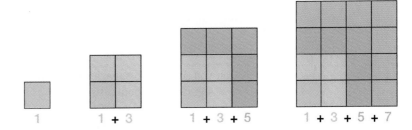

1   1 + 3   1 + 3 + 5   1 + 3 + 5 + 7

Each consecutive odd number of dots can be added to the previous square arrangement to form another square. Thus, the sum of the first n odd numbers is n^2.

Generalizing patterns, however, must be done with caution because with a sequence of only 3 or 4 numbers, a case could be made for more than one pattern. For example, consider the sequence 1, 2, 4, ... What are the next 4 numbers in the sequence? It can be seen that 1 is doubled to get 2 and 2 is doubled to get 4. Following that pattern, the next four numbers would be 8, 16, 32, 64. If, however, it is noted that the difference between the first and second term is 1 and the difference between the second and third term is 2, then a case could be made that the difference is increasing by one. Thus, the next four terms would be 7, 11, 16, 22. Another case could be made for the differences

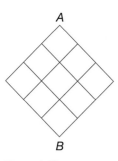

Figure 1.18

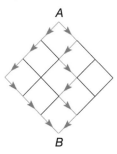

Figure 1.19

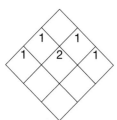

Figure 1.20

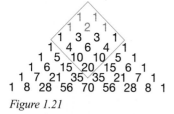

Figure 1.21

Children's Literature
www.wiley.com/college/musser
See "There Was an Old Lady
Who Swallowed a Fly"
by Simms Taback.

alternating between 1 and 2. In that case, the next four terms would be 5, 7, 8, 10. Thus, from the initial three numbers of 1, 2, 4, at least three different patterns are possible:

1, 2, 4, 8, 16, 32, 64, . . .	Doubling
1, 2, 4, 7, 11, 16, 22, . . .	Difference increasing by 1
1, 2, 4, 5, 7, 8, 10, . . .	Difference alternating between 1 and 2

Problem

How many different downward paths are there from *A* to *B* in the grid in Figure 1.18? A path must travel on the lines.

Step 1 Understand the Problem

What do we mean by different and downward? Figure 1.19 illustrates two paths. Notice that each such path will be 6 units long. *Different* means that they are not exactly the same; that is, some part or parts are different.

Step 2 Devise a Plan

Let's look at each point of intersection in the grid and see how many different ways we can get to each point. Then perhaps we will notice a pattern (Figure 1.20). For example, there is only one way to reach each of the points on the two outside edges; there are two ways to reach the middle point in the row of points labeled 1, 2, 1; and so on. Observe that the point labeled 2 in Figure 1.20 can be found by adding the two 1s above it.

Step 3 Carry Out the Plan

To see how many paths there are to any point, observe that you need only *add* the number of paths required to arrive at the point or points immediately above. To reach a point beneath the pair 1 and 2, the paths to 1 and 2 are extended downward, resulting in $1 + 2 = 3$ paths to that point. The resulting number pattern is shown in Figure 1.21. Notice, for example, that $4 + 6 = 10$ and $20 + 15 = 35$. (This pattern is part of what is called **Pascal's triangle**. It is used again in Chapter 11.) The surrounded portion of this pattern applies to the given problem; thus the answer to the problem is 20.

Step 4 Look Back

Can you see how to solve a similar problem involving a larger square array, say a 4×4 grid? How about a 10×10 grid? How about a rectangular grid?

A pattern of numbers arranged in a particular order is called a number **sequence**, and the individual numbers in the sequence are called **terms** of the sequence. The **counting numbers**, 1, 2, 3, 4, . . . , give rise to many sequences. (An **ellipsis**, the three periods after the 4, means "and so on.") Several sequences of counting numbers follow.

SEQUENCE	NAME
2, 4, 6, 8, . . .	The **even** (counting) **numbers**
1, 3, 5, 7, . . .	The **odd** (counting) **numbers**
1, 4, 9, 16, . . .	The **square** (counting) **numbers**
1, 3, 3^2, 3^3, . . .	The **powers** of three
1, 1, 2, 3, 5, 8, . . .	The **Fibonacci sequence** (after the two 1s, each term is the sum of the two preceding terms)

NCTM Standard
All students should analyze how both repeating and growing patterns are generated.

Inductive reasoning is used to draw conclusions or make predictions about a large collection of objects or numbers, based on a small representative subcollection. For example, inductive reasoning can be used to find the ones digit of the 400th term of the sequence 8, 12, 16, 20, 24, ... By continuing this sequence for a few more terms, 8, 12, 16, 20, 24, 28, 32, 36, 40, 44, 48, 52, 56, 60, . . . , one can observe that the ones digit of every fifth term starting with the term 24 is a four. Thus, the ones digit of the 400th term must be a four.

Reflection from Research
In classrooms where problem solving is valued and teachers have knowledge of children's mathematical thinking, children see mathematics as a problem-solving endeavor in which communicating mathematical thinking is important (Franke & Carey, 1997).

Additional Problems Where the Strategy "Look for a Pattern" Is Useful

1. Find the ones digit in 3^{99}.

Step 1 Understand the Problem

The number 3^{99} is the product of 99 threes. Using the exponent key on one type of scientific calculator yields the result $\boxed{1.717925065^{47}}$. This shows the first digit, but not the ones (last) digit, since the 47 indicates that there are 47 places to the right of the decimal. (See the discussion on scientific notation in Chapter 4 for further explanation.) Therefore, we will need to use another method.

Step 2 Devise a Plan

Consider $3^1, 3^2, 3^3, 3^4, 3^5, 3^6, 3^7, 3^8$. Perhaps the ones digits of these numbers form a pattern that can be used to predict the ones digit of 3^{99}.

Step 3 Carry Out the Plan

$3^1 = \mathbf{3}$, $3^2 = \mathbf{9}$, $3^3 = 2\mathbf{7}$, $3^4 = 8\mathbf{1}$, $3^5 = 24\mathbf{3}$, $3^6 = 72\mathbf{9}$, $3^7 = 218\mathbf{7}$, $3^8 = 656\mathbf{1}$. The ones digits form the sequence 3, 9, 7, 1, 3, 9, 7, 1. Whenever the exponent of the 3 has a factor of 4, the ones digit is a 1. Since 100 has a factor of 4, 3^{100} must have a ones digit of 1. Therefore, the ones digit of 3^{99} must be 7, since 3^{99} precedes 3^{100} and 7 precedes 1 in the sequence 3, 9, 7, 1.

Step 4 Look Back

Ones digits of other numbers involving exponents might be found in a similar fashion. Check this for several of the numbers from 4 to 9.

2. Which whole numbers, from 1 to 50, have an odd number of factors? For example, 15 has 1, 3, 5, and 15 as factors, and hence has an even number of factors: four.

3. In the next diagram, the left "H"-shaped array is called the 32-H and the right array is the 58-H.

0	1	2	3	4	5	6	7	8	9
10	11	12	13	14	15	16	17	18	19
20	㉑	22	㉓	24	25	26	27	28	29
30	㉛	㉜	㉝	34	35	36	37	38	39
40	㊶	42	㊸	44	45	46	㊼	48	㊾
50	51	52	53	54	55	56	(57)	(58)	(59)
60	61	62	63	64	65	66	(67)	68	(69)
70	71	72	73	74	75	76	77	78	79
80	81	82	83	84	85	86	87	88	89
90	91	92	93	94	95	96	97	98	99

a. Find the sums of the numbers in the 32-H. Do the same for the 58-H and the 74-H. What do you observe?

b. Find an H whose sum is 497.

c. Can you predict the sum in any H if you know the middle number? Explain.

Children's Literature
www.wiley.com/college/musser
See "Patterns in Peru" by Cindy
Neuschwander.

CLUES

The Look for a Pattern strategy may be appropriate when

- A list of data is given.
- A sequence of numbers is involved.
- Listing special cases helps you deal with complex problems.
- You are asked to make a prediction or generalization.
- Information can be expressed and viewed in an organized manner, such as in a table.

Review the preceding three problems to see how these clues may have helped you select the Look for a Pattern strategy to solve these problems.

Reflection from Research
Problem-solving abililty develops
with age, but the relative
difficulty inherent in each
problem is grade independent
(Christou & Philippou, 1998).

Strategy 5   Make a List

The Make a List strategy is often combined with the Look for a Pattern strategy to suggest a solution to a problem. For example, here is a list of all the squares of the numbers 1 to 20 with their ones digits in boldface.

$$\mathbf{1}, \quad \mathbf{4}, \quad \mathbf{9}, \quad 1\mathbf{6}, \quad 2\mathbf{5}, \quad 3\mathbf{6}, \quad 4\mathbf{9}, \quad 6\mathbf{4}, \quad 8\mathbf{1}, \quad 10\mathbf{0},$$
$$12\mathbf{1}, \quad 14\mathbf{4}, \quad 16\mathbf{9}, \quad 19\mathbf{6}, \quad 22\mathbf{5}, \quad 25\mathbf{6}, \quad 28\mathbf{9}, \quad 32\mathbf{4}, \quad 36\mathbf{1}, \quad 40\mathbf{0}$$

The pattern in this list can be used to see that the ones digits of squares must be one of 0, 1, 4, 5, 6, or 9. This list suggests that a perfect square can never end in a 2, 3, 7, or 8.

NCTM Standard
Instructional programs should
enable all students to build new
mathematical knowledge
through problem solving.

Problem

The number 10 can be expressed as the sum of four odd numbers in three ways: (i) $10 = 7 + 1 + 1 + 1$, (ii) $10 = 5 + 3 + 1 + 1$, and (iii) $10 = 3 + 3 + 3 + 1$. In how many ways can 20 be expressed as the sum of eight odd numbers?

Step 1   Understand the Problem

Recall that the odd numbers are the numbers 1, 3, 5, 7, 9, 11, 13, 15, 17, 19, ... Using the fact that 10 can be expressed as the sum of four odd numbers, we can form various combinations of those sums to obtain eight odd numbers whose sum is 20. But does this account for all possibilities?

Step 2   Devise a Plan

Instead, let's make a list starting with the largest possible odd number in the sum and work our way down to the smallest.

Step 3   Carry Out the Plan

$$20 = 13 + 1 + 1 + 1 + 1 + 1 + 1 + 1$$
$$20 = 11 + 3 + 1 + 1 + 1 + 1 + 1 + 1$$
$$20 = 9 + 5 + 1 + 1 + 1 + 1 + 1 + 1$$
$$20 = 9 + 3 + 3 + 1 + 1 + 1 + 1 + 1$$

$$20 = 7 + 7 + 1 + 1 + 1 + 1 + 1 + 1$$
$$20 = 7 + 5 + 3 + 1 + 1 + 1 + 1 + 1$$
$$20 = 7 + 3 + 3 + 3 + 1 + 1 + 1 + 1$$
$$20 = 5 + 5 + 5 + 1 + 1 + 1 + 1 + 1$$
$$20 = 5 + 5 + 3 + 3 + 1 + 1 + 1 + 1$$
$$20 = 5 + 3 + 3 + 3 + 3 + 1 + 1 + 1$$
$$20 = 3 + 3 + 3 + 3 + 3 + 3 + 1 + 1$$

Reflection from Research
Correct answers are not a safe indicator of good thinking. Teachers must examine more than answers and must demand from students more than answers (Sowder, Threadgill-Sowder, Moyer, & Moyer, 1983).

| Step 4 | Look Back

Could you have used the three sums to 10 to help find these 11 sums to 20? Can you think of similar problems to solve? For example, an easier one would be to express 8 as the sum of four odd numbers, and a more difficult one would be to express 40 as the sum of 16 odd numbers. We could also consider sums of even numbers, expressing 20 as the sum of six even numbers.

Additional Problems Where the Strategy "Make a List" Is Useful

1. In a dart game, three darts are thrown. All hit the target (Figure 1.22). What scores are possible?

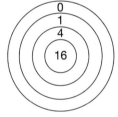

Figure 1.22

| Step 1 | Understand the Problem

Assume that all three darts hit the board. Since there are four different numbers on the board, namely, 0, 1, 4, and 16, three of these numbers, with repetitions allowed, must be hit.

| Step 2 | Devise a Plan

We should make a systematic list by beginning with the smallest (or largest) possible sum. In this way we will be more likely to find all sums.

| Step 3 | Carry Out the Plan

$0 + 0 + 0 = 0$	$0 + 0 + 1 = 1,$	$0 + 1 + 1 = 2,$
$1 + 1 + 1 = 3,$	$0 + 0 + 4 = 4,$	$0 + 1 + 4 = 5,$
$1 + 1 + 4 = 6,$	$0 + 4 + 4 = 8,$	$1 + 4 + 4 = 9,$
$4 + 4 + 4 = 12,$	$\ldots,$	$16 + 16 + 16 = 48$

| Step 4 | Look Back

Several similar problems could be posed by changing the numbers on the dartboard, the number of rings, or the number of darts. Also, using geometric probability, one could ask how to design and label such a game to make it a fair skill game. That is, what points should be assigned to the various regions to reward one fairly for hitting that region?

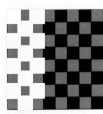

Figure 1.23

2. How many squares, of all sizes, are there on an 8×8 checkerboard? (See Figure 1.23; the sides of the squares are on the lines.)

3. It takes 1230 numerical characters to number the pages of a book. How many pages does the book contain?

CLUES

The Make a List strategy may be appropriate when

- Information can easily be organized and presented.
- Data can easily be generated.
- Listing the results obtained by using Guess and Test.
- Asked "in how many ways" something can be done.
- Trying to learn about a collection of numbers generated by a rule or formula.

Review the preceding three problems to see how these clues may have helped you select the Make a List strategy to solve these problems.

The problem-solving strategy illustrated next could have been employed in conjunction with the Make a List strategy in the preceding problem.

Strategy 6	Solve a Simpler Problem

Like the Make a List strategy, the Solve a Simpler Problem strategy is frequently used in conjunction with the Look for a Pattern strategy. The Solve a Simpler Problem strategy involves reducing the size of the problem at hand and making it more manageable to solve. The simpler problem is then generalized to the original problem.

Problem

In a group of nine coins, eight weigh the same and the ninth is heavier. Assume that the coins are identical in appearance. Using a pan balance, what is the smallest number of balancings needed to identify the heavy coin?

Step 1	Understand the Problem

Coins may be placed on both pans. If one side of the balance is lower than the other, that side contains the heavier coin. If a coin is placed in each pan and the pans balance, the heavier coin is in the remaining seven. We could continue in this way, but if we missed the heavier coin each time we tried two more coins, the last coin would be the heavy one. This would require four balancings. Can we find the heavier coin in fewer balancings?

Step 2	Devise a Plan

To find a more efficient method, let's examine the cases of three coins and five coins before moving to the case of nine coins.

Step 3	Carry Out the Plan

Figure 1.24

Figure 1.25

Three coins: Put one coin on each pan (Figure 1.24). If the pans balance, the third coin is the heavier one. If they don't, the one in the lower pan is the heavier one. Thus, it only takes one balancing to find the heavier coin.

Five coins: Put two coins on each pan (Figure 1.25). If the pans balance, the fifth coin is the heavier one. If they don't, the heavier one is in the lower pan. Remove the two coins in the higher pan and put one of the two coins in the lower pan on the other pan. In this case, the lower pan will have the heavier coin. Thus, it takes at most two balancings to find the heavier coin.

Figure 1.26

Nine coins: At this point, patterns should have been identified that will make this solution easier. In the three-coin problem, it was seen that a heavy coin can be found in a group of three as easily as it can in a group of two. From the five-coin problem, we know that by balancing groups of coins together, we could quickly reduce the number of coins that needed to be examined. These ideas are combined in the nine-coin problem by breaking the nine coins into three groups of three and balancing two groups against each other (Figure 1.26). In this first balancing, the group with the heavy coin is identified. Once the heavy coin has been narrowed to three choices, then the three-coin balancing described above can be used.

The minimum number of balancings needed to locate the heavy coin out of a set of nine coins is two.

Step 4 | Look Back

In solving this problem by using simpler problems, no numerical patterns emerged. However, patterns in the balancing process that could be repeated with a larger number of coins did emerge.

Additional Problems Where the Strategy "Solve a Simpler Problem" Is Useful

1. Find the sum $\dfrac{1}{2} + \dfrac{1}{2^2} + \dfrac{1}{2^3} + \cdots + \dfrac{1}{2^{10}}$.

Step 1 | Understand the Problem

This problem can be solved directly by getting a common denominator, here 2^{10}, and finding the sum of the numerators.

Step 2 | Devise a Plan

Instead of doing a direct calculation, let's combine some previous strategies. Namely, make a list of the first few sums and look for a pattern.

Step 3 | Carry Out the Plan

$$\dfrac{1}{2}, \quad \dfrac{1}{2} + \dfrac{1}{4} = \dfrac{3}{4}, \quad \dfrac{1}{2} + \dfrac{1}{4} + \dfrac{1}{8} = \dfrac{7}{8}, \quad \dfrac{1}{2} + \dfrac{1}{4} + \dfrac{1}{8} + \dfrac{1}{16} = \dfrac{15}{16}$$

The pattern of sums, $\dfrac{1}{2}, \dfrac{3}{4}, \dfrac{7}{8}, \dfrac{15}{16}$, suggests that the sum of the 10 fractions is $\dfrac{2^{10} - 1}{2^{10}}$, or $\dfrac{1023}{1024}$.

Step 4 | Look Back

Algebraic Reasoning
Using a variable, the sum to the right can be expressed more generally as follows:

$$\dfrac{1}{2} + \dfrac{1}{2^2} + \cdots + \dfrac{1}{2^n} = \dfrac{2^n - 1}{2^n}.$$

This method of combining the strategy of Solve a Simpler Problem with Make a List and Look for a Pattern is very useful. For example, what is the sum $\dfrac{1}{2} + \dfrac{1}{2^2} + \cdots + \dfrac{1}{2^{100}}$? Because of the large denominators, you wouldn't want to add these fractions directly.

2. Following the arrows in Figure 1.27, how many paths are there from *A* to *B*?

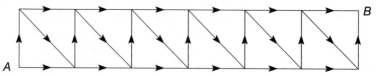

Figure 1.27

3. There are 20 people at a party. If each person shakes hands with each other person, how many handshakes will there be?

CLUES

The Solve a Simpler Problem strategy may be appropriate when

- The problem involves complicated computations.
- The problem involves very large or very small numbers.
- A direct solution is too complex.
- You want to gain a better understanding of the problem.
- The problem involves a large array or diagram.

Review the preceding three problems to see how these clues may have helped you select the Solve a Simpler Problem strategy to solve these problems.

Combining Strategies to Solve Problems

Reflection from Research
The development of a disposition toward realistic mathematical modeling and interpreting of word problems should permeate the entire curriculum from the outset (Verschaffel & DeCorte, 1997).

As shown in the previous four-step solution, it is often useful to employ several strategies to solve a problem. For example, in Section 1.1, a pizza problem similar to the following was posed: What is the maximum number of pieces you can cut a pizza into using four straight cuts? This question can be extended to the more general question: What is the maximum number of pieces you can cut a pizza into using n straight cuts? To answer this, consider the sequence in Figure 1.9: 1, 2, 4, 7, 11. To identify patterns in a sequence, observing how successive terms are related can be helpful. In this case, the second term of 2 can be obtained from the first term of 1 by either adding 1 or multiplying by 2. The third term, 4, can be obtained from the second term, 2, by adding 2 or multiplying by 2. Although multiplying by 2 appears to be a pattern, it fails as we move from the third term to the fourth term. The fourth term can be found by adding 3 to the third term. Thus, the sequence appears to be the following:

Extending the difference sequence, we obtain the following

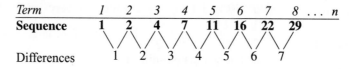

Algebraic Reasoning
In order to generalize patterns, one must first identify what is staying the same (the initial 1) and what is changing (the difference is increasing by one) with each step. Secondly, one must notice the relationship between what is changing and the step number.

Starting with 1 in the sequence, dropping down to the difference line, then back up to the number in the sequence line, we find the following:

1st Term: **1** $= 1$

2nd Term: **2** $= 1 + 1$

3rd Term: **4** $= 1 + (1 + 2)$

4th Term: **7** $= 1 + (1 + 2 + 3)$

5th Term: **11** $= 1 + (1 + 2 + 3 + 4)$, and so forth

Recall that earlier we saw that $1 + 2 + 3 + \ldots + n = \dfrac{n(n + 1)}{2}$. Thus, the nth term in the sequence is $1 + [1 + 2 + \ldots + (n - 1)] = 1 + \dfrac{(n - 1)n}{2}$. Notice that as a check, the eighth term in the sequence is $1 + \dfrac{7 \cdot 8}{2} = 1 + 28 = 29$. Hence, to solve the original problem, we used Draw a Picture, Look for a Pattern, and Use a Variable.

It may be that a pattern does not become obvious after one set of differences. Consider the following problem where several differences are required to expose the pattern.

Problem If 10 points are placed on a circle and each pair of points is connected with a segment, what is the maximum number of regions created by these segments?

Step 1 Understand the Problem

This problem can be better understood by drawing a picture. Since drawing 10 points and all of the joining segments may be overwhelming, looking at a simpler problem of circles with 1, 2, or 3 points on them may help in further understanding the problem. The first three cases are in Figure 1.28.

Figure 1.28

Step 2 Devise a Plan

So far, the number of regions are 1, 2, and 4 respectively. Here, again, this could be the start of the pattern, 1, 2, 4, 8, 16, ... Let's draw three more pictures to see if this is the case. Then the pattern can be generalized to the case of 10 points.

Step 3 Carry Out the Plan

The next three cases are shown in Figure 1.29.

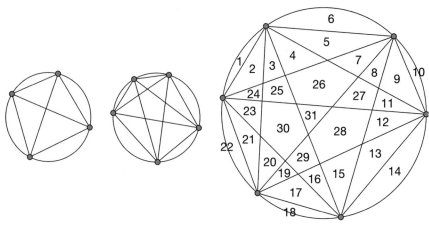

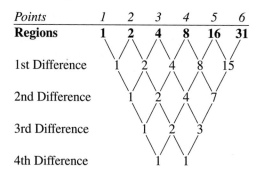

Figure 1.29

Making a list of the number of points on the circle and the corresponding number of regions will help us see the pattern.

Points	1	2	3	4	5	6
Regions	1	2	4	8	16	31

While the pattern for the first five cases makes it appear as if the number of regions are just doubling with each additional point, the 31 regions with 6 points ruins this pattern. Consider the differences between the numbers in the pattern and look for a pattern in the differences.

Points	*1*	*2*	*3*	*4*	*5*	*6*
Regions	**1**	**2**	**4**	**8**	**16**	**31**
1st Difference		1	2	4	8	15
2nd Difference			1	2	4	7
3rd Difference				1	2	3
4th Difference					1	1

Because the first, second, and third difference did not indicate a clear pattern, the fourth difference was computed and revealed a pattern of all ones. This observation is used to extend the pattern by adding four 1s to the two 1s in the fourth difference to make a sequence of six 1s. Then we work up until the Regions sequence has ten numbers as shown next.

Points	*1*	*2*	*3*	*4*	*5*	*6*	*7*	*8*	*9*	*10*
Regions	**1**	**2**	**4**	**8**	**16**	**31**	**57**	**99**	**163**	**256**
1st Difference		1	2	4	8	15	26	42	64	93
2nd Difference			1	2	4	7	11	16	22	29
3rd Difference				1	2	3	4	5	6	7
4th Difference					1	1	1	1	1	1

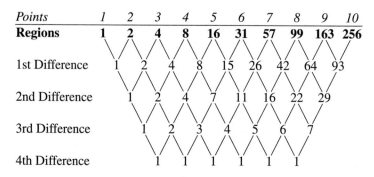

By finding successive differences, it can be seen that the solution to our problem is 256 regions.

| Step 4 | Look Back

By using a combination of Draw a Picture, Solve a Simpler Problem, Make a List, and Look for a Pattern, the solution was found. It can also be seen that it is important when looking for such patterns to realize that we may have to look at many terms and many differences to be able to find the pattern.

Recapitulation

When presenting the problems in this chapter, we took great care in organizing the solutions using Pólya's four-step approach. However, it is not necessary to label and display each of the four steps every time you work a problem. On the other hand, it is good to get into the habit of recalling the four steps as you plan and as you work through a problem. In this chapter we have introduced several useful problem-solving strategies. In each of the following chapters, a new problem-solving strategy is introduced. These strategies will be especially helpful when you are making a plan. As you are planning to solve a problem, think of the strategies as a collection of tools. Then an important part of solving a problem can be viewed as selecting an appropriate tool or strategy.

We end this chapter with a list of suggestions that students who have successfully completed a course on problem solving felt were helpful tips. Reread this list periodically as you progress through the book.

Suggestions from Successful Problem Solvers

- Accept the challenge of solving a problem.
- Rewrite the problem in your own words.
- Take time to explore, reflect, think. . . .
- Talk to yourself. Ask yourself lots of questions.
- If appropriate, try the problem using simple numbers.
- Many problems require an incubation period. If you get frustrated, do not hesitate to take a break—your subconscious may take over. But do return to try again.
- Look at the problem in a variety of ways.
- Run through your list of strategies to see whether one (or more) can help you get a start.
- Many problems can be solved in a variety of ways—you only need to find one solution to be successful.
- Do not be afraid to change your approach, strategy, and so on.
- Organization can be helpful in problem solving. Use the Pólya four-step approach with a variety of strategies.
- Experience in problem solving is very valuable. *Work lots of problems*; your confidence will grow.
- If you are not making much progress, do not hesitate to go back to make sure that you really understand the problem. This review process may happen two or three times in a problem since understanding usually grows as you work toward a solution.
- There is nothing like a breakthrough, a small *aha!*, as you solve a problem.

Reflection from Research
Having children write their own story problems helps students to discern between relevant and irrelevant attributes in a problem and to focus on the various parts of a problem, such as the known and unknown quantities (Whitin & Whitin, 2008).

Reflection from Research
The unrealistic expectations of teachers, namely lack of time and support, can cause young students to struggle with problem solving (Buschman, 2002).

- Always, always look back. Try to see precisely what the key step was in your solution.
- Make up and solve problems of your own.
- Write up your solutions neatly and clearly enough so that you will be able to understand your solution if you reread it in 10 years.
- Develop good problem-solving helper skills when assisting others in solving problems. Do not give out solutions; instead, provide meaningful hints.
- By helping and giving hints to others, you will find that you will develop many new insights.
- Enjoy yourself! Solving a problem is a positive experience.

MATHEMATICAL MORSEL

Sophie Germain was born in Paris in 1776, the daughter of a silk merchant. At the age of 13, she found a book on the history of mathematics in her father's library. She became enthralled with the study of mathematics. Even though her parents disapproved of this pursuit, nothing daunted her—she studied at night wrapped in a blanket, because her parents had taken her clothing away from her to keep her from getting up. They also took away her heat and light. This only hardened her resolve until her father finally gave in and she, at last, was allowed to study to become a mathematician.

Section 1.2   EXERCISE / PROBLEM SET A

Use any of the six problem-solving strategies introduced thus far to solve the following.

1. a. Complete this table and describe the pattern in the 'Answer' column.

SUM	ANSWER
1	1
1 + 3	4
1 + 3 + 5	
1 + 3 + 5 + 7	
1 + 3 + 5 + 7 + 9	

  b. How many odd whole numbers would have to be added to get a sum of 81? Check your guess by adding them.
  c. How many odd whole numbers would have to be added to get a sum of 169? Check your guess by adding them.
  d. How many odd whole numbers would have to be added to get a sum of 529? (You do not need to check.)

2. Find the missing term in each pattern.
  a. 256, 128, 64, _____, 16, 8
  b. $1, \dfrac{1}{3}, \dfrac{1}{9},$ _____ $, \dfrac{1}{81}$

  c. 7, 9, 12, 16, _____
  d. 127,863; 12,789; _____; 135; 18

3. Sketch a figure that is next in each sequence.

a.

b.

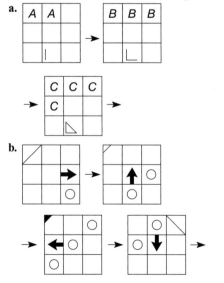

4. Consider the following differences. Use your calculator to verify that the statements are true.

$$6^2 - 5^2 = 11$$
$$56^2 - 45^2 = 1111$$
$$556^2 - 445^2 = 111,111$$

a. Predict the next line in the sequence of differences. Use your calculator to check your answer.
b. What do you think the eighth line will be?

5. Look for a pattern in the first two number grids. Then use the pattern you observed to fill in the missing numbers of the third grid.

6. The **triangular numbers** are the whole numbers that are represented by certain triangular arrays of dots. The first five triangular numbers are shown.

1   2   3   4   5

a. Complete the following table and describe the pattern in the 'Number of Dots' column.

NUMBER	NUMBER OF DOTS (TRIANGULAR NUMBERS)
1	1
2	3
3	
4	
5	
6	

b. Make a sketch to represent the seventh triangular number.
c. How many dots will be in the tenth triangular number?
d. Is there a triangular number that has 91 dots in its shape? If so, which one?
e. Is there a triangular number that has 150 dots in its shape? If so, which one?
f. Write a formula for the number of dots in the *n*th triangular number.
g. When the famous mathematician Carl Friedrich Gauss was in fourth grade, his teacher challenged him to add the first one hundred counting numbers. Find this sum.

$$1 + 2 + 3 + \ldots + 100$$

7. In a group of 12 coins identical in appearance, all weigh the same except one that is heavier. What is the minimum number of weighings required to determine the counterfeit coin? Use the Chapter 1 eManipulative activity *Counterfeit Coin* on our Web site for eight or nine coins to better understand the problem.

8. If 20 points are placed on a circle and every pair of points is joined with a segment, what is the total number of segments drawn?

9. Find reasonable sixth, seventh, and eighth terms of the following sequences:
a. 1, 4, 9, 17, 29, _____, _____, _____
b. 3, 7, 13, 21, 31, _____, _____, _____

10. As mentioned in this section, the square numbers are the counting numbers 1, 4, 9, 16, 25, 36, ... Each square number can be represented by a square array of dots as shown in the following figure, where the second square number has four dots, and so on. The first four square numbers are shown.

a. Find two triangular numbers (refer to Problem 6) whose sum equals the third square number.
b. Find two triangular numbers whose sum equals the fifth square number.
c. What two triangular numbers have a sum that equals the 10th square number? the 20th square number? the *n*th square number?
d. Find a triangular number that is also a square number.
e. Find five pairs of square numbers whose difference is a triangular number.

11. Would you rather work for a month (30 days) and get paid 1 million dollars or be paid 1 cent the first day, 2 cents the second day, 4 cents the third day, 8 cents the fourth day, and so on? Explain.

12. Find the perimeters and then complete the table.

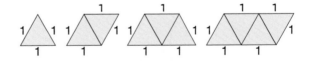

number of triangles	1	2	3	4	5	6	10		*n*
perimeter								40	

13. The integers greater than 1 are arranged as shown.

```
        2   3   4   5
    9   8   7   6
        10  11  12  13
    17  16  15  14
            ·   ·   ·
```

    a. In which column will 100 fall?
    b. In which column will 1000 fall?
    c. How about 1999?
    d. How about 99,997?

14. How many cubes are in the 100th collection of cubes in this sequence?

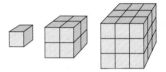

 15. The Fibonacci sequence is 1, 1, 2, 3, 5, 8, 13, 21, . . . , where each successive number beginning with 2 is the sum of the preceding two; for example, $13 = 5 + 8, 21 = 8 + 13$, and so on. Observe the following pattern.

$$1^2 + 1^2 = 1 \times 2$$
$$1^2 + 1^2 + 2^2 = 2 \times 3$$
$$1^2 + 1^2 + 2^2 + 3^2 = 3 \times 5$$

Write out six more terms of the Fibonacci sequence and use the sequence to predict what $1^2 + 1^2 + 2^2 + 3^2 + \ldots + 144^2$ is without actually computing the sum. Then use your calculator to check your result.

 16. Write out 16 terms of the Fibonacci sequence and observe the following pattern:

$$1 + 2 = 3$$
$$1 + 2 + 5 = 8$$
$$1 + 2 + 5 + 13 = 21$$

Use the pattern you observed to predict the sum

$$1 + 2 + 5 + 13 + \ldots + 610$$

without actually computing the sum. Then use your calculator to check your result.

 17. Pascal's triangle is where each entry other than a 1 is obtained by adding the two entries in the row above it.

```
        1
      1   1
    1   2   1
  1   3   3   1
1   4   6   4   1
  ·   ·   ·   ·   ·   ·
```

    a. Find the sums of the numbers on the diagonals in Pascal's triangle as are indicated in the following figure.

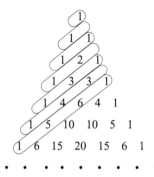

    b. Predict the sums along the next three diagonals in Pascal's triangle without actually adding the entries. Check your answers by adding entries on your calculator.

18. Answer the following questions about Pascal's triangle (see Problem 17).
    a. In the triangle shown here, one number, namely 3, and the six numbers immediately surrounding it are encircled. Find the sum of the encircled seven numbers.

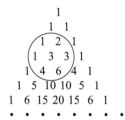

    b. Extend Pascal's triangle by adding a few rows. Then draw several more circles anywhere in the triangle like the one shown in part (a). Explain how the sums obtained by adding the seven numbers inside the circle are related to one of the numbers outside the circle.

19. Consider the following sequence of shapes. The sequence starts with one square. Then at each step squares are attached around the outside of the figure, one square per exposed edge in the figure.

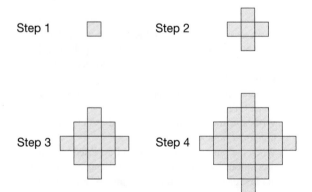

a. Draw the next two figures in the sequence.
b. Make a table listing the number of unit squares in the figure at each step. Look for a pattern in the number of unit squares. (*Hint:* Consider the number of squares attached at each step.)
c. Based on the pattern you observed, predict the number of squares in the figure at step 7. Draw the figure to check your answer.
d. How many squares would there be in the 10th figure? in the 20th figure? in the 50th figure?

20. In a dart game, only 4 points or 9 points can be scored on each dart. What is the largest score that it is *not* possible to obtain? (Assume that you have an unlimited number of darts.)

21. If the following four figures are referred to as stars, the first one is a three-pointed star and the second one is a six-pointed star. (*Note:* If this pattern of constructing a new equilateral triangle on each side of the existing

equilateral triangle is continued indefinitely, the resulting figure is called the **Koch curve** or **Koch snowflake**.)

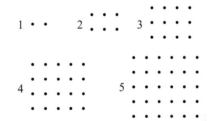

a. How many points are there in the third star?
b. How many points are there in the fourth star?

22. Using the Chapter 1 eManipulative activity *Color Patterns* on our Web site, describe the color patterns for the first three computer exercises.

23. Looking for a pattern can be frustrating if the pattern is not immediately obvious. Create your own sequence of numbers that follows a pattern but that has the capacity to stump some of your fellow students. Then write an explanation of how they might have been able to discover your pattern.

Section 1.2 **EXERCISE / PROBLEM SET B**

1. Find the missing term in each pattern.
  a. 10, 17, _____, 37, 50, 65
  b. $1, \dfrac{3}{2},$ _____ $, \dfrac{7}{8}, \dfrac{9}{16}$
  c. 243, 324, 405, _____, 567
  d. 234; _____; 23,481; 234,819; 2,348,200

2. Sketch a figure that is next in each sequence.

  a.

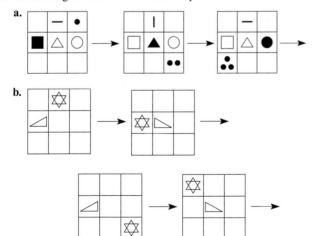

  b.

3. The **rectangular numbers** are whole numbers that are represented by certain rectangular arrays of dots. The first five rectangular numbers are shown.

a. Complete the following table and describe the pattern in the 'Number of Dots' column.

NUMBER	NUMBER OF DOTS (RECTANGULAR NUMBERS)
1	2
2	6
3	
4	
5	
6	

b. Make a sketch to represent the seventh rectangular number.
c. How many dots will be in the tenth rectangular number?
d. Is there a rectangular number that has 380 dots in its shape? If so, which one?
e. Write a formula for the number of dots in the *n*th rectangular number.
f. What is the connection between triangular numbers (see Problem 6 in Part A) and rectangular numbers?

4. The **pentagonal numbers** are whole numbers that are represented by pentagonal shapes. The first four pentagonal numbers are shown.

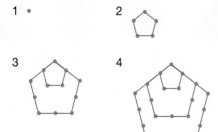

1 •   2

3   4

a. Complete the following table and describe the pattern in the 'Number of Dots' column.

NUMBER	NUMBER OF DOTS (PENTAGONAL NUMBERS)
1	1
2	5
3	
4	
5	

b. Make a sketch to represent the fifth pentagonal number.
c. How many dots will be in the ninth pentagonal number?
d. Is there a pentagonal number that has 200 dots in its shape? If so, which one?
e. Write a formula for the number of dots in the nth pentagonal number.

5. Consider the following process.
   i. Choose a whole number.
   ii. Add the squares of the digits of the number to get a new number.
   Repeat step 2 several times.
   a. Apply the procedure described to the numbers 12, 13, 19, 21, and 127.
   b. What pattern do you observe as you repeat the steps over and over?
   c. Check your answer for part (b) with a number of your choice.

6. How many triangles are in the picture?

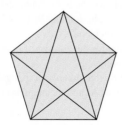

7. What is the smallest number that can be expressed as the sum of two squares in two different ways? (You may use one square twice.)

8. How many cubes are in the 10th collection of cubes in this sequence?

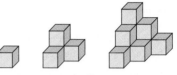

9. The 2×2 array of numbers $\begin{bmatrix} 4 & 5 \\ 5 & 6 \end{bmatrix}$ has a sum of 4×5,

and the 3×3 array $\begin{bmatrix} 6 & 7 & 8 \\ 7 & 8 & 9 \\ 8 & 9 & 10 \end{bmatrix}$ has a sum of 9×8.

   a. What will be the sum of the similar 4×4 array starting with 7?
   b. What will be the sum of a similar 100×100 array starting with 100?

10. The Fibonacci sequence was defined to be the sequence 1, 1, 2, 3, 5, 8, 13, 21, . . . , where each successive number is the sum of the preceding two. Observe the following pattern.

$$1 + 1 = 3 - 1$$
$$1 + 1 + 2 = 5 - 1$$
$$1 + 1 + 2 + 3 = 8 - 1$$
$$1 + 1 + 2 + 3 + 5 = 13 - 1$$

Write out six more terms of the Fibonacci sequence, and use the sequence to predict the answer to

$$1 + 1 + 2 + 3 + 5 + \ldots + 144$$

without actually computing the sum. Then use your calculator to check your result.

11. Write out 16 terms of the Fibonacci sequence.
   a. Notice that the fourth term in the sequence (called F_4) is odd: $F_4 = 3$. The sixth term in the sequence (called F_6) is even: $F_6 = 8$. Look for a pattern in the terms of the sequence, and describe which terms are even and which are odd.
   b. Which of the following terms of the Fibonacci sequence are even and which are odd: $F_{38}, F_{51}, F_{150}, F_{200}, F_{300}$?
   c. Look for a pattern in the terms of the sequence and describe which terms are divisible by 3.
   d. Which of the following terms of the Fibonacci sequence are multiples of 3: $F_{48}, F_{75}, F_{196}, F_{379}, F_{1000}$?

12. Write out 16 terms of the Fibonacci sequence and observe the following pattern.

$$1 + 3 = 5 - 1$$
$$1 + 3 + 8 = 13 - 1$$
$$1 + 3 + 8 + 21 = 34 - 1$$

Use the pattern you observed to predict the answer to

$$1 + 3 + 8 + 21 + \ldots + 377$$

without actually computing the sum. Then use your calculator to check your result.

13. Investigate the "Tower of Hanoi" problem on the Chapter 1 eManipulative activity *Tower of Hanoi* on our Web site to answer the following questions:
  a. Determine the fewest number of moves required when you start with two, three, and four disks.
  b. Describe the general process to move the disks in the fewest number of moves.
  c. What is the minimum number of moves that it should take to move six disks?

14. While only 19 years old, Carl Friedrich Gauss proved in 1796 that every positive integer is the sum of at the most three triangular numbers (see Problem 6 in Part A).
  a. Express each of the numbers 25 to 35 as a sum of no more than three triangular numbers.
  b. Express the numbers 74, 81, and 90 as sums of no more than three triangular numbers.

15. Answer the following for Pascal's triangle.
  a. In the following triangle, six numbers surrounding a central number, 4, are circled. Compare the products of alternate numbers moving around the circle; that is, compare $3 \cdot 1 \cdot 10$ and $6 \cdot 1 \cdot 5$.

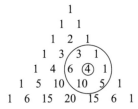

  b. Extend Pascal's triangle by adding a few rows. Then draw several more circles like the one shown in part (a) anywhere in the triangle. Find the products as described in part (a). What patterns do you see in the products?

16. A certain type of gutter comes in 6-foot, 8-foot, and 10-foot sections. How many different lengths can be formed using three sections of gutter?

17. Consider the sequence of shapes shown in the following figure. The sequence starts with one triangle. Then at each step, triangles are attached to the outside of the preceding figure, one triangle per exposed edge.

Step 1   Step 2

Step 3   Step 4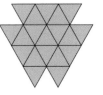

a. Draw the next two figures in the sequence.
b. Make a table listing the number of triangles in the figure at each step. Look for a pattern in the number of triangles. (*Hint:* Consider the number of triangles added at each step.)
c. Based on the pattern you observed, predict the number of triangles in the figure at step 7. Draw the figure to check your answer.
d. How many triangles would there be in the 10th figure? in the 20th figure? in the 50th figure?

18. How many equilateral triangles of all sizes are there in the $3 \times 3 \times 3$ equilateral triangle shown next?

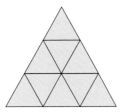

19. Refer to the following figures to answer the questions. (NOTE: If this pattern is continued indefinitely, the resulting figure is called the **Sierpinski triangle** or the **Sierpinski gasket**.)

a. How many black triangles are there in the fourth figure?
b. How many white triangles are there in the fourth figure?
c. If the pattern is continued, how many black triangles are there in the *n*th figure?
d. If the pattern is continued, how many white triangles are there in the *n*th figure?

20. If the pattern illustrated next is continued,
  a. find the total number of 1 by 1 squares in the thirtieth figure.
  b. find the perimeter of the twenty-fifth figure.
  c. find the total number of toothpicks used to construct the twentieth figure.

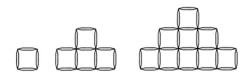

21. Find reasonable sixth, seventh, and eighth terms of the following sequences:
  a. 1, 3, 4, 7, 11, _____, _____, _____
  b. 0, 1, 4, 12, 29, _____, _____, _____

22. Many board games involve throwing two dice and summing of the numbers that come up to determine how many squares to move. Make a list of all the different sums that can appear. Then write down how many ways each different sum can be formed. For example, 11 can be formed in two ways: from a 5 on the first die and a 6 on the second OR a 6 on the first die and a 5 on the second. Which sum has the greatest number of combinations? What conclusion could you draw from that?

23. There is an old riddle about a frog at the bottom of a 20-foot well. If he climbs up 3 feet each day and slips back 2 feet each night, how many days will it take him to reach the 20-foot mark and climb out of the well? The answer isn't 20. Try doing the problem with a well that is only 5 feet deep, and keep track of all the frog's moves. What strategy are you using?

 Analyzing Student Thinking

24. Marietta extended the pattern 2, 4, 8 to be 2, 4, 8, 16, 32, ... Pascuel extended the same pattern to be 2, 4, 8, 14, 22, ... They asked you who was correct. How should you respond?

25. Eula is asked to find the following sum: 1 + 3 + 5 + 7 + ⋯ + 97 + 99. She decided to "solve a simpler problem" but doesn't know where to start. What would you suggest?

26. When Mickey counted the number of outcomes of rolling two 4-sided, tetrahedral dice (see Figure 12.89 for an example of a tetrahedron), he decided to "make a list" and got (1,1), (2,2), (3,3), (4,4), (1,2), (3,4), (2,4), (4,1). He started to get confused about which ones he had listed and which ones were left. How would you help him create a more systematic list?

27. Bridgette says that she knows how to see patterns like 3, 7, 11, 15, 19, . . . and 5, 12, 19, 26, 33, . . . because "you are just adding the same amount each time." However, she can't see the pattern in 3, 5, 9, 15, 23 because the difference between the numbers is changing. How could you help her see this new pattern?

28. Jeremy is asked to find the number of rectangles of all possible dimensions in the figure below and decides to "solve a simpler problem."

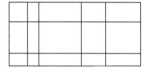

What simpler problem would you suggest he use?

29. After solving several simpler problems, Janell commented that she often makes a list of solutions of the simpler problems and then looks for a pattern in that list. She asks if it is okay to use more than one type of strategy when solving the same problem. How should you respond?

Problems Related to the NCTM Standards and Curriculum Focal Points

1. The Focal Points for Grade 3 state "Apply increasingly sophisticated strategies . . . to solve multiplication and division problems." Find a problem in this problem set that illustrates this statement and explain your reasoning.

2. The NCTM Standards state "Instructional programs should enable all students to build new mathematical knowledge through problem solving." Explain some new mathematical knowledge that you have learned by solving problems in this section.

3. The NCTM Standards state "All students should represent, analyze, and generalize a variety of patterns with tables, graphs, and, when possible, symbolic rules." Explain how tables, graphs, and symbolic rules could be used to represent and analyze the pattern in Problem 11 of Problem Set A.

END OF CHAPTER MATERIAL

Place the whole numbers 1 through 9 in the circles in the accompanying triangle so that the sum of the numbers on each side is 17.

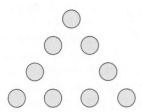

Strategy: Guess and Test

Having solved a simpler problem in this chapter, you might easily be able to conclude that 1, 2, and 3 must be in the corners. Then the remaining six numbers, 4, 5, 6, 7, 8, and 9, must produce three pairs of numbers whose sums are 12, 13, and 14. The only two possible solutions are as shown.

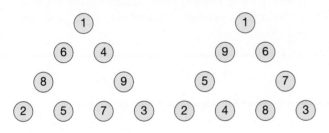

Solution for Additional Problems

Guess and Test

1. $s = 1, u = 3, n = 6, f = 9, w = 0, i = 7, m = 2$
2. $0 = (4 - 4) + (4 - 4)$
$1 = (4 + 4) \div (4 + 4)$
$2 = (4 \div 4) + (4 \div 4)$
$3 = (4 + 4 + 4) \div 4$
$4 = 4 + 4 \times (4 - 4)$
$5 = (4 \times 4 + 4) \div 4$
$6 = ((4 + 4) \div 4) + 4$
$7 = 4 + 4 - (4 \div 4)$
$8 = ((4 \times 4) \div 4) + 4$
$9 = 4 + 4 + (4 \div 4)$
There are many other possible answers.

3.

Draw a Picture

1. 5
2. Yes; make one cut, then lay the logs side by side for the second cut.
3. 12

Use a Variable

1. 55, 5050, 125,250
2. $(2m + 1) + (2m + 3) + (2m + 5) + (2m + 7) + (2m + 9)$
$= 10m + 25 = 5(2m + 5)$
3. 10°, 80°, 90°

Look for a Pattern

1. 7
2. Square numbers
3. a. 224; 406; 518   **b.** 71
    c. The sum is seven times the middle number.

Make a List

1. 48, 36, 33, 32, 24, 21, 20, 18, 17, 16, 12, 9, 8, 6, 5, 4, 3, 2, 1, 0
2. 204
3. 446

Solve a Simpler Problem

1. $\dfrac{1023}{1024}$
2. 377
3. 190

People in Mathematics

Carl Friedrich Gauss (1777–1885)
Carl Friedrich Gauss, according to the historian E. T. Bell, "lives everywhere in mathematics." His contributions to geometry, number theory, and analysis were deep and wide-ranging. Yet he also made crucial contributions in applied mathematics. When the tiny planet Ceres was discovered in 1800, Gauss developed a technique for calculating its orbit, based on meager observations of its direction from Earth at several known times. Gauss contributed to the modern theory of electricity and magnetism, and with the physicist W. E. Weber constructed one of the first practical electric telegraphs. In 1807 he became director of the astronomical observatory at Gottingen, where he served until his death. At age 18, Gauss devised a method for constructing a 17-sided regular polygon, using only a compass and straightedge. Remarkably, he then derived a general rule that predicted which regular polygons are likewise constructible.

Sophie Germain (1776–1831)
Sophie Germain, as a teenager in Paris, discovered mathematics by reading books from her father's library. At age 18, Germain wished to attend the prestigious Ecole Polytechnique in Paris, but women were not admitted. So she studied from classroom notes supplied by sympathetic male colleagues, and she began submitting written work using the pen name Antoine LeBlanc. This work won her high praise, and eventually she was able to reveal her true identity. Germain is noted for her theory of the vibration patterns of elastic plates and for her proof of Fermat's last theorem in some special cases. Of Sophie Germain, Carl Gauss wrote, "When a woman, because of her sex, encounters infinitely more obstacles than men . . . yet overcomes these fetters and penetrates that which is most hidden, she doubtless has the most noble courage, extraordinary talent, and superior genius."

CHAPTER REVIEW

Review the following terms and problems to determine which require learning or relearning—page numbers are provided for easy reference.

SECTION 1.1 The Problem-Solving Process and Strategies

VOCABULARY/NOTATION

Exercise   4
Problem   4
Pólya's four-step process   4
Strategy   4
Random Guess and Test   6

Systematic Guess and Test   6
Inferential Guess and Test   6
Cryptarithm   7
Tetromino   10
Variable or unknown   11

Equation   15
Solution of an equation   15
Solve an equation   15

PROBLEMS

For each of the following, (i) determine a reasonable strategy to use to solve the problem, (ii) state a clue that suggested the strategy, and (iii) write out a solution using Pólya's four-step process.

1. Fill in the circles using the numbers 1 through 9 once each where the sum along each of the five rows totals 17.

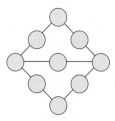

2. In the following arithmagon, the number that appears in a square is the product of the numbers in the circles on each side of it. Determine what numbers belong in the circles.

3. The floor of a square room is covered with square tiles. Walking diagonally across the room from corner to corner, Susan counted a total of 33 tiles on the two diagonals. What is the total number of tiles covering the floor of the room?

SECTION 1.2 Three Additional Strategies

VOCABULARY/NOTATION

Pascal's triangle 22	Ellipsis 22	Powers 22
Sequence 22	Even numbers 22	Fibonacci sequence 22
Terms 22	Odd numbers 22	Inductive reasoning 23
Counting numbers 22	Square numbers 22	

PROBLEMS

For each of the following, (i) determine a reasonable strategy to use to solve the problem, (ii) state a clue that suggested the strategy, and (iii) write out a solution using Pólya's four-step process.

1. Consider the following products. Use your calculator to verify that the statements are true.

$$1 \times (1) = 1^2$$
$$121 \times (1 + 2 + 1) = 22^2$$
$$12321 \times (1 + 2 + 3 + 2 + 1) = 333^2$$

Predict the next line in the sequence of products. Use your calculator to check your answer.

2. a. How many cubes of all sizes are in a $2 \times 2 \times 2$ cube composed of eight $1 \times 1 \times 1$ cubes?
   b. How many cubes of all sizes are in an $8 \times 8 \times 8$ cube composed of 512 $1 \times 1 \times 1$ cubes?

3. a. What is the smallest number of whole-number gram weights needed to weigh any whole-number amount from 1 to 12 grams on a scale allowing the weights to be placed on either or both sides?
   b. How about from 1 to 37 grams?
   c. What is the most you can weigh using six weights in this way?

CHAPTER TEST

KNOWLEDGE

1. List the four steps of Pólya's problem-solving process.

2. List the six problem-solving strategies you have learned in this chapter.

SKILL

3. Identify the unneeded information in the following problem.

Birgit took her $5 allowance to the bookstore to buy some back-to-school supplies. The pencils cost $.10, the erasers cost $.05 each, and the clips cost 2 for $.01. If she bought 100 items altogether at a total cost of $1, how many of each item did she buy?

4. Rewrite the following problem in your own words.

If you add the square of Ruben's age to the age of Angelita, the sum is 62; but if you add the square of Angelita's age to the age of Ruben, the sum is 176. Can you say what the ages of Ruben and Angelita are?

5. Given the following problem and its numerical answer, write the solution in a complete sentence.

Amanda leaves with a basket of hard-boiled eggs to sell. At her first stop she sold half her eggs plus half an egg. At her second stop she sold half her eggs plus half an egg. The same thing occurs at her third, fourth, and fifth stops. When she finishes, she has no eggs in her basket. How many eggs did she start with?
Answer: 31

UNDERSTANDING

6. Explain the difference between an *exercise* and a *problem*.

7. List at least two characteristics of a problem that would suggest using the Guess and Test strategy.

8. List at least two characteristics of a problem that would suggest using the Use a Variable strategy.

PROBLEM SOLVING / APPLICATION

For each of the following problems, read the problem carefully and solve it. Identify the strategy you used.

9. Can you rearrange the 16 numbers in this 4 × 4 array so that each row, each column, and each of the two diagonals total 10? How about a 2 × 2 array containing two 1s and two 2s? How about the corresponding 3 × 3 array?

1	1	1	1
2	2	2	2
3	3	3	3
4	4	4	4

10. In three years, Chad will be three times my *present* age. I will then be half as old as he. How old am I now?

11. There are six baseball teams in a tournament. The teams are lettered A through F. Each team plays each of the other teams twice. How many games are played altogether?

12. A fish is 30 inches long. The head is as long as the tail. If the head was twice as long and the tail was its present length, the body would be 18 inches long. How long is each portion of the fish?

13. The Orchard brothers always plant their apple trees in square arrays, like those illustrated. This year they planted 31 more apple trees in their square orchard than last year. If the orchard is still square, how many apple trees are there in the orchard this year?

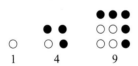

14. Arrange 10 people so that there are five rows each containing 4 persons.

15. A milk crate holds 24 bottles and is shaped like the one shown below. The crate has four rows and six columns. Is it possible to put 18 bottles of milk in the crate so that each row and each column of the crate has an even number of bottles in it? If so, how? (*Hint:* One row has 6 bottles in it and the other three rows have 4 bottles in them.)

16. Otis has 12 coins in his pocket worth $1.10. If he only has nickels, dimes, and quarters, what are all of the possible coin combinations?

17. Show why 3 always divides evenly into the sum of any three consecutive whole numbers.

18. If 14 toothpicks are arranged to form a triangle so none of the toothpicks are broken or bent and all 14 toothpicks are used, how many different-shaped triangles can be formed?

19. Together a baseball and a football weigh 1.25 pounds, the baseball and a soccer ball weigh 1.35 pounds, and the football and the soccer ball weigh 1.6 pounds. How much does each of the balls weigh? Explain your reasoning.

20. In the figure below, there are 7 chairs arranged around 5 tables. How many chairs could be placed around a similar arrangement of 31 triangular tables?

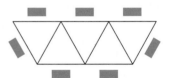

21. Carlos' father pays Carlos his allowance each week using patterns. He pays a different amount each day according to some pattern. Carlos must identify the pattern in order to receive his allowance. Help Carlos complete the pattern for the missing days in each week below.

a. 5¢, 9¢, 16¢, 26¢, _____, _____, _____
b. 1¢, 6¢, 15¢, 30¢, 53¢, _____, _____
c. 4¢, 8¢, 16¢, 28¢, _____, _____, _____

Sets, Whole Numbers, and Numeration

The Mayan Numeration System

The Maya people lived mainly in southeastern Mexico, including the Yucatan Peninsula, and in much of northwestern Central America, including Guatemala and parts of Honduras and El Salvador. Earliest archaeological evidence of the Maya civilization dates to 9000 B.C.E., with the principal epochs of the Maya cultural development occurring between 2000 B.C.E. and C.E. 1700.

Knowledge of arithmetic, calendrical, and astronomical matters was more highly developed by the ancient Maya than by any other New World peoples. Their numeration system was simple, yet sophisticated. Their system utilized three basic numerals: a dot, •, to represent 1; a horizontal bar, —, to represent 5; and a conch shell, ⬭, to represent 0. They used these three symbols, in combination, to represent the numbers 0 through 19.

For numbers greater than 19, they initially used a base 20 system. That is, they grouped in twenties and displayed their numerals vertically. Three Mayan numerals are shown together with their values in our system and the place values initially used by the Mayans.

The sun, and hence the solar calendar, was very important to the Maya. They calculated that a year consisted of 365.2420 days. (Present calculations measure our year as 365.2422 days long.) Since 360 had convenient factors and was close to 365 days in their year and 400 in their numeration system, they made a place value system where the column values from right to left were 1, 20, 20 · 18 (= 360), $20^2 \cdot 18$ (= 7200), $20^3 \cdot 18$ (= 144,000), and so on. Interestingly, the Maya could record all the days of their history simply by using the place values through 144,000. The Maya were also able to use larger numbers. One Mayan hieroglyphic text recorded a number equivalent to 1,841,641,600.

Finally, the Maya, famous for their hieroglyphic writing, also used the 20 ideograms pictured here, called head variants, to represent the numbers 0–19.

The Mayan numeration system is studied in this chapter along with other ancient numeration systems.

STRATEGY **7**
Draw a Diagram

Often there are problems where, although it is not necessary to draw an actual picture to represent the problem situation, a diagram that represents the essence of the problem is useful. For example, if we wish to determine the number of times two heads can turn up when we toss two coins, we could literally draw pictures of all possible arrangements of two coins turning up heads or tails. However, in practice, a simple tree diagram is used like the one shown next.

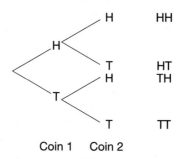

Outcomes when two coins are tossed

This diagram shows that there is one way to obtain two heads out of four possible outcomes. Another type of diagram is helpful in solving the next problem.

INITIAL PROBLEM

A survey was taken of 150 college freshmen. Forty of them were majoring in mathematics, 30 of them were majoring in English, 20 were majoring in science, 7 had a double major of mathematics and English, and none had a double (or triple) major with science. How many students had majors other than mathematics, English, or science?

CLUES

The Draw a Diagram strategy may be appropriate when

• The problem involves sets, ratios, or probabilities.
• An actual picture can be drawn, but a diagram is more efficient.
• Relationships among quantities are represented.

A solution of this Initial Problem is on page 82.

INTRODUCTION

Much of elementary school mathematics is devoted to the study of numbers. Children first learn to count using the **natural numbers** or **counting numbers** 1, 2, 3, . . . (the ellipsis, or three periods, means "and so on"). This chapter develops the ideas that lead to the concepts central to the system of **whole numbers** 0, 1, 2, 3, . . . (the counting numbers together with zero) and the symbols that are used to represent them. First, the notion of a one-to-one correspondence between two sets is shown to be the idea central to the formation of the concept of number. Then operations on sets are discussed. These operations form the foundation of addition, subtraction, multiplication, and division of whole numbers. Finally, the Hindu–Arabic numeration system, our system of symbols that represent numbers, is presented after its various attributes are introduced by considering other ancient numeration systems.

> ### Key Concepts from NCTM Curriculum Focal Points

- **PREKINDERGARTEN:** Developing an understanding of whole numbers, including concepts of correspondence, counting, cardinality, and comparison.
- **KINDERGARTEN:** Representing, comparing, and ordering whole numbers and joining and separating sets. Ordering objects by measurable attributes.
- **GRADE 1:** Developing an understanding of whole number relationships, including grouping in tens and ones.
- **GRADE 2:** Developing an understanding of the base-ten numeration system and place-value concepts.
- **GRADE 6:** Writing, interpreting, and using mathematical expressions and equations.

2.1   SETS AS A BASIS FOR WHOLE NUMBERS

STARTING POINT

After forming a group of students, use a diagram like the one at the right to place the names of each member of your group in the appropriate region. All members of the group will fit somewhere in the rectangle. Discuss the attributes of a person whose name is in the shaded region. Discuss the attributes of a person whose name is not in any of the circles.

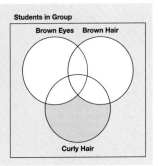

Sets

Algebraic Reasoning
When solving algebraic equations, we are looking for all values/numbers that make an equation true. This set of numbers is called the solution set.

A collection of objects is called a **set** and the objects are called **elements** or **members** of the set. Sets can be defined in three common ways: (1) a verbal description, (2) a listing of the members separated by commas, with braces ("{" and "}") used to enclose the list of elements, and (3) **set-builder notation**. For example, the verbal description "the set of all states in the United States that border the Pacific Ocean" can be represented in the other two ways as follows:

1. *Listing:* {Alaska, California, Hawaii, Oregon, Washington}.
2. *Set-builder:* {$x \mid x$ is a U.S. state that borders the Pacific Ocean}. (This set-builder notation is read: "The set of all x such that x is a U.S. state that borders the Pacific Ocean.")

Sets are usually denoted by capital letters such as A, B, C, and so on. The symbols "$\in$" and "$\notin$" are used to indicate that an object **is or is not an element of a set**, respectively. For example, if S represents the set of all U.S. states bordering the Pacific, then Alaska $\in S$ and Michigan $\notin S$. The set without elements is called the **empty set** (or **null set**) and is denoted by { } or the symbol $\varnothing$. The set of all U.S. states bordering Antarctica is the empty set.

Two sets A and B are **equal**, written $A = B$, if and only if they have precisely the same elements. Thus {$x \mid x$ is a state that borders Lake Michigan} = {Illinois, Indiana, Michigan, Wisconsin}. Notice that two sets, A and B, are equal if every element of A is in B, and vice versa. If A does not equal B, we write $A \neq B$.

There are two inherent rules regarding sets: (1) The same element is not listed more than once within a set, and (2) the order of the elements in a set is immaterial. Thus, by rule 1, the set {a, a, b} would be written as {a, b} and by rule 2. {a, b} = {b, a}, {x, y, z} = {y, z, x}, and so on.

The concept of a 1-1 correspondence, read "one-to-one correspondence," is needed to formalize the meaning of a whole number.

DEFINITION

One-to-One Correspondence

A **1-1 correspondence** between two sets A and B is a pairing of the elements of A with the elements of B so that each element of A corresponds to exactly one element of B, and vice versa. If there is a 1-1 correspondence between sets A and B, we write $A \sim B$ and say that A and B are **equivalent** or **matching** sets.

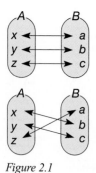

Figure 2.1

Figure 2.1 shows two 1-1 correspondences between two sets, A and B.

There are four other possible 1-1 correspondences between A and B. Notice that equal sets are always equivalent, since each element can be matched with itself, but that equivalent sets are not necessarily equal. For example, {1, 2} $\sim$ {a, b}, but {1, 2} $\neq$ {a, b}. The two sets A = {a, b} and B = {a, b, c} are not equivalent. However, they do satisfy the relationship defined next.

DEFINITION

Subset of a Set: $A \subseteq B$

Set A is said to be a **subset** of B, written $A \subseteq B$, if and only if every element of A is also an element of B.

The set consisting of New Hampshire is a subset of the set of all New England states and {a, b, c} $\subseteq$ {a, b, c, d, e, f}. Since every element in a set A is in A, $A \subseteq A$ for all sets A. Also, {a, b, c} $\nsubseteq$ {a, b, d} because c is in the set {a, b, c} but not in the set {a, b, d}. Using similar reasoning, you can argue that $\varnothing \subseteq A$ for any set A since it is impossible to find an element in $\varnothing$ that is not in A.

If $A \subseteq B$ and B has an element that is not in A, we write $A \subset B$ and say that A is a **proper subset** of B. Thus $\{a, b\} \subset \{a, b, c\}$, since $\{a, b\} \subseteq \{a, b, c\}$ and c is in the second set *but* not in the first.

Circles or other closed curves are used in **Venn diagrams** (named after the English logician John Venn) to illustrate relationships between sets. These circles are usually pictured within a rectangle, U, where the rectangle represents the **universal set** or **universe**, the set comprised of all elements being considered in a particular discussion. Figure 2.2 displays sets A and B inside a universal set U.

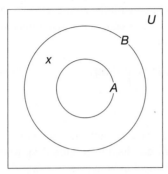

Figure 2.2

Set A is comprised of everything inside circle A, and set B is comprised of everything inside circle B, including set A. Hence A is a *proper* subset of B since $x \in B$, but $x \notin A$. The idea of proper subset will be used later to help establish the meaning of the concept "less than" for whole numbers.

 Check for Understanding: Exercise/Problem Set A #1–9

Finite and Infinite Sets

There are two broad categories of sets: finite and infinite. Informally, a set is **finite** if it is empty or can have its elements listed (where the list eventually ends), and a set is **infinite** if it goes on without end. A little more formally, a set is finite if (1) it is empty or (2) it can be put into a 1-1 correspondence with a set of the form $\{1, 2, 3, \ldots, n\}$, where n is a counting number. On the other hand, a set is infinite if it is *not* finite.

Example 2.1 Determine whether the following sets are finite or infinite.

a. $\{a, b, c\}$
b. $\{1, 2, 3, \ldots\}$
c. $\{2, 4, 6, \ldots, 20\}$

Reflection from Research
While many students will agree that two infinite sets such as the set of counting numbers and the set of even numbers are equivalent, the same students will argue that the set of counting numbers is larger due to its inclusion of the odd numbers (Wheeler, 1987).

SOLUTION
a. $\{a, b, c\}$ is finite since it can be matched with the set $\{1, 2, 3\}$.
b. $\{1, 2, 3, \ldots\}$ is an infinite set.
c. $\{2, 4, 6, \ldots, 20\}$ is a finite set since it can be matched with the set $\{1, 2, 3, \ldots, 10\}$. (Here, the ellipsis means to continue the pattern until the last element is reached.) ∎

NOTE: The small solid square (∎) is used to mark the end of an example or mathematical argument.

An interesting property of every infinite set is that it can be matched with a proper subset of itself. For example, consider the following 1-1 correspondence:

$$A = \{1, 2, 3, 4, \ldots, n, \ldots\}$$

$$B = \{2, 4, 6, 8, \ldots, 2n, \ldots\}.$$

Algebraic Reasoning
Due to the nature of infinite sets, a variable is commonly used to illustrate matching elements in two sets when showing 1-1 correspondences.

Note that $B \subset A$ and that each element in A is paired with exactly one element in B, and vice versa. Notice that matching n with $2n$ indicates that we never "run out" of elements from B to match with the elements from set A. Thus an alternative definition is that a set is infinite if it is equivalent to a proper subset of itself. In this case, a set is finite if it is not infinite.

✓ **Check for Understanding:** Exercise/Problem Set A #10–11

Operations on Sets

Two sets A and B that have no elements in common are called **disjoint sets**. The sets $\{a, b, c\}$ and $\{d, e, f\}$ are disjoint (Figure 2.3), whereas $\{x, y\}$ and $\{y, z\}$ are not disjoint, since y is an element in both sets.

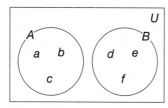

Figure 2.3

There are many ways to construct a new set from two or more sets. The following operations on sets will be very useful in clarifying our understanding of whole numbers and their operations.

DEFINITION

Union of Sets: $A \cup B$

The **union** of two sets A and B, written $A \cup B$, is the set that consists of all elements belonging either to A or to B (or to both).

Informally, $A \cup B$ is formed by putting all the elements of A and B together. The next example illustrates this definition.

Example 2.2   Find the union of the given pairs of sets.

a. $\{a, b\} \cup \{c, d, e\}$
b. $\{1, 2, 3, 4, 5\} \cup \varnothing$
c. $\{m, n, q\} \cup \{m, n, p\}$

SOLUTION
a. $\{a, b\} \cup \{c, d, e\} = \{a, b, c, d, e\}$
b. $\{1, 2, 3, 4, 5\} \cup \varnothing = \{1, 2, 3, 4, 5\}$
c. $\{m, n, q\} \cup \{m, n, p\} = \{m, n, p, q\}$ ■

Notice that although *m* is a member of both sets in Example 2.2(c), it is listed only once in the union of the two sets. The union of sets *A* and *B* is displayed in a Venn diagram by shading the portion of the diagram that represents $A \cup B$ (Figure 2.4).

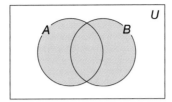

Figure 2.4   Shaded region is $A \cup B$.

The notion of set union is the basis for the addition of whole numbers, but only when disjoint sets are used. Notice how the sets in Example 2.2(a) can be used to show that $2 + 3 = 5$.

Another useful set operation is the intersection of sets.

DEFINITION

Intersection of Sets: $A \cap B$

The **intersection** of sets *A* and *B*, written $A \cap B$, is the set of all elements common to sets *A* and *B*.

Thus $A \cap B$ is the set of elements shared by *A* and *B*. Example 2.3 illustrates this definition.

Example 2.3   Find the intersection of the given pairs of sets.

a. $\{a, b, c\} \cap \{b, d, f\}$
b. $\{a, b, c\} \cap \{a, b, c\}$
c. $\{a, b\} \cap \{c, d\}$

SOLUTION
a. $\{a, b, c\} \cap \{b, d, f\} = \{b\}$ since *b* is the only element in both sets.
b. $\{a, b, c\} \cap \{a, b, c\} = \{a, b, c\}$ since *a*, *b*, *c* are in both sets.
c. $\{a, b\} \cap \{c, d\} = \varnothing$ since there are no elements common to the given two sets. ■

Figure 2.5 displays $A \cap B$. Observe that two sets are disjoint if and only if their intersection is the empty set. Figure 2.3 shows a Venn diagram of two sets whose intersection is the empty set.

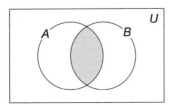

Figure 2.5   Shaded region is $A \cap B$.

In many situations, instead of considering elements of a set A, it is more productive to consider all elements in the universal set *other than* those in A. This set is defined next.

DEFINITION

Complement of a Set: $\overline{A}$

The **complement** of a set A, written $\overline{A}$, is the set of all elements in the universe, U, that are *not* in A.

The set $\overline{A}$ is shaded in Figure 2.6.

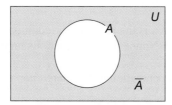

Figure 2.6   Shaded region is $\overline{A}$.

Example 2.4   Find the following sets.

a. $\overline{A}$ where $U = \{a, b, c, d\}$ and $A = \{a\}$
b. $\overline{B}$ where $U = \{1, 2, 3, \ldots\}$ and $B = \{2, 4, 6, \ldots\}$
c. $\overline{A} \cup \overline{B}$ and $\overline{A \cap B}$ where $U = \{1, 2, 3, 4, 5\}$, $A = \{1, 2, 3\}$, and $B = \{3, 4\}$

SOLUTION
a. $\overline{A} = \{b, c, d\}$
b. $\overline{B} = \{1, 3, 5, \ldots\}$
c. $\overline{A} \cup \overline{B} = \{4, 5\} \cup \{1, 2, 5\} = \{1, 2, 4, 5\}$
$\overline{A \cap B} = \overline{\{3\}} = \{1, 2, 4, 5\}$ ∎

The next set operation forms the basis for subtraction.

DEFINITION

Difference of Sets: $A - B$

The set **difference** (or **relative complement**) of set B from set A, written $A - B$, is the set of all elements in A that are not in B.

In set-builder notation, $A - B = \{x \mid x \in A \text{ and } x \notin B\}$. Also, as can be seen in Figure 2.7, $A - B$ can be viewed as $A \cap \overline{B}$. Example 2.5 provides some examples of the difference of one set from another.

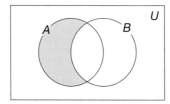

Figure 2.7   Shaded region is $A - B$.

Example 2.5   Find the difference of the given pairs of sets.

a. $\{a, b, c\} - \{b, d\}$
b. $\{a, b, c\} - \{e\}$
c. $\{a, b, c, d\} - \{b, c, d\}$

SOLUTION
a. $\{a, b, c\} - \{b, d\} = \{a, c\}$
b. $\{a, b, c\} - \{e\} = \{a, b, c\}$
c. $\{a, b, c, d\} - \{b, c, d\} = \{a\}$ ■

In Example 2.5(c), the second set is a subset of the first. These sets can be used to show that $4 - 3 = 1$.

Another way of combining two sets to form a third set is called the Cartesian product. The Cartesian product, named after the French mathematician René Descartes, forms the basis of whole-number multiplication and is also useful in probability and geometry. To define the Cartesian product, we need to have the concept of ordered pair. An **ordered pair**, written (a, b), is a pair of elements where one of the elements is designated as first (a in this case) and the other is second (b here). The notion of an ordered pair differs from that of simply a set of two elements because of the preference in order. For example, $\{1, 2\} = \{2, 1\}$ as sets, because they have the same elements. But $(1, 2) \neq (2, 1)$ *as ordered pairs*, since the order of the elements is different. Two ordered pairs (a, b) and (c, d) are equal if and only if $a = c$ and $b = d$.

DEFINITION

Cartesian Product of Sets: $A \times B$

The **Cartesian product** of set A with set B, written $A \times B$ and read "A cross B," is the set of all ordered pairs (a, b), where $a \in A$ and $b \in B$.

In set-builder notation, $A \times B = \{(a, b) \mid a \in A \text{ and } b \in B\}$.

Example 2.6   Find the Cartesian product of the given pairs of sets.

a. $\{x, y, z\} \times \{m, n\}$
b. $\{7\} \times \{a, b, c\}$

SOLUTION
a. $\{x, y, z\} \times \{m, n\} = \{(x, m), (x, n), (y, m), (y, n), (z, m), (z, n)\}$
b. $\{7\} \times \{a, b, c\} = \{(7, a), (7, b), (7, c)\}$ ■

Notice that when finding a Cartesian product, all possible pairs are formed where the first element comes from the first set and the second element comes from the second set. Also observe that in part (a) of Example 2.6, there are three elements in the first set, two in the second, and six in their Cartesian product, and that $3 \times 2 = 6$. Similarly, in part (b), these sets can be used to find the whole-number product $1 \times 3 = 3$.

All of the operations on sets that have been introduced in this subsection result in a new set. For example, $A \cap B$ is an operation on two sets that results in the set of all elements that are common to set A and B. Similarly, $C - D$ is an operation on set C that results in the set of elements C that are not also in set D. On the other hand, expressions such as $A \subseteq B$ or $x \notin C$ are not operations; they are statements that are either true or false. Table 2.1 lists all such set statements and operations.

TABLE 2.1

STATEMENTS	OPERATIONS
$A \subseteq B$	$A \cup B$
$A \subset B$	$A \cap B$
$A \sim B$	$\overline{A}$
$x \in B$	$A - B$
$A = B$	$A \times B$
$A \not\subseteq B$	
$x \notin A$	
$A \neq B$	

Venn diagrams are often used to solve problems, as shown next.

Example 2.7   Thirty elementary teachers were asked which high school courses they appreciated: algebra or geometry. Seventeen appreciated algebra and 15 appreciated geometry; of these, 5 said that they appreciated both. How many appreciated neither?

SOLUTION Since there are two courses, we draw a Venn diagram with two overlapping circles labeled A for algebra and G for geometry [Figure 2.8(a)]. Since 5 teachers appreciated both algebra and geometry, we place a 5 in the intersection of A and G [Figure 2.8(b)]. Seventeen must be in the A circle; thus 12 must be in the remaining part of A [Figure 2.8(c)]. Similarly, 10 must be in the G circle outside the intersection [Figure 2.8(d)]. Thus we have accounted for $12 + 5 + 10 = 27$ teachers. This leaves 3 of the 30 teachers who appreciated neither algebra nor geometry. ■

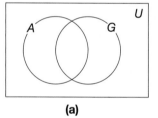
(a)

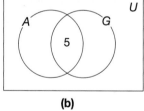
(b)

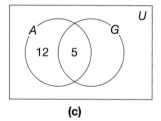
(c)

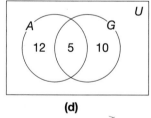
(d)

Figure 2.8   (a)–(d)

✔ **Check for Understanding:** Exercise/Problem Set A #12–32

MATHEMATICAL MORSEL

There are several theories concerning the rationale behind the shapes of the 10 digits in our Hindu–Arabic numeration system. One is that the number represented by each digit is given by the number of angles in the original digit. Count the "angles" in each digit below. (Here an "angle" is less than 180°.) Of course, zero is round, so it has no angles.

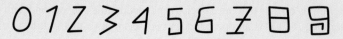

| **Section 2.1** | EXERCISE / PROBLEM SET A |

EXERCISES

1. Indicate the following sets by the listing method.
   a. Whole numbers between 5 and 9
   b. Even counting numbers less than 15
   c. Even counting numbers less than 151

2. Which of the following sets are equal to $\{4, 5, 6\}$?
   a. $\{5, 6\}$ b. $\{5, 4, 6\}$
   c. Whole numbers greater than 3
   d. Whole numbers less than 7
   e. Whole numbers greater than 3 or less than 7
   f. Whole numbers greater than 3 and less than 8
   g. $\{e, f, g\}$

3. True or false?
   a. $7 \in \{6, 7, 8, 9\}$
   b. $5 \notin \{2, 3, 4, 6\}$
   c. $\{1, 2, 3\} \subseteq \{1, 2, 3\}$
   d. $\{1, 2, 5\} \subset \{1, 2, 5\}$
   e. $\{2\} \nsubseteq \{1, 2\}$

4. Find four 1-1 correspondences between A and B other than the two given in Figure 2.1.

5. Determine which of the following sets are equivalent to the set $\{x, y, z\}$.
   a. $\{w, x, y, z\}$ b. $\{1, 5, 17\}$ c. $\{w, x, z\}$
   d. $\{a, b, a\}$ e. $\{\Box, \triangle, O\}$

6. Which of the following pairs of sets are equal?
   a. $\{a, b\}$ and "First two letters of the alphabet"
   b. $\{7, 8, 9, 10\}$ and "Whole numbers greater than 7"
   c. $\{7, a, b, 8\}$ and $\{a, b, c, 7, 8\}$
   d. $\{x, y, x, z\}$ and $\{z, x, y, z\}$

7. List all the subsets of $\{a, b, c\}$.

8. List the proper subsets of $\{O, \triangle\}$.

9. Let $A = \{v, x, z\}$, $B = \{w, x, y\}$, and $C = \{v, w, x, y, z\}$. In the following, choose all of the possible symbols ($\in$, $\notin$, $\subset$, $\subseteq$, $\nsubseteq$, $\sim$, or $=$) that would make a true statement.
   a. z _____ B b. B _____ C c. $\varnothing$ _____ A
   d. A _____ B e. v _____ C f. B _____ B

10. Determine which of the following sets are finite. For those sets that are finite, how many elements are in the set?
    a. {ears on a typical elephant}
    b. $\{1, 2, 3, \ldots, 99\}$ c. $\{0, 1, 2, 3, \ldots, 200\}$
    d. Set of points belonging to a line segment
    e. Set of points belonging to a circle

11. Since the set $A = \{3, 6, 9, 12, 15, \ldots\}$ is infinite, there is a proper subset of A that can be matched to A. Find two such proper subsets and describe how each is matched to A.

12. Given $A = \{2, 4, 6, 8, 10, \ldots\}$, and $B = \{4, 8, 12, 16, 20, \ldots\}$, answer the following questions.
    a. Find the set $A \cup B$.   b. Find the set $A \cap B$.
    c. Is B a subset of A? Explain.
    d. Is A equivalent to B? Explain.
    e. Is A equal to B? Explain.
    f. Is B a proper subset of A? Explain.

13. True or false?
    a. For all sets X and Y, either $X \subseteq Y$ or $Y \subseteq X$.
    b. If A is an infinite set and $B \subseteq A$, then B also is an infinite set.
    c. For all finite sets A and B, if $A \cap B = \varnothing$, then the number of elements in $A \cup B$ equals the number of elements in A plus the number of elements in B.

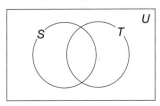

14. The regions $A \cap B$ and $A \cup B$ can each be formed by shading the set A in one direction and the set B in another direction. The region with shading in both directions is $A \cap B$ and the entire shaded region is $A \cup B$. Use the Chapter 2 eManipulative activity *Venn Diagrams* on our Web site to do the following:
    a. Find the region $(A \cup B) \cap C$.
    b. Find the region $A \cup (B \cap C)$.
    c. Based on the results of parts a and b, what conclusions can you draw about the placement of parentheses?

15. Draw a Venn diagram like the following one for each part. Then shade each Venn diagram to represent each of the sets indicated.

[Venn diagram with two overlapping circles S and T inside a rectangle labeled U]

    a. $\bar{S}$ b. $\bar{S} \cap T$ c. $(S - T) \cup (T - S)$

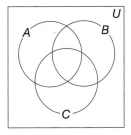

16. A Venn diagram can be used to illustrate more than two sets. Shade the regions that represent each of the following sets. The Chapter 2 eManipulative activity *Venn Diagrams* on our Web site may help in solving this problem.

[Venn diagram with three overlapping circles A, B, and C inside a rectangle labeled U]

    a. $A \cap (B \cap C)$ b. $A - (B \cap C)$ c. $A \cup (B - C)$

17. Represent the following shaded regions using the symbols
A, B, C, ∪, ∩, and −. The Chapter 2 eManipulative activity
Venn Diagrams on our Web site can be used in solving this
problem.

a.
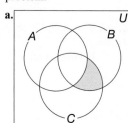

b.
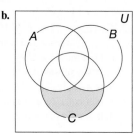

c.
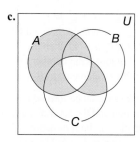

18. Draw Venn diagrams that represent sets *A* and *B* as
described as follows:
a. *A* ⊂ *B*   **b.** *A* ∩ *B* = ∅

19. In the drawing, *C* is the interior of the circle, *T* is the
interior of the triangle, and *R* is the interior of the rectangle.
Copy the drawing on a sheet of paper, then shade in each of
the following regions.

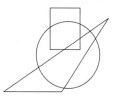

a. *C* ∪ *T*   **b.** *C* ∩ *R*   **c.** (*C* ∩ *T*) ∪ *R*
d. (*C* ∪ *R*) ∪ *T*   **e.** (*C* ∩ *R*) ∩ *T*   **f.** *C* ∩ (*R* ∩ *T*)

20. Let *W* = {women who have won Nobel Prizes},
A = {Americans who have won Nobel Prizes}, and
C = {winners of the Nobel Prize in chemistry}. Describe
the elements of the following sets.
a. *W* ∪ *A*   **b.** *W* ∩ *A*   **c.** *A* ∩ *C*

21. Let *A* = {*a, b, c*}, *B* = {*b, c*}, and *C* = {*e*}. Find each of
the following.
a. *A* ∩ *B*   **b.** *B* ∪ *C*   **c.** *A* − *B*

22. Find each of the following differences.
a. {○, △, /, □} − {△, □}
b. {0, 1, 2, . . .} − {12, 13, 14, . . .}
c. {people} − {married people}
d. {*a, b, c, d*} − { }

23. Let *A* = {2, 4, 6, 8, 10, . . .} and *B* = {4, 8, 12, 16, . . .}.
a. Find *A* − *B*.
b. Find *B* − *A*.
c. Based on your observations in part a and b, describe a
general case for which *A* − *B* = ∅.

24. Given *A* = {0, 1, 2, 3, 4, 5}, *B* = {0, 2, 4, 6, 8, 10}, and
C = {0, 4, 8}, find each of the following.
a. *A* ∪ *B*   **b.** *B* ∪ *C*   **c.** *A* ∩ *B*
d. *B* ∩ *C*   **e.** *B* − *C*   **f.** (*A* ∪ *B*) − *C*
g. *A* ∩ ∅

25. Let *M* = the set of the months of the year, *J* = {January,
June, July}, *S* = {June, July, August}, *W* = {December,
January, February}. List the members of each of the
following:
a. *J* ∪ *S*   **b.** *J* ∩ *W*
c. *S* ∩ *W*   **d.** *J* ∩ (*S* ∪ *W*)
e. *M* − (*S* ∪ *W*)   **f.** *J* − *S*

26. Let *A* = {3, 6, 9, 12, 15, 18, 21, 24, . . .} and *B* = {6, 12,
18, 24, . . .}.
a. Is *B* ⊆ *A*?
b. Find *A* ∪ *B*.
c. Find *A* ∩ *B*.
d. In general, when *B* ⊆ *A*, what is true about *A* ∪ *B*?
about *A* ∩ *B*?

27. Verify that $\overline{A \cup B} = \overline{A} \cap \overline{B}$ in two different ways as
follows:
a. Let *U* = {1, 2, 3, 4, 5, 6}, *A* = {2, 3, 5}, and *B* = {1, 4}.
List the elements of the sets $\overline{A \cup B}$ and $\overline{A} \cap \overline{B}$. Do the
two sets have the same members?
b. Draw and shade a Venn diagram for each of the
sets $\overline{A \cup B}$ and $\overline{A} \cap \overline{B}$. Do the two Venn diagrams
look the same? NOTE: The equation $\overline{A \cup B} = \overline{A} \cap \overline{B}$
is one of two laws called **DeMorgan's laws**.

28. Find the following Cartesian products.
a. {*a*} × {*b, c*}
b. {5} × {*a, b, c*}
c. {*a, b*} × {1, 2, 3}
d. {2, 3} × {1, 4}
e. {*a, b, c*} × {5}
f. {1, 2, 3} × {*a, b*}

29. Determine how many ordered pairs will be in the
following sets.
a. {1, 2, 3, 4} × {*a, b*}
b. {*m, n, o*} × {1, 2, 3, 4}

30. If *A* has two members, how many members does
B have when *A* × *B* has the following number of
members? If an answer is not possible,
explain why.
a. 4   **b.** 8   **c.** 9
d. 50   **e.** 0   **f.** 23

31. The Cartesian product, $A \times B$, is given in each of the following parts. Find A and B.
  a. $\{(a, 2), (a, 4), (a, 6)\}$
  b. $\{(a, b), (b, b), (b, a), (a, a)\}$

32. True or false?
  a. $\{(4, 5), (6, 7)\} = \{(6, 7), (4, 5)\}$
  b. $\{(a, b), (c, d)\} = \{(b, a), (c, d)\}$
  c. $\{(4, 5), (7, 6)\} = \{(7, 6), (5, 4)\}$
  d. $\{(5, 6), (7, 4)\} \subseteq \{4, 5, 6\} \times \{5, 7, 9\}$

PROBLEMS

33. a. If X has five elements and Y has three elements, what is the greatest number of elements possible in $X \cap Y$? in $X \cup Y$?
  b. If X has x elements and Y has y elements with x greater than or equal to y, what is the greatest number of elements possible in $X \cap Y$? in $X \cup Y$?

34. How many different 1-1 correspondences are possible between $A = \{1, 2, 3, 4\}$ and $B = \{a, b, c, d\}$?

35. How many subsets does a set with the following number of members have?
  a. 0   **b.** 1   **c.** 2   **d.** 3   **e.** 5   **f.** n

36. If it is possible, give examples of the following. If it is not possible, explain why.
  a. Two sets that are not equal but are equivalent
  b. Two sets that are not equivalent but are equal

37. a. When does $D \cap E = D$?   **b.** When does $D \cup E = D$?
  c. When does $D \cap E = D \cup E$?

38. Carmen has 8 skirts and 7 blouses. Show how the concept of Cartesian product can be used to determine how many different outfits she has.

39. How many matches are there if 32 participants enter a single-elimination tennis tournament (one loss eliminates a participant)?

40. Can you show a 1-1 correspondence between the points on base $\overline{AB}$ of the given triangle and the points on the two sides $\overline{AC}$ and $\overline{CB}$? Explain how you can or why you cannot.

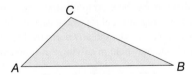

41. Can you show a 1-1 correspondence between the points on chord $\overline{AB}$ and the points on arc $\widehat{ACB}$? Explain how you can or why you cannot.

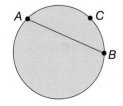

42. A poll of 100 registered voters designed to find out how voters kept up with current events revealed the following facts.

> 65 watched the news on television.
> 39 read the newspaper.
> 39 listened to radio news.
> 20 watched TV news and read the newspaper.
> 27 watched TV news and listened to radio news.
> 9 read the newspaper and listened to radio news.
> 6 watched TV news, read the newspaper, and listened to radio news.

  a. How many of the 100 people surveyed did not keep up with current events by the three sources listed?
  b. How many of the 100 people surveyed read the paper but did *not* watch TV news?
  c. How many of the 100 people surveyed used only one of the three sources listed to keep up with current events?

43. At a convention of 375 butchers (B), bakers (A), and candlestick makers (C), there were

> 50 who were both B and A but not C
> 70 who were B but neither A nor C
> 60 who were A but neither B nor C
> 40 who were both A and C but not B
> 50 who were both B and C but not A
> 80 who were C but neither A nor B

How many at the convention were A, B, and C?

44. A student says that $A - B$ means you start with all the elements of A and you take away all the elements of B. So $A \times B$ must mean you take all the elements of A and multiply them times all the elements of B. Do you agree with the student? How would you explain your reasoning?

| Section 2.1 | EXERCISE / PROBLEM SET B |

EXERCISES

1. Indicate the following sets by the listing method.
   a. Whole numbers greater than 8
   b. Odd whole numbers less than 100
   c. Whole numbers less than 0

2. Represent the following sets using set-builder notation:
   a. {Alabama, Alaska, . . . Maine, Maryland, . . . Wisconsin, Wyoming}
   b. $\{1, 6, 11, 16, 21, \ldots\}$
   c. $\{a, b, c, d, \ldots x, y, z\}$
   d. $\{1, 3, 5, 7, 9\}$

3. True or false?
   a. $\frac{2}{3} \in \{1, 2, 3\}$
   b. $1 \notin \{0, 1, 2\}$
   c. $\{4, 3\} \subset \{2, 3, 4\}$
   d. $\varnothing \subseteq \{\ \}$
   e. $\{1, 2\} \nsubseteq \{2\}$

4. Show three different 1-1 correspondences between $\{1, 2, 3, 4\}$ and $\{x, y, z, w\}$.

5. Write a set that is equivalent to, but not equal to the set $\{a, b, c, d, e, f\}$.

6. Which of the following sets are equal to $\{4, 5, 6\}$?
   a. $\{5, 6\}$ **b.** $\{3, 4, 5\}$
   c. Whole numbers greater than 3
   d. Whole numbers less than 7
   e. Whole numbers greater than 3 or less than 7
   f. Whole numbers greater than 3 and less than 8
   g. $\{e, f, g\}$ **h.** $\{4, 5, 6, 5\}$

7. List all subsets of $\{\bigcirc, \triangle, \square\}$. Which are proper subsets?

8. How many proper subsets does $R = \{r, s, t, u, v\}$ have?

9. Let $A = \{1, 2, 3, 4, 5\}, B = \{3, 4, 5\}$, and $C = \{4, 5, 6\}$. In the following, choose all of the possible symbols $(\in, \notin, \subset, \subseteq, \nsubseteq, \sim, \text{or} =)$ that would make a true statement.
   a. 2 _____ A **b.** B _____ A **c.** C _____ B
   d. 6 _____ C **e.** A _____ A **f.** $B \cap C$ _____ A

10. Show that the following sets are finite by giving the set of the form $\{1, 2, 3, \ldots, n\}$ that matches the given set.
   a. $\{121, 122, 123, \ldots, 139\}$
   b. $\{1, 3, 5, \ldots, 27\}$

11. Show that the following sets are infinite by matching each with a proper subset of itself.
   a. $\{2, 4, 6, \ldots, n, \ldots\}$
   b. $\{50, 51, 52, 53, \ldots, n, \ldots\}$

12. Let $A = \{0, 10, 20, 30, \ldots\}$ and $B = \{5, 15, 25, 35, \ldots\}$. Decide which of the following are true and which are false. Explain your answers.
   a. A equals B.   **b.** B is equivalent to A.   **c.** $A \cap B \neq \varnothing$.
   d. B is equivalent to a proper subset of A.
   e. There is a proper subset of B that is equivalent to a proper subset of A.
   f. $A \cup B$ is all multiples of 5.

13. True or false?
   a. The empty set is a subset of every set.
   b. The set $\{105, 110, 115, 120, \ldots\}$ is an infinite set.
   c. If A is an infinite set and $B \subseteq A$, then B is a finite set.

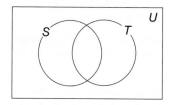

14. Use Venn diagrams to determine which, if any, of the following statements are true for all sets A, B, and C: The Chapter 2 eManipulative *Venn Diagrams* on our Web site may help in determining which statements are true.
   a. $A \cup (B \cup C) = (A \cup B) \cup C$
   b. $A \cup (B \cap C) = (A \cup B) \cap C$
   c. $A \cap (B \cap C) = (A \cap B) \cap C$
   d. $A \cap (B \cup C) = (A \cap B) \cup C$

15. Draw a Venn diagram like the following for each part. Then shade each Venn diagram to represent each of the sets indicated.

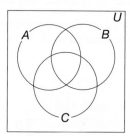

   a. $T - S$ **b.** $\overline{S} \cup \overline{T}$ **c.** $(S - T) \cap (T - S)$

16. A Venn diagram can be used to illustrate more than two sets. Shade the regions that represent each of the following sets. The Chapter 2 eManipulative activity *Venn Diagrams* on our Web site may help in solving this problem.

   a. $(A \cup B) \cap C$ **b.** $\overline{A} \cap (\overline{B} \cap \overline{C})$ **c.** $(A \cup B) - (B \cap C)$

17. Represent the following shaded regions using the symbols $A, B, C, \cup, \cap,$ and $-$. The Chapter 2 eManipulative activity *Venn Diagrams* on our Web site can be used in solving this problem.

a.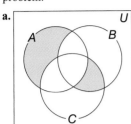

b.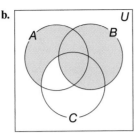

c.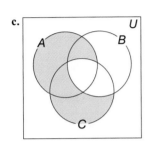

18. Draw Venn diagrams that represent sets A and B as described below.
  a. $A \cap B \neq \varnothing$
  b. $A \cup B = A$

19. Make 6 copies of the diagram and shade regions in parts a–f.

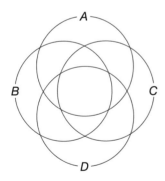

  a. $(A \cap B) \cap C$
  b. $(C \cap D) - (A \cup B)$
  c. $(A \cap B) \cap (C \cap D)$
  d. $(B \cap C) \cap D$
  e. $(A \cap D) \cup (C \cap B)$
  f. $(A \cap B) \cup (C \cap A)$

20. Let $A = \{a, b, c, d, e\}, B = \{c, d, e, f, g\},$ and $C = \{a, e, f, h\}$. List the members of each set.
  a. $A \cup B$
  b. $A \cap B$
  c. $(A \cup B) \cap C$
  d. $A \cup (B \cap C)$

21. If A is the set of all sophomores in a school and B is the set of students who belong to the orchestra, describe the following sets in words.
  a. $A \cup B$ **b.** $A \cap B$ **c.** $A - B$ **d.** $B - A$

22. Find each of the following differences.
  a. $\{h, i, j, k\} - \{k\}$
  b. $\{3, 10, 13\} - \{\ \}$
  c. {two-wheeled vehicles} $-$ {two-wheeled vehicles that are not bicycles}
  d. $\{0, 2, 4, 6, \ldots, 20\} - \{12, 14, 16, 18, 20\}$

23. In each of the following cases, find $B - A$.
  a. $A \cap B = \varnothing$ **b.** $A = B$ **c.** $B \subseteq A$

24. Let $R = \{a, b, c\}, S = \{c, d, e, f\}, T = \{x, y, z\}$. List the elements of the following sets.
  a. $R \cup S$ **b.** $R \cap S$ **c.** $R \cup T$ **d.** $R \cap T$
  e. $S \cup T$ **f.** $S \cap T$ **g.** $T \cup \varnothing$

25. Let $A = \{50, 55, 60, 65, 70, 75, 80\}$
  $B = \{50, 60, 70, 80\}$
  $C = \{60, 70, 80\}$
  $D = \{55, 65\}$
  List the members of each set.
  a. $A \cup (B \cap C)$ **b.** $(A \cup B) \cap C$
  c. $(A \cap C) \cup (C \cap D)$ **d.** $(A \cap C) \cap (C \cup D)$
  e. $(B - C) \cap A$ **f.** $(A - D) \cap (B - C)$

26. a. If $x \in X \cap Y$, is $x \in X \cup Y$? Justify your answer.
  b. If $x \in X \cup Y$, is $x \in X \cap Y$? Justify your answer.

27. Verify that $\overline{A \cap B} = \overline{A} \cup \overline{B}$ in two different ways as follows:
  a. Let $U = \{2, 4, 6, 8, 10, 12, 14, 16\}, A = \{2, 4, 8, 16\},$ and $B = \{4, 8, 12, 16\}$. List the elements of the sets $\overline{A \cap B}$ and $\overline{A} \cup \overline{B}$. Do the two sets have the same members?
  b. Draw and shade a Venn diagram for each of the sets $\overline{A \cap B} = \overline{A} \cup \overline{B}$. Do the two Venn diagrams look the same?

  NOTE: The equation $\overline{A \cap B} = \overline{A} \cup \overline{B}$ is one of the two laws called **DeMorgan's laws**.

28. Find the following Cartesian products.
  a. $\{a, b, c\} \times \{1\}$ **b.** $\{1, 2\} \times \{p, q, r\}$
  c. $\{p, q, r\} \times \{1, 2\}$ **d.** $\{a\} \times \{1\}$

29. Determine how many ordered pairs will be in $A \times B$ under the following conditions.
  a. A has one member and B has four members.
  b. A has two members and B has four members.
  c. A has three members and B has seven members.

30. Find sets A and B so that $A \times B$ has the following number of members.
  a. 1   **b.** 2   **c.** 3   **d.** 4
  e. 5   **f.** 6   **g.** 7   **h.** 0

31. The Cartesian product, $X \times Y$, is given in each of the following parts. Find X and Y.
  a. $\{(b, c), (c, c)\}$
  b. $\{(2, 1), (2, 2), (2, 3), (5, 1), (5, 2), (5, 3)\}$

32. True or false?
  a. $\{(3, 4), (5, 6)\} = \{(3, 4), (6, 5)\}$
  b. $\{(a, c), (d, b)\} = \{a, c, d, b\}$
  c. $\{(c, d), (a, b)\} = \{(c, a), (d, b)\}$
  d. $\{(4, 5), (6, 7)\} \subseteq \{4, 5, 6\} \times \{5, 7, 9\}$

PROBLEMS

33. How many 1-1 correspondences are there between the following pairs of sets?
  a. Two 2-member sets
  b. Two 4-member sets
  c. Two 6-member sets
  d. Two sets each having m members

34. Find sets (when possible) satisfying each of the following conditions.
  a. Number of elements in A plus number of elements in B is greater than number of elements in $A \cup B$.
  b. Number of elements in I plus number of elements in J is less than number of elements in $I \cup J$.
  c. Number of elements in E plus number of elements in F equals number of elements in $E \cup F$.
  d. Number of elements in G plus number of elements in K equals number of elements in $G \cap K$.

35. Your house can be painted in a choice of 7 exterior colors and 15 interior colors. Assuming that you choose only 1 color for the exterior and 1 color for the interior, how many different ways of painting your house are there?

36. Show a 1-1 correspondence between the points on the given circle and the triangle in which it is inscribed. Explain your procedure.

37. Show a 1-1 correspondence between the points on the given triangle and the circle that circumscribes it. Explain your procedure.

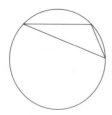

38. A schoolroom has 13 desks and 13 chairs. You want to arrange the desks and chairs so that each desk has a chair with it. How many such arrangements are there?

39. A university professor asked his class of 42 students when they had studied for his class the previous weekend. Their responses were as follows:

9 had studied on Friday.
18 had studied on Saturday.
30 had studied on Sunday.
3 had studied on both Friday and Saturday.
10 had studied on both Saturday and Sunday.
6 had studied on both Friday and Sunday.
2 had studied on Friday, Saturday, and Sunday.

Assuming that all 42 students responded and answered honestly, answer the following questions.
  a. How many students studied on Sunday but not on either Friday or Saturday?
  b. How many students did all of their studying on one day?
  c. How many students did not study at all for this class last weekend?

40. At an automotive repair shop, 50 cars were inspected. Suppose that 23 cars needed new brakes and 34 cars needed new exhaust systems.
  a. What is the least number of cars that could have needed both?
  b. What is the greatest number of cars that could have needed both?
  c. What is the greatest number of cars that could have needed neither?

41. If A is a proper subset of B, and A has 23 elements, how many elements does B have? Explain.

Analyzing Student Thinking
42. Kylee says that if two sets are equivalent, they must be equal. Jake says that if two sets are equal, then they must be equivalent. Who is correct? Explain.

43. Tonia determines that a set with three elements has as many proper subsets as it has nonempty subsets. Is she correct? Explain.

44. Amanda says that the sets $\{1, 2, 3, \ldots\}$ and $\{2, 4, 6, \ldots\}$ cannot be matched because the first set has many numbers that the second one does not. Is she correct? Explain.

45. LeNae says that $A \cup B$ must always have more elements than either A or B. Is she correct? Explain.

46. Marshall says that $A \cap B$ always has fewer elements than either A or B. Is he correct? Explain.

47. Michael asserts that if A and B are infinite sets, $A \cap B$ must be an infinite set. Is he correct? Explain.

48. DeDee says that B must be a subset of A to be able to find the set $A - B$. How should you respond?

Problems Relating to the NCTM Standards and Curriculum Focal Points

1. The Focal Points for Prekindergarten state "Developing an understanding of whole numbers, including concepts of correspondence, counting, cardinality, and comparisons." How does the idea of 1-1 correspondence introduced in this chapter relate to this focal point for young children?

2. The NCTM Standards state "Students should count with understanding and recognize 'how many' in sets of objects."

Discuss how the concept of "how many" is highlighted as students count objects in equivalent sets.

3. The NCTM Standards state "Instructional programs should enable students to select, apply, and translate among mathematical representations to solve problems." Explain how Venn diagrams can be used as a representation to solve problems.

2.2 WHOLE NUMBERS AND NUMERATION

STARTING POINT

Today our numeration system has the symbol "2" to represent the number of eyes a person has. The symbols "1" and "0" combine to represent the number of toes a person has, "10." The Roman numeration system used the symbol "X" to represent the number of toes and "C" to represent the number of years in a century.

Using only the three symbols at the right, devise your own numeration system and show how you can use your system to represent all of the quantities 0, 1, 2, 3, 4, . . . , 100.

Children's Literature
www.wiley.com/college/musser
See "Uno, Dos, Tres: One, Two, Three" by Pat Mora.

NCTM Standard
All students should develop understanding of the relative position and magnitude of whole numbers and of ordinal and cardinal numbers and their connections.

Reflection from Research
There is a clear separation of development in young children concerning the cardinal and ordinal aspects of numbers. Despite the fact that they could utilize the same counting skills, the understanding of ordinality by young children lags well behind the understanding of cardinality (Bruce & Threlfall, 2004).

Numbers and Numerals

As mentioned earlier, the study of the set of whole numbers, $W = \{0, 1, 2, 3, 4, \ldots\}$, is the foundation of elementary school mathematics. But what precisely do we mean by the whole number 3? A **number** is an idea, or an abstraction, that represents a quantity. The symbols that we see, write, or touch when representing numbers are called **numerals**. There are three common uses of numbers. The most common use of whole numbers is to describe how many elements are in a finite set. When used in this manner, the number is referred to as a **cardinal number**. A second use is concerned with order. For example, you may be second in line, or your team may be fourth in the standings. Numbers used in this way are called **ordinal numbers**. Finally, **identification numbers** are used to name such things as telephone numbers, bank account numbers, and social security numbers. In this case, the numbers are used in a numeral sense in that only the symbols, rather than their values, are important. Before discussing our system of numeration or symbolization, the concept of cardinal number will be considered.

What is the number 3? What do you think of when you see the sets in Figure 2.9?

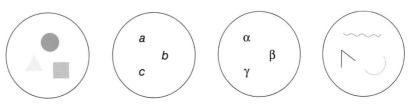

Figure 2.9

First, there are no common elements. One set is made up of letters, one of shapes, one of Greek letters, and so on. Second, each set can be matched with every other set. Now imagine all the infinitely many sets that can be matched with these sets. Even though the sets will be made up of various elements, they will all share the common attribute that they are equivalent to the set $\{a, b, c\}$. The common *idea* that is associated with all of these equivalent sets is the number 3. That is, *the number 3 is the attribute common to all sets that match the set* $\{a, b, c\}$. Similarly, the whole number 2 is the common idea associated with all sets equivalent to the set $\{a, b\}$. All other nonzero whole numbers can be conceptualized in a similar manner. Zero is the idea, or number, one imagines when asked: "How many elements are in the empty set?"

Although the preceding discussion regarding the concept of a whole number may seem routine for you, there are many pitfalls for children who are learning the concept of numerousness for the first time. Chronologically, children first learn how to *say* the counting chant "one, two, three, ..." However, saying the chant and *understanding* the concept of number are not the same thing. Next, children must learn how to match the counting chant words they are saying with the objects they are counting. For example, to count the objects in the set $\{\triangle, \bigcirc, \square\}$, a child must correctly assign the words "one, two, three" to the objects in a 1-1 fashion. Actually, children first learning to count objects fail this task in two ways: (1) They fail to assign a word to each object, and hence their count is too small; or (2) they count one or more objects at least twice and end up with a number that is too large. To reach the final stage in understanding the concept of number, children must be able to observe several equivalent sets, as in Figure 2.9, and realize that, when they count each set, they arrive at the same word. Thus this word is used to name the attribute common to all such sets.

The symbol $n(A)$ is used to represent the **number of elements in a finite set** A. More precisely, (1) $n(A) = m$ if $A \sim \{1, 2, \ldots, m\}$, where m is a counting number, and (2) $n(\varnothing) = 0$. Thus

$$n(\{a, b, c\}) = 3 \text{ since } \{a, b, c\} \sim \{1, 2, 3\}, \text{ and}$$
$$n(\{a, b, c, \ldots, z\}) = 26 \text{ since}$$
$$\{a, b, c, \ldots, z\} \sim \{1, 2, 3, \ldots, 26\},$$

and so on, for other finite sets.

 Check for Understanding: Exercise/Problem Set A #1–4

Ordering Whole Numbers

Children may get their first introduction to ordering whole numbers through the counting chant "one, two, three, ..." For example, "two" is less than "five," since "two" comes before "five" in the counting chant.

A more meaningful way of comparing two whole numbers is to use 1-1 correspondences. We can say that 2 is less than 5, since any set with two elements matches a proper subset of any set with five elements (Figure 2.10).

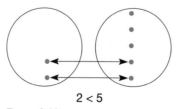

2 < 5

Figure 2.10

The general set formulation of "less than" follows.

> ## DEFINITION
>
> ### *Ordering Whole Numbers*
>
> Let $a = n(A)$ and $b = n(B)$. Then $a < b$ (read "*a* **is less than** *b*") or $b > a$ (read "*b* **is greater than** *a*") if A is equivalent to a proper subset of B.

The "greater than" and "less than" signs can be combined with the equal sign to produce the following symbols: $a \le b$ (*a* **is less than or equal to** *b*) and $b \ge a$ (*b* **is greater than or equal to** *a*).

A third common way of ordering whole numbers is through the use of the whole-number "line" (Figure 2.11). Actually, the **whole-number line** is a sequence of equally spaced marks where the numbers represented by the marks begin on the left with 0 and increase by one each time we move one mark to the right.

Reflection from Research
Most counting mistakes made by young children can be attributed to not keeping track of objects that have already been counted and objects that still need to be counted (Fuson, 1988).

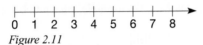

Figure 2.11

| **Example 2.8** | Determine the greater of the two numbers 3 and 8 in three different ways. |

SOLUTION

a. *Counting Chant:* One, two, *three*, four, five, six, seven, *eight*. Since "three" precedes "eight," eight is greater than three.
b. *Set Method:* Since a set with three elements can be matched with a proper subset of a set with eight elements, $3 < 8$ and $8 > 3$ [Figure 2.12(a)].
c. *Whole-Number Line:* Since 3 is to the left of 8 on the number line, 3 is less than 8 and 8 is greater than 3 [Figure 2.12(b)]. ■

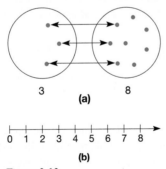

Figure 2.12

✔ **Check for Understanding:** Exercise/Problem Set A #5–6

Children's Literature
www.wiley.com/college/musser
See "Count on Your Fingers African Style" by Claudia Zaslavsky.

Numeration Systems

To make numbers more useful, systems of symbols, or numerals, have been developed to represent numbers. In fact, throughout history, many different numeration systems have evolved. The following discussion reviews various ancient numeration systems with an eye toward identifying features of those systems that are incorporated in our present system, the Hindu–Arabic numeration system.

The Tally Numeration System   The **tally numeration system** is composed of single strokes, one for each object being counted (Figure 2.13).

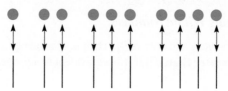

Figure 2.13

The next six such tally numerals are

Reflection from Research
Teaching other numeration systems, such as the Chinese system, can reinforce a student's conceptual knowledge of place value (Uy, 2002).

An advantage of this system is its simplicity; however, two disadvantages are that (1) large numbers require many individual symbols, and (2) it is difficult to read the numerals for such numbers. For example, what number is represented by these tally marks?

The tally system was improved by the introduction of **grouping**. In this case, the fifth tally mark was placed across every four to make a group of five. Thus the last tally numeral can be written as follows:

⅃⅃⅃⅃ ⅃⅃⅃⅃ ⅃⅃⅃⅃ ⅃⅃⅃⅃ ⅃⅃⅃⅃ ⅃⅃⅃⅃ ⅃⅃⅃⅃ ‖

Grouping makes it easier to recognize the number being represented; in this case, there are 37 tally marks.

The Egyptian Numeration System   The **Egyptian numeration system**, which developed around 3400 B.C.E., involves grouping by ten. In addition, this system introduced new symbols for powers of 10 (Figure 2.14).

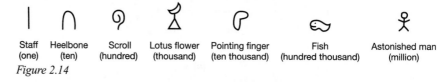

| Staff (one) | Heelbone (ten) | Scroll (hundred) | Lotus flower (thousand) | Pointing finger (ten thousand) | Fish (hundred thousand) | Astonished man (million) |

Figure 2.14

Examples of some Egyptian numerals are shown in Figure 2.15. Notice how this system required far fewer symbols than the tally system once numbers greater than 10 were represented. This system is also an **additive system**, since the values for the various individual numerals are added together.

| 321 | 1034 | 1,120,013 |

Figure 2.15

Notice that the order in which the symbols are written is immaterial. A major disadvantage of this system is that computation is cumbersome. Figure 2.16 shows, in Egyptian numerals, the addition problem that we write as $764 + 598 = 1362$. Here 51 individual Egyptian numerals are needed to express this addition problem, whereas our system requires only 10 numerals!

999999∩∩∩∩∩|||||+99999∩∩∩∩∩∩∩∩∩∩|||||||||=𐤀999∩∩∩∩∩||

Figure 2.16

The Roman Numeration System The **Roman numeration system**, which developed between 500 B.C.E. and C.E. 100, also uses grouping, additivity, and many symbols. The basic Roman numerals are listed in Table 2.2.

TABLE 2.2

ROMAN NUMERAL	VALUE
I	1
V	5
X	10
L	50
C	100
D	500
M	1000

Roman numerals are made up of combinations of these basic numerals, as illustrated next.

CCLXXXI (equals 281)   MCVIII (equals 1108)

Notice that the values of these Roman numerals are found by adding the values of the various basic numerals. For example, MCVIII means $1000 + 100 + 5 + 1 + 1 + 1$, or 1108. Thus the Roman system is an additive system.

Two new attributes that were introduced by the Roman system were a subtractive principle and a multiplicative principle. Both of these principles allow the system to use fewer symbols to represent numbers. The Roman numeration system is a **subtractive system** since it permits simplifications using combinations of basic Roman numerals: IV (I to the left of V means five minus one) for 4 rather than using IIII, IX (ten minus one) for 9 instead of VIIII, XL for 40, XC for 90, CD for 400, and CM for 900 (Table 2.3).

TABLE 2.3

ROMAN NUMERAL	VALUE
IV	4
IX	9
XL	40
XC	90
CD	400
CM	900

Thus, when reading from left to right, if the values of the symbols in any pair of symbols increase, group the pair together. The value of this pair, then, is the value of the larger numeral less the value of the smaller. One may wonder if IC is an acceptable way to write 99. The answer is no because of the additional restriction that only I's, X's and C's may be subtracted, but only from the next two larger numerals in each case. Thus, the symbols shown in Table 2.3 are the only numerals where the subtraction principle is applied. To evaluate a complex Roman numeral, one looks to see whether any of these subtractive pairs are present, groups them together mentally, and then adds values from left to right. For example,

in   MCMXLIV

think   M   CM   XL   IV, which is $1000 + 900 + 40 + 4$.

Notice that without the subtractive principle, 14 individual Roman numerals would be required to represent 1944 instead of the 7 numerals used in MCMXLIV. Also, because of the subtractive principle, the Roman system is a **positional** system, since the position of a numeral can affect the value of the number being represented. For example, VI is six, whereas IV is four.

NCTM Standard
All students should develop a sense of whole numbers and represent and use them in flexible ways including relating, composing, and decomposing numbers.

| **Example 2.9** | Express the following Roman numerals in our numeration system: |

a. MCCCXLIV
b. MMCMXCIII
c. CCXLIX

SOLUTION
a. *Think:* MCCC   XL   IV, or 1300 + 40 + 4 = 1344
b. *Think:* MM   CM   XC   III, or 2000 + 900 + 90 + 3 = 2993
c. *Think:* CC   XL   IX, or 200 + 40 + 9 = 249   ∎

The Roman numeration system also utilized a horizontal bar above a numeral to represent 1000 times the number. For example, $\overline{V}$ meant 5 times 1000, or 5000; $\overline{XI}$ meant 11,000; and so on. Thus the Roman system was also a **multiplicative system**. Although expressing numbers using the Roman system requires fewer symbols than the Egyptian system, it still requires many more symbols than our current system and is cumbersome for doing arithmetic. In fact, the Romans used an abacus to perform calculations instead of paper/pencil methods as we do (see the Focus On at the beginning of Chapter 3).

The Babylonian Numeration System   The **Babylonian numeration system**, which evolved between 3000 and 2000 B.C.E., used only two numerals, a one and a ten (Figure 2.17). For numbers up to 59, the system was simply an additive system. For example, 37 was written using three tens and seven ones (Figure 2.18).

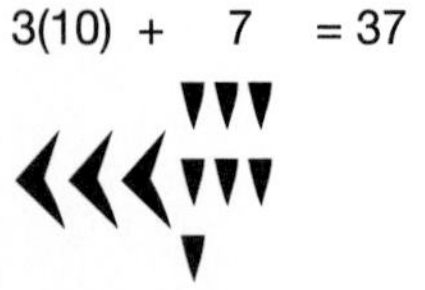

However, even though the Babylonian numeration system was developed about the same time as the simpler Egyptian system, the Babylonians used the sophisticated notion of **place value**, where symbols represent different values depending on the place in which they were written. The symbol ▼ could represent 1 or 1 · 60 or 1 · 60 · 60 depending on where it is placed. Since the position of a symbol in a place-value system affects its value, place-value systems are also positional. Thus, the Babylonian numeration system is another example of a positional system. Figure 2.19 displays three Babylonian numerals that illustrate this place-value attribute, which is based on 60. Notice the subtle spacing of the numbers in Figure 2.19(a) to assist in understanding that the ▼ represents a 1 · 60 and not a 1. Similarly, the symbol, ◀▼▼ in Figure 2.19(b) is spaced slightly to the left to indicate that it represents a 12(60) instead of just 12. Finally, the symbols in Figure 2.19(c) have 2 spaces to indicate ▼▼ is multiplied by 60 · 60 and ◀▼ is multiplied by 60.

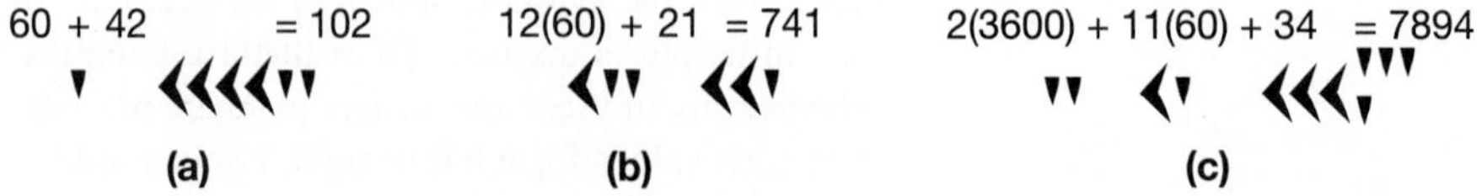

One   Ten
Figure 2.17

3(10) + 7 = 37

Figure 2.18

60 + 42   = 102   12(60) + 21 = 741   2(3600) + 11(60) + 34 = 7894

(a)   (b)   (c)

Figure 2.19

Unfortunately, in its earliest development, this system led to some confusion. For example, as illustrated in Figure 2.20, the numerals representing 74 ($= 1 \cdot 60 + 14$) and 3614 ($= 1 \cdot 60 \cdot 60 + 0 \cdot 60 + 14$) differed only in the spacing of symbols. Thus, there was a chance for misinterpretation. From 300 B.C.E. on, a separate symbol made up of two small triangles arranged one above the other was used to serve as a **placeholder** to indicate a vacant place (Figure 2.21). This removed some of the ambiguity. However, two Babylonian tens written next to each other could still be interpreted as 20, or 610, or even 3660. Although their placeholder acts much like our zero, the Babylonians did not recognize zero as a number.

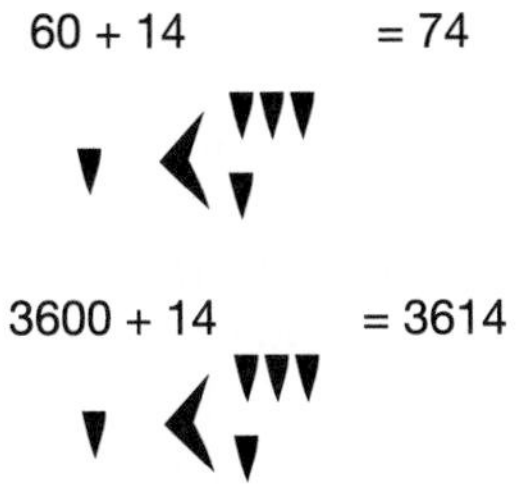

60 + 14 = 74
3600 + 14 = 3614

Figure 2.20

60 + 14 = 74
3600 + 0(60) + 14 = 3614

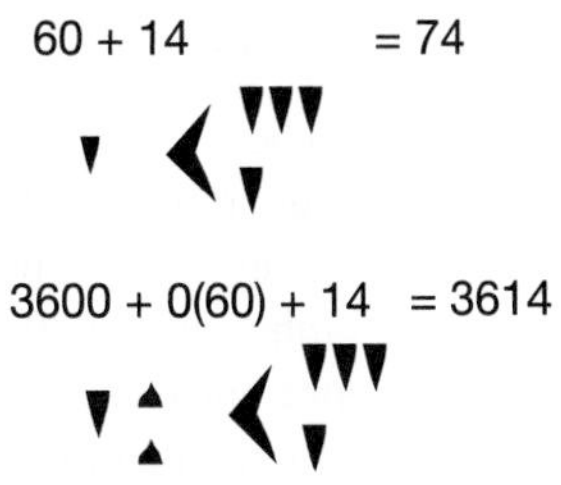

Figure 2.21

Example 2.10 Express the following Babylonian numerals in our numeration system.

a.
b.
c.

SOLUTION

a.
2(60) + 11 = 131
b.
3600 + 0(60) + 1 = 3601
c.
21(60) + 15 = 1275

■

The Mayan Numeration System

The **Mayan numeration system**, which developed between C.E. 300 and C.E. 900, was a vertical place-value system, and it introduced a symbol for **zero**. The system used only three elementary numerals (Figure 2.22).

Reflection from Research
Zero is an important number that should be carefully integrated into early number experiences. If children do not develop a clear understanding of zero early on, misconceptions can arise that might be detrimental to the further development of their understanding of number properties and subsequent development of algebraic thinking (Anthony & Walshaw, 2004).

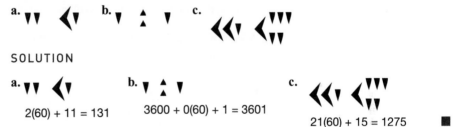

one
five
zero

Figure 2.22

Several Mayan numerals are shown in Figure 2.22 together with their respective values. The symbol for twenty in Figure 2.23 illustrates the use of place value in that the "dot" represents one "twenty" and the represents zero "ones."

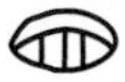

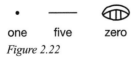

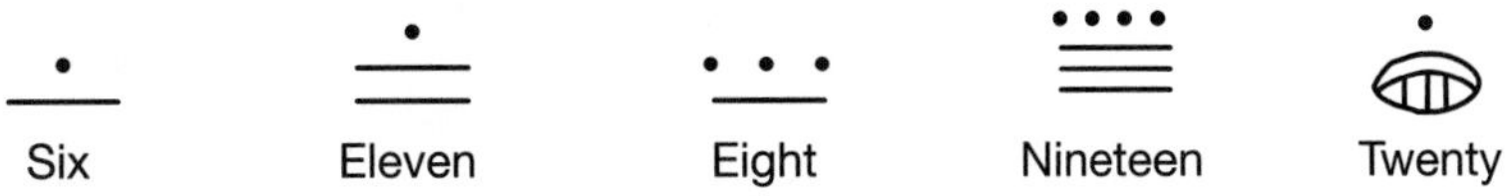

Six
Eleven
Eight
Nineteen
Twenty

Figure 2.23

Various place values for this system are illustrated in Figure 2.24.

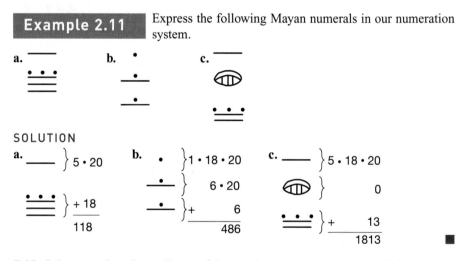

$\left.\begin{array}{c}\bullet\end{array}\right\}$ $18 \cdot 20^2$

$\left.\dfrac{\bullet}{}\right\}$ $18 \cdot 20$

$\left.\text{(eye)}\right\}$ 20

$\left.\begin{array}{c}\bullet\ \bullet\ \bullet\end{array}\right\}$ 1

Figure 2.24

The bottom section represents the number of ones (3 here), the second section from the bottom represents the number of 20s (0 here), the third section from the bottom represents the number of $18 \cdot 20$s (6 here), and the top section represents the number of $18 \cdot 20 \cdot 20$s (1 here). Reading from top to bottom, the value of the number represented is $1(18 \cdot 20 \cdot 20) + 6(18 \cdot 20) + 0(20) + 3(1)$, or 9363. (See the Focus On at the beginning of this chapter for additional insight into this system.)

Notice that in the Mayan numeration system, you must take great care in the way the numbers are spaced. For example, two horizontal bars could represent $5 + 5$ as $=$ or $5 \cdot 20 + 5$ as $\overline{\overline{}}$, depending on how the two bars are spaced. Also notice that the place-value feature of this system is somewhat irregular. After the ones place comes the 20s place. Then comes the $18 \cdot 20$s place. Thereafter, though, the values of the places are increased by multiplying by 20 to obtain $18 \cdot 20^2$, $18 \cdot 20^3$, $18 \cdot 20^4$, and so on.

Example 2.11   Express the following Mayan numerals in our numeration system.

a. b. c.

SOLUTION

a. $\left.\overline{}\right\}\ 5 \cdot 20$

$\left.\overline{\overline{\bullet\bullet\bullet}}\right\}\ +\ 18$

118

b. $\left.\bullet\right\}\ 1 \cdot 18 \cdot 20$

$\left.\overline{\bullet}\right\}\ 6 \cdot 20$

$\left.\overline{\bullet}\right\}\ +\ 6$

486

c. $\left.\overline{}\right\}\ 5 \cdot 18 \cdot 20$

$\left.\text{(eye)}\right\}\ 0$

$\left.\overline{\overline{\bullet\bullet\bullet}}\right\}\ +\ 13$

1813

Table 2.4 summarizes the attributes of the number systems we have studied.

TABLE 2.4

SYSTEM	ADDITIVE	SUBTRACTIVE	MULTIPLICATIVE	POSITIONAL	PLACE VALUE	HAS A ZERO
Tally	Yes	No	No	No	No	No
Egyptian	Yes	No	No	No	No	No
Roman	Yes	Yes	Yes	Yes	No	No
Babylonian	Yes	No	Yes	Yes	Yes	No
Mayan	Yes	No	Yes	Yes	Yes	Yes

✓ **Check for Understanding:** Exercise/Problem Set A #7–14

MATHEMATICAL MORSEL

When learning the names of two-digit numerals, some children suffer through a "reversals" stage, where they may write 21 for twelve or 13 for thirty-one. The following story from the December 5, 1990, *Grand Rapids* [Michigan] *Press* stresses the importance of eliminating reversals. "It was a case of mistaken identity. A transposed address that resulted in a bulldozer blunder. City orders had called for demolition on Tuesday of a boarded-up house at 451 Fuller Ave. S.E. But when the dust settled, 451 Fuller stood untouched. Down the street at 415 Fuller S.E., only a basement remained."

| Section 2.2 | EXERCISE / PROBLEM SET A |

EXERCISES

1. In the following paragraph, numbers are used in various ways. Specify whether each number is a cardinal number, an ordinal number, or an identification number. Linda dialed 314-781-9804 to place an order with a popular mail-order company. When the sales representative answered, Linda told her that her customer number was 13905. Linda then placed an order for 6 cotton T-shirts, stock number 7814, from page 28 of the catalog. For an extra $10 charge, Linda could have next-day delivery, but she chose the regular delivery system and was told her package would arrive November 20.

2. Define each of the following numbers in a way similar to the way in which the number three was defined in this section. (*Hint:* You may decide "impossible.")
   a. 7   **b.** 1   **c.** −3   **d.** 0

3. Explain how to count the elements of the set $\{a, b, c, d, e, f\}$.

4. Which number is larger, 5 or 8? Which numeral is larger?

5. Use the set method as illustrated in Figure 2.10 to explain why 7 > 3.

6. Place < , or > in the blanks to make each statement true. Indicate how you would verify your choice.
   a. 3 _____ 7   **b.** 11 _____ 9   **c.** 21 _____ 12

7. Change to Egyptian numerals.
   a. 9   **b.** 23   **c.** 453   **d.** 1231

8. Change to Roman numerals.
   a. 76   **b.** 49   **c.** 192   **d.** 1741

9. Change to Babylonian numerals.
   a. 47   **b.** 76   **c.** 347   **d.** 4192

10. Change to Mayan numerals.
   a. 17   **b.** 51   **c.** 275   **d.** 401

11. Change to numerals we use.
   a. ⟨▼▼   **b.** ▼ ⟨▼ ⟨   **c.** ▼▲⟨▼▼▼   **d.** MCMXCI
   e. CMLXXVI   **f.** MMMCCXLV   **g.** ∩∩∩∩II
   h. 9999IIII   **i.** 𝍦𝍦𝍦∩   **j.** $\underline{\overset{\cdots\cdots}{=}}$
   k. $\underline{\overset{\cdot\;\;\cdot}{=}}$ **l.** $\underline{\underset{\cdots}{\overset{\cdot}{=}}}$

12. Perform each of the following numeral conversions.
   a. Roman numeral DCCCXXIV to a Babylonian numeral
   b. Mayan numeral to a Roman numeral
   c. Babylonian numeral ▼⟨⟨⟨⟨▼▼▼▼ to a Mayan numeral

13. Imagine representing 246 in the Mayan, Babylonian, and Egyptian numeration systems.
   a. In which system is the greatest number of symbols required?
   b. In which system is the smallest number of symbols required?
   c. Do your answers for parts (a) and (b) hold true for other numbers as well?

14. In 2010, the National Football League's championship game was Super Bowl XLIV. What was the first year of the Super Bowl?

PROBLEMS

15. Some children go through a reversal stage; that is, they confuse 13 and 31, 27 and 72, 59 and 95. What numerals would give Roman children similar difficulties? How about Egyptian children?

16. a. How many Egyptian numerals are needed to represent the following problems?

    i. 59 + 88   **ii.** 150 − 99

    iii. 7897 + 934   **iv.** 9698 − 5389

    b. State a general rule for determining the number of Egyptian numerals needed to represent an addition (or subtraction) problem written in our numeral system.

17. A newspaper advertisement introduced a new car as follows: IV Cams, XXXII Valves, CCLXXX Horsepower, coming December XXVI—the new 1999 Lincoln Mark VII. Write the Roman numeral that represents the model year of the car.

18. Linda pulled out one full page from the Sunday newspaper. If the left half was numbered A4 and the right half was numbered A15, how many pages were in the A section of the newspaper?

19. Determine which of the following numbers is larger.

$$1993 \times (1 + 2 + 3 + 4 + \cdots + 1994)$$
$$1994 \times (1 + 2 + 3 + 4 + \cdots + 1993)$$

20. You have five coins that appear to be identical and a balance scale. One of these coins is counterfeit and either heavier or lighter than the other four. Explain how the counterfeit coin can be identified and whether it is lighter or heavier than the others with only three weighings on the balance scale.

(*Hint:* Solve a simpler problem—given just three coins, can you find the counterfeit in two weighings?)

21. One system of numeration in Greece in about 300 B.C.E., called the Ionian system, was based on letters of the alphabet. The different symbols used for numbers less than 1000 are as follows:

$$\alpha \quad \beta \quad \gamma \quad \delta \quad \epsilon \quad \varsigma \quad \xi \quad \eta \quad \theta \quad \iota \quad \kappa \quad \lambda \quad \mu \quad \nu$$
1   2   3   4   5   6   7   8   9   10   20   30   40   50

$$\xi \quad o \quad \pi \quad \varsigma \quad \rho \quad \sigma \quad \tau \quad \upsilon \quad \phi \quad \chi \quad \psi \quad \omega \quad \chi$$
60   70   80   90   100   200   300   400   500   600   700   800   900

To represent multiples of 1000 an accent mark was used. For example, $'\epsilon$ was used to represent 5000. The accent mark might be omitted if the size of the number being represented was clear without it.

a. Express the following Ionian numerals in our numeration system.

    i. $\mu\beta$ **ii.** $\chi\kappa\epsilon$ **iii.** $\gamma\phi\lambda\gamma$ **iv.** $\pi' \theta\omega\alpha$

b. Express each of the following numerals in the Ionian numeration system.

    i. 85   **ii.** 744   **iii.** 2153   **iv.** 21,534

c. Was the Ionian system a place-value system?

| Section 2.2 | **EXERCISE / PROBLEM SET B**

EXERCISES

1. Write sentences that show the number 45 used in each of the following ways.
    a. As a cardinal number
    b. As an ordinal number
    c. As an identification number

2. Decide whether the word in parentheses is being used in the "number sense" (as an idea) or in the "numeral sense" (as a symbol for an idea).
    a. Camel is a five-letter word.   (camel)
    b. A camel is an animal with four legs.   (camel)
    c. Tim is an Anglo-Saxon name.   (Tim)
    d. Tim was an Anglo-Saxon.   (Tim)

3. Explain why each of the following sets can or cannot be used to count the number of elements in {a, b, c, d}.
    a. {4}   **b.** {0, 1, 2, 3}   **c.** {1, 2, 3, 4}

4. Which is more abstract: number or numeral? Explain.

5. Determine the greater of the two numbers 4 and 9 in three different ways.

6. Use the definition of "less than" given in this section to explain why there are exactly five whole numbers that are less than 5.

7. Change to Egyptian numerals.
    a. 2431   **b.** 10,352

8. Change to Roman numerals.
   a. 79   **b.** 3054

9. Change to Babylonian numerals.
   a. 117   **b.** 3521

10. Change to Mayan numerals.
   a. 926   **b.** 37,865

11. Express each of the following numerals in our numeration system.
   a.   **b.**

   c. MCCXLVII   **d.**

12. Complete the following chart expressing the given numbers in the other numeration system.

	Babylonian	Egyptian	Roman	Mayan
a.				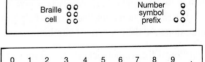
b.			CXLIV	
c.		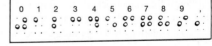		
d.	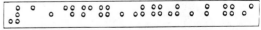			

13. Is it possible for a numeration system to be positional and not place-value? Explain why or why not. If possible, give an example.

14. After the credits for a film, the Roman numeral MCMLXXXIX appears, representing the year in which the film was made. Express the year in our numeration system.

PROBLEMS

15. What is the largest number that you can enter on your calculator
   a. if you may use the same digit more than once?
   b. if you must use a different digit in each place?

16. The following Chinese numerals are part of one of the oldest numeration systems known.

   一 1   十 10
   二 2   百 100
   三 3   千 1000
   四 4
   五 5
   六 6
   七 7
   八 8
   九 9

The numerals are written vertically. Some examples follow

   十 二   represents 12

   二 十   represents 20

   三 百 六 十 七   represents 367

   a. Express each of the following numerals in this Chinese numeration system: 80, 19, 52, 400, 603, 6031.
   b. Is this system a positional system? an additive system? a multiplicative system?

17. Two hundred persons are positioned in 10 rows, each containing 20 persons. From each of the 20 columns thus formed, the shortest is selected, and the tallest of these 20 (short) persons is tagged A. These persons now return to their initial places. Next, the tallest person in each row is selected and from these 10 (tall) persons the shortest is tagged B. Which of the two tagged persons is the taller (if they are different people)?

18. Braille numerals are formed using dots in a two-dot by three-dot Braille cell. Numerals are preceded by a backwards "L" dot symbol. The following shows the basic elements for Braille numerals and two examples.

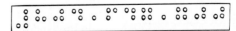

One billion, four hundred sixty-seven million, seventy thousand, two hundred seventy-nine.

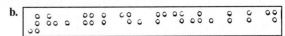

Eight hundred four million, six hundred forty-seven thousand, seven hundred.

Express these Braille numerals in our numeration system.

   a.

   b.

19. The heights of five famous human-made structures are related as follows:
- The height of the Statue of Liberty is 65 feet more than half the height of the Great Pyramid at Giza.
- The height of the Eiffel Tower is 36 feet more than three times the height of Big Ben.
- The Great Pyramid at Giza is 164 feet taller than Big Ben.
- The Leaning Tower of Pisa is 137 feet shorter than Big Ben.
- The total of all of the heights is nearly half a mile. In fact, the sum of the five heights is 2264 feet.

Find the height of each of the five structures.

20. Can an 8×8 checkerboard with two opposite corner squares removed be exactly covered (without cutting) by thirty-one 2×1 dominoes? Give details.

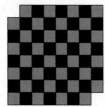

Analyzing Student Thinking

21. Tammie asserts that if $n(A) \leq n(B)$ where A and B are finite sets, then $A \subseteq B$. Is she correct? Explain.

22. Which way is a child most likely to first learn the ordering of whole numbers less than 10: **(i)** using the counting chant; **(ii)** using the set method; **(iii)** using the number line method? Explain.

23. Anthony thinks that we should all use the tally numeration system instead of the Hindu–Arabic system because the Tally system is so easy. How should you respond?

24. When asked to express 999 in the Egyptian numeration system, Misti says that it will require twenty-seven numerals and Victor says that it will require a lot more. Which student is correct? Explain.

25. When teaching the Roman numeration system, you show your students that it is additive, subtractive, and multiplicative. Shalonda asks, "Why can't you do division in the Roman system?" How should you respond?

26. Natalie asks if the symbol comprised of two small triangles, one atop the other, in the Babylonian numeration system is zero. How should you respond?

27. Blanca says that since zero means nothing, she doesn't have to use a numeral for zero in the Mayan numeration system. Instead, she can simply leave a blank space. Is she correct? Explain.

Problems Relating to the NCTM Standards and Curriculum Focal Points

1. The Focal Points for Prekindergarten state "Developing an understanding of whole numbers, including concepts of correspondence, counting, cardinality, and comparison." Explain how the concept of cardinality (cardinal number) introduced in this section could be used to help young children understand the concept of number.

2. The Focal Points for Kindergarten state "Representing, comparing, and ordering whole numbers and joining and separating sets. Ordering objects by measurable attributes."

What is a concept about representing numbers introduced in this section that would be important for a kindergartener to understand? Explain.

3. The NCTM Standards state "All students should develop a sense of whole numbers and represent and use them in flexible ways including relating, composing, and decomposing numbers." Explain how numbers in the Babylonian and Mayan systems could be composed and decomposed.

2.3   THE HINDU–ARABIC SYSTEM

STARTING POINT

In the land of Odd, they only use quarters, nickels, and pennies for their coins. Martina, who lives in Odd, likes to carry as few coins as possible. What is the minimum number of coins Martina could carry for each of the following amounts of money? How many of each coin would she have in each case?

68¢   39¢   83¢   97¢

If Martina always exchanges her money to have a minimum number of coins, what is the maximum number of nickels that she would have after an exchange? Why?

Children's Literature
www.wiley.com/college/musser
See "Anno's Counting House"
by Mitsumasa Anno.

The Hindu–Arabic Numeration System

The **Hindu–Arabic numeration system** that we use today was developed about C.E. 800. The following list features the basic numerals and various attributes of this system.

1. *Digits, 0, 1, 2, 3, 4, 5, 6, 7, 8, 9:* These 10 symbols, or **digits**, can be used in combination to represent all possible numbers.

2. *Grouping by tens (decimal system):* Grouping into sets of 10 is a basic principle of this system, probably because we have 10 "digits" on our two hands. (The word *digit* literally means "finger" or "toe.") Ten ones are replaced by one ten, ten tens are replaced by one hundred, ten hundreds are replaced by one thousand, and so on. Figure 2.25 shows how grouping is helpful when representing a collection of objects. The number of objects grouped together is called the **base** of the system; thus our Hindu–Arabic system is a base ten system.

   NOTE: Recall that an element is listed only once in a set. Although all the dots in Figure 2.25 look the same, they are assumed to be unique, individual elements here and in all such subsequent figures.

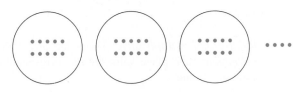

3 tens and 4

Figure 2.25

The following two models are often used to represent multidigit numbers.

a. **Bundles of sticks** can be any kind of sticks banded together with rubber bands. Each 10 loose sticks are bound together with a rubber band to represent 10, then 10 bundles of 10 are bound together to represent 100, and so on (Figure 2.26).

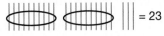

Figure 2.26

b. **Base ten pieces** (also called **Dienes blocks**) consist of individual cubes, called "units," "longs," made up of ten units, "flats," made up of ten longs, or one hundred units, and so on (Figure 2.27). Inexpensive two-dimensional sets of base ten pieces can be made using grid paper cutouts.

Reflection from Research
Results from research suggest that base ten blocks should be used in the development of students' place-value concepts (Fuson, 1990).

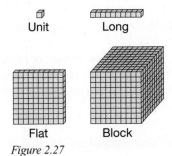

Figure 2.27

3. *Place value (hence positional):* Each of the various places in the numeral 6523, for example, has its own value.

thousand	hundred	ten	one
6	5	2	3

The 6 represents 6 thousands, the 5 represents 5 hundreds, the 2 represents 2 tens, and the 3 represents 3 ones due to the place-value attribute of the Hindu–Arabic system.

The following device is used to represent numbers written in place value. A **chip abacus** is a piece of paper or cardboard containing lines that form columns, on which chips or markers are used to represent unit values. Conceptually, this model is more abstract than the previous models because markers represent different values, depending on the columns in which the markers appear (Figure 2.28).

100	10	1		100	10	1		100	10	1		100	10	1
	••			••					••			•••	••	:::

Twenty	Two hundred	Two	Three hundred twenty-six

Figure 2.28

4. *Additive and multiplicative.* The value of a Hindu–Arabic numeral is found by *multiplying* each place value by its corresponding digit and then *adding* all the resulting products.

Place values:	thousand	hundred	ten	one
Digits:	6	5	2	3
Numeral value:	$6 \times 1000 + 5 \times 100 + 2 \times 10 + 3 \times 1$			
Numeral:	6523			

Expressing a numeral as the sum of its digits times their respective place values is called the numeral's **expanded form** or **expanded notation**. The expanded form of 83,507 is

$$8 \times 10,000 + 3 \times 1000 + 5 \times 100 + 0 \times 10 + 7 \times 1.$$

Because $7 \times 1 = 7$, we can simply write 7 in place of 7×1 when expressing 83,507 in expanded form.

Example 2.12   Express the following numbers in expanded form.

a. 437   **b.** 3001

SOLUTION
a. $437 = 4(100) + 3(10) + 7$
b. $3001 = 3(1000) + 0(100) + 0(10) + 1$ or $3(1000) + 1$ ∎

Notice that our numeration system requires fewer symbols to represent numbers than did earlier systems. Also, the Hindu–Arabic system is far superior when performing computations. The computational aspects of the Hindu–Arabic system will be studied in Chapter 3.

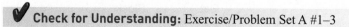

Check for Understanding: Exercise/Problem Set A #1–3

Numbers and Counting

Base-10 blocks can show numbers.

Base-10 block	Base-10 shorthand	Name	Value
	■	cube	1
	|	long	10
	▢	flat	100
	▢	big cube	1,000

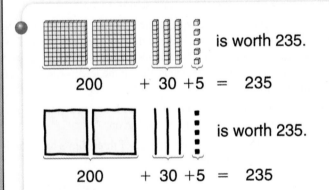

is worth 235.

200 + 30 + 5 = 235

is worth 235.

200 + 30 + 5 = 235

Try It Together

Use blocks to show 46 and 64. Is the 6 worth more in 46 or 64?

eleven MRB 11

Naming Hindu–Arabic Numerals

Reflection from Research
Children are able to recognize and read one- and two-digit numerals prior to being able to write them (Baroody, Gannon, Berent, & Ginsburg, 1983).

Associated with each Hindu–Arabic numeral is a word name. Some of the English names are as follows:

0 zero	10 ten
1 one	11 eleven
2 two	12 twelve
3 three	13 thirteen (three plus ten)
4 four	14 fourteen (four plus ten)
5 five	21 twenty-one (two tens plus one)
6 six	87 eighty-seven (eight tens plus seven)
7 seven	205 two hundred five (two hundreds plus five)
8 eight	1,374 one thousand three hundred seventy-four
9 nine	23,100 twenty-three thousand one hundred

Here are a few observations about the naming procedure.

1. The numbers 0, 1, . . . , 12 all have unique names.

2. The numbers 13, 14, . . . , 19 are the "teens," and are composed of a combination of earlier names, with the ones place named first. For example, "thirteen" is short for "three ten," which means "ten plus three," and so on.

3. The numbers 20, . . . , 99 are combinations of earlier names but *reversed* from the teens in that the tens place is named first. For example, 57 is "fifty-seven," which means "five tens plus seven," and so on. The method of naming the numbers from 20 to 90 is better than the way we name the teens, due to the left-to-right agreement with the way the numerals are written.

4. The numbers 100, . . . , 999 are combinations of hundreds and previous names. For example, 538 is read "five hundred thirty-eight," and so on.

NCTM Standard
All students should connect number words and numerals to the quantities they represent, using various physical models and representations.

5. In numerals containing more than three digits, groups of three digits are usually set off by commas. For example, the number

123,456,789,987,654,321

quadrillion trillion billion million thousand

is read "one hundred twenty-three quadrillion four hundred fifty-six trillion seven hundred eighty-nine billion nine hundred eighty-seven million six hundred fifty-four thousand three hundred twenty-one." (Internationally, the commas are omitted and single spaces are used instead. Also, in some countries, commas are used in place of decimal points.) Notice that the word *and* does not appear in any of these names: it is reserved to separate the decimal portion of a numeral from the whole-number portion.

Figure 2.29 graphically displays the three distinct ideas that children need to learn in order to understand the Hindu–Arabic numeration system.

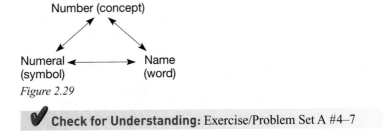

Number (concept)

Numeral   Name
(symbol)   (word)

Figure 2.29

✔ **Check for Understanding:** Exercise/Problem Set A #4–7

Nondecimal Numeration Systems

Our Hindu–Arabic system is based on grouping by ten. To understand our system better and to experience some of the difficulties children have when learning our numeration system, it is instructive to study similar systems, but with different place values. For example, suppose that a Hindu–Arabic-like system utilized one hand (five digits) instead of two (ten digits). Then, grouping would be done in groups of five. If sticks were used, bundles would be made up of five each (Figure 2.30). Here seventeen objects are represented by three bundles of five each with two left over. This can be expressed by the equation $17_{\text{ten}} = 32_{\text{five}}$, which is read "seventeen base ten equals three two base five." (Be careful not to read 32_{five} as "thirty-two," because thirty-two means "three tens and two," not "three fives and two.") The subscript words "ten" and "five" indicate that the grouping was done in tens and fives, respectively. For simplicity, the subscript "ten" will be omitted; hence 37 will always mean 37_{ten}. (With this agreement, the numeral 24_{five} could also be written 24_5 since the subscript "5" means the usual base ten 5.) The 10 digits $0, 1, 2, \ldots, 9$ are used in base ten; however, only the five digits 0, 1, 2, 3, 4 are necessary in base five. A few examples of base five numerals are illustrated in Figure 2.31.

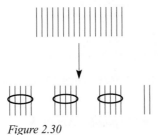

Figure 2.30

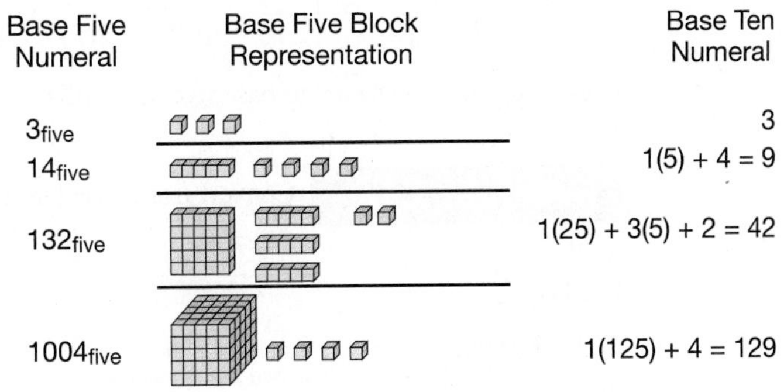

Base Five Numeral	Base Five Block Representation	Base Ten Numeral
3_{five}		3
14_{five}		$1(5) + 4 = 9$
132_{five}		$1(25) + 3(5) + 2 = 42$
1004_{five}		$1(125) + 4 = 129$

Figure 2.31

Reflection from Research
Students experience more success counting objects that can be moved around than they do counting pictured objects that cannot be moved (Wang, Resnick, & Boozer, 1971).

Counting using base five names differs from counting in base ten. The first ten base five numerals appear in Figure 2.32. Interesting junctures in counting come after a number has a 4 in its ones column. For example, what is the next number (written in base five) after 24_{five}? after 34_{five}? after 44_{five}? after 444_{five}?

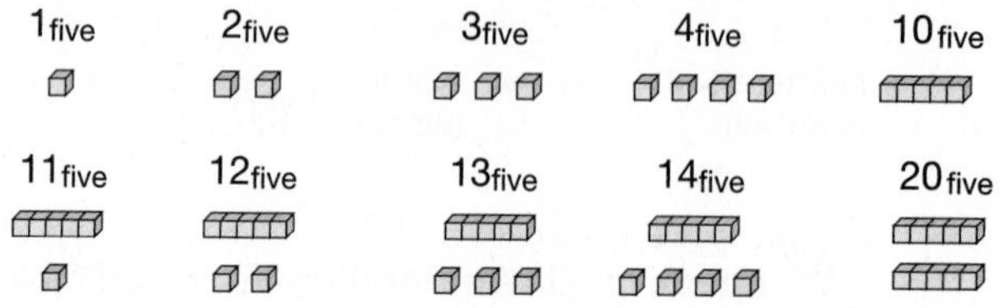

1_{five} 2_{five} 3_{five} 4_{five} 10_{five}

11_{five} 12_{five} 13_{five} 14_{five} 20_{five}

Figure 2.32

Figure 2.33 shows how to find the number after 24_{five} using multibase pieces.

Exchange these for a long

24_{five} $24_{five} + 1_{five}$ 30_{five}

Figure 2.33

Converting numerals from base five to base ten can be done using (1) multibase pieces or (2) place values and expanded notation.

Example 2.13   Express 123_{five} in base ten.

SOLUTION
a. *Using Base Five Pieces:* See Figure 2.34.

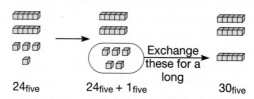
Base Five Pieces

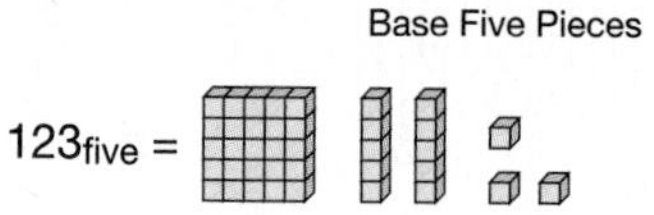

$123_{five} = $

Base ten values $25 + 10 + 3 = 38$. Thus $123_{five} = 38$.
Figure 2.34

b. *Using Place Value and Expanded Notation*

Place values
in base ten $\longrightarrow$

$$123_{five} = \frac{25 \mid 5 \mid 1}{1 \mid 2 \mid 3} = 1(25) + 2(5) + 3(1) = 38$$

Converting from base ten to base five also utilizes place value.

Example 2.14   Convert from base ten to base five.

a. 97
b. 341

SOLUTION
a. $97 = \dfrac{25 \mid 5 \mid 1}{? \mid ? \mid ?}$ ← *Base five place values expressed using base ten numerals*

Algebraic Reasoning
The process described for converting 97 to a base five number is really solving the equation $97 = 25x + 5y + z$ where x, y, and z are less than 5. The solution is $x = 3$, $y = 4$, and $z = 2$. Although an equation was not used, the reasoning is still algebraic.

Think: How many 25s are in 97? There are three since $3 \cdot 25 = 75$ with 22 remaining. How many 5s in the remainder? There are four since $4 \cdot 5 = 20$. Finally, since $22 - 20 = 2$, there are two 1s.

$$97 = 3(25) + 4(5) + 2 = 342_{\text{five}}$$

b. A more systematic method can be used to convert 341 to its base five numeral. First, find the highest power of 5 that will divide into 341; that is, which is the greatest among 1, 5, 25, 125, 625, 3125, and so on, that will divide into 341? The answer in this case is 125. The rest of that procedure uses long division, each time dividing the remainder by the next smaller place value.

$$
\begin{array}{llll}
\quad\ 2 & \quad\ 3 & \quad\ 3 & \ 1 \\
125\overline{)341} & 25\overline{)91} & 5\overline{)16} & \\
\ \ 250 & \ \ 75 & \ \ 15 & \\
\ \ \ \ 91 & \ \ 16 & \ \ \ \ 1 &
\end{array}
$$

Therefore, $341 = 2(125) + 3(25) + 3(5) + 1$, or 2331_{five}. More simply, $341 = 2331_{\text{five}}$, where 2, 3, and 3 are the quotients from left to right and 1 is the final remainder. ∎

When expressing place values in various bases, **exponents** can provide a convenient shorthand notation. The symbol a^m represents the product of m factors of a. Thus $5^3 = 5 \cdot 5 \cdot 5$, $7^2 = 7 \cdot 7$, $3^4 = 3 \cdot 3 \cdot 3 \cdot 3$, and so on. Using this exponential notation, the first several place values of base five, in reverse order, are $1, 5, 5^2, 5^3, 5^4$. Although we have studied only base ten and base five thus far, these same place-value ideas can be used with any base greater than one. For example, in base two the place values, listed in reverse order, are $1, 2, 2^2, 2^3, 2^4, \ldots$; in base three the place values are $1, 3, 3^2, 3^3, 3^4, \ldots$. The next two examples illustrate numbers expressed in bases other than five and their relationship to base ten.

Example 2.15 Express the following numbers in base ten.

a. 11011_{two}
b. 1234_{eight}
c. $1ET_{\text{twelve}}$
(NOTE: Base twelve has twelve basic numerals: 0 through 9, T for ten, and E for eleven.)

SOLUTION

a. $11011_{\text{two}} = \begin{array}{c|c|c|c|c} 2^4 & 2^3 & 2^2 & 2 & 1 \\ \hline 1 & 1 & 0 & 1 & 1 \end{array} = 1(16) + 1(8) + 0(4) + 1(2) + 1(1) = 27$

b. $1234_{\text{eight}} = \begin{array}{c|c|c|c} 8^3 & 8^2 & 8 & 1 \\ \hline 1 & 2 & 3 & 4 \end{array} = 1(8^3) + 2(8^2) + 3(8) + 4(1) = 512 + 128 + 24 + 4 = 668$

c. $1ET_{\text{twelve}} = \begin{array}{c|c|c} 12^{12} & 12 & 1 \\ \hline 1 & E & T \end{array} = 1(12^2) + E(12) + T(1) = 144 + 132 + 10 = 286$ ∎

Converting from base ten to other bases is accomplished by using grouping just as we did in base five.

Example 2.16 Convert from base ten to the given base.

a. 53 to base two
b. 1982 to base twelve

SOLUTION

a. $53 = \dfrac{2^5 \mid 2^4 \mid 2^3 \mid 2^2 \mid 2 \mid 1}{\ ?\ \mid\ ?\ \mid\ ?\ \mid\ ?\ \mid ? \mid ?}$

Think: What is the largest power of 2 contained in 53?

Answer: $2^5 = 32$. Now we can find the remaining digits by dividing by decreasing powers of 2.

$$
\begin{array}{ccccccc}
& 1 & & 1 & & 0 & & 1 & & 0 & 1\\
32\overline{)53} & & 16\overline{)21} & & 8\overline{)5} & & 4\overline{)5} & & 2\overline{)1} & \\
& 32 & & 16 & & 0 & & 4 & & 0 & \\
\cline{2-2}\cline{4-4}\cline{6-6}\cline{8-8}\cline{10-10}
& 21 & & 5 & & 5 & & 1 & & 1 &
\end{array}
$$

Therefore, $53 = 110101_{two}$.

b. $1982 = \dfrac{12^3\,(=1728) \mid 12^2\,(=144) \mid 12^1\,(=12) \mid 1}{\qquad ? \qquad\mid\qquad ? \qquad\mid\quad ? \quad\mid\ ?}$

$$
\begin{array}{cccc}
1 & 1 & 9 & 2\\
1728\overline{)1982} & 144\overline{)254} & 12\overline{)110} & 1\overline{)2}\\
1728 & 144 & 108 & 2\\
\cline{1-1}\cline{2-2}\cline{3-3}\cline{4-4}
254 & 110 & 2 & 0
\end{array}
$$

Therefore, $1982 = 1192_{twelve}$. ∎

 Check for Understanding: Exercise/Problem Set A #8–25

MATHEMATICAL MORSEL

Consider the three cards shown here. Choose any number from 1 to 7 and note which cards your number is on. Then add the numbers in the upper right-hand corner of the cards containing your number. What did you find? This "magic" can be justified mathematically using the binary (base two) numeration system.

Section 2.3 **EXERCISE / PROBLEM SET A**

EXERCISES

1. Write each of the following numbers in expanded notation.
  a. 70   **b.** 300
  c. 984   **d.** 60,006,060

2. Write each of the following expressions in standard place-value form.
  a. $1(1000) + 2(100) + 7$
  b. $5(100,000) + 3(100)$

  c. $8(10^6) + 7(10^4) + 6(10^2) + 5(1)$
  d. $2(10^9) + 3(10^4) + 3(10^3) + 4(10)$

3. State the place value of the digit 2 in each numeral.
  a. 6234
  b. 5142
  c. 2168

4. Words and their roots often suggest numbers. Using this idea, complete the following chart. (*Hint:* Look for a pattern.)

WORD	LATIN ROOT	MEANING OF ROOT	POWER OF 10
Billion	bi	2	9
Trillion	tri	3	(a)
Quadrillion	quater	(b)	15
(c)	quintus	5	18
Sextillion	sex	6	21
(d)	septem	7	(e)
Octillion	octo	8	27
Nonillion	novem	(f)	(g)
(h)	decem	10	33

5. Write these numerals in words.
   a. 2,000,000,000   **b.** 87,000,000,000,000
   c. 52,672,405,123,139

6. The following numbers are written in words. Rewrite each one using Hindu–Arabic numerals.
   a. Seven million six hundred three thousand fifty-nine
   b. Two hundred six billion four hundred fifty-three thousand

7. List three attributes of our Hindu–Arabic numeration system.

8. Write a base four numeral for the following set of base four pieces. Represent the blocks on the Chapter 2 eManipulative activity *Multibase Blocks* on our Web site and make all possible trades first.

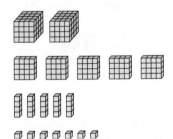

9. Represent each of the following numerals with multibase pieces. Use the Chapter 2 eManipulative activity *Multibase Blocks* on our Web site to assist you.
   a. 134_{five} **b.** 1011_{two} **c.** 3211_{four}

10. To express 69 with the fewest pieces of base three blocks, flats, longs, and units, you need _____ blocks, _____ flats, _____ longs, and _____ units. The Chapter 2 eManipulative activity *Multibase Blocks* on our Web site may help in the solution.

11. Represent each of the following with bundling sticks and chips on a chip abacus. (The Chapter 2 eManipulative *Chip Abacus* on our Web site may help in understanding how the chip abacus works.)
   a. 24   **b.** 221_{five} **c.** 167_{eight}

12. a. Draw a sketch of 62 pennies and trade for nickels and quarters. Write the corresponding base five numeral.
   b. Write the base five numeral for 93 and 2173.

13. How many different symbols would be necessary for a base twenty-three system?

14. What is wrong with the numerals 85_{eight} and 24_{three}?

15. True or false?
   a. $7_{\text{eight}} = 7$ **b.** $30_{\text{four}} = 30$
   c. $200_{\text{three}} = 200_{\text{nine}}$

16. a. Write out the base five numerals in order from 1 to 100_{five}.
   b. Write out the base two numerals in order from 1 to 10000_{two}.
   c. Write out the base three numerals in order from 1 to 1000_{three}.
   d. In base six, write the next four numbers after 254_{six}.
   e. What base four numeral follows 303_{four}?

17. Write each of the following base seven numerals in expanded notation.
   a. 15_{seven} **b.** 123_{seven} **c.** 5046_{seven}

18. a. What is the largest three-digit base four number?
   b. What are the five base four numbers that follow it? Give your answers in base four numeration.

19. Use the Chapter 2 dynamic spreadsheet *Base Converter* on our Web site to convert the base ten numbers 2400 and 2402, which both have four digits, to a base seven number. What do you notice about the number of digits in the base seven representations of these numbers? Why is this?

20. Convert each base ten numeral into a numeral in the base requested.
   a. 395 in base eight   **b.** 748 in base four
   c. 54 in base two

21. The base twelve numeration system has the following twelve symbols: 0, 1, 2, 3, 4, 5, 6, 7, 8, 9, T, E. Change each of the following numerals to base ten numerals. Use the Chapter 2 dynamic spreadsheet *Base Converter* on our Web site to check your answers.
   a. 142_{twelve} **b.** 234_{twelve} **c.** 503_{twelve}
   d. $T9_{\text{twelve}}$ **e.** $T0E_{\text{twelve}}$ **f.** $ETET_{\text{twelve}}$

22. The hexadecimal numeration system, used in computer programming, is a base sixteen system that uses the symbols 0, 1, 2, 3, 4, 5, 6, 7, 8, 9, A, B, C, D, E, and F. Change each of the following hexadecimal numerals to base ten numerals.
   a. 213_{sixteen} **b.** $1C2B_{\text{sixteen}}$

23. Write each of the following base ten numerals in base sixteen (hexadecimal) numerals.
   a. 375   **b.** 2941   **c.** 9520   **d.** 24,274

24. Write each of the following numbers in base six and in base twelve.
   a. 74   **b.** 128   **c.** 210   **d.** 2438

25. Find the missing base.
   a. $35 = 120$ _____   **b.** $41_{\text{six}} = 27$ _____
   c. $52_{\text{seven}} = 34$ _____

PROBLEMS

26. What bases make these equations true?
  a. $32 = 44$ _____   **b.** $57_{\text{eight}} = 10$ _____
  c. $31_{\text{four}} = 11$ _____   **d.** $15_x = 30_y$

27. The set of even whole numbers is the set $\{0, 2, 4, 6, \ldots\}$. What can be said about the ones digit of every even number in the following bases?
  a. 10   **b.** 4   **c.** 2   **d.** 5

28. Mike used 2989 digits to number the pages of a book. How many pages does the book have?

29. The sum of the digits in a two-digit number is 12. If the digits are reversed, the new number is 18 greater than the original number. What is the number?

30. To determine a friend's birth date, ask him or her to perform the following calculations and tell you the result: Multiply the number of the month in which you were born by 4 and add 13 to the result. Then multiply that answer by 25 and subtract 200. Add your birth date (day of month) to that answer and then multiply by 2. Subtract 40 from the result and then multiply by 50. Add the last two digits of your birth year to that answer and, finally, subtract 10,500.
  a. Try this sequence of operations with your own birth date. How does place value allow you to determine a birth date from the final answer? Try the sequence again with a different birth date.
  b. Use expanded notation to explain why this technique always works.

Section 2.3 **EXERCISE / PROBLEM SET B**

EXERCISES

1. Write each of the following numbers in expanded form.
  a. 409   **b.** 7094
  c. 746   **d.** 840,001

2. Write each expression in place-value form.
  a. $3(1000) + 7(10) + 5$
  b. $7(10,000) + 6(100)$
  c. $6(10^5) + 3(10^3) + 9(1)$
  d. $6(10^7) + 9(10^5)$

3. State the place value of the digit 0 in each numeral.
  a. 40,762   **b.** 9802   **c.** 0

4. The names of the months in the premodern calendar, which had a different number of months than we do now, was based on the Latin roots for bi, tri, quater, etc. in Part A Exercise 4. Consider the names of the months on the premodern calendar. These names suggest the number of the month. What was September's number on the premodern calendar? What was October's number? November's? If December were the last month of the premodern calendar year, how many months made up a year?

5. Write these numerals in words.
  a. 32,090,047
  b. 401,002,560,300
  c. 98,000,000,000,000,000

6. The following numbers are written in words. Rewrite each one using Hindu–Arabic numerals.
  a. Twenty-seven million sixty-nine thousand fourteen
  b. Twelve trillion seventy million three thousand five

7. Explain how the Hindu–Arabic numeration system is multiplicative and additive.

8. Write a base three numeral for the following set of base three pieces. Represent the blocks on the Chapter 2 eManipulative activity *Multibase Blocks* on our Web site and make all possible trades first.

9. Represent each of the following numerals with multibase pieces. Use the Chapter 2 eManipulative *Multibase Blocks* on our Web site to assist you.
  a. 221_{three}
  b. 122_{four}
  c. 112_{four}
  d. List these three numbers from smallest to largest.
  e. Explain why you can't just compare the first digit in the different base representations to determine which is larger.

10. To express 651 with the smallest number of base eight pieces (blocks, flats, longs, and units), you need _____ blocks, _____ flats, _____ longs, and _____ units.

11. Represent each of the following with bundling sticks and chips on a chip abacus. (The Chapter 2 eManipulative *Chip Abacus* on our Web site may help in understanding how the chip abacus works.)
  a. 38   **b.** 52_{six} **c.** 1032_{five}

12. Suppose that you have 10 "longs" in a set of multibase pieces in each of the following bases. Make all possible exchanges and write the numeral the pieces represent in that base.
    a. Ten longs in base eight
    b. Ten longs in base six
    c. Ten longs in base three

13. If all the letters of the alphabet were used as our single-digit numerals, what would be the name of our base system? If a represented zero, b represented one, and so on, what would be the base ten numeral for the "alphabet" numeral zz?

14. Explain why a base six numeration system doesn't use more than six different symbols.

15. True or false?
    a. $8_{\text{nine}} = 8_{\text{eleven}}$
    b. $30_{\text{five}} = 30_{\text{six}}$
    c. $30_{\text{eight}} = 40_{\text{six}}$

16. a. Write out the first 20 base four numerals.
    b. How many base four numerals precede 2000_{four}?
    c. Write out the base six numerals in order from 1 to 100_{six}.
    d. What base nine numeral follows 888_{nine}?

17. Write each of the following base three numerals in expanded notation.
    a. 22_{three}
    b. 212_{three}
    c. 12110_{three}

18. a. What is the largest six-digit base two number?
    b. What are the next three base two numbers? Give your answers in base two numeration.

19. Find two different numbers whose base 10 representations have a different number of digits but their base three representations each has 4 digits. The Chapter 2 dynamic spreadsheet *Base Converter* on our Web site can assist in solving this problem.

20. Convert each base ten numeral into its numeral in the base requested.
    a. 142 in base twelve
    b. 72 in base two
    c. 231 in base eight

21. Find the base ten numerals for each of the following. Use the Chapter 2 dynamic spreadsheet *Base Converter* on our Web site to check your answers.
    a. 342_{five} b. $TE0_{\text{twelve}}$ c. 101101_{two}

22. Using the hexidecimal digits described in Part A, Exercise 22, rewrite the following hexidecimal numerals as base ten numerals.
    a. $A4_{\text{sixteen}}$ b. $420E_{\text{sixteen}}$

23. Convert these base two numerals into base eight numerals. Can you state a shortcut? [*Hint:* Look at part (d).]
    a. 1001_{two} b. 110110_{two}
    c. 10101010_{two} d. 101111_{two}

24. Convert the following base five numerals into base nine numerals.
    a. 12_{five} b. 204_{five} c. 1322_{five}

25. Find the missing base.
    a. $28 = 34$ _____
    b. $28 = 26$ _____
    c. $23_{\text{twelve}} = 43$ _____

PROBLEMS

26. Under what conditions can this equation be true: $a_b = b_a$? Explain.

27. Propose new names for the numbers 11, 12, 13, . . . , 19 so that the naming scheme is consistent with the numbers 20 and above.

28. A certain number has four digits, the sum of which is 10. If you exchange the first and last digits, the new number will be 2997 larger. If you exchange the middle two digits of the original number, your new number will be 90 larger. This last enlarged number plus the original number equals 2558. What is the original number?

29. What number is twice the product of its two digits?

30. As described in the Mathematical Morsel, the three cards shown here can be used to read minds. Have a person think of a number from 1 to 7 (say, 6) and tell you what card(s) it is on (cards A and B). You determine the person's number

by adding the numbers in the upper right-hand corner $(4 + 2 = 6)$.

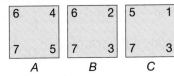

a. How does this work?
b. Prepare a set of four such magic cards for the numbers 1–15.

31. a. Assuming that you can put weights only on one pan, show that the gram weights 1, 2, 4, 8, and 16 are sufficient to weigh each whole-gram weight up to 31 grams using a pan balance. (*Hint:* Base two.)
    b. If weights can be used on either pan, what would be the fewest number of gram weights required to weigh 31 grams, and what would they weigh?

32. What is a real-world use for number bases 2 and 16?

Analyzing Student Thinking

33. Jason asks why the class studied other numeration systems like the Roman system and base 5. How should you respond?

34. Brandi asks why you are teaching the Hindu–Arabic numeration system using a chip abacus. How should you respond?

35. Jamie read the number 512 as "five hundred and twelve." Is she correct? If not, why not?

36. The number 43 is read "forty-three" and means "4 tens plus 3 ones." Since 13 is "1 ten and 3 ones," Juan asks if he could call the number "onety-three." How should you respond?

37. After studying base two, Gladys marvels at its simplicity and asks why we don't use base two rather than base 10. How should you respond?

38. After asking Riann to name the numeral $1,000,000_2$, she says "one million." Is she correct? Explain.

Problems Relating to the NCTM Standards and Curriculum Focal Points

1. The Focal Points for Grade 1 state "Developing an understanding of whole number relationships, including grouping in tens and ones." What is something discussed in this section that will help students accomplish this?

2. The Focal Points for Grade 2 state "Developing an understanding of the base-ten numeration system and place-value concepts." Identify and explain two mathematical ideas that you think will be difficult for students to understand

regarding the base-ten numeration system and place-value concepts.

3. The NCTM Standards state "All students should connect number words and numerals to the quantities they represent, using various physical models and representations." Identify some of the physical models and representations discussed in this section that could be used to meet this standard.

END OF CHAPTER MATERIAL

Solution of Initial Problem

A survey was taken of 150 college freshmen. Forty of them were majoring in mathematics, 30 of them were majoring in English, 20 were majoring in science, 7 had a double major of mathematics and English, and none had a double (or triple) major with science. How many students had majors other than mathematics, English, or science?

Strategy: Draw a Diagram

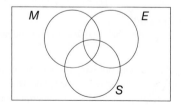

A Venn diagram with three circles, as shown here, is useful in this problem. There are to be 150 students within the rectangle, 40 in the mathematics circle, 30 in the English circle, 20 in the science circle, and 7 in the intersection of the mathematics and English circles but outside the science circle.

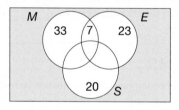

There are $33 + 7 + 23 + 20$, or 83, students accounted for, so there must be $150 - 83$, or 67, students outside the three circles. Those 67 students were the ones who did not major in mathematics, English, or science.

Additional Problems Where the Strategy "Draw a Diagram" Is Useful

1. A car may be purchased with the following options:
Radio: AM/FM, AM/FM Cassette, AM/FM Cassette/CD
Sunroof: Pop-up, Sliding
Transmission: Standard, Automatic
How many different cars can a customer select among these options?

2. One morning a taxi driver travels the following routes: North: 5 blocks; West: 3 blocks; North: 2 blocks; East: 5 blocks; and South: 2 blocks. How far is she from where she started?

3. For every 50 cars that arrive at a highway intersection, 25 turn right to go to Allentown, 10 go straight ahead to Boston, and the rest turn left to go to Canton. Half of the cars that arrive at Boston turn right to go to Denton, and one of every five that arrive at Allentown turns left to go to Denton. If 10,000 cars arrive at Denton one day, how many cars arrived at Canton?

People in Mathematics

Emmy Noether (1882–1935)

Emmy Noether was born and educated in Germany and graduated from the University of Erlangen, where her father, Max Noether, taught mathematics. There were few professional opportunities for a woman mathematician, so Noether spent the next eight years doing research at home and teaching for her increasingly disabled father. Her work, which was in algebra, in particular, ring theory, attracted the attention of the mathematicians Hilbert and Klein, who invited her to the University of Gottingen. Initially, Noether's lectures were announced under Hilbert's name, because the university refused to admit a woman lecturer. Conditions improved, but in 18 years at Gottingen, she was routinely denied the promotions that would have come to a male mathematician of her ability. When the Nazis came to power in 1933, she was dismissed from her position. She immigrated to the United States and spent the last two years of her life at Bryn Mawr College. Upon her death, Albert Einstein wrote in the *New York Times* that "In the judgment of the most competent living mathematicians, Fraulein Noether was the most significant creative mathematical genius thus far produced since the higher education of women began."

David Hilbert (1862–1943)

David Hilbert attended the gymnasium in his home town of Königsberg and then went on to the University of Königsberg where he received his doctorate in 1885. He moved on and became a professor of mathematics at the University of Gottingen, where, in 1895, he was appointed to the chair of mathematics. He spent the rest of his career at Gottingen. Hilbert's work in geometry has been considered to have had the greatest influence in that area second only to Euclid. However, Hilbert is perhaps most famous for surveying the spectrum of unsolved problems in 1900 from which he selected 23 for special attention. He felt these 23 were crucial for progress in mathematics in the coming century. Hilbert's vision was proved to be prophetic. Mathematicians took up the challenge, and a great deal of progress resulted from attempts to solve "Hilbert's Problems." Hilbert made important contributions to the foundations of mathematics and attempted to prove that mathematics was self-consistent. He became one of the most influential mathematicians of his time. Yet, when he read or heard new ideas in mathematics, they seemed "so difficult and practically impossible to understand," until he worked the ideas through for himself.

CHAPTER REVIEW

Review the following terms and problems to determine which require learning or relearning—page numbers are provided for easy reference.

SECTION 2.1 Sets As a Basis for Whole Numbers

VOCABULARY/NOTATION

Natural numbers   45
Counting numbers   45
Whole numbers   45
Set ({ . . . })   45
Element (member)   45
Set-builder notation { . . . | . . . }   45
Is an element of (∈)   46
Is not an element of (∉)   46
Empty set (∅) or null set   46

Equal sets (=)   46
Is not equal to (≠)   46
1-1 correspondence   46
Equivalent sets (~)   46
Matching sets   46
Subset (⊆)   46
Proper subset (⊂)   47
Venn diagram   47
Universal set (U)   47

Finite set   47
Infinite set   47
Disjoint sets   48
Union (∪)   48
Intersection (∩)   49
Complement ($\overline{A}$)   50
Set difference (−)   50
Ordered pair   51
Cartesian product (×)   51

EXERCISES

1. Describe three different ways to define a set.

2. True or false?

   a. $1 \in \{a, b, 1\}$ **b.** $a \notin \{1, 2, 3\}$
   c. $\{x, y\} \subset \{x, y, z\}$ **d.** $\{a, b\} \subseteq \{a, b\}$
   e. $\varnothing = \{ \}$ **f.** $\{a, b\} \sim \{c, d\}$
   g. $\{a, b\} = \{c, d\}$
   h. $\{1, 2, 3\} \cap \{2, 3, 4\} = \{1, 2, 3, 4\}$
   i. $\{2, 3\} \cup \{1, 3, 4\} = \{2, 3, 4\}$
   j. $\{1, 2\}$ and $\{2, 3\}$ are disjoint sets
   k. $\{4, 3, 5, 2\} - \{2, 3, 4\} = \{5\}$
   l. $\{a, 1\} \times \{b, 2\} = \{(a, b), (1, 2)\}$

3. What set is used to determine the number of elements in the set $\{a, b, c, d, e, f, g\}$?

4. Explain how you can distinguish between finite sets and infinite sets.

5. A poll at a party having 23 couples revealed that there were

   i. 25 people who liked both country-western and ballroom dancing.
   ii. 8 who liked only country-western dancing.
   iii. 6 who liked only ballroom dancing.

   How many did not like either type of dancing?

SECTION 2.2 Whole Numbers and Numeration

VOCABULARY/NOTATION

Number   59
Numeral   59
Cardinal number   59
Ordinal number   59
Identification number   59
Number of a set [$n(A)$]   60
Less than (<), greater than (>)   61
Less than or equal to (≤)   61

Greater than or equal to (≥)   61
Whole-number line   61
Tally numeration system   62
Grouping   62
Egyptian numeration system   62
Additive numeration system   62
Roman numeration system   63
Subtractive numeration system   63

Positional numeration system   64
Multiplicative numeration system   64
Babylonian numeration system   64
Place-value   64
Placeholder   65
Mayan numeration system   65
Zero   65

EXERCISES

1. Is the expression "house number" literally correct? Explain.

2. Give an example of a situation where each of the following is useful:

   a. cardinal number
   b. ordinal number
   c. identification number

3. True or false?

   a. $n(\{a, b, c, d\}) = 4$ **b.** $7 \leq 7$
   c. $3 \geq 4$ **d.** $5 < 50$
   e. ||| is three in the tally system
   f. ∩ ||| = ||| ∩ in the Egyptian system
   g. IV = VI in the Roman system
   h. ⋮ = ••• in the Mayan system

4. Express each of the following in our system.

a. 𝟡∩| **b.** CXIV   **c.** ⋮⋮

5. Express 37 in each of the following systems:

a. Egyptian   **b.** Roman   **c.** Mayan

6. Using examples, distinguish between a positional numeration system and a place-value numeration system.

SECTION 2.3 The Hindu–Arabic System

VOCABULARY/NOTATION

Hindu–Arabic numeration system   71

Digits   71

Base   71

Bundles of sticks   71

Base ten pieces (Dienes blocks)   71

Chip abacus   72

Expanded form   72

Expanded notation   72

Exponents   77

EXERCISES

1. Explain how each of the following contributes to formulating the Hindu–Arabic numeration system.

  a. Digits

  b. Grouping by ten

  c. Place value

  d. Additive and multiplicative attributes

2. Explain how the names of 11, 12, . . . , 19 are inconsistent with the names of 21, 22, . . . , 29.

3. True or false?

  a. $100 = 212_{\text{five}}$ **b.** $172_{\text{nine}} = 146$

  c. $11111_{\text{two}} = 2222_{\text{three}}$ **d.** $18_{\text{twelve}} = 11_{\text{nineteen}}$

4. What is the value of learning different number bases?

CHAPTER TEST

KNOWLEDGE

1. Identify each of the following as always true, sometimes true, or never true. If it is sometimes true, give one true and one false example. (Note: If a statement is sometimes true, then it is considered to be mathematically false.)

  a. If $A \sim B$ then $A = B$.

  b. If $A \subset B$, then $A \subseteq B$.

  c. $A \cap B \subseteq A \cup B$.

  d. $n(\{a, b\} \times \{x, y, z\}) = 6$.

  e. If $A \cap B = \varnothing$, then $n(A - B) < n(A)$.

  f. $\{2, 4, 6, \ldots, 2000000\} \sim \{4, 8, 12, \ldots\}$.

  g. The range of a function is a subset of the codomain of the function.

  h. VI = IV in the Roman numeration system.

  i. ÷ represents one hundred six in the Mayan numeration system.

  j. $123 = 321$ in the Hindu–Arabic numeration system.

2. How many different symbols would be necessary for a base nineteen system?

3. Explain what it means for two sets to be disjoint.

SKILL

4. For $A = \{a, b, c\}$, $B = \{b, c, d, e\}$, $C = \{d, e, f, g\}$, $D = \{e, f, g\}$, find each of the following.

  a. $A \cup B$ **b.** $A \cap C$

  c. $A \cap B$ **d.** $A \times D$

  e. $C - D$ **f.** $(B \cap D) \cup (A \cap C)$

5. Write the equivalent Hindu–Arabic base ten numeral for each of the following numerals.

  a. ∩∩∩|| (Egyptian)   **b.** CMXLIV (Roman)

  c. : (Mayan)   **d.**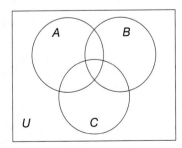

  e. 10101_{two} **f.** ET_{twelve}

6. Express the following in expanded form.

  a. 759   **b.** 7002   **c.** 1001001_{two}

7. Shade the region in the following Venn diagram to represent the set $A - \overline{(B \cup C)}$.

8. Rewrite the base ten number 157 in each of the following number systems that were described in this chapter.

  Babylonian

  Roman

  Egyptian

  Mayan

9. Write a base five numeral for the following set of base five blocks. (Make all possible trades first.)

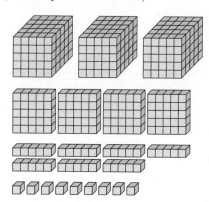

10. Represent the shaded region using the appropriate set notation.

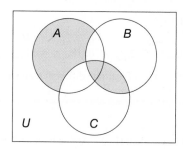

UNDERSTANDING

11. Use the Roman and Hindu–Arabic systems to explain the difference between a *positional* numeration system and a *place-value* numeration system.

12. Determine conditions, if any, on nonempty sets A and B so that the following equalities will be true.

    a. $A \cup B = B \cup A$ **b.** $A \cap B = B \cap A$
    c. $A - B = B - A$ **d.** $A \times B = B \times A$

13. If (a, b) and (c, d) are in $A \times B$, name four elements in $B \times A$.

14. Explain two distinctive features of the Mayan number system as compared to the other three non-Hindu–Arabic number systems described in this chapter.

15. Given the universal set of $\{1, 2, 3, \ldots, 20\}$ and sets A, B, and C as described, place all of the numbers from the universal set in the appropriate location on the following Venn diagram.

    $A = \{2, 4, 0, 1, 3, 5, 6\}$,
    $B = \{10, 11, 12, 1, 2, 7, 6, 14\}$,
    $C = \{18, 19, 6, 11, 16, 12, 9, 8\}$

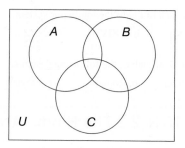

16. Let $A = \{x \mid x$ is a letter in the alphabet$\}$ and $B = \{10, 11, 12, \ldots, 40\}$. Is it possible to have 1-1 correspondence between sets A and B? If so, describe the correspondence. If not, explain why not.

17. Represent the numeral 1212_{three} with base three blocks and chips on a chip abacus.

PROBLEM SOLVING / APPLICATION

18. If $n(A) = 71$, $n(B) = 53$, $n(A \cap B) = 27$, what is $n(A \cup B)$?

19. Find the smallest values for a and b so that $21_b = 25_a$.

20. A number in some base b has two digits. The sum of the digits is 6 and the difference of the digits is 2. The number is equal to 20 in the base 10. What is the base, b, of the number?

21. What is the largest Mayan number that can be represented with exactly 4 symbols? Explain.

22. A third-grade class of 24 students counted the number of students in their class with the characteristics of brown eyes, brown hair, and curly hair. The students found the following:

    12 students had brown eyes
    19 students had brown hair
    12 students had curly hair
    5 students had brown eyes and curly hair
    10 students had brown eyes and brown hair
    7 students had brown, curly hair
    3 students had brown eyes with brown, curly hair

    To answer questions a–c, we will classify all eyes as either brown or blue. Similarly all hair will be either curly or straight. The color of the hair will be either brown or non-brown.

    a. How many students have brown eyes with straight, non-brown hair?

    b. How many students have curly brown hair and blue eyes?

    c. How many students straight-haired, blue-eyed students are in the class?

23. To write the numbers 10, 11, 12, 13, 14, 15 in the Hindu–Arabic system requires 12 symbols. If the same numbers were written in the Babylonian, Mayan, or Roman systems, which system would require the most symbols? Explain.

Whole Numbers: Operations and Properties

CHAPTER 3

Calculation Devices Versus Written Algorithms:
A Debate Through Time

The Hindu–Arabic numeration system can be traced back to 250 B.C.E. However, it wasn't until about C.E. 800 when a complete Hindu system was described in a book by the Persian mathematician al-Khowarizimi. Although the Hindu–Arabic numerals, as well as the Roman numeral system, were used to represent numbers, they were not used for computations, mainly because of the lack of inexpensive, convenient writing equipment such as paper and pencil. In fact, the Romans used a sophisticated abacus or "sand tray" made of a board with small pebbles (calculi) that slid in grooves as their calculator. Another form of the abacus was a wooden frame with beads sliding on thin rods, much like those used by the Chinese as shown in the Focus On for Chapter 4.

From about C.E. 1100 to 1500 there was a great debate among Europeans regarding calculation. Those who advocated the use of Roman numerals along with the abacus were called the *abacists*. Those who advocated using the Hindu–Arabic numeration system together with written algorithms such as the ones we use today were called *algorists*. About 1500, the algorists won the argument and by the eighteenth century, there was no trace of the abacus in western Europe. However, parts of the world, notably, China, Japan, Russia, and some Arabian countries, continued to use a form of the abacus.

It is interesting, though, that in the 1970s and 1980s, technology produced the inexpensive, handheld calculator,

An algorist racing an abacist

which rendered many forms of written algorithms obsolete. Yet the debate continues regarding what role the calculator should play in arithmetic. Could it be that a debate will be renewed between algorists and the modern-day abacists (or "calculatorists")? Is it possible that we may someday return to being "abacists" by using our Hindu–Arabic system to record numbers while using calculators to perform all but simple mental calculations? Let's hope that it does not take us 400 years to decide the appropriate balance between written and electronic calculations!

STRATEGY 8
Use Direct Reasoning

The Use Direct Reasoning strategy is used virtually all the time in conjunction with other strategies when solving problems. Direct reasoning is used to reach a valid conclusion from a series of statements. Often, statements involving direct reasoning are of the form "If A then B." Once this statement is shown to be true, statement B will hold whenever statement A does. (An expanded discussion of reasoning is contained in the Logic section near the end of the book.) In the following initial problem, no computations are required. That is, a solution can be obtained merely by using direct reasoning, and perhaps by drawing pictures.

INITIAL PROBLEM

In a group of nine coins, eight weigh the same and the ninth is either heavier or lighter. Assume that the coins are identical in appearance. Using a pan balance, what is the smallest number of balancings needed to identify the heavy coin?

CLUES

The Use Direct Reasoning strategy may be appropriate when

- A proof is required.
- A statement of the form "If . . . , then . . ." is involved.
- You see a statement that you want to imply from a collection of known conditions.

A solution of this Initial Problem is on page 128.

INTRODUCTION

T he whole-number operations of addition, subtraction, multiplication, and division and their corresponding properties form the foundation of arithmetic. Because of their primary importance, this entire chapter is devoted to the study of how to introduce and develop these concepts independent of computational procedures. First, addition is introduced by considering the union of disjoint sets. Then the key properties of addition are developed and applied to a sequence for learning the basic addition facts. Then, subtraction is introduced and shown to be closely related to addition. Next, multiplication is introduced as a shortcut for addition and, here again, properties of multiplication are developed and applied to a sequence for learning the basic multiplication facts. Division of whole numbers, without and with remainders, is introduced next, both as an extension of subtraction and as the inverse of multiplication. Finally, exponents are introduced to simplify multiplication and to serve as a convenient notation for representing large numbers.

Key Concepts from NCTM Curriculum Focal Points

- **KINDERGARTEN:** Representing, comparing and ordering whole numbers and joining and separating sets.
- **GRADE 1:** Developing understandings of addition and subtraction and strategies for basic addition facts and related subtraction facts.
- **GRADE 2:** Developing quick recall of addition facts and related subtraction facts and fluency with multidigit addition and subtraction.
- **GRADE 3:** Developing understandings of multiplication and division and strategies for basic multiplication facts and related division facts.
- **GRADE 4:** Developing quick recall of multiplication facts and related division facts and fluency with whole number multiplication.

3.1   ADDITION AND SUBTRACTION

STARTING POINT

Discuss how a 6-year-old would find the answer to the question "What is 7 + 2?" If the 6-year-old were then asked "What is 2 + 7?", how would he find the answer to that question? Is there a difference? Why or why not?

Addition and Its Properties

Finding the sum of two whole numbers is one of the first mathematical ideas a child encounters after learning the counting chant "one, two, three, four, . . ." and the concept of number. In particular, the question "How many is 3 and 2?" can be answered using both a set model and a measurement model.

Set Model   To find "3 + 2" using a set model, one must represent two disjoint sets: one set, A, with three objects and another set, B, with 2 objects. Recall that $n(A)$ denotes the number of elements in set A. In Figure 3.1, $n(A) = 3$ and $n(B) = 2$.

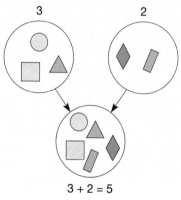

$$3 + 2 = 5$$

Figure 3.1

With sets, addition can be viewed as combining the contents of the two sets to form the union and then counting the number of elements in the union, $n(A \cup B) = 5$. In this case, $n(A) + n(B) = n(A \cup B)$. The example in Figure 3.1 suggests the following general definition of addition.

DEFINITION

Addition of Whole Numbers

Let a and b be any two whole numbers. If A and B are disjoint sets with $a = n(A)$ and $b = n(B)$, then $a + b = n(A \cup B)$.

The number $a + b$, read "a **plus** b," is called the **sum** of a and b, and a and b are called **addends** or **summands** of $a + b$.

When using sets to discuss addition, care must be taken to use disjoint sets. In Figure 3.2, the sets A and B are not disjoint because $n(A \cap B) = 1$.

This nonempty intersection makes it so $n(A) + n(B) \neq n(A \cup B)$ and so it is not an example of addition using the set model. However, Figure 3.2 gives rise to a more general statement about the number of elements in the union of two sets. It is $n(A) + n(B) - n(A \cap B) = n(A \cup B)$. The following example illustrates how to properly use disjoint sets to model addition.

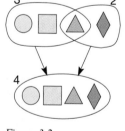

Figure 3.2

Example 3.1   Use the definition of addition to compute 4 + 5.

SOLUTION Let $A = \{a, b, c, d\}$ and $B = \{e, f, g, h, i\}$. Then $n(A) = 4$ and $n(B) = 5$. Also, A and B have been chosen to be disjoint.

Therefore, $4 + 5 = n(A \cup B)$
$$= n(\{a, b, c, d\} \cup \{e, f, g, h, i\})$$
$$= n(\{a, b, c, d, e, f, g, h, i\})$$
$$= 9.$$ ■

Addition is called a **binary operation** because two ("bi") numbers are combined to produce a unique (one and only one) number. Multiplication is another example of a binary operation with numbers. Intersection, union, and set difference are binary operations using sets.

Measurement Model   Addition can also be represented on the whole-number line pictured in Figure 3.3. Even though we have drawn a solid arrow starting at zero and pointing to the right to indicate that the collection of whole numbers is unending, the whole numbers are represented by the equally spaced points labeled 0, 1, 2, 3, and so on. The magnitude of each number is represented by its distance from 0. The number line will be extended and filled in in later chapters.

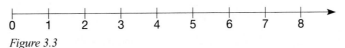

Figure 3.3

Addition of whole numbers is represented by directed arrows of whole-number lengths. The procedure used to find the sum 3 + 4 using the number line is illustrated in Figure 3.4. Here the sum, 7, of 3 and 4 is found by placing arrows of lengths 3 and 4 end to end, starting at zero. Notice that the arrows for 3 and 4 are placed end to end and are disjoint, just as in the set model.

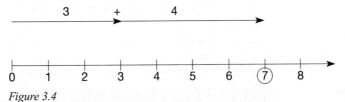

Figure 3.4

Next we examine some fundamental properties of addition of whole numbers that can be helpful in simplifying computations.

Properties of Whole-Number Addition   The fact that one always obtains a whole number when adding two whole numbers is summarized by the closure property.

PROPERTY

Closure Property for Whole-Number Addition

The sum of any two whole numbers is a whole number.

When an operation on a set satisfies a closure property, the set is said to be **closed** with respect to the given operation. Knowing that a set is closed under an operation is helpful when checking certain computations. For example, consider the set of all even whole numbers, {0, 2, 4, . . .}, and the set of all odd whole numbers, {1, 3, 5, . . .}. The set of even numbers is closed under addition since the sum of two even numbers is even. Therefore, if one is adding a collection of even numbers and obtains an odd sum, an error has been made. The set of odd numbers is *not* closed under addition since the sum 1 + 3 is *not* an odd number.

Many children learn how to add by "counting on." For example, to find 9 + 1, a child will count on 1 more from 9, namely, think "nine, then ten." However, if asked to find 1 + 9, a child might say "1, then 2, 3, 4, 5, 6, 7, 8, 9, 10." Not only is this inefficient, but the child might lose track of counting on 9 more from 1. The fact that 1 + 9 = 9 + 1 is useful in simplifying this computation and is an instance of the following property.

NCTM Standard
All students should illustrate general principles and properties of operations, such as commutativity, using specific numbers.

PROPERTY

Commutative Property for Whole-Number Addition

Let *a* and *b* be any whole numbers. Then

$$a + b = b + a$$

Problem-Solving Strategy
Draw a Picture

Note that the root word of *commutative* is *commute*, which means "to interchange." Figure 3.5 illustrates this property for 3 + 2 and 2 + 3.

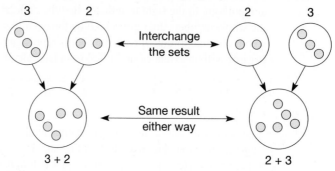

Figure 3.5

Now suppose that a child knows all the addition facts through the fives, but wants to find 6 + 3. A simple way to do this is to rewrite 6 + 3 as 5 + 4 by taking one from 6 and adding it to 3. Since the sum 5 + 4 is known to be 9, the sum 6 + 3 is 9. In summary, this argument shows that 6 + 3 can be thought of as 5 + 4 by following this reasoning: 6 + 3 = (5 + 1) + 3 = 5 + (1 + 3) = 5 + 4. The next property is most useful in simplifying computations in this way.

Algebraic Reasoning
When solving algebraic equations, we often need to "combine like terms." The commutative and associative properties make this possible. For example, (3 + 2x) + (4 + 5x) is simplified by changing the order and grouping of the terms to be (3 + 4) + (2x + 5x).

> ## PROPERTY
>
> ### Associative Property for Whole-Number Addition
>
> Let a, b, and c be any whole numbers. Then
>
> $$(a + b) + c = a + (b + c).$$

The root word of *associative* is *associate*, which means "to unite," or, in this case, "reunite." The example in Figure 3.6 illustrates this property.

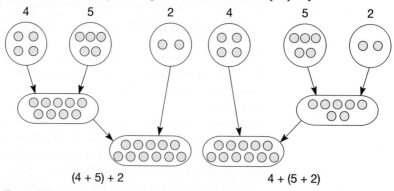

$(4 + 5) + 2$ $4 + (5 + 2)$

Figure 3.6

Since the empty set has no elements, $A \cup \{ \ \} = A$. A numerical counterpart to this statement is one such as 7 + 0 = 7. In general, adding zero to any number results in the same number. This concept is stated in generality in the next property.

> ## PROPERTY
>
> ### Identity Property for Whole-Number Addition
>
> There is a unique whole number, namely 0, such that for all whole numbers a,
>
> $$a + 0 = a = 0 + a.$$

Because of this property, zero is called the **additive identity** or the **identity for addition**.

The previous properties can be applied to help simplify computations. They are especially useful in learning the basic addition facts (that is, all possible sums of the digits 0 through 9). Although drilling using flash cards or similar electronic devices is helpful for learning the facts, an introduction to learning the facts via the following thinking strategies will pay rich dividends later as students learn to perform multidigit addition mentally.

Reflection from Research
When students are taught strategies for thinking and working in mathematics, instead of just basic facts, their computational accuracy, efficiency, and flexibility can be improved (Crespo, Kyriakides, & McGee, 2005).

Thinking Strategies for Learning the Addition Facts
The addition table in Figure 3.7 has 100 empty spaces to be filled. The sum of $a + b$ is placed in the intersection of the row labeled a and the column labeled b. For example, since $4 + 1 = 5$, a 5 appears in the intersection of the row labeled 4 and the column labeled 1.

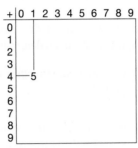
Figure 3.7

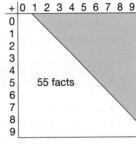
Figure 3.8

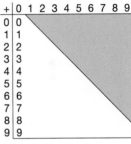
Figure 3.9

1. *Commutativity:* Because of commutativity and the symmetry of the table, a child will automatically know the facts in the shaded region of Figure 3.8 as soon as the child learns the remaining 55 facts. For example, notice that the sum $4 + 1$ is in the unshaded region, but its corresponding fact $1 + 4$ is in the shaded region.

2. *Adding zero:* The fact that $a + 0 = a$ for all whole numbers fills in 10 of the remaining blank spaces in the "zero" column (Figure 3.9)—45 spaces to go.

3. *Counting on by 1 and 2:* Children find sums like $7 + 1$, $6 + 2$, $3 + 1$, and $9 + 2$ by counting on. For example, to find $9 + 2$, think 9, then 10, 11. This thinking strategy fills in 17 more spaces in the columns labeled 1 and 2 (Figure 3.10)—28 facts to go.

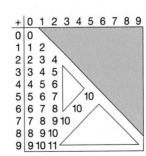
Figure 3.10   Figure 3.11

4. *Combinations to ten:* Combinations of the ten fingers can be used to find $7 + 3$, $6 + 4$, $5 + 5$, and so on. Notice that now we begin to have some overlap. There are 25 facts left to learn (Figure 3.11).

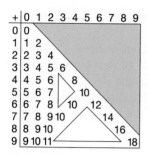

Figure 3.12

5. *Doubles:* $1 + 1 = \mathbf{2}, 2 + 2 = \mathbf{4}, 3 + 3 = \mathbf{6}$, and so on. These sums, which appear on the main left-to-right downward diagonal, are easily learned as a consequence of counting by twos: namely, 2, 4, 6, 8, 10, . . . (Figure 3.12). Now there are 19 facts to be determined.

6. *Adding ten:* When using base ten pieces as a model, adding 10 amounts to laying down a "long" and saying the new name. For example, $3 + 10$ is 3 units and 1 long, or 13; $7 + 10$ is seventeen, and so on.

7. *Associativity:* The sum $9 + 5$ can be thought of as $10 + 4$, or 14, because $9 + 5 = 9 + (1 + 4) = (9 + 1) + 4$. Similarly, $8 + 7 = 10 + 5 = 15$, and so on. The rest of the addition table can be filled using associativity (sometimes called *regrouping*) combined with adding 10.

8. *Doubles ± 1 and ± 2:* This technique overlaps with the others. Many children use it effectively. For example, $7 + 8 = 7 + 7 + 1 = 14 + 1 = 15$, or $8 + 7 = 8 + 8 - 1 = 15; 5 + 7 = 5 + 5 + 2 = 10 + 2 = 12$, and so on.

By using thinking strategies 6, 7, and 8, the remaining basic addition facts needed to complete the table in Figure 3.12 can be determined.

Example 3.2   Use thinking strategies in three different ways to find the sum of $9 + 7$.

SOLUTION
a. $9 + 7 = 9 + (1 + 6) = (9 + 1) + 6 = 10 + 6 = 16$
b. $9 + 7 = (8 + 1) + 7 = 8 + (1 + 7) = 8 + 8 = 16$
c. $9 + 7 = (2 + 7) + 7 = 2 + (7 + 7) = 2 + 14 = 16$ ∎

NCTM Standard
All students should develop fluency with basic number combinations for addition and subtraction.

Thus far we have been adding single-digit numbers. However, thinking strategies can be applied to multidigit addition also. Figure 3.13 illustrates how multidigit addition is an extension of single-digit addition. The only difference is that instead of adding units each time, we might be adding longs, flats, and so on. Mentally combine similar pieces, and then exchange as necessary.

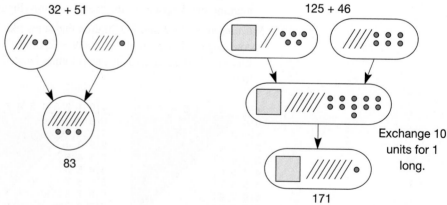

Figure 3.13

The next example illustrates how thinking strategies can be applied to multidigit numbers.

Example 3.3   Using thinking strategies, find the following sums.

a. $42 + 18$ **b.** $37 + (42 + 13)$ **c.** $51 + 39$

SOLUTION

a. $42 + 18 = (40 + 2) + (10 + 8)$ *Addition*
$ = (40 + 10) + (2 + 8)$ *Commutativity and associativity*
$ = 50 + 10$ *Place value and combination to 10*
$ = 60$ *Addition*

b. $37 + (42 + 13) = 37 + (13 + 42)$
$ = (37 + 13) + 42$
$ = 50 + 42$
$ = 92$

c. $51 + 39 = (50 + 1) + 39$
$ = 50 + (1 + 39)$
$ = 50 + 40$
$ = 90$ ■

The use of other number bases can help you simulate how these thinking strategies are experienced by students when they learn base ten arithmetic. Perhaps the two most powerful thinking strategies, especially when used together, are associativity and combinations to the base (base ten above). For example, $7_{nine} + 6_{nine} = 7_{nine} + (2_{nine} + 4_{nine}) = (7_{nine} + 2_{nine}) + 4_{nine} = 14_{nine}$ (since the sum of 7_{nine} and 2_{nine} is one of the base in base nine), $4_{six} + 5_{six} = 3_{six} + 1_{six} + 5_{six} = 13_{six}$ (since $1_{six} + 5_{six}$ is one of the base in base six), and so on.

Example 3.4   Compute the following sums using thinking strategies.

a. $7_{eight} + 3_{eight}$ **b.** $5_{seven} + 4_{seven}$ **c.** $9_{twelve} + 9_{twelve}$

SOLUTION

a. $7_{eight} + 3_{eight} = 7_{eight} + (1_{eight} + 2_{eight}) = (7_{eight} + 1_{eight}) + 2_{eight} = 10_{eight} + 2_{eight} = 12_{eight}$
b. $5_{seven} + 4_{seven} = 5_{seven} + (2_{seven} + 2_{seven}) = (5_{seven} + 2_{seven}) + 2_{seven} = 10_{seven} + 2_{seven} = 12_{seven}$
c. $9_{twelve} + 9_{twelve} = 9_{twelve} + (3_{twelve} + 6_{twelve}) = (9_{twelve} + 3_{twelve}) + 6_{twelve} = 10_{twelve} + 6_{twelve} = 16_{twelve}$

Notice how associativity and combinations to the base are used. ■

✔ **Check for Understanding:** Exercise/Problem Set A #1–7

Subtraction

The Take-Away Approach   There are two distinct approaches to subtraction. The take-away approach is often used to introduce children to the concept of subtraction. The problem "If you have 5 coins and spend 2, how many do you have left?" can be solved with a set model using the take-away approach. Also, the problem "If you walk 5 miles from home and turn back to walk 2 miles toward home, how many miles are you from home?" can be solved with a measurement model using the take-away approach (Figure 3.14).

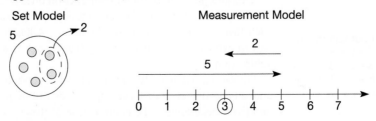

Figure 3.14

This approach can be stated using sets.

Subtraction of Whole Numbers: Take-Away Approach

Let a and b be any whole numbers and A and B be sets such that $a = n(A)$, $b = n(B)$, and $B \subseteq A$. Then

$$a - b = n(A - B).$$

NCTM Standard

All students should understand various meanings of addition and subtraction of whole numbers and the relationship between the two operations.

The number "$a - b$" is called the **difference** and is read "a minus b," where a is called the **minuend** and b the **subtrahend**. To find $7 - 3$ using sets, think of a set with seven elements, say $\{a, b, c, d, e, f, g\}$. Then, using set difference, take away a subset of three elements, say $\{a, b, c\}$. The result is the set $\{d, e, f, g\}$, so $7 - 3 = 4$.

The Missing-Addend Approach   The second method of subtraction, which is called the missing-addend approach, is often used when making change. For example, if an item costs 76 cents and 1 dollar is tendered, a clerk will often hand back the change by adding up and saying "76 plus *four* is 80, and *twenty* is a dollar" as four pennies and two dimes are returned. This method is illustrated in Figure 3.15.

Reflection from Research

Children frequently have difficulty with missing-addend problems when they are not related to word problems. A common answer to $5 + ? = 8$ is 13 (Kamii, 1985).

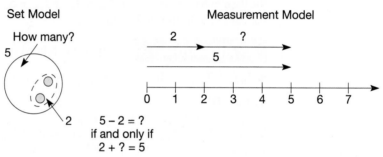

Figure 3.15

Since $2 + \mathbf{3} = 5$ in each case in Figure 3.15, we know that $5 - 2 = \mathbf{3}$.

Subtraction of Whole Numbers: Missing-Addend Approach

Let a and b be any whole numbers. Then $a - b = c$ if and only if $a = b + c$ for some whole number c.

In this alternative definition of subtraction, c is called the **missing addend**. The missing-addend approach to subtraction is very useful for learning subtraction facts because it shows how to relate them to the addition facts via **four-fact families** (Figure 3.16).

This alternative definition of subtraction does not guarantee that there is an answer for every whole-number subtraction problem. For example, there is no whole number c such that $3 = 4 + c$, so the problem $3 - 4$ has no whole-number answer. Another way of expressing this idea is to say that the set of whole numbers is *not* closed under subtraction.

Notice that we have two approaches to subtraction, (i) take away and (ii) missing addend and that each of these approaches can be modeled in two ways using (i) sets and (ii) measurement. The combination of these four methods can be visualized in a two-dimensional diagram (Figure 3.17).

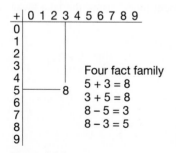

Figure 3.16

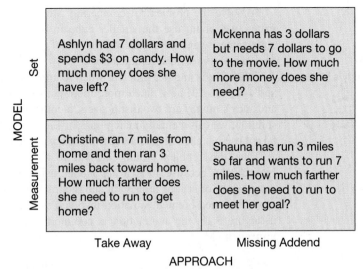

Figure 3.17

The reason for learning to add and subtract is to solve problems in the real world. For example, consider the next two problems.

1. Monica was 59″ tall last year. She had a growth spurt and is now 66″ tall. How much did she grow during this past year?

To solve this problem, we can use the lower right square in Figure 3.17 because we are dealing with her height (measurement) and we want to know how many more inches 66 is than 59 (missing addend).

2. Monica joined a basketball team this year. One of her teammates is 70″ tall. How much taller is that teammate than Monica?

There is a new aspect to this problem. Instead of considering how much taller Monica is than she was last year, you are asked to *compare* her height with another player. More generally, you might want to compare her height to all the members of her team. This way of viewing subtraction adds a third dimension, **comparison**, to the 2-by-2 square in Figure 3.17. (Figure 3.18)

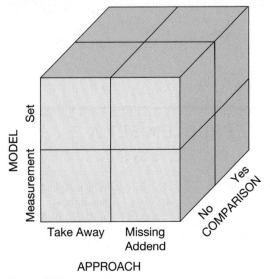

Figure 3.18

To solve the problem of comparing Monica's height with the rest of her team-mates, we would use the smaller cube in the lower right back of the 2-by-2-by-2 cube since it uses the *measurement model* and *missing addend approach* involving the *comparison* with several teammates.

Following is another problem where comparison comes into play: If Larry has $7 and Judy has $3, how much more money does Larry have? Because Larry's money and Judy's money are two distinct sets, a comparison view would be used. To find the solution, we can mentally match up 3 of Larry's dollars with 3 of Judy's dollars and take those matched dollars away from Larry's (see Figure 3.19).

Larry's Money   Judy's Money

Figure 3.19

Thus, this problem would correlate to the smaller cube in the top back left of Figure 3.18 because it is a *set model* using *take-away approach* involving the *comparison* of sets of money. In subtraction situations where there is more than one set or one measurement situation involved as illustrated by the back row of the cube in Figure 3.18, the subtraction is commonly referred to as using the **comparison approach**.

✔ **Check for Understanding:** Exercise/Problem Set A #8–14

MATHEMATICAL MORSEL

Benjamin Franklin was known for his role in politics and as an inventor. One of his mathematical discoveries was an 8-by-8 square made up of the counting numbers from 1 to 64. Check out the following properties:

1. All rows and columns total 260.

2. All half-rows and half-columns total 130.

3. The four corners total 130.

4. The sum of the corners in any 4-by-4 or 6-by-6 array is 130.

5. Every 2-by-2 array of four numbers totals 130.

(NOTE: There are 49 of these 2-by-2 arrays!)

Section 3.1   EXERCISE / PROBLEM SET A

EXERCISES

1. **a.** Draw a figure similar to Figure 3.1 to find $4 + 3$.
   b. Find $3 + 5$ using a number line.

2. For which of the following pairs of sets is it true that $n(D) + n(E) = n(D \cup E)$? When not true, explain why not.
   a. $D = \{1, 2, 3, 4\}$, $E = \{7, 8, 9, 10\}$
   b. $D = \{\ \}$, $E = \{1\}$
   c. $D = \{a, b, c, d\}$, $E = \{d, c, b, a\}$

3. Which of the following sets are closed under addition? Why or why not?
   a. $\{0, 10, 20, 30, \ldots\}$
   b. $\{0\}$
   c. $\{0, 1, 2\}$
   d. $\{1, 2\}$
   e. Whole numbers greater than 17

4. Identify the property or properties being illustrated.
   a. $1279 + 3847$ must be a whole number.
   b. $7 + 5 = 5 + 7$
   c. $53 + 47 = 50 + 50$
   d. $1 + 0 = 1$
   e. $1 + 0 = 0 + 1$
   f. $(53 + 48) + 7 = 60 + 48$

5. Use the Chapter 3 eManipulative *Number Bars* on our Web site to model $7 + 2$ and $2 + 7$ on the same number line. Sketch what is represented on the computer and describe how the two problems are different. How are they similar?

6. What property or properties justify that you get the same answer to the following problem whether you add "up" (starting with $9 + 8$) or "down" (starting with $3 + 8$)?

$$3$$
$$8$$
$$+\ 9$$

7. Addition can be simplified using the associative property of addition. For example,

$$26 + 57 = 26 + (4 + 53) = (26 + 4) + 53$$
$$= 30 + 53 = 83.$$

Complete the following statements.
   a. $39 + 68 = 40 +$ _____ $=$ _____
   b. $25 + 56 = 30 +$ _____ $=$ _____
   c. $47 + 23 = 50 +$ _____ $=$ _____

8. a. Complete the following addition table in base five. Remember to use the thinking strategies.

+	0	1	2	3	4
0					
1					
2			(base five)		
3					
4					

   b. For each of the following subtraction problems in base five, rewrite the problem using the missing-addend approach and find the answer in the table.
   i. $13_{\text{five}} - 4_{\text{five}}$ **ii.** $11_{\text{five}} - 3_{\text{five}}$
   iii. $12_{\text{five}} - 4_{\text{five}}$ **iv.** $10_{\text{five}} - 2_{\text{five}}$

9. Complete the following four-fact families in *base five*.
   a. $3_{\text{five}} + 4_{\text{five}} = 12_{\text{five}}$ **b.** _____

   _____ $4_{\text{five}} + 1_{\text{five}} = 10_{\text{five}}$

   _____   _____

   _____   _____

   c. _____

   _____

   $11_{\text{five}} - 4_{\text{five}} = 2_{\text{five}}$

   _____

10. In the following figure, centimeter strips are used to illustrate $3 + 8 = 11$. What two subtraction problems are

also being represented? What definition of subtraction is being demonstrated?

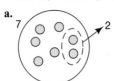

11. For the following figures, identify the problem being illustrated, the model, and the conceptual approach being used.
   a.

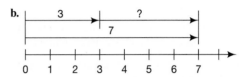

   b.

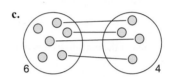

   c.

12. Using different-shaped boxes for variables provides a transition to algebra as well as a means of stating problems. Try some whole numbers in the boxes to determine whether these properties hold.
   a. Is subtraction closed?

$$\square - \triangle \overset{?}{=} \bigcirc$$

   b. Is subtraction commutative?

$$\square - \triangle \overset{?}{=} \triangle - \square$$

   c. Is subtraction associative?

$$(\square - \triangle) - \bigcirc \overset{?}{=} \square - (\triangle - \bigcirc)$$

   d. Is there an identity element for subtraction?

$$\square - \triangle = \square \text{ and } \triangle - \square = \square$$

13. Each situation described next involves a subtraction problem. In each case, briefly name the small cube portion of Figure 3.18 that correctly classifies the problem. Typical answers may be *set, take-away, no comparison* or *measurement, missing-addend, comparison*. Finally, write an equation to fit the problem.
   a. An elementary teacher started the year with a budget of $200 to be spent on manipulatives. By the end of December, $120 had been spent. How much money remained in the budget?
   b. Doreen planted 24 tomato plants in her garden and Justin planted 18 tomato plants in his garden. How many more plants did Doreen plant?

c. Tami is saving money for a trip to Hawaii over spring break. The package tour she is interested in costs $1795. From her part-time job she has saved $1240 so far. How much more money must she save?

14. a. State a subtraction word problem involving $8 - 3$, the missing addend approach, the set model, without comparison.

b. State a subtraction word problem involving $8 - 3$, the take-away approach, the measurement model, with comparison.

c. Sketch the set model representation of the situation described in part a.

d. Sketch the measurement model representation of the situation described in part b.

PROBLEMS

15. A given set contains the number 1. What other numbers must also be in the set if it is closed under addition?

16. The number 100 can be expressed using the nine digits 1, 2, . . . , 9 with plus and minus signs as follows:

$$1 + 2 + 3 - 4 + 5 + 6 + 78 + 9 = 100$$

Find a sum of 100 using each of the nine digits and only three plus or minus signs.

17. Complete the following magic square in which the sum of each row, each column, and each diagonal is the same. When completed, the magic square should contain each of the numbers 10 through 25 exactly once.

25			
		19	17
18	16		
	23		10

18. Magic squares are not the only magic figures. The following figure is a magic hexagon. What is "magic" about it?

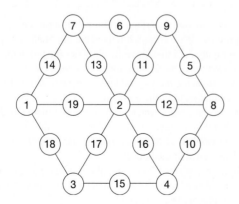

19. A **palindrome** is any number that reads the same backward and forward. For example, 262 and 37673 are palindromes. In the accompanying example, the process of reversing the digits and adding the two numbers has been repeated until a palindrome is obtained.

$$
\begin{array}{r}
67 \\
+ 76 \\
\hline
143 \\
+ 341 \\
\hline
484
\end{array}
$$

a. Try this method with the following numbers.
  i. 39   **ii.** 87   **iii.** 32

b. Find a number for which the procedure takes more than three steps to obtain a palindrome.

20. Mr. Morgan has five daughters. They were all born the number of years apart as the youngest daughter is old. The oldest daughter is 16 years older than the youngest. What are the ages of Mr. Morgan's daughters?

21. Use the Chapter 3 eManipulative activity, *Number Puzzles* exercise 2, on our Web site to arrange the numbers 1, 2, 3, 4, 5, 6, 7, 8, 9 in the circles below so the sum of the numbers along each line of four is 23.

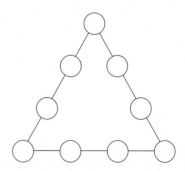

| Section 3.1 | EXERCISE / PROBLEM SET B |

EXERCISES

1. Show that $2 + 6 = 8$ using two different types of models.

2. For which of the following pairs of sets is it true that $n(D) + n(E) = n(D \cup E)$? When not true, explain why not.
   a. $D = \{a, c, e, g\}, E = \{b, d, f, g\}$
   b. $D = \{\ \}, E = \{\ \}$
   c. $D = \{1, 3, 5, 7\}, E = \{2, 4, 6\}$

3. Which of the following sets are closed under addition? Why or why not?
   a. $\{0, 3, 6, 9, \ldots\}$
   b. $\{1\}$
   c. $\{1, 5, 9, 13, \ldots\}$
   d. $\{8, 12, 16, 20, \ldots\}$
   e. Whole numbers less than 17

4. Each of the following is an example of one of the properties for addition of whole numbers. Fill in the blank to complete the statement, and identify the property.
   a. $5 + \underline{\quad} = 5$
   b. $7 + 5 = \underline{\quad} + 7$
   c. $(4 + 3) + 6 = 4 + (\underline{\quad} + 6)$
   d. $(4 + 3) + 6 = \underline{\quad} + (4 + 3)$
   e. $(4 + 3) + 6 = (3 + \underline{\quad}) + 6$
   f. $2 + 9$ is a $\underline{\quad}$ number.

5. Show that the commutative property of whole number addition holds for the following examples in other bases by using a different number line for each base.
   a. $3_{\text{five}} + 4_{\text{five}} = 4_{\text{five}} + 3_{\text{five}}$ **b.** $5_{\text{nine}} + 7_{\text{nine}} = 7_{\text{nine}} + 5_{\text{nine}}$

6. Without performing the addition, determine which sum (if either) is larger. Explain how this was accomplished and what properties were used.

3261	4187
4287	5291
+ 5193	+ 3263

7. Look for easy combinations of numbers to compute the following sums mentally. Show and identify the properties you used to make the groupings.
   a. $94 + 27 + 6 + 13$ **b.** $5 + 13 + 25 + 31 + 47$

8. **a.** Complete the following addition table in base six. Remember to use the thinking strategies.

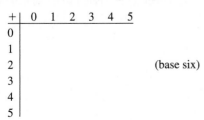

9. Using the addition table for base six given in Exercise 8, write the following four-fact families in base six.
   a. $2_{\text{six}} + 3_{\text{six}} = 5_{\text{six}}$ **b.** $11_{\text{six}} - 5_{\text{six}} = 2_{\text{six}}$

10. Rewrite each of the following subtraction problems as an addition problem.
    a. $x - 156 = 279$ **b.** $279 - 156 = x$ **c.** $279 - x = 156$

11. For the following figures, identify the problem being illustrated, the model, and the conceptual approach being used.

a.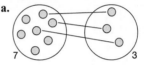

b.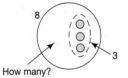
How many?

c.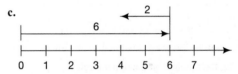

b. For each of the following subtraction problems in base six, rewrite the problem using the missing–addend approach and find the answer in the table.
   i. $13_{\text{six}} - 5_{\text{six}}$ **ii.** $5_{\text{six}} - 4_{\text{six}}$
   iii. $12_{\text{six}} - 4_{\text{six}}$ **iv.** $10_{\text{six}} - 2_{\text{six}}$

12. For each of the following, determine whole numbers x, y, and z that make the statement true.
    a. $x - 0 = 0 - x = x$ **b.** $x - y = y - x$
    c. $(x - y) - z = x - (y - z)$
    Which, if any, are true for all whole numbers x, y, and z?

13. Each situation described next involves a subtraction problem. In each case, briefly name the small cube portion of Figure 3.18 that correctly classifies the problem. Typical answers may be *set, take-away, no comparison* or *measurement, missing-addend, comparison*. Finally, write an equation to fit the problem.
    a. Robby has accumulated a collection of 362 sports cards. Chris has a collection of 200 cards. How many more cards than Chris does Robby have?
    b. Jack is driving from St. Louis to Kansas City for a meeting, a total distance of 250 miles. After 2 hours he notices that he has traveled 114 miles. How far is he from Kansas City at that time?
    c. An elementary school library consists of 1095 books. As of May 8, 105 books were checked out of the library. How many books were still available for checkout on May 8?

14. a. State a subtraction word problem involving $9 - 5$, the missing addend approach, the measurement model, without comparison.

b. State a subtraction word problem involving $9 - 5$, the take-away approach, the set model, with comparison.

c. Sketch the measurement model representation of the situation described in part a.

d. Sketch the set model representation of the situation described in part b.

PROBLEMS

15. Suppose that S is a set of whole numbers closed under addition. S contains 3, 27, and 72.

a. List six other elements in S.   **b.** Why must 24 be in S?

16. A given set contains the number 5. What other numbers must also be in the set if it is closed under addition?

17. The next figure can provide practice in addition and subtraction. The figure is completed by filling the upper two circles with the sums obtained by adding diagonally.

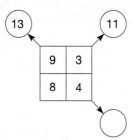

$9 + 4 = 13$ and $8 + 3 = 11$

The circle at the lower right is filled in one of two ways:

i. Adding the numbers in the upper circles:

$$13 + 11 = 24$$

ii. Adding across the rows, adding down the columns, and then adding the results in each case:

$$12 + 12 = 24 \text{ and } 17 + 7 = 24$$

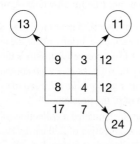

a. Fill in the missing numbers for the following figure.

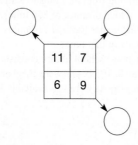

b. Fill in the missing numbers for the following figure.

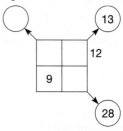

c. Use variables to show why the sum of the numbers in the upper two circles will always be the same as the sum of the two rows and the sum of the two columns.

18. Arrange numbers 1 to 10 around the outside of the circle shown so that the sum of any two adjacent numbers is the same as the sum of the two numbers on the other ends of the spokes. As an example, 6 and 9, 8 and 7 might be placed as shown, since $6 + 9 = 8 + 7$.

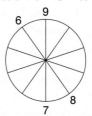

19. Place the numbers 1–16 in the cells of the following magic square so that the sum of each row, column, and diagonal is the same.

	2		
5			8
	7	6	
		15	1

20. Use the Chapter 3 eManipulative activity, *Number Puzzles* exercise 3, on our Web site to arrange the numbers 1, 2, 3, 4, 5, 6, 7, 8, 9 in the circles below so the sum of the numbers along each line of three is 15.

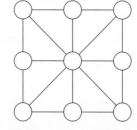

21. Shown here is a magic triangle discovered by the mental calculator Marathe. What is its magic?

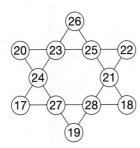

22. The property "If $a + c = b + c$, then $a = b$" is called the **additive cancellation property**. Is this property true for all whole numbers? If it is, how would you convince your students that it is always true? If not, give a counter example.

Analyzing Student Thinking
23. Kaitlyn doesn't understand why the definition of Addition of Whole Numbers insists that sets A and B must be disjoint. What can you say to help her?

24. Enrique says, "I think of closure as a bunch of numbers locked in a room and the operation, like addition, comes along and links any two of the numbers together. As long as the link is in the room, the room can be said to be closed with respect to addition. If the link is found outside of the room, then the set is not closed." Is his reasoning mathematically correct? Explain.

25. Monique prefers using rote memory to learn the addition facts rather than using thinking strategies. What case can be made to convince her that there is value in using thinking strategies? Explain.

26. Theresa prefers using the number line for addition rather than the set model. Can she use the number line model to interpret the properties of whole-number addition? Explain.

27. Severino says, "When I added 27 and 36, I made the 27 a 30, then I added the 30 and the 36 and got 66, and then subtracted the 3 from the beginning and got 63." Patricia says, "But when I added 27 and 36, I added the 20 and the 30 and got 50, then I knew 6 plus 6 was 12 so 6 plus 7 was 13, and then I added 50 and 13 and got 63." Can you follow the students' reasonings here? How would you describe some of their techniques?

28. Kayla claims that $7_{eight} + 3_{eight} = 10_{eight}$ since $7 + 3 = 10$. How should you respond?

29. Your classroom has 21 students and there are 9 boys. You ask two students to use these numbers to determine how many girls are in the classroom. Conner says, "9 plus 10 is 19, 19 plus 2 is 21, so there are $10 + 2 = 12$ girls." Chandler says that Conner is wrong because he did not use "take-away." How should you respond?

30. Darren happens to see your copy of this book on your desk open to Figure 3.18. He says, "What is that used for?" How should you respond?

Problems Relating to the NCTM Standards and Curriculum Focal Points

1. The Focal Points for Kindergarten state "Representing, comparing and ordering whole numbers and joining and separating sets." Where are the ideas of joining and separating sets addressed in this section?

2. The Focal Points for Grade 1 state "Developing understandings of addition and subtraction and strategies for basic addition facts and related subtraction facts."

Identify 3 examples from this section that address this focal point.

3. The NCTM Standards state "All students should illustrate general principles and properties of operations, such as commutativity, using specific numbers." Explain why understanding "properties of operations" is worthwhile for young children to know.

3.2 MULTIPLICATION AND DIVISION

STARTING POINT

The ways of thinking about the operations in the following two word problems are conceptually different. Discuss what the difference is and how it might impact the way students solve the problem.

Joshua has 12 cups of flour to make cookies. Each batch of cookies calls for 3 cups of flour. How many batches can Joshua make?

Emily made 12 loaves of bread to share with her 3 neighbors. If she gives the same amount of bread to each neighbor, how many loaves does each neighbor get?

Children's Literature
www.wiley.com/college/musser
See "Amanda Bean's Amazing
Dream: A Mathematical Story"
by Cindy Neuschwander.

Multiplication and Its Properties

There are many ways to view multiplication.

Repeated-Addition Approach   Consider the following problems: There are five children, and each has three silver dollars. How many silver dollars do they have altogether? The silver dollars are about 1 inch wide. If the silver dollars are laid in a single row with each dollar touching the next, what is the length of the row? These problems can be modeled using the set model and the measurement model (Figure 3.20).

Reflection from Research
When multiplication is
represented by repeated
addition, students have a great
deal of difficulty keeping track
of the two sets of numbers. For
instance, when considering how
many sets of three there are in
fifteen, students need to keep
track of counting up the threes
and how many sets of three they
count (Steffe, 1988).

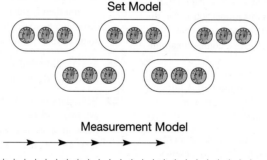

Figure 3.20

These models look similar to the ones that we used for addition, since we are merely adding repeatedly. They show that $3 + 3 + 3 + 3 + 3 = 15$, or that $5 \times 3 = 15$.

DEFINITION

Multiplication of Whole Numbers: Repeated-Addition Approach

Let a and b be any whole numbers where $a \neq 0$. Then

$$ab = \underbrace{b + b \ldots + b}_{a \text{ addends}}$$

If $a = 1$, then $ab = 1 \cdot b = b$; also $0 \cdot b = 0$ for all b.

Children's Literature
www.wiley.com/college/musser
See "One Hundred Hungry
Ants" by Elinor Pinczes.

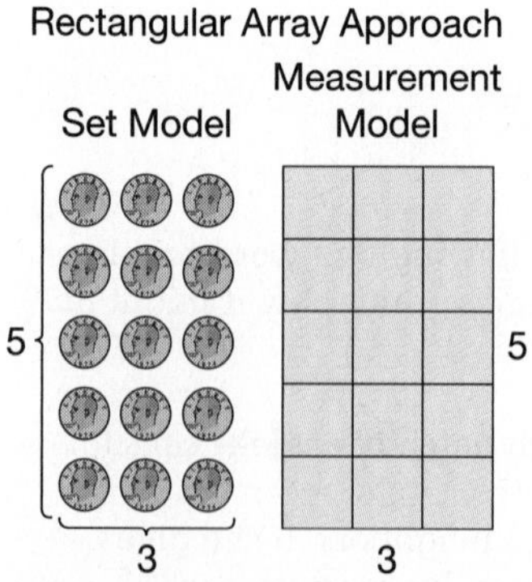

Since multiplication combines two numbers to form a single number, it is a binary operation. The number ab, read "a times b," is called the **product** of a and b. The numbers a and b are called **factors** of ab. The product ab can also be written as "$a \cdot b$" and "$a \times b$." Notice that $0 \cdot b = 0$ for all b. That is, the product of zero and any whole number is zero.

Rectangular Array Approach
Measurement
Set Model   Model

5 {   } 5
        3   3

Figure 3.21

Rectangular Array Approach   If the silver dollars in the preceding problem are arranged in a rectangular array, multiplication can be viewed in a slightly different way (Figure 3.21).

ALTERNATIVE DEFINITION

Multiplication of Whole Numbers: Rectangular Array Approach

Let a and b be any whole numbers. Then ab is the number of elements in a rectangular array having a rows and b columns.

Cartesian Product Approach A third way of viewing multiplication is an abstraction of this array approach.

ALTERNATIVE DEFINITION

Multiplication of Whole Numbers: Cartesian Product Approach

Let a and b be any whole numbers. If $a = n(A)$ and $b = n(B)$, then

$$ab = n(A \times B).$$

For example, to compute $2 \cdot 3$, let $2 = n(\{a, b\})$ and $3 = n(\{x, y, z\})$. Then $2 \cdot 3$ is the number of ordered pairs in $\{a, b\} \times \{x, y, z\}$. Because $\{a, b\} \times \{x, y, z\} = \{(a, x), (a, y), (a, z), (b, x), (b, y), (b, z)\}$ has six ordered pairs, we conclude that $2 \cdot 3 = 6$. Actually, by arranging the pairs in an appropriate row and column configuration, this approach can also be viewed as the array approach, as illustrated next (Figure 3.22).

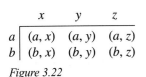

	x	y	z
a	(a, x)	(a, y)	(a, z)
b	(b, x)	(b, y)	(b, z)

Figure 3.22

Tree Diagram Approach Another way of modeling this approach is through the use of a **tree diagram** (Figure 3.23). Tree diagrams are especially useful in the field of probability, which we study in Chapter 11.

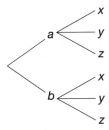

Figure 3.23

Reflection from Research
Children can solve a variety of multiplicative problems long before being formally introduced to multiplication and division (Mulligan & Mitchelmore, 1995).

Properties of Whole-Number Multiplication You have probably observed that whenever you multiplied any two whole numbers, your product was always a whole number. This fact is summarized by the following property.

PROPERTY

Closure Property for Multiplication of Whole Numbers

The product of two whole numbers is a whole number.

When two odd whole numbers are multiplied together, the product is odd; thus the set of odd numbers is closed under multiplication. Closure is a useful idea, since if we are multiplying two (or more) odd numbers and the product we calculate is even, we can conclude that our product is incorrect. The set $\{2, 5, 8, 11, 14, \ldots\}$ is not closed under multiplication, since $2 \cdot 5 = 10$ and 10 is not in the set.

The next property can be used to simplify learning the basic multiplication facts. For example, by the repeated-addition approach, 7×2 represents $2 + 2 + 2 + 2 + 2 + 2 + 2$, whereas 2×7 means $7 + 7$. Since $7 + 7$ was learned as an addition fact, viewing 7×2 as 2×7 makes this computation easier.

PROPERTY

Commutative Property for Whole-Number Multiplication

Let a and b be any whole numbers. Then

$$ab = ba.$$

Problem-Solving Strategy
Draw a Picture

Reflection from Research
If multiplication is viewed as computing area, children can see the commutative property relatively easily, but if multiplication is viewed as computing the price of a number of items, the commutative property is not obvious (Vergnaud, 1981).

The example in Figure 3.24 should convince you that the commutative property for multiplication is true.

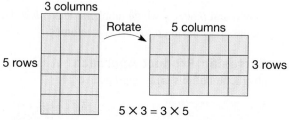

Figure 3.24

The product $5 \cdot (2 \cdot 13)$ is more easily found if it is viewed as $(5 \cdot 2) \cdot 13$. Regrouping to put the 5 and 2 together can be done because of the next property.

PROPERTY

Associative Property for Whole-Number Multiplication

Let a, b, and c be any whole numbers. Then

$$a(bc) = (ab)c.$$

To illustrate the validity of the associative property for multiplication, consider the three-dimensional models in Figure 3.25.

Problem-Solving Strategy
Draw a Picture

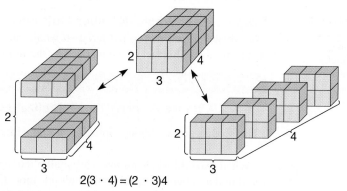

Figure 3.25

The next property is an immediate consequence of each of our definitions of multiplication.

PROPERTY

Identity Property for Whole-Number Multiplication

The number 1 is the unique whole-number such that for every whole number a,

$$a \cdot 1 = a = 1 \cdot a.$$

Because of this property, the number 1 is called the **multiplicative identity** or the **identity for multiplication**.

Reflection from Research
The array representation for multiplication can be used to introduce key ideas of multiplication, but students need to be taught to recognize what the array represents in multiplication (Barmby, Harries, Higgins, & Suggate, 2009).

There is one other important property of the whole numbers. This property, distributivity, combines both multiplication and addition. Study the array model in Figure 3.26. This model shows that the *product of a sum*, $3(2 + 4)$, can be expressed as the *sum of products*, $(3 \cdot 2) + (3 \cdot 4)$. This relationship holds in general.

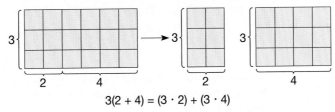

$$3(2 + 4) = (3 \cdot 2) + (3 \cdot 4)$$

Figure 3.26

NCTM Standard
All students should understand and use properties of operations such as the distributivity of multiplication over addition.

PROPERTY

Distributive Property of Multiplication over Addition

Let a, b, and c be any whole numbers. Then

$$a(b + c) = ab + ac.$$

Algebraic Reasoning
The distributive property is commonly used to "combine like terms" in problems like $3x + 2x = (3 + 2)x = 5x$. Becoming comfortable with the distributive property with numbers develops a foundation for applying the property in algebra.

Because of commutativity, we can also write $(b + c)a = ba + ca$. Notice that the distributive property "distributes" the a to the b *and* the c.

Example 3.5

Rewrite each of the following expressions using the distributive property.

a. $3(4 + 5)$ **b.** $5 \cdot 7 + 5 \cdot 3$

c. $am + an$ **d.** $31 \cdot 76 + 29 \cdot 76$

e. $a(b + c + d)$

SOLUTION

a. $3(4 + 5) = 3 \cdot 4 + 3 \cdot 5$ **b.** $5 \cdot 7 + 5 \cdot 3 = 5(7 + 3)$

c. $am + an = a(m + n)$ **d.** $31 \cdot 76 + 29 \cdot 76 = (31 + 29)76$

e. $a(b + c + d) = a(b + c) + ad = ab + ac + ad$ ■

Let's summarize the properties of whole-number addition and multiplication.

PROPERTIES

Whole-Number Properties

PROPERTY	ADDITION	MULTIPLICATION
Closure	Yes	Yes
Commutativity	Yes	Yes
Associativity	Yes	Yes
Identity	Yes (zero)	Yes (one)
Distributivity of multiplication over addition	Yes	

In addition to these properties, we highlight the following property.

> **PROPERTY**
>
> ### Multiplication Property of Zero
>
> For every whole number, a,
>
> $$a \cdot 0 = 0 \cdot a = 0.$$

Using the missing-addend approach to subtraction, we will show that $a(b - c) = ab - ac$ whenever $b - c$ is a whole number. In words, multiplication distributes over subtraction.

Let $\qquad b - c = n$

Then $\qquad\qquad b = c + n$ *Missing addend*

$\qquad\qquad\qquad ab = a(c + n)$ *Multiplication*

$\qquad\qquad\qquad ab = ac + an$ *Distributivity*

Therefore, $\ ab - ac = an$ *Missing addend from the first equation*

But $\qquad\quad b - c = n$

So, substituting $b - c$ for n, we have

$$ab - ac = a(b - c).$$

> **PROPERTY**
>
> ### Distributivity of Multiplication over Subtraction
>
> Let a, b, and c be any whole numbers where $b \geq c$. Then
>
> $$a(b - c) = ab - ac.$$

The following discussion shows how the properties are used to develop thinking strategies for learning the multiplication facts.

Thinking Strategies for Learning the Multiplication Facts
The multiplication table in Figure 3.27 has $10 \times 10 = 100$ unfilled spaces.

Figure 3.27

Figure 3.28

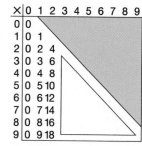

Figure 3.29

1. *Commutativity:* As in the addition table, because of commutativity, only 55 facts in the unshaded region in Figure 3.28 have to be found.

2. *Multiplication by 0:* $a \cdot 0 = 0$ for all whole numbers a. Thus the first column is all zeros (Figure 3.29).

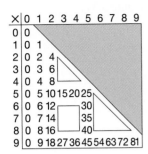

Figure 3.30

3. *Multiplication by 1:* $1 \cdot a = a \cdot 1 = a$. Thus the column labeled "1" is the same as the left-hand column outside the table (Figure 3.29).

4. *Multiplication by 2:* $2 \cdot a = a + a$, which are the doubles from addition (Figure 3.29).

We have filled in 27 facts using thinking strategies 1, 2, 3, and 4. Therefore, 28 facts remain to be found out of our original 55.

5. *Multiplication by 5:* The counting chant by fives, namely 5, 10, 15, 20, and so on, can be used to learn these facts (see the column and/or row headed by a 5 in Figure 3.30).

6. *Multiplication by 9:* The multiples of 9 are 9, 18, 27, 36, 45, 54, 63, 72, and 81 (Figure 3.30). Notice how the tens digit is one less than the number we are multiplying by 9. For example, the tens digit of $3 \cdot 9$ is 2 (one less than 3). Also, the sum of the digits of the multiples of 9 is 9. Thus $3 \cdot 9 = 27$ since $2 + 7 = 9$. The multiples of 5 and 9 eliminate 13 more facts, so 15 remain.

7. *Associativity and distributivity:* The remaining facts can be obtained using these two properties. For example, $8 \times 4 = 8 \times (2 \times 2) = (8 \times 2) \times 2 = 16 \times 2 = 32$ or $8 \times 4 = 8(2 + 2) = 8 \cdot 2 + 8 \cdot 2 = 16 + 16 = 32$.

In the next example we consider how knowledge of the basic facts and the properties can be applied to multiplying a single-digit number by a multidigit number.

Example 3.6   Compute the following products using thinking strategies.

a. 2×34 **b.** $5(37 \cdot 2)$ **c.** $7(25)$

SOLUTION
a. $2 \times 34 = 2(30 + 4) = 2 \cdot 30 + 2 \cdot 4 = 60 + 8 = 68$
b. $5(37 \cdot 2) = 5(2 \cdot 37) = (5 \cdot 2) \cdot 37 = 370$
c. $7(25) = (4 + 3)25 = 4 \cdot 25 + 3 \cdot 25 = 100 + 75 = 175$ ■

✔ **Check for Understanding:** Exercise/Problem Set A #1–10

Division

Just as with addition, subtraction, and multiplication, we can view division in different ways. Consider these two problems.

1. A class of 20 children is to be divided into four teams with the same number of children on each team. How many children are on each team?

2. A class of 20 children is to be divided into teams of four children each. How many teams are there?

Each of these problems is based on a different conceptual way of viewing division. A general description of the first problem is that you have a certain number of objects that you are dividing into or "sharing" among a specified number of groups and are asking how many objects are in each group. Because of its sharing nature, this type of division is referred to as **sharing division**. A general description of the second problem is that you have a certain number of objects and you are "measuring out" a

NCTM Standard
All students should develop fluency with basic number combinations for multiplication and division and use combinations to mentally compute related problems, such as 30×50.

Reflection from Research
Multiplication is usually introduced before division and separated from it, whereas children spontaneously relate them and do not necessarily find division more difficult than multiplication (Mulligan & Mitchelmore, 1997).

specified number of objects to be in each group and asking how many groups there are. This type of division is called **measurement division** (Figure 3.31).

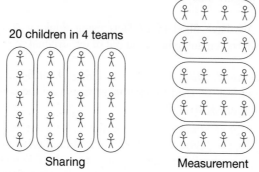

20 children in 4 teams — Sharing

20 children 4 per team — Measurement

Figure 3.31

When dealing with whole numbers, the difference between these two types of division may seem very subtle, but these differences become more apparent when considering the division of decimals or fractions.

The following examples will help clarify the distinction between sharing and measurement division.

Example 3.7   Classify each of the following division problems as examples of either sharing or measurement division.

a. A certain airplane climbs at a rate of 300 feet per second. At this rate, how long will it take the plane to reach a cruising altitude of 27,000 feet?

b. A group of 15 friends pooled equal amounts of money to buy lottery tickets for a $1,987,005 jackpot. If they win, how much should each friend receive?

c. Shauna baked 54 cookies to give to her friends. She wants to give each friend a plate with 6 cookies on it. How many friends can she give cookies to?

SOLUTION

a. Since every 300 feet can be viewed as a single group corresponding to 1 second, we are interested in finding out how many groups of 300 feet there are in 27,000 feet. Thus this is a measurement division problem.

b. In this case, each friend represents a group and we are interested in how much money goes to each group. Therefore, this is an example of a sharing division problem.

c. Since every group of cookies needs to be of size 6, we need to determine how many groups of size 6 there are in 54 cookies. This is an example of a measurement division problem.   ■

Missing-Factor Approach   Figure 3.32 shows that multiplication and division are related. This suggests the following definition of division.

DEFINITION

Division of Whole Numbers: Missing-Factor Approach

If a and b are any whole numbers with $b \neq 0$, then $a \div b = c$ if and only if $a = bc$ for some whole number c.

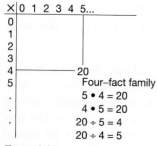

Four–fact family
$5 \cdot 4 = 20$
$4 \cdot 5 = 20$
$20 \div 5 = 4$
$20 \div 4 = 5$

Figure 3.32

ACTIVITY

2 There are 12 counters. Group the counters 3 at a time.

Step 1 Count out 12 counters.

Step 2 Make equal groups of 3 until all the counters are gone.

There are 4 equal groups of 3.
So, $12 \div 4 = 3$.

Think About It

1. Explain how you divided 12 counters into equal groups.

2. When you divided the counters into groups of 3, how did you find the number of equal groups?

 **CHECK What You Know**

3. Make equal groups to find the number of counters in each group.

4. Find the number of equal groups of 5.

5. Copy the chart. Then use counters to help complete.

Number of Counters	Number of Equal Groups	Number in Each Group	Division Sentence
9	3	3	$9 \div 3 = 3$
14	2	▢	▢
15	▢	5	▢
6	▢	3	▢

6. **WRITING IN ►MATH** Can 13 counters be divided equally into groups of 3? Explain.

252 **Chapter 6** Develop Division Concepts and Facts

The symbol $a \div b$ is read "*a divided by b*." Also, a is called the **dividend**, b is called the **divisor**, and c is called the **quotient** or **missing factor**. The basic facts multiplication table can be used to learn division facts (Figure 3.32).

| **Example 3.8** | Find the following quotients. |

a. $24 \div 8$ **b.** $72 \div 9$ **c.** $52 \div 4$ **d.** $0 \div 7$

SOLUTION
a. $24 \div 8 = 3$, since $24 = 8 \times 3$
b. $72 \div 9 = 8$, since $72 = 9 \times 8$
c. $52 \div 4 = 13$, since $52 = 13 \times 4$
d. $0 \div 7 = 0$, since $0 = 7 \times 0$ ∎

The division problem in Example 3.8(d) can be generalized as follows and verified using the missing-factor approach.

Reflection from Research
Fourth- and fifth-grade students most frequently defined division as undoing multiplication (Graeber & Tirosh, 1988).

PROPERTY

Division Property of Zero

If $a \neq 0$, then $0 \div a = 0$.

Next, consider the situation of *dividing by zero*. Suppose that we extend the missing-factor approach of division to dividing by zero. Then we have the following two cases.

Algebraic Reasoning
Notice how variables are used to represent any number in order to show that this explanation works for any number.

Case 1: $a \div 0$, where $a \neq 0$. If $a \div 0 = c$, then $a = 0 \cdot c$, or $a = 0$. But $a \neq 0$. Therefore, $a \div 0$ is undefined.

Case 2: $0 \div 0$. If $0 \div 0 = c$, then $0 = 0 \cdot c$. But any value can be selected for c, so there is no *unique* quotient c. Thus division by zero is said to be indeterminate, or undefined, here. These two cases are summarized by the following statement.

Division by 0 is undefined.

Reflection from Research
Second- and third-grade students tend to use repeated addition to solve simple multiplication AND division problems. In a division problem, such as $15 \div 5$, they will repeatedly add the divisor until they reach the quotient ($5 + 5 = 10$; $10 + 5 = 15$), often using their fingers to keep track of the number of times they use 5 (Mulligan & Mitchelmore, 1995).

Now consider the problem $37 \div 4$. Although $37 \div 4$ does not have a whole-number answer, there are applications where it is of interest to know how many groups of 4 are in 37 with the possibility that there is something left over. For example, if there are 37 fruit slices to be divided among four children so that each child gets the same number of slices, how many would each child get? We can find as many as 9 fours in 37 and then have 1 remaining. Thus each child would get nine fruit slices with one left undistributed. This way of looking at division of whole numbers, but with a remainder, is summarized next.

> ### The Division Algorithm
>
> If a and b are any whole numbers with $b \neq 0$, then there exist unique whole numbers q and r such that $a = bq + r$, where $0 \leq r < b$.

Here b is called the **divisor**, q is called the **quotient**, and r is the **remainder**. Notice that the remainder is always less than the divisor. Also, when the remainder is 0, this result coincides with the usual definition of whole-number division.

Example 3.9   Find the quotient and remainder for these problems.

a. $57 \div 9$ **b.** $44 \div 13$ **c.** $96 \div 8$

SOLUTION

a. $9 \times 6 = 54$, so $57 = 6 \cdot 9 + 3$. The quotient is 6 and the remainder is 3 (Figure 3.33).

Problem-Solving Strategy
Draw a Picture

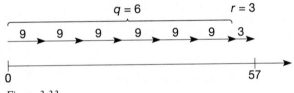

Figure 3.33

b. $13 \times 3 = 39$, so $44 = 3 \cdot 13 + 5$. The quotient is 3 and the remainder is 5.
c. $8 \times 12 = 96$, so $96 = 12 \cdot 8 + 0$. The quotient is 12 and the remainder is 0.   ∎

Reflection from Research
The Dutch approach to written division calculations involves repeated subtraction using increasingly larger chunks. This approach, which has helped Dutch students to outperform students from other nations, builds progressively on intuitive strategies (Anghileri, Beishuizen, & Van Putten, 2002).

Repeated-Subtraction Approach   Figure 3.34 suggests alternative ways of viewing division.

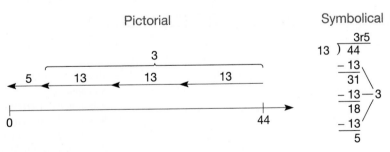

Figure 3.34

In Figure 3.34, 13 was subtracted from 44 three successive times until a number less than 13 was reached, namely 5. Thus 44 divided by 13 has a quotient of 3 and a remainder of 5. This example shows that division can be viewed as repeated subtraction. In general, to find $a \div b$ using the repeated-subtraction approach, subtract b successively from a and from the resulting differences until a remainder r is reached, where $r < b$. The number of times b is subtracted is the quotient q.

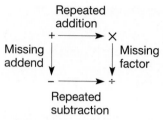

Figure 3.35 provides a visual way to remember the main interconnections among the four basic whole-number operations. For example, multiplication of whole numbers is defined by using the repeated-addition approach, subtraction is defined using the missing-addend approach, and so on. An important message in this diagram is that success in subtraction, multiplication, and division begins with a solid foundation in addition.

Figure 3.35

 Check for Understanding: Exercise/Problem Set A #11–17

MATHEMATICAL MORSEL

The following note appeared in a newspaper.

"What is 241,573,142,393,627,673,576,957,439,048 times 45,994, 811,347,886,846,310,221,728,895,223,034,301,839? The answer is 71 consecutive 1s—one of the biggest numbers a computer has ever factored. The 71-digit number was factored in 9.5 hours of a Cray super-computer's time at Los Alamos National Laboratory in New Mexico, besting the previous high—69 digits—by two.

Why bother? The feat might affect national security. Some computer systems are guarded by cryptographic codes once thought to be beyond factoring. The work at Los Alamos could help intelligence experts break codes."

See whether you can find an error in the article and correct it.

| Section 3.2 | EXERCISE / PROBLEM SET A |

EXERCISES

1. What multiplication problems are suggested by the following diagrams?

   a.

   b.

   c.

2. Illustrate 3×2 using the following combinations of models and approaches.

   a. Set model; Cartesian product approach

   b. Set model; rectangular array approach

   c. Set model; repeated-addition approach

   d. Measurement model; rectangular array approach

   e. Measurement model; repeated-addition approach

3. Each situation described next involves a multiplication problem. In each case tell whether the problem situation is best represented by the repeated-addition approach, the rectangular array approach, or the Cartesian product approach, and why. Then write an appropriate equation to fit the situation.

a. A rectangular room has square tiles on the floor. Along one wall, Kurt counts 15 tiles and along an adjacent wall he counts 12 tiles. How many tiles cover the floor of the room?

b. Jack has three pairs of athletic shorts and eight different T-shirts. How many different combinations of shorts and T-shirts could he wear to play basketball?

c. A teacher provided three number-2 pencils to each student taking a standardized test. If a total of 36 students were taking the test, how many pencils did the teacher need to have available?

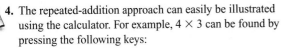

4. The repeated-addition approach can easily be illustrated using the calculator. For example, 4×3 can be found by pressing the following keys:

$$3 \boxed{+} 3 \boxed{+} 3 \boxed{+} 3 \boxed{=} \boxed{12}$$

or if the calculator has a constant key, by pressing

$$3 \boxed{+} \boxed{=} \boxed{=} \boxed{=} \boxed{12} \text{ or}$$

$$3 \boxed{+} \boxed{+} \boxed{=} \boxed{=} \boxed{=} \boxed{12}$$

Find the following products using one of these techniques.

a. 3×12 **b.** 4×17
c. 7×93 **d.** 143×6 (Think!)

5. Which of the following sets are closed under multiplication? If the set is not closed, explain why not.

a. $\{2, 4\}$ **b.** $\{0, 2, 4, 6, \ldots\}$
c. $\{0, 3\}$ **d.** $\{0, 1\}$
e. $\{1\}$ **f.** $\{0\}$
g. $\{5, 7, 9, \ldots\}$
h. $\{0, 7, 14, 21, \ldots\}$
i. $\{0, 1, 2, 4, 8, 16, \ldots, 2^k, \ldots\}$
j. Odd whole numbers

6. Identify the property of whole numbers being illustrated.

a. $4 \cdot 5 = 5 \cdot 4$
b. $6(3 + 2) = (3 + 2)6$
c. $5(2 + 9) = 5 \cdot 2 + 5 \cdot 9$
d. $1(x + y) = x + y$

7. Rewrite each of the following expressions using the distributive property for multiplication over addition or for multiplication over subtraction.

a. $4(60 + 37)$
b. $(21 + 35) \cdot 6$
c. $37 \cdot (60 - 22)$
d. $5x + 2x$
e. $5(a + 1) - 3(a + 1)$

8. The distributive property of multiplication over addition can be used to perform some calculations mentally. For example, to find $13 \cdot 12$, you can think

$$13(12) = 13(10 + 2) = 13(10) + 13(2)$$
$$= 130 + 26 + 156.$$

How could each of the following products be rewritten using the distributive property so that it is more easily computed mentally?

a. $45(11)$ **b.** $39(102)$
c. $23(21)$ **d.** $97(101)$

9. a. Compute 374×12 without using the 4 key. Explain.
    b. Compute 374×12 without using the 2 key. Explain.

10. Compute using thinking strategies. Show your reasoning.
    a. $5(23 \times 4)$ **b.** 12×25

11. a. Complete the following multiplication table in *base five*.

×	0	1	2	3	4	
0						
1						
2						(base five)
3						
4						

b. Using the table in part (a), complete the following four-fact families in *base five*.

    i. $2_{\text{five}} \times 3_{\text{five}} = 11_{\text{five}}$
    _____
    _____
    _____

    ii. _____
    _____
    $22_{\text{five}} \div 3_{\text{five}} = 4_{\text{five}}$
    _____

    iii. _____
    _____
    $13_{\text{five}} \div 2_{\text{five}} = 4_{\text{five}}$

12. Identify each of the following problems as an example of either sharing or measurement division. Justify your answers.

a. Gabriel bought 15 pints of paint to redo all the doors in his house. If each door requires 3 pints of paint, how many doors can Gabriel paint?

b. Hideko cooked 12 tarts for her family of 4. If all of the family members receive the same amount, how many tarts will each person receive?

c. Ms. Ivanovich needs to give 3 straws to each student in her class for their art activity. If she uses 51 straws, how many students does she have in her class?

13. a. Write a sharing division problem that would have the equation $15 \div 3$ as part of its solution.

    b. Write a measurement division problem that would have the equation $15 \div 3$ as part of its solution.

14. Rewrite each of the following division problems as a multiplication problem.
    a. $48 \div 6 = 8$ **b.** $51 \div x = 3$
    c. $x \div 13 = 5$

15. How many division problems without remainder are possible where one member of the given set is divided by another (possibly the same) member of the same set? List the problems. Remember, division by zero is not defined. For example, in $\{1, 2, 4\}$ there are six problems: $1 \div 1$, $2 \div 2$, $4 \div 4$, $4 \div 1$, $2 \div 1$, and $4 \div 2$.
    a. $\{0\}$ **b.** $\{0, 1\}$
    c. $\{0, 1, 2, 3, 4\}$ **d.** $\{0, 2, 4, 6\}$
    e. $\{0, 1, 2, 3, \ldots, 9\}$ **f.** $\{3, 4, 5, \ldots, 11\}$

16. Use the Chapter 3 eManipulative, *Rectangular Division*, on our Web site to investigate the three problems from Example 3.9. Explain why the remainder is always smaller than the divisor in terms of this rectangle division model.

17. In general, each of the following is false if x, y, and z are whole numbers. Give an example (other than dividing by zero) where each statement is false.
    a. $x \div y$ is a whole number.
    b. $x \div y = y \div x$
    c. $(x \div y) \div z = x \div (y \div z)$
    d. $x \div y = x = y \div x$ for some y
    e. $x \div (y + z) = x \div y + x \div z$

PROBLEMS

18. A square dancing contest has 213 teams of 4 pairs each. How many dancers are participating in the contest?

19. A stamp machine dispenses twelve 32¢ stamps. What is the total cost of the twelve stamps?

20. If the American dollar is worth 121 Japanese yen, how many dollars can 300 yen buy?

21. An estate valued at $270,000 was left to be split equally among three heirs. How much did each one get (before taxes)?

22. Shirley meant to add 12349 $\boxed{+}$ 29746 on her calculator. After entering 12349, she pushed the $\boxed{\times}$ button by mistake. What could she do next to keep from reentering 12349? What property are you using?

23. Suppose that A is a set of whole numbers closed under addition. Is A necessarily closed under multiplication? (If you think so, give reasons. If you think not, give a counterexample, that is, a set A that is closed under addition but not multiplication.)

24. **a.** Use the numbers from 1 to 9 once each to complete this magic square. (The row, column, and diagonal sums are all equal.) (*Hint:* First determine the SUM OF EACH ROW.)

		8
	5	

    b. Can you make a multiplicative magic square? (The row, column, and diagonal products are equal.) (NOTE: The numbers 1 through 9 will not work in this case.)

25. Predict the next three lines in this pattern, and check your work.

$$\begin{aligned}
1 &= 1 \\
3 + 5 &= 8 \\
7 + 9 + 11 &= 27 \\
13 + 15 + 17 + 19 &= 64 \\
21 + 23 + 25 + 27 + 29 &= 125
\end{aligned}$$

26. Using the digits 1 through 9 once each, fill in the boxes to make the equations true.

27. Take any number. Add 10, multiply by 2, add 100, divide by 2, and subtract the original number. The answer will be the number of minutes in an hour. Why?

28. Jason, Wendy, Kevin, and Michelle each entered a frog in an annual frog-jumping contest. Each of their frogs—Hippy, Hoppy, Bounce, and Pounce—placed first, second, or third in the contest and earned a blue, red, or white ribbon, respectively. Use the following clues to determine who entered which frog and the order in which the frogs placed.
    a. Michelle's frog finished ahead of both Bounce and Hoppy.
    b. Hippy and Hoppy tied for second place.
    c. Kevin and Wendy recaptured Hoppy when he escaped from his owner.
    d. Kevin admired the blue ribbon Pounce received but was quite happy with the red ribbon his frog received.

29. A café sold tea at 30 cents a cup and cakes at 50 cents each. Everyone in a group had the same number of cakes and the same number of cups of tea. (NOTE: This is not to say that the number of cakes is the same as the number of teas.) The bill came to $13.30. How many cups of tea did each have?

30. A creature from Mars lands on Earth. It reproduces itself by dividing into three new creatures each day. How many creatures will populate Earth on day 30 if there is one creature on the first day?

31. There are eight coins and a balance scale. The coins are alike in appearance, but one of them is counterfeit and lighter than the other seven. Find the counterfeit coin using two weighings on the balance scale.

32. Determine whether the property "If $ac = bc$, then $a = b$" is true for all whole numbers. If not, give a counter-example. (NOTE: This property is called the **multiplicative cancellation property** when $c \neq 0$.)

Section 3.2 | EXERCISE / PROBLEM SET B

EXERCISES

1. What multiplication problems are suggested by the following diagrams?

   a.

   b.

   c.

2. Illustrate 4×6 using the following combinations of models and approaches.
   a. Set model; rectangular array approach
   b. Measurement model; rectangular array approach
   c. Set model; repeated addition approach
   d. Measurement model; repeated addition approach
   e. Set model; Cartesian product approach

3. Each situation described next involves a multiplication problem. In each case state whether the problem situation is best represented by the repeated-addition approach, the rectangular array approach, or the Cartesian product approach, and why. Then write an appropriate equation to fit the situation.
   a. At the student snack bar, three sizes of beverages are available: small, medium, and large. Five varieties of soft drinks are available: cola, diet cola, lemon-lime, root beer, and orange. How many different choices of soft drink does a student have, including the size that may be selected?
   b. At graduation students file into the auditorium four abreast. A parent seated near the door counts 72 rows of students who pass him. How many students participated in the graduation exercise?
   c. Kirsten was in charge of the food for an all-school picnic. At the grocery store she purchased 25 eight-packs of hot dog buns for 70 cents each. How much did she spend on the hot dog buns?

4.  Use a calculator to find the following without using an $\boxed{X}$ key. Explain your method.
   a. 4×39
   b. 231×3
   c. 5×172
   d. 6×843

5. **a.** Is the set of whole numbers with 3 removed
   i. closed under addition? Why?
   ii. closed under multiplication? Why?
   b. Answer the same questions for the set of whole numbers with 7 removed.

6. Identify the property of whole number multiplication being illustrated.
   a. $3(5 - 2) = 3 \cdot 5 - 3 \cdot 2$
   b. $6(7 \cdot 2) = (6 \cdot 7) \cdot 2$
   c. $(4 + 7) \cdot 0 = 0$
   d. $(5 + 6) \cdot 3 = 5 \cdot 3 + 6 \cdot 3$

7. Rewrite each of the following expressions using the distributive property for multiplication over addition or for multiplication over subtraction.
   a. $3(29 + 30 + 6)$
   b. $5(x - 2y)$
   c. $3a + 6a - 4a$
   d. $x(x + 2) + 3(x + 2)$
   e. $37(60 - 22)$

8. The distributive property of multiplication over subtraction can be used to perform some calculations mentally. For example, to find 7(99), you can think

$$7(99) = 7(100 - 1) = 7(100) - 7(1)$$
$$= 700 - 7 = 693.$$

   How could each of the following products be rewritten using the distributive property so that it is more easily computed mentally?
   a. $14(19)$
   b. $25(38)$
   c. $35(98)$
   d. $27(999)$

9. a. Compute 463×17 on your calculator *without* using the 7 key.
   b. Find another way to do it.
   c. Calculate 473×17 without using the 7 key.

10. Compute using thinking strategies. Show your reasoning.
   a. 8×85
   b. $12(125)$

11. a. Complete the following multiplication table in base eight. Remember to use the thinking strategies.

$\times$	0	1	2	3	4	5	6	7
0								
1								
2								
3								
4								
5								
6								
7								

(base eight)

   b. Rewrite each of the following division problems in *base eight* using the missing-factor approach, and find the answer in the table.
   i. $61_{\text{eight}} \div 7_{\text{eight}}$ **ii.** $17_{\text{eight}} \div 3_{\text{eight}}$
   iii. $30_{\text{eight}} \div 6_{\text{eight}}$ **iv.** $16_{\text{eight}} \div 2_{\text{eight}}$
   v. $44_{\text{eight}} \div 6_{\text{eight}}$ **vi.** $25_{\text{eight}} \div 7_{\text{eight}}$

12. Identify each of the following problems as an example of either sharing or measurement division. Justify your answers.
   a. For Amberly's birthday, her mother brought 60 cupcakes to her mathematics class. There were 28 students in class that day. If she gives each student the same number of cupcakes, how many will each receive?
   b. Tasha needs 2 cups of flour to make a batch of cookies. If she has 6 cups of flour, how many batches of cookies can she make?
   c. Maria spent $45 on three shirts at the store. If the shirts all cost the same, how much did each shirt cost?

13. a. Write a measurement division problem that would have the equation $91 \div 7$ as part of its solution.
   b. Write a sharing division problem that would have the equation $91 \div 7$ as part of its solution.

14. Rewrite each of the following division problems as a multiplication problem.
   a. $24 \div x = 12$
   b. $x \div 3 = 27$
   c. $a \div b = x$

15. Find the quotient and remainder for each problem.
   a. $7 \div 3$ **b.** $3 \div 7$ **c.** $7 \div 1$
   d. $1 \div 7$ **e.** $15 \div 5$ **f.** $8 \div 12$

16. How many possible remainders (including zero) are there when dividing by the following numbers? How many possible quotients are there?
   a. 2   **b.** 12
   c. 62   **d.** 23

17. Which of the following properties hold for division of whole numbers?
   a. Closure
   b. Commutativity
   c. Associativity
   d. Identity

PROBLEMS

18. A school has 432 students and 9 grades. What is the average number of students per grade?

19. Twelve thousand six hundred people attended a golf tournament. If attendees paid $30 a piece and were distributed equally among the 18 holes, how much revenue is collected per hole?

20. Compute mentally.

$$(2348 \times 7{,}653{,}214) + (7652 \times 7{,}653{,}214)$$

(*Hint:* Use distributivity.)

21. If a subset of the whole numbers is closed under multiplication, is it necessarily closed under addition? Discuss.

22. Is there a subset of the whole numbers with more than one element that is closed under division? Discuss.

23. Complete the pattern and give a justification for your answers. If necessary, check your answers using your calculator.

$$12{,}345{,}679 \times 9 = 111{,}111{,}111$$
$$12{,}345{,}679 \times 18 = 222{,}222{,}222$$
$$12{,}345{,}679 \times 27 = \underline{\quad}$$
$$12{,}345{,}679 \times 63 = \underline{\quad}$$
$$12{,}345{,}679 \times 81 = \underline{\quad}$$

24. Solve this problem posed by this Old English children's rhyme.

> As I was going to St. Ives
> I met a man with seven wives;
> Every wife had seven sacks;
> Every sack had seven cats;
> Every cat had seven kits.
> Kits, cats, sacks, and wives.
> How many were going to St. Ives?

How many wives, sacks, cats, and kits were met?

25. Write down your favorite three-digit number twice to form a six-digit number (e.g., 587,587). Is your six-digit number divisible by 7? How about 11? How about 13? Does this always work? Why? (*Hint:* Expanded form.)

26. Find a four-digit whole number equal to the cube of the sum of its digits.

27. Delete every third counting number starting with 3.

$$1, 2, 4, 5, 7, 8, 10, 11, 13, 14, 16, 17$$

Write down the cumulative sums starting with 1.

$$1, 3, 7, 12, 19, 27, 37, 48, 61, 75, 91, 108$$

Delete every second number from this last sequence, starting with 3. Then write down the sequence of cumulative sums. Describe the resulting sequence.

28. Write, side by side, the numeral 1 an even number of times. Take away from the number thus formed the number obtained by writing, side by side, a series of 2s half the length of the first number. For example,

$$1111 - 22 = 1089 = 33 \times 33.$$

Will you always get a perfect square? Why or why not?

29. Four men, one of whom committed a crime, said the following:

> Bob: Charlie did it.
> Charlie: Eric did it.
> Dave: I didn't do it.
> Eric: Charlie lied when he said I did it.

a. If only one of the statements is true, who was guilty?
b. If only one of the statement is false, who was guilty?

30. Andrew and Bert met on the street and had the following conversation:

> A: How old are your three children?
> B: The product of their ages is 36.
> A: That's not enough information for me to know their ages.
> B: The sum of their ages is your house number.

> A: That's still not quite enough information.
> B: The oldest child plays the piano.
> A: Now I know!

Assume that the ages are whole numbers and that twins have the same age. How old are the children? (*Hint:* Make a list after Bert's first answer.)

31. Three boxes contain black and white marbles. One box has all black marbles, one has all white marbles, and one has a mixture of black and white. All three boxes are mislabeled. By selecting only one marble, determine how you can correctly label the boxes. (*Hint:* Notice that "all black" and "all white" are the "same" in the sense that they are the same color.)

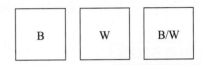

32. If a and b are whole numbers and $ab = 0$, what conclusion can you draw about a or b? Defend your conclusion with a convincing argument.

 Analyzing Student Thinking

33. Pascuel claims that the rectangular array approach is the same as the Cartesian product approach. Is there a difference? If so, what is it?

34. Phyllis claims that the tree diagram approach for multiplication can only be used to model multiplying two numbers, but not more than two. Is she correct? Explain.

35. Maurice rewrites $6(7 \cdot 3)$ as $(6 \cdot 7) \times (6 \cdot 3)$ and says that he used distributivity. Is he correct in using the distributive property this way? How should you respond to this student?

36. Before you can respond to Maurice in #35, Taylor shouts, "No, that is an application of the associative property for multiplication." How should you respond to this student?

37. Breanne claims that the multiplication property of zero should be called the identity property of zero because when you multiply by zero you get zero. Is her claim reasonable? Explain.

38. Olga says she can't see how distributivity can be used as a thinking strategy. How should you respond?

39. Ervin says that $a + 0 = a$ and $a - 0 = a$. Thus, since $a \times 0 = 0$, it must be true that $a \div 0 = 0$. How could you help him better understand this situation?

40. A student asks you if "4 divided by 12" and "4 divided into 12" mean the same thing. How should you respond?

Problems Relating to the NCTM Standards and Curriculum Focal Points

1. The Focal Points for Grade 3 state "Developing understandings of multiplication and division and strategies for basic multiplication facts and related division facts." Based on what is presented in this section, what are some key underlying concepts of multiplication and division?

2. The NCTM Standards state "All students should understand and use properties of operations such as the distributivity of

multiplication over addition." Describe some examples where students could use such properties.

3. The NCTM Standards state "All students should understand situations that entail multiplication and division, such as equal groupings of objects and sharing equally." Describe at least 2 situations that involve equal groupings of objects or sharing equally.

3.3   ORDERING AND EXPONENTS

STARTING POINT   You are teaching a unit on exponents and a student asks you what 4^0 means. One student volunteers that it is 0 since exponents are a shortcut for multiplication. How do you respond in a meaningful way?

NCTM Standard
All students should describe quantitative change, such as a student's growing two inches in one year.

Ordering and Whole-Number Operations

In Chapter 2, whole numbers were ordered in three different, though equivalent, ways using (1) the counting chant, (2) the whole-number line, and (3) a 1-1 correspondence. Now that we have defined whole-number addition, there is another, more useful way to define "less than." Notice that $3 < 5$ and $3 + 2 = 5$, $4 < 9$ and $4 + 5 = 9$, and $2 < 11$ and $2 + 9 = 11$. This idea is presented in the next definition of **"less than."**

DEFINITION

"Less Than" for Whole Numbers

For any two whole numbers a and b, $a < b$ (or $b > a$) if and only if there is a nonzero whole number n such that $a + n = b$.

For example, $7 < 9$ since $7 + 2 = 9$ and $13 > 8$ since $8 + 5 = 13$. The symbols "$\leq$" and "$\geq$" mean **less than or equal to** and **greater than or equal to,** respectively.
One useful property of "less than" is the transitive property.

PROPERTY

Transitive Property of "Less Than" for Whole Numbers

For all whole numbers a, b, and c, if $a < b$ and $b < c$, then $a < c$.

The transitive property can be verified using any of our definitions of "less than." Consider the number line in Figure 3.36.

Problem-Solving Strategy
Draw a Diagram

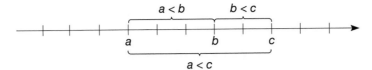

Figure 3.36

Since $a < b$, we have a is to the left of b, and since $b < c$, we have b is to the left of c. Hence a is to the left of c, or $a < c$.

The following is a more formal argument to verify the transitive property. It uses the definition of "less than" involving addition.

$a < b$ means $a + n = b$ for some nonzero whole number n.
$b < c$ means $b + m = c$ for some nonzero whole number m.
Adding m to $a + n$ and b, we obtain

$$a + n + m = b + m.$$

Thus $a + n + m = c$ since $b + m = c$.
Therefore, $a < c$ since $a + (n + m) = c$ and $n + m$ is a nonzero whole number.

NOTE: The transitive property of "less than" holds if "$<$" (and "$\leq$") are replaced with "greater than" for "$>$" (and "$\geq$") throughout.

There are two additional properties involving "less than." The first involves addition (or subtraction).

Algebraic Reasoning
When finding values of x that make the expression $x - 3 < 6$ true, this property can be used by adding 3 on both sides as follows: $x - 3 + 3 < 6 + 3$. Thus it can be seen that all values of x that satisfy $x < 9$ will make the original expression true.

Problem-Solving Strategy
Draw a Diagram

> ## PROPERTY
>
> ### Less Than and Addition for Whole Numbers
>
> If $a < b$, then $a + c < b + c$.

As was the case with transitivity, this property can be verified formally using the definition of "less than." An informal justification using the whole number line follows (Figure 3.37).

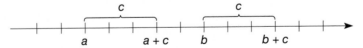

Figure 3.37

Notice that $a < b$, since a is to the left of b. Then the same distance, c, is added to each to obtain $a + c$ and $b + c$, respectively. Since $a + c$ is left of $b + c$, we have $a + c < b + c$.

In the case of "less than" and multiplication, we have to assume that $c \neq 0$. The proof of this property is left for the problem set.

> ## PROPERTY
>
> ### Less Than and Multiplication for Whole Numbers
>
> If $a < b$ and $c \neq 0$, then $ac < bc$.

Since c is a nonzero whole number, it follows that $c > 0$. In Chapter 8, where negative numbers are first discussed, this property will have to be modified to include negatives.

✔ **Check for Understanding:** Exercise/Problem Set A #1–4

Exponents

Just as multiplication can be defined as repeated addition and division may be viewed as repeated subtraction, the concept of exponent can be used to simplify situations involving repeated multiplication.

Children's Literature
www.wiley.com/college/musser
See "The King's Chessboard"
by David Birch.

DEFINITION

Whole-Number Exponent

Let a and m be any two whole numbers where $m \neq 0$. Then

$$a^m = \underbrace{a \cdot a \cdots a}_{m \text{ factors}}.$$

The number m is called the **exponent** or **power** of a, and a is called the **base**. The number a^m is read "a to the power m" or "a to the mth power." For example, 5^2, read "5 to the second power" or "5 squared," is $5 \cdot 5 = 25$; 2^3, read "2 to the third power" or "2 cubed," equals $2 \cdot 2 \cdot 2 = 8$; and $3^4 = 3 \cdot 3 \cdot 3 \cdot 3 = 81$.

There are several properties of exponents that permit us to represent numbers and to do many calculations quickly.

Example 3.10 Rewrite each of the following expressions using a single exponent.

a. $2^3 \cdot 2^4$ **b.** $3^5 \cdot 3^7$

SOLUTION
a. $2^3 \cdot 2^4 = (2 \cdot 2 \cdot 2) \cdot (2 \cdot 2 \cdot 2 \cdot 2) = 2^7$
b. $3^5 \cdot 3^7 = (3 \cdot 3 \cdot 3 \cdot 3 \cdot 3) \cdot (3 \cdot 3 \cdot 3 \cdot 3 \cdot 3 \cdot 3 \cdot 3) = 3^{12}$ ∎

In Example 3.10(a) the exponents of the factors were 3 and 4, and the exponent of the product is $3 + 4 = 7$. Also, in (b) the exponents 5 and 7 yielded an exponent of $5 + 7 = 12$ in the product.

The fact that exponents are added in this way can be shown to be valid in general. This result is stated next as a theorem. A **theorem** is a statement that can be proved based on known results.

THEOREM

Let a, m, and n be any whole numbers where m and n are nonzero. Then
$$a^m \cdot a^n = a^{m+n}.$$

Algebraic Reasoning
Notice how algebraic reasoning is used when proving statements involving variables such as in the proof at the right.

PROOF

$$a^m \cdot a^n = \underbrace{a \cdot a \cdots a}_{m \text{ factors}} \cdot \underbrace{a \cdot a \cdots a}_{n \text{ factors}} = \underbrace{a \cdot a \cdots a}_{m + n \text{ factors}} = a^{m+n}$$

∎

The next example illustrates another way of rewriting products of numbers having the same exponent.

Example 3.11   Rewrite the following expressions using a single exponent.
a. $2^3 \cdot 5^3$ **b.** $3^2 \cdot 7^2 \cdot 11^2$

SOLUTION
a. $2^3 \cdot 5^3 = (2 \cdot 2 \cdot 2)(5 \cdot 5 \cdot 5) = (2 \cdot 5)(2 \cdot 5)(2 \cdot 5) = (2 \cdot 5)^3$
b. $3^2 \cdot 7^2 \cdot 11^2 = (3 \cdot 3)(7 \cdot 7)(11 \cdot 11) = (3 \cdot 7 \cdot 11)(3 \cdot 7 \cdot 11) = (3 \cdot 7 \cdot 11)^2$ ■

The results in Example 3.11 suggest the following theorem.

THEOREM

Let a, b, and m be any whole numbers where m is nonzero. Then
$$a^m \cdot b^m = (ab)^m.$$

PROOF

$$a^m \cdot b^m = \underbrace{a \cdot a \cdots a}_{m \text{ factors}} \cdot \underbrace{b \cdot b \cdots b}_{m \text{ factors}} = \underbrace{(a\,b)(ab) \cdots (ab)}_{m \text{ pairs of factors}} = (ab)^m.$$
    ■

The next example shows how to simplify expressions of the form $(a^m)^n$.

Example 3.12   Rewrite the following expressions with a single exponent.
a. $(5^3)^2$ **b.** $(7^8)^4$

SOLUTION
a. $(5^3)^2 = 5^3 \cdot 5^3 = 5^{3+3} = 5^6 = 5^{3 \cdot 2}$
b. $(7^8)^4 = 7^8 \cdot 7^8 \cdot 7^8 \cdot 7^8 = 7^{32} = 7^{8 \cdot 4}$ ■

In general, we have the next theorem.

THEOREM

Let a, m, and n be any whole numbers where m and n are nonzero. Then
$$(a^m)^n = a^{mn}.$$

The proof of this theorem is similar to the proofs of the previous two theorems.

The previous three properties involved exponents and multiplication. However, notice that $(2 + 3)^3 \neq 2^3 + 3^3$, so there is *not* a corresponding property involving sums or differences raised to powers.

The next example concerns the division of numbers involving exponents with the same base number.

Example 3.13   Rewrite the following quotients with a single exponent.
a. $5^7 \div 5^3$ **b.** $7^8 \div 7^5$

SOLUTION
a. $5^7 \div 5^3 = 5^4$, since $5^7 = 5^3 \cdot 5^4$. Therefore, $5^7 \div 5^3 = 5^{7-3}$.
b. $7^8 \div 7^5 = 7^3$, since $7^8 = 7^5 \cdot 7^3$. Therefore, $7^8 \div 7^5 = 7^{8-5}$.   ■

In general, we have the following result.

> ## THEOREM
>
> Let a, m, and n be any whole numbers where $m > n$ and a, m, and n are nonzero. Then
>
> $$a^m \div a^n = a^{m-n}.$$

PROOF $a^m \div a^n = c$ if and only if $a^m = a^n \cdot c$. Since $a^n \cdot a^{m-n} = a^{n+(m-n)} = a^m$, we have $c = a^{m-n}$. Therefore, $a^m \div a^n = a^{m-n}$.   ∎

Problem-Solving Strategy
Look for a Pattern

Notice that we have not yet defined a^0. Consider the following pattern

$$
\begin{aligned}
a^3 &= a \cdot a \cdot a & &\searrow \div a \\
a^2 &= a \cdot a & &\searrow \div a \\
a^1 &= a & &\searrow \div a \\
a^0 &= 1 & &\searrow
\end{aligned}
$$

$\uparrow$ ⎡The exponents are decreasing by 1 each time⎤ **when** ⎡the numbers are divided by a each time⎤ $\uparrow$

Extending this pattern, we see that the following definition is appropriate.

> ## DEFINITION
>
> ### *Zero as an Exponent*
>
> $a^0 = 1$ for all whole numbers $a \neq 0$.

Notice that 0^0 is not defined. To see why, consider the following two patterns.

Problem-Solving Strategy
Look for a Pattern

PATTERN 1	PATTERN 2
$3^0 = 1$	$0^3 = 0$
$2^0 = 1$	$0^2 = 0$
$1^0 = 1$	$0^1 = 0$
$0^0 = ?$	$0^0 = ?$

Pattern 1 suggests that 0^0 should be 1 and pattern 2 suggests that 0^0 should be 0. Thus to avoid such an inconsistency, 0^0 is undefined.

 Check for Understanding: Exercise/Problem Set A #5–12

Order of Operations

Now that the operations of addition, subtraction, multiplication, and division as well as exponents have been introduced, a point of confusion may occur when more than one operation is in the same expression. For example, does it matter which operation is performed first in an expression such as $3 + 4 \times 5$? If the 3 and 4 are added first, the result is $7 \times 5 = 35$, but if the 4 and 5 are multiplied first, the result is $3 + 20 = 23$.

Since the expression $3 + 5 + 5 + 5 + 5 \,(= 23)$ can be written as $3 + 4 \times 5$, it seems reasonable to do the multiplication, 4×5, first. Similarly, since $4 \cdot 5 \cdot 5 \cdot 5 \,(= 500)$ can be rewritten as $4 \cdot 5^3$, it seems reasonable to do exponents before multiplication. Also, to prevent confusion, parentheses are used to indicate that all operations within a pair of parentheses are done first. To eliminate any ambiguity, mathematicians have agreed that the proper **order of operations** shall be P̲arentheses, E̲xponents, M̲ultiplication *and* D̲ivision, A̲ddition *and* S̲ubtraction (PEMDAS). Although multiplication is listed before division, these operations are done left to right in order of appearance. Similarly, addition and subtraction are done left to right in order of appearance. The pneumonic device P̲lease E̲xcuse M̲y D̲ear A̲unt S̲ally is often used to remember this order.

| **Example 3.13** | Use the proper order of operations to simplify the following expressions. |

a. $5^3 - 4 \cdot (1 + 2)^2$ **b.** $11 - 4 \div 2 \cdot 5 + 3$

SOLUTION

$$\textbf{a. } 5^3 - 4 \cdot (1 + 2)^2 = 5^3 - 4 \cdot 3^2$$
$$= 125 - 4 \cdot 9$$
$$= 125 - 36$$
$$= 89$$

$$\textbf{b. } 11 - 4 \div 2 \cdot 5 + 3 = 11 - 2 \cdot 5 + 3$$
$$= 11 - 10 + 3$$
$$= 1 + 3$$
$$= 4$$

✔ **Check for Understanding:** Exercise/Problem Set A #13–14

MATHEMATICAL MORSEL

John von Neumann was a brilliant mathematician who made important contributions to several scientific fields, including the theory and application of high-speed computing machines. George Pólya of Stanford University admitted that "Johnny was the only student I was ever afraid of. If in the course of a lecture I stated an unsolved problem, the chances were he'd come to me as soon as the lecture was over, with the complete solution in a few scribbles on a slip of paper." At the age of 6, von Neumann could divide two eight-digit numbers in his head, and when he was 8 he had mastered the calculus. When he invented his first electronic computer, someone suggested that he race it. Given a problem like "What is the smallest power of 2 with the property that its decimal digit fourth from the right is a 7," the machine and von Neumann started at the same time and von Neumann won!

| Section 3.3 | EXERCISE / PROBLEM SET A |

EXERCISES

1. Find the nonzero whole number n in the definition of "less than" that verifies the following statements.
  a. $12 < 31$ **b.** $53 > 37$

2. Using the definitions of $<$ and $>$ given in this section, write four inequality statements based on the fact that $2 + 8 = 10$.

3. The statement $a < x < b$ is equivalent to writing $a < x$ and $x < b$ and is called a **compound inequality**. We often read $a < x < b$ as "x is between a and b." For the questions that follow, assume that a, x, and b are whole numbers.
  If $a < x < b$ and c is a nonzero whole number, is it always true that $a + c < x + c < b + c$? Try several examples to test your conjecture.

4. Does the transitive property hold for the following? Explain.
   a. =   **b.** ≠

5. Using exponents, rewrite the following expressions in a simpler form.
   a. $3 \cdot 3 \cdot 3 \cdot 3$ **b.** $2 \cdot 2 \cdot 3 \cdot 2 \cdot 3 \cdot 2$
   c. $6 \cdot 7 \cdot 6 \cdot 7 \cdot 6$ **d.** $x \cdot y \cdot x \cdot y \cdot y \cdot y$
   e. $a \cdot b \cdot b \cdot a$ **f.** $5 \cdot 6 \cdot 5 \cdot 5 \cdot 6 \cdot 6$

6. Evaluate each of the following without a calculator and order them from largest to smallest.
   $$5^2 \quad 4^3 \quad 3^4 \quad 2^5$$

7. Write each of the following expressions in expanded form, without exponents.
   a. $3x^2y^5z$ **b.** $7 \cdot 5^3$ **c.** $(7 \cdot 5)^3$

8. Rewrite each with a single exponent.
   a. $5^3 \cdot 5^4$ **b.** $3^{12} \div 3^2$
   c. $2^7 \cdot 5^7$ **d.** $8 \cdot 2^5$
   e. $25^3 \div 5^2$ **f.** $9^2 \cdot 12^3 \cdot 2$

9. Express 5^{14} in three different ways using the numbers 2, 5, 7 and exponents. (You may use a number more than once.)

10. Let $a, b, n \in W$ and $n \geq 1$. Determine if $(a + b)^n = a^n + b^n$ is always true, sometimes true, or never true. Justify your conclusion.

11. Find x.
    a. $3^7 \cdot 3^x = 3^{13}$ **b.** $(3^x)^4 = 3^{20}$
    c. $3^x \cdot 2^x = 6^x$

12. Use the $\boxed{y^x}$, $\boxed{x^y}$, or $\boxed{\wedge}$ key on your calculator to evaluate the following.
    a. 6^8 **b.** $(3 \cdot 5)^4$ **c.** $3 \cdot 5^4$

13. Simplify each of the following expressions.
    a. $15 - 3(7 - 2)$
    b. $2 \cdot 5^2$
    c. $3^2 \cdot 4 - 2(5 - 3)^3$
    d. $\dfrac{6 + 2(3^3 - 4^2)^2 + 4^2}{6 \cdot (3^3 - 4^2)}$

14. For each of the following:
    i. Show that the expression is not equal to the numerical value.
    ii. Insert parentheses in the expression so it will be equal to the numerical value.
    a. $2 \cdot 3^2 - 4$; 10   **b.** $4^2 - 3 \cdot 4 \div 2$; 26

PROBLEMS

15. Let $a, m,$ and n be whole numbers where a is not zero. Prove the following property: $(a^m)^n = a^{m \cdot n}$.

16. Using properties of exponents, *mentally* determine the larger of the following pairs.
    a. 6^{10} and 3^{20} **b.** 9^9 and 3^{20} **c.** 12^{10} and 3^{20}

17. The price of a certain candy bar doubled over a period of five years. Suppose that the price continued to double every five years and that the candy bar cost 25 cents in 2000.
    a. What would be the price of the candy bar in the year 2015?
    b. What would be the price of the candy bar in the year 2040?
    c. Write an expression representing the price of the candy bar after n five-year periods.

18. Verify the transitive property of "less than" using the 1-1 correspondence definition.

19. Observe the following pattern in the sums of consecutive whole numbers. Use your calculator to verify that the statements are true.
    $$2 + 3 + 4 = 1^3 + 2^3$$
    $$5 + 6 + 7 + 8 + 9 = 2^3 + 3^3$$
    $$10 + 11 + 12 + 13 + 14 + 15 + 16 = 3^3 + 4^3$$

    a. Write the next two lines in this sequence of sums.
    b. Express $9^3 + 10^3$ as a sum of consecutive whole numbers.
    c. Express $12^3 + 13^3$ as a sum of consecutive whole numbers.
    d. Express $n^3 + (n + 1)^3$ as a sum of consecutive whole numbers.

20. Pizzas come in four different sizes, each with or without a choice of four ingredients. How many ways are there to order a pizza?

21. The perfect square 49 is special in that each of the two nonzero digits forming the number is itself a perfect square.
    a. Explain why there are no other 2-digit squares with this property.
    b. What 3-digit perfect squares can you find that are made up of one 1-digit square and one 2-digit square?
    c. What 4-digit perfect squares can you find that are made up of two 1-digit squares and one 2-digit square?
    d. What 4-digit perfect squares can you find that are made up of one 3-digit square and one 1-digit square?
    e. What 4-digit perfect squares can you find that are made up of two 2-digit squares?
    f. What 4-digit perfect squares can you find that are made up of four 1-digit squares?

22. When asked to find four whole numbers such that the product of any two of them is one less than the square of a whole number, one mathematician said, "2, 4, 12, and 22." A second mathematician said, "2, 12, 24, and 2380." Which was correct?

23. **a.** Give a formal proof of the property of less than and addition. (*Hint:* See the proof in the paragraph following Figure 3.37.)
    b. State and prove the corresponding property for subtraction.

| **Section 3.3** | EXERCISE / PROBLEM SET B |

EXERCISES

1. Find the nonzero whole number n in the definition of "less than" that verifies the following statements.
 a. $17 < 26$ **b.** $113 > 49$

2. Using the definitions of $<$ and $>$ given in this section, write four inequality statements based on the fact that $29 + 15 = 44$.

3. If $a < x < b$ and c is a nonzero whole number, is it always true that $ac < xc < bc$? Try several examples to test your conjecture.

4. Does the transitive property hold for the following? Explain.
 a. $>$ **b.** $\leq$

5. Using exponents, rewrite the following expressions in a simpler form.
 a. $4 \cdot 4 \cdot 4 \cdot 4 \cdot 4 \cdot 4 \cdot 4$
 b. $4 \cdot 3 \cdot 3 \cdot 4 \cdot 4 \cdot 3 \cdot 3 \cdot 3 \cdot 3$
 c. $y \cdot 2 \cdot x \cdot y \cdot x \cdot x$
 d. $a \cdot b \cdot a \cdot b \cdot a \cdot b \cdot a \cdot b$

6. Evaluate each of the following without a calculator and arrange them from smallest to largest.

$$5^3 \quad 6^2 \quad 3^5 \quad 2^7$$

7. Write each of the following expressions in expanded form, without exponents.
 a. $10ab^4$ **b.** $(2x)^5$ **c.** $2x^5$

8. Write the following with only one exponent.
 a. $x^3 \cdot x^6$ **b.** $a^{15} \div a^3$ **c.** $x^5 y^5$
 d. $2^3 \cdot 16$ **e.** $128 \div 2^3$ **f.** $3^7 \cdot 9^5 \cdot 27^2$

9. Express 7^{20} in three different ways using the numbers 7, 2, 5 and exponents. (You may use a number more than once.)

10. Let $a, b, m, n \in W$ and a is not zero. Determine if $a^n \cdot a^m = a^{n \cdot m}$ is always true, sometimes true, or never true. Justify your conclusion.

11. Find the value of x that makes each equation true.
 a. $2^x \div 2^5 = 2^7$
 b. $(6^x)^2 = 36^x$
 c. $5^7 \cdot 3^x = 15^x$

12. Use the $\boxed{y^x}$, $\boxed{x^y}$, or $\boxed{\wedge}$ key on your calculator to evaluate the following.
 a. $3^7 + 2^4$ **b.** $2 \cdot 5^6 - 3 \cdot 2^3$ **c.** $\dfrac{9^3 \cdot 12^4}{3^8}$

13. Simplify each of the following expressions.
 a. $2 \cdot 3^2 - 2^2 \cdot 3$
 b. $\dfrac{2(4-1)^3}{15 - 2 \cdot 3^1(7+5)^0}$
 c. $5^2 - 4^2 + (6-4)^5 \div 2^3$
 d. $4 \times 2^3 - 6^4 \div (2^3 \cdot 3^2)$

14. For each of the following:
 i. Show that the expression is not equal to the numerical value.
 ii. Insert parentheses in the expression so it will be equal to the numerical value.
 a. $22 - 2 \cdot 7 - 3$; 137
 b. $17 + 2 \cdot 3^2 + 5 \div 5$; 8

PROBLEMS

15. a. How does the sum $1 + 2 + 3$ compare to the sum $1^3 + 2^3 + 3^3$?

 b. Try several more such examples and determine the relationship between $1 + 2 + 3 + \cdots + n$ and $1^3 + 2^3 + 3^3 + \cdots + n^3$.

 c. Use the pattern you observed to find the sum of the first 10 cubes, $1^3 + 2^3 + 3^3 + \cdots + 10^3$, without evaluating any of the cubes.

16. Order these numbers from smallest to largest using properties of exponents and mental methods.

$$3^{22} \quad 4^{14} \quad 9^{10} \quad 8^{10}$$

17. A pad of 200 sheets of paper is approximately 15 mm thick. Suppose that one piece of this paper were folded in half, then

folded in half again, then folded again, and so on. If this folding process was continued until the piece of paper had been folded in half 30 times, how thick would the folded paper be?

18. Suppose that you can order a submarine sandwich with or without each of seven condiments.
 a. How many ways are there to order a sandwich?
 b. How many ways can you order exactly two condiments?
 c. Exactly seven?
 d. Exactly one?
 e. Exactly six?

19. a. If $n^2 = 121$, what is n?
 b. If $n^2 = 1,234,321$, what is n?
 c. If $n^2 = 12,345,654,321$, what is n?
 d. If $n^2 = 123,456,787,654,321$, what is n?

20. 12 is a factor of $10^2 - 2^2$, 27 is a factor of $20^2 - 7^2$, and 84 is a factor of $80^2 - 4^2$. Check to see whether these three statements are correct. Using a variable, prove why this works in general.

21. a. Verify that the property of less than and multiplication holds where $a = 3$, $b = 7$, and $c = 5$.
 b. Show that the property does not hold if $c = 0$.
 c. Give a formal proof of the property. (*Hint:* Use the fact that the product of two nonzero whole numbers is nonzero.)
 d. State the corresponding property for division.

22. Let a, m, and n be whole numbers where $m > n$ and a is not zero. Prove the following property: $a^m \div a^n = a^{m-n}$.

Analyzing Student Thinking
23. Brooke claims that because "less than and addition for whole numbers" is a property, so too should "less than and subtraction for whole numbers" be a property. How should you respond?

24. A student asks why there is not a property of "less than and division for whole numbers." How should you respond?

25. Jarell was asked to simplify the expression $3^2 \cdot 3^4$ and wrote $3^2 \cdot 3^4 = 9^6$. How would you convince him that this answer is

incorrect? That is, give the correct answer *and* explain *why* the student's method is incorrect.

26. Viridiana observes $0 + 0 = 0 \times 0$ and $2 + 2 = 2 \times 2$ and assumes that addition and multiplication are the same. Is she correct? Explain.

27. Abbi was asked to simplify the expression $8^5 \div 2^2$ and wrote $8^5 \div 2^2 = 4^3$. How would you convince her that this answer is incorrect?

28. Cho rewrote $(3^2)^2$ as $3^{(2^2)}$ (a form of associativity, perhaps). Was she correct or incorrect? She also rewrote $(2^3)^2$ as $2^{(3^2)}$. Is this right or wrong? How should you respond?

29. Ayumi writes $a^m \cdot b^n = (ab)^{m+n}$. Is this statement correct or incorrect? Explain.

30. Gavin says that because of distributivity, the following equation is true: $(a + b)^m = a^m + b^m$. What could you say to help him better understand the situation?

31. Bailey wrote the following using "Please Excuse My Dear Aunt Sally." Explain where she may have misinterpreted this acronym.

$(5 - 3)^3 + 17 = 5^3 - 3^3 + 17 = 125 - 27 + 17 = 115.$

Problems Relating to the NCTM Standards and Curriculum Focal Points

1. The Focal Points for Kindergarten state "Representing, comparing and ordering whole numbers and joining and separating sets." Compare the definition of ordering in the section to the discussion of ordering in Section 2.2. Which way of looking at ordering is more appropriate for kindergarteners and which is more abstract?

2. The NCTM Standards state "All students should develop an understanding of large numbers and recognize and

appropriately use exponential, scientific, and calculator notation." Describe some examples of scientific notation discussed in this section.

3. The NCTM Standards state "All students should describe quantitative change, such as a student's growing two inches in one year." Explain how an understanding of quantitative change is related to the discussion of the properties of less than in this section.

END OF CHAPTER MATERIAL

Solution of Initial Problem

In a group of nine coins, eight weigh the same and the ninth is either heavier or lighter. Assume that the coins are identical in appearance. Using a pan balance, what is the smallest number of balancings needed to identify the counterfeit coin?

Strategy: Use Direct Reasoning
Three balancings are sufficient. Separate the coins into three groups of three coins each.

 A   *B*   *C*

Balance group A against group B. If they balance, we can deduce that the counterfeit coin is in group C. We then need to determine if the coin is heavier or lighter. Balance group C against group A. Based on whether group C goes up or down, we can deduce whether group C is light or heavy, respectively.

If the coins in group A do not balance the coins in group B, then we can conclude that either A is light or B is heavy (or vice versa). We now balance group A against group C. If they balance, we know that group B has the counterfeit coin. If group A and C do not balance, then group A has the counterfeit coin. We also know whether group A or B is light or heavy depending on which one went down on the first balancing.

In two balancings, we know which group of three coins contains the counterfeit one and whether the counterfeit coin is heavy or light. The third balancing will exactly identify the counterfeit coin.

From the group of three coins that has the counterfeit coin, select two coins and balance them against each other. This will determine which coin is the counterfeit one. Thus, the counterfeit coin can be found in three balancings.

Additional Problems Where the Strategy "Use Direct Reasoning" Is Useful

1. The sum of the digits of a three-digit palindrome is odd. Determine whether the middle digit is odd or is even.

2. Jose's room in a hotel was higher than Michael's but lower than Ralph's. Andre's room is on a floor between Ralph's and Jose's. If it weren't for Michael, Clyde's room would be the lowest. List the rooms from lowest to highest.

3. Given an 8-liter jug of water and empty 3-liter and 5-liter jugs, pour the water so that two of the jugs have 4 liters.

People in Mathematics

John Von Neumann (1903–1957)
John von Neumann was one of the most remarkable mathematicians of the twentieth century. His logical power was legendary. It is said that during and after World War II the U.S. government reached many scientific decisions simply by asking von Neumann for his opinion. Paul Halmos, his one-time assistant, said, "The most spectacular thing about Johnny was not his power as a mathematician, which was great, but his rapidity; he was very, very fast. And like the modern computer, which doesn't memorize logarithms, but computes them, Johnny didn't bother to memorize things. He computed them." Appropriately, von Neumann was one of the first to realize how a general-purpose computing machine—a computer—should be designed. In the 1950s he invented a "theory of automata," the basis for subsequent work in artificial intelligence.

Julia Bowman Robinson (1919–1985)
Julia Bowman Robinson spent her early years in Arizona, near Phoenix. She said that one of her earliest memories was of arranging pebbles in the shadow of a giant saguaro—"I've always had a basic liking for the natural numbers." In 1948, Robinson earned her doctorate in mathematics at Berkeley; she went on to contribute to the solution of "Hilbert's tenth problem." In 1975 she became the first woman mathematician elected to the prestigious National Academy of Sciences. Robinson also served as president of the American Mathematical Society, the main professional organization for research mathematicians. "Rather than being remembered as the first woman this or that, I would prefer to be remembered simply for the theorems I have proved and the problems I have solved."

CHAPTER REVIEW

Review the following terms and exercises to determine which require learning or relearning—page numbers are provided for easy reference.

SECTION 3.1 Addition and Subtraction
VOCABULARY/NOTATION

EXERCISES

1. Show how to find $5 + 4$ using

    a. a set model.   **b.** a measurement model.

2. Name the property of addition that is used to justify each of the following equations.

    a. $7 + (3 + 9) = (7 + 3) + 9$
    b. $9 + 0 = 9$
    c. $13 + 27 = 27 + 13$
    d. $7 + 6$ is a whole number

3. Identify and use thinking strategies that can be used to find the following addition facts.

    a. $5 + 6$
    b. $7 + 9$

4. Illustrate the following using $7 - 3$.

    a. The take-away approach
    b. The missing-addend approach

5. Show how the addition table for the facts 1 through 9 can be used to solve subtraction problems.

6. Which of the following properties hold for whole number subtraction?

    a. Closure   **b.** Commutative
    c. Associative   **d.** Identity

SECTION 3.2 Multiplication and Division

VOCABULARY/NOTATION

Repeated-addition approach   104
Times   104
Product   104
Factor   104
Rectangular array approach   104
Cartesian product approach   105
Tree diagram approach   105
Closure for multiplication   105
Commutativity for multiplication   105
Associativity for multiplication   106
Identity for multiplication   106

Multiplicative identity   106
Distributive property   107
Multiplication property of zero   108
Distributivity of multiplication over subtraction   108
Thinking strategies for multiplication facts   108
Sharing division   109
Measurement division   110
Missing-factor approach   110
Divided by   112

Dividend   112
Divisor   112
Quotient   112
Missing factor   112
Division property of zero   112
Division by zero   112
Division algorithm   113
Divisor   113
Quotient   113
Remainder   113
Repeated-subtraction approach   113

EXERCISES

1. Illustrate 3×5 using each of the following approaches.

    a. Repeated addition with the set model
    b. Repeated addition with the measurement model
    c. Rectangular array with the set model
    d. Rectangular array with the measurement model

2. Name the property of multiplication that is used to justify each of the following equations.

    a. $37 \times 1 = 37$
    b. $26 \times 5 = 5 \times 26$
    c. $2 \times (5 \times 17) = (2 \times 5) \times 17$
    d. 4×9 is a whole number

3. Show how the distributive property can be used to simplify these calculations.

    a. $7 \times 27 + 7 \times 13$ **b.** $8 \times 17 - 8 \times 7$

4. Use and name the thinking strategies that can be used to find the following addition facts.

    a. 6×7 **b.** 9×7

5. Show how $17 \div 3$ can be found using

    a. repeated subtraction with the set model.
    b. repeated subtraction with the measurement model.

6. Show how the multiplication table for the facts 1 through 9 can be used to solve division problems.

7. Calculate the following if possible. If impossible, explain why.

    a. $7 \div 0$ **b.** $0 \div 7$ **c.** $0 \div 0$

8. Apply the division algorithm and apply it to the calculation $39 \div 7$.

9. Which of the following properties hold for whole-number division?

   a. Closure   **b.** Commutative
   c. Associative   **d.** Identity

10. Label the following diagram and comment on its value.

SECTION 3.3 Ordering and Exponents

VOCABULARY/NOTATION

Less than   120
Less than or equal to   120
Greater than or equal to   120
Transitive property of less
   than   120

Property of less than and addition
   (subtraction)   121
Property of less than and multiplication
   (division)   121
Exponent   122

Power   122
Base   122
Theorem   122
Zero as an exponent   124
Order of operations   124

EXERCISES

1. Describe how addition is used to define "less than" ("greater than").

2. For whole numbers a, b, and c, if $a < b$, what can be said about

   a. $a + c$ and $b + c$?   **b.** $a \times c$ and $b \times c$?

3. Rewrite 5^4 using the definition of exponent.

4. Rewrite the following using properties of exponents.

   a. $(7^3)^4$ **b.** $3^5 \times 7^5$ **c.** $5^7 \div 5^3$ **d.** $4^{12} \times 4^{13}$

5. Explain how to motivate the definition of zero as an exponent.

CHAPTER TEST

KNOWLEDGE

1. True or false?

   a. $n(A \cup B) = n(A) + n(B)$ for all finite sets A and B.
   b. If $B \subseteq A$, then $n(A - B) = n(A) - n(B)$ for all finite sets A and B.
   c. Commutativity does not hold for subtraction of whole numbers.
   d. Distributivity of multiplication over subtraction does not hold in the set of whole numbers.
   e. The symbol m^a, where m and a are nonzero whole numbers, represents the product of m factors of a.
   f. If a is the divisor, b is the dividend, and c is the quotient, then $ab = c$.
   g. The statement "$a + b = c$ if and only if $c - b = a$" is an example of the take-away approach to subtraction.
   h. Factors are to multiplication as addends are to addition.
   i. If $n \neq 0$ and $b + n = a$, then $a < b$.
   j. If $n(A) = a$ and $n(B) = b$, then $A \times B$ contains exactly ab ordered pairs.

2. Complete the following table for the operations on the set of whole numbers. Write True in the box if the indicated property holds for the indicated operation on whole numbers and write False if the indicated property does not hold for the indicated operation on whole numbers.

	ADD	SUBTRACT	MULTIPLY	DIVIDE
Closure				
Commutative				
Associative				
Identity				

3. Identify the property of whole numbers being illustrated.

   a. $a \cdot (b \cdot c) = a \cdot (c \cdot b)$
   b. $(3 + 2) \cdot 1 = 3 + 2$
   c. $(4 + 7) + 8 = 4 + (7 + 8)$
   d. $(2 \cdot 3) \cdot 5 = 2 \cdot (3 \cdot 5)$
   e. $(6 - 5) \cdot 2 = 6 \cdot 2 - 5 \cdot 2$
   f. $m + (n + p) = m + (p + n)$

SKILL

4. Find the following sums and products using thinking strategies. Show your work.

   a. $39 + 12$ **b.** $47 + 87$
   c. $5(73 \cdot 2)$ **d.** 12×33

5. Find the quotient and remainder when 321 is divided by 5.

6. Rewrite the following using a single exponent in each case.

  a. $3^7 \cdot 3^{12}$

  b. $5^{31} \div 5^7$

  c. $(7^3)^5$

  d. $4^5/2^8$

  e. $7^{12} \cdot 2^{12} \cdot 14^3$

  f. $(12^8/12^5)^4 \cdot (3^6)^2$

7. Perform the following calculations by applying appropriate properties. Which properties are you using?

  a. $13 \cdot 97 + 13 \cdot 3$

  b. $(194 + 86) + 6$

  c. $7 \cdot 23 + 23 \cdot 3$

  d. $25(123 \cdot 8)$

8. Classify each of the following division problems as examples of either sharing or measurement division.

  a. Martina has 12 cookies to share between her three friends and herself. How many cookies will each person receive?

  b. Coach Massey had 56 boys sign up to play intramural basketball. If he puts 7 boys on each team, how many teams will he have?

  c. Eduardo is planning to tile around his bathtub. If he wants to tile 48 inches up the wall and the individual tiles are 4 inches wide, how many rows of tile will he need?

9. Each of the following situations involves a subtraction problem. In each case, tell whether the problem is best represented by the take-away approach or the missing-addend approach, and why. Then write an equation that could be used to answer the question.

  a. Ovais has 137 basketball cards and Quinn has 163 basketball cards. How many more cards does Quinn have?

  b. Regina set a goal of saving money for a $1500 down payment on a car. Since she started, she has been able to save $973. How much more money does she need to save in order to meet her goal?

  c. Riley was given $5 for his allowance. After he spent $1.43 on candy at the store, how much did he have left to put into savings for a new bike?

UNDERSTANDING

10. Using the following table, find $A - B$.

+	A	B	C
A	C	A	B
B	A	B	C
C	B	C	A

11. a. Using the definition of an exponent, provide an explanation to show that $(7^3)^4 = 7^{12}$.

  b. Use the fact that $a^m \cdot a^n = a^{m+n}$ to explain why $(7^3)^4 = 7^{12}$.

12. Show why $3 \div 0$ is undefined.

13. Explain in detail why $a^m \cdot b^m = (a \cdot b)^m$.

14. Explain why $(a \cdot b)^c \neq a \cdot b^c$ for all $a, b, c, \in W$.

15. If we make up another operation, say Ω, and we give it a table using the letters A, B, C, D as the set on which this symbol is operating, determine whether this operation is commutative.

Ω	A	B	C	D
A	B	B	B	B
B	B	C	D	A
C	B	A	C	D
D	B	D	A	C

Then create your own 4 × 4 table for a new operation @, operating on the same four numbers, A, B, C, D. Make sure your operation is commutative. Can you see something that would always be true in the table of a commutative operation?

PROBLEM SOLVING/APPLICATION

16. Which is the smallest set of whole numbers that contains 2 and 3 and is closed under addition and multiplication?

17. If the product of two numbers is even and their sum is odd, what can you say about the two numbers?

18. Illustrate the following approaches for 4 × 3 using the measurement model. Please include a written description to clarify the illustration.

  a. Repeated-addition approach

  b. Rectangular array approach

19. Use a set model to illustrate that the associative property for whole-number addition holds.

20. Illustrate the missing-addend approach for the subtraction problem $8 - 5$ by using

  a. the set model.

  b. the measurement model.

21. Use the rectangular array approach to illustrate that the commutative property for whole-number multiplication holds.

22. Find a whole number less than 100 that is both a perfect square and a perfect cube.

23. Find two examples where $a, b \in W$ and $a \cdot b = a + b$.

Whole-Number Computation—Mental, Electronic, and Written

CHAPTER 4

FOCUS ON   *Computational Devices from the Abacus to the Computer*

The abacus was one of the earliest computational devices. The Chinese abacus, or suan-pan, was composed of a frame together with beads on fixed rods.

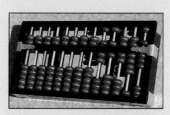

In 1617, Napier invented lattice rods, called Napier's bones. To multiply, appropriate rods were selected, laid side by side, and then appropriate "columns" were added—thus only addition was needed to multiply.

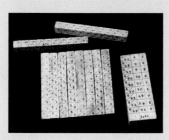

About 1594, Napier invented logarithms. Using logarithms, multiplication can be performed by adding respective logarithms. The slide rule, used extensively by engineers and scientists through the 1960s, was designed to use properties of logarithms.

In 1642, Pascal invented the first mechanical adding machine.

In 1671, Leibniz developed his "reckoning machine," which could also multiply and divide.

In 1812, Babbage built his Difference Engine, which was the first "computer."

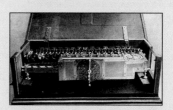

By 1946, ENIAC (Electronic Numerical Integrator and Computer) was developed. It filled a room, weighed over 30 tons, and had nearly 20,000 vacuum tubes. Chips permitted the manufacture of microcomputers, such as the Apple and DOS-based computers in the late 1970s, the Apple Macintosh and Windows-based versions in the 1980s, to laptop computers in the 1990s.

Chip manufacture also allowed calculators to become more powerful to the point that the dividing line between calculator and computer has become blurred.

STRATEGY 9
Use Indirect Reasoning

Occasionally, in mathematics, there are problems that are not easily solved using direct reasoning. In such cases, indirect reasoning may be the best way to solve the problem. A simple way of viewing **indirect reasoning** is to consider an empty room with only two entrances, say A and B. If you want to use direct reasoning to prove that someone entered the room through A, you would watch entrance A. However, you could also prove that someone entered through A by watching entrance B. If a person got into the room and did not go through B, the person had to go through entrance A. In mathematics, to prove that a condition, say "A," is true, one assumes that the condition "not A" is true and shows the latter condition to be impossible.

INITIAL PROBLEM

The whole numbers 1 through 9 can be used once, each being arranged in a 3×3 square array so that the sum of the numbers in each of the rows, columns, and diagonals is 15. Show that 1 cannot be in one of the corners.

```
      2 ┌───┬───┬───┐ 5
        │   │   │   │   6
    1   ├───┼───┼───┤ 7
      3 │   │   │   │ 8
    4   ├───┼───┼───┤
        │   │   │   │ 9
        └───┴───┴───┘
```

CLUES

The Use Indirect Reasoning strategy may be appropriate when

- Direct reasoning seems too complex or does not lead to a solution.
- Assuming the negation of what you are trying to prove narrows the scope of the problem.
- A proof is required.

  A solution of this Initial Problem is on page 176.

INTRODUCTION

NCTM Standard
All students should select appropriate methods and tools for computing with whole numbers from among mental computation, estimation, calculators, and paper and pencil according to the context and nature of the computation and use the selected method or tool.

In the past, much of elementary school mathematics was devoted to learning written methods for doing addition, subtraction, multiplication, and division. Due to the availability of electronic calculators and computers, less emphasis is being placed on doing written calculations involving numbers with many digits. Instead, an emphasis is being placed on developing skills in the use of all three types of computations: mental, written, and electronic (calculators/computers). Then, depending on the size of the numbers involved, the number of operations to be performed, the accuracy desired in the answer, and the time required to do the calculations, the appropriate mode(s) of calculation will be selected and employed.

In this chapter you will study all three forms of computation: mental, electronic (calculators), and written.

Key Concepts from NCTM Curriculum Focal Points

- **GRADE 1:** Developing an understanding of whole number relationships, including grouping in tens and ones.
- **GRADE 2:** Developing quick recall of addition facts and related subtraction facts and fluency with multidigit addition and subtraction.
- **GRADE 4:** Developing quick recall of multiplication facts and related division facts and fluency with whole number multiplication.
- **GRADE 5:** Developing an understanding of and fluency with division of whole numbers.
- **GRADES 4 AND 5:** Students select appropriate methods and apply them accurately to estimate products and calculate them mentally, depending on the context and numbers involved.

4.1   MENTAL MATH, ESTIMATION, AND CALCULATORS

STARTING POINT

Compute each of the following mentally and write a sentence for each problem describing your thought processes. After a discussion with classmates, determine some common strategies.

$$32 \cdot 26 - 23 \cdot 32 \qquad (16 \times 9) \times 25 \qquad 25 + (39 + 105)$$
$$49 + 27 \qquad 152 - 87 \qquad 46 \times 99 \qquad 252 \div 12$$

Mental Math

Children's Literature
www.wiley.com/college/musser
See "A Million Fish More or Less" by Patricia C. McKissack.

The availability and widespread use of calculators and computers have permanently changed the way we compute. Consequently, there is an increasing need to develop students' skills in estimating answers when checking the reasonableness of results obtained electronically. Computational estimation, in turn, requires a good working knowledge of mental math. Thus this section begins with several techniques for doing calculations mentally.

In Chapter 3 we saw how the thinking strategies for learning the basic arithmetic facts could be extended to multidigit numbers, as illustrated next.

Example 4.1   Calculate the following mentally.

a. $15 + (27 + 25)$ **b.** $21 \cdot 17 - 13 \cdot 21$ **c.** $(8 \times 7) \times 25$
d. $98 + 59$ **e.** $87 + 29$ **f.** $168 \div 3$

SOLUTION

a. $15 + (27 + 25) = (27 + 25) + 15 = 27 + (25 + 15) = 27 + 40 = 67$. Notice how commutativity and associativity play a key role here.
b. $21 \cdot 17 - 13 \cdot 21 = 21 \cdot 17 - 21 \cdot 13 = 21 (17 - 13) = 21 \cdot 4 = 84$. Observe how commutativity and distributivity are useful here.
c. $(8 \times 7) \times 25 = (7 \times 8) \times 25 = 7 \times (8 \times 25) = 7 \times 200 = 1400$. Here commutativity is used first; then associativity is used to group the 8 and 25 since their product is 200.
d. $98 + 59 = 98 + (2 + 57) = (98 + 2) + 57 = 157$. Associativity is used here to form 100.
e. $87 + 29 = 80 + 20 + 7 + 9 = 100 + 16 = 116$ using associativity and commutativity.
f. $168 \div 3 = (150 \div 3) + (18 \div 3) = 50 + 6 = 56$. ∎

Observe that part (f) makes use of **right distributivity of division over addition**; that is, whenever the three quotients are whole numbers, $(a + b) \div c = (a \div c) + (b \div c)$. Right distributivity of division over subtraction also holds.

The calculations in Example 4.1 illustrate the following important mental techniques.

Properties   Commutativity, associativity, and distributivity play an important role in simplifying calculations so that they can be performed mentally. Notice how useful these properties were in parts (a), (b), (c), (d), and (e) of Example 4.1. Also, the solution in part (f) uses right distributivity.

Compatible Numbers   **Compatible numbers** are numbers whose sums, differences, products, or quotients are easy to calculate mentally. Examples of compatible numbers are 86 and 14 under addition (since $86 + 14 = 100$), 25 and 8 under multiplication (since $25 \times 8 = 200$), and 600 and 30 under division (since $600 \div 30 = 20$). In part (a) of Example 4.1, adding 15 to 25 produces a number, namely 40, that is easy to add to 27. Notice that numbers are compatible with *respect to an operation*. For example, 86 and 14 are compatible with respect to addition but not with respect to multiplication.

Example 4.2   Calculate the following mentally using properties and/or compatible numbers.

a. $(4 \times 13) \times 25$ **b.** $1710 \div 9$ **c.** 86×15

SOLUTION

a. $(4 \times 13) \times 25 = 13 \times (4 \times 25) = 1300$
b. $1710 \div 9 = (1800 - 90) \div 9 = (1800 \div 9) - (90 \div 9) = 200 - 10 = 190$
c. $86 \times 15 = (86 \times 10) + (86 \times 5) = 860 + 430 = 1290$ (Notice that 86×5 is half of 86×10.) ∎

Compensation   The sum $43 + (38 + 17)$ can be viewed as $38 + 60 = 98$ using commutativity, associativity, and the fact that 43 and 17 are compatible numbers. Finding the answer to $43 + (36 + 19)$ is not as easy. However, by reformulating the sum $36 + 19$ mentally as $37 + 18$, we obtain the sum $(43 + 37) + 18 = 80 + 18 = 98$. This process of reformulating a sum, difference, product, or quotient to one that is more readily obtained mentally is called **compensation**. Some specific techniques using compensation are introduced next.

In the computations of Example 4.1(d), 98 was *increased* by 2 to 100 and then 59 was *decreased* by 2 to 57 (a compensation was made) to maintain the same sum. This technique, **additive compensation**, is an application of associativity. Similarly, additive compensation is used when $98 + 59$ is rewritten as $97 + 60$ or $100 + 57$. The problem $47 - 29$ can be thought of as $48 - 30 (= 18)$. This use of compensation in subtraction is called the **equal additions method** since the same number (here 1) is added to both 47 and 29 to maintain the same difference. This compensation is performed to make the subtraction easier by subtracting 30 from 48. The product 48×5 can be found using **multiplicative compensation** as follows: $48 \times 5 = 24 \times 10 = 240$. Here, again, associativity can be used to justify this method.

Left-to-Right Methods   To add 342 and 136, first add the hundreds $(300 + 100)$, then the tens $(40 + 30)$, and then the ones $(2 + 6)$, to obtain 478. To add 158 and 279, one can think as follows: $100 + 200 = 300, 300 + 50 + 70 = 420, 420 + 8 + 9 = 437$. Alternatively, $158 + 279$ can be found as follows: $158 + 200 = 358, 358 + 70 = 428, 428 + 9 = 437$. Subtraction from left to right can be done in a similar manner. Research has found that people who are excellent mental calculators utilize this left-to-right method to reduce memory load, instead of mentally picturing the usual right-to-left written method. The multiplication problem 3×123 can be thought of mentally as $3 \times 100 + 3 \times 20 + 3 \times 3$ using distributivity. Also, 4×253 can be thought of mentally as $800 + 200 + 12 = 1012$ or as $4 \times 250 + 4 \times 3 = 1000 + 12 = 1012$.

Multiplying Powers of 10   These special numbers can be multiplied mentally in either standard or exponential form. For example, $100 \times 1000 = 100,000, 10^4 \times 10^5 = 10^9, 20 \times 300 = 6000$, and $12,000 \times 110,000 = 12 \times 11 \times 10^7 = 1,320,000,000$.

Multiplying by Special Factors   Numbers such as 5, 25, and 99 are regarded as special factors because they are convenient to use mentally. For example, since $5 = 10 \div 2$, we have $38 \times 5 = 38 \times 10 \div 2 = 380 \div 2 = 190$. Also, since $25 = 100 \div 4$, $36 \times 25 = 3600 \div 4 = 900$. The product 46×99 can be thought of as $46(100 - 1) = 4600 - 46 = 4554$. Also, dividing by 5 can be viewed as dividing by 10, then multiplying by 2. Thus $460 \div 5 = (460 \div 10) \times 2 = 46 \times 2 = 92$.

Example 4.3   Calculate mentally using the indicated method.

a. $197 + 248$ using additive compensation
b. 125×44 using multiplicative compensation
c. $273 - 139$ using the equal additions method
d. $321 + 437$ using a left-to-right method
e. 3×432 using a left-to-right method
f. 456×25 using the multiplying by a special factor method

SOLUTION
a. $197 + 248 = 197 + 3 + 245 = 200 + 245 = 445$
b. $125 \times 44 = 125 \times 4 \times 11 = 500 \times 11 = 5500$
c. $273 - 139 = 274 - 140 = 134$
d. $321 + 437 = 758$ [*Think:* $(300 + 400) + (20 + 30) + (1 + 7)$]
e. $3 \times 432 = 1296$ [*Think:* $(3 \times 400) + (3 \times 30) + (3 \times 2)$]
f. $456 \times 25 = 114 \times 100 = 11,400$ (*Think:* $25 \times 4 = 100$. Thus $456 \times 25 = 114 \times 4 \times 25 = 114 \times 100 = 11,400$.)   ■

✔ Check for Understanding: Exercise/Problem Set A #1–7

Computational Estimation

The process of estimation takes on various forms. The number of beans in a jar may be estimated using no mathematics, simply a "guesstimate." Also, one may estimate how long a trip will be, based simply on experience. **Computational estimation** is the process of finding an approximate answer (an estimate) to a computation, often using mental math. With the use of calculators becoming more commonplace, computational estimation is an essential skill. Next we consider various types of computational estimation.

Front-End Estimation   Three types of front-end estimation will be demonstrated.

Range Estimation   Often it is sufficient to know an interval or **range**—that is, a low value and a high value—that will contain an answer. The following example shows how ranges can be obtained in addition and multiplication.

Example 4.4   Find a range for answers to these computations by using only the leading digits.

a. $\begin{array}{r} 257 \\ + 576 \\ \hline \end{array}$ b. $\begin{array}{r} 294 \\ \times 53 \\ \hline \end{array}$

SOLUTION

a.
Sum	Low Estimate	High Estimate
257	200	300
+ 576	+ 500	+ 600
	700	900

Thus a range for the answer is from 700 to 900. Notice that you have to look at only the digits having the largest place values (2 + 5 = 7, or 700) to arrive at the low estimate, and these digits each increased by one (3 + 6 = 9, or 900) to find the high estimate.

b.
Product	Low Estimate	High Estimate
294	200	300
× 53	× 50	× 60
	10,000	18,000

Due to the nature of multiplication, this method gives a wide range, here 10,000 to 18,000. Even so, this method will catch many errors. ■

One-Column/Two-Column Front-End   We can estimate the sum 498 + 251 using the **one-column front-end estimation method** as follows: To estimate 498 + 251, think 400 + 200 = 600 (the estimate). Notice that this is simply the low end of the range estimate. The one-column front-end estimate always provides low estimates in addition problems as well as in multiplication problems. In the case of 376 + 53 + 417, the one-column estimate is 300 + 400 = 700, since there are no hundreds in 53. The two-column front-end estimate also provides a low estimate for sums and products. However, this estimate is closer to the exact answer than one obtained from using only one column. For example, in the case of 372 + 53 + 417, the **two-column front-end estimation method** yields 370 + 50 + 410 = 830, which is closer to the exact answer 842 than the 700 obtained using the one-column method.

Front-End with Adjustment   This method enhances the one-column front-end estimation method. For example, to find 498 + 251, think 400 + 200 = 600 and 98 + 51 is about 150. Thus the estimate is $600 + 150 = 750$. Unlike one-column or two-column front-end estimates, this technique may produce either a low estimate or a high estimate, as in this example.

Keep in mind that one estimates to obtain a "rough" answer, so all of the preceding forms of front-end estimation belong in one's estimation repertoire.

Example 4.5   Estimate using the method indicated.

a. 503×813 using one-column front-end
b. 1200×35 using range estimation
c. $4376 - 1889$ using two-column front-end
d. $3257 + 874$ using front-end adjustment

SOLUTION
a. To estimate 503×813 using the one-column front-end method, think $500 \times 800 = 400{,}000$. Using words, think "5 hundreds times 8 hundreds is 400,000."
b. To estimate a range for 1200×35, think $1200 \times 30 = 36{,}000$ and $1200 \times 40 = 48{,}000$. Thus a range for the answer is from 36,000 to 48,000. One also could use $1000 \times 30 = 30{,}000$ and $2000 \times 40 = 80{,}000$. However, this yields a wider range.
c. To estimate $4376 - 1889$ using the two-column front-end method, think $4300 - 1800 = 2500$. You also can think $43 - 18 = 25$ and then append two zeros after the 25 to obtain 2500.
d. To estimate $3257 + 874$ using front-end with adjustment, think 3000, but since $257 + 874$ is about 1000, adjust to 4000.   ■

Reflection from Research
To be confident and successful estimators, children need numerous opportunities to practice estimation and to learn from their experiences. Thus, the skills required by students to develop a comfort level with holistic, or range-based, estimation need to be included throughout a young child's education (Onslow, Adams, Edmunds, Waters, Chapple, Healey, & Eady, 2005).

Rounding   Rounding is perhaps the best-known computational estimation technique. The purpose of rounding is to replace complicated numbers with simpler numbers. Here, again, since the objective is to obtain an estimate, any of several rounding techniques may be used. However, some may be more appropriate than others, depending on the word problem situation. For example, if you are estimating how much money to take along on a trip, you would round up to be sure that you had enough. When calculating the amount of gas needed for a trip, one would round the miles per gallon estimate down to ensure that there would be enough money for gas. Unlike the previous estimation techniques, rounding is often applied to an answer as well as to the individual numbers before a computation is performed.

Several different methods of rounding are illustrated next. What is common, however, is that each method rounds to a particular place. You are asked to formulate rules for the following methods in the problem set.

Round Up (Down)   The number 473 **rounded up** to the nearest tens place is 480 since 473 is between 470 and 480 and 480 is *above* 473 (Figure 4.1). The number 473 **rounded down** to the nearest tens place is 470. Rounding down is also called truncating (**truncate** means "to cut off"). The number 1276 truncated to the hundreds place is 1200.

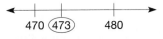

Figure 4.1

Round a 5 Up   The most common rounding technique used in schools is the round a 5 up method. This method can be motivated using a number line. Suppose that we wish to round 475 to the nearest ten (Figure 4.2).

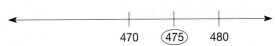

Figure 4.2

Since 475 is midway between 470 and 480, we have to make an agreement concerning whether we round 475 to 470 or to 480. The **round a 5 up** method always rounds such numbers up, so 475 rounds to 480. In the case of the numbers 471 to 474, since they are all nearer 470 than 480, they are rounded to 470 when rounding to the nearest ten. The numbers 476 to 479 are rounded to 480.

One disadvantage of this method is that estimates obtained when several 5s are involved tend to be on the high side. For example, the "round a 5 up" to the nearest ten estimate applied to the addends of the sum $35 + 45 + 55 + 65$ yields $40 + 50 + 60 + 70 = 220$, which is 20 more than the exact sum 200.

Round to the Nearest Even   Rounding to the nearest even can be used to avoid errors of accumulation in rounding. For example, if $475 + 545\ (= 1020)$ is estimated by rounding up to the tens place or rounding a 5 up, the answer is $480 + 550 = 1030$. By rounding down, the estimate is $470 + 540 = 1010$. Since 475 is between 480 and 470 and the 8 in the tens place is even, and 545 is between 550 and 540 and the 4 is even, **round to the nearest even** method yields $480 + 540 = 1020$.

Example 4.6   Estimate using the indicated method. (The symbol "$\approx$" means "is approximately.")

a. Estimate $2173 + 4359$ by rounding down to the nearest hundreds place.
b. Estimate $3250 - 1850$ by rounding to the nearest even hundreds place.
c. Estimate $575 - 398$ by rounding a 5 up to the nearest tens place.

SOLUTION
a. $2173 + 4359 \approx 2100 + 4300 = 6400$
b. $3250 - 1850 \approx 3200 - 1800 = 1400$
c. $575 - 398 \approx 580 - 400 = 180$ ■

Round to Compatible Numbers   Another rounding technique can be applied to estimate products such as 26×37. A reasonable estimate of 26×37 is $25 \times 40 = 1000$. The numbers 25 and 40 were selected since they are estimates of 26 and 37, respectively, and are compatible with respect to multiplication. (Notice that the rounding up technique would have yielded the considerably higher estimate of $30 \times 40 = 1200$, whereas the exact answer is 962.) This **round to compatible numbers** technique allows one to round either up or down to compatible numbers to simplify calculations, rather than rounding to specified places. For example, a reasonable estimate of 57×98 is $57 \times 100\ (= 5700)$. Here, only the 98 needed to be rounded to obtain an estimate mentally. The division problem $2716 \div 75$ can be estimated mentally by considering $2800 \div 70\ (= 40)$. Here 2716 was rounded up to 2800 and 75 was rounded down to 70 because $2800 \div 70$ easily leads to a quotient since 2800 and 70 are compatible numbers with respect to division.

Example 4.7   Estimate by rounding to compatible numbers in two different ways.

a. 43×21 **b.** $256 \div 33$

SOLUTION
a. $43 \times 21 \approx 40 \times 21 = 840$ **b.** $256 \div 33 \approx 240 \div 30 = 8$
$\quad 43 \times 21 \approx 43 \times 20 = 860$ $\quad 256 \div 33 \approx 280 \div 40 = 7$
(The exact answer is 903.)   (The exact answer is 7 with remainder 25.)   ■

Rounding is a most useful and flexible technique. It is important to realize that the main reasons to round are (1) to simplify calculations while obtaining reasonable answers and (2) to report numerical results that can be easily understood. Any of the methods illustrated here may be used to estimate.

The ideas involving mental math and estimation in this section were observed in children who were facile in working with numbers. The following suggestions should help develop number sense in all children.

1. Learn the basic facts using thinking strategies, and extend the strategies to multi-digit numbers.

2. Master the concept of place value.

3. Master the basic addition and multiplication properties of whole numbers.

4. Develop a habit of using the front-end and left-to-right methods.

5. Practice mental calculations often, daily if possible.

6. Accept approximate answers when exact answers are not needed.

7. Estimate prior to doing exact computations.

8. Be flexible by using a variety of mental math and estimation techniques.

> ✔ **Check for Understanding:** Exercise/Problem Set A #8–15

Reflection from Research
Students in classrooms where calculators are used tend to have more positive attitudes about mathematics than students in classrooms where calculators are not used (Reys & Reys, 1987).

Figure 4.3

Using a Calculator

Although a basic calculator that costs less than $10 is sufficient for most elementary school students, there are features on $15 to $30 calculators that simplify many complicated calculations. The TI-34 II, manufactured by Texas Instruments, is shown in Figure 4.3. The TI-34 II, which is designed especially for elementary and middle schools, performs fraction as well as the usual decimal calculations, can perform long division with remainders directly, and has the functions of a scientific calculator. One nice feature of the TI-34 II is that it has two lines of display, which allows the student to see the input and output at the same time.

The ON key turns the calculator on. The DEL key is an abbreviation for "delete" and allows the user to delete one character at a time from the right if the cursor is at the end of an expression or delete the character under the cursor. Pressing the CLEAR key will clear the current entry. The previous entry can be retrieved by pressing the ▲ key.

Three types of logic are available in calculators: arithmetic, algebraic, and reverse Polish notation. Reverse Polish notation is considerably more complicated and not as common as the other two, so we will only discuss arithmetic and algebraic logic.

(NOTE: For ease of reading, we will write numerals without the usual squares around them to indicate that they are keys.)

Arithmetic Logic   In arithmetic logic, the calculator performs operations in the order they are entered. For example, if 3 ⊞ 4 ⊠ 5 ⊟ is entered, the calculations are performed as follows: $(3 + 4) \times 5 = 7 \times 5 = 35$. That is, the operations are performed from left to right as they are entered.

Algebraic Logic   If your calculator has algebraic logic and the expression 3 ⊞ 4 ⊠ 5 ⊟ is entered, the result is different; here the calculator evaluates expressions according to the usual mathematical convention for order of operations.

If a calculator has parentheses, they can be inserted to be sure that the desired operation is performed first. In a calculator using algebraic logic, the calculation $13 - 5 \times 4 \div 2 + 7$ will result in $13 - 10 + 7 = 10$. If one wishes to calculate $13 - 5$ first, parentheses must be inserted. Thus $(13 - 5) \times 4 \div 2 + 7 = 23$.

Reflection from Research

Young people in the workplace believe that menial tasks, such as calculations, are low order tasks that should be undertaken by technology and that their role is to identify problems and solve them using technology to support that solution. Thus, mathematics education may need to reshift its focus from accuracy and precision relying on arduous calculations to one that will better fit the contemporary workplace and life beyond schools (Zevenbergen, 2004).

Example 4.8   Use the order of operations to mentally calculate the following and then enter them into a calculator to compare results.

a. $(4 + 2 \times 5) \div 7 + 3$
b. $8 \div 2^2 + 3 \times 2^2$
c. $17 - 4(5 - 2)$
d. $40 \div 5 \times 2^3 - 2 \times 3$

SOLUTION

a. $(4 + 2 \times 5) \div 7 + 3 = (4 + 10) \div 7 + 3$
$$= (14 \div 7) + 3$$
$$= 2 + 3 = 5$$

b. $8 \div 2^2 + 3 \times 2^2 = (8 \div 4) + (3 \times 4)$
$$= 2 + 12 = 14$$

c. $17 - 4(5 - 2) = 17 - (4 \times 3)$
$$= 17 - 12 = 5$$

d. $40 \div 5 \times 2^3 - 2 \times 3 = [(40 \div 5) \times 2^3] - (2 \times 3)$
$$= 8 \times 8 - 2 \times 3$$
$$= 64 - 6 = 58$$ ∎

Now let's consider some features that make a calculator helpful both as a computational and a pedagogical device. Several keystroke sequences will be displayed to simulate the variety of calculator operating systems available.

Parentheses   As mentioned earlier when we were discussing algebraic logic, one must always be attentive to the order of operations when several operations are present. For example, the product $2 \times (3 + 4)$ can be found in two ways. First, by using commutativity, the following keystrokes will yield the correct answer:

$$3 \boxplus 4 \boxeq \boxtimes 2 \boxeq \boxed{\qquad 14}.$$

Alternatively, the parentheses keys may be used as follows:

$$2 \boxtimes \boxed{(} 3 \boxplus 4 \boxed{)} \boxeq \boxed{\qquad 14}.$$

Parentheses are needed, since pressing the keys $2 \boxtimes 3 \boxplus 4 \boxeq$ on a calculator with algebraic logic will result in the answer 10. Distributivity may be used to simplify calculations. For example, $753 \cdot 8 + 753 \cdot 9$ can be found using $753 \boxtimes \boxed{(} 8 \boxplus 9 \boxed{)}$ $\boxeq$ instead of $753 \boxtimes 8 \boxplus 753 \boxtimes 9 \boxeq$.

Constant Functions   In Chapter 3, multiplication was viewed as repeated addition; in particular, $5 \times 3 = 3 + 3 + 3 + 3 + 3 = 15$. Repeated operations are carried out in different ways depending on the model of calculator. For example, the following keystroke sequence is used to calculate 5×3 on one calculator that has a built-in constant function:

$$3 \boxplus \boxeq \boxeq \boxeq \boxeq \boxed{\qquad 15}.$$

Numbers raised to a whole-number power can be found using a similar technique. For example, 3^5 can be calculated by replacing the $\boxplus$ with a $\boxtimes$ in the preceding examples. A constant function can also be used to do repeated subtraction to find a quotient and a remainder in a division problem. For example, the following sequence can be used to find $35 \div 8$:

$$35 \boxminus 8 \boxeq \boxeq \boxeq \boxeq \boxed{\qquad 3}.$$

The remainder (3 here) is the first number displayed that is less than the divisor (8 here), and the number of times the equal sign was pressed is the quotient (4 here).

Because of the two lines of display, the TI-34 II can handle most of these examples by typing in the entire expression. For example, representing 5×3 as repeated addition is entered into the TI-34 II as

$$3 \boxplus 3 \boxplus 3 \boxplus 3 \boxplus 3 \boxminus$$

The entire expression of $3 + 3 + 3 + 3 + 3$ appears on the first line of display and the result $\boxed{15}$ appears on the second line of display.

Exponent Keys There are three common types of exponent keys: $\boxed{x^2}$, $\boxed{y^x}$, and $\boxed{\wedge}$. The x^2 key is used to find squares in one of two ways:

$$3 \; \boxed{x^2} \; \boxminus \; \boxed{9} \quad \text{or} \quad 3 \; \boxed{x^2} \; \boxed{9}.$$

The $\boxed{y^x}$ and $\boxed{\wedge}$ keys are used to find more general powers and have similar keystrokes. For example, 7^3 may be found as follows:

$$7 \; \boxed{y^x} \; 3 \; \boxminus \; \boxed{343} \quad \text{or} \quad 7 \; \boxed{\wedge} \; 3 \; \boxed{343}.$$

Memory Functions Many calculators have a memory function designated by the keys $\boxed{M+}$, $\boxed{M-}$, $\boxed{MR}$, or $\boxed{STO}$, $\boxed{RCL}$, $\boxed{SUM}$. Your calculator's display will probably show an "M" to remind you that there is a nonzero number in the memory. The problem $5 \times 9 + 7 \times 8$ may be found as follows using the memory keys:

$$5 \; \boxtimes \; 9 \; \boxminus \; \boxed{M+} \; 7 \; \boxtimes \; 8 \; \boxminus \; \boxed{M+} \; \boxed{MR} \; \boxed{101} \quad \text{or}$$

$$5 \; \boxtimes \; 9 \; \boxminus \; \boxed{SUM} \; 7 \; \boxtimes \; 8 \; \boxminus \; \boxed{SUM} \; \boxed{RCL} \; \boxed{101}.$$

It is a good practice to clear the memory for each new problem using the all clear key.

The TI-34 II has five memory locations—*A, B, C, D,* and *E*—which can be accessed by pressing the $\boxed{STO\Rightarrow}$ key and then using the right arrow key, $\boxed{\Rightarrow}$, to select the desired variable. The following keystrokes are used to evaluate the expression above.

$$5 \; \boxtimes \; 9 \; \boxed{STO\Rightarrow} \; \boxminus \; \text{and} \; 7 \; \boxtimes \; 8 \; \boxed{STO\Rightarrow} \; \boxed{\Rightarrow} \; \boxminus$$

The above keys will store the value 45 in the memory location *A* and the value 56 in the memory location *B*. The values *A* and *B* can then be added together as follows.

$$\boxed{MEMVAR} \; \boxminus \; \boxplus \; \boxed{MEMVAR} \; \boxed{\Rightarrow} \; \boxminus \; \boxminus$$

This will show $A + B$ on the first line of the calculator display and $\boxed{101}$ on the second line of the display.

Additional special keys will be introduced throughout the book as the need arises.

Scientific Notation Input and output of a calculator are limited by the number of places in the display (generally 8, 10, or 12). Two basic responses are given when a number is too large to fit in the display. Simple calculators either provide a partial answer with an "E" (for "error"), or the word "ERROR" is displayed. Many scientific calculators automatically express the answer in **scientific notation** (that is, as the product of a decimal number greater than or equal to 1 but less than 10, and the appropriate power of 10). For example, on the TI-34 II, the product of 123,456,789 and 987 is displayed $\boxed{1.2185185 \times 10^{11}}$. (NOTE: Scientific notation is discussed in more detail in Chapter 9 after decimals and negative numbers have been studied.)

If an exact answer is needed, the use of the calculator can be combined with paper and pencil and distributivity as follows:

$$123{,}456{,}789 \times 987 = 123{,}456{,}789 \times 900 + 123{,}456{,}789 \times$$
$$80 + 123{,}456{,}789 \times 7$$
$$= 111{,}111{,}110{,}100 + 9{,}876{,}543{,}120$$
$$+ 864{,}197{,}523.$$

Now we can obtain the product by adding:

$$
\begin{array}{r}
111{,}111{,}110{,}100 \\
9{,}876{,}543{,}120 \\
+ \quad 864{,}197{,}523 \\
\hline
121{,}851{,}850{,}743.
\end{array}
$$

Calculations with numbers having three or more digits will probably be performed on a calculator (or computer) to save time and increase accuracy. Even so, it is prudent to estimate your answer when using your calculator.

 Check for Understanding: Exercise/Problem Set A #16–24

MATHEMATICAL MORSEL

In his fascinating book *The Great Mental Calculators*, author Steven B. Smith discusses various ways that the great mental calculators did their calculations. In his research, he found that all auditory calculators (people who are given problems verbally and perform computations mentally) except one did their multiplications from left to right to minimize their short-term memory load.

Section 4.1   EXERCISE / PROBLEM SET A

EXERCISES

1. Calculate mentally using properties.
  a. $(37 + 25) + 43$
  b. $47 \cdot 15 + 47 \cdot 85$
  c. $(4 \times 13) \times 25$
  d. $26 \cdot 24 - 21 \cdot 24$

2. Find each of these differences mentally using equal additions. Write out the steps that you thought through.
  a. $43 - 17$ **b.** $62 - 39$
  c. $132 - 96$ **d.** $250 - 167$

3. Calculate mentally left to right.
  a. $123 + 456$ **b.** $342 + 561$
  c. $587 - 372$ **d.** $467 - 134$

4. Calculate mentally using the indicated method.
  a. $198 + 387$ (additive compensation)
  b. 84×5 (multiplicative compensation)
  c. 99×53 (special factor)
  d. $4125 \div 25$ (special factor)

5. Calculate mentally.
  a. $58{,}000 \times 5{,}000{,}000$
  b. $7 \times 10^5 \times 21{,}000$
  c. $13{,}000 \times 7{,}000{,}000$
  d. $4 \times 10^5 \times 3 \times 10^6 \times 7 \times 10^3$
  e. $5 \times 10^3 \times 7 \times 10^7 \times 4 \times 10^5$
  f. $17{,}000{,}000 \times 6{,}000{,}000{,}000$

6. The sum $26 + 38 + 55$ can be found mentally as follows: $26 + 30 = 56, 56 + 8 = 64, 64 + 50 = 114, 114 + 5 = 119$. Find the following sums mentally using this technique.

a. $32 + 29 + 56$

b. $54 + 28 + 67$

c. $19 + 66 + 49$

d. $62 + 84 + 27 + 81$

7. In division you can sometimes simplify the problem by multiplying or dividing both the divisor and dividend by the same number. This is called **division compensation**. For example,

$$72 \div 12 = (72 \div 2) \div (12 \div 2) = 36 \div 6 = 6 \text{ and}$$
$$145 \div 5 = (145 \times 2) \div (5 \times 2) = 290 \div 10 = 29$$

Calculate the following mentally using this technique.

a. $84 \div 14$ **b.** $234 \div 26$ **c.** $120 \div 15$ **d.** $168 \div 14$

8. Before granting an operating license, a scientist has to estimate the amount of pollutants that should be allowed to be discharged from an industrial chimney. Should she overestimate or underestimate? Explain.

9. Estimate each of the following using the four front-end methods: (i) range, (ii) one-column, (iii) two-column, and (iv) with adjustment.

a.   3741
   + 1252

b.   1591
     346
     589
   + 163

c.   2347
      58
    192
  + 5783

10. Find a range estimate for these products.

a. 37×24 **b.** 157×231 **c.** 491×8

11. Estimate using compatible number estimation.

a. 63×97 **b.** 51×212 **c.** $3112 \div 62$

d. 103×87 **e.** 62×58 **f.** $4254 \div 68$

12. Round as specified.

a. 373 to the nearest tens place

b. 650 using round a 5 up method to the hundreds place

c. 1123 up to the tens place

d. 457 to the nearest tens place

e. 3457 to the nearest thousands place

13. Cluster estimation is used to estimate sums and products when several numbers cluster near one number. For example, the addends in $789 + 810 + 792$ cluster around 800. Thus $3 \times 800 = 2400$ is a good estimate of the sum. Estimate the following using cluster estimation.

a. $347 + 362 + 354 + 336$

b. $61 \times 62 \times 58$

c. $489 \times 475 \times 523 \times 498$

d. $782 + 791 + 834 + 812 + 777$

14. Here are four ways to estimate 26×12:

$$26 \times 10 = 260 \quad 30 \times 12 = 360$$
$$25 \times 12 = 300 \quad 30 \times 10 = 300$$

Estimate the following in four ways.

a. 31×23 **b.** 35×46

c. 48×27 **d.** 76×12

15. Estimate the following values and check with a calculator.

a. 656×74 is between _____ 000 and _____ 000.

b. 491×3172 is between _____ 00000 and _____ 00000.

c. 143^2 is between _____ 0000 and _____ 0000.

16. Guess what whole numbers can be used to fill in the blanks. Use your calculator to check.

a. _____ $^6 = 4096$

b. _____ $^4 = 28{,}561$

17. Guess which is larger. Check with your calculator.

a. 5^4 or 4^5?   **b.** 7^3 or 3^7?

c. 7^4 or 4^7?   **d.** 6^3 or 3^6?

18. Some products can be found most easily using a combination of mental math and a calculator. For example, the product $20 \times 47 \times 139 \times 5$ can be found by calculating 47×139 on a calculator and then multiplying your result by 100 mentally ($20 \times 5 = 100$). Calculate the following using a combination of mental math and a calculator.

a. $17 \times 25 \times 817 \times 4$

b. $98 \times 2 \times 673 \times 5$

c. $674 \times 50 \times 889 \times 4$

d. $783 \times 8 \times 79 \times 125$

19. Compute the quotient and remainder (a whole number) for the following problems on a calculator without using repeated subtraction. Describe the procedure you used.

a. $8)\overline{103}$ **b.** $17)\overline{543}$

c. $123)\overline{849}$ **d.** $894)\overline{107{,}214}$

20. $1233 = 12^2 + 33^2$ and $8833 = 88^2 + 33^2$. How about 10,100 and 5,882,353? (*Hint:* Think 588 2353.)

21. Determine whether the following equation is true for $n = 1$, 2, or 3.

$$1^n + 6^n + 8^n = 2^n + 4^n + 9^n$$

22. Notice that $153 = 1^3 + 5^3 + 3^3$. Determine which of the following numbers have the same property.

a. 370   **b.** 371   **c.** 407

23. Determine whether the following equation is true when n is 1, 2, or 3.

$$1^n + 4^n + 5^n + 5^n + 6^n + 9^n =$$
$$2^n + 3^n + 3^n + 7^n + 7^n + 8^n$$

24. Simplify the following expressions using a calculator.

a. $135 - 7(48 - 33)$

b. $32 \cdot 51^2$

c. $13^2 \cdot 34 - 3(45 - 37)^3$

d. $\dfrac{26 + 4(31^3 - 172^2)^2 + 2 \cdot 401}{26 \cdot (31^3 - 172^2)}$

PROBLEMS

25. Five of the following six numbers were rounded to the nearest thousand, then added to produce an estimated sum of 87,000. Which number was not included?

5228   14,286   7782   19,628   9168   39,228

26. True or false?

$$493,827,156^2 = 246,913,578 \times 987,654,312$$

27. Place a multiplication sign or signs so that the product in each problem is correct; for example, in 1 2 3 4 5 6 = 41,472, the multiplication sign should be between the 2 and the 3 since $12 \times 3456 = 41,472$.
a. 1 3 5 7 9 0 = 122,130
b. 6 6 6 6 6 6 = 439,956
c. 7 8 9 3 4 5 6 = 3,307,824
d. 1 2 3 4 5 6 7 = 370,845

28. Develop a method for finding a range for subtraction problems for three-digit numbers.

29. Find $13,333,333^2$.

30. Calculate $99 \cdot 36$ and $99 \cdot 23$ and look for a pattern. Then predict $99 \cdot 57$ and $99 \cdot 63$ mentally and check with a calculator.

31. a. Calculate 25^2, 35^2, 45^2, and 55^2 and look for a pattern. Then find 65^2, 75^2, and 95^2 mentally and check your answers.
b. Using a variable, prove that your result holds for squaring numbers that have a 5 as their ones digit.

32. George Bidder was a calculating prodigy in England during the nineteenth century. As a nine-year-old, he was asked: If the moon were 123,256 miles from the Earth and sound traveled at the rate of 4 miles a minute, how long would it be before inhabitants of the moon could hear the battle of Waterloo? His answer—21 days, 9 hours, 34 minutes—was given in 1 minute. Was he correct? Try to do this calculation in less than 1 minute using a calculator. (NOTE: The moon is about 240,000 miles from Earth and sound travels about 12.5 miles per second.)

33. Found in a newspaper article: What is

241,573,142,393,627,673,576,957,439,048 × 45,994,811,347,886,846,310,221,728,895,223, 034,301,839?

The answer is 71 consecutive 1s—one of the biggest numbers a computer has ever factored. This factorization

bested the previous high, the factorization of a 69-digit number. Find a mistake here, and suggest a correction.

34. Some mental calculators use the following fact: $(a + b)(a - b) = a^2 - b^2$. For example, $43 \times 37 = (40 + 3)(40 - 3) = 40^2 - 3^2 = 1600 - 9 = 1591$. Apply this technique to find the following products mentally.
a. 54×46
b. 81×79
c. 122×118
d. 1210×1190

35. Fermat claimed that

$$100,895,598,169 = 898,423 \times 112,303.$$

Check this on your calculator.

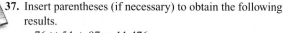

36. Show how to find $439,268 \times 6852$ using a calculator that displays only eight digits.

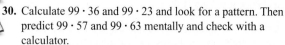

37. Insert parentheses (if necessary) to obtain the following results.
a. $76 \times 54 + 97 = 11,476$
b. $4 \times 13^2 = 2704$
c. $13 + 59^2 \times 47 = 163,620$
d. $79 - 43 \div 2 + 17^2 = 307$

38. a. Find a shortcut.

$$24 \times 26 = 624$$
$$62 \times 68 = 4216$$
$$73 \times 77 = 5621$$
$$41 \times 49 = 2009$$
$$86 \times 84 = 7224$$
$$57 \times 53 = \underline{\quad}$$

b. Prove that your result works in general.
c. How is this problem related to Problem 31?

39. Develop a set of rules for the round a 5 up method.

40. There are eight consecutive odd numbers that when multiplied together yield 34,459,425. What are they?

41. Jill goes to get some water. She has a 5-liter pail and a 3-liter pail and is supposed to bring exactly 1 liter back. How can she do this?

| Section 4.1 | **EXERCISE / PROBLEM SET B** |

EXERCISES

1. Calculate mentally using properties.
 a. $52 \cdot 14 - 52 \cdot 4$ **b.** $(5 \times 37) \times 20$
 c. $(56 + 37) + 44$ **d.** $23 \cdot 4 + 23 \cdot 5 + 7 \cdot 9$

2. Find each of these differences mentally using equal additions. Write out the steps that you thought through.
 a. $56 - 29$ **b.** $83 - 37$
 c. $214 - 86$ **d.** $542 - 279$

3. Calculate mentally using the left-to-right method.
 a. $246 + 352$ **b.** $49 + 252$
 c. $842 - 521$ **d.** $751 - 647$

4. Calculate mentally using the method indicated.
 a. $359 + 596$ (additive compensation)
 b. 76×25 (multiplicative compensation)
 c. 4×37 (halving and doubling)
 d. 37×98 (special factor)
 e. $1240 \div 5$ (special factor)

5. Calculate mentally.
 a. $32,000 \times 400$ **b.** $6000 \times 12,000$
 c. $4000 \times 5000 \times 70$ **d.** $5 \times 10^4 \times 30 \times 10^5$
 e. $12,000 \times 4 \times 10^7$ **f.** $23,000,000 \times 5,000,000$

6. Often subtraction can be done more easily in steps. For example, $43 - 37$ can be found as follows: $43 - 37 = (43 - 30) - 7 = 13 - 7 = 6$. Find the following differences using this technique.
 a. $52 - 35$ **b.** $173 - 96$
 c. $241 - 159$ **d.** $83 - 55$

7. The **halving and doubling** method can be used to multiply two numbers when one factor is a power of 2. For example, to find 8×17, find 4×34 or $2 \times 68 = 136$. Find the following products using this method.
 a. 16×21 **b.** 4×72
 c. 8×123 **d.** 16×211

8. In determining an evacuation zone, a scientist must estimate the distance that lava from an erupting volcano will flow. Should she overestimate or underestimate? Explain.

9. Estimate each of the following using the four front-end methods: (i) one-column, (ii) range, (iii) two-column, and (iv) with adjustment.

a. 4652	**b.**	2659	**c.**	15923
8134		3752		672
		79		2341
	+	143	+	251

10. Find a range estimate for these products.
 a. 57×1924 **b.** 1349×45 **c.** $547 \times 73,951$

11. Estimate using compatible number estimation.
 a. 84×49 **b.** $5527 \div 82$
 c. $2315 \div 59$ **d.** 78×81
 e. 207×73 **f.** $6401 \div 93$

12. Round as specified.
 a. 257 down to the nearest tens place
 b. 650 to the nearest even hundreds place
 c. 593 to the nearest tens place
 d. 4157 to the nearest hundreds place
 e. 7126 to the nearest thousands place

13. Estimate using cluster estimation.
 a. $547 + 562 + 554 + 556$ **b.** $31 \times 32 \times 35 \times 28$
 c. $189 + 175 + 193 + 173$ **d.** $562 \times 591 \times 634$

14. Estimate the following products in two different ways and explain each method.
 a. 52×39 **b.** 17×74
 c. 88×11 **d.** 26×42

 15. Estimate the following values and check with a calculator.
 a. 324×56 is between _____ 000 and _____ 000.
 b. 5714×13 is between _____ 000 and _____ 000.
 c. 256^3 is between _____ 000000 and _____ 000000.

 16. Guess what whole numbers can be used to fill in the blanks. Use your calculator to check.
 a. _____ $^4 = 6561$
 b. _____ $^5 = 16,807$

 17. Guess which is larger. Check with your calculator.
 a. 6^4 or 5^5 **b.** 3^8 or 4^6
 c. 5^4 or 9^3 **d.** 8^5 or 6^6

18. Compute the following products using a combination of mental math and a calculator. Explain your method.
 a. $20 \times 14 \times 39 \times 5$
 b. $40 \times 27 \times 25 \times 23$
 c. $647 \times 50 \times 200 \times 89$
 d. $25 \times 91 \times 2 \times 173 \times 2$

19. Find the quotient and remainder using a calculator. Check your answers.
 a. $18,114 \div 37$ **b.** $381,271 \div 147$
 c. $9,346,870 \div 1349$ **d.** $817,293 \div 749$

 20. Check to see that $1634 = 1^4 + 6^4 + 3^4 + 4^4$. Then determine which of the following four numbers satisfy the same property.
 a. 8208   **b.** 9474   **c.** 1138   **d.** 2178

21. It is easy to show that $3^2 + 4^2 = 5^2$, and $5^2 + 12^2 = 13^2$. However, in 1966 two mathematicians claimed the following:

$$27^5 + 84^5 + 110^5 + 133^5 = 144^5.$$

True or false?

22. Verify the following patterns.

$$3^2 + 4^2 = 5^2$$
$$10^2 + 11^2 + 12^2 = 13^2 + 14^2$$
$$21^2 + 22^2 + 23^2 + 24^2 = 25^2 + 26^2 + 27^2$$

23. For which of the values $n = 1, 2, 3, 4$ is the following true?

$$1^n + 5^n + 8^n + 12^n + 18^n + 19^n =$$
$$2^n + 3^n + 9^n + 13^n + 16^n + 20^n$$

24. Simplify each of the following expressions using a calculator.
a. $42 \cdot 63^2 - 52^2 \cdot 23$
b. $\dfrac{72(43 - 31)^3}{162 - 2 \cdot 3^2(27 + 115)^0}$
c. $35^2 - 24^2 + (26 - 14)^5 \div 2^3$
d. $14 \times 23^3 - 36^4 \div 12^3 \cdot 3^2$

PROBLEMS

25. Notice how by starting with 55 and continuing to raise the digits to the third power and adding, 55 reoccurs in three steps.

$$55 \longrightarrow 5^3 + 5^3 = 250 \longrightarrow 2^3 + 5^3$$
$$= 133 \longrightarrow 1^3 + 3^3 + 3^3 = 55$$

Check to see whether this phenomenon is also true for these three numbers:
a. 136   **b.** 160   **c.** 919

26. What is interesting about the quotient obtained by dividing 987,654,312 by 8? (Do this mentally.)

27. Using distributivity, show that $(a - b)^2 = a^2 - 2ab + b^2$. How can this idea be used to compute the following squares mentally? (*Hint:* 99 = 100 − 1.)
a. 99^2 **b.** 999^2 **c.** 9999^2

28. Fill in the empty squares to produce true equations.

3	×	5	×	☐	=	135

(× × × ×)

☐	×	☐	×	☐	=	56

(× × × ×)

☐	×	8	×	1	=	48

(‖ ‖ ‖ ‖)

126	×	160	×	18	=	☐

29. Discuss the similarities/differences of using (i) special factors and (ii) multiplicative compensation when calculating 36×5 mentally.

30. Find $166,666,666^2$.

31. Megan tried to multiply 712,000 by 864,000 on her calculator and got an error message. Explain how she can use her calculator (and a little thought) to find the exact product.

32. What is the product of 777,777,777 and 999,999,999?

33. Explain how you could calculate 342×143 even if the 3 and 4 keys did not work.

34. Find the missing products by completing the pattern. Check your answers with a calculator.

$$11 \times 11 = 121$$
$$111 \times 111 = 12321$$
$$1111 \times 1111 = \underline{\hspace{1cm}}$$
$$11111 \times 11111 = \underline{\hspace{1cm}}$$
$$111111 \times 111111 = \underline{\hspace{1cm}}$$

35. Use your calculator to find the following products.

$$12 \times 11 \qquad 24 \times 11 \qquad 35 \times 11$$

Look at the middle digit of each product and at the first and last digits. Write a rule that you can use to multiply by 11. Now try these problems using your rule and check your answers with your calculator.

$$54 \times 11 \qquad 62 \times 11 \qquad 36 \times 11$$

Adapt your rule to handle

$$37 \times 11 \qquad 59 \times 11 \qquad 76 \times 11.$$

36. When asked to multiply 987,654,321 by 123,456,789, one mental calculator replied, "I saw in a flash that $987,654,321 \times 81 = 80,000,000,001$, so I multiplied 123,456,789 by 80,000,000,001 and divided by 81." Determine whether his reasoning was correct. If it was, see whether you can find the answer using your calculator.

37. a. Find a pattern for multiplying the following pairs.

$$32 \times 72 = 2304 \qquad 43 \times 63 = 2709$$
$$73 \times 33 = 2409$$

Try finding these products mentally.

$$17 \times 97 \qquad 56 \times 56 \qquad 42 \times 62$$

b. Prove why your method works.

38. Have you always wanted to be a calculating genius? Amaze yourself with the following problems.
a. To multiply 4,109,589,041,096 by 83, simply put the 3 in front of it and the 8 at the end of it. Now check your answer.

b. After you have patted yourself on the back, see whether you can find a fast way to multiply

7,894,736,842,105,263,158 by 86.

(NOTE: This works only in special cases.)

39. Develop a set of rules for the round to the nearest even method.

40. Find the ones digits.
 a. 2^{10} **b.** 432^{10} **c.** 3^6 **d.** 293^6

41. A magician had his subject hide an odd number of coins in one hand and an even number of coins in another. He then told the subject to multiply the number of coins in the right hand by 2 and the number of coins in the left hand by 3 and to announce the sum of these two numbers. The magician immediately then correctly stated which hand had the odd number of coins. How did he do it?

Analyzing Student Thinking

42. Jessica calculated $84 - 28$ as $84 - 30 = 54$ and $54 + 2 = 56$. Is her method valid? Explain.

43. Kalil tells you that multiplying by 5 is a lot like dividing by 2. For example, $48 \times 5 = 240$, but it is easier just to go

$48 \div 2 = 24$ and then affix a zero at the end. Will his method always work? Explain.

44. Kalil also says that dividing by 5 is the same as multiplying by 2 and "dropping" a zero. Does this work? Explain.

45. To work the problem $125 \div 5$, Paula did the following: $(100 \div 5) + (25 \div 5) = 20 + 5 = 25$. She said that she used a form of distributivity. Do you agree? Why or why not?

46. Alyssa was asked to find a reasonable range for the sum $158 + 547$. She said 600 to 700. How should you respond?

47. Jared was asked which method would give the best estimate for addition of numbers with at least 3 digits: one-column front-end or two-column front-end. He said that it didn't matter because an estimate is an estimate. Is he correct? Explain.

48. Nicole multiplied 3472 and 259 on her calculator and she wrote down the answer of 89,248. How can you see immediately using estimation that she made an error? Can you see how she made the error?

49. Kysha was asked to calculate the product of 987,654,321 and 123 on her 10 digit calculator. She said that it was impossible. How should you respond?

Problems Relating to the NCTM Standards and Curriculum Focal Points

1. The Focal Points for Grades 4 and 5 state "Students select appropriate methods and apply them accurately to estimate products and calculate them mentally, depending on the context and numbers involved." Provide examples from this section that would be appropriate for a fourth or fifth grader to "estimate products" and to "calculate mentally."

2. The NCTM Standards state "All students should select appropriate methods and tools for computing with whole numbers from among mental computation, estimation, calculators, and paper and pencil according to the context

and nature of the computation and use the selected method or tool." Describe a different real-world situation where each of the following would be most appropriate: a) mental computation, b) estimation, c) calculators, d) paper and pencil.

3. The NCTM Standards state "All students should develop and use strategies to estimate the results of whole-number computations and to judge the reasonableness of such results." Provide an example of how estimation can assist in determining the reasonableness of a problem's solution.

 **4.2   WRITTEN ALGORITHMS FOR WHOLE-NUMBER OPERATIONS**

STARTING POINT   When a class of students was given the problem $48 + 35$, the following three responses were typical of what the students did.

Nick		Trevor		Courtney	
48	*I combined 40 and*	1	*8 + 5 is 13*	48	*48 plus 30 is 78.*
+ 35	*30 to get 70*	48	*Carry the 1*	+ 35	*Now I add the 5*
70	*8 + 5 = 13*	+ 35	*write down 3*	83	*and get 83.*
13	*70 and 13 is 83*	83	*4 + 3 + 1 = 8*		
83			*write down 8*		

Which of these methods demonstrates the best (least) understanding of place value? Which method is the best? Justify.

Section 4.1 was devoted to mental and calculator computation. This section presents the common written algorithms as well as some alternative ones that have historical interest and can be used to help students better understand how their algorithms work.

Algorithms for the Addition of Whole Numbers

Children's Literature
www.wiley.com/college/musser
See "The King's
Commissioners" by Aileen
Friedman.

An **algorithm** is a systematic, step-by-step procedure used to find an answer, usually to a computation. The common written algorithm for addition involves two main procedures: (1) adding single digits (thus using the basic facts) and (2) carrying (regrouping or exchanging).

A development of our **standard addition algorithm** is used in Figure 4.4 to find the sum 134 + 325.

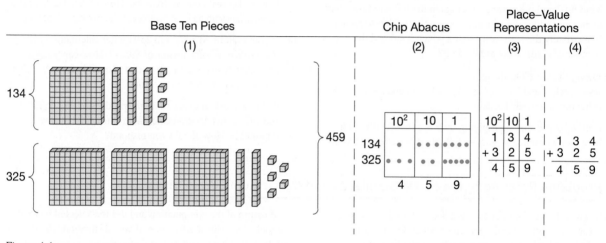

Figure 4.4

Reflection from Research
Students in upper grades can develop shortcut strategies for addition and subtraction, but younger students need careful instruction to support the discovery of such shortcut strategies (Torbeyns, De Smedt, Ghesquiere, & Vershaffel, 2009).

Observe how the left-to-right sequence in Figure 4.4 becomes progressively more abstract. When one views the base ten pieces (1), the hundreds, tens, and ones are distinguishable due to their sizes and the number of each type of piece. In the chip abacus (2), the chips all look the same. However, representations are distinguished by the number of chips in each column and by the column containing the chips (i.e., place value). In the place-value representation (3), the numbers are distinguished by the digits and the place values of their respective columns. Representation (4) is the common "add in columns" algorithm. The place-value method can be justified using expanded form and properties of whole-number addition as follows.

$$134 + 325 = (1 \cdot 10^2 + 3 \cdot 10 + 4) + (3 \cdot 10^2 + 2 \cdot 10 + 5) \quad \textit{Expanded form}$$
$$= (1 \cdot 10^2 + 3 \cdot 10^2) + (3 \cdot 10 + 2 \cdot 10) \quad \textit{Associativity and}$$
$$+ (4 + 5) \quad \textit{commutativity}$$
$$= (1 + 3)10^2 + (3 + 2)10 + (4 + 5) \quad \textit{Distributivity}$$
$$= 4 \cdot 10^2 + 5 \cdot 10 + 9 \quad \textit{Addition}$$
$$= 459 \quad \textit{Simplified form}$$

Note that 134 + 325 can be found working from left to right (add the hundreds first, etc.) or from right to left (add the ones first, etc.).

An addition problem when regrouping is required is illustrated in Figure 4.5 to find the sum 37 + 46. Notice that grouping 10 units together and exchanging them for a long with the base 10 pieces is not as abstract as exchanging 10 ones for one 10 in the chip abacus. The abstraction occurs because the physical size of the 10 units is maintained

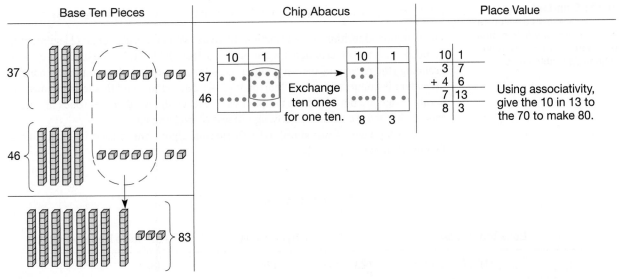

Figure 4.5

with the one long of the base 10 pieces but is not maintained when we exchange 10 dots in the ones column for only one dot in the tens column of the chip abacus.

The procedure illustrated in the place-value representation can be refined in a series of steps to lead to our standard carrying algorithm for addition. Intermediate algorithms that build on the physical models of base 10 pieces and place-value representations lead to our standard addition algorithm and are illustrated next.

Reflection from Research
Students who initially used invented strategies for addition and subtraction demonstrated knowledge of base ten number concepts before students who relied primarily on standard algorithms (Carpenter, Franke, Jacobs, Fennema, & Empson, 1997).

(a) **INTERMEDIATE ALGORITHM 1**

$$
\begin{array}{r}
568 \\
+\ 394 \\
\hline
12 \quad \text{\textit{sum of ones}} \\
150 \quad \text{\textit{sum of tens}} \\
800 \quad \text{\textit{sum of hundreds}} \\
\hline
962 \quad \text{\textit{final sum}}
\end{array}
$$

(b) **INTERMEDIATE ALGORITHM 2**

$$
\begin{array}{r}
568 \\
+\ 394 \\
\hline
12 \\
15 \\
8 \\
\hline
962
\end{array}
$$

(c) **STANDARD ALGORITHM**

$$
\begin{array}{r}
^{1\ 1} \\
568 \\
+\ 394 \\
\hline
962
\end{array}
$$

The preceding intermediate algorithms are easier to understand than the standard algorithm. However, they are less efficient and generally require more time and space.

Throughout history many other algorithms have been used for addition. One of these, the **lattice method for addition**, is illustrated next.

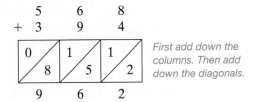

First add down the columns. Then add down the diagonals.

Notice how the lattice method is very much like intermediate algorithm 2. Other interesting algorithms are contained in the problem sets.

 Check for Understanding: Exercise/Problem Set A #1–11

NCTM Standard
All students should develop and
use strategies for whole-number
computations, with a focus on
addition and subtraction.

Algorithms for the Subtraction of Whole Numbers

The common algorithm for subtraction involves two main procedures: (1) subtracting numbers that are determined by the addition facts table and (2) exchanging or regrouping (the reverse of the carrying process for addition). Although this exchanging procedure is commonly called "borrowing," we choose to avoid this term because the numbers that are borrowed are not paid back. Hence the word *borrow* does not represent to children the actual underlying process of exchanging.

A development of our **standard subtraction algorithm** is used in Figure 4.6 to find the difference $357 - 123$.

Concrete Models

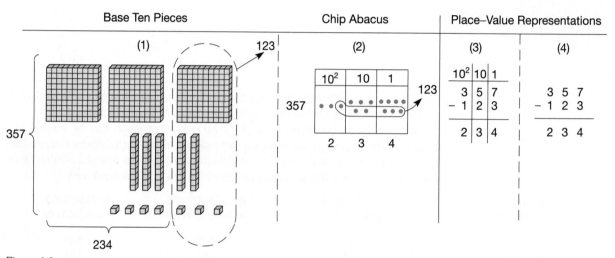

Figure 4.6

Notice that in the example in Figure 4.6, the answer will be the same whether we subtract from left to right or from right to left. In either case, the base 10 blocks are used by first representing 357 and then taking away 123. Since there are 7 units from which 3 can be taken and there are 5 longs from which 2 can be removed, the use of the blocks is straightforward. The problem $423 - 157$ is done differently because we cannot take 7 units away from 3 units directly. In this problem, a long is broken into 10 units to create 13 units and a flat is exchanged from 10 longs and combined with the remaining long to create 11 longs (see Figure 4.7). Once these exchanges have been made, 157 can be taken away to leave 266.

In Figure 4.7, the representations of the base 10 blocks, chip abacus, and place-value model become more and more abstract. The place-value procedure is finally shortened to produce our standard subtraction algorithm. Even though the standard algorithm is abstract, a connection with the base 10 blocks can be seen when exchanging 1 long for 10 units because this action is equivalent to a "borrow."

$$
\begin{array}{r}
423 \\
-\ 157 \\
\end{array}
\quad
\begin{array}{c}
make \\
exchanges \\
\longrightarrow
\end{array}
\quad
\begin{array}{r}
{\scriptstyle 3\ 11\ 13} \\
\cancel{4}\,\cancel{2}\,\cancel{3} \\
+\ 1\ 5\ 7 \\
\hline
2\ 6\ 6
\end{array}
$$

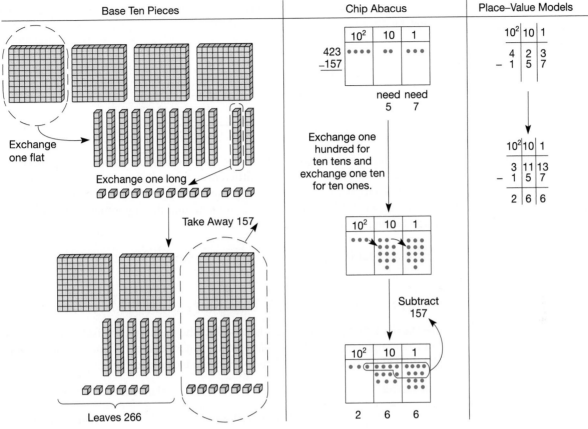

Figure 4.7

One nontraditional algorithm that is especially effective in any base is called the **subtract-from-the-base algorithm**. This algorithm is illustrated in Figure 4.8 using base ten pieces to find $323 - 64$.

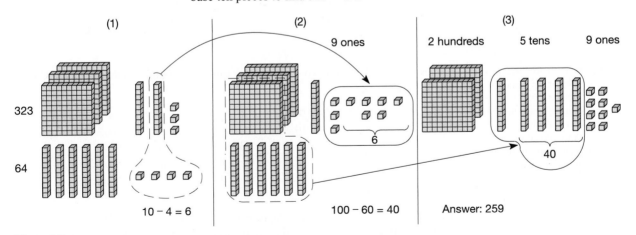

Figure 4.8

In (1), observe that the 4 is subtracted from the 10 (instead of finding $13 - 4$, as in the standard algorithm). The difference, $10 - 4 = 6$, is then combined with the 3 units in (2) to form 9 units. Then the 6 longs are subtracted from 1 flat (instead of finding $11 - 6$). The difference, $10 - 6 = 4$ longs, is then combined with the 1 long in (3) to obtain 5 longs (or 50). Thus, since two flats remain, $323 - 64 = 259$. The following illustrates this process symbolically.

$$
\begin{array}{cccc}
 & & 10 & 10 \\
 & 1\ 10 & 2\ 1\ 10 & 2\ 1\ 10 \\
323 & 3\ 2\ 3 & \cancel{3}\ 2\ 3 & \cancel{3}\ 2\ 3 \\
-\ 64 \rightarrow & -\ \ 6\ 4 \rightarrow & -\ \ 6\ 4 \rightarrow & -\ \ 6\ 4 \\
\hline
 & 9 & 5\ 9 & 2\ 5\ 9
\end{array}
$$

$$\underbrace{(10 - 4) + 3} \qquad \underbrace{(10 - 6) + 1}$$

Reflection from Research
Having students create their own computational algorithms for large number addition and subtraction is a worthwhile activity (Cobb, Yackel, & Wood, 1988).

The advantage of this algorithm is that we only need to know the addition facts and *differences from 10* (as opposed to differences from all the teens). As you will see later in this chapter, this method can be used in any base (hence the name *subtract-from-the-base*). After a little practice, you may find this algorithm to be easier and faster than our usual algorithm for subtraction.

 Check for Understanding: Exercise/Problem Set A #12–19

Algorithms for the Multiplication of Whole Numbers

The standard multiplication algorithm involves the multiplication facts, distributivity, and a thorough understanding of place value. A development of our **standard multiplication algorithm** is used in Figure 4.9 to find the product 3×213.

Concrete Model	Place Value Representations		
	Horizontal Format		Vertical Format

Concrete Model:

	10^2	10	1
213	• •	•	• • •
213	• •	•	• • •
213	• •	•	• • •
	6	3	9

Horizontal Format:

$3(213) = 3(200 + 10 + 3)$	Expanded form
$= 3 \times 200 + 3 \times 10 + 3 \times 3$	Distributivity
$= 600 + 30 + 9$	Multiplication
$= 639$	Addition

Vertical Format:

$$
\begin{array}{rl}
213 & \\
\times\ \ \ 3 & \\
\hline
9 & 3 \times 3 \\
30 & 3 \times 10 \\
\underline{600} & 3 \times 200 \\
639 &
\end{array}
$$

Figure 4.9

Reflection from Research
Teachers should help students to develop a conceptual understanding of how multidigit multiplication and division relates to and builds upon place value and basic multiplication combinations (Fuson, 2003).

Next, the product of a two-digit number times a two-digit number is found. Calculate 34×12.

$$
\begin{aligned}
34 \times 12 &= 34(10 + 2) & \textit{Expanded form}\\
&= 34 \cdot 10 + 34 \cdot 2 & \textit{Distributivity}\\
&= (30 + 4)10 + (30 + 4)2 & \textit{Expanded form}\\
&= 30 \cdot 10 + 4 \cdot 10 + 30 \cdot 2 + 4 \cdot 2 & \textit{Distributivity}\\
&= 300 + 40 + 60 + 8 & \textit{Multiplication}\\
&= 408 & \textit{Addition}
\end{aligned}
$$

The product 34×12 also can be represented pictorially (Figure 4.10).

It is worthwhile to note how the Intermediate Algorithm 1 closely connects to the base block representation of 34×12. The numbers in the algorithm have been color coded with the regions in the rectangular array in Figure 4.10 to make the connection more apparent. The intermediate algorithms assist in the transition from the concrete blocks to the abstract standard algorithm.

7-4 **Multiply Two-Digit Numbers**

► GET READY to Learn

A coyote travels 27 miles per hour. How far would a coyote travel in 12 hours?

MAIN IDEA

I will multiply two-digit numbers.

Math Online

macmillanmh.com
• Extra Examples
• Personal Tutor
• Self-Check Quiz

There is more than one way to multiply two-digit numbers.

Real-World EXAMPLE

① **MEASUREMENT** A coyote travels 27 miles each hour. Multiply 27 × 12 to find how far a coyote can travel in 12 hours.

One Way:	Partial Products		Another Way:	Paper and Pencil

One Way: Partial Products

```
    27
  × 12
    14     Multiply 2 × 7.
    40     Multiply 2 × 20.
    70     Multiply 10 × 7.
 + 200     Multiply 10 × 20.
   324     Add partial products.
```

```
           20        7
      ┌──────────┬──────┐
   10 │   200    │  70  │
      │          │      │
      ├──────────┼──────┤
    2 │    40    │  14  │
      └──────────┴──────┘
```

Another Way: Paper and Pencil

Step 1 Multiply the ones.
```
     1
    27
  × 12
    54  ←  2 × 27
```

Step 2 Multiply the tens.
```
     1
    27
  × 12
    54   ←  2 × 27
   270   ←  10 × 27
```

Step 3 Add the products.
```
     1
    27
  × 12
    54
  +270
   324   ←  Add.
```

So, a coyote can travel 324 miles in 12 hours.

284 Chapter 7 Multiply by Two-Digit Numbers

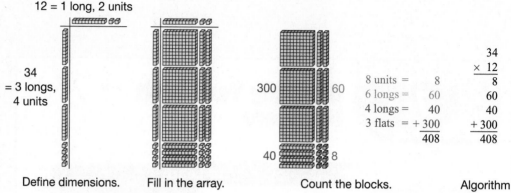

12 = 1 long, 2 units

34 = 3 longs, 4 units

300   60

40   8

8 units =	8
6 longs =	60
4 longs =	40
3 flats =	+ 300
	408

$$\begin{array}{r} 34 \\ \times\ 12 \\ \hline 8 \\ 60 \\ 40 \\ +300 \\ \hline 408 \end{array}$$

Define dimensions.   Fill in the array.   Count the blocks.   Algorithm

Figure 4.10

Algebraic Reasoning

In Figure 4.10, the model of a rectangular array can be used to multiply expressions such as $x + 2$ and $x + 3$. Tiles that look similar to base ten blocks are placed with an $x + 2$ down the side and $x + 3$ across the top. When the rectangle is filled in, the product of $(x + 2)(x + 3)$ is seen to be $x^2 + 5x + 6$.

(a) INTERMEDIATE ALGORITHM 1

$$\begin{array}{r} 34 \\ \times\ 12 \\ \hline 8 \\ 60 \\ 40 \\ 300 \\ \hline 408 \end{array}$$

(b) INTERMEDIATE ALGORITHM 2

$$\begin{array}{r} 34 \\ \times\ 12 \\ \hline 68 \\ 340 \\ \hline 408 \end{array}$$

68   Think 2×34

340   Think 10×34

(c) STANDARD ALGORITHM

$$\begin{array}{r} 34 \\ \times\ 12 \\ \hline 68 \end{array}$$ Think 2×4
     Think 2×3

34 ← Think 1×4, but in
         tens place
         Think 1×3, but in
408   hundreds place

One final complexity in the standard multiplication algorithm is illustrated next. Calculate 857×9.

(a) INTERMEDIATE ALGORITHM

$$\begin{array}{r} 857 \\ \times\quad 9 \\ \hline 63 \\ 450 \\ 7200 \\ \hline 7713 \end{array}$$

63 ← 9×7

450 ← 9×50

7200 ← 9×800

(b) INTERMEDIATE ALGORITHM

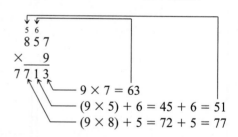

$$\begin{array}{r} 5\ 6 \\ 8\ 5\ 7 \\ \times\quad 9 \\ \hline 7\ 7\ 1\ 3 \end{array}$$

$9 \times 7 = 63$

$(9 \times 5) + 6 = 45 + 6 = 51$

$(9 \times 8) + 5 = 72 + 5 = 77$

Notice the complexity involved in explaining the standard algorithm!

The **lattice method for multiplication** is an example of an extremely simple multiplication algorithm that is no longer used, perhaps because we do not use paper with lattice markings on it and it is too time-consuming to draw such lines.

To calculate 35×4967, begin with a blank lattice and find products of the digits in intersecting rows and columns. The 18 in the completed lattice was obtained by multiplying its row value, 3, by its column value, 6 (Figure 4.11). The other values are filled in similarly. Then the numbers are added down the diagonals as in lattice addition. The answer, read counterclockwise from left to right, is 173,845.

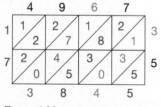

Figure 4.11

 Check for Understanding: Exercise/Problem Set A #20–28

Algorithms for the Division of Whole Numbers

Reflection from Research
A weak understanding of the place value system and a procedure-oriented performance of algorithms cause students to struggle to understand the traditional long division algorithm (Lee, 2007).

The long-division algorithm is the most complicated procedure in the elementary mathematics curriculum. Because of calculators, the importance of written long division using multidigit numbers has greatly diminished. However, the long-division algorithm involving one- and perhaps two-digit divisors continues to have common applications. The main idea behind the long-division algorithm is the division algorithm, which was given in Section 3.2. It states that if a and b are any whole numbers with $b \neq 0$, there exist unique whole numbers q and r such that $a = bq + r$, where $0 \leq r < b$. For example, if $a = 17$ and $b = 5$, then $q = 3$ and $r = 2$ since $17 = 5 \cdot 3 + 2$. The purpose of the long division algorithm is to find the quotient, q, and remainder, r, for any given divisor, b, and dividend, a.

To gain an understanding of the division algorithm, we will use base ten blocks and a fundamental definition of division. Find the quotient and remainder of 461 divided by 3. This can be thought of as 461 divided into groups of size 3. As you read this example, notice how the manipulation of the base ten blocks parallels the written algorithm. The following illustrates **long division using base ten blocks**.

Thought One

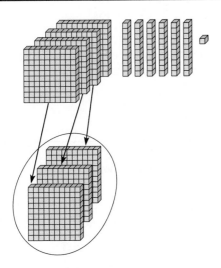

$$\begin{array}{r} 1 \\ 3\overline{)461} \\ \underline{3} \\ 1 \end{array}$$

Think: One group of three flats, which is 100 groups of 3, leaves one flat left over.

Thought Two

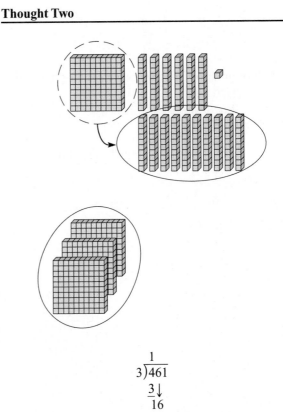

$$\begin{array}{r} 1 \\ 3\overline{)461} \\ \underline{3}{\downarrow} \\ 16 \end{array}$$

Think: Convert the one leftover flat to 10 longs and add it to the existing 6 longs to make 16 longs.

Thought Three

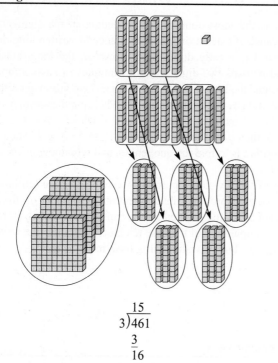

$$\begin{array}{r} 15 \\ 3\overline{)461} \\ \underline{3} \\ 16 \\ \underline{15} \\ 1 \end{array}$$

Think: Five groups of 3 longs, which is 50 groups of 3, leaves 1 long left over.

Thought Four

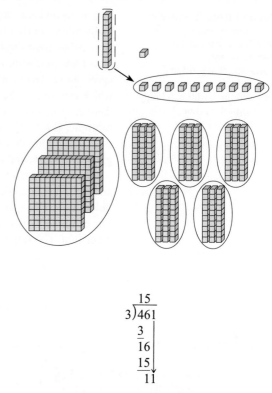

$$\begin{array}{r} 15 \\ 3\overline{)461} \\ \underline{3} \\ 16 \\ \underline{15} \\ 11 \end{array}$$

Think: Convert the one leftover long into 10 units and add it to the existing 1 unit to make 11 units.

Thought Five

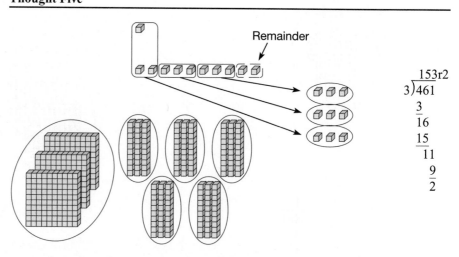

$$\begin{array}{r} 153\text{r}2 \\ 3\overline{)461} \\ \underline{3} \\ 16 \\ \underline{15} \\ 11 \\ \underline{9} \\ 2 \end{array}$$

Think: Three groups of 3 units each leaves 2 units left over. Since there is one group of flats (hundreds), five groups of longs (tens), and three groups of units (ones) with 2 left over, the quotient is 153 with a remainder of 2.

We will arrive at the final form of the long-division algorithm by working through various levels of complexity to illustrate how one can gain an understanding of the algorithm by progressing in small steps.

Find the quotient and remainder for 5739 ÷ 31.

The **scaffold method** is a good one to use first.

Reflection from Research
When solving arithmetic problems, students who move directly from using concrete strategies to algorithms, without being allowed to generate their own abstract strategies, are less likely to develop a conceptual understanding of multidigit numbers (Ambrose, 2002).

$$
\begin{array}{r}
31\overline{)5739} \\
-\ 3100 \\
\hline
2639 \\
-\ 1550 \\
\hline
1089 \\
-\ 930 \\
\hline
159 \\
155 \\
\hline
4
\end{array}
$$

100(31)

50(31)

30(31)

+   5(31)

185(31)

How many 31s in 5739? *Guess:* 100

How many 31s in 2639? *Guess:* 50

How many 31s in 1089? *Guess:* 30

How many 31s in 159? *Guess:* 5

Since 4 < 31, we stop and add 100 + 50 + 30 + 5. Therefore, the quotient is 185 and remainder is 4.

Check: $31 \cdot 185 + 4 = 5735 + 4 = 5739$.

As just shown, various multiples of 31 are subtracted successively from 5739 (or the resulting difference) until a remainder less than 31 is found. The key to this method is how well one can estimate the appropriate multiples of 31. In the scaffold method, it is better to estimate too low rather than too high, as in the case of the 50. However, 80 would have been the optimal guess at that point. Thus, although the quotient and remainder can be obtained using this method, it can be an inefficient application of the Guess and Test strategy.

The next example illustrates how division by a single digit can be done more efficiently.

Find the quotient and remainder for 3159 ÷ 7.

INTERMEDIATE ALGORITHM

Start here:

$$
\begin{array}{r}
451 \\
1 \\
50 \\
400 \\
7\overline{)3159} \\
-\ 2800 \\
\hline
359 \\
-\ 350 \\
\hline
9 \\
-\ 7 \\
\hline
2
\end{array}
$$

Think: How many 7s in 3100? 400

Think: How many 7s in 350? 50

Think: How many 7s in 9? 1

Therefore, the quotient is the sum 400 + 50 + 1, or 451, and the remainder is 2.
Check: $7 \cdot 451 + 2 = 3157 + 2 = 3159$.

Now consider division by a two-digit divisor. Find the quotient and remainder for 1976 ÷ 32.

INTERMEDIATE ALGORITHM

$$
\begin{array}{r}
61 \\
\overline{1} \\
60 \\
32\overline{)1976} \\
-\ 1920 \\
\overline{56} \\
-\ \ 32 \\
\overline{24}
\end{array}
$$

Think: How many 32s in 1976? 60

Think: How many 32s in 56? 1

Therefore, the quotient is 61 and the remainder is 24.
Check: $32 \cdot 61 + 24 = 1952 + 24 = 1976$.

Next we will employ rounding to help estimate the appropriate quotients. Find the quotient and remainder of $4238 \div 56$.

$$
\begin{array}{r}
5 \\
\overline{70} \\
56\overline{)4238} \\
-\ 3920 \\
\overline{318} \\
-\ \ 280 \\
\overline{38}
\end{array}
$$

Think: How many 60s in 4200? 70
$70 \times 56 = 3920$
Think: How many 60s in 310? 5
$5 \times 56 = 280$

Therefore, the quotient is $70 + 5 = 75$ and the remainder is 38.
Check: $56 \cdot 75 + 38 = 4200 + 38 = 4238$.

Observe how we rounded the divisor up to 60 and the dividend *down* to 4200 in the first step. This up/down rounding assures us that the quotient at each step will not be too large.

This algorithm can be simplified further to our **standard algorithm for division** by reducing the "think" steps to divisions with single-digit divisors. For example, in place of "How many 60s in 4200?" one could ask equivalently, "How many 6s in 420?" Even easier, "How many 6s in 42?" Notice also that in general, the *divisor should be rounded up and the dividend should be rounded down.*

| **Example 4.9** | Find the quotient and remainder for $4238 \div 56$. |

SOLUTION

$$
\begin{array}{r}
75 \\
56\overline{)4238} \\
392 \\
\hline
\end{array}
$$
$\left\{ \begin{array}{l} \textit{Think:} \text{ How many 6s in 42? 7} \\ \text{Put the 7 above the 3 since we are actually finding} \\ 4230 \div 56. \\ \text{The 392 is } 7 \cdot 56. \end{array} \right.$

$$
\begin{array}{r}
318 \\
-\ 280 \\
\hline
38
\end{array}
$$
$\left\{ \begin{array}{l} \textit{Think:} \text{ How many 6s in 31? 5} \\ \text{Put the 5 above the 8 since we are finding } 318 \div 56. \\ \text{The 280 is } 5 \cdot 56. \end{array} \right.$

The quotient and remainder for $4238 \div 56$ can be found using a calculator. The TI-34 II does long division with remainder directly using 4238 ⎡2nd⎤ ⎡INT÷⎤ 56 ⎡=⎤. The result for this problem is shown in Figure 4.12 as it appears on the second line of the calculator's display. To find the quotient and remainder using a standard calculator, press these keys: 4238 ⎡÷⎤ 56 ⎡=⎤. Your display should read 75.678571 (perhaps with fewer or more decimal places). Thus the whole-number quotient is 75. From the relationship $a = bq + r$, we see that $r = a - bq$ is the remainder. In this case $r = 4238 - 56 \cdot 75$, or 38.

Algebraic Reasoning
Solving equations like $x^3 - 2x^2 - 3x + 6 = 0$ can be done by factoring. One way to factor is a type of algebraic long division. The standard division algorithm provides a foundation for this type of algebraic reasoning.

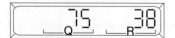

Figure 4.12

As the preceding calculator example illustrates, calculators virtually eliminate the need for becoming skilled in performing involved long divisions and other tedious calculations.

In this section, each of the four basic operations was illustrated by different algorithms. The problem set contains examples of many other algorithms. Even today, other countries use algorithms different from our "standard" algorithms. Also, students may even invent "new" algorithms. Since computational algorithms are aids for simplifying calculations, it is important to understand that *all correct algorithms are acceptable*. Clearly, computation in the future will rely less and less on written calculations and more and more on mental and electronic calculations.

 Check for Understanding: Exercise/Problem Set A #29–34

MATHEMATICAL MORSEL

Have someone write down a three-digit number using three different digits hidden from your view. Then have the person form all of the other five three-digit numbers that can be obtained by rearranging his or her three digits. Add these six numbers together with a seventh number, which is any other one of the six. The person tells you the sum, and then you, in turn, tell him or her the seventh number.

Here is how. Add the thousands digit of the sum to the remaining three-digit number (if the sum was 3635, you form 635 + 3 = 638). Then take the remainder upon division of this new number by nine (638 ÷ 9 leaves a remainder of 8). Multiply the remainder by 111 (8 × 111 = 888) and add this to the previous number (638 + 888 = 1526). Finally, add the thousands digit (if there is one) to the remaining number (1526 yields 526 + 1 = 527, the seventh number!).

Section 4.2   EXERCISE / PROBLEM SET A

EXERCISES

1. Using the Chapter 4 eManipulative activity *Base Blocks—Addition* on our Web site, model the following addition problems using base ten blocks. Sketch how the base ten blocks would be used.
   a. 327 + 61   **b.** 347 + 86

2. The physical models of base ten blocks and the chip abacus have been used to demonstrate addition. Bundling sticks can also be used. Sketch 15 + 32 using the following models.
   a. Chip abacus   **b.** Bundling sticks

3. Give a reason or reasons for each of the following steps to justify the addition process.

$$17 + 21 = (1 \cdot 10 + 7) + (2 \cdot 10 + 1)$$
$$= (1 \cdot 10 + 2 \cdot 10) + (7 + 1)$$
$$= 3 \cdot 10 + 8$$
$$= 38$$

4. There are many ways of providing intermediate steps between the models for computing sums (base ten blocks,

chip abacus, etc.) and the algorithm for addition. One of these is to represent numbers in their expanded forms. Consider the following examples:

$$246 = 2 \text{ hundreds} + 4 \text{ tens} + 6$$
$$+\ 352 = 3 \text{ hundreds} + 5 \text{ tens} + 2$$
$$= 5 \text{ hundreds} + 9 \text{ tens} + 8$$
$$= 598$$

$$547 = 5(10)^2 + 4(10) + 7$$
$$+\ 296 = 2(10)^2 + 9(10) + 6$$

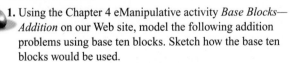

$$= 843$$

Use this expanded form of the addition algorithm to compute the following sums.

a.	351	**b.**	564
	+ 635		+ 345

5. Use the Intermediate Algorithm 1 to compute the following sums.
   a. $598 + 396$
   b. $322 + 799 + 572$

6. An alternative algorithm for addition, called **scratch addition**, is shown next. Using it, students can do more complicated additions by doing a series of single-digit additions. This method is sometimes more effective with students having trouble with the standard algorithm. For example, to compute $78 + 56 + 38$:

   $$\begin{array}{r} 7\;\;8 \\ 5\;\;\cancel{6} \\ +\;3\;\;\;8^{4} \\ \end{array}$$
   Add the number in the units place starting at the top. When the sum is ten or more, scratch a line through the last number added and write down the unit. The scratch represents 10.

   $$\begin{array}{r} {}^{2}\;\;\;\;\; \\ 7\;\;8 \\ 5\;\;\cancel{6} \\ +\;3\;\;\;8^{4} \\ \hline 2 \end{array}$$
   Continue adding units (adding 4 and 8). Write the last number of units below the line. Count the number of scratches, and write above the second column.

   $$\begin{array}{r} {}^{2}\;\;\;\;\; \\ 7\;\;8 \\ \cancel{5}\;\;\cancel{6} \\ +\;\;\;3^{4}\;\;8^{4} \\ \hline 1\;\;7\;\;2 \end{array}$$
   Repeat the procedure for each column.

   Compute the following additions using the scratch algorithm.
   a.
   $$\begin{array}{r} 734 \\ 468 \\ +\;\;27 \\ \end{array}$$
   b.
   $$\begin{array}{r} 1364 \\ 7257 \\ +\;4813 \\ \end{array}$$

7. Compute the following sums using the lattice method.
   a.
   $$\begin{array}{r} 482 \\ +\;269 \\ \end{array}$$
   b.
   $$\begin{array}{r} 567 \\ +\;765 \\ \end{array}$$

8. Give an advantage and a disadvantage of each of the following methods for addition.
   a. Intermediate algorithm **b.** Lattice

9. Add the following numbers. Then turn this page upside down and add it again. What did you find? What feature of the numerals 1, 6, 8, 9 accounts for this?
   $$\begin{array}{r} 986 \\ 818 \\ 969 \\ 989 \\ 696 \\ 616 \end{array}$$

10. Without performing the addition, tell which sum, if either, is greater.
    $$\begin{array}{rr} 23{,}456 & 20{,}002 \\ 23{,}400 & 32 \\ 23{,}000 & 432 \\ +\;20{,}002 & +\;65{,}432 \end{array}$$

11. Without calculating the actual sums, select the smallest sum, the middle sum, and the largest sum in each group. Mark them *A*, *B*, and *C*, respectively. Use your estimating powers.
    a. _____ $283 + 109$ _____ $161 + 369$ _____ $403 + 277$
    b. _____ $629 + 677$ _____ $723 + 239$ _____ $275 + 631$
    Now check your estimate with a calculator.

12. Using the Chapter 4 eManipulative activity *Base Blocks—Subtraction* on our Web site, model the following subtraction problems using base ten blocks. Sketch how the base ten blocks would be used.
    a.
    $$\begin{array}{r} 87 \\ -\;35 \end{array}$$
    b.
    $$\begin{array}{r} 483 \\ -\;\;57 \end{array}$$

13. Sketch solutions to the following problems, using bundling sticks and a chip abacus
    a.
    $$\begin{array}{r} 57 \\ -\;37 \end{array}$$
    b.
    $$\begin{array}{r} 34 \\ -\;29 \end{array}$$

14. 9342 is usually thought of as 9 thousands, 3 hundreds, 4 tens, and 2 ones, but in subtracting 6457 from 9342 using the customary algorithm, we regroup and think of 9342 as
    _____ thousands, _____ hundreds, _____ tens, and _____ ones.

15. Order these computations from easiest to hardest.
    a.
    $$\begin{array}{r} 809 \\ -\;306 \end{array}$$
    b.
    $$\begin{array}{r} 8 \\ -\;3 \end{array}$$
    c.
    $$\begin{array}{r} 82 \\ -\;67 \end{array}$$

16. To perform some subtractions, it is necessary to reverse the rename and regroup process of addition. Perform the following subtraction in expanded form and follow regrouping steps.
    $$\begin{array}{r} 732 \\ -\;378 \end{array} \quad \begin{array}{r} 700 + 30 + 2 \\ -\;(300 + 70 + 8) \end{array} \quad \text{or}$$
    $$\begin{array}{r} 700 + 20 + 12 \\ -\;(300 + 70 + \;\;8) \end{array} \;\text{or}\; \begin{array}{r} 600 + 120 + 12 \\ -\;(300 + \;\;70 + \;\;8) \\ \hline 300 + \;\;50 + \;\;4 = 354 \end{array}$$

    Use expanded form with regrouping as necessary to perform the following subtractions.
    a. $652 - 175$ **b.** $923 - 147$ **c.** $8257 - 6439$

17. The **cashier's algorithm** for subtraction is closely related to the missing-addend approach to subtraction; that is, $a - b = c$ if and only if $a = b + c$. For example, you buy $23 of school supplies and give the cashier a $50 bill. While

handing you the change, the cashier would say "$23, $24, $25, $30, $40, $50." How much change did you receive?

    What cashier said: $23, $24, $25, $30, $40, $50
    Money received: 0, $1, $1, $5, $10, $10

Now you are the cashier. The customer owes you $62 and gives you a $100 bill. What will you say to the customer, and how much will you give back?

18. Subtraction by **adding the complement** goes as follows:

$$
\begin{array}{r}
619 \\
-\ 476 \\
\end{array}
\qquad
\begin{array}{r}
619 \\
+\ 523 \\
\hline
\cancel{1}142 \\
+\quad 1 \\
\hline
143 \\
\end{array}
$$

The complement of 476 is 523
since $476 + 523 = 999$.
(The sum in each place is 9.)
Cross out the leading digit.
Add 1.
Answer = 143

Find the following differences using this algorithm.
a. $\begin{array}{r}537 \\ -\ 179\end{array}$ **b.** $\begin{array}{r}86{,}124 \\ -\ 38{,}759\end{array}$

19. A subtraction algorithm, popular in the past, is called the **equal-additions algorithm**. Consider this example.

$$
\begin{array}{r}
436 \\
-\ 282 \\
\end{array}
\qquad\qquad
\begin{array}{r}
4\cdot 10^2 + 3\cdot 10 + 6 \\
-\ (2\cdot 10^2 + 8\cdot 10 + 2) \\
\end{array}
$$

$$
\begin{array}{r}
4\cdot 10^2 + \mathbf{13}\cdot 10 + 6 \\
-\ (\mathbf{3\cdot 10^2} +\ 8\cdot 10 + 2) \\
\hline
1\cdot 10^2 +\ 5\cdot 10 + 4 = 154 \\
\end{array}
\qquad
\begin{array}{r}
\overset{13}{4\overset{}{3}6} \\
-\ \overset{3}{2}82 \\
\hline
1\,5\,4 \\
\end{array}
$$

To subtract $8\cdot 10$ from $3\cdot 10$, add ten 10s to the minuend and $1\cdot 10^2$ (or ten 10s) to the subtrahend. The problem is changed, but the answer is the same. Use the equal-additions algorithm to find the following differences.
a. $421 - 286$ **b.** $92{,}863 - 75{,}387$

20. Consider the product of 27×33.
  a. Sketch how base ten blocks can be used in a rectangular array to model this product.
  b. Find the product using the Intermediate Algorithm 1.
  c. Describe the relationship between the solutions in parts a. and b.

21. Show how to find 28×34 on this grid paper.

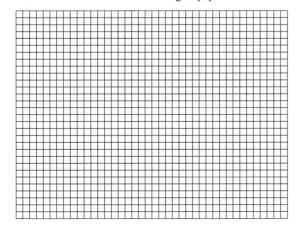

22. The pictorial representation of multiplication can be adapted as follows to perform 23×16.

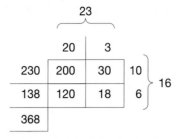

Use this method to find the following products.
a. 15×36 **b.** 62×35

23. Justify each step in the following proof that $72 \times 10 = 720$.

$$
\begin{aligned}
72 \times 10 &= (70 + 2) \times 10 \\
&= 70 \times 10 + 2 \times 10 \\
&= (7 \times 10) \times 10 + 2 \times 10 \\
&= 7 \times (10 \times 10) + 2 \times 10 \\
&= 7 \times 100 + 2 \times 10 \\
&= 700 + 20 \\
&= 720
\end{aligned}
$$

24. Solve the following problems using the lattice method for multiplication and an intermediate algorithm.
a. 23×62 **b.** 17×45

25. Study the pattern in the following left-to-right multiplication.

$$
\begin{array}{r}
731 \\
\times\ 238 \\
\hline
1462 \\
2139 \\
5848 \\
\hline
173978 \\
\end{array}
\qquad
\begin{array}{l}
(2\cdot 731) \\
(3\cdot 731) \\
(8\cdot 731) \\
\end{array}
$$

Use this algorithm to do the following computations.
a. 75×47 **b.** 364×421

26. The **Russian peasant algorithm** for multiplying 27×51 is illustrated as follows:

HALVING		DOUBLING
27	×	51
13	×	102
~~6~~	~~×~~	~~204~~
3	×	408
1	×	816

Notice that the numbers in the first column are halved (disregarding any remainder) and that the numbers in the second column are doubled. When 1 is reached in the halving column, the process is stopped. Next, each row with an even number in the halving column is crossed out and the remaining numbers in the doubling column are added. Thus

$$27 \times 51 = 51 + 102 + 408 + 816 = 1377.$$

Use the Russian peasant algorithm to compute the following products.
a. 68×35 **b.** 38×62

27. The use of finger numbers and systems of finger computation has been widespread through the years. One such system for multiplication uses the finger positions shown for computing the products of numbers from 6 through 10.

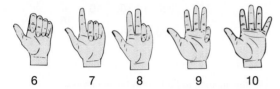

6	7	8	9	10

The two numbers to be multiplied are each represented on a different hand. The sum of the raised fingers is the number of tens, and the product of the closed fingers is the number of ones. For example, $1 + 3 = 4$ fingers raised, and $4 \times 2 = 8$ fingers down.

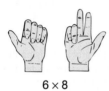

6×8

Use this method to compute the following products.
a. 7×8 **b.** 6×7 **c.** 6×10

28. The **duplication algorithm for multiplication** combines a succession of doubling operations, followed by addition. This algorithm depends on the fact that any number can be written as the sum of numbers that are powers of 2. To compute 28×36, the 36 is repeatedly doubled as shown.

$$
\begin{array}{rrr}
& 1 \times 36 = & 36 \\
& 2 \times 36 = & 72 \\
\rightarrow & 4 \times 36 = & 144 \\
\rightarrow & 8 \times 36 = & 288 \\
\rightarrow & 16 \times 36 = & 576 \\
& \uparrow & \\
& \text{powers of 2} &
\end{array}
$$

This process stops when the next power of 2 in the list is greater than the number by which you are multiplying. Here we want 28 of the 36s, and since $28 = (16 + 8 + 4)$, the product of $28 \times 36 = (16 + 8 + 4) \cdot 36$. From the last column, you add $144 + 288 + 576 = 1008$.

Use the duplication algorithm to compute the following products.
a. 25×62 **b.** 35×58 **c.** 73×104

29. Use the scaffold method in the Chapter 4 dynamic spreadsheet *Scaffold Division* on our Web site to find the

following quotients. Write down how the scaffold method was used.
a. $899 \div 13$ **b.** $5697 \div 23$

30. A third-grade teacher prepared her students for division this way:

$$
\begin{array}{cc}
20 \div 4 & 20 \\
& \underline{-\ 4}\ \checkmark \\
& 16 \\
& \underline{-\ 4}\ \checkmark \\
& 12 \\
& \underline{-\ 4}\ \checkmark \quad 20 \div 4 = 5 \\
& 8 \\
& \underline{-\ 4}\ \checkmark \\
& 4 \\
& \underline{-\ 4}\ \checkmark \\
& 0
\end{array}
$$

How would her students find $42 \div 6$?

31. Without using the divide key, find the quotient for each of the following problems.
a. $24 \div 4$ **b.** $56 \div 7$
c. Describe how the calculator was used to find the quotients.

32. When asked to find the quotient and remainder of $431 \div 17$, one student did the following with a calculator:

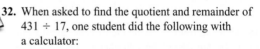

Display

$431\ \boxed{\div}\ 17\ \boxed{=}\ \boxed{25.35294}\ \boxed{-}$

Display

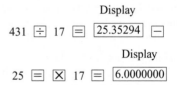

$25\ \boxed{=}\ \boxed{\times}\ 17\ \boxed{=}\ \boxed{6.0000000}$

a. Try this method on the following pairs.
   (i) $1379 \div 87$
   (ii) $69{,}431 \div 139$
   (iii) $1{,}111{,}111 \div 333$

b. Does this method always work? Explain.

33. Sketch how base ten blocks can be used to model $762 \div 5$.

34. When performing the division problem $2137 \div 14$ using the standard algorithm, the first few steps look like what is shown here. The next step is to "bring down" the 3. Explain how that process of "bringing down" the 3 is modeled using base ten blocks.

$$
\begin{array}{r}
1 \\
14\overline{)2137} \\
\underline{14} \\
7
\end{array}
$$

PROBLEMS

35. Larry, Curly, and Moe each add incorrectly as follows.

Larry: 29
       $+\ 83$
       1012

Curly: $\overset{2}{2}9$
       $+\ 83$
       121

Moe: 29
     $+\ 83$
     102

How would you explain their mistakes to each of them?

36. Use the digits 1 to 9 to make an addition problem and answer. Use each digit only once.

37. Place the digits 2, 3, 4, 6, 7, 8 in the boxes to obtain the following sums.

a. The greatest sum   **b.** The least sum

38. Arrange the digits 1, 2, 3, 4, 5, 6, 7 such that they add up to 100. (For example, $12 + 34 + 56 + 7 = 109$.)

39. Given next is an addition problem.

a. Replace seven digits with 0s so that the sum of the numbers is 1111.

$$999$$
$$777$$
$$555$$
$$333$$
$$+\ 111$$

b. Do the same problem by replacing (i) eight digits with 0s, (ii) nine digits with 0s, (iii) ten digits with 0s.

40. Consider the following array:

```
 1   2   3   4   5   6   7   8   9  10
11  12  13  14  15  16  17  18  19  20
21  22  23  24  25  26  27  28  29  30
31  32  33  34  35  36  37  38  39  40
41  42  43  44  45  46  47  48  49  50
51  52  53  54  55  56  57  58  59  60
```

Compare the pair 26, 37 with the pair 36, 27.
a. Add: $26 + 37 = $ _____. $36 + 27 = $ _____.
   What do you notice about the answers?
b. Subtract: $37 - 26 = $ _____. $36 - 27 = $ _____.
   What do you notice about the answers?
c. Are your findings true for any two such pairs?
d. What similar patterns can you find?

41. The x's in half of each figure can be counted in two ways.

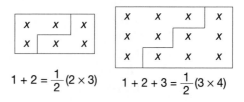

$$1 + 2 = \frac{1}{2}(2 \times 3) \qquad 1 + 2 + 3 = \frac{1}{2}(3 \times 4)$$

a. Draw a similar figure for $1 + 2 + 3 + 4$.
b. Express that sum in a similar way. Is the sum correct?
c. Use this idea to find the sum of whole numbers from 1 to 50 and from 1 to 75.

42. In the following problems, each letter represents a different digit and any of the digits 0 through 9 can be used. However, both additions have the same result. What are the problems?

```
   ZZZ          ZZZ
   KKK          PPP
 + LLL        + QQQ
  RSTU         RSTU
```

43. Following are some problems worked out by students. Each student has a particular error pattern. Find that error, and tell what answer that student will get for the last problem.

Bob:

```
   22        312        82        84
 ×  4       ×  2      × 37      × 26
   28        314       254
```

Jennifer:

```
                 2          2
   34           26         36        25
 ×  2         ×  4       ×  4      ×  6
   68           84        124
```

Suzie:

```
    2          2          3
   27         34         54        29
 ×  4       ×  5       ×  8      ×  4
  168        250        642
```

Tom:

```
                          1
   313        211        433       517
 ×   4       × 15      × 226     × 463
  1252        215       878
```

What instructional procedures might you use to help each of these students?

44. The following is an example of the **German low-stress algorithm.** Find 5314×79 using this method and explain how it works.

$$
\begin{array}{r}
4967 \times 35 \\
\hline
21 \\
1835 \\
2730 \\
1245 \\
20 \\
\hline
173845
\end{array}
$$

45. Select any four-digit number. Arrange the digits to form the largest possible number and the smallest possible number. Subtract the smallest number from the largest number. Use the digits in the difference and start the process over again. Keep repeating the process. What do you discover?

Section 4.2　EXERCISE / PROBLEM SET B

EXERCISES

1. Sketch how base ten blocks could be used to solve the following problems. You may may find the Chapter 4 eManipulative activity *Base Blocks—Addition* on our Web site to be useful in this process.

 a. 258 **b.** 627
  + 149   + 485

2. Sketch the solution to $46 + 55$ using the following models.
 a. Bundling sticks **b.** Chip abacus

3. Give a reason for each of the following steps to justify the addition process.

$$
\begin{aligned}
38 + 56 &= (3 \cdot 10 + 8) + (5 \cdot 10 + 6) \\
&= (3 \cdot 10 + 5 \cdot 10) + (8 + 6) \\
&= (3 \cdot 10 + 5 \cdot 10) + 14 \\
&= (3 \cdot 10 + 5 \cdot 10) + 1 \cdot 10 + 4 \\
&= (3 \cdot 10 + 5 \cdot 10 + 1 \cdot 10) + 4 \\
&= (3 + 5 + 1) \cdot 10 + 4 \\
&= 9 \cdot 10 + 4 \\
&= 94
\end{aligned}
$$

4. Use the expanded form of the addition algorithm (see Part A, Exercise 4) to compute the following sums.
 a. 478 **b.** 1965
  + 269   + 857

5. Use the Intermediate Algorithm 2 to compute the following sums.
 a. $347 + 679$ **b.** $3538 + 784$
 c. Describe the advantages and disadvantages of Intermediate Algorithm 2 versus Intermediate Algorithm 1.

6. Another scratch method involves adding from left to right, as shown in the following example.

$$
\begin{array}{r}
987 \\
+ 356 \\
\hline
12
\end{array}
\qquad
\begin{array}{r}
9\ 8\ 7 \\
+ 3\ 5\ 6 \\
\hline
1\ \not{2}\ 3 \\
{\scriptstyle 3}
\end{array}
\qquad
\begin{array}{r}
9\ 8\ 7 \\
+ 3\ 5\ 6 \\
\hline
1\ \not{2}\ \not{3} \\
{\scriptstyle 3\ 4}
\end{array}
\qquad
\begin{array}{r}
987 \\
+ 356 \\
\hline
1343
\end{array}
$$

First the hundreds column was added. Then the tens column was added and, because of carrying, the 2 was scratched

out and replaced by a 3. The process continued until the sum was complete. Apply this method to compute the following sums.

 a. 475 **b.** 856 **c.** 179
  + 381   + 907   + 356

7. Compute the following sums using the lattice method.
 a. 982 **b.** 4698
  + 659   + 5487

8. Give an advantage and a disadvantage of each of the following methods for addition.
 a. Expanded form
 b. Standard algorithm

9. In Part A, Exercise 9, numbers were listed that add to the same sum whether they were read right side up or upside down. Find another 6 three-digit numbers that have the same sum whether read right side up or upside down.

10. Gerald added 39,642 and 43,728 on his calculator and got 44,020 as the answer. How could he tell, mentally, that his sum is wrong?

11. Without calculating the actual sums, select the smallest sum, the middle sum, and the largest sum in each group. Mark them *A*, *B*, and *C*, respectively.
 a. _____ $284 + 625$ _____ $593 + 237$ _____ $304 + 980$
 b. _____ $427 + 424$ _____ $748 + 611$ _____ $272 + 505$

12. Sketch how base ten blocks could be used to solve the following problems. You may find the Chapter 4 eManipulative activity *Base Blocks—Subtraction* on our Web site to be useful in this process.
 a. $536 - 54$
 b. $625 - 138$

13. Sketch the solution to the following problems using bundling sticks and a chip abacus.
 a. $42 - 27$
 b. $324 - 68$

14. To subtract 999 from 1111, regroup and think of 1111 as _____ hundreds, _____ tens, and _____ ones.

15. Order these computations from easiest to hardest.

   a.   81   b.   80   c.   8819
       − 36   − 30   − 3604

16. Use the expanded form with regrouping (see Part A, Exercise 16) to perform the following subtractions.
   a. 455 − 278
   b. 503 − 147
   c. 3426 − 652

17. Use the cashiers algorithm (see Part A, Exercise 17) to describe what the cashier would say to the customer in each of the following cases. How much change does the customer receive?
   a. Customer owes: $28; Cashier receives: $40
   b. Customer owes: $33; Cashier receives: $100

18. Use the adding the complement algorithm described in Part A, Exercise 18 to find the differences in parts a and b.

   a.   3479
       − 2175

   b.   6,002,005
       − 4,187,269

   c. Explain how the method works with three-digit numbers.

19. Use the equal-additions algorithm described in Part A, Exercise 19 to find the differences in parts a and b.
   a. 3476 − 558
   b. 50,004 − 36,289
   c. Will this algorithm work in general? Why or why not?

20. Consider the product of 42 × 24.
   a. Sketch how base ten blocks can be used in a rectangular array to model this product.
   b. Find the product using the Intermediate Algorithm 1.
   c. Describe the relationship between the solutions in parts a and b.

21. Show how to find 17 × 26 on this grid paper.

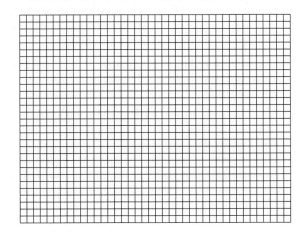

22. Use the pictorial representation shown in Part A, Exercise 22 to find the products in parts a and b.
   a. 23 × 48
   b. 34 × 52
   c. How do the numbers within the grid compare with the steps of Intermediate Algorithm 1?

23. Justify each step in the following proof that shows 573 × 100 = 57,300.

$$
\begin{aligned}
573 \times 100 &= (500 + 70 + 3) \times 100 \\
&= 500 \times 100 + 70 \times 100 + 3 \times 100 \\
&= (5 \times 100) \times 100 + (7 \times 10) \times 100 \\
&\quad + 3 \times 100 \\
&= 5 \times (100 \times 100) + 7 \times (10 \times 100) \\
&\quad + 3 \times 100 \\
&= 5 \times 10,000 + 7 \times 1000 + 300 \\
&= 50,000 + 7000 + 300 \\
&= 57,300
\end{aligned}
$$

24. Solve the following problems using the lattice method for multiplication and an intermediate algorithm.
   a. 237 × 48
   b. 617 × 896

25. Use the left-to-right multiplication algorithm shown in Part A, Exercise 25 to find the following products.
   a. 276 × 43
   b. 768 × 891

26. Use the Russian peasant algorithm for multiplication algorithm shown in Part A, Exercise 26 to find the following products.
   a. 44 × 83
   b. 31 × 54

27. Use the finger multiplication method described in Part A, Exercise 27 to find the following products. Explain how the algorithm was used in each case.
   a. 9 × 6   b. 7 × 9   c. 8 × 8

28. Use the duplication algorithm for multiplication algorithm shown in Part A, Exercise 28 to find the products in parts a, b, and c.
   a. 14 × 43
   b. 21 × 67
   c. 43 × 73
   d. Which property justifies the algorithm?

29. Use the scaffold method to find the following quotients. Show how the scaffold method was used.
   a. 749 ÷ 22
   b. 3251 ÷ 14

30. a. Use the method described in Part A, Exercise 30 to find the quotient 63 ÷ 9 and describe how the method was used.
   b. Which approach to division does this method illustrate?

31. Without using the divide key, use a calculator to find the quotient and remainder for each of the following problems.
a. 3)39   **b.** 8)89   **c.** 6)75
d. Describe how the calculator was used to find the remainders.

32. Find the quotient and remainder to the problems in parts a, b, and c using a calculator and the method illustrated in Part A, Exercise 32. Describe how the calculator was used.
a. $18,114 \div 37$
b. $381,271 \div 47$
c. $9,346,870 \div 349$
d. Does this method always work? Explain.

33. Sketch how to use base ten blocks to model the operation $673 \div 4$.

34. When finding the quotient for $527 \div 3$ using the standard division algorithm, the first few steps are shown here.

$$
\begin{array}{r}
1 \\
3\overline{)527} \\
-\,3 \\
\hline
2
\end{array}
$$

Explain how the process of subtracting 3 from 5 is modeled with base ten blocks.

PROBLEMS

35. Peter, Jeff, and John each perform subtraction incorrectly as follows:

Peter: $\begin{array}{r} 503 \\ -\,269 \\ \hline 366 \end{array}$ Jeff: $\begin{array}{r} {}^{4}{}^{10}\,^{13} \\ \cancel{5}\,\cancel{0}\,\cancel{3} \\ -\,2\,6\,9 \\ \hline 2\,4\,4 \end{array}$ John: $\begin{array}{r} {}^{3}\,^{9}{} \\ ^{4}\,\cancel{\cancel{1}0}\,^{13} \\ \cancel{5}\,0\,\cancel{3} \\ -\,2\,6\,9 \\ \hline 1\,3\,4 \end{array}$

How would you explain their mistakes to each of them?

36. Let A, B, C, and D represent four consecutive whole numbers. Find the values for A, B, C, and D if the four boxes are replaced with A, B, C, and D in an unknown order.

$$
\begin{array}{r}
A\,,\ B\ \ C\ \ D \\
D\,,\ C\ \ B\ \ A \\
+\ \ \square\ \square\ \square\ \square \\
\hline
1\ \ 2\,,\ 3\ \ 0\ \ 0
\end{array}
$$

37. Place the digits 3, 5, 6, 2, 4, 8 in the boxes to obtain the following differences.
a. The greatest difference
b. The least difference

$$
\begin{array}{r}
\square\ \square\ \square \\
-\ \square\ \square\ \square \\
\hline
\end{array}
$$

38. a. A college student, short of funds and in desperate need, writes the following note to his father:

$$
\begin{array}{r}
\text{SEND} \\
+\ \text{MORE} \\
\hline
\text{MONEY}
\end{array}
$$

If each letter in this message represents a different digit, how much MONEY (in cents) is he asking for?

b. The father, considering the request, decides to send some money along with some important advice.

$$
\begin{array}{r}
\text{SAVE} \\
+\ \text{MORE} \\
\hline
\text{MONEY}
\end{array}
$$

However, the father had misplaced the request and could not recall the amount. If he sent the largest amount of MONEY (in cents) represented by this sum, how much did the college student receive?

39. Consider the sums

$$
\begin{aligned}
1 + 11 &= \\
1 + 11 + 111 &= \\
1 + 11 + 111 + 1111 &=
\end{aligned}
$$

a. What is the pattern?
b. How many addends are there the first time the pattern no longer works?

40. Select any three-digit number whose first and third digits are different. Reverse the digits and find the difference between the two numbers. By knowing only the hundreds digit in this difference, it is possible to determine the other two digits. How? Explain how the trick works.

41. Choose any four-digit number, reverse its digits, and add the two numbers. Is the sum divisible by 11? Will this always be true?

42. Select any number larger than 100 and multiply it by 9. Select one of the digits of this result as the "missing digit." Find the sum of the remaining digits. Continue adding digits in resulting sums until you have a one-digit number. Subtract that number from 9. Is that your missing digit? Try it again with another number. Determine which missing digits this procedure will find.

43. Following are some division exercises done by students.

Carol:

$$
\begin{array}{cccc}
233 & 221 & 231 & \\
2\overline{)176} & 4\overline{)824} & 3\overline{)813} & 4\overline{)581}
\end{array}
$$

Steve:

$$
\begin{array}{cccc}
14 & 97 & 37 & \\
4\overline{)164} & 3\overline{)237} & 5\overline{)365} & 6\overline{)414} \\
\underline{160} & \underline{210} & \underline{350} & \\
4 & 27 & 15 & \\
\underline{4} & \underline{27} & &
\end{array}
$$

Tracy:

$$
\begin{array}{cccc}
75r5 & 47r4 & 53r5 & \\
6\overline{)4235} & 8\overline{)3260} & 7\overline{)3526} & 9\overline{)3642} \\
\underline{42} & \underline{32} & \underline{35} & \\
35 & 60 & 26 & \\
\underline{30} & \underline{56} & \underline{21} & \\
5 & 4 & 5 &
\end{array}
$$

Determine the error pattern and tell what each student will get for the last problem.
What instructional procedures might you use to help each of these students?

44. Three businesswomen traveling together stopped at a motel to get a room for the night. They were charged $30 for the room and agreed to split the cost equally. The manager later realized that he had overcharged them by $5. He gave the refund to his son to deliver to the women. This smart son, realizing it would be difficult to split $5 equally, gave the women $3 and kept $2 for himself. Thus, it cost each woman $9 for the room. Therefore, they spent $27 for the room plus the $2 "tip." What happened to the other dollar?

45. Show that a perfect square is obtained by adding 1 to the product of two whole numbers that differ by 2. For example, $8(10) + 1 = 9^2$, $11 \times 13 + 1 = 12^2$, etc.

 Analyzing Student Thinking

46. A student's father was curious about why his daughter was learning addition using base ten pieces when he had not learned it that way. How should you respond?

47. Is it okay for a student to use the lattice method for addition or must all of your students eventually use the standard algorithm? Explain.

48. When finding the difference $123 - 67$, why might the subtract-from-the-base algorithm be easier for some students?

49. What is one advantage and one disadvantage of having your students use base ten blocks to model the standard multiplication algorithm? Explain.

50. After two subtraction algorithms were shared in class, Nicholas asked why they needed two different methods and which of them he was supposed to learn. How should you respond?

51. A student found $4005 - 37$ as follows:

$$
\begin{array}{r}
4005 \\
- \quad 37 \\
\hline
2078
\end{array}
$$

Diagnose what the student was doing wrong.

52. Natasha asked what the advantages of the lattice method are as compared to the standard multiplication algorithm. How would you respond?

53. Andres found the product of 46 and 53 horizontally as follows: $(40 + 6)(50 + 3) = 40 \times 50 + 40 \times 3 + 6 \times 50 + 6 \times 3 = 2000 + 120 + 300 + 18 = 2438$. Will this method always work? Explain.

54. When using the standard division algorithm to solve $621 \div 3$, Dylan found that quotient to be 27 instead of 207. How could base 10 pieces be used to clarify this misunderstanding?

Problems Relating to the NCTM Standards and Curriculum Focal Points

1. The Focal Points for Grade 2 state "Developing quick recall of addition facts and related subtraction facts and fluency with multidigit addition and subtraction." Explain how the "quick recall" of addition and subtraction facts influences a student's ability to be fluent in multidigit addition and subtraction.

2. The Focal Points for Grade 5 state "Developing an understanding of and fluency with division of whole numbers." Describe a key element of understanding whole number division that will contribute to fluency with the algorithm.

3. The NCTM Standards state "All students should develop and use strategies for whole-number computation." Describe a whole number computation strategy from this section that you think a student might "develop" on their own and justify your conclusion.

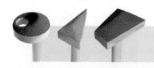

4.3   ALGORITHMS IN OTHER BASES

Abe liked working with numbers in other bases, but wasn't sure that he could do the four basic operations. Suppose he wanted to add 34_{seven} and 65_{seven}. Do you think that it is possible? If so, how would you help Abe understand it? How is it different from or similar to adding numbers in base ten?

All of the algorithms you have learned can be used in any base. In this section we apply the algorithms in base five and then let you try them in other bases in the problem set. The purpose for doing this is to help you see where, how, and why your future students might have difficulties in learning the standard algorithms.

Operations in Base Five

Addition   Addition in base five is facilitated using the thinking strategies *in base five*. These thinking strategies may be aided by referring to the base five number line shown in Figure 4.13, in which $2_{five} + 4_{five} = 11_{five}$ is illustrated. This number line also provides a representation of counting in base five. (All numerals on the number line are written in base five with the subscripts omitted.)

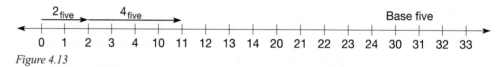

Figure 4.13

Example 4.10   Find $342_{five} + 134_{five}$ using the following methods.

a. Lattice method   **b.** Intermediate algorithm   **c.** Standard algorithm

SOLUTION

a. Lattice Method   **b. Intermediate Algorithm**   **c. Standard Algorithm**

$$
\begin{array}{rccc}
 & 3 & 4 & 2_{five} \\
+ & 1 & 3 & 4_{five}
\end{array}
$$

| 0 \\ 4 | 1 \\ 2 | 1 \\ 1 |

1   0   3 1_{five}

b. Intermediate Algorithm

$$
\begin{array}{r}
342_{five} \\
+134_{five} \\
\hline
11_{five} \\
120_{five} \\
400_{five} \\
\hline
1031_{five}
\end{array}
$$

c. Standard Algorithm

$$
\begin{array}{r}
1\ 1\ 1\ \ \\
3\ 4\ 2_{five} \\
+1\ 3\ 4_{five} \\
\hline
1\ 0\ 3\ 1_{five}
\end{array}
$$

Be sure to use thinking strategies when adding in base five. It is helpful to find sums to five first; for example, think of $4_{five} + 3_{five}$ as $4_{five} + (1_{five} + 2_{five}) = (4_{five} + 1_{five}) + 2_{five} = 12_{five}$ and so on.

✔ **Check for Understanding:** Exercise/Problem Set A #1–6

Subtraction   There are two ways to apply a subtraction algorithm successfully. One is to know the addition facts table forward and *backward*. The other is to use the missing-addend approach repeatedly. For example, to find $12_{five} - 4_{five}$, think "What number plus 4_{five} is 12_{five}?" To answer this, one could count up "10_{five}, 11_{five}, 12_{five}." Thus $12_{\text{five}} - 4_{\text{five}} = 3_{\text{five}}$ (one for each of 10_{five}, 11_{five}, and 12_{five}). A base five number line can also illustrate $12_{\text{five}} - 4_{\text{five}} = 3_{\text{five}}$. The missing-addend approach is illustrated in Figure 4.14 and the take-away approach is illustrated in Figure 4.15.

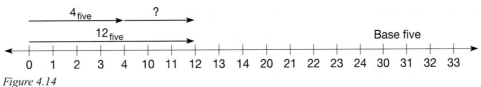

Figure 4.14

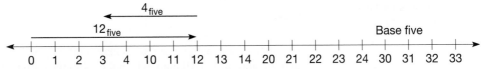

Figure 4.15

A copy of the addition table for base five is included in Figure 4.16 to assist you in working through Example 4.11. (All numerals in Figure 4.16 are written in base five with the subscripts omitted.)

+	0	1	2	3	4
0	0	1	2	3	4
1	1	2	3	4	10
2	2	3	4	10	11
3	3	4	10	11	12
4	4	10	11	12	13

Figure 4.16

Example 4.11   Calculate $412_{\text{five}} - 143_{\text{five}}$ using the following methods.

SOLUTION

a. Standard Algorithm
Think:

$$
\begin{array}{r}
412_{\text{five}} \\
-\ 143_{\text{five}} \\
\end{array}
\longrightarrow
\begin{array}{r}
\overset{3\ \ 10\ 12}{4\ 1\ 2}_{\text{five}} \\
-\ 1\ 4\ 3_{\text{five}} \\
\hline
2\ 1\ 4_{\text{five}}
\end{array}
$$

Third step $3_{\text{five}} - 1_{\text{five}}$

Second step $10_{\text{five}} - 4_{\text{five}}$

First step $12_{\text{five}} - 3_{\text{five}}$

b. Subtract-from-the-Base
Think:

$$
\begin{array}{r}
412_{\text{five}} \\
-\ 143_{\text{five}} \\
\end{array}
\longrightarrow
\begin{array}{r}
\overset{3\ \ 10}{\underset{0\ \ 10}{4\ 1\ 2}}_{\text{five}} \\
-\ 1\ 4\ 3_{\text{five}} \\
\hline
2\ 1\ 4_{\text{five}}
\end{array}
$$

Third step $3_{\text{five}} - 1_{\text{five}}$

Second step $(10_{\text{five}} - 4_{\text{five}}) + 0_{\text{five}}$

First step $(10_{\text{five}} - 3_{\text{five}}) + 2_{\text{five}}$ ∎

Notice that to do subtraction in base five using the subtract-from-the-base algorithm, you only need to know two addition combinations to five, namely $1_{\text{five}} + 4_{\text{five}} = 10_{\text{five}}$ and $2_{\text{five}} + 3_{\text{five}} = 10_{\text{five}}$. These two, in turn, lead to the four subtraction facts you need to know, namely $10_{\text{five}} - 4_{\text{five}} = 1_{\text{five}}$, $10_{\text{five}} - 1_{\text{five}} = 4_{\text{five}}$, $10_{\text{five}} - 3_{\text{five}} = 2_{\text{five}}$, and $10_{\text{five}} - 2_{\text{five}} = 3_{\text{five}}$.

✔ **Check for Understanding:** Exercise/Problem Set A #7–11

Multiplication   To perform multiplication efficiently, one must know the multiplication facts. The multiplication facts for base five are displayed in Figure 4.17. The entries in this multiplication table can be visualized by referring to the number line shown in Figure 4.18.

Algebraic Reasoning
To find $3 \cdot 4$ in base 5, one must solve $12 = 5a + b$ where $a, b < 5$. Although this is typically done mentally, algebraic reasoning is required to complete this base 5 multiplication table.

×	0	1	2	3	4
0	0	0	0	0	0
1	0	1	2	3	4
2	0	2	4	11	13
3	0	3	11	14	22
4	0	4	13	22	31

Figure 4.17

The number line includes a representation of $4_{\text{five}} \times 3_{\text{five}} = 22_{\text{five}}$ using the repeated-addition approach. (All numerals in the multiplication table and number line are written in base five with subscripts omitted.)

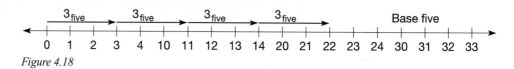

Figure 4.18

Example 4.12   Calculate $43_{\text{five}} \times 123_{\text{five}}$ using the following methods.

SOLUTION

a. Lattice Method

        1   2   3 $_{\text{five}}$

1 | 0/4 | 1/3 | 2/2 | 4

1 | 0/3 | 1/1 | 1/4 | 3 $_{\text{five}}$

     4   4   4 $_{\text{five}}$

b. Intermediate Algorithm

$$
\begin{array}{rl}
123_{\text{five}} & \\
\times\ 43_{\text{five}} & \\
\hline
14 & 3 \cdot 3 \\
110 & 3 \cdot 20 \\
300 & 3 \cdot 100 \\
220 & 40 \cdot 3 \\
1300 & 40 \cdot 20 \\
4000 & 40 \cdot 100 \\
\hline
11444_{\text{five}} &
\end{array}
$$

c. Standard Algorithm

$$
\begin{array}{r}
123_{\text{five}} \\
\times 43_{\text{five}} \\
\hline
424 \\
1102 \\
\hline
11444_{\text{five}}
\end{array}
$$

Notice how efficient the lattice method is. Also, instead of using the multiplication table, you could find single-digit products using repeated addition and thinking strategies. For example, you could find $4_{\text{five}} \times 2_{\text{five}}$ as follows.

$$4_{\text{five}} \times 2_{\text{five}} = 2_{\text{five}} \times 4_{\text{five}} = 4_{\text{five}} + 4_{\text{five}} = 4_{\text{five}} + (1 + 3)_{\text{five}}$$
$$= (4 + 1)_{\text{five}} + 3_{\text{five}} = 13_{\text{five}}$$

Although this may look like it would take a lot of time, it would go quickly mentally, especially if you imagine base five pieces.

✔ **Check for Understanding:** Exercise/Problem Set A #12–14

Division   As shown in Section 3.2, division can be displayed using a number line. Figure 4.19 displays $23_{\text{five}} \div 4_{\text{five}}$ using the repeated subtraction approach. (All numerals below the number line without subscripts are assumed to be base 5.)

Figure 4.19

Figure 4.19 shows that $23_{\text{five}} \div 4_{\text{five}}$ has a quotient of 3_{five} with a remainder of 1_{five}.

Doing long division in other bases points out the difficulties of learning this algorithm and, especially, the need to become proficient at approximating multiples of numbers.

Example 4.13   Find the quotient and remainder for $1443_{\text{five}} \div 34_{\text{five}}$ using the following methods.

SOLUTION
a. Scaffold Method

$$
\begin{array}{r}
34_{\text{five}}\overline{)1443_{\text{five}}} \\
-\ 1230 \qquad 20_{\text{five}} \\
\hline
213 \\
-\ 212 \qquad 3_{\text{five}} \\
\hline
1 \qquad 23_{\text{five}}
\end{array}
$$

b. Standard Long-Division Algorithm

$$
\begin{array}{r}
23_{\text{five}} \\
34_{\text{five}}\overline{)1443_{\text{five}}} \\
-\ 123 \qquad (2_{\text{five}} \times 34_{\text{five}}) \\
\hline
213 \\
-\ 212 \qquad (3_{\text{five}} \times 34_{\text{five}}) \\
\hline
1
\end{array}
$$

Quotient: 23_{five}
Remainder: 1_{five}
In the scaffold method, the first estimate, namely 20_{five}, was selected because $2_{\text{five}} \times 3_{\text{five}}$ is 11_{five}, which is less than 14_{five}.   ∎

In summary, doing computations in other number bases can provide insights into how computational difficulties arise, whereas our own familiarity and competence with our algorithms in base ten tend to mask the trouble spots that children face.

✔ **Check for Understanding:** Exercise/Problem Set A #15–18

MATHEMATICAL MORSEL

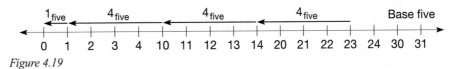

George Parker Bidder (1806–1878), who lived in Devonshire, England, was blessed with an incredible memory as well as being a calculating prodigy. When he was 10 he was read a number backward and he immediately gave the number back in its correct form. An hour later, he repeated the original number, which was

2,563,721,987,653,461,598,746,231,905,607,541,127,975,231.

Furthermore, his brother memorized the entire Bible and could give the chapter and verse of any quoted text. Also, one of Bidder's sons could multiply 15-digit numbers in his head.

Section 4.3	EXERCISE / PROBLEM SET A

EXERCISES

1. Create a number line to illustrate the following operations.
   a. $12_{four} + 3_{four}$ **b.** $4_{six} + 15_{six}$

2. Use multibase blocks to illustrate each of the following base four addition problems. The Chapter 4 eManipulative activity *Multibase Blocks* on our Web site may be helpful in the solution process.
   a. $1_{four} + 2_{four}$ **b.** $11_{four} + 23_{four}$
   c. $212_{four} + 113_{four}$ **d.** $2023_{four} + 3330_{four}$

3. Use bundling sticks or chip abacus for the appropriate base to illustrate the following problems.
   a. $41_{six} + 33_{six}$
   b. $555_{seven} + 66_{seven}$
   c. $3030_{four} + 322_{four}$

4. Write out a base six addition table. Use your table and the intermediate algorithm to compute the following sums.
   a. $32_{six} + 23_{six}$ **b.** $45_{six} + 34_{six}$
   c. $145_{six} + 541_{six}$ **d.** $355_{six} + 211_{six}$

5. Use the lattice method to compute the following sums.
   a. $46_{seven} + 13_{seven}$ **b.** $13_{four} + 23_{four}$

6. Use the standard algorithm to compute the following sums.
   a. $213_{five} + 433_{five}$ **b.** $716_{eight} + 657_{eight}$

7. Create a number line to illustrate the following operations.
   a. $12_{four} - 3_{four}$ **b.** $14_{six} - 5_{six}$

8. Use multibase blocks to illustrate each of the following base four subtraction problems. The Chapter 4 eManipulative activity *Multibase Blocks* on our Web site may be helpful in the solution process.
   a. $31_{four} - 12_{four}$ **b.** $123_{four} - 32_{four}$
   c. $1102_{four} - 333_{four}$

9. Use bundling sticks or chip abacus for the appropriate base to illustrate the following problems.
   a. $41_{six} - 33_{six}$ **b.** $555_{seven} - 66_{seven}$
   c. $3030_{four} - 102_{four}$

10. Solve the following problems using both the standard algorithm and the subtract-from-the-base algorithm.
    a. $36_{eight} - 17_{eight}$ **b.** $1010_{two} - 101_{two}$
    c. $32_{four} - 13_{four}$

11. Find $10201_{three} - 2122_{three}$ using "adding the complement." What is the complement of a base three number?

12. Create a number line to illustrate the following operations.
    a. $2_{four} \times 13_{four}$ **b.** $3_{six} \times 5_{six}$

13. Sketch the rectangular array of multibase pieces and find the products of the following problems.
    a. $23_{four} \times 3_{four}$
    b. $23_{five} \times 12_{five}$

14. Solve the following problems using the lattice method, an intermediate algorithm, and the standard algorithm.
    a. 31_{four} **b.** 43_{five} **c.** 22_{four}
    $\times \underline{2_{four}}$ $\times \underline{3_{five}}$ $\times \underline{3_{four}}$

15. Create a number line to illustrate the following operations.
    a. $22_{four} \div 3_{four}$ **b.** $24_{six} \div 5_{six}$

16. Use the scaffold method of division to compute the following numbers. (*Hint:* Write out a multiplication table in the appropriate base to help you out.)
    a. $22_{six} \div 2_{six}$ **b.** $4044_{seven} \div 51_{seven}$
    c. $13002_{four} \div 33_{four}$

17. Solve the following problems using the missing-factor definition of division. (*Hint:* Use a multiplication table for the appropriate base.)
    a. $21_{four} \div 3_{four}$ **b.** $23_{six} \div 3_{six}$
    c. $24_{eight} \div 5_{eight}$

18. Sketch how to use base seven blocks to illustrate the operation $534_{seven} \div 4_{seven}$.

PROBLEMS

19. 345 _____ + 122 _____ = 511 _____ is an addition problem done in base _____.

20. Jane has $10 more than Bill, Bill has $17 more than Tricia, and Tricia has $21 more than Steve. If the total amount of all their money is $115, how much money does each have?

21. Without using a calculator, determine which of the five numbers is a perfect square. There is exactly one.

22. What single number can be added separately to 100 and 164 to make them both perfect square numbers?

39,037,066,087
39,037,066,084
39,037,066,082
38,336,073,623
38,414,432,028

23. What is wrong with the following problem in base four? Explain.

$$1022_{four}$$
$$+ \ 413_{four}$$

24. Write out the steps you would go through to mentally subtract 234_{five} from 421_{five} using the standard subtraction algorithm.

Section 4.3 **EXERCISE / PROBLEM SET B**

EXERCISES

1. Create a number line to illustrate the following operations.
  a. $12_{seven} + 6_{seven}$ **b.** $4_{eight} + 16_{eight}$

2. Use multibase blocks to illustrate each of the following base five addition problems. The Chapter 4 eManipulative activity *Multibase Blocks* on our Web site may be helpful in the solution process.
  a. $12_{five} + 20_{five}$ **b.** $24_{five} + 13_{five}$
  c. $342_{five} + 13_{five}$ **d.** $2134_{five} + 1330_{five}$

3. Use bundling sticks or chip abacus for the appropriate base to illustrate the following problems.
  a. $32_{four} + 33_{four}$ **b.** $54_{eight} + 55_{eight}$
  c. $265_{nine} + 566_{nine}$

4. Use an intermediate algorithm to compute the following sums.
  a. $78_{nine} + 65_{nine}$ **b.** $TE_{twelve} + EE_{twelve}$

5. Use the lattice method to compute the following sums.
  a. $54_{six} + 34_{six}$
  b. $1T8_{eleven} + 499_{eleven}$

6. Use the standard algorithm to compute the following sums.
  a. $79_{twelve} + 85_{twelve}$ **b.** $T1_{eleven} + 99_{eleven}$

7. Create a number line to illustrate the following operations.
  a. $12_{seven} - 3_{seven}$ **b.** $14_{eight} - 5_{eight}$

8. Use multibase blocks to illustrate each of the following base five subtraction problems. The Chapter 4 eManipulative activity *Multibase Blocks* on our Web site may be helpful in the solution process.
  a. $32_{five} - 14_{five}$ **b.** $214_{five} - 32_{five}$
  c. $301_{five} - 243_{five}$

9. Use bundling sticks or chip abacus for the appropriate base to illustrate the following problems.
  a. $123_{five} - 24_{five}$ **b.** $253_{eight} - 76_{eight}$
  c. $1001_{two} - 110_{two}$

10. Solve the following problems using both the standard algorithm and the subtract-from-the-base algorithm.
  a. $45_{seven} - 36_{seven}$ **b.** $99_{twelve} - 7T_{twelve}$
  c. $100_{eight} - 77_{eight}$

11. Find $1001010_{two} - 111001_{two}$ by "adding the complement."

12. Create a number line to illustrate the following operations.
  a. $2_{seven} \times 13_{seven}$ **b.** $3_{eight} \times 5_{eight}$

13. Sketch the rectangular array of multibase pieces and find the products of the following problems.
  a. $32_{six} \times 13_{six}$ **b.** $34_{seven} \times 21_{seven}$

14. Solve the following problems using the lattice method, an intermediate algorithm, and the standard algorithm.

  a. 11011_{two} **b.** 43_{twelve} **c.** 66_{seven}
  $\times \ \underline{1101_{two}}$ $\times \ \underline{23_{twelve}}$ $\times \ \underline{66_{seven}}$

15. Create a number line to illustrate the following operations.
  a. $22_{seven} \div 3_{seven}$ **b.** $23_{eight} \div 5_{eight}$

16. Use the scaffold method of division to compute the following numbers. (*Hint:* Write out a multiplication table in the appropriate base to help you out.)
  a. $14_{five} \div 3_{five}$ **b.** $2134_{six} \div 14_{six}$
  c. $61245_{seven} \div 354_{seven}$

17. Solve the following problems using the missing-factor definition of division. (*Hint:* Use a multiplication table for the appropriate base.)
  a. $42_{seven} \div 5_{seven}$ **b.** $62_{nine} \div 7_{nine}$
  c. $92_{twelve} \div E_{twelve}$

18. Sketch how to use base four blocks to illustrate the operation $3021_{four} \div 11_{four}$.

PROBLEMS

19. $320 \underline{\quad} - 42 \underline{\quad} = 256 \underline{\quad}$ is a correct subtraction problem in what base?

20. Betty has three times as much money as her brother Tom. If each of them spends $1.50 to see a movie, Betty will have nine times as much money left over as Tom. How much money does each have before going to the movie?

21. To stimulate his son in the pursuit of mathematics, a math professor offered to pay his son $8 for every equation correctly solved and to fine him $5 for every incorrect solution. At the end of 26 problems, neither owed any money to the other. How many did the boy solve correctly?

22. Prove: If n is a whole number and n^2 is odd, then n is odd. (*Hint:* Use indirect reasoning. Either n is even or it is odd. Assume that n is even and reach a contradiction.)

Analyzing Student Thinking

23. Antolina asks why they have to be doing algorithms in other bases. How should you respond?

24. Ralph asks if it is okay to use the base 5 addition table when subtracting in base 5 or does he have to memorize the table first?

25. You ask a student to make up a subtraction problem in base four. The student writes the following:

$$1022_{four}$$
$$- \ 413_{four}$$

Is this a reasonable base four subtraction problem? Explain.

26. When doing a multiplication problem in base 5, Veronica uses the intermediate algorithm. Geoff doesn't want to use it because it has too many steps. How should you respond in this situation?

27. One of your students says that she is having difficulty doing division in base 5 using the standard algorithm. Suggest how you might help the student.

28. When Sherry did the subtraction problem $342_{six} - 135_{six}$, she "borrowed" from the 4 to get 12 in the ones columns as shown.

$$3 \ \overset{3}{\cancel{4}} \ \overset{1}{2}_{six}$$
$$- \ 1 \ 3 \ 5_{six}$$

She got confused when she subtracted $12 - 5$ and got 7 because the digit "7" is not in base 6. However, when she converted 7 to 11_{six} she didn't know what to do with both ones. Where is Sherry's misunderstanding and how would you help her clarify her thinking?

Problems Relating to the NCTM Standards and Curriculum Focal Points

1. The Focal Points for Grade 1 state "Developing an understanding of whole number relationships, including grouping in tens and ones." Explain how working with algorithms in other bases can help in developing a better understanding of "whole number relationships" and "grouping in tens and ones."

2. The Focal Points for Grade 2 state "Developing quick recall of addition facts and related subtraction facts and fluency with multidigit addition and subtraction." Some of the multidigit addition problems in this section suggested that you complete an addition table first. How is this suggestion related to this focal point?

3. The Focal Points for Grade 4 state "Developing quick recall of multiplication facts and related division facts and fluency with whole number multiplication." Explain how the "quick recall" of multiplication facts influences a student's ability to be fluent in whole number multiplication.

END OF CHAPTER MATERIAL

Solution of Initial Problem

The whole numbers 1 through 9 can be used once, each arranged in a 3×3 square array so that the sum of the numbers in each of the rows, columns, and diagonals is 15. Show that 1 cannot be in one of the corners.

Strategy: Use Indirect Reasoning

Suppose that 1 could be in a corner as shown in the following figure. Each row, column, and diagonal containing 1 must have a sum of 15. This means that there must be three pairs of numbers among 2 through 9 whose sum is 14. Hence the sum of all three pairs is 42. However, the largest six numbers—9, 8, 7, 6, 5, and 4—have a sum of 39, so that it is impossible to find three pairs whose sum is 14. Therefore, it is impossible to have 1 in a corner.

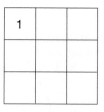

Additional Problems Where the Strategy "Use Indirect Reasoning" Is Useful

1. If x represents a whole number and $x^2 + 2x + 1$ is even, prove that x cannot be even.

2. If n is a whole number and n^4 is even, then prove that n is even.

3. For whole numbers x and y, if $x^2 + y^2$ is a square, then prove that x and y cannot both be odd.

People in Mathematics

Grace Brewster Murray Hopper (1906–1992)
Grace Brewster Murray Hopper recalled that as a young girl, she disassembled one of her family's alarm clocks. When she was unable to reassemble the parts, she dismantled another clock to see how those parts fit together. This process continued until she had seven clocks in pieces. This attitude of exploration foreshadowed her innovations in computer programming. Trained in mathematics, Hopper worked with some of the first computers and invented the business language COBOL. After World War II she was active in the Navy, where her experience in computing and programming began. In 1985 she was promoted to the rank of rear admiral. Known for her common sense and spirit of invention, she kept a clock on her desk that ran (and kept time) counterclockwise. Whenever someone argued that a job must be done in the traditional manner, she just pointed to the clock. Also, to encourage risk taking, she once said, "I do have a maxim—I teach it to all youngsters: A ship in port is safe, but that's not what ships are built for."

John Kemeny (1926–1992)
John Kemeny was born in Budapest, Hungary. His family immigrated to the United States, and he attended high school in New York City. He entered Princeton where he studied mathematics and philosophy. As an undergraduate, he took a year off to work on the Manhattan Project. While he and Tom Kurtz were teaching in the mathematics department at Dartmouth in the mid-1960s, they created BASIC, an elementary computer language. Kemeny made Dartmouth a leader in the educational uses of computers in his era. Kemeny's first faculty position was in philosophy. "The only good job offer I got was from the Princeton philosophy department," he said, explaining that his degree was in logic, and he studied philosophy as a hobby in college. Kemeny had the distinction of having served as Einstein's mathematical assistant while still a young graduate student at Princeton. Einstein's assistants were always mathematicians. Contrary to popular belief, Einstein did need help in mathematics. He was very good at it, but he was not an up-to-date research mathematician.

CHAPTER REVIEW

Review the following terms and exercises to determine which require learning or relearning—page numbers are provided for easy reference.

SECTION 4.1 Mental Math, Estimation, and Calculators

VOCABULARY/NOTATION

EXERCISES

1. Calculate the following mentally, and name the property(ies) you used.

a. $97 + 78$ **b.** $267 \div 3$

c. $(16 \times 7) \times 25$ **d.** $16 \times 9 - 6 \times 9$

e. 92×15 **f.** 17×99

g. $720 \div 5$ **h.** $81 - 39$

2. Estimate using the techniques given.

a. Range: $157 + 371$

b. One-column front-end: 847×989

c. Front-end with adjustment: $753 + 639$

d. Compatible numbers: 23×56

3. Round as indicated.

a. Up to the nearest 100: 47,943

b. To the nearest 10: 4751

c. Down to the nearest 10: 576

4. Insert parentheses (wherever necessary) to produce the indicated results.

a. $3 + 7 \times 5 = 38$

b. $7 \times 5 - 2 + 3 = 24$

c. $15 + 48 \div 3 \times 4 = 19$

5. Fill in the following without using a calculator.

a. $5 \boxed{+} 2 \boxed{\times} 3 \boxed{=}$ [_____]

b. $8 \boxed{-} 6 \boxed{\div} 3 \boxed{=}$ [_____]

c. $2 \boxed{\times} \boxed{(} 3 \boxed{+} 2 \boxed{)} \boxed{=}$ [_____]

d. $2 \boxed{y^x} 3 \boxed{=}$ [_____]

e. $3 \boxed{\text{STO}} 7 \boxed{+} \boxed{\text{RCL}} \boxed{=}$ [_____]

f. $3 \boxed{\times} 5 \boxed{=} \boxed{\text{STO}} 8 \boxed{\div} 2 \boxed{=} \boxed{+} \boxed{\text{RCL}} \boxed{=}$ [_____]

SECTION 4.2 Written Algorithms for Whole-Number Operations

VOCABULARY/NOTATION

Algorithm   150
Standard addition algorithm   150
Lattice method for addition   151
Standard subtraction algorithm   152

Subtract-from-the-base algorithm   153
Standard multiplication
    algorithm   154
Lattice method for multiplication   156

Long division using base ten
    blocks   157
Scaffold method for division   159
Standard algorithm for division   160

EXERCISES

1. Find $837 + 145$ using

a. the lattice method.

b. an intermediate algorithm.

c. the standard algorithm.

2. Find $451 - 279$ using

a. the standard algorithm.

b. a nonstandard algorithm.

3. Find 72×43 using

a. an intermediate algorithm.

b. the standard algorithm.

c. the lattice method.

4. Find $253 \div 27$ using

a. the scaffold method.   **b.** an intermediate algorithm.

c. the standard algorithm.   **d.** a calculator.

SECTION 4.3 Algorithms in Other Bases

VOCABULARY/NOTATION

Operations in base five   170

EXERCISES

1. Find $413_{\text{six}} + 254_{\text{six}}$ using

a. the lattice method.

b. an intermediate algorithm.

c. the standard algorithm.

2. Find $234_{\text{seven}} - 65_{\text{seven}}$ using

a. the standard algorithm.

b. a nonstandard algorithm.

3. Find $21_{\text{four}} \times 32_{\text{four}}$ using

a. an intermediate algorithm.

b. the standard algorithm.

c. the lattice method.

4. Find $213_{\text{five}} \div 41_{\text{five}}$ using

a. repeated subtraction   **b.** the scaffold method.

c. the standard algorithm.

CHAPTER TEST

KNOWLEDGE

1. True or false?

   a. An algorithm is a technique that is used exclusively for doing algebra.

   b. Intermediate algorithms are helpful because they require less writing than their corresponding standard algorithms.

   c. There is only one computational algorithm for each of the four operations: addition, subtraction, multiplication, and division.

   d. Approximating answers to computations by rounding is useful because it increases the *speed* of computation.

SKILL

2. Compute each of the following using an intermediate algorithm.

   a. $376 + 594$ **b.** 56×73

3. Compute the following using the lattice method.

   a. $568 + 493$ **b.** 37×196

4. Compute the following mentally. Then, explain how you did it.

   a. $54 + 93 + 16 + 47$ **b.** $9223 - 1998$

   c. $3497 - 1362$ **d.** 25×52

5. Find $7496 \div 32$ using the standard division algorithm, and check your results using a calculator.

6. Estimate the following using (i) one-column front-end, (ii) range estimation, (iii) front-end with adjustment, and (iv) rounding to the nearest 100.

   a. $546 + 971 + 837 + 320$

   b. 731×589

UNDERSTANDING

7. Compute 32×21 using expanded form; that is, continue the following.

$$32 \times 21 = (30 + 2)(20 + 1) = \ldots$$

8. In the standard multiplication algorithm, why do we "shift over one to the left" as illustrated in the 642 in the following problem?

$$
\begin{array}{r}
321 \\
\times\ \ 23 \\
\hline
963 \\
+\ 642\ \ \\
\hline
\end{array}
$$

9. To check an addition problem where one has "added down the column," one can "add up the column." Which properties guarantee that the sum should be the same in both directions?

10. Sketch how a chip abacus could be used to perform the following operation.

$$374 + 267$$

11. Use an appropriate intermediate algorithm to compute the following quotient and remainder.

$$7261 \div 43$$

12. Sketch how base ten blocks could be used to find the quotient and remainder of the following.

$$538 \div 4$$

13. Sketch how base four blocks could be used to find the following difference.

$$32_{\text{four}} - 13_{\text{four}}$$

14. Sketch how a chip abacus could be used to find the following sum.

$$278_{\text{nine}} + 37_{\text{nine}}$$

15. Sketch how base ten blocks could be used to model the following operations and explain how the manipulations of the blocks relate to the standard algorithm.

   a. $357 + 46$ **b.** $253 - 68$ **c.** $789 \div 5$

16. Compute 492×37 using an intermediate algorithm and a standard algorithm. Explain how the distributive property is used in each of these algorithms.

17. State some of the advantages and disadvantages of the standard algorithm versus the lattice algorithm for multiplication.

18. State some of the advantages and disadvantages of the standard subtraction algorithm versus the subtract-from the-base algorithm.

19. Show how to find 17×23 on the following grid paper and explain how the solution on the grid paper can be related to the intermediate algorithm for multiplication.

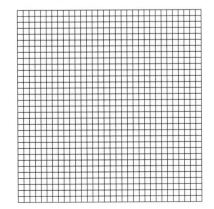

PROBLEM SOLVING/APPLICATION

20. If each different letter represents a different digit, find the number "HE" such that $(HE)^2 = SHE$. (NOTE: "HE" means $10 \cdot H + E$ due to place value.)

21. Find values for a, b, and c in the lattice multiplication problem shown. Also find the product.

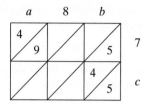

22. Find digits represented by A, B, C, and D so that the following operation is correct.

$$\begin{array}{r} ABA \\ + \underline{BAB} \\ CDDC \end{array}$$

Number Theory

FOCUS ON **Famous Unsolved Problems**

Number theory provides a rich source of intriguing problems. Interestingly, many problems in number theory are easily understood, but still have never been solved. Most of these problems are statements or conjectures that have never been proven right or wrong. The most famous "unsolved" problem, known as Fermat's Last Theorem, is named after Pierre de Fermat who is pictured below. It states "There are no nonzero whole numbers *a*, *b*, *c*, where $a^n + b^n = c^n$, for *n* a whole number greater than two."

Fermat left a note in the margin of a book saying that he did not have room to write up a proof of what is now called Fermat's Last Theorem. However, it remained an unsolved problem for over 350 years because mathematicians were unable to prove it. In 1993, Andrew Wiles, an English mathematician on the Princeton faculty, presented a "proof" at a conference at Cambridge University. However, there was a hole in his proof. Happily, Wiles and Richard Taylor produced a valid proof in 1995, which followed from work done by Serre, Mazur, and Ribet beginning in 1985.

The following list contains several such problems that are still unsolved. If you can solve any of them, you will surely become famous, at least among mathematicians.

1. **Goldbach's conjecture.** *Every even number greater than 4 can be expressed as the sum of two odd primes.* For example, 6 = 3 + 3, 8 = 3 + 5, 10 = 5 + 5, 12 = 5 + 7, and so on. It is interesting to note that if Goldbach's conjecture is true, then every odd number greater than 7 can be written as the sum of three odd primes.

2. **Twin prime conjecture.** *There is an infinite number of pairs of primes whose difference is two.* For example, (3, 5), (5, 7), and (11, 13) are such prime pairs. Notice that 3, 5, and 7 are three prime numbers where 5 − 3 = 2 and 7 − 5 = 2. It can easily be shown that this is the only such triple of primes.

3. **Odd perfect number conjecture.** *There is no odd perfect number; that is, there is no odd number that is the sum of its proper factors.* For example, 6 = 1 + 2 + 3; hence 6 is a perfect number. It has been shown that the even perfect numbers are all of the form $2^{p-1}(2p - 1)$, where 2^{p-1} is a prime.

4. **Ulam's conjecture.** *If a nonzero whole number is even, divide it by 2. If a nonzero whole number is odd, multiply it by 3 and add 1. If this process is applied repeatedly to each answer, eventually you will arrive at 1.* For example, the number 7 yields this sequence of numbers: 7, 22, 11, 34, 17, 52, 26, 13, 40, 20, 10, 5, 16, 8, 4, 2, 1. Interestingly, there is a whole number less than 30 that requires at least 100 steps before it arrives at 1. It can be seen that 2^n requires *n* steps to arrive at 1. Hence one can find numbers with as many steps (finitely many) as one wishes.

Problem-Solving Strategies

1. Guess and Test
2. Draw a Picture
3. Use a Variable
4. Look for a Pattern
5. Make a List
6. Solve a Simpler Problem
7. Draw a Diagram
8. Use Direct Reasoning
9. Use Indirect Reasoning
10. **Use Properties of Numbers**

STRATEGY 10
Use Properties of Numbers

Understanding the intrinsic nature of numbers is often helpful in solving problems. For example, knowing that the sum of two even numbers is even and that an odd number squared is odd may simplify checking some computations. The solution of the initial problem will seem to be impossible to a naive problem solver who attempts to solve it using, say, the Guess and Test strategy. On the other hand, the solution is immediate for one who understands the concept of divisibility of numbers.

INITIAL PROBLEM

A major fast-food chain held a contest to promote sales. With each purchase a customer was given a card with a whole number less than 100 on it. A $100 prize was given to any person who presented cards whose numbers totaled 100. The following are several typical cards. Can you find a winning combination?

$$\boxed{3} \quad \boxed{9} \quad \boxed{12} \quad \boxed{15} \quad \boxed{18} \quad \boxed{27} \quad \boxed{51} \quad \boxed{72} \quad \boxed{84}$$

Can you suggest how the contest could be structured so that there would be at most 1000 winners throughout the country? (*Hint:* What whole number divides evenly in each sum?)

CLUES

The Use Properties of Numbers strategy may be appropriate when

- Special types of numbers, such as odds, evens, primes, and so on, are involved.
- A problem can be simplified by using certain properties.
- A problem involves lots of computation.

A solution of this Initial Problem is on page 210.

INTRODUCTION

Number theory is a branch of mathematics that is devoted primarily to the study of the set of counting numbers. In this chapter, those aspects of the counting numbers that are useful in simplifying computations, especially those with fractions (Chapter 6), are studied. The topics central to the elementary curriculum that are covered in this chapter include primes, composites, and divisibility tests as well as the notions of greatest common factor and least common multiple.

Key Concepts from NCTM Curriculum Focal Points

- **GRADE 3**: Developing understandings of multiplication and division and strategies for basic multiplication facts and related division facts.
- **GRADE 4**: Developing quick recall of multiplication facts and related division facts and fluency with whole number multiplication.
- **GRADE 5**: Developing an understanding of and fluency with addition and subtraction of fractions and decimals.

5.1   PRIMES, COMPOSITES, AND TESTS FOR DIVISIBILITY

STARTING POINT

On a piece of paper, sketch all of the possible rectangles that can be made up of exactly 12 squares. An example of a rectangle consisting of 6 squares is shown at the right.

Repeat these sketches for 13 squares. Why can more rectangles be made with 12 squares than with 13 squares? How are the dimensions of the rectangles related to the number of squares?

Primes and Composites

Prime numbers are building blocks for the counting numbers 1, 2, 3, 4, ...

NCTM Standard
All students should use factors, multiples, prime factorization, and relatively prime numbers to solve problems.

> **DEFINITION**
>
> ### *Prime and Composite Numbers*
>
> A counting number with exactly two different factors is called a **prime number**, or a **prime**. A counting number with more than two factors is called a **composite number**, or a **composite**.

For example, 2, 3, 5, 7, 11 are primes, since they have only themselves and 1 as factors; 4, 6, 8, 9, 10 are composites, since they each have more than two factors; 1 is neither prime nor composite, since 1 is its only factor.

Reflection from Research
Talking, drawing, and writing about types of numbers such as factors, primes, and composites, allows students to explore and explain their ideas about generalizations and patterns dealing with these types of numbers (Whitin & Whitin, 2002).

An algorithm used to find primes is called the **Sieve of Eratosthenes** (Figure 5.1).

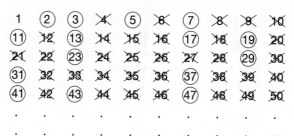

Figure 5.1

The directions for using this procedure are as follows: Skip the number 1. Circle 2 and cross out every second number after 2. Circle 3 and cross out every third number after 3 (even if it had been crossed out before). Continue this procedure with 5, 7, and each succeeding number that is not crossed out. The circled numbers will be the primes and the crossed-out numbers will be the composites, since prime factors cause them to be crossed out. Again, notice that 1 is neither prime nor composite.

Composite numbers have more than two factors and can be expressed as the product of two smaller numbers. Figure 5.2 shows how a composite can be expressed as the product of smaller numbers using **factor trees**.

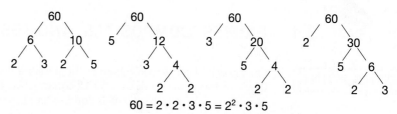

$$60 = 2 \cdot 2 \cdot 3 \cdot 5 = 2^2 \cdot 3 \cdot 5$$

Figure 5.2

Notice that 60 was expressed as the product of two factors in several different ways. However, when we kept factoring until we reached primes, each method led us to the same **prime factorization**, namely $60 = 2 \cdot 2 \cdot 3 \cdot 5$. This example illustrates the following important results.

THEOREM

Fundamental Theorem of Arithmetic

Each composite number can be expressed as the product of primes in exactly one way (except for the order of the factors).

Algebraic Reasoning
To factor an expression such as $x^2 - 5x - 24$, it is important to be able to factor 24 into pairs of factors.

Example 5.1   Express each number as the product of primes.

a. 84   **b.** 180   **c.** 324

SOLUTION

a. $84 = 4 \times 21 = 2 \cdot 2 \cdot 3 \cdot 7 = 2^2 \cdot 3 \cdot 7$
b. $180 = 10 \times 18 = 2 \cdot 5 \cdot 2 \cdot 3 \cdot 3 = 2^2 \cdot 3^2 \cdot 5$
c. $324 = 4 \times 81 = 2 \cdot 2 \cdot 3 \cdot 3 \cdot 3 \cdot 3 = 2^2 \cdot 3^4$

■

LESSON 1

Factors and Multiples

OBJECTIVE: Find factors and multiples using arrays and number lines.

Learn

A factor is a number multiplied by another number to find a product. Every whole number greater than 1 has at least two factors, that number and 1.

$$18 = 1 \times 18 \qquad 7 = 7 \times 1 \qquad 342 = 1 \times 342$$
$$\uparrow \quad \uparrow$$
factor factor

Many numbers can be broken into factors in different ways.

$$16 = 1 \times 16 \qquad 16 = 4 \times 4 \qquad 16 = 2 \times 8$$

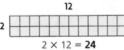

Activity Materials ■ square tiles ■ grid paper

Make arrays to show all the factors of 24.

- Use all 24 tiles to make an array. Record the array on grid paper. Write the factors shown by the array.

12
2

$2 \times 12 = 24$
Factors: 2, 12

- Make as many different arrays as you can with 24 tiles. Record the arrays on grid paper and write the factors shown.

8
3

$3 \times 8 = 24$
Factors: 3, 8

6
4

$4 \times 6 = 24$
Factors: 4, 6

24
1

$1 \times 24 = 24$
Factors: 1, 24

So, the factors of 24 listed from least to greatest are 1, 2, 3, 4, 6, 8, 12, and 24.

- Can you arrange the tiles in each array another way and show the same factors? Explain.

ERROR ALERT

Don't forget to list 1 and the number itself as factors.

372

Next, we will study shortcuts that will help us find prime factors. When division yields a zero remainder, as in the case of $15 \div 3$, for example, we say that 15 is divisible by 3, 3 is a divisor of 15, or 3 divides 15. In general, we have the following definition.

Children's Literature
www.wiley.com/college/musser
See "The Doorbell Rang"
by Pat Hutchins.

DEFINITION

Divides

Let a and b be any whole numbers with $a \neq 0$. We say that a **divides** b, and write $a \mid b$, if and only if there is a whole number x such that $ax = b$. The symbol $a \nmid b$ means that a **does not divide** b.

In words, a divides b if and only if a is a factor of b. When a divides b, we can also say that a is a **divisor** of b, a is a **factor** of b, b is a **multiple** of a, and b **is divisible by** a.

We can also say that $a \mid b$ if b objects can be arranged in a rectangular array with a rows. For example, $4 \mid 12$ because 12 dots can be placed in a rectangular array with 4 rows, as shown in Figure 5.3(a). On the other hand, $5 \nmid 12$ because if 12 dots are placed in an array with 5 rows, a rectangular array cannot be formed [Figure 5.3(b)].

Does not make an entire column.

(a)   (b)

Figure 5.3

Algebraic Reasoning
Each time we ask ourselves if $a \mid b$, we are solving the equation $ax = b$. For example, we use algebraic reasoning when we decide if a statement like $7 \mid 91$ is true because we are looking for a whole number x that will make $7x = 91$ true.

| **Example 5.2** | Determine whether the following are true or false. Explain. |

a. $3 \mid 12$.   **b.** 8 is a divisor of 96.
c. 216 is a multiple of 6.   **d.** 51 is divisible by 17.
e. 7 divides 34.   **f.** $(2^2 \cdot 3) \mid (2^3 \cdot 3^2 \cdot 5)$.

SOLUTION
a. True. $3 \mid 12$, since $3 \cdot 4 = 12$.
b. True. 8 is a divisor of 96, since $8 \cdot 12 = 96$.
c. True. 216 is a multiple of 6, since $6 \cdot 36 = 216$.
d. True. 51 is divisible by 17, since $17 \cdot 3 = 51$.
e. False. $7 \nmid 34$, since there is no whole number x such that $7x = 34$.
f. True. $(2^2 \cdot 3) \mid (2^3 \cdot 3^2 \cdot 5)$, since $(2^2 \cdot 3)(2 \cdot 3 \cdot 5) = (2^3 \cdot 3^2 \cdot 5)$.   ∎

 Check for Understanding: Exercise/Problem Set A #1–6

Reflection from Research
When students are allowed to use calculators to generate data and are encouraged to examine the data for patterns, they often discover divisibility rules on their own (Bezuszka, 1985).

Tests for Divisibility

Some simple tests can be employed to help determine the factors of numbers. For example, which of the numbers 27, 45, 38, 70, and 111, 110 are divisible by 2, 5, or 10? If your answers were found simply by looking at the ones digits, you were applying tests for divisibility. The tests for divisibility by 2, 5, and 10 are stated next.

Children's Literature
www.wiley.com/college/musser
See "The Great Divide" by
Dayle Ann Dodds.

THEOREM

Tests for Divisibility by 2, 5, and 10

A number is divisible by 2 if and only if its ones digit is 0, 2, 4, 6, or 8.
A number is divisible by 5 if and only if its ones digit is 0 or 5.
A number is divisible by 10 if and only if its ones digit is 0.

Now notice that $3 \mid 27$ and $3 \mid 9$. It is also true that $3 \mid (27 + 9)$ and that $3 \mid (27 - 9)$. This is an instance of the following theorem.

THEOREM

Let a, m, n, and k be whole numbers where $a \neq 0$.

a. If $a \mid m$ and $a \mid n$, then $a \mid (m + n)$.
b. If $a \mid m$ and $a \mid n$, then $a \mid (m - n)$ for $m \geq n$.
c. If $a \mid m$, then $a \mid km$.

PROOF

a. If $a \mid m$, then $ax = m$ for some whole number x.
    If $a \mid n$, then $ay = n$ for some whole number y.
Therefore, adding the respective sides of the two equations, we have $ax + ay = m + n$, or

$$a (x + y) = m + n.$$

Since $x + y$ is a whole number, this last equation implies that $a \mid (m + n)$. Part (b) can be proved simply by replacing the plus signs with minus signs in this discussion. The proof of (c) follows from the definition of divides. ∎

Part (a) in the preceding theorem can also be illustrated using the rectangular array description of *divides*. In Figure 5.4, $3 \mid 9$ is represented by a rectangle with 3 rows of 3 blue dots. $3 \mid 12$ is represented by a rectangle of 3 rows of 4 black dots. By placing the 9 blue dots and the 12 black dots together, there are $(9 + 12)$ dots arranged in 3 rows, so $3 \mid (9 + 12)$.

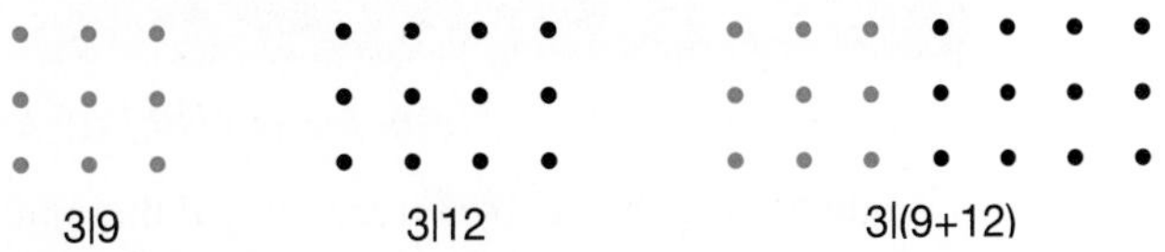

3|9   3|12   3|(9+12)
Figure 5.4

Using this result, we can verify the tests for divisibility by 2, 5, and 10. The main idea of the proof of the test for 2 is now given for an arbitrary three-digit number (the same idea holds for any number of digits).

Let $r = a \cdot 10^2 + b \cdot 10 + c$ be any three-digit number.
Observe that $a \cdot 10^2 + b \cdot 10 = 10(a \cdot 10 + b)$.
Since $2 \mid 10$, it follows that $2 \mid 10(a \cdot 10 + b)$ or $2 \mid (a \cdot 10^2 + b \cdot 10)$ for any digits a and b.

Algebraic Reasoning
To the right, notice how the variables a, b, and c represent the digits 0, 1, 2, . . . , 9. In this way, all three-digit numbers may be represented (where $a \neq 0$). Then, rearranging sums using properties and techniques of algebra shows that the digit c is the one that determines whether a number is even or not.

Thus if $2 \mid c$ (where c is the ones digit), then $2 \mid [10(a \cdot 10 + b) + c]$.
Thus $2 \mid (a \cdot 10^2 + b \cdot 10 + c)$, or $2 \mid r$.
Conversely, let $2 \mid (a \cdot 10^2 + b \cdot 10 + c)$. Since $2 \mid (a \cdot 10^2 + b \cdot 10)$, it follows that
$2 \mid [(a \cdot 10^2 + b \cdot 10 + c) - (a \cdot 10^2 + b \cdot 10)]$ or $2 \mid c$.

Therefore, we have shown that 2 divides a number if and only if 2 divides the number's ones digit. One can apply similar reasoning to see why the tests for divisibility for 5 and 10 hold.

The next two tests for divisibility can be verified using arguments similar to the test for 2. Their verifications are left for the problem set.

THEOREM

Tests for Divisibility by 4 and 8

A number is divisible by 4 if and only if the number represented by its last two digits is divisible by 4.
A number is divisible by 8 if and only if the number represented by its last three digits is divisible by 8.

Notice that the test for 4 involves two digits and $2^2 = 4$. Also, the test for 8 requires that one consider the last three digits and $2^3 = 8$.

Example 5.3
Determine whether the following are true or false. Explain.

a. $4 \mid 1432$ **b.** $8 \mid 4204$
c. $4 \mid 2{,}345{,}678$ **d.** $8 \mid 98{,}765{,}432$

SOLUTION
a. True. $4 \mid 1432$, since $4 \mid 32$.
b. False. $8 \nmid 4204$, since $8 \nmid 204$.
c. False. $4 \nmid 2{,}345{,}678$, since $4 \nmid 78$.
d. True. $8 \mid 98{,}765{,}432$, since $8 \mid 432$.   ∎

The next two tests for divisibility provide a simple way to test for factors of 3 or 9.

THEOREM

Tests for Divisibility by 3 and 9

A number is divisible by 3 if and only if the sum of its digits is divisible by 3.
A number is divisible by 9 if and only if the sum of its digits is divisible by 9.

Example 5.4
Determine whether the following are true or false. Explain.

a. $3 \mid 12{,}345$ **b.** $9 \mid 12{,}345$ **c.** $9 \mid 6543$

SOLUTION
a. True. $3 \mid 12{,}345$, since $1 + 2 + 3 + 4 + 5 = 15$ and $3 \mid 15$.
b. False. $9 \nmid 12{,}345$, since $1 + 2 + 3 + 4 + 5 = 15$ and $9 \nmid 15$.
c. True. $9 \mid 6543$, since $9 \mid (6 + 5 + 4 + 3)$.   ∎

The following justification of the test for divisibility by 3 in the case of a three-digit number can be extended to prove that this test holds for any whole number.

Let $r = a \cdot 10^2 + b \cdot 10 + c$ be any three-digit number. We will show that if $3 \mid (a + b + c)$, then $3 \mid r$. Rewrite r as follows:

$$r = a \cdot (99 + 1) + b \cdot (9 + 1) + c$$
$$= a \cdot 99 + a \cdot 1 + b \cdot 9 + b \cdot 1 + c$$
$$= a \cdot 99 + b \cdot 9 + a + b + c$$
$$= (a \cdot 11 + b)9 + a + b + c.$$

Since $3 \mid 9$, it follows that $3 \mid (a \cdot 11 + b)9$. Thus if $3 \mid (a + b + c)$, where $a + b + c$ is the sum of the digits of r, then $3 \mid r$ since $3 \mid [(a \cdot 11 + b)9 + (a + b + c)]$. On the other hand, if $3 \mid r$, then $3 \mid (a + b + c)$, since $3 \mid [r - (a \cdot 11 + b)9]$ and $r - (a \cdot 11 + b)9 = a + b + c$.

The test for divisibility by 9 can be justified in a similar manner.

The following is a test for divisibility by 11.

THEOREM

Test for Divisibility by 11

A number is divisible by 11 if and only if 11 divides the difference of the sum of the digits whose place values are odd powers of 10 and the sum of the digits whose place values are even powers of 10.

When using the divisibility test for 11, first compute the sums of the two different sets of digits, and then subtract the smaller sum from the larger sum.

Example 5.5

Determine whether the following are true or false. Explain.

a. $11 \mid 5346$ **b.** $11 \mid 909{,}381$ **c.** $11 \mid 76{,}543$

SOLUTION
a. True. $11 \mid 5346$, since $5 + 4 = 9$, $3 + 6 = 9$, $9 - 9 = 0$, and $11 \mid 0$.
b. True. $11 \mid 909{,}381$, since $0 + 3 + 1 = 4$, $9 + 9 + 8 = 26$, $26 - 4 = 22$, and $11 \mid 22$.
c. False. $11 \nmid 76{,}543$, since $6 + 4 = 10$, $7 + 5 + 3 = 15$, $15 - 10 = 5$, and $11 \nmid 5$. ∎

The justification of this test for divisibility by 11 is left for Problem 44 in Part A of the Exercise/Problem Set. Also, a test for divisibility by 7 is given in Exercise 10 in Part A of the Exercise/Problem Set.

One can test for divisibility by 6 by applying the tests for 2 and 3.

THEOREM

Test for Divisibility by 6

A number is divisible by 6 if and only if both of the tests for divisibility by 2 and 3 hold.

This technique of applying two tests simultaneously can be used in other cases also. For example, the test for 10 can be thought of as applying the tests for 2 and 5 simultaneously. By the test for 2, the ones digit must be 0, 2, 4, 6, or 8, *and* by the test for 5 the ones digit must be 0 or 5. Thus a number is divisible by 10 if and only if its ones digit is zero. Testing for divisibility by applying two tests can be done in general.

THEOREM

A number is divisible by the product, ab, of two nonzero whole numbers a and b if it is divisible by both a and b, and a and b have only the number 1 as a common factor.

According to this theorem, a test for divisibility by 36 would be to test for 4 and test for 9, since 4 and 9 both divide 36 and 4 and 9 have only 1 as a common factor. However, the test "a number is divisible by 24 if and only if it is divisible by 4 and 6" is not valid, since 4 and 6 have a common factor of 2. For example, $4 \mid 36$ and $6 \mid 36$, but $24 \nmid 36$. The next example shows how to use tests for divisibility to find the prime factorization of a number.

Example 5.6   Find the prime factorization of 5148.

SOLUTION First, since the sum of the digits of 5148 is 18 (which is a multiple of 9), we know that $5148 = 9 \cdot 572$. Next, since $4 \mid 72$, we know that $4 \mid 572$. Thus $5148 = 9 \cdot 572 = 9 \cdot 4 \cdot 143 = 3^2 \cdot 2^2 \cdot 143$. Finally, since in 143, $1 + 3 - 4 = 0$ is divisible by 11, the number 143 is divisible by 11, so $5148 = 2^2 \cdot 3^2 \cdot 11 \cdot 13$. ∎

We can also use divisibility tests to help decide whether a particular counting number is prime. For example, we can determine whether 137 is prime or composite by checking to see if it has any prime factors less than 137. None of 2, 3, or 5 divides 137. How about 7? 11? 13? How many prime factors must be considered before we know whether 137 is a prime? Consider the following example.

Example 5.7   Determine whether 137 is a prime.

SOLUTION First, by the tests for divisibility, none of 2, 3, or 5 is a factor of 137. Next try 7, 11, 13, and so on.

$$7 \times 19 < 137 \text{ and } 7 \times 20 > 137, \text{ so } 7 \nmid 137$$
$$11 \times 12 < 137 \text{ and } 11 \times 13 > 137, \text{ so } 11 \nmid 137$$
$$13 \times 10 < 137 \text{ and } 13 \times 11 > 137, \text{ so } 13 \nmid 137$$
$$17 \times 8 < 137 \text{ and } 17 \times 9 > 137, \text{ so } 17 \nmid 137$$

column 1
column 2

Notice that the numbers in column 1 form an increasing list of primes and the numbers in column 2 are decreasing. Also, the numbers in the two columns "cross over" between 11 and 13. Thus, if there is a prime factor of 137, it will appear in column 1 first and reappear later as a factor of a number in column 2. Thus, as soon as the crossover is reached, there is no need to look any further for prime factors. Since the crossover point was passed in testing 137 and no prime factor of 137 was found, we conclude that 137 is prime. ∎

Example 5.7 suggests that to determine whether a number n is prime, we need only search for prime factors p, where $p^2 \leq n$. Recall that $y = \sqrt{x}$ (read "the **square root** of x") means that $y^2 = x$ where $y \geq 0$. For example, $\sqrt{25} = 5$ since $5^2 = 25$. Not all whole numbers have whole-number square roots. For example, using a calculator, $\sqrt{25} \approx 5.196$, since $5.196^2 \approx 27$. (A more complete discussion of the square root is contained in Chapter 9.) Thus the search for prime factors of a number n by considering only those primes p where $p^2 \leq n$ can be simplified even further by using the $\sqrt{x}$ key on a calculator and checking only those primes p where $p \leq \sqrt{n}$.

THEOREM

Prime Factor Test

To test for prime factors of a number n, one need only search for prime factors p of n, where $p^2 \leq n$ (or $p \leq \sqrt{n}$).

Example 5.8

Determine whether the following numbers are prime or composite.

a. 299   **b.** 401

SOLUTION

a. Only the prime factors 2 through 17 need to be checked, since $17^2 < 299 < 19^2$ (check this on your calculator). None of 2, 3, 5, 7, or 11 is a factor, but since $299 = 13 \cdot 23$, the number 299 is composite.
b. Only primes 2 through 19 need to be checked, since $\sqrt{401} \approx 20$. Since none of the primes 2 through 19 are factors of 401, we know that 401 is a prime. (The tests for divisibility show that 2, 3, 5, and 11 are not factors of 401. A calculator, tests for divisibility, or long division can be used to check 7, 13, 17, and 19.)   ∎

✔ **Check for Understanding:** Exercise/Problem Set A #7–14

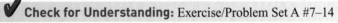

MATHEMATICAL MORSEL

Finding large primes is a favorite pastime of some mathematicians. Before the advent of calculators and computers, this was certainly a time-consuming endeavor. Three anecdotes about large primes follow.

- Euler once announced that 1,000,009 was prime. However, he later found that it was the product of 293 and 3413. At the time of this discovery, Euler was 70 and blind.
- Fermat was once asked whether 100,895,598,169 was prime. He replied shortly that it had two factors, 898,423 and 112,303.
- For more than 200 years the Mersenne number $2^{67} - 1$ was thought to be prime. In 1903, Frank Nelson Cole, in a speech to the American Mathematical Society, went to the blackboard and without uttering a word, raised 2 to the power 67 (by hand, using our usual multiplication algorithm!) and subtracted 1. He then multiplied 193,707,721 by 761,838,257,287 (also by hand). The two numbers agreed! When asked how long it took him to crack the number, he said, "Three years of Sunday."

| Section 5.1 | EXERCISE / PROBLEM SET A |

EXERCISES

1. Using the Chapter 5 eManipulative activity *Sieve of Eratosthenes* on our Web site, find all primes less than 100.

2. Find a factor tree for each of the following numbers.
   a. 36   **b.** 54   **c.** 102   **d.** 1000

3. A factor tree is not the only way to find the prime factorization of a composite number. Another method is to divide the number first by 2 as many times as possible, then by 3, then by 5, and so on, until all possible divisions by prime numbers have been performed. For example, to find the prime factorization of 108, you might organize your work as follows to conclude that $108 = 2^2 \times 3^3$.

$$
\begin{array}{r}
3 \\
3\overline{\smash{\big)}9} \\
3\overline{\smash{\big)}27} \\
2\overline{\smash{\big)}54} \\
2\overline{\smash{\big)}108}
\end{array}
$$

   Use this method to find the prime factorization of the following numbers.
   a. 216   **b.** 2940   **c.** 825   **d.** 198,198

4. Determine which of the following are true. If true, illustrate it with a rectangular array. If false, explain.
   a. $3 \mid 9$ **b.** $12 \mid 6$
   c. 3 is a divisor of 21.   **d.** 6 is a factor of 3.
   e. 4 is a factor of 16.   **f.** $0 \mid 5$
   g. $11 \mid 11$ **h.** 48 is a multiple of 16.

5. If 21 divides m, what else must divide m?

6. If the variables represent counting numbers, determine whether each of the following is true or false.
   a. If $x \nmid y$ and $x \nmid z$, then $x \nmid (y + z)$.
   b. If $2 \mid a$ and $3 \mid a$, then $6 \mid a$.

7. **a.** Show that $8 \mid 123{,}152$ using the test for divisibility by 8.
   b. Show that $8 \mid 123{,}152$ by finding x such that $8x = 123{,}152$.
   c. Is the x that you found in part (b) a divisor of 123,152? Prove it.

8. Which of the following are multiples of 3? of 4? of 9?
   a. 123,452   **b.** 1,114,500

9. Use the test for divisibility by 11 to determine which of the following numbers are divisible by 11.
   a. 2838   **b.** 71,992   **c.** 172,425

10. A test for divisibility by 7 is illustrated as follows. Does 7 divide 17,276?

Test:	17276	
$-$	12	Subtract 2×6 from 172
	1715	
$-$	10	Subtract 2×5 from 171
	161	
$-$	2	Subtract 2×1 from 16
	14	

    Since $7 \mid 14$, we also have $7 \mid 17{,}276$. Use this test to see whether the following numbers are divisible by 7.
    a. 8659   **b.** 46,187   **c.** 864,197,523

11. True or false? Explain.
    a. If a counting number is divisible by 9, it must be divisible by 3.
    b. If a counting number is divisible by 3 and 11, it must be divisible by 33.

12. Decide whether the following are true or false using only divisibility ideas given in this section (do not use long division or a calculator). Give a reason for your answers.
    a. $6 \mid 80$ **b.** $15 \mid 10{,}000$
    c. $4 \mid 15{,}000$ **d.** $12 \mid 32{,}304$

13. Which of the following numbers are composite? Why?
    a. 12   **b.** 123   **c.** 1234   **d.** 12,345

14. To determine if 467 is prime, we must check to see if it is divisible by any numbers other than 1 and itself. List all of the numbers that must be checked as possible factors to see if 467 is prime.

PROBLEMS

15. **a.** Write 36 in prime factorization form.
    b. List the divisors of 36.
    c. Write each divisor of 36 in prime factorization form.
    d. What relationship exists between your answer to part (a) and each of your answers to part (c)?
    e. Let $n = 13^2 \times 29^5$. If m divides n, what can you conclude about the prime factorization of m?

16. Justify the tests for divisibility by 5 and 10 for any three-digit number by reasoning by analogy from the test for divisibility by 2.

17. The symbol 4! is called four **factorial** and means $4 \times 3 \times 2 \times 1$; thus $4! = 24$. Which of the following statements are true?
    a. $6 \mid 6!$ **b.** $5 \mid 6!$ **c.** $11 \mid 6!$
    d. $30 \mid 30!$ **e.** $40 \mid 30!$ **f.** $30 \mid (30! + 1)$

    [Do not multiply out parts (d) to (f).]

18. a. Does $8 \mid 7!$?   **b.** Does $7 \mid 6!$?
  c. For what counting numbers n will n divide $(n - 1)!$?

19. There is one composite number in this set: 331, 3331, 33,331, 333,331, 3,333,331, 33,333,331, 333, 333,331. Which one is it? (*Hint:* It has a factor less than 30.)

20. Show that the formula $p(n) = n^2 + n + 17$ yields primes for $n = 0, 1, 2,$ and 3. Find the smallest whole number n for which $p(n) = n^2 + n + 17$ is not a prime.

21. a. Compute $n^2 + n + 41$, where $n = 0, 1, 2, \ldots, 10$, and determine which of these numbers is prime.
  b. On another piece of paper, continue the following spiral pattern until you reach 151. What do you notice about the main upper left to lower right diagonal?

		etc.	
53	52	51	50
	43	42	49
	44	41	48
	45	46	47

22. In his book *The Canterbury Puzzles* (1907), Dudeney mentioned that 11 was the only number consisting entirely of ones that was known to be prime. In 1918, Oscar Hoppe proved that the number 1,111,111,111,111,111,111 (19 ones) was prime. Later it was shown that the number made up of 23 ones was also prime. Now see how many of these "repunit" numbers up to 19 ones you can factor.

23. Which of the following numbers can be written as the sum of two primes, and why?

$$7, 17, 27, 37, 47, \ldots$$

24. One of Fermat's theorems states that every prime of the form $4x + 1$ is the sum of two square numbers in one and only one way. For example, $13 = 4(3) + 1$, and $13 = 4 + 9$, where 4 and 9 are square numbers.
  a. List the primes less than 100 that are of the form $4x + 1$, where x is a whole number.
  b. Express each of these primes as the sum of two square numbers.

25. The primes 2 and 3 are consecutive whole numbers. Is there another such pair of consecutive primes? Justify your answer.

26. Two primes that differ by 2 are called **twin primes**. For example, 5 and 7, 11 and 13, 29 and 31 are twin primes. Using the Chapter 5 eManipulative activity *Sieve of Eratosthenes* on our Web site to display all primes less than 200, find all twin primes less than 200.

27. One result that mathematicians have been unable to prove true or false is called Goldbach's conjecture. It claims that each even number greater than 2 can be expressed as the sum of two primes. For example.

$$4 = 2 + 2, \quad 6 = 3 + 3, \quad 8 = 3 + 5,$$
$$10 = 5 + 5, \quad 12 = 5 + 7.$$

  a. Verify that Goldbach's conjecture holds for even numbers through 40.
  b. Assuming that Goldbach's conjecture is true, show how each odd whole number greater than 6 is the sum of three primes.

28. For the numbers greater than 5 and less than 50, are there at least two primes between every number and its double? If not, for which number does this not hold?

29. Find two whole numbers with the smallest possible difference between them that when multiplied together will produce 1,234,567,890.

30. Find the largest counting number that divides every number in the following sets.
  a. $\{1 \cdot 2 \cdot 3, 2 \cdot 3 \cdot 4, 3 \cdot 4 \cdot 5, \ldots\}$
  b. $\{1 \cdot 3 \cdot 5, 2 \cdot 4 \cdot 6, 3 \cdot 5 \cdot 7, \ldots\}$
  Can you explain your answer in each case?

31. Find the smallest counting number that is divisible by the numbers 2 through 10.

32. What is the smallest counting number divisible by 2, 4, 5, 6, and 12?

33. Fill in the blank. The sum of three consecutive counting numbers always has a divisor (other than 1) of _____. Prove.

34. Choose any two numbers, say 5 and 7. Form a sequence of numbers as follows: 5, 7, 12, 19, and so on, where each new term is the sum of the two preceding numbers until you have 10 numbers. Add the 10 numbers. Is the seventh number a factor of the sum? Repeat several times, starting with a different pair of numbers each time. What do you notice? Prove that your observation is always true.

35. a. $5! = 5 \cdot 4 \cdot 3 \cdot 2 \cdot 1$ is divisible by 2, 3, 4, and 5. Prove that $5! + 2, 5! + 3, 5! + 4,$ and $5! + 5$ are all composite.
  b. Find 1000 consecutive numbers that are composite.

36. The customer said to the cashier, "I have 5 apples at 27 cents each and 2 pounds of potatoes at 78 cents per pound. I also have 3 cantaloupes and 6 lemons, but I don't remember the price for each." The cashier said, "That will be $3.52." The customer said, "You must have made a mistake." The cashier checked and the customer was correct. How did the customer catch the mistake?

37. There is a three-digit number with the following property: If you subtract 7 from it, the difference is divisible by 7; if you subtract 8 from it, the difference is divisible by 8; and if you subtract 9 from it, the difference is divisible by 9. What is the number?

38. Paula and Ricardo are serving cupcakes at a school party. If they arrange the cupcakes in groups of 2, 3, 4, 5, or 6, they always have exactly one cupcake left over. What is the smallest number of cupcakes they could have?

39. Prove that all six-place numbers of the form *abcabc* (e.g., 416,416) are divisible by 13. What other two numbers are always factors of a number of this form?

40. a. Prove that all four-digit palindromes are divisible by 11.
b. Is this also true for every palindrome with an even number of digits? Prove or disprove.

41. The annual sales for certain calculators were $2567 one year and $4267 the next. Assuming that the price of the calculators was the same each of the two years, how many calculators were sold in each of the two years?

42. Observe that 7 divides 2149. Also check to see that 7 divides 149,002. Try this pattern on another four-digit number using 7. If it works again, try a third. If that one also works, formulate a conjecture based on your three examples and prove it. (*Hint:* $7 \mid 1001$.)

43. How long does this list continue to yield primes?

$$17 + 2 = 19$$
$$19 + 4 = 23$$
$$23 + 6 = 29$$
$$29 + 8 = 37$$

44. Justify the test for divisibility by 11 for four-digit numbers by completing the following: Let $a \cdot 10^3 + b \cdot 10^2 + c \cdot 10 + d$ be any four-digit number. Then

$$a \cdot 10^3 + b \cdot 10^2 + c \cdot 10 + d$$
$$= a(1001 - 1) + b(99 + 1) + c(11 - 1) + d$$
$$= \cdots .$$

45. If p is a prime greater than 5, then the number $111 \ldots 1$, consisting of $p - 1$ ones, is divisible by p. For example, $7 \mid 111,111$, since $7 \times 15,873 = 111,111$. Verify the initial sentence for the next three primes.

46. a. Find the largest n such that $3^n \mid 24!$.
b. Find the smallest n such that $3^6 \mid n!$.
c. Find the largest n such that $12^n \mid 24!$.

47. Do Problem 20 using a spreadsheet to create a table of values, n and $p(n)$, for $n = 1, 2, \ldots 20$. Once the smallest value of n is found, evaluate $p(n + 1)$ and $p(n + 2)$. Are they prime or composite?

Section 5.1	EXERCISE / PROBLEM SET B

EXERCISES

1. An efficient way to find all the primes up to 100 is to arrange the numbers from 1 to 100 in six columns. As with the Sieve of Eratosthenes, cross out the multiples of 2, 3, 5, and 7. What pattern do you notice?
(*Hint:* Look at the columns and diagonals.)

1	2	3	4	5	6
7	8	9	10	11	12
13	14	15	16	17	18
19	20	21	22	23	24
25	26	27	28	29	30
31	32	33	34	35	36
37	38	39	40	41	42
43	44	45	46	47	48
49	50	51	52	53	54
55	56	57	58	59	60
61	62	63	64	65	66
67	68	69	70	71	72
73	74	75	76	77	78
79	80	81	82	83	84
85	86	87	88	89	90
91	92	93	94	95	96
97	98	99	100		

2. Find a factor tree for each of the following numbers.
a. 192   **b.** 380   **c.** 1593   **d.** 3741

3. Factor each of the following numbers into primes.
a. 39   **b.** 1131   **c.** 55
d. 935   **e.** 3289   **f.** 5889

4. Use the definition of *divides* to show that each of the following is true. (*Hint:* Find x that satisfies the definition of *divides*.)
a. $7 \mid 49$ **b.** $21 \mid 210$
c. $3 \mid (9 \times 18)$ **d.** $2 \mid (2^2 \times 5 \times 7)$
e. $6 \mid (2^4 \times 3^2 \times 7^3 \times 13^5)$
f. $100,000 \mid (2^7 \times 3^9 \times 5^{11} \times 17^8)$
g. $6000 \mid (2^{21} \times 3^{17} \times 5^{89} \times 29^{37})$
h. $22 \mid (121 \times 4)$
i. $p^3 q^5 r \mid (p^5 q^{13} r^7 s^2 t^{27})$ **j.** $7 \mid (5 \times 21 + 14)$

5. If 24 divides b, what else must divide b?

6. a. Prove in two different ways that 2 divides 114.
b. Prove in two different ways that $3 \mid 336$.

7. Which of the following are multiples of 3? of 4? of 9?
a. 2,199,456   **b.** 31,020,417

8. Use the test for divisibility by 11 to determine which of the following numbers are divisible by 11.
a. 945,142   **b.** 6,247,251   **c.** 385,627

9. Use the test for divisibility by 7 shown in Part A, Exercise 9 to determine which of the following numbers are divisible by 7.
a. 3,709,069   **b.** 275,555   **c.** 39,486

10. True or false? Explain.
a. If a counting number is divisible by 6 and 8, it must be divisible by 48.
b. If a counting number is divisible by 4, it must be divisible by 8.

11. If the variables represent counting numbers, determine whether each of the following is true or false.
a. If $2 \mid a$ and $6 \mid a$, then $12 \mid a$.
b. $6 \mid xy$, then $6 \mid x$ or $6 \mid y$.

12. Decide whether the following are true or false using only divisibility ideas given in this section (do not use long division or a calculator). Give a reason for your answers.
a. $24 \mid 325,608$ **b.** $45 \mid 13,075$
c. $40 \mid 1,732,800$ **d.** $36 \mid 677,916$

13. Which of the following numbers are composite? Why?
a. 123,456   **b.** 1,234,567   **c.** 123,456,789

14. To determine if 769 is prime, we must check to see if it is divisible by any numbers other than 1 and itself. List all of the numbers that must be checked as possible factors to see if 769 is prime.

PROBLEMS

15. A calculator may be used to test for divisibility of one number by another, where n and d represent counting numbers.
a. If $n \div d$ gives the answer 176, is it necessarily true that $d \mid n$?
b. If $n \div d$ gives the answer 56.3, is it possible that $d \mid n$?

16. Justify the test for divisibility by 9 for any four-digit number. (*Hint:* Reason by analogy from the test for divisibility by 3.)

17. Justify the tests for divisibility by 4 and 8.

18. Find the first composite number in this list.

$$3! - 2! + 1! = 5 \text{ Prime}$$
$$4! - 3! + 2! - 1! = 19 \text{ Prime}$$
$$5! - 4! + 3! - 2! + 1! = 101 \text{ Prime}$$

Continue this pattern. (*Hint:* The first composite comes within the first 10 such numbers.)

19. In 1845, the French mathematician Bertrand made the following conjecture: Between any whole number greater than 1 and its double there is at least one prime. In 1911, the Russian mathematician Tchebyshev proved the conjecture true. Using the Chapter 5 eManipulative activity *Sieve of Eratosthenes* on our Web site to display all primes less than 200, find three primes between each of the following numbers and its double.
a. 30   **b.** 50   **c.** 100

20. The numbers 2, 3, 5, 7, 11, and 13 are not factors of 211. Can we conclude that 211 is prime without checking for more factors? Why or why not?

21. It is claimed that the formula $n^2 - n + 41$ yields a prime for all whole-number values for n. Decide whether this statement is true or false.

22. In 1644, the French mathematician Mersenne asserted that $2^n - 1$ was prime only when $n = 2, 3, 5, 7, 13, 17, 19, 31, 67, 127$, and 257. As it turned out, when $n = 67$ and $n = 257$, $2^n - 1$ was a composite, and $2^n - 1$ was also prime when $n = 89$ and $n = 107$. Show that Mersenne's assertion was correct concerning $n = 3, 5, 7$, and 13.

23. It is claimed that every prime greater than 3 is either one more or one less than a multiple of 6. Investigate. If it seems true, prove it. If it does not, find a counterexample.

24. Is it possible for the sum of two odd prime numbers to be a prime number? Why or why not?

25. Mathematician D. H. Lehmer found that there are 209 consecutive composites between 20,831,323 and 20,831,533. Pick two numbers at random between 20,831,323 and 20,831,533 and prove that they are composite.

26. Prime triples are consecutive primes whose difference is 2. One such triple is 3, 5, 7. Find more or prove that there cannot be any more.

27. A seventh-grade student named Arthur Hamann made the following conjecture: Every even number is the difference of two primes. Express the following even numbers as the difference of two primes.
a. 12   **b.** 20   **c.** 28

28. The numbers 1, 7, 13, 31, 37, 43, 61, 67, and 73 form a 3×3 additive magic square. (An **additive magic square** has the same sum in all three rows, three columns, and two main diagonals.) Find it.

29. Can you find whole numbers a and b such that $3^a = 5^b$? Why or why not?

30. I'm a two-digit number less than 40. I'm divisible by only one prime number. The sum of my digits is a prime, and the difference between my digits is another prime. What numbers could I be?

31. What is the smallest counting number divisible by 2, 4, 6, 8, 10, 12, and 14?

32. What is the smallest counting number divisible by the numbers 1, 2, 3, 4, . . . 24, 25? (*Hint:* Give your answer in prime factorization form.)

33. The sum of five consecutive counting numbers has a divisor (other than 1) of _____. Prove.

34. Take any number with an even number of digits. Reverse the digits and add the two numbers. Does 11 divide your result? If yes, try to explain why.

35. Take a number. Reverse its digits and subtract the smaller of the two numbers from the larger. Determine what number always divides such differences for the following types of numbers.
a. A two-digit number   **b.** A three-digit number
c. A four-digit number

36. Choose any three digits. Arrange them three ways to form three numbers. *Claim:* The sum of your three numbers has a factor of 3. True or false?

$$\begin{array}{r} Example: \quad 371 \\ 137 \\ + 713 \\ \hline 1221 \end{array}$$
and $1221 = 3 \times 407$

37. Someone spilled ink on a bill for 36 sweatshirts. If only the first and last digits were covered and the other three digits were, in order, 8, 3, 9 as in ?83.9?, how much did each cost?

38. Determine how many zeros are at the end of the numerals for the following numbers in base ten.
a. 10!   **b.** 100!   **c.** 1000!

39. Find the smallest number n with the following property: If n is divided by 3, the quotient is the number obtained by moving the last digit (ones digit) of n to become the first digit. All of the remaining digits are shifted one to the right.

40. A man and his grandson have the same birthday. If for six consecutive birthdays the man is a whole number of times as old as his grandson, how old is each at the sixth birthday?

41. Let m be any odd whole number. Then m is a divisor of the sum of any m consecutive whole numbers. True or false? If true, prove. If false, provide a counterexample.

42. A merchant marked down some pads of paper from $2 and sold the entire lot. If the gross received from the sale was $603.77, how many pads did she sell?

43. How many prime numbers less than 100 can be written using the digits 1, 2, 3, 4, 5 if
a. no digit is used more than once?
b. a digit may be used twice?

44. Which of the numbers in the set

$$\{9, 99, 999, 9999, \ldots\}$$

are divisible by 7?

45. Two digits of this number were erased: 273*49*5. However, we know that 9 and 11 divide the number. What is it?

46. This problem appeared on a Russian mathematics exam: Show that all the numbers in the sequence 100001, 10000100001, 1000010000100001, ... are composite. Show that 11 divides the first, third, fifth numbers in this sequence, and so on, and that 111 divides the second. An American engineer claimed that the fourth number was the product of

21401 and 4672725574038601.

Was he correct?

47. The Fibonacci sequence, 1, 1, 2, 3, 5, 8, 13, . . . , is formed by adding any two consecutive numbers to find the next term. Prove or disprove: The sum of any ten consecutive Fibonacci numbers is a multiple of 11.

48. Do Part A Problem 21(a) using a spreadsheet to create a table of values, n and $p(n)$, for $n = 1, 2, \ldots 20$.

Analyzing Student Thinking

49. Courtney asserts that if the Sieve of Eratosthenes can be used to find all the primes, then it should also be able to find all the composite numbers. Is she correct? Explain.

50. One of the theorems in this section states "If $a \mid m$ and $a \mid n$, then $a \mid (m + n)$ when a is nonzero." A student suggests that "If $a \mid (m + n)$, then $a \mid m$ or $a \mid n$." Is the student correct? Explain.

51. Christa asserts that the test for divisibility by 9 is similar to the test for divisibility by 3 because every power of 10 is one more than a multiple of 9. Is she correct? Explain.

52. Brooklyn says to you that to find all of the prime factors of 113, she only has to check to see if any of 2, 3, 5, 7 is a factor of 113. How do you respond?

53. A student says that she is confused by the difference between $a \mid b$, which means "a divides b," and a/b, which is read "a divided by b." How would you help her resolve her confusion?

54. Kelby notices that if 2 | 36 and 9 | 36, then 18 | 36 since 18 = 2 × 9. He also notices that 4 | 36 and 6 | 36 but 24 ∤ 36. How could you help him understand why one case works and the other does not?

55. Lorena claims that since a number is divisible by 5 if its ones digit is a 5 then the number 357 is divisible by 7 because the last digit is a 7. How would you respond?

56. Suppose a student said that the sum of the digits of the number 354 is 12 and therefore 354 is divisible by any number that divides into 12, like 2, 3, 4, and 6. Would you agree with the student? Explain.

Problems Relating to the NCTM Standards and Curriculum Focal Points

1. The Focal Points for Grade 3 state "Developing understandings of multiplication and division strategies for basic multiplication facts and related division facts." Explain how the ideas of prime and composite numbers are related to multiplication and division facts.

2. The NCTM Standards state "All students should use factors, multiples, prime factorization, and relatively prime numbers to solve problems." Describe a problem involving fractions where factors, multiples, prime factorization, or relatively prime numbers are needed to solve the problem.

5.2 COUNTING FACTORS, GREATEST COMMON FACTOR, AND LEAST COMMON MULTIPLE

STARTING POINT

Following recess, the 1000 students of Wilson School lined up for the following activity: The first student opened all of the 1000 lockers in the school. The second student closed all lockers with even numbers. The third student "changed" all lockers that were numbered with multiples of 3 by closing those that were open and opening those that were closed. The fourth student changed each locker whose number was a multiple of 4, and so on. After all 1000 students had completed the activity, which lockers were open? Why?

Problem-Solving Strategy
Look for a Pattern

Children's Literature
www.wiley.com/college/musser
See "Sea Squares" by
Joy Hulme.

Counting Factors

In addition to finding prime factors, it is sometimes useful to be able to find how many factors (not just prime factors) a number has. The fundamental theorem of arithmetic is helpful in this regard. For example, to find all the factors of 12, consider its prime factorization $12 = 2^2 \cdot 3^1$. All factors of 12 must be made up of products of at most 2 twos and 1 three. All such combinations are contained in the table to the left. Therefore, 12 has six factors, namely, 1, 2, 3, 4, 6, and 12.

EXPONENT OF 2	EXPONENT OF 3	FACTOR
0	0	$2^0 \cdot 3^0 = 1$
1	0	$2^1 \cdot 3^0 = 2$
2	0	$2^2 \cdot 3^0 = 4$
0	1	$2^0 \cdot 3^1 = 3$
1	1	$2^1 \cdot 3^1 = 6$
2	1	$2^2 \cdot 3^1 = 12$

The technique used in this table can be used with any whole number that is expressed as the product of primes with their respective exponents. To find the number of factors of $2^3 \cdot 5^2$, a similar list could be constructed. The exponents of 2 would range from 0 to 3 (four possibilities), and the exponents of 5 would range from 0 to 2 (three possibilities). In all there would be $4 \cdot 3$ combinations, or 12 factors of $2^3 \cdot 5^2$, as shown in the following table.

EXPONENTS OF	5		
2	0	1	2
0	$2^0 5^0$	$2^0 5^1$	$2^0 5^2$
1	$2^1 5^0$	$2^1 5^1$	$2^1 5^2$
2	$2^2 5^0$	$2^2 5^1$	$2^2 5^2$
3	$2^3 5^0$	$2^3 5^1$	$2^3 5^2$

This method for finding the number of factors of any number can be summarized as follows.

THEOREM

Suppose that a counting number n is expressed as a product of *distinct* primes with their respective exponents, say $n = (p_1^{n_1})(p_2^{n_2}) \cdots (p_m^{n_m})$. Then the number of factors of n is the product $(n_1 + 1) \cdot (n_2 + 1) \cdots (n_m + 1)$.

Example 5.9

Find the number of factors.

a. 144   **b.** $2^3 \cdot 5^7 \cdot 7^4$ **c.** $9^5 \cdot 11^2$

SOLUTION

a. $144 = 2^4 \cdot 3^2$. So, the number of factors of 144 is $(4 + 1)(2 + 1) = 15$.
b. $2^3 \cdot 5^7 \cdot 7^4$ has $(3 + 1)(7 + 1)(4 + 1) = 160$ factors.
c. $9^5 \cdot 11^2 = 3^{10} \cdot 11^2$ has $(10 + 1)(2 + 1) = 33$ factors. (NOTE: 9^5 had to be rewritten as 3^{10}, since 9 was not prime.) ■

Notice that the number of factors does not depend on the prime factors, but rather on their respective exponents.

 Check for Understanding: Exercise/Problem Set A #1–2

Greatest Common Factor

The concept of greatest common factor is useful when simplifying fractions.

Algebraic Reasoning
The concept of greatest common factor (applied to 6, 15, and 12 in $6x - 15y + 12$) is useful when factoring or simplifying such expressions.

DEFINITION

Greatest Common Factor

The **greatest common factor** (GCF) of two (or more) nonzero whole numbers is the largest whole number that is a factor of both (all) of the numbers. The GCF of a and b is written **GCF(a, b)**.

There are two elementary ways to find the greatest common factor of two numbers: the set intersection method and the prime factorization method. The GCF (24, 36) is found next using these two methods.

Set Intersection Method

Step 1

Find all factors of 24 and 36. Since $24 = 2^3 \cdot 3$, there are $4 \cdot 2 = 8$ factors of 24, and since $36 = 2^2 \cdot 3^2$, there are $3 \cdot 3 = 9$ factors of 36. The set of factors of 24 is $\{1, 2, 3, 4, 6, 8, 12, 24\}$, and the set of factors of 36 is $\{1, 2, 3, 4, 6, 9, 12, 18, 36\}$.

Step 2

Find all common factors of 24 and 36 by taking the intersection of the two sets in step 1.
$$\{1, 2, 3, 4, 6, 8, 12, 24\} \cap \{1, 2, 3, 4, 6, 9, 12, 18, 36\} = \{1, 2, 3, 4, 6, 12\}$$

Step 3

Find the largest number in the set of common factors in step 2. The largest number in $\{1, 2, 3, 4, 6, 12\}$ is 12. Therefore, 12 is the GCF of 24 and 36. (NOTE: The set intersection method can also be used to find the GCF of more than two numbers in a similar manner.)

While the set intersection method can be cumbersome and at times less efficient than other methods, it is conceptually a natural way to think of the greatest common factor. The "common" part of the greatest common factor is the "intersection" part of the set intersection method. Once students have a good understanding of what the greatest common factor is by using the set intersection method, the prime factorization method, which is often more efficient, can be introduced.

Prime Factorization Method

Step 1

Express the numbers 24 and 36 in their prime factor exponential form: $24 = 2^3 \cdot 3$ and $36 = 2^2 \cdot 3^2$.

Step 2

The GCF will be the number $2^m 3^n$ where m is the smaller of the exponents of the 2s and n is the smaller of the exponents of the 3s. For $2^3 \cdot 3$ and $2^2 \cdot 3^2$, m is the smaller of 3 and 2, and n is the smaller of 1 and 2. Therefore, the GCF of $2^3 \cdot 3^1$ and $2^2 \cdot 3^2$ is $2^2 \cdot 3^1 = 12$. Review this method so that you see why it always yields the largest number that is a factor of both of the given numbers.

Example 5.10   Find GCF(42, 24) in two ways.

SOLUTION

Set Intersection Method
$42 = 2 \cdot 3 \cdot 7$, so 42 has $2 \cdot 2 \cdot 2 = 8$ factors.
$24 = 2^3 \cdot 3$, so 24 has $4 \cdot 2 = 8$ factors.
Factors of 42 are 1, 2, 3, 6, 7, 14, 21, 42.
Factors of 24 are 1, 2, 3, 4, 6, 8, 12, 24.
Common factors are 1, 2, 3, 6.
GCF(42, 24) = 6.

Prime Factorization Method
$42 = 2 \cdot 3 \cdot 7$ and $24 = 2^3 \cdot 3$.
$GCF(42, 24) = 2 \cdot 3 = 6$.
Notice that only the common primes (2 and 3) are used, since the exponent on the 7 is zero in the prime factorization of 24. ∎

Earlier in this chapter we obtained the following result: If $a \mid m$, $a \mid n$, and $m \geq n$, then $a \mid (m - n)$. In words, if a number divides each of two numbers, then it divides their difference. Hence, if c is a common factor of a and b, where $a \geq b$, then c is also a common factor of b and $a - b$. Since every common factor of a and b is also a common factor of b and $a - b$, the pairs (a, b) and $(a - b, b)$ have the same common factors. So $GCF(a, b)$ and $GCF(a - b, b)$ must also be the same.

THEOREM

If a and b are whole numbers, with $a \geq b$, then

$$GCF(a, b) = GCF(a - b, b).$$

The usefulness of this result is illustrated in the next example.

Example 5.11   Find the GCF(546, 390).

SOLUTION
$$\begin{aligned}
GCF(546, 390) &= GCF(546 - 390, 390) \\
&= GCF(156, 390) \\
&= GCF(390 - 156, 156) \\
&= GCF(234, 156) \\
&= GCF(78, 156) \\
&= GCF(78, 78) \\
&= 78
\end{aligned}$$
∎

Using a calculator, we can find the GCF(546, 390) as follows:

$$546 \boxminus 390 \boxminus 156$$
$$390 \boxminus 156 \boxminus 234$$
$$234 \boxminus 156 \boxminus 78$$
$$156 \boxminus 78 \ \boxminus 78$$

Therefore, since the last two numbers in the last line are equal, then the GCF(546, 390) = 78. Notice that this procedure may be shortened by storing 156 in the calculator's memory.

This calculator method can be refined for very large numbers or in exceptional cases. For example, to find GCF(1417, 26), 26 must be subtracted many times to produce a number that is less than (or equal to) 26. Since division can be viewed as repeated subtraction, long division can be used to shorten this process as follows:

$$\begin{array}{r} 54 \text{ R } 13 \\ 26 \overline{)1417} \end{array}$$

Here 26 was "subtracted" from 1417 a total of 54 times to produce a remainder of 13. Thus GCF(1417, 26) = GCF(13, 26). Next, divide 13 into 26.

$$\begin{array}{r} 2 \text{ R } 0 \\ 13\overline{)26} \end{array}$$

Thus GCF(13, 26) = 13, so GCF(1417, 26) = 13. Each step of this method can be justified by the following theorem.

THEOREM

If a and b are whole numbers with $a \geq b$ and $a = bq + r$, where $r < b$, then

$$GCF(a, b) = GCF(r, b).$$

Thus, to find the GCF of any two numbers, this theorem can be applied repeatedly until a remainder of zero is obtained. The final divisor that leads to the zero remainder is the GCF of the two numbers. This method is called the **Euclidean algorithm**.

Example 5.12   Find the GCF(840, 3432).

SOLUTION

$$\begin{array}{r} 4 \text{ R } 72 \\ 840\overline{)3432} \end{array}$$

$$\begin{array}{r} 11 \text{ R } 48 \\ 72\overline{)840} \end{array}$$

$$\begin{array}{r} 1 \text{ R } 24 \\ 48\overline{)72} \end{array}$$

$$\begin{array}{r} 2 \text{ R } 0 \\ 24\overline{)48} \end{array}$$

Therefore, GCF(840, 3432) = 24. ■

 A calculator also can be used to calculate the GCF(3432, 840) using the Euclidean algorithm.

$$3432 \div 840 = \boxed{4.085714286}$$
$$3432 - 4 \times 840 = \boxed{72.}$$
$$840 \div 72 = \boxed{11.66666667}$$
$$840 - 11 \times 72 = \boxed{48.}$$
$$72 \div 48 = \boxed{1.5}$$
$$72 - 1 \times 48 = \boxed{24.}$$
$$48 \div 24 = \boxed{2.}$$

Therefore, 24 is the GCF(3432, 840). Notice how this method parallels the one in Example 5.12.

 Check for Understanding: Exercise/Problem Set A #3–8

Least Common Multiple

The least common multiple is useful when adding or subtracting fractions.

DEFINITION

Least Common Multiple

The **least common multiple (LCM)** of two (or more) nonzero whole numbers is the smallest nonzero whole number that is a multiple of each (all) of the numbers. The LCM of a and b is written **LCM(a, b)**.

For the GCF, there are three elementary ways to find the least common multiple of two numbers: the set intersection method, the prime factorization method, and the build-up method. The LCM(24, 36) is found next using these three methods.

Set Intersection Method

Step 1

List the first several nonzero multiples of 24 and 36. The set of nonzero multiples of 24 is {24, 48, 72, 96, 120, 144, . . .}, and the set of nonzero multiples of 36 is {36, 72, 108, 144, . . .}. (Note: The set of multiples of any nonzero whole number is an infinite set.)

Step 2

Find the first several common multiples of 24 and 36 by taking the intersection of the two sets in step 1:
{24, 48, 72, 96, 120, 144, . . .} ∩ {36, 72, 108, 144, . . .} = {72, 144, . . .}.

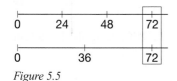

Figure 5.5

Step 3

Find the smallest number in the set of common multiples in step 2. The smallest number in {72, 144, . . .} is 72. Therefore, 72 is the LCM of 24 and 36 (Figure 5.5).

Similar to the methods for finding the greatest common factor, the "intersection" part of the set intersection method illustrates the "common" part of the least common multiple. Thus, the set intersection method is a natural way to introduce the least common multiple.

Prime Factorization Method

Step 1

Express the numbers 24 and 36 in their prime factor exponential form: $24 = 2^3 \cdot 3$ and $36 = 2^2 \cdot 3^2$.

Step 2

The LCM will be the number $2^r 3^s$, where r is the larger of the exponents of the twos and s is the larger of the exponents of the threes. For $2^3 \cdot 3^1$ and $2^2 \cdot 3^2$, r is the larger of 3 and 2 and s is the larger of 1 and 2. That is, the LCM of $2^3 \cdot 3^1$ and $2^2 \cdot 3^2$ is $2^3 \cdot 3^2$, or 72. Review this procedure to see why it always yields the smallest number that is a multiple of both of the given numbers.

Build-up Method

Step 1

As in the prime factorization method, express the numbers 24 and 36 in their prime factor exponential form: $24 = 2^3 \cdot 3$ and $36 = 2^2 \cdot 3^2$.

Step 2

Select the prime factorization of one of the numbers and build the LCM from that as follows. Beginning with $24 = 2^3 \cdot 3$, compare it to the prime factorization of $36 = 2^2 \cdot 3^2$. Because $2^2 \cdot 3^2$ has more threes than $2^3 \cdot 3^1$, build up the $2^3 \cdot 3^1$ to have the same number of threes as $2^2 \cdot 3^2$, making the LCM $2^3 \cdot 3^2$. If there are more than two numbers for which the LCM is to be found, continue to compare and build with each subsequent number.

Example 5.13   Find the LCM(42, 24) in three ways.

SOLUTION

Set Intersection Method
Multiples of 42 are 42, 84, 126, 168, ...
Multiples of 24 are 24, 48, 72, 96, 120, 144, 168, ...
Common multiples are 168, ...
LCM(42, 24) = 168.

Prime Factorization Method
$42 = 2 \cdot 3 \cdot 7$ and $24 = 2^3 \cdot 3$.
LCM(42, 24) = $2^3 \cdot 3 \cdot 7 = 168$.

Build-up Method
$42 = 2 \cdot 3 \cdot 7$ and $24 = 2^3 \cdot 3$.
Beginning with $24 = 2^3 \cdot 3$, compare to $2 \cdot 3 \cdot 7$ and build $2^3 \cdot 3$ up to $2^3 \cdot 3 \cdot 7$.
LCM(42, 24) = $2^3 \cdot 3 \cdot 7 = 168$.

Notice that *all* primes from either number are used when forming the least common multiple. ■

 Check for Understanding: Exercise/Problem Set A #9–11

Extending the Concepts of GCF and LCM

These methods can also be applied to find the GCF and LCM of several numbers.

Example 5.14   Find the (a) GCF and (b) LCM of the three numbers $2^5 \cdot 3^2 \cdot 5^7$, $2^4 \cdot 3^4 \cdot 5^3 \cdot 7$, and $2 \cdot 3^6 \cdot 5^4 \cdot 13^2$.

SOLUTION

a. The GCF is $2^1 \cdot 3^2 \cdot 5^3$ (use the common primes and the smallest respective exponents).

b. Using the build-up method, begin with $2^5 \cdot 3^2 \cdot 5^7$. Then compare it to $2^4 \cdot 3^4 \cdot 5^3 \cdot 7$ and build up the LCM to $2^5 \cdot 3^4 \cdot 5^7 \cdot 7$. Now compare with $2 \cdot 3^6 \cdot 5^4 \cdot 13^2$ and build up $2^5 \cdot 3^4 \cdot 5^7 \cdot 7$ to $2^5 \cdot 3^6 \cdot 5^7 \cdot 7 \cdot 13^2$. ■

If you are trying to find the GCF of several numbers that are not in prime-factored exponential form, as in Example 5.14, you may want to use a computer program. By considering examples in exponential notation, one can observe that the GCF of a, b, and c can be found by finding GCF(a, b) first and then GCF(GCF(a, b), c). This idea can be extended to as many numbers as you wish. Thus one can use the Euclidean algorithm by finding GCFs of numbers, two at a time. For example, to find GCF(24, 36, 160), find GCF(24, 36), which is 12, and then find GCF(12, 160), which is 4.

Finally, there is a very useful connection between the GCF and LCM of two numbers, as illustrated in the next example.

Example 5.15   Find the GCF and LCM of a and b, for the numbers $a = 2^5 \cdot 3^7 \cdot 5^2 \cdot 7$ and $b = 2^3 \cdot 3^2 \cdot 5^6 \cdot 11$.

SOLUTION Notice in the following solution that the products of the factors of a and b, which are in bold type, make up the GCF, and the products of the remaining factors, which are circled, make up the LCM.

$$\text{GCF} = 2^3 \cdot 3^2 \cdot 5^2$$
$$a = \textcircled{2^5} \cdot \textcircled{3^7} \cdot \mathbf{5^2} \cdot \textcircled{7} \quad b = \mathbf{2^3} \cdot \mathbf{3^2} \cdot \textcircled{5^6} \cdot \textcircled{11}$$
$$\text{LCM} = 2^5 \cdot 3^7 \cdot 5^6 \cdot 7 \cdot 11$$

Hence

$$\begin{aligned}
\text{GCF}(a, b) \times \text{LCM}(a, b) &= (2^3 \cdot 3^2 \cdot 5^2)(2^5 \cdot 3^7 \cdot 5^6 \cdot 7 \cdot 11) \\
&= (2^5 \cdot 3^7 \cdot 5^2 \cdot 7) \cdot (2^3 \cdot 3^2 \cdot 5^6 \cdot 11) \\
&= a \times b.
\end{aligned}$$ ■

Example 5.15 illustrates that *all* of the prime factors and their exponents from the original number are accounted for in the GCF and LCM. This relationship is stated next.

THEOREM

Let a and b be any two whole numbers. Then

$$\text{GCF}(a, b) \times \text{LCM}(a, b) = ab.$$

Also, $\text{LCM}(a, b) = \dfrac{ab}{GCF(a, b)}$ is a consequence of this theorem. So if the GCF of two numbers is known, the LCM can be found using the GCF.

Example 5.16 Find the LCM(36, 56).

SOLUTION GCF(36, 56) = 4. Therefore, LCM = $\dfrac{36 \cdot 56}{4}$ = 9 · 56 = 504. ∎

This technique applies only to the case of finding the GCF and LCM of *two* numbers.

We end this chapter with an important result regarding the primes by proving that there is an infinite number of primes.

THEOREM

There is an infinite number of primes.

Problem-Solving Strategy
Use Indirect Reasoning

PROOF

Either there is a finite number of primes or there is an infinite number of primes. We will use indirect reasoning. Let us *assume* that there is only a *finite* number of primes, say 2, 3, 5, 7, 11, · · ·, p, where p is the greatest prime. Let $N = (2 \cdot 3 \cdot 5 \cdot 7 \cdot 11 \cdots p) + 1$. This number, N, must be 1, prime, or composite. Clearly, N is greater than 1. Also, N is greater than any prime. But then, if N is composite, it must have a prime factor. Yet whenever N is divided by a prime, the remainder is always 1 (think about this)! Therefore, N is neither 1, nor a prime, nor a composite. But that is impossible. Using indirect reasoning, we conclude that there must be an infinite number of primes. ∎

There are also infinitely many composite numbers (for example, the even numbers greater than 2).

✔ **Check for Understanding:** Exercise/Problem Set A #12–17

MATHEMATICAL MORSEL

On April 12, 2009, a new large Mersenne prime was found. Mersenne primes are special primes that take on a certain form. Typically each new prime that is found is larger than the previous ones. However, in 2009 that was not the case. On August 23, 2008, the prime $2^{43112609} - 1$ was found and verified to have 12,978,189 digits. The prime found in 2009 only has 12,837,064 digits, a difference of over 140,000 digits. If the largest prime, found in 2008, were written out in a typical newsprint size, it would fill about 670 pages of a newspaper. Why search for such large primes? One reason is that it requires trillions of calculations and hence can be used to test computer speed and reliability. Also, it is important in writing messages in code. Besides, as a computer expert put it, "It's like Mount Everest; why do people climb mountains?" To keep up on the ongoing race to find a bigger prime, visit the Web site www.mersenne.org.

Section 5.2 **EXERCISE / PROBLEM SET A**

EXERCISES

1. How many factors does each of the following numbers have?
  a. $2^2 \times 3$ **b.** $3^3 \times 5^2$ **c.** $5^2 \times 7^3 \times 11^4$

2. a. Factor 36 into primes.
  b. Factor each divisor of 36 into primes.
  c. What relationship exists between the prime factors in part (b) and the prime factors in part (a)?
  d. Let $x = 7^4 \times 17^2$. If n is a divisor of x, what can you say about the prime factorization of n?
  e. How many factors does $x = 7^4 \cdot 17^2$ have? List them.

3. Use the set intersection method to find the GCFs.
  a. GCF(12, 18)   **b.** GCF(42, 28)   **c.** GCF(60, 84)

4. Use the prime factorization method to find the GCFs.
  a. GCF(8, 18)   **b.** GCF(36, 42)   **c.** GCF(24, 66)

5. Using a calculator method, find the following.
  a. GCF(138, 102)
  b. GCF(484, 363)
  c. GCF(297, 204)
  d. GCF(222, 2222)

6. Using the Euclidean algorithm, find the following GCFs.
  a. GCF(24, 54)
  b. GCF(39, 91)
  c. GCF(72, 160)
  d. GCF(5291, 11951)

7. Use any method to find the following GCFs.
  a. GCF(51, 85)   **b.** GCF(45, 75)
  c. GCF(42, 385)   **d.** GCF(117, 195)

8. Two counting numbers are **relatively prime** if the greatest common factor of the two numbers is 1. Which of the following pairs of numbers are relatively prime?
  a. 4 and 9   **b.** 24 and 123   **c.** 12 and 45

9. Use the set intersection method to find the following LCMs.
  a. LCM(24, 30)   **b.** LCM(42, 28)   **c.** LCM(12, 14)

10. Use the (i) prime factorization method and the (ii) build-up method to find the following LCMs.
  a. LCM(6, 8)   **b.** LCM(4, 10)
  c. LCM(7, 9)   **d.** LCM(8, 10)

11. Find the following LCMs using any method.
  a. LCM(60, 72)   **b.** LCM(35, 110)   **c.** LCM(45, 27)

12. Use the any method to find the following GCFs.
  a. GCF(12, 60, 90)   **b.** GCF(55, 75, 245)
  c. GCF(1105, 1729, 3289)   **d.** GCF(1421, 1827, 2523)
  e. GCF($3^3 \cdot 5^5 \cdot 11^9, 3^4 \cdot 5^3 \cdot 11^7, 3^7 \cdot 5^7 \cdot 11^7, 3^{11} \cdot 5^6 \cdot 11^5$)
  f. GCF($2^3 \cdot 3^4 \cdot 11^2 \cdot 13, 2^2 \cdot 3^6 \cdot 7 \cdot 13^2, 2^4 \cdot 3^5 \cdot 5^3 \cdot 13$)

13. Use any method to find the following LCMs.
  a. LCM(2, 3, 5)   **b.** LCM(8, 12, 18)
  c. LCM($3^3 \cdot 5^5 \cdot 11^9, 3^{11} \cdot 5^6 \cdot 11^5, 2^4 \cdot 3^5 \cdot 5^3 \cdot 13$)
  d. LCM($2^3 \cdot 3^4 \cdot 11^2 \cdot 13, 2^2 \cdot 3^6 \cdot 7 \cdot 13^2, 3^7 \cdot 5^7 \cdot 11^7$)

14. Another method of finding the LCM of two or more numbers is shown. Find the LCM(27, 36, 45, 60). Use this method to find the following LCMs.

2	27	36	45	60	Divide all even numbers by 2. If not
2	27	18	45	30	divisible by 2, bring down. Repeat
3	27	9	45	15	until none are divisible by 2.
3	9	3	15	5	Proceed to the next prime number
3	3	1	5	5	and repeat the process.
5	1	1	5	5	Continue until the last row is all 1s.
	1	1	1	1	LCM $= 2^2 \cdot 3^3 \cdot 5$ (see the left column)

  a. LCM(21, 24, 63, 70)
  b. LCM(20, 36, 42, 33)
  c. LCM(15, 35, 42, 80)

15. a. For $a = 91, b = 39$ find GCF(a, b) and $a \cdot b$. Use these two values to find LCM(a, b).
  b. For $a = 3^6 \cdot 7^3 \cdot 11^5, b = 2^3 \cdot 3^4 \cdot 7^5$ find LCM(a, b) and $a \cdot b$. Use these values to find GCF(a, b).

16. For each of the pairs of numbers in parts a–c below **(i)** sketch a Venn diagram with the prime factors of a and b in the appropriate locations.

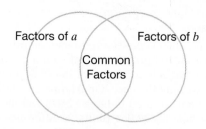

  (ii) find GCF(a, b) and LCM(a, b).
  Use the Chapter 5 eManipulative *Factor Tree* on our Web site to better understand the use of the Venn diagram.
  a. $a = 63, b = 90$
  b. $a = 48, b = 40$
  c. $a = 16, b = 49$

17. Which is larger, GCF(12, 18) or LCM(12, 18)?

PROBLEMS

18. The factors of a number that are less than the number itself are called **proper factors**. The Pythagoreans classified numbers as deficient, abundant, or perfect, depending on the sum of their proper factors.

   a. A number is **deficient** if the sum of its proper factors is less than the number. For example, the proper factors of 4 are 1 and 2. Since $1 + 2 = 3 < 4$, 4 is a deficient number. What other numbers less than 25 are deficient?

   b. A number is **abundant** if the sum of its proper factors is greater than the number. Which numbers less than 25 are abundant?

   c. A number is **perfect** if the sum of its proper factors is equal to the number. Which number less than 25 is perfect?

19. A pair of whole numbers is called **amicable** if each is the sum of the proper divisors of the other. For example, 284 and 220 are amicable, since the proper divisors of 220 are 1, 2, 4, 5, 10, 11, 20, 22, 44, 55, 110, which sum to 284, whose proper divisors are 1, 2, 4, 71, 142, which sum to 220.

   Determine which of the following pairs are amicable.
   a. 1184 and 1210
   b. 1254 and 1832
   c. 5020 and 5564

20. Two numbers are said to be **betrothed** if the sum of all proper factors greater than 1 of one number equals the other, and vice versa. For example, 48 and 75 are betrothed, since

$$48 = 3 + 5 + 15 + 25,$$
proper factors of 75 except for 1,

   and

$$75 = 2 + 3 + 4 + 6 + 8 + 12 + 16 + 24,$$
proper factors of 48 except for 1.

   Determine which of the following pairs are betrothed.
   a. (140, 195)   **b.** (1575, 1648)   **c.** (2024, 2295)

21. In the following problems, you are given three pieces of information. Use them to answer the question.
   a. $\text{GCF}(a, b) = 2 \times 3$, $\text{LCM}(a, b) = 2^2 \times 3^3 \times 5$, $b = 2^2 \times 3 \times 5$. What is a?
   b. $\text{GCF}(a, b) = 2^2 \times 7 \times 11$, $\text{LCM}(a, b) = 2^5 \times 3^2 \times 5 \times 7^3 \times 11^2$, $b = 2^5 \times 3^2 \times 5 \times 7 \times 11$. What is a?

22. What is the smallest whole number having exactly the following number of divisors?
   a. 1   **b.** 2   **c.** 3   **d.** 4
   e. 5   **f.** 6   **g.** 7   **h.** 8

23. Find six examples of whole numbers that have the following number of factors. Then try to characterize the set of numbers you found in each case.
   a. 2   **b.** 3   **c.** 4   **d.** 5

24. Euclid (300 B.C.E.) proved that $2^{n-1}(2^n - 1)$ produced a perfect number [see Exercise 13(c)] whenever $2^n - 1$ is prime, where $n = 1, 2, 3, \ldots$. Find the first four such perfect numbers. (NOTE: Some 2000 years later, Euler proved that this formula produces all even perfect numbers.)

25. Find all whole numbers x such that $\text{GCF}(24, x) = 1$ and $1 \le x \le 24$.

26. George made enough money by selling candy bars at 15 cents each to buy several cans of pop at 48 cents each. If he had no money left over, what is the fewest number of candy bars he could have sold?

27. Three chickens and one duck sold for as much as two geese, whereas one chicken, two ducks, and three geese were sold together for $25. What was the price of each bird in an exact number of dollars?

28. Which, if any, of the numbers in the set $\{10, 20, 40, 80, 160, \ldots\}$ is a perfect square?

29. What is the largest three-digit prime all of whose digits are prime?

30. Take any four-digit palindrome whose digits are all nonzero and not all the same. Form a new palindrome by interchanging the unlike digits. Add these two numbers.

$$\begin{array}{r} \text{Example:} \quad 8{,}448 \\ +4{,}884 \\ \hline 13{,}332 \end{array}$$

   a. Find a whole number greater than 1 that divides *every* such sum.
   b. Find the *largest* such whole number.

31. Fill in the following 4×4 additive magic square, which is comprised entirely of primes.

3	61	19	37
43	31	5	—
—	—	—	29
—	—	23	—

32. What is the least number of cards that could satisfy the following three conditions?

   If all the cards are put in two equal piles, there is one card left over.

   If all the cards are put in three equal piles, there is one card left over.

   If all the cards are put in five equal piles, there is one card left over.

33. Show that the number 343 is divisible by 7. Then prove or disprove: Any three-digit number of the form $100a + 10b + a$, where $a + b = 7$, is divisible by 7.

34. In the set $\{18, 96, 54, 27, 42\}$, find the pair(s) of numbers with the greatest GCF and the pair(s) with the smallest LCM.

35. Using the Chapter 5 eManipulative *Fill 'n Pour* on our Web site, determine how to use container A

and container B to measure the described target amount.
   a. Container A = 8 ounces
   Container B = 12 ounces
   Target = 4 ounces
   b. Container A = 7 ounces
   Container B = 11 ounces
   Target = 1 ounce

| Section 5.2 | EXERCISE / PROBLEM SET B |

EXERCISES

1. How many factors does each of the following numbers have?
   a. $2^2 \times 3^2$
   b. $7^3 \times 11^3$
   c. $7^{11} \times 19^6 \times 79^{23}$
   d. 12^4
   e. How many factors does $x = 11^5 \cdot 13^3$ have? List them.

2. **a.** Factor 120 into primes.
   b. Factor each divisor of 120 into primes.
   c. What relationship exists between the prime factors in part (b) and the prime factors in part (a)?
   d. Let $x = 11^5 \times 13^3$. If n is a divisor of x, what can you say about the prime factorization of n?

3. Use the set intersection method to find the GCFs.
   a. GCF(24, 16) **b.** GCF(48, 64) **c.** GCF(54, 72)

4. Use the prime factorization method to find the following GCFs.
   a. GCF(36, 54)
   b. GCF(16, 51)
   c. GCF(136, 153)

5. Using a calculator method, find the following.
   a. GCF(276, 54) **b.** GCF(111, 111111)
   c. GCF(399, 102) **d.** GCF(12345, 54323)

6. Using the Euclidean algorithm and your calculator, find the GCF for each pair of numbers.
   a. 2244 and 418
   b. 963 and 657
   c. 7286 and 1684

7. Use any method to find the following GCFs.
   a. GCF(38, 68) **b.** GCF(60, 126)
   c. GCF(56, 120) **d.** GCF(338, 507)

8. **a.** Show that 83,154,367 and 4 are relatively prime.
   b. Show that 165,342,985 and 13 are relatively prime.
   c. Show that 165,342,985 and 33 are relatively prime.

9. Use the set intersection method to find the following LCMs.
   a. LCM(15, 18) **b.** LCM(26, 39) **c.** LCM(36, 45)

10. Use the (1) prime factorization method and the (2) build-up method to find the following LCMs.
   a. LCM(15, 21) **b.** LCM(14, 35)
   c. LCM(75, 100) **d.** LCM(130, 182)

11. Find the following LCMs using any method.
   a. LCM(21, 51)
   b. LCM(111, 39)
   c. LCM(125, 225)

12. Use any method to find the following GCFs.
   a. GCF(15, 35, 42) **b.** GCF(28, 98, 154)
   c. GCF(1449, 1311, 1587) **d.** GCF(2737, 3553, 3757)
   e. GCF($5^4 \cdot 7^3 \cdot 13^6, 5^6 \cdot 7^5 \cdot 11^2 \cdot 13^4, 5^4 \cdot 7^7 \cdot 13^{11}, 5^3 \cdot 7^6 \cdot 13^8$)
   f. GCF($3^4 \cdot 5 \cdot 7^4 \cdot 11^2, 2^2 \cdot 3^3 \cdot 7^7 \cdot 13^3, 3^5 \cdot 7^2 \cdot 11 \cdot 13^2$)

13. Use the any method to find the following LCMs.
   a. LCM(4, 5, 6) **b.** LCM(9, 15, 25)
   c. LCM($3^3 \cdot 5^5 \cdot 7^4, 5^2 \cdot 7^6 \ 11^4, 3^4 \cdot 7^3 \cdot 11^3$)
   d. LCM($2^3 \cdot 5^4 \cdot 11^3, 3^8 \cdot 7^2 \cdot 13^7, 2^4 \cdot 5^2 \cdot 7^5 \cdot 13^3$)

14. Use the method described in Part A, Exercise 14 to find the following LCMs.
   a. LCM(12, 14, 45, 35)
   b. LCM(54, 40, 44, 50)
   c. LCM(39, 36, 77, 28)

15. **a.** For $a = 49$, $b = 84$ find GCF(a, b) and $a \cdot b$. Use these two values to find LCM(a, b).
   b. Given LCM(a, b) = $2^7 \cdot 5^4 \cdot 7^5 \cdot 11^4$ and $a \cdot b = 2^7 \cdot 5^7 \cdot 7^9 \cdot 11^4$, find GCF($a, b$).
   c. Find two different candidates for a and b in part b.

16. For each of the pairs of numbers in parts $a - c$ below
   (i) sketch a Venn diagram with the prime factors of a and b in the appropriate locations.

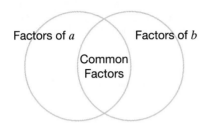

Factors of a Factors of b

Common
Factors

(ii) find GCF(a, b) and LCM(a, b).

Use the Chapter 5 eManipulative *Factor Tree* on our Web site to better understand the use of the Venn diagram.
   a. $a = 30$, $b = 24$
   b. $a = 4$, $b = 27$
   c. $a = 18$, $b = 45$

17. Let a and b represent two nonzero whole numbers. Which is larger, GCF(a, b) or LCM(a, b)?

PROBLEMS

18. Identify the following numbers as deficient, abundant, or perfect. (See Part A, Problem 18a)
   a. 36   **b.** 28
   c. 60   **d.** 51

19. Determine if the following pairs of numbers are amicable. (See Part A, Problem 19)
   a. 1648, 1576
   b. 2620, 2924
   c. If 17,296 is one of a pair of amicable numbers, what is the other one? Be sure to check your work.

20. Determine if the following pairs of numbers are betrothed. (See Part A, Problem 20).
   a. (248, 231)
   b. (1050, 1925)
   c. (1575, 1648)

21. a. Complete the following table by listing the factors for the given numbers. Include 1 and the number itself as factors.
   b. What kind of numbers have only two factors?
   c. What kind of numbers have an odd number of factors?

NUMBER	FACTORS	NUMBER OF FACTORS
1	1	1
2	1, 2	2
3		
4		
5		
6		
7		
8		
9		
10		
11		
12		
13		
14		
15		
16		

22. Let the letters p, q, and r represent different primes. Then p^2qr^3 has 24 divisors. So would p^{23}. Use p, q, and r to describe all whole numbers having exactly the following number of divisors.
   a. 2   **b.** 3   **c.** 4   **d.** 5   **e.** 6   **f.** 12

23. Let a and b represent whole numbers. State the conditions on a and b that make the following statements true.
   a. GCF(a, b) = a **b.** LCM(a, b) = a
   c. GCF(a, b) = $a \times b$ **d.** LCM(a, b) = $a \times b$

24. If GCF(x, y) = 1, what is GCF(x^2, y^2)? Justify your answer.

25. It is claimed that every perfect number greater than 6 is the sum of consecutive odd cubes beginning with 1. For example, $28 = 1^3 + 3^3$. Determine whether the preceding statement is true for the perfect numbers 496 and 8128.

26. Plato supposedly guessed (and may have proved) that there are only four relatively prime whole numbers that satisfy both of the following equations simultaneously.

$$x^2 + y^2 = z^2 \text{ and } x^3 + y^3 + z^3 = w^3$$

If $x = 3$ and $y = 4$ are two of the numbers, what are z and w?

27. Tilda's car gets 34 miles per gallon and Naomi's gets 8 miles per gallon. When traveling from Washington, D.C., to Philadelphia, they both used a whole number of gallons of gasoline. How far is it from Philadelphia to Washington, D.C.?

28. Three neighborhood dogs barked consistently last night. Spot, Patches, and Lady began with a simultaneous bark at 11 P.M. Then Spot barked every 4 minutes, Patches every 3 minutes, and Lady every 5 minutes. Why did Mr. Jones suddenly awaken at midnight?

29. The numbers 2, 5, and 9 are factors of my locker number and there are 12 factors in all. What is my locker number, and why?

30. Which number less than 70 has the greatest number of factors?

31. The theory of biorhythm states that there are three "cycles" to your life:

    The physical cycle: 23 days long
    The emotional cycle: 28 days long
    The intellectual cycle: 33 days long

    If your cycles are together one day, in how many days will they be together again?

32. Show that the number 494 is divisible by 13. Then prove or disprove: Any three-digit number of the form $100a + 10b + a$, where $a + b = 13$, is divisible by 13.

33. A **Smith number** is a counting number the sum of whose digits is equal to the sum of all the digits of its prime factors. Prove that 4,937,775 (which was discovered by Harold Smith) is a Smith number.

34. **a.** Draw a 2×3 rectangular array of squares. If one diagonal is drawn in, how many squares will the diagonal go through?
    b. Repeat for a 4×6 rectangular array.
    c. Generalize this problem to an $m \times n$ array of squares.

35. Ramanujan observed that 1729 was the smallest number that was the sum of two cubes in two ways. Express 1729 as the sum of two cubes in two ways.

36. The Euclidian algorithm is an iterative process of finding the remainder over and over again in order to find the GCF. Use the dynamic spreadsheet *Euclidean* on our Web site to identify two numbers that will require the Euclidean algorithm at least 10 steps to find the GCF. (*Hint:* The numbers are not necessarily large, but they can be found by thinking of doing the algorithm backward.)

Analyzing Student Thinking

37. Colby used the ideas in this section to claim that $8^3 \cdot 9^4$ has $(3 + 1)(4 + 1) = 20$ factors. Is he correct? Explain.

38. Eva is confused by the terms LCM and GCF. She says that the LCM of two numbers is greater than the GCF of two numbers. How can you help her understand this apparent contradiction?

39. A student noticed the terms LCD and GCD in another math book. What do you think these abbreviations stand for?

40. Brett knows that all primes have exactly two factors, but does not think that there is anything special about whole numbers that have exactly three factors. How should you respond?

41. Vivian says that her older brother told her that the GCF and LCM are useful when studying fractions. Is the older brother correct in both cases? Explain.

42. Cecilia says that she prefers to use the Set Intersection method to find the GCF of two numbers, but Mandy prefers the Prime Factorization Method. How can you help the students see the value of learning both methods?

43. In the theorem proving that there is an infinite number of primes, it considers $(2 \cdot 3 \cdot 5 \cdot 7 \cdot 11 \cdot \ldots \cdot p) + 1$. One of your students says that $2 \cdot 3 \cdot 5 \cdot 7 \cdot 11 \cdot 13 \cdot +1$ is not a prime because it is equal to $59 \cdot 509$. Is the student correct? Does this invalidate the theorem? Explain.

Problems Relating to the NCTM Standards and Curriculum Focal Points

1. The Focal Points for Grade 4 state "Developing quick recall of multiplication facts and related division facts and fluency with whole number multiplication." How does having a "quick recall" of multiplication and division facts influence the process of finding LCMs and GCFs?

2. The Focal Points for Grade 5 state "Developing an understanding of and fluency with addition and subtraction of fractions and decimals." What does addition and subtraction of fractions and decimals have to do with LCMs and GCFs?

3. The NCTM Standards state "All students should use factors, multiples, prime factorization, and relatively prime numbers to solve problems." Factors, multiples, and prime factorizations are all used to find LCMs and GCFs. What are some examples of LCMs and GCFs being used to solve problems in algebra?

END OF CHAPTER MATERIAL

Solution of Initial Problem

A major fast-food chain held a contest to promote sales. With each purchase a customer was given a card with a whole number less than 100 on it. A $100 prize was given to any person who presented cards whose numbers totaled 100. The following are several typical cards. Can you find a winning combination?

| 3 | 9 | 12 | 15 | 18 | 22 | 51 | 72 | 84 |

Can you suggest how the contest could be structured so that there would be at most 1000 winners throughout the country?

Strategy: Use Properties of Numbers

Perhaps you noticed something interesting about the numbers that were on sample cards—they are all multiples of 3. From work in this chapter, we know that the sum of two (hence any number of) multiples of 3 is a multiple of 3. Therefore, any combination of the given numbers will produce a sum that is a multiple of 3. Since 100 is not a multiple of 3, it is impossible to win with the given numbers. Although there are several ways to control the number of winners, a simple way is to include only 1000 cards with the number 1 on them.

Additional Problems Where the Strategy "Use Properties of Numbers" Is Useful

1. How old is Mary?
- She is younger than 75 years old.
- Her age is an odd number.
- The sum of the digits of her age is 8.
- Her age is a prime number.
- She has three great-grandchildren.

2. A folding machine folds letters at a rate of 45 per minute and a stamping machine stamps folded letters at a rate of 60 per minute. What is the fewest number of each machine required so that all machines are kept busy?

3. Find infinitely many natural numbers each of which has exactly 91 factors.

People in Mathematics

Srinivasa Ramanujan (1887–1920) Srinivasa Ramanujan developed a passion for mathematics when he was a young man in India. Working from numerical examples, he arrived at astounding results in number theory. Yet he had little formal training beyond high school and had only vague notions of the principles of mathematical proof. In 1913 he sent some of his results to the English mathematician George Hardy, who was astounded at the raw genius of the work. Hardy arranged for the poverty-stricken young man to come to England. Hardy became his mentor and teacher but later remarked, "I learned from him much more than he learned from me." After several years in England, Ramanujan's health declined. He went home to India in 1919 and died of tuberculosis the following year. On one occasion, Ramanujan was ill in bed. Hardy went to visit, arriving in taxicab number 1729. He remarked to Ramanujan that the number seemed rather dull, and he hoped it wasn't a bad omen. "No," said Ramanujan, "it is a very interesting number; it is the smallest number expressible as a sum of cubes in two different ways."

Constance Bowman Reid (1918–) Constance Bowman Reid, Julia Bowman Robinson's older sister, became a high school English and journalism teacher. She gave up teaching after marriage to become a freelance writer. She coauthored *Slacks and Calluses*, a book about two young teachers who, in 1943, decided to help the war effort during their summer vacation by working on a B-24 bomber production line. Reid became fascinated with number theory because of discussions with her mathematician sister. Her first popular exposition of mathematics in a 1952 *Scientific American* article was about finding perfect numbers using a computer. One of the readers complained that *Scientific American* articles should be written by recognized authorities, not by housewives! Reid has written the popular books *From Zero to Infinity*, *A Long Way from Euclid*, and *Introduction to Higher Mathematics* as well as biographies of mathematicians. She also wrote *Julie: A Life of Mathematics*, which contains an autobiography of Julia Robinson and three articles about Julia's work by outstanding mathematical colleagues.

CHAPTER REVIEW

Review the following terms and exercises to determine which require learning or relearning—page numbers are provided for easy reference.

SECTION 5.1 Primes, Composites, and Tests for Divisibility

VOCABULARY/NOTATION

Prime number 183	Fundamental Theorem of	Factor 186
Composite number 183	Arithmetic 184	Multiple 186
Sieve of Eratosthenes 184	Divides $(a \mid b)$ 186	Is divisible by 186
Factor tree 184	Does not divide $(a \nmid b)$ 186	Square root 191
Prime factorization 184	Divisor 186	Prime Factor Test 191

EXERCISES

1. Find the prime factorization of 17,017.

2. Find all the composite numbers between 90 and 100 inclusive.

3. True or false?
  a. 51 is a prime number.
  b. 101 is a composite number.
  c. $7 \mid 91$.
  d. 24 is a divisor of 36.

  e. 21 is a factor of 63.
  f. 123 is a multiple of 3.
  g. 81 is divisible by 27.
  h. $\sqrt{169} = 13$.

4. Using tests for divisibility, determine whether 2, 3, 4, 5, 6, 8, 9, 10, or 11 are factors of 3,963,960.

5. Invent a test for divisibility by 25.

SECTION 5.2 Counting Factors, Greatest Common Factor, and Least Common Multiple

VOCABULARY/NOTATION

Greatest common factor	Euclidean algorithm 201	Least common multiple
[GCF (a, b)] 198		[LCM (a, b)] 202

EXERCISES

1. How many factors does $3^5 \cdot 7^3$ have?

2. Find GCF(144, 108) using the prime factorization method.

3. Find GCF(54, 189) using the Euclidean algorithm.

4. Find LCM(144, 108).

5. Given that there is an infinite number of primes, show that there is an infinite number of composite numbers.

6. Explain how the four numbers 81, 135, GCF(81, 135), and LCM(81, 135) are related.

CHAPTER TEST

KNOWLEDGE

1. True or false?
   a. Every prime number is odd.
   b. The Sieve of Eratosthenes is used to find primes.
   c. A number is divisible by 6 if it is divisible by 2 and 3.
   d. A number is divisible by 8 if it is divisible by 4 and 2.
   e. If $a \neq b$, then GCF(a, b) < LCM(a, b).
   f. The number of factors of n can be determined by the exponents in its prime factorization.
   g. The prime factorization of a and b can be used to find the GCF and LCM of a and b.
   h. The larger a number, the more prime factors it has.
   i. The number 12 is a multiple of 36.
   j. Every counting number has more multiples than factors.

2. Write a complete sentence that conveys the meaning of and correctly uses each of the following terms or phrases.
   a. divided into   b. divided by   c. divides

SKILL

3. Find the prime factorization of each of the following numbers.
   a. 120   b. 10,800   c. 819

4. Test the following for divisibility by 2, 3, 4, 5, 6, 8, 9, 10, and 11.
   a. 11,223,344   b. 6,543,210   c. $2^3 \cdot 3^4 \cdot 5^6$

5. Determine the number of factors for each of the following numbers.
   a. 360   b. 216   c. 900

6. Find the GCF and LCM of each of the following pairs of numbers.
   a. 144, 120   b. 147, 70
   c. $2^3 \cdot 3^5 \cdot 5^7$, $2^7 \cdot 3^4 \cdot 5^3$ d. 2419, 2173
   e. 45, 175, 42, 60

7. Use the Euclidean algorithm to find GCF(6273, 1025).

8. Find the LCM(18, 24) by using the (i) set intersection method, (ii) prime factorization method, and (iii) build-up method.

UNDERSTANDING

9. Explain how the Sieve of Eratosthenes can be used to find composite numbers.

10. Is it possible to find nonzero whole numbers x and y such that $7^x = 11^y$? Why or why not?

11. Show that the sum of any four consecutive counting numbers must have a factor of 2.

12. a. Show why the following statement is not true. "If $4 \mid m$ and $6 \mid m$ then $24 \mid m$."
    b. Devise a divisibility test for 18.

13. Given that $a \cdot b = 270$ and GCF(a, b) = 3, find LCM(a, b).

14. Use rectangular arrays to illustrate why $4 \mid 8$ but $3 \nmid 8$.

15. If $n = 2 \cdot 3 \cdot 2 \cdot 7 \cdot 2 \cdot 3$ and $m = 2 \cdot 2^2 \cdot 3^2 \cdot 7$, how are m and n related? Justify your answer.

PROBLEM-SOLVING/APPLICATION

16. Find the smallest number that has factors of 2, 3, 4, 5, 6, 7, 8, 9, and 10.

17. The primes 2 and 5 differ by 3. Prove that this is the only pair of primes whose difference is 3.

18. If $a = 2^2 \cdot 3^3$ and the LCM(a, b) is 1080, what is the (a) smallest and (b) the largest that b can be?

19. Find the longest string of consecutive composite numbers between 1 and 50. What are those numbers?

20. Identify all of the numbers between 1 and 20 that have an odd number of divisors. How are these numbers related?

21. What is the maximum value of n that makes the statement $2^n \mid 15 \cdot 14 \cdot 13 \cdot 12 \cdots 3 \cdot 2 \cdot 1$ true?

22. Find two pairs of numbers a and b such that GCF(a, b) = 15 and LCM(a, b) = 180.

23. When Alpesh sorts his marbles, he notices that if he puts them into groups of 5, he has 1 left over. When he puts them in groups of 7, he also has 1 left over, but in groups of size 6, he has none left over. What is the smallest number of marbles that he could have?

Fractions

FOCUS ON *Fractions—A Historical Sketch*

The first extensive treatment of fractions known to us appears in the Ahmes (or Rhind) Papyrus (1600 B.C.E.), which contains the work of Egyptian mathematicians.

The Egyptians expressed fractions as unit fractions (that is, fractions in which the numerator is 1). Thus, if they wanted to describe how much fish each person would get if they were dividing 5 fish among 8 people, they wouldn't write it as $\frac{5}{8}$ but would express it as $\frac{1}{2} + \frac{1}{8}$. Of course, the Egyptians used hieroglyphics to represent these unit fractions.

$$\frac{1}{5} = \text{(hieroglyph)} \quad \frac{1}{10} = \text{(hieroglyph)} \quad \frac{1}{21} = \text{(hieroglyph)}$$

Although the (symbol) symbol looks similar to the zero in

the (symbol) Mayan number system, the Egyptians used it

to denote the unit fraction with the denominator of the fraction written below the (symbol).

Because of its common use, the Egyptians did not write $\frac{2}{3}$ as the sum $\frac{1}{2} + \frac{1}{6}$, but rather wrote it as a unit fraction with a denominator of $\frac{3}{2}$. Therefore, $\frac{2}{3}$ was written as the reciprocal of $\frac{3}{2}$ with the special symbol shown here.

$$\frac{2}{3} = \text{(symbol)} = \frac{1}{\frac{3}{2}}$$

Our present way of expressing fractions is probably due to the Hindus. Brahmagupta (circa C.E. 630) wrote the symbol $\frac{2}{3}$ (with no bar) to represent "two-thirds." The Arabs introduced the "bar" to separate the two parts of a fraction, but this first attempt did not catch on. Later, due to typesetting constraints, the bar was omitted and, at times, the fraction "two-thirds" was written as 2/3.

The name *fraction* came from the Latin word *fractus*, which means "to break." The term *numerator* comes from the Latin word *numerare*, which means "to number" or to count and the name *denominator* comes from *nomen* or name. Therefore, in the fraction two-thirds $\left(\frac{2}{3}\right)$, the denominator tells the reader the name of the objects (thirds) and the numerator tells the number of the objects (two).

STRATEGY 11
Solve an Equivalent Problem

One's point of view or interpretation of a problem can often change a seemingly difficult problem into one that is easily solvable. One way to solve the next problem is by drawing a picture or, perhaps, by actually finding some representative blocks to try various combinations. On the other hand, another approach is to see whether the problem can be restated in an equivalent form, say, using numbers. Then if the equivalent problem can be solved, the solution can be interpreted to yield an answer to the original problem.

INITIAL PROBLEM

A child has a set of 10 cubical blocks. The lengths of the edges are 1 cm, 2 cm, 3 cm, . . . , 10 cm. Using all the cubes, can the child build two towers of the same height by stacking one cube upon another? Why or why not?

CLUES

The Solve an Equivalent Problem strategy may be appropriate when

- You can find an equivalent problem that is easier to solve.
- A problem is related to another problem you have solved previously.
- A problem can be represented in a more familiar setting.
- A geometric problem can be represented algebraically, or vice versa.
- Physical problems can easily be represented with numbers or symbols.

A solution of this Initial Problem is on page 259.

INTRODUCTION

C hapters 2 to 5 have been devoted to the study of the system of whole numbers. Understanding the system of whole numbers is necessary to ensure success in mathematics later. This chapter is devoted to the study of fractions. Fractions were invented because it was not convenient to describe many problem situations using only whole numbers. As you study this chapter, note the importance that the whole numbers play in helping to make fraction concepts easy to understand.

Key Concepts from NCTM Curriculum Focal Points

- **GRADE 3:** Developing an understanding of fractions and fraction equivalence.
- **GRADE 5:** Developing an understanding of and fluency with addition and subtraction of fractions and decimals.
- **GRADE 6:** Developing an understanding of and fluency with multiplication and division of fractions and decimals.

6.1   THE SET OF FRACTIONS

STARTING POINT

For each of the following visual representations of fractions, there is a corresponding incorrect symbolic expression. Discuss what aspects of the visual representation might lead a student to the *incorrect* expression.

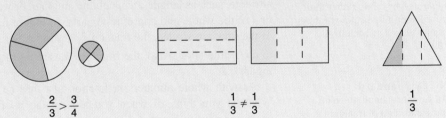

$$\frac{2}{3} > \frac{3}{4} \qquad\qquad \frac{1}{3} \neq \frac{1}{3} \qquad\qquad \frac{1}{3}$$

Children's Literature
www.wiley.com/college/musser
See "Eating Fractions" by Bruce McMillan.

Algebraic Reasoning
While the equation $x - 6 = 2$ can be solved using whole numbers, an equation such as $3x = 2$ has a fraction as a solution.

The Concept of a Fraction

There are many times when whole numbers do not fully describe a mathematical situation. For example, using whole numbers, try to answer the following questions that refer to Figure 6.1: (1) How much pizza is left? (2) How much of the stick is shaded? (3) How much paint is left in the can?

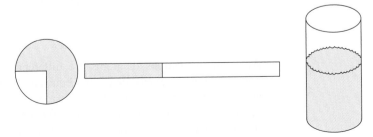

Figure 6.1

Although it is not easy to provide whole-number answers to the preceding questions, the situations in Figure 6.1 can be conveniently described using fractions. Reconsider the preceding questions in light of the subdivisions added in Figure 6.2. Typical answers to these questions are (1) "Three-fourths of the pizza is left," (2) "Four-tenths of the stick is shaded," (3) "The paint can is three-fifths full."

Figure 6.2

The term *fraction* is used in two distinct ways in elementary mathematics. Initially, fractions are used as numerals to indicate the number of parts of a whole to be considered. In Figure 6.2, the pizza was cut into 4 equivalent pieces, and 3 remain. In this case we use the fraction $\frac{3}{4}$ to represent the 3 out of 4 equivalent pieces (i.e., equivalent in size). The use of a fraction as a numeral in this way is commonly called the "part-to-whole" model. Succinctly, if a and b are whole numbers, where $b \neq 0$, then the fraction $\frac{a}{b}$ or a/b, represents a of b equivalent parts; a is called the **numerator** and b is called the **denominator**. The term *equivalent parts* means equivalent in some attribute, such as length, area, volume, number, or weight, depending on the composition of the whole and appropriate parts. In Figure 6.2, since 4 of 10 equivalent parts of the stick are shaded, the fraction $\frac{4}{10}$ describes the shaded part when it is compared to the whole stick. Also, the fraction $\frac{3}{5}$ describes the filled portion of the paint can in Figure 6.2.

As with whole numbers, a fraction also has an *abstract* meaning as a number. What do you think of when you look at the relative amounts represented by the shaded regions in Figure 6.3?

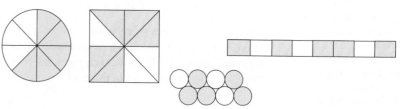

Figure 6.3

Although the various diagrams are different in size and shape, they share a common attribute—namely, that 5 of 8 equivalent parts are shaded. That is, the same *relative amount* is shaded. This attribute can be represented by the fraction $\frac{5}{8}$. Thus, in addition to representing parts of a whole, a fraction is viewed as a number representing a relative amount. Hence we make the following definition.

DEFINITION

Fractions

A **fraction** is a number that can be represented by an ordered pair of whole numbers $\dfrac{a}{b}$ (or a/b), where $b \neq 0$. In set notation, the **set of fractions** is

$$F = \left\{ \dfrac{a}{b} \,\middle|\, a \text{ and } b \text{ are whole numbers, } b \neq 0 \right\}.$$

Before proceeding with the computational aspects of fractions as numbers, it is instructive to comment further on the complexity of this topic—namely, viewing fractions as numerals and as numbers. Recall that the whole number three was the attribute common to all sets that match the set $\{a, b, c\}$. Thus if a child who understands the concept of a whole number is shown a set of three objects, the child will answer the question "How many objects?" with the word "three" regardless of the size, shape, color, and so on of the objects themselves. That is, it is the "numerousness" of the set on which the child is focusing.

With fractions, there are two attributes that the child must observe. First, when considering a fraction *as a number*, the focus is on relative amount. For example, in Figure 6.4, the relative amount represented by the various shaded regions is described by the fraction $\frac{1}{4}$ (which is considered as a number). Notice that $\frac{1}{4}$ describes the relative amount shaded without regard to size, shape, arrangement, orientation, number of equivalent parts, and so on; thus it is the "numerousness" of a fraction on which we are focusing.

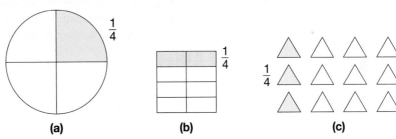

Figure 6.4

Second, when considering a fraction as a *numeral* representing a part-to-whole relationship, many numerals can be used for the relationship. For example, the three diagrams in Figure 6.4 can be labeled differently (Figure 6.5).

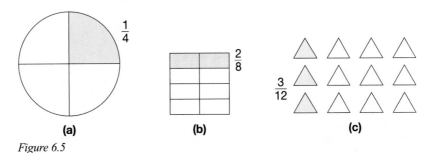

Figure 6.5

In Figures 6.5(b) and (c), the shaded regions have been renamed using the fractions $\frac{2}{8}$ and $\frac{3}{12}$, respectively, to call attention to the different subdivisions. The notion of fraction as a numeral displaying a part-to-whole relationship can be merged with the concept of fraction as a number. That is, the fraction (number) $\frac{1}{4}$ can also be thought of and represented by any of the fractions $\frac{2}{8}$, $\frac{3}{12}$, $\frac{4}{16}$, and so on. Figure 6.6 brings this into sharper focus.

On a more general note, a model such as those in Figure 6.6, which use geometric shapes or "regions" to represent fractions, is called a **region model**.

NCTM Standard
All students should understand and represent commonly used fractions, such as $\frac{1}{4}$, $\frac{1}{3}$, and $\frac{1}{2}$.

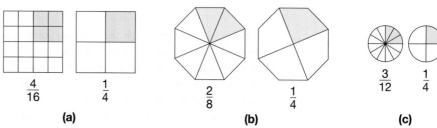

Figure 6.6

In each of the pairs of diagrams in Figure 6.6, the same relative amount is shaded, although the subdivisions into equivalent parts and the sizes of the diagrams are different. As suggested by the shaded regions, the fractions $\frac{4}{16}$, $\frac{2}{8}$, and $\frac{3}{12}$ all represent the same relative amount as $\frac{1}{4}$.

Two fractions that represent the same relative amount are said to be **equivalent fractions**.

The diagrams in Figure 6.6 were different shapes and sizes. **Fraction strips**, which can be constructed out of paper or cardboard, can be used to visualize fractional parts (Figure 6.7). The advantage of this model is that the unit strips are the same size—only the shading and number of subdivisions vary.

Figure 6.7

It is useful to have a simple test to determine whether fractions such as $\frac{2}{8}$, $\frac{3}{12}$, and $\frac{4}{16}$ represent the same relative amount without having to draw a picture of each representation. Two approaches can be taken. First, observe that $\frac{2}{8} = \frac{1 \cdot 2}{4 \cdot 2}$, $\frac{3}{12} = \frac{1 \cdot 3}{4 \cdot 3}$, and $\frac{4}{16} = \frac{1 \cdot 4}{4 \cdot 4}$. These equations illustrate the fact that $\frac{2}{8}$ can be obtained from $\frac{1}{4}$ by equally subdividing each portion of a representation of $\frac{1}{4}$ by 2 [Figure 6.6(b)]. A similar argument can be applied to the equations $\frac{3}{12} = \frac{1 \cdot 3}{4 \cdot 3}$ [Figure 6.6(c)] and $\frac{4}{16} = \frac{1 \cdot 4}{4 \cdot 4}$ [Figure 6.6(a)]. Thus it appears that any fraction of the form $\frac{1 \cdot n}{4 \cdot n}$, where n is a counting number, represents the same relative amount as $\frac{1}{4}$, or that $\frac{an}{bn} = \frac{a}{b}$, in general. When $\frac{an}{bn}$ is replaced with $\frac{a}{b}$, where $n \neq 1$, we say that $\frac{an}{bn}$ has been **simplified**.

Reflection from Research
A child's understanding of fractions needs to coordinate the knowledge of notation and the knowledge of some part-whole relations. However, these two types of knowledge develop independently (Saxe, Taylor, McIntosh, & Gearhart, 2005).

To determine whether $\frac{3}{12}$ and $\frac{4}{16}$ are equal, we can simplify each of them: $\frac{3}{12} = \frac{1}{4}$ and $\frac{4}{16} = \frac{1}{4}$. Since they both equal $\frac{1}{4}$, we can write $\frac{3}{12} = \frac{4}{16}$. Alternatively, we can view $\frac{3}{12}$ and $\frac{4}{16}$ as $\frac{3 \cdot 16}{12 \cdot 16}$ and $\frac{4 \cdot 12}{16 \cdot 12}$ instead. Since the numerators $3 \cdot 16 = 48$ and $4 \cdot 12 = 48$ are equal and the denominators are the same, namely $12 \cdot 16$, the two fractions $\frac{3}{12}$ and $\frac{4}{16}$ must be equal. As the next diagram suggests, the numbers $3 \cdot 16$ and $4 \cdot 12$ are called the cross-products of the fractions $\frac{3}{12}$ and $\frac{4}{16}$.

$$\frac{3}{12} \bowtie \frac{4}{16}$$

The technique, which can be used for any pair of fractions, leads to the following definition of fraction equality.

DEFINITION

Fraction Equality

Let $\frac{a}{b}$ and $\frac{c}{d}$ be any fractions. Then $\frac{a}{b} = \frac{c}{d}$ if and only if $ad = bc$.

Algebraic Reasoning
Although established on the principles of equivalent fractions, the process of cross multiplication is commonly used when solving proportions algebraically.

In words, two fractions are **equal fractions** if and only if their **cross-products**, that is, products ad and bc obtained by **cross-multiplication**, are equal. The first method described for determining whether two fractions are equal is an immediate consequence of this definition, since $a(bn) = b(an)$ by associativity and commutativity. This is summarized next.

THEOREM

Let $\frac{a}{b}$ be any fraction and n a nonzero whole number. Then

$$\frac{a}{b} = \frac{an}{bn} = \frac{na}{nb}.$$

It is important to note that this theorem can be used in two ways: (1) to replace the fraction $\frac{a}{b}$ with $\frac{an}{bn}$ and (2) to replace the fraction $\frac{an}{bn}$ with $\frac{a}{b}$. Occasionally, the term *reducing* is used to describe the process in (2). However, the term *reducing* can be misleading, since fractions are not reduced in size (the relative amount they represent) but only in complexity (the numerators and denominators are smaller).

Example 6.1 Verify the following equations using the definition of fraction equality or the preceding theorem.

a. $\dfrac{5}{6} = \dfrac{25}{30}$ **b.** $\dfrac{27}{36} = \dfrac{54}{72}$ **c.** $\dfrac{16}{48} = \dfrac{1}{3}$

SOLUTION

a. $\dfrac{5}{6} = \dfrac{5 \cdot 5}{6 \cdot 5} = \dfrac{25}{30}$ by the preceding theorem.

b. $\dfrac{54}{72} = \dfrac{27 \cdot 2}{36 \cdot 2} = \dfrac{27}{36}$ by simplifying. Alternatively, $\dfrac{27}{36} = \dfrac{3 \cdot 9}{4 \cdot 9} = \dfrac{3}{4}$ and $\dfrac{54}{72} = \dfrac{3 \cdot 18}{4 \cdot 18} = \dfrac{3}{4}$, so $\dfrac{32}{36} = \dfrac{54}{72}$.

c. $\dfrac{16}{48} = \dfrac{1}{3}$, since their cross-products, $16 \cdot 3$ and $48 \cdot 1$, are equal. ∎

Fraction equality can readily be checked on a calculator using an alternative version of cross-multiplication—namely, $\dfrac{a}{b} = \dfrac{c}{d}$ if and only if $\dfrac{ad}{b} = c$. Thus the equality $\dfrac{20}{36} = \dfrac{30}{54}$ can be checked by pressing 20 ☒ 54 ÷ 36 ⊟ [30]. Since 30 obtained in this way is equal to the numerator of $\dfrac{30}{54}$, the two fractions are equal.

Since $\dfrac{a}{b} = \dfrac{an}{bn}$ for $n = 1, 2, 3, \ldots$, every fraction has an infinite number of representations (numerals). For example,

$$\frac{1}{2} = \frac{2}{4} = \frac{3}{6} = \frac{4}{8} = \frac{5}{10} = \frac{6}{12} = \cdots$$

are different numerals for the number $\frac{1}{2}$. In fact, another way to view a fraction as a number is to think of the idea that is common to all of its various representations. That is, the fraction $\frac{2}{3}$, as a *number*, is the idea that one associates with the set of all fractions, as *numerals*, that are equivalent to $\frac{2}{3}$, namely $\frac{2}{3}, \frac{4}{6}, \frac{6}{9}, \frac{8}{12}, \ldots$. Notice that the term *equal* refers to fractions as numbers, while the term *equivalent* refers to fractions as numerals.

Every whole number is a fraction and hence has an infinite number of fraction representations. For example,

$$1 = \frac{1}{1} = \frac{2}{2} = \frac{3}{3} = \ldots, 2 = \frac{2}{1} = \frac{4}{2} = \frac{6}{3} = \ldots, 0 = \frac{0}{1} = \frac{0}{2} = \ldots,$$

and so on. Thus the set of fractions extends the set of whole numbers.

A fraction is written in its **simplest form** or **lowest terms** when its numerator and denominator have no common prime factors.

Name the fraction represented by the shaded sections in two ways.

❶ ❹

❷ ❺

❸ ❻

Writing + Math **Journal**
Which is greater, $2\frac{1}{2}$ or $3\frac{1}{3}$? Explain.

Chapter 8 • Lesson 8   319

Example 6.2   Find the simplest form of the following fractions.

a. $\dfrac{12}{18}$ **b.** $\dfrac{36}{56}$ **c.** $\dfrac{9}{31}$ **d.** $(2^3 \cdot 3^5 \cdot 5^7)/(2^6 \cdot 3^4 \cdot 7)$

SOLUTION

a. $\dfrac{12}{18} = \dfrac{2 \cdot 6}{3 \cdot 6} = \dfrac{2}{3}$

b. $\dfrac{36}{56} = \dfrac{18 \cdot 2}{28 \cdot 2} = \dfrac{18}{28} = \dfrac{9 \cdot 2}{14 \cdot 2} = \dfrac{9}{14}$ or $\dfrac{36}{56} = \dfrac{2 \cdot 2 \cdot 3 \cdot 3}{2 \cdot 2 \cdot 2 \cdot 7} = \dfrac{3 \cdot 3}{2 \cdot 7} = \dfrac{9}{14}$

c. $\dfrac{9}{31}$ is in simplest form, since 9 and 31 have only 1 as a common factor.

d. To write $(2^3 \cdot 3^5 \cdot 5^7)/(2^6 \cdot 3^4 \cdot 7)$ in simplest form, first find the GCF of $2^3 \cdot 3^5 \cdot 5^7$ and $2^6 \cdot 3^4 \cdot 7$:

$$\text{GCF}(2^3 \cdot 3^5 \cdot 5^7, 2^6 \cdot 3^4 \cdot 7) = 2^3 \cdot 3^4.$$

Then

$$\dfrac{2^3 \cdot 3^5 \cdot 5^7}{2^6 \cdot 3^4 \cdot 7} = \dfrac{(3 \cdot 5^7)(2^3 \cdot 3^4)}{(2^3 \cdot 7)(2^3 \cdot 3^4)} = \dfrac{3 \cdot 5^7}{2^3 \cdot 7}.$$ ∎

Reflection from Research
When dealing with improper fractions, like $\dfrac{12}{11}$, students struggle to focus on the whole, $\dfrac{11}{11}$, and not the number of parts, 12 (Tzur, 1999).

Fractions with numerators greater than or equal to their denominators fall into two categories. The fractions $\frac{1}{1}, \frac{2}{2}, \frac{3}{3}, \frac{4}{4}, \ldots$, in which the numerators and denominators are equal, represent the whole number 1. Fractions where the numerators are greater than the denominators are called **improper fractions**. For example, $\frac{7}{2}, \frac{8}{5},$ and $\frac{117}{35}$ are improper fractions. The fraction $\frac{7}{2}$ would mean that an object was divided into 2 equivalent parts and 7 such parts are designated. Figure 6.8 illustrates a model for $\frac{7}{2}$ because seven halves are shaded where one shaded circle represents one unit. The diagram in Figure 6.8 illustrates that $\frac{7}{2}$ can also be viewed as 3 wholes plus $\frac{1}{2}$, or $3\frac{1}{2}$. A combination of a whole number with a fraction juxtaposed to its right is called a **mixed number**. Mixed numbers will be studied in Section 6.2.

Figure 6.8

The TI-34 II calculator can be used to convert improper fractions to mixed numbers. For example, to convert $\dfrac{1234}{378}$ to a mixed number in its simplest form on a fraction calculator, press 1234 $\boxed{/}$ 378 $\boxed{\text{2nd}}$ $\boxed{A^b\!/_c \triangleleft\!\triangleright\, ^d\!/_e}$ $\boxed{=}$ $\boxed{3\cup100/378}$. (If the fraction mode is set as A $\cup$ $^b\!/_c$, the $\boxed{A^b\!/_c \triangleleft\!\triangleright\, ^d\!/_e}$ button will not need to be used.) Pressing $\boxed{\text{SIMP}}$ $\boxed{=}$ yields the result $3\dfrac{50}{189}$, which is in simplest form. For calculators without the fraction function, 1234 $\boxed{\div}$ 378 $=$ $\boxed{3.2645502}$ shows the whole-number part, namely 3, together with a decimal fraction. The calculation 1234 $\boxed{-}$ 3 $\boxed{\times}$ 378 $\boxed{=}$ $\boxed{100}$ gives the numerator of the fraction part; thus $\dfrac{1234}{378} = 3\dfrac{100}{378}$, which is $3\dfrac{50}{189}$ in simplest form.

✔ **Check for Understanding:** Exercise/Problem Set A #1–11

Ordering Fractions

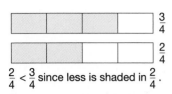

$\frac{2}{4} < \frac{3}{4}$ since less is shaded in $\frac{2}{4}$.

Figure 6.9

The concepts of less than and greater than in fractions are extensions of the respective whole-number concepts. Fraction strips can be used to order fractions (Figure 6.9).

Next consider the three pairs of fractions on the **fraction number line** in Figure 6.10.

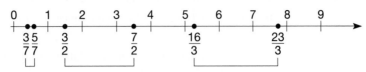

Figure 6.10

Reflection from Research
Young children have a very difficult time believing that a fraction such as one-eighth is smaller than one-fifth because the number eight is larger than five (Post, Wachsmuth, Lesh, & Behr, 1985).

As it was in the case of whole numbers, the smaller of two fractions is to the left of the larger fraction on the fraction number line. Also, the three examples in Figure 6.10 suggest the following definition, where fractions having common denominators can be compared simply by comparing their numerators (which are whole numbers).

Children's Literature
www.wiley.com/college/musser
See "Fraction Action" by
Loreen Leedy.

DEFINITION

Less Than for Fractions

Let $\frac{a}{c}$ and $\frac{b}{c}$ be any fractions. Then $\frac{a}{c} < \frac{b}{c}$ if and only if $a < b$.

NOTE: Although the definition is stated for "less than," a corresponding statement holds for "**greater than**." Similar statements hold for "**less than or equal to**" and "**greater than or equal to**."

For example, $\frac{3}{7} < \frac{5}{7}$, since $3 < 5$; $\frac{4}{13} < \frac{10}{13}$, since $4 < 10$; and so on. The numbers $\frac{2}{7}$ and $\frac{4}{13}$ can be compared by getting a common denominator.

$$\frac{2}{7} = \frac{2 \cdot 13}{7 \cdot 13} = \frac{26}{91} \quad \text{and} \quad \frac{4}{13} = \frac{4 \cdot 7}{13 \cdot 7} = \frac{28}{91}$$

Since $\frac{26}{91} < \frac{28}{91}$, we conclude that $\frac{2}{7} < \frac{4}{13}$.

This last example suggests a convenient shortcut for comparing any two fractions. To compare $\frac{2}{7}$ and $\frac{4}{13}$, we compared $\frac{26}{91}$ and $\frac{28}{91}$ and, eventually, 26 and 28. But $26 = 2 \cdot 13$ and $28 = 7 \cdot 4$. In general, this example suggests the following theorem.

THEOREM

Cross-Multiplication of Fraction Inequality

Let $\frac{a}{b}$ and $\frac{c}{d}$ be any fractions. Then $\frac{a}{b} < \frac{c}{d}$ if and only if $ad < bc$.

Notice that this theorem reduces the ordering of fractions to the ordering of whole numbers. Also, since $\frac{a}{b} < \frac{c}{d}$ if and only if $\frac{c}{d} > \frac{a}{b}$, we can observe that $\frac{c}{d} > \frac{a}{b}$ if and only if $bc > ad$.

Example 6.3   Arrange in order.

a. $\frac{7}{8}$ and $\frac{9}{11}$ **b.** $\frac{17}{32}$ and $\frac{19}{40}$

SOLUTION

a. $\frac{7}{8} < \frac{9}{11}$ if and only if $7 \cdot 11 < 8 \cdot 9$. But $77 > 72$; therefore, $\frac{7}{8} > \frac{9}{11}$.

b. $17 \cdot 40 = 680$ and $32 \cdot 19 = 608$. Since $32 \cdot 19 < 17 \cdot 40$, we have $\frac{19}{40} < \frac{17}{32}$.   ■

Children's Literature
www.wiley.com/college/musser
See "Inchworm and a Half" by
Elinor Pinczes.

Often fractions can be ordered mentally using your "fraction sense." For example, fractions like $\frac{4}{5}, \frac{7}{8}, \frac{11}{12}$, and so on are close to 1, fractions like $\frac{1}{15}, \frac{1}{14}, \frac{1}{10}$, and so on are close to 0, and fractions like $\frac{6}{14}, \frac{8}{15}, \frac{11}{20}$, and so on are close to $\frac{1}{2}$. Thus $\frac{4}{7} < \frac{12}{13}$, since $\frac{4}{7} \approx \frac{1}{2}$ and $\frac{12}{13} \approx 1$. Also, $\frac{1}{11} < \frac{7}{13}$, since $\frac{1}{11} \approx 0$ and $\frac{7}{13} \approx \frac{1}{2}$.

Keep in mind that this procedure is just a shortcut for finding common denominators and comparing the numerators.

Cross-multiplication of fraction inequality can also be adapted to a calculator as follows: $\frac{a}{b} < \frac{c}{d}$ if and only if $\frac{ad}{b} < c$ (or $\frac{a}{b} > \frac{c}{d}$ if and only if $\frac{ad}{b} > c$). To order $\frac{17}{32}$ and $\frac{19}{40}$ using a fraction calculator, press 17 $\boxed{/}$ 32 $\boxed{\times}$ 40 $\boxed{=}$ $\boxed{21 \cup 8/32}$, or $21\frac{1}{4}$. Since $21\frac{1}{4} > 19$, we conclude that $\frac{17}{32} > \frac{19}{40}$. On a decimal calculator, the following sequence leads to a similar result: 17 $\boxed{\times}$ 40 $\boxed{\div}$ 32 $\boxed{=}$ $\boxed{21.25}$. Since 21.25 is greater than 19, $\frac{17}{32} > \frac{19}{40}$. Ordering fractions using decimal equivalents, which is shown next, will be covered in Chapter 7. In this case, 17 $\boxed{\div}$ 32 $\boxed{=}$ $\boxed{0.53125}$ and 19 $\boxed{\div}$ 40 $\boxed{=}$ $\boxed{0.475}$. Therefore, $\frac{19}{40} < \frac{17}{32}$, since $0.475 < 0.53125$. Finally, one could have ordered these two fractions mentally by observing that $\frac{19}{40}$ is less than $\frac{1}{2}(= \frac{20}{40})$, whereas $\frac{17}{32}$ is greater than $\frac{1}{2}(= \frac{16}{32})$.

Reflection from Research
A variety of alternative approaches and forms of presenting fractions will help students build a foundation that will allow them to later deal in more systematic ways with equivalent fractions, convert fractions from one representation to another, and move back and forth between division of whole numbers and rational numbers (Flores & Klein, 2005).

On the whole-number line, there are gaps between the whole numbers (Figure 6.11).

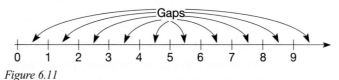

Figure 6.11

However, when fractions are introduced to make up the fraction number line, many new fractions appear in these gaps (Figure 6.12).

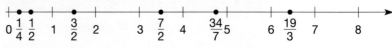

Figure 6.12

Unlike the case with whole numbers, it can be shown that there is a fraction between any two fractions. For example, consider $\frac{3}{4}$ and $\frac{5}{6}$. Since $\frac{3}{4} = \frac{18}{24}$ and $\frac{5}{6} = \frac{20}{24}$, we have that $\frac{19}{24}$ is between $\frac{3}{4}$ and $\frac{5}{6}$. Now consider $\frac{18}{24}$ and $\frac{19}{24}$. These equal $\frac{36}{48}$ and $\frac{38}{48}$, respectively; thus $\frac{37}{48}$ is between $\frac{3}{4}$ and $\frac{5}{6}$ also. Continuing in this manner, one can show that there are infinitely many fractions between $\frac{3}{4}$ and $\frac{5}{6}$. From this it follows that there are *infinitely* many fractions between any two different fractions.

Example 6.4   Find a fraction between these pairs of fractions.

a. $\frac{7}{11}$ and $\frac{8}{11}$ **b.** $\frac{9}{13}$ and $\frac{12}{17}$

SOLUTION

a. $\frac{7}{11} = \frac{14}{22}$ and $\frac{8}{11} = \frac{16}{22}$. Hence $\frac{15}{22}$ is between $\frac{7}{11}$ and $\frac{8}{11}$.

b. $\frac{9}{13} = \frac{9 \cdot 17}{13 \cdot 17} = \frac{153}{13 \cdot 17}$ and $\frac{12}{17} = \frac{12 \cdot 13}{17 \cdot 13} = \frac{156}{17 \cdot 13}$. Hence both $\frac{154}{13 \cdot 17}$ and $\frac{155}{13 \cdot 17}$ are between $\frac{9}{13}$ and $\frac{12}{17}$. ∎

Sometimes students incorrectly add numerators and denominators to find the sum of two fractions. It is interesting, though, that this simple technique does provide an easy way to find a fraction between two given fractions. For example, for fractions $\frac{2}{3}$ and $\frac{3}{4}$, the number $\frac{5}{7}$ satisfies $\frac{2}{3} < \frac{5}{7} < \frac{3}{4}$ since $2 \cdot 7 < 3 \cdot 5$ and $5 \cdot 4 < 7 \cdot 3$. This idea is generalized next.

THEOREM

Let $\frac{a}{b}$ and $\frac{c}{d}$ be any fractions, where $\frac{a}{b} < \frac{c}{d}$. Then

$$\frac{a}{b} < \frac{a+c}{b+d} < \frac{c}{d}.$$

Algebraic Reasoning
Commutativity and distributivity are introduced when children realize expressions like $2 + 5 = 5 + 2$ or $2(4 + 6) = 2 \cdot 4 + 2 \cdot 6$ will work for any numbers. These properties are also used to simplify algebraic expressions like those used in the proof at the right.

PROOF

Let $\frac{a}{b} < \frac{c}{d}$. Then we have $ad < bc$. From this inequality, it follows that $ad + ab < bc + ab$, or $a(b + d) < b(a + c)$. By cross-multiplication of fraction inequality, this last inequality implies $\frac{a}{b} < \frac{a+c}{b+d}$, which is "half" of what we are to prove. The other half can be proved in a similar fashion. ∎

To find a fraction between $\frac{9}{13}$ and $\frac{12}{17}$ using this theorem, add the numerators and denominators to obtain $\frac{21}{30}$. This theorem shows that there is a fraction between any two fractions. The fact that there is a fraction between any two fractions is called the **density property** of fractions.

 Check for Understanding: Exercise/Problem Set A #12–15

MATHEMATICAL MORSEL

Although decimals are prevalent in our monetary system, we commonly use the fraction terms "a quarter" and a "half dollar." It has been suggested that this tradition was based on the Spanish milled dollar coin and its fractional parts that were used in our American colonies. Its fractional parts were called "bits" and each bit had a value of $12\frac{1}{2}$ cents (thus a quarter is known as "two bits"). A familiar old jingle (which seems impossible today) is "Shave and a haircut, two-bits." Some also believe that this fraction system evolved from the British shilling and pence. A shilling was one-fourth of a dollar and a sixpence was one-eighth of a dollar, or $12\frac{1}{2}$ cents.

EXERCISE / PROBLEM SET A

EXERCISES

1. What fraction is represented by the shaded portion of each diagram?

a.

b.

c.  **d.**

2. In addition to fraction strips, a region model, and a set model, fractions can also be represented on the number line by selecting a unit length and subdividing the interval into equal parts. For example, to locate the fraction $\frac{3}{4}$, subdivide the interval from 0 to 1 into four parts and mark off three as shown.

Represent the following fractions using the given models.

   i. $\frac{4}{5}$ **ii.** $\frac{3}{8}$

a. Region model   **b.** Set model
c. Fraction strips   **d.** Number line

3. In this section fractions were represented using equivalent parts. Another representation uses a set model. In the following set of objects, four out of the total of five objects are triangles.

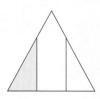

We could say that $\frac{4}{5}$ of the objects are triangles. This interpretation of fractions compares part of a set with all of the set. Draw pictures to represent the following fractions using sets of nonequivalent objects.

a. $\frac{3}{5}$ **b.** $\frac{3}{7}$ **c.** $\frac{1}{3}$

4. Does the following picture represent $\frac{1}{3}$? Explain.

5. Using the diagram below, represent each of the following as a fraction of all shapes shown.

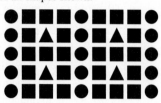

a. What fraction is made of circular shapes?
b. What fraction is made of square shapes?
c. What fraction is not made of triangular shapes?

6. Fill in the blank with the correct fraction.

a. 10 cents is _____ of a dollar.
b. 15 minutes is _____ of an hour.
c. If you sleep eight hours each night, you spend _____ of a day sleeping.
d. Using the information in part (c), what part of a year do you sleep?

7. Use the area model illustrated on the Chapter 6 eManipulative activity *Equivalent Fractions* on our Web site to show that $\frac{5}{8} = \frac{15}{24}$. Explain how the eManipulative was used to do this.

8. Determine whether the following pairs are equal by writing each in simplest form.

a. $\frac{5}{8}$ and $\frac{625}{1000}$ **b.** $\frac{11}{18}$ and $\frac{275}{450}$ **c.** $\frac{24}{36}$ and $\frac{50}{72}$ **d.** $\frac{14}{98}$ and $\frac{8}{56}$

9. Determine which of the following pairs are equal.

a. $\frac{349}{568}, \frac{569}{928}$ **b.** $\frac{734}{957}, \frac{468}{614}$ **c.** $\frac{156}{558}, \frac{52}{186}$ **d.** $\frac{882}{552}, \frac{147}{92}$

10. Rewrite in simplest form.

a. $\frac{21}{28}$ **b.** $\frac{49}{56}$ **c.** $\frac{108}{156}$ **d.** $\frac{220}{100}$

11. Rewrite as a mixed number in simplest form.
a. $\frac{525}{96}$ **b.** $\frac{1234}{432}$

12. a. Arrange each of the following from smallest to largest.

   i. $\frac{11}{17}, \frac{13}{17}, \frac{12}{17}$ **ii.** $\frac{1}{5}, \frac{1}{6}, \frac{1}{7}$
   b. What patterns do you observe?

13. Arrange each of the following from smallest to largest.

   a. $\frac{14}{27}, \frac{3}{7}, \frac{9}{20}$ **b.** $\frac{6}{13}, \frac{17}{39}, \frac{25}{51}$

14. The Chapter 6 eManipulative *Comparing Fractions* on our Web site uses number lines and common denominators to compare fractions. The eManipulative will have you plot two fractions, $\frac{a}{b}$ and $\frac{c}{d}$, on a number line. Do a few examples and plot $\frac{a+c}{b+d}$ on the number line as well. How does the fraction $\frac{a + c}{b + d}$ compare to $\frac{a}{b}$ and $\frac{c}{d}$? Does this relationship appear to hold for all fractions $\frac{a}{b}$ and $\frac{c}{d}$?

15. Order the following sets of fractions from smaller to larger and find a fraction between each pair

a. $\frac{17}{23}, \frac{51}{68}$ **b.** $\frac{43}{567}, \frac{50}{687}$ **c.** $\frac{214}{897}, \frac{597}{2511}$ **d.** $\frac{93}{2811}, \frac{3}{87}$

PROBLEMS

16. According to Bureau of the Census data, in 2005 in the United States there were about

113,000,000 total households
58,000,000 married-couple households
5,000,000 family households with a male head of household
14,000,000 family households with a female head of household
30,000,000 households consisting of one person

(NOTE: Figures have been rounded to simplify calculations.)

a. What fraction of U.S. households in 2005 were married couple households? To what fraction with a denominator of 100 is this fraction closest?

b. What fraction of U.S. households in 2005 consisted of individuals living alone? To what fraction with a denominator of 100 is this closest?

c. What fraction of U.S. family households were headed by a woman in 2005? To what fraction with a denominator of 100 is this fraction closest?

17. What is mathematically inaccurate about the following sales "pitches"?
a. "Save $\frac{1}{2}$, $\frac{1}{3}$, $\frac{1}{4}$, and even more!"
b. "You'll pay only a fraction of the list price!"

18. In 2000, the United States generated 234,000,000 tons of waste and recycled 68,000,000 tons. In 2003, 236,000,000 tons of waste were generated and 72,000,000 tons were recycled. In which year was a greater fraction of the waste recycled?

19. The shaded regions in the figures represent the fractions $\frac{1}{2}$ and $\frac{1}{3}$, respectively.

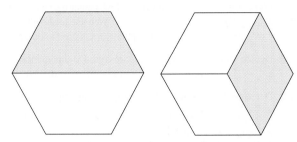

Trace the outline of a figure like those shown and shade in portions that represent the following fractions.
a. $\frac{1}{2}$ (different from the one shown)
b. $\frac{1}{3}$ (different from the one shown)
c. $\frac{1}{4}$ **d.** $\frac{1}{6}$ **e.** $\frac{1}{12}$ **f.** $\frac{1}{24}$

20. A student simplifies $\frac{286}{583}$ by "canceling" the 8s, obtaining $\frac{26}{53}$, which equals $\frac{286}{583}$. He uses the same method with $\frac{28,886}{58,883}$, simplifying it to $\frac{26}{53}$ also. Does this always work with similar fractions? Why or why not?

21. I am a proper fraction. The sum of my numerator and denominator is a one-digit square. Their product is a cube. What fraction am I?

22. True or false? Explain.
a. The greater the numerator, the greater the fraction.
b. The greater the denominator, the smaller the fraction.
c. If the denominator is fixed, the greater the numerator, the greater the fraction.
d. If the numerator is fixed, the greater the denominator, the smaller the fraction.

23. The fraction $\frac{12}{18}$ is simplified on a fraction calculator and the result is $\frac{2}{3}$. Explain how this result can be used to find the GCF(12, 18). Use this method to find the following.
a. GCF(72, 168)
b. GCF(234, 442)

24. Determine whether the following are correct or incorrect. Explain.
a. $\frac{a\cancel{b} + c}{\cancel{b}} = a + c$ **b.** $\frac{a + b}{a + c} = \frac{b}{c}$
c. $\frac{\cancel{a}b + \cancel{a}c}{\cancel{a}d} = \frac{b + c}{d}$

25. Three-fifths of a class of 25 students are girls. How many are girls?

26. The Independent party received one-eleventh of the 6,186,279 votes cast. How many votes did the party receive?

27. Seven-eighths of the 328 adults attending a school bazaar were relatives of the students. How many attendees were not relatives?

28. The school library contains about 5280 books. If five-twelfths of the books are for the primary grades, how many such books are there in the library?

29. Talia walks to school at point B from her house at point A, a distance of six blocks. For variety she likes to try different routes each day. How many different paths can she take if she always moves closer to B? One route is shown.

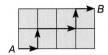

30. If you place a 1 in front of the number 5, the new number is 3 times as large as the original number.
   a. Find another number (not necessarily a one-digit number) such that when you place a 1 in front of it, the result is 3 times as large as the original number.
   b. Find a number such that when you place a 1 in front of it, the result is 5 times as large as the original number. Is there more than one such number?
   c. Find a number such that, when you place a 2 in front of it, the result is 6 times as large as the original number. Can you find more than one such number?

d. Find a number such that, when you place a 3 in front of it, the result is 5 times as large as the original number. Can you find more than one such number?

31. After using the Chapter 6 eManipulative activity *Comparing Fractions* on our Web site, identify two fractions between $\frac{4}{7}$ and $\frac{1}{2}$.

| Section 6.1 | **EXERCISE / PROBLEM SET B** |

EXERCISES

1. What fraction is represented by the shaded portion of each diagram?

a.

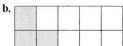

b.

c.

d.

2. Represent the following fractions using the given models.
   i. $\dfrac{7}{10}$ **ii.** $\dfrac{8}{3}$
   a. Region model   **b.** Set model
   c. Fraction strips   **d.** Number line (see Part A, Exercise 2)

3. Use the set model with non-equivalent parts as described in Part A, Exercise 3 to represent the following fractions.
   a. $\dfrac{5}{6}$ **b.** $\dfrac{2}{9}$ **c.** $\dfrac{3}{4}$

4. Does the following picture represent $\frac{3}{4}$? Explain.

5. Using the diagram, represent each of the following as a fraction of all the dots.

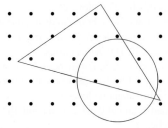

   a. The part of the collection of dots inside the circle
   b. The part of the collection of dots inside both the circle and the triangle
   c. The part of the collection of dots inside the triangle but outside the circle

6. True or false? Explain.
   a. 5 days is $\frac{1}{6}$ of a month.
   b. 4 days is $\frac{4}{7}$ of a week.
   c. 1 month is $\frac{1}{12}$ of a year.

7. Use the area model illustrated on the Chapter 6 eManipulative activity *Equivalent Fractions* on our Web site to show that $\frac{3}{2} = \frac{9}{6}$. Explain how the eManipulative was used to do this.

8. Decide which of the following are true. Do this mentally.
   a. $\frac{7}{6} = \frac{29}{64}$ **b.** $\frac{3}{12} = \frac{20}{84}$ **c.** $\frac{7}{9} = \frac{63}{81}$ **d.** $\frac{7}{12} = \frac{105}{180}$

9. Determine which of the following pairs are equal.
   a. $\frac{693}{858}, \frac{42}{52}$ **b.** $\frac{873}{954}, \frac{184}{212}$ **c.** $\frac{48}{84}, \frac{756}{1263}$ **d.** $\frac{468}{891}, \frac{156}{297}$

10. Rewrite in simplest form.
   a. $\frac{189}{153}$ **b.** $\frac{294}{63}$ **c.** $\frac{480}{672}$ **d.** $\frac{3335}{230}$

11. Rewrite as a mixed number in simplest form.
   a. $\frac{2232}{444}$ **b.** $\frac{8976}{144}$

12. For each of the following, arrange from smallest to largest and explain how this ordering could be done mentally.
   a. $\frac{5}{11}, \frac{5}{9}, \frac{5}{13}$ **b.** $\frac{7}{8}, \frac{6}{7}, \frac{8}{9}$

13. Arrange each of the following from smallest to largest.

a. $\frac{4}{7}, \frac{7}{13}, \frac{14}{25}$ **b.** $\frac{3}{11}, \frac{7}{23}, \frac{2}{9}, \frac{5}{18}$

14. Use the Chapter 6 eManipulative *Comparing Fractions* on our Web site to plot several pairs of fractions, $\frac{a}{b}$ and $\frac{c}{d}$, with small denominators on a number line. For each example, plot $\frac{ad + bc}{2bd}$ on the number line as well. How does the fraction $\frac{ad + bc}{2bd}$ relate to $\frac{a}{b}$ and $\frac{c}{d}$? Does this relationship appear to hold for all fractions $\frac{a}{b}$ and $\frac{c}{d}$? Explain.

15. Determine whether the following pairs are equal. If they are not, order them and find a fraction between them.

a. $\frac{231}{654}$ and $\frac{308}{872}$ **b.** $\frac{1516}{2312}$ and $\frac{2653}{2890}$ **c.** $\frac{516}{892}$ and $\frac{1376}{2376}$

PROBLEMS

16. According to the Bureau of the Census data on living arrangements of Americans 15 years of age and older in 2005 there were about

230,000,000 people over 15
20,000,000 people from 25–34 years old
4,000,000 people from 25–34 living alone
17,000,000 people over 75 years old
7,000,000 people over 75 living alone
3,000,000 people over 75 living with other persons

(NOTE: Figures have been rounded to simplify calculations.)

a. In 2005, what fraction of people over 15 in the United States were from 25 to 34 years old? To what fraction with a denominator of 100 is this fraction closest?

b. In 2005, what fraction of 25 to 34 years olds were living alone? To what fraction with a denominator of 100 is this fraction closest?

c. In 2005, what fraction of people over 15 in the United States were over 75 years old? To what fraction with a denominator of 100 is this fraction closest?

d. In 2005, what fraction of people over 75 were living alone? To what fraction with a denominator of 100 is this fraction closest?

17. Frank ate 12 pieces of pizza and Dave ate 15 pieces. "I ate $\frac{1}{4}$ more," said Dave. "I ate $\frac{1}{5}$ less," said Frank. Who was right?

18. Mrs. Wills and Mr. Roberts gave the same test to their fourth-grade classes. In Mrs. Wills's class, 28 out of 36 students passed the test. In Mr. Roberts's class, 26 out of 32 students passed the test. Which class had the higher passing rate?

19. The shaded regions in the following figures represent the fractions $\frac{1}{2}$ and $\frac{1}{6}$, respectively.

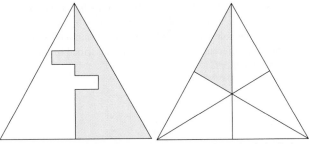

Trace outlines of figures like the ones shown and shade in portions that represent the following fractions.

a. $\frac{1}{2}$ (different from the one shown)

b. $\frac{1}{3}$ **c.** $\frac{1}{4}$ **d.** $\frac{1}{8}$ **e.** $\frac{1}{9}$

20. A popular math trick shows that a fraction like $\frac{16}{64}$ can be simplified by "canceling" the 6s and obtaining $\frac{1}{4}$. There are many other fractions for which this technique yields a correct answer.

a. Apply this technique to each of the following fractions and verify that the results are correct.

i. $\frac{16}{64}$ **ii.** $\frac{19}{95}$ **iii.** $\frac{26}{65}$ **iv.** $\frac{199}{995}$ **v.** $\frac{26666}{66665}$

b. Using the pattern established in parts (iv) and (v) of part (a), write three more examples of fractions for which this method of simplification works.

21. Find a fraction less than $\frac{1}{12}$. Find another fraction less than the fraction you found. Can you continue this process? Is there a "smallest" fraction greater than 0? Explain.

22. What is wrong with the following argument?

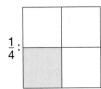

Therefore, $\frac{1}{4} > \frac{1}{2}$, since the area of the shaded square is greater than the area of the shaded rectangle.

23. Use a method like the one in Part A, Problem 23, find the following.

a. LCM(224, 336)   **b.** LCM(861, 1599)

24. If the same number is added to the numerator and denominator of a proper fraction, is the new fraction greater than, less than, or equal to the original fraction? Justify your answer. (Be sure to look at a variety of fractions.)

25. Find 999 fractions between $\frac{1}{3}$ and $\frac{1}{2}$ such that the difference between pairs of numbers next to each other is the same. (*Hint:* Find convenient equivalent fractions for $\frac{1}{3}$ and $\frac{1}{2}$.)

26. About one-fifth of a federal budget goes for defense. If the total budget is $400 billion, how much is spent on defense?

27. The U.S. Postal Service delivers about 170 billion pieces of mail each year. If approximately 90 billion of these are first class, what fraction describes the other classes of mail delivered?

28. Tuition in public universities is about two-ninths of tuition at private universities. If the average tuition at private universities is about $12,600 per year, what should you expect to pay at a public university?

29. A hiker traveled at an average rate of 2 kilometers per hour (km/h) going up to a lookout and traveled at an average rate of 5 km/h coming back down. If the entire trip (not counting a lunch stop at the lookout) took approximately 3 hours and 15 minutes, what is the total distance the hiker walked? Round your answer to the nearest tenth of a kilometer.

30. Five women participated in a 10-kilometer (10 K) Volkswalk, but started at different times. At a certain time in the walk the following descriptions were true.

   1. Rose was at the halfway point (5 K).
   2. Kelly was 2 K ahead of Cathy.
   3. Janet was 3 K ahead of Ann.
   4. Rose was 1 K behind Cathy.
   5. Ann was 3.5 K behind Kelly.

   a. Determine the order of the women at that point in time. That is, who was nearest the finish line, who was second closest, and so on?

   b. How far from the finish line was Janet at that time?

31. Pattern blocks 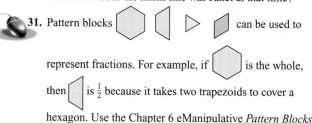 can be used to represent fractions. For example, if ⬡ is the whole, then ◊ is $\frac{1}{2}$ because it takes two trapezoids to cover a hexagon. Use the Chapter 6 eManipulative *Pattern Blocks*

on our Web site to determine representations of the following fractions. In each case, you will need to identify what the whole and what the part is.

   a. $\frac{1}{3}$ in two different ways.   **b.** $\frac{1}{6}$ **c.** $\frac{1}{4}$ **d.** $\frac{1}{12}$

32. Refer to the Chapter 6 eManipulative activities *Parts of a Whole* and *Visualizing Fractions* on our Web site. Conceptually, what are some of the advantages of having young students use such activities?

Analyzing Student Thinking

33. David claims that an improper fraction is always greater than a proper fraction. Is his statement true or false? Explain.

34. How would you respond to a student who says that fractions don't change in value if you multiply the top and bottom by the same number or add the same number to the top and bottom?

35. Brandon claims that he cannot find a number between $\frac{3}{4}$ and $\frac{3}{5}$ because they are "right next to each other." How should you respond?

36. Rafael asserts that $\frac{2}{8} > \frac{1}{4}$ since 2 > 1 and 8 > 4. How should you respond?

37. Regarding two fractions, Collin says that the one with the larger numerator is the larger. Is he correct? Explain.

38. You have a student who says she knows how to divide a circle into pieces to illustrate what $\frac{2}{3}$ means but wonders how she can divide a circle to show $\frac{3}{2}$. What could you say to help her understand the situation?

39. Hailey says that if $ab < cd$, then $\frac{a}{b} < \frac{c}{d}$. Is she correct? Explain.

Problems Relating to the NCTM Standards and Curriculum Focal Points

1. The Focal Points for Grade 3 state "Developing an understanding of fractions and fraction equivalence." Based on the discussions in this section, explain at least three main concepts essential to understanding fractions and fraction equivalence.

2. The NCTM Standards state "All students should understand and represent commonly used fractions such as $\frac{1}{4}, \frac{1}{3}$, and $\frac{1}{2}$."

What are some examples from this section that show some possible fraction representations?

3. The NCTM Standards state "All students should develop understanding of fractions as parts of unit wholes, as part of a collection, as locations on number lines, and as division of whole numbers." Provide an example of each of the four different views of fractions described in this NCTM statement.

6.2 FRACTIONS: ADDITION AND SUBTRACTION

Some students initially view the addition of fractions as adding the numerators and adding the denominators as follows: $\frac{3}{4} + \frac{1}{2} = \frac{4}{6}$. Using this example, discuss why such a method for addition is unreasonable.

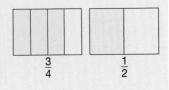

NCTM Standard
All students should use visual models, benchmarks, and equivalent forms to add and subtract commonly used fractions and decimals.

Reflection from Research
A curriculum for teaching fractions that focuses on the use of physical models, pictures, verbal symbols, and written symbols allows students to better conceptually understand fraction ideas (Cramer, Post, & delMas, 2002).

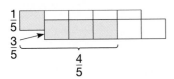

Figure 6.14

Addition and Its Properties

Addition of fractions is an extension of whole-number addition and can be motivated using models. To find the sum of $\frac{1}{5}$ and $\frac{3}{5}$, consider the following measurement models: the region model and number-line model in Figure 6.13.

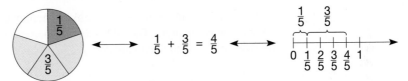

Region Model   Number–Line Model

Figure 6.13

The idea illustrated in Figure 6.13 can be applied to any pair of fractions that have the same denominator. Figure 6.14 shows how fraction strips, which are a blend of these two models, can be used to find the sum of $\frac{1}{5}$ and $\frac{3}{5}$. That is, the sum of two fractions with the same denominator can be found by adding the numerators, as stated next.

DEFINITION

Addition of Fractions with Common Denominators

Let $\frac{a}{b}$ and $\frac{c}{b}$ be any fractions. Then

$$\frac{a}{b} + \frac{c}{b} = \frac{a+c}{b}.$$

Figure 6.15 illustrates how to add fractions when the denominators are not the same.

Similarly, to find the sum $\frac{2}{7} + \frac{3}{5}$, use the equality of fractions to express the fractions with common denominators as follows:

$$\frac{2}{7} + \frac{3}{5} = \frac{2 \cdot 5}{7 \cdot 5} + \frac{3 \cdot 7}{5 \cdot 7}$$
$$= \frac{10}{35} + \frac{21}{35}$$
$$= \frac{31}{35}.$$

This procedure can be generalized as follows.

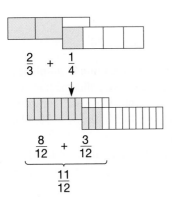

Figure 6.15

> ## THEOREM
>
> ### Addition of Fractions with Unlike Denominators
>
> Let $\dfrac{a}{b}$ and $\dfrac{c}{d}$ be any fractions. Then
>
> $$\frac{a}{b} + \frac{c}{d} = \frac{ad + bc}{bd}.$$

PROOF

$$\frac{a}{b} + \frac{c}{d} = \frac{ad}{bd} + \frac{bc}{bd} \qquad \textit{Equality of fractions}$$

$$= \frac{ad + bc}{bd} \qquad \textit{Addition with common denominators} \qquad \blacksquare$$

In words, to add fractions with unlike denominators, find equivalent fractions with common denominators. Then the sum will be represented by the sum of the numerators over the common denominator.

Reflection from Research
The most common error when adding two fractions is to add the denominators as well as the numerators; for example, $\frac{1}{2} + \frac{1}{4}$ becomes $\frac{2}{6}$ (Bana, Farrell, & McIntosh, 1995).

Example 6.5   Find the following sums and simplify.

a. $\frac{3}{7} + \frac{2}{7}$ **b.** $\frac{5}{9} + \frac{3}{4}$ **c.** $\frac{17}{15} + \frac{5}{12}$

SOLUTION

a. $\dfrac{3}{7} + \dfrac{2}{7} = \dfrac{3+2}{7} = \dfrac{5}{7}$

b. $\dfrac{5}{9} + \dfrac{3}{4} = \dfrac{5\cdot 4}{9\cdot 4} + \dfrac{9\cdot 3}{9\cdot 4} = \dfrac{20}{36} + \dfrac{27}{36} = \dfrac{47}{36}$

c. $\dfrac{17}{15} + \dfrac{5}{12} = \dfrac{17\cdot 12 + 15\cdot 5}{15\cdot 12} = \dfrac{204 + 75}{180} = \dfrac{279}{180} = \dfrac{31}{20}$ $\qquad\blacksquare$

In Example 6.5(c), an alternative method can be used. Rather than using $15 \cdot 12$ as the common denominator, the least common multiple of 12 and 15 can be used. The $\mathrm{LCM}(15, 12) = 2^2 \cdot 3 \cdot 5 = 60$. Therefore,

$$\frac{17}{15} + \frac{5}{12} = \frac{17\cdot 4}{15\cdot 4} + \frac{5\cdot 5}{12\cdot 5} = \frac{68}{60} + \frac{25}{60} = \frac{93}{60} = \frac{31}{20}.$$

Although using the LCM of the denominators (called the **least common denominator** and abbreviated LCD) simplifies paper-and-pencil calculations, using this method does not necessarily result in an answer in simplest form as in the previous case. For example, to find $\frac{3}{10} + \frac{8}{15}$, use 30 as the common denominator since $\mathrm{LCM}(10, 15) = 30$. Thus $\frac{3}{10} + \frac{8}{15} = \frac{9}{30} + \frac{16}{30} = \frac{25}{30}$, which is not in simplest form.

Calculators and computers can also be used to calculate the sums of fractions. A common four-function calculator can be used to find sums, as in the following example.

A fraction calculator can be used to find sums as follows: To calculate $\frac{23}{48} + \frac{38}{51}$, press 23 ⟦/⟧ 48 ⟦+⟧ 38 ⟦/⟧ 51 ⟦=⟧ 1∪183/816. This mixed number can be simplified by pressing ⟦SIMP⟧ ⟦=⟧ to obtain 1∪61/272. The sum $\frac{237}{496} + \frac{384}{517}$ may not fit on a common fraction calculator display. In this case, the common denominator approach to addition can be used instead, namely $\frac{a}{b} + \frac{c}{d} = \frac{ad + bc}{bd}$. Here

$$
\begin{aligned}
ad &= 237 \times 517 & &= 122529 \\
bc &= 496 \times 384 & &= 190464 \\
ad + bc &= 122529 + 190464 &&= 312993 \\
bd &= 496 \times 517 & &= 256432.
\end{aligned}
$$

Therefore, the sum is $\frac{312993}{256432}$. Notice that the latter method may be done on any four-function calculator.

The following properties of fraction addition can be used to simplify computations. For simplicity, all properties are stated using common denominators, since any two fractions can be expressed with the same denominator.

PROPERTY

Closure Property for Fraction Addition

The sum of two fractions is a fraction.

This follows from the equation $\frac{a}{c} + \frac{b}{c} = \frac{a + b}{c}$, since $a + b$ and c are both whole numbers and $c \neq 0$.

PROPERTY

Commutative Property for Fraction Addition

Let $\frac{a}{b}$ and $\frac{c}{b}$ be any fractions. Then

$$\frac{a}{b} + \frac{c}{b} = \frac{c}{b} + \frac{a}{b}.$$

Problem-Solving Strategy
Draw a Picture

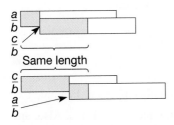

Figure 6.16

Figure 6.16 provides a visual justification using fraction strips. The following is a formal proof of this commutativity.

$$
\begin{aligned}
\frac{a}{b} + \frac{c}{b} &= \frac{a + c}{b} & &\textit{Addition of fractions} \\
&= \frac{c + a}{b} & &\textit{Commutative property of whole-number addition} \\
&= \frac{c}{b} + \frac{a}{b} & &\textit{Addition of fractions}
\end{aligned}
$$

> ## PROPERTY
>
> ### Associative Property for Fraction Addition
>
> Let $\dfrac{a}{b}, \dfrac{c}{b}$, and $\dfrac{e}{b}$ be any fractions. Then
>
> $$\left[\frac{a}{b} + \frac{c}{b}\right] + \frac{e}{b} = \frac{a}{b} + \left[\frac{c}{b} + \frac{e}{b}\right].$$

The associative property for fraction addition is easily justified using the associative property for whole-number addition.

> ## PROPERTY
>
> ### Additive Identity Property for Fraction Addition
>
> Let $\dfrac{a}{b}$ be any fraction. There is a unique fraction, $\dfrac{0}{b}$, such that
>
> $$\frac{a}{b} + \frac{0}{b} = \frac{a}{b} = \frac{0}{b} + \frac{a}{b}.$$

The following equations show how this additive identity property can be justified using the corresponding property in whole numbers.

$$\frac{a}{b} + \frac{0}{b} = \frac{a + 0}{b} \qquad \textit{Addition of fractions}$$

$$= \frac{a}{b} \qquad \textit{Additive identity property of whole-number addition}$$

The fraction $\dfrac{0}{b}$ is also written as $\dfrac{0}{1}$ or 0. It is shown in the problem set that this is the only fraction that serves as an additive identity.

The preceding properties can be used to simplify computations.

Example 6.6   Compute: $\dfrac{3}{5} + \left[\dfrac{4}{7} + \dfrac{2}{5}\right]$.

SOLUTION

$$\frac{3}{5} + \left[\frac{4}{7} + \frac{2}{5}\right] = \frac{3}{5} + \left[\frac{2}{5} + \frac{4}{7}\right] \qquad \textit{Commutativity}$$

$$= \left[\frac{3}{5} + \frac{2}{5}\right] + \frac{4}{7} \qquad \textit{Associativity}$$

$$= 1 + \frac{4}{7} \qquad \textit{Addition}$$

∎

The number $1 + \frac{4}{7}$ can be expressed as the mixed number $1\frac{4}{7}$. As in Example 6.6, any mixed number can be expressed as a sum. For example, $3\frac{2}{5} = 3 + \frac{2}{5}$. Also, any mixed number can be changed to an improper fraction, and vice versa, as shown in the next example.

Example 6.7

a. Express $3\frac{2}{5}$ as an improper fraction.

b. Express $\frac{36}{7}$ as a mixed number.

SOLUTION

a. $3\frac{2}{5} = 3 + \frac{2}{5} = \frac{15}{5} + \frac{2}{5} = \frac{17}{5}$

$$\left[\text{Shortcut: } 3\frac{2}{5} = \frac{5 \cdot 3 + 2}{5} = \frac{17}{5} \right]$$

b. $\frac{36}{7} = \frac{35}{7} + \frac{1}{7} = 5 + \frac{1}{7} = 5\frac{1}{7}$ ■

 Check for Understanding: Exercise/Problem Set A #1–8

Problem-Solving Strategy
Draw a Picture

Subtraction

Subtraction of fractions can be viewed in two ways as we did with whole-number subtraction—either as (1) take-away or (2) using the missing-addend approach.

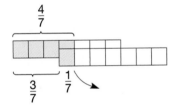

$\frac{4}{7}$

$\frac{3}{7}$ $\frac{1}{7}$

Figure 6.17

Example 6.8   Find $\frac{4}{7} - \frac{1}{7}$.

SOLUTION   From Figure 6.17, $\frac{4}{7} - \frac{1}{7} = \frac{3}{7}$. ■

This example suggests the following definition.

DEFINITION

Subtraction of Fractions with Common Denominators

Let $\frac{a}{b}$ and $\frac{c}{b}$ be any fractions with $a \geq c$. Then

$$\frac{a}{b} - \frac{c}{b} = \frac{a - c}{b}.$$

Now consider the subtraction of fractions using the missing-addend approach. For example, to find $\frac{4}{7} - \frac{1}{7}$, find a fraction $\frac{n}{7}$ such that $\frac{4}{7} = \frac{1}{7} + \frac{n}{7}$. The following argument shows that the missing-addend approach leads to the take-away approach.

If $\frac{a}{b} - \frac{c}{b} = \frac{n}{b}$, and the missing-addend approach holds, then $\frac{a}{b} = \frac{c}{b} + \frac{n}{b}$, or $\frac{a}{b} = \frac{c + n}{b}$. This implies that $a = c + n$ or $a - c = n$.

That is, $\frac{a}{b} - \frac{c}{b} = \frac{a - c}{b}$.

Also, it can be shown that the missing-addend approach is a consequence of the take-away approach.

If fractions have different denominators, subtraction is done by first finding common denominators, then subtracting as before.

$$\text{Suppose that } \frac{a}{b} \ge \frac{c}{d}. \text{ Then } \frac{a}{b} - \frac{c}{d} = \frac{ad}{bd} - \frac{bc}{bd} = \frac{ad - bc}{bd}.$$

Therefore, fractions with unlike denominators may be subtracted as follows.

THEOREM

Subtraction of Fractions with Unlike Denominators

Let $\dfrac{a}{b}$ and $\dfrac{c}{d}$ be any fractions, where $\dfrac{a}{b} \ge \dfrac{c}{d}$. Then

$$\frac{a}{b} - \frac{c}{d} = \frac{ad - bc}{bd}.$$

Example 6.9   Find the following differences.

a. $\dfrac{4}{7} - \dfrac{3}{8}$ **b.** $\dfrac{25}{12} - \dfrac{7}{18}$ **c.** $\dfrac{7}{10} - \dfrac{8}{15}$

SOLUTION

NCTM Standard
All students should develop and use strategies to estimate computations involving fractions and decimals in situations relevant to students' experience.

a. $\dfrac{4}{7} - \dfrac{3}{8} = \dfrac{4 \cdot 8}{7 \cdot 8} - \dfrac{7 \cdot 3}{7 \cdot 8} = \dfrac{32 - 21}{56} = \dfrac{11}{56}$

b. $\dfrac{25}{12} - \dfrac{7}{18}$. NOTE: LCM(12, 18) = 36.

$\dfrac{25}{12} - \dfrac{7}{18} = \dfrac{25 \cdot 3}{12 \cdot 3} - \dfrac{7 \cdot 2}{18 \cdot 2} = \dfrac{75 - 14}{36} = \dfrac{61}{36}$

c. $\dfrac{7}{10} - \dfrac{8}{15} = \dfrac{21}{30} - \dfrac{16}{30} - \dfrac{5}{36} = \dfrac{1}{6}$ ■

✔ **Check for Understanding:** Exercise/Problem Set A #8–14

Mental Math and Estimation for Addition and Subtraction

Mental math and estimation techniques similar to those used with whole numbers can be used with fractions.

Example 6.10   Calculate mentally.

a. $\left(\dfrac{1}{5} + \dfrac{3}{4} \right) + \dfrac{4}{5}$ **b.** $3\dfrac{4}{5} + 2\dfrac{2}{5}$ **c.** $40 - 8\dfrac{3}{7}$

SOLUTION

a. $\left(\dfrac{1}{5} + \dfrac{3}{4} \right) + \dfrac{4}{5} = \dfrac{4}{5} + \left(\dfrac{1}{5} + \dfrac{3}{4} \right) = \left(\dfrac{4}{5} + \dfrac{1}{5} \right) + \dfrac{3}{4} = 1\dfrac{3}{4}$

Commutativity and associativity were used to be able to add $\dfrac{4}{5}$ and $\dfrac{1}{5}$, since they are compatible fractions (their sum is 1).

b. $3\frac{4}{5} + 2\frac{2}{5} = 4 + 2\frac{1}{5} = 6\frac{1}{5}$

This is an example of additive compensation, where $3\frac{4}{5}$ was increased by $\frac{1}{5}$ to 4 and consequently $2\frac{2}{5}$ was decreased by $\frac{1}{5}$ to $2\frac{1}{5}$.

c. $40 - 8\frac{3}{7} = 40\frac{4}{7} - 9 = 31\frac{4}{7}$

Here $\frac{4}{7}$ was added to both 40 and $8\frac{3}{7}$ $\left(\text{since } 8\frac{3}{7} + \frac{4}{7} = 9\right)$, an example of the equal-additions method of subtraction. This problem could also be viewed as $39\frac{7}{7} - 8\frac{3}{7} = 31\frac{4}{7}$.

NCTM Standard
All students should develop and use strategies to estimate the results of rational-number computations and judge the reasonableness of the results.

Example 6.11　Estimate using the indicated techniques.

a. $3\frac{3}{7} + 6\frac{2}{5}$ using range estimation

b. $15\frac{4}{5} - 7\frac{3}{8}$ using front-end with adjustment

c. $3\frac{5}{6} + 5\frac{1}{8} + 8\frac{3}{8}$ rounding to the nearest $\frac{1}{2}$ or whole

Algebraic Reasoning
When solving algebraic expressions that involve fractions, it is worthwhile to be able to estimate the result of computations so the reasonableness of the algebraic solution can be evaluated.

SOLUTION

a. $3\frac{3}{7} + 6\frac{2}{5}$ is between $3 + 6 = 9$ and $4 + 7 = 11$.

b. $15\frac{4}{5} - 7\frac{3}{8} \approx 8\frac{1}{2}$ since $15 - 7 = 8$ and $\frac{4}{5} - \frac{3}{8} \approx \frac{1}{2}$.

c. $3\frac{5}{6} + 5\frac{1}{8} + 8\frac{3}{8} \approx 4 + 5 + 8\frac{1}{2} = 17\frac{1}{2}$.

Check for Understanding: Exercise/Problem Set A #15–19

MATHEMATICAL MORSEL

Around 2900 B.C.E. the Great Pyramid of Giza was constructed. It covered 13 acres and contained over 2,000,000 stone blocks averaging 2.5 tons each. Some chamber roofs are made of 54-ton granite blocks, 27 feet long and 4 feet thick, hauled from a quarry 600 miles away and set into place 200 feet above the ground. The relative error in the lengths of the sides of the square base was $\frac{1}{14,000}$ and in the right angles was $\frac{1}{27,000}$. This construction was estimated to have required 100,000 laborers working for about 30 years.

Section 6.2 EXERCISE / PROBLEM SET A

EXERCISES

1. Illustrate the problem $\frac{2}{5} + \frac{1}{3}$ using the following models.
   a. A region model   **b.** A number-line model

2. Find $\frac{5}{9} + \frac{7}{12}$ using four different denominators.

3. Using rectangles or circles as the whole, represent the following problems. The Chapter 6 eManipulative activity *Adding Fractions* on our Web site will help you understand these representations.
   a. $\frac{2}{3} + \frac{1}{6}$ **b.** $\frac{1}{4} + \frac{3}{8}$ **c.** $\frac{3}{4} + \frac{2}{3}$

4. Find the following sums and express your answer in simplest form.
   a. $\frac{1}{8} + \frac{5}{8}$ **b.** $\frac{1}{4} + \frac{1}{2}$ **c.** $\frac{3}{7} + \frac{1}{3}$
   d. $\frac{8}{9} + \frac{1}{12} + \frac{3}{16}$ **e.** $\frac{8}{13} + \frac{4}{51}$ **f.** $\frac{9}{22} + \frac{89}{121}$
   g. $\frac{61}{100} + \frac{7}{1000}$ **h.** $\frac{7}{10} + \frac{20}{100}$ **i.** $\frac{143}{1000} + \frac{759}{100,000}$

5. Change the following mixed numbers to improper fractions.
   a. $3\frac{5}{6}$ **b.** $2\frac{7}{8}$ **c.** $5\frac{1}{5}$ **d.** $7\frac{1}{9}$

6. Find the sum for the following pairs of mixed numbers. Answers should be written as mixed numbers.
   a. $2\frac{2}{3}, 1\frac{1}{4}$ **b.** $7\frac{5}{7}, 5\frac{2}{3}$ **c.** $22\frac{1}{6}, 15\frac{11}{12}$

7. To find the sum $\frac{2}{5} + \frac{3}{4}$ on a scientific calculator, press 2 ÷
   5 + 3 ÷ 4 = 1.15 . The whole-number part of the
   sum is 1. Subtract it: − 1 = 0.15 . This represents the fraction part of the answer in decimal form. Since the denominator of the sum should be $5 \times 4 = 20$, multiply by 20: × 20 = 3 . This is the numerator of the fraction part of the sum. Thus $\frac{2}{5} + \frac{3}{4} = 1\frac{3}{20}$. Find the simplest form of the sums using this method.
   a. $\frac{3}{7} + \frac{5}{8}$ **b.** $\frac{3}{8} + \frac{4}{5}$

8. Compute the following. Use a fraction calculator if available.
   a. $\frac{3}{4} + \frac{7}{10}$ **b.** $\frac{5}{6} + \frac{5}{8}$

9. On a number line, demonstrate the following problems using the take-away approach.
   a. $\frac{7}{10} - \frac{3}{10}$ **b.** $\frac{5}{12} - \frac{1}{12}$ **c.** $\frac{2}{3} - \frac{1}{4}$

10. Perform the following subtractions.
    a. $\frac{9}{11} - \frac{5}{11}$ **b.** $\frac{3}{7} - \frac{2}{9}$ **c.** $\frac{4}{5} - \frac{3}{4}$
    d. $\frac{13}{18} - \frac{8}{27}$ **e.** $\frac{21}{51} - \frac{7}{39}$ **f.** $\frac{11}{100} - \frac{99}{1000}$

11. Find the difference for the following pairs of mixed numbers. Answers should be written as mixed numbers.
    a. $2\frac{2}{3}, 1\frac{1}{4}$ **b.** $7\frac{5}{7}, 5\frac{2}{3}$ **c.** $22\frac{1}{6}, 15\frac{11}{12}$

12. Find the simplest form of the following differences using the method described in #7.
    a. $\frac{25}{8} - \frac{4}{5}$ **b.** $\frac{3}{5} - \frac{4}{7}$

13. Compute the following. Use a fraction calculator if available.
    a. $\frac{5}{6} - \frac{8}{15}$ **b.** $\frac{7}{9} - \frac{3}{5}$

14. An alternative definition of "less than" for fractions is as follows:

    $$\frac{a}{b} < \frac{c}{d} \text{ if and only if}$$
    $$\frac{a}{b} + \frac{m}{n} = \frac{c}{d} \text{ for a}$$
    nonzero $\frac{m}{n}$

    Use this definition to confirm the following statements.
    a. $\frac{3}{7} < \frac{5}{7}$ **b.** $\frac{1}{3} < \frac{1}{2}$

15. Use the properties of fraction addition to calculate each of the following sums mentally.
    a. $(\frac{3}{7} + \frac{1}{9}) + \frac{4}{7}$
    b. $1\frac{9}{13} + \frac{5}{6} + \frac{4}{13}$
    c. $(2\frac{2}{5} + 3\frac{5}{8}) + (1\frac{4}{5} + 2\frac{3}{8})$

16. Find each of these differences mentally using the equal-additions method. Write out the steps that you thought through.
    a. $8\frac{2}{7} - 2\frac{6}{7}$ **b.** $9\frac{1}{8} - 2\frac{5}{8}$
    c. $11\frac{3}{7} - 6\frac{5}{7}$ **d.** $8\frac{1}{6} - 3\frac{5}{6}$

17. Estimate each of the following using (i) range and (ii) front-end with adjustment estimation.
    a. $6\frac{7}{11} + 7\frac{3}{9}$ **b.** $9\frac{1}{8} - 6\frac{4}{7}$ **c.** $8\frac{2}{11} + 2\frac{7}{11} + 5\frac{2}{9}$

18. Estimate each of the following using "rounding to the nearest whole number or $\frac{1}{2}$."
    a. $9\frac{7}{9} + 3\frac{6}{13}$ **b.** $9\frac{5}{8} - 5\frac{4}{9}$ **c.** $7\frac{2}{11} + 5\frac{3}{13} + 2\frac{7}{12}$

19. Estimate using cluster estimations: $5\frac{1}{3} + 4\frac{4}{5} + 5\frac{6}{7}$.

PROBLEMS

20. Sally, her brother, and another partner own a pizza restaurant. If Sally owns $\frac{1}{3}$ and her brother owns $\frac{1}{4}$ of the restaurant, what part does the third partner own?

21. John spent a quarter of his life as a boy growing up, one-sixth of his life in college, and one-half of his life as a teacher. He spent his last six years in retirement. How old was he when he died?

22. Rafael ate one-fourth of a pizza and Rocco ate one-third of it. What fraction of the pizza did they eat?

23. Greg plants two-fifths of his garden in potatoes and one-sixth in carrots. What fraction of the garden remains for his other crops?

24. About eleven-twelfths of a golf course is in fairways, one-eighteenth in greens, and the rest in tees. What part of the golf course is in tees?

25. David is having trouble when subtracting mixed numbers. What might be causing his difficulty? How might you help David?

$$3\tfrac{2}{5} = 2\tfrac{12}{5}$$
$$-\ \tfrac{3}{5} = \ \tfrac{3}{5}$$
$$2\tfrac{9}{5} = 3\tfrac{4}{5}$$

26. a. The divisors (other than 1) of 6 are 2, 3, and 6. Compute $\tfrac{1}{2} + \tfrac{1}{3} + \tfrac{1}{6}$.
b. The divisors (other than 1) of 28 are 2, 4, 7, 14, and 28. Compute $\tfrac{1}{2} + \tfrac{1}{4} + \tfrac{1}{7} + \tfrac{1}{14} + \tfrac{1}{28}$.
c. Will this result be true for 496? What other numbers will have this property?

27. Determine whether $\dfrac{1+3}{5+7} = \dfrac{1+3+5}{7+9+11}$. Is $\dfrac{1+3+5+7}{9+11+13+15}$ also the same fraction? Find two other such fractions. Prove why this works. (*Hint:* $1+3 = 2^2$, $1+3+5 = 3^2$, etc.)

28. Find this sum: $\dfrac{1}{2} + \dfrac{1}{2^2} + \dfrac{1}{2^3} + \ldots + \dfrac{1}{2^{100}}$.

29. In the first 10 games of the baseball season, Jim has 15 hits in 50 times at bat. The fraction of his times at bat that were hits is $\tfrac{15}{50}$. In the next game he is at bat 6 times and gets 3 hits.
a. What fraction of at-bats are hits in this game?
b. How many hits does he now have this season?

c. How many at-bats does he now have this season?
d. What is his record of hits/at-bats this season?
e. In this setting "baseball addition" can be defined as
$$\frac{a}{b} \oplus \frac{c}{d} = \frac{a+c}{b+d}$$
(Use $\oplus$ to distinguish from ordinary $+$.)

Using this definition, do you get an equivalent answer when fractions are replaced by equivalent fractions?

30. Fractions whose numerators are 1 are called **unitary fractions**. Do you think that it is possible to add unitary fractions with different odd denominators to obtain 1? For example, $\tfrac{1}{2} + \tfrac{1}{3} + \tfrac{1}{6} = 1$, but 2 and 6 are even. How about the following sum?

$$\tfrac{1}{3} + \tfrac{1}{5} + \tfrac{1}{7} + \tfrac{1}{9} + \tfrac{1}{15} + \tfrac{1}{21} + \tfrac{1}{27} +$$
$$\tfrac{1}{35} + \tfrac{1}{63} + \tfrac{1}{105} + \tfrac{1}{135}$$

31. The Egyptians were said to use only unitary fractions with the exception of $\tfrac{2}{3}$. It is known that every unitary fraction can be expressed as the sum of two unitary fractions in more than one way. Represent the following fractions as the sum of two different unitary fractions. (NOTE: $\tfrac{1}{2} = \tfrac{1}{4} + \tfrac{1}{4}$, but $\tfrac{1}{2} = \tfrac{1}{3} + \tfrac{1}{6}$ is requested.)
a. $\tfrac{1}{5}$ **b.** $\tfrac{1}{7}$ **c.** $\tfrac{1}{17}$

32. At a round-robin tennis tournament, each of eight players plays every other player once. How many matches are there?

33. New lockers are being installed in a school and will be numbered from 0001 to 1000. Stick-on digits will be used to number the lockers. A custodian must calculate the number of packages of numbers to order. How many 0s will be needed to complete the task? How many 9s?

| Section 6.2 | **EXERCISE / PROBLEM SET B**

EXERCISES

1. Illustrate $\tfrac{3}{4} + \tfrac{2}{3}$ using the following models.
a. A region model
b. A number-line model

2. Find $\tfrac{5}{8} + \tfrac{1}{6}$ using four different denominators.

3. Using rectangles as the whole, represent the following problems. (The Chapter 6 eManipulative activity *Adding Fractions* on our Web site will help you understand this process.)
a. $\tfrac{3}{4} - \tfrac{1}{3}$ **b.** $3\tfrac{1}{3} - 1\tfrac{5}{6}$

4. Find the following sums and express your answer in simplest form. (Leave your answers in prime factorization form.)
a. $\dfrac{1}{2^2 \times 3^2} + \dfrac{1}{2 \times 3^3}$
b. $\dfrac{1}{3^2 \times 7^3} + \dfrac{1}{5^3 \times 7^2 \times 29}$
c. $\dfrac{1}{5^4 \times 7^5 \times 13^2} + \dfrac{1}{3^2 \times 5 \times 13^3}$
d. $\dfrac{1}{17^3 \times 53^5 \times 67^{13}} + \dfrac{1}{11^5 \times 17^2 \times 67^9}$

5. Change the following improper fractions to mixed numbers.
   a. $\frac{35}{3}$ **b.** $\frac{19}{4}$ **c.** $\frac{49}{6}$ **d.** $\frac{17}{5}$

6. Calculate the following and express as mixed numbers in simplest form.
   a. $7\frac{5}{8} + 13\frac{2}{3}$ **b.** $11\frac{3}{5} + 9\frac{8}{9}$

7. Using a scientific calculator, find the simplest form of each sum.
   a. $\frac{19}{135} + \frac{51}{75}$ **b.** $\frac{37}{52} + \frac{19}{78}$

8. Compute the following. Use a fraction calculator if available.
   a. $\frac{7}{6} + \frac{4}{5}$ **b.** $\frac{4}{9} + \frac{5}{12}$

9. On a number line, demonstrate the following problems using the missing-addend approach.
   a. $\frac{9}{12} - \frac{5}{12}$ **b.** $\frac{2}{3} - \frac{1}{5}$ **c.** $\frac{3}{4} - \frac{1}{3}$

10. **a.** Compute the following problems.
       i. $\frac{7}{8} - (\frac{2}{3} - \frac{1}{6})$ **ii.** $(\frac{7}{8} - \frac{2}{3}) - \frac{1}{6}$
    b. The results of i and ii illustrate that a property of fraction addition does not hold for fraction subtraction. What property is it?

11. Calculate the following and express as mixed numbers in simplest form.
    a. $11\frac{3}{5} - 9\frac{8}{9}$ **b.** $13\frac{2}{3} - 7\frac{5}{8}$

12. Find the simplest form of the following differences using the method described in Exercise/Problem Set A, #7.
    a. $\frac{23}{14} - \frac{4}{9}$ **b.** $\frac{37}{52} - \frac{19}{78}$

13. Compute the following. Use a fraction calculator if available.
    a. $\frac{7}{6} - \frac{3}{5}$ **b.** $\frac{4}{5} - \frac{2}{7}$

14. Prove that $\frac{2}{5} < \frac{5}{8}$ in two ways.

15. Use properties of fraction addition to calculate each of the following sums mentally.
    a. $(\frac{2}{5} + \frac{5}{8}) + \frac{3}{5}$ **b.** $\frac{4}{9} + (\frac{2}{15} + 2\frac{5}{9})$
    c. $(1\frac{3}{4} + 3\frac{5}{11}) + (1\frac{8}{11} + 2\frac{1}{4})$

16. Find each of these differences mentally using the equal-additions method. Write out the steps that you thought through.
    a. $5\frac{2}{9} - 2\frac{7}{9}$ **b.** $9\frac{1}{6} - 2\frac{5}{6}$
    c. $21\frac{3}{7} - 8\frac{5}{7}$ **d.** $5\frac{3}{11} - 2\frac{6}{11}$

17. Estimate each of the following using (i) range and (ii) front-end with adjustment estimation.
    a. $5\frac{8}{9} + 6\frac{3}{13}$ **b.** $7\frac{4}{5} - 5\frac{6}{7}$ **c.** $8\frac{2}{11} + 2\frac{8}{9} + 7\frac{3}{13}$

18. Estimate each of the following using "rounding to the nearest whole number or $\frac{1}{2}$" estimation.
    a. $5\frac{8}{9} + 6\frac{4}{7}$ **b.** $7\frac{4}{5} - 5\frac{5}{9}$ **c.** $8\frac{2}{11} + 2\frac{7}{12} + 7\frac{3}{13}$

19. Estimate using cluster estimation.
    $$6\frac{1}{8} + 6\frac{2}{11} + 5\frac{8}{9} + 6\frac{3}{13}$$

PROBLEMS

20. Grandma was planning to make a red, white, and blue quilt. One-third was to be red and two-fifths was to be white. If the area of the quilt was to be 30 square feet, how many square feet would be blue?

21. A recipe for cookies will prepare enough for three-sevenths of Ms. Jordan's class of 28 students. If she makes three batches of cookies, how many extra students can she feed?

22. Karl wants to fertilize his 6 acres. If it takes $8\frac{2}{3}$ bags of fertilizer for each acre, how much fertilizer does Karl need to buy?

23. During one evening Kathleen devoted $\frac{2}{5}$ of her study time to mathematics, $\frac{3}{20}$ of her time to Spanish, $\frac{1}{3}$ of her time to biology, and the remaining 35 minutes to English. How much time did she spend studying her Spanish?

24. A man measures a room for a wallpaper border and finds he needs lengths of 10 ft. $6\frac{3}{8}$ in., 14 ft. $9\frac{3}{4}$ in., 6 ft. $5\frac{1}{2}$ in., and 3 ft. $2\frac{7}{8}$ in. What total length of wallpaper border does he need to purchase? (Ignore amount needed for matching and overlap.)

25. Following are some problems worked by students. Identify their errors and determine how they would answer the final question.

Amy:

$$7\frac{1}{6} = 7\frac{\overset{6}{\cancel{7}}}{6}$$
$$- 5\frac{2}{3} = 5\frac{4}{6}$$
$$\overline{1\frac{2}{6} = 1\frac{1}{3}}$$

$$5\frac{1}{3} = 8\frac{\overset{4}{2}}{6} \overset{6}{}$$
$$- 2\frac{1}{2} = 2\frac{3}{6}$$
$$\overline{2\frac{3}{6} = 2\frac{1}{2}}$$

$$5\frac{3}{8}$$
$$- 2\frac{1}{2}$$
$$\overline{}$$

Robert:

$$9\frac{1}{6} = 9\frac{55}{48}$$
$$- 2\frac{7}{8} = 2\frac{23}{48}$$
$$\overline{7\frac{32}{48}}$$

$$6\frac{1}{3} = 6\frac{19}{3}$$
$$- 1\frac{2}{3} = 1\frac{5}{3}$$
$$\overline{5\frac{14}{3}}$$

$$5\frac{1}{3}$$
$$- 1\frac{4}{5}$$
$$\overline{}$$

What concept of fractions might you use to help these students?

26. Consider the sum of fractions shown next.
    $$\frac{1}{3} + \frac{1}{5} + \frac{8}{15}$$
    The denominators of the first two fractions differ by two.

a. Verify that 8 and 15 are two parts of a Pythagorean triple. What is the third number of the triple?

b. Verify that the same result holds true for the following sums:

   i. $\frac{1}{7} + \frac{1}{9}$ **ii.** $\frac{1}{11} + \frac{1}{13}$ **iii.** $\frac{1}{19} + \frac{1}{21}$

c. How is the third number in the Pythagorean triple related to the other two numbers?

d. Use a variable to explain why this result holds. For example, you might represent the two denominators by n and $n + 2$.

27. Find this sum:

$$\frac{1}{1 \times 3} + \frac{1}{3 \times 5} + \frac{1}{5 \times 7} + \cdots + \frac{1}{21 \times 23}$$

28. The unending sum $\frac{1}{2} + \frac{1}{4} + \frac{1}{8} + \frac{1}{16} + \cdots$, where each term is a fixed multiple (here $\frac{1}{2}$) of the preceding term, is called an **infinite geometric series**. The **sum** of the first two terms is $\frac{3}{4}$.

a. Find the sum of the first three terms, first four terms, first five terms.

b. How many terms must be added in order for the sum to exceed $\frac{99}{100}$?

c. Guess the sum of the geometric series.

29. By giving a counterexample, show for fractions that
a. subtraction is not closed.
b. subtraction is not commutative.
c. subtraction is not associative.

30. The triangle shown is called the **harmonic triangle**. Observe the pattern in the rows of the triangle and then answer the questions that follow.

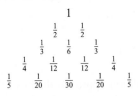

a. Write down the next two rows of the triangle.
b. Describe the pattern in the numbers that are first in each row.
c. Describe how each fraction in the triangle is related to the two fractions directly below it.

31. There is at least one correct subtraction equation of the form $a - b = c$ in each of the following. Find all such equations. For example, in the row $\frac{1}{4}$ $\frac{2}{3}$ $\frac{1}{7}$ $\frac{11}{21}$ $\frac{2}{15}$, a correct equation is $\frac{2}{3} - \frac{1}{7} - \frac{11}{21}$.

   a. $\frac{11}{21}$ $\frac{7}{12}$ $\frac{3}{4}$ $\frac{5}{9}$ $\frac{4}{5}$ $\frac{5}{12}$ $\frac{1}{3}$ $\frac{1}{12}$ **b.** $\frac{2}{3}$ $\frac{3}{5}$ $\frac{3}{7}$ $\frac{6}{12}$ $\frac{1}{6}$ $\frac{1}{3}$ $\frac{1}{9}$

32. If one of your students wrote $\frac{1}{4} + \frac{2}{3} = \frac{3}{7}$, how would you convince him or her that this is incorrect?

33. A classroom of 25 students was arranged in a square with five rows and five columns. The teacher told the students that they could rearrange themselves by having each student move to a new seat directly in front or back, or directly to the right or left—no diagonal moves were permitted. Determine how this could be accomplished (if at all). (*Hint:* Solve an equivalent problem—consider a 5×5 checkerboard.)

Analyzing Student Thinking

34. Cristobal says that you don't necessarily have to find the LCD to add two fractions and that any common denominator will do. Is he correct? Explain.

35. Whitley claims that she can add two fractions without finding a common denominator. How should you respond?

36. To add $3\frac{1}{4}$ and $5\frac{2}{7}$, a student claims that you have to change these two mixed numbers into improper fractions first. Is the student correct? Explain.

37. Instead of adding $\frac{3}{4}$ and $\frac{7}{8}$ first as shown in the problem $\left(\frac{3}{4} + \frac{7}{8}\right) + \frac{1}{4}$, Kalin adds $\frac{3}{4}$ and $\frac{1}{4}$ first. Is this okay? Explain.

38. You asked Marcos to determine whether certain fractions were closer to 0, $\frac{1}{2}$, or to 1. He answered that since fractions were always small, they would all be close to 0. How would you respond to him?

39. Brenda asks why she needs to find a common denominator when adding or subtracting fractions. How should you respond?

40. Marilyn said her family made two square pizzas at home, one $8''$ on a side and the other $12''$ on a side. She ate $\frac{1}{4}$ of the small pizza and $\frac{1}{6}$ of the larger pizza. So Marilyn says she ate $\frac{5}{12}$ of the pizza. Do you agree? Explain.

Problems Relating to the NCTM Standards and Curriculum Focal Points

1. The Focal Points for Grade 3 state "Developing an understanding of and fluency with addition and subtraction of fractions and decimals." Based on the discussions in this section, explain at least one main concept essential to understanding addition and subtraction of fractions.

2. The NCTM Standards state "All students use visual models, benchmarks, and equivalent forms to add and subtract commonly used fractions and decimals." Explain what is meant by "visual models" when adding and subtracting fractions.

3. The NCTM Standards state "All students should develop and use strategies to estimate computations involving fractions and decimals in situations relevant to students' experience." List and explain some examples of strategies to estimate fraction computations.

6.3 FRACTIONS: MULTIPLICATION AND DIVISION

Write a word problem for each of the following expressions. Each word problem should have the corresponding expression as part of its solution.

$$\text{(a) } 3 \div \frac{1}{2} \qquad \text{(b) } \frac{1}{3} \div 4 \qquad \text{(c) } \frac{5}{8} \div \frac{1}{4}$$

An example of a word problem for the expression $4 \times \frac{2}{3}$ is the following:

Darius has been given the job of painting 4 doors. He knows that it takes $\frac{2}{3}$ of a quart of paint to paint each door. How much paint does he need to buy?

Reflection from Research
In the teaching of fractions, even low performing students seem to benefit from task-based participant instruction where students are given tasks or problems to solve on their own or in groups. Such instruction allows students to be engaged in the mathematical practices of problem solving (Empson, 2003).

Multiplication and Its Properties

Extending the repeated-addition approach of whole-number multiplication to fraction multiplication is an interesting challenge. Consider the following cases.

Case 1: A Whole Number Times a Fraction

$$3 \times \frac{1}{4} = \frac{1}{4} + \frac{1}{4} + \frac{1}{4} = \frac{3}{4}$$
$$6 \times \frac{1}{2} = \frac{1}{2} + \frac{1}{2} + \frac{1}{2} + \frac{1}{2} + \frac{1}{2} + \frac{1}{2} = 3$$

Here repeated addition works well since the first factor is a whole number.

Case 2: A Fraction Times a Whole Number

$$\frac{1}{2} \times 6$$

Here, we cannot apply the repeated-addition approach directly, since that would literally say to add 6 one-half times. But if multiplication is to be commutative, then $\frac{1}{2} \times 6$ would have to be equal to $6 \times \frac{1}{2}$, or 3, as in case 1. Thus a way of interpreting $\frac{1}{2} \times 6$ would be to view the $\frac{1}{2}$ as taking "one-half of 6" or "one of two equal parts of 6," namely 3. Similarly, $\frac{1}{4} \times 3$ could be modeled by finding "one-fourth of 3" on the fraction number line to obtain $\frac{3}{4}$ (Figure 6.18).

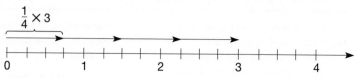

Figure 6.18

In the following final case, it is impossible to use the repeated-addition approach, so we apply the new technique of case 2.

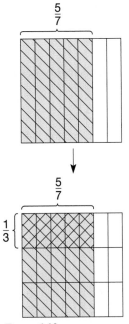

Figure 6.19

Reflection from Research

Students who only view fractions like $\frac{3}{4}$ as "three out of 4 parts" struggle to handle fraction multiplication problems such as $\frac{2}{3}$ of $\frac{9}{10}$. Students who can more flexibly view $\frac{3}{4}$ as "three fourths of one whole or three units of one fourth" can better solve multiplication of two proper fractions (Mack, 2001).

Case 3: A Fraction of a Fraction

$$\frac{1}{3} \times \frac{5}{7} \quad \text{means} \quad \frac{1}{3} \text{ of } \frac{5}{7}$$

First picture $\frac{5}{7}$. Then take one of the three equivalent parts of $\frac{5}{7}$ (Figure 6.19).

After subdividing the region in Figure 6.19 horizontally into seven equivalent parts and vertically into three equal parts, the shaded region consists of 5 of the 21 smallest rectangles (each small rectangle represents $\frac{1}{21}$). Therefore,

$$\frac{1}{3} \times \frac{5}{7} = \frac{5}{21}$$

Similarly, $\frac{2}{3} \times \frac{5}{7}$ would comprise 10 of the smallest rectangles, so

$$\frac{2}{3} \times \frac{5}{7} = \frac{10}{21}.$$

This discussion should make the following definition of fraction multiplication seem reasonable.

DEFINITION

Multiplication of Fractions

Let $\dfrac{a}{b}$ and $\dfrac{c}{d}$ be any fractions. Then

$$\frac{a}{b} \cdot \frac{c}{d} = \frac{ac}{bd}.$$

Example 6.12   Compute the following products and express the answers in simplest form.

a. $\frac{2}{3} \cdot \frac{5}{13}$ **b.** $\frac{3}{4} \cdot \frac{28}{15}$ **c.** $2\frac{1}{3} \cdot 7\frac{2}{5}$

SOLUTION

a. $\dfrac{2}{3} \cdot \dfrac{5}{13} = \dfrac{2 \cdot 5}{3 \cdot 13} = \dfrac{10}{39}$

b. $\dfrac{3}{4} \cdot \dfrac{28}{15} = \dfrac{3 \cdot 28}{4 \cdot 15} = \dfrac{84}{60} = \dfrac{21 \cdot 4}{15 \cdot 4} = \dfrac{21}{15} = \dfrac{7 \cdot 3}{5 \cdot 3} = \dfrac{7}{5}$

c. $2\dfrac{1}{3} \cdot 7\dfrac{2}{5} = \dfrac{7}{3} \cdot \dfrac{37}{5} = \dfrac{259}{15}$, or $17\dfrac{4}{15}$ ∎

Two mixed numbers were multiplied in Example 6.12(c). Children may *incorrectly* multiply mixed numbers as follows:

$$2\tfrac{2}{3} \cdot 3\tfrac{1}{2} = (2 \cdot 3) + (\tfrac{2}{3} \cdot \tfrac{1}{2})$$
$$= 6\tfrac{1}{3}.$$

However, Figure 6.20 shows that multiplying mixed numbers is more complex.

In Example 6.12(b), the product was easy to find but the process of simplification required several steps.

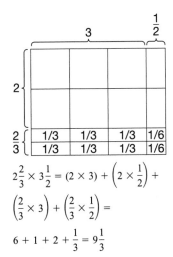

$$2\tfrac{2}{3} \times 3\tfrac{1}{2} = (2 \times 3) + \left(2 \times \tfrac{1}{2}\right) +$$

$$\left(\tfrac{2}{3} \times 3\right) + \left(\tfrac{2}{3} \times \tfrac{1}{2}\right) =$$

$$6 + 1 + 2 + \tfrac{1}{3} = 9\tfrac{1}{3}$$

Figure 6.20

When using a fraction calculator, the answers are usually not given in simplest form. For example, on the TI-34 II, Example 6.12(b) is obtained:

$$3 \boxed{/} 4 \boxed{\times} 28 \boxed{/} 15 \boxed{=} 1 \boxed{\cup 24/60}$$

This mixed number is simplified one step at a time by pressing the simplify key repeatedly as follows:

$$\boxed{\text{SIMP}} \boxed{=} \boxed{1\cup 12/30} \boxed{\text{SIMP}} \boxed{=} \boxed{1\cup 6/15} \boxed{\text{SIMP}} \boxed{=} \boxed{1\cup 2/5}$$

The display of the original result on the TI-34 II may be the improper fraction $\boxed{84/60}$, depending on how the $\boxed{\text{FracMode}}$ has been set.

The next example shows how one can simplify first (a good habit to cultivate) and then multiply.

Example 6.13   Compute and simplify: $\dfrac{3}{4} \cdot \dfrac{28}{15}$.

SOLUTION   Instead, simplify, and then compute.

$$\frac{3}{4} \cdot \frac{28}{15} = \frac{3 \cdot 28}{4 \cdot 15} = \frac{3 \cdot 28}{15 \cdot 4} = \frac{3}{15} \cdot \frac{28}{4} = \frac{1}{5} \cdot \frac{7}{1} = \frac{7}{5}.$$

Another way to calculate this product is

$$\frac{3}{4} \cdot \frac{28}{15} = \frac{3 \cdot 2 \cdot 2 \cdot 7}{2 \cdot 2 \cdot 3 \cdot 5} = \frac{7}{5}.$$

∎

The equation $\dfrac{a}{b} \cdot \dfrac{c}{d} = \dfrac{a}{d} \cdot \dfrac{c}{b}$ is a simplification of the essence of the procedure in Example 6.13. That is, we simply interchange the two denominators to expedite the simplification process. This can be justified as follows:

$$\frac{a}{b} \cdot \frac{c}{d} = \frac{ac}{bd} \qquad \textit{Multiplication of fractions}$$

$$= \frac{ac}{bd} \qquad \textit{Commutativity for whole-number multiplication}$$

$$= \frac{a}{d} \cdot \frac{c}{b}. \qquad \textit{Multiplication of fractions}$$

You may have seen the following even shorter method.

Example 6.14   Compute and simplify.

a. $\frac{18}{13} \cdot \frac{39}{72}$ **b.** $\frac{50}{15} \cdot \frac{39}{55}$

SOLUTION

a. $\dfrac{18}{13} \cdot \dfrac{39}{72} = \dfrac{18}{\cancel{13}_{1}} \cdot \dfrac{\overset{3}{\cancel{39}}}{72} = \dfrac{\overset{1}{\cancel{18}}}{\cancel{13}_{1}} \cdot \dfrac{\overset{3}{\cancel{39}}}{\cancel{72}_{4}} = \dfrac{3}{4}$

b. $\dfrac{50}{15} \cdot \dfrac{39}{55} = \dfrac{\overset{10}{\cancel{50}}}{\cancel{15}_{3}} \cdot \dfrac{39}{55} = \dfrac{\overset{2}{\cancel{10}}}{3} \cdot \dfrac{39}{\cancel{55}_{11}} = \dfrac{2}{\cancel{3}_{1}} \cdot \dfrac{\overset{13}{\cancel{39}}}{11} = \dfrac{26}{11}$

∎

The definition of fraction multiplication together with the corresponding properties for whole-number multiplication can be used to verify properties of fraction multiplication. A verification of the multiplicative identity property for fraction multiplication is shown next.

$$\frac{a}{b} \cdot 1 = \frac{a}{b} \cdot \frac{1}{1}$$ *Recall that* $1 = \frac{1}{1} = \frac{2}{2} = \frac{3}{3} = \ldots.$

$$= \frac{a \cdot 1}{b \cdot 1}$$ *Fraction multiplication*

$$= \frac{a}{b}$$ *Identity for whole-number multiplication*

It is shown in the problem set that 1 is the only multiplicative identity.

The properties of fraction multiplication are summarized next. Notice that fraction multiplication has an additional property, different from any whole-number properties—namely, the multiplicative inverse property.

Reflection from Research
Although there are inherent dangers in using rules without meaning, teachers can introduce rules that are both useful and mathematically meaningful to enhance children's understanding of fractions (Ploger & Rooney, 2005).

PROPERTY

Properties of Fraction Multiplication

Let $\dfrac{a}{b}, \dfrac{c}{d}$, and $\dfrac{e}{f}$ be any fractions.

Closure Property for Fraction Multiplication

The product of two fractions is a fraction.

Commutative Property for Fraction Multiplication

$$\frac{a}{b} \cdot \frac{c}{d} = \frac{c}{d} \cdot \frac{a}{b}$$

Associative Property for Fraction Multiplication

$$\left(\frac{a}{b} \cdot \frac{c}{d}\right) \cdot \frac{e}{f} = \frac{a}{b}\left(\frac{c}{d} \cdot \frac{e}{f}\right)$$

Multiplicative Identity Property for Fraction Multiplication

$$\frac{a}{b} \cdot 1 = \frac{a}{b} = 1 \cdot \frac{a}{b}. \quad \left(1 = \frac{m}{m}, m \neq 0\right)$$

Multiplicative Inverse Property for Fraction Multiplication

For every nonzero fraction $\dfrac{a}{b}$, there is a unique fraction $\dfrac{b}{a}$ such that

$$\frac{a}{b} \cdot \frac{b}{a} = 1.$$

Algebraic Reasoning
Being comfortable with the multiplicative inverse property is very valuable when solving equations like $\frac{2}{3}x = \frac{5}{7}$. This property allows one to isolate x by multiplying both sides of this equation by $\frac{3}{2}$ to get $\frac{3}{2} \cdot \frac{2}{3}x = \frac{3}{2} \cdot \frac{5}{7}$ or $x = \frac{15}{14}$.

When $\dfrac{a}{b} \neq 0$, $\dfrac{b}{a}$ is called the **multiplicative inverse** or **reciprocal** of $\dfrac{a}{b}$. The multiplicative inverse property is useful for solving equations involving fractions.

Example 6.15   Solve: $\dfrac{3}{7}x = \dfrac{5}{8}$.

SOLUTION

$$\frac{3}{7}x = \frac{5}{8}$$

$$\frac{7}{3}\left(\frac{3}{7}x\right) = \frac{7}{3}\cdot\frac{5}{8} \qquad \textit{Multiplication}$$

$$\left(\frac{7}{3}\cdot\frac{3}{7}\right)x = \frac{7}{3}\cdot\frac{5}{8} \qquad \textit{Associative property}$$

$$1\cdot x = \frac{35}{24} \qquad \textit{Multiplicative inverse property}$$

$$x = \frac{35}{24} \qquad \textit{Multiplicate identity property}$$

∎

Finally, as with whole numbers, distributivity holds for fractions. This property can be verified using distributivity in the whole numbers.

PROPERTY

Distributive Property of Fraction Multiplication over Addition

Let $\dfrac{a}{b}$, $\dfrac{c}{d}$, and $\dfrac{e}{f}$ be any fractions. Then

$$\frac{a}{b}\left(\frac{c}{d} + \frac{e}{f}\right) = \frac{a}{b}\times\frac{c}{d} + \frac{a}{b}\times\frac{e}{f}.$$

Distributivity of multiplication over subtraction also holds; that is,

$$\frac{a}{b}\left(\frac{c}{d} - \frac{e}{f}\right) = \frac{a}{b}\times\frac{c}{d} - \frac{a}{b}\times\frac{e}{f}.$$

 Check for Understanding: Exercise/Problem Set A #1–10

Division

Division of fractions is a difficult concept for many children (and adults), in part because of the lack of simple concrete models. We will view division of fractions as an extension of whole-number division. Several other approaches will be used in this section and in the problem set. These approaches provide a *meaningful way* of learning fraction division. Such approaches are a departure from simply memorizing the rote procedure of "invert and multiply," which offers no insight into fraction division.

By using common denominators, division of fractions can be viewed as an extension of whole-number division. For example, $\frac{6}{7} \div \frac{2}{7}$ is just a measurement division problem where we ask the question, "How many groups of size $\frac{2}{7}$ are in $\frac{6}{7}$?" The answer to this question is the equivalent measurement division problem of $6 \div 2$, where the question is asked, "How many groups of size 2 are in 6?" Since there are *three* 2s in 6, there are *three* $\frac{2}{7}$s in $\frac{6}{7}$. Figure 6.21 illustrates this visually. In general, the division

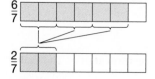

Figure 6.21

of fractions in which the divisor is not a whole number can be viewed as a measurement division problem. On the other hand, if the division problem has a divisor that is a whole number, then it should be viewed as a sharing division problem.

> ### Example 6.16   Find the following quotients.
>
> **a.** $\frac{12}{13} \div \frac{4}{13}$ **b.** $\frac{6}{17} \div \frac{3}{17}$ **c.** $\frac{16}{19} \div \frac{2}{19}$
>
> **SOLUTION**
>
> **a.** $\frac{12}{13} \div \frac{4}{13} = 3$, since there are three $\frac{4}{13}$ in $\frac{12}{13}$.
>
> **b.** $\frac{6}{17} \div \frac{3}{17} = 2$, since there are two $\frac{3}{17}$ in $\frac{6}{17}$.
>
> **c.** $\frac{16}{19} \div \frac{2}{19} = 8$, since there are eight $\frac{2}{19}$ in $\frac{16}{19}$.

Reflection from Research
Until students understand operations with fractions, they often have misconceptions that multiplication always results in a larger answer and division in a smaller answer (Greer, 1988).

Notice that the answers to all three of these problems can be found simply by dividing the numerators in the correct order. ∎

In the case of $\frac{12}{13} \div \frac{5}{13}$, we ask ourselves, "How many $\frac{5}{13}$ make $\frac{12}{13}$?" But this is the same as asking, "How many 5s (including fractional parts) are in 12?" The answer is 2 and $\frac{2}{5}$ fives or $\frac{12}{5}$ fives. Thus $\frac{12}{13} \div \frac{5}{13} = \frac{12}{5}$. Generalizing this idea, fraction division is defined as follows.

> ### DEFINITION
>
> **Division of Fraction with Common Denominators**
>
> Let $\frac{a}{b}$ and $\frac{c}{b}$ be any fractions with $c \neq 0$. Then
>
> $$\frac{a}{b} \div \frac{c}{b} = \frac{a}{c}.$$

To divide fractions with different denominators, we can rewrite the fractions so that they have the same denominator. Thus we see that

$$\frac{a}{b} \div \frac{c}{d} = \frac{ad}{bd} \div \frac{bc}{bd} = \frac{ad}{bc} \left(= \frac{a}{b} \times \frac{d}{c} \right)$$

using division with common denominators. For example,

$$\frac{3}{7} \div \frac{5}{9} = \frac{27}{63} \div \frac{35}{63} = \frac{27}{35}.$$

Notice that the quotient $\frac{a}{b} \div \frac{c}{d}$ is equal to the product $\frac{a}{b} \times \frac{d}{c}$, since they are both equal to $\frac{ab}{bc}$. Thus a procedure for dividing fractions is to invert the divisor and multiply.

Another interpretation of division of fractions using the missing-factor approach refers directly to multiplication of fractions.

Example 6.17   Find: $\dfrac{21}{40} \div \dfrac{7}{8}$.

SOLUTION

Let $\dfrac{21}{40} \div \dfrac{7}{8} = \dfrac{e}{f}$. If the missing-factor approach holds, then $\dfrac{21}{40} = \dfrac{7}{8} \times \dfrac{e}{f}$. Then
$\dfrac{7 \times e}{8 \times f} = \dfrac{21}{40}$ and we can take $e = 3$ and $f = 5$. Therefore, $\dfrac{e}{f} = \dfrac{3}{5}$, or $\dfrac{21}{40} \div \dfrac{7}{8} = \dfrac{3}{5}$.   ∎

In Example 6.17 we have the convenient situation where one set of numerators and denominators divides evenly into the other set. Thus a short way of doing this problem is

$$\frac{21}{40} \div \frac{7}{8} = \frac{21 \div 7}{40 \div 8} = \frac{3}{5},$$

since $21 \div 7 = 3$ and $40 \div 8 = 5$. This "divide-the-numerators-and-denominators approach" can be adapted to a more general case, as the following example shows.

Example 6.18   Find: $\dfrac{21}{40} \div \dfrac{6}{11}$.

SOLUTION

$$\begin{aligned}
\frac{21}{40} \div \frac{6}{11} &= \frac{21 \times 6 \times 11}{40 \times 6 \times 11} \div \frac{6}{11} \\
&= \frac{(21 \times 6 \times 11) \div 6}{(40 \times 6 \times 11) \div 11} \\
&= \frac{21 \times 11}{40 \times 6} \\
&= \frac{231}{240} = \frac{21}{40} \times \frac{11}{6}
\end{aligned}$$

∎

Notice that this approach leads us to conclude that $\frac{21}{40} \div \frac{6}{11} = \frac{21}{40} \times \frac{11}{6}$. Generalizing from these examples and results using the common-denominator approach, we are led to the following familiar "invert-the-divisor-and-multiply" procedure.

THEOREM

Division of Fractions with Unlike Denominators— Invert the Divisor and Multiply

Let $\dfrac{a}{b}$ and $\dfrac{c}{d}$ be any fractions with $c \neq 0$. Then

$$\frac{a}{b} \div \frac{c}{d} = \frac{a}{b} \times \frac{d}{c}.$$

A more visual way to understand why you "invert and multiply" in order to divide fractions is described next. Consider the problem $3 \div \frac{1}{2}$. Viewing it as a measurement division problem, we ask "How many groups of size $\frac{1}{2}$ are in 3?" Let each rectangle in

Figure 6.22 represent *one whole*. Since each of the rectangles can be broken into *two* halves and there are three rectangles, there are $3 \times 2 = 6$ one-halfs in 3. Thus we see that $3 \div \frac{1}{2} = 3 \times 2 = 6$.

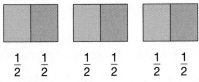

$$\frac{1}{2} \quad \frac{1}{2} \qquad \frac{1}{2} \quad \frac{1}{2} \qquad \frac{1}{2} \quad \frac{1}{2}$$

Figure 6.22

The problem $4 \div \frac{2}{3}$ should also be approached as a measurement division problem for which the question is asked, "How many groups of size $\frac{2}{3}$ are in 4?" In order to answer this question, we must first determine how many groups of size $\frac{2}{3}$ are in *one whole*. Let each rectangle in Figure 6.23 represent one whole and divide each of them into three equal parts.

Reflection from Research
As children are given opportunities to create fractional amounts from wholes (partitioning) and wholes from fractional amounts (iterating), they will naturally develop images that can be used as tools for working with fractions and fraction operations (Siebert & Gaskin, 2006).

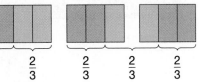

$$\frac{2}{3} \qquad \frac{2}{3} \qquad \frac{2}{3} \qquad \frac{2}{3} \qquad \frac{2}{3} \qquad \frac{2}{3}$$

Figure 6.23

As shown in Figure 6.23, there is *one* group of size $\frac{2}{3}$ in the rectangle and *one-half* of a group of size $\frac{2}{3}$ in the rectangle. Therefore, each rectangle has $1\frac{1}{2}$ groups of size $\frac{2}{3}$ in it. In this case there are 4 rectangles, so there are $4 \times 1\frac{1}{2} = 6$ groups of size $\frac{2}{3}$ in 4. Since $1\frac{1}{2}$ can be rewritten as $\frac{3}{2}$, the expression $4 \times 1\frac{1}{2}$ is equivalent to $4 \times \frac{3}{2}$. Thus, $4 \div \frac{2}{3} = 4 \times \frac{3}{2} = 6$.

In a similar way, this visual approach can be extended to handle problems with a dividend that is not a whole number.

Example 6.19 Find the following quotients using the most convenient division method.

a. $\frac{17}{11} \div \frac{4}{11}$ **b.** $\frac{3}{4} \div \frac{5}{7}$ **c.** $\frac{6}{25} \div \frac{2}{5}$ **d.** $\frac{5}{19} \div \frac{13}{11}$

SOLUTION

a. $\dfrac{17}{11} \div \dfrac{4}{11} = \dfrac{17}{4}$, using the common-denominator approach.

b. $\dfrac{3}{4} \div \dfrac{5}{7} = \dfrac{3}{4} \times \dfrac{7}{5} = \dfrac{21}{20}$, using the invert-the-divisor-and-multiply approach.

c. $\dfrac{6}{25} \div \dfrac{2}{5} = \dfrac{6 \div 2}{25 \div 5} = \dfrac{3}{5}$, using the divide-numerators-and-denominators approach.

d. $\dfrac{5}{19} \div \dfrac{13}{11} = \dfrac{5}{19} \times \dfrac{11}{13} = \dfrac{55}{247}$, using the invert-the-divisor-and-multiply approach. ∎

In summary, there are three equivalent ways to view the division of fractions:

1. The common-denominator approach.
2. The divide-the-numerators-and-denominators approach
3. The invert-the-divisor-and-multiply approach

Now, through the division of fractions, we can perform the division of any whole numbers without having to use remainders. (Of course, we still cannot divide by zero.) That is, if a and b are whole numbers and $b \neq 0$, then $a \div b = \dfrac{a}{1} \div \dfrac{b}{1} = \dfrac{a}{1} \times \dfrac{1}{b} = \dfrac{a}{b}$. This approach is summarized next.

> **For all whole numbers a and b, $b \neq 0$,**
> $$a \div b = \frac{a}{b}.$$

Example 6.20   Find $17 \div 6$ using fractions.

SOLUTION

$$17 \div 6 = \tfrac{17}{6} = 2\tfrac{5}{6}$$ ∎

There are many situations in which the answer $2\tfrac{5}{6}$ is more useful than 2 with a remainder of 5. For example, suppose that 17 acres of land were to be divided among 6 families. Each family would receive $2\tfrac{5}{6}$ acres, rather than each receiving 2 acres with 5 acres remaining unassigned.

Expressing a division problem as a fraction is a useful idea. For example, **complex fractions** such as $\dfrac{\frac{1}{2}}{\frac{3}{5}}$ may be written in place of $\tfrac{1}{2} \div \tfrac{3}{5}$. Although fractions are comprised of whole numbers in elementary school mathematics, numbers other than whole numbers are used in numerators and denominators of "fractions" later. For example, the "fraction" $\dfrac{\sqrt{2}}{\pi}$ is simply a symbolic way of writing the quotient $\sqrt{2} \div \pi$ (numbers such as $\sqrt{2}$ and π are discussed in Chapter 9).

Complex fractions are used to divide fractions, as shown next.

Example 6.21   Find $\tfrac{1}{2} \div \tfrac{3}{5}$ using a complex fraction.

SOLUTION

$$\tfrac{1}{2} \div \tfrac{3}{5} = \frac{\frac{1}{2}}{\frac{3}{5}} \cdot \frac{\frac{5}{3}}{\frac{5}{3}} = \frac{\frac{1}{2} \cdot \frac{5}{3}}{1} = \frac{5}{6}$$

Notice that the multiplicative inverse of the denominator $\tfrac{3}{5}$ was used to form a complex fraction form of one. ∎

✓ Check for Understanding: Exercise/Problem Set A #11–19

Mental Math and Estimation for Multiplication and Division

Mental math and estimation techniques similar to those used with whole numbers can be used with fractions.

Example 6.22 Calculate mentally.

a. $(25 \times 16) \times \dfrac{1}{4}$ **b.** $24\dfrac{4}{7} \div 4$ **c.** $\dfrac{4}{5} \times 15$

SOLUTION

a. $(25 \times 16) \times \dfrac{1}{4} = 25 \times \left(16 \times \dfrac{1}{4} \right) = 25 \times 4 = 100.$

Associativity was used to group 16 and $\dfrac{1}{4}$ together, since they are compatible numbers. Also, 25 and 4 are compatible with respect to multiplication.

b. $24\dfrac{4}{7} \div 4 = \left(24 + \dfrac{4}{7} \right) \div 4 = (24 \div 4) + \left(\dfrac{4}{7} \div 4 \right) = 6 + \dfrac{1}{7} = 6\dfrac{1}{7}$

Right distributivity can often be used when dividing mixed numbers, as illustrated here.

c. $\dfrac{4}{5} \times 15 = \left(4 \times \dfrac{1}{5} \right) \times 15 = 4 \times \left(\dfrac{1}{5} \times 15 \right) = 4 \times 3 = 12$

The calculation also can be written as $\dfrac{4}{5} \times 15 = 4 \times \dfrac{15}{5} = 4 \times 3 = 12$. This

product also can be found as follows: $\dfrac{4}{5} \times 15 = \left(\dfrac{4}{5} \times 5 \right) \times 3 = 4 \times 3 = 12.$ ■

Example 6.23 Estimate using the indicated techniques.

a. $5\dfrac{1}{8} \times 7\dfrac{5}{6}$ using range estimation   **b.** $4\dfrac{3}{8} \times 9\dfrac{1}{16}$ rounding to the nearest $\dfrac{1}{2}$ or whole

c. $14\dfrac{8}{9} \div 2\dfrac{3}{8}$

SOLUTION

a. $5\dfrac{1}{8} \times 7\dfrac{5}{6}$ is between $5 \times 7 = 35$ and $6 \times 8 = 48$.

b. $4\dfrac{3}{8} \times 9\dfrac{1}{16} \approx 4\dfrac{1}{2} \times 9 = 36 + 4\dfrac{1}{2} = 40\dfrac{1}{2}$

c. $14\dfrac{8}{9} \div 2\dfrac{3}{8} \approx 15 \div 2\dfrac{1}{2} = 6$ ■

✔ **Check for Understanding:** Exercise/Problem Set A #20–23

MATHEMATICAL MORSEL

The Hindu mathematician Bhaskara (1119–1185) wrote an arithmetic text called the *Lilavat* (named after his wife). The following is one of the problems contained in this text. "A necklace was broken during an amorous struggle. One-third of the pearls fell to the ground, one-fifth stayed on the couch, one-sixth were found by the girl, and one-tenth were recovered by her lover; six pearls remained on the string. Say of how many pearls the necklace was composed."

Section 6.3 | EXERCISE / PROBLEM SET A

EXERCISES

1. Use a number line to illustrate how $\frac{1}{3} \times 5$ is different from $5 \times \frac{1}{3}$.

2. Use the Chapter 6 eManipulative activity *Multiplying Fractions* on our Web site or the rectangular area model to sketch representations of the following multiplication problems.
  a. $\frac{1}{3} \times \frac{2}{5}$ **b.** $\frac{3}{8} \times \frac{5}{6}$ **c.** $\frac{2}{3} \times \frac{7}{10}$

3. What multiplication problems are represented by each of the following area models? What are the products?

a. 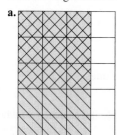 **b.**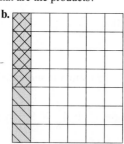

4. Find reciprocals for the following numbers.
  a. $\frac{11}{21}$ **b.** $\frac{9}{3}$ **c.** $13\frac{4}{9}$ **d.** 108

5. a. Insert the appropriate equality or inequality symbol in the following statement:
$$\frac{3}{4} \underline{\quad} \frac{3}{2}$$
  b. Find the reciprocals of $\frac{3}{4}$ and $\frac{3}{2}$ and complete the following statement, inserting either < or > in the center blank.
$$\text{reciprocal of } \frac{3}{4} \underline{\quad} \text{reciprocal of } \frac{3}{2}$$
  c. What do you notice about ordering reciprocals?

6. Identify which of the properties of fractions could be applied to simplify each of the following computations.
  a. $\frac{5}{7} \times \frac{2}{9} \times \frac{7}{5}$ **b.** $(\frac{3}{5} \times \frac{2}{11}) + (\frac{2}{5} \times \frac{2}{11})$ **c.** $(\frac{8}{5} \times \frac{3}{13}) \times \frac{13}{3}$

7. Perform the following operations and express your answer in simplest form.
  a. $\frac{4}{7} \times \frac{3}{8}$ **b.** $\frac{6}{25} \times \frac{5}{9} \times \frac{3}{2}$
  c. $\frac{2}{5} \times \frac{9}{13} + \frac{2}{5} \times \frac{4}{13}$ **d.** $\frac{11}{12} \times \frac{5}{13} + \frac{5}{13} \times \frac{7}{12}$
  e. $\frac{4}{7} \times \frac{3}{14}$ **f.** $\frac{2}{9} \times \frac{4}{3} \times \frac{5}{7}$
  g. $\frac{7}{15} \times 3\frac{1}{2} \times \frac{3}{5}$ **h.** $\frac{1}{3} \times (\frac{5}{4} - \frac{1}{4}) \times \frac{5}{6}$

8. Calculate using a fraction calculator if available.
  a. $\frac{7}{6} \times \frac{4}{5}$ **b.** $\frac{3}{8} \times \frac{4}{5}$

9. Find the following products.
  a. $5\frac{1}{3} \times 2\frac{1}{6}$ **b.** $3\frac{7}{8} \times 2\frac{3}{4}$ **c.** $3\frac{3}{4} \times 2\frac{2}{5}$

10. We usually think of the distributive property for fractions as "multiplication of fractions distributes over addition of fractions." Which of the following variations of the distributive property for fractions holds for arbitrary fractions?
  a. Addition over subtraction
  b. Division over multiplication

11. Suppose that the following unit square represents the whole number 1. ☐ We can use squares like this one to represent division problems like $3 \div \frac{1}{2}$, by asking how many $\frac{1}{2}$s are in 3. ▨ ▨ ▨ $3 \div \frac{1}{2} = 6$, since there are six one-half squares in the three squares. Draw similar figures and calculate the quotients for the following division problems.
  a. $4 \div \frac{1}{3}$ **b.** $2\frac{1}{2} \div \frac{1}{4}$ **c.** $3 \div \frac{3}{4}$

12. Using the Chapter 6 eManipulative activity *Dividing Fractions* on our Web site, construct representations of the following division problems. Sketch each representation.

a. $\frac{7}{4} \div \frac{1}{2}$ **b.** $\frac{3}{4} \div \frac{2}{3}$ **c.** $2\frac{1}{4} \div \frac{5}{8}$

13. Use the common-denominator method to divide the following fractions.

a. $\frac{15}{17} \div \frac{3}{17}$ **b.** $\frac{4}{7} \div \frac{3}{7}$ **c.** $\frac{33}{51} \div \frac{39}{51}$

14. Use the fact that the numerators and denominators divide evenly to simplify the following quotients.

a. $\frac{15}{16} \div \frac{3}{4}$ **b.** $\frac{21}{27} \div \frac{7}{9}$ **c.** $\frac{39}{56} \div \frac{3}{8}$ **d.** $\frac{17}{24} \div \frac{17}{12}$

15. The missing-factor approach can be applied to fraction division, as illustrated.

$$\frac{4}{7} \div \frac{2}{5} = \boxed{} \ \text{so} \ \frac{2}{5} \times \boxed{} = \frac{4}{7}$$

Since we want $\frac{4}{7}$ to be the result, we insert that in the box. Then if we put in the reciprocal of $\frac{2}{5}$, we have

$$\frac{2}{5} \times \boxed{\frac{5}{2} \times \frac{4}{7}} = \frac{4}{7} \ \text{so}$$

$$\frac{4}{7} \div \frac{2}{5} = \boxed{\frac{5}{2} \times \frac{4}{7}} = \frac{20}{14} = \frac{10}{7}$$

Use this approach to do the following division problems.

a. $\frac{3}{5} \div \frac{2}{7}$ **b.** $\frac{13}{6} \div \frac{3}{7}$ **c.** $\frac{12}{13} \div \frac{6}{5}$

16. Find the following quotients using the most convenient of the three methods for division. Express your answer in simplest form.

a. $\frac{5}{7} \div \frac{4}{9}$ **b.** $\frac{33}{14} \div \frac{11}{7}$ **c.** $\frac{5}{13} \div \frac{3}{13}$ **d.** $\frac{3}{11} \div \frac{8}{22}$

17. Perform the following operations and express your answer in simplest form.

a. $\frac{7}{11} \div \frac{11}{7}$ **b.** $\frac{1}{3} + \frac{5}{4}(\frac{1}{4} \div \frac{5}{6})$ **c.** $\frac{7}{8} \div \frac{21}{4}$

18. Calculate using a fraction calculator if available.

a. $\frac{3}{8} \div \frac{5}{6}$ **b.** $\frac{4}{5} \div \frac{2}{7}$

19. Find the following quotients.

a. $8\frac{1}{3} \div 2\frac{1}{10}$ **b.** $6\frac{1}{4} \div 1\frac{2}{3}$ **c.** $16\frac{2}{3} \div 2\frac{7}{9}$

20. Change each of the following complex fractions into ordinary fractions.

a. $\dfrac{\frac{7}{9}}{\frac{13}{14}}$ **b.** $\dfrac{\frac{2}{3}}{\frac{3}{2}}$

21. Calculate mentally using properties.

a. $15 \times \frac{3}{7} + 6 \times \frac{3}{7}$ **b.** $35 \times \frac{6}{7} - 35 \times \frac{3}{7}$

c. $(\frac{2}{5} \times \frac{3}{8}) \times \frac{5}{2}$ **d.** $3\frac{5}{9} \times 54$

22. Estimate using compatible numbers.

a. $29\frac{1}{3} \times 4\frac{2}{3}$ **b.** $57\frac{1}{5} \div 7\frac{4}{5}$

c. $70\frac{3}{5} \div 8\frac{5}{8}$ **d.** $31\frac{1}{4} \times 5\frac{3}{4}$

23. Estimate using cluster estimation.

a. $12\frac{1}{4} \times 11\frac{5}{6}$ **b.** $5\frac{1}{10} \times 4\frac{8}{9} \times 5\frac{4}{11}$

24. Here is a shortcut for multiplying by 25:

$$25 \times 36 = \frac{100}{4} \times 36 = 100 \times \frac{36}{4} = 900.$$

Use this idea to find the following products mentally.

a. 25×44 **b.** 25×120 **c.** 25×488 **d.** 1248×25

PROBLEMS

25. The introduction of fractions allows us to solve equations of the form $ax = b$ by dividing whole numbers. For example, $5x = 16$ has as its solution $x = \frac{16}{5}$ (which is 16 divided by 5). Solve each of the following equations and check your results.

a. $31x = 15$ **b.** $67x = 56$ **c.** $102x = 231$

26. Another way to find a fraction between two given fractions $\frac{a}{b}$ and $\frac{c}{d}$ is to find the average of the two fractions. For example, the average of $\frac{1}{2}$ and $\frac{2}{3}$ is $\frac{1}{2}(\frac{1}{2} + \frac{2}{3}) = \frac{7}{12}$. Use this method to find a fraction between each of the given pairs.

a. $\frac{7}{8}, \frac{8}{9}$ **b.** $\frac{7}{12}, \frac{11}{16}$

27. You buy a family-size box of laundry detergent that contains 40 cups. If your washing machine calls for $1\frac{1}{4}$ cups per wash load, how many loads of wash can you do?

28. In April of 2007, about 250/999 of the oil refined in the United States was produced in the United States. If the United States produced 4,201,000 barrels per day in April of 2007, how much oil was being refined at that time? (Source: *U.S. Energy Information Administration*)

29. All but $\frac{1}{16}$ of the students enrolled at a particular elementary school participated in "Family Fun Night" activities. If a total of 405 students were involved in the evening's activities, how many students attend the school?

30. The directions for Weed-Do-In weed killer recommend mixing $2\frac{1}{2}$ ounces of the concentrate with 1 gallon of water. The bottle of Weed-Do-In contains 32 ounces of concentrate.

a. How many gallons of mixture can be made from the bottle of concentrate?

b. Since the weed killer is rather expensive, one gardener decided to stretch his dollar by mixing only $1\frac{3}{4}$ ounces of concentrate with a gallon of water. How many more gallons of mixture can be made this way?

31. A number of employees of a company enrolled in a fitness program on January 2. By March 2, $\frac{4}{5}$ of them were still participating. Of those, $\frac{5}{6}$ were still participating on May 2 and of those, $\frac{9}{10}$ were still participating on July 2. Determine the number of employees who originally enrolled in the program if 36 of the original participants were still active on July 2.

32. Each morning Tammy walks to school. At one-third of the way she passes a grocery store, and halfway to school she passes a bicycle shop. At the grocery store, her watch says 7:40 and at the bicycle shop it says 7:45. When does Tammy reach her school?

33. A recipe that makes 3 dozen peanut butter cookies calls for $1\frac{1}{4}$ cups of flour.
   a. How much flour would you need if you doubled the recipe?
   b. How much flour would you need for half the recipe?
   c. How much flour would you need to make 5 dozen cookies?

34. A softball team had three pitchers: Gale, Ruth, and Sandy. Gale started in $\frac{3}{8}$ of the games played in one season. Sandy started in one more game than Gale, and Ruth started in half as many games as Sandy. In how many of the season's games did each pitcher start?

35. A piece of office equipment purchased for $60,000 depreciates in value each year. Suppose that each year the value of the equipment is $\frac{1}{20}$ less than its value the preceding year.
   a. Calculate the value of the equipment after 2 years.
   b. When will the piece of equipment first have a value less than $40,000?

36. If a nonzero number is divided by one more than itself, the result is one-fifth. If a second nonzero number is divided by one more than itself, the answer is one-fifth of the number itself. What is the product of the two numbers?

37. Carpenters divide fractions by 2 in the following way:
$\frac{11}{16} \div 2 = \frac{11}{16 \times 2} = \frac{11}{32}$ (doubling the denominator)

   a. How would they find $\frac{11}{16} \div 5$?
   b. Does $\dfrac{a}{b} \div n = \dfrac{a}{b \times n}$ always?
   c. Find a quick mental method for finding $5\frac{3}{8} \div 2$. Do the same for $10\frac{9}{16} \div 2$.

38. a. Following are examples of student work in multiplying fractions. In each case, identify the error and answer the given problem as the student would.

Sam: $\frac{1}{2} \times \frac{2}{3} = \frac{3}{6} \times \frac{4}{6} = \frac{12}{6} = 2$
         $\frac{3}{4} \times \frac{1}{8} = \frac{6}{8} \times \frac{1}{8} = \frac{6}{8} = \frac{3}{4}$ $\frac{3}{4} \times \frac{1}{6} = ?$

Sandy: $\frac{3}{8} \times \frac{5}{6} = \frac{3}{8} \times \frac{6}{5} = \frac{18}{40} = \frac{9}{20}$
         $\frac{2}{5} \times \frac{2}{3} = \frac{2}{5} \times \frac{3}{2} = \frac{6}{10} = \frac{3}{5}$ $\frac{5}{6} \times \frac{3}{8} = ?$

   b. Each student is confusing the multiplication algorithm with another algorithm. Which one?

39. Mr. Chen wanted to buy all the grocer's apples for a church picnic. When he asked how many apples the store had, the grocer replied, "If you added $\frac{1}{4}$, $\frac{1}{5}$, and $\frac{1}{6}$ of them, it would make 37." How many apples were in the store?

40. Seven years ago my son was one-third my age at that time. Seven years from now he will be one-half my age at that time. How old is my son?

41. Try a few examples on the Chapter 6 eManipulative *Dividing Fractions* on our Web site. Based on these examples, answer the following question: "When dividing 1 whole by $\frac{3}{5}$, it can be seen that there is 1 group of $\frac{3}{5}$ and a part of a group of $\frac{3}{5}$. Why is the part of a group described as $\frac{2}{3}$ and not $\frac{2}{5}$?"

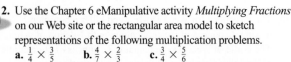

Section 6.3   EXERCISE / PROBLEM SET B

EXERCISES

1. Use a number line to illustrate how $\frac{3}{5} \times 2$ is different from $2 \times \frac{3}{5}$.

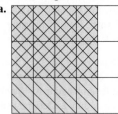

2. Use the Chapter 6 eManipulative activity *Multiplying Fractions* on our Web site or the rectangular area model to sketch representations of the following multiplication problems.
   a. $\frac{1}{4} \times \frac{3}{5}$ **b.** $\frac{4}{7} \times \frac{2}{3}$ **c.** $\frac{3}{4} \times \frac{5}{6}$

3. What multiplication problems are represented by each of the following area models? What are the products?

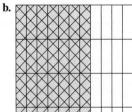

4. a. What is the reciprocal of the reciprocal of $\frac{4}{13}$?
   b. What is the reciprocal of the multiplicative inverse of $\frac{4}{13}$?

5. a. Order the following numbers from smallest to largest.
$$\frac{5}{8} \quad \frac{3}{16} \quad \frac{7}{5} \quad \frac{9}{10}$$
   b. Find the reciprocals of the given numbers and order them from smallest to largest.
   c. What do you observe about these two orders?

6. Identify which of the properties of fractions could be applied to simplify each of the following computations.

   a. $\left(\dfrac{3}{8} \times \dfrac{7}{6}\right) + \left(\dfrac{3}{8} \times \dfrac{5}{6}\right)$ **b.** $\dfrac{6}{11} \times \left(\dfrac{11}{3} \times \dfrac{2}{7}\right)$

   c. $\dfrac{6}{13} \times \dfrac{2}{5} \times \dfrac{13}{6} \times \dfrac{15}{2}$

7. Perform the following operations and express your answer in simplest form.
   a. $\frac{3}{5} \times \frac{4}{9}$
   b. $\frac{2}{7} \times \frac{21}{10}$
   c. $\frac{7}{100} \times \frac{11}{10,000}$
   d. $\frac{4}{9} \times \frac{8}{11} + \frac{7}{9} \times \frac{8}{11}$
   e. $\frac{3}{5} \times \frac{2}{3} + \frac{4}{7}$
   f. $\frac{3}{5} + \frac{2}{3} \times \frac{4}{7}$
   g. $\frac{3}{5} \times (\frac{2}{3} + \frac{4}{7})$
   h. $7\frac{2}{5} \times 5\frac{4}{7}$

8. Calculate using a fraction calculator if available.
   a. $2 \times \frac{3}{8}$
   b. $\frac{3}{7} \times 5$

9. Calculate the following and express as mixed numbers in simplest form.
   a. $8\frac{1}{4} \times 3\frac{4}{5}$
   b. $7\frac{5}{8} \times 13\frac{2}{3}$
   c. $11\frac{3}{5} \times 9\frac{8}{9}$

10. Which of the following variations of the distributive property for fractions holds for arbitrary fractions?
    a. Multiplication over subtraction
    b. Subtraction over addition

11. Draw squares similar to those show in Part A, Exercise 7 to illustrate the following division problems and calculate the quotients.
    a. $2 \div \frac{2}{3}$
    b. $4 \div \frac{2}{5}$
    c. $1\frac{3}{4} \div \frac{1}{2}$

12. Using the Chapter 6 eManipulative activity *Dividing Fractions* on our Web site, construct representations of the following division problems. Sketch each representation.
    a. $\frac{5}{6} \div \frac{1}{3}$
    b. $\frac{4}{3} \div \frac{2}{5}$
    c. $2\frac{1}{3} \div \frac{5}{6}$

13. Use the common-denominator method to divide the following fractions.
    a. $\frac{5}{8} \div \frac{3}{8}$
    b. $\frac{12}{13} \div \frac{4}{13}$
    c. $\frac{13}{15} \div \frac{28}{30}$

14. Use the fact that the numerators and denominators divide evenly to simplify the following quotients.
    a. $\frac{12}{15} \div \frac{4}{5}$
    b. $\frac{18}{24} \div \frac{9}{6}$
    c. $\frac{30}{39} \div \frac{6}{13}$
    d. $\frac{28}{33} \div \frac{14}{11}$

15. Use the method described in Part A, Exercise 11 to find the following quotients.
    a. $\frac{3}{4} \div \frac{6}{9}$
    b. $\frac{10}{7} \div \frac{8}{11}$
    c. $\frac{5}{6} \div \frac{2}{3}$

16. Find the following quotients using the most convenient of the three methods for division. Express your answer in simplest form.
    a. $\frac{48}{63} \div \frac{12}{21}$
    b. $\frac{8}{11} \div \frac{4}{11}$
    c. $\frac{9}{4} \div \frac{3}{5}$
    d. $\frac{3}{7} \div \frac{5}{8}$

17. Perform the following operations and express your answer in simplest form.
    a. $\frac{9}{11} \div \frac{2}{3}$
    b. $\frac{17}{100} \div \frac{9}{10,000}$
    c. $\frac{6}{35} \div \frac{4}{21}$

18. Calculate using a fraction calculator if available.
    a. $\frac{7}{9} \div 14$
    b. $12 \div \frac{2}{3}$

19. Calculate the following and express as mixed numbers in simplest form.
    a. $11\frac{3}{5} \div 9\frac{8}{9}$
    b. $7\frac{5}{8} \div 13\frac{2}{3}$
    c. $4\frac{3}{4} \div 3\frac{8}{11}$

20. Change each of the following complex fractions into ordinary fractions.
    a. $\frac{\frac{2}{3}}{\frac{2}{3}}$
    b. $\frac{1\frac{4}{7}}{3\frac{7}{8}}$

21. Calculate mentally using properties.
    a. $52 \cdot \frac{7}{8} - 52 \cdot \frac{3}{8}$
    b. $(\frac{2}{5} + \frac{5}{8}) + \frac{3}{5}$
    c. $(\frac{3}{7} \times \frac{1}{9}) \times \frac{7}{3}$
    d. $23 \cdot \frac{3}{7} + 7 + 23 \cdot \frac{4}{7}$

22. Estimate using compatible numbers.
    a. $19\frac{1}{3} \times 5\frac{3}{5}$
    b. $77\frac{1}{5} \times 23\frac{4}{5}$
    c. $54\frac{3}{5} \div 7\frac{5}{8}$
    d. $25\frac{2}{3} \times 3\frac{3}{4}$

23. Estimate using cluster estimation.
    a. $5\frac{2}{3} \times 6\frac{1}{8}$
    b. $3\frac{1}{10} \times 2\frac{8}{9} \times 3\frac{2}{11}$

24. Make up your own shortcuts for multiplying by 50 and 75 (see Part A, Exercise 24) and use them to compute the following products mentally. Explain your shortcut for each part.
    a. 50×246
    b. $84,602 \times 50$
    c. 75×848
    d. 420×75

PROBLEMS

25. Solve the following equations involving fractions.
    a. $\frac{2}{5}x = \frac{3}{7}$
    b. $\frac{1}{6}x = \frac{5}{12}$
    c. $\frac{2}{9}x = \frac{7}{9}$
    d. $\frac{5}{3}x = \frac{1}{10}$

26. Find a fraction between $\frac{2}{7}$ and $\frac{3}{8}$ in two different ways.

27. According to a report, approximately 57 billion aluminum cans were recycled in the United States in 2010. That amount was about $\frac{5}{11}$ of the total number of aluminum cans sold in the United States. How many aluminum cans were sold in the United States in 2010?

28. Kids belonging to a Boys and Girls Club collected cans and bottles to raise money by returning them for the deposit. If 54 more cans than bottles were collected and the number of bottles was $\frac{5}{11}$ of the total number of beverage containers collected, how many bottles were collected?

29. Mrs. Martin bought $20\frac{1}{4}$ yards of material to make 4 bridesmaid dresses and 1 dress for the flower girl. The flower girl's dress needs only half as much material as a bridesmaid dress. How much material is needed for a bridesmaid dress? For the flower girl's dress?

30. In a cost-saving measure, Chuck's company reduced all salaries by $\frac{1}{8}$ of their present salaries. If Chuck's monthly salary was $2400, what will he now receive? If his new salary is $2800, what was his old salary?

31. If you place one full container of flour on one pan of a balance scale and a similar container $\frac{3}{4}$ full and a $\frac{1}{3}$-pound weight on the other pan, the pans balance. How much does the full container of flour weigh?

32. A young man spent $\frac{1}{4}$ of his allowance on a movie. He spent $\frac{11}{18}$ of the remainder on after-school snacks. Then from the money remaining, he spent $3.00 on a magazine, which left him $\frac{1}{24}$ of his original allowance to put into savings. How much of his allowance did he save?

33. An airline passenger fell asleep halfway to her destination. When she awoke, the distance remaining was half the distance traveled while she slept. How much of the entire trip was she asleep?

34. A recipe calls for $\frac{2}{3}$ of a cup of sugar. You find that you only have $\frac{1}{2}$ a cup of sugar left. What fraction of the recipe can you make?

35. The following students are having difficulty with division of fractions. Determine what procedure they are using, and answer their final question as they would.

Abigail: $\frac{4}{6} \div \frac{2}{6} = \frac{2}{6}$ Harold: $\frac{2}{3} \div \frac{3}{8} = \frac{3}{2} \times \frac{3}{8} = \frac{9}{16}$

$\quad\quad\quad \frac{6}{10} \div \frac{2}{10} = \frac{3}{10}$ $\quad\quad\quad \frac{3}{4} \div \frac{5}{6} = \frac{4}{3} \times \frac{5}{6} = \frac{20}{18}$

$\quad\quad\quad \frac{8}{12} \div \frac{2}{12} =$ $\quad\quad\quad\quad \frac{5}{8} \div \frac{3}{4} =$

36. A chicken and a half lays an egg and a half in a day and a half. How many eggs do 12 chickens lay in 12 days?
a. How long will it take 3 chickens to lay 2 dozen eggs?
b. How many chickens will it take to lay 36 eggs in 6 days?

37. Fill in the empty squares with different fractions to produce equations.

38. If the sum of two numbers is 18 and their product is 40, find the following without finding the two numbers.
a. The sum of the reciprocals of the two numbers
b. The sum of the squares of the two numbers [*Hint:* What is $(x + y)^2$?]

39. Observe the following pattern:

$$3 + 1\frac{1}{2} = 3 \times 1\frac{1}{2}$$
$$4 + 1\frac{1}{3} = 4 \times 1\frac{1}{3}$$
$$5 + 1\frac{1}{4} = 5 \times 1\frac{1}{4}$$

a. Write the next two equations in the list.
b. Determine whether this pattern will always hold true. If so, explain why.

40. Using the alternative definition of "less than," prove the following statements. Assume that the product of two fractions is a fraction in part (c).

a. If $\frac{a}{b} < \frac{c}{d}$ and $\frac{c}{d} < \frac{e}{f}$, then $\frac{a}{b} < \frac{e}{f}$.

b. If $\frac{a}{b} < \frac{c}{d}$, then $\frac{a}{b} + \frac{e}{f} < \frac{c}{d} + \frac{e}{f}$.

c. If $\frac{a}{b} < \frac{c}{d}$, then $\frac{a}{b} \times \frac{e}{f} < \frac{c}{d} \times \frac{e}{f}$ for any nonzero $\frac{e}{f}$.

41. How many guests were present at a dinner if every two guests shared a bowl of rice, every three guests shared a bowl of broth, every four guests shared a bowl of fowl, and 65 bowls were used altogether?

42. a. Does $2\frac{3}{4} + 5\frac{7}{8} = 2\frac{7}{8} + 5\frac{3}{4}$? Explain.
b. Does $2\frac{3}{4} \times 5\frac{7}{8} = 2\frac{7}{8} \times 5\frac{3}{4}$? Explain.

Analyzing Student Thinking

43. Devonnie asserts that she needs to find common denominators to multiply fractions. Is she correct? Explain.

44. When asked to simplify $\frac{12}{27} \times \frac{9}{24}$, Cameron did the following:

$$\frac{9}{27} \times \frac{12}{24} = \frac{1}{3} \times \frac{1}{2} = \frac{1}{6}.$$

Is his method okay? Explain.

45. Damon asks you if you can draw a picture to explain what $\frac{3}{4}$ of $\frac{5}{7}$ means. What would you draw?

46. Hans asks if you can illustrate what $8 \div \frac{3}{4}$ means. What would you draw?

47. Robbyn noticed that $9 \div 6 = \frac{9}{6}$ whereas $6 \div 9 = \frac{6}{9}$. She wonders if turning a division problem around will always give answers that are reciprocals. How would you respond?

48. Katrina said that dividing always makes numbers smaller, for example, $10 \div 5 = 2$ and 2 is smaller than 10. She wonders how $6 \div \frac{1}{2}$ could give a result that is bigger than 6. How could you help Katrina make sense of this situation?

49. To estimate $6\frac{1}{9} \times 4\frac{5}{8}$ Blair uses range estimation, but Paulo uses rounding. Should one method be preferred over the other? Explain.

Problems Relating to the NCTM Standards and Curriculum Focal Points

1. The Focal Points for Grade 6 state "Developing an understanding of and fluency with multiplication and division of fractions and decimals." Find one example in this section that would assist in understanding multiplication or division of fractions.

2. The Focal Points for Grade 3 state "Developing an understanding of fractions and fraction equivalence." What role does an understanding of fraction equivalence play in understanding division of fractions?

3. The NCTM Standards state "All students should develop and use strategies to estimate computations involving fractions and decimals in situations relevant to students' experience." List and explain some examples of strategies to estimate fraction multiplication.

END OF CHAPTER MATERIAL

Solution of Initial Problem

A child has a set of 10 cubical blocks. The lengths of the edges are 1 cm, 2 cm, 3 cm, ..., 10 cm. Using all the cubes, can the child build two towers of the same height by stacking one cube upon another? Why or why not?

Strategy: Solve an Equivalent Problem

This problem can be restated as an equivalent problem: Can the numbers 1 through 10 be put into two sets whose sums are equal? Answer—No! If the sums are *equal* in each set and if these two sums are added together, the resulting sum would be even. However, the sum of 1 through 10 is 55, an odd number! *Additional Problems Where the Strategy "Solve an Equivalent Problem" Is Useful*

1. How many numbers are in the set $\{11, 18, 25, \ldots, 396\}$?
2. Which is larger: 2^{30} or 3^{20}?
3. Find eight fractions equally spaced between 0 and $\frac{1}{3}$ on the number line.

People in Mathematics

Evelyn Boyd Granville (1924–) Evelyn Boyd Granville was a mathematician in the Mercury and Apollo space programs, specializing in orbit and trajectory computations. She says that if she had foreseen the space program and her role in it, she would have been an astronomer. Granville grew up in Washington, D.C., at a time when the public schools were racially segregated. She was fortunate to attend an African-American high school with high standards and was encouraged to apply to the best colleges. In 1949, she graduated from Yale with a Ph.D. in mathematics, one of two African-American women to receive doctorates in mathematics that year and the first ever to do so. After the space program, she joined the mathematics faculty at California State University. She has written (with Jason Frand) the text *Theory and Application of Mathematics for Teachers*. "I never encountered any problems in combining career and private life. Black women have always had to work."

Paul Erdos (1913–1996) Paul Erdos was one of the most prolific mathematicians of the modern era. Erdos (pronounced "air-dish") authored or coauthored approximately 900 research papers. He was called an "itinerant mathematician" because of his penchant for traveling to mathematical conferences around the world. His achievements in number theory are legendary. At one mathematical conference, he was dozing during a lecture of no particular interest to him. When the speaker mentioned a problem in number theory, Erdos perked up and asked him to explain the problem again. The lecture then proceeded, and a few minutes later Erdos interrupted to announce that he had the solution! Erdos was also known for posing problems and offering monetary awards for their solution, from $25 to $10,000. He also was known for the many mathematical prodigies he discovered and "fed" problems to.

CHAPTER REVIEW

Review the following terms and exercises to determine which require learning or relearning—page numbers are provided for easy reference.

SECTION 6.1 The Set of Fractions

VOCABULARY/NOTATION

Numerator   218
Denominator   218
Fraction (*a/b*)   219
Set of fractions (*F*)   219
Region model   220
Equivalent fractions   220
Fraction strips   220

Simplified   220
Equal fractions   221
Cross-product   221
Cross-multiplication   221
Simplest form   222
Lowest terms   222
Improper fraction   224

Mixed number   224
Fraction number line   225
Less than (<)   225
Greater than (>)   225
Less than or equal to (≤)   225
Greater than or equal to (≥)   225
Density property   227

EXERCISES

1. Explain why a child might think that $\frac{1}{4}$ is greater than $\frac{1}{2}$.

2. Draw a sketch to show why $\frac{3}{4} = \frac{6}{8}$.

3. Explain the difference between an improper fraction and a mixed number.

4. Determine whether the following are equal. If not, determine the smaller of the two.
   a. $\frac{24}{56}, \frac{8}{19}$ **b.** $\frac{12}{28}, \frac{15}{35}$

5. Express each fraction in Exercise 4 in simplest form.

6. Illustrate the density property using $\frac{2}{5}$ and $\frac{5}{12}$.

SECTION 6.2 Fractions: Addition and Subtraction

VOCABULARY/NOTATION

Least common denominator (LCD)   234

EXERCISES

1. Use fraction strips to find the following.
   a. $\frac{1}{6} + \frac{5}{12}$ **b.** $\frac{7}{8} - \frac{3}{4}$

2. Find the following sum/difference, and express your answers in simplest form.
   a. $\frac{12}{27} + \frac{13}{15}$ **b.** $\frac{17}{25} - \frac{7}{15}$

3. Name the property of addition that is used to justify each of the following equations.
   a. $\frac{3}{7} + \frac{2}{7} = \frac{2}{7} + \frac{3}{7}$ **b.** $\frac{4}{15} + \frac{0}{15} = \frac{4}{15}$

   c. $\frac{2}{5} + \left(\frac{3}{5} + \frac{4}{7} \right) = \left(\frac{2}{5} + \frac{3}{5} \right) + \frac{4}{7}$

   d. $\frac{2}{5} + \frac{3}{7}$ is a fraction

4. Which of the following properties hold for fraction subtraction?
   a. Closure   **b.** Commutative
   c. Associative   **d.** Identity

5. Calculate mentally, and state your method.
   a. $5\frac{3}{8} + 3\frac{7}{8}$ **b.** $31 - 4\frac{7}{8}$ **c.** $\left(\frac{2}{7} + \frac{3}{5} \right) + \frac{5}{7}$

6. Estimate using the techniques given.
   a. Range: $5\frac{2}{3} + 7\frac{1}{6}$

   b. Rounding to the nearest $\frac{1}{2}$: $17\frac{1}{8} + 24\frac{2}{5}$

   c. Front-end with adjustment: $9\frac{3}{4} + 7\frac{2}{3} + 5\frac{1}{6}$

SECTION 6.3 Fractions: Multiplication and Division

VOCABULARY/NOTATION

Multiplicative inverse   247   Reciprocal   247   Complex fraction   252

EXERCISES

1. Use a model to find $\dfrac{2}{3} \times \dfrac{4}{5}$.

2. Find the following product/quotient, and express your answers in simplest form.

   a. $\dfrac{16}{25} \times \dfrac{15}{36}$ **b.** $\dfrac{17}{19} \div \dfrac{34}{57}$

3. Name the property of multiplication that is used to justify each of the following equations.

   a. $\dfrac{6}{7} \times \dfrac{7}{6} = 1$ **b.** $\dfrac{7}{5}\left(\dfrac{3}{4} \times \dfrac{5}{7}\right) = \left(\dfrac{7}{5} \times \dfrac{3}{4}\right)\dfrac{5}{7}$

   c. $\dfrac{5}{9} \times \dfrac{6}{6} = \dfrac{5}{9}$ **d.** $\dfrac{2}{5} \times \dfrac{3}{7}$ is a fraction

   e. $\dfrac{3}{8}\left(\dfrac{8}{3} \times \dfrac{4}{7}\right) = \left(\dfrac{3}{8} \times \dfrac{8}{3}\right)\dfrac{4}{7}$

4. State the distributive property of fraction multiplication over addition and give an example to illustrate its usefulness.

5. Find $\dfrac{12}{25} \div \dfrac{1}{5}$ in two ways.

6. Which of the following properties hold for fraction division?
   a. Closure
   b. Commutative
   c. Associative
   d. Identity

7. Calculate mentally and state your method.

   a. $\dfrac{2}{3} \times (5 \times 9)$

   b. $25 \times 2\dfrac{2}{5}$

8. Estimate using the techniques given.

   a. Range: $5\dfrac{2}{3} \times 7\dfrac{1}{6}$

   b. Rounding to the nearest $\dfrac{1}{2}$: $3\dfrac{3}{5} \times 4\dfrac{1}{7}$

CHAPTER TEST

KNOWLEDGE

1. True or false?
   a. Every whole number is a fraction.
   b. The fraction $\dfrac{17}{51}$ is in simplest form.
   c. The fractions $\dfrac{2}{12}$ and $\dfrac{15}{20}$ are equivalent.
   d. Improper fractions are always greater than 1.
   e. There is a fraction less than $\dfrac{2}{1,000,000}$ and greater than $\dfrac{1}{1,000,000}$.
   f. The sum of $\dfrac{5}{7}$ and $\dfrac{3}{8}$ is $\dfrac{8}{15}$.
   g. The difference $\dfrac{4}{7} - \dfrac{5}{6}$ does not exist in the set of fractions.
   h. The quotient $\dfrac{6}{11} \div \dfrac{7}{13}$ is the same as the product $\dfrac{11}{6} \cdot \dfrac{7}{13}$.

2. Select two possible meanings of the fraction $\dfrac{3}{4}$ and explain each.

3. Identify a property of an operation that holds in the set of fractions but does not hold for the same operation on whole numbers.

SKILL

4. Write the following fractions in simplest form.
   a. $\dfrac{12}{18}$ **b.** $\dfrac{34}{36}$ **c.** $\dfrac{34}{85}$ **d.** $\dfrac{123,123}{567,567}$

5. Write the following mixed numbers as improper fractions, and vice versa.
   a. $3\dfrac{5}{11}$ **b.** $\dfrac{91}{16}$ **c.** $5\dfrac{2}{7}$ **d.** $\dfrac{123}{11}$

6. Determine the smaller of each of the following pairs of fractions.
   a. $\dfrac{3}{4}, \dfrac{10}{13}$ **b.** $\dfrac{7}{2}, \dfrac{7}{3}$ **c.** $\dfrac{16}{92}, \dfrac{18}{94}$

7. Perform the following operations and write your answer in simplest form.
   a. $\dfrac{4}{9} + \dfrac{5}{12}$ **b.** $\dfrac{7}{15} - \dfrac{8}{25}$ **c.** $\dfrac{4}{5} \cdot \dfrac{15}{16}$ **d.** $\dfrac{8}{7} \div \dfrac{7}{8}$

8. Use properties of fractions to perform the following computations in the easiest way. Write answers in simplest form.
   a. $\dfrac{5}{2} \cdot \left(\dfrac{3}{4} \cdot \dfrac{2}{5}\right)$ **b.** $\dfrac{4}{7} \cdot \dfrac{3}{5} + \dfrac{4}{5} \cdot \dfrac{3}{5}$
   c. $\left(\dfrac{13}{17} + \dfrac{5}{11}\right) + \dfrac{4}{17}$ **d.** $\dfrac{3}{8} \cdot \dfrac{5}{7} - \dfrac{4}{9} \cdot \dfrac{3}{8}$

9. Estimate the following and describe your method of estimation.

   a. $35\frac{4}{5} \div 9\frac{2}{7}$ **b.** $3\frac{5}{8} \times 14\frac{2}{3}$ **c.** $3\frac{4}{9} + 13\frac{1}{5} + \frac{3}{13}$

UNDERSTANDING

10. Using a carton of 12 eggs as a model, explain how the fractions $\frac{6}{12}$ and $\frac{12}{24}$ are distinguishable.

11. Show how the statement "$\frac{a}{b} < \frac{b}{c}$ if and only if $a < b$" can be used to verify the statement "$\frac{a}{b} < \frac{c}{d}$ if and only if $ad < bc$," where b and d are nonzero.

12. Verify the distributive property of fraction multiplication over subtraction using the distributive property of whole-number multiplication over subtraction.

13. Make a drawing that would show why $\frac{2}{3} > \frac{3}{5}$.

14. Use rectangles to explain the process of adding $\frac{1}{4} + \frac{2}{3}$.

15. Use the area model to illustrate $\frac{3}{5} \times \frac{3}{4}$.

16. Write a word problem for each of the following.

   a. $2 \times \frac{3}{4}$ **b.** $2 \div \frac{1}{3}$ **c.** $\frac{2}{5} \div 3$

17. If ⬡⬡ is one whole, then shade the following regions:

   a. $\frac{1}{4}$ **b.** $\frac{2}{3}$ of $\frac{1}{4}$

PROBLEM SOLVING/APPLICATION

18. Notice that $\frac{2}{3} < \frac{3}{4} < \frac{4}{5}$. Show that this sequence continues indefinitely—namely, that $\frac{n}{n+1} < \frac{n+1}{n+2}$ when $n \geq 0$.

19. An auditorium contains 315 occupied seats and was $\frac{7}{9}$ filled. How many empty seats were there?

20. Upon his death, Mr. Freespender left $\frac{1}{2}$ of his estate to his wife, $\frac{1}{8}$ to each of his two children, $\frac{1}{16}$ to each of his three grandchildren, and the remaining $15,000 to his favorite university. What was the value of his entire estate?

21. Find three fractions that are greater than $\frac{2}{5}$ and less than $\frac{3}{7}$.

22. Inga was making a cake that called for 4 cups of flour. However, she could only find a two-thirds measuring cup. How many two-thirds measuring cups of flour will she need to make her cake?

Decimals, Ratio, Proportion, and Percent

FOCUS ON   *The Golden Ratio*

The **golden ratio**, also called the **divine proportion**, was known to the Pythagoreans in 500 B.C.E. and has many interesting applications in geometry. The golden ratio may be found using the Fibonacci sequence, 1, 1, 2, 3, 5, 8, . . . , a_n, . . . , *where a_n is obtained by* adding the previous two numbers. That is, $1 + 1 = 2$, $1 + 2 = 3$, $2 + 3 = 5$, and so on. If the quotient of each consecutive pair of numbers, $\dfrac{a_n}{a_{n-1}}$, is formed, the numbers produce a new sequence. The first several terms of this new sequence are 1, 2, 1.5, 1.66 . . . , 1.6, 1.625, 1.61538 . . . , 1.61904 . . . , ... These numbers approach a decimal 1.61803 . . . , which is the golden ratio, technically $\phi = \dfrac{1 + \sqrt{5}}{2}$. (Square roots are discussed in Chapter 9.)

Following are a few of the remarkable properties associated with the golden ratio.

1. *Aesthetics.* In a golden rectangle, the ratio of the length to the width is the golden ratio, ϕ. Golden rectangles were deemed by the Greeks to be especially pleasing to the eye. The Parthenon at Athens can be surrounded by such a rectangle.

Along these lines, notice how index cards are usually dimensioned 3×5 and 5×8, two pairs of numbers in the Fibonacci sequence whose quotients approximate ϕ.

2. *Geometric fallacy.* If one cuts out the square shown next on the left and rearranges it into the rectangle shown at right, a surprising result regarding the areas is obtained. (Check this!)

    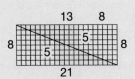

Notice that the numbers 5, 8, 13, and 21 occur. If these numbers from the Fibonacci sequence are replaced by 8, 13, 21, and 34, respectively, an even more surprising result occurs. These surprises continue when using the Fibonacci sequence. However, if the four numbers are replaced with 1, ϕ, $\phi + 1$, and $2\phi + 1$, respectively, all is in harmony.

3. *Surprising places.* Part of Pascal's triangle is shown.

$$
\begin{array}{ccccccccc}
 & & & & 1 & & & & \\
 & & & 1 & & 1 & & & \\
 & & 1 & & 2 & & 1 & & \\
 & 1 & & 3 & & 3 & & 1 & \\
1 & & 4 & & 6 & & 4 & & 1 \\
\end{array}
$$
· · · · · ·

However, if carefully rearranged, the Fibonacci sequence reappears.

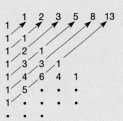

These are but a few of the many interesting relationships that arise from the golden ratio and its counterpart, the Fibonacci sequence.

STRATEGY 12

Work Backward

Normally, when you begin to solve a problem, you probably start at the beginning of the problem and proceed "forward" until you arrive at an answer by applying appropriate strategies. At times, though, rather than start at the beginning of a problem statement, it is more productive to begin at the end of the problem statement and work backward. The following problem can be solved quite easily by this strategy.

INITIAL PROBLEM

A street vendor had a basket of apples. Feeling generous one day, he gave away one-half of his apples plus one to the first stranger he met, one-half of his remaining apples plus one to the next stranger he met, and one-half of his remaining apples plus one to the third stranger he met. If the vendor had one left for himself, with how many apples did he start?

CLUES

The Work Backward strategy may be appropriate when

- The final result is clear and the initial portion of a problem is obscure.
- A problem proceeds from being complex initially to being simple at the end.
- A direct approach involves a complicated equation.
- A problem involves a sequence of reversible actions.

A solution of this Initial Problem is on page 313.

INTRODUCTION

I n Chapter 6, the set of fractions was introduced to permit us to deal with parts of a whole. In this chapter we introduce decimals, which are a convenient numeration system for fractions, and percents, which are representations of fractions convenient for commerce. Then the concepts of ratio and proportion are developed because of their importance in applications throughout mathematics.

Key Concepts from NCTM Curriculum Focal Points

- **GRADE 2:** Developing an understanding of the base-ten numeration system and place-value concepts.
- **GRADE 4:** Developing an understanding of decimals, including the connections between fractions and decimals.
- **GRADE 5:** Developing an understanding of and fluency with addition and subtraction of fractions and decimals.
- **GRADE 6:** Developing an understanding of and fluency with multiplication and division of fractions and decimals.
- **GRADE 7:** Developing an understanding of and applying proportionality, including similarity.

7.1   DECIMALS

STARTING POINT

The numbers .1, .10, and .100 are all equal but can be represented differently. Use base ten blocks to represent .1, .10, and .100 and demonstrate that they are, in fact, equal.

NCTM Standard
All students should understand the place-value structure of the base ten number system and be able to represent and compare whole numbers and decimals.

Children's Literature
www.wiley.com/college/musser
See "If the World Were a Village" by David J. Smith.

Decimals

Decimals are used to represent fractions in our usual base ten place-value notation. The method used to express decimals is shown in Figure 7.1.

$\div10$	$\div10$	$\div10$	$\div10$	$\div10$	$\div10$
1000	100	10	1	$\frac{1}{10}$	$\frac{1}{100}$	$\frac{1}{1000}$
3	4	5	7	9	6	8
thousands	hundreds	tens	ones	tenths	hundredths	thousandths

Figure 7.1

In the figure the number 3457.968 shows that the **decimal point** is placed between the ones column and the tenths column to show where the whole-number portion ends and where the decimal (or fractional) portion begins. Decimals are read as if they were written as fractions and the decimal point is read "and." The number 3457.968 is written in its **expanded form** as

Reflection from Research
Students often have misconceptions regarding decimals. Some students see the decimal point as something that separates two whole numbers (Greer, 1987).

$$3(1000) + 4(100) + 5(10) + 7(1) + 9\left(\frac{1}{10}\right) + 6\left(\frac{1}{100}\right) + 8\left(\frac{1}{1000}\right)$$

From this form one can see that $3457.968 = 3457\frac{968}{1000}$ and so is read "three thousand four hundred fifty-seven *and* nine hundred sixty-eight thousandths." Note that the word *and* should only be used to indicate where the decimal point is located.

Figure 7.2 shows how a **hundreds square** can be used to represent tenths and hundredths. Notice that the large square represents 1, one vertical strip represents 0.1, and each one of the smallest squares represents 0.01.

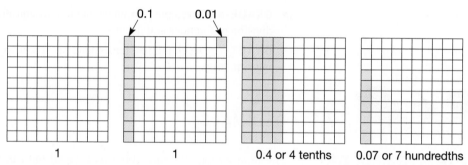

Figure 7.2

A number line can also be used to picture decimals. The number line in Figure 7.3 shows the location of various decimals between 0 and 1.

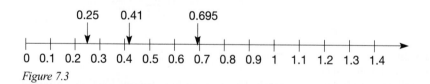

Figure 7.3

| **Example 7.1** | Rewrite each of these numbers in decimal form, and state the decimal name. |

a. $\frac{7}{100}$ **b.** $\frac{123}{10,000}$ **c.** $1\frac{7}{8}$

SOLUTION

a. $\frac{7}{100} = 0.07$, read "seven hundredths"

b. $\frac{123}{10,000} = \frac{100}{10,000} + \frac{20}{10,000} + \frac{3}{10,000} = \frac{1}{100} + \frac{2}{1000} + \frac{3}{10,000} = 0.0123$, read "one hundred twenty-three ten thousandths"

c. $1\frac{7}{8} = 1 + \frac{7}{8} = 1 + \frac{7 \cdot 5 \cdot 5 \cdot 5}{2 \cdot 2 \cdot 2 \cdot 5 \cdot 5 \cdot 5} = 1 + \frac{875}{1000} =$

$1 + \frac{800}{1000} + \frac{70}{1000} + \frac{5}{1000} = 1 + \frac{8}{10} + \frac{7}{100} + \frac{5}{1000} = 1.875$, read "one and eight hundred seventy-five thousandths" ∎

All of the fractions in Example 7.1 have denominators whose only prime factors are 2 or 5. Such fractions can always be expressed in decimal form, since they have equivalent fractional forms whose denominators are powers of 10. This idea is illustrated in Example 7.2.

Example 7.2 Express as decimals.

a. $\frac{3}{2^4}$ **b.** $\frac{7}{2^3 \cdot 5}$ **c.** $\frac{43}{1250}$

SOLUTION

Reflection from Research
Students should be encouraged to express decimal fractions with meaningful language (rather than using "point"). It is sometimes helpful to have students break fractions down into compositions of tenths; for instance, 0.35 would be read three tenths plus five hundredths rather than 35 hundredths (Resnick, Nesher, Leonard, Magone, Omanson, & Peled, 1989).

a. $\frac{3}{2^4} = \frac{3 \cdot 5^4}{2^4 \cdot 5^4} = \frac{1875}{10,000} = 0.1875$

b. $\frac{7}{2^3 \cdot 5} = \frac{7 \cdot 5^2}{2^3 \cdot 5^3} = \frac{175}{1000} = 0.175$

c. $\frac{43}{1250} = \frac{43}{2 \cdot 5^4} = \frac{43 \cdot 2^3}{2^4 \cdot 5^4} = \frac{344}{10,000} = 0.0344$ ∎

The decimals we have been studying thus far are called **terminating decimals**, since they can be represented using a finite number of nonzero digits to the right of the decimal point. We will study nonterminating decimals later in this chapter. The following result should be clear, based on the work we have done in Example 7.2.

THEOREM

Fractions with Terminating Decimal Representations

Let $\frac{a}{b}$ be a fraction in simplest form. Then $\frac{a}{b}$ has a terminating decimal representation if and only if b contains only 2s and/or 5s in its prime factorization (since b can be expanded to a power of 10).

 Check for Understanding: Exercise/Problem Set A #1–7

Reflection from Research
Students mistakenly identify a number such as 0.1814 as being larger than 0.3 because 0.1814 has more digits (Hiebert & Wearne, 1986).

Ordering Decimals

Terminating decimals can be compared using a hundreds square, using a number line, by comparing them in their fraction form, or by comparing place values one at a time from left to right just as we compare whole numbers.

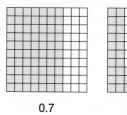

Example 7.3 Determine the larger of each of the following pairs of numbers in the four ways mentioned in the preceding paragraph.

a. 0.7, 0.23   **b.** 0.135, 0.14

SOLUTION

a. Hundreds Square: See Figure 7.4. Since more is shaded in the 0.7 square, we conclude that 0.7 > 0.23.

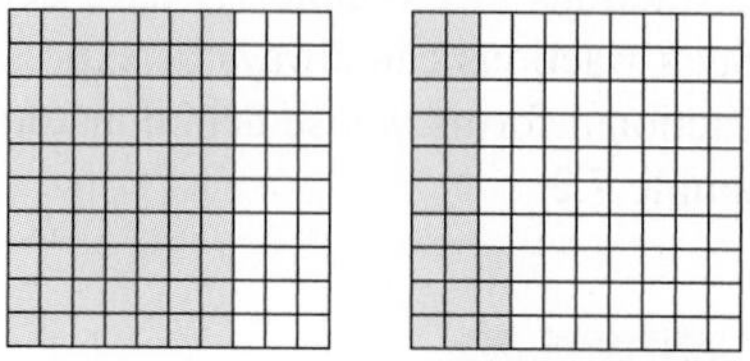

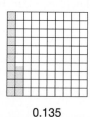

0.7   0.23

Figure 7.4

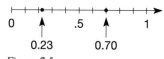

Figure 7.5

Number Line: See Figure 7.5. Since 0.7 is to the right of 0.23, we have 0.7 > 0.23.

Fraction Method: First, $0.7 = \frac{7}{10}$, $0.23 = \frac{23}{100}$. Now $\frac{7}{10} = \frac{70}{100}$ and $\frac{70}{100} > \frac{23}{100}$ since 70 > 23. Therefore, 0.7 > 0.23.

Place-Value Method: 0.7 > 0.23, since 7 > 2. The reasoning behind this method is that since 7 > 2, we have 0.7 > 0.2. Furthermore, in a terminating decimal, the digits that appear after the 2 cannot contribute enough to make a decimal as large as 0.3 yet have 2 in its tenths place. This technique holds for all terminating decimals.

b. Hundreds Square: The number 0.135 is one tenth plus three hundredths plus five thousandths. Since $\frac{5}{1000} = \frac{1}{200} = \frac{1}{2} \cdot \frac{1}{100}$, $13\frac{1}{2}$ squares on a hundreds square must be shaded to represent 0.135. The number 0.14 is represented by 14 squares on a hundreds square. See Figure 7.6. Since an extra half of a square is shaded in 0.14, we have 0.14 > 0.135.

Number Line: See Figure 7.7. Since 0.14 is to the right of 0.135 on the number line, 0.14 > 0.135.

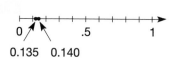

0.135   0.14   0.135   0.140

Figure 7.6   *Figure 7.7*

Fraction Method: $0.135 = \frac{135}{1000}$ and $0.14 = \frac{14}{100} = \frac{140}{1000}$. Since 140 > 135, we have 0.14 > 0.135. Many times children will write 0.135 > 0.14 because they know 135 > 14 and believe that this situation is the same. It is not! Here we are comparing *decimals*, not whole numbers. A decimal comparison can be turned into a whole-number comparison by getting common denominators or, equivalently, by having the same number of decimal places. For example, 0.14 > 0.135 since $\frac{140}{1000} > \frac{135}{1000}$, or 0.140 > 0.135.

Place-Value Method: 0.14 > 0.135, since (1) the tenths are equal (both are 1), but (2) the hundredths place in 0.14, namely 4, is greater than the hundredths place in 0.135, namely 3. ∎

✔ **Check for Understanding:** Exercise/Problem Set A #8–11

NCTM Standard
All students should use models, benchmarks, and equivalent forms to judge the size of fractions.

Mental Math and Estimation

The operations of addition, subtraction, multiplication, and division involving decimals are similar to the corresponding operations with whole numbers. In particular, place value plays a key role. For example, to find the sum $3.2 + 5.7$ mentally, one may add the whole-number parts, $3 + 5 = 8$, and then the tenths, $0.2 + 0.7 = 0.9$, to obtain 8.9. Observe that the whole-number parts were added first, then the tenths—that is, the addition took place from left to right. In the case of finding the sum $7.6 + 2.5$, one could add the tenths first, $0.6 + 0.5 = 1.1$, then combine this sum with $7 + 2 = 9$ to obtain the sum $9 + 1.1 = 10.1$. Thus, as with whole numbers, decimals may be added from left to right or right to left.

Before developing algorithms for operations involving decimals, some mental math and estimation techniques similar to those that were used with whole numbers and fractions will be extended to decimal calculations.

| **Example 7.4** | Use compatible (decimal) numbers, properties, and/or compensation to calculate the following mentally. |

a. $1.7 + (3.2 + 4.3)$ **b.** $(0.5 \times 6.7) \times 4$ **c.** 6×8.5
d. $3.76 + 1.98$ **e.** $7.32 - 4.94$ **f.** $17 \times 0.25 + 0.25 \times 23$

Reflection from Research
Students often have difficulty understanding the equivalence between a decimal fraction and a common fraction (for instance, that 0.4 is equal to 2/5). Research has found that this understanding can be enhanced by teaching the two concurrently by using both a decimal fraction and a common fraction to describe the same situation (Owens, 1990).

SOLUTION
a. $1.7 + (3.2 + 4.3) = (1.7 + 4.3) + 3.2 = 6 + 3.2 = 9.2$. Here 1.7 and 4.3 are compatible numbers with respect to addition, since their sum is 6.
b. $(0.5 \times 6.7) \times 4 = 6.7 \times (0.5 \times 4) = 6.7 \times 2 = 13.4$. Since $0.5 \times 4 = 2$, it is more convenient to use commutativity and associativity to find 0.5×4 rather than to find 0.5×6.7 first.
c. Using distributivity, $6 \times 8.5 = 6(8 + 0.5) = 6 \times 8 + 6 \times 0.5 = 48 + 3 = 51$.
d. $3.76 + 1.98 = 3.74 + 2 = 5.74$ using additive compensation.
e. $7.32 - 4.94 = 7.38 - 5 = 2.38$ by equal additions.
f. $17 \times 0.25 + 0.25 \times 23 = 17 \times 0.25 + 23 \times 0.25 = (17 + 23) \times 0.25 = 40 \times 0.25 = 10$ using distributivity and the fact that 40 and 0.25 are compatible numbers with respect to multiplication.   ∎

Since common decimals have fraction representations, the **fraction equivalents** shown in Table 7.1 can often be used to simplify decimal calculations.

TABLE 7.1

DECIMAL	FRACTION
0.05	$\frac{1}{20}$
0.1	$\frac{1}{10}$
0.125	$\frac{1}{8}$
0.2	$\frac{1}{5}$
0.25	$\frac{1}{4}$
0.375	$\frac{3}{8}$
0.4	$\frac{2}{5}$
0.5	$\frac{1}{2}$
0.6	$\frac{3}{5}$
0.625	$\frac{5}{8}$
0.75	$\frac{3}{4}$
0.8	$\frac{4}{5}$
0.875	$\frac{7}{8}$

| **Example 7.5** | Find these products using fraction equivalents. |

a. 68×0.5 **b.** 0.25×48 **c.** 0.2×375
d. 0.05×280 **e.** 56×0.125 **f.** 0.75×72

SOLUTION
a. $68 \times 0.5 = 68 \times \frac{1}{2} = 34$ **b.** $0.25 \times 48 = \frac{1}{4} \times 48 = 12$

c. $0.2 \times 375 = \frac{1}{5} \times 375 = 75$ **d.** $0.05 \times 280 = \frac{1}{20} \times 280 = \frac{1}{2} \times 28 = 14$

e. $56 \times 0.125 = 56 \times \frac{1}{8} = 7$

f. $0.75 \times 72 = \frac{3}{4} \times 72 = 3 \times \frac{1}{4} \times 72 = 3 \times 18 = 54$ ∎

Multiplying and dividing decimals by powers of 10 can be performed mentally in a fashion similar to the way we multiplied and divided whole numbers by powers of 10.

Example 7.6 Find the following products and quotients by converting to fractions.

a. 3.75×10^4 **b.** 62.013×10^5 **c.** $127.9 \div 10$ **d.** $0.53 \div 10^4$

SOLUTION

a. $3.75 \times 10^4 = \frac{375}{100} \times \frac{10,000}{1} = 37,500$

b. $62.013 \times 10^5 = \frac{62013}{1000} \times \frac{100,000}{1} = 6,201,300$

c. $127.9 \div 10 = \frac{1279}{10} \div 10 = \frac{1279}{10} \times \frac{1}{10} = 12.79$

d. $0.53 \div 10^4 = \frac{53}{100} \div 10^4 = \frac{53}{100} \times \frac{1}{10,000} = 0.000053$ ∎

Notice that in Example 7.6(a), multiplying by 10^4 was equivalent to moving the decimal point of 3.75 four places to the right to obtain 37,500. Similarly, in part (b), because of the 5 in 10^5, moving the decimal point five places to the right in 62.013 results in the correct answer, 6,201,300. When dividing by a power of 10, the decimal point is moved to the left an appropriate number of places. These ideas are summarized next.

THEOREM

Multiplying/Dividing Decimals by Powers of 10

Let n be any decimal number and m represent any nonzero whole number. *Multiplying* a number n by 10^m is equivalent to forming a new number by moving the decimal point of n to the right m places. *Dividing* a number n by 10^m is equivalent to forming a new number by moving the decimal point of n to the left m places.

Multiplying/dividing by powers of 10 can be used with multiplicative compensation to multiply some decimals mentally. For example, to find the product $0.003 \times 41,000$, one can multiply 0.003 by 1000 (yielding 3) and then divide 41,000 by 1000 (yielding 41) to obtain the product $3 \times 41 = 123$.

Previous work with whole-number and fraction computational estimation can also be applied to estimate the results of decimal operations.

Example 7.7 Estimate each of the following using the indicated estimation techniques.

a. $\$1.57 + \$4.36 + \$8.78$ using (i) range, (ii) front-end with adjustment, and (iii) rounding techniques

b. 39.37×5.5 using (i) range and (ii) rounding techniques

SOLUTION

a. Range: A low estimate for the range is $\$1 + \$4 + \$8 = \$13$, and a high estimate is $\$2 + \$5 + \$9 = \$16$. Thus a range estimate of the sum is \$13 to \$16.

Front-end: The one-column front-end estimate is simply the low estimate of the range, namely \$13. The sum of 0.57, 0.36, and 0.78 is about \$1.50, so a good estimate is \$14.50.

Rounding: Rounding to the nearest whole or half yields an estimate of $\$1.50 + \$4.50 + \$9.00 = \$15.00$.

b. Range: A low estimate is $30 \times 5 = 150$, and a high estimate is $40 \times 6 = 240$. Hence a range estimate is 150 to 240.

Rounding: One choice for estimating this product is to round 39.37×5.5 to 40×6 to obtain 240. A better estimate would be to round to $40 \times 5.5 = 220$. ∎

Decimals can be rounded to any specified place as was done with whole numbers.

Example 7.8   Round 56.94352 to the nearest.

a. tenth   **b.** hundredth
c. thousandth   **d.** ten thousandth

SOLUTION
a. First, $56.9 < 56.94352 < 57.0$. Since 56.94352 is closer to 56.9 than to 57.0, we round to 56.9 (Figure 7.8).

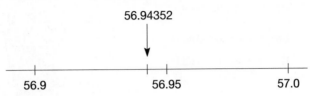

Figure 7.8

b. $56.94 < 56.94352 < 56.95$ and 56.94352 is closer to 56.94 (since $352 < 500$), so we round to 56.94.
c. $56.943 < 56.94352 < 56.944$ and 56.94352 is closer to 56.944, since $52 > 50$. Thus we round up to 56.944.
d. $56.9435 < 56.94352 < 56.9436$. Since $56.94352 < 56.94355$, and 56.94355 is the halfway point between 56.94350 and 56.94360, we round down to 56.9435.   ∎

For decimals ending in a 5, we can use the "round a 5 up" method, as is usually done in elementary school. For example, 1.835, rounded to hundredths, would round to 1.84.

Perhaps the most useful estimation technique for decimals is rounding to numbers that will, in turn, yield compatible whole numbers or fractions.

Example 7.9   Estimate.

a. 203.4×47.8 **b.** $31 \div 1.93$ **c.** 75×0.24
d. $124 \div 0.74$ **e.** $0.0021 \times 44{,}123$ **f.** $3847.6 \div 51.3$

SOLUTION
a. $203.4 \times 47.8 \approx 200 \times 50 = 10{,}000$
b. $31 \div 1.93 \approx 30 \div 2 = 15$
c. $75 \times 0.24 \approx 75 \times \frac{1}{4} \approx 76 \times \frac{1}{4} = 19$. (Note that 76 and $\frac{1}{4}$ are compatible, since 76 has a factor of 4.)
d. $124 \div 0.74 \approx 124 \div \frac{3}{4} = 124 \times \frac{4}{3} \approx 123 \times \frac{4}{3} = 164$. (123 and $\frac{3}{4}$, hence $\frac{4}{3}$, are compatible, since 123 has a factor of 3.)
e. $0.0021 \times 44{,}123 = 0.21 \times 441.23 \approx \frac{1}{5} \times 450 = 90$. (Here multiplicative compensation was used by *multiplying* 0.0021 by 100 and *dividing* 44,123 by 100.)
f. $3847.6 \div 51.3 \approx 38.476 \div 0.513 \approx 38 \div \frac{1}{2} = 76$; alternatively, $3847.6 \div 51.3 \approx 3500 \div 50 = 70$ ∎

✔ **Check for Understanding:** Exercise/Problem Set A #12–17

MATHEMATICAL MORSEL

Decimal notation has evolved over the years without universal agreement. Consider the following list of decimal expressions for the fraction $\frac{3142}{1000}$.

NOTATION	DATE INTRODUCED
3 142	1522, Adam Riese (German)
3 | 142 ⎫ 3,142 ⎭	1579, François Vieta (French)
0 | 1 | 2 | 3 3 | 1 | 4 | 2	1585, Simon Stevin (Dutch)
3 · 142	1614, John Napier (Scottish)

Today, Americans use a version of Napier's "decimal point" notation (3.142, where the point is on the line), the English retain the original version (3 · 142, where the point is in the middle of the line), and the French and Germans retain Vieta's "decimal comma" notation (3,142). Hence the issue of establishing a universal decimal notation remains unresolved to this day.

Section 7.1   ## EXERCISE / PROBLEM SET A

EXERCISES

1. Write each of the following sums in decimal form.
   a. $7(10) + 5 + 6(\frac{1}{10}) + 3(\frac{1}{1000})$
   b. $6(\frac{1}{10})^2 + 3(\frac{1}{10})^3$
   c. $3(10)^2 + 6 + 4(\frac{1}{10})^2 + 2(\frac{1}{10})^3$

2. Write each of the following decimals (i) in its expanded form and (ii) as a fraction.
   a. 0.45   **b.** 3.183   **c.** 24.2005

3. Write the following expressions as decimal numbers.
   a. Seven hundred forty-six thousand
   b. Seven hundred forty-six thousandths
   c. Seven hundred forty-six million

4. Write the following numbers in words.
   a. 0.013   **b.** 68,485.532
   c. 0.0082   **d.** 859.080509

5. A student reads the number 3147 as "three thousand one hundred and forty-seven." What is wrong with this reading?

6. Determine, without converting to decimals, which of the following fractions has a terminating decimal representation.
   a. $\frac{21}{45}$ **b.** $\frac{62}{125}$ **c.** $\frac{63}{90}$
   d. $\frac{326}{400}$ **e.** $\frac{39}{60}$ **f.** $\frac{54}{130}$

7. Decide whether the following fractions terminate in their decimal form. If a fraction terminates, tell in how many places and explain how you can tell from the fraction form.
   a. $\frac{4}{3}$ **b.** $\frac{7}{8}$
   c. $\frac{1}{15}$ **d.** $\frac{3}{16}$

8. Arrange the following numbers in order from smallest to largest.
   a. 0.58, 0.085, 0.85
   b. 781.345, 781.354, 780.9999
   c. 4.9, 4.09, 4.99, 4.099

9. One method of comparing two fractions is to find their decimal representations by calculator and compare them. For example, divide the numerator by the denominator.

   $$\frac{7}{12} = \boxed{0.58333333} \qquad \frac{9}{16} = \boxed{0.56250000}$$

   Thus $\frac{9}{16} < \frac{7}{12}$. Use this method to compare the following fractions.
   a. $\frac{5}{9}$ and $\frac{19}{34}$ **b.** $\frac{38}{52}$ and $\frac{18}{25}$

10. Order each of the following from smallest to largest as simply as possible by using any combination of these three methods: (i) common denominator, (ii) cross-multiplication, and (iii) converting to decimal.

a. $\dfrac{7}{8}, \dfrac{4}{5}, \dfrac{9}{10}$ b. $\dfrac{27}{25}, \dfrac{43}{40}, \dfrac{539}{500}$ c. $\dfrac{3}{5}, \dfrac{5}{8}, \dfrac{7}{9}$

11. The legal limit of blood alcohol content to drive a car is 0.08. Three drivers are tested at a police checkpoint. Juan had a level of .061, Lucas had a level of .1, and Amy had a level of .12. Who was arrested and who was let go?

12. Calculate mentally. Describe your method.
    a. $18.43 - 9.96$ b. $1.3 \times 5.9 + 64.1 \times 1.3$
    c. $4.6 + (5.8 + 2.4)$ d. $(0.25 \times 17) \times 8$
    e. $51.24 \div 10^3$ f. $21.28 + 17.79$
    g. $8(9.5)$ h. 0.15×10^5

13. Calculate mentally by using fraction equivalents.
    a. 0.25×44 b. 0.75×80 c. 35×0.4
    d. 0.2×65 e. 65×0.8 f. 380×0.05

14. Find each of the following products and quotients.
    a. $(6.75)(1{,}000{,}000)$ b. $19.514 \div 100{,}000$
    c. $(2.96 \times 10^{16})(10^{12})$ d. $\dfrac{2.96 \times 10^{16}}{10^{12}}$

15. Estimate, using the indicated techniques.
    a. $4.75 + 5.91 + 7.36$; range and rounding to the nearest whole number
    b. 74.5×6.1; range and rounding
    c. $3.18 + 4.39 + 2.73$; front-end with adjustment
    d. 4.3×9.7; rounding to the nearest whole number

16. Estimate by rounding to compatible numbers and fraction equivalents.
    a. $47.1 \div 2.9$
    b. 0.23×88
    c. 126×0.21
    d. $56{,}324 \times 0.25$
    e. $14{,}897 \div 750$
    f. 0.59×474

17. Round the following.
    a. 97.26 to the nearest tenth
    b. 345.51 to the nearest ten
    c. 345.00 to the nearest ten
    d. 0.01826 to the nearest thousandth
    e. 0.01826 to the nearest ten thousandth
    f. 0.498 to the nearest tenth
    g. 0.498 to the nearest hundredth

PROBLEMS

18. The numbers shown next can be used to form an additive magic square:

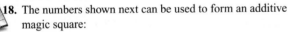

10.48,   15.72,   20.96,   26.2,   31.44,
36.68,   41.92,   47.16,   52.4.

Use your calculator to determine where to place the numbers in the nine cells of the magic square.

19. Suppose that classified employees went on strike for 22 working days. One of the employees, Kathy, made $9.74

per hour before the strike. Under the old contract, she worked 240 six-hour days per year. If the new contract is for the same number of days per year, what increase in her hourly wage must Kathy receive to make up for the wages she lost during the strike in one year?

20. Decimals are just fractions whose denominators are powers of 10. Change the three decimals in the following sum to fractions and add them by finding a common denominator.

$$0.6 + 0.783 + 0.29$$

In what way(s) is this easier than adding fractions such as $\dfrac{2}{7}, \dfrac{5}{6},$ and $\dfrac{3}{4}$?

| Section 7.1 | **EXERCISE / PROBLEM SET B** |

EXERCISES

1. Write each of the following sums in decimal form.
    a. $5\left(\frac{1}{10}\right)^2 + 7(10) + 3\left(\frac{1}{10}\right)^5$
    b. $8\left(\frac{1}{10}\right) + 3(10)^3 + 9\left(\frac{1}{10}\right)^2$
    c. $5\left(\frac{1}{10}\right)^3 + 2\left(\frac{1}{10}\right)^2 + \left(\frac{1}{10}\right)^6$

2. Write each of the following decimals (i) in its expanded form and (ii) as a fraction.
    a. 0.525
    b. 34.007
    c. 5.0102

3. Write the following expressions as decimal numerals.
   a. Seven hundred forty-six millionths
   b. Seven hundred forty-six thousand and seven hundred forty-six millionths
   c. Seven hundred forty-six million and seven hundred forty-six thousandths

4. Write the following numbers in words.
   a. 0.000000078   **b.** 7,589.12345
   c. 187,213.02003   **d.** 1,001,002,003.00100002

5. A student reads 0.059 as "point zero five nine thousandths." What is wrong with this reading?

6. Determine which of the following fractions have terminating decimal representations.
   a. $\dfrac{2^4 \cdot 11^{16} \cdot 17^{19}}{5^{12}}$ **b.** $\dfrac{2^3 \cdot 3^{11} \cdot 7^9 \cdot 11^{16}}{7^{13} \cdot 11^9 \cdot 5^7}$ **c.** $\dfrac{2^3 \cdot 3^9 \cdot 11^{17}}{2^8 \cdot 3^4 \cdot 5^7}$

7. Decide whether the following fractions terminate in their decimal form. If a fraction terminates, tell in how many places and explain how you can tell from the fraction form.
   a. $\dfrac{1}{11}$ **b.** $\dfrac{17}{625}$ **c.** $\dfrac{3}{12,800}$ **d.** $\dfrac{17}{2^{19} \times 5^{23}}$

8. Arrange the following from smallest to largest.
   a. 3.08, 3.078, 3.087, 3.80
   b. 8.01002, 8.010019, 8.0019929
   c. 0.5, 0.505, 0.5005, 0.55

9. Order each of the following from smallest to largest by changing each fraction to a decimal.
   a. $\frac{5}{7}, \frac{4}{5}, \frac{10}{13}$ **b.** $\frac{4}{11}, \frac{3}{7}, \frac{2}{5}$ **c.** $\frac{5}{9}, \frac{7}{13}, \frac{11}{18}$ **d.** $\frac{3}{5}, \frac{11}{18}, \frac{17}{29}$

10. Order each of the following from smallest to largest as simply as possible by using any combinations of the three following methods: (i) common denominators, (ii) cross-multiplication, and (iii) converting to a decimal.
   a. $\frac{5}{8}, \frac{1}{2}, \frac{17}{23}$ **b.** $\frac{13}{16}, \frac{2}{3}, \frac{3}{4}$ **c.** $\frac{8}{5}, \frac{26}{15}, \frac{50}{31}$

11. According to state law, the amount of radon released from wastes cannot exceed a 0.033 working level. A study of two locations reported a 0.0095 working level at one location and 0.0039 at a second location. Does either of these locations fail to meet state standards?

12. Calculate mentally.
   a. $7 \times 3.4 + 6.6 \times 7$ **b.** $26.53 - 8.95$
   c. $0.491 \div 10^2$ **d.** $5.89 + 6.27$
   e. $(5.7 + 4.8) + 3.2$ **f.** 67.32×10^3
   g. $0.5 \times (639 \times 2)$ **h.** 6.5×12

13. Calculate mentally using fraction equivalents.
   a. 230×0.1 **b.** 36×0.25 **c.** 82×0.5
   d. 125×0.8 **e.** 175×0.2 **f.** 0.6×35

14. Find each of the following products and quotients. Express your answers in scientific notation.
   a. 12.6416×100 **b.** $\dfrac{7.8752}{10,000,000}$
   c. $(8.25 \times 10^{20})(10^7)$ **d.** $\dfrac{8.25 \times 10^{20}}{10^7}$

15. Estimate, using the indicated techniques.
   a. 34.7×3.9; range and rounding to the nearest whole number
   b. $15.71 + 3.23 + 21.95$; two-column front-end
   c. 13.7×6.1; one-column front-end and range
   d. $3.61 + 4.91 + 1.3$; front-end with adjustment

16. Estimate by rounding to compatible numbers and fraction equivalents.
   a. $123.9 \div 5.3$ **b.** 87.4×7.9
   c. $402 \div 1.25$ **d.** $34,546 \times 0.004$
   e. $0.0024 \times 470,000$ **f.** $3591 \div 0.61$

17. Round the following as specified.
   a. 321.0864 to the nearest hundredth
   b. 12.16231 to the nearest thousandth
   c. 4.009055 to the nearest thousandth
   d. 1.9984 to the nearest tenth
   e. 1.9984 to the nearest hundredth

PROBLEMS

18. Determine whether each of the following is an additive magic square. If not, change one entry so that your resulting square is magic.

   a.

2.4	5.4	1.2
1.8	3	4.2
4.8	1.4	3.6

   b.

0.438	0.073	0.584
0.511	0.365	0.219
0.146	0.657	0.292

19. Solve the following cryptarithm where $D = 5$.

   DONALD
   + GERALD
   ROBERT

Analyzing Student Thinking

20. Joseph read 357.8 as "three hundred and fifty seven and eight tenths." Did he read it correctly? Explain.

21. Brigham says the fraction $\dfrac{42}{150}$ should be a repeating decimal because the factors of the denominator include

a 3 as well as 2s and 5s. But on his calculator 42 ÷ 150 seems to terminate. What could you say to clarify this confusion?

22. Mary Lou said she knows that when fractions are written as decimals they either repeat or terminate. So $\frac{12}{17}$ must not be a fraction because when she divided 12 by 17 on her calculator, she got a decimal that did not repeat or terminate. How would you react to this?

23. Camille tells you that 6.45 is greater than 6.5 because 45 is great than 5. How would you respond to this?

24. Caroline is rounding decimals to the nearest hundredth. She rounds 19.67472 to 19.675, then rounds 19.675 to 19.68. Is her method correct? Explain.

25. Looking at the same problem that Caroline had in 24, Amir comes up with the answer 19.66. When his teacher asks him how he got the answer, he says, "Because of the 4, I had to round down." What is Amir's misconception?

26. Merilee said her calculator changed $\frac{2}{3}$ to 0.6666667, so obviously it does not repeat. Therefore it must be a terminating decimal. How would you respond to Merilee?

27. When asked to find a decimal number between 0.19 and 0.20, Alondra said there is none since 19 and 20 are consecutive whole numbers. How should you respond?

Problems Relating to the NCTM Standards and Curriculum Focal Points

1. The Focal Points for Grade 2 state "Developing an understanding of the base-ten numeration system and place-value concepts." Explain how the base-ten representation of whole numbers is extended to represent non-whole numbers.

2. The Focal Points for Grade 4 state, "Developing an understanding of decimals, including the connections between fractions and decimals." Explain how fractions and decimals are connected.

3. The NCTM Standards state "All students should use models, benchmarks, and equivalent forms to judge the size of fractions." Explain how decimal representations of numbers can be used to judge the size of fractions.

7.2   OPERATIONS WITH DECIMALS

STARTING POINT

Researchers have coined the phrase "multiplication makes bigger" to describe the student misconception that in any multiplication problem, the product is always larger than either of the factors. What is a problem or situation where "multiplication makes bigger" does not hold?

Similarly, "division makes smaller" is used to describe the student misconception that in a division problem, the quotient is always smaller than the dividend. What is a problem or situation where this does not hold? Discuss where the misconception "multiplication makes bigger, division makes smaller" might come from.

Algorithms for Operations with Decimals

Algorithms for adding, subtracting, multiplying, and dividing decimals are simple extensions of the corresponding whole-number algorithms.

Addition

Example 7.10   Add:

a. 3.56 + 7.95   **b.** 0.0094 + 80.183

SOLUTION We will find these sums in two ways: using fractions and using a decimal algorithm.

Fraction Approach

1	$\frac{1}{10}$	$\frac{1}{10^2}$
3	5	6
7	9	5
11	5	1

a. $3.56 + 7.95 = \dfrac{356}{100} + \dfrac{795}{100}$

$= \dfrac{1151}{100}$

$= 11.51$

b. $0.0094 + 80.183 = \dfrac{94}{10,000} + \dfrac{80,183}{1000}$

$= \dfrac{94}{10,000} + \dfrac{801,830}{10,000}$

$= \dfrac{801,924}{10,000}$

$= 80.1924$

10	1	$\frac{1}{10}$	$\frac{1}{10^2}$	$\frac{1}{10^3}$	$\frac{1}{10^4}$
		0	0	9	4
8	0	1	8	3	
8	0	1	9	2	4

Figure 7.9

Decimal Approach As with whole-number addition, arrange the digits in columns according to their corresponding place values and add the numbers in each column, regrouping when necessary (Figure 7.9).

This decimal algorithm can be stated more simply as "align the decimal points, add the numbers in columns as if they were whole numbers, and insert a decimal point in the answer immediately beneath the decimal points in the numbers being added." This algorithm can easily be justified by writing the two summands in their expanded form and applying the various properties for fraction addition and/or multiplication. ■

Subtraction

Example 7.11 Subtract:

a. $14.793 - 8.95$ **b.** $7.56 - 0.0008$

SOLUTION Here we could again use the fraction approach as we did with addition. However, the usual subtraction algorithm is more efficient.

a.

Step 1: Align Decimal Points	Step 2: Subtract as if Whole Numbers	Step 3: Insert Decimal Point in Answer
14.793 − 8.95	14793 − 8950 5843	14.793 − 8.95 5.843

(NOTE: Step 2 is performed mentally—there is no need to rewrite the numbers without the decimal points.)

b. Rewrite 7.56 as 7.5600.

$$7.5600$$
$$- 0.0008$$
$$7.5592$$

■

Now let's consider how to multiply decimals.

Multiplication

Example 7.12 Multiply 437.09×3.8.

SOLUTION Refer to fraction multiplication.

$$437.09 \times 3.8 = \frac{43,709}{100} \times \frac{38}{10} = \frac{43,709 \times 38}{100 \times 10}$$

$$= \frac{1,660,942}{1000} = 1660.942$$

■

Reflection from Research
Students tend to assume that adding a zero to the end of a decimal fraction is the same as adding a zero to the end of a whole number. The most common error on a test item for which students were to write the number ten times bigger than 437.56 was 437.560 (Hiebert & Wearne, 1986).

Decimals and Percents

Lattice Multiplication with Decimals

Example Find 34.5 * 2.05 using lattice multiplication.

Step 1: Make a magnitude estimate. 34.5 * 2.05 ≈ 35 * 2 = 70
The product will be in the tens. (The symbol ≈ means *is about equal to*.)

Step 2: Draw the lattice and write the factors, including the decimal points, at the top and right side. In the factor above the grid, the decimal point should be above a column line. In the factor on the right side of the grid, the decimal point should be to the right of a row line.

Step 3: Find the products inside the lattice.

Step 4: Add along the diagonals, moving from right to left.

Step 5: Locate the decimal point in the answer as follows. Slide the decimal point in the factor above the grid down along the column line. Slide the decimal point in the factor on the right side of the grid across the row line. When the decimal points meet, slide the decimal point down along the diagonal line. Write a decimal point at the end of the diagonal line.

Step 6: Compare the result with the estimate.

The product, 70.725, is very close to the estimate of 70.

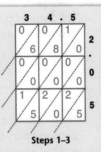

Steps 1–3

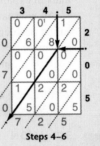

Steps 4–6

Example Find 73.4 * 10.5 using lattice multiplication.

A good magnitude estimate is 73.4 * 10.5 ≈ 73 * 10 = 730. (The symbol ≈ means *is about equal to*.)

The product, 770.70, is close to the estimate of 730.

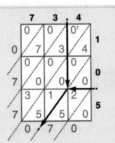

Did You Know?

The lattice method of multiplication was used by Persian scholars as long ago as the year 1010. It was often called the "grating" method.

Check Your Understanding

Draw a lattice for each problem and multiply.

1. 32.5 * 2.5   2. 4.02 * 17   3. 8.1 * 23.4

Check your answers on page 434.

  forty

Observe that when multiplying the two fractions in Example 7.12, we multiplied 43,709 and 38 (the original numbers "without the decimal points"). Thus the procedure illustrated in Example 7.12 suggests the following algorithm for multiplication.

Multiply the numbers "without the decimal points":

$$
\begin{array}{r}
43{,}709 \\
\times \quad\quad 38 \\
\hline
1{,}660{,}942
\end{array}
$$

Insert a decimal point in the answer as follows: The number of digits to the right of the decimal point in the answer is the sum of the number of digits to the right of the decimal points in the numbers being multiplied.

$$
\begin{array}{r}
437.09 \\
\times \quad\quad 3.8 \\
\hline
1660.942
\end{array}
$$

   (2 digits to the right of the decimal point)
   (1 digit to the right of the decimal point)
   (2 + 1 digits to the right of the decimal point)

Notice that there are three decimal places in the answer, since the product of the two denominators (100 and 10) is 10^3. This procedure can be justified by writing the decimals in expanded form and applying appropriate properties.

An alternative way to place the decimal point in the answer of a decimal multiplication problem is to do an approximate calculation. For example, 437.09 × 3.8 is approximately 400 × 4 or 1600. Hence the answer should be in the thousands—namely, 1660.942, not 16,609.42 or 16.60942, and so on.

Example 7.13   Compute: 57.98 × 1.371 using a calculator.

SOLUTION First, the answer should be a little less than 60 × 1.4, or 84. Using a calculator we find 57.98 ⊠ 1.371 ⊟ 79.49058. Notice that the answer is close to the estimate of 84. ∎

Division

Example 7.14   Divide 154.63 ÷ 4.7.

SOLUTION First let's estimate the answer: 155 ÷ 5 = 31, so the answer should be approximately 31. Next, we divide using fractions.

$$
154.63 \div 4.7 = \frac{15{,}463}{100} \div \frac{47}{10} = \frac{15{,}463}{100} \div \frac{470}{100}
$$

$$
= \frac{15{,}463}{470} = 32.9 \qquad\blacksquare
$$

Reflection from Research
Division of decimals tends to be quite difficult for students, especially when the division problem requires students to add zeros as place holders in either the dividend or the quotient (Trafton & Zawojewski, 1984).

Notice that in the fraction method, we replaced our original problem in decimals with an equivalent problem involving whole numbers:

$$
154.63 \div 4.7 \longrightarrow 15{,}463 \div 470.
$$

Similarly, the problem 1546.3 ÷ 47 also has the answer 32.9 by the missing-factor approach. Thus, as this example suggests, any decimal division problem can be replaced with an equivalent one having a whole-number divisor. This technique is usually used when performing the long-division algorithm with decimals, as illustrated next.

Algebraic Reasoning
The problem $154.63 \div 4.7$ is equivalent to $1546.3 \div 47$ because they both have the same solution. The latter problem is preferred because it is easier to compute. This is similar to the algebraic process of converting $3x + 7 = 19$ into the equivalent equation $3x = 12$. Both equations have the same solution but the solution is easier to see in the latter equation.

Example 7.15   Compute: $4.7\overline{)154.63}$.

SOLUTION   Replace with an equivalent problem where the divisor is a whole number.

$$47\overline{)1546.3}$$

Note: Both the divisor and dividend have been multiplied by 10. Now divide as if it is whole-number division. The decimal point in the dividend is temporarily omitted.

$$
\begin{array}{r}
329 \\
47\overline{)15463} \\
-141 \\
\hline
136 \\
-94 \\
\hline
423 \\
-423 \\
\hline
0
\end{array}
$$

Replace the decimal point in the dividend, and place a decimal point in the quotient directly above the decimal point in the dividend. This can be justified using division of fractions.

$$
\begin{array}{r}
32.9 \\
47\overline{)1546.3}
\end{array}
$$

Check: $4.7 \times 32.9 = 154.63$.   ■

The "moving the decimal points" step to obtain a whole-number divisor in Example 7.15 can be justified as follows:

> Let a and b be decimals.
> If $a \div b = c$, then $a = bc$.
> Then $a \cdot 10^n = bc \cdot 10^n = (b \cdot 10^n) c$ for any n.
> Thus $(a \cdot 10^n) \div (b \cdot 10^n) = c$.

This last equation shows we can multiply both a and b (the dividend and divisor) by the same power of 10 to make the divisor a whole number. This technique is similar to equal-additions subtraction except that division and multiplication are involved here.

✔ **Check for Understanding:** Exercise/Problem Set A #1–4

Scientific Notation

Multiplying and dividing large numbers can sometimes be assisted by first expressing them in scientific notation. In Section 4.1, scientific notation was discussed in the context of using a scientific calculator. Numbers are said to be in **scientific notation** when expressed in the form $a \times 10^n$, where $1 \leq a < 10$ and n is any whole number (the case when n can be negative will be discussed in Chapter 8). The number a is called the **mantissa** and n the **characteristic** of $a \times 10^n$. The following table provides some examples of numbers written in scientific notation.

	SCIENTIFIC NOTATION	STANDARD NOTATION
Diameter of Jupiter	1.438×10^8 meters	143,800,000 meters
Total amount of gold in Earth's crust	1.2×10^{16} kilograms	12,000,000,000,000,000 kilograms
Distance from Earth to Jupiter	5.88×10^{11} meters	588,000,000,000 meters

Once large numbers are expressed in scientific notation they can be multiplied and divided more easily as shown in the following example.

Example 7.16 Compute the following using scientific notation.

a. $54{,}500{,}000{,}000 \times 346{,}000{,}000$ **b.** $1{,}200{,}000{,}000{,}000 \div 62{,}500{,}000$

SOLUTION

a. $54{,}500{,}000{,}000 \times 346{,}000{,}000 = (5.45 \times 10^{10}) \times (3.46 \times 10^8)$
$$= (5.45 \times 3.46) \times (10^{10} \times 10^8)$$
$$= 18.857 \times 10^{18}$$
$$= 1.8857 \times 10^1 \times 10^{18}$$
$$= 1.8857 \times 10^{19}$$

b. $\dfrac{1{,}200{,}000{,}000{,}000}{62{,}500{,}000} = \dfrac{1.2 \times 10^{12}}{6.25 \times 10^7}$
$$= \dfrac{1.2}{6.25} \times \dfrac{10^{12}}{10^7}$$
$$= 0.192 \times 10^5$$
$$= 0.192 \times 10 \times 10^4$$
$$= 1.92 \times 10^4$$

Check for Understanding: Exercise/Problem Set A #5–11

Classifying Repeating Decimals

In Example 7.2 we observed that fractions in simplest form whose denominators are of the form $2^m \cdot 5^n$ have terminating decimal representations. Fractions of this type can also be converted into decimals using a calculator or the long-division algorithm for decimals.

Example 7.17 Express $\frac{7}{40}$ in decimal form **(a)** using a calculator and **(b)** using the long-division algorithm.

SOLUTION

a. $7 \boxed{\div} 40 \boxed{=} \boxed{0.175}$

b.
$$
\begin{array}{r}
0.175 \\
40\overline{)7.000} \\
-4\,0 \\
\hline
3\,00 \\
-2\,80 \\
\hline
200 \\
-200 \\
\hline
0
\end{array}
$$

Therefore, $\frac{7}{40} = 0.175$.

Now, let's express $\frac{1}{3}$ as a decimal. Using a calculator, we obtain

$$1 \boxed{\div} 3 \boxed{=} \boxed{0.333333333}$$

This display shows $\frac{1}{3}$ as a terminating decimal, since the calculator can display only finitely many decimal places. However, the long-division method adds some additional insight to this situation.

$$
\begin{array}{r}
0.333\ldots \\
3\overline{)1.000} \\
-\underline{9} \\
10 \\
-\underline{9} \\
10 \\
-\underline{9} \\
1
\end{array}
$$

Using long division, we see that the decimal in the quotient will never terminate, since every remainder is 1. Similarly, the decimal for $\frac{1}{11}$ is 0.0909.... Instead of writing dots, a horizontal bar may be placed above the **repetend**, the first string of repeating digits. Thus

$$\frac{1}{3} = 0.\overline{3}, \qquad \frac{1}{11} = 0.\overline{09},$$

$$\frac{2}{7} = 0.\overline{285714}, \qquad \frac{2}{9} = 0.\overline{2},$$

$$\text{and} \quad \frac{40}{99} = 0.\overline{40}.$$

(Use your calculator or the long-division algorithm to check that these are correct.) Decimals having a repetend are called **repeating decimals**. (NOTE: Terminating decimals are those repeating decimals whose repetend is zero.) The number of digits in the repetend is called the **period** of the decimal. For example, the period of $\frac{1}{11}$ is 2. To gain additional insight into why certain decimals repeat, consider the next example.

> **Example 7.18**   Express $\frac{6}{7}$ as a decimal.

SOLUTION

Problem-Solving Strategy
Look for a Pattern

$$
\begin{array}{r}
0.857142 \\
7\overline{)6.000000} \\
-\underline{56} \\
40 \\
-\underline{35} \\
50 \\
-\underline{49} \\
10 \\
-\underline{7} \\
30 \\
-\underline{28} \\
20 \\
-\underline{14} \\
6
\end{array}
$$

When dividing by 7, there are seven possible remainders—0, 1, 2, 3, 4, 5, 6. Thus, when dividing by 7, either a 0 will appear as a remainder (and the decimal terminates) or one of the other nonzero remainders must eventually *reappear* as a remainder. At that point, the decimal will begin to repeat. Notice that the remainder 6 appears for a second time, so the decimal will begin to repeat at that point. Therefore, $\frac{6}{7} = 0.\overline{857142}$. Similarly, $\frac{1}{13}$ will begin repeating no later than the 13th remainder, $\frac{7}{23}$ will begin repeating by the 23rd remainder, and so on. ∎

By considering several examples where the denominator has factors other than 2 or 5, the following statement will be apparent.

THEOREM

Fractions with Repeating, Nonterminating Decimal Representations

Let $\dfrac{a}{b}$ be a fraction written in simplest form. Then $\dfrac{a}{b}$ has a repeating decimal representation that does not terminate if and only if b has a prime factor other than 2 or 5.

Earlier we saw that it was easy to express any terminating decimal as a fraction. But suppose that a number has a repeating, nonterminating decimal representation. Can we find a fractional representation for that number?

Algebraic Reasoning
In the solution of Example 7.19, a letter is used to represent a specific number, namely $n = 0.\overline{34}$, rather than to represent many possible numbers as a variable does. Using a letter in this way allows one to manipulate the number in order to find its fractional representation.

Example 7.19　Express $0.\overline{34}$ in its fractional form.

SOLUTION　Let $n = 0.\overline{34}$. Thus $100n = 34.\overline{34}$.

$$\begin{aligned} \text{Then} \qquad 100n &= 34.343434\ldots \\ -\qquad n &= .343434\ldots \\ \hline \text{so} \qquad 99n &= 34 \\ \text{or} \qquad n &= \frac{34}{99}. \end{aligned}$$

∎

This procedure can be applied to any repeating decimal that does not terminate, except that instead of multiplying n by 100 each time, you must multiply n by 10^m, where m is the number of digits in the repetend. For example, to express $17.\overline{531}$ in its fractional form, let $n = 17.\overline{531}$ and multiply both n and $17.\overline{531}$ by 10^3, since the repetend $.\overline{531}$ has three digits. Then $10^3 n - n = 17{,}531.\overline{531} - 17.\overline{531} = 17{,}514$. From this we find that $n = \frac{17{,}514}{999}$.

Finally, we can state the following important result that links fractions and repeating decimals.

THEOREM

Every fraction has a repeating decimal representation, and every repeating decimal has a fraction representation.

The following diagram provides a visual summary of this theorem.

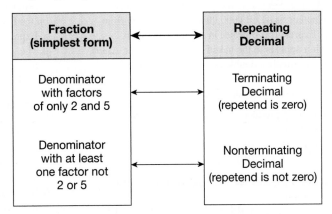

✔ **Check for Understanding:** Exercise/Problem Set A #12–14

MATHEMATICAL MORSEL

Debugging is a term used to describe the process of checking a computer program for errors and then correcting the errors. According to legend, the process of debugging was adopted by Grace Hopper, who designed the computer language COBOL. When one of her programs was not running as it should, it was found that one of the computer components had malfunctioned and that a real bug found among the components was the culprit. Since then, if a program did not run as it was designed to, it was said to have a "bug" in it. Thus it had to be "debugged."

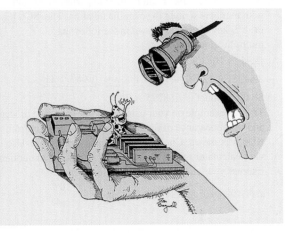

Section 7.2   EXERCISE / PROBLEM SET A

EXERCISES

1. a. Perform the following operations using the decimal algorithms of this section.

   i. $38.52 + 9.251$ **ii.** $534.51 - 48.67$

  b. Change the decimals in part (a) to fractions, perform the computations, and express the answers as decimals.

2. a. Perform the following operations using the algorithms of this section.

   i. 5.23×0.034 **ii.** $8.272 \div 1.76$

  b. Change the decimals in part (a) to fractions, perform the computations, and express the answers as decimals.

3. Find answers on your calculator *without* using the decimal-point key. (*Hint:* Locate the decimal point by doing approximate calculations.) Check using a written algorithm.

  a. 48.62×52.7 **b.** $123,658.57 \div 17.9$

4. By thinking about the process of the division algorithm for decimals, determine which of the following division problems have the same quotient. NOTE: You don't need to complete the algorithm in order to answer this question.

  a. $56 \overline{)1680}$ **b.** $0.056 \overline{)0.168}$ **c.** $0.56 \overline{)0.168}$

5. It is possible to write any decimal as a number between 1 and 10 (including 1) times a power of 10. This scientific notation is particularly useful in expressing large numbers. For example,

$$6321 = 6.321 \times 10^3 \quad \text{and}$$
$$760,000,000 = 7.6 \times 10^8.$$

Write each of the following in scientific notation.

  a. 59   **b.** 4326

  c. 97,000   **d.** 1,000,000

  e. 64,020,000   **f.** 71,000,000,000

6. The nearest star (other than the sun) is Alpha Centauri, which is the brightest star in the constellation Centaurus.
   a. Alpha Centauri is 41,600,000,000,000,000 meters from our sun. Express this distance in scientific notation.
   b. Although it appears to the naked eye to be one star, Alpha Centauri is actually a double star. The two stars that comprise it are about 3,500,000,000 meters apart. Express this distance in scientific notation.

7. Find the following products, and express answers in scientific notation.
   a. $(6.2 \times 10^1) \times (5.9 \times 10^4)$
   b. $(7.1 \times 10^2) \times (8.3 \times 10^6)$

8. Find the following quotients, and express the answers in scientific notation.
   a. $\dfrac{1.612 \times 10^5}{3.1 \times 10^2}$
   b. $\dfrac{8.019 \times 10^9}{9.9 \times 10^5}$
   c. $\dfrac{9.02 \times 10^5}{2.2 \times 10^3}$

9. A scientific calculator can be used to perform calculations with numbers written in scientific notation. The $\boxed{\text{SCI}}$ key or $\boxed{\text{EE}}$ key is used as shown in the following multiplication example:
   $(3.41 \times 10^{12})(4.95 \times 10^8)$.
   3.41 $\boxed{\text{SCI}}$ 12 $\boxed{\times}$ 4.95 $\boxed{\text{SCI}}$ 8 $\boxed{=}$ $\boxed{1.68795\ 21}$
   So the product is 1.68795×10^{21}.
   Try this example on your calculator. The sequence of steps and the appearance of the result may differ slightly from what was shown. Consult your manual if necessary. Use your calculator to find the following products and quotients. Express your answers in scientific notation.
   a. $(7.19 \times 10^6)(1.4 \times 10^8)$
   b. $\dfrac{6.4 \times 10^{24}}{5.0 \times 10^{10}}$

10. The Earth's oceans have a total volume of approximately 1,286,000,000 cubic kilometers. The volume of fresh water on the Earth is approximately 35,000,000 cubic kilometers.
    a. Express each of these volumes in scientific notation.
    b. The volume of salt water in the oceans is about how many times greater than the volume of fresh water on the Earth?

11. The distance from Earth to Mars is 399,000,000 kilometers. Use this information and scientific notation to answer the following questions.
    a. If you traveled at 88 kilometers per hour (55 miles per hour), how many hours would it take to travel from Earth to Mars?
    b. How many years would it take to travel from Earth to Mars?
    c. In order to travel from Earth to Mars in a year, how fast would you have to travel in kilometers per hour?

12. Write each of the following using a bar over the repetend.
    a. 0.7777 . . .
    b. 0.47121212 . . .
    c. 0.181818 . . .

13. Write out the first 12 decimal places of each of the following.
    a. $0.3\overline{174}$
    b. $0.31\overline{74}$
    c. $0.317\overline{4}$

14. Express each of the following repeating decimals as a fraction in simplest form.
    a. $0.\overline{16}$
    b. $0.3\overline{87}$
    c. $0.7\overline{25}$

PROBLEMS

15. The star Deneb is approximately 1.5×10^{19} meters from Earth. A light year, the distance that light travels in one year, is about 9.46×10^{15} meters. What is the distance from Earth to Deneb measured in light years?

16. Is the decimal expansion of 151/7,018,923,456,413 terminating or nonterminating? How can you tell without computing the decimal expansion?

17. Give an example of a fraction whose decimal expansion terminates in the following numbers of places.
    a. 3   b. 4   c. 8   d. 17

18. From the fact that $0.\overline{1} = \frac{1}{9}$, mentally convert the following decimals into fractions.
    a. $0.\overline{3}$ b. $0.\overline{5}$ c. $0.\overline{7}$ d. $2.\overline{8}$ e. $5.\overline{9}$

19. From the fact that $0.\overline{01} = \frac{1}{99}$, mentally convert the following decimals into fractions.
    a. $0.\overline{03}$ b. $0.\overline{05}$ c. $0.\overline{07}$
    d. $0.\overline{37}$ e. $0.\overline{64}$ f. $5.\overline{97}$

20. From the fact that $0.\overline{001} = \frac{1}{999}$, mentally convert the following decimals into fractions.
    a. $0.\overline{003}$ b. $0.\overline{005}$ c. $0.\overline{007}$
    d. $0.\overline{019}$ e. $0.\overline{827}$ f. $3.\overline{217}$

21. a. Use the pattern you have discovered in Problems 19 to 21 to convert the following decimals into fractions. Do mentally.
       i. $0.\overline{23}$ ii. $0.\overline{010}$ iii. $0.\overline{769}$
       iv. $0.\overline{9}$ v. $0.\overline{57}$ vi. $0.\overline{1827}$
    b. Verify your answers by using the method taught in the text for converting repeating decimals into fractions using a calculator.

22. a. Give an example of a fraction whose decimal representation has a repetend containing exactly five digits.
    b. Characterize all fractions whose decimal representations are of the form $0.\overline{abcde}$, where a, b, c, d, and e are arbitrary digits 0 through 9 and not all five digits are the same.

23. **a.** What is the 11th digit to the right of the decimal in the decimal expansion of $\frac{1}{13}$?

   b. What is the 33rd digit of $\frac{1}{13}$?

   c. What is the 2731st digit of $\frac{1}{13}$?

   d. What is the 11,000,000th digit of $\frac{1}{13}$?

24. From the observation that $100 \times \frac{1}{71} = \frac{100}{71} = 1\frac{29}{71}$, what conclusion can you draw about the relationship between the decimal expansions of $\frac{1}{71}$ and $\frac{29}{71}$?

25. It may require some ingenuity to calculate the following number on an inexpensive four-function calculator. Explain why, and show how one can, in fact, calculate it.

$$\frac{364 \times 363 \times 362 \times 361 \times 360 \times 359}{365 \times 365 \times 365 \times 365 \times 365 \times 365}$$

26. Gary cashed a check from Joan for $29.35. Then he bought two magazines for $1.95 each, a book for $5.95, and a tape for $5.98. He had $21.45 left. How much money did he have before cashing the check?

27. Each year a car depreciates to about 0.8 of its value the year before. What was the original value of a car that is worth $16,000 at the end of 3 years?

28. A regional telephone company advertises calls for $.11 a minute. How much will an hour and 21 minute call cost?

29. Juanita's family's car odometer read 32,576.7 at the beginning of the trip and 35,701.2 at the end. If $282.18 worth of gasoline at $2.89 per gallon was purchased during the trip, how many miles per gallon (to the nearest mile) did they average?

30. In 2007, the exchange rate for the Japanese yen was 121 yen per U.S. dollar. How many dollars should one receive in exchange for 10,000 yen (round to the nearest hundredth)?

31. A typical textbook measures 8 inches by 10 inches. There are exactly 2.54 centimeters per inch. What are the dimensions of a textbook in centimeters?

32. Inflation causes prices to increase about .03 per year. If a textbook costs $115 in 2010, what would you expect the book to cost in 2014 (round to the nearest dollar)?

33. Sport utility vehicles advertise the following engine capacities: a 2.4-liter 4-cylinder, a 3.5-liter V-6, a 4.9-liter V-8, and a 6.8-liter V-10. Compare the capacities of these engines in terms of liters per cylinder.

34. Three nickels, one penny, and one dime are placed as shown. You may move only one coin at a time, to an adjacent empty square. Move the coins so that the penny and the dime have exchanged places and the lower middle square is empty. Try to find the minimum number of such moves.

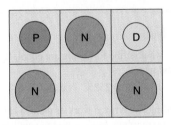

| Section 7.2 | **EXERCISE / PROBLEM SET B** |

EXERCISES

1. Perform the following operations using the decimal algorithms of this section.
   a. $7.482 + 94.3$ **b.** $100.63 - 72.495$
   c. $0.08 + 0.1234$ **d.** $24 - 2.099$

2. Perform the following operations using the decimal algorithms of this section.
   a. 16.4×2.8 **b.** 0.065×1.92
   c. $44.4 \div 0.3$ **d.** $129.168 \div 4.14$

3. Find answers on your calculator *without* using the decimal-point key. (*Hint:* Locate the decimal point by doing approximate calculations.) Check using a written algorithm.
   a. 473.92×49.12 **b.** $537,978.4146 \div 1379.4$

4. By thinking about the process of the division algorithm for decimals, determine which of the following division problems have the same quotient. NOTE: You don't need to complete the algorithm in order to answer this question.
   a. $5.6\overline{)16.8}$ **b.** $0.056\overline{)1.68}$ **c.** $0.56\overline{)16.8}$

5. Write each of the following numbers in scientific notation.
   a. 860   **b.** 4520
   c. 26,000,000   **d.** 315,000
   e. 1,084,000,000   **f.** 54,000,000,000,000

6. **a.** The longest human life on record was more than 122 years, or about 3,850,000,000 seconds. Express this number of seconds in scientific notation.
   b. Some tortoises have been known to live more than 150 years, or about 4,730,000,000 seconds. Express this number of seconds in scientific notation.
   c. The oldest living plant is probably a bristlecone pine tree in Nevada; it is about 4900 years old. Its age in seconds would be about 1.545×10^{11} seconds. Express this number of seconds in standard form and write a name for it.

7. Perform the following operations, and express answers in scientific notation.
   a. $(2.3 \times 10^2) \times (3.5 \times 10^4)$ **b.** $(7.3 \times 10^3) \times (8.6 \times 10^6)$

8. Find the following quotients, and express the answers in scientific notation.

a. $\dfrac{1.357 \times 10^{27}}{2.3 \times 10^3}$ b. $\dfrac{4.894689 \times 10^{23}}{5.19 \times 10^{18}}$ c. $\dfrac{5.561 \times 10^7}{6.7 \times 10^2}$

9. Use your calculator to find the following products and quotients. Express your answers in scientific notation.
a. $(1.2 \times 10^{10})(3.4 \times 10^{12})(8.5 \times 10^{17})$
b. $\dfrac{(4.56 \times 10^9)(7.0 \times 10^{21})}{(1.2 \times 10^6)(2.8 \times 10^{10})}$
c. $(3.6 \times 10^{18})^3$

10. At a height of 8.488 kilometers, the highest mountain in the world is Mount Everest in the Himalayas. The deepest part of the oceans is the Marianas Trench in the Pacific Ocean, with a depth of 11.034 kilometers. What is the vertical distance from the top of the highest mountain in the world to the deepest part of the oceans?

11. The amount of gold in the Earth's crust is about 120,000,000,000,000 kilograms.

a. Express this amount of gold in scientific notation.
b. The market value of gold in March 2007 was about $20,700 per kilogram. What was the total market value of all the gold in the Earth's crust at that time?
c. The total U.S. national debt in March 2007 was about 8.6×10^{12}. How many times would the value of the gold pay off the national debt?
d. If there were about 300,000,000 people in the United States in March 2007, how much do each of us owe on the national debt?

12. Write each of the following using a bar over the repetend.
a. 0.35 b. $0.141414\ldots$ c. $0.45315961596\ldots$

13. Write out the first 12 decimal places of each of the following.
a. $0.3\overline{174}$ b. $0.3\overline{174}$ c. $0.\overline{1159123}$

14. Express each of the following decimals as fractions.
a. $0.\overline{5}$ b. $0.\overline{78}$ c. $0.\overline{123}$
d. $0.1\overline{24}$ e. $0.01\overline{78}$ f. $0.123\overline{456}$

PROBLEMS

15. Determine whether the following are equal. If not, which is smaller, and why?

$$0.25\overline{25} \qquad 0.2\overline{525}$$

16. Without doing any written work or using a calculator, order the following numbers from largest to smallest.

$$x = 0.00000456789 \div 0.00000987654$$
$$y = 0.00000456789 \times 0.00000987654$$
$$z = 0.00000456789 + 0.00000987654$$

17. Look for a pattern in each of the following sequences of decimal numbers. For each one, write what you think the next two terms would be.
a. $11.5, 14.7, 17.9, 21.1, \ldots$
b. $24, 33.6, 47.04, 65.856, \ldots$
c. $0.5, 0.05, 0.055, 0.0055, 0.00555, \ldots$
d. $0.5, 0.6, 1.0, 1.9, 3.5, 6.0, \ldots$
e. $1.0, 0.5, 0.\overline{6}, 0.75, 0.8, \ldots$

18. In Chapter 3 a palindrome was defined to be a number such as 343 that reads the same forward and backward. A process of reversing the digits of any number and adding until a palindrome is obtained was described. The same technique works for decimal numbers, as shown next.

7.95	
+59.7	Step 1
67.65	
+56.76	Step 2
124.41	
+14.421	Step 3
138.831	A palindrome

a. Determine the number of steps required to obtain a palindrome from each of the following numbers.
   i. 16.58   ii. 217.8   iii. 1.0097   iv. 9.63
b. Find a decimal number that requires exactly four steps to give a palindrome.

19. a. Express each of the following as fractions.
   i. $0.\overline{1}$ ii. $0.\overline{01}$ iii. $0.\overline{001}$ iv. $0.\overline{0001}$
b. What fraction would you expect to be given by $0.\overline{000000001}$?
c. What would you expect the decimal expansion of $\frac{1}{90}$ to be?

20. Change $0.\overline{9}$ to a fraction. Can you explain your result?

21. Consider the decimals: $a_1 = 0.9$, $a_2 = 0.99$, $a_3 = 0.999$, $a_4 = 0.9999, \ldots, a_n = 0.999\ldots9$ (with n digits of 9).
a. Give an argument that $0 < a_n < a_{n+1} < 1$ for each n.
b. Show that there is a term a_n in the sequence such that

$$1 - a_n < \frac{1}{10^{100}}.$$

(Find a value of n that works.)
c. Give an argument that the sequence of terms gets arbitrarily close to 1. That is, for any distance d, no matter how small, there is a term a_n in the sequence such that $1 - d < a_n < 1$.

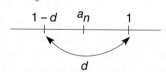

d. Use parts (a) to (c) to explain why $0.\overline{9} = 1$.

22. a. Write $\frac{1}{7}, \frac{2}{7}, \frac{3}{7}, \frac{4}{7}, \frac{5}{7}$, and $\frac{6}{7}$ in their decimal expansion form. What do the repetends for each expansion have in common?

b. Write $\frac{1}{13}, \frac{2}{13}, \frac{3}{13}, \ldots, \frac{11}{13}$, and $\frac{12}{13}$ in decimal expansion form. What observations can you make about the repetends in these expansions?

23. Characterize all fractions a/b, $a < b$, whose decimal expansions consist of n random digits to the right of the decimal followed by a five-digit repetend. For example, suppose that $n = 7$; then $0.213567\overline{451139}$ would be the decimal expansion of such a fraction.

24. If $\frac{9}{23} = 0.\overline{3913043478260869565217}$, what is the 999th digit to the right of the decimal?

25. Name the digit in the 4321st place of each of the following decimals.

a. $0.\overline{142857}$ **b.** $0.1234567891011121314\ldots$

26. What happened to the other $\frac{1}{4}$?

$$
\begin{array}{r}
16.5 \\
\times 12.5 \\
\hline
8.25 \\
33 \\
165 \\
\hline
206.25
\end{array}
\qquad
\begin{array}{r}
16\frac{1}{2} \\
\times 12\frac{1}{2} \\
\hline
32 \\
160 \\
8\frac{1}{4} \quad \text{(one half of } 16\frac{1}{2}\text{)} \\
6\frac{1}{4} \quad \text{(one half of } 12\frac{1}{2}\text{)} \\
\hline
206\frac{1}{2}
\end{array}
$$

27. The weight in grams, to the nearest hundredth, of a particular sample of toxic waste was 28.67 grams.

a. What is the minimum amount the sample could have weighed? (Write out your answer to the ten-thousandths place.)

b. What is the maximum amount? (Write out your answer to the ten-thousandths place.)

28. A map shows a scale of 1 in. = 73.6 mi.

a. How many miles would 3.5 in. represent?

b. How many inches would represent 576 miles (round to the nearest tenth)?

29. If you invest $7500 in a mutual fund at $34.53 per share, how much profit would you make if the price per share increases to $46.17?

30. A casino promises a payoff on its slot machines of 93 cents on the dollar. If you insert 188 quarters one at a time, how much would you expect to win?

31. Your family takes a five-day trip logging the following miles and times: (503 mi, 9 hr), (480 mi, 8.5 hr), (465 mi, 7.75 hr), (450 mi, 8.75 hr), and (490 mi, 9.75 hr). What was the average speed (to the nearest mile per hour) of the trip?

32. The total value of any sum of money that earns interest at 9% per year doubles about every 8 years. What amount of money invested now at 9% per year will accumulate to about $120,000 in about 40 years (assuming no taxes are paid on the earnings and no money is withdrawn)?

33. An absentminded bank teller switched the dollars and cents when he cashed a check for Mr. Spencer, giving him dollars instead of cents, and cents instead of dollars. After buying a 5-cent newspaper, Mr. Spencer discovered that he had left exactly twice as much as his original check. What was the amount of the check?

 Analyzing Student Thinking

34. Bhumi adds 6.45 and 2.3 and states that the answer is 6.68. What mistake did the student make and how would you help her understand her misconception?

35. Kaisa multiplies 7.2 and 3.5 and gets 2.52, which is clearly wrong. What mistake did she make?

36. Tyler says that 50 times 4.68 is the same as .5 times 468. Thus, he simply takes half of 468 to get the answer. Is his method acceptable? Explain.

37. To find 0.33 times 24, a student takes one-third of 24 and says the answer is 8. Is she correct? Explain.

38. When changing $7.\overline{452}$ to a fraction, Henry set $n = 7.\overline{452}$ and multiplied both sides by 100. However, when he subtracted, he got another repeating decimal. How could you help?

39. Lauren asserts that $3.1211211121111\ldots$ is a repeating decimal. How should you respond?

40. A student says that the sum of two repeating decimals must be a repeating decimal. How should you respond?

41. Barry says he can't find the product of $12{,}750{,}000{,}000{,}000 \times 3{,}987{,}000{,}000$ on a standard calculator that has a ten digit display. How should you respond?

Problems Relating to the NCTM Standards and Curriculum Focal Points

1. The Focal Points for Grade 5 state "Developing an understanding of and fluency with addition and subtraction of fractions and decimals." Part of understanding addition and subtraction of decimals is knowing why the decimal point needs to be lined up. Explain why this is so.

2. The Focal Points for Grade 6 state "Developing an understanding of and fluency with multiplication and division of fractions and decimals." Explain your understanding of why the placement of the decimal point in the multiplication of decimal numbers is determined by counting the number of digits to the right of the decimal in the numbers in the problem.

3. The NCTM Standards state "All students should understand the place-value structure of the base ten number system and be able to represent and compare whole numbers and decimals." Explain how the "structure of the base ten number system" is used to write numbers in scientific notation.

7.3 Ratio and Proportion

STARTING POINT

For his construction project, José needed to cut some boards into two pieces A and B so that piece A is $\frac{1}{3}$ as big as piece B. For this situation, discuss the following questions:

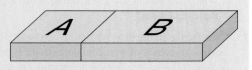

1. Piece A is how much of the board? Repeat for the following two situations:

2. Piece B is _____ times as big as piece A? Piece A is $\frac{3}{4}$ as big as piece B

3. What is the ratio of piece A to piece B? Piece A is $\frac{2}{5}$ as big as piece B

Ratio

The concept of ratio occurs in many places in mathematics and in everyday life, as the next example illustrates.

Example 7.20

a. In Washington School, the ratio of students to teachers is $17:1$, read "17 to 1."
b. In Smithville, the ratio of girls to boys is $3:2$.
c. A paint mixture calls for a $5:3$ ratio of blue paint to red paint.
d. The ratio of centimeters to inches is $2.54:1$. ∎

In this chapter the numbers used in ratios will be whole numbers, fractions, or decimals representing fractions. Ratios involving real numbers are studied in Chapter 9.

In English, the word *per* means "for every" and indicates a ratio. For example, rates such as miles per gallon (gasoline mileage), kilometers per hour (speed), dollars per hour (wages), cents per ounce (unit price), people per square mile (population density), and percent are all ratios.

DEFINITION

Children's Literature
www.wiley.com/college/musser
See "Beanstalk: The Measure of a Giant" by Ann McCallum.

Ratio

A **ratio** is an ordered pair of numbers, written $a:b$, with $b \neq 0$.

Unlike fractions, there are instances of ratios in which b could be zero. For example, the ratio of men to women on a starting major league baseball team could be reported as 9:0. However, since such applications are rare, the definition of the ratio $a:b$ excludes cases in which $b = 0$.

Ratios allow us to compare the relative sizes of two quantities. This comparison can be represented by the ratio symbol $a:b$ or as the quotient $\frac{a}{b}$. Quotients occur quite naturally when we interpret ratios. In Example 7.20(a), there are $\frac{1}{17}$ as many teachers as students in Washington School. In part (b) there are $\frac{3}{2}$ as many girls as boys in Smithville. We could also say that there are $\frac{2}{3}$ as many boys as girls, or that the ratio of boys to girls is $2:3$. This is illustrated in Figure 7.10.

$G\ G\ G$
$B\ B$

Figure 7.10

Algebraic Reasoning
A common ratio used in algebra is that of slope. The slope is the ratio of the "change in y" compared to the "change in x." More generally, the slope is the ratio of the amount one variable changes with respect to the amount of change in another variable.

Reflection from Research
Children understand and can work with part-whole relationships of quantities even before they start school. However, this concept is often not introduced in schools for at least the first 2 years (Irwin, 1996).

Notice that there are several ratios that we can form when comparing the population of boys and girls in Smithville, namely $2:3$ (boys to girls), $3:2$ (girls to boys), $2:5$ (boys to children), $5:3$ (children to girls), and so on. Some ratios give a **part-to-part** comparison, as in Example 7.20(c). In mixing the paint, we would use 5 units of blue paint and 3 units of red paint. (A unit could be any size—milliliter, teaspoon, cup, and so on.) Ratios can also represent the comparison of **part-to-whole** or **whole-to-part**. In Example 7.20(b) the ratio of boys (part) to children (whole) is $2:5$. Notice that the part-to-whole ratio, $2:5$, is the same concept as the fraction of the children that are boys, namely $\frac{2}{5}$. The comparison of all the children to the boys can be expressed in a whole-to-part ratio as $5:2$, or as the fraction $\frac{5}{2}$.

In Example 7.20(b), the ratio of girls to boys indicates only the *relative* sizes of the populations of girls and boys in Smithville. There could be 30 girls and 20 boys, 300 girls and 200 boys, or some other pair of numbers whose ratio is equivalent. It is important to note that ratios always represent relative, rather than absolute, amounts. In many applications, it is useful to know which ratios represent the same relative amounts. Consider the following example.

Example 7.21 In class 1 the ratio of girls to boys is $8:6$. In class 2 the ratio is $4:3$. Suppose that each class has 28 students. Do these ratios represent the same relative amounts?

SOLUTION Notice that the classes can be grouped in different ways (Figure 7.11).

Class 1: *GGGG*   *GGGG* | *GGGG*   *GGGG*
       BBB   *BBB* | *BBB*   *BBB*   Ratio 8:6

Class 2: *GGGG* | *GGGG* | *GGGG* | *GGGG*
       BBB | *BBB* | *BBB* | *BBB*   Ratio 4:3

Figure 7.11

The subdivisions shown in Figure 7.11 do not change the relative number of girls to boys in the groups. We see that in both classes there are 4 girls for every 3 boys. Hence we say that, as ordered pairs, the ratios $4:3$ and $8:6$ are equivalent, since they represent the same relative amount. They are equivalent to the ratio $16:12$. ■

From Example 7.21 it should be clear that the ratios $a:b$ and $ar:br$, where $r \neq 0$, represent the same relative amounts. Using an argument similar to the one used with fractions, we can show that the ratios $a:b$ and $c:d$ represent the same relative amounts if and only if $ad = bc$. Thus we have the following definition.

DEFINITION

Equality of Ratios

Let $\dfrac{a}{b}$ and $\dfrac{c}{d}$ be any two ratios. Then $\dfrac{a}{b} = \dfrac{c}{d}$ if and only if $ad = bc$.

Just as with fractions, this definition can be used to show that if n is a nonzero number, then $\dfrac{an}{bn} = \dfrac{a}{b}$, or $an:bn = a:b$. In the equation $\dfrac{a}{b} = \dfrac{c}{d}$, a and d are called the **extremes**, since a and d are at the "extremes" of the equation $a:b = c:d$, while b and c are called the **means**. Thus the equality of ratios states that two ratios are equal if and only if the product of the means equals the product of the extremes.

✔ **Check for Understanding:** Exercise/Problem Set A #1–5

Proportion

Reflection from Research
Sixth-grade students "seem able to generalize the arithmetic that they know well, but they have difficulty generalizing the arithmetic with which they are less familiar. In particular, middle school students would benefit from more experiences with a rich variety of multiplicative situations, including proportionality, inverse variation and exponentiation" (Swafford & Langrall, 2000).

Children's Literature
www.wiley.com/college/musser
See "What's Faster than a Speeding Cheetah?" by Robert E. Wells.

The concept of proportion is useful in solving problems involving ratios.

> ### DEFINITION
>
> ### *Proportion*
>
> A **proportion** is a statement that two given ratios are equal.

The equation $\dfrac{10}{12} = \dfrac{5}{6}$ is a proportion since $\dfrac{10}{12} = \dfrac{5 \cdot 2}{6 \cdot 2} = \dfrac{5}{6}$. Also, the equation $\dfrac{14}{21} = \dfrac{22}{33}$ is an example of a proportion, since $14 \cdot 33 = 21 \cdot 22$. In general, $\dfrac{a}{b} = \dfrac{c}{d}$ is a proportion if and only if $ad = bc$. The next example shows how proportions are used to solve everyday problems.

| **Example 7.22** | Adams School orders 3 cartons of chocolate milk for every 7 students. If there are 581 students in the school, how many cartons of chocolate milk should be ordered? |

SOLUTION Set up a proportion using the ratio of cartons to students. Let n be the unknown number of cartons. Then

$$\frac{3 \text{ (cartons)}}{7 \text{ (students)}} = \frac{n \text{ (cartons)}}{581 \text{ (students)}}.$$

NCTM Standard
The so-called cross-multiplication method can be developed meaningfully if it arises naturally in students' work, but it can also have unfortunate side effects when students do not adequately understand when the method is appropriate to use.

Using the cross-multiplication property of ratios, we have that

$$3 \times 581 = 7 \times n,$$

so

$$n = \frac{3 \times 581}{7} = 249.$$

The school should order 249 cartons of chocolate milk. ∎

In Example 7.22, the number of cartons of milk was compared with the number of students. Ratios involving different units (here cartons to students) are called **rates**. Commonly used rates include miles per gallon, cents per ounce, and so on.

When solving proportions like the one in Example 7.22, it is important to set up the ratios in a consistent way according to the units associated with the numbers. In our solution, the ratios $3:7$ and $n:581$ represented ratios of *cartons of chocolate milk* to *students in the school*. The following proportion could also have been used.

$$\frac{3 \left(\begin{array}{c} \text{cartons of chocolate} \\ \text{milk in the ratio} \end{array} \right)}{n \left(\begin{array}{c} \text{cartons of chocolate} \\ \text{milk in school} \end{array} \right)} = \frac{7 \left(\begin{array}{c} \text{students} \\ \text{in the ratio} \end{array} \right)}{581 \left(\begin{array}{c} \text{students} \\ \text{in school} \end{array} \right)}$$

Here the numerators show the original ratio. (Notice that the proportion $\dfrac{3}{n} = \dfrac{581}{7}$ would *not* correctly represent the problem, since the units in the numerators and denominators would not correspond.)

In general, the following proportions are equivalent (i.e., have the same solutions). This can be justified by cross-multiplication.

$$\frac{a}{b} = \frac{c}{d} \qquad \frac{a}{c} = \frac{b}{d} \qquad \frac{b}{a} = \frac{d}{c} \qquad \frac{c}{a} = \frac{d}{b}$$

Thus there are several possible correct proportions that can be established when equating ratios.

Algebraic Reasoning
The proportion in Example 7.23 can be solved by reasoning that since there are 2.5 times as many people, there will need to be 2.5 times as many eggs. Such reasoning is algebraic even if the typical cross-multiplication techniques are not used.

Example 7.23   A recipe calls for 1 cup of mix, 1 cup of milk, the whites from 4 eggs, and 3 teaspoons of oil. If this recipe serves 6 people, how many eggs are needed to make enough for 15 people?

SOLUTION   When solving proportions, it is useful to list the various pieces of information as follows:

	ORIGINAL RECIPE	NEW RECIPE
Number of eggs	4	x
Number of people	6	15

Thus $\dfrac{4}{6} = \dfrac{x}{15}$. This proportion can be solved in two ways.

CROSS-MULTIPLICATION	EQUIVALENT RATIOS
$\dfrac{4}{6} = \dfrac{x}{15}$	$\dfrac{4}{6} = \dfrac{x}{15}$
$4 \cdot 15 = 6x$	$\dfrac{4}{6} = \dfrac{2 \cdot 2}{2 \cdot 3} = \dfrac{2}{3} = \dfrac{2 \cdot 5}{3 \cdot 5} = \dfrac{10}{15} = \dfrac{x}{15}$
$60 = 6x$	Thus $x = 10$.
$10 = x$	

Notice that the table in Example 7.23 showing the number of eggs and people can be used to set up three other equivalent proportions:

$$\frac{4}{x} = \frac{6}{15} \qquad \frac{x}{4} = \frac{15}{6} \qquad \frac{6}{4} = \frac{15}{x}.$$ ■

NCTM Standard
All students should solve simple problems involving rates and derived measurements for such attributes as velocity and density.

Example 7.24   If your car averages 29 miles per gallon, how many gallons should you expect to buy for a 609-mile trip?

SOLUTION

Reflection from Research
Students often see no difference in meaning between expressions such as 5 km per hour and 5 hours per km. The meanings of the numerator and denominator with respect to rate are not correctly understood (Bell, 1986).

	AVERAGE	TRIP
Miles	29	609
Gallons	1	x

Therefore, $\dfrac{29}{1} = \dfrac{609}{x}$, or $\dfrac{x}{1} = \dfrac{609}{29}$. Thus $x = 21$.   ■

Example 7.25   In a scale drawing, 0.5 centimeter represents 35 miles.

a. How many miles will 4 centimeters represent?
b. How many centimeters will represent 420 miles?

SOLUTION

a.

	SCALE	ACTUAL
Centimeters	0.5	4
Miles	35	x

Thus, $\dfrac{0.5}{35} = \dfrac{4}{x}$. Solving, we obtain $x = \dfrac{35 \cdot 4}{0.5}$, or $x = 280$.

b.

	SCALE	ACTUAL
Centimeters	0.5	y
Miles	35	420

Thus, $\dfrac{0.5}{35} = \dfrac{y}{420}$, or $\dfrac{0.5 \times 420}{35} = y$. Therefore, $y = \dfrac{210}{35} = 6$ centimeters. ■

NCTM Standard
All students should develop, analyze, and explain methods for solving problems involving proportions such as scaling and finding equivalent ratios.

Example 7.25 could have been solved mentally by using the following mental technique called **scaling up/scaling down**, that is, by multiplying/dividing each number in a ratio by the same number. In Example 7.25(a) we can scale up as follows:

$$0.5 \text{ centimeter} : 35 \text{ miles} = 1 \text{ centimeter} : 70 \text{ miles}$$
$$= 2 \text{ centimeters} : 140 \text{ miles}$$
$$= 4 \text{ centimeters} : 280 \text{ miles}.$$

Similarly, the number of centimeters representing 420 miles in Example 7.25(b) could have been found mentally by scaling up as follows:

$$35 \text{ miles} : 0.5 \text{ centimeter} = 70 \text{ miles} : 1 \text{ centimeter}$$
$$= 6 \times 70 \text{ miles} : 6 \times 1 \text{ centimeters}.$$

Thus, 420 miles is represented by 6 centimeters.

In Example 7.23, to solve the proportion $4:6 = x:15$, the ratio $4:6$ was scaled down to $2:3$, then $2:3$ was scaled up to $10:15$. Thus $x = 10$.

Example 7.26   Two neighbors were trying to decide whether their property taxes were fair. The assessed value of one house was $175,800 and its tax bill was $2777.64. The other house had a tax bill of $3502.85 and was assessed at $189,300. Were the two houses taxed at the same rate?

SOLUTION   Since the ratio of property taxes to assessed values should be the same, the following equation should be a proportion:

$$\frac{2777.64}{175{,}800} = \frac{3502.85}{189{,}300}$$

Equivalently, we should have $2777.64 \times 189{,}300 = 175{,}800 \times 3502.85$. Using a calculator, $2777.64 \times 189{,}300 = 525{,}807{,}252$ and $3502.85 \times 175{,}800 = 615{,}801{,}030$. Thus, the two houses are not taxed the same, since $525{,}807{,}252 \neq 615{,}801{,}030$.

An alternative solution to this problem would be to determine the tax rate per $1000 for each house.

First house: $\dfrac{2777.64}{175{,}800} = \dfrac{r}{1000}$ yields $r = \$15.80$ per $1000.

Second house: $\dfrac{3502.85}{189{,}3000} = \dfrac{r}{1000}$ yields $r = \$18.50$ per $1000.

Thus, it is likely that two digits of one of the tax rates were accidentally interchanged when calculating one of the bills. ∎

✔ **Check for Understanding:** Exercise/Problem Set A #6–11

MATHEMATICAL MORSEL

The famous mathematician Pythagoras founded a school that bore his name. As lore has it, to lure a young student to study at this school, he agreed to pay the student a penny for every theorem the student mastered. The student, motivated by the penny-a-theorem offer, studied intently and accumulated a huge sum of pennies. However, he so enjoyed the geometry that he begged Pythagoras for more theorems to prove. Pythagoras agreed to provide him with more theorems, but for a price—namely, a penny a theorem. Soon, Pythagoras had all his pennies back, in addition to a sterling student.

Section 7.3   EXERCISE / PROBLEM SET A

EXERCISES

1. The ratio of girls to boys in a particular classroom is 6:5.
   a. What is the ratio of boys to girls?
   b. What fraction of the total number of students are boys?
   c. How many boys are in the class?
   d. How many boys are in the class if there are 33 students?

2. Explain how each of the following rates satisfies the definition of ratio. Give an example of how each is used.
   a. 250 miles/11.6 gallons
   b. 25 dollars/3.5 hours
   c. 1 dollar (American)/0.65 dollar (Canadian)
   d. 2.5 dollars/0.96 pound

3. Write a fraction in the simplest form that is equivalent to each ratio.
   a. 16 to 64
   b. 30 to 75
   c. 82.5 to 16.5

4. Determine whether the given ratios are equal.
   a. 3:4 and 15:22
   b. 11:6 and 66:36

5. When blood cholesterol levels are tested, sometimes a cardiac risk ratio is calculated.

   $$\text{Cardiac risk ratio} = \frac{\text{total cholesterol level}}{\text{high-density lipoprotein level (HDL)}}$$

   For women, a ratio between 3.0 and 4.5 is desirable. A woman's blood test yields an HDL cholesterol level of 60 mg/dL and a total cholesterol level of 225 mg/dL. What is her cardiac risk ratio, expressed as a one-place decimal? Is her ratio in the normal range?

6. Solve each proportion for n.
   a. $\dfrac{n}{70} = \dfrac{6}{21}$ **b.** $\dfrac{n}{84} = \dfrac{3}{14}$ **c.** $\dfrac{7}{n} = \dfrac{42}{48}$ **d.** $\dfrac{12}{n} = \dfrac{18}{45}$

7. Solve each proportion for x. Round each answer to two decimal places.

a. $16:125 = x:5$ b. $\dfrac{9}{7} = \dfrac{10.8}{x}$

c. $\dfrac{35.2}{19.6} = \dfrac{5}{3x}$ d. $\dfrac{x}{4-x} = \dfrac{3}{4}$

e. $\dfrac{3\frac{1}{4}}{2\frac{1}{4}} = \dfrac{x}{1\frac{1}{2}}$ f. $\dfrac{2x}{x+10} = \dfrac{0.04}{1.85}$

8. Write three other proportions for the given proportion.

$$\dfrac{36 \text{ cents}}{18 \text{ ounces}} = \dfrac{42 \text{ cents}}{21 \text{ ounces}}$$

9. Solve these proportions mentally by scaling up or scaling down.
a. 24 miles for 2 gallons is equal to _____ miles for 16 gallons.
b. \$13.50 for 1 day is equal to _____ for 6 days.

c. 300 miles in 12 hours is equal to _____ miles in 8 hours. (*Hint:* Scale down to 4 hours, then scale up to 8 hours.)
d. 20 inches in 15 hours is equal to 16 inches in _____ hours.
e. 32 cents for 8 ounces is equal to _____ cents for 12 ounces.

10. If you are traveling 100 kilometers per hour, how fast are you traveling in mph? For this exercise, use 50 mph = 80 kph (kilometers per hour). (The exact metric equivalent is 80.4672 kph.)

11. Which of the following is the better buy?
a. 67 cents for 58 ounces or 17 cents for 15 ounces
b. 29 ounces for 13 cents or 56 ounces for 27 cents
c. 17 ounces for 23 cents, 25 ounces for 34 cents, or 73 ounces for 96 cents

PROBLEMS

12. Grape juice concentrate is mixed with water in a ratio of 1 part concentrate to 3 parts water. How much grape juice can be made from a 10-ounce can of concentrate?

13. A crew clears brush from $\frac{1}{2}$ acre of land in 3 days. How long will it take the same crew to clear the entire plot of $2\frac{3}{4}$ acres?

14. A recipe for peach cobbler calls for 6 small peaches for 4 servings. If a large quantity is to be prepared to serve 10 people, about how many peaches would be needed?

15. Dan used a 128-ounce bottle of liquid laundry detergent over a period of $6\frac{1}{2}$ weeks. About how many ounces of liquid laundry detergent will he probably purchase in a year's time if this use of detergent is typical?

16. If a 92-year-old man has averaged 8 hours per 24-hour day sleeping, how many years of his life has he been asleep?

17. A man who weighs 175 pounds on Earth would weigh 28 pounds on the moon. How much would his 30-pound dog weigh on the moon?

18. Suppose that you drive an average of 4460 miles every half-year in your car. At the end of $2\frac{3}{4}$ years, how far will your car have gone?

19. Becky is climbing a hill that has a 17° slope. For every 5 feet she gains in altitude, she travels about 16.37 horizontal feet. If at the end of her uphill climb she has traveled 1 mile horizontally, how much altitude has she gained?

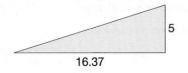

20. The *Spruce Goose*, a wooden flying boat built for Howard Hughes, had the world's largest wingspan, 319 ft 11 in. according to the *Guinness Book of World Records*. It flew only once in 1947, for a distance of about 1000 yards. Shelly wants to build a scale model of the 218 ft 8 in.–long *Spruce Goose*. If her model will be 20 inches long, what will its wingspan be (to the nearest inch)?

21. Jefferson School has 1400 students. The teacher–pupil ratio is 1:35.
a. How many additional teachers will have to be hired to reduce the ratio to 1:20?
b. If the teacher–pupil ratio remains at 1:35 and if the cost to the district for one teacher is \$33,000 per year, how much will be spent per pupil per year?
c. Answer part (b) for a ratio of 1:20.

22. An **astronomical unit (AU)** is a measure of distance used by astronomers. In October 1985 the relative distance from Earth to Mars in comparison with the distance from Earth to Pluto was 1:12.37.
a. If Pluto was 30.67 AU from Earth in October 1985, how many astronomical units from Earth was Mars?
b. Earth is always about 1 AU from the sun (in fact, this is the basis of this unit of measure). In October 1985, Pluto was about 2.85231×10^9 miles from Earth. About how many miles is Earth from the sun?
c. In October 1985 about how many miles was Mars from Earth?

23. According to the "big-bang" hypothesis, the universe was formed approximately 10^{10} years ago. The analogy of a 24-hour day is often used to put the passage of this amount

of time into perspective. Imagine that the universe was formed at midnight 24 hours ago and answer the following questions.

a. To how many years of actual time does 1 hour correspond?

b. To how many years of actual time does 1 minute correspond?

c. To how many years of actual time does 1 second correspond?

d. The Earth was formed, according to the hypothesis, approximately 5 billion years ago. To what time in the 24-hour day does this correspond?

e. Earliest known humanlike remains have been determined by radioactive dating to be approximately 2.6 million years old. At what time of the 24-hour day did the creatures who left these remains die?

f. Intensive agriculture and the growth of modern civilization may have begun as early as 10,000 years ago. To what time of the 24-hour day does this correspond?

24. Cary was going to meet Jane at the airport. If he traveled 60 mph, he would arrive 1 hour early, and if he traveled 30 mph, he would arrive 1 hour late. How far was the airport? (*Recall:* Distance = rate · time.)

25. Seven children each had a different number of pennies. The ratio of each child's total to the next poorer was a whole number. Altogether they had $28.79. How much did each have?

26. Two baseball batters, Eric and Morgan, each get 31 hits in 69 at-bats. In the next week, Eric slumps to 1 hit in 27 at-bats and Morgan bats 4 for 36 (1 out of 9). Without doing any calculations, which batter do you think has the higher average? Check your answer by calculating the two averages (the number of hits divided by the number of times at bat).

27. A woman has equal numbers of pennies, nickels, and dimes. If the total value of the coins is $12.96, how many dimes does she have?

28. A man walked into a store to buy a hat. The hat he selected cost $20. He said to his father, "If you will lend me as much money as I have in my pocket, I will buy that $20 hat." The father agreed. Then they did it again with a $20 pair of slacks and again with a $20 pair of shoes. The man was finally out of money. How much did he have when he walked into the store?

29. What is the largest sum of money in U.S. coins that you could have without being able to give change for a nickel, dime, quarter, half-dollar, or dollar?

30. Beginning with 100, each of two persons, in turn, subtracts a single-digit number. The player who ends at zero is the loser. Can you explain how to play so that one player always wins?

31. How can you cook something for exactly 15 minutes if all you have are a 7-minute and an 11-minute egg timer?

32. Twelve posts stand equidistant along a race track. Starting at the first post, a runner reaches the eighth post in 8 seconds. If she runs at a constant velocity, how many seconds are needed to reach the twelfth post?

33. Melvina was planning a long trip by car. She knew she could average about 180 miles in 4 hours, but she was trying to figure out how much farther she could get each day if she and her friend (who drives about the same speed) shared the driving and they drove for 10 hours per day. She figured they could travel an extra 450 miles, so altogether they could do 630 miles a day. Is she on track? How would you explain this?

Section 7.3 EXERCISE / PROBLEM SET B

EXERCISES

1. Write a ratio based on each of the following.

a. Two-fifths of Ted's garden is planted in tomatoes.

b. The certificate of deposit you purchased earns $6.18 interest on every $100 you deposit.

c. Three out of every four voters surveyed favor ballot measure 5.

d. There are five times as many boys as girls in Mr. Wright's physics class.

e. There are half as many sixth graders in Fremont School as eighth graders.

f. Nine of every 16 students in the hot-lunch line are girls.

2. Explain how each of the following rates satisfies the definition of ratio. Give an example of how each is used.

a. 1580 people/square mile

b. 450 people/year

c. 360 kilowatt-hours/4 months

d. 355 calories/6 ounces

3. Write a fraction in the simplest form that is equivalent to each ratio.

a. 17 to 119

b. 26 to 91

c. 97.5 to 66.3

4. Determine whether the given ratios are equal.
  a. $5:8$ and $15:25$
  b. $7:12$ and $36:60$

5. In one analysis of people of the world, it was reported that of every 1000 people of the world the following numbers speak the indicated language as their native tongue.

> 165 speak Mandarin
>
> 86 speak English
>
> 83 speak Hindi/Urdu
>
> 64 speak Spanish
>
> 58 speak Russian
>
> 37 speak Arabic

  a. Find the ratio of Spanish speakers to Russian speakers.
  b. Find the ratio of Arabic speakers to English speakers.
  c. The ratio of which two groups is nearly $2:1$?
  d. Find the ratio of persons who speak Mandarin, English, or Hindi/Urdu to the total group of 1000 people.
  e. What fraction of persons in the group of 1000 world citizens are *not* accounted for in this list? These persons speak one of the more than 200 other languages spoken in the world today.

6. Solve for the unknown in each of the following proportions.
  a. $\dfrac{\frac{3}{5}}{6} = \dfrac{D}{25}$ **b.** $\dfrac{B}{8} = \dfrac{2\frac{1}{4}}{18}$ **c.** $\dfrac{X}{100} = \dfrac{4.8}{1.5}$
  d. $\dfrac{57.4}{39.6} = \dfrac{7.4}{P}$ (to one decimal place)

7. Solve each proportion for x. Round your answers to two decimal places where decimal answers do not terminate.
  a. $\dfrac{7}{5} = \dfrac{x}{40}$ **b.** $\dfrac{12}{35} = \dfrac{40}{x}$ **c.** $2:9 = x:3$
  d. $\dfrac{3}{4}:8 = 9:x$ **e.** $\dfrac{15}{32} = \dfrac{x}{x+2}$ **f.** $\dfrac{3x}{4} = \dfrac{12-x}{6}$

8. Write three other proportions for each given proportion.

$$\frac{35 \text{ miles}}{2 \text{ hours}} = \frac{87.5 \text{ miles}}{5 \text{ hours}}$$

9. Solve these proportions mentally by scaling up or scaling down.
  a. 26 miles for 6 hours is equal to _____ miles for 24 hours.
  b. 84 ounces for each 6 square inches is equal to _____ ounces for each 15 square inches.
  c. 40 inches in 12 hours is equal to _____ inches in 9 hours.
  d. $27.50 for 1.5 days is equal to _____ for 6 days.
  e. 750 people for each 12 square miles is equal to _____ people for each 16 square miles.

10. If you are traveling 55 mph, how fast are you traveling in kph?

11. Determine which of the following is the better buy.
  a. 60 ounces for 29 cents or 84 ounces for 47 cents
  b. $45 for 10 yards of material or $79 for 15 yards
  c. 18 ounces for 40 cents, 20 ounces for 50 cents, or 30 ounces for 75 cents (*Hint:* How much does $1 purchase in each case?)

PROBLEMS

12. Three car batteries are advertised with warranties as follows.

> Model *XA*: 40-month warranty, $34.95
>
> Model *XL*: 50-month warranty, $39.95
>
> Model *XT*: 60-month warranty, $49.95

Considering only the warranties and the prices, which model of car battery is the best buy?

13. Cari walked 3.4 kilometers in 45 minutes. At that rate, how long will it take her to walk 11.2 kilometers? Round to the nearest minute.

14. A family uses 5 gallons of milk every 3 weeks. At that rate, how many gallons of milk will they need to purchase in a year's time?

15. A couple was assessed property taxes of $1938.90 on a home valued at $168,600. What might Frank expect to pay in property taxes on a home he hopes to purchase in the same neighborhood if it has a value of $181,300? Round to the nearest dollar.

16. By reading just a few pages at night before falling asleep, Randy finished a 248-page book in $4\frac{1}{2}$ weeks. He just started a new book of 676 pages. About how long should it take him to finish the new book if he reads at the same rate?

17. a. If 1 inch on a map represents 35 miles, how many miles are represented by 3 inches? 10 inches? n inches?
  b. Los Angeles is about 1000 miles from Portland. About how many inches apart would Portland and Los Angeles be on this map?

18. A farmer calculates that out of every 100 seeds of corn he plants, he harvests 84 ears of corn. If he wants to harvest 7200 ears of corn, how many seeds must he plant?

19. A map is drawn to scale such that $\frac{1}{8}$ inch represents 65 feet. If the shortest route from your house to the grocery store measures $23\frac{7}{16}$ inches, how many miles is it to the grocery store?

20. a. If $1\frac{3}{4}$ cups of flour are required to make 28 cookies, how many cups are required for 88 cookies?
  b. If your car gets 32 miles per gallon, how many gallons do you use on a 160-mile trip?
  c. If your mechanic suggests 3 parts antifreeze to 4 parts water, and if your radiator is 14 liters, how many liters of antifreeze should you use?
  d. If 11 ounces of roast beef cost $1.86, how much does roast beef cost per pound?

21. Two professional drag racers are speeding down a $\frac{1}{4}$-mile track. If the lead driver is traveling 1.738 feet for every 1.670 feet that the trailing car travels, and if the trailing car is going 198 miles per hour, how fast in miles per hour is the lead car traveling?

22. In 1994, the Internal Revenue Service audited 107 of every 10,000 individual returns.
 a. In a community in which 12,500 people filed returns, how many returns might be expected to be audited?
 b. In 1996, 163 returns per 10,000 were audited. How many more of the 12,500 returns would be expected to be audited for 1996 than for 1994?

23. a. A baseball pitcher has pitched a total of 25 innings so far during the season and has allowed 18 runs. At this rate, how many runs, to the nearest hundredth, would he allow in nine innings? This number is called the pitcher's **earned run average**, or ERA.
 b. Randy Johnson of the Arizona Diamondbacks had an ERA of 2.64 in 2000. At that rate, how many runs would he be expected to allow in 100 innings pitched? Round your answer to the nearest whole number.

24. Many tires come with $\frac{13}{32}$ inch of tread on them. The first $\frac{2}{32}$ inch wears off quickly (say, during the first 1000 miles). From then on the tire wears uniformly (and more slowly). A tire is considered "worn out" when only $\frac{2}{32}$ inch of tread is left.
 a. How many 32nds of an inch of usable tread does a tire have after 1000 miles?
 b. A tire has traveled 20,000 miles and has $\frac{5}{32}$ inch of tread remaining. At this rate, how many total miles should the tire last before it is considered worn out?

25. In classroom A, there are 12 boys and 15 girls. In classroom B, there are 8 boys and 6 girls. In classroom C, there are 4 boys and 5 girls.
 a. Which two classrooms have the same boys-to-girls ratio?
 b. On one occasion classroom A joined classroom B. What was the resulting boys-to-girls ratio?
 c. On another occasion classroom C joined classroom B. What was the resulting ratio of boys to girls?
 d. Are your answers to parts (b) and (c) equivalent? What does this tell you about adding ratios?

26. An old picture frame has dimensions 33 inches by 24 inches. What one length must be cut from each dimension so that the ratio of the shorter side to the longer side is $\frac{2}{3}$?

27. The Greek musical scale, which very closely resembles the 12-note tempered scale used today, is based on ratios of frequencies. To hear the first and fifth tones of the scale is equivalent to hearing the ratio $\frac{3}{2}$, which is the ratio of their frequencies.

 a. If the frequency of middle C is 256 vibrations per second, find the frequencies of each of the other notes given. For example, since G is a fifth above middle C, it follows that G : 256 = 3 : 2 or G = 384 vibrations/second. (NOTE: Proceeding beyond B would give sharps, below F, flats.)
 b. Two notes are an octave apart if the frequency of one is double the frequency of the other. For example, the frequency of C above middle C is 512 vibrations per second. Using the values found in part (a), find the frequencies of the corresponding notes in the octave above middle C (in the following range).

256512
C   DEFGABC

 c. The aesthetic effect of a chord depends on the ratio of its frequencies. Find the following ratios of seconds.

D : C   E : D   A : G

 What simple ratio are these equivalent to?
 d. Find the following ratio of fourths.

F : C   G : D   A : E

 What simple ratio are these equivalent to?

28. Ferne, Donna, and Susan have just finished playing three games. There was only one loser in each game. Ferne lost the first game, Donna lost the second game, and Susan lost the third game. After each game, the loser was required to double the money of the other two. After three rounds, each woman had $24. How much did each have at the start?

29. A ball, when dropped from any height, bounces $\frac{1}{3}$ of the original height. If the ball is dropped, bounces back up, and continues to bounce up and down so that it has traveled 106 feet when it strikes the ground for the fourth time, what is the original height from which it was dropped?

30. Mary had a basket of hard-boiled eggs to sell. She first sold half her eggs plus half an egg. Next she sold half her eggs and half an egg. The same thing occurred on her third, fourth, and fifth times. When she finished, she had no eggs in her basket. How many did she have when she started?

31. Joleen had a higher batting average than Maureen for the first half of the season, and Joleen also had a higher batting average than Maureen for the second half of the season. Does it follow that Joleen had a better batting average than Maureen for the entire season? Why or why not?

32. A box contains three different varieties of apples. What is the smallest number of apples that must be taken to be sure of getting at least 2 of one kind? How about at least 3 of one kind? How about at least 10 of a kind? How about at least n of a kind?

33. Ms. Price has three times as many girls as boys in her class. Ms. Lippy has twice as many girls as boys. Ms. Price has 60 students in her class and Ms. Lippy has 135 students. If the classes were combined into one, what would be the ratio of girls to boys?

Analyzing Student Thinking

34. Carlos says that if the ratio of oil to vinegar in a salad dressing is 3 : 4, that means that 75% of the dressing is oil. How should you respond?

35. Scott heard that the ratio of boys to girls in his class next year was going to be 5 : 4. He asks, "Does that mean that there are going to be 5 boys in my class?" How should you respond?

36. Ashlee writes that for ratios a/b and c/d, if $a/b = c/d$, then $a/c = b/d$. Is she correct? Explain.

37. Caleb used scaling up to find how many miles would be represented by 8 meters if 0.25 centimeters represents 12 miles as follows: 0.25 cm : 12 miles = 100 cm : 48 miles = 800 cm : 384 miles. Is this correct? Explain.

38. When mixing orange juice concentrate, the ratio of juice to water is 1 : 3. Micala thought that using 2 cans of juice would require using 4 cans of water or a ratio of 2 : 4 to have the same flavor. What is Micala's misunderstanding?

39. Sabrina noticed that 60% of her English class was girls and so she concluded that the ratio of girls to boys was 3 : 5. Is she correct? Explain.

40. Marvin is trying to find the height of a tree in the school yard. He is using the proportion

$$\frac{\text{Marvin's height}}{\text{Marvin's shadow length}} = \frac{\text{tree's height}}{\text{tree's shadow length}}$$

His height is 4 feet. His shadow length is 15 inches. The length of the tree's shadow is 12 feet. Marvin used the proportion $\dfrac{4}{15} = \dfrac{\text{tree's height}}{12}$. But that gave the tree's height as being shorter than Marvin's! What went wrong?

Problems Relating to the NCTM Standards and Curriculum Focal Points

1. The Focal Points for Grade 7 state "Developing an understanding of and applying proportionality, including similarity." A student says that because he needs 3 cans of water to mix with 1 can of orange juice then he will need 5 cans of water to mix with 3 cans of orange juice. Explain what aspect of proportionality this student does not understand.

2. The NCTM Standards state "All students should solve simple problems involving rates and derived measurements for such attributes as velocity and density." Provide two examples that satisfy this statement and justify your choices.

3. The NCTM Standards state "All students should develop, analyze, and explain methods for solving problems involving proportions such as scaling and finding equivalent ratios." Explain what is meant by the method of "scaling" for solving proportion problems.

7.4   PERCENT

STARTING POINT If the wholesale price of a jacket is marked up 40% to obtain the retail price and the retail price is then marked down 40% to a sale price, are the wholesale price and the sale price the same? If not, explain why not and determine which is larger.

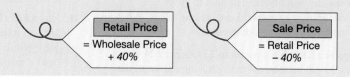

Converting Percents

Like ratios, percents are used and seen commonly in everyday life.

Example 7.27

a. The Dow Jones stock index declined by 1.93%.
b. The BYU basketball team made 41.3% of the three-point shots they attempted.

c. A spring clearance sale advertised jeans at 30% off the retail price.
d. The land prices in Mapleton today are up 150% from 5 years ago.

In each case, the percent represents a ratio, a fraction, or a decimal. The percent in part b represents the fact that a basketball team made 247 out of 598 three-point shots, a ratio of $\frac{247}{598}$ or about .413. Thus, it was reported that they made 41.3%. The jeans sale described in part c offered buyers a discount of \$18 off of \$60. This fraction $\frac{18}{60}$ is equal to 0.3 or 30%. ∎

The word **percent** has a Latin origin that means "per hundred." Thus 25 percent means 25 per hundred, $\frac{25}{100}$, or 0.25. The symbol "%" is used to represent percent. So 420% means $\frac{420}{100}$, 4.20, or 420 per hundred. In general, $n\%$ represents the ratio $\frac{n}{100}$.

Since percents are alternative representations of fractions and decimals, it is important to be able to convert among all three forms, as suggested in Figure 7.12.

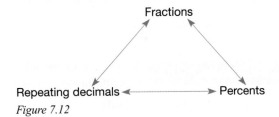

Figure 7.12

Since we have studied converting fractions to decimals, and vice versa, there are only four cases of conversion left to consider in Figure 7.12.

Case 1: Percents to Fractions

Use the definition of *percent*. For example, $63\% = \frac{63}{100}$ by the meaning of *percent*.

Case 2: Percents to Decimals

Since we know how to convert fractions to decimals, we can use this skill to convert percents to fractions and then to decimals. For example, $63\% = \frac{63}{100} = 0.63$ and $27\% = \frac{27}{100} = 0.27$. These two examples suggest the following shortcut, which eliminates the conversion to a fraction step. Namely, to convert a percent directly to a decimal, "drop the % symbol and move the number's decimal point two places to the *left*." Thus $31\% = 0.31$, $213\% = 2.13$, $0.5\% = .005$, and so on. These examples can also be seen visually in Figure 7.13 on a 10-by-10 grid, where 31% is represented by shading 31 out of 100 squares, 213% is represented by shading 213 squares (2 full grids and 13 squares on a third grid), and 0.5% is represented by shading half of 1 square on the grid.

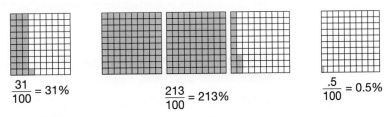

$\frac{31}{100} = 31\%$ $\frac{213}{100} = 213\%$ $\frac{.5}{100} = 0.5\%$

Figure 7.13

NCTM Standard
All students should recognize
and generate equivalent forms
of commonly used fractions,
decimals, and percents.

Case 3: Decimals to Percents

Here we merely reverse the shortcut in case 2. For example, $0.83 = 83\%$, $5.1 = 510\%$, and $0.0001 = 0.01\%$ where the percents are obtained from the decimals by "moving the decimal point two places to the *right* and writing the % symbol on the *right* side."

Case 4: Fractions to Percents

Some fractions that have terminating decimals can be converted to percents by expressing the fraction with a denominator of 100. For example, $\frac{17}{100} = 17\%$, $\frac{2}{5} = \frac{4}{100} = \frac{40}{100} = 40\%$, $\frac{3}{25} = \frac{12}{100} = 12\%$, and so on. Also, fractions can be converted to decimals (using a calculator or long division), and then case 3 can be applied.

A calculator is useful when converting fractions to percents. For example,

$$3 \boxed{\div} 13 \boxed{=} \boxed{0.23076923}$$

shows that $\frac{3}{13} \approx 0.23$ or 23%. Also,

$$5 \boxed{\div} 9 \boxed{=} \boxed{0.555555556}$$

shows that $\frac{5}{9} \approx 56\%$.

NCTM Standard
All students should work
flexibly with fractions, decimals,
and percents to solve problems.

Example 7.28 Write each of the following in all three forms: decimal, percent, fraction (in simplest form).

a. 32% **b.** 0.24 **c.** 450% **d.** $\frac{1}{16}$

SOLUTION

a. $32\% = 0.32 = \frac{32}{100} = \frac{8}{25}$

b. $0.24 = 24\% = \frac{24}{100} = \frac{6}{25}$

c. $450\% = \frac{450}{100} = 4.5 = 4\frac{1}{2}$

d. $\frac{1}{16} = \frac{1}{2^4} = \frac{1 \cdot 5^4}{2^4 \cdot 5^4} = \frac{625}{10,000} = 0.0625 = \frac{6.25}{100} = 6.25\%$ ∎

✔ **Check for Understanding:** Exercise/Problem Set A #1–2

TABLE 7.2

PERCENT	FRACTION
5%	$\frac{1}{20}$
10%	$\frac{1}{10}$
20%	$\frac{1}{5}$
25%	$\frac{1}{4}$
$33\frac{1}{3}$	$\frac{1}{3}$
50%	$\frac{1}{2}$
$66\frac{2}{3}$	$\frac{2}{3}$
75%	$\frac{3}{4}$

Mental Math and Estimation Using Fraction Equivalents

Since many commonly used percents have convenient fraction equivalents, it is often easier to find the percent of a number mentally, using fractions (Table 7.2). Also, as was the case with proportions, percentages of numbers can be estimated by choosing compatible fractions.

Example 7.29 Find the following percents mentally, using fraction equivalents.

a. 25% × 44 **b.** 75% × 24 **c.** 50% × 76
d. $33\frac{1}{3}\%$ × 93 **e.** 38% × 50 **f.** 84% × 25

SOLUTION

a. $25 \times 44 = \frac{1}{4} \times 44 = 11$ **b.** $75\% \times 24 = \frac{3}{4} \times 24 = 18$

c. $50\% \times 76 = \frac{1}{2} \times 76 = 38$ **d.** $33\frac{1}{3}\% \times 93 = \frac{1}{3} \times 93 = 31$

e. $38\% \times 50 = 38 \times 50\% = 38 \times \frac{1}{2} = 19$

f. $84\% \times 25 = 84 \times 25\% = 84 \times \frac{1}{4} = 21$ ■

Example 7.30 Estimate the following percents mentally, using fraction equivalents.

a. $48\% \times 73$ **b.** $32\% \times 95$ **c.** $24\% \times 71$
d. $123\% \times 54$ **e.** $0.45\% \times 57$ **f.** $59\% \times 81$

SOLUTION

a. $48\% \times 73 \approx 50\% \times 72 = 36$. (Since $50\% > 48\%$, 73 was rounded down to 72 to compensate.)

b. $32\% \times 95 \approx 33\frac{1}{3} \times 93 = \frac{1}{3} \times 93 = 31$. (Since $33\frac{1}{3}\% > 32\%$, 95 was rounded down to 93, which is a multiple of 3.)

c. $24\% \times 71 \approx \frac{1}{4} \times 72 = \frac{1}{4} \times 8 \times 9 = 18$

d. $123\% \times 54 \approx 125\% \times 54 \approx \frac{5}{4} \times 56 = 5 \times 14 = 70$; alternatively,

$123\% \times 54 = 123 \times 54\% \approx 130 \times 50\% = 130 \times \frac{1}{2} = 65$

e. $0.45\% \times 57 \approx 0.5\% \times 50 = 0.5 \times 50\% = 0.25$

f. $59\% \times 81 \approx 60\% \times 81 \approx \frac{3}{5} \times 80 = 3 \times 16 = 48$ ■

 Check for Understanding: Exercise/Problem Set A #3–8

Reflection from Research
Students who work on decimal problems that are given in familiar, everyday contexts increase their knowledge much more significantly than those who work on noncontextualized problems (Irwin, 2001).

Solving Percent Problems

Since percents can be expressed as fractions using a denominator of 100, percent problems involve three pieces of information: a percent, p, and two numbers, a and n, as the numerator and denominator of a fraction. The relationship between these numbers is shown in the proportion

$$\frac{p}{100} = \frac{a}{n}.$$

This proportion can be rewritten as the equation $\frac{p}{100} \cdot n = a$. Related to these three quantities, there are three common types of problems involving percents and each type is determined by what piece of information is unknown: p, a, or n.

The following questions illustrate three common types of problems involving percents.

a. A car was purchased for \$13,000 with a 20% down payment. How much was the down payment?

b. One hundred sixty-two seniors, 90% of the senior class, are going on the class trip. How many seniors are there?

c. Susan scored 48 points on a 60-point test. What percent did she get correct?

There are three approaches to solving percent problems such as the preceding three problems. The first of the three approaches is the grid approach and relies on the 10-by-10 grids introduced earlier in this section. This approach is more concrete and aids in understanding the underlying concept of percents. The more common approaches, proportions and equations, are more powerful and can be used to solve a broader range of problems.

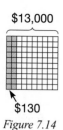

$13,000

$130

Figure 7.14

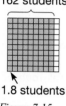

162 students

1.8 students

Figure 7.15

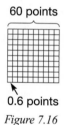

60 points

0.6 points

Figure 7.16

100%

50%

0%

Figure 7.17

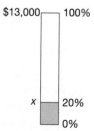

$13,000 ⌐ 100%

x ⌐ 20%

0%

Figure 7.18

Grid Approach   Since *percent* means "per hundred," solving problems to find a missing percent can be visualized by using the 10-by-10 grids introduced earlier in the section.

Example 7.31   Answer the preceding three problems using the grid approach.

SOLUTION

a. A car was purchased for $13,000 with a 20% down payment. How much was the down payment?

Let the grid in Figure 7.14 represent the total cost of the car, or $13,000. Since the down payment was 20%, shade 20 out of 100 squares. The solution can be found by reasoning that since 100 squares represent $13,000, then 1 square represents $\frac{13,000}{100} = \$130$ and therefore 20 squares represent the down payment of 20 × $130 = $2600.

b. One hundred sixty-two seniors, 90% of the senior class, are going on the class trip. How many seniors are there?

Let the grid in Figure 7.15 represent the total class size. Since 90% of the students will go on the class trip, shade 90 of the 100 squares. The reasoning used to solve this problem is that since 90 squares represent 162 students, then 1 square represents $\frac{162}{90} = 1.8$ students. Thus 100 squares, the whole class, is 100 × 1.8 = 180 students.

c. Susan scored 48 points on a 60-point test. What percent did she get correct?

Let the grid in Figure 7.16 represent all 60 points on the test. In this case, the percent is not given, so determining how many squares should be shaded to represent Susan's score of 48 points becomes the focus of the problem. Reasoning with the grid, it can be seen that since 100 squares represent 60 points, then 1 square represents 0.6 points. Thus 10 squares is 6 points and 80 squares is Susan's 6 × 8 = 48 point score. Thus she got 80% correct. ∎

Proportion Approach   Since percents can be written as a ratio, solving percent problems may be done using proportions. For problems involving percents between 0 and 100, it may be helpful to think of a fuel gauge that varies from empty (0%) to full (100%) (Figure 7.17). The next example shows how this visual device leads to solving a proportion.

Example 7.32   Answer the preceding three problems using the proportion approach.

SOLUTION

a. A car was purchased for $13,000 with a 20% down payment. How much was the down payment (Figure 7.18)?

	DOLLARS	PERCENT
Down payment	x	20
Purchase price	13,000	100

Thus $\dfrac{x}{13{,}000} = \dfrac{20}{100}$, or $x = \dfrac{13{,}000}{5} = \$2600.$

b. One hundred sixty-two seniors, 90% of the senior class, are going on the class trip. How many seniors are there (Figure 7.19)?

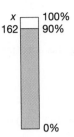

Figure 7.19

	SENIORS	PERCENT
Class trip	162	90
Class total	x	100

Thus $\dfrac{162}{x} = \dfrac{90}{100}$, or $x = 162\left(\dfrac{10}{9}\right) = 180.$

c. Susan scored 48 points on a 60-point test. What percent did she get correct (Figure 7.20)?

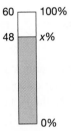

Figure 7.20

	TEST	PERCENT
Score	48	x
Total	60	100

Thus $\dfrac{48}{60} = \dfrac{x}{100}$, or $x = 100 \cdot \dfrac{4}{5} = 80.$ ■

Notice how (a), (b), and (c) lead to the following generalization:

$$\frac{\text{Part}}{\text{Whole}} = \frac{\text{percent}}{100}.$$

In other examples, if the "part" is larger than the "whole," the percent is larger than 100%.

Algebraic Reasoning
As can be seen here, equations and variables can be used to solve percent problems that are commonly found in daily life.

Equation Approach   An equation can be used to represent each of the problems in Example 7.32 as follows:

$$\text{(a) } 20\% \cdot 13{,}000 = x$$
$$\text{(b) } 90\% \cdot x = 162$$
$$\text{(c) } x\% \cdot 60 = 48.$$

The following equations illustrate these three forms, where x represents an unknown and takes the place of p, n, or a depending on what is given and what is unknown in the problem.

TRANSLATION OF PROBLEM	EQUATION
(a) $p\%$ of n is x	$\left(\dfrac{p}{100}\right)n = x$
(b) $p\%$ of x is a	$\left(\dfrac{p}{100}\right)x = a$
(c) $x\%$ of n is a	$\left(\dfrac{x}{100}\right)n = a$

Once we have obtained one of these three equations, the solution, x, can be found. In equation (a), we multiply $\dfrac{p}{100}$ and n. In equations (b) and (c) we solve for the missing factor x.

> **Example 7.33**   Solve the problems in Example 7.32 using the equation approach.

SOLUTION

a. $20\% \cdot 13{,}000 = 0.20(13{,}000) = \$2600$

b. $90\% \cdot x = 162$ or $0.9x = 162$. Thus, by the missing-factor approach, $x = 162 \div (0.9)$, or $x = 180$.   *Check:* $90\%(180) = 162$.

c. $x\% \cdot 60 = 48$, or $\dfrac{x}{100}(60) = 48$. By the missing-factor approach,

$$\frac{x}{100} = \frac{48}{60} = \frac{8}{10}, \text{ or } x = 80. \qquad Check: 80\%(60) = 48. \qquad \blacksquare$$

 A calculator can also be used to solve percent problems once the correct equations or proportions are set up. (Problems can be done using fewer keystrokes if your calculator has a percent key.) The following key sequences can be used to solve the equations arising from Example 7.31.

a. $20\% \times 13000 = x$.

$$20 \;\boxed{\%}\; \boxed{\times}\; \boxed{13000}\; \boxed{=}\; \boxed{\qquad 2600}$$

NOTE: With some calculators, the 13000 must be keyed in before the 20%. Also, the $\boxed{=}$ may not be needed in this case.

b. $90\% \times x = 162$ (or $x = 162 \div 90\%$):

$$162\; \boxed{\div}\; 90\; \boxed{\%}\; \boxed{=}\; \boxed{\qquad 180}$$

NOTE: Some calculators do not require the $\boxed{=}$ here.

c. $x\% \times 60 = 48$ (or $\dfrac{x}{100} = 48 \div 60$):

$$48\; \boxed{\div}\; 60\; \boxed{\times}\; 100\; \boxed{=}\; \boxed{\qquad 80}$$

As mentioned earlier, the proportion and equation approaches are more powerful because they can be used with a broader range of problems. For example, in Example 7.32(a), if the car costs \$13,297 instead of \$13,000 and the down payment was 22.5% instead of 20%, then the proportion and equation approaches could be used in an identical manner. However, the visualization aspect of the grid approach becomes less effective because the problems no longer deal with whole numbers.

We end this section on percent with several applications.

Reflection from Research
When presented with algebraic relationships expressed in words (e.g., There are 3 times as many girls as boys), many students translate this relationship as $3g = b$ rather than $3b = g$ (Lopez-Real, 1995).

> **Example 7.34**   Rachelle bought a dress whose original price was \$125 but was discounted 10%. What was the discounted price? Also, what is a quick way to mark down several items 10% using a calculator?

SOLUTION   The original price is \$125. The discount is $(10\%)(125)$, or \$12.50. The new price is $\$125 - \$12.50 = \$112.50$. In general, if the original price was n, the discount would be $(10\%)n$. Then the new price would be $n - (10\%)n = n - (0.1)n = 0.9n$. $\blacksquare$

If many prices were to be discounted 10%, the new prices could be found by multiplying the old price by 0.9, or 90%. If your calculator has a percent key, the solution to the original problem would be

$$125 \boxed{\times} \; 90 \; \boxed{\%} \; \boxed{=} \; \boxed{112.50}.$$

(NOTE: It is not necessary to use the percent key; we could simply multiply by 0.9.)

Example 7.35   A television set is put on sale at 28% off the regular price. The sale price is $379. What was the regular price?

SOLUTION   The sale price is 72% of the regular price (since 100% − 28% = 72%). Let P be the regular price. Then, in proportion form,

$$\frac{72}{100} = \frac{379}{P} \left(\frac{\text{sale price}}{\text{regular price}} \right)$$

$$72 \times P = 379 \times 100 = 37{,}900$$

$$P = \frac{37{,}900}{72} = \$526.39, \text{ rounding to the nearest cent.}$$

Check: $(0.72)(526.39) = 379$, rounding to the nearest dollar.   ■

Example 7.36   Suppose that Irene's credit-card balance is $576. If the monthly interest rate is 1.5% (i.e., 18% per year), what will this debt be at the end of 5 months if she makes no payments to reduce her balance?

SOLUTION   The amount of interest accrued by the end of the first month is 1.5% × 576, or $8.64, so the balance at the end of the first month is $576 + $8.64, or $584.64. The interest at the end of the second month would be (1.5%)(584.64), or $8.77 (rounding to the nearest cent), so the balance at the end of the second month would be $593.41. Continuing in this manner, the balance at the end of the fifth month would be $620.52. Can you see why this is called compound interest?   ■

A much faster way to solve this problem is to use the technique illustrated in Example 7.34. The balance at the end of a month can be found by multiplying the balance from the end of the previous month by 1.015 (this is equal to 100% + 1.5%). Then, using your calculator, the computation for the balance after five months would be

$$576(1.015)(1.015)(1.015)(1.015)(1.015) = 576(1.015)^5 = 620.52.$$

Algebraic Reasoning
One of the common techniques in algebra is generalizing patterns. In the calculator example at the right, the pattern of repeatedly multiplying by 1.015 is generalized to using exponents, $(1.015)^x$, which simplifies the expression.

If your calculator has a constant function, your number of key presses would be reduced considerably. Here is a sequence of steps that works on many calculators.

$$1.015 \; \boxed{\times} \; \boxed{=} \; \boxed{=} \; \boxed{=} \; \boxed{=} \; \boxed{\times} \; 576 \; \boxed{=} \; \boxed{620.5155862}$$

(On some calculators you may have to press the $\boxed{\times}$ key twice after entering 1.015 to implement the constant function to repeat multiplication.) Better yet, if your calculator has a $\boxed{y^x}$ (or $\boxed{x^y}$ or $\boxed{\wedge}$) key, the following keystrokes can be used.

$$1.015 \; \boxed{y^x} \; 5 \; \boxed{\times} \; 576 \; \boxed{=} \; \boxed{620.5155862}$$

The balance at the end of a year is

$$1.015 \; \boxed{y^x} \; 12 \; \boxed{\times} \; 576 \; \boxed{=} \; \boxed{688.6760668},$$

or $688.68.

Example 7.36 illustrates a problem involving interest. Most of us encounter interest through savings, loans, credit cards, and so on. With a calculator that has an exponential key, such as $\boxed{y^x}$ or $\boxed{x^y}$, calculations that formerly were too time-consuming for the average consumer are now merely a short sequence of keystrokes. However, it is important that one understand how to set up a problem so that the calculator can be correctly used. Our last two examples illustrate how a calculator with an exponential key can be used to show the effect of compound interest.

Example 7.37   Parents want to establish a college fund for their 8-year-old daughter. The father received a bonus of $10,000. The $10,000 is deposited in a tax-deferred account guaranteed to yield at least $7\frac{3}{4}\%$ compounded quarterly. How much will be available from this account when the child is 18?

SOLUTION There are several aspects to this problem. First, one needs to understand what *compounded quarterly* means. *Compounded quarterly* means that earned interest is added to the principal amount every 3 months. Since the annual rate is $7\frac{3}{4}\%$, the quarterly rate is $\frac{1}{4}(7\frac{3}{4}\%) = 1.9375\%$. Following the ideas in Example 7.36, the principal, which is $10,000, will amount to $10,000(1.019375) = \$10,193.75$ at the end of the first quarter.

Next, one needs to determine the number of quarters (of a year) that the $10,000 will earn interest. Since the child is 8 and the money is needed when she is 18, this account will grow for 10 years (or 40 quarters). Again, following Example 7.36, after 40 quarters the $10,000 will amount to $10,000(1.019375)^{40} \approx \$21,545.63$. If the interest rate had simply been $7\frac{3}{4}\%$ per year not compounded, the $10,000 would have earned $10,000(7\frac{3}{4}\%) = \$775$ per year for each of the 10 years, or would have amounted to $\$10,000 + 10(\$775) = \$17,750$. Thus, the compounding quarterly amounted to an extra $3795.63. ■

Our last example shows you how to determine how much to save now for a specific amount at a future date.

Example 7.38   You project that you will need $20,000 before taxes in 15 years. If you find a tax-deferred investment that guarantees you 10% interest, compounded semiannually, how much should you set aside now?

SOLUTION As you may have observed while working through Examples 7.36 and 7.37, if P is the amount of your initial principal, r is the interest rate for a given period, and n is the number of payment periods for the given rate, then your final amount, A, will be given by the equation $A = P(1 + r)^n$. In this example, $A = \$20,000$, $r = \frac{1}{2}(10\%)$, since *semiannual* means "every half-year," and $n = 2 \times 15$, since there are $2 \times 15 = 30$ half-years in 15 years. Thus

$$20,000 = P[1 + \tfrac{1}{2}(0.10)]^{30} \quad \text{or} \quad P = \frac{20,000}{[1 + \tfrac{1}{2}(0.10)]^{30}}. \quad ■$$

 A calculator can be used to find the dollar value for P.

$$20000 \boxed{\div} \boxed{(} 1.05 \boxed{y^x} 30 \boxed{)} \boxed{=} \boxed{4627.548973}$$

Thus $4627.55 needs to be set aside now at 10% interest compounded semiannually to have $20,000 available in 15 years.

 Check for Understanding: Exercise/Problem Set A #9–13

MATHEMATICAL MORSEL

Two students were finalists in a free-throw shooting contest. In the two parts of the contest, the challenger had to shoot 25 free-throws in the first part, then 50 in the second part, while the champion shot 50 free-throws first and 25 second. In the first part, Vivian made 20 of 25, or 80%, and Joan made 26 of 50, or 52%. Then Vivian made 9 of 50, or 18%, and Joan made 4 of 25, or 16%. Since Vivian had a higher percentage in both parts, she declared herself to be the winner. However, Joan cried "Foul!" and claimed the totals should be counted. In that case, Vivian made 29 of 75 and Joan made 30 of 75. Who should win? This mathematical oddity can arise when data involving ratios are combined (Simpson's paradox).

Section 7.4   **EXERCISE / PROBLEM SET A**

EXERCISES

1. Each of the following grids has some shaded squares. Write the percent of squares shaded and convert that percent to a decimal and a fraction in lowest terms.

a.   **b.**   **c.**

2. Fill in this chart.

FRACTION	DECIMAL	PERCENT
_____	_____	50%
_____	0.35	_____
$\frac{1}{4}$	_____	_____
$\frac{1}{8}$	_____	_____
_____	0.0125	_____
_____	_____	125%
_____	0.75	_____

3. a. Mentally calculate each of the following.
   i. 10% of 50   **ii.** 10% of 68.7
   iii. 10% of 4.58   **iv.** 10% of 32,900

   b. Mentally calculate each of the following. Use the fact that 5% is half of 10%.
   i. 5% of 240
   ii. 5% of 18.6
   iii. 5% of 12,000
   iv. 5% of 62.56

c. Mentally calculate each of the following. Use the fact that 15% is 10% + 5%.
   i. 15% of 90
   ii. 15% of 50,400
   iii. 15% of 7.2
   iv. 15% of 0.066

4. Complete the following statements mentally.
   a. 126 is 50% of _____.   **b.** 36 is 25% of _____.
   c. 154 is $66\frac{2}{3}$% of _____.   **d.** 78 is 40% of _____.
   e. 50 is 125% of _____.   **f.** 240 is 300% of _____.

5. Solve mentally.
   a. 56 is _____% of 100.   **b.** 38 is _____% of 50.
   c. 17 is _____% of 25.   **d.** 7.5 is _____% of 20.
   e. 75 is _____% of 50.   **f.** 40 is _____% of 30.

6. Mentally find the following percents using fraction equivalents.
   a. 50% of 64   **b.** 25% of 148   **c.** 75% of 244
   d. $33\frac{1}{3}$% of 210   **e.** 20% of 610   **f.** 60% of 450

7. Estimate.
   a. 39% of 72   **b.** 58.7% of 31   **c.** 123% of 59
   d. 0.48% of 207   **e.** 18% of 76   **f.** 9.3% of 315
   g. 0.97% of 63   **h.** 412% of 185

8. A generous tip at a restaurant is 20%. Mentally estimate the amount of tip to leave for each of the following check amounts.
   a. $23.72   **b.** $13.10   **c.** $67.29   **d.** $32.41

9. As discussed in this section, percent problems can be solved using three different methods: (i) grids, (ii) proportions, and (iii) equations. For each of the following problems (i) set up a grid with appropriate shading, (ii) set up a proportion similar to the one below, and (iii) set up an equation. Select one of these methods to solve the problem.

$$\frac{\text{Part}}{\text{Whole}} = \frac{\text{percent}}{100}$$

Finally, enter the proportion that you have determined into the Chapter 7 eManipulative activity *Percent Gauge* on our Web site and check your solution.

a. 42 is what percent of 75?
b. 17% of 964 is what number?
c. 156.6 is 37% of what number?
d. $8\frac{3}{4}$ is what percent of $12\frac{1}{3}$?
e. 225% of what number is $12\frac{1}{3}$?

10. Answer the following and round to one decimal place.
a. Find 24% of 140.
b. Find $3\frac{1}{2}$% of 78.
c. Find 32.7% of 252.
d. What percent of 23 is 11.2?
e. What percent of 1.47 is 0.816?
f. 21 is 17% of what number?

g. What percent of $\frac{1}{4}$ is $\frac{1}{12}$?
h. 512 is 240% of what number?
i. 140% of a number is 0.65. Find the number.
j. Find $\frac{1}{2}$% of 24.6.

11. Use your calculator to find the following percents.
a. 63% of 90 is _____.
b. 27.5% of 420 is _____.
c. 31.3% of 1200 is _____.
d. 147 is 42% of _____.
e. 3648 is 128% of _____.
f. 0.5% of _____ is 78.4.

12. Calculate the following using a percent key.
a. 150% of 86
b. 63% of 49
c. 40% of what number is 75?
d. 65 is what percent of 104?
e. A discount of 15% on $37
f. A mark up of 28% on $50

13. Compute each of the following to the nearest cent.
a. 33.3% of $62.75
b. 5.6% of $138.53
c. 91% of $543.87
d. 66.7% of $374.68

PROBLEMS

14. A 4200-pound automobile contains 357 pounds of rubber. What percent of the car's total weight is rubber? Set up a proportion to solve this problem in the Chapter 7 eManipulative activity *Percent Gauge* on our Web site. Describe the setup and the solution.

15. The senior class consists of 2780 students. If 70% of the students will graduate, how many students will graduate? Set up a proportion to solve this problem in the Chapter 7 eManipulative activity *Percent Gauge* on our Web site. Describe the setup and the solution.

16. An investor earned $208.76 in interest in one year on an account that paid 4.25% simple interest.
a. What was the value of the account at the end of that year?
b. How much more interest would the account have earned at a rate of 5.33%?

17. Suppose that you have borrowed $100 at the daily interest rate of 0.04839%. How much would you save by paying the entire $100.00 15 days before it is due?

18. A basketball team played 35 games. They lost 2 games. What percent of the games played did they lose? What percent did they win?

19. In 1997, total individual charitable contributions increased by 73% from 1990 contributions.
a. If a total of $9.90 × 10^{10} was donated to charity in 1997, what amount was donated to charity in 1990?

b. The average charitable contribution increased from $1958 to $3041 over the same period. What was the percent increase in average charitable contributions from 1990 to 1997?

20. The following pie chart shows the sources of U.S. energy production in 1999 in quadrillion BTUs.

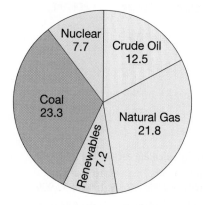

a. How much energy was produced, from all sources, in the United States in 1999?
b. What percent of the energy produced in the United States in 1999 came from each of the sources? Round your answers to the nearest tenth of a percent.

21. A clothing store advertised a coat at a 15% discount. The original price was $115.00, and the sale price was $100. Was the price consistent with the ad? Explain.

22. Rosemary sold a car and made a profit of $850, which was 17% of the selling price. What was the selling price?

23. Complete the following. Try to solve them mentally before using written or calculator methods.
    a. 30% of 50 is 6% of _____.
    b. 40% of 60 is 5% of _____.
    c. 30% of 80 is _____% of 160.

24. A car lot is advertising an 8% discount on a particular automobile. You pay $4485.00 for the car. What was the original price of the car?

25. a. The continents of Asia, Africa, and Europe together have an area of 8.5×10^{13} square meters. What percent of the surface area of the Earth do these three continents comprise if the total surface area of the Earth is about 5.2×10^{14} square meters?
    b. The Pacific Ocean has an area of about 1.81×10^{14} square meters. What percent of the surface of the Earth is covered by the Pacific Ocean?
    c. If all of the oceans are taken together, they make up about 70% of the surface of the Earth. How many square meters of the Earth's surface are covered by ocean?
    d. What percent of the landmass of the Earth is contained in Texas, with an area of about 6.92×10^{11} square meters?

26. The nutritional information on a box of cereal indicates that one serving provides 3 grams of protein, or 4% of U.S. recommended daily allowances (RDA). One serving with milk provides 7 grams, or 15% U.S. RDA. Is the information provided consistent? Explain.

27. A pair of slacks was made of material that was expected to shrink 10%. If the manufacturer makes the 32-inch inseam of the slacks 10% longer, what will the inseam measure after shrinkage?

28. Which results in a higher price: a 10% markup followed by a 10% discount, or a 10% discount followed by a 10% markup?

29. Joseph has 64% as many baseball cards as Cathy. Martin has 50% as many cards as Joseph. Martin has _____% as many cards as Cathy.

30. Your optimal exercise heart rate for cardiovascular benefits is calculated as follows: Subtract your age from 220. Then find 70% of this difference and 80% of this difference. The optimal rate is between the latter two numbers. Find the optimal heart rate range for a 50-year-old.

31. In an advertisement for a surround-sound decoder, it was stated that "our unit provides six outputs of audio information—that's 40% more than the competition." Explain why the person writing this ad does not understand the mathematics involved.

32. A heart doctor in Florida offers patients discounts for adopting good health habits. He offers 10% off if a patient stops smoking and another 5% off if a patient lowers her blood pressure or cholesterol a certain percentage. If you qualify for both discounts, would you rather the doctor (i) add them together and take 15% off your bill, or (ii) take 10% off first and then take 5% off the resulting discounted amount? Explain.

33. The population in one country increased by 4.2% during 2004, increased by 2.8% in 2005, and then decreased by 2.1% in 2006. What was the net percent change in population over the three-year period? Round your answer to the nearest tenth of a percent.

34. Monica has a daisy with nine petals. She asks Jerry to play the following game: They will take turns picking either one petal or two petals that are next to each other. The player who picks the last petal wins. Does the first player always win? Can the first player ever win? Discuss.

35. A clothing store was preparing for its semiannual 20% off sale. When it came to marking down the items, the salespeople wondered if they should (i) deduct the 20% from the selling price and then add the 6% sales tax, or (ii) add the 6% tax and then deduct the 20% from the total. Which way is correct, and why?

36. Elaine wants to deposit her summer earnings of $12,000 in a savings account to save for retirement. The bank pays 7% interest per year compounded semiannually (every 6 months). How much will her tax-deferred account be worth at the end of 3 years?

37. Assuming an inflation rate of 11%, how much would a woman earning $35,000 per year today need to earn five years from now to have the same buying power? Round your answer to the nearest thousand.

38. A couple wants to increase their savings for their daughter's college education. How much money must they invest now at 8.25% compounded annually in order to have accumulated $20,000 at the end of 10 years?

39. The consumer price index (CPI) is used by the government to relate prices to inflation. In July 2001, the CPI was 177.5, which means that prices were 77.5% higher than prices for the 1982–1984 period. If the CPI in July 2000 was 172.8, what was the percent increase from July 2000 to July 2001?

40. The city of Taxaphobia imposed a progressive income tax rate; that is, the more you earn, the higher the rate you pay. The rate they chose is equal to the number of thousands of dollars you earn. For example, a person who earns $13,000 pays 13% of her earnings in taxes. If you could name your own salary less than $100,000, what would you want to earn? Explain.

41. Wages were found to have risen to 108% from the previous year. If the current average wage is $9.99, what was the average wage last year?

42. A man's age at death was $\frac{1}{29}$ of the year of his birth. How old was he in 1949?

43. Your rectangular garden, which has whole-number dimensions, has an area of 72 square feet. However, you have absentmindedly forgotten the actual dimensions. If you want to fence the garden, what possible lengths of fence might be needed?

44. The pilot of a small plane must make a round trip between points A and B, which are 300 miles apart. The plane has an airspeed of 150 mph, and the pilot wants to make the trip in the minimum length of time. This morning there is a tailwind of 50 mph blowing from A to B and therefore a headwind of 50 mph from B to A. However, the weather forecast is for no wind tomorrow. Should the pilot make the trip today and take advantage of the tailwind in one direction or should the pilot wait until tomorrow, assuming that there will be no wind at all? That is, on which day will travel time be shorter?

| Section 7.4 | **EXERCISE / PROBLEM SET B** |

EXERCISES

1. Each of the following grids has some shaded squares. Write the percent of squares shaded and convert that percent to a decimal and a fraction in lowest terms.

  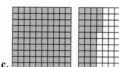

a.   b.   c.

2. Fill in this chart.

FRACTION	DECIMAL	PERCENT
___	___	66.66%
___	0.003	___
$\frac{1}{40}$	___	___
___	0.05	___
___	___	1.6%
$\frac{1}{100}$	___	___
___	0.00001	___
___	___	0.0085%

3. Mentally complete the following sets of information.
  a. A school's enrollment of seventh-, eighth-, and ninth-graders is 1000 students. 40% are seventh- graders = _____ of 1000 students. 35% are eighth-graders = _____ of 1000 students. _____% are ninth-graders = _____ of 1000 students.
  b. 10% interest rate: 10 cents on every _____; $1.50 on every _____; $4.00 on every _____.
  c. 6% sales tax: $_____ on $1.00; $_____ on $6.00; $_____ on $0.50; $_____ on $7.50.

4. Mentally complete the following statements.
  a. 196 is 200% of _____.
  b. 25% of 244 is _____.
  c. 39 is _____% of 78.
  d. 731 is 50% of _____.
  e. 40 is _____% of 32.
  f. 40% of 355 is _____.
  g. $166\frac{1}{3}$% of 300 is _____.
  h. 4.2 is _____% of 4200.
  i. 210 is 60% of_____.

5. Find mentally.
  a. 10% of 16
  b. 1% of 1000
  c. 20% of 150
  d. 200% of 75
  e. 15% of 40
  f. 10% of 440
  g. 15% of 50
  h. 300% of 120

6. Find mentally, using fraction equivalents.
  a. 50% of 180
  b. 25% of 440
  c. 75% of 320
  d. $33\frac{1}{3}$ of 210
  e. 40% of 250
  f. $12\frac{1}{2}$ of 400
  g. $66\frac{2}{3}$ of 660
  h. 20% of 120

7. Estimate.
  a. 21% of 34
  b. 42% of 61
  c. 24% of 57
  d. 211% of 82
  e. 16% of 42
  f. 11.2% of 431
  g. 48% of 26
  h. 39.4% of 147

8. It is common practice to leave a 15% tip when eating in a restaurant. Mentally estimate the amount of tip to leave for each of the following check amounts.
  a. $11.00
  b. $14.87
  c. $35.06
  d. $23.78

9. Write a percent problem for each proportion and then solve it using either grids or equations. Check your solution by inputting the original proportion into the Chapter 7 eManipulative activity *Percent Gauge* on our Web site.

  a. $\frac{67}{95} = \frac{x}{100}$ **b.** $\frac{18.4}{x} = \frac{112}{100}$

  c. $\frac{x}{3.5} = \frac{16\frac{2}{3}}{100}$ **d.** $\frac{2.8}{0.46} = \frac{x}{100}$

  e. $\frac{4200}{x} = \frac{0.05}{100}$

10. Find each missing number in the following percent problems. Round to the nearest tenth.
  a. 48% of what number is 178?
  b. 14.36 is what percent of 35?

c. What percent of 2.4 is 5.2?

d. $83\frac{1}{3}$ of 420 is what number?

e. 6 is $\frac{1}{4}$% of what number?

f. What percent of $16\frac{3}{4}$ is $12\frac{2}{3}$?

11. Use your calculator to find the following percents.

a. 3.5% of _____ is 154.

b. 36.3 is _____% of 165.

c. 7.5 is 0.6% of _____.

d. 87.5 is 70% of _____.

e. 221 is _____% of 34.

12. Calculate, using a percent key.

a. 34% of 90

b. 126% of 72

c. 30% of what number is 57?

d. 50 is what percent of 80?

e. $90 marked up 13%

f. $120 discounted 12%

13. Compute each of the following to the nearest cent.

a. 65% of $298.54   b. 52.7% of $211.53

c. 35.2% of $2874.65   d. 49.5% of $632.09

PROBLEMS

14. A mathematics test had 80 questions, each worth the same value. Wendy was correct on 55 of the questions. Using the Chapter 7 eManipulative activity *Percent Gauge* on our Web site, determine what percent of the questions Wendy got correct. Describe how you used the eManipulative to find the solution.

15. A retailer sells a shirt for $21.95. If the retailer marked up the shirt about 70%, what was his cost for the shirt? Use the Chapter 7 eManipulative activity *Percent Gauge* on our Web site to find the solution and describe how the eManipulative was used to accomplish this.

16. In 1995, 87,000 taxpayers reported incomes of more than $1,000,000. In 1997, the number of taxpayers reporting incomes of more than $1,000,000 had increased to 144,000. By what percent did the number of taxpayers earning more than $1,000,000 increase between 1995 and 1997? Round your answer to the nearest whole number.

17. Frank's salary is $240 per week. He saves $28 a week. What percent of his salary does he save?

18. It is common practice to pay salespeople extra money, called a **commission**, on the amount of sales. Bill is paid $315.00 a week, plus 6% commission on sales. Find his total earnings if his sales are $575.

19. The following pie chart (or circle chart) shows a student's relative expenditures. If the student's resources are $8000.00, how much is spent on each item?

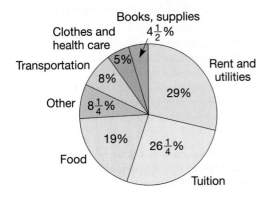

20. In a class of 36 students, 13 were absent on Friday. What percent of the class was absent?

21. A volleyball team wins 105 games, which is 70% of the games played. How many games were played?

22. The mass of all the bodies in our solar system, excluding the sun, is about 2.67×10^{27} kg. The mass of Jupiter is about 1.9×10^{27} kg.

a. What percent of the total mass of the solar system, excluding the sun, does Jupiter contain?

b. The four largest planets together (Jupiter, Saturn, Neptune, and Uranus) account for nearly all of the mass of the solar system, excluding the sun. If the masses of Saturn, Neptune, and Uranus are 5.7×10^{26} kg, 1.03×10^{26} kg, and 8.69×10^{25} kg, respectively, what percent of the total mass of the solar system, excluding the sun, do these four planets contain?

23. Henry got a raise of $80, which was 5% of his salary. What was his salary? Calculate mentally.

24. A CD store is advertising all CDs at up to 35% off. What would be the price range for CDs originally priced at $12.00?

25. Shown in the following table are data on the number of registered motor vehicles in the United States and fuel consumption in the United States in 1990 and 1998.

	VEHICLE REGISTRATIONS (MILLIONS)	MOTOR FUEL CONSUMPTION (THOUSANDS OF BARRELS PER DAY)
1990	188.8	8532
1998	211.6	10,104

a. By what percent did the number of vehicle registrations increase between 1990 and 1998?

b. By what percent did the consumption of motor fuel increase between 1990 and 1998?

c. Are these increases proportional? Explain.

26. A refrigerator and range were purchased and a 5% sales tax was added to the purchase price. If the total bill was $834.75, how much did the refrigerator and range cost?

27. Susan has $20.00. Sharon has $25.00. Susan claims that she has 20% less than Sharon. Sharon replies. "No. I have 25% more than you." Who is right?

28. Following is one tax table from a recent income tax form.

IF YOUR TAXABLE INCOME IS:	YOUR TAX IS:
Not over $500	4.2% of taxable income
Over $500 but not over $1000	$21.00 + 5.3% of excess over $500
Over $1000 but not over $2000	$47.50 + 6.5% of excess over $1000
Over $2000 but not over $3000	$112.50 + 7.6% of excess over $2000
Over $3000 but not over $4000	$188.50 + 8.7% of excess over $3000
Over $4000 but not over $5000	$275.50 + 9.8% of excess over $4000
Over $5000	$373.50 + 10.8% of excess over $5000

a. Given the following taxable income figures, compute the tax owed (to the nearest cent). (i) $3560, (ii) $8945, (iii) $2990.
b. If your tax was $324.99, what was your taxable income?

29. The price of coffee was 50 cents a pound 10 years ago. If the current price of coffee is $4.25 a pound, what percent increase in price does this represent?

30. A bookstore had a spring sale. All items were reduced by 20%. After the sale, prices were marked up at 20% over sale price. How do prices after the sale differ from prices before the sale?

31. A department store marked down all of its summer clothing 25%. The following week the remaining items were marked down again 15% off the sale price. When Jorge bought two tank tops on sale, he presented a coupon that gave him an additional 20% off. What percent of the original price did Jorge save?

32. A fishing crew is paid 43% of the value of their catch.
a. If they catch $10,500 worth of fish, what is the crew paid?
b. If the crew is paid $75,000 for a year's work, what was the total catch worth?
c. Suppose that the owner has the following expenses for a year:

ITEM	EXPENSE
Insurance	$12,000
Fuel	20,000
Maintenance	7,500
Miscellaneous	5,000

How much does he need to make to pay all his expenses and the crew?
d. If the fish are selling to the processors for an average of 22 cents/pound, how many pounds of fish does the owner need to sell to pay his expenses in part (c)?

33. Alan has thrown 24 passes and completed 37.5% of them. How many consecutive passes will Alan have to complete if he wants to have a completion average above 58%?

34. Beaker A has a quantity of water and beaker B has an equal quantity of wine. A milliliter of A is placed in B and B is mixed thoroughly. Then a milliliter of the mixture in B is placed in A and mixed. Which is greater, the percentage of wine in A or the percentage of water in B? Explain.

35. A girl bought some pencils, erasers, and paper clips at the stationery store. The pencils cost 10 cents each, the erasers cost 5 cents each, and the clips cost 2 for 1 cent. If she bought 100 items altogether at a total cost of $1, how many of each item did she buy?

36. If you add the square of Tom's age to the age of Carol, the sum is 62; but if you add the square of Carol's age to the age of Tom, the result is 176. Determine the ages of Tom and Carol.

37. Suppose that you have 5 chains each consisting of 3 links. If a single chain of 15 links is to be formed by cutting and welding, what is the fewest number of cuts that need to be made?

38. A pollster found that $36.72\overline{3672}\%$ of her sample voted Republican. What is the smallest number of people that could have been in the sample?

39. Think of any whole number. Add 20. Multiply by 10. Find 20% of your last result. Find 50% of the last number. Subtract the number you started with. What is your result? Repeat. Did you get a similar result? If yes, prove that this procedure will always lead to a certain result.

40. Eric deposited $32,000 in a savings account to save for his children's college education. The bank pays 8% tax-deferred interest per year compounded quarterly. How much will his account be worth at the end of 18 years?

41. Jim wants to deposit money in an account to save for a new stereo system in two years. He wants to have $4000 available at that time. The following rates are available to him:
1. 6.2% simple interest
2. 6.1% compounded annually
3. 5.58% compounded semiannually
4. 5.75% compounded quarterly
a. Which account(s) should he choose if he wants to invest the smallest amount of money now?
b. How much money must he invest to accumulate $4000 in two years' time?

42. Suppose that you have $1000 in a savings account that pays 4.8% interest per year. Suppose, also, that you owe $500 at 1.5% per month interest.

a. If you pay the interest on your loan for one month so that you can collect one month's interest on $500 in your savings account, what is your net gain or loss?

b. If you pay the loan back with $500 from your savings account rather than pay one month's interest on the loan, what is your net gain or loss?

c. What strategy do you recommend?

43. One-fourth of the world's population is Chinese and one-fifth of the rest is Indian. What percent of the world's population is Indian?

44. A **cevian** is a line segment that joins a vertex of a triangle and a point on the opposite side. How many triangles are formed if eight cevians are drawn from one vertex of a triangle?

Analyzing Student Thinking

45. Martina says that if the sale price of a shirt during a 60% off sale is $27.88, then the amount saved must be $27.88 times $\frac{60}{40}$. How should you respond?

46. Which of the following fractions are easily converted into percents?

$$\frac{7}{50} \quad \frac{13}{25} \quad \frac{4}{9} \quad \frac{3}{10}$$

Hugo says, "Only $\frac{3}{10}$." Is he correct? Explain.

47. To solve the problem "What percent of 60 is 30?" Bertrand writes $\frac{x}{100} = \frac{30}{60}$. Can his method lead to a correct solution? Explain.

48. An iPod is on sale for $159.20 and its normal price is $199. A student says that the percent discount is 39.8%. Is the student correct? If not, where did the student go wrong?

49. Andrew's parents put $1000 in a college savings account that is yielding 3% compound interest. He says that after 10 years, the account would be worth $1300 since 3% of $1000 is $30 and ten times $30 is $300. Is he correct? If not, how can you help him calculate the correct answer?

50. Yoko poses the scenario of a car dealer paying General Motors $17,888 for a new car and trying to sell it for 20% over cost. She claims that if it doesn't sell, the dealer can mark it down 20% and still come out even. Is her analysis correct? Explain.

51. Jerry says that if a store has a sale for 35% off and the sale price of a treadmill is $137, then he can figure out what the original price was by taking 35% of $137 and adding it back onto the $137. So the original price should be $184.95. But the answer doesn't check. Explain what mistake Jerry is making.

Problems Relating to the NCTM Standards and Curriculum Focal Points

1. The Focal Points for Grade 7 state "Use ratio and proportionality to solve a wide variety of percent problems." Explain how ratio and proportionality can be used to solve percent problems.

2. The NCTM Standards state "All students should recognize and generate equivalent forms of commonly used fractions, decimals, and percents." Describe two examples of "equivalent forms of commonly used fractions, decimals, and percents."

3. The NCTM Standards state "All students should work flexibly with fractions, decimals, and percents to solve problems." What is meant by "work flexibly"?

END OF CHAPTER MATERIAL

Solution of Initial Problem

A street vendor had a basket of apples. Feeling generous one day, he gave away one-half of his apples plus one to the first stranger he met, one-half of his remaining apples plus one to the next stranger he met, and one-half of his remaining apples plus one to the third stranger he met. If the vendor had one left for himself, with how many apples did he start?

Strategy: Work Backward

The vendor ended up with 1 apple. In the previous step, he gave away half of his apples plus 1 more. Thus he must have had 4 apples since the one he had plus the one he gave away was 2,

and 2 is half of 4. Repeating this procedure, 4 + 1 = 5 and 2 · 5 = 10; thus he must have had 10 apples when he met the second stranger. Repeating this procedure once more, 10 + 1 = 11 and 2 · 11 = 22. Thus he had 22 apples when he met the first stranger.

Check:

Start with 22.
Give away one-half (11) plus one, or 12.
10 remain.
Give away one-half (5) plus one, or 6.
4 remain.
Give away one-half (2) plus one, or 3.
1 remains.

Additional Problems Where the Strategy "Work Backward" Is Useful

1. On a class trip to the world's tallest building, the class rode up several floors, then rode down 18 floors, rode up 59 floors, rode down 87 floors, and ended up on the first floor. How many floors did they ride up initially?

2. At a sports card trading show, one trader gave 3 cards for 5. Then she traded 7 cards for 2. Finally, she bought 4 and traded 2 for 9. If she ended up with 473 cards, how many did she bring to the show?

3. Try the following "magic" trick: Multiply a number by 6. Then add 9. Double this result. Divide by 3. Subtract 6. Then divide by 4. If the answer is 13, what was your original number?

People in Mathematics

David Blackwell (1919–2010)
When David Blackwell entered college at age 16, his ambition was to become an elementary teacher. Six years later, he had a doctorate in mathematics and was nominated for a fellowship at the Institute for Advanced Study at Princeton. The position included an honorary membership in the faculty at nearby Princeton University, but the university objected to the appointment of an African American as a faculty member. The director of the institute insisted on appointing Blackwell, and eventually won out. From Princeton, Blackwell taught at Howard University and at Berkeley. He made important contributions to statistics, probability, game theory, and set theory. "Why do you want to share something beautiful with someone else? It's because of the pleasure he will get, and in transmitting it you will appreciate its beauty all over again. My high school geometry teacher really got me interested in mathematics. I hear it suggested from time to time that geometry might be dropped from the curriculum. I would really hate to see that happen. It is a beautiful subject."

Sonya Kovalevskaya (1850–1891)
As a young woman, Sonya Kovalevskaya hoped to study in Berlin under the great mathematician Karl Weierstrass. But women were barred from attending the university. She approached Weierstrass directly. Skeptical, he assigned her a set of difficult problems. When Kovalevskaya returned the following week with solutions, he agreed to teach her privately and was influential in seeing that she was granted her degree—even though she never officially attended the university. Kovalevskaya is known for her work in differential equations and for her mathematical theory of the rotation of solid bodies. In addition, she was editor of a mathematical journal, wrote two plays (with Swedish writer Anne Charlotte Leffler), a novella, and memoirs of her childhood. Of her literary and mathematical talents, she wrote, "The poet has to perceive that which others do not perceive, to look deeper than others look. And the mathematician must do the same thing."

CHAPTER REVIEW

Review the following terms and exercises to determine which require learning or relearning—page numbers are provided for easy reference.

SECTION 7.1 Decimals

VOCABULARY/NOTATION

Decimal   265

Decimal point   266

Expanded form   266

Hundreds square   266

Terminating decimal   267

Fraction equivalents   269

EXERCISES

1. Write 37.149 in expanded form.

2. Write 2.3798 in its word name.

3. Determine which of the following fractions have a terminating decimal representation.

a. $\dfrac{7}{2^3}$ **b.** $\dfrac{5^3}{3^2 \cdot 2^5}$ **c.** $\dfrac{17}{2^{13}}$

4. Explain how to determine the smaller of 0.24 and 0.3 using the following techniques.
   a. A hundreds square
   b. The number line
   c. Fractions
   d. Place value

5. Calculate mentally and explain what techniques you used.
   a. $(0.25 \times 12.3) \times 8$
   b. $1.3 \times 2.4 + 2.4 \times 2.7$
   c. $15.73 + 2.99$
   d. $27.51 - 19.98$

6. Estimate using the techniques given.
   a. Range: $2.51 \times 3.29 \times 8.07$
   b. Front-end with adjustment: $2.51 + 3.29 + 8.2$
   c. Rounding to the nearest tenth: $8.549 - 2.352$
   d. Rounding to compatible numbers: $421.7 \div 52.937$

SECTION 7.2 Operations with Decimals

VOCABULARY/NOTATION

Scientific notation 279	Characteristic 279	Repeating decimal 281
Mantissa 279	Repetend ($.\overline{abcd}$) 281	Period 281

EXERCISES

1. Calculate the following using (i) a standard algorithm and (ii) a calculator.

   a. $16.179 + 4.83$
   b. $84.25 - 47.761$
   c. 41.5×3.7
   d. $154.611 \div 4.19$

a. $\dfrac{5}{13}$

b. $\dfrac{132}{333}$

c. $\dfrac{46}{92}$

2. Determine which of the following fractions have repeating decimals. For those that do, express them as a decimal with a bar over their repetend.

3. Find the fraction representation in simplest form for each of the following decimals.

   a. $3.\overline{674}$ **b.** $24.1\overline{32}$

SECTION 7.3 Ratio and Proportion

VOCABULARY/NOTATION

Ratio 288	Whole-to-part 289	Proportion 290
Part-to-part 289	Extremes 289	Rates 290
Part-to-whole 289	Means 289	Scaling up/scaling down 292

EXERCISES

1. How do the concepts ratio and proportion differ?

2. Determine whether the following are proportions. Explain your method.

   a. $\dfrac{7}{13} = \dfrac{9}{15}$ **b.** $\dfrac{12}{15} = \dfrac{20}{25}$

3. Describe two ways to determine whether $\dfrac{a}{b} = \dfrac{c}{d}$ is a proportion.

4. Which is the better buy? Explain.
   a. 58 cents for 24 oz or 47 cents for 16 oz
   b. 7 pounds for $3.45 or 11 pounds for $5.11

5. Solve: If $3\frac{1}{4}$ cups of sugar are used to make a batch of candy for 30 people, how many cups are required for 40 people?

SECTION 7.4 Percent

VOCABULARY/NOTATION

Percent   299
Grid approach   302

Proportion approach   302

Equation approach   303

EXERCISES

1. Write each of the following in all three forms: decimal, percent, and fraction (in simplest form).

   a. 56%   **b.** 0.48   **c.** $\frac{1}{8}$

2. Calculate mentally using fraction equivalents.

   a. $48 \times 25\%$ **b.** $33\frac{1}{3}\% \times 72$

   c. $72 \times 75\%$ **d.** $20\% \times 55$

3. Estimate using fraction equivalents.

   a. $23\% \times 81$ **b.** $49\% \times 199$
   c. $32\% \times 59$ **d.** $67\% \times 310$

4. Solve:

   a. A car was purchased for $17,120 including a 7% sales tax. What was the price of the car before tax?
   b. A soccer player has been successful 60% of the times she kicks toward goal. If she has taken 80 kicks, what percent will she have if she kicks 11 out of the next 20?

CHAPTER TEST

KNOWLEDGE

1. True or false?

   a. The decimal 0.034 is read "thirty-four hundredths."
   b. The expanded form of 0.0271 is $\frac{2}{100} + \frac{7}{1000} + \frac{1}{10,000}$.
   c. The fraction $\frac{27}{125}$ has a terminating decimal representation.
   d. The repetend of $0.03\overline{74}$ is "374."
   e. The fraction $\frac{27}{225}$ has a repeating, nonterminating decimal representation.
   f. Forty percent equals two-fifths.
   g. The ratios $m : n$ and $p : q$ are equal if and only if $mq = np$.
   h. If $p\%$ of n is x, then $\frac{100x}{n} = p$.

2. Write the following in expanded form.

   a. 32.198   **b.** .000342

3. What does the "cent" part of the word *percent* mean?

4. In a bag of 23 Christmas candies there were 14 green candies and 9 red candies. Express the following types of ratios.

   a. Part to part   **b.** Part to whole

SKILL

5. Compute the following problems without a calculator. Find approximate answers first.

   a. $3.71 + 13.809$ **b.** $14.3 - 7.961$
   c. 7.3×11.41 **d.** $6.5 \div 0.013$

6. Determine which number in the following pairs is larger using (i) the fraction representation, and (ii) the decimal representation.

   a. 0.103 and 0.4   **b.** 0.0997 and 0.1

7. Express each of the following fractions in its decimal form.

   a. $\frac{2}{7}$ **b.** $\frac{5}{8}$ **c.** $\frac{7}{48}$ **d.** $\frac{4}{9}$

8. Without converting, determine whether the following fractions will have a terminating or nonterminating decimal representation.

   a. $\frac{9}{16}$ **b.** $\frac{17}{78}$ **c.** $\frac{2^3}{2^7 \cdot 5^3}$

9. Express each of the following decimals in its simplest fraction form.

   a. $0.\overline{36}$ **b.** $0.3\overline{6}$ **c.** 0.3636

10. Express each of the following in all three forms: decimal, fraction, and percent.

    a. 52%   **b.** 1.25   **c.** $\frac{17}{25}$

11. The ratio of boys to girls is $3:2$ and there are 30 boys and girls altogether. How many boys are there?

12. Estimate the following and describe your method.

    a. 53×0.48
    b. $1469.2 \div 26.57$
    c. $33 \div 0.76$
    d. 442.78×18.7

13. Arrange the following from smallest to largest.

    $$\frac{1}{3}, \quad 0.3, \quad 3\%, \quad \frac{2}{7}$$

UNDERSTANDING

14. Without performing any calculations, explain why $\frac{1}{123456789}$ must have a repeating, nonterminating decimal representation.

15. Suppose that the percent key and the decimal point key on your calculator are both broken. Explain how you could still use your calculator to solve problems like "Find 37% of 58."

16. Write a word problem involving percents that would have the following proportion or equation as part of its solution.

   a. $80\% \cdot x = 48$

   b. $\dfrac{x}{100} = \dfrac{35}{140}$

17. When adding 1.3 and 0.2, the sum has 1 digit to the right of the decimal. When multiplying 1.3 and 0.2, the product has 2 digits to the right of the decimal. Explain why the product has 2 digits to the right of the decimal and not just 1.

PROBLEM-SOLVING/APPLICATION

18. What is the 100th digit in $0.\overline{564793}$?

19. If the cost of a new car is $12,000 (plus 5% sales tax) and a down payment of 20% (including the tax) is required, how much money will a customer need to drive out in a new car?

20. A television set was to be sold at a 13% discount, which amounted to $78. How much would the set sell for after the discount?

21. A photograph measuring 3 inches by $2\frac{1}{2}$ inches is to be enlarged so that the smaller side, when enlarged, will be 8 inches. How long will the enlarged longer side be?

22. Find three numbers between 5.375 and 5.3751.

23. Dr. Fjeldsted has 91 students in his first-quarter calculus class. If the ratio of math majors to non-math majors is 4 to 9, how many math majors are in the class?

24. In a furniture store advertisement it was stated "our store offers six new sofa styles—that's 40% more than the competition." Explain why the person writing this advertisement does not understand the mathematics involved.

25. A refrigerator was on sale at the appliance store for 20% off. Marcus received a coupon from the store for an additional 30% off any current price in the store. If he uses the coupon to buy the refrigerator, the price would be $487.20 before taxes. What was the original price?

Integers

FOCUS ON │ *A Brief History of Negative Numbers*

No trace of the recognition of negative numbers can be found in any of the early writings of the Egyptians, Babylonians, Hindus, Chinese, or Greeks. Even so, computations involving subtractions, such as $(10 - 6) \cdot (5 - 2)$, were performed correctly where rules for multiplying negatives were applied.

An approximate timeline of the introduction of negative numbers follows:

200 B.C.E.   The first mention of negative numbers can be traced to the Chinese in 200 B.C.E.

300 C.E.   In the fourth century in his text *Arithmetica*, Diophantus spoke of the equation $4x + 20 = 4$ as "absurd," because x would have to be -4.

630 C.E.   The Hindu Brahmagupta spoke of "negative" and "affirmative" quantities, although these numbers always appeared as subtrahends.

1300 C.E.   The Chinese mathematician Chu Shi-Ku gave the "rule of signs" in his algebra text.

1545 C.E.   In his text *Ars Magna*, the Italian mathematician Cardano recognized negative roots and clearly stated rules of negatives.

Various notations have been used to designate negative numbers. The Hindus placed a dot or small circle over or beside a number to denote that it was negative; for example, 6̇ or 6̣ represented -6. In Chu Shih-Chieh's book on algebra, *Precious Mirror of Four Elements*, published in 1303, both zeros and negative terms are introduced as shown next.

Each box in the figure, consisting of a group of squares containing signs, represents a "matrix" form of writing an algebraic expression. The frequent occurrence of the sign "0" for zero can be clearly seen. (In these cases, it means that terms corresponding to those squares do not occur in the equation.)

In the right column of the figure, the symbol ⋕ can be seen in two locations. The diagonal line slashed through the two vertical lines indicate that it is a negative value. Thus ⋕ represents -2. The slash to represent a negative is also used in other boxes in the figure. The Chinese were also known to use red to denote positive and black to denote negative integers.

In this chapter we use black chips and red chips to motivate the concepts underlying positive ("in the black") and negative ("in the red") numbers much as the Chinese may have done, although with the colors reversed.

STRATEGY 13
Use Cases

Many problems can be solved more easily by breaking the problem into various cases. For example, consider the following statement: The square of any whole number n is a multiple of 4 or one more than a multiple of 4. To prove this, we need only consider two cases: n is even or n is odd. If n is even, then $n = 2x$ and $n^2 = 4x^2$, which is a multiple of 4. If n is odd, then $n = 2x + 1$ and $n^2 = 4x^2 + 4x + 1$, which is one more than a multiple of 4. The following problem can be solved easily by considering various cases.

INITIAL PROBLEM

A pentominoe consists of 5 congruent squares joined at complete sides. For example,

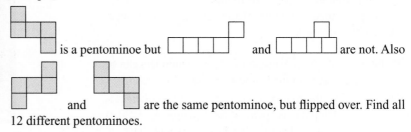

is a pentominoe but ⬚⬚⬚⬚ and ⬚⬚⬚⬚ are not. Also

and are the same pentominoe, but flipped over. Find all 12 different pentominoes.

CLUES

The Use Cases strategy may be appropriate when

- A problem can be separated into several distinct cases.
- A problem involves distinct collections of numbers such as odds and evens, primes and composites, and positives and negatives.
- Investigations in specific cases can be generalized.

A solution of this Initial Problem is on page 351.

Children's Literature
www.wiley.com/college/musser
See "50 Below Zero"
by Robert Munsch.

INTRODUCTION

Whole numbers and fractions are useful in solving many problems and applications in society. However, there are many situations where negative numbers are useful. For example, negative numbers are very helpful in describing temperature below zero, elevation below sea level, losses in the stock market, and an overdrawn checking account. In this chapter we study the integers, the set of numbers that consists of the whole numbers, together with the negative numbers that are the opposites of the nonzero whole numbers. The four basic operations of the integers are introduced together with order relationships.

Key Concepts from NCTM Curriculum Focal Points

- **GRADE 5:** Students should explore contexts that they can describe with negative numbers (e.g., situations of owing money or measuring elevations above and below sea level).
- **GRADE 7:** By applying properties of arithmetic and considering negative numbers in everyday contexts, students explain why the rules of adding, subtracting, multiplying, and dividing with negative numbers make sense.

8.1 ADDITION AND SUBTRACTION

STARTING POINT

In the above introduction, temperature, elevation, stocks, and banking are presented as situations where positive and negative numbers are used. Using one of these scenarios, write a word problem for each of the following expressions.

$$-30 + 14 \qquad -30 - 14 \qquad -30 + (-14)$$

Integers and the Integer Number Line

Algebraic Reasoning
As can be seen in the introduction at the right, the use of integers allows one to solve a larger selection of equation types. Two examples of these equations are: $3 - x = 5$ and $8 + x = 2$.

Reflection from Research
An understanding of integers is crucial to an understanding of future work in algebra (Sheffield & Cruikshank, 1996).

The introduction to this chapter lists several situations in which negative numbers are useful. There are other situations in mathematics in which negative numbers are needed. For example, the subtraction problem $4 - 7$ has no answer when using whole numbers. Also, the equation $x + 7 = 4$ has no whole-number solution. To remedy these situations, we introduce a new set of numbers, the integers. Our approach here will be to introduce the integers using a physical model. This model is related to a procedure that was used in accounting. Numerals written in black ink represent amounts above zero ("in the black" is positive) and in red ink represent accounts below zero ("in the red" is negative). We will use the integers to represent these situations.

DEFINITION

Integers

The set of **integers** is the set

$$I = \{\ldots, -3, -2, -1, 0, 1, 2, 3, \ldots\}.$$

The numbers $1, 2, 3, \ldots$ are called **positive integers** and the numbers $-1, -2, -3, \ldots$ are called **negative integers**. Zero is neither a positive nor a negative integer.

Children's Literature
www.wiley.com/college/musser
See "Exactly the Opposite" by
Tana Hoban.

In a set model, chips can be used to represent integers. However, *two* colors of chips must be used, one color to represent positive integers (black) and a second to represent negative integers (red) (Figure 8.1). One black chip represents a credit of 1 and one red chip represents a debit of 1. Thus *one black chip and one red chip cancel each other*, or "make a zero" so they are called a **zero pair** [Figure 8.2(a)]. Using this concept, each integer can be represented by chips in many different ways [Figure 8.2(b)].

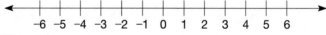

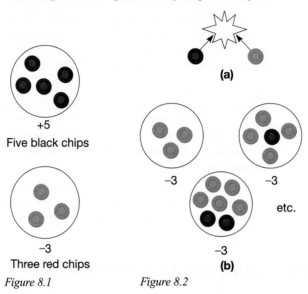

Figure 8.1   Figure 8.2

An extension from the examples in Figure 8.2 is that each integer has infinitely many representations using chips. (Recall that every fraction also has an infinite number of representations.)

Another way to represent the integers is to use a measurement model, the **integer number line** (Figure 8.3). The integers are equally spaced and arranged

$$\xleftarrow{\quad} \overset{\displaystyle -6\ -5\ -4\ -3\ -2\ -1\ \ 0\ \ 1\ \ 2\ \ 3\ \ 4\ \ 5\ \ 6}{|\ \ |\ \ |\ \ |\ \ |\ \ |\ \ |\ \ |\ \ |\ \ |\ \ |\ \ |\ \ |\ \ |} \xrightarrow{\quad}$$

Figure 8.3

symmetrically to the right and left of zero on the number line. This symmetry leads to a useful concept associated with positive and negative numbers. This concept, the opposite of a number, can be defined using either the measurement model or the set model of integers. The **opposite** of the integer a, written $-a$ or $(-a)$, is defined as follows.

Set Model   The opposite of a is the integer that is represented by the same number of chips as a, but of the opposite color (Figure 8.4).

Reflection from Research
It is important to introduce
children to negative numbers
using manipulatives
(Thompson, 1988).

4 and −4 are
opposites of each other.

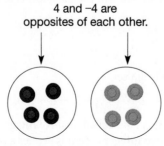

Figure 8.4

Measurement Model   The opposite of a is the integer that is its mirror image about 0 on the integer number line (Figure 8.5).

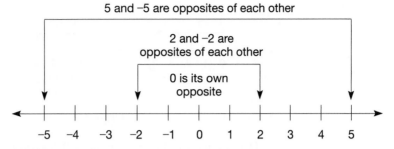

5 and −5 are opposites of each other

2 and −2 are opposites of each other

0 is its own opposite

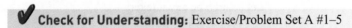

Figure 8.5

The opposite of a positive integer is negative, and the opposite of a negative integer is positive. Also, the opposite of zero is zero. The concept of opposite will be seen to be very useful later in this section when we study subtraction.

✔ **Check for Understanding:** Exercise/Problem Set A #1–5

Addition and Its Properties

Consider the following situation. In a football game, a running back made 12 running attempts and was credited with the following yardage for each attempt: 12, 7, −6, 8, 13, −1, 17, −5, 32, 16, 14, −7. What was his total yardage for the game? Integer addition can be used to answer this question. The definition of addition of integers can be motivated using both the set model and the measurement model.

Set Model   Addition means to put together or form the union of two disjoint sets (Figure 8.6).

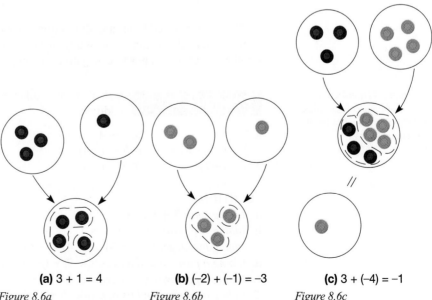

(a) 3 + 1 = 4   **(b)** (−2) + (−1) = −3   **(c)** 3 + (−4) = −1

Figure 8.6a   *Figure 8.6b*   *Figure 8.6c*

Measurement Model Addition means to put directed arrows end to end starting at zero. Note that positive integers are represented by arrows pointing to the right and negative integers by arrows pointing to the left (Figure 8.7).

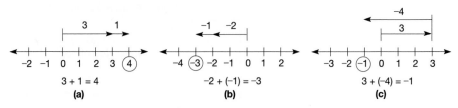

Figure 8.7a   Figure 8.7b   Figure 8.7c

The examples in Figures 8.6 and 8.7 lead to the following definition of integer addition.

DEFINITION

Addition of Integers

Let a and b be any integers.

1. *Adding zero:* $a + 0 = 0 + a = a$.
2. *Adding two positives:* If a and b are positive, they are added as whole numbers.
3. *Adding two negatives:* If a and b are positive (hence $-a$ and $-b$ are negative), then $(-a) + (-b) = -(a + b)$, where $a + b$ is the whole-number sum of a and b.
4. *Adding a positive and a negative:*
   a. If a and b are positive and $a \geq b$, then $a + (-b) = a - b$, where $a - b$ is the whole-number difference of a and b.
   b. If a and b are positive and $a < b$, then $a + (-b) = -(b - a)$, where $b - a$ is the whole-number difference of a and b.

These rules for addition are abstractions of what most people do when they add integers—namely, compute mentally using whole numbers and then determine whether the answer is positive, negative, or zero.

Children's Literature
www.wiley.com/college/musser
See "The Phantom Tollbooth"
by Norman Juster.

Example 8.1

Calculate the following using the definition of integer addition.

a. $3 + 0$ **b.** $3 + 4$
c. $(-3) + (-4)$ **d.** $7 + (-3)$
e. $3 + (-7)$ **f.** $5 + (-5)$

SOLUTION
a. *Adding zero:* $3 + 0 = 3$
b. *Adding two positives:* $3 + 4 = 7$
c. *Adding two negatives:* $(-3) + (-4) = -(3 + 4) = -7$
d. *Adding a positive and a negative:* $7 + (-3) = 7 - 3 = 4$
e. *Adding a positive and a negative:* $3 + (-7) = -(7 - 3) = -4$
f. *Adding a number and its opposite:* $5 + (-5) = 0$ ∎

The problems in Example 8.1 have interpretations in the physical world. For example, $(-3) + (-4)$ can be thought of as the temperature dropping 3 degrees one hour and 4 degrees the next for a total of 7 degrees. In football, $3 + (-7)$ represents a gain of 3 and a loss of 7 for a net loss of 4 yards.

The integer models and the rules for the addition of integers can be used to justify the following properties of integers.

PROPERTIES

Properties of Integer Addition

Let a, b, and c be any integers.

Closure Property for Integer Addition

$$a + b \text{ is an integer.}$$

Commutative Property for Integer Addition

$$a + b = b + a$$

Associative Property for Integer Addition

$$(a + b) + c = a + (b + c)$$

Identity Property for Integer Addition

0 is the unique integer such that $a + 0 = a = 0 + a$ for all a.

Additive Inverse Property for Integer Addition

For each integer a there is a unique integer, written $-a$, such that $a + (-a) = 0$. The integer $-a$ is called the **additive inverse** of a.

Reflection from Research
Students should be able to make generalizations to integers from their experience with arithmetic (Thompson & Dreyfus, 1988).

In words, this property states that any number plus its additive inverse is zero. A useful result that is a consequence of the additive inverse property is **additive cancellation**.

THEOREM

Additive Cancellation for Integers

Let a, b, and c be any integers. If $a + c = b + c$, then $a = b$.

Algebraic Reasoning
When solving an equation such as $x + 4 = 3$, the additive inverse of 4, namely -4, is added to both sides of the equation as follows: $x + 4 + (-4) = 3 + (-4)$. This shows that $x = -1$.

Algebraic Reasoning
In the proof at the right, variables are used to represent integers. Since the variables can take on the value of any integer, the proof holds for all integers.

PROOF

Let $a + c = b + c$. Then

$$
\begin{array}{ll}
(a + c) + (-c) = (b + c) + (-c) & \textit{Addition} \\
a + [c + (-c)] = b + [c + (-c)] & \textit{Associativity} \\
a + 0 = b + 0 & \textit{Additive inverse} \\
a = b & \textit{Additive identity}
\end{array}
$$

Thus, if $a + c = b + c$, then $a = b$. ∎

Observe that $-a$ need not be negative. For example, the opposite of -7, written $-(-7)$, is 7, a positive number. In general, if a is positive, then $-a$ is negative; if a is negative, then $-a$ is positive; and if a is zero, then $-a$ is zero. As shown in

Figure 8.8, using colored chips or a number line, it can be seen that $-(-a) = a$ for any integer a. (NOTE: The three small dots are used to allow for enough chips to represent any integer a, not necessarily just -3 and 3 as suggested by the black and red chips.)

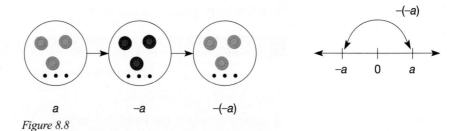

Figure 8.8

THEOREM

Let a be any integer. Then $-(-a) = a$.

PROOF

Notice that $a + (-a) = 0$ and $-(-a) + (-a) = 0$.
Therefore, $a + (-a) = -(-a) + (-a)$.
Finally, $a = -(-a)$, since the $(-a)$s can be canceled by additive cancellation. ∎

Properties of integer addition, together with thinking strategies, are helpful in doing computations. For example,

$$3 + (-10) = 3 + [(-3) + (-7)]$$
$$= [3 + (-3)] + (-7) = 0 + (-7) = -7$$

and

$$(-7) + 21 = (-7) + (7 + 14)$$
$$= [(-7) + 7] + 14 = 0 + 14 = 14.$$

Problem-Solving Strategy
Look for a Pattern

Each preceding step can be justified using a property or the definition of integer addition. When one does the preceding problem mentally, not all the steps need to be carried out. However, it is important to understand how the properties are being applied.

✔ **Check for Understanding:** Exercise/Problem Set A #6–12

Subtraction

Subtraction of integers can be viewed in several ways.

Pattern

THE FIRST COLUMN REMAINS 4.	$4 - 2 = 2$
	$4 - 1 = 3$
THE SECOND COLUMN DECREASES BY 1 EACH TIME.	$4 - 0 = 4$
	$4 - (-1) = 5$
	$4 - (-2) = 6$

1 MORE
1 MORE
1 MORE
1 MORE

Take-Away

Example 8.2   Calculate the following differences.

a. $6 - 2$
b. $-4 - (-1)$
c. $-2 - (-3)$
d. $2 - 5$

SOLUTION
   See Figure 8.9.

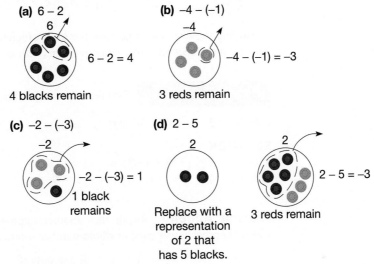

Figure 8.9

Adding the Opposite   Let's reexamine the problem in Example 8.2(d). The difference $2 - 5$ can be found in yet another way using the chip model (Figure 8.10).

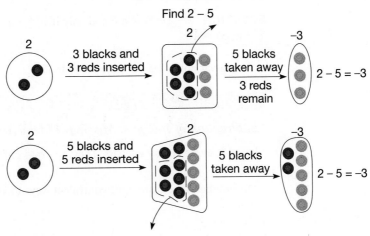

Figure 8.10

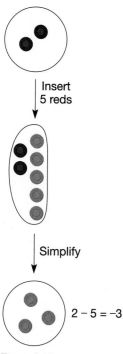

Insert
5 reds

Simplify

$2 - 5 = -3$

Figure 8.11

This second method in Figure 8.10 can be simplified. The process of inserting 5 blacks and 5 reds and then removing 5 blacks can be accomplished by inserting 5 reds, since we would just turn around and take the 5 blacks away once they were inserted.

Simplified Second Method   Find $2 - 5$. The simplified method in Figure 8.11 finds $2 - 5$ by finding $2 + (-5)$. Thus the method of subtraction replaces a subtraction problem with an equivalent addition problem—namely, adding the opposite.

DEFINITION

Subtraction of Integers: Adding the Opposite

Let a and b be any integers. Then

$$a - b = a + (-b).$$

Adding the opposite is perhaps the most efficient method for subtracting integers because it replaces any subtraction problem with an equivalent addition problem.

Example 8.3   Find the following differences by adding the opposite.

a. $(-8) - 3$ **b.** $4 - (-5)$

SOLUTION
a. $(-8) - 3 = (-8) + (-3) = -11$
b. $4 - (-5) = 4 + [-(-5)] = 4 + 5 = 9$ ■

Missing Addend   Recall that another approach to subtraction, the missing-addend approach, was used in whole-number subtraction. For example,

$$7 - 3 = n \qquad \text{if and only if} \qquad 7 = 3 + n.$$

In this way, subtraction can be done by referring to addition. This method can also be extended to integer subtraction.

Example 8.4   Find $7 - (-3)$.

SOLUTION $7 - (-3) = n$ if and only if $7 = -3 + n$. But $-3 + 10 = 7$. Therefore, $7 - (-3) = 10$.   ■

Using variables, we can state the following.

ALTERNATIVE DEFINITION

Subtraction of Integers: Missing-Addend Approach

Let a, b, and c be any integers. Then $a - b = c$ if and only if $a = b + c$.

In summary, there are three equivalent ways to view subtraction in the integers.

1. Take-away
2. Adding the opposite
3. Missing addend

STUDENT PAGE SNAPSHOT

4 Model Subtraction

OBJECTIVE: Model subtraction of integers.

Quick Review

Subtract.
1. 9 − 7   2. 18 − 3
3. 29 − 14   4. 37 − 18
5. 55 − 27

Investigate

Materials ■ two-color counters

You can use counters to find the difference of integers.

A Find ⁻3 − ⁻1. Use red counters to represent ⁻3.

B Take away 1 red counter. The remaining counters represent the difference ⁻3 − ⁻1.

$$^-3 - ^-1 = ^-2$$

C Find 3 − 7. Use yellow counters to represent 3.

D Adding a red counter paired with a yellow counter does not change the value of 3. Show another way to model 3 that includes 7 yellow counters.

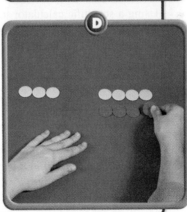

E Use your model to find 3 − 7. Take away 7 yellow counters. The remaining counters represent the difference 3 − 7.

$$3 - 7 = ^-4$$

Draw Conclusions

1. Why was it necessary to use pairs of red and yellow counters in Step D?

2. **Synthesis** How could you model the difference ⁻2 − 5?

262

From Lesson 4 "Model Subtraction" from HSP MATH: Problem Solving and Reading Strategies Practice Workbook, Student Edition (National), Grade 6 (2009 Edition), copyright ©2009 by Houghton Mifflin Harcourt Publishing Company.

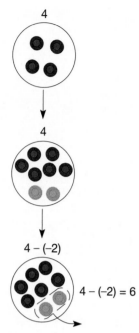

4

4

4 – (–2)

4 – (–2) = 6

Figure 8.12

Notice that both the take-away and the missing-addend approaches are extensions of whole-number subtraction. The adding-the-opposite approach is new because the additive inverse property is a property the integers have but the whole numbers do not. As one should expect, all of these methods yield the same answer. The following argument shows that adding the opposite is a consequence of the missing-addend approach.

Let $a - b = c$.

Then $a = b + c$ by the missing-addend approach.

Hence $a + (-b) = b + c + (-b) = c$, or
$$a + (-b) = c.$$

Therefore, $a - b = a + (-b)$.

It can also be shown that the missing-addend approach follows from adding the opposite.

Example 8.5   Find $4 - (-2)$ using all three methods of subtraction.

SOLUTION

a. Take-Away: See Figure 8.12

b. Adding the Opposite: $4 - (-2) = 4 + [-(-2)] = 4 + 2 = 6$.

c. Missing Addend: $4 - (-2) = c$ if and only if $4 = (-2) + c$. But $4 = -2 + 6$. Therefore, $c = 6$.   ■

Using a scientific calculator to do integer computation requires an understanding of the difference between subtracting a number and a negative number. On a calculator the subtraction key is ⊟ and the negative key is (−). The number −9 is found by pressing (−) 9 [− 9]. To calculate $(-18) - (-3)$, press these keys: (−) 18 ⊟ (−) 3 = [− 15]. (NOTE: On some calculators there is a change-of-sign key +/− instead of a negative key (−). In those cases a −9 is entered as 9 +/− .)

As you may have noticed, the "−" symbol has three different meanings. Therefore, it should be read in a way that distinguishes among its uses. First, the symbol "−7" is read "negative 7" (*negative* means "less than zero"). Second, since it also represents the opposite or additive inverse of 7, "−7" can be read "the opposite of 7" or "the additive inverse of 7." Remember that "opposite" and "additive inverse" are not synonymous with "negative integers." For example, the opposite or additive inverse of −5 is 5 and 5 is a positive integer. In general, the symbol "−a" should be read "the opposite of a" or "the additive inverse of a." It is confusing to children to call it "negative a" since $-a$ may be positive, zero, or negative, depending on the value of a. Third, "$a - b$" is usually read "a minus b" to indicate subtraction.

✔ **Check for Understanding:** Exercise/Problem Set A #13–17

MATHEMATICAL MORSEL

Shaquille O'Neal is listed as one of the 50 Greatest Players to play professional basketball. He is big, strong, quick and even has a tattoo of Superman to go along with his skills. He does, however, have one glaring weakness—making free throws. Over his career, he has made slightly more than 52% of all of his free throws. In fact, during the 2004–2005 season he only made 46%. Rick Barry is also listed as one of the 50 Greatest Players to play professional basketball. He is the only man to lead the NCAA, NBA, and ABA in single-season scoring. He is different than O'Neal, however, because he made 90% of his free throws and he did it by shooting them underhanded. When O'Neal was asked if he would let Barry teach him his technique, he responded, "Rick Barry's résumé is not good enough to come into my office to be qualified for a job. I will shoot negative 30 percent before I shoot underhanded."

| Section 8.1 | EXERCISE / PROBLEM SET A |

EXERCISES

1. Which of the following are integers? If they are, identify as positive, negative, or neither.
   a. 25   **b.** -7 **c.** 0

2. Represent the opposites of each of the numbers represented by the following models, where B = black chip and R = red chip.
   a. *BBBBR*
   b. *RBBRRRRR*
   c.
   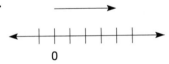
   d.
   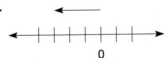

3. Use the set model and number-line model to represent each of the following integers.
   a. 3   **b.** -5 **c.** 0

4. Write the opposite of each integer.
   a. 3   **b.** -4 **c.** 0
   d. -168 **e.** 56   **f.** -1235

5. Given I = integers, $N = \{-1, -2, -3, -4, \ldots\}$, $P = \{1, 2, 3, 4, \ldots\}$, W = whole numbers, list the members of the following sets.
   a. $N \cup W$ **b.** $N \cup P$ **c.** $N \cap P$

6. Show how you could find the following sums (i) using a number-line model and (ii) using black and red chips. Look at the Chapter 8 eManipulative activity *Chips Plus* on our Web site to gain a better understanding of how to use the black and red chips.
   a. $5 + (-3)$ **b.** $(-3) + (-2)$

7. Use thinking strategies to compute the following sums. Identify your strategy.
   a. $-14 + 6$ **b.** $17 + (-3)$

8. Fill in each empty square so that the number in the square will be the sum of the pair of numbers beneath the square.

   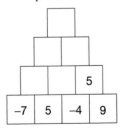

9. True or false?
   a. The set of negative integers is closed with respect to addition.
   b. The set of additive inverses of the whole numbers is equal to the set of integers.
   c. $-(-a)$ is always positive.
   d. The set of additive inverses of the negative integers is a proper subset of the whole numbers.

10. Identify the property illustrated by the following equations.
    a. $3 + [6 + (-3)] = 3 + (-3 + 6)$
    b. $[3 + (-3)] + 6 = 0 + 6$

11. Apply the properties and thinking strategies to compute the following sums mentally.
    a. $-126 + (635 + 126)$
    b. $84 + (-67) + (-34)$

12. The existence of additive inverses in the set of integers enables us to solve equations of the form $x + b = c$. For example, to solve $x + 15 = 8$, add (-15) to both sides; $x + 15 + (-15) = 8 + (-15)$ or $x = -7$. Solve the following equations using this technique.
    a. $x + 21 = 16$ **b.** $(-5) + x = 7$
    c. $65 + x = -13$ **d.** $x + 6 = -5$

13. The Chapter 8 eManipulative activity *Chips Minus* on our Web site demonstrates how to use black and red chips to model integer subtraction. After doing a few examples on the eManipulative, sketch how the chip model could be used to do the following problems.
    a. $3 - 7$ **b.** $4 - (-5)$

14. Calculate.
    a. $3 - 7$ **b.** $8 - (-4)$
    c. $(-2) + 3$ **d.** $(-7) - (-8)$

15. Find the following using your calculator and the ⊟ key. Check mentally.
    a. $-27 + 53$ **b.** $(-51) - (-46)$
    c. $123 - (-247)$ **d.** $-56 - 72$

16. Write out in words (use *minus, negative, opposite*).
    a. $5 - 2$ **b.** -6 (two possible answers)   **c.** -3

17. The **absolute value** of an integer a, written $|a|$, is defined to be the distance from a to zero on the integer number line. For example, $|3| = 3$, $|0| = 0$, and $|-7| = 7$. Evaluate the following absolute values.
    a. $|5|$ **b.** $|-17|$ **c.** $|5 - 7|$
    d. $|5| - |7|$ **e.** $-|7 - 5|$ **f.** $|-(7 - 5)|$

PROBLEMS

18. Dixie had a balance of $115 in her checking account at the beginning of the month. She deposited $384 in the account and then wrote checks for $153, $86, $196, $34, and $79. Then she made a deposit of $123. If at any time during the month the account is overdrawn, a $10 service charge is deducted. At the end of the month, what was Dixie's balance?

19. Which of the following properties hold for integer subtraction? If the property holds, give an example. If it does not hold, disprove it by a counterexample.
    a. Closure
    b. Commutative
    c. Associative
    d. Identity

20. Assume that the adding-the-opposite approach is true, and prove that the missing-addend approach is a consequence of it. (*Hint:* Assume that $a - b = c$, and show that $a = b + c$ using the adding-the-opposite approach.)

21. **a.** If possible, for each of the following statements find a pair of integers a and b that satisfy the equation or inequality.
    i. $|a + b| = |a| + |b|$
    ii. $|a + b| < |a| + |b|$
    iii. $|a + b| > |a| + |b|$
    iv. $|a + b| \leq |a| + |b|$

    b. Which of these conditions will hold for all pairs of integers?

22. Complete the magic square using the following integers.

    $10, 7, 4, 1, -5, -8, -11, -14$

	-2	

23. **a.** Let A be a set that is closed under subtraction. If 4 and 9 are elements of A, show that each of the following are also elements of A.
    i. 5   **ii.** -5 **iii.** 0
    iv. 13   **v.** 1   **vi.** -3

    b. List all members of A.
    c. Repeat part (b) if 4 and 8 are given as elements of A.
    d. Make a generalization about your findings.

24. Fill in each empty square so that the number in a square will be the sum of the pair of numbers beneath the square.

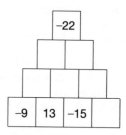

25. A student suggests the following algorithm for calculating 72 − 38.

$$
\begin{array}{r}
72 \\
-\ 38 \\
\hline
-\ 6 \\
40 \\
\hline
34
\end{array}
$$

    Two minus eight equals negative six.

    Seventy minus thirty equals forty.
    Forty plus negative six equals thirty-four,
    which therefore is the result.

As a teacher, what is your response? Does this procedure always work? Explain.

26. A **squared rectangle** is a rectangle whose interior can be divided into two or more squares. One example of a squared rectangle follows. The number written inside a square gives the length of a side of that square. Determine the dimensions of the unlabeled squares.

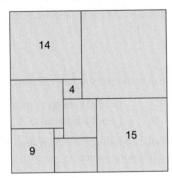

27. Place the numbers −6, −5, −4, −3, −2, −1, 0, 1, 2, 3, 4, 5, 6, 7 one in each of the regions of the 7 circles below so that the sum of the three numbers in each circle is 0. Refer to the Chapter 8 eManipulative *Circle 0* on our Web site to aid in the solution process.

28. Using the black and red chip model, how would you explain to students why you were inserting 5 black and 5 red chips into the circle in order to subtract 8 from 3?

Section 8.1	**EXERCISE / PROBLEM SET B**

EXERCISES

1. Which of the following are integers? Identify those that are as positive, negative, or neither.
   a. $\frac{3}{4}$ **b.** 556   **c.** −252/5

2. Identify each of the integers represented by the following models, where B = black chip and R = red chip.
   a. *BBBRR*   **b.** *BRRRRBRR*
   c.

        0

   d.

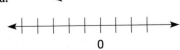

        0

3. Use the set model and number-line model to represent each of the following integers.
   a. −3   **b.** 6

4. What is the opposite or additive inverse of each of the following (a and b represent integers)?
   a. a **b.** $-b$
   c. $a + b$ **d.** $a - b$

5. Given I = integers, $N = \{-1, -2, -3, -4, \ldots\}$, $P = \{1, 2, 3, 4, \ldots\}$, W = whole numbers, list the members of the following sets.
   a. $N \cap I$ **b.** $P \cap I$ **c.** $I \cap W$

6. Show how you could find the following sums (i) using a number-line model and (ii) using black and red chips. Look at the Chapter 8 eManipulative activity *Chips Plus* on our Web site to gain a better understanding of how to use the black and red chips.
   a. $4 + (-7)$ **b.** $(-3) + (-5)$

7. Use thinking strategies to compute the following sums. Identify your strategy.
   a. $14 + (-6)$ **b.** $21 + (-41)$

8. Fill in each empty square so that the number in the square will be the sum of the pair of numbers beneath the square.

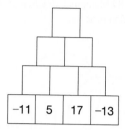

| -11 | 5 | 17 | -13 |

9. If p is an arbitrary negative integer and q is an arbitrary integer, which of the following is true?
a. $-p$ is negative
b. $-q$ is negative
c. $-q$ is positive
d. $-p$ is positive

10. Identify the property illustrated by the following equations.
a. $3 + [(-3) + 6] = [3 + (-3)] + 6$
b. $0 + 6 = 6$

11. Apply the properties and thinking strategies to compute the following sums mentally.
a. $-165 + 3217 + 65$
b. $173 + (-43) + (-97)$

12. For each of the following equations, find the integer that satisfies the equation.
a. $x + (-3) = -10$
b. $x + 5 = -8$
c. $6 + -x = -3$
d. $-5 + -x = -2$

13. The Chapter 8 eManipulative activity *Chips Minus* on our Web site demonstrates how to use black and red chips to model integer subtraction. After doing a few examples on the eManipulative, sketch how the chip model could be used to do the following problems.
a. $(-3) - (-6)$ **b.** $0 - (-4)$

14. Calculate the following sums and differences.
a. $13 - 27$ **b.** $38 - (-14)$
c. $(-21) + 35$ **d.** $-26 - (-32)$

15. Find the following using your calculator and the $\boxed{(-)}$ key. Check mentally.
a. $-119 + 351 + (-463)$
b. $-98 - (-42)$
c. $632 - (-354)$
d. $-752 - (-549) + (-352)$

16. Write out in words (use *minus, negative, opposite*).
a. $-(-5)$
b. $10 - [-(-2)]$
c. $-p$

17. An alternate definition of absolute value is

$$|a| = \begin{cases} a \text{ if } a \text{ is positive or zero.} \\ -a \text{ if } a \text{ is negative.} \end{cases}$$

(NOTE: $-a$ is the opposite of a.) Using this definition, calculate the following values.
a. $|-3|$
b. $|7|$
c. $|x|$ if $x < 0$
d. $|-x|$ if $-x > 0$
e. $-|x|$ if $x < 0$
f. $-|-x|$ if $-x > 0$

PROBLEMS

18. Write an addition statement for each of the following sentences and then find the answer.
a. In a series of downs, a football team gained 7 yards, lost 4 yards, lost 2 yards, and gained 8 yards. What was the total gain or loss?
b. In a week, a given stock gained 5 points, dropped 12 points, dropped 3 points, gained 18 points, and dropped 10 points. What was the net change in the stock's worth?
c. A visitor in an Atlantic City casino won $300, lost $250, and then won $150. Find the gambler's overall gain or loss.

19. Under what conditions is the following equation true?

$$(a - b) - c = (a - c) - b$$

a. Never   **b.** Always
c. Only when $b = c$ **d.** Only when $b = c = 0$

20. On a given day, the following Fahrenheit temperature extremes were recorded. Find the range between the high and low temperature in each location.

CITY	HIGH	LOW
Philadelphia	65	37
Cheyenne	35	-9
Bismarck	-2	-13

21. A student claims that if $a \neq 0$, then $|a| = -a$ is never true, since absolute value is always positive. Explain why the student is wrong. What two concepts is the student confusing?

22. Switch two numbers to produce an additive magic square.

140	−56	−42	−28
−14	70	56	28
42	14	0	84
98	112	126	−70

23. If a is an element of $\{-3, -2, -1, 0, 1, 2\}$ and b is an element of $\{-5, -4, -3, -2, -1, 0, 1\}$, find the smallest and largest values for the following expressions.

a. $a + b$ **b.** $b - a$ **c.** $|a + b|$

24. Fill in each empty square so that a number in a square will be the sum of the pair of numbers beneath the square.

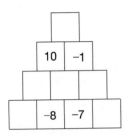

25. a. Demonstrate a 1-1 correspondence between the sets given.
   i. Positive integers and negative integers
   ii. Positive integers and whole numbers
   iii. Whole numbers and integers
   b. What does part (iii) tell you about the number of whole numbers compared to the number of integers?

26. A **squared square** is a square whose interior can be subdivided into two or more squares. One example of a squared square follows. The number written inside a square

gives the length of a side of that square. Determine the dimensions of the unlabeled squares.

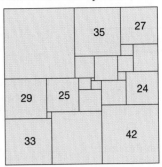

27. In the additive inverse property there is the phrase "there is a unique integer." How would you explain the meaning of that phrase to students?

Analyzing Student Thinking

28. Jarell wonders if, in theory, every integer can have an infinite number of representations using black chips and red chips. How should you respond?

29. When asked, Brandi claims that whole number addition and integer addition have the same properties. Is she correct? Explain.

30. Misti said that her brother helped her learn the following rule: To add two numbers with different signs like 4 and −6, first subtract the numbers and take the sign of the larger number. Explain how this rule can cause confusion.

31. Chandler, performing the subtraction problem $4 - (-3)$, says "A negative times a negative is positive, so this problem means $4 + 3$." How should you respond?

32. Kylee claims that the sum of a positive integer and a negative integer is positive. Is she correct? Explain.

33. Because "−3" means "negative 3," many students assume that "$-n$" is also a negative number. How would you explain to students that "$-n$" is sometimes positive, sometimes negative, and sometimes neither?

34. Brooke says that if a negative integer is represented by red chips and black chips, there must be more red chips than black chips. Is she correct? Explain.

Problems Relating to the NCTM Standards and Curriculum Focal Points

1. The Focal Points for Grade 5 state "Students should explore contexts that they can describe with negative numbers (e.g., situations of owing money or measuring elevations above and below sea level)." Write two problems about integers that involve some real-world context.

2. The Focal Points for Grade 7 state "By applying properties of arithmetic and considering negative numbers in everyday contexts, students explain why the rules of adding, subtracting, multiplying, and dividing with negative numbers make sense." *Explain* one rule of adding or subtracting integers by using everyday contexts of negative numbers.

8.2 MULTIPLICATION, DIVISION, AND ORDER

STARTING POINT

Recall that for positive exponents, the following properties hold:

$$7^4 = 7 \cdot 7 \cdot 7 \cdot 7 \qquad 7^0 = 1 \qquad 7^5 \div 7^3 = 7^{5-3} = 7^2 \qquad 7^5 \cdot 7^3 = 7^{5+3} = 7^8$$

It is important that the properties of negative exponents are consistent with the properties of the exponents above. If the properties were consistent, what would 7^{-2} be equal to? Justify your conclusion. (*Hint*: Consider $7^3 \div 7^5$ or $7^2 \cdot 7^{-2}$.)

Reflection from Research
If students understand multiplication as repeated addition, then a positive times a negative, such as 7×-6, can be taught as "seven negative 6s" (Bley & Thornton, 1989).

Multiplication and Its Properties

Integer multiplication can be viewed as extending whole-number multiplication. Recall that the first model for whole-number multiplication was repeated addition, as illustrated here:

$$3 \times 4 = 4 + 4 + 4 = 12.$$

Now suppose that you were selling tickets and you accepted three bad checks worth \$4 each. A natural way to think of your situation would be $3 \times (-4) = (-4) + (-4) + (-4) = -12$ (Figure 8.13).

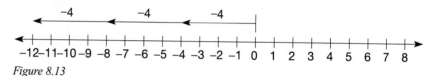

Figure 8.13

Rules for integer multiplication can be motivated using the following pattern.

THE FIRST COLUMN REMAINS 3 THROUGHOUT.	$3 \times 4 = 12$	*3 LESS*
	$3 \times 3 = 9$	*3 LESS*
THE SECOND COLUMN IS	$3 \times 2 = 6$	*3 LESS*
DECREASING BY 1 EACH	$3 \times 1 = 3$	*ETC.*
TIME.	$3 \times 0 = 0$	
	$3 \times (-1) = ?$	
	$3 \times (-2) = ?$	
	$3 \times (-3) = ?$	
	$3 \times (-4) = ?$	

This pattern extended suggests that $3 \times (-1) = -3, 3 \times (-2) = -6, 3 \times (-3) = -9$, and so on. A similar pattern can be used to suggest what the product of two negative integers should be, as follows.

THE FIRST COLUMN REMAINS (−3).	$(-3) \times 3 = -9$	
	$(-3) \times 2 = -6$	*3 MORE*
	$(-3) \times 1 = -3$	*3 MORE*
	$(-3) \times 0 = 0$	*3 MORE*
THE SECOND COLUMN	$(-3) \times (-1) = ?$	*ETC.*
DECREASES BY 1 EACH	$(-3) \times (-2) = ?$	
TIME.	$(-3) \times (-3) = ?$	

Problem-Solving Strategy
Look for a Pattern

This pattern suggests that $(-3)(-1) = 3, (-3)(-2) = 6, (-3)(-3) = 9$, and so on.

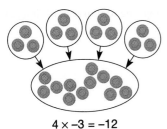

$4 \times -3 = -12$

Figure 8.14

Integer multiplication can also be modeled using black and red chips. Since 4×3 can be thought of as "combine 4 groups of 3 black chips," the operation 4×-3 can be thought of as "combine 4 groups of 3 red chips" (see Figure 8.14).

Notice that the sign on the second number in the operation determines the color of chips being used. Since the first number in 4×-3 is positive, we *combined* 4 groups of -3. How would the situation of -4×3 be handled? In this case the first number (4) is negative, which indicates that we should "*take away* 4 groups of 3 black chips" rather than combine. When the first number is positive, the groups are *combined* into a new set that has a value of 0. When the first number is negative, the groups are *taken away* from a set that has a value of 0. In order to take something away from a set with a value of 0, we must add some chips with a value of 0 to the set. This is done by adding an equal number of red and black chips to the set. After taking away 4 groups of 3 black chips, the resulting set has 12 red chips or a value of -12 (Figure 8.15).

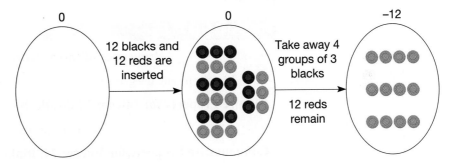

Figure 8.15

The number-line model, the patterns, and the black and red chips model all lead to the following definition.

DEFINITION

Multiplication of Integers

Let a and b be any integers.

1. *Multiplying by 0:* $a \cdot 0 = 0 = 0 \cdot a$.

2. *Multiplying two positives:* If a and b are positive, they are multiplied as whole numbers.

3. *Multiplying a positive and a negative:* If a is positive and b is positive (thus $-b$ is negative), then

$$a(-b) = -(ab),$$

where ab is the whole-number product of a and b. That is, the product of a positive and a negative is negative.

4. *Multiplying two negatives:* If a and b are positive, then

$$(-a)(-b) = ab,$$

where ab is the whole-number product of a and b. That is, the product of two negatives is positive.

Example 8.6   Calculate the following using the definition of integer multiplication.

a. $5 \cdot 0$
b. $5 \cdot 8$
c. $5(-8)$
d. $(-5)(-8)$

SOLUTION
a. *Multiplying by zero:* $5 \cdot 0 = 0$
b. *Multiplying two positives:* $5 \cdot 8 = 40$
c. *Multiplying a positive and a negative:* $5(-8) = -(5 \cdot 8) = -40$
d. *Multiplying two negatives:* $(-5)(-8) = 5 \cdot 8 = 40$ ∎

The definition of multiplication of integers can be used to justify the following properties.

PROPERTIES

Properties of Integer Multiplication

Let a, b, and c be any integers.

Closure Property for Integer Multiplication

ab is an integer.

Commutative Property for Integer Multiplication

$$ab = ba$$

Associative Property for Integer Multiplication

$$(ab)c = a(bc)$$

Identity Property for Integer Multiplication

1 is the unique integer such that $a \cdot 1 = a = 1 \cdot a$ for all a.

As in the system of whole numbers, our final property, the distributive property, connects addition and multiplication.

PROPERTY

Distributivity of Multiplication over Addition of Integers

Let a, b, and c be any integers. Then

$$a(b + c) = ab + ac.$$

Using the preceding properties of addition and multiplication of integers, some important results that are useful in computations can be justified.

THEOREM

Let a be any integer. Then

$$a(-1) = -a.$$

PROOF   First, $a \cdot 0 = 0$ by definition.

But
$$
\begin{aligned}
a \cdot 0 &= a[1 + (-1)] &\quad& \textit{Additive inverse} \\
&= a(1) + a(-1) &\quad& \textit{Distributivity} \\
&= a + a(-1). &\quad& \textit{Multiplicative identity}
\end{aligned}
$$

Therefore, $a + a(-1) = 0$

Then $a + a(-1) = a + (-a)$ *Additive inverse*

Finally $a(-1) = -a$ *Additive cancellation*   ■

Stating the preceding result in words, we have "the product of negative one and any integer is the opposite (or additive inverse) of that integer." Notice that, on the integer number line, multiplication by -1 is equivalent geometrically to reflecting an integer about the origin (Figure 8.16).

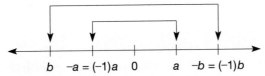

$\quad b \quad -a = (-1)a \quad 0 \qquad a \quad -b = (-1)b$

Figure 8.16

THEOREM

Let a and b be any integers. Then
$$(-a)b = -(ab).$$

PROOF

$$
\begin{aligned}
(-a)b &= [(-1)a]b &\quad& (-1)a = -a \\
&= (-1)(ab) &\quad& \textit{Associativity for multiplication} \\
&= -(ab) &\quad& (-1)a = -a
\end{aligned}
$$

Using commutativity with this result gives $a(-b) = -(ab)$.   ■

THEOREM

Let a and b be any integers. Then
$$(-a)(-b) = ab \text{ for all integers } a, b.$$

PROOF

$$
\begin{aligned}
(-a)(-b) &= [(-1)a][(-1)b] &\quad& (-1)a = -a \\
&= [(-1)(-1)](ab) &\quad& \textit{Associativity and commutativity} \\
&= 1ab &\quad& \textit{Definition of integer multiplication} \\
&= ab &\quad& \textit{Multiplicative identity}
\end{aligned}
$$ ■

NOTE: The three preceding results encompass more than just statements about multiplying by negative numbers. For example, $(-a)(-b) = ab$ is read "the opposite of a times the opposite of b is ab." The numbers a and b may be positive, negative, or zero; hence $(-a)$ and $(-b)$ also may be negative, positive, or zero. Thus there is a subtle but important difference between these results and parts 3 and 4 of the definition of multiplication of integers.

Example 8.7   Calculate the following products.

a. $3(-1)$ **b.** $(-3)5$ **c.** $(-3)(-4)$ **d.** $(-1)(-7)$ **e.** $(-x)(-y)(-z)$

SOLUTION
a. $3(-1) = -3$, since $a(-1) = -a$.
b. $(-3)5 = -(3 \cdot 5) = -15$, since $(-a)b = -(ab)$.
c. $(-3)(-4) = (3 \cdot 4) = 12$, since $(-a)(-b) = ab$.
d. $(-1)(-7)$ can be found in two ways: $(-1)(-7) = -(-7) = 7$, since $(-1)a = -a$, and $(-1)(-7) = 1 \cdot 7 = 7$, since $(-a)(-b) = ab$.
e. $(-x)(-y)(-z) = xy(-z)$, since $(-a)(-b) = ab$; and $xy(-z) = -(xyz)$, since $a(-b) = -(ab)$. ∎

Finally, the next property will be useful in integer division.

PROPERTY

Multiplicative Cancellation Property

Let a, b, c be any integers with $c \neq 0$. If $ac = bc$, then $a = b$.

Notice that the condition $c \neq 0$ is necessary, since $3 \cdot 0 = 2 \cdot 0$, but $3 \neq 2$.

The multiplicative cancellation property is truly a *property* of the integers (and whole numbers and counting numbers) because it cannot be proven from any of our previous properties. However, in a system where nonzero numbers have multiplicative inverses (such as the fractions), it is a theorem. The following property is equivalent to the multiplicative cancellation property.

Algebraic Reasoning
This property makes it possible to solve equations such as $(x - 2)(x + 3) = 0$. Because of this property, it is known that either $x - 2 = 0$ or $x + 3 = 0$.

PROPERTY

Zero Divisors Property

Let a and b be integers. Then $ab = 0$ if and only if $a = 0$ or $b = 0$ or a and b both equal zero.

 Check for Understanding: Exercise/Problem Set A #1–7

Division

Recall that to find $6 \div 3$ in the whole numbers, we sought the whole number c, where $6 = 3 \cdot c$. Division of integers can be viewed as an extension of whole-number division using the missing-factor approach.

DEFINITION

Division of Integers

Let a and b be any integers, where $b \neq 0$. Then $a \div b = c$ if and only if $a = b \cdot c$ for a unique integer c.

| **Example 8.8** | Find the following quotients (if possible). |

a. $12 \div (-3)$ **b.** $(-15) \div (-5)$ **c.** $(-8) \div 2$ **d.** $7 \div (-2)$

SOLUTION

a. $12 \div (-3) = c$ if and only if $12 = (-3) \cdot c$. From multiplication, $12 = (-3)(-4)$. Since $(-3) \cdot c = (-3)(-4)$, by multiplicative cancellation, $c = -4$.

b. $(-15) \div (-5) = c$ if and only if $-15 = (-5) \cdot c$. From multiplication, $-15 = (-5) \cdot 3$. Since $(-5) \cdot c = (-5) \cdot 3$, by multiplicative cancellation, $c = 3$.

c. $(-8) \div 2 = c$ if and only if $(-8) = 2 \cdot c$. Thus $c = -4$, since $2(-4) = -8$.

d. $7 \div (-2) = c$ if and only if $7 = (-2) \cdot c$. There is no such integer c. Therefore, $7 \div (-2)$ is undefined in the integers. ■

Considering the results of this example, the following generalizations can be made about the division of integers: Assume that b divides a; that is, that b is a factor of a.

1. *Dividing by 1:* $a \div 1 = a$.

2. *Dividing two positives (negatives):* If a and b are both positive (or both negative), then $a \div b$ is positive.

3. *Dividing a positive and a negative:* If one of a or b is positive and the other is negative, then $a \div b$ is *negative*.

4. *Dividing zero by a nonzero integer:* $0 \div b = 0$, where $b \neq 0$, since $0 = b \cdot 0$. As with whole numbers, division by zero is undefined for integers.

| **Example 8.9** | Calculate. |

a. $0 \div 5$ **b.** $40 \div 5$ **c.** $40 \div (-5)$ **d.** $(-40) \div (-5)$

SOLUTION

a. *Dividing into zero:* $0 \div 5 = 0$

b. *Dividing two positives:* $40 \div 5 = 8$

c. *Dividing a positive and negative:* $40 \div (-5) = -8$ and $(-40) \div 5 = -8$

d. *Dividing two negatives:* $(-40) \div (-5) = 8$ ■

The negative-sign key can be used to find $-306 \times (-76) \div 12$ as follows:

$$\boxed{(-)} \ 306 \ \boxed{\times} \ \boxed{(-)} \ 76 \ \boxed{\div} \ 12 \ \boxed{=} \ \boxed{1938}$$

However, this calculation can be performed without the negative-sign key by observing that there are an even number (two) of negative integers multiplied together. Thus the product is positive. In the case of an odd number of negative factors, the product is negative.

 Check for Understanding: Exercise/Problem Set A #8–11

Negative Exponents and Scientific Notation

When studying whole numbers, exponents were introduced as a shortcut for multiplication. As the following pattern suggests, there is a way to extend our current definition of exponents to include integer exponents.

$$a^3 = a \cdot a \cdot a$$
$$a^2 = a \cdot a \quad \Big) \div a$$
$$a^1 = a \quad \Big) \div a$$
$$a^0 = 1 \quad \Big) \div a$$
$$a^{-1} = \frac{1}{a} \quad \Big) \div a$$
$$a^{-2} = \frac{1}{a^2} \quad \Big) \div a$$
$$a^{-3} = \frac{1}{a^3} \quad \Big) \div a$$
$$\vdots$$

etc.

Problem-Solving Strategy
Look for a Pattern

This pattern leads to the next definition.

DEFINITION

Negative Integer Exponent

Let a be any nonzero number and n be a positive integer. Then

$$a^{-n} = \frac{1}{a^n}.$$

Algebraic Reasoning
Negative integer exponents give students a way to see that $\frac{1}{7^3} \cdot 7^3 = 1$. Because $\frac{1}{7^3} = 7^{-3}$, $\frac{1}{7^3} \cdot 7^3 = 7^{-3} \cdot 7^3 = 7^{-3+3} = 7^0 = 1$.

Knowing this fact is a tool for solving an equation like $7^3 x = 2401$.

For example, $7^{-3} = \frac{1}{7^3}$, $2^{-5} = \frac{1}{2^5}$, $3^{-10} = \frac{1}{3^{10}}$, and so on. Also, $\frac{1}{4^{-3}} = \frac{1}{1/4^3} = 4^3$.

The last sentence indicates how the definition leads to the statement $a^{-n} = \frac{1}{a^n}$ *for all integers n*.

It can be shown that the theorems on whole-number exponents given in Section 3.3 can be extended to integer exponents. That is, for any nonzero numbers a and b, and integers m and n, we have

$$a^m \cdot a^n = a^{m+n}$$
$$a^m \cdot b^m = (ab)^m$$
$$(a^m)^n = a^{mn}$$
$$\frac{a^m}{a^n} = a^{m-n}.$$

NCTM Standard
All students should develop an understanding of large numbers and recognize and appropriately use exponential, scientific, and calculator notations.

In Section 7.2, scientific notation was introduced in terms of very large numbers and positive exponents. With the introduction of negative exponents, we can now use scientific notation to represent very small numbers. The following table provides some examples of small numbers written in scientific notation.

	SCIENTIFIC NOTATION	STANDARD NOTATION
Mass of a human egg	1.5×10^{-9} kilograms	0.0000000015 kilograms
Diameter of a proton	1×10^{-11} meters	0.00000000001 meters
Diameter of human hair	7.9×10^{-4} centimeters	0.00079 centimeters

Example 8.10   Convert as indicated.

a. 7.2×10^{-14} to standard notation   **b.** 0.0000961 to scientific notation

SOLUTION

a. $7.2 \times 10^{-14} = 0.000000000000072$ **b.** $0.0000961 = 9.61 \times 10^{-5}$ ■

Conversions from standard notation to scientific notation can be performed on most scientific calculators. For example, the following keystrokes convert 38,500,000 to scientific notation.

38500000 [2nd] [Sci] [3.85^{07}]

The raised "07" represents 10^7. Since the number of digits displayed by calculators differs, one needs to keep these limitations in mind when converting between scientific and standard notations.

Scientific notation is used to solve problems involving very large and very small numbers, especially in science and engineering.

Example 8.11   The diameter of Jupiter is about 1.438×10^8 meters, and the diameter of Earth is about 1.27×10^7 meters. What is the ratio of the diameter of Jupiter to the diameter of Earth?

SOLUTION

$$\frac{1.438 \times 10^8}{1.27 \times 10^7} = \frac{1.438}{1.27} \times \frac{10^8}{10^7} \approx 1.13 \times 10 = 11.3$$ ■

When performing calculations involving numbers written in scientific notation, it is customary to express the answer in scientific notation. For example, the product $(5.4 \times 10^7)(3.5 \times 10^6)$ is written as follows:

$$(5.4 \times 10^7)(3.5 \times 10^6) = 18.9 \times 10^{13}$$
$$= 1.89 \times 10^{14}.$$

 Check for Understanding: Exercise/Problem Set A #12–20

Ordering Integers

The concepts of *less than* and *greater than* in the integers are defined to be extensions of ordering in the whole numbers. In the following, ordering is viewed in two equivalent ways, the number-line approach and the addition approach. Let a and b be any integers.

Number-Line Approach   The integer a **is less than** the integer b, written $a < b$, if a is to the left of b on the integer number line. Thus, by viewing the number line, one can see that $-3 < 2$ (Figure 8.17). Also, $-4 < -1$, $-2 < 3$, and so on.

$-3 < 2$

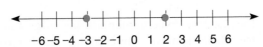

Figure 8.17

Addition Approach The integer a **is less than** the integer b, written $a < b$, if and only if there is a *positive* integer p such that $a + p = b$. Thus $-5 < -3$, since $-5 + 2 = -3$, and $-7 < 2$, since $-7 + 9 = 2$. Equivalently, $a < b$ if and only if $b - a$ is positive (since $b - a = p$). For example, $-27 < -13$, since $-13 - (-27) = 14$, which is positive.

The integer a **is greater than** the integer b, written $a > b$, if and only if $b < a$. Thus, the discussion of greater than is analogous to that of less than. Similar definitions can be made for $\leq$ and $\geq$.

Example 8.12	Order the following integers from the smallest to largest using the number-line approach.

$$2, 11, -7, 0, 5, -8, -13.$$

SOLUTION See Figure 8.18.

$$-13 < -8 < -7 < 0 < 2 < 5 < 11$$

Figure 8.18 ∎

Example 8.13	Determine the smallest integer in the set $\{3, 0, -5, 9, -8\}$ using the addition approach.

SOLUTION $-8 < -5$, since $(-8) + 3 = -5$. Also, since any negative integer is less than 0 or any positive integer, -8 must be the smallest. ∎

The following results involving ordering, addition, and multiplication extend similar ones for whole numbers.

PROPERTY

Properties of Ordering Integers

Let a, b, and c be any integers, p a positive integer, and n a negative integer.

Transitive Property for Less Than

$$\text{If } a < b \text{ and } b < c, \text{ then } a < c.$$

Property of Less Than and Addition

$$\text{If } a < b, \text{ then } a + c < b + c.$$

Property of Less Than and Multiplication by a Positive

$$\text{If } a < b, \text{ then } ap < bp.$$

Property of Less Than and Multiplication by a Negative

$$\text{If } a < b, \text{ then } an > bn.$$

The first three properties for ordering integers are extensions of similar statements in the whole numbers. However, the fourth property deserves special attention because it involves multiplying both sides of an inequality by a *negative* integer. For example, $2 < 5$ but $2(-3) > 5(-3)$. [Note that 2 *is less than* 5 but that $2(-3)$ *is greater than* $5(-3)$.] Similar properties hold where $<$ is replaced by $\leq$, $>$, and $\geq$. The last two properties, which involve multiplication and ordering, are illustrated in Example 8.14 using the number-line approach.

Example 8.14

a. $-2 < 3$ and $4 > 0$; thus $(-2) \cdot 4 < 3 \cdot 4$ by the property of less than and multiplication by a positive (Figure 8.19).

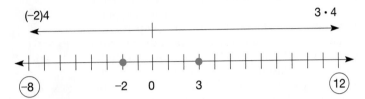

Figure 8.19

b. $-2 < 3$ and $-4 < 0$; thus $(-2)(-4) > 3(-4)$ by the property of less than and multiplication by a negative (Figure 8.20).

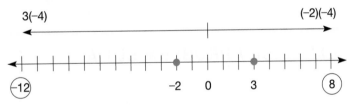

Figure 8.20

Notice how -2 was to the left of 3, *but* $(-2)(-4)$ is to the *right* of $(3)(-4)$. ∎

To see why the property of less than and multiplication by a negative is true, recall that multiplying an integer a by -1 is geometrically the same as reflecting a across the origin on the integer number line. Using this idea in all cases leads to the following general result.

If $a < b$, then $(-1)a > (-1)b$ (Figure 8.21).

Algebraic Reasoning
When asked to solve an inequality like $-x > 5$, one might know that multiplying both sides of the inequality by a negative number will impact the direction of the inequality symbol, making the solution $x < -5$. The discussion at the right, however, helps clarify why this is so.

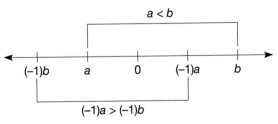

Figure 8.21

To justify the statement "if $a < b$ and $n < 0$, then $an > bn$," suppose that $a < b$ and $n < 0$. Since n is negative, we can express n as $(-1)p$, where p is positive. Then $ap < bp$ by the property of less than and multiplication by a positive. But if $ap < bp$, then $(-1)ap > (-1)bp$, or $a\,[(-1)p] > b\,[(-1)p]$, which, in turn, yields $an > bn$. Informally, this result says that "multiplying an inequality by a negative number 'reverses' the inequality."

✔ **Check for Understanding:** Exercise/Problem Set A #21–23

MATHEMATICAL MORSEL

In January 1999, a 16-year-old high school student from Cork County, Ireland, named Sarah Flannery, caused quite a stir in the technology world. She devised an advanced mathematical code used to encrypt information sent electronically. Her algorithm uses the properties of 2×2 matrices and is said to be up to 30 times faster than the previous algorithm, Rivest, Shamir, and Adlemann (RSA), which was created by three students at Massachusetts Institute of Technology in 1977. She named her algorithm the Cayley-Purser algorithm, after nineteenth-century mathematician Arthur Cayley and Michael Purser, a Trinity College professor who gave her the initial ideas and inspired her. Because such an advancement can have a significant impact in the computer and banking industries, Sarah had computer firms offering her consulting jobs and prestigious universities inviting her to sign up when she graduated.

Section 8.2   EXERCISE / PROBLEM SET A

EXERCISES

1. Write one addition and one multiplication equation represented by each number-line model.

a.

b.

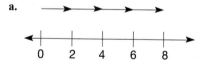

c.

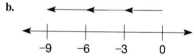

2. a. Extend the following patterns by writing the next three equations.

i. $6 \times 3 = 18$
$6 \times 2 = 12$
$6 \times 1 = 6$
$6 \times 0 = 0$

ii. $9 \times 3 = 27$
$9 \times 2 = 18$
$9 \times 1 = 9$
$9 \times 0 = 0$

b. What rule of multiplication of negative numbers is suggested by the equations you have written?

3. Find the following products.
a. $6(-5)$ **b.** $(-2)(-16)$
c. $-(-3)(-5)$ **d.** $-3(-7-6)$

4. Represent the following products using black and red chips and give the results.
a. $3 \times (-2)$ **b.** $(-3) \times (-4)$

5. The uniqueness of additive inverses and other properties of integers enable us to give another justification that $(-3)4 = -12$. By definition, the additive inverse of $3(4)$ is $-(3 \cdot 4)$. Provide reasons for each of the following equations.

$$(-3)(4) + 3 \cdot 4 = (-3 + 3) \cdot 4$$
$$= 0 \cdot 4$$
$$= 0$$

Thus we have shown that $(-3)4$ is also the additive inverse of $3 \cdot 4$ and hence is equal to $-(3 \cdot 4)$.

6. Provide reasons for each of the following steps.

$$a(b - c) = a[b + (-c)]$$
$$= ab + a(-c)$$
$$= ab + [-(ac)]$$
$$= ab - ac$$

Which property have you justified?

7. Make use of the $\boxed{(-)}$ key on a calculator to calculate each of the following.
   a. -36×72 b. $-51 \times (-38)$
   c. $-128 \times (-765)$

8. Solve the following equations using the missing factor approach.
   a. $-3x = -9$ b. $-15x = 1290$

9. Find each quotient.
   a. $-18 \div 3$ b. $-45 \div (-9)$
   c. $75 \div (-5)$

10. Make use of the $\boxed{(-)}$ key on a calculator to calculate each of the following.
    a. $-658 \div 14$ b. $3588 \div (-23)$
    c. $-108,697 \div (-73)$

11. Consider the statement $(x + y) \div z = (x \div z) + (y \div z)$. Is this a true statement in the integers for the following values of x, y, and z?
    a. $x = 16, y = -12, z = 4$
    b. $x = -20, y = 36, z = -4$
    c. $x = -42, y = -18, z = -6$
    d. $x = -12, y = -8, z = 2$

12. Extend the meaning of a whole-number exponent.

$$a^n = \underbrace{a \cdot a \cdot a \cdots a,}_{n \text{ factors}}$$

where a is any integer. Use this definition to find the following values.
   a. 2^4 b. $(-3)^3$ c. $(-2)^4$
   d. $(-5)^2$ e. $(-3)^5$ f. $(-2)^6$

13. If a is an integer and $a \neq 0$, which of the following expressions are always positive and which are always negative?
   a. a b. $-a$ c. a^2
   d. $(-a)^2$ e. $-(a)^2$ f. a^3

14. Write each of the following as a fraction without exponents.
   a. 10^{-2} b. 4^{-3} c. 2^{-6} d. 5^{-3}

15. a. Simplify $4^{-2} \cdot 4^6$ by expressing it in terms of whole-number exponents and simplifying.
    b. Simplify $4^{-2} \cdot 4^6$ by applying $a^m \cdot a^n = a^{m+n}$.
    c. Repeat parts (a) and (b) to simplify $5^{-4} \cdot 5^{-2}$.
    d. Does it appear that the property $a^m \cdot a^n = a^{m+n}$ still applies for integer exponents?

16. a. Simplify $\dfrac{3^{-2}}{3^5}$ by expressing it in terms of whole-number exponents and simplifying.
    b. Simplify the expression in part (a) by applying
    $$\frac{a^m}{a^n} = a^{m-n}.$$

c. Repeat parts (a) and (b) to simplify $\dfrac{6^3}{6^{-7}}$.

d. Does it appear that the property $\dfrac{a^m}{a^n} = a^{m-n}$ still applies for integer exponents?

17. Use the definition of integer exponents and properties of exponents to find a numerical value for the following expressions.
    a. $3^{-2} \cdot 3^5$ b. $\dfrac{6^{-3}}{6^{-4}}$ c. $(3^{-4})^{-2}$

18. Each of the following numbers is written in scientific notation. Rewrite each in standard decimal form.
    a. 3.7×10^{-5} b. 2.45×10^{-8}

19. Express each of the following numbers in scientific notation.
    a. 0.0004
    b. 0.0000016
    c. 0.000000000495

20. You can use a scientific calculator to perform arithmetic operations with numbers written in scientific notation. If the exponent is negative, use your $\boxed{+/-}$ or $\boxed{CHS}$ or $\boxed{(-)}$ key to change the sign.

For example, see the following multiplication problem.

$$(1.6 \times 10^{-4})(2.7 \times 10^{-8})$$

$1.6 \boxed{SCI}\ 4\ \boxed{+/-}\ \boxed{\times}\ 2.7\ \boxed{SCI}\ 8\ \boxed{+/-}\ \boxed{=}$

$\boxed{4.32 - 12}$

(NOTE: The sequence of steps or appearance of the answer in the display window may be slightly different on your calculator.)

Use your calculator to evaluate each of the following. Express your results in scientific notation.
   a. $(7.6 \times 10^{10})(9.5 \times 10^{-36})$
   b. $(2.4 \times 10^{-6})(3.45 \times 10^{-20})$
   c. $\dfrac{1.2 \times 10^{-15}}{4.8 \times 10^{-6}}$
   d. $\dfrac{(7.5 \times 10^{-12})(8 \times 10^{-17})}{(1.5 \times 10^9)}$
   e. $\dfrac{480,000,000}{0.0000006}$
   f. $\dfrac{0.000000000000123}{0.0000006}$

21. Show that each of the following is true by using the number-line approach.
    a. $-3 < 2$
    b. $-6 < -2$
    c. $-3 > -12$

22. Write each of the following lists of integers in increasing order from left to right.

a. $-5, 5, 2, -2, 0$ **b.** $12, -6, -8, 3, -5$
c. $-2, -3, -5, -8, -11$ **d.** $23, -36, 45, -72, -108$

23. Complete the following statements by inserting $<$, $=$, or $>$ in the blanks to produce true statements.

a. If $x < 4$, then $x + 2$ _____ 6.
b. If $x > -2$, then $x - 6$ _____ -8.

PROBLEMS

24. Fill in each empty square so that a number in a square is the product of the two numbers beneath it.

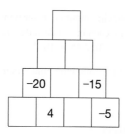

25. a. Which of the following integers when substituted for x make the given inequality true: $-6, -10, -8, -7$?

$$3x + 5 < -16$$

b. Is there a largest integer value for x that makes the inequality true?
c. Is there a smallest integer value for x that makes the inequality true?

26. a. The rules of integer addition can be summarized in a table as follows:

+	+	−
+	+	?
−		

Positive + positive = positive (+ sign)
Positive + negative = positive or negative or zero (? sign)
Complete the table.

b. Make a similar table for
   i. subtraction.
   ii. multiplication.
   iii. division (when possible).

27. a. If possible, find an integer x to satisfy the following conditions.
   i. $|x| > x$ **ii.** $|x| = x$
   iii. $|x| < x$ **iv.** $|x| \geq x$

b. Which, if any, of the conditions in part (a) will hold for all integers?

28. A student suggests that she can show $(-1)(-1) = 1$ using the fact that $-(-1) = 1$. Is her reasoning correct? If yes, what result will she apply? If not, why not?

29. A student does not believe that $-10 < -5$. He argues that a debt of $10 is greater than a debt of $5. How would you convince him that the inequality is true?

30. In a multiplicative magic square, the product of the integers in each row, each column, and each diagonal is the same number. Complete the multiplication magic square given.

31. If $0 < x < y$ where x and y are integers, prove that $x^2 < y^2$.

32. There are 6.022×10^{23} atoms in 12.01 grams of carbon. Find the mass of one atom of carbon. Express your answer in scientific notation.

33. Hair on the human body can grow as fast as 0.0000000043 meter per second.
   a. At this rate, how much would a strand of hair grow in one month of 30 days? Express your answer in scientific notation.
   b. About how long would it take for a strand of hair to grow to be 1 meter in length?

34. A farmer goes to market and buys 100 animals at a total cost of $1000. If cows cost $50 each, sheep cost $10 each, and rabbits cost 50 cents each, how many of each kind does he buy?

35. Prove or disprove: The square of any whole number is a multiple of 3 or one more than a multiple of 3.

36. A shopper asked for 50 cents worth of apples. The shopper was surprised when she received five more than the previous week. Then she noticed that the price had dropped 10 cents per dozen. What was the new price per dozen?

37. Assume that if $ac = bc$ and $c \neq 0$, then $a = b$. Prove that if $ab = 0$, then $a = 0$ or $b = 0$. (*Hint:* Assume that $b \neq 0$. Then $ab = 0 = 0 \cdot b \ldots$.)

| Section 8.2 | EXERCISE / PROBLEM SET B |

EXERCISES

1. Illustrate the following products on an integer number line.
   a. $2 \times (-5)$ **b.** $3 \times (-4)$ **c.** $5 \times (-2)$

2. Extend the following patterns by writing the next three equations. What rule of multiplication of negative numbers is suggested by the equations you have written?
   a. $-5 \times 3 = -15$ **b.** $-8 \times 3 = -24$
   $\ -5 \times 2 = -10$ $\ -8 \times 2 = -16$
   $\ -5 \times 1 = -5$ $\ -8 \times 1 = -8$
   $\ -5 \times 0 = 0$ $\ -8 \times 0 = 0$

3. Find the following products.
   a. $(-2)(-5)(-3)$
   b. $(-10)(7)(-6)$
   c. $5[(-2)(13) + 5(-4)]$
   d. $-23[(-2)(6) + (-3)(-4)]$

4. Represent the following products using black and red chips and give the results.
   a. $(-3) \times 4$ **b.** $(2) \times (-4)$ **c.** $(-2) \times (-1)$

5. The following argument shows another justification for $(-3)(-4) = 12$. Provide reasons for each of the following equations.

$$(-3)(-4) + (-3) \cdot 4 = (-3)(-4 + 4)$$
$$= (-3) \cdot 0$$
$$= 0$$

Therefore, $(-3)(-4)$ is the additive inverse of $(-3)4 = -12$. But the additive inverse of -12 is 12, so $(-3)(-4) = 12$.

6. Expand each of the following products.
   a. $-6(x + 2)$ **b.** $-5(x - 11)$
   c. $-3(x - y)$ **d.** $x(a - b)$
   e. $-x(a - b)$ **f.** $(x - 3)(x + 2)$

7. Compute using a calculator.
   a. $(-36)(52)$
   b. $(-83)(-98)$
   c. $(127)(-31)(-57)$
   d. $(-39)(-92)(-68)$

8. Solve the following equations using the missing-factor approach.
   a. $11x = -374$ **b.** $-9x = -8163$

9. Find each quotient.
   a. $(-5 + 5) \div (-2)$ **b.** $[144 \div (-12)] \div (-3)$
   c. $144 \div [-12 \div (-3)]$

10. Compute using a calculator.
   a. $-899 \div 29$
   b. $-5904 \div (-48)$
   c. $7308 \div (-126)$
   d. $[-1848 \div (-56)] \div (-33)$

11. Consider the statement $x \div (y + z) = (x \div y) + (x \div z)$. Is this statement true for the following values of x, y, and z?
   a. $x = 12, y = -2, z = -4$
   b. $x = 18, y = 2, z = -3$

12. Are the following numbers positive or negative?
   a. $(-2)^5$ **b.** $(-2)^8$ **c.** $(-5)^3$
   d. $(-5)^{16}$ **e.** $(-1)^{20}$ **f.** $(-1)^{33}$
   g. a^n if $a < 0$ and n is even
   h. a^n if $a < 0$ and n is odd

13. If a is an integer and $a \neq 0$, which expressions are always positive and which are always negative?
   a. a^3 **b.** $(-a)^3$ **c.** $-(a^3)$
   d. a^4 **e.** $(-a)^4$ **f.** $-(a^4)$

14. Write each of the following as a fraction without exponents.
   a. 4^{-2} **b.** 2^{-5} **c.** 7^{-3}

15. a. Simplify $(3^2)^{-3}$ by expressing it in terms of whole-number exponents and simplifying.
   b. Simplify $(3^2)^{-3}$ by applying $(a^m)^n = a^{mn}$.
   c. Repeat parts (a) and (b) to simplify $(5^{-3})^{-2}$.
   d. Does it appear that the property $(a^m)^n = a^{mn}$ still applies for integer exponents?

16. a. Simplify $(2^{-3})(4^{-3})$ by expressing it in terms of whole-number exponents and simplifying.
   b. Simplify $(2^{-3})(4^{-3})$ by applying $(a^m)(b^m) = (ab)^m$.
   c. Repeat parts (a) and (b) to simplify $(3^{-4})(5^{-4})$.
   d. Does it appear that the property $(a^m)(b^m) = (ab)^m$ still applies for integer exponents?

17. Apply the properties of exponents to express the following values in a simpler form.

   a. $\dfrac{5^{-2} \cdot 5^3}{5^{-4}}$

   b. $\dfrac{(3^{-2})^{-5}}{3^{-6}}$

   c. $\dfrac{8^3}{2^3 \cdot 4^{-2}}$

   d. $\dfrac{2^6 \cdot 3^2}{(3^{-2})^{-2} \cdot 4^5}$

18. Each of the following numbers is written in scientific notation. Rewrite each in standard decimal form.
   a. 9.0×10^{-6}
   b. 1.26×10^{-13}

19. Express each of the following numbers in scientific notation.
  a. 0.000000691
  b. 0.0000000000003048
  c. 0.00000000000000000008071

20. Use your calculator to evaluate each of the following. Express your answers in scientific notation.
  a. $(9.62 \times 10^{-12})(2.8 \times 10^{-9})$
  b. $\dfrac{3.74 \times 10^{-6}}{8.5 \times 10^{-30}}$
  c. $(4.35 \times 10^{-40})(7.8 \times 10^{19})$
  d. $\dfrac{(1.38 \times 10^{12})(4.5 \times 10^{-16})}{1.15 \times 10^{10}}$
  e. $(62,000)(0.00000000000033)$
  f. $\dfrac{0.000000000000000232}{0.000000145}$

21. Show that each of the following inequalities is true by using the addition approach.
  a. $-7 < -3$ **b.** $-6 < 5$ **c.** $-17 > -23$

22. Fill in the blanks with the appropriate symbol—$<$, $>$, or $=$ —to produce true statements.
  a. -4 _____ 9
  b. 3 _____ -2
  c. -4 _____ -5
  d. 0 _____ -2
  e. $3 + (-5)$ _____ $2 \times (-3)$
  f. $(-12) \div (-2)$ _____ $-2 - (-3)$
  g. $15 - (-6)$ _____ $(-3) \times (-7)$
  h. $5 + (-5)$ _____ $(-3) \times (-6)$

23. Complete the following statements by inserting $<$, $=$, or $>$ in the blanks to produce true statements.
  a. If $x < -3$, then $4x$ _____ -12.
  b. If $x > -6$, then $-2x$ _____ 12.

PROBLEMS

24. Fill in each empty square so that a number in a square is the product of the two numbers beneath it.

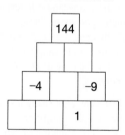

25. a. Which of the following integers when substituted for x make the given inequality true: $-4, -3, -2, -1$?
$$5x - 3 \geq -18$$
  b. Is there a largest integer value for x that makes the inequality true?
  c. Is there a smallest integer value for x that makes the inequality true?

26. a. Is there a largest whole number? integer? negative integer? positive integer? If yes, what is it?
  b. Is there a smallest whole number? integer? negative integer? positive integer? If yes, what is it?

27. Use absolute-value notation to write the following two parts of the definition of integer multiplication.
  a. If p is positive and q is negative, then $pq =$ _____.
  b. If p is negative and q is negative, then $pq =$ _____.

28. Use the absolute-value notation to express the answers for these division problems.
  a. If p is positive and q is negative, then $p \div q =$ _____.
  b. If both of p and q are negative, then $p \div q =$ _____.

29. If $x < y$, where x and y are integers, is it always true that $x^2 < y^2$? Prove or give a counterexample.

30. If $x < y$, where x and y are integers, is it always true that $z - y < z - x$, if z is an integer? Prove or give a counterexample.

31. The mass of one electron is 9.11×10^{-28} grams. A uranium atom contains 92 electrons. Find the total mass of the electrons in a uranium atom. Express your answer in scientific notation.

32. A rare gas named "krypton" glows orange when heated by an electric current. The wavelength of the light it emits is about 605.8 nanometers, and this wavelength is used to define the exact length of a meter. If one nanometer is 0.000000001 meter, what is the wavelength of krypton in meters? Express your answer in scientific notation.

33. The mass of one molecule of hemoglobin can be described as 0.11 attogram.
  a. If 1 attogram $= 10^{-21}$ kilogram, what is the mass in kilograms of one molecule of hemoglobin?
  b. The mass of a molecule of hemoglobin can be specified in terms of other units, too. For example, the mass of a molecule of hemoglobin might be given as 68,000 daltons. Determine the number of kilograms in 1 dalton.

34. Red blood corpuscles in the human body are constantly disintegrating and being replaced. About 73,000 of them disintegrate and are replaced every 3.16×10^{-2} second.
  a. How many red blood corpuscles break down in 1 second? Express your answer in scientific notation.
  b. There are approximately 25,000,000,000,000 red blood corpuscles in the blood of an adult male at any given time. About how long does it take for all of these red blood corpuscles to break down and be replaced?

35. Prove or disprove: If $x^2 + y^2 = z^2$ for whole numbers x, y, and z, either x or y is a multiple of 3.

36. A woman born in the first half of the nineteenth century (1800 to 1849) was X years old in the year X^2. In what year was she born?

37. Assume that the statement "If $ab = 0$, then $a = 0$ or $b = 0$" is true. Prove the multiplication cancellation property. [*Hint:* If $ac = bc$, where $c \neq 0$, then $ac - bc = 0$, or $(a - b)c = 0$. Since $(a - b)c = 0$, what can you conclude based on the statement assumed here?]

Analyzing Student Thinking

38. After finding that $(-x)(-y)(-z) = -xyz$, Olga asks, "How do you know the answer is negative if you don't know what x, y, or z are?" How should you respond?

39. Anthony says that for integers a and b, $(a + b)(a + b) = a^2 + b^2$. Is this statement always true, never true, or sometimes true?

40. Given the problem $(-a) \div (-b)$, Jeannette says that since there are two negative signs, the answer is positive. Is she correct? Explain.

41. Bailey looks at the problem $(-a) \div (-b)$, and says that since there are two negative signs, you can forget them. So the answer is $a \div b$. Is she correct? Explain.

42. Juan changes 3.47×10^{-7} to its decimal standard form and has 7 zeros between the decimal point and the 3. Is he correct? Explain.

43. Tonya says that if $7x > -28$, then $x < -4$ because when you have a negative, you reverse the inequality. How should you respond?

44. Joe and Misha are using their calculators to do the problem -7^2. Joe types the negative sign, the seven, the exponent character ^, and then 2. He gets the answer -49. Misha's calculator won't allow her to type the negative sign first, so she types 7, then the negative sign, then the exponent character ^, and then 2. Her calculator says the answer is 49. Explain why there is a difference in the results.

Problems Relating to the NCTM Standards and Curriculum Focal Points

1. The Focal Points for Grade 7 state "By applying properties of arithmetic and considering negative numbers in everyday contexts, students explain why the rules of adding, subtracting, multiplying, and dividing with negative numbers make sense." Using contexts, explain one of the properties of multiplication.

2. The NCTM Standards state "All students should develop an understanding of large numbers and recognize and appropriately use exponential, scientific, and calculator notations." Explain how exponents are used in scientific notation to represent large and small numbers.

3. The NCTM Standards state "All students should develop meaning for integers and represent and compare quantities with them." Describe an example where integers can be used to compare quantities.

END OF CHAPTER MATERIAL

Solution of Initial Problem

Find the 12 different pentominoes.

Strategy: Use Cases

Cases can be used to solve this problem by fixing a certain number of squares as a case and moving the remaining squares around to see the different configurations for that case.

Case 3: 3 in a row

Case 1: 5 in a row

Case 2: 4 in a row

Case 4: 2 in a row

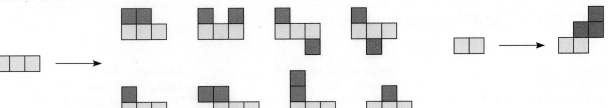

Additional Problems Where the Strategy "Use Cases" Is Useful

1. If the sum of three consecutive numbers is even, prove that two of the numbers must be odd.

2. If m and n are integers, under what circumstances will $m^2 - n^2$ be positive?

3. Show that the square of any whole number is either a multiple of 5, one more than a multiple of 5, or one less than a multiple of 5.

People in Mathematics

Grace Chisholm Young (1868–1944) Grace Chisholm Young, who was born in England, became the first woman to receive a doctoral degree in Germany. She married William Young, a mathematician who had been her tutor in England. Both had done important mathematical research independently, but together they produced 220 mathematical papers, several books, and six children. Their joint papers were usually published under Will's name alone because of prejudice against women mathematicians. In a letter to Grace, Will wrote, "Our papers ought to be published under our joint names, but if this were done, neither of us get the benefit of it." Between 1914 and 1916, she did publish work on the foundations of calculus under her own name. Their daughter Cecily describes their collaboration: "My mother had decision and initiative and the stamina to carry an undertaking to its conclusion. If not for [her skill] my father's genius would probably have been abortive, and would not have eclipsed hers and the name she had already made for herself."

Martin Gardner (1914–2010) Martin Gardner wrote the lively and thoughtful "Mathematical Games" column in *Scientific American* magazine for more than 20 years, yet he was not a mathematician—his main interests were philosophy and religion. Readers were served an eclectic blend of diversions—logical puzzles, number problems, card tricks, game theory, and much more. Perhaps more than anyone else in our time, Gardner succeeded in popularizing mathematics, which he called "a kind of game that we play with the universe." There are 14 book collections of his *Scientific American* features, and he authored more than 60 books in all. He wrote, "A good mathematical puzzle, paradox, or magic trick can stimulate a child's imagination much faster than a practical application (especially if the application is remote from the child's experience), and if the game is chosen carefully, it can lead almost effortlessly into significant mathematical ideas." Douglas Hofstadter said, "Martin Gardner is one of the greatest intellects produced in this country in [the twentieth] century."

CHAPTER REVIEW

Review the following terms and exercises to determine which require learning or relearning—page numbers are provided for easy reference.

SECTION 8.1 Addition and Subtraction
VOCABULARY/NOTATION

Integers 321	Integer number line 322	Take-away 327
Positive integers 321	Opposite 322	Adding the opposite 327
Negative integers 321	Additive inverse 325	Missing-addend approach 328
Zero pair 322	Additive cancellation 325	

EXERCISES

1. Explain how to represent integers in two ways using the following:
   a. A set model   **b.** A measurement model

2. Show how to find $7 + (-4)$ using (a) colored chips and (b) the integer number line.

3. Name the property of addition of integers that is used to justify each of the following equations.
   a. $(-7) + 0 = -7$
   b. $(-3) + 3 = 0$
   c. $4 + (-5) = (-5) + 4$
   d. $(7 + 4) + (-4) = 7 + [4 + (-4)]$
   e. $(-9) + 7$ is an integer

4. Show how to find $3 - (-2)$ using each of the following approaches.
   a. Take-away
   b. Adding the opposite
   c. Missing addend

5. Which of the following properties hold for integer subtraction?
   a. Closure
   b. Commutative
   c. Associative
   d. Identity

SECTION 8.2 Multiplication, Division, and Order

VOCABULARY/NOTATION

Less than, greater than   343, 344

EXERCISES

1. Explain how you can provide motivation for the following.
   a. $5(-2) = -10$
   b. $(-5)(-2) = 10$

2. Name the property of multiplication of integers that is used to justify each of the following equations.
   a. $(-3)(-4) = (-4)(-3)$
   b. $(-5)[2(-7)] = [(-5)(2)](-7)$
   c. $(-5)(-7)$ is an integer
   d. $(-8) \times 1 = -8$
   e. If $(-3)n = (-3)7$, then $n = 7$.

3. Explain how $(-a)(-b) = ab$ is a generalization of $(-3)(-4) = 3 \times 4$.

4. If $3n = 0$, what can you conclude? What property can you cite for justification?

5. Explain how integer division is related to integer multiplication.

6. Which of the following properties hold for integer division?
   a. Closure
   b. Commutative
   c. Associative
   d. Identity

7. Without doing the indicated calculations, determine whether the answers are positive, negative, or zero. Explain your reasoning.
   a. $(-3)(-7)(-5) \div (-15)$
   b. $(-27) \div 3 \times (-4) \div (-3)$
   c. $35(-4) \div 5 \times 0 \times (-2)$

8. Explain how you can motivate the fact that $7^{-4} = \dfrac{1}{7^4}$.

9. Convert as indicated.
   a. 0.000079 to scientific notation
   b. 3×10^{-4} to standard notation
   c. 458.127 to scientific notation
   d. 2.39×10^7 to standard notation

10. Explain how to determine the smaller of -17 and -21 using the following techniques.
   a. The number-line approach
   b. The addition approach

11. Complete the following, and name the property you used as a justification.
   a. If $(-3) < 4$, then $(-3)(-2)$ _____ $4(-2)$.
   b. If $-5 < 7$ and $7 < 9$, then -5 _____ 9.
   c. If $-3 < 7$, then $(-3)2$ _____ $7 \cdot 2$.
   d. If $-4 < 5$, then $(-4) + 3$ _____ $5 + 3$.

CHAPTER TEST

KNOWLEDGE

1. True or false?
   a. The sum of any two negative integers is negative.
   b. The product of any two negative integers is negative.
   c. The difference of any two negative integers is negative.
   d. The result of any positive integer subtracted from any negative integer is negative.
   e. If $a < b$, then $ac < bc$ for integers a, b, and nonzero integer c.
   f. The opposite of an integer is negative.
   g. If $c = 0$ and $ac = bc$, then $a = b$.
   h. The sum of an integer and its additive inverse is zero.

2. What does the notation a^{-n} mean, where a is not zero and n is a positive integer?

3. Which of the following is a property of the integers but not of the whole numbers? (circle all that apply)
   a. Additive identity   b. Additive inverse
   c. Closure for subtraction

4. Identify three different approaches to the subtraction of integers.

SKILL

5. Compute each of the following problems without using a calculator.
   a. $37 + (-43)$
   b. $(-7)(-6)$
   c. $45 - (-3)$
   d. $16 \div (-2)$
   e. $(-13) - 17$
   f. $(-24) \div (-8)$
   g. $(-13)(4)$
   h. $[-24 - (-27)] \times (-4)$

6. Evaluate each of the following expressions in two ways to check the fact that $a(b + c)$ and $ab + ac$ are equal.
   a. $a = 3, b = -4, c = 2$ b. $a = -3, b = -5, c = -2$

7. Express the following in scientific notation.
   a. $(9.7 \times 10^8)(8.5 \times 10^3)$ b. $(5.5 \times 10^{-7}) \div (9.1 \times 10^{-2})$

8. Solve for n in the following expression.
$$\frac{(2^5)^{-2} \cdot 2^3}{2^{-3}} = 2^n$$

UNDERSTANDING

9. Name the property or properties that can be used to simplify these computations.
   a. $(-37 + 91) + (-91)$ b. $[(-2)17] \cdot 5$
   c. $(-31)17 + (-31)83$ d. $(-7)13 + 13(17)$

10. Compute using each of the three approaches: (i) take-away, (ii) adding the opposite, and (iii) missing addend.
    a. $8 - (-5)$ b. $(-2) - (-7)$

11. If a and b are negative and c is positive, determine whether the following are positive or negative.
    a. $(-a)(-c)$ b. $(-a)b$
    c. $(c - b)(c - a)$ d. $a(b - c)$

12. Illustrate the following operations using a (i) number line, and (ii) black and red chips.
    a. $8 + -3$ b. $-2 + 4$ c. $3 + -5$

13. Illustrate with black and red chips the operation $-2 - 3$ using the (i) take-away and the (ii) missing-addend approaches.

14. a. Building from the fact that $3 \times 4 = 12$, use patterns to illustrate why $-2 \times 4 = -8$.
    b. Building from the fact established in part (a), use patterns to illustrate why $-2 \times -4 = 8$.

15. Explain whether or not $a(b \cdot c)$ is equal to $(a \cdot b) \times (a \cdot c)$.

PROBLEM SOLVING/APPLICATION

16. If $30 \le a \le 60$ and $-60 \le b \le -30$, where a and b are integers, find the largest and smallest possible *integer* values for the following expressions.
    a. $a + b$ b. $a - b$ c. ab d. $a \div b$

17. Complete this *additive* magic square of integers using 9, $-12, 3, -6, 6, -3, 12, -9$.

18. Complete this *multiplicative* magic square of integers.

19. Find all values of a and b such that $a - b = b - a$.

20. On Hideki's history exams, he gets 4 points for each problem answered correctly, he loses 2 points for each incorrect answer, and he gets 0 points for each question left blank. On a 25-question test, Hideki received a score of 70.
    a. What is the largest number of questions that he could have answered correctly?
    b. What is the fewest number of questions that he could have answered correctly?
    c. What is the largest number of questions that he could have left blank?

Rational Numbers, Real Numbers, and Algebra

FOCUS ON

The Pythagoreans and Irrational Numbers

Pythagoras (circa 570 B.C.E.) was one of the most famous of all Greek mathematicians. After his studies and travels, he founded a school in southern Italy. This school, an academy of philosophy, mathematics, and natural science, developed into a closely knit brotherhood with secret rites and observances. The society was dispersed, but the brotherhood continued to exist for at least two centuries after the death of Pythagoras.

Much of the work of the Pythagoreans was done in whole numbers, but they also believed that *all* measurements could be done with fractions. However, the hypotenuse, c, of the right triangle where $a = b = 1$ caused them some alarm.

They could not find a fraction to measure c and still fit the Pythagorean theorem, $a^2 + b^2 = c^2$. One feeble attempt was to say that $c = \dfrac{7}{5}$. Then $c^2 = \dfrac{49}{25}$ (or *almost* 2).

Hippasus is attributed with the discovery of numbers that could not be expressed as a fraction—the ratio of two whole numbers. This discovery caused a scandal among the Pythagoreans, since their theory did not allow for such a number. Legend has it that Hippasus, a Pythagorean, was drowned because he shared the secret of incommensurables with others outside the society. Actually, according to Aristotle, the Pythagoreans gave the first proof (using an indirect proof) that there is no fraction whose square is 2. Thus, there was no fraction for c in the triangle below. The number whose square is 2 and other numbers that can't be written as fractions came to be known as irrational numbers.

By 300 B.C.E. many other irrational numbers were known, such as $\sqrt{3}$, $\sqrt{5}$, $\sqrt{6}$, and $\sqrt{8}$. Eudoxus, a Greek mathematician, developed a geometric method for handling irrationals. In the first century B.C.E., the Hindus began to treat irrationals like other numbers, replacing expressions such as $5\sqrt{2} + 4\sqrt{2}$ with $9\sqrt{2}$ and so on. Finally, in the late nineteenth century, irrationals were fully accepted as numbers.

Not only are irrationals inexpressible as fractions, they cannot be expressed exactly as decimals. For example, $\pi = 3.141592654\ldots$ has been calculated to over one billion places, but it has no exact decimal representation. This may seem strange to you at first, but if you have difficulty grasping the concept of an irrational number, keep in mind that many famous mathematicians throughout history had similar difficulties.

$a = 1$

c

$90°$

$b = 1$

STRATEGY 14
Solve an Equation

Often, when applying the Use a Variable strategy to solve a problem, the representation of the problem will be an equation. The following problem yields such an equation. Techniques for solving simple equations are given in Section 9.2.

INITIAL PROBLEM

A man's boyhood lasted $\frac{1}{6}$ of his life, he then played soccer for $\frac{1}{12}$ of his life, and he married after $\frac{1}{8}$ more of his life. A daughter was born 9 years after his marriage, and her birth coincided with the halfway point of his life. How old was the man when he died?

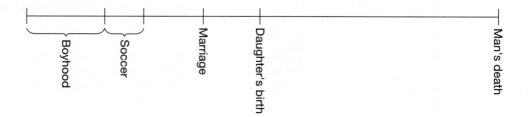

CLUES

The Solve an Equation strategy may be appropriate when

- A variable has been introduced.
- The words *is*, *is equal to*, or *equals* appear in a problem.
- The stated conditions can easily be represented with an equation.

A solution of this Initial Problem is on page 428.

INTRODUCTION

In this book we have introduced number systems much the same as they are developed in the school curriculum. The counting numbers came first. Then zero was included to form the whole numbers. Because of the need to deal with parts of a whole, fractions were introduced. Since there was a need to have numbers to represent amounts less than zero, the set of integers was introduced. The relationships among these sets are illustrated in Figure 9.1, where each arrow represents "is a subset of." For example, the set of counting numbers is a subset of the set of whole numbers, and so on. Recall that as number systems, both the fractions and integers extend the system of whole numbers.

NCTM Standard
All students should understand the meaning and effects of arithmetic operations with fractions, decimals, and integers.

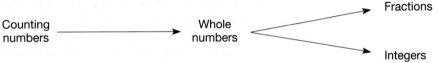

Figure 9.1

It is the objective of this chapter to introduce our final number systems, first the rational numbers and then the real numbers. Both of these are extensions of our existing number systems. The set of rational numbers is composed of the fractions and their opposites, and the real numbers include all of the rational numbers together with additional numbers such as π and $\sqrt{2}$. Finally, we use the real numbers to solve equations and inequalities, and we graph functions.

Key Concepts from NCTM Curriculum Focal Points

- **GRADE 5:** Using patterns, models, and relationships as contexts for writing and solving simple equations and inequalities.
- **GRADE 6:** Writing, interpreting, and using mathematical expressions and equations.
- **GRADE 7:** Developing an understanding of operations on all rational numbers and solving linear equations.
- **GRADE 8:** Analyzing and representing linear functions and solving linear equations and systems of linear equations.

9.1   THE RATIONAL NUMBERS

STARTING POINT   The fraction $\frac{2}{3}$ can be thought of as the number $0.\overline{6}$, which lies on the number line between 0 and 1. It can also be thought of as one whole broken into 3 parts where 2 of those parts are of interest. How are the symbols $-\frac{2}{3}$ and $\frac{-2}{3}$ related to each other or to either of the meanings described to the right?

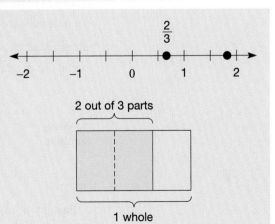

Rational Numbers: An Extension of Fractions and Integers

There are many reasons for needing numbers that have both reciprocals, as fractions do, and opposites, as integers do. For example, the fraction $\frac{2}{3}$ satisfies the equation $3x = 2$, since $3(\frac{2}{3})$, and -3 satisfies the equation $x + 3 = 0$, since $-3 + 3 = 0$. However, there is neither a fraction nor an integer that satisfies the equation $3x = -2$. To find such a number, we need the set of rational numbers.

There are various ways to introduce a set of numbers that extends both the fractions and the integers. Using models, one could merge the shaded-region model for fractions with the black and red chip model for integers. The resulting model would represent rational numbers by shading parts of wholes—models with black shaded parts to represent positive rational numbers and with red shaded parts to represent negative rational numbers.

For the sake of efficiency and mathematical clarity, we will introduce the rational numbers abstractly by focusing on the two properties we wish to extend, namely, that every nonzero number has a reciprocal and that every number has an opposite. There are two directions we can take. First, we could take all the fractions together with their opposites. This would give us a new collection of numbers, namely the fractions and numbers such as $-\frac{2}{3}, -\frac{5}{7}, -\frac{11}{2}$. A second approach would be to take the integers and form all possible "fractions" where the numerators are *integers* and the denominators are *nonzero integers*. We adopt this second approach, in which a rational number will be defined to be a *ratio* of integers. The set of rational numbers defined in this way will include the opposites of the fractions.

DEFINITION

Rational Numbers

The set of **rational numbers** is the set

$$Q = \left\{ \frac{a}{b} \mid a \text{ and } b \text{ are integers, } b \neq 0 \right\}.$$

Examples of rational numbers are $\frac{2}{3}, \frac{-5}{7}, \frac{4}{-9}, \frac{0}{1}$, and $\frac{-7}{-9}$. Mixed numbers such as $-3\frac{1}{4} = \frac{-13}{4}, -5\frac{2}{7} = \frac{-37}{7}$, and $2\frac{1}{3} = \frac{7}{3}$ are also rational numbers, since they can be expressed in the form $\frac{a}{b}$, where a and b are integers, $b \neq 0$. Notice that every fraction is a rational number; for example, in the case when $a \geq 0$ and $b > 0$ in $\frac{a}{b}$. Also, every integer is a rational number, for example, in the case when $b = 1$ in $\frac{a}{b}$. Thus we can extend our diagram in Figure 9.1 to include the set of rational numbers (Figure 9.2).

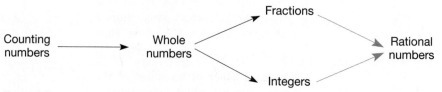

Figure 9.2

Equality of rational numbers and the four basic operations are defined as natural extensions of their counterparts for fractions and integers.

DEFINITION

Equality of Rational Numbers

Let $\dfrac{a}{b}$ and $\dfrac{c}{d}$ be any rational numbers. Then $\dfrac{a}{b} = \dfrac{c}{d}$ if and only if $ad = bc$.

The equality-of-rational-numbers definition is used to find equivalent representations of rational numbers (1) to simplify rational numbers and (2) to obtain common denominators to facilitate addition, subtraction, and comparing rational numbers.

As with fractions, each rational number has an infinite number of representations. That is, by the definition of equality of rational numbers, $\dfrac{1}{2} = \dfrac{2}{4} = \dfrac{3}{6} = \cdots = \dfrac{-1}{-2} = \dfrac{-2}{-4} = \dfrac{-3}{-6} = \cdots$. The rational number $\dfrac{1}{2}$ can then be viewed as the idea represented by all of its various representations. Similarly, the number $\dfrac{-2}{3}$ should come to mind when any of the representations $\dfrac{-2}{3}, \dfrac{2}{-3}, \dfrac{-4}{6}, \dfrac{4}{-6}, \dfrac{-6}{9}, \dfrac{6}{-9}, \ldots$ are considered.

By using the definition of equality of rational numbers, it can be shown that the following theorem holds for rational numbers.

THEOREM

Let $\dfrac{a}{b}$ be any rational number and n any nonzero integer. Then

$$\frac{a}{b} = \frac{an}{bn} = \frac{na}{nb}.$$

A rational number $\dfrac{a}{b}$ is said to be in **simplest form** or in **lowest terms** if a and b have no common prime factors and b is *positive*. For example, $\dfrac{2}{3}, \dfrac{-5}{7},$ and $\dfrac{-3}{10}$ are in simplest form, whereas $\dfrac{5}{-7}, \dfrac{4}{6},$ and $\dfrac{-3}{81}$ are not because of the -7 in $\dfrac{5}{-7}$, and because $\dfrac{4}{6} = \dfrac{2}{3}$ and $\dfrac{-3}{81} = \dfrac{-1}{27}$.

Example 9.1

Determine whether the following pairs are equal. Then express them in simplest form.

a. $\dfrac{5}{-7}, \dfrac{-5}{7}$ **b.** $\dfrac{-20}{-12}, \dfrac{5}{3}$ **c.** $\dfrac{16}{-30}, \dfrac{-18}{35}$ **d.** $\dfrac{-15}{36}, \dfrac{20}{-48}$

SOLUTION

a. $\dfrac{5}{-7} = \dfrac{-5}{7}$, since $5 \cdot 7 = (-7)(-5)$. The simplest form is $\dfrac{-5}{7}$.

b. $\dfrac{-20}{-12} = \dfrac{(-4)5}{(-4)3} = \dfrac{5}{3}$ due to simplification. The simplest form is $\dfrac{5}{3}$.

c. $\dfrac{16}{-30} \neq \dfrac{-18}{35}$, since $16 \cdot 35 = 560$ and $(-30) \cdot (-18) = 540$.

d. $\dfrac{-15}{36} = \dfrac{20}{-48}$, since $(-15)(-48) = 720 = 36 \times 20$. The simplest form is $\dfrac{-5}{12}$. ∎

✔ **Check for Understanding:** Exercise/Problem Set A #1–5

Addition and Its Properties

Addition of rational numbers is defined as an extension of fraction addition.

Reflection from Research
Helping students to develop an understanding of the magnitude and relationships of rational number quantities and their operations is more effective than simply teaching students the rules for operations with rational numbers (Moss, 2003).

DEFINITION

Addition of Rational Numbers

Let $\dfrac{a}{b}$ and $\dfrac{c}{d}$ be any rational numbers. Then

$$\frac{a}{b} + \frac{c}{d} = \frac{ad + bc}{bd}.$$

It follows from this definition that $\dfrac{a}{b} + \dfrac{c}{b} = \dfrac{a + c}{b}$ also.

Example 9.2   Find these sums.

a. $\dfrac{3}{7} + \dfrac{-5}{7}$ **b.** $\dfrac{-2}{5} + \dfrac{4}{-7}$ **c.** $\dfrac{-2}{5} + \dfrac{0}{5}$ **d.** $\dfrac{5}{6} + \dfrac{-5}{6}$

SOLUTION

a. $\dfrac{3}{7} + \dfrac{-5}{7} = \dfrac{3 + (-5)}{7} = \dfrac{-2}{7}$

b. $\dfrac{-2}{5} + \dfrac{4}{-7} = \dfrac{(-2)(-7) + 5 \cdot 4}{5(-7)} = \dfrac{14 + 20}{-35} = \dfrac{34}{-35} = \dfrac{-34}{35}$

c. $\dfrac{-2}{5} + \dfrac{0}{5} = \dfrac{-2 + 0}{5} = \dfrac{-2}{5}$

d. $\dfrac{5}{6} + \dfrac{-5}{6} = \dfrac{5 + (-5)}{6} = \dfrac{0}{6}$

Example 9.2(c) suggests that just as with the integers, the rationals have an additive identity. Also, Example 9.2(d) suggests that there is an additive inverse for each rational number. These two observations will be substantiated in the rest of this paragraph.

$$\frac{a}{b} + \frac{0}{b} = \frac{a + 0}{b} \qquad \textit{Addition of rational numbers}$$

$$= \frac{a}{b} \qquad \textit{Identity property for integer addition}$$

Thus $\dfrac{0}{b}$ is an identity for addition of rational numbers; moreover, it can be shown to be unique. For this reason, we write $\dfrac{0}{b}$ as 0, where b can represent any nonzero integer.

Next, let's consider additive inverses.

$$\frac{a}{b} + \frac{-a}{b} = \frac{a + (-a)}{b} \qquad \textit{Addition of rational numbers}$$

$$= \frac{0}{b} \qquad \textit{Additive inverse property for integer addition}$$

Thus the rational number $\dfrac{-a}{b}$ is an additive inverse of $\dfrac{a}{b}$. Moreover, it can be shown that each rational number has a unique additive inverse.

Notice that $\dfrac{-a}{b} = \dfrac{a}{-b}$, since $(-a)(-b) = ab = ba$. Therefore, $\dfrac{a}{-b}$ is the additive inverse of $\dfrac{a}{b}$ also. The symbol $-\dfrac{a}{b}$ is used to represent this additive inverse. We summarize this in the following result.

THEOREM

Let $\dfrac{a}{b}$ be any rational number. Then

$$-\frac{a}{b} = \frac{-a}{b} = \frac{a}{-b}.$$

Algebraic Reasoning
From this theorem, it can be seen that the solutions of $2x = -3$ and $-2x = 3$ are equal.

We can represent the rational numbers on a line that extends both the fraction number line and the integer number line. Since every fraction and every integer is a rational number, we can begin to form the rational number line from the combination of the fraction number line and the integer number line (Figure 9.3).

Reflection from Research
Rational number is an area of the mathematical curriculum in which students must meaningfully construct large portions of knowledge rather than simply receiving it from textbooks and teachers (Moseley, 2005).

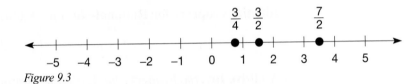

Figure 9.3

Just as in the case of fractions, we cannot label the entire fraction portion of the line, since there are infinitely many fractions between each pair of fractions. Furthermore, this line does not represent the rational numbers, since the additive inverses of the fractions are not yet represented. The additive inverses of the nonzero fractions, called the negative rational numbers, can be located by reflecting each nonzero fraction across zero (Figure 9.4). In particular, $-\frac{2}{3}, -\frac{5}{7}, -\frac{13}{4}$, and so on, are examples of negative rational numbers. In general, $\dfrac{a}{b}$ is a **positive rational number** if a and b are both positive or both negative integers, and $\dfrac{a}{b}$ is a **negative rational number** if one of a or b is positive and the other is negative.

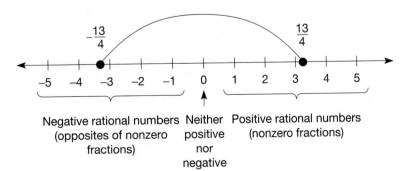

Figure 9.4

Next we list all the properties of rational-number addition. These properties can be verified using similar properties of integers.

PROPERTIES

Rational-Number Addition

Let $\dfrac{a}{b}, \dfrac{c}{d}$, and $\dfrac{e}{f}$ be any rational numbers.

Closure Property for Rational-Number Addition

$$\frac{a}{b} + \frac{c}{d} \text{ is a rational number.}$$

Commutative Property for Rational-Number Addition

$$\frac{a}{b} + \frac{c}{d} = \frac{c}{d} + \frac{a}{b}$$

Associative Property for Rational-Number Addition

$$\left(\frac{a}{b} + \frac{c}{d}\right) + \frac{e}{f} = \frac{a}{b} + \left(\frac{c}{d} + \frac{e}{f}\right)$$

Identity Property for Rational-Number Addition

$$\frac{a}{b} + 0 = \frac{a}{b} = 0 + \frac{a}{b} \qquad \left(0 = \frac{0}{m}, m \neq 0\right)$$

Additive Inverse Property for Rational-Number Addition

For every rational number $\dfrac{a}{b}$ there exists a unique rational number $-\dfrac{a}{b}$ such that

$$\frac{a}{b} + \left(-\frac{a}{b}\right) = 0 = \left(-\frac{a}{b}\right) + \frac{a}{b}.$$

Example 9.3 Apply properties of rational-number addition to calculate the following sums. Try to do them mentally before looking at the solutions.

a. $\left(\dfrac{3}{4} + \dfrac{5}{6}\right) + \dfrac{1}{4}$ **b.** $\left(\dfrac{5}{7} + \dfrac{3}{8}\right) + \dfrac{-6}{16}$

SOLUTION

a.
$$\left(\frac{3}{4} + \frac{5}{6}\right) + \frac{1}{4} = \frac{1}{4} + \left(\frac{3}{4} + \frac{5}{6}\right) \quad \textit{Commutativity}$$

$$= \left(\frac{1}{4} + \frac{3}{4}\right) + \frac{5}{6} \quad \textit{Associativity}$$

$$= 1 + \frac{5}{6} \quad \textit{Addition}$$

$$= 1\frac{5}{6} \quad \text{or} \quad \frac{11}{6} \quad \textit{Addtion}$$

NCTM Standard
All students should use the associative and commutative properties of addition and multiplication and the distributive property of multiplication over addition to simplify computations with integers, fractions, and decimals.

b. $\left(\dfrac{5}{7} + \dfrac{3}{8}\right) + \dfrac{-6}{16} = \dfrac{5}{7} + \left(\dfrac{3}{8} + \dfrac{-6}{16}\right)$ *Associativity*

$= \dfrac{5}{7} + 0$ *Additive inverse*

$= \dfrac{5}{7}.$ *Additive identity* ∎

The following two theorems are extensions of corresponding integer results. Their verifications are left for Problems 37 in Part A and 34 in Part B.

THEOREM
Additive Cancellation for Rational Numbers

Let $\dfrac{a}{b}, \dfrac{c}{d},$ and $\dfrac{e}{f}$ be any rational numbers.

If $\dfrac{a}{b} + \dfrac{e}{f} = \dfrac{c}{d} + \dfrac{e}{f}$, then $\dfrac{a}{b} = \dfrac{c}{d}.$

THEOREM
Opposite of the Opposite for Rational Numbers

Let $\dfrac{a}{b}$ be any rational number. Then

$$-\left(-\dfrac{a}{b}\right) = \dfrac{a}{b}.$$

✔ **Check for Understanding:** Exercise/Problem Set A #6–11

Subtraction

Since there is an additive inverse for each rational number, subtraction can be defined as an extension of integer subtraction.

DEFINITION
Subtraction of Rational Numbers: Adding the Opposite

Let $\dfrac{a}{b}$ and $\dfrac{c}{d}$ be any rational numbers. Then

$$\dfrac{a}{b} - \dfrac{c}{d} = \dfrac{a}{b} + \left(-\dfrac{c}{d}\right).$$

The following discussion shows that this definition extends fraction subtraction.

Algebraic Reasoning
Variables are used to show that the definition $\dfrac{a}{b} - \dfrac{c}{d} = \dfrac{a}{b} + \left(-\dfrac{c}{d}\right)$ leads naturally to the equation $\dfrac{a}{b} - \dfrac{c}{b} = \dfrac{a-c}{b}.$

Common Denominators

$$\dfrac{a}{b} - \dfrac{c}{b} = \dfrac{a}{b} + \left(-\dfrac{c}{b}\right) = \dfrac{a}{b} + \left(\dfrac{-c}{b}\right) = \dfrac{a+(-c)}{b} = \dfrac{a-c}{b}$$

That is,

$$\dfrac{a}{b} - \dfrac{c}{b} = \dfrac{a-c}{b}.$$

Thus, rational numbers with common denominators can be subtracted as is done with fractions, namely by subtracting numerators.

Unlike Denominators

$$\frac{a}{b} - \frac{c}{d} = \frac{ad}{bd} - \frac{bc}{bd} = \frac{ad - bc}{bd} \qquad \textit{Using common denominators}$$

Example 9.4   Calculate the following differences and express the answers in simplest form.

a. $\dfrac{3}{10} - \dfrac{4}{5}$ **b.** $\dfrac{8}{27} - \dfrac{-1}{12}$

SOLUTION

a. $\dfrac{3}{10} - \dfrac{4}{5} = \dfrac{3}{10} - \dfrac{8}{10} = \dfrac{3 - 8}{10} = \dfrac{-5}{10} = \dfrac{-1}{2}$

b. $\dfrac{8}{27} - \left(\dfrac{-1}{12}\right) = \dfrac{32}{108} - \left(\dfrac{-9}{108}\right) = \dfrac{32}{108} + \left[-\left(\dfrac{-9}{108}\right)\right] = \dfrac{41}{108}$ ■

The fact that the missing-addend approach to subtraction is equivalent to the adding-the-opposite approach is discussed in the Problem Set (Problem 34 in Part A).

A fraction calculator can be used to find sums and differences of rational numbers just as we did with fractions, except that the $\boxed{(-)}$ key may have to be used. For example $\dfrac{5}{27} - \left(\dfrac{-7}{15}\right)$ can be found as follows: 5 $\boxed{/}$ 27 $\boxed{-}$ $\boxed{(-)}$ 7 $\boxed{/}$ 15 $\boxed{=}$ $\boxed{88/135}$. On some calculators, there is a change-of-sign key $\boxed{+/-}$ instead of a negative key $\boxed{(-)}$. In those cases, a -7 is entered as 7 $\boxed{+/-}$. Notice that the keystrokes 7 $\boxed{/}$ $\boxed{(-)}$ 15 would also be correct because $\dfrac{-7}{15} = \dfrac{7}{-15}$. Using a decimal calculator, the numerator, $5 \cdot 15 + 27 \cdot 7$, and the denominator, $27 \cdot 15$, can be calculated. The result, $\dfrac{264}{405}$, can be simplified to $\dfrac{88}{135}$.

✔ **Check for Understanding:** Exercise/Problem Set A #12–14

Multiplication and Its Properties

Multiplication of rational numbers extends fraction multiplication as follows.

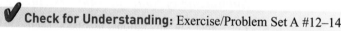

DEFINITION

Multiplication of Rational Numbers

Let $\dfrac{a}{b}$ and $\dfrac{c}{d}$ be any rational numbers. Then

$$\frac{a}{b} \cdot \frac{c}{d} = \frac{ac}{bd}.$$

A fraction calculator can be used to find products of rational numbers. For example, $\dfrac{-24}{35} \cdot \dfrac{-15}{16}$ can be found as follows: $\boxed{(-)}$ 24 $\boxed{/}$ 35 $\boxed{\times}$ $\boxed{(-)}$ 15 $\boxed{/}$ 16 $\boxed{=}$ $\boxed{360/560}$, which simplifies to $\dfrac{9}{14}$. Also, this product can be found as follows using a decimal calculator. 24 $\boxed{\times}$ 15 $\boxed{=}$ $\boxed{360}$ (the numerator) and 35 $\boxed{\times}$ 16 $\boxed{=}$ $\boxed{560}$ (the denominator); the product is 360/560 (since the product of two negative numbers is positive, the two $\boxed{(-)}$ keys were omitted).

Reasoning by analogy to fraction multiplication, the following properties can be verified using the definition of rational-number multiplication and the corresponding properties of integer multiplication.

PROPERTIES

Rational-Number Multiplication

Let $\dfrac{a}{b}, \dfrac{c}{d}$, and $\dfrac{e}{f}$ be any rational numbers.

Closure Property for Rational-Number Multiplication

$$\frac{a}{b} \cdot \frac{c}{d} = \frac{ac}{bd} \text{ is a rational number.}$$

Commutative Property for Rational-Number Multiplication

$$\frac{a}{b} \cdot \frac{c}{d} = \frac{c}{d} \cdot \frac{a}{b}$$

Associative Property for Rational-Number Multiplication

$$\left(\frac{a}{b} \cdot \frac{c}{d}\right)\frac{e}{f} = \frac{a}{b}\left(\frac{c}{d} \cdot \frac{e}{f}\right)$$

Identity Property for Rational-Number Multiplication

$$\frac{a}{b} \cdot 1 = \frac{a}{b} = 1 \cdot \frac{a}{b} \qquad \left(1 = \frac{m}{m}, m \neq 0\right)$$

Multiplicative Inverse Property for Rational-Number Multiplication

For every nonzero rational number $\dfrac{a}{b}$ there exists a unique rational number $\dfrac{b}{a}$ such that $\dfrac{a}{b} \cdot \dfrac{b}{a} = 1$.

Algebraic Reasoning
The multiplicative inverse property is utilized when isolating a variable in an equation like $\dfrac{2}{3}x = 4$. Both sides of the equation are multiplied by the multiplicative inverse of $\dfrac{2}{3}$, which is $\dfrac{3}{2}$. This produces $\dfrac{3}{2} \cdot \dfrac{2}{3}x = \dfrac{3}{2} \cdot 4$ or $x = 6$.

Recall that the multiplicative inverse of a number is also called the **reciprocal** of the number. Notice that the reciprocal of the reciprocal of any nonzero rational number is the original number.

It can be shown that distributivity also holds in the set of rational numbers. The verification of this fact takes precisely the same form as it did in the set of fractions and will be left for the Problem Set (Problem 35 in Part A).

PROPERTY

Distributive Property of Multiplication over Addition of Rational Numbers

Let $\dfrac{a}{b}$, $\dfrac{c}{d}$, and $\dfrac{e}{f}$ be any rational numbers. Then

$$\frac{a}{b}\left(\frac{c}{d}+\frac{e}{f}\right)=\frac{a}{b}\cdot\frac{c}{d}+\frac{a}{b}\cdot\frac{e}{f}.$$

The distributive property of multiplication over subtraction also holds.

Example 9.5   Use properties of rational numbers to compute the following problems (mentally if possible).

a. $\dfrac{2}{3}\cdot\dfrac{5}{7}+\dfrac{2}{3}\cdot\dfrac{2}{7}$ **b.** $\dfrac{-3}{5}\left(\dfrac{13}{37}\cdot\dfrac{10}{3}\right)$ **c.** $\dfrac{4}{5}\cdot\dfrac{7}{8}-\dfrac{1}{4}\cdot\dfrac{4}{5}$

SOLUTION

a. $\dfrac{2}{3}\cdot\dfrac{5}{7}+\dfrac{2}{3}\cdot\dfrac{2}{7}=\dfrac{2}{3}\left(\dfrac{5}{7}+\dfrac{2}{7}\right)=\dfrac{2}{3}\left(\dfrac{7}{7}\right)=\dfrac{2}{3}$

b. $\dfrac{-3}{5}\left(\dfrac{13}{37}\cdot\dfrac{10}{3}\right)=\left(\dfrac{13}{37}\cdot\dfrac{10}{3}\right)\left(\dfrac{-3}{5}\right)=\dfrac{13}{37}\left(\dfrac{10}{3}\cdot\dfrac{-3}{5}\right)=\dfrac{-26}{37}$

NOTE: Just as with fractions, we could simplify before multiplying as follows.

$$\frac{-3}{5}\left(\frac{13}{37}\cdot\frac{10}{3}\right)=\frac{\overset{-1}{-3}}{\overset{}{5}}\left(\frac{13}{37}\cdot\frac{\overset{2}{10}}{\overset{}{3}}\right)=\frac{-26}{37}$$

c. $\dfrac{4}{5}\cdot\dfrac{7}{8}-\dfrac{1}{4}\cdot\dfrac{4}{5}=\dfrac{4}{5}\cdot\dfrac{7}{8}-\dfrac{4}{5}\cdot\dfrac{1}{4}=\dfrac{4}{5}\left(\dfrac{7}{8}-\dfrac{1}{4}\right)=\dfrac{4}{5}\cdot\dfrac{5}{8}=\dfrac{1}{2}$ ■

✔ **Check for Understanding:** Exercise/Problem Set A #15–20

Division

Division of rational numbers is the natural extension of fraction division, namely, "invert the divisor and multiply" or "multiply by the reciprocal of the divisor."

DEFINITION

Division of Rational Numbers

Let $\dfrac{a}{b}$ and $\dfrac{c}{d}$ be any rational numbers where $\dfrac{c}{d}$ is nonzero. Then

$$\frac{a}{b}\div\frac{c}{d}=\frac{a}{b}\times\frac{d}{c}.$$

The common-denominator approach to fraction division also holds for rational-number division, as illustrated next.

$$\frac{a}{b} \div \frac{c}{b} = \frac{a}{b} \times \frac{b}{c} = \frac{a}{c}, \text{ that is, } \frac{a}{b} \div \frac{c}{b} = \frac{a}{c}$$

Also, since $a \div b$ can be represented as $\frac{a}{b}$, the numerator and denominator of the quotient of two rationals can also be found by dividing numerators and denominators in order from left to right. That is,

$$\frac{a}{b} \div \frac{c}{d} = \frac{a}{b} \times \frac{d}{c} = \frac{a}{c} \times \frac{d}{b} = \frac{a}{c} \div \frac{b}{d} = \frac{a \div c}{b \div d};$$

in summary, $\frac{a}{b} \div \frac{c}{d} = \frac{a \div c}{b \div d}$. When c is a divisor of a, the rational number $\frac{a}{c}$ equals the integer $a \div c$ and, if d is a divisor of b, $\frac{b}{d}$ equals $b \div d$.

So, as with fractions, there are three equivalent ways to divide rational numbers.

NCTM Standard
All students should develop and analyze algorithms for computing with fractions, decimals, and integers, and develop fluency in their use.

THEOREM

Three Methods of Rational-Number Division

Let $\frac{a}{b}$ and $\frac{c}{d}$ be any rational numbers where $\frac{c}{d}$ is nonzero. Then the following are equivalent.

1. $\dfrac{a}{b} \div \dfrac{c}{d} = \dfrac{a}{b} \times \dfrac{d}{c}$

2. $\dfrac{a}{b} \div \dfrac{c}{b} = \dfrac{a}{c}$

3. $\dfrac{a}{b} \div \dfrac{c}{d} = \dfrac{a \div c}{b \div d}$

Example 9.6	Express the following quotients in simplest form using the most appropriate of the three methods of rational-number division.

a. $\dfrac{12}{-25} \div \dfrac{4}{5}$ **b.** $\dfrac{13}{17} \div \dfrac{-4}{9}$ **c.** $\dfrac{-18}{23} \div \dfrac{-6}{23}$

SOLUTION

a. $\dfrac{12}{-25} \div \dfrac{4}{5} = \dfrac{12 \div 4}{-25 \div 5} = \dfrac{3}{-5} = \dfrac{-3}{5}$ by dividing the numerators and denominators using method (3) of the previous theorem, since $4 \mid 12$ and $5 \mid 25$.

b. $\dfrac{13}{17} \div \dfrac{-4}{9} = \dfrac{13}{17} \times \dfrac{-9}{4} = \dfrac{-117}{68}$ by multiplying by the reciprocal using method (1).

c. $\dfrac{-18}{23} \div \dfrac{-6}{23} = \dfrac{-18}{-6} = 3$ by the common-denominator approach using method (2), since the denominators are equal.   ■

Figure 9.5 shows how rational numbers are extensions of the fractions and the integers.

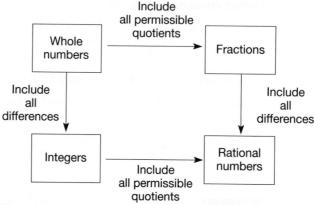

Figure 9.5

> ✔ **Check for Understanding:** Exercise/Problem Set A #21–23

Ordering Rational Numbers

There are three equivalent ways to order rationals in much the same way as the fractions were ordered.

Number-Line Approach $\dfrac{a}{b} < \dfrac{c}{d}\left(\text{or } \dfrac{c}{d} > \dfrac{a}{b}\right)$ if and only if $\dfrac{a}{b}$ is to the left of $\dfrac{c}{d}$ on the rational-number line.

Common-Positive-Denominator Approach $\dfrac{a}{b} < \dfrac{c}{d}$ if and only if $a < c$ and $b > 0$. Look at some examples where $a < c$ and $b < 0$. What can be said about $\dfrac{a}{b}$ and $\dfrac{c}{d}$ in these cases? In particular, consider the pair $\dfrac{3}{-5}$ and $\dfrac{4}{-5}$ to see why a positive denominator is required in this approach.

Addition Approach $\dfrac{a}{b} < \dfrac{c}{d}$ if and only if there is a *positive* rational number $\dfrac{p}{q}$ such that $\dfrac{a}{b} + \dfrac{p}{q} = \dfrac{c}{d}$. An equivalent form of the addition approach is $\dfrac{a}{b} < \dfrac{c}{d}$ if and only if $\dfrac{c}{d} - \dfrac{a}{b}$ is positive.

> **Example 9.7**   Order the following pairs of numbers using one of the three approaches to ordering.
>
> **a.** $\dfrac{-3}{7}, \dfrac{5}{2}$ **b.** $\dfrac{-7}{13}, \dfrac{-2}{13}$ **c.** $\dfrac{-5}{7}, \dfrac{-3}{4}$

SOLUTION

a. Using the number line, all negatives are to the left of all positives, hence $\dfrac{-3}{7} < \dfrac{5}{2}$.

b. Since $-7 < -2$, we have $\dfrac{-7}{13} < \dfrac{-2}{13}$ by the common-positive-denominator approach.

c. $\dfrac{-5}{7} - \left(\dfrac{-3}{4}\right) = \dfrac{-5}{7} + \dfrac{3}{4} = \dfrac{-20}{28} + \dfrac{21}{28} = \dfrac{1}{28}$, which is positive.

Therefore, $\dfrac{-3}{4} < \dfrac{-5}{7}$ by the addition approach. Alternately, using the common-positive-denominator approach, $\dfrac{-3}{4} = \dfrac{-21}{28} < \dfrac{-20}{28} = \dfrac{-5}{7}$.   ∎

As was done with fractions, the common-positive-denominator approach to ordering can be used to develop a shortcut for determining which of two rationals is smaller.

Suppose that $\dfrac{a}{b} < \dfrac{c}{d}$, where $b > 0$ and $d > 0$.

Then $\dfrac{ad}{bd} < \dfrac{bc}{bd}$. Since $bd > 0$, we conclude that $ad < bc$.

Similarly, if $ad < bc$, where $b > 0$ and $d > 0$, then $\dfrac{ad}{bd} < \dfrac{bc}{bd}$, so, $\dfrac{a}{b} < \dfrac{c}{d}$.

We can summarize this as follows.

THEOREM

Cross-Multiplication of Rational-Number Inequality

Let $\dfrac{a}{b}$ and $\dfrac{c}{d}$ be any rational numbers, where $b > 0$ and $d > 0$. Then

$$\frac{a}{b} < \frac{c}{d} \text{ if and only if } ad < bc.$$

Cross-multiplication of inequality can be applied immediately when the two rational numbers involved are in simplest form, since their denominators will be positive.

To compare $\dfrac{-37}{56}$ and $\dfrac{63}{-95}$, first rewrite both numbers with a positive denominator: $\dfrac{-37}{56}$ and $\dfrac{-63}{95}$. Now $(-37)95 = -3515$, and $(-63)(56) = -3528$, and $-3528 < -3515$. Therefore, $\dfrac{-63}{95} < \dfrac{-37}{56}$. Of course, one could also compare the two numbers using their decimal representations: $\dfrac{-37}{56} \approx -0.6607$, $\dfrac{63}{-95} \approx -0.6632$, and $-0.6632 < -0.6607$. Therefore, $\dfrac{63}{-95} < \dfrac{-37}{56}$. One could also use the fact that $\dfrac{a}{b} < \dfrac{c}{d}$ if and only if $\dfrac{ad}{b} < c$ $\left(\dfrac{a}{b} > \dfrac{c}{d} \text{ if and only if } \dfrac{ad}{b} > c\right)$, where $b, d > 0$, as we did with fractions.

The following relationships involving order, addition, and multiplication are extensions of similar ones involving fractions and integers. The verification of these is left for the Problem Set (Problems 36 Part A and 36–38 Part B).

PROPERTIES

Ordering Rational Numbers

Transitive Property for Less Than
Property of Less Than and Addition
Property of Less Than and Multiplication by a Positive
Property of Less Than and Multiplication by a Negative
Density Property

Similar properties hold for $>$, $\leq$, and $\geq$. Applications of these properties are given in Section 9.2.

 Check for Understanding: Exercise/Problem Set A #24–31

MATHEMATICAL MORSEL

As reported on the *Air Force Link* Web page on November 18, 2003, 12-year-old seventh-grader Killie Rick, at the Mary Help of Christians school in Fairborn, Ohio, found a new way to subtract mixed numbers using the idea of negative numbers. Following is one of Killie's solutions.

$$8\ 2/5 - 5\ 3/5 = 3 - 1/5 = 2 + 5/5 - 1/5 = 2\ 4/5$$

Instead of "borrowing from the whole number" before subtracting the fractions, Killie simply subtracted 3/5 from 2/5 to obtain $-1/5$ and proceeded from there. Her teacher, Colin McCabe, presented Killie with a certificate "in recognition of her mathematical ingenuity in the discovery of a new method of solution to mixed number subtraction." McCabe said he intends to teach what he calls "Killie's Way" to students in his future classes. "I think a lot of credit should go to the teacher," said Anne Steck, the school's principal. "I know lots of math teachers who would've looked at Killie's work and just said it was wrong." Her principal added that it is not so surprising that Killie said math is her favorite subject now.

Section 9.1   EXERCISE / PROBLEM SET A

EXERCISES

1. Explain how the following numbers satisfy the definition of a rational number.

　a. $-\dfrac{2}{3}$　　**b.** $-5\dfrac{1}{6}$　　**c.** 10

2. Let W = the set of whole numbers
　　　F = the set of (nonnegative) fractions
　　　I = the set of integers
　　　N = the set of negative integers
　　　Q = the set of rational numbers
List all the sets that have the following properties.
　a. -5 is an element of the set.
　b. $-\dfrac{3}{4}$ is an element of the set.

3. Which of the following are equal to -3?

$$\frac{-3}{1}, \frac{3}{1}, \frac{3}{-1}, -\frac{3}{1}, \frac{-3}{-1}, -\frac{-3}{1}, -\frac{-3}{-1}$$

4. Determine which of the following pairs of rational numbers are equal (try to do mentally first).

　a. $\dfrac{-3}{5}$ and $\dfrac{63}{-105}$　　**b.** $\dfrac{-18}{-24}$ and $\dfrac{45}{60}$

5. Rewrite each of the following rational numbers in simplest form.

　a. $\dfrac{5}{-7}$　**b.** $\dfrac{21}{-35}$　**c.** $\dfrac{-8}{-20}$　**d.** $\dfrac{-144}{180}$

6. Add the following rational numbers. Express your answers in simplest form.

　a. $\dfrac{4}{9} + \dfrac{-5}{9}$　　**b.** $\dfrac{-5}{12} + \dfrac{11}{-12}$
　c. $\dfrac{-2}{5} + \dfrac{13}{20}$　　**d.** $\dfrac{-7}{8} + \dfrac{1}{12} + \dfrac{2}{3}$

7. Apply the properties of rational-number addition to calculate the following sums. Do mentally, if possible.

　a. $\dfrac{5}{7} + \left(\dfrac{9}{7} + \dfrac{5}{8}\right)$　　**b.** $\left(\dfrac{5}{9} + \dfrac{3}{5}\right) + \dfrac{4}{9}$

8. Find the additive inverses of each of the following numbers.

　a. -2　　**b.** $\dfrac{5}{3}$

9. Using a fraction calculator, if available, calculate the following and express in simplest form.

　a. $\dfrac{25}{33} + \dfrac{-23}{39}$　　**b.** $-\dfrac{15}{28} + \dfrac{21}{44}$

10. Let W = the set of whole numbers
F = the set of (nonnegative) fractions
I = the set of integers
N = the set of negative integers
Q = the set of rational numbers
List all the sets that have the following properties.
a. The set is closed under addition.
b. The set has the additive inverse property.

11. State the property that justifies each statement.

a. $\dfrac{-2}{3} + \left(\dfrac{1}{6} + \dfrac{3}{4}\right) = \left(\dfrac{-2}{3} + \dfrac{1}{6}\right) + \dfrac{3}{4}$

b. $\dfrac{3}{-5} + \left(\dfrac{-5}{8} + \dfrac{4}{7}\right) = \left(\dfrac{-5}{8} + \dfrac{4}{7}\right) + \dfrac{3}{-5}$

12. Perform the following subtractions. Express your answers in simplest form.

a. $\dfrac{5}{6} - \dfrac{1}{6}$ **b.** $\dfrac{3}{4} - \dfrac{-5}{4}$

c. $\dfrac{-4}{7} - \dfrac{-9}{7}$ **d.** $\dfrac{-7}{12} - \dfrac{5}{18}$

13. Using a fraction calculator, if available, calculate the following and express in simplest form.

a. $\dfrac{47}{57} - \dfrac{19}{-72}$ **b.** $\dfrac{-16}{39} - \dfrac{21}{26}$

14. Let W = the set of whole numbers
F = the set of (nonnegative) fractions
I = the set of integers
N = the set of negative integers
Q = the set of rational numbers
List all the sets that have the following properties.
a. The set is closed under subtraction.
b. The set has an identity property for subtraction.

15. Perform each of the following multiplications. Express your answers in simplest form.

a. $\dfrac{2}{3} \cdot \dfrac{7}{9}$ **b.** $\dfrac{-5}{6} \cdot \dfrac{7}{3}$ **c.** $\dfrac{-3}{10} \cdot \dfrac{-25}{27}$ **d.** $\dfrac{-2}{5} \cdot \dfrac{-15}{24}$

16. Use the properties of rational numbers to compute the following (mentally, if possible).

a. $-\dfrac{3}{5} \cdot \left(\dfrac{11}{17} \cdot \dfrac{5}{3}\right)$ **b.** $\left(-\dfrac{3}{7} \cdot \dfrac{10}{12}\right) \cdot \dfrac{6}{10}$

c. $\dfrac{2}{3} \cdot \left(\dfrac{3}{2} + \dfrac{5}{7}\right)$ **d.** $\dfrac{5}{9} \cdot \dfrac{2}{7} + \dfrac{2}{7} \cdot \dfrac{4}{9}$

17. Using a fraction calculator, if available, calculate the following and express in simplest form.

a. $\dfrac{-65}{72} \times \dfrac{7}{48}$ **b.** $-\dfrac{16}{65} \times \dfrac{39}{40}$

18. Let W = the set of whole numbers
F = the set of (nonnegative) fractions
I = the set of integers
N = the set of negative integers
Q = the set of rational numbers
List all the sets that have the following properties.
a. The set is closed under multiplication.
b. The set has an identity property for multiplication.

19. State the property that justifies each statement.

a. $\left(\dfrac{5}{6} \cdot \dfrac{7}{8}\right) \cdot \dfrac{-8}{3} = \left(\dfrac{7}{8} \cdot \dfrac{5}{6}\right) \cdot \dfrac{-8}{3}$

b. $\dfrac{1}{4}\left(\dfrac{8}{3} + \dfrac{-5}{4}\right) = \dfrac{1}{4}\left(\dfrac{8}{3}\right) + \dfrac{1}{4}\left(\dfrac{-5}{4}\right)$

20. Calculate the following in two ways: (i) exactly as written and (ii) calculating an answer using all positive numbers and then determining whether the answer is positive or negative.

a. $(-37)(-43)(-57)$

b. $\left(\dfrac{-14}{15}\right)\left(-\dfrac{35}{18}\right)\left(\dfrac{27}{-49}\right)$

21. Find the following quotients using the most appropriate of the three methods of rational-number division. Express your answer in simplest form.

a. $\dfrac{-40}{27} \div \dfrac{-10}{9}$ **b.** $\dfrac{-1}{4} \div \dfrac{3}{2}$ **c.** $\dfrac{-3}{8} \div \dfrac{5}{6}$ **d.** $\dfrac{21}{25} \div \dfrac{-3}{5}$

22. Using a fraction calculator, if available, calculate the following and express in simplest form.

a. $\dfrac{43}{57} \div \dfrac{37}{72}$ **b.** $-\dfrac{18}{49} \div \dfrac{15}{-28}$

23. Calculate the following in two ways: (i) exactly as written and (ii) calculating an answer using all positive numbers and then determining whether the answer is positive or negative.

a. $\dfrac{(-55)(-49)}{-35}$ **b.** $\dfrac{-33}{(-21)(-55)} \div \left(\dfrac{15}{-28}\right)$

24. Order the following pairs of rational numbers from smaller to larger using any of the approaches.

a. $\dfrac{-9}{11}, \dfrac{-3}{11}$ **b.** $\dfrac{-1}{3}, \dfrac{2}{5}$ **c.** $\dfrac{-5}{6}, \dfrac{-9}{10}$ **d.** $\dfrac{-10}{9}, \dfrac{-9}{8}$

25. Using a calculator and cross-multiplication of inequality, order the following pairs of rational numbers.

a. $\dfrac{-232}{356}, \dfrac{-152}{201}$ **b.** $\dfrac{-761}{532}, \dfrac{-500}{345}$

26. State the property that justifies each statement.

a. If $\dfrac{4}{9} < \dfrac{5}{9}$, then $\dfrac{4}{9} + \dfrac{3}{5} < \dfrac{5}{9} + \dfrac{3}{5}$

b. If $\dfrac{3}{4} < \dfrac{7}{8}$, then $\dfrac{3}{4} \cdot \left(-\dfrac{2}{5}\right) > \dfrac{7}{8}\left(-\dfrac{2}{5}\right)$

27. The property of less than and addition for ordering rational numbers can be used to solve simple inequalities. For example,

$$x + \frac{3}{5} < \frac{-7}{10}$$

$$x + \frac{3}{5} + \left(-\frac{3}{5}\right) < \frac{-7}{10} + \left(-\frac{3}{5}\right)$$

$$x < -\frac{13}{10}.$$

Solve the following inequalities.

a. $x + \frac{1}{2} < -\frac{5}{6}$ **b.** $x - \frac{2}{3} < \frac{-3}{4}$

28. Some inequalities with rational numbers can be solved by applying the property of less than and multiplication by a positive for ordering rational numbers. For example,

$$\frac{2}{3}x < -\frac{5}{6}$$

$$\left(\frac{3}{2}\right)\left(\frac{2}{3}x\right) < \left(\frac{3}{2}\right)\left(-\frac{5}{6}\right)$$

$$x < -\frac{5}{4}.$$

Solve the following inequalities.

a. $\frac{5}{4}x < \frac{15}{8}$ **b.** $\frac{3}{2}x < -\frac{9}{8}$

29. When the property of less than and multiplication by a negative for ordering rational numbers is applied to solve inequalities, we need to be careful to change the inequality sign. For example,

$$-\frac{2}{3}x < \frac{5}{-6}$$

$$\left(-\frac{3}{2}\right)\left(-\frac{2}{3}x\right) > \left(-\frac{3}{2}\right)\left(-\frac{5}{6}\right)$$

$$x > \frac{5}{4}.$$

Solve each of the following inequalities.

a. $-\frac{3}{4}x < -\frac{15}{16}$ **b.** $-\frac{3}{5}x < \frac{9}{10}$

30. Order the following pairs of numbers, and find a number between each pair.

a. $\frac{-37}{76}, \frac{-43}{88}$ **b.** $\frac{59}{-97}, \frac{-68}{113}$

31. The set of rational numbers also has the density property. Recall some of the methods we used for fractions, and find three rational numbers between each pair of given numbers.

a. $\frac{-3}{4}$ and $\frac{-1}{2}$ **b.** $\frac{-5}{6}$ and $\frac{-7}{8}$

PROBLEMS

32. Using the definition of equality of rational numbers, prove that $\frac{a}{b} = \frac{an}{bn}$, where n is any nonzero integer.

33. Using the corresponding properties of integers and reasoning by analogy from fraction properties, prove the following properties of rational-number multiplication.
    a. Closure   **b.** Commutativity
    c. Associativity   **d.** Identity
    e. Inverse

34. **a.** Complete the following statement for the missing-addend approach to subtraction.

$$\frac{a}{b} - \frac{c}{d} = \frac{e}{f} \text{ if and only if } \underline{\qquad}$$

   b. Assuming the adding-the-opposite approach, prove that the missing-addend approach is true.
   c. Assume that the missing-addend approach is true, and prove that the adding-the-opposite approach is true.

35. Verify the distributive property of multiplication over addition for rational numbers: If $\frac{a}{b}, \frac{c}{d}$, and $\frac{e}{f}$ are rational numbers, then

$$\frac{a}{b}\left(\frac{c}{d} + \frac{e}{f}\right) = \frac{a}{b}\cdot\frac{c}{d} + \frac{a}{b}\cdot\frac{e}{f}.$$

36. Verify the following statement.

$$\text{If } \frac{a}{b} < \frac{c}{d}, \text{ then } \frac{a}{b} + \frac{e}{f} < \frac{c}{d} + \frac{e}{f}.$$

37. Prove that additive cancellation holds for the rational numbers.

$$\text{If } \frac{a}{b} + \frac{e}{f} = \frac{c}{d} + \frac{e}{f}, \text{ then } \frac{a}{b} = \frac{c}{d}.$$

38. Using a 5-minute and an 8-minute hourglass timer, how can you measure 6 minutes?

Section 9.1 EXERCISE / PROBLEM SET B

EXERCISES

1. Explain how the following numbers satisfy the definition of a rational number.
   a. $\frac{7}{3}$ **b.** $7\frac{1}{8}$ **c.** -3

2. Let W = the set of whole numbers
   F = the set of (nonnegative) fractions
   I = the set of integers
   N = the set of negative integers
   Q = the set of rational numbers
   List all the sets that have the following properties.
   a. 0 is an element of the set.
   b. $\frac{5}{8}$ is an element of the set.

3. Which of the following are equal to $\frac{5}{6}$?
$$-\frac{5}{6}, \frac{-5}{6}, \frac{5}{-6}, \frac{-5}{-6}, -\frac{-5}{6}, -\frac{5}{-6}$$

4. Determine whether the following statements are true or false.
   a. $\frac{-32}{22} = \frac{48}{-33}$ **b.** $\frac{-75}{-65} = \frac{21}{18}$

5. Rewrite each of the following rational numbers in simplest form.
   a. $\frac{4}{-6}$ **b.** $\frac{-60}{-84}$ **c.** $\frac{64}{-144}$ **d.** $\frac{96}{-108}$

6. Add the following rational numbers. Express your answers in simplest form.
   a. $\frac{3}{10} + \frac{-8}{10}$ **b.** $\frac{-5}{4} + \frac{1}{9}$
   c. $\frac{-5}{6} + \frac{5}{12} + \frac{-1}{4}$ **d.** $\frac{-3}{8} + \frac{5}{12}$

7. Apply the properties of rational-number addition to calculate the following sums. Do mentally, if possible.
   a. $\left(\frac{3}{11} + \frac{-18}{66}\right) + \frac{17}{23}$ **b.** $\left(\frac{3}{17} + \frac{6}{29}\right) + \frac{3}{-17}$

8. Find the additive inverses of each of the following numbers.
   a. $\frac{2}{-7}$ **b.** $-\frac{5}{16}$

9. Using a fraction calculator, if available, calculate the following and express in simplest form.
   a. $\frac{13}{27} + \frac{-21}{31}$ **b.** $\frac{24}{-35} + \frac{-15}{49}$

10. Let W = the set of whole numbers
   F = the set of (nonnegative) fractions
   I = the set of integers

N = the set of negative integers
Q = the set of rational numbers
List all the sets that have the following properties.
a. The set has the commutative property of addition.
b. The set has the identity property for addition.

11. State the property that justifies each statement.
   a. $\frac{-2}{5} + 0 = 0 + \frac{-2}{5} = \frac{-2}{5}$ **b.** $-\frac{3}{5} + \left(\frac{3}{5}\right) = 0$

12. Perform the following subtractions. Express your answers in simplest form.
   a. $\frac{8}{9} - \frac{2}{9}$ **b.** $\frac{-3}{7} - \frac{3}{4}$
   c. $\frac{2}{9} - \frac{-7}{12}$ **d.** $\frac{-13}{24} + \frac{-11}{24}$

13. Using a fraction calculator, if available, calculate the following and express in simplest form.
   a. $\frac{-15}{22} - \frac{-31}{48}$ **b.** $\frac{25}{36} - \frac{28}{-45}$

14. Let W = the set of whole numbers
   F = the set of (nonnegative) fractions
   I = the set of integers
   N = the set of negative integers
   Q = the set of rational numbers
   List all the sets that have the following properties.
   a. The set has the commutative property of subtraction.
   b. The set has an inverse property for subtraction.

15. Multiply the following rational numbers. Express your answers in simplest form.
   a. $\frac{3}{5} \cdot \frac{-10}{21}$ **b.** $\frac{-6}{11} \cdot \frac{-33}{18}$
   c. $\frac{5}{12} \cdot \frac{48}{-15} \cdot \frac{-9}{8}$ **d.** $\frac{-6}{11} \cdot \frac{-22}{21} \cdot \frac{7}{-12}$

16. Apply the properties of rational numbers to compute the following (mentally, if possible).
   a. $\frac{-3}{5} \cdot \left(\frac{14}{9}\right) - \frac{-3}{5} \cdot \left(\frac{5}{9}\right)$
   b. $\frac{3}{7}\left(\frac{-11}{21}\right) + \left(\frac{-3}{7}\right)\left(\frac{-11}{21}\right)$
   c. $\left(\frac{2}{7}\right) \cdot \frac{5}{-6} + \left(\frac{5}{7}\right) \cdot \frac{5}{-6}$
   d. $\left(\frac{-9}{7} \cdot \frac{23}{-27}\right) \cdot \left(\frac{-7}{9}\right)$

17. Using a fraction calculator, if available, calculate the following and express in simplest form.

a. $\dfrac{67}{42} \times \dfrac{51}{59}$ **b.** $\dfrac{25}{-42} \times \dfrac{-91}{156}$

18. Let W = the set of whole numbers
 F = the set of (nonnegative) fractions
 I = the set of integers
 N = the set of negative integers
 Q = the set of rational numbers
 List all the sets that have the following properties.
 a. The set has multiplicative inverses for each nonzero element.
 b. The set has the commutative property for multiplication.

19. State the property that justifies each statement.

a. $-\dfrac{2}{3}\left(\dfrac{3}{2}\cdot\dfrac{3}{5}\right) = \left(-\dfrac{2}{3}\cdot\dfrac{3}{2}\right)\cdot\dfrac{3}{5}$

b. $\dfrac{-7}{9}\left(\dfrac{3}{2}+\dfrac{-4}{5}\right) = \dfrac{-7}{9}\left(\dfrac{-4}{5}+\dfrac{3}{2}\right)$

20. Calculate the following in two ways: (i) exactly as written and (ii) calculating an answer using all positives numbers and then determining whether the answer is positive or negative.

a. $(-43)^2(-36)^3$ **b.** $\left(-\dfrac{18}{25}\right)\left(\dfrac{-45}{-91}\right)\left(\dfrac{28}{-81}\right)$

21. Find the following quotients using the most appropriate of the three methods of rational-number division. Express your answer in simplest form.

a. $\dfrac{-8}{9} \div \dfrac{2}{9}$ **b.** $\dfrac{12}{15} \div \dfrac{-4}{3}$

c. $\dfrac{-10}{9} \div \dfrac{-5}{4}$ **d.** $\dfrac{-13}{24} \div \dfrac{-39}{-48}$

22. Using a fraction calculator, if available, calculate the following and express in simplest form.

a. $\dfrac{213}{76} \div \dfrac{-99}{68}$ **b.** $\dfrac{21}{-44} \div \left(-\dfrac{35}{132}\right)$

23. Calculate the following in two ways: (i) exactly as written and (ii) calculating an answer using all positive numbers

and then determining whether the answer is positive or negative.

a. $\dfrac{(-1111)(-23)(49)}{-77}$ **b.** $\dfrac{(-35)(-91)}{(-36)(-24)} \div \left(\dfrac{49}{-144}\right)$

24. Put the appropriate symbol, $<$, $=$, or $>$, between each pair of rational numbers to make a true statement.

a. $-\dfrac{5}{6}$ ___ $-\dfrac{11}{12}$ **b.** $-\dfrac{1}{3}$ ___ $\dfrac{5}{4}$

c. $-\dfrac{12}{15}$ ___ $\dfrac{36}{-45}$ **d.** $-\dfrac{3}{12}$ ___ $\dfrac{-4}{20}$

25. Using a calculator and cross-multiplication of inequality, order the following pairs of rational numbers.

a. $\dfrac{475}{652}, \dfrac{-308}{-421}$ **b.** $\dfrac{372}{487}, \dfrac{-261}{-319}$

26. State the property that justifies each statement.

a. If $\dfrac{-3}{5} < \dfrac{-1}{5}$, then $\left(\dfrac{-3}{5}\right) + \left(\dfrac{-5}{6}\right) < \left(\dfrac{-1}{5}\right) + \left(\dfrac{-5}{6}\right)$

b. If $\dfrac{5}{11} < \dfrac{6}{11}$, then $\dfrac{5}{11}\cdot\left(\dfrac{-1}{3}\right) > \dfrac{6}{11}\cdot\left(\dfrac{-1}{3}\right)$

27. Solve the following inequalities.

a. $x - \dfrac{6}{5} < \dfrac{-12}{7}$ **b.** $x + \left(\dfrac{-3}{7}\right) > \dfrac{-4}{5}$

28. Solve the following inequalities.

a. $\dfrac{1}{6}x < \dfrac{-5}{12}$ **b.** $\dfrac{2}{5}x < -\dfrac{7}{8}$

29. Solve the following inequalities.

a. $-\dfrac{1}{3}x < -\dfrac{5}{6}$ **b.** $\dfrac{-3}{7}x > \dfrac{8}{5}$

30. Order the following pairs of numbers and find a number between each pair.

a. $\dfrac{-113}{217}, \dfrac{-163}{314}$ **b.** $\dfrac{-812}{779}, \dfrac{545}{-522}$

31. Find three rational numbers between each pair of given numbers.

a. $\dfrac{-5}{4}$ and $\dfrac{-6}{5}$ **b.** $\dfrac{-1}{10}$ and $\dfrac{-1}{11}$

PROBLEMS

32. The closure property for rational-number addition can be verified as follows:

$$\dfrac{a}{b} + \dfrac{c}{d} = \dfrac{ad + bc}{bd} \text{ by definition of addition.}$$

$ab + bc$ and bd are both integers by closure properties of integer addition and multiplication and $bd \neq 0$. Therefore, by the definition of rational number,

$\dfrac{ad + bc}{bd}$ is a rational number.

In a similar way, verify the following properties of rational-number addition.

a. Commutative
b. Associative

33. Which of the following properties hold for subtraction of rational numbers? Verify the property or give a counterexample.
    a. Closure   **b.** Commutative   **c.** Associative
    d. Identity   **e.** Inverse

34. Using additive cancellation, prove $-\left(-\dfrac{a}{b}\right) = \dfrac{a}{b}$.

35. The positive rational numbers can be defined as those a/b where $ab > 0$. Determine whether the following are true or false. If true, prove; if false, give a counterexample.
    a. The sum of two positive rationals is a positive rational.
    b. The difference of two positive rationals is a positive rational.
    c. The product of two positive rationals is a positive rational.
    d. The quotient of two positive rationals is a positive rational.

36. Given: $\dfrac{a}{b}\cdot\left(\dfrac{c}{d}+\dfrac{e}{f}\right) = \dfrac{a}{b}\cdot\dfrac{c}{d}+\dfrac{a}{b}\cdot\dfrac{e}{f}$

    Prove: $\dfrac{a}{b}\cdot\left(\dfrac{c}{d}-\dfrac{e}{f}\right) = \dfrac{a}{b}\cdot\dfrac{c}{d}-\dfrac{a}{b}\cdot\dfrac{e}{f}$

37. Prove: If $\dfrac{a}{b} < \dfrac{c}{d}$ and $\dfrac{c}{d} < \dfrac{e}{f}$, then $\dfrac{a}{b} < \dfrac{e}{f}$.

38. Prove each of the following statements.
    a. If $\dfrac{a}{b} < \dfrac{c}{d}$ and $\dfrac{e}{f} > 0$, then $\dfrac{a}{b}\cdot\dfrac{e}{f} < \dfrac{c}{d}\cdot\dfrac{e}{f}$.
    b. If $\dfrac{a}{b} < \dfrac{c}{d}$ and $\dfrac{e}{f} < 0$, then $\dfrac{a}{b}\cdot\dfrac{e}{f} > \dfrac{c}{d}\cdot\dfrac{e}{f}$.

39. Prove: If $\dfrac{a}{b} < \dfrac{c}{d}$, then there is an $\dfrac{e}{f}$ such that $\dfrac{a}{b} < \dfrac{e}{f} < \dfrac{c}{d}$.

40. José discovered what he thought was a method for generating a **Pythagorean triple**, that is, three whole numbers a, b, c such that $a^2 + b^2 = c^2$. Here are his rules: Take any odd number (say, 11). Square it (121). Subtract 1 and divide by 2 (60). Add 1 (61). (Note: $11^2 + 60^2 = 121 + 3600 = 3721 = 61^2$.)

Try another example. Prove that José's method always works by using a variable.

41. Explain how you know why the sum of two rational numbers, say $\dfrac{3}{7}$ and $\dfrac{2}{5}$, will be a rational number. In other words, explain why the closure property holds for rational number addition.

Analyzing Student Thinking
42. Rock asks why 2/3 is a fraction but −2/3 is not. How would you respond?

43. Maria simplified 210/63 and got 10/3, which she said was in simplest form. Karl says that 3 1/3 is in simplest form. How should you respond?

44. Cody says that the properties of rational number addition are the same as the properties of fraction addition. Is he correct? Explain.

45. Kelsey says that −3/−4 is negative because both −3 and −4 are negative. How should you respond?

46. To calculate $\dfrac{-5}{24} - \dfrac{-1}{9}$, Pierce did the following:

    $$\dfrac{(-5)\cdot 9}{24\cdot 9} - \dfrac{(-1)\cdot 24}{9\cdot 24} = \dfrac{-45}{216} - \dfrac{-24}{216} = \dfrac{-21}{216}.$$
    Is his method correct? Explain.

47. Marina works a problem as follows:
    $$2/5 \times 1/7 - 2/5 \times 3/7 =$$
    $$(2/5 - 2/5) \times (1/7 - 3/7) = 0.$$
    Is she correct? If not, what mistake did she make?

48. Duncan calculates 12/35 ÷ −2/7 as follows: $[12 \div (-2)]/(35 \div 7) = -6/5$. Is he correct? Explain.

Problems Relating to the NCTM Standards and Curriculum Focal Points

1. The Focal Points for Grade 7 state "Developing an understanding of operations on all rational numbers and solving linear equations." Provide one example of an understanding of rational number operations that goes beyond the understanding of operations on fractions and integers.

2. The NCTM Standards state "All students should use the associative and commutative properties of addition and multiplication and the distributive property of multiplication

over addition to simplify computations with integers, fractions, and decimals." Give two examples of how the properties described in this standard could be used to simplify computations with rational numbers.

3. The NCTM Standards state "All students should develop and analyze algorithms for computing with fractions, decimals, and integers, and develop fluency in their use." Explain what it means to "develop algorithms" as opposed to memorizing algorithms.

9.2   THE REAL NUMBERS

In Chapter 7, it was stated that fractions could be written as terminating or repeating decimals. The same is true for rational numbers. (Remember that terminating decimals are those decimals that repeat zero.) What are some examples of nonterminating, nonrepeating decimal numbers?

$$-\frac{3}{8} = -0.375$$

$$\frac{13}{5} = 4.333333\ldots$$

$$-\frac{5}{7} = -0.714285\overline{714285}$$

Real Numbers: An Extension of Rational Numbers

Algebraic Reasoning
As can be seen in the discussion at the right, there is a close connection between different sets of numbers and the solutions of algebraic equations. Thus, a good understanding of the attributes of different number systems is an essential part of algebraic reasoning.

Every repeating decimal (this includes terminating decimals because of the repeating zero) can be written as a rational number $\frac{a}{b}$ where a and b are integers. Therefore, numbers with decimal representations that do not repeat are not rational numbers. What type of numbers are such decimals? Let's approach this question from another point of view.

The equation $x - 3 = 0$ has a whole-number solution, namely 3. However, the equation $x + 3 = 0$ does not have a *whole*-number solution. But the equation $x + 3 = 0$ does have an *integer* solution, namely -3. Now consider the equation $3x = 2$. This equation has neither a whole-number nor an integer solution. But the *fraction* $\frac{2}{3}$ is a solution of $3x = 2$. What about the equation $-3x = 2$? We must move to the set of *rationals* to find its solution, namely $-\frac{2}{3}$. Since solving equations plays an important role in mathematics, we want to have a number system that will allow us to solve many types of equations. Mathematicians encountered great difficulty when attempting to solve the equation $x^2 = 2$ using rational numbers. Because of its historical significance, we give a proof to show that it is actually *impossible* to find a rational number whose square is 2.

THEOREM

There is no rational number whose square is 2.

Problem-Solving Strategy
Use Indirect Reasoning

PROOF   Use indirect reasoning. Suppose that there is a rational number $\frac{a}{b}$ such that $\left(\frac{a}{b}\right)^2 = 2$. Then we have the following.

$$\left(\frac{a}{b}\right)^2 = 2$$

$$\frac{a^2}{b^2} = 2$$

$$a^2 = 2b^2$$

Now the argument will become a little subtle. By the Fundamental Theorem of Arithmetic, the numbers a^2 and $2b^2$ have the same prime factorization. Because squares have prime factors that occur in pairs, a^2 must have an *even* number of prime factors in its prime factorization. Similarly, b^2 has an even number of prime factors in its prime factorization. But 2 is a prime also, so $2 \cdot b^2$ has an *odd* number of prime factors in its prime factorization. (Note that b^2 contributes an even number of prime factors, and the factor 2 produces one more, hence an odd number of prime factors.) Recapping, we have (i) $a^2 = 2b^2$, (ii) a^2 has an even number of prime factors in its prime factorization, and (iii) $2b^2$ has an odd number of prime factors in its prime factorization. According to the Fundamental Theorem of Arithmetic, it is impossible for a number to have an even number of prime factors *and* an odd number of prime factors in its prime factorization. Thus there is *no* rational number whose square is 2. ∎

Using similar reasoning, it can be shown that for every prime p there is no rational number, $\dfrac{a}{b}$, whose square is p. We leave that verification for the problem set.

Using a calculator, one can show that the square of the rational number 1.414213562 is very close to 2. However, we have proved that *no* rational number squared is exactly 2. Consequently, we have a need for a new system of numbers that will include infinite nonrepeating decimals, such as 0.020020002 . . . , as well as numbers that are solutions to equations such as $x^2 = p$, where p is a prime.

DEFINITION

Real Numbers

The set of **real numbers**, R, is the set of all numbers that have an infinite decimal representation.

Children's Literature
www.wiley.com/college/musser
See "Sir Cumference and the Dragon of Pi" by Cindy Neuschwander.

Thus the real numbers contain all the rationals (which are the infinite *repeating* decimals, positive, negative, or zero) together with a new set of numbers called, appropriately, the irrational numbers. The set of **irrational numbers** is the set of numbers that have infinite *nonrepeating* decimal representations. Figure 9.6 shows the different types of decimals. Since irrational numbers have infinite nonrepeating decimal representations, rational-number approximations (using finite decimals) have to be used to perform approximate computations in some cases.

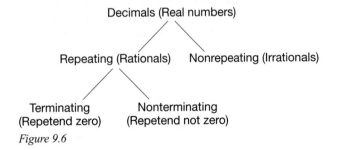

Figure 9.6

| **Example 9.8** | Determine whether the following decimals represent rational or irrational numbers. |

a. 0.273   **b.** 3.14159 . . .   **c.** $-15.\overline{76}$

SOLUTION
a. 0.273 is a rational number, since it is a terminating decimal.
b. 3.14159 . . . should be considered to be irrational, since the three dots indicate an infinite decimal and there is no repetend indicated.
c. $-15.\overline{76}$ is rational, since it is a repeating decimal. ∎

Now we can extend our diagram in Figure 9.2 to include the real numbers (Figure 9.7).

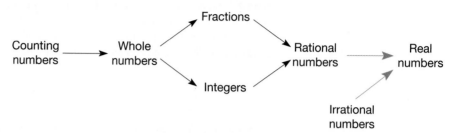

Figure 9.7

In terms of a number line, the points representing real numbers completely fill in the gaps in the rational number line. In fact, the points in the gaps represent irrational numbers (Figure 9.8).

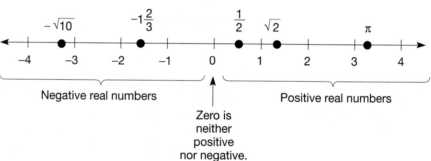

Figure 9.8

Let's take this geometric representation of the real numbers one step further. The Pythagorean theorem from geometry states that in a right triangle whose sides have lengths a and b and whose hypotenuse has length c, the equation $a^2 + b^2 = c^2$ holds (Figure 9.9).

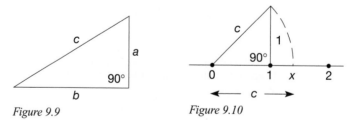

Figure 9.9   Figure 9.10

Now consider the construction in Figure 9.10. The length c is found by using the Pythagorean theorem:

$$1^2 + 1^2 = c^2 \quad \text{or} \quad c^2 = 2.$$

Moreover, the length of the segment from 0 to x is c also, since the dashed arc in Figure 9.10 is a portion of a circle. Thus $x = c$ where $c^2 = 2$. Since we know the number whose square is 2 is not rational, c must have an infinite *nonrepeating* decimal representation. To represent c with numerals other than an infinite nonrepeating decimal, we need the concept of square root.

NCTM Standard
All students should understand
and use the inverse relationships
of addition and subtraction,
multiplication and division, and
squaring and finding square
roots to simplify computations
and solve problems.

Since both $(-3)^2$ and 3^2 equal 9, -3 and 3 are called *square roots* of 9. The symbol $\sqrt{a}$ represents the *nonnegative* square root of a, called the **principal square root**. For example, $\sqrt{4} = 2$, $\sqrt{25} = 5$, $\sqrt{144} = 12$, and so on. We can also write symbols such as $\sqrt{2}$, $\sqrt{3}$, and $\sqrt{17}$. These numbers are not rational, so they have infinite nonrepeating decimal representations. Thus it is necessary to leave them written as $\sqrt{2}$, $\sqrt{3}$, $\sqrt{17}$, and so on. According to the definition, though, we know that $(\sqrt{2})^2 = 2$, $(\sqrt{3})^2 = 3$, $(\sqrt{17})^2 = 17$.

DEFINITION

Square Root

Let a be a nonnegative real number. Then the **square root** of a (i.e., the principal square root of a), written $\sqrt{a}$, is defined as

$$\sqrt{a} = b \quad \text{where } b^2 = a \quad \text{and} \quad b \geq 0.$$

Calculators can be used to find square roots. First, a $\boxed{\sqrt{}}$ key can be used. For example, to find $\sqrt{3}$ press $\boxed{\sqrt{}}$ 3 $\boxed{=}$ $\boxed{1.732050808}$ or simply 3 $\boxed{\sqrt{}}$. (Some calculators have "$\sqrt{}$" as a second function.) The $\boxed{\sqrt[x]{y}}$ key may also be used where x is 2 for square root. To find $\sqrt{3}$ using $\boxed{\sqrt[x]{y}}$, press 2 $\boxed{\sqrt[x]{y}}$ 3 $\boxed{=}$ $\boxed{1.732050808}$. Notice that this entered in the same way that it would be read, namely "the second root of three." Some calculators, however, use the following syntax: 3 $\boxed{\sqrt[x]{y}}$ 2, where the y is entered first. NOTE: The calculator-displayed number is an *approximation* to $\sqrt{3}$.

One can observe that there are infinitely many irrational numbers, namely $\sqrt{p}$, where p is a prime. However, the fact that there are many more irrationals will be developed in the problem set. The number pi (π), of circle fame, was proved to be irrational around 1870; π is the ratio of the circumference to the diameter in any circle.

Using the decimal representation of real numbers, addition, multiplication, subtraction, and division of real numbers can be defined as extensions of similar operations in the rationals. The following properties hold (although it is beyond the scope of this book to prove them).

PROPERTIES

Real-Number Operations

ADDITION	MULTIPLICATION
Closure	Closure
Commutativity	Commutativity
Associativity	Associativity
Identity (0)	Identity (1)
Inverse $(-a)$	Inverse $\left(\dfrac{1}{a} \text{ for } a \neq 0\right)$

Distributivity of Multiplication over Addition

Also, subtraction is defined by $a - b = a + (-b)$, and division is defined by $a \div b = a \cdot \dfrac{1}{b}$, where $b \neq 0$. "Less than" and "greater than" can be defined as extensions of ordering in the rationals, namely $a < b$ if and only if $a + p = b$ for some positive real number p. The following order properties also hold. Similar properties hold for $>$, $\leq$, and $\geq$.

PROPERTIES

Ordering Real Numbers

Transitive Property of Less Than
Property of Less Than and Addition
Property of Less Than and Multiplication by a Positive
Property of Less Than and Multiplication by a Negative
Density Property

You may have observed that the system of real numbers satisfies all of the properties that we have identified for the system of rational numbers. The main property that distinguishes the two systems is that the real numbers are "complete" in the sense that this is the set of numbers that finally fills up the entire number line. Even though the rational numbers are dense, there are still infinitely many gaps in the rational-number line, namely, the points that represent the irrationals. Together, the rationals and irrationals comprise the entire real number line.

 Check for Understanding: Exercise/Problem Set A #1–17

Rational Exponents

Now that we have the set of real numbers, we can extend our study of exponents to rational exponents. We begin by generalizing the definition of square root to more general types of roots. For example, since $(-2)^3 = -8$, -2 is called the cube root of -8. Because of negative numbers, the definition must be stated in two parts.

Children's Literature
www.wiley.com/college/musser
See "The King's Chessboard"
by David Birch.

DEFINITION

nth Root

Let a be a real number and n be a positive integer.

1. If $a \geq 0$, then $\sqrt[n]{a} = b$ if and only if $b^n = a$ and $b \geq 0$.
2. If $a < 0$ and n is odd, then $\sqrt[n]{a} = b$ if and only if $b^n = a$.

Algebraic Reasoning
An understanding of rational exponents is a valuable tool for solving equations like $x^4 = 81$. Taking the 4th root of both sides of the equation yields $x = \sqrt[4]{81} = 3$.

Example 9.9

Where possible, write the following values in simplest form by applying the previous two definitions.

a. $\sqrt[4]{81}$ **b.** $\sqrt[5]{-32}$ **c.** $\sqrt[6]{-64}$

SOLUTION

a. $\sqrt[4]{81} = b$ if and only if $b^4 = 81$. Since $3^4 = 81$, we have $\sqrt[4]{81} = 3$.

b. $\sqrt[5]{32} = b$ if and only if $b^5 = -32$. Since $(-2)^5 = -32$, we have $\sqrt[5]{-32} = -2$.

c. It is tempting to begin to apply the definition and write $\sqrt[6]{-64} = b$ if and only if $b^6 = -64$. However, since b^6 must always be positive or zero, there is no real number b such that $\sqrt[6]{-64} = b$. ∎

The number a in $\sqrt[n]{a}$ is called the **radicand** and n is called the **index**. The symbol $\sqrt[n]{a}$ is read **the nth root of a** and is called a **radical**. Notice that $\sqrt[n]{a}$ has not been defined for the case when n is even and a is negative. The reason is that $b^n \geq 0$ for any real number b when n is an even positive integer. For example, there is no real number b such that $b = \sqrt{-1}$, for if there were, then b^2 would equal -1. This is impossible since, by the property of less than and multiplication by a positive (or negative), it can be shown that the square of any nonzero real number is positive.

Roots of real numbers can be calculated by using the $\boxed{\sqrt[x]{y}}$ key. For example, to find $\sqrt[5]{30}$, enter it into the calculator just as it is read: the fifth root of thirty, or $5 \boxed{\sqrt[x]{y}} 30 \boxed{=} \boxed{1.9743505}$. (NOTE: Some calculators require that you press the second function key, $\boxed{\text{2nd}}$, to get to the $\boxed{\sqrt[x]{y}}$ function.) Also, as a good mental check, since $2^5 = 32$, a good estimate of $\sqrt[5]{30}$ is a number somewhat less than 2. Hence, the calculator display of 1.9743505 is a reasonable approximation for $\sqrt[5]{30}$.

Using the concept of radicals, we can now proceed to define rational exponents. What would be a good definition of $3^{1/2}$? If the usual additive property of exponents is to hold, then $3^{1/2} \cdot 3^{1/2} = 3^{1/2+1/2} = 3^1 = 3$. But $\sqrt{3} \cdot \sqrt{3} = 3$. Thus $3^{1/2}$ should represent $\sqrt{3}$. Similarly, $5^{1/3} = \sqrt[3]{5}$, $2^{1/7} = \sqrt[7]{2}$ and so on. We summarize this idea in the next definition.

DEFINITION

Unit Fraction Exponent

Let a be any real number and n any positive integer. The

$$a^{1/n} = \sqrt[n]{a}$$

where

1. n is arbitrary when $a \geq 0$, and
2. n must be odd when $a < 0$.

For example, $(-8)^{1/3} = \sqrt[3]{-8} = -2$, and $81^{1/4} = \sqrt[4]{81} = 3$.

The combination of this last definition with the definitions for integer exponents leads us to this final definition of **rational exponent**. For example, taking into account the previous definition and our earlier work with exponents, a natural way to think of $27^{2/3}$ would be $(27^{1/3})^2$. For the sake of simplicity, we restrict our definition to rational exponents of nonnegative real numbers.

DEFINITION

Rational Exponents

Let a be a nonnegative number and $\dfrac{m}{n}$ be a rational number in simplest form. Then

$a^{m/n} = (a^{1/n})^m = (a^m)^{1/n}$.

Example 9.10 Express the following values without exponents.

a. $9^{3/2}$ **b.** $16^{5/4}$ **c.** $125^{-4/3}$

SOLUTION

a. $9^{3/2} = (9^{1/2})^3 = 3^3 = 27$ **b.** $16^{5/4} = (16^{1/4})^5 = 2^5 = 32$

c. $125^{-4/3} = (125^{1/3})^{-4} = 5^{-4} = \dfrac{1}{5^4} = \dfrac{1}{625}$ ∎

The following properties hold for rational exponents.

PROPERTIES

Rational Exponents

Let a, b represent positive real numbers and m, n positive rational exponents. Then

$$a^m a^n = a^{m+n}$$
$$a^m b^m = (ab)^m$$
$$(a^m)^n = a^{mn}$$
$$a^m \div a^n = a^{m-n}.$$

Real-number exponents are defined using more advanced mathematics, and they have the same properties as rational exponents.

 An exponent key such as $\boxed{\wedge}$ or $\boxed{y^x}$ can be used to calculate real exponents. For example, to calculate $3^{\sqrt{2}}$, press 3 $\boxed{\wedge}$ $\boxed{\sqrt{}}$ 2 $\boxed{=}$ $\boxed{4.7288044}$.

 Check for Understanding: Exercise/Problem Set A #18–21

Algebra

Solving Equations and Inequalities   In Chapter 1, variables and equations were introduced along with some basic methods for solving those equations. The solutions to those equations, however, were restricted to whole numbers. Now that all of the real numbers have been introduced, we will take a second look at solving equations along with inequalities.

An **inequality** is a sentence whose verb is one of the following: $<, \leq, >, \geq,$ or $\neq$. Recall that a conditional equation is one that is only true for certain values of x. Examples of conditional equations and inequalities follow.

EQUATIONS	INEQUALITIES
$x + 7 = 3$	$2x + 4 < -17$
$\dfrac{1}{3}x + \dfrac{2}{3} = \dfrac{2}{7}x - \dfrac{4}{13}$	$(\sqrt{2})x - \dfrac{2}{5} \leq 8x - \dfrac{1}{\sqrt{3}}$

Solutions to conditional equations and inequalities are the values of x that make the statement true. Solutions are often written in set notation. For example, the solution set of the equation $x + 7 = 3$ is $\{-4\}$ and of $x + 7 < 4$ is $\{x \mid x < -3\}$.

One of the important concepts in solving equations is understanding the meaning of the equals sign. Many view the equals sign in the equation $2 + 6 = \square$ as the indicator to do the addition. Instead the equals sign means that the value of what is on the left is the same as the value on the right. In solving equations, the values on both sides of the equals sign must be maintained to be the same. To solidify this understanding we introduce the **balancing method**. This method requires that the numbers are represented by identically weighted objects like coins. Thus, the next three examples address equations of the form $ax + b = cx + d$ where a, b, c, d, and x are whole numbers.

Form 1: $x + b = d$

$$x + b = d$$
$$Solve: x + 4 = 7.$$

Concrete/Pictorial Representation	**Abstract Representation**

Problem-Solving Strategy
Draw a Picture

$$x + 4 = 7$$

There are four coins and some more hidden from view behind the square. Altogether they balance seven coins. How many coins are hidden?

Reflection from Research
The use of objects and containers as models for variables helps students solve linear equations. These models not only positively influenced students' achievement, but also their attitude toward the algebra (Quinlan, 1995).

(NOTE: Throughout this section we are assuming that the coins are identical.)

Remove four coins from each side.

Subtract 4 from both sides [equivalently add (-4) to both sides].
$$x + 4 + (-4) = 7 + (-4)$$
$$x + 0 = 3$$
$$x = 3$$

There are three coins hidden.

Form 2: $ax + b = d$

$$ax + b = d$$
$$Solve: 3x + 6 = 12.$$

Concrete/Pictorial Representation	**Abstract Representation**

$$3x + 6 = 12$$

Remove six coins from each side.

Subtract 6 from both sides [equivalently add (-6) to both sides].
$$3x + 6 + (-6) = 12 + (-6)$$
$$3x = 6$$

Divide both sides by 3 (equivalently, multiply both sides by $\frac{1}{3}$).

Divide the coins into three equal piles (one pile for each square).

$$\left(\frac{1}{3}\right)3x = \left(\frac{1}{3}\right)6$$

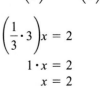

$$\left(\frac{1}{3} \cdot 3\right)x = 2$$
$$1 \cdot x = 2$$
$$x = 2$$

Each square hides two coins.

Form 3: $ax + b = cx + d$

$$ax + b = cx + d$$
Solve: $4x + 5 = 2x + 13$.

Algebraic Reasoning	**Concrete/Pictorial Representation**	**Abstract Representation**

Algebraic Reasoning
Because of the abstract nature of equations, developing algebraic reasoning through concrete representations can be valuable. Inherent in these physical models is the idea of determining the contents of the box that will maintain the balance or equality. This same idea is important in reasoning about equations.

Abstract Representation

$$4x + 5 = 2x + 13$$

Remove five coins from each pan. (We could have removed the coins behind two squares from each pan also.)

Subtract 5 from both sides [equivalently, add (-5) to both sides].

$$4x + 5 + (-5) = 2x + 13 + (-5)$$
$$4x = 2x + 8$$

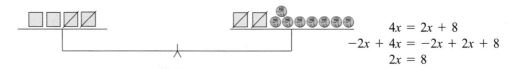

Remove all the coins behind two squares from each pan. Remember, all squares hide the same number of coins.

Subtract $2x$ from both sides, [equivalently, add $(-2x)$ to both sides].

$$4x = 2x + 8$$
$$-2x + 4x = -2x + 2x + 8$$
$$2x = 8$$

Divide the coins into two equal piles (one for each square).

Multiply both sides by $\frac{1}{2}$ (equivalently, divide both sides by 2).

$$2x = 8$$
$$\frac{1}{2}(2x) = \frac{1}{2} \cdot 8$$
$$x = 4$$

Each square hides four coins.

(NOTE: In the preceding three examples, all the coefficients of x were chosen to be positive. However, the same techniques we have applied hold for negative coefficients also.)

The previous examples show that to solve equations of the form $ax + b = cx + d$, you should add the appropriate values to each side to obtain another equation of the form $mx = n$. Then multiply both sides by $\frac{1}{m}$ (or, equivalently, divide by m) to yield the solution $x = \frac{n}{m}$.

Now that some properties of equality have been demonstrated using the balancing method, we will extend them to handle $ax + b = cx + d$ where $a, b, c, d,$ and x are *real numbers*. In this general equation, $a, b, c,$ and d are fixed real numbers where a and c are called **coefficients** of the variable x; they are numbers multiplied by a variable.

Example 9.11   Solve these equations.

a. $5x = 7x - 4\sqrt{2}$ **b.** $\dfrac{2}{3}x + \dfrac{5}{7} = \dfrac{9}{4}x - \dfrac{2}{11}$

SOLUTION

a.

$$5x = 7x - 4\sqrt{2}$$

$$(-7x) + 5x = (-7x) + 7x - 4\sqrt{2}$$

$$-2x = -4\sqrt{2}$$

$$\left(-\frac{1}{2}\right) \cdot -2x = \left(-\frac{1}{2}\right) \cdot -4\sqrt{2}$$

$$x = 2\sqrt{2}$$

To check, substitute $2\sqrt{2}$ for x into the initial equation:

Check: $5 \cdot 2\sqrt{2} = \mathbf{10\sqrt{2}}$, and $7 \cdot 2\sqrt{2} - 4\sqrt{2} = \mathbf{10\sqrt{2}}$

b. This solution incorporates some shortcuts.

$$\frac{2}{3}x + \frac{5}{7} = \frac{9}{4}x - \frac{2}{11}$$

$$\frac{2}{3}x = \frac{9}{4}x - \frac{2}{11} - \frac{5}{7}$$

$$\frac{2}{3}x - \frac{9}{4}x = -\frac{69}{77}$$

$$\frac{-19}{12}x = \frac{-69}{77}$$

$$x = \left(-\frac{12}{19}\right)\left(-\frac{69}{77}\right) = \frac{828}{1463}$$

Check: $\dfrac{2}{3} \cdot \dfrac{828}{1463} + \dfrac{5}{7} = \dfrac{552}{1463} + \dfrac{5}{7} = \dfrac{\mathbf{1597}}{\mathbf{1463}}$ and

$\dfrac{9}{4} \cdot \dfrac{828}{1463} - \dfrac{2}{11} = \dfrac{1863}{1463} - \dfrac{2}{11} = \dfrac{\mathbf{1597}}{\mathbf{1463}}$ ∎

In the solution of Example 9.11(a), the same term was added to both sides of the equation or both sides were multiplied by the same number until an equation of the form $x = a$ (or $a = x$) resulted. In the solution of Example 9.11(b), terms were moved from one side to the other, changing signs when addition was involved and inverting when multiplication was involved. This method is called **transposing**.

Solving Inequalities   We will examine inequalities that are similar in form to the equations we have solved, namely $ax + b \le cx + d$ where a, b, c, d, and x are all real numbers. We will use the following properties of order.

Property of less than and addition: If $a < b$, then $a + c < b + c$.

Property of less than and multiplication by a positive: If $a < b$ and $c > 0$, then $ac < bc$.

Property of less than and multiplication by a negative: If $a < b$ and $c < 0$, then $ac > bc$.

Notice that in the third property, the property of less than and multiplication by a negative, the inequality $a < b$ "reverses" to the inequality $ac > bc$, since c is *negative*. Also, similar corresponding properties hold for "greater than," "less than or equal to," and "greater than or equal to."

Example 9.12　Solve these inequalities.

a. $3x - 4 < x + 12$　　**b.** $\frac{1}{3}x - 7 > \frac{3}{5}x + 3$

SOLUTION

a.
$$3x - 4 < x + 12 \qquad \text{\textit{Property of less than and addition}}$$
$$3x + (-4) + 4 < x + 12 + 4$$
$$3x < x + 16 \qquad \text{\textit{Property of less than and addition}}$$
$$(-x) + 3x < (-x) + x + 16$$
$$2x < 16$$
$$\frac{1}{2}(2x) < \frac{1}{2}(16) \qquad \text{\textit{Property of less than and multiplication by a positive}}$$
$$x < 8$$

b.
$$\frac{1}{3}x - 7 > \frac{3}{5}x + 3$$
$$\frac{1}{3}x - 7 + 7 > \frac{3}{5}x + 3 + 7 \qquad \text{\textit{Property of greater than and addition}}$$
$$\frac{1}{3}x > \frac{3}{5}x + 10$$
$$-\frac{3}{5}x + \frac{1}{3}x > -\frac{3}{5}x + \frac{3}{5}x + 10 \qquad \text{\textit{Property of greater than and addition}}$$
$$-\frac{4}{15}x > 10$$
$$\left(-\frac{15}{4}\right)\left(-\frac{4}{15}x\right) < \left(-\frac{15}{4}\right)10 \qquad \text{\textit{Property of greater than and multiplication by a negative}}$$
$$x < \frac{-75}{2} = -37.5 \qquad\blacksquare$$

Solutions of equations can be checked by substituting the solutions back into the initial equation. In Example 9.11(a), the substitution of 3 into the equation $5x + 11 = 7x + 5$ yields $5 \cdot 3 + 11 = 7 \cdot 3 + 5$, or $26 = 26$. Thus 3 is a solution of this equation. The process of checking inequalities is more involved. Usually, there are infinitely many numbers in the solution set of an inequality. Since there are infinitely many numbers to check, it is reasonable to check only a few (perhaps two or three) well-chosen numbers. For example, let's consider Example 9.12(b). The solution set for the inequality $\frac{1}{3}x - 7 > \frac{3}{5}x + 3$ is $\{x \mid x < -37.5\}$ (Figure 9.11).

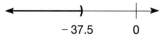

$$-37.5 \qquad 0$$

Figure 9.11

To check the solution, substitute into the inequality one "convenient" number from the solution set and one outside the solution set. Here -45 (in the solution set) and 0 (not in the solution set) are two convenient values.

1. In $\frac{1}{3}x - 7 > \frac{3}{5}x + 3$, substitute 0 for x: $\frac{1}{3} \cdot 0 - 7 > \frac{3}{5} \cdot 0 + 3$, or $-7 > 3$, which is false. Therefore, 0 does *not* belong to the solution set.

2. To test -45: $\frac{1}{3}(-45) - 7 > \frac{3}{5}(-45) + 3$, or $-22 > -24$ which is true. Therefore, -45 does belong to the solution set.

You may want to check several other numbers. Although this method is not a complete check, it should add to your confidence that your solution set is correct.

Algebra has important uses in addition to solving equations and inequalities. For example, the problem-solving strategy Use a Variable is another application of algebra that is very useful.

| **Example 9.13** | Prove that the sum of any five consecutive whole numbers has a factor of 5. |

SOLUTION Let $x, x + 1, x + 2, x + 3, x + 4$ represent any five consecutive whole numbers.

Then $x + (x + 1) + (x + 2) + (x + 3) + (x + 4) = 5x + 10 = 5(x + 2)$, which has a factor of 5. ■

✔ **Check for Understanding:** Exercise/Problem Set A #22–25

MATHEMATICAL MORSEL

Throughout history there have been many interesting approximations of π as well as many ways of computing them. The value of pi to seven decimal places can easily be remembered using the mnemonic "May I have a large container of coffee?", where the number of letters in each word yields 3.1415926.

1. Found in an Egyptian papyrus: $\pi \approx \left(2 \times \frac{8}{9}\right)^2$.

2. Due to Archimedes: $\pi \approx \frac{22}{7}$, $\pi \approx \frac{355}{113}$.

3. Due to Wallis:

$$\pi = 2 \cdot \frac{2}{1} \cdot \frac{2}{3} \cdot \frac{4}{3} \cdot \frac{4}{5} \cdot \frac{6}{5} \cdot \frac{6}{7} \cdot \frac{8}{7} \cdots.$$

4. Due to Gregory:

$$\pi = 4\left(1 - \frac{1}{3} + \frac{1}{5} - \frac{1}{7} + \cdots\right).$$

5. Due to Euler and Bernoulli:

$$\pi = 6\left(\frac{1}{1^2} + \frac{1}{2^2} - \frac{1}{3^2} + \cdots\right).$$

6. In 1989, Gregory V. and David V. Chudnovsky calculated π to 1,011,196,691 places.

| **Section 9.2** | **EXERCISE / PROBLEM SET A** |

EXERCISES

1. Which of the following numbers are rational, and which are irrational? Assume that the decimal patterns continue.
 a. 6.233233323333 . . .   **b.** $\sqrt{49}$
 c. $\sqrt{61}$ **d.** -25.235723572357 . . .
 e. 7.121231234 . . .   **f.** $\sqrt{37}$
 g. $\sqrt{64}$ **h.** 4.233233233 . . .

2. The number π is given as an example of an irrational number. Often the value $\frac{22}{7}$ is used for π. Does $\pi = \frac{22}{7}$? Why or why not?

3. Use the Pythagorean theorem to find the lengths of the given segments drawn on the following square lattices.
 a.

1 unit

 b.

 c.

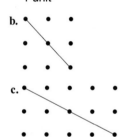

4. Construct the lengths $\sqrt{2}$, $\sqrt{3}$, $\sqrt{4}$, $\sqrt{5}$, . . . as follows.
 a. First construct a right triangle with both legs of length 1. What is the length of the hypotenuse?
 b. This hypotenuse is a leg of the next right triangle. The other leg has length 1. What is the length of the hypotenuse of this triangle?
 c. Continue drawing right triangles, using the hypotenuse of the preceding triangle as a leg of the next triangle until you have constructed one with length $\sqrt{7}$.

5. Use the Pythagorean theorem to find the length of the indicated side of the following right triangles. (NOTE: The square-like symbol indicates the 90° angle.)
 a.

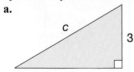

 b.

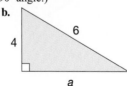

 c.

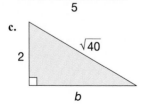

6. Simplify the following square roots.
 a. $\sqrt{48}$ **b.** $\sqrt{63}$ **c.** $\sqrt{162}$

7. Estimate the following values; then check with a calculator.
 a. $\sqrt{361}$ **b.** $\sqrt{729}$

8. **a.** Which property of real numbers justifies the following statement?

$$2\sqrt{3} + 5\sqrt{3} = (2 + 5)\sqrt{3} = 7\sqrt{3}$$

 b. Can this property be used to simplify $5\pi + 3\pi$? Explain.
 c. Can this property be used to simplify $2\sqrt{3} + 7\sqrt{5}$? Explain.

9. Compute the following pairs of expressions.
 a. $\sqrt{4} \times \sqrt{9}$, $\sqrt{4 \times 9}$ **b.** $\sqrt{4} \times \sqrt{25}$, $\sqrt{4 \times 25}$
 c. $\sqrt{9} \times \sqrt{16}$, $\sqrt{9 \times 16}$ **d.** $\sqrt{9} \times \sqrt{25}$, $\sqrt{9 \times 25}$
 e. What conclusion do you draw about $\sqrt{a}$, $\sqrt{b}$, and $\sqrt{a \times b}$? (NOTE: a and b must be nonnegative.)

10. Compute the following pairs.
 a. $\dfrac{\sqrt{16}}{\sqrt{4}}$, $\sqrt{\dfrac{16}{4}}$ **b.** $\dfrac{\sqrt{36}}{\sqrt{4}}$, $\sqrt{\dfrac{36}{4}}$
 c. $\dfrac{\sqrt{256}}{\sqrt{64}}$, $\sqrt{\dfrac{256}{64}}$ **d.** $\dfrac{\sqrt{441}}{\sqrt{49}}$, $\sqrt{\dfrac{441}{49}}$
 e. What conclusion do you draw about $\sqrt{a}$, $\sqrt{b}$, and $\sqrt{\dfrac{a}{b}}$? (NOTE: $a \geq 0$ and $b > 0$.)

11. Arrange the following real numbers in increasing order.
 0.56 $0.5\overline{6}$ $0.5\overline{66}$ 0.565565556 . . .
 $0.\overline{566}$ 0.56656665 . . .
 0.565566555666 . . .

12. Find an irrational number between $0.\overline{37}$ and $0.\overline{38}$.

13. Find four irrational numbers between 3 and 4.

14. Since the square roots of some numbers are irrational, their decimal representations do not repeat. Approximations of these decimal representations can be made by a process of squeezing. For example, from Figure 9.9, we see that $1 < \sqrt{2} < 2$. To improve this approximation, find two numbers between 1 and 2 that "squeeze" $\sqrt{2}$. Since $(1.4)^2 = 1.96$ and $(1.5)^2 = 2.25$, $1.4 < \sqrt{2} < 1.5$. To obtain a closer approximation, we could continue the squeezing process by choosing numbers close to 1.4 (since 1.96 is closer to 2 than 2.25). Since $(1.41)^2 = 1.9881$ and $(1.42)^2 = 2.0164$, $1.41 < \sqrt{2} < 1.42$, or $\sqrt{2} \approx 1.41$. Use the squeezing process to approximate square roots of the following to the nearest hundredth.
 a. 7   **b.** 15.6   **c.** 0.036

15. Find $\sqrt{13}$ using the following **divide and average** method: Make a guess, say r_1. Then find $13 \div r_1 = s_1$. Then find the average of r_1 and s_1 by computing $(r_1 + s_1)/2 = r_2$. Now find $13 \div r_2 = s_2$. Continue this procedure until r_n and s_n differ by less than 0.00001.

16. Using a calculator with a square-root key, enter the number 2. Press the square-root key several times consecutively. What do you observe about the numbers displayed? Continue to press the square-root key until no new numbers appear in the display. What is this number?

17. Using the square-root key on your calculator, find the square roots of the following numbers. Then order the given number and its square root in increasing order. What do you observe?
a. 0.3   b. 0.5

18. Express the following values without exponents.
a. $25^{1/2}$ b. $32^{1/5}$ c. $9^{5/2}$
d. $(-27)^{4/3}$ e. $16^{3/4}$ f. $25^{-3/2}$

19. Write the following radicals in simplest form if they are real numbers.
a. $\sqrt[3]{-27}$ b. $\sqrt[4]{-16}$ c. $\sqrt[5]{32}$

20. Calculate the following to three decimal places.
a. $625^{0.5}$ b. $37^{0.37}$ c. $11111^{1.7}$ d. $7^{8.23}$

21. Determine the larger of each pair.
a. $\sqrt[4]{64}$, 1.41^3 b. $\sqrt[3]{37}$, 1.35^4

22. Solve the following two problems using the balance beam approach. The problems are exercises 2 and 3 in the Chapter 9 eManipulative activity *Balance Beam Algebra* on our Web site. Sketch the steps used on the balance beam and the corresponding steps using symbols.
a. $2x + 3 = 7$ b. $3x + 4 = x + 8$

23. Solve the following equations using any method.
a. $x + 15 = 7$ b. $x + (-21) = -16$
c. $x + \frac{11}{9} = \frac{2}{3}$ d. $x + 2\sqrt{2} = 5\sqrt{2}$

24. Solve the following equations.
a. $2x - 5 = 13$ b. $3x + 7 = 22$
c. $-5x + 13 = -12$ d. $\frac{2}{3}x + \frac{1}{6} = \frac{11}{22}$
e. $-\frac{3}{5}x - \frac{1}{4} = \frac{9}{20}$ f. $3x + \pi = 7\pi$

25. Solve these inequalities.
a. $3x - 6 < 6x + 5$ b. $2x + 3 \geq 5x - 9$
c. $\frac{2}{3}x - \frac{1}{4} > \frac{1}{9}x + \frac{3}{4}$ d. $\frac{6}{5}x - \frac{1}{3} \leq \frac{3}{10}x + \frac{2}{5}$

PROBLEMS

26. Prove that $\sqrt{3}$ is not rational. (*Hint:* Reason by analogy from the proof that there is no rational number whose square is 2.)

27. Show why, when reasoning by analogy from the proof that $\sqrt{2}$ is irrational, an indirect proof does not lead to a contradiction when you try to show that $\sqrt{9}$ is irrational.

28. Prove that $\sqrt[3]{2}$ is irrational.

29. a. Show that $5\sqrt{3}$ is an irrational number. (*Hint:* Assume that it is rational, say a/b, isolate $\sqrt{3}$, and show that a contradiction occurs.)
b. Using a similar argument, show that the product of any nonzero rational number with an irrational number is an irrational number.

30. a. Prove that $1 + \sqrt{3}$ is an irrational number.
b. Show, similarly, that $m + n\sqrt{3}$ is an irrational number for all rational numbers m and n ($n \neq 0$).

31. Show that the following are irrational numbers.
a. $6\sqrt{2}$ b. $2 + \sqrt{3}$ c. $5 + 2\sqrt{3}$

32. A student says to his teacher, "You proved to us that $\sqrt{a} \cdot \sqrt{b} = \sqrt{ab}$. Reasoning by analogy, we get $\sqrt{a} + \sqrt{b} = \sqrt{a + b}$. Therefore, $\sqrt{9} + \sqrt{16} = \sqrt{25}$ or $3 + 4 = 5$. Right?" Comment!

33. A student says to her teacher, "You proved that $\sqrt{a} \cdot \sqrt{b} = \sqrt{ab}$. Therefore, $-1 = (\sqrt{-1})^2 = \sqrt{-1}\sqrt{-1} = \sqrt{(-1)(-1)} = \sqrt{1} = 1$, so that $-1 = 1$." What do you say?

34. Recall that a Pythagorean triple is a set of three nonzero whole numbers (a, b, c) where $a^2 + b^2 = c^2$. For example, $(3, 4, 5)$ is a Pythagorean triple. Show that there are infinitely many Pythagorean triples.

35. A **primitive Pythagorean triple** is a Pythagorean triple whose members have only 1 as a common prime factor. For example, $(3, 4, 5)$ is primitive, whereas $(6, 8, 10)$ is not. It has been shown that all primitive Pythagorean triples are given by the three equations:

$$a = 2uv \qquad b = u^2 - v^2 \qquad c = u^2 + v^2,$$

where u and v are relatively prime, one of u or v is even and the other is odd, and $u > v$. Generate five primitive triples using these equations.

36. You have three consecutive integers less than 20. Add two of them together, divide by the third, and the answer is the smallest of the three integers. What are the numbers?

37. Can a rational number plus its reciprocal ever be an integer? If yes, say precisely when.

38. If you are given two straight pieces of wire, is it possible to cut one of them into two pieces so that the length of one of the three pieces is the average of the lengths of the other two? Explain.

39. Messrs. Carter, Farrell, Milne, and Smith serve the little town of Milford as architect, banker, druggist, and grocer, though not necessarily respectively. The druggist earns exactly twice as much as the grocer, the architect earns exactly twice as much as the druggist, and the banker earns exactly twice as much as the architect. Although Carter is older than anyone who makes more money than Farrell, Farrell does not make twice as much as Carter. Smith earns exactly $3776 more than Milne. Who is the druggist?

40. At a contest, two persons were asked their ages. Then, to test their arithmetical powers, they were asked to add the two ages together. One gave 44 as the answer and the other gave 1280. The first had subtracted one age from the other, while the second person had multiplied them together. What were their ages?

Section 9.2 **EXERCISE / PROBLEM SET B**

EXERCISES

1. Which of the following numbers are rational, and which are irrational?
  a. $2.375375\ldots$ **b.** $3.0120123\ldots$
  c. $\sqrt{169}$ **d.** 2π
  e. $3.\overline{12}$
  g. $\dfrac{35}{0.72}$ **h.** $5.626626662\ldots$
  f. $\sqrt{7}$

2. The number $\sqrt{2}$ is often given as 1.414. Doesn't this show that $\sqrt{2}$ is rational, since it has a terminating decimal representation? Discuss.

3. Use the Pythagorean theorem to find the lengths of the given segments drawn on the following square lattices.

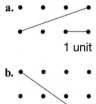

1 unit

4. Construct $\sqrt{8}$, $\sqrt{9}$, $\sqrt{10}$, $\sqrt{11}$ as follows.
  a. First construct a right triangle with both legs of length 2. What is the length of the hypotenuse?
  b. This hypotenuse is a leg of the next right triangle. The other leg has length 1. What is the length of the hypotenuse of this triangle?
  c. Continue drawing right triangles, using the hypotenuse of the preceding triangle as a leg of the next triangle until you have constructed one with length $\sqrt{11}$.

5. Use the Pythagorean theorem to find the missing lengths in the following diagrams.

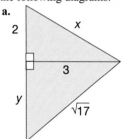

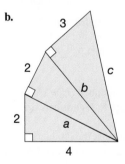

6. Simplify the following square roots.
  a. $\sqrt{40}$ **b.** $\sqrt{80}$ **c.** $\sqrt{180}$

 7. Estimate the following values; then check with a calculator.
  a. $\sqrt{3136}$ **b.** $\sqrt{5041}$

8. Use properties to simplify the following expressions. Explain how the properties were used in the simplification.
  a. $4\sqrt{3} - \sqrt{3}$
  b. $5\sqrt{7} + (\sqrt{35} + 7\sqrt{7})$
  c. $\sqrt{32} + \sqrt{50}$

9. Compute and simplify the following using Set A, Exercise 9e.
  a. $\sqrt{18} \times \sqrt{2}$ **b.** $\sqrt{27} \times \sqrt{3}$
  c. $\sqrt{60} \times \sqrt{15}$ **d.** $\sqrt{18} \times \sqrt{32}$

10. Compute and simplify the following using Part A, Exercise 10.

a. $\dfrac{\sqrt{75}}{\sqrt{3}}$ b. $\dfrac{\sqrt{96}}{\sqrt{6}}$ c. $\dfrac{\sqrt{147}}{\sqrt{12}}$ d. $\dfrac{\sqrt{45}}{\sqrt{125}}$

11. Arrange the following real numbers in increasing order.

0.876 $0.8\overline{76}$ $0.8\overline{76}$ 0.876787677876 . . .

$0.8\overline{766}$ 0.8766876667 . . .

0.8767876677887666 . . .

12. Find an irrational number between $0.\overline{5777}$ and $0.\overline{5778}$.

13. Find three irrational numbers between 2 and 3.

14. Use the squeezing process described in Part A, Exercise 14 to approximate the following square roots to the nearest hundredth.

a. $\sqrt{5}$ b. $\sqrt{19.2}$ c. $\sqrt{0.05}$

d. Explain the relationship between the solutions to part a and part c.

15. Use the divide and average method shown in Part A, Exercise 15 to find $\sqrt{24}$. Continue until r_n and s_n differ by less than 0.00001.

16. On your calculator, enter a positive number less than 1. Repeatedly press the square-root key. The displayed numbers should be increasing. Will they ever reach 1?

17. Using the square key on your calculator, find the squares of the following numbers. Then order the given number and its square in increasing order. What do you observe?

a. 0.71   b. 0.98

18. Express the following values without exponents.

a. $36^{1/2}$ b. $9^{3/2}$ c. $27^{2/3}$ d. $(-32)^{3/5}$ e. $(81)^{3/4}$ f. $(-243)^{6/5}$

19. Write the following radicals in simplest form if they are real numbers.

a. $\sqrt[5]{-32}$ b. $\sqrt[3]{-216}$ c. $\sqrt[6]{-64}$

20. Use a scientific calculator to calculate approximations of the following values. (They will require several steps and/or the use of the memory.)

a. $\sqrt{2^{4/3}}$ b. $\sqrt{3}^{\sqrt{2}}$ c. $\sqrt{17}^{\sqrt{17}}$ d. $391^{0.31}$

21. Determine the larger of each pair.

a. $\sqrt[5]{7^2}$, $\sqrt[13]{7^5}$ b. $\pi^{\sqrt{2}}$, $(\sqrt{2})^{\pi}$

22. Solve the following two problems using the balance beam approach. The problems are exercises 4 and 5 in the Chapter 9 eManipulative activity *Balance Beam Algebra* on our Web site. Sketch the steps used on the balance beam and the corresponding steps using symbols.

a. $4x + 1 = 9$ b. $4x + 2 = 2x + 8$

23. Solve the following equations.

a. $3x + \sqrt{6} = 2x - 3\sqrt{6}$ b. $x - \sqrt{2} = 9\sqrt{3}$

c. $5x - \sqrt{3} = 4\sqrt{3}$ d. $2\pi x - 6 = 5\pi x + 9$

24. Solve the following equations.

a. $x + 9 = -5$ b. $x - (-\frac{3}{4}) = \frac{5}{6}$ c. $3x - 4 = 9$

d. $\frac{1}{2}x + 1 = \frac{5}{2}$ e. $6 = 3x - 9$ f. $-2 = (\frac{-5}{12})x + 3$

25. Solve the following inequalities.

a. $x - \frac{2}{3} > \frac{5}{6}$ b. $-2x + 4 \le 11$

c. $3x + 5 \ge 6x - 7$ d. $\frac{3}{2}x - 2 < \frac{5}{6}x + \frac{1}{3}$

PROBLEMS

26. True or false? $\sqrt{p}$ is irrational for any prime p. If true, prove. If false, give a counterexample.

27. Prove that $\sqrt{6}$ is irrational. (*Hint:* You should use an indirect proof as we did for $\sqrt{2}$; however, this case requires a little additional reasoning.)

28. Prove that $\sqrt{p^7 q^5}$ is not rational where p and q are primes.

29. Prove or disprove: $\sqrt[n]{2}$ is irrational for any whole number $n \ge 2$.

30. Let p represent any prime. Determine whether the following are rational or irrational, and prove your assertion.

a. $\sqrt[3]{p}$ b. $\sqrt[3]{p^2}$

31. a. Let r be a nonzero rational number and p and q be two irrational numbers. Determine whether the following expressions are rational or irrational. Prove your assertion in each case.

(i) $r + p$ (ii) $r \cdot p$ (iii) $p + q$ (iv) $p \cdot q$

b. What if $r = 0$? Would this change your answers in part (a)? Explain.

32. Give an example that shows that each of the following can occur.

a. The sum of two irrational numbers may be an irrational number.

b. The sum of two irrational numbers may be a rational number.

c. The product of two irrational numbers may be an irrational number.

d. The product of two irrational numbers may be a rational number.

33. Is the set of irrational numbers

a. closed under addition?

b. closed under subtraction?

c. closed under multiplication?

d. closed under division?

34. Take *any* two real numbers whose sum is 1 (fractions, decimals, integers, etc. are appropriate). Square the larger and add the smaller. Then square the smaller and add the larger.
a. What will be true?   **b.** Prove your assertion.

35. The tempered musical scale, first employed by Johann Sebastian Bach, divides the octave into 12 equally spaced intervals:

$$C\ C^{\#}\ D\ D^{\#}\ E\ F\ F^{\#}\ G\ G^{\#}\ A\ A^{\#}\ B\ C^{oct.}$$

The fact that the intervals are equally spaced means that the ratios of the frequencies between any adjacent notes are the same. For example,

$$C^{\#}{:}C\ =\ k \qquad \text{and} \qquad D{:}C^{\#}\ =\ k.$$

From this we see that $C^{\#} = k \cdot C$ and $D = k \cdot C^{\#} = k(k \cdot C) = k^2 C$. Continuing this pattern, we can show that $C^{oct} = k^{12} \cdot C$ (verify this). It is also true that two notes are an octave apart if the frequency of one is double the other. Thus $C^{oct} = 2 \cdot C$. Therefore, $k^{12} = 2$ or $k = \sqrt[12]{2}$. In tuning instruments, the frequency of A above middle C is 440 cycles per second. From this we can find the other frequencies of the octave:

$$A^{\#} = \sqrt[12]{2} \cdot 440 = 466.16$$

$$G^{\#} = 440 / \left(\sqrt[12]{2} \right) = 415.31.$$

a. Find the remaining frequencies to the nearest hundredth of a cycle.
b. In the Greek scale, a fifth (C to G, F to C) had a ratio of $\frac{3}{2}$. How does the tempered scale compare?
c. Also in the Greek scale, a fourth (C to F, D to G) had a ratio of $\frac{4}{3}$. How close is the tempered scale to this ratio?

36. Two towns A and B are 3 miles apart. It is proposed to build a new school to serve 200 students in town A and 100 students in town B. How far from A should the school be built if the total distance traveled by all 300 students is to be as small as possible?

37. *Calendar calculus:*
a. Mark any 4 × 4 array of dates on a calendar.

		1	2	3	4	5
6	7	8	9	10	11	12
13	14	15	16	17	18	19
20	21	22	23	24	25	26
27	28	29	30	31		

b. Circle any numeral in the 4 × 4 array, say 15. Then cross out all other numerals in the same row and column as 15.
c. Circle any numeral not crossed out, say 21. Then cross out all other numerals in the same row and column as 21.

d. Continue until there are four circled numbers. Their sum should be 76 (this is true for this particular 4 × 4 array).

Try this with another 4 × 4 calendar array. Are all such sums the same there? Does this work for 3 × 3 calendar arrays? How about $n \times n$ arrays if we make bigger calendars?

38. Two numbers are reciprocals of each other. One number is 9 times as large as the other. Find the two numbers.

39. The following problem was given as a challenge to Fibonacci: Three men are to share a pile of money in the fractions $\frac{1}{2}, \frac{1}{3}, \frac{1}{6}$. Each man takes some money from the pile until there is nothing left. The first man returns one-half of what he took, the second returns one-third, and the third one-sixth. When the returned amount is divided equally among the men, it is found that they each have what they are entitled to. How much money was in the original pile, and how much did each man take from the original pile?

40. Chad was the same age as Shelly, and Holly was 4 years older than both of them. Chad's dad was 20 when Chad was born, and the average age of the four of them is 39. How old is Chad?

 Analyzing Student Thinking
41. Sadi asserts that the sum of two irrational numbers must be irrational due to closure of addition of real numbers. How should you respond?

42. Romona asks you how it could be that 0.9999999 . . . equals 1 as it says in her book. How should you respond?

43. Lars says that $\sqrt{9} = -3$ since $(-3)^2 = 9$. Is he correct? Explain.

44. Ian says that $27^{-5/3}$ must be negative because $-5/3$ is negative. How should you respond?

45. Fatima wants you to show her some numbers other than π that are real but not rational. What would you show her?

46. Zachery claims that $8^{-2/3}$ is the same as $8^{3/2}$ because when you have a negative exponent, you use the reciprocal. How would you respond to Zachery?

47. Suppose you give your students some problems that involve the Pythagorean Theorem. Tanner comes up to you and says that he prefers to work with whole numbers, but some of his answers are not whole numbers. Identify four sets of three whole numbers that you could give Tanner to use.

Problems Relating to the NCTM Standards and Curriculum Focal Points

1. The Focal Points for Grade 5 state "Use patterns, models, and relationships as contexts for writing and solving simple equations and inequalities." Describe an example of a model that can be used to solve simple equations.

2. The Focal Points for Grade 6 state "Writing, interpreting, and using mathematical expressions and equations." What is the difference between a mathematical expression and mathematical equation?

3. The NCTM Standards state "All students should understand and use the inverse relationships of addition and subtraction, multiplication and division, and squaring and finding square roots to simplify computations and solve problems." Explain why squaring and square roots are considered inverse relationships.

9.3   RELATIONS AND FUNCTIONS

STARTING POINT

Describe a possible relationship between the two sets of numbers at the right. Include a description of how the numbers might be matched up. Compare your relationship with a classmate's. What are the similarities or differences between the two relationships?

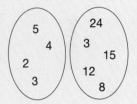

Relations and functions are central to mathematics. Relations are simply the description of relationships between two sets. Functions, which will be described later in this section, are specific types of relations.

Children's Literature
www.wiley.com/college/musser
See "Anno's Magic Seeds" by
Mitsumasa Anno.

Relations

Relationships between objects or numbers can be analyzed using ideas from set theory. For example, on the set {1, 2, 3, 4}, we can express the relationship "*a* is a divisor of *b*" by listing all the ordered pairs (*a, b*) for which the relationship is true, namely {(1, 1), (1, 2), (1, 3), (1, 4), (2, 2), (2, 4), (3, 3), (4, 4)}. In this section we study properties of relations.

Relations are used in mathematics to represent a relationship between two numbers or objects. For example, when we say, "3 is less than 7," "2 is a factor of 6," and "Triangle *ABC* is similar to triangle *DEF*," we are expressing relationships between pairs of numbers in the first two cases and triangles in the last case. More generally, the concept of relation can be applied to arbitrary sets. A set of ordered pairs can be used to show that certain pairs of objects are related. For example, the set {(Hawaii, 50), (Alaska, 49), (New Mexico, 48)} lists the newest three states of the United States and their number of statehood. This relation can be verbally described as "_____ was state number _____ to join the United States"; for example, "Alaska was state number 49 to join the United States."

A diagrammatic way of denoting relationships is through the use of **arrow diagrams**. For example, in Figure 9.12, each arrow can be read "_____ was the vice-president under _____" where the arrow points to the president.

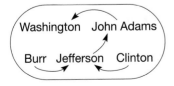

Figure 9.12

When a relation can be described on a single set, an arrow diagram can be used on that set in two ways. For example, the relation "is a factor of" on the set {2, 4, 6, 8} is represented in two equivalent ways in Figure 9.13, using one set in part (a) and two copies of a set in part (b). The advantage of using two sets in an arrow diagram is that relations between *two different* sets can be pictured, as in the case of the newest states (Figure 9.14).

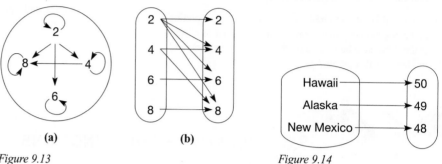

(a) (b)

Figure 9.13   *Figure 9.14*

Formally, a **relation** R from set A to set B is a subset of $A \times B$, the Cartesian product of A and B. If $A = B$, we say that R is a relation on A. In our example about the states, set A consists of the three newest states and B consists of the numbers 48, 49, and 50. In the preceding paragraph, "is a factor of," the sets A and B were the same, namely, the set {2, 4, 6, 8}. This last relation is represented by the following set of ordered pairs.

$$R = \{(2, 2), (2, 4), (2, 6), (2, 8), (4, 4), (4, 8), (6, 6), (8, 8)\}$$

Notice that R is a subset of $\{2, 4, 6, 8\} \times \{2, 4, 6, 8\}$.

In the case of a relation R on a set A, that is, where $R \subseteq A \times A$, there are three useful properties that a relation may have.

Reflexive Property   A relation R on a set A is said to be **reflexive** if $(a, a) \in R$ for all $a \in A$. We say that R is reflexive if every element in A is related to itself. For example, the relation "is a factor of" on the set $A = \{2, 4, 6, 8\}$ is reflexive, since every number in A is a factor of itself. In general, in an arrow diagram, a relation is reflexive if every element in A has an arrow pointing to itself. Thus the relation depicted in Figure 9.15(a) is reflexive and the one depicted in Figure 9.15(b) is not.

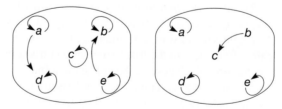

(a) Reflexive relation   **(b) Not reflexive (since neither b nor**
c is related to itself)

Figure 9.15

Symmetric Property   A relation R on a set A is said to be **symmetric** if whenever $(a, b) \in R$, then $(b, a) \in R$ also; in words, if a is related to b, then b is related to a. Let R be the relation "is the opposite of" on the set $A = \{1, -1, 2, -2\}$.

Then $R = \{(1, -1), (-1, 1), (2, -2), (-2, 2)\}$; that is, R has all possible ordered pairs (a, b) from $A \times A$ if a is the opposite of b. The arrow diagram of this relation is shown in Figure 9.16.

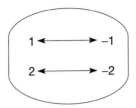

Figure 9.16

Notice that for a relation to be symmetric, whenever an arrow points in one direction, it must point in the opposite direction also. Thus the relation "is the opposite of" is symmetric on the set $\{1, -1, 2, -2\}$. The relation "is a factor of" on the set $\{2, 4, 6, 8\}$ is *not* symmetric, since 2 is a factor of 4, but 4 is not a factor of 2. Notice that this fact can be seen in Figure 9.13(a), since there is an arrow pointing from 2 to 4, but not conversely.

Transitive Property   A relation R on a set A is **transitive** if whenever $(a, b) \in R$ and $(b, c) \in R$, then $(a, c) \in R$. In words, a relation is transitive if for all a, b, c in A, if a is related to b and b is related to c, then a is related to c. Consider the relation "is a factor of" on the set $\{2, 4, 6, 8, 12\}$. Notice that 2 is a factor of 4 and 4 is a factor of 8 *and* 2 is a factor of 8. Also, 2 is a factor of 4 and 4 is a factor of 12 *and* 2 is a factor of 12. The last case to consider, involving 2, 6, and 12, is also true. Thus "is a factor of" is a transitive relation on the set $\{2, 4, 6, 8, 12\}$. In an arrow diagram, a relation is transitive if whenever there is an "a to b" arrow and a "b to c" arrow, there is also an "a to c" arrow (Figure 9.17).

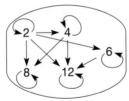

(a) Transitive relation

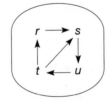

(b) Not a transitive relation, since $(r, s) \in R$ and $(s, u) \in R$, but $(r, u) \notin R$ (there is no arrow from r to u)

Figure 9.17

Now consider the relation "has the same ones digit as" on the set of numbers $\{1, 2, 3, \ldots, 40\}$. Clearly, every number has the same ones digit as itself; thus this relation is reflexive; it is also symmetric and transitive. Any relation on a set that is reflexive, symmetric, and transitive is called an **equivalence relation**. Thus the relation "has the same ones digit as" is an equivalence relation on the set $\{1, 2, 3, \ldots, 40\}$. There are many equivalence relations in mathematics. Some common ones are "is equal to" on any set of numbers and "is congruent to" and "is similar to" on sets of geometric shapes.

An important attribute of an equivalence relation R on a set A is that the relation imparts a subdivision, or partitioning, of the set A into a collection of nonempty, pairwise disjoint subsets (i.e., the intersection of any two subsets is $\varnothing$). For example, if the numbers that are related to each other in the preceding paragraph are collected

Reflection from Research
Most middle school students do not understand that the equal sign represents a relation. This lack of understanding greatly inhibits students' equation-solving performance (Knuth, Stephens, McNeil, & Alibali, 2006).

into sets, the relation R on the set $\{1, 2, 3, \ldots, 40\}$ is represented by the following set of nonempty, pairwise disjoint subsets.

$$\big\{\{1, 11, 21, 31\}, \{2, 12, 22, 32\}, \ldots, \{10, 20, 30, 40\}\big\}$$

That is, all of the elements having the same ones digit are grouped together.

Formally, a **partition** of a set A is a collection of nonempty, pairwise disjoint subsets of A whose union is A. It can be shown that every equivalence relation on a set A gives rise to a unique partition of A *and*, conversely, that every partition of A yields a corresponding equivalence relation. The partition associated with the relation "has the same shape as" on a set of shapes is shown in Figure 9.18. Notice how all the squares are grouped together, since they have the "same shape."

Figure 9.18

✔ **Check for Understanding:** Exercise/Problem Set A #1–6

Functions

As was mentioned earlier, functions are specific types of relations. The underlying concept of function is described in the following definition.

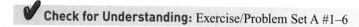

DEFINITION

Function

A function is a relation that matches each element of a first set to an element of a second set in such a way that no element in the first set is assigned to two different elements in the second set.

Algebraic Reasoning
Functions are a fundamental part of algebraic thinking. Functions are used to describe relationships between things such as time and distance. They are often represented as equations.

The concept of a function is found throughout mathematics and society. Simple examples in society include (1) to each person is assigned his or her social security number, (2) to each item in a store is assigned a unique bar code number, and (3) to each house on a street is assigned a unique address.

Of the examples that we examined earlier in the section, the relation defined by "_____ is a factor of _____ " is not a function because 2, being in the first set, is a factor of many numbers and would therefore be related to more than one number in the second set. The arrow diagram in Figure 9.13(b) also illustrates this point because the 2 in the first set has 4 arrows coming from it. The relation defined by "_____ was the vice-president under _____ " is also not a function because George Clinton was the vice-president from 1805 to 1812 under two presidents, Thomas Jefferson and James Madison. The relation "_____ was state number _____ to join the United States," however, would be a function because each state is related to only one number.

The remainder of this section will list several other examples of functions followed by a description of notation and representations of functions. In Section 9.4, graphs of important types of functions that model applications in society will be studied.

1. Recall that a sequence is a list of numbers, called terms, arranged in order, where the first term is called the **initial term**. For example, the sequence of consecutive even counting numbers listed in *increasing order* is 2, 4, 6, 8, 10, ... Another way of showing this sequence is by using arrows:

$$1 \rightarrow 2, 2 \rightarrow 4, 3 \rightarrow 6, 4 \rightarrow 8, 5 \rightarrow 10, \ldots$$

Here, the arrows assign to each counting number its double. Using a variable, this assignment can be represented as $n \rightarrow 2n$. Not only is this assignment an example of a function, a function is formed whenever each counting number is assigned to one and only one element.

Some special sequences can be classified by the way their terms are found. In the sequence 2, 4, 6, 8, . . . , each term after the first can be found by adding 2 to the preceding term. This type of sequence, in which successive terms differ by the same number, is called an arithmetic sequence. Using variables, an **arithmetic sequence** has the form

$$a, a + d, a + 2d, \ldots$$

Here a is the initial term and d is the amount by which successive terms differ. The number d is called the **common difference** of the sequence.

In the sequence 1, 3, 9, 27, . . . , each term after the first can be found by multiplying the preceding term by 3. This is an example of a geometric sequence. By using variables, a **geometric sequence** has the form

$$a, ar, ar^2, ar^3, \ldots$$

The number r, by which each successive term is multiplied, is called the **common ratio** of the sequence. Table 9.1 displays the terms for general arithmetic and geometric sequences.

TABLE 9.1

TERM	1	2	3	4	. . .	N	. . .
Arithmetic sequence	a	$a + d$	$a + 2d$	$a + 3d$	. . .	$a + (n-1)d$	. . .
Geometric sequence	a	ar	ar^2	ar^3	. . .	ar^{n-1}	. . .

Using this table, the 400th term of the arithmetic sequence 8, 12, 16, . . . is found by observing that $a = 8$ and $d = 4$; thus the 400th term is $8 + (400 - 1)\,4 = 1604$. The 10th term of the geometric sequence 4, 8, 16, 32, . . . is found by observing that $a = 4$ and $r = 2$; thus the 10th term is $4 \cdot 2^{10-1} = 2048$.

Example 9.14   Determine whether the following sequences are arithmetic, geometric, or neither. Then determine the common difference or ratio where applicable, and find the tenth term.

a. 5, 10, 20, 40, 80, . . .   **b.** 7, 20, 33, 46, 59, . . .   **c.** 2, 3, 6, 18, 108, 1944, . . .

SOLUTION

a. The sequence 5, 10, 20, 40, 80, . . . can be written as 5, $5 \cdot 2$, $5 \cdot 2^2$, $5 \cdot 2^3$, $5 \cdot 2^4$, . . . Thus it is a geometric sequence whose common ratio is 2. The 10th term is $5 \cdot 2^9 = 2560$.

b. The consecutive terms of the sequence 7, 20, 33, 46, 59, . . . have a common difference of 13. Thus this is an arithmetic sequence whose 10th term is $7 + 9(13) = 124$.

c. The sequence 2, 3, 6, 18, 108, 1944, . . . is formed by taking the product of two successive terms to find the next term. For example, $6 \cdot 18 = 108$. This sequence is neither arithmetic nor geometric. Using exponential notation, its terms are 2, 3, 2×3, 2×3^2, $2^2 \times 3^3$, $2^3 \times 3^5$, $2^5 \times 3^8$, $2^8 \times 3^{13}$, $2^{13} \times 3^{21}$, $2^{21} \times 3^{34}$ (the 10th term). ∎

2. Rectangular numbers are numbers that can be represented in arrays where the number of dots on the shorter side is one less than the number of dots on the longer side (Figure 9.19). The first six rectangular numbers are 2, 6, 12, 20, 30, and 42. The length of the shorter side of the nth array is n and the length of the longer side is $n + 1$. Thus the nth rectangular number is $n(n + 1)$, or $n^2 + n$.

2	• •	1×2
6	• • • • • •	2×3
12	• • • • • • • • • • • •	3×4
20	• • • • • • • • • • • • • • • • • • • •	4×5

Figure 9.19

Figure 9.20

Algebraic Reasoning
Since sequences have an infinite number of elements, variables are used to represent the general term.

3. Figure 9.20 displays a $3 \times 3 \times 3$ cube that is composed of three layers of nine unit cubes for a total of 27 of the unit cubes. Table 9.2 shows several instances where a larger cube is formed from unit cubes. In general, if there are n unit cubes along any side of a larger cube, the larger cube is made up of n^3 unit cubes.

TABLE 9.2

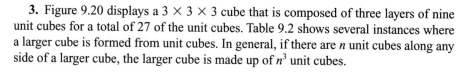

Number of unit cubes on a side	1	2	3	4	5	6	. . .
Number of unit cubes in the larger cube	1	8	27	64	125	216	. . .

TABLE 9.3

NUMBER OF SPLITS	NUMBER OF AMOEBAS
1	2
2	4
3	8
4	16
.	.
.	.
.	.
n	2^n

4. Amoebas regenerate themselves by splitting into two amoebas. Table 9.3 shows the relationship between the number of splits and the number of amoebas after that split, starting with one amoeba. Notice how the number of amoebas grows rapidly. The rapid growth as described in this table is called **exponential growth**.

✔ **Check for Understanding:** Exercise/Problem Set A #7–9

Function Notation and Representations

A function, f, that assigns an element of set A to an element of set B is written $f: A \to B$. If $a \in A$, then the **function notation** for the element in B that is assigned to *a* is *f(a)*, read "*f* of *a*" or "*f* at *a*" (Figure 9.21). Consider how each of the preceding examples 1 to 4 satisfies the definition of a function.

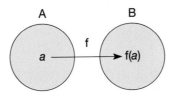

Figure 9.21

1. *Even numbers:* Assigned to each counting number *n* is its double, namely 2*n*; that is, $f(n) = 2n$.

Algebraic Reasoning
A variable is used to designate functions that are defined on infinite sets as shown to the right.

2. *Rectangular numbers:* If there are *n* dots in the shorter side, there are $n + 1$ dots in the longer side. Since the number of dots in the *n*th rectangular number is $n(n + 1)$, we can write $f(n) = n(n + 1)$. So $f(n) = n(n + 1)$ is the function that produces rectangular numbers.

3. *Cube:* Assigned to each number *n* is its cube; that is, $f(n) = n^3$.

4. *Amoebas:* Assigned to each number of splits, *n*, is the number of amoebas, 2^n. Thus $f(n) = 2^n$.

NOTE: We are not required to use an *f* to represent a function and an *n* as the variable in $f(n)$. For example, the rectangular number function may be written $r(x) = x(x + 1)$ or $R(t) = t(t + 1)$. The function for the cube could be written $C(r) = r^3$. That is, a function may be represented by any upper- or lowercase letter. However, the variable is usually represented by a lowercase letter.

NCTM Standard
All students should identify and describe situations with constant or varying rates of change and compare them.

> ### Example 9.15   Express the following relationships using function notation.
>
> **a.** The cost of a taxi ride given that the rate is $1.75 plus 75 cents per quarter mile
> **b.** The degree measure in Fahrenheit as a function of degrees Celsius, given that in Fahrenheit it is 32° more than 1.8 times the degrees measured in Celsius
> **c.** The amount of muscle weight, in terms of body weight, given that for each 5 pounds of body weight, there are about 2 pounds of muscle
> **d.** The value of a $1000 investment after *t* years at 7% interest, compounded annually, given that the amount will be 1.07^t times the initial principal

SOLUTION
a. $C(m) = 1.75 + 4m(0.75)$, where *m* is the number of miles traveled
b. $F(c) = 1.8c + 32$, where *c* is degrees Celsius
c. $M(b) = \frac{2}{5}b$, where *b* is the body weight
d. $P(t) = 1000(1.07^t)$, where *t* is the number of years   ∎

If *f* represents a function from set *A* to set *B*, set *A* is called the **domain** of *f* and set *B* is called the **codomain**. The doubling function, $f(n) = 2n$, can be defined to have the set of counting numbers as its domain and codomain. Notice that only the even numbers are used in the codomain in this function. The set of all elements in the codomain that the function pairs with an element of the domain is called the **range** of the function. The doubling function as already described has domain {1, 2, 3, . . .}, codomain {1, 2, 3, . . .}, and range {2, 4, 6, . . .} (Figure 9.22).

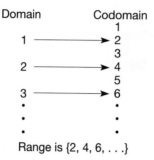

Range is {2, 4, 6, . . .}

Figure 9.22

Notice that the range must be a subset of the codomain. However, the codomain and range may be equal. For example, if $A = \{a, e, i, o, u\}$, $B = \{1, 2, 3, 4, 5\}$, and the function g assigns to each letter in A its alphabetical order among the five letters, then $g(a) = 1$, $g(e) = 2$, $g(i) = 3$, $g(o) = 4$, and $g(u) = 5$ (Figure 9.23). Here the range of g is B. The notation $g\colon A \to B$ is used to indicate the domain, A, and codomain, B, of the function g.

A function can assign more than one element from the domain to the same element in the codomain. For example, for sets A and B in the preceding paragraph, a letter could be assigned to 1 if it is in the first half of the alphabet and to 2 if it is in the second half. Thus a, e, and i would be assigned to 1 and o and u would be assigned to 2.

Functions as Arrow Diagrams   Since functions are examples of relations, functions can be represented as arrow diagrams when sets A and B are finite sets with few elements. The arrow diagram associated with the function in Figure 9.23 is shown in Figure 9.24. To be a function, exactly one arrow must leave each element in the domain and point to one element in the codomain. However, not all elements in the codomain have to be hit by an arrow. For example, in the function shown in Figure 9.23, if B is changed to {1, 2, 3, 4, 5, . . .}, the numbers 6, 7, 8, ... would not be hit by an arrow. Here the codomain of the function would be the set of counting numbers and the range would be the set {1, 2, 3, 4, 5}.

Reflection from Research
When using a table of values to teach functions, the order in which numbers appear in the table impacts the students' abilities to find generalizations. Randomly generated numbers force students to think about the relation between the input and output rather than the relation between sequential outputs (Warren, Cooper, & Lamb, 2006).

Domain   Codomain
a ──────────▶ 1
e ──────────▶ 2
i ──────────▶ 3
o ──────────▶ 4
u ──────────▶ 5

Figure 9.23

A	B
a	1
e	2
i	3
o	4
u	5

Figure 9.24

Figure 9.25

Functions as Tables   The function in Figure 9.23, where B is the set {1, 2, 3, 4, 5}, also can be defined using a table (Figure 9.25). Notice how when one defines a function in this manner, it is implied that the codomain and range are the same, namely set B.

LESSON 5.2 Functions and Ordered Pairs

Key Ideas

The input and output of a function machine can be thought of as an ordered pair, which can be graphed.

Look at the function machine below. In this case, x is the input and y is the output.

In the function rule, if you put in 2 for x, you get 7 for y because $2 + 5 = 7$. We can think of the pair of numbers (2, 7) as an ordered pair of numbers produced by the function rule $x \longrightarrow +5 \longrightarrow y$. Notice that we write the x first and the y second.

Copy each list of ordered pairs, but replace the x or y with the correct number. The first one is done for you. **Algebra**

1 $x \longrightarrow +5 \longrightarrow y$

(7, 12); (12, y); (15, y); (0, y); (x, 7)

2 $x \longrightarrow -9 \longrightarrow y$

(11, y); (20, y); (25, y); (x, 0); (x, 8); (x, 9)

3 $x \longrightarrow ×0 \longrightarrow y$

(7, y); (12, y); (50, y); (2,589, y); (x, 0)

Draw and complete these function-machine tables on a sheet of paper.

4

$x \longrightarrow -7 \longrightarrow y$

in	out
9	▨
11	▨
14	▨
▨	21

5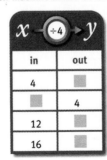

$x \longrightarrow ÷4 \longrightarrow y$

in	out
4	▨
▨	4
12	▨
16	▨

6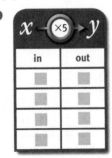

$x \longrightarrow ×5 \longrightarrow y$

in	out
▨	▨
▨	▨
▨	▨
▨	▨

198

🅖 **Textbook** This lesson is available in the **eTextbook.**

Functions as Machines   A dynamic way of visualizing the concept of function is through the use of a machine. The "input" elements are the elements of the domain and the "output" elements are the elements of the range. The function machine in Figure 9.26 takes any number put into the machine, squares it, and then outputs the square. For example, if 3 is an input, its corresponding output is 9. In this case, 3 is an element of the domain and 9 is an element of the range.

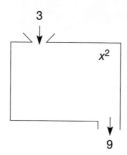

Figure 9.26

Functions as Ordered Pairs   The function in Figure 9.24 also can be expressed as the set of ordered pairs $\{(a, 1), (e, 2), (i, 3), (o, 4), (u, 5)\}$. This method of defining a function by listing its ordered pairs is practical if there is a small finite number of pairs that define the function. Functions having an infinite domain can be defined using this ordered-pair approach by using set-builder notation. For example, the squaring function $f: A \rightarrow B$, where $A = B$ is the set of whole numbers and $f(n) = n^2$, is $\{(a, b)|b = a^2, a$ any whole number$\}$, that is, the set of all ordered pairs of whole numbers, (a, b), where $b = a^2$.

Functions as Graphs   The ordered pairs of a function can be represented as points on a two-dimensional coordinate system (graphing functions will be studied in depth in Section 9.4). Briefly, a horizontal line is usually used for elements in the domain of the function and a vertical line is used for the codomain. Then the ordered pair $(x, f(x))$ is plotted. Five of the ordered pairs associated with the squaring function, $f(x) = x^2$, where the domain of f is the set of whole numbers, are illustrated in Figure 9.27. Graphing is especially useful when a function consists of infinitely many ordered pairs.

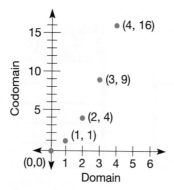

Figure 9.27

Functions as Formulas   In Chapter 13 we derive formulas for finding areas of certain plane figures. For example, the formula for finding the area of a circle is $A = \pi r^2$, where r is the radius of the circle. To reinforce the fact that the area of a circle, A, is a function of the radius, we sometimes write this formula as $A(r) = \pi r^2$.

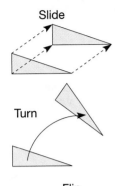

Slide

Turn

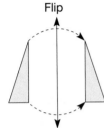

Flip

Figure 9.28

Usually, formulas are used to define a function whenever the domain has infinitely many elements. In the formula $A(r) = \pi r^2$; we have that the domain of the area function is any number used to measure lengths, not simply the whole numbers: $A(1) = \pi, A(2) = 4\pi, A(0.5) = (0.5)^2\pi = 0.25\pi$, and so on.

Functions as Geometric Transformations   Certain aspects of geometry can be studied more easily through the use of functions. For example, geometric shapes can be slid, turned, and flipped to produce other shapes (Figure 9.28). Such transformations can be viewed as functions that assign to each point in the plane a unique point in the plane. Geometric transformations of the plane are studied in Chapter 16.

Example 9.16   Identify the domain, codomain, and range of the following functions.

a. $a \rightarrow 1$
$\quad\ b \rightarrow 2$
$\qquad\quad 3$

b.
x	y
1	11
2	21
3	31
4	41

c. $g: R \rightarrow S$, where $g(x) = x^2$, R and S are the counting numbers.

d.

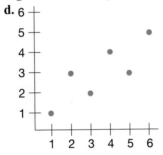

SOLUTION

a. Domain: $\{a, b\}$, codomain: $\{1, 2, 3\}$, range: $\{1, 2\}$
b. Domain: $\{1, 2, 3, 4\}$, codomain: $\{11, 21, 31, 41\}$, range = codomain
c. Domain: $\{1, 2, 3, 4, \ldots\}$, codomain = domain, range: $\{1, 4, 9, 16, \ldots\}$
d. Domain: $\{1, 2, 3, 4, 5, 6\}$, codomain = domain, range: $\{1, 2, 3, 4, 5\}$ ∎

 Check for Understanding: Exercise/Problem Set A #10–15

Reflection from Research
Students may be able to complete a task using one representation of a function but be unable to complete the same task when given a different representation of the function (Goldenberg, Harvey, Lewis, Umiker, West, & Zodhiates, 1988).

MATHEMATICAL MORSEL

Suppose that a large sheet of paper one-thousandth of an inch thick is torn in half and the two pieces are put on a pile. Then these two pieces are torn in half and put together to form a pile of four pieces. The first three terms of a pattern is shown next. If this process is continued a total of 50 times, the last pile will be over 17 million miles high!

"Yeah Houston..... you're not going to believe this . . . . ."

NUMBER OF TEARS	THICKNESS IN INCHES
1	$0.002 = 0.001 \times 2$
2	$0.004 = 0.001 \times 2^2$
3	$0.008 = 0.001 \times 2^3$

| Section 9.3 | **EXERCISE / PROBLEM SET A** |

EXERCISES

1. List the ordered-pair representation for each of the relations in the arrow diagrams or the sets listed below.

a.

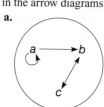

b.

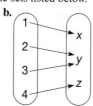

c. Set: {1, 2, 3, 4, 5, 6}
   Relation: "Has the same number of factors as"
d. Set: {2, 4, 6, 8, 10, 12}
   Relation: "Is a multiple of"

2. a. Make an arrow diagram for the relation "is greater than" on the following two sets.

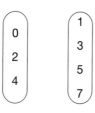

b. Make an arrow diagram for the relation "is younger than" on the following two sets.

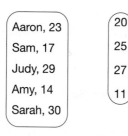

3. Name the relations suggested by the following ordered pairs [e.g., (Hawaii, 50) has the name "is state number"].
a. (Lincoln, 16)
   (Madison, 4)
   (Reagan, 40)
   (McKinley, 25)
b. (Atlanta, GA)
   (Dover, DE)
   (Austin, TX)
   (Harrisburg, PA)

4. Determine whether the relations represented by the following sets of ordered pairs are reflexive, symmetric, or transitive. Which are equivalence relations?
a. {(1, 1), (2, 1), (2, 2), (3, 1), (3, 2), (3, 3)}
b. {(1, 2), (1, 3), (2, 3), (2, 1), (3, 2), (3, 1)}
c. {(1, 1), (1, 3), (2, 2), (3, 2), (1, 2)}

5. Determine whether the relations represented by the following diagrams are reflexive, symmetric, or transitive. Which are equivalence relations?

a.

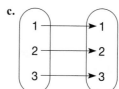

b.

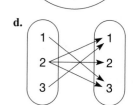

c.

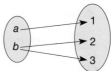

d.

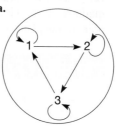

6. Determine whether the relations represented by the following sets and descriptions are reflexive, symmetric, or transitive. Which are equivalence relations? Describe the partition for each equivalence relation.
a. "Less than" on the set {1, 2, 3, 4, . . .}
b. "Has the same number of factors as" on the set {1, 2, 3, 4, . . .}
c. "Has the same tens digit as" on the set collection {1, 2, 3, 4, . . .}

7. Which of the following arrow diagrams represent functions? If one does not represent a function, explain why not.

a.   **b.**

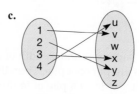

c.   **d.**

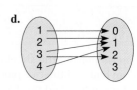

8. Which of the following relations describe a function? If one does not, explain why not.
a. Each U.S. citizen → his or her birthday
b. Each vehicle registered in Michigan → its current license plate
c. Each college graduate → his or her degree
d. Each shopper in a grocery store → number of items purchased

9. Which of the following relations, listed as ordered pairs, could belong to a function? For those that cannot, explain why not.

   a. {(7, 4) (6, 3) (5, 2) (4, 1)}
   b. {(red, 3) (blue, 4) (green, 5) (yellow, 6) (black, 5)}
   c. {(1, 1) (1, 2) (3, 4) (4, 4)}
   d. {(1, 1) (2, 1) (3, 1) (4, 1)}
   e. {(a, b) (b, b) (d, e) (b, c) (d, f)}

10. List the ordered pairs for these functions using the domain specified. Find the range for each function.

    a. $C(t) = 2t^3 - 3t$, with domain {0, 2, 4}
    b. $a(x) = x + 2$, with domain {1, 2, 9}
    c. $P(n) = \left(\dfrac{n+1}{n}\right)^n$ with domain {1, 2, 3}

11. Using the function machines, find all possible missing whole-number inputs or outputs.

    a. 5

    $x^3 - x^2$

    b. 2

    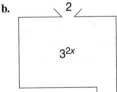

    3^{2x}

    c.

    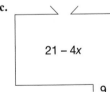

    $21 - 4x$

    9

    d.

    $\dfrac{12}{x^2}$

    3

12. The following functions are expressed in one of the following forms: a formula, an arrow diagram, a table, or a set of ordered pairs. Express each function in each of the other three forms.

    a. $f(x) = x^3 - x$ for $x \in \{0, 1, 4\}$
    b. {(1, 1), (4, 2), (9, 3)}

c.

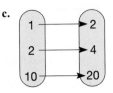

d.

x	f(x)
5	55
6	66
7	77

13. Inputs into a function are not always single numbers or single elements of the domain. For example, a function can be defined to accept as input the length and width of a rectangle and to output its perimeter.

    $$P(l, w) = 2l + 2w$$
    $$\text{or } P{:}(l, w) \rightarrow 2l + 2w$$

    For each function defined, evaluate $f(2, 5)$, $f(3, 3)$, and $f(1, 4)$.
    a. $f(x, y) = x^2 + y^2$
    b. $f{:}(a, b) \rightarrow 3a + 1$

    c. (m, n)

    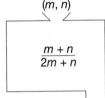

    $\dfrac{m+n}{2m+n}$

    d. $f{:}(x, y) \rightarrow x$ or y, whichever is larger

14. Oregon's 1991 state income tax rate for single persons was expressed as follows, where i = taxable income.

TAX RATE (T_i)	TAXABLE INCOME (i)
$0.05i$	$i \le 2000$
$100 + 0.07(i - 2000)$	$2000 < i \le 5000$
$310 + 0.09(i - 5000)$	$i > 5000$

    a. Calculate $T(4000)$, $T(1795)$, $T(26,450)$, and $T(2000)$.
    b. Find the income tax on persons with taxable incomes of $49,570 and $3162.
    c. A single person's tax calculated by this formula was $1910.20. What was that person's taxable income?

15. A 6% sales tax function applied to any price p can be described as follows: $f(p)$ is $0.06p$ rounded to the nearest cent, where half-cents are rounded up. For example, $0.06(1.25) = 0.075$, so $f(1.25) = 0.08$, since 0.075 is rounded up to 0.08. Use the 6% sales tax function to find the correct tax on the following amounts.

    a. $7.37   **b.** $9.25
    c. $11.15   **d.** $76.85

PROBLEMS

16. Fractions are numbers of the form $\frac{a}{b}$, where a and b are whole numbers and $b \neq 0$. Fraction equality is defined as $\frac{a}{b} = \frac{c}{d}$ if and only if $ad = bc$. Determine whether fraction equality is an equivalence relation. If it is, describe the equivalence class that contains $\frac{1}{2}$.

17. a. The function $f(n) = \frac{9}{5}n + 32$ can be used to convert degrees Celsius to degrees Fahrenheit. Calculate $f(0)$, $f(100), f(50)$, and $f(-40)$.
   b. The function $g(m) = \frac{5}{9}(m - 32)$ can be used to convert degrees Fahrenheit to degrees Celsius. Calculate $g(32)$, $g(212), g(104)$, and $g(-40)$.
   c. Is there a temperature where the degrees Celsius equals the degrees Fahrenheit? If so, what is it?

18. Find the 458th number in the sequence $21, 29, 37, 45, \ldots$.

19. A fitness club charges an initiation fee of $85 plus $35 per month.
   a. Write a formula for a function, $C(x)$, that gives the total cost for using the fitness club facilities after x months.
   b. Calculate $C(18)$ using the formula you wrote in part (a). Explain in words what you have found.
   c. When will the total amount spent by a club member first exceed $1000?

20. The second term of a certain geometric sequence is 1200 and the fifth term of the sequence is 150.
   a. Find the common ratio, r, for this geometric sequence.
   b. Write out the first six terms of the sequence.

21. Consider the following sequence of toothpick figures.

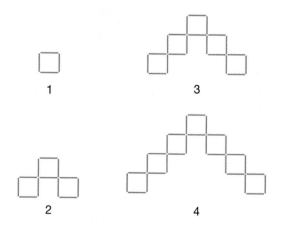

   a. Let $T(n)$ be the function representing the total number of toothpicks in the nth figure. Complete the following table, which gives one representation of the function T.

n	T(n)
1	4
2	
3	
4	
5	
6	
7	
8	

   b. What kind of sequence do the numbers in the second column form?
   c. Represent the function T in another way by writing a formula for $T(n)$.
   d. Find $T(20)$ and $T(150)$.
   e. What are the domain and range of the function T?

22. Consider the following sequence of toothpick figures.

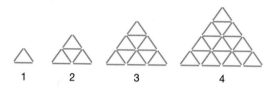

1	2	3	4

   a. Let $T(n)$ be the function representing the total number of toothpicks in the nth figure. Complete the following table, which gives one representation of the function T.

n	T(n)
1	3
2	
3	
4	
5	
6	
7	
8	

   b. Do the numbers in column 2 form a geometric or arithmetic sequence, or neither?
   c. Represent the function T in another way by writing a formula for $T(n)$.
   d. Find $T(15)$ and $T(100)$.
   e. What are the domain and range of the function T?

23. Suppose that $100 is earning interest at an annual rate of 5%.
   a. If the interest earned on the $100 is simple interest, the same amount of interest is earned each year. The interest is 5% of $100, or $5 per year. Complete a table like the one following to show the value of the account after 10 years.

NUMBER OF YEARS, n	ANNUAL INTEREST EARNED	VALUE OF ACCOUNT
0	0	100
1	5	105
2	5	110
3		
4		
5		
.		
.		
.		
10		

b. What kind of sequence, arithmetic or geometric, do the numbers in the third column form? What is the value of d or r? Write a function $A(n)$ that gives the value of the account after n years.

24. a. If the interest earned on the $100 is compound interest and is compounded annually, the amount of interest earned at the end of a year is 5% of the current balance. After the first year the interest is calculated using the original $100 plus any accumulated interest. Complete a table like the one following to show the value of the account after n years.

NUMBER OF YEARS, n	ANNUAL INTEREST EARNED	VALUE OF ACCOUNT
0	0	100
1	0.05(100) = 5	105
2	0.05(105) = 5.25	110.25
3		
4		
5		
.		
.		
.		
10		

b. What kind of sequence, arithmetic or geometric, do the numbers in the third column form? What is the value of d or r? Write a function $A(n)$ that gives the value of the account after n years.
c. Over a period of 10 years, how much more interest is earned when interest is compounded annually than when simple interest is earned? (NOTE: Generally, banks do pay compound interest rather than simple interest.)

25. A clown was shot out of a cannon at ground level. Her height above the ground at any time t was given by the function $h(t) = -16t^2 + 64t$. Find her height when $t = 1, 2,$ and 3. How many seconds of flight will she have?

26. Suppose that you want to find out my telephone number (it consists of seven digits) by asking me questions that I can only answer "yes" or "no." What method of interrogation leads to the correct answer after the smallest number of questions? (*Hint:* Use base two.)

27. Determine whether the following sequences are arithmetic sequences, geometric sequences, or neither. Determine the common difference (ratio) and 200th term for the arithmetic (geometric) sequences.
a. 7, 12, 17, 22, 27, . . .
b. 14, 28, 56, 112, . . .
c. 4, 14, 24, 34, 44, . . .
d. 1, 11, 111, 1111, . . .

28. How many numbers are in this collection?
1, 4, 7, 10, 13, . . . , 682

29. The representation of a function as a machine can be seen in the Chapter 9 eManipulative *Function Machine* on our Web site. Use this eManipulative to find the rules to two different functions. Describe each of the functions that were found and the process by which the function was found.

Section 9.3	**EXERCISE / PROBLEM SET B**

EXERCISES

1. List the ordered-pair representation for each of the relations in the arrow diagrams or the sets listed below.

a.

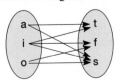

b.

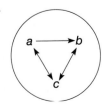

c. Set: {1, 2, 3, 4, 5, 6, 7, 8}
   Relation: "Has more factors than"
d. Set: {3, 6, 9, 12, 15}
   Relation: "Is a factor of"

2. a. Make an arrow diagram for the relation "is an NFL team representing" on the following two sets.

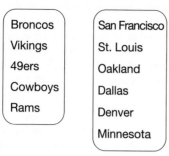

b. Make an arrow diagram for the relation "has a factor of" on the following two sets.

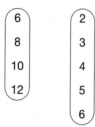

3. Name the relations suggested by the following ordered pairs. Refer to Part A, Exercise 3 for an example.
  a. (George III, England) **b.** (21, 441)
  (Philip, Spain) (12, 144)
  (Louis XIV, France) (38, 1444)
  (Alexander, Macedonia) (53, 2809)

4. Determine which of the reflexive, symmetric, or transitive properties hold for these relations. Which are equivalence relations?
  a. {(1, 2), (1, 3), (1, 4), (2, 3), (2, 4), (3, 4)}
  b. {(1, 2), (2, 3), (1, 4), (2, 4), (4, 2), (2, 1), (4, 1), (3, 2)}
  c. {(1, 1), (2, 2), (3, 3)}

5. Determine whether the relations represented by the following arrow diagrams are reflexive, symmetric, or transitive. Which are equivalence relations?

a.

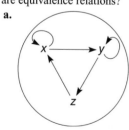

b.

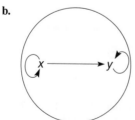

c.

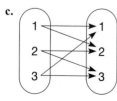

d.

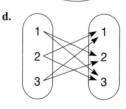

6. Determine whether the relations represented by the following sets and descriptions are reflexive, symmetric, or transitive. Which are equivalence relations? Describe the partition for each equivalence relation.
  a. "Has the same shape as" on the set of all triangles
  b. "Is a factor of" on the set {1, 2, 3, 4, . . .}
  c. "Has the primary residence in the same state as" on the set of all people in the United States

7. Which of the following arrow diagrams represent functions? If one does not represent a function, explain why not.

a.

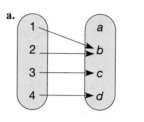

b.

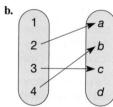

c.

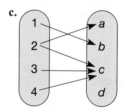

d.

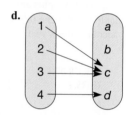

8. Which of the following relations describe a function? If one does not, explain why not.
  a. Each registered voter in California → his or her polling place
  b. Each city in the United States → its zip code
  c. Each type of plant → its genus
  d. Each pet owner in the United States → his or her pet

9. Which of the following relations, listed as ordered pairs, could belong to a function? For those that cannot, explain why not.
  a. {(Bob, m), (Sue, s), (Joe, s), (Jan, s), (Sue, m)}
  b. {(dog, 3), (horse, 7), (cat, 4)}, (mouse, 3), (bird, 7)}
  c. {(a, x), (c, y), (x, a), (y, y), (b, z)}
  d. {(1, x), (a, x), (Joe, y), (Bob, x)}
  e. {(1, 2), (2, 3), (2, 1), (3, 3), (3, 1)}

10. List the ordered pairs for these functions using the domains specified. Find the range for each function.
  a. $f(x) = 2x^2 + 4$, with domain: {0, 1, 2}
  b. $g(y) = (y + 2)^2$, with domain: {7, 2, 1}
  c. $h(t) = 2^t - 3$, with domain: {2, 3}

11. Using the following function machines, find all possible missing whole-number inputs or outputs.

a.

b.

c.

d.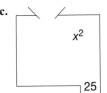

12. The functions shown next are expressed in one of the following forms: a formula, an arrow diagram, a table, or a set of ordered pairs. Express each function in each of the three other forms.

a.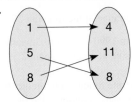

b.

x	$f(x)$
3	$\frac{1}{3}$
4	$\frac{1}{4}$
1	1
$\frac{1}{2}$	2

c. $\{(4, 12), (2, 6), (7, 21)\}$
d. $f(x) = x^2 - 2x + 1$ for $x \in \{2, 3, 4, 5\}$

13. The output of a function is not always a single number. It may be an ordered pair or a set of numbers. Several examples follow. Assume in each case that the domain is the set of natural numbers or ordered pairs of natural numbers, as appropriate.
    a. $f: n \rightarrow \{$all factors of $n\}$. Find $f(7)$ and $f(12)$.
    b. $f(n) = (n + 1, n - 1)$. Find $f(3)$ and $f(20)$.
    c. $f: n \rightarrow \{$natural numbers greater than $n\}$. Find $f(6)$ and $f(950)$.
    d. $f(n, m) = \{$natural numbers between n and $m\}$. Find $f(2, 6)$ and $f(10, 11)$.

14. Some functions expressed in terms of a formula use different formulas for different parts of the domain. Such a function is said to be defined piecewise. For example, suppose that f is a function with a domain of $\{1, 2, 3, \ldots\}$ and

$$f(x) = \begin{cases} 2x & \text{for } x \leq 5 \\ x + 1 & \text{for } x > 5 \end{cases}$$

This notation means that if an element of the domain is 5 or less, the formula $2x$ is used. Otherwise, the formula $x + 1$ is used.
    a. Evaluate each of the following: $f(3), f(10), f(25), f(5)$.
    b. Sketch an example of what a function machine might look like for f.

15. A cell phone plan costs $40 a month plus 45 cents a minute for minutes beyond 700. A cost function for this plan is:

DOLLARS	MINUTES (m)
40	$m \leq 700$
$40 + .45(m - 700)$	$m > 700$

Use this function to find the monthly cost for the following number of minutes.
    a. 546 minutes
    b. 743 minutes
    c. 1191 minutes

PROBLEMS

16. A spreadsheet allows a user to input many different values from the domain and see the corresponding outputs of the range in a table format. Using the Chapter 9 dynamic spreadsheet *Function Machines and Tables* on our Web site, find two different values of x that produce the same output of the function $f(x) = x^2 - 2x - 3$. Would such an example be inconsistent with the definition of a function? Why or why not?

17. Determine whether the following sequences are arithmetic sequences, geometric sequences, or neither. Determine the common difference (ratio) and 200th term for the arithmetic (geometric) sequences.
    a. 5, 50, 500, 5000, . . .   b. 8, 16, 32, 64, . . .
    c. 12, 23, 34, 45, 56, . . .
    d. 1, 12, 123, 1234, . . .

18. Find a reasonable 731st number in this collection: 2, 9, 16, 23, 30, ...

19. How many numbers are in this arithmetic sequence? 16, 27, 38, 49, . . . , 1688.

20. The volume of a cube whose sides have length s is given by the formula $V(s) = s^3$.
   a. Find the volume of cubes whose sides have length 3; 5; 11.
   b. Find the lengths of the sides of cubes whose volumes are 64; 216; 2744.

21. If the interest rate of a $1000 savings account is 5% and no additional money is deposited, the amount of money in the account at the end of t years is given by the function $a(t) = (1.05)^t \cdot 1000$.
   a. Calculate how much will be in the account after 2 years; after 5 years; after 10 years.
   b. What is the minimum number of years that it will take to more than double the account?

22. A rectangular parking area for a business will be enclosed by a fence. The fencing for the front of the lot, which faces the street, will cost $10 more per foot than the fencing for the other three sides. Use the dimensions shown to answer the following questions.

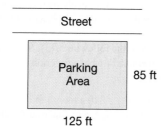

Street

Parking Area   85 ft

125 ft

   a. Write a formula for a function, $F(x)$, that gives the total cost of fencing for the lot if fencing for the three sides costs x per foot.
   b. Calculate $F(11.50)$ using the formula you wrote in part (a). Explain in words what you have found.
   c. Suppose that no more than $9000 can be spent on this fence. What is the most expensive fencing that can be used?

23. The third term of a certain geometric sequence is 36 and the seventh term of the sequence is 2916.
   a. Find the common ratio, r, of the sequence.
   b. Write out the first seven terms of the sequence.

24. Consider the following sequence of toothpick figures.

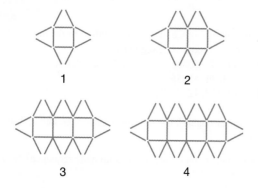

1   2

3   4

   a. Let $T(n)$ be the function representing the total number of toothpicks in the nth figure. Complete the following table, which gives one representation of the function T.

n	$T(n)$
1	12
2	
3	
4	
5	
6	
7	
8	

   b. What kind of sequence, arithmetic or geometric, do the numbers in the second column form? What is the value of d or r?
   c. Represent the function T in another way by writing a formula for $T(n)$.
   d. Find $T(25)$ and $T(200)$.
   e. What are the domain and range of the function T?

25. The population of Mexico in 1990 was approximately 88,300,000 and was increasing at a rate of about 2.5% per year.
   a. Complete a table like the one following to predict the population in subsequent years, assuming that the population continues to increase at the same rate.

YEAR	INCREASE IN POPULATION	POPULATION OF MEXICO
1990	0	88,300,000
1991	0.025 × 88,300,000 = 2,207,500	90,507,500
1992	0.025 × 90,507,500 = 2,262,688	92,770,188
1993		
1994		
1995		
1996		
1997		
1998		
1999		
2000		
2001		
2002		

   b. What kind of sequence, geometric or arithmetic, do the figures in the third column form? What is the value of r or d?
   c. Use the sequence you established to predict the population of Mexico in the year 2010 and in the year 2015. (NOTE: This means assuming that the growth rate remains the same, which may not be a valid assumption.)
   d. Write a function, $P(n)$, that will give the estimated population of Mexico n years after 1990.

26. The 114th term of an arithmetic sequence is 341 and its 175th term is 524. What is its 4th term?

27. Write a 10-digit numeral such that the first digit tells the number of zeros in the numeral, the second digit tells the number of ones, the third digit tells the number of twos, and so on. For example, the numeral 9000000001 is not correct because there are not nine zeros and there is one 1.

28. Equations are equivalent if they have the same solution set. For example, $3x - 2 = 7$ and $2x + 4 = 10$ are equivalent since they both have $\{3\}$ as their solution set. Explain the connection between the notion of equivalent equations and equivalence classes.

Analyzing Student Thinking

29. Alfonso says the sequence 1, 11, 111, 1111, . . . must be geometric because the successive differences 10, 100, 1000, etc. are powers of 10. Is he correct? Explain.

30. Iris was working with the formula $C(m) = 1.75 + 4m(0.75)$ that represented the cost of a taxi ride (C) per mile traveled (m), given that the rate charged is $1.75 plus 75 cents per quarter mile. She was struggling to understand where the 4 in the formula comes from. What could you say to help her understand the origin of the 4?

31. Bryce and Luke were asked to graph the sequence $\frac{1}{3}$, 1, 3, . . . using the ordered pairs $(1, \frac{1}{3})$, (2, 1), (3, 3), ... Bryce thought that these points were on a straight line but Luke disagreed. Who is correct? Explain.

32. Garrett said that if a sequence begins 1, 3, . . . , the next term can be a 5 because it is going up by twos. The two other members of his group each came up with different results. What are two possible sequences that the other members of Garrett's group might have found? Explain your reasoning.

33. Nicha looked at the set of ordered pairs, (1,b), (2,a), (3,c), (4,c), (2,d) and said that they could not represent a relation because the 2 is mapped to two different elements: a and d. Is she correct? Explain.

34. Arielle said that since every number is equal to itself, the reflexive property must always be true for all relations. What are some examples of relations you could show to Arielle to help her see that the reflexive property doesn't hold for all relations?

35. Hayden looked at the set of ordered pairs, {(1,d), (2,c), (3,b), (4,d)} and said that it could not represent a function because 1 and 4 both mapped to d. Is he correct? Explain.

Problems Relating to the NCTM Standards and Curriculum Focal Points

1. The Focal Points for Grade 6 state "Writing, interpreting, and using mathematical expressions and equations." Identify 2 examples from this section that address this focal point.

2. The NCTM Standards state "All students should represent and analyze patterns and functions using words, tables, and graphs." Represent the pattern 1, 3, 6, 10, 15, 21, . . . in words, a table, and a graph.

3. The NCTM Standards state "All students should identify and describe situations with constant or varying rates of change and compare them." Find a function from this problem set that illustrates a varying rate of change and a similar function that has a constant rate of change. What elements of the functions make the rates of change different?

9.4   FUNCTIONS AND THEIR GRAPHS

STARTING POINT

Tanika and Marcelle each went for a bike ride down a different road. The graphs below represent each girl's bicycle speed as she traveled along her respective road. Describe the possible roads and/or bike-riding scenarios that would correspond to these graphs.

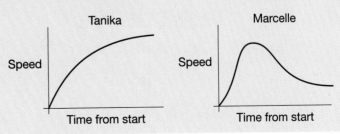

The Cartesian Coordinate System

The concept of a function was introduced in Section 9.3. Here we see how functions can be displayed using graphs on a coordinate system. This section has several goals: to emphasize the importance of functions by showing how they represent many types of physical situations, to help develop skills in graphing functions, and to help you learn how to use a graph to develop a better understanding of the corresponding function.

Children's Literature
www.wiley.com/college/musser
See "The Fly on the Ceiling" by
Julie Glass.

Suppose that we choose two perpendicular real number lines l and m in the plane and use their point of intersection, O, as a reference point called the **origin** [Figure 9.29(a)]. To locate a point P relative to point O, we use the directed real-number distances x and y that indicate the position of P left/right of and above/below the origin O, respectively. If P is to the right of line m, then x is positive [Figure 9.29(b)].

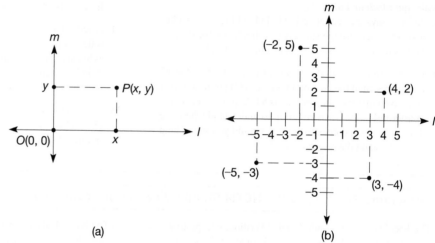

(a)   (b)

Figure 9.29

If P is to the left of line m, then x is negative. If P is on line m, then x is zero. Similarly, y is positive, negative, or zero, respectively, according to whether P is above, below, or on line l. The pair of real numbers x and y are called the **coordinates** of point P. We identify a point simply by giving its coordinates in an ordered pair (x, y). That is, by "the point (x, y)" we mean the point whose coordinates are x and y, respectively. In an ordered pair of coordinates, the first number is called the **x-coordinate**, and the second is the **y-coordinate**. Figure 9.30 shows the various possible cases for the coordinates of points in the plane.

NCTM Standard
All students should make and
use coordinate systems to specify
locations and to describe paths.

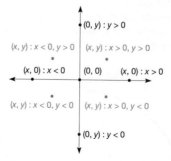

Figure 9.30

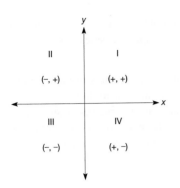

Figure 9.31

NCTM Standard

All students should use symbolic algebra to represent situations and to solve problems, especially those that involve linear relationships.

We say that lines *l* and *m* determine a **coordinate system** for the plane. Customarily, the horizontal line *l* is called the *x*-**axis**, and the vertical line *m* is called the *y*-**axis** for the coordinate system. Observe in Figure 9.31 that *l* and *m* have been relabeled as the *x*-axis and *y*-axis and that they divide the plane into four disjoint regions, called **quadrants**. (The axes are not part of any of the quadrants.) The points in quadrants I and IV have positive *x*-coordinates, while the points in quadrants II and III have negative *x*-coordinates. Similarly, the points in quadrants I and II have positive *y*-coordinates, while the points in quadrants III and IV have negative *y*-coordinates (Figure 9.31).

The following example provides a simple application of coordinates in mapmaking.

Example 9.17   Plot the points with the following coordinates.

$P_1 (-7, 5), P_2 (-5, 5), P_3 (-4, 3), P_4 (0, 3), P_5 (3, 4), P_6 (6, 4), P_7 (7, 3),$
$P_8 (5, -1), P_9 (6, -2), P_{10} (6, -7), P_{11} (-8, -7), P_{12} (-8, -3)$

Connect the points, in succession, P_1 to P_2, P_2 to P_3, . . . , P_{12} to P_1 with line segments to form a polygon (Figure 9.32).

SOLUTION

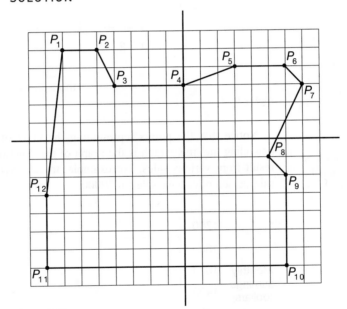

Figure 9.32

Notice that the polygon in Figure 9.32 is a simplified map of Oregon. Cartographers use computers to store maps of regions in coordinate form. They can then print maps in a variety of sizes. In the Problem Set we will investigate altering the size of a two-dimensional figure using coordinates.

✔ **Check for Understanding:** Exercise/Problem Set A #1–3

Graphs of Linear Functions

As the name suggests, **linear functions** are functions whose graphs are lines. The next example involves a linear function and its graph.

Example 9.18 A salesperson is given a monthly salary of $1200 plus a 5% commission on sales. Graph the salesperson's total earnings as a function of sales.

SOLUTION Let s represent the dollar amount of the salesperson's monthly sales. The total earnings can be represented as a function of sales, s, as follows: $E(s) = 1200 + (0.05)s$. Several values of this function are shown in Table 9.4. Using these values, we can plot the function $E(s)$ (Figure 9.33). The mark on the vertical axis below 1200 is used to indicate that this portion of the graph is not the same scale as on the rest of the axis.

TABLE 9.4

SALES, s	EARNINGS, $E(s)$
1000	1250
2000	1300
3000	1350
4000	1400
5000	1450

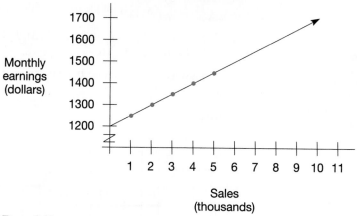

Figure 9.33

Notice that the points representing the pairs of values lie on a line. Thus, by extending the line, which is the graph of the function, we can see what salaries will result from various sales. For example, to earn $1650, Figure 9.34 shows that the salesperson must have sales of $9000.

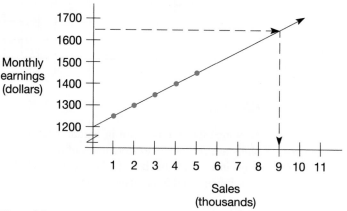

Figure 9.34

A *linear function* has the algebraic form $f(x) = ax + b$, where a and b are constants. In the function $E(s) = (0.05)s + 1200$, the value of a is 0.05 and of b is 1200.

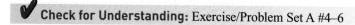 **Check for Understanding:** Exercise/Problem Set A #4–6

Graphs of Quadratic Functions

A **quadratic function** is a function of the form $f(x) = ax^2 + bx + c$, where a, b, and c are constants and $a \neq 0$. The next example presents a problem involving a quadratic function.

Algebraic Reasoning
In looking at different types of functions, an important connection is the ability to move flexibly between the table, graph, and equation of the same function. For example, by looking at an equation, can you tell what the graph will look like and visa versa?

Example 9.19   A ball is tossed up vertically at a velocity of 50 feet per second from a point 5 feet above the ground. It is known from physics that the height of the ball above the ground, in feet, is given by the position function $p(t) = -16t^2 + 50t + 5$, where t is the time in seconds. At what time, t, is the ball at its highest point?

SOLUTION   Table 9.5 lists several values for t with the corresponding function values from $p(t) = -16t^2 + 50t + 5$. Figure 9.35 shows a graph of the points in the table. Unfortunately, it is unclear from the graph of these four points what the highest point will be. One way of getting a better view of this situation would be to plot several more points between 1 and 2, say $t = 1.1, 1.2, 1.3, \ldots, 1.9$. However, this can be tedious. Instead, Figure 9.36 shows how a graphics calculator can be used to get an estimate of this point.

Reflection from Research
The emergence of the graphing calculator has caused an emphasis to be placed on the graphical representation of functions (Adams, 1993).

TABLE 9.5

t	$p(t)$
0	5
1	39
2	41
3	11

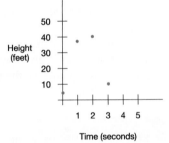

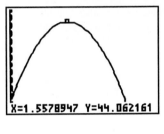

Figure 9.35   *Figure 9.36*

By moving the cursor (the "☐") to what appears to be the highest point on the graph, the calculator's display screen shows that the value $t = 1.5578947$ corresponds to that point. It can be shown *mathematically* that $t = \frac{25}{16} = 1.5625$ seconds is the exact time when the ball is at its highest point, 44.0625 feet.   ■

 Check for Understanding: Exercise/Problem Set A #7–8

Graphs of Exponential Functions

Amoebas have the interesting property that they split in two over time intervals. Therefore, the number of amoebas is a function of the number of splits. Table 9.6

TABLE 9.6

NUMBER OF SPLITS	NUMBER OF AMOEBAS
0	1
1	$2 (= 2^1)$
2	$4 (= 2^2)$
3	$8 (= 2^3)$
4	$16 (= 2^4)$
5	$32 (= 2^5)$

lists the first several ordered pairs of this function, and Figure 9.37 shows the corresponding graph.

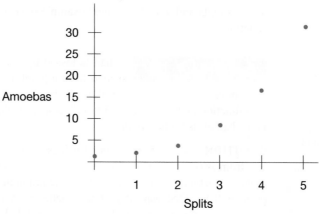

Figure 9.37

NCTM Standard
All students should model and solve contextualized problems using various representations, such as graphs and equations.

This functional relationship can be represented as the formula $f(x) = 2^x$, where $x = 0, 1, 2, \ldots$. This is an example of an **exponential function**, since, in the function rule, the variable appears as the exponent.

Exponential growth also appears in the study of compound interest. For an initial principal of P_0, an interest rate of r, compounded annually, and time t, in years, the amount of principal is given by the equation $P(t) = P_0(1 + r)^t$. In particular, if \$100 is deposited at 6% interest, the value of the investment after t years is given by $P(t) = 100 (1.06)^t$. Figure 9.38 shows a portion of the graph of this function.

Example 9.20   How long does it take to double your money when the interest rate is 6% compounded annually? (Assume that your money is in a tax-deferred account so that you don't have to pay taxes until the money is withdrawn.)

SOLUTION If a horizontal line is drawn through \$200 in Figure 9.38, it will intersect the graph of the function approximately above the 12. Thus it takes about 12 years to double the \$100 investment. (A more precise estimate that can be obtained from the formula is 11.9 years.)

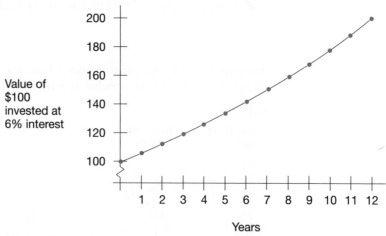

Figure 9.38

Interestingly, it takes only seven more years to add another $100 to the account and five more to add the next $100. This acceleration in accumulating principal illustrates the power of compounding, in particular, and of exponential growth, in general.

A similar phenomenon, decay, occurs in nature. Radioactive materials decay at an exponential rate. For example, the half-life of uranium-238 is 4.5 billion years. The formula for calculating the amount of ^{238}U after t billion years is $U(t) = (0.86)^t$. Figure 9.39 shows part of the graph of this function.

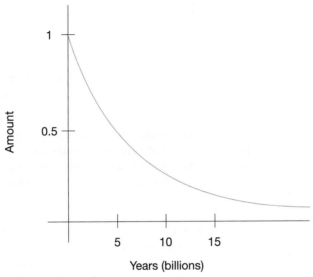

Figure 9.39

This graph in Figure 9.39 shows that although uranium decays rapidly at first, relatively speaking, it lingers around a long time.

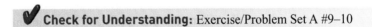

✔ **Check for Understanding:** Exercise/Problem Set A #9–10

Graphs of Other Common Functions

Cubic Functions The following example illustrates a cubic function.

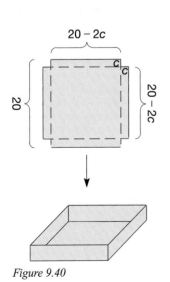

Figure 9.40

Example 9.21 A box is to be constructed from a piece of cardboard 20 cm-by-20 cm square by cutting out square corners and folding up the resulting sides (Figure 9.40). Estimate the maximum volume of a box that can be formed in this way.

SOLUTION When a corner of dimensions 1 cm-by-1 cm is cut out, a box of dimensions 1 cm-by-18 cm by 18 cm is formed. Its volume is $1 \times 18 \times 18 = 324$. In general, if the corner is c by c, the volume of the resulting box is given by $V(c) = c(20 - 2c)(20 - 2c)$. Table 9.7 shows several sizes of corners together with the resulting box volumes. Using these values, we can sketch the graph of the function $V(c)$ (Figure 9.41).

TABLE 9.7

CORNERS	VOLUME
1 cm by 1 cm	324 cm^3
2 cm by 2 cm	512 cm^3
3 cm by 3 cm	588 cm^3
4 cm by 4 cm	576 cm^3
5 cm by 5 cm	500 cm^3

NCTM Standard
All students should investigate how a change in one variable relates to the change in a second variable.

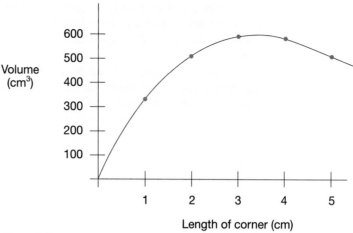

Figure 9.41

The five points in the table are shown in the graph in Figure 9.41. From the graph it appears that when the corner measures about 3.5 by 3.5, the maximum volume is achieved, $V(3.5) = (3.5)(13)(13) \approx 592$ cm^3. It can be shown mathematically that the value $c = 3\frac{1}{3}$ actually leads to the maximum volume of about 593.   ■

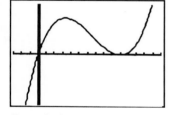

Figure 9.42

The function $V(c) = c(20 - 2c)(20 - 2c)$ can be rewritten as $V(c) = 4c^3 - 80c^2 + 400c$, a **cubic function**. Actually, the graph in Figure 9.41 looks similar to the quadratic function pictured earlier in this section. However, if the function $V(c) = 4c^3 - 80c^2 + 400c$ were allowed to take on all real-number values, its graph would take the shape as shown from a graphics calculator in Figure 9.42. (This shape is characteristic of all cubic functions.)

However, in Example 9.21, only a portion of this graph is shown, since the values of c are limited to $0 < c < 10$, the only lengths that produce corners that lead to a box.

Step Functions   The sales tax or the amount of postage are examples of step functions. Table 9.8 shows a typical sales tax, in cents, for sales up to $1.15. The graph in Figure 9.43 displays this information.

TABLE 9.8

AMOUNT (CENTS)	TAX (CENTS)
0–15	0
16–35	1
36–55	2
56–75	3
76–95	4
96–115	5

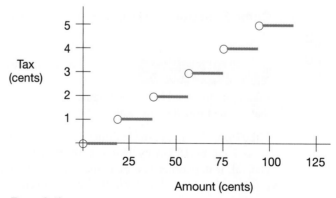

Figure 9.43

The open circles indicate that those points are *not* part of the graph. Otherwise, the endpoints are included in a segment. Notice that although the steps in this function are pictured as line segments, they could actually be pictured as a series of dots, one for each cent in the amount. A similar graph, which can be drawn for postage stamp rates, must use a line segment, since the weights of envelopes vary continuously. A function such as the one pictured in Figure 9.43 is called a **step function**, since its values are pictured in a series of line segments, or steps.

Graphs and Their Functions   Thus far we have studied several special types of functions: linear, quadratic, exponential, cubic, and step. Rather than starting with a function and constructing the graph, this subsection will develop your graphical sense by first displaying a graph and then analyzing it to predict what type of function would produce the graph.

Algebraic Reasoning
The example at the right highlights that algebraic reasoning is not just about solving equations but also deals with reasoning about the relationship between quantities like time and height or height and volume.

Example 9.22   Water is poured at a constant rate into the three containers shown in Figure 9.44. Which graph corresponds to which container?

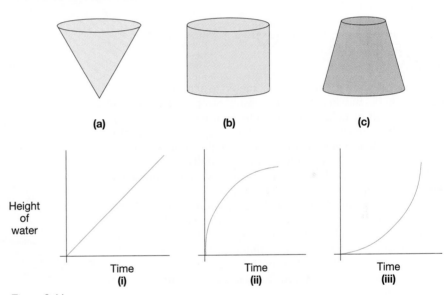

Figure 9.44

SOLUTION   Since the bottom of the figure in (a) is the narrowest, if water is poured into it at a constant rate, its height will rise faster initially and will slow in time. Graph (ii) is steeper initially to indicate that water is rising faster. Then it levels off slowly as the container is being filled. Thus graph (ii) best represents the height of water in container (a) as it is being filled. Container (b) should fill at a constant rate; thus graph (i) best represents its situation. Since the bottom of (c) is larger than its top, the water's height will rise more slowly at first, as in (iii). ∎

Finally, since a function assigns to each element in its domain only one element in its codomain, there is a simple visual test to see whether a graph represents a function. The **vertical line test** states that a graph can represent a function if every vertical line that can be drawn intersects the graph in at most one point. Review the graphs of functions in this section to see that they pass this test by moving a vertical pencil across the graph as suggested in Figure 9.45.

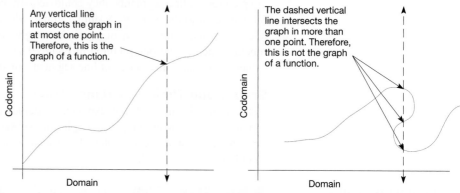

Figure 9.45

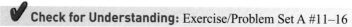
✔ **Check for Understanding:** Exercise/Problem Set A #11–16

MATHEMATICAL MORSEL

Functions are used to try to predict the price action of the stock market. Since the action is the result of the psychological frame of mind of millions of individuals, price movements do not seem to conform to a nice smooth curve. One stock market theory, the Elliott wave theory, postulates that prices move in waves, 5 up and 3 down. Interestingly, when these waves are broken into smaller subdivisions, numbers of the Fibonacci sequence, such as 3, 5, 8, 13, 21, 34, and 55, arise naturally. Another interesting mathematical relationship associated with this theory is the concept of self-similarity. That is, when a smaller wave is enlarged, its structure is supposed to look exactly like the larger wave containing it. If the stock market behaved exactly as Elliott had postulated it should, everyone would become rich by playing the market. Unfortunately, it is not that easy.

Section 9.4 EXERCISE / PROBLEM SET A

EXERCISES

1. Plot the following points on graph paper. Indicate in which quadrant or on which axis the point lies.

　　a. $(3, 2)$

　　b. $(-3, 2)$

　　c. $(3, -2)$

　　d. $(3, 0)$

　　e. $(-3, -2)$

　　f. $(0, 3)$

2. In which of the four quadrants will a point have the following characteristics?

　　a. Negative y-coordinate

　　b. Positive x-coordinate and negative y-coordinate

　　c. Negative x-coordinate and negative y-coordinate

3. On a coordinate system, shade the region consisting of all points that satisfy both of the following conditions:

$$-3 \leq x \leq 2 \quad \text{and} \quad 2 \leq y \leq 4.$$

4. Make a table of at least five values for each of the following linear functions, and sketch the graph of each function. How does the coefficient of the *x* affect the graph? How does the constant term affect the graph?

a. $f(x) = 2x + 3$
b. $m(x) = 40 - 5x$
c. $g(x) = 7.2x - 4.5$

5. a. Sketch the graph of each of the following linear functions. Compare your graphs. A graphics calculator would be helpful.

   i. $f(x) = 2x - 3$ **ii.** $f(x) = \frac{1}{2}x - 3$

   iii. $f(x) = 4x - 3$ **iv.** $f(x) = \frac{2}{3}x - 3$

b. How is the graph of the line affected by the coefficient of *x*?
c. How would a negative coefficient of *x* affect the graph of the line? Try graphing the following functions to test your conjecture.

   i. $f(x) = (-2)x - 3$ **ii.** $f(x) = (-\frac{3}{4})x - 3$

6. Use the Chapter 9 eManipulative activity *Function Grapher* on our Web site to graph the function $f(x) = ax + 2$ (enter *ax* as *a* * *x*). Move the slider for *a* back and forth to answer the following questions.
a. What happens to the shape of the graph as *a* gets larger?
b. What does the graph look like when $a = 0$?
c. How does the graph change when *a* is negative?

7. a. Sketch the graph of each function. Use a graphics calculator if available.

   i. $f(x) = x^2$ **ii.** $f(x) = x^2 + 2$

   iii. $f(x) = x^2 - 2$ **iv.** $f(x) = (x - 2)^2$

   v. $f(x) = (x + 2)^2$

b. Taking the graph in part (i) as a standard, what effect does the constant 2 have on the graph in each of the other parts of part (a)?
c. Use the pattern you observed in part (a) to sketch graphs of $f(x) = x^2 + 4$ and $f(x) = (x - 3)^2$. Use a graphics calculator to check your prediction.

8. Use the Chapter 9 eManipulative activity *Function Grapher* on our Web site to graph the function $f(x) = (x - b)^2 + c$. Move the slider for *b* and *c* back and forth to answer the following questions.
a. How does *b* affect the position of the graph?
b. How does *c* affect the position of the graph?

9. a. Sketch the graph of each of the following exponential functions. Use a graphics calculator if available. Compare your graphs.

   i. $f(x) = 2^x$ **ii.** $f(x) = 5^x$

   iii. $f(x) = (\frac{1}{2})^x$ **iv.** $f(x) = (\frac{3}{4})^x$

b. How is the shape of the graph of each function affected by the value of the base of the function?
c. Use the pattern you observed in part (a) to predict the shapes of the graphs of $f(x) = 10^x$ and $f(x) = (0.95)^x$. Check your prediction by sketching their graphs.

10. Use the Chapter 9 eManipulative activity *Function Grapher* on our Web site to graph the function $f(x) = a^x$. Move the slider for *a* back and forth to answer the following questions.
a. What happens to the shape of the graph as *a* gets larger?
b. What does the graph look like when $a = 1$?
c. How does the graph look different when $0 < a < 1$?

11. Make a table of at least five values for each of the following functions and sketch their graphs.
a. $h(x) = x^3 - 3x^2$ **b.** $s(x) = 2 - x^3$

12. In March, 2007, the first-class postal rates were:

   39 cents w≤1 oz
   63 cents 1<w≤2
   87 cents 2<w≤3
   $1.11 3<w≤4
   $1.35 4<w≤5
   $1.59 5<w≤6
   $1.83 6<w≤7
   $2.07 7<w≤8
   $2.31 8<w≤9
   $2.55 9<w≤10
   $2.79 10<w≤11
   $3.03 11<w≤12
   $3.27 12<w≤13

a. If $P(w)$ gives the rate for a parcel weighing *w* ounces, find each of the following.

   i. $P(0.5)$ **ii.** $P(5.5)$ **iii.** $P(11.9)$ **iv.** $P(12.1)$

b. Specify the domain and range for *P* based on the previous list.
c. Sketch the graph of the first-class rates as a function of weight for $0 < w \le 6$.
d. Suppose that you have 20 pieces weighing $\frac{3}{4}$ oz each that you wish to mail first class to the same destination. Explain why it is cheaper to package them together in one bundle than to mail them separately.

13. The **greatest integer function** of *x*, denoted $f(x) = [\![x]\!]$, is defined to be the greatest integer that is less than or equal to *x*. For example, $[\![3.5]\!] = 3$, $[\![-3.9]\!] = -4$, and $[\![17]\!] = 17$.
a. Evaluate the following.

   i. $[\![2.4]\!]$ **ii.** $[\![7.98]\!]$

   iii. $[\![-4.2]\!]$ **iv.** $[\![0.3]\!]$

b. Sketch the graph of $f(x) = [\![x]\!]$ for $-3 \le x \le 3$.

14. Sketch the graph of each of the following step functions.
a. $f(x) = [\![x + 1]\!]$ for $0 \le x \le 4$
b. $f(x) = [\![2 - x]\!]$ for $-1 \le x \le 3$
c. $f(x) = 5 - [\![x]\!]$ for $0 \le x \le 5$
d. $f(x) = 6 \left[\!\left[\dfrac{x}{2} \right]\!\right]$ for $2 \le x \le 6$

15. Which type of function best fits each of the following graphs: linear, quadratic, cubic, exponential, or step?

a.

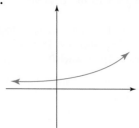

b.

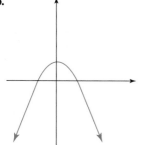

c.

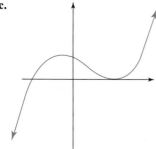

16. Determine which of the following graphs represent functions. (*Hint:* Use the vertical line test.) For those that are functions, specify the domain and range.

a.

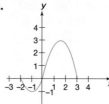

b.

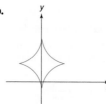

c.

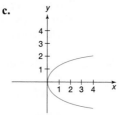

d.

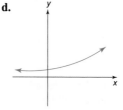

PROBLEMS

17. Consider the function f whose graph is shown next

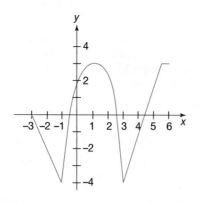

a. Find the following: (i) $f(1)$, (ii) $f(-1)$, and (iii) $f(4.5)$.
b. Specify the domain and range of the function.
c. For which value(s) of x is $f(x) = 2$?

18. As you stand on a beach and look out toward the ocean, the distance that you can see is a function of the height of your eyes above sea level. The following formula and graph represent this relationship, where h is the height of your eyes in *feet* and d is the distance you can see *in miles*.

$$d(h) = 1.2\sqrt{h}$$

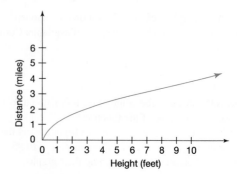

a. Use the formula to calculate the approximate values of $d(4)$ and $d(5.5)$. Use the graph to check your answers.

b. A child's eyes are about 3 feet 3 inches from the ground. How far can she see out to the horizon?

c. Specify the domain and range of the function.

19. The Institute for Aerobics Research recommends an optimal heart rate for exercisers who want to get the maximum benefit from their workouts. The rate is a function of the age of the exerciser and should be between 65% and 80% of the difference between 220 and the person's age. That is, if a is the age in years, then the minimum heart rate for 1 minute is

$$r(a) = 0.65(220 - a)$$

and the maximum is

$$R(a) = 0.8(220 - a).$$

a. Sketch the graphs of the functions r and R on the same set of axes.

b. A woman 30 years old begins a new exercise program. To benefit from the program, into what range should her heart rate fall?

c. How are the recommended heart rates affected as the age of the exerciser increases? How does your graph display this information?

20. The following graph shows the relationship between the length of the shadow of a 100-meter-tall building and the number of hours that have passed since noon.

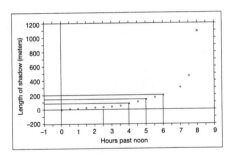

a. If L represents the length of the shadow and n represents the number of hours since noon, why is L a function of n? What type of function does the graph appear to represent?

b. Use the graph to approximate $L(5)$, $L(8)$, and $L(2.5)$ to the nearest 50.

c. After how many hours is the shadow 100 meters long? When is it twice as long?

d. Why do you think the graph stops at $n = 8$?

21. A man standing at a window 55 feet above the ground leans out and throws a ball straight up into the air with a speed of 70 feet per second. The height, s, of the ball above the ground, as a function of the number of seconds elapsed, t, is given as $s(t) = -16t^2 + 70t + 55$.

a. Sketch a graph of the function for $0 \le t \le 6$. If available, use a graphics calculator.

b. Use your graph to determine when the ball is about 90 feet above the ground. (NOTE: There are two times when this occurs. Use the formula as a check.)

c. About when does the ball hit the ground?

d. About how high does the ball go before it starts back down?

22. The population of the world is growing exponentially. A formula that can be used to make rough predictions of world population based on the population in 1990 and 2001 is given as

$$P(t) = 5.284e^{.0139t},$$

where $P(t)$ is the world population in billions, t is the number of years since 1990, and e is an irrational number approximately equal to 2.718. (NOTE: Scientific calculators have a key to calculate e.)

a. Sketch the graph of the function P. A graphics calculator will be helpful.

b. Use the formula to predict the world population in 2006.

c. Use your graph to predict when the world population will reach 8 billion.

d. Use your graph to estimate the current doubling time for the world population. That is, about how many years are required for the 1990 population to double?

23. A bicyclist pedals at a constant rate along a route that is essentially flat but has one hill, as shown next.

Which of the following graphs best describes what happens to the speed of the cyclist as she travels along the route?

a.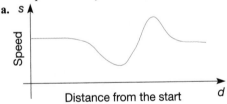

b.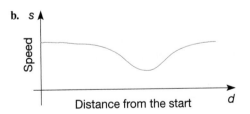

c.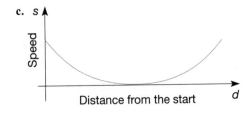

24. Three people on the first floor of a building wish to take the elevator up to the top floor. The maximum weight that the elevator can carry is 300 pounds. Also, one of the three people must be in the elevator to operate it. If the people weigh 130, 160, and 210 pounds, how can they get to the top floor?

25. Use the Chapter 9 dyamic spreadsheet *Cubic* on our Web site to graph $f(x) = ax^3 + bx^2 + cx + d$. Set $a = b = c = d = 1$ and enter different values of b. Explain the impact of the coefficient b on the shape of the graph of a cubic function.

Section 9.4 | EXERCISE / PROBLEM SET B

EXERCISES

1. Plot the following points on graph paper. Indicate in which quadrant or on which axis the point lies.
a. $(-3, 0)$
b. $(6, 4)$
c. $(-2, 3)$
d. $(0, 5)$
e. $(-1, -4)$
f. $(3, -2)$

2. In which of the four quadrants will a point have the following characteristics?
a. Negative x-coordinate and positive y-coordinate
b. Positive x-coordinate and positive y-coordinate
c. Positive x-coordinate

3. A region in the coordinate plane is shaded where each mark on the axes represents one unit. Describe this region algebraically. That is, describe the values of the coordinates of the region using equations and/or inequalities.

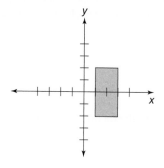

4. Make a table of at least five values for each of the following linear functions and sketch their graphs.
a. $f(x) = 3x - 2$
b. $g(x) = -\frac{3}{4}x + 9$
c. $h(x) = 120x + 25$

5. a. Sketch the graph of each of the following linear equations. Use a graphics calculator if available. Compare your graphs.
  i. $f(x) = x + 2$ **ii.** $f(x) = x - 4$
  iii. $f(x) = x + 6.5$ **iv.** $f(x) = x$
b. How is the graph of the line affected by the value of the constant term of the function?

6. Use the Chapter 9 eManipulative activity *Function Grapher* on our Web site to graph the function $f(x) = x + b$. Move the slider for b back and forth to answer the following questions.
a. What does the graph look like when $b = 0$?
b. How does the value of b affect the graph of $f(x) = x + b$?

7. a. Sketch a graph of each of the following quadratic equations. Use a graphics calculator if available.
  i. $f(x) = x^2$ **ii.** $f(x) = 2x^2$
  iii. $f(x) = \frac{1}{2}x^2$ **iv.** $f(x) = -3x^2$
b. What role does the coefficient of x^2 play in determining the shape of the graph?
c. Use the pattern you observed in part (a) and in Exercise 5 to predict the shape of the graphs of $f(x) = 5x^2$ and $f(x) = \frac{1}{3}x^2 + 2$.

8. Use the Chapter 9 eManipulative activity *Function Grapher* on our Web site to graph the function $f(x) = ax^2$ (enter ax as $a * x$). Move the slider for a back and forth to answer the following questions.
a. What happens to the shape of the graph as a gets larger?
b. What does the graph look like when $a = 0$?
c. How does the graph change when a is negative?

9. a. Draw graphs of each of the following pairs of exponential functions. Compare the graphs you obtain. Use a graphics calculator if available.
  i. $f(x) = (\frac{1}{3})^x$ and $f(x) = 3^{-x}$
  ii. $f(x) = (\frac{2}{5})^x$ and $f(x) = 2.5^{-x}$
  iii. $f(x) = 10^x$ and $f(x) = (0.1)^{-x}$
b. What interesting observation can be made about the pairs in part (a)?

10. Use the Chapter 9 eManipulative activity *Function Grapher* on our Web site to graph the function $f(x) = 2^{(cx)}$ (enter cx as $c * x$). Move the slider for c back and forth to answer the following questions.
a. What happens to the shape of the graph as c gets larger?
b. What does the graph look like when $c = 0$?
c. How does the graph change when c is negative?

11. Make a table of at least five values for each of the following functions and sketch their graphs.
a. $f(x) = x^3 - 3x$ **b.** $f(x) = \frac{2}{3}x^3 - 4$

Line Graphs and Cropping   What we have seen regarding bar graphs also applies to line graphs. Recall the data of average teacher salaries displayed in the line graph in Figure 10.7. That graph makes it appear as if the increase was fairly significant. Suppose, however, that the teachers' union wants to make a case for better teacher pay. This increase may be made less dramatic by extending the scale of the vertical axis and using larger increments, as in Figure 10.27.

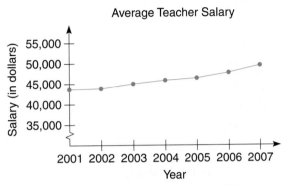

Figure 10.27   Source: National Education Association.

Example 10.6   Draw two line graphs of the unemployment data (see Table 10.9) from Example 10.5 that give different impressions of the situation.

SOLUTION

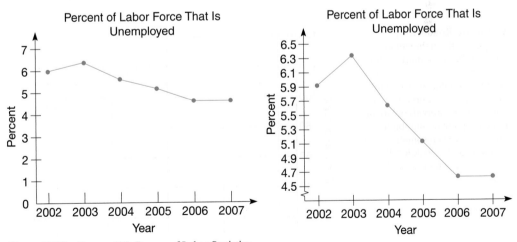

Figure 10.28   Source: U.S. Bureau of Labor Statistics.

The graph on the left in Figure 10.28 suggests that the rate of unemployment is decreasing slowly, whereas the graph on the right gives the impression that unemployment is decreasing more rapidly through 2006.   ∎

Figure 10.29 shows the values of a stock from January 11 through January 20. The stock appears to be a good buy because it is on an upward trend. Notice that the graph is rising above the edge of the vertical scale. Graphs that do this or even go to the edge of the scale make the trend appear more dramatic.

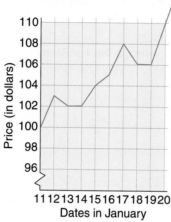

Figure 10.29

This kind of scale manipulation is part of a larger phenomenon called cropping. **Cropping** refers to the choice of the window that the graph uses to view the data. Suppose we wish to present the price of a certain company's stock. We may choose which time period and vertical axis to display. In other words, when we show a picture we have to choose a window in which to frame it. Figure 10.30 shows the value of the stock over the previous five months; the stock price is plotted every 10 days.

Algebraic Reasoning
Comparing the behavior of the graph of the stock market over a period of days versus a period of months is similar to examining the local (small interval) versus global (large interval) behavior of the graph of an algebraic equation. We can sometimes see things when we look locally that we don't see when we look globally.

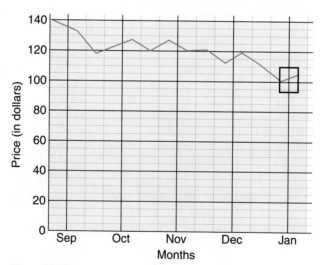

Figure 10.30

The data from Figure 10.29 are now contained in the box of Figure 10.30. Thus, this graph gives a very different perception regarding the value of the stock. This different perception is caused by the change in the vertical scale as well as the horizontal scale.

The downward trend in Figure 10.30 would be more apparent if we choose the vertical scale to be between 100 and 140. The data from Figure 10.30 are shown in Figure 10.31.

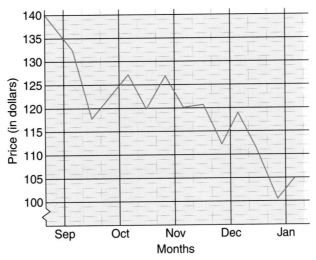

Figure 10.31

Notice how by changing the vertical axis, we get a very different impression of the price trend of the company's stock.

Three-Dimensional Effects   Three-dimensional effects, which are often found in newspapers and magazines, make a graph more attractive but can also obscure the true picture of the data. These graphs are difficult to draw unless you have computer graphing software.

The data for average teacher salary shown in Figure 10.7 are shown using a bar graph with three-dimensional effects in Figure 10.32.

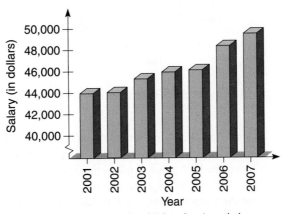

Figure 10.32   Source: National Education Association.

The perspective of the graph makes it difficult to see exact values. For example, the average salary in 2007 was $49,294, but to glance at the graph it could be estimated to be as much as $48,000.

Line charts with three-dimensional effects may also reduce the amount of visible information, as shown in Figure 10.33.

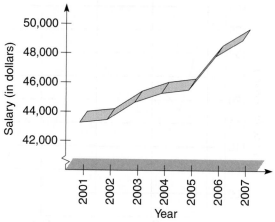

Figure 10.33

The upward trend is still apparent, but the exact values are very difficult to read. This is a graph of the same data as shown in Figures 10.32 and 10.7.

Consider the pictographs of cotton bales showing the increased exports of cotton from 1990 to 2005 [Figure 10.34(a)].

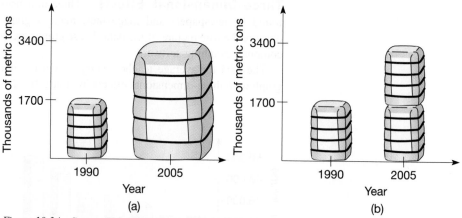

Figure 10.34 *Source:* U.S. Department of Agriculture.

The amount of cotton exported in 2005 (3,397,000 metric tons) is twice as much as that exported in 1990 (1,696,000 metric tons). At first glance, it might seem appropriate to make one bale twice as tall as the other. However, looking at the pictures of the two bales in Figure 10.34(a), we get the impression that the taller one is much more than twice the volume of the other. In addition to making the height of the larger twice the height of the smaller, the large bale's width and depth have been doubled. Thus, the bale on the right in Figure 10.34(a) represents a volume that is $2 \times 2 \times 2 = 8$ times as large as the one on the left. The pictograph in Figure 10.34(b) shows how a 3-D pictograph could be constructed without deception.

Circle Graphs   Circle graphs allow for visual comparisons of the relative sizes of fractional parts. The graph in Figure 10.35 shows the relative sizes of the vitamin content in a serving of cornflakes and milk. Four vitamins are present—B_1, B_2, A, and C. We can conclude that most of the vitamin content is B_1 and B_2, that less vitamin A is present, and that the vitamin C content is the least. However, the graph is deceptive, in that it gives no indication whatsoever of the actual amount of these four vitamins, either by weight (say in grams) or by percentage of minimum daily requirement. Thus, although the circle graph is excellent for picturing relative amounts, it does not necessarily indicate absolute amounts.

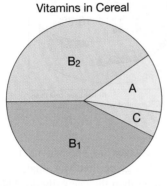

Figure 10.35

Circle graphs or pie charts can also be manipulated to reinforce a particular message or to mislead. It is very common to take a sector of the "pie" and **explode** it (that is, move it slightly away from the center; Figure 10.36).

This gives the sector more emphasis and may make it seem larger than it is. Making it three-dimensional and exploding the sector makes the largest sector seem even larger still. The graph in Figure 10.37 is a good example of the dominant effect of the exploded sector representing the share of stocks owned by individuals.

NCTM Standard
Draw inferences from charts, tables, and graphs that summarize data from real-world situations.

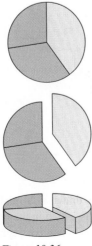

Figure 10.36

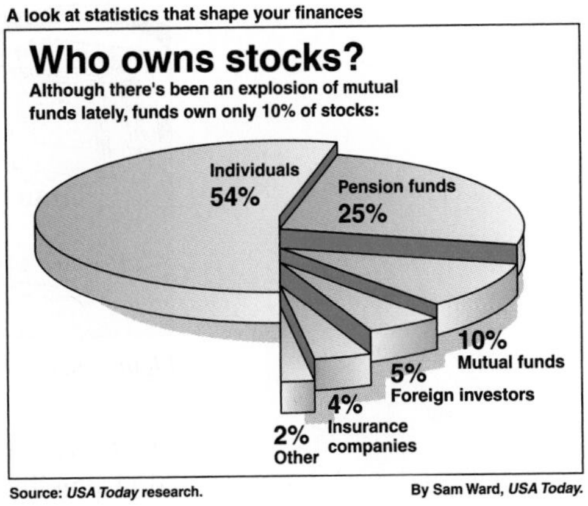

A look at statistics that shape your finances

Who owns stocks?
Although there's been an explosion of mutual funds lately, funds own only 10% of stocks:

Individuals
54%

Pension funds
25%

10%
Mutual funds

5%
Foreign investors

4% Insurance
companies

2%
Other

Source: *USA Today* research.   By Sam Ward, *USA Today.*

Copyright 1994, USA TODAY. Reprinted with permission.

Figure 10.37

A third way in which circle graphs can be deceptive is illustrated in the following example.

Example 10.7   Figure 10.38 shows what looks like a circle graph embedded in a picture of a hamburger. It conceals a misleading piece of distortion. Can you spot it?

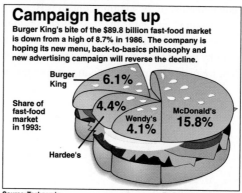

Campaign heats up

Burger King's bite of the $89.8 billion fast-food market is down from a high of 8.7% in 1986. The company is hoping its new menu, back-to-basics philosophy and new advertising campaign will reverse the decline.

Burger King — 6.1%

Share of fast-food market in 1993:

4.4%

Wendy's 4.1%

McDonald's 15.8%

Hardee's

Source: Technomic   By Bob Laud, *USA Today.*
Copyright 1994, USA TODAY. Reprinted with permission.

Figure 10.38

SOLUTION The percentages do not add up to 100%. There are only a total of 30.4%. The impression is given that McDonald's and the other chains have a much larger share of the market than they actually do. This graph also provides an example of a pictorial embellishment, which we will now discuss as another source of misleading graphs. ∎

Deceptive Pictorial Embellishments   Pictorial embellishments in both two-dimensional and three-dimensional situations can also lead to confusion and be deceptive. Figure 10.39 displays a bar chart embedded into a gasoline pump nozzle, which compares the price of gas in the Netherlands, the United States, and Venezuela.

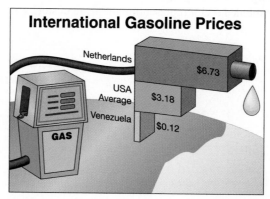

International Gasoline Prices

Netherlands $6.73

USA Average $3.18

Venezuela $0.12

GAS

Figure 10.39

The chart has visual appeal but is drawn in a misleading way. The length of the bar corresponding to the Netherlands is 1 inch in the original graph, which is to represent a price of $6.73 per gallon. Thus a 1-inch bar represents $6.73 but the nozzle on the end of the bar makes it appear even longer. The length of the bar for the United States was 1/2 inch in the original graph so that an inch represents only $3.18 × 2 = $6.36. The length of the Venezuela bar was 1/16 inch in the original graph, giving a scale of $0.12 × 16 = $1.92 per inch. These discrepancies in the lengths of the bars, while slight, create a visual image that is not consistent with the numerical values they represent.

Figure 10.40 gives a variation on a bar chart. The graph displays the responses to the question "Would you date a person who disliked dogs?" This graph could possibly be a pictograph if it displayed the value of each heart. Since it does not, it must be interpreted as a bar graph where the lengths of the bars are a visual picture of the percent being represented. The curved bars in this graph make it very difficult to compare the lengths. Another misleading attribute of the graph is the increasing size of the hearts on the "wouldn't date" bar. The large broken heart at the end misleadingly dominates the graph.

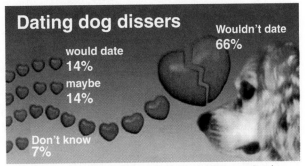

Copyright 2007, USA TODAY. Reprinted with permission. Source: American Kennel Club.

Figure 10.40

Example 10.8   The three-dimensional bar chart in Figure 10.41 compares the number of days of work missed each year by employees. What is misleading about it?

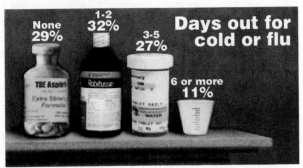

Copyright 2007, USA TODAY. Reprinted with permission. Source: Impulse Research for SinuCleanse.

Figure 10.41

SOLUTION The heights of the different medicine containers accurately represent their corresponding numbers. For example, the bottle representing "None" is about 3.8 cm tall and the one representing "1–2" days of work missed is about 4.2 cm tall. Thus the ratio of heights is $\frac{4.2}{3.8} \approx 1.1$ and the ratio of percentages is $\frac{32}{29} \approx 1.1$. However, the widths and shapes of the containers are all different giving the impression that the narrower container on the right represents a smaller amount than it really does.   ■

Any graph may be embedded in a picture to make it more eyecatching and provide emphasis so that you interpret the graph in a desired way. Figure 10.42 shows a line graph of the number of babies delivered by midwives. This shows a strong increasing trend.

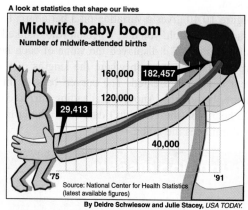

A look at statistics that shape our lives

Midwife baby boom
Number of midwife-attended births

160,000   182,457

120,000

29,413

40,000

'75   '91

Source: National Center for Health Statistics
(latest available figures)

By Deidre Schwiesow and Julie Stacey, *USA TODAY.*

Copyright 1993, USA TODAY. Reprinted with permission.

Figure 10.42

By making the line of the graph the arm of the midwife, the eye is directed upward from the infant at the left of the graph up the arm to the midwife. This exaggerates the increasing nature of the graph.

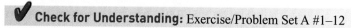 **Check for Understanding:** Exercise/Problem Set A #1–12

Samples and Bias

All of the examples of misleading statistics that we have looked at thus far have dealt with the way in which the data were presented. However, this assumes that the data were accurate to begin with, which may not be the case, depending on how the data were gathered. One of the most common uses of statistics is gathering and analyzing information about specific groups of people or objects. In the following, we will look at how this information is gathered and analyzed and how bias can enter this process.

As President William Jefferson Clinton was facing the possibility of impeachment during the summer and fall of 1998, one of the interesting controversies of the process was conflict between public opinion polls and the opinions of the members of the House of Representatives. A question that naturally arises regarding the public opinion polls is, "How is such information gathered?" Do the pollsters contact *every* voter in the United States? If they only contact a subset of the voters, how is that subset selected? Is the information collected from voters in the East or in the West, Republicans or Democrats, young voters or older voters? How all of these questions are addressed will determine the quality of the data collected.

The entire group in question is called the **population**, and the subset of the population that is actually observed, questioned, or analyzed is called a **sample**. If a sample is carefully chosen, we may assume that it is representative of the population and shares the main characteristics of the group. The results we obtain from the sample, such as means or percentages, can then be used as estimates for values we would find in the population. However, a great deal of care should be taken in selecting a sample.

NCTM Standard
All students should use observations about differences between two or more samples to make conjectures about the populations from which the samples were taken.

Reflection from Research
Students struggle to differentiate between the out-of-school definition of *sample*, and the more technical definition that applies when it is being used to represent a population in order to draw conclusions about that population (Watson & Moritz, 2000).

Example 10.9   Suppose you wish to determine voter opinion regarding the ballot measure to fund the proposed new library. To determine this, you survey potential voters among the pedestrians on Main Street during the lunch hour. What is the population and what is the sample?

SOLUTION The population consists of people who are going to vote in the upcoming election. The sample consists of those interviewed on the street who say they will be voting in the election.   ∎

If a sample is not representative of the population, we will draw an erroneous conclusion. A **bias** is a flaw in the sampling procedure that makes it more likely that the sample will not be representative of the population. As an example, suppose a late-night news program wished to have a call-in telephone poll on a gun control issue with a 50-cent cost of participation. Such a telephone poll has many sources of bias. An important source is the fact that it takes an effort and some expense to participate. This means that people who have strong opinions about gun control and are willing to part with 50 cents are more likely to participate. Other sources of bias include the fact that there is nothing to prevent nonresidents from participating or to prevent people from voting more than once. There are other forms of bias that can also affect the result, such as the way questions are worded. In this section, we will discuss how to analyze surveys and polls and how to choose samples that are free of bias.

Example 10.10   Suppose you wish to determine voter opinion regarding the elimination of the capital gains tax (a profit made on an investment is called a capital gain). To determine this, you survey potential voters near Wall Street in New York City. Identify a source of bias in this poll.

SOLUTION One source of bias in choosing this sample is that many people involved in trading stocks work on Wall Street and their income could be enhanced by the elimination of the capital gains tax. The percentage of people in this sample that favor elimination is likely to be much higher than that of the population as a whole.   ∎

The population and sample need not always consist of people, as we see in the next example.

Example 10.11   To test the reliability of a lot (a unit of production) of automobile components produced at a certain factory, the first 30 components of a lot of 1000 are tested for defects. Describe the population, the sample, and any potential sources of bias.

SOLUTION The population is the lot of 1000 automobile components that are produced at the factory. The sample is the set of the first 30 produced from the lot. Bias results from the fact that the first 30 are chosen. It is possible that these 30 were made with special care or that they were made at the start of the process when defects are more likely.   ∎

A summary of the common errors that occur when surveys are conducted is provided in Table 10.10.

TABLE 10.10 Common Sources of Bias in Surveys

TYPE OF ERROR	DESCRIPTION
Faulty sampling	The chosen sample is not representative.
Faulty questions	Questions worded so as to influence the answers.
Faulty interviewing	Failure to interview all of the chosen sample. Misreading the questions. Misinterpreting the answers.
Lack of understanding or knowledge	The person being interviewed does not understand what is being asked or does not have the information needed.
False answers	The person being interviewed intentionally gives incorrect information.

 Check for Understanding: Exercise/Problem Set A #13–14

MATHEMATICAL MORSEL

Several presidential election polls went statistically awry in the twentieth century. A spectacular failure was the 1935 *Literary Digest* poll predicting that Alfred Landon would defeat Franklin Roosevelt in the 1936 election. So devastated was the Literary Digest by its false prediction that it subsequently ceased publication. The *Literary Digest* poll used voluntary responses from a preselected sample—but only 23% of the people in the sample responded. Evidently, the majority of those who did were more enthusiastic about their candidate (Landon) than were the majority of the entire sample. Thus the sampling error was so large that a false prediction resulted. A study by J. H. Powell showed that if the data were analyzed and weighted according to how the respondents represented the general population, they would have picked Roosevelt.

The Dewey–Truman 1948 Gallup poll also used a biased sample. Interviewers were allowed to select individuals based on certain quotas (e.g., sex, race, and age). However, the people selected tended to be more prosperous than average, which produced a sample biased toward Republican candidates. Also, the poll was conducted three weeks before the election, when Truman was gaining support and Dewey was slipping.

Nowadays, sampling procedures are done with extreme care to produce representative samples of public opinion.

EXERCISE / PROBLEM SET A

EXERCISES

1. The world record time for the mile run is given in the following table:
   a. Draw a line graph of this data using 3:30.0 as the baseline for the graph.
   b. What effect does having 3:30.0 as the baseline as opposed to 0 have on the impression made by the graph?

YEAR	WORLD RECORD FOR MILE RUN
1950	4:01.4 (4 min 1.4 sec)
1955	3:58.0
1960	3:54.5
1965	3:53.6
1970	3:51.1
1975	3:49.4
1980	3:48.8
1985	3:46.3
1990	3:46.3
1995	3:44.4
2000	3:43.1

2. Since 1900, the death rate related to certain causes (other than old age) in the United States has fallen, while it has risen for several other causes. For heart disease, the death rate per 100,000 population was as follows:

1960	1970	1980	1990	2000
229	492.7	412.1	321.8	257.6

Source: U.S. National Center for Health Statistics.

   a. Draw a bar graph for this data using the same distance between each of the bars.
   b. Draw a line graph for the data having the years as the baseline with the usual spacing.
   c. Which graphing approach do you prefer? Why?

3. The following graphs represent the average wages of employees in a given company.

   i.

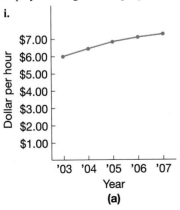

   (a)

   ii.

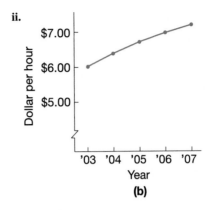

   (b)

   a. Do these graphs represent the same data?
   b. What is the difference between these graphs?
   c. Which graph would you use if you were the leader of a labor union seeking increased wages?
   d. Which graph would you use if you were seeking to impress prospective employees with wages?

4. Health-care costs became a major issue in the last decade for both employers and employees. The following graph shows changes that occurred during this period.

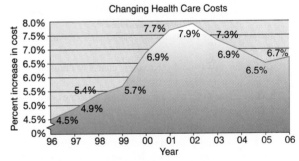

Source: U.S. Centers for Medicare and Medicaid Services.

   Redo the graph, showing percentage of change without shortening the vertical scale.

5. Create a 3-D bar chart for the following data.

YEAR	NEW CAR SALES ($\times$ 1000)
1994	8,991
1996	8,527
1998	8,142
2000	8,846
2002	8,103
2004	7,506
2006	7,781

Source: Ward's Motor Vehicle Facts & Figures.

6. Use the following pie chart for Meat Consumption per Person, 2006, to create an "exploded" 3-D pie chart to emphasize the amount of red meat consumed per person.

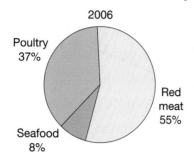

2006

Poultry
37%

Red meat
55%

Seafood
8%

7. Using perspective with pie charts can be deceiving.

52 weeks ending June 13, 1992, in millions of units

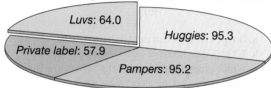

Luvs: 64.0

Huggies: 95.3

Private label: 57.9

Pampers: 95.2

52 weeks ending Dec. 11, 1993, in millions of units

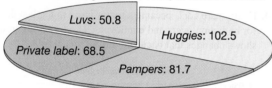

Luvs: 50.8

Huggies: 102.5

Private label: 68.5

Pampers: 81.7

Source: Company reports, Nielson Marketing Research, *Investors Business Daily.*

a. Use the data from these two pie charts to draw two new pie charts in the usual manner.
b. How do the pie charts you drew compare to the original ones?
c. Do the comparative pieces seem the same as before?

Use the following for Exercises 8 and 9.

The following pictorial embellishment of a circle graph was taken from the May 17, 1993, issue of *Fortune* magazine. In it,

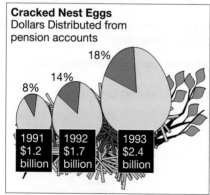

Cracked Nest Eggs
Dollars Distributed from pension accounts

18%

14%

8%

| 1991 $1.2 billion | 1992 $1.7 billion | 1993 $2.4 billion |

Credit: Keehan for Fortune
Source: Fidelity Investments © 1993 Time Inc. All rights reserved.

the ovals that represent the "nest eggs" have lengths that are in proportion to the total amounts in the pension accounts. This tends to exaggerate the amounts they represent. That is, the area of the third oval is actually *four* times the area of the first oval although the amount it represents is only *two* times as great.

8. Create a set of three pie charts based on the data from the pictograph. Make all the circles the same size. How does making the circles the same size affect the impression about the amounts involved?

9. Create a segmented bar chart based on the data from the pictograph. Make each of the bars proportional in height to the amounts in the pension accounts.

10. Discuss the misleading attributes of the following graph and what could be done to the graph to make it more mathematically accurate.

64%   Who makes the kids lunch?

21%

11%

4%

MOM   the Kids   Dad   other

11. a. Which of the following pictographs would be correct to show that sales have doubled from the left figure to the right figure?

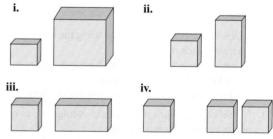

i.

ii.

iii.

iv.

b. What is misleading about the other(s)?

12. Identify three ways in which bar graphs can be deceptive.

In Exercises 13 and 14 identify the population being studied and the sample that is actually observed.

13. A light bulb company says that its light bulbs last 2000 hours. To test this, a package of 8 bulbs is purchased and the bulbs are kept lit until they burn out. Five of the bulbs burn out before 2000 hours.

14. The registrar's office is interested in the percentage of full-time students who commute on a regular basis. One hundred students are randomly selected and briefly interviewed; 75 of these students commute on a regular basis.

PROBLEMS

15. Pictographs are often drawn incorrectly even if there is no intent to distort the data. Suppose we want to show that the number of women in the work force today is twice what it was at some time in the past. One way this could be done is to have two pictures of women representing the number of women in the work force and draw the one for today twice as tall as the one for the past, similar to what was done with the cotton bales in Figure 10.34. The problem is that most people tend to respond to graphics by comparing areas; we are also used to interpreting depth and perspective in drawings depicting three-dimensional objects.

Suppose we want to compare the revenue of two companies. Suppose company A had revenues of $5,000,000 last year and company B had $10,000,000.

a. If we want to use the area of circles to represent the revenues of the companies, what should be the radius of the circle for company B if the radius of the circle for company A is 1 inch? Explain.

b. If we want to use the volume of spheres to represent the revenues of the companies, what should be the radius of the sphere for company B if the radius of the sphere for company A is 1 inch? Explain.

16. One indicator of the changes in the world economy is the change in imports and exports. Redo the following graph about aluminum imports so the fluctuation from year to year seems more extreme.

ALUMINUM IMPORTS

Pounds (in millions)

2004: 11,221
2005: 12,607
2006: 12,322

Source: The Aluminum Association.

17. Prepare a vertical bar chart for the data on the federal tax burden per capita in such a way that the changes are very dramatic.

The Federal Tax Burden per Capita

FISCAL YEARS 1999–2004					
1999	2000	2001	2002	2003	2004
$6796	$7404	$7440	$6632	$6229	$6369

Source: Tax Foundation.

18. Redraw the graph on the increases in the federal tax burden per capita, 1999–2004, to de-emphasize the changes.

19. Redo the following graph so that agriculture prices from 2000 to 2007 don't appear to change so much.

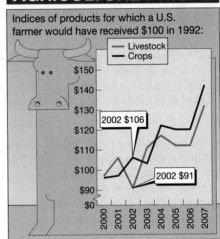

Source: U.S. Dept. of Agriculture.

In Problems 20 and 21 identify the population being studied, the sample actually observed, and discuss any sources of bias.

20. A biologist wants to estimate the number of fish in a lake. As part of the study, 250 fish are caught, tagged, and released back into the lake. Later, 500 fish are caught and examined; 18 of these fish are found to be tagged and the rest are untagged.

21. A drug company wishes to claim that 9 out of 10 doctors recommend the active ingredients in their product. They commission a study of 20 doctors. If at least 18 doctors say they recommend the active ingredients in the product, the company will feel free to make this claim. If not, the company will commission another study.

Section 10.2 | EXERCISE / PROBLEM SET B

EXERCISES

1. **Harness Racing Records for the Mile**

TROTTERS	
1921	1:57.8
1922	1:57
1922	1:56.8
1937	1:56.6
1937	1:56
1938	1:55.2
1969	1:54.8
1980	1:54.6
1982	1:54
1987	1:52.2
1994	1:51.4
2002	1:50.4
2004	1:50.2

Source: Information Please almanac.

a. Draw a line graph of the data on Trotters using 1:50.0 as the baseline for the graph.
b. What effect does having the baseline at 1:50.0 as opposed to 0 have on the impression made by the graph?

2. Redraw the bar graph from Figure 10.24 with horizontal bars, but this time reverse the order of the bars from how they appear in Figure 10.25.
a. What is the visual impression regarding profits in this graph?
b. Which graph would you use? Why?

3. The following data represents the prices of gasoline in the United States from 2001 to 2007.

YEAR	GAS PRICE
2001	$1.46
2002	$1.39
2003	$1.60
2004	$1.90
2005	$2.31
2006	$2.61
2007	$2.80

a. Construct a line graph as if you were a representative of an oil company. Explain the reasoning for your construction.
b. Construct a line graph as if you were representing a consumer advocacy group. Explain the reasoning for your construction.

4. From 2000 to 2006, the average annual wages and salary in the transportation industry are shown in the following graph. Redo the graph with a full vertical scale.

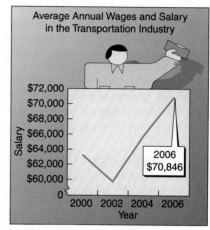

Source: U.S. Bureau of Economic Analysis.

5. Create a 3-D line chart for the following data on the projected number of landfills in the United States.

YEARS	LANDFILLS
1985	6000
1990	3300
1995	2600
2000	1500
2005	1100

6. Use the pie chart from Exercise 6, Part A, to create an "exploded" 3-D pie chart to emphasize the amount of poultry consumed per person. Rotate the pie chart further to emphasize the poultry.

7. A circle graph with equal-sized sectors is shown in (i). The same graph is shown in (ii), but drawn as if three-dimensional and in perspective.

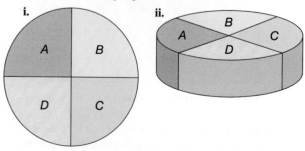

Explain how the perspective version is deceptive.

For Exercises 8 and 9 refer to the graph used for Exercise 8 in Part A.

8. Create a set of three pie charts based on the data in the pictograph. Make the area of each circle proportional to the amount in the pension fund. That is, the area of the circle for 1993 should be twice the area of the circle for 1991.

9. Create a proportional bar graph based on the data from the pictograph. In a proportional bar chart, all bars are the same height. How does making the bars all the same height affect the impression about the amount of funds distributed?

10. Identify any misleading features of the following graph and discuss what could be done to correct them.

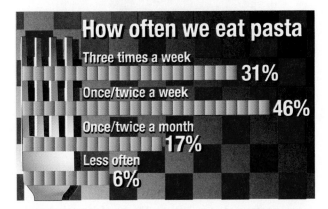

11. CD sales of a certain singing group tripled from March to June. Is the following graph an accurate representation of the increase in sales? Why or why not?

CD Sales

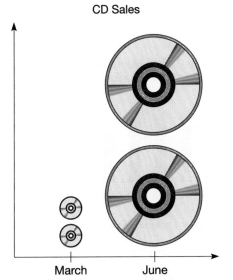

March   June

12. Identify three ways in which circle graphs can be deceptive.

In Exercises 13 and 14 identify the population being studied and the sample that is actually observed.

13. A chest of 1000 gold coins is to be presented to the king. The royal minter believes the king will not notice if only one of the coins is counterfeit. The king is suspicious and has 20 coins taken from the top of the chest and tested to see if they are pure gold.

14. The mathematics department is concerned about the amount of time students regularly set aside for studying. A questionnaire is distributed in three classes having a total of 82 students.

PROBLEMS

15. The following graphs appeared together in an environmental publication. Estimate values from each graph, combine them into a single set of numbers, and produce a single bar graph.

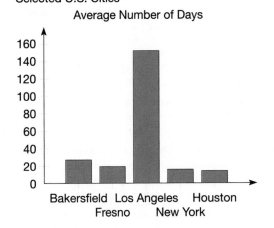

Smog Levels Above Standards, Selected U.S. Cities
Average Number of Days

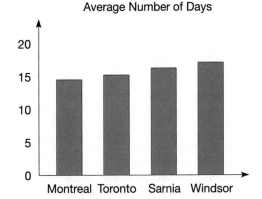

Smog Levels Above Standards, Selected Canadian Cities
Average Number of Days

Use the following graph for Problems 16 and 17.

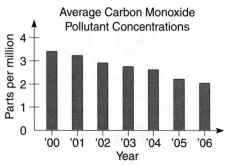

Average Carbon Monoxide Pollutant Concentrations

Source: U.S. Environmental Protection Agency.

16. Redraw the graph on Average Carbon Monoxide Pollutant Concentrations to emphasize the changes and make the decreases less dramatic.

17. Redraw the graph on Average Carbon Monoxide Pollutant Concentrations to emphasize the changes and make the decreases more dramatic.

18. Gun control has been a major political issue for many years. The following graph shows the number of robberies committed with firearms from 1998 to 2007.

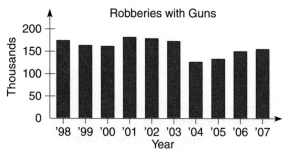

Robberies with Guns

Source: U.S. Federal Bureau of Investigation.

   a. Redo the graph so the decrease appears even greater.

   b. Redo the graph so the decrease is not so obvious.

19. During the 1980s and early 1990s, many changes occurred with respect to the work force, including downsizing and hiring of temporary employees. As a result, job security became a significant concern. The following graph shows the changes in attitude among workers.

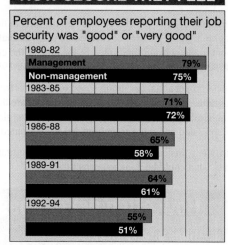

HOW SECURE THEY FEEL

Percent of employees reporting their job security was "good" or "very good"

Redo the graph so that

a. the downward trend is less obvious.

b. the trend is apparently even worse than it is.

In Problems 20 and 21 identify the population being studied, the sample actually observed, and discuss any sources of bias.

20. A college professor is up for promotion. Teaching performance, as judged through student evaluations, is a significant factor in the decision. The professor is asked to choose one of his classes for student evaluations. The day of the evaluations he passes out questionnaires and then remains in the room to answer any questions about the form and filling it out.

21. There are two candidates for student body president of a college. Candidate Johnson believes that the student body resources should be used to enhance the social atmosphere of the college and that the number one priority should be dances, concerts, and other social events. Candidate Jackson believes that sports should be the number one priority and wants to subsidize student sporting events and enlarge the recreation facility. A poll is taken by the student newspaper. One interviewer goes to a coffeehouse near the college one evening and asks students which candidate they prefer. Another interviewer goes to the gym and asks students which candidate they prefer.

Analyzing Student Thinking

22. Siope says that you must always begin the vertical axis of a vertical bar graph at zero. How should you respond?

23. Cesar wants to draw a graph representing how he spends each hour of the day. He says that he can't use a circle graph because there are 24 hours in a day, not 100. How should you respond?

24. A three-dimensional bar chart represents a given amount. All three dimensions of the bar are doubled. Looking at the two graphs, Santos says that the new graph appears to be twice as large as the original graph. Is he correct? Explain.

25. Joel noticed that when part of the vertical axis of a graph is cut out, the graph looks very different. He asks if graphs

that are constructed this way are necessarily designed with the intent to deceive. How would you respond?

26. Otis is creating a pictograph to show that the pencil sales at the school bookstore have tripled in a week. He knows he could draw one pencil for the first week and 3 of the same sized pencils for the second week. He wonders if it would be deceptive to instead draw a pencil that is three times as

long but the same diameter to represent the tripling in sales. How should you respond?

27. Anita wants to conduct a survey about whether the city should raise taxes to build a new playground at the park. She asks you if it would work to gather her data by interviewing people at the park because they are familiar with the facilities. How should you respond?

Problems Relating to the NCTM Standards and Curriculum Focal Points

1. The Focal points for Grade 7 state "Students use proportions to make estimates relating to a population on the basis of a sample." Explain how proportions are used to generalize from a sample to the whole population.

2. The Focal points for Grade 8 state "Analyzing and summarizing data sets." Explain how graphs are used to analyze and summarize data sets.

3. The NCTM Standards state "Draw inferences from charts, tables, and graphs that summarize data from real-world situations." Give two examples where faulty inferences are drawn because of the way a graph is constructed.

10.3   ANALYZING DATA

STARTING POINT

Two girls are arguing over who is on the taller basketball team. The table lists the heights in inches of the players on the two teams. Identify ways that you could help these girls settle their disagreement about the heights of their respective teams. Some might say that the taller team is the team with the two tallest players on it. Describe another way to determine which team is the taller one by taking all players into account.

TEAM 1	TEAM 2
64	69
70	61
65	70
63	70
75	62
64	71
73	65
67	70
64	66
66	67

NCTM Standard
All students should find, use, and interpret measures of center and spread, including mean and interquartile range.

Measuring Central Tendency

Suppose that two fifth-grade classes take a reading test, yielding the following scores. Scores are given in year-month equivalent form. For example, a score of 5.3 means that the student is reading at the fifth-year, third-month level, where years mean years in school.

Class 1: 5.3, 4.9, 5.2, 5.4, 5.6, 5.1, 5.8, 5.3, 4.9, 6.1, 6.2, 5.7, 5.4, 6.9, 4.3, 5.2, 5.6, 5.9, 5.3, 5.8

Class 2: 4.7, 5.0, 5.5, 4.1, 6.8, 5.0, 4.7, 5.6, 4.9, 6.3, 7.8, 3.6, 8.4, 5.4, 4.7, 4.4, 5.6, 3.7, 6.2, 7.5

How did the two classes compare on the reading test? This question is complicated, since there are many ways to compare the classes. To answer it, we need several new concepts.

Since we wish to compare the classes as a whole, we need to take the overall performances into account rather than individual scores. Numbers that give some indication of the overall "average" of some data are called **measures of central tendency**. The three measures of central tendency that we study in this chapter are the mode, median, and mean.

Mode, Median, Mean To compare these two classes, we first begin by putting the scores from the two classes in increasing order.

Class 1: 4.3, 4.9, 4.9, 5.1, 5.2, 5.2, 5.3, 5.3, 5.3, 5.4, 5.4, 5.6, 5.6, 5.7, 5.8, 5.8, 5.9, 6.1, 6.2, 6.9

Class 2: 3.6, 3.7, 4.1, 4.4, 4.7, 4.7, 4.7, 4.9, 5.0, 5.0, 5.4, 5.5, 5.6, 5.6, 6.2, 6.3, 6.8, 7.5, 7.8, 8.4

The most frequently occurring score in class 1 is 5.3 (it occurs three times), while in class 2 it is 4.7 (it also occurs three times). Each of the numbers 5.3 and 4.7 is called the mode score for its respective list of scores.

DEFINITION

Mode

In a list of numbers, the number that occurs most frequently is called the **mode**. There can be more than one mode, for example, if several numbers occur most frequently. If each number appears equally often, there is no mode.

The mode for a class gives us some very rough information about the general performance of the class. It is unaffected by all the other scores. On the basis of the mode scores *only*, it appears that class 1 scored higher than class 2.

The median score for a class is the "middle score" or "halfway" point in a list of the scores that is arranged in increasing (or decreasing) order. The median of the data set 7, 11, 13, 17, 23 is 13. For the data set 7, 11, 13, 17, there is no middle score; thus the median is taken to be the average of 11 and 13 (the two middle scores), or 12. The following precise definition states how to find the median of any data set.

DEFINITION

Median

Suppose that $x_1, x_2, x_3, \ldots, x_n$ is a collection of numbers in increasing order; that is, $x_1 \leq x_2 \leq x_3 \leq \cdots \leq x_n$. If n is odd, the **median** of the numbers is the middle score in the list; that is, the median is the number with subscript $\frac{n+1}{2}$. If n is even, the **median** is the arithmetic average of the two middle scores; that is, the median is one-half of the sum of the two numbers with subscripts $\frac{n}{2}$ and $\frac{n}{2} + 1$.

Since there is an even number of scores (20) in each class, we average the tenth and eleventh scores. The median for class 1 is 5.4. For class 2, the median is 5.2 (verify). On the basis of the median scores *only*, it appears that class 1 scored higher than class 2. Notice that the median does not take into account the magnitude of any scores except the score (or scores) in the middle. Hence it is not affected by extreme scores. Also, the median is not necessarily a member of the original set of scores if there are an even number of scores.

Example 10.12 Find the mode and median for each collection of numbers.

a. 1, 2, 3, 3, 4, 6, 9   **b.** 1, 1, 2, 3, 4, 5, 10
c. 0, 1, 2, 3, 4, 4, 5, 5   **d.** 1, 2, 3, 4

SOLUTION

a. The mode is 3, since it occurs more often than any other number. The median is also 3, since it is the middle score in this ordered list of numbers.

b. The mode is 1 and the median is 3.

c. There are two modes, 4 and 5. Here we have an even number of scores. Hence we average the two middle scores to compute the median. The median is $\frac{3+4}{2} = 3.5$. Note that the median is not one of the scores in this case.

d. The median is $\frac{2+3}{2} = 2.5$. There is no mode, since each number occurs equally often. ∎

From Example 10.12 we observe that the mode can be equal to, less than, or greater than the median [see parts (a), (b), and (c), respectively].

A third, and perhaps the most useful, measure of central tendency is the mean, also called the **arithmetic average**.

Algebraic Reasoning
In order to define the mean for any size data set, a variable, x, is used to represent the numbers in the collection and the subscript, n, is used to represent the number of elements in the data set. The use of variables streamlines the definition and represents all possible cases.

Reflection from Research
A difficult concept for students is that the mean is not necessarily a member of the data set (Brown & Silver, 1989).

DEFINITION

Mean

Suppose that $x_1, x_2, \ldots, x_n$ is a collection of numbers. The **mean** of the collection is

$$\bar{x} = \frac{x_1 + x_2 + \cdots + x_n}{n}.$$

The mean for each class is obtained by summing all the scores and dividing the sum by the total number of scores. For our two fifth-grade classes, we can compute the means as in Table 10.11.

TABLE 10.11

CLASS	SUM OF SCORES	MEAN
1	109.9	$\frac{109.9}{20} = 5.495$
2	109.9	$\frac{109.9}{20} = 5.495$

On the basis of the mean scores, the classes performed equivalently. That is, the "average student" in each class scored 5.495 on the reading test. This means that if all the students had equal scores (and the class total was the same), each student would have a score of 5.495. The mean takes every score into account and hence is affected by extremely high or low scores. Among the mean, median, and mode, any one of the three can be the largest or smallest measure of central tendency.

The mean of a data set can be found using the T1–34 II calculator. For example, to find the mean of 5, 5, 13, 15, and 17, first press [2nd] [STAT] [ENTER]. This will put the calculator in statistics mode with one variable. Both values of 5 can be entered separately or entered once with a frequency of 2. Enter the data as follows:

$$[DATA]\ 5\ [\blacktriangledown]\ 2\ [\blacktriangledown]\ 13\ [\blacktriangledown]\ [\blacktriangledown]\ 15\ [\blacktriangledown]\ [\blacktriangledown]\ 17\ [ENTER]$$

Once the data are entered, the mean is computed by pressing [STATVAR] and then pressing the right arrow once so that $\bar{x}$ is underlined. Since $\bar{x}$ is the symbol commonly used to represent the mean, the second line of the display is [11], which is the mean of the five numbers above.

Reflection from Research
It is worthwhile to demonstrate the need for other measures of central tendency by pointing out the main weakness of the mean—the extent to which its value can be affected by extreme scores (Bohan & Moreland, 1981).

Example 10.13 Find the mean, median, and mode for the following sets of data that represent the monthly salaries of two small companies. What do you observe about the mode, median, and mean for the two sets of data?

Company A: $3,300, $2,500, $4,200, $3,100, $6,200, $3,300, $3,500, $5,100
Company B: $2,500, $9,200, $3,100, $5,100, $3,300, $3,500, $4,200, $3,300,

SOLUTION
Company A:
First list the numbers from smallest to largest.

$2,400, $3,100, $3,300, $3,300, $3,500, $4,200, $5,100, $6,200

From this list the mode and median are easily identified.

$$\text{Mode} = \$3,300$$

$$\text{Median} = \frac{\$3,300 + \$3,500}{2} = \$3,400$$

$$\text{Mean} =$$

$$\frac{\$2,500 + \$3,100 + 2 \cdot \$3,300 + \$3,500 + \$4,200 + \$5,100 + \$6,200}{8} = \$3,900$$

Company B:
If this data set is also ordered, it can be seen that this set of numbers is the same as the previous data set except for the largest value.

$2,500, $3,100, $3,300, $3,300, $3,500, $4,200, $5,100, $9,200

Changing only the largest value in the data set did not change the mode or median so they are the same as for the previous set of numbers.

$$\text{Mode} = \$3,300$$
$$\text{Median} = \$3,400$$
$$\text{Mean} = \$4,275$$

If the owner of company B wanted to promote how much her employees are paid, she would likely choose the mean as the measure of central tendency because one employee's high salary makes the company mean higher. If an employee representative wanted to make a different point, they would choose the mode or median salary because they are less affected by one large salary.

NCTM Standard
All students should discuss and understand the correspondence between data sets and their graphical representations, especially histograms, stem-and-leaf plots, box plots, and scatterplots.

Box and Whisker Plots   A popular application of the median is a **box and whisker plot** or simply a **box plot**. To construct a box and whisker plot, we first find the lowest score, the median, the highest score, and two additional statistics, namely the lower and upper quartiles. We define the lower and upper quartiles using the median. To find the lower and upper quartiles, arrange the scores in increasing order. With an even number of scores, say $2n$, the **lower quartile** is the median of the n smallest scores. The **upper quartile** is the median of the n largest scores. With an odd number of scores, say $2n + 1$, the lower quartile is the median of the n smallest scores, and the upper quartile is the median of the n largest scores.

We will use the reading test scores from class 1 as an illustration:

$$4.3, 4.9, 4.9, 5.1, 5.2, 5.2, 5.3, 5.3, 5.3, 5.4,$$
$$5.4, 5.6, 5.6, 5.7, 5.8, 5.8, 5.9, 6.1, 6.2, 6.9$$

Lowest score = 4.3
Lower quartile = median of 10 lowest scores = 5.2
Median = 5.4
Upper quartile = median of 10 highest scores = 5.8
Highest score = 6.9

Next, we plot these five statistics on a number line, then make a box from the lower quartile to the upper quartile, indicating the median with a line crossing the box. Finally, we connect the lowest score to the lower quartile with a line segment, one "whisker," and the upper quartile to the highest score with another line segment, the other whisker (Figure 10.43). The box represents about 50% of the scores, and each whisker represents about 25%.

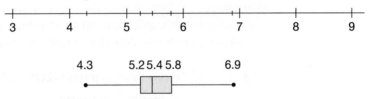

Figure 10.43

The difference between the upper and lower quartiles is called the **interquartile range (IQR)**. This statistic is useful for identifying extremely small or large values of the data, called outliers. An **outlier** is commonly defined as any value of the data that lies more than 1.5 IQR units below the lower quartile or more than 1.5 IQR units above the upper quartile. For the class scores, IQR = 5.8 − 5.2 = 0.6, so that 1.5 IQR units = (1.5)(0.6) = 0.9. Hence any score below 5.2 − 0.9 = 4.3 or above 5.8 + 0.9 = 6.7 is an outlier. Thus 6.9 is an outlier for these data; that is, it is an unusually large value given the relative closeness of the rest of the data. Later in this section, we will see an explanation of outliers using z-scores. Often outliers are indicated using an asterisk. In the case of the earlier reading test scores, 6.9 was identified to be an outlier. This is indicated in Figure 10.44. When there are outliers, the whiskers end at the value farthest away from the box that is still within 1.5 IQR units from the end.

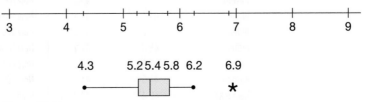

Figure 10.44

We can visually compare the performances of class 1 and class 2 on the reading test by comparing their box and whisker plots. The reading scores from class 2 are 3.6, 3.7, 4.1, 4.4, 4.7, 4.7, 4.7, 4.9, 5.0, 5.0, 5.4, 5.5, 5.6, 5.6, 6.2, 6.3, 6.8, 7.5, 7.8, and 8.4. Thus we have

> Lowest score = 3.6
> Lower quartile = 4.7
> Median = 5.2
> Upper quartile = 6.25
> Highest score = 8.4
> 1.5 IQR = 2.325.

The box and whisker plots for both classes appear with outliers in Figure 10.45.

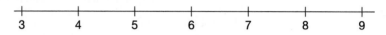

NCTM Standard
All students should describe the shape and important features of a set of data and compare related data sets, with an emphasis on how the data are distributed.

Figure 10.45

From the two box and whisker plots, we see that the scores for class 2 are considerably more widely spread; the box is wider, and the distances to the extreme scores are greater.

> **Example 10.14** Teacher salary averages for 2005–2006 are given in Table 10.12. Construct a stem and leaf plot as well as box and whisker plots for the data. How do the salaries compare?

TABLE 10.12 Teacher Salary Averages in 2005–2006 (× $1000)

STATE	ELEMENTARY TEACHERS	SECONDARY TEACHERS	STATE	ELEMENTARY TEACHERS	SECONDARY TEACHERS
Alabama	40.0	40.8	Louisiana	40.0	40.0
Alaska	53.6	53.6	Maine	40.8	40.6
Arizona	44.7	44.7	Maryland	54.1	54.6
Arkansas	42.8	42.8	Massachusetts	56.4	56.4
California	59.8	59.8	Michigan	54.7	54.7
Colorado	44.4	44.4	Minnesota	48.5	48.5
Connecticut	59.1	60.4	Mississippi	40.1	41.3
Delaware	54.1	54.4	Missouri	40.5	40.4
DC	59.0	59.0	Montana	39.8	39.8
Florida	43.3	43.3	Nebraska	40.4	40.4
Georgia	47.7	49.2	Nevada	44.0	45.1
Hawaii	49.3	49.3	New Hampshire	45.3	45.3
Idaho	41.2	41.1	New Jersey	57.2	59.3
Illinois	53.2	61.2	New Mexico	41.2	42.8
Indiana	48.3	47.2	New York	57.4	57.4
Iowa	41.2	40.8	North Carolina	43.9	43.9
Kansas	41.5	41.5	North Dakota	38.1	37.1
Kentucky	42.4	43.2	Ohio	50.3	50.3

STATE	ELEMENTARY TEACHERS	SECONDARY TEACHERS	STATE	ELEMENTARY TEACHERS	SECONDARY TEACHERS
Oklahoma	38.1	39.5	Utah	40.0	40.0
Oregon	49.9	50.3	Vermont	46.6	46.6
Pennsylvania	54.0	54.0	Virginia	43.8	43.8
Rhode Island	54.7	54.7	Washington	46.4	46.2
South Carolina	40.9	41.8	West Virginia	38.1	38.8
South Dakota	34.8	34.5	Wisconsin	46.4	46.4
Tennessee	42.1	43.6	Wyoming	43.2	43.3
Texas	41.3	42.2			

Source: National Education Association.

SOLUTION The stem and leaf plot is given in Table 10.13, where the statistics for constructing the box and whisker plots are shown in boldface type.

TABLE 10.13

ELEMENTARY TEACHERS	STEM	SECONDARY TEACHERS
8	34.	**1**
	35.	
	36.	
	37.	1
1 1 1	38.	8
8	39.	5 8
9 8 5 4 1 0 0 0	40.	0 0 4 4 6 8 8
5 3 2 2 2	41.	**1** 3 5 8
8 4 1	42.	2 8 8
9 8 3 2	43.	2 3 3 6 8 9
7 4 **0**	44.	**4** 7
3	45.	1 3
6 4 4	46.	2 4 6
7	47.	2
5 3	48.	5
9 3	49.	2 3
3	50.	3 3
	51.	
	52.	
6 **2**	53.	**6**
7 7 1 1 0	54.	0 4 6 7 7
	55.	
4	56.	4
4 2	57.	4
	58.	
8 1 0	59.	0 3 8
	60.	4
	61.	**2**

Thus we have the following quartile statistics for constructing the box and whisker plots (Table 10.14). Using the statistics in Table 10.14, we can construct the box and whisker plots (Figure 10.46).

TABLE 10.14

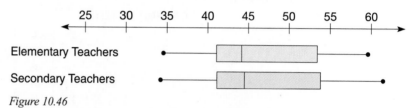

	ELEMENTARY TEACHERS	SECONDARY TEACHERS
Lowest data value	34.8	34.1
Lower quartile	40.9	41.1
Median	44	44.4
Upper quartile	53.2	53.6
Highest data value	59.8	61.2
Interquartile range	12.3	12.5
1.5 * IQR	18.45	18.75
Outliers	$<40.9 - 18.45 = 22.45$	$<41.1 - 18.75 = 22.35$
	$>53.2 + 18.45 = 71.65$	$>53.6 + 18.75 = 72.35$

Since the box and whisker plot for the secondary teachers lies to the right of that of the elementary teachers, we see that secondary teachers were generally paid more.

Notice how the box and whisker plots of Figure 10.46 give us a *direct visual comparison* of the statistics in Table 10.14.

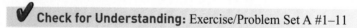

Figure 10.46

Percentiles   When constructing box and whisker plots, we used medians and quartiles. Medians essentially divide the data so that 50% of the data are equal to or below the median. Similarly, quartiles divide the data into fourths. In other words, one-fourth of the data points are equal to or below the lower quartile and the other three-fourths of the data points are above it. The upper quartile is equal to or above three-fourths of the data and below the remaining one-fourth of the data. If we were to divide the data into 100 equal parts, **percentiles** could be used to mark the dividing points in the data. For example, the first percentile would separate the bottom 1% of the data from the top 99% and the 37th percentile would separate the bottom 37% of the data from the upper 63%. Formally, a number is in the ***n*th percentile** of some data if it is greater than or equal to *n*% of the data.

Percentiles are frequently used in connection with scores on large standardized tests like the ACT and SAT or when talking about the height and weight of babies. The doctor may say that your baby is in the 70th percentile for height and the 45th percentile for weight. This would mean that the baby is taller than 70% and heavier than 45% of the babies of the same age. Percentiles will be discussed later in this section.

✔ **Check for Understanding:** Exercise/Problem Set A #1–11

Measuring Dispersion

Statistics that give an indication of how the data are "spread out" or distributed are called **measures of dispersion**. The **range** of the scores is simply the difference of the largest and smallest scores. For the class 1 scores at the beginning of this section, the range is $6.9 - 4.3 = 2.6$. For class 2, the range of the scores is $8.4 - 3.6 = 4.8$. The range gives us limited information about the distribution of scores, since it takes only the extremes into account, ignoring the intervening scores.

Variance and Standard Deviation   Perhaps the most common measures of dispersion are the variance and the standard deviation.

DEFINITION

Variance

Algebraic Reasoning
An understanding of what each variable represents is essential for understanding the equation for variance.

The **variance** of a collection of numbers is the arithmetic average of the squared differences between each number and the mean of the collection of numbers. Symbolically, for the numbers, $x_1, x_2, \ldots, x_n$, with mean $\bar{x}$, the variance is

$$\frac{(x - \bar{x})^2 + (x_2 - \bar{x})^2 + \cdots + (x_n - \bar{x})^2}{n}.$$

To find the variance of a set of numbers, use the following procedure.

1. Find the mean, $\bar{x}$.
2. For each number x, find the difference between the number and the mean, namely $x - \bar{x}$.
3. Square all the differences in step 2, namely $(x - \bar{x})^2$.
4. Find the arithmetic average of all the squares in step 3. This average is the variance.

Example 10.15   Find the variance for the numbers 5, 7, 7, 8, 10, 11.

SOLUTION   The mean, $\bar{x} = \dfrac{5 + 7 + 7 + 8 + 10 + 11}{6} = 8.$

	STEP 1 $\bar{x}$	STEP 2 $x - \bar{x}$	STEP 3 $(x - \bar{x})^2$
5	8	−3	9
7	8	−1	1
7	8	−1	1
8	8	0	0
10	8	2	4
11	8	3	9

Step 4: $\dfrac{9 + 1 + 1 + 0 + 4 + 9}{6} = 4$, the variance.   ■

DEFINITION

Standard Deviation

The **standard deviation** is the square root of the variance.

Example 10.16   Find the standard deviation for the data in Example 10.15.

SOLUTION   The standard deviation is the square root of the variance, 4. Hence the standard deviation is 2.   ■

In general, the greater the standard deviation, the more the scores are spread out.

Finding the standard deviation for a collection of data is a straightforward task when using a calculator that possesses the appropriate statistical keys. Usually, a calculator must be set in its statistics or standard deviation mode. Then, after the data are entered one at a time, the mean and standard deviation can be found simply by pressing appropriate keys. For example, assuming that the calculator is in its statistics mode, enter the data 3, 4, 7, 8, 9 using the $\boxed{\Sigma +}$ key as follows:

$$3 \boxed{\Sigma +} \, 4 \boxed{\Sigma +} \, 7 \boxed{\Sigma +} \, 8 \boxed{\Sigma +} \, 9 \boxed{\Sigma +}$$

Pressing the $\boxed{n}$ key yields the number 5, which is the number of data entered. Pressing $\boxed{\bar{x}}$ yields 6.2, the mean of our data. Pressing $\boxed{\sigma_n}$ yields 2.315167381, the standard deviation. Squaring this result yields the variance, 5.36.

NOTE: When the key representing standard deviation is pressed in the preceding example, a number greater than 2.315167381 appears on some calculators. This difference is due to two different interpretations of standard deviation. If *all n* of the data for some experiment are used in calculating the standard deviation, then $\boxed{\sigma_n}$ is the correct choice. However, if only *n* pieces of data from a large collection of numbers (more than *n*) are used, the variance is calculated with an *n* − 1 in the denominator. Some calculators have a $\boxed{\sigma_n - 1}$ key to distinguish this case. Computing the standard deviation on the TI–34 II is identical to computing the mean described earlier in this section except in the final step we select *Sx* or *σx*.

Let us return to our comparison of the two fifth-grade classes on their reading test. Table 10.15 gives the variance and standard deviation for each class, rounded to two decimal places.

TABLE 10.15

CLASS	VARIANCE	STANDARD DEVIATION
1	0.29	0.54
2	1.67	1.29

Comparing the classes on the basis of the standard deviation shows that the scores in class 2 were more widely distributed than were the scores in class 1, since the greater the standard deviation, the larger the spread of scores. Hence class 2 is more heterogeneous in reading ability than is class 1. This finding may mean that more reading groups are needed in class 2 than in class 1 if students are grouped by ability. Although it is difficult to give a general rule of thumb about interpreting the standard deviation, it does allow us to compare several sets of data to see which set is more homogeneous. In summary, comparing the two classes on the basis of the mean scores, the classes performed equivalently on the reading. However, on the basis of the standard deviation, class 2 is more heterogeneous than class 1.

In addition to obtaining information about the entire class, we can use the mean and standard deviation to compare an individual student's performances on different tests relative to the class as a whole. Example 10.17 illustrates how we might do this.

Example 10.17 Adrienne made the following scores on two achievement tests. On which test did she perform better relative to the class?

	TEST 1	TEST 2
Adrienne	45	40
Mean	30	25
Standard deviation	10	15

SOLUTION Comparing Adrienne's scores only to the means seems to suggest that she performed equally well on both tests, since her score is 15 points higher than the mean in each case. However, using the standard deviation as a unit of distance, we see that she was 1.5 (15 divided by 10) standard deviations above the mean on test 1 and only 1 (15 divided by 15) standard deviation above the mean on test 2. Hence she performed better on test 1, relative to the whole class. ■

We are able to make comparisons as in Example 10.17 more easily if we use z-scores.

DEFINITION

z-score

The **z-score**, z, for a particular score, x, is $z = \dfrac{x - \bar{x}}{s}$, where $\bar{x}$ is the mean of all the scores and s is the standard deviation.

The z-score of a number indicates how many standard deviations the number is away from the mean. Numbers above the mean have positive z-scores, and numbers below the mean have negative z-scores.

Example 10.18   Compute Adrienne's z-score for tests 1 and 2 in Example 10.17.

SOLUTION For test 1, her z-score is $\dfrac{45 - 30}{10} = 1.5$, and for test 2, her z-score is $\dfrac{40 - 25}{15} = 1$. ■

Notice that Adrienne's z-score tells us how far her score was above the mean, measured in multiples of the standard deviation. Example 10.19 illustrates several other features of z-scores.

Example 10.19   Find the z-scores for the data 1, 1, 2, 3, 4, 9, 12, 18.

SOLUTION We first find the mean, $\bar{x}$, and the standard deviation, s.

$$\bar{x} = \frac{1 + 1 + 2 + 3 + 4 + 9 + 12 + 18}{8} = \frac{50}{8} = 6.25$$

$$s = 5.78 \text{ to two places (verify)}$$

Hence we can find the z-scores for each number in the set of data (Table 10.16). ■

TABLE 10.16

SCORE	Z-SCORE
1	$\dfrac{1 - 6.25}{5.78} = -0.91$
2	$\dfrac{2 - 6.25}{5.78} = -0.74$
3	$\dfrac{3 - 6.25}{5.78} = -0.56$
4	$\dfrac{4 - 6.25}{5.78} = -0.39$
9	$\dfrac{9 - 6.25}{5.78} = 0.48$
12	$\dfrac{12 - 6.25}{5.78} = 0.99$
18	$\dfrac{18 - 6.25}{5.78} = 2.03$

The computations in Table 10.16 suggest the following observations.

Case 1: If $x > \bar{x}$, then $x - \bar{x} > 0$, so $z = \dfrac{x - \bar{x}}{s} > 0$.

Conclusion: x is greater than the mean if and only if the z-score of x is positive.

Case 2: If $x = \bar{x}$, then $z = \dfrac{x - \bar{x}}{s} = \dfrac{\bar{x} - \bar{x}}{s} = 0$.

Conclusion: The z-score of the mean is 0.

Case 3: If $x < \bar{x}$, then $x - \bar{x} < 0$, so $z = \dfrac{x - \bar{x}}{s} < 0$.

Conclusion: x is less than the mean if and only if the z-score of x is negative.

✔️ **Check for Understanding:** Exercise/Problem Set A #12–15

Distributions

Large amounts of data are commonly organized in increasing order and pictured in relative frequency form in a histogram. The **relative frequency** that a number occurs is the percentage of the total amount of data that the number represents. For example, in a collection of 100 numbers, if the number 14 appears 6 times, the relative frequency of 14 is 6%. A graph of the data versus the relative frequency of each number in the data is called a **distribution**. Two hypothetical distributions are discussed in Example 10.20.

Example 10.20 For the data in Figures 10.47 and 10.48, identify the mode and describe any observable symmetry of the data.

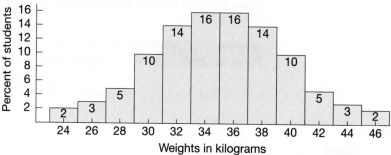

Figure 10.47

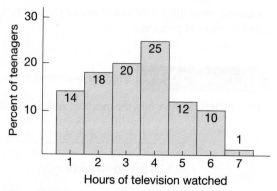

Figure 10.48

SOLUTION The distribution in Figure 10.47 has two modes, 35 and 36 kilograms. The modes are indicated by the "peaks" of the histogram. The distribution is also symmetrical, since there is a vertical line that would serve as a "mirror" line of symmetry, namely a line through 35 on the horizontal axis. The distribution in Figure 10.48 has only one mode (4 hours) and is not symmetrical.   ∎

In Figure 10.47 students' weights were rounded to the nearest 2 kilograms, producing 12 possible values from 24 to 46. Suppose, instead, that very accurate weights were obtained for the students, say to the nearest gram (one one-thousandth of a kilogram). Suppose, also, that a smooth curve was used to connect the midpoints of the "steps" of the histogram. One possibility is shown in Figure 10.49. The curve shows a symmetrical "bell-shaped" distribution with one mode.

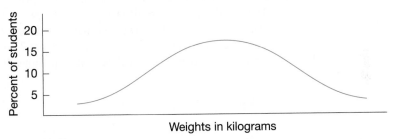

Figure 10.49

Distributions of physical measurements such as heights and weights for one sex, for large groups of data, frequently are smooth bell-shaped curves, such as the curve in Figure 10.49. There is a geometrical, or visual, way to interpret the median, mean, and mode for such smooth distributions. The vertical line through the median cuts the region between the curve and the horizontal axis into two regions of equal area (Figure 10.50). (NOTE: This characterization of the median does not always hold for histograms because they are not "smooth.")

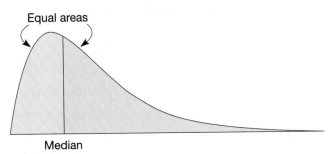

Figure 10.50

The mean is the point on the horizontal axis where the distribution would balance (Figure 10.51). This characterization of the mean holds for all distributions, histograms as well as smooth curves. Since the mode is the most frequently occurring value of the data, the highest point or points of the graph occur above the mode(s).

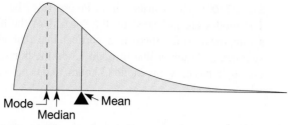

Figure 10.51

A special type of smooth, bell-shaped distribution is the **normal distribution**. The normal distribution is symmetrical, with the mean, median, and mode all being equal. Figure 10.52 shows the general shape of the normal distribution. (The technical definition of the normal distribution is more complicated than we can go into here.) An interesting feature of the normal distribution is that it is completely determined by the mean, $\bar{x}$, and the standard deviation, s. The "peak" is always directly above the mean. The standard deviation determines the shape, in the following way. The larger the standard deviation, the lower and flatter is the curve. That is, if two normal distributions are represented using the same horizontal and vertical scales, the one with the larger standard deviation will be lower and flatter (Figure 10.53).

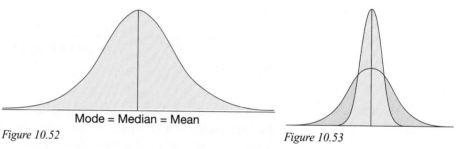

Figure 10.52

Figure 10.53

The distribution of the weights in Figure 10.47 is essentially normal, so we could determine everything about the curve from the mean and the standard deviation as follows:

1. About 68% of the data are between $\bar{x} - s$ and $\bar{x} + s$.
2. About 95% of the data are between $\bar{x} - 2s$ and $\bar{x} + 2s$.
3. About 99.7% of the data are between $\bar{x} - 3s$ and $\bar{x} + 3s$ (Figure 10.54).

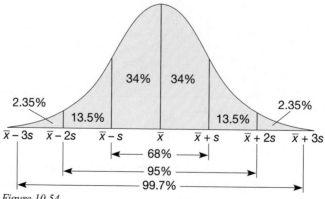

Figure 10.54

We can picture our results about *z*-scores for normal distributions in Figure 10.55.

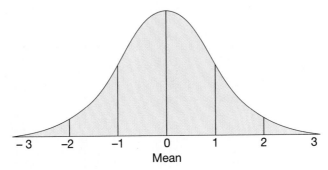

Figure 10.55

From Figures 10.54 and 10.55, we see the following:

1. About 68% of the scores are within one *z*-score of the mean.

2. About 95% of the scores are within two *z*-scores of the mean.

3. About 99.7% of the scores are within three *z*-scores of the mean.

z-scores of 2 or more in a normal distribution are very high (higher than 97.5% of all other scores—50% below the mean plus 47.5% up to $z = 2$). Also, *z*-scores of 3 or more are extremely high. On the other hand, *z*-scores of -2 or less from a normal distribution are lower than 97.5% of all scores.

A *z*-score of 2 in a normal distribution is very high; in fact, it is about the 97.5 percentile. By comparing the graphs in Figures 10.54 and 10.55, it can be seen that a *z*-score of 2 is above 97.5% of the scores. On the other hand, a *z*-score of -1 is between the 15th and 16th percentiles. Now that we see this connection between *z*-scores and percentiles, we could compute what percentile a score on the SAT would be in.

Example 10.21 In 2009, the mean and standard deviation for the math portion of the SAT were 515 and 116 respectively. If Quinn scored 696 on the math portion, what percentile was he in?

SOLUTION Since Quinn scored a 696, his *z*-score would be computed using the mean of 515 and standard deviation of 116 for that year. This would give him a *z*-score of

$$z = \frac{696 - 515}{116} \approx 1.5603$$

We can now refer to the percentiles and *z*-scores in Table 10.17 to see that Quinn's score on the math SAT in 2009 was about the 94th percentile and, therefore, it was higher than 94% of the other scores.

TABLE 10.17

PERCENTILE	z-SCORE	PERCENTILE	z-SCORE	PERCENTILE	z-SCORE
1	−2.326	34	−0.412	67	0.44
2	−2.054	35	−0.385	68	0.468
3	−1.881	36	−0.358	69	0.496
4	−1.751	37	−0.332	70	0.524
5	−1.645	38	−0.305	71	0.553
6	−1.555	39	−0.279	72	0.583
7	−1.476	40	−0.253	73	0.613
8	−1.405	41	−0.228	74	0.643
9	−1.341	42	−0.202	75	0.674
10	−1.282	43	−0.176	76	0.706
11	−1.227	44	−0.151	77	0.739
12	−1.175	45	−0.126	78	0.772
13	−1.126	46	−0.1	79	0.806
14	−1.08	47	−0.075	80	0.842
15	−1.036	48	−0.05	81	0.878
16	−0.994	49	−0.025	82	0.915
17	−0.954	50	0	83	0.954
18	−0.915	51	0.025	84	0.994
19	−0.878	52	0.05	85	1.036
20	−0.842	53	0.075	86	1.08
21	−0.806	54	0.1	87	1.126
22	−0.772	55	0.126	88	1.175
23	−0.739	56	0.151	89	1.227
24	−0.706	57	0.176	90	1.282
25	−0.674	58	0.202	91	1.341
26	−0.643	59	0.228	92	1.405
27	−0.613	60	0.253	93	1.476
28	−0.583	61	0.279	94	1.555
29	−0.553	62	0.305	95	1.645
30	−0.524	63	0.332	96	1.751
31	−0.496	64	0.358	97	1.881
32	−0.468	65	0.385	98	2.054
33	−0.44	66	0.412	99	2.326

Tabulated values of z-scores for a normal distribution can be used to explain the relatively unlikely occurrence of outliers. For example, for data from a normal distribution, small outliers have z-scores less than −2.6 and are smaller than 99.5% of the data. Similarly, large outliers from a normal distribution have z-scores greater than 2.6 and are larger than 99.5% of the data. Thus outliers represent very rare observations. The normal distribution is a very commonly occurring distribution for many large collections of data. Hence the mean, standard deviation, and z-scores are especially important statistics.

✔ **Check for Understanding:** Exercise/Problem Set A #16–18

MATHEMATICAL MORSEL

Did it rain a lot or didn't it? Sometimes the answer to that question depends on how you want to measure it. For example, during October 1994 in Portland, Oregon, the most commonly occurring daily precipitation total (the mode) was 0 inches. In the same month the median daily precipitation total was 0 inches. These measures would seem to indicate that it was a dry month. But was it? The mean daily precipitation in October of 1994 was 0.27 inches. By most standards, this measure would indicate that it did rain a lot. How could this happen? How could two measures say it was dry and another measure indicate that it was wet? Here's how. On 21 of the days in that October, there was no measurable rain and yet on three of the 10 days that it did rain, it rained 2.33, 2.44, and 2.44 inches.

OCTOBER 1994

DAY OF MONTH	1	2	3	4	5	6	7	8	9	10	
DAILY PRECIPITATION	0	0	0	0	0	0	0	0	0	0	
DAY OF MONTH	11	12	13	14	15	16	17	18	19	20	
DAILY PRECIPITATION	0	0	.12	.13	0	0	T	0	T	.03	
DAY OF MONTH	21	22	23	24	25	26	27	28	29	30	31
DAILY PRECIPITATION	13	0	T	0	.09	2.33	2.44	.24	0	.46	2.44

| Section 10.3 | **EXERCISE / PROBLEM SET A** |

EXERCISES

1. Calculate the mean, median, and mode for each collection of data.
   a. 8, 9, 9, 10, 11, 12
   b. 17, 2, 10, 29, 14, 13
   c. 4.2, 3.8, 9.7, −4.8, 0, −10.0
   d. 29, 42, −65, −73, 48, 17, 0, 0, −36

2. Calculate the mean, median, and mode for each collection of data.
   a. $-2 + \sqrt{7}, \sqrt{7}, 3 + \sqrt{7}, -4 + \sqrt{7}, 5 + \sqrt{7}, 3 + \sqrt{7}$
   b. $-2\pi, 4\pi, 0, 6\pi, 10\pi, 4\pi$
   c. 7.37, 5.37, 10.37, 2.37, 8.37, 5.37

3. Scores for Mrs. McClellan's class on mathematics and reading tests are given in the following table.

Which student is the "average" student for the group?

STUDENT	MATHEMATICS TEST SCORE	READING TEST SCORE
Rob	73	87
Doug	83	58
Myron	62	90
Alan	89	70
Ed	96	98

4. All the students in a school were weighed. Their average weight was 31.4 kilograms, and their total weight was 18,337.6 kilograms. How many students are in the school?

5. A class of 24 students took a 75-point test. If the mean was 63, is it possible that 18 of the students got a score of 59 or lower? Explain.

6. Which of the following situations are possible regarding the mean, median, and mode for a set of data? Give examples.
   a. Mean = median = mode
   b. Mean < median = mode

7. Make a box and whisker plot for the following heights of children, in centimeters.

   120, 121, 121, 124, 126, 128, 132, 134, 140, 142, 147, 150, 152, 160

8. **a.** Make box and whisker plots on the same number line for the following test scores.

   Class 1: 57, 58, 59, 60, 62, 72, 75,
   76, 76, 79, 80, 80, 81, 86,
   86, 86, 87, 93, 93, 93
   Class 2: 66, 67, 68, 75, 77, 77, 79,
   82, 83, 84, 85, 85, 87, 87,
   90, 90, 92, 92, 92, 95

   b. Which class performed better on the test? Explain.

9. Use quartiles and medians to answer the following questions about the data in Exercise 8 of Part A.
   a. What score is above 75% of the scores in class 1?
   b. What score is at the 50th percentile of class 2?
   c. What score is at the 25th percentile of class 1?

10. Given in the table are projected changes in the U.S. population for the period 1986–2010. For example, the population of Alaska is expected to increase 38.7%. Make a box and whisker plot for states east of the Mississippi River (in boldface) and beneath it a box and whisker plot for states west of the Mississippi River. What trends, if any, do your box and whisker plots reveal?

Projected Population Changes (1986–2010)

STATE	PERCENT CHANGE	STATE	PERCENT CHANGE	STATE	PERCENT CHANGE
AK	38.7	LA	1.0	OH	−3.3
AL	13.2	MA	7.1	OK	6.2
AR	10.3	MD	25.2	OR	10.5
AZ	51.4	ME	11.1	PA	−6.4
CA	34.4	MI	−0.6	RI	10.9
CO	23.6	MN	8.4	SC	22.9
CT	10.4	MO	8.6	SD	1.9
DE	23.3	MS	14.6	TN	13.8
FL	43.8	MT	−3.1	TX	30.3
GA	42.3	NC	26.5	UT	27.8
HI	41.2	ND	−10.4	VA	25.9
IA	−17.4	NE	−4.3	VT	12.0
ID	7.4	NH	37.5	WA	17.4
IL	−0.5	NJ	16.0	WI	−4.1
IN	−1.8	NM	45.0	WV	−16.5
KS	4.2	NV	46.7	WY	−4.1
KY	−0.5	NY	2.1		

Source: U.S. Bureau of the Census.

11. Thirty-two major league baseball players have hit more than 450 home runs in their careers as of 2007.

PLAYER	HOME RUNS
Barry Bonds	762
Hank Aaron	755
Babe Ruth	714
Willie Mays	660
Ken Griffey, Jr.	630
Sammy Sosa	609
Frank Robinson	586
Mark McGwire	583
Alex Rodriguez	583
Harmon Killebrew	573
Rafael Palmeiro	569
Jim Thome	564
Reggie Jackson	563
Mike Schmidt	548
Manny Ramirez	546
Mickey Mantle	536
Jimmie Foxx	534
Willie McCovey	521
Frank Thomas	521
Ted Williams	521
Ernie Banks	512
Eddie Matthews	512
Mel Ott	511
Carlos Delgodo	509
Gary Sheffield	509
Eddie Murray	504
Lou Gehrig	493
Fred McGriff	493
Stan Musial	475
Willie Stargell	475
Dave Winfield	465
Jose Canseco	462
Carl Yastrzemski	452

Source: baseball-reference.com

   a. Make a stem and leaf plot and a box and whisker plot of the data.
   b. Outliers between 1.5 and 3.0 IQR are called **mild outliers**, and those greater than 3.0 IQR are called **extreme outliers**. What outliers, mild or extreme, occur?

12. Compute the variance and standard deviation for each collection of data.
   a. 4, 4, 4, 4, 4
   b. −4, −3, −2, −1, 0, 1, 2, 3, 4
   c. 14.6, −18.7, 29.3, 15.4, −17.5

13. Compute the variance and standard deviation for each collection of data. What do you observe?
   a. 1, 2, 3, 4, 5   **b.** 3, 6, 9, 12, 15
   c. 5, 10, 15, 20, 25   **d.** −6, −12, −18, −24, −30
   e. Use the Chapter 10 dynamic spreadsheet *Standard Deviation* on our Web site to find the standard deviation for the sets of data 3, 8, 13, 18, 23 and 31, 36, 41, 46, 51. Describe how the data and results in part (c) compare to these sets of data and their standard deviations.

14. Compute the mean, median, mode, variance, and standard deviation for the data in the following histogram.

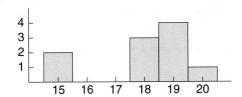

15. Compute the *z*-scores for the following test scores.

STUDENT	SCORE	STUDENT	SCORE
Larry	59	Lou	62
Curly	43	Jerry	65
Moe	71	Dean	75
Bud	89		

16. Suppose a class test has scores with a normal distribution.
   a. If you have a score that is 1 standard deviation above the mean, what percent of the rest of the class has a score below yours? What is your *z*-score?

b. If you have a score that is 2 standard deviations above the mean, what percent of the rest of the class has a score below yours? What is your *z*-score?

17. In a class with test scores in a normal distribution, a teacher can "grade on a curve" using the following guideline for assigning grades:

   A: *z*-score > 2
   B: $1 <$ *z*-score ≤ 2
   C: $-1 <$ *z*-score ≤ 1
   D: $-2 <$ *z*-score ≤ -1
   F: *z*-score ≤ -2

On a 100-point test with a mean of 85 and a standard deviation of 5, find the test scores that would yield each grade.

18. On the critical reasoning portion of the SAT in 2009 the mean was 501 and the standard deviation was 112. If Marcella had a score of 725 on the exam,
   a. What percentile is she in?
   b. What percent of all of the students who took the exam had a score lower than hers?

PROBLEMS

19. If the average (mean) mid-twenties male weighs 169 pounds and a weight of 150 is in the 31st percentile, what is the standard deviation of the weights in this age group?

20. Vince's 2009 ACT reading score was below 33% of all of the scores. If the mean and standard deviation for all ACT reading scores in 2009 were 21.4 and 6.2 respectively, what was Vince's score?

21. Use the Chapter 10 dynamic spreadsheet *Standard Deviation* on our Web site to find two sets of data where the standard deviation of one set is twice the standard deviation of the other. What process did you use to find the sets of data?

22. The class average on a reading test was 27.5 out of 40 possible points. The 19 girls in the class scored 532 points. How many total points did the 11 boys score?

23. When 100 students took a test, the average score was 77.1. Two more students took the test. The sum of their scores was 125. What is the new average?

24. The mean score for a set of 35 mathematics tests was 41.6, with a standard deviation of 4.2. What was the sum of all the scores?

25. Here are Mr. Emery's class scores for two tests. On which test did Lora do better relative to the entire class?

STUDENT	TEST 1 SCORE	TEST 2 SCORE
Lora	85	89
Verne	72	93
Harvey	89	96
Lorna	75	65
Jim	79	79
Betty	86	60

26. At a shoe store, which statistic would be most helpful to the manager when reordering shoes: mean, median, or mode? Explain.

27. a. On the same axes, draw a graph of two normal distributions with the same means but different variances. Which graph has a higher "peak"?
   b. On the same axes, draw a graph of two normal distributions with different means but equal variances. Which graph is farther to the right?

28. Reading test scores for Smithville had an average of 69.2. Nationally, the average was 60.3 with a standard deviation of 7.82. In Miss Brown's class, the average was 75.9.
  a. What is the z-score for Smithville's average score?

b. What is the z-score for Miss Brown's class average?
c. Assume that the distribution of all scores was a normal distribution. Approximately what percent of students in the country scored lower than Miss Brown's average?

Section 10.3 | EXERCISE / PROBLEM SET B

EXERCISES

1. Calculate the mean, median, and mode for each collection of data. Give exact answers.
  a. $-10, -9, -8, -7, 0, 0, 7, 8, 9, 10$
  b. $-5, -3, -1, 0, 3, 6$
  c. $-6.5, -6.3, -6.1, 6.0, 6.3, 6.6$
  d. $3 + \sqrt{2}, 4 + \sqrt{2}, 5 + \sqrt{2}, 6 + \sqrt{2}, 7 + \sqrt{2}$

2. Calculate the mean, median, and mode for each collection of data. Give exact answers.
  a. $\sqrt{2}, 3\sqrt{2}, -8\sqrt{2}, 4\sqrt{2}, 3\sqrt{2}, 0$
  b. $-3 + \pi, -8 + \pi, -15 + \pi, \pi, 4 + \pi, 4 + \pi, 18 + \pi$
  c. $\sqrt{2} + \pi, 2\sqrt{2} + \pi, \pi, -3\sqrt{2} + \pi, \sqrt{3} + \pi, \sqrt{3} + \pi$

3. Jamie made the following grades during fall term at State University. What was his grade point average? (A = 4 points, B = 3 points, C = 2, D = 1, F = 0.)

COURSE	CREDITS	GRADE
English	2	B
Chemistry	3	C
Mathematics	4	A
History	3	B
French	3	C

4. The students in a class were surveyed about their TV watching habits. The average number of hours of TV watched in a week was 23.4 hours. If the total hours of TV watching for the whole class was 608.4, how many students are in the class?

5. Twenty-seven students averaged 70 on their midterm. Could 21 of them have scored above 90? Explain.

6. Which of the following situations are possible regarding the mean, median, and mode for a set of data? Give examples.
  a. Mean < median < mode   **b.** Mean = median < mode

7. a. From the box and whisker plot for 80 test scores, find the lowest score, the highest score, the lower quartile, the upper quartile, and the median.

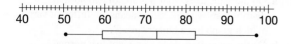

  b. Approximately how many scores are between the lowest score and the lower quartile? between the lower quartile and the upper quartile? between the lower quartile and the highest score?

8. a. Consider the following double stem and leaf plot.

	CLASS 1			CLASS 2
	9 6	0	5 7	
	8 7 6 4 1	1	2 3 4	
8 8 7 6 5 5 3 2 2 2 2 1		2	2 5 6 7 8 8 9	
	9 9 6 4 4 3 2	3	1 2 3 4 4 5 6 7	
	9 6 5 1	4	2 3 5 6 7 8 9	

Construct a box and whisker plot for each class on the same number line for the test scores.
  b. Which class performed better? Explain.

9. Use quartiles and medians to answer the following questions about the data in Exercise 8 of Part B.
  a. What score is below 75% of the scores in class 1?
  b. What score is above 75% of the scores in class 2?
  c. What score is at the 25th percentile of class 2?

10. Given in the table are school expenditures per student by state in 2006.

School Expenditures, 2006 ($\times$ 100)

STATE	EXPENDITURES PER STUDENT	STATE	EXPENDITURES PER STUDENT
AK	77	MT	86
AL	115	NC	93
AR	65	ND	72
AZ	80	NE	104
CA	83	NH	150
CO	82	NJ	84
CT	131	NM	146
DC	116	NV	74
DE	138	NY	87
FL	78	OH	97
GA	86	OK	69
HI	99	OR	86
IA	65	PA	107
ID	91	RI	126
IL	89	SC	81
IN	84	SD	78
KS	86	TN	70
KY	77	TX	75
LA	85	UT	55
MA	108	VA	128
MD	109	VT	95
ME	126	WA	80
MI	96	WI	94
MN	92	WV	100
MO	72	WY	114
MS	83		

Source: National Education Association.

a. Make a stem and leaf plot of the data, using one-digit stems.

b. What gaps or clusters occur?

c. Which, if any, data values are outliers (using IQR units)? What explanation is there for the occurrence of outliers in these data?

d. Make a box and whisker plot for states east of the Mississippi River (see Exercise 10 in Part A), and beneath it a box and whisker plot for states west of the Mississippi River. What trends, if any, do your box and whisker plots reveal?

11. Twenty-four baseball pitchers have won 300 or more games in their careers, as of 2009.

PITCHER	VICTORIES	PITCHER	VICTORIES
Cy Young	511	Eddie Plank	326
Walter Johnson	417	Don Sutton	324
Grover Alexander	373	Nolan Ryan	324
Christy Mathewson	373	Phil Niekro	318
James Galvin	364	Gaylord Perry	314
Warren Spahn	363	Tom Seaver	311
Charles Nichols	361	Charles Radbourne	309
Roger Clemens	355	Mickey Welch	308
Greg Maddux	355	Tom Glavine	305
Tim Keefe	342	Randy Johnson	305
Steve Carlton	329	"Lefty" Grove	300
John Clarkson	328	Early Wynn	300

Source: baseball-reference.com

a. Make a stem and leaf plot and a box and whisker plot of the data.

b. What outliers, mild or extreme, occur?

12. Compute the variance and standard deviation for each collection of data. Round to the nearest tenth.

a. 5, 5, 5, 5, 5, 5, 5   b. 8.7, 3.8, 9.2, 14.7, 26.3

c. 1, 3, 5, 7, 9, 11   d. −13.8, −12.3, −9.7, −15.4, −19.7

13. Use the Chapter 10 dynamic spreadsheet *Standard Deviation* on our Web site to compute the standard deviations described below.

a. Compute the variance and standard deviation for the data 2, 4, 6, 8, and 10.

b. Add 0.7 to each element of the data in part (a) and compute the variance and standard deviation.

c. Subtract 0.5 from each data value in part (a) and compute the variance and standard deviation.

d. Given that the variance and standard deviation of the set of data a, b, c, and d is 16 and 4, respectively, what are the variance and standard deviation of the set $a + x$, $b + x$, $c + x$, $d + x$, where x is any real number?

14. Compute the mean, median, mode, variance, and standard deviation for the distribution represented by this histogram.

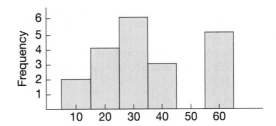

15. Compute the z-scores for the following data.

8, 10, 4, 3, 6, 9, 2, 1, 15, 20

16. a. What percentile is the median score?

b. In a normal distribution, what percentile has a z-score of 1? 2? −1? −2?

17. Using the grade breakdown shown in Exercise 17 of Part A, answer the following problem. On a 100-point test with a mean of 75 and a standard deviation of 10, find the test scores that would yield each grade.

18. Sabino took the ACT in 2009 and received a composite score of 22. If the mean and standard deviation for that year were, respectively, 21.1 and 5.1,

a. What percentile is he in?

b. What percent of all of the students who took the exam had a score better than his?

PROBLEMS

19. Using the information from Part A, Problem 19, determine what percent of the males age 20–29 weigh less than 200 pounds.

20. Assume a certain distribution with mean 65 and standard deviation 10. Find the 50th percentile score. Find the 16th percentile and the 84th percentile scores.

21. Dorian's score of 558 on the writing portion of the 2009 SAT exam placed him in the 72nd percentile. If the mean on this exam was 493, what was the standard deviation?

22. The average height of a class of students is 134.7 cm. The sum of all the heights is 3771.6 cm. There are 17 boys in the class. How many girls are in the class?

23. The average score on a reading test for 58 students was 87.3. Twelve more students took the test. The average of the 12 students was 90.7. What was the average for all students?

24. Suppose that the variance for a set of data is zero. What can you say about the data?

25. a. Give two sets of data with the same means but different variances.

b. Give two sets of data with the same variances but different means.

26. Amy's z-score on her reading test was 1.27. The class average was 60, the median was 58.5, and the variance was 6.2. What was Amy's "raw" score (i.e., her score before converting to z-scores)?

27. a. Can two different numbers in a distribution have the same z-score?

b. Can all of the z-scores for a distribution be equal?

28. a. For the distribution given here by the histogram, find the median according to the following definition: The median is the number through which a vertical line divides the area under the graph into two equal areas. (Recall that the area of a rectangle is the product of the length of the base and the height.)

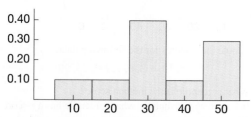

b. Find the median according to the definition in Section 10.1. Are the two "medians" equal?

29. The **unbiased standard deviation**, s_{n-1}, is computed in exactly the same way as the standard deviation, s, except that instead of dividing by n, we divide by $n - 1$. That is, s_{n-1} is equal to

$$\sqrt{\frac{(x_1 - \bar{x})^2 + (x_2 - \bar{x})^2 + \cdots + (x_n - \bar{x})^2}{n - 1}}$$

where $x_1, \ldots, x_n$ are the data and $\bar{x}$ is the mean. The unbiased standard deviation of a sample is a better estimate of the true standard deviation for a normal distribution.

a. Compute s_{n-1} and s for the following data: 1, 2, 3, 4, 5.

b. True or false? $s_{n-1} \geq s$ for all sets of data. Explain.

Analyzing Student Thinking

30. Over the summer the third-grade classroom was painted lavender. Amber took a poll of her third-grade classmates in September to see how they liked the new color. They were asked to respond on a five-point scale with 1 meaning they really did not like the new color, 3 being neutral, and 5 meaning they really liked it. Amber announced the results as follows: The median was 5, but the mean was 3.9, so it seemed people were pretty neutral about it. How would you respond?

31. Spike looks at the data 5, 6, 7, 8, 8, 9, 4, 9 and says that the median is 8. How should you respond?

32. Santos states that a set with four numbers cannot have a median because there is no middle number. Is he correct? Explain.

33. Valicia claims that a set of data cannot have all of the mean, median, and mode the same number. Is she correct? Explain.

34. In trying to understand z-scores, Oneil claims that there will be more data points between z-scores of 2 and 10 than there are between 0 and 2 because there is a bigger gap between 2 and 10 than between 0 and 2. How should you respond?

35. Mckay claims that in a box and whisker plot, the whiskers are always longer than the box. How should you respond?

36. Whitney asserts that if the range of the test scores of two classes is the same, then scores have the same standard deviation. How should you respond?

Problems Relating to the NCTM Standards and Curriculum Focal Points

1. The Focal Points for Grade 4 state "Students solve problems by making frequency tables, bar graphs, picture graphs, and line plots. They apply their understanding of place value to develop and use stem-and-leaf plots." Explain the role that place value plays in constructing stem-and-leaf plots.

2. The Focal Points for Grade 8 state "Analyzing and summarizing data sets." Describe at least 4 different topics

from this section that can be used to analyze and summarize data sets.

3. The NCTM Standards state "All students should use measures of center, focusing on the median, and understand what each does or does not indicate about the data set." Describe what each of the mean, median, and mode do or do not indicate about a data set.

END OF CHAPTER MATERIAL

Solution of Initial Problem

A servant was asked to perform a job that would take 30 days. The servant would be paid 1000 gold coins. The servant replied, "I will happily complete the job, but I would rather be paid 1

copper coin on the first day, 2 copper coins on the second day, 4 on the third day, and so on, with the payment of copper coins doubling each day." The king agreed to the servant's method of payment. If a gold coin is worth 1000 copper coins, did the king make the right decision? How much was the servant paid?

Strategy: Look for a Formula

Make a table.

DAY	PAYMENT (COPPER COINS)	TOTAL PAYMENT TO DATE
1	$1 = 2^0$	1
2	$2 = 2^1$	$1 + 2 = 3$
3	$4 = 2^2$	$1 + 2 + 4 = 7$
4	$8 = 2^3$	$1 + 2 + 4 + 8 = 15$
5	$16 = 2^4$	$1 + 2 + 4 + 8 + 16 = 31$
$\vdots$	$\vdots$	$\vdots$
n	2^{n-1}	$1 + 2 + 4 + 8 + \cdots + 2^{n-1} = S$

From our table, we see on the nth day, where n is a whole number from 1 to 30, the servant is paid 2^{n-1} copper coins. His total payment through n days is $1 + 2 + 4 + \cdots + 2^{n-1}$ copper coins. Hence we wish to find a formula for $1 + 2 + \cdots + 2^{n-1}$. From the table it appears that this sum is $2^n - 1$. (Check this for $n = 1, 2, 3, 4, 5$.) Notice that this formula allows us to make a quick calculation of the value of S for any whole number n. In particular, for $n = 30$, $S = 2^{30} - 1$, so the servant would be paid $2^{30} - 1$ copper coins altogether. Using a calculator, $2^{30} - 1 = 1{,}073{,}741{,}823$. Hence the servant is paid the equivalent of 1,073,741.823 gold coins. The king made a very costly error!

Additional Problems Where the Strategy "Look for a Formula" Is Useful

1. Hector's parents suggest the following allowance arrangements for a 30-week period: a penny a day for the first week, 3 cents a day for the second week, 5 cents a day for the third week, and so on, or $2 a week. Which deal should he take?
2. Jack's beanstalk increases its height by $\frac{1}{2}$ the first day, $\frac{1}{3}$ the second day, $\frac{1}{4}$ the third day, and so on.
   What is the smallest number of days it would take to become at least 100 times as tall as its original height?
3. How many different (nonzero) angles are formed in a fan of rays like the one pictured below, but one having 100 rays?

People in Mathematics

Mina Rees (1902–1997)
Mina Rees graduated from Hunter College, a women's school where mathematics was one of the most popular majors. "I wanted to be in the mathematics department, not because of its practical uses at all; it was because it was such fun!" Ironically, much of her recognition in mathematics has been for practical results. During World War II, she served on the National Defense Research Committee, working on wartime applications of mathematics. Later, she was director of mathematical sciences in the Office of Naval Research. Rees also taught for many years at Hunter College and the City College of New York, where she served as president. After her retirement, she was active in the applications of research to social problems. "I have always found that mathematics was an advantage when I was dean or president of a college. If your habit is to organize things a certain way, the way a mathematician does, then you are apt to have an organization that is easier to present and explain."

Andrew Gleason (1921–2008)
Andrew Gleason said that he had always had a knack for solving problems. As a young man, he worked in cryptanalysis during World War II. The work involved problems in statistics and probability, and Gleason, despite having only a bachelor's degree, found that he understood the problems better than many experienced mathematicians. After the war, he made his mark in the mathematical world when he contributed to the solution of Hilbert's famous Fifth Problem. Gleason was a longtime professor of mathematics at Harvard. "[As part of the School Mathematics Project] I worked with a group of kids who had just finished the first grade. One day I produced some squared paper and said, 'Here's how you multiply.' I drew a 3 × 4 rectangle and said, 'This is 3 times 4; we count the squares and get 12. So 3 × 4 is 12.' Then I did another, 4 × 5. Then I gave each kid some paper and said, 'You do some.' They were very soon doing two-digit problems."

CHAPTER REVIEW

Review the following terms and exercises to determine which require learning or relearning—page numbers are provided for easy reference.

SECTION 10.1 Organizing and Picturing Information

VOCABULARY/NOTATION

Line plot (or dot plot)　438
Frequency　438
Stem and leaf plot　438
Gap　439
Cluster　439
Back-to-back stem and leaf plot　439

Histogram　440
Bar graph　440
Line graph　444
Circle graph　445
Pie chart　445
Pictograph　446

Pictorial embellishments　447
Scatterplot　449
Outlier　450
Regression line　450
Correlation　450

EXERCISES

1. Construct a back-to-back stem and leaf plot for the following two data sets:

   Class 1: 72, 74, 76, 74, 23, 78, 37, 79, 80, 23, 81, 90, 82, 39, 94, 96, 41, 94, 94
   Class 2: 17, 99, 25, 97, 29, 40, 39, 97, 40, 95, 92, 89, 40, 49, 40, 85, 52, 80, 52, 51

2. Construct a histogram for the data for class 1 in Exercise 1 using intervals 0–9, 10–19, . . . , 90–100.

3. Draw a multiple-bar graph to represent the following two data sets.

	2002	2003	2004	2005	2006
MEAN SALARIES OF ELEMENTARY TEACHERS (× $1000)	44.2	45.5	46.4	47.2	48.6
MEAN SALARIES OF SECONDARY TEACHERS (× $1000)	45.3	46.1	47.1	47.9	49.3

Source: NEA.

4. Draw a double-line graph representing the data sets in Exercise 3.

5. Draw a circle graph to display the following data: Fruit, 30%; Vegetable, 40%; Meat, 10%; Milk, 10%; Others, 10%.

6. The manager of a sporting goods store notes that high levels of rainfall have a negative effect on sales of beach equipment and apparel. Sales in thousands of dollars and summer rainfall in inches measured for various years are recorded in the following table.

RAIN (IN INCHES)	SALES (IN THOUSANDS OF DOLLARS)
10	300
22	120
20	160
2	360
21	180
5	320
18	340

Make a scatterplot of these data. Identify any outliers. Sketch a regression line. If the predicted rainfall for the coming summer is 15 inches, what is the best prediction for sales? If the sales in one year were $260,000, what is the best guess for rainfall that summer?

SECTION 10.2 Misleading Graphs and Statistics

VOCABULARY/NOTATION

Scaling　462
Cropping　466
Three-dimensional effects　467

Explode　469
Deceptive pictorial embellishments　470

Population　472
Sample　472
Bias　473

EXERCISES

1. From 2000 to 2007 the number of new car leases in the United States has fluctuated, as shown in the following graph. Redo the graph with a full vertical scale.

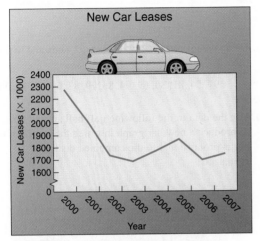

Source: U.S. Bureau of Transportation Statistics.

2. Health-care reform has become a major political issue. The following graph shows health-care spending as a percentage of the gross domestic product (GDP). The GDP is the value of all goods and services produced in the national economy.

a. Redo the graph so the increase appears even greater.

b. Redo the graph so the increase is not so dramatic.

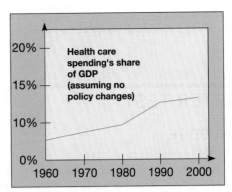

3. Use the data in Problem 1 of Section 10.2 Exercise 10 to construct a circle graph. Construct a second circle graph of this same data with the sector representing "the kids" exploded.

4. On the first page of this chapter evaluate the graph about "college seniors' plans." Discuss what aspects of the pictorial embellishment might be misleading.

5. We wish to determine the opinion of the voters in a certain town with regard to allowing in-line skating in the town square. A survey is taken of adult passersby near the local high school one late afternoon. What is the population in this case? What is the sample? What sources of bias might there be in the sampling procedure?

6. In the following scenario, identify and discuss any sources of bias in the sampling method.

A Minnesota-based toothpaste company claims that 90% of dentists prefer the formula in its toothpaste to any other. To prove this, they conduct a study. They send questionnaires to 100 dentists in the Minneapolis–St. Paul area asking if they prefer this formula to others.

SECTION 10.3 Analyzing Data

VOCABULARY/NOTATION

Measures of central tendency 481	Upper quartile 485	Variance 489
Mode 482	Interquartile range (IQR) 485	Standard deviation 489
Median 482	Outlier 485	z-score 491
Arithmetic average 483	Percentile 488	Relative frequency 492
Mean 483	nth percentile 488	Distribution 492
Box and whisker plot 485	Measures of dispersion 488	Normal distribution 494
Lower quartile 485	Range 488	

EXERCISES

1. Determine the mode, median, and mean of the data set: 1, 2, 3, 5, 9, 9, 13, 14, 14, 14.

2. Construct the box and whisker plot for the data in Exercise 1.

3. Find the range, variance, and standard deviation of the data set in Exercise 1.

4. Find the z-scores for 2, 5, and 14 for the data set in Exercise 1.

5. What is the usefulness of the *z*-score of a number?

6. In a normal distribution, approximately what percent of the data are within 1 standard deviation of the mean?

7. On a test whose scores form a normal distribution, approximately how many of the scores have a *z*-score between –2 and 2?

8. Find the percentile of 2, 5, and 14 for the data set in Exercise 1.

CHAPTER TEST

KNOWLEDGE

1. True or false?

    a. The mode of a collection of data is the middle score.

    b. The range is the last number minus the first number in a collection of data.

    c. A *z*-score is the number of standard deviations away from the median.

    d. The median is always greater than the mean.

    e. A circle graph is effective in displaying relative amounts.

    f. Pictographs can be used to mislead by displaying two dimensions when only one of the dimensions represents the data.

    g. Every large group of data has a normal distribution.

    h. In a normal distribution, more than half of the data are contained within 1 standard deviation from the mean.

    i. When determining the opinion of a voting population, the larger the sample the better.

    j. A score in the 37th percentile is greater than 63% of all of the scores.

    k. When the vertical axis of a bar graph is cropped or compressed, it is done to mislead the reader.

2. Identify three measures of central tendency and two measures of dispersion.

3. Identify the kinds of information that bar graphs and line graphs are good for picturing and circle graphs are not. Conversely, identify the kinds of information that circle graphs are good for picturing but bar and line graphs are not.

SKILL

4. If a portion of a circle graph is to represent 30%, what will be the measure of the corresponding central angle?

5. Find the mean, median, mode, and range of the following data: 5, 7, 3, 8, 10, 3.

6. If a collection of data has a mean of 17 and a standard deviation of 3, what numbers would have *z*-scores of –2, –1, 1, and 2?

7. Calculate the standard deviation for the following data: 15, 1, 9, 13, 17, 8, 3.

8. On a football team with a mean weight of 220 pounds and a standard deviation of the weights being 35 pounds, what percentile is a 170-pound receiver or a 290-pound lineman?

9. Using the following scores, construct a box and whisker plot.

    97, 54, 81, 80, 69, 94, 86, 79, 82, 64, 84, 72, 78

10. Use the data in the following golf ball advertisement to produce a new bar graph in which the length of each bar is proportional to the combined distances it represents.

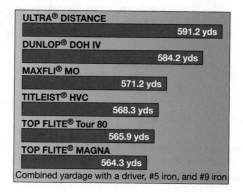

ULTRA® DISTANCE — 591.2 yds
DUNLOP® DOH IV — 584.2 yds
MAXFLI® MO — 571.2 yds
TITLEIST® HVC — 568.3 yds
TOP FLITE® Tour 80 — 565.9 yds
TOP FLITE® MAGNA — 564.3 yds
Combined yardage with a driver, #5 iron, and #9 iron

11. A statistics professor gives an 80-point test to his class, with the following scores:

    35, 44, 48, 55, 56, 57, 60, 61, 62, 62, 63, 64, 67, 70, 71, 71, 75

To provide an example of how histograms might be constructed, she is considering two options.

    a. Grouping the data into subintervals of length 10, beginning with 71–80, 61–70, etc.

    b. Grouping the data into subintervals of length 8, beginning with 73–80, 65–72, etc.

Draw the histogram for each option.

12. A sociologist working for a large school system is interested in demographic information on the families having children in the schools served by the system. Two hundred students are randomly selected from the school system's database and a questionnaire is sent to the home address in care of the parents or guardian. Identify the population being studied and the sample that was actually observed.

UNDERSTANDING

13. If possible, give a single list of data such that the mean equals the mode and the mode is less than the median. If impossible, explain why.

14. If possible, give a collection of data for which the standard deviation is zero and the mean is nonzero. If impossible, explain why.

15. Give a reason justifying the use of each histogram constructed in Problem 11. Why might the professor use the first one? Why might she use the second one?

16. Explain how pictographs can be deceptive.

17. Give an example of two sets of data with the same means and different standard deviations.

18. Explain how line graphs can be deceptive.

19. What type of graph would be best for displaying the data in the following table? Justify your answer and construct the graph.

Percent of High School Graduates Enrolled in College

YEAR	MALE	FEMALE
1997	63.5	70.3
1998	62.4	68.1
1999	61.4	64.4
2000	59.9	66.2
2001	60.1	63.5
2002	62.1	68.4
2003	61.2	66.5
2004	61.4	71.5
2005	66.5	70.4
2006	65.8	66.1

Source: U.S. National Center for Educational Statistics.

20. Redraw the following graph of the increases in the federal tax burden per capita, 1999–2004, to deemphasize the changes. Manipulate the horizontal and/or vertical axes so that the changes appear less dramatic.

The Federal Tax Burden per Capita, Fiscal Years 1999–2004

1999	2000	2001	2002	2003	2004
$6796	$7404	$7441	$6632	$6229	$6369

Source: Tax Foundation.

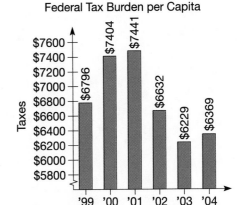

Federal Tax Burden per Capita

PROBLEM-SOLVING/APPLICATION

21. In a distribution, the number 7 has a z-score of -2 and the number 19 has a z-score of 1. What is the mean of the distribution?

22. If the mean of the numbers 1, 3, x, 7, 11 is 9, what is x?

23. On which test did Ms. Brown's students perform the best compared to the national averages? Explain.

	MS. BROWN'S CLASS AVERAGE	NATIONAL AVERAGE	AVERAGE DEVIATION
Reading	77.9	75.2	12.3
Mathematics	75.2	74.1	14.2
Science	74.3	70.3	13.6
Social studies	71.7	69.3	10.9

24. Identify any possible sources of bias in the sampling procedure in the following scenario.

A soft-drink company produces a lemon-lime drink that it says people prefer by a margin of two-to-one over its main competitor, a cola. To prove this claim, it sets up a booth in a large shopping mall where customers are allowed to try both drinks. The customers are filmed for a possible television commercial. They are asked which drink they prefer.

25. On the first page of this chapter evaluate the graph about "Perennial playoff teams." Discuss what aspects of the graph might be misleading.

Probability

Probability in the Everyday World

I t is generally agreed that the science of probability began in the sixteenth century from the so-called *problem of the points*. The problem is to determine the division of the stakes of two equally skilled players when a game of chance is interrupted before either player has obtained the required number of points in order to win. However, real progress on this subject began in 1654 when Chevalier de Mere, an experienced gambler whose theoretical understanding of the problem did not match his observations, approached the mathematician Blaise Pascal (see the following illustration) for assistance.

ments, advisers assign probabilities to future prices in an effort to decide among various investment opportunities. Another important use of probability is in actuarial science, which is used to determine insurance premiums. Probability also continues to play a role in games of chance such as dice and cards.

Pascal communicated with Fermat about the problem and, remarkably, each solved the problem by different means. Thus, in this correspondence, Pascal and Fermat laid the foundations of probability.

Now, probability is recognized in many aspects of our lives. For example, when you were conceived, you could have had any of 8,388,608 different sets of characteristics based on 23 pairs of chromosomes. In school, if you guess at random on a 10-item true/false test, there is only about a 17% probability that you will answer 7 or more questions correctly. In the manufacturing process, quality control is becoming the buzzword. Thus it is important to know the probability that certain parts will fail when deciding to revamp a production process or offer a warranty. In invest-

One very popular application of probability is the famous "birthday problem." Simply stated, in a group of people, what is the probability of two people having the same month and day of birth? Surprisingly, the probability of such matching birth dates is about 0.5 when there are 23 people and almost 0.9 when there are 40 people. An interesting application of this problem is the birthdays of the 43 American presidents through George W. Bush: Presidents Polk and Harding were both born on November 2.

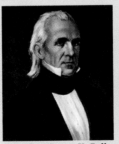 

President James K. Polk
Born: November 2, 1795

President Warren G. Harding
Born: November 2, 1865

STRATEGY 16

Do a Simulation

A simulation is a representation of an experiment using some appropriate objects (slips of paper, dice, etc.) or perhaps a computer program. The purpose of a simulation is to run many replications of an experiment that may be difficult or impossible to perform. As you will see, to solve the following Initial Problem, it is easier to simulate the problem than to perform the actual experiment many times by questioning five strangers repeatedly.

INITIAL PROBLEM

At a party, a friend bets you that at least two people in a group of five strangers will have the same astrological sign. Should you take the bet? Why or why not?

CLUES

The Do a Simulation strategy may be appropriate when

- A problem involves a complicated probability experiment.
- An actual experiment is too difficult or impossible to perform.
- A problem has a repeatable process that can be done experimentally.
- Finding the actual answer requires techniques not previously developed.

A solution of this Initial Problem is on page 570.

INTRODUCTION

In this chapter we discuss the fundamental concepts and principles of probability. Probability is the branch of mathematics that enables us to predict the likelihood of uncertain occurrences. There are many applications and uses of probability in the sciences (meteorology and medicine, for example), in sports and games, and in business, to name a few areas. Because of its widespread usefulness, the study of probability is an essential component of a comprehensive mathematics curriculum. In the first section of this chapter we develop the main concepts of probability. In the second section some counting procedures are introduced that lead to more sophisticated methods for computing probabilities. In the third section, simulations are developed and several applications of probability are presented. Finally, in the last section, additional counting methods referred to as permutations and combinations are discussed. These methods are used to determine probabilities on large sets.

> ### Key Concepts from NCTM Curriculum Focal Points
>
> - **GRADE 7:** Students understand that when all outcomes of an experiment are equally likely, the theoretical probability of an event is the fraction of outcomes in which the event occurs.
> - **GRADE 7:** Students use theoretical probability and proportions to make approximate predictions.

11.1   PROBABILITY AND SIMPLE EXPERIMENTS

STARTING POINT

A red cube, a white cube, and a blue cube are placed in a box. One cube is randomly drawn, its color is recorded, and it is returned to the box. A second cube is drawn and its color recorded. What are the chances (probability) of drawing a red cube? (*Hint:* Drawing a red cube could be done on the first draw, the second draw, or both draws.)

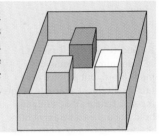

Children's Literature
www.wiley.com/college/musser
See "A Very Improbable
Story: A Math Adventure"
by Edward Einhorn.

Reflection from Research
When teachers use contexts
(e.g., a lottery) for teaching
probability concepts, many
elementary students have
difficulty learning the
mathematical concepts because
their personal experiences
interfere (e.g., "It's impossible to
win the lottery because no one
in my family has ever won.")
(Taylor & Biddulph, 1994).

Simple Experiments

Probability is the mathematics of chance. Example 11.1 illustrates how probability is commonly used and reported.

Example 11.1

a. The probability of precipitation today is 80%.
   Interpretation: On days in the past with atmospheric conditions like today's, it rained at some time on 80% of the days.
b. The odds that a patient improves using drug X are 60 : 40.
   Interpretation: In a group of 100 patients who have had the same symptoms as the patient being treated, 60 of them improved when administered drug X, and 40 did not.
c. The chances of winning the lottery game "Find the Winning Ticket" are 1 in 150,000.
   Interpretation: If 150,000 lottery tickets are printed, only one of the tickets is the winning ticket. If more tickets are printed, the fraction of winning tickets is approximately $\frac{1}{150,000}$. ∎

Probability tells us the relative frequency with which we expect an event to occur. Thus it can be reported as a fraction, decimal, percent, or ratio. The greater the probability, the more likely the event is to occur. Conversely, the smaller the probability, the less likely the event is to occur.

To study probability in a mathematically precise way, we need special terminology and notation. An **experiment** is the act of making an observation or taking a measurement. An **outcome** is one of the possible things that can occur as a result of an experiment. The set of all the possible outcomes is called the **sample space**. Finally, an **event** is any subset of the sample space.

Since a sample space is a set, it is commonly represented in set notation with the letter S. Similarly, because an event is a subset, in set notation, it is frequently represented with letters like A, B, C, or the generic letter E for event. These concepts are illustrated in Example 11.2.

Example 11.2

a. Experiment: Toss a fair coin and record whether the top side is heads or tails.

Sample Space: There are two possible outcomes when tossing a coin, heads or tails. Hence the sample space is $S = \{H, T\}$, where H and T are abbreviations for heads and tails, respectively.

Event: Since an event is simply a subset of the sample space, we will first consider all the subsets of the sample space S. The subsets are $\{\}$, $\{H\}$, $\{T\}$, $\{H, T\}$. It is not always the case that we can describe in words an event associated with each subset, but in this case we can. The events are as follows:

A = getting a heads = $\{H\}$
B = getting a tails = $\{T\}$
C = getting either a heads or a tails = $\{H, T\}$
D = getting neither a heads nor a tails = $\{\}$

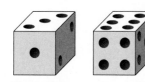

Figure 11.1

Reflection from Research
"Some numbers come up more often, but all dice are fair" is a typical example of the inconsistencies that students hold about the fairness of dice. Students also hold inconsistent beliefs about strategies that can be used to test the fairness of dice (Watson & Moritz, 2003).

b. Experiment: Roll a standard six-sided die with one, two, three, four, five, and six dots on the six faces (Figure 11.1). Record the number of dots showing on the top face.

Sample Space: There are six outcomes:—1, 2, 3, 4, 5, 6—where numerals represent the number of dots. Thus the sample space is $S = \{1, 2, 3, 4, 5, 6\}$.

Event: For this experiment, there are many more events than for the previous example of tossing a single coin. In fact, there are $2^6 = 64$ possible events. Each event is a subset of S. Some of the events are:

A = getting a prime number of dots = $\{2, 3, 5\}$
B = getting an even number of dots = $\{2, 4, 6\}$
C = getting more than 4 dots = $\{5, 6\}$

c. Experiment: Spin a spinner as shown in Figure 11.2 once and record the color of the indicated region.

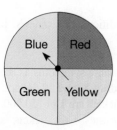

Figure 11.2

Sample Space: There are 4 different colored regions (outcomes) on this spinner, so the sample space is $S = \{R, Y, G, B\}$. It is important to note that the regions on the spinner are the same size. If they were not the same size, we would have to approach the sample space differently.

Event: Some of the possible events for this experiment are:

A = pointing to the red region = {R}
B = pointing to a blue or green region = {B, G}
C = pointing to a region with a primary color = {R, Y, B}

d. Experiment: A single card is drawn from a standard deck of playing cards. The suit and type of card are recorded.

Sample Space: There are 4 suits [diamonds (♦), hearts (♥), spades (♠), and clubs (♣)] and 13 cards (2, 3, 4, 5, 6, 7, 8, 9, 10, jack, queen, king, and ace) in each suit for a total of 52 possible outcomes.

$$S = \{2♦, 3♦, 4♦, 5♦, 6♦, 7♦, 8♦, 9♦, 10♦, J♦, Q♦, K♦, A♦,$$
$$2♥, 3♥, 4♥, 5♥, 6♥, 7♥, 8♥, 9♥, 10♥, J♥, Q♥, K♥, A♥,$$
$$2♠, 3♠, 4♠, 5♠, 6♠, 7♠, 8♠, 9♠, 10♠, J♠, Q♠, K♠, A♠,$$
$$2♣, 3♣, 4♣, 5♣, 6♣, 7♣, 8♣, 9♣, 10♣, J♣, Q♣, K♣, A♣\}$$

Event: This sample space of 52 elements has 2^{52} = 4,503,599,627,370,496 different subsets (events). Some of the events are:

A = drawing a diamond = {2♦, 3♦, 4♦, 5♦, 6♦, 7♦, 8♦, 9♦,
    10♦, J♦, Q♦, K♦, A♦}
B = drawing a face card = {J♦, Q♦, K♦, J♥, Q♥, K♥, J♠, Q♠, K♠,
    J♣, Q♣, K♣}
C = drawing a diamond or face card = {2♦, 3♦, 4♦, 5♦, 6♦, 7♦, 8♦,
    9♦, 10♦, J♦, Q♦, K♦, A♦, J♥, Q♥, K♥,
    J♠, Q♠, K♠, J♣, Q♣, K♣}
D = drawing a diamond face card = {J♦, Q♦, K♦}

Notice that $D = A \cap B$ and $C = A \cup B$.   ■

✔ **Check for Understanding:** Exercise/Problem Set A #1–6

NCTM Standard
All students should describe events as likely or unlikely and discuss the degree of likelihood using such words as *certain*, *equally likely*, and *impossible*.

Computing Probabilities in Simple Experiments

The probability of an event, E, is the fraction (decimal, percent, or ratio) indicating the relative frequency with which event E should occur in a given sample space S. Two events are **equally likely** if they occur with equal relative frequency (i.e., equally often).

DEFINITION

Probability of an Event with Equally Likely Outcomes

Suppose that all of the outcomes in the nonempty sample space S of an experiment are equally likely to occur. Let E be an event, $n(E)$ be the number of outcomes in E, and $n(S)$ the number of outcomes in S. Then the **probability of event E**, denoted **$P(E)$**, is

$$P(E) = \frac{\text{number of elements in } E}{\text{number of elements in } S},$$

or in symbols

$$P(E) = \frac{n(E)}{n(S)}.$$

Using this definition, we can compute the probabilities of some of the events described in Example 11.2.

Example 11.3

a. What is the probability of getting tails when tossing a fair coin?

b. For the experiment of rolling a standard six-sided die and recording the number of dots on the top face, what is the probability of getting a prime number?

c. On the spinner found in Figure 11.2, what is the probability of pointing to a primary color?

d. For the experiment of drawing a card from a standard deck of playing cards, what is the probability of getting a diamond? What is the probability of getting a diamond face card?

SOLUTION

a. While the probability of getting tails might seem like common sense, we will discuss it in terms of the definition in order to lay the groundwork for more complicated probabilities. The sample space for this experiment is $S = \{H, T\}$, where each of the outcomes is equally likely. The event of getting tails corresponds to the subset $B = \{T\}$. Thus the probability of getting tails is

$$P(B) = \frac{n(B)}{n(S)} = \frac{1}{2}.$$

b. Since all of the outcomes in the sample space $S = \{1, 2, 3, 4, 5, 6\}$ are equally likely and the event of getting a prime number is subset $A = \{2, 3, 5\}$, the probability of getting a prime is

$$P(A) = \frac{n(A)}{n(S)} = \frac{3}{6} = \frac{1}{2}.$$

c. Since each region is exactly the same size, each color has an equally likely chance of being selected. The event of pointing to a primary color is subset $C = \{R, Y, B\}$ and $S = \{R, Y, G, B\}$, so the probability of pointing to a primary color is

$$P(C) = \frac{n(C)}{n(S)} = \frac{3}{4}.$$

d. Since each card in the deck has an equally likely chance of being drawn, we can again use the previous definition. The event of getting a diamond is represented by subset A, which consists of 13 cards, and the event of getting a diamond face card is subset $D = \{J\blacklozenge, Q\blacklozenge, K\blacklozenge\}$. Thus the probability of drawing a diamond is

$$P(A) = \frac{n(A)}{n(S)} = \frac{13}{52} = \frac{1}{4}$$

and the probability of a diamond face card is

$$P(D) = \frac{n(D)}{n(S)} = \frac{3}{52}.$$ ∎

Reflection from Research
When discussing the terms certain, possible, and impossible, it was found that children had difficulty generating examples of certain and would often suggest a new category: almost certain (Nugent, 1990).

These examples provide a sense of the types of numbers that probabilities can take on. By using the fact that $\varnothing \subseteq E \subseteq S$, we can determine the range for $P(E)$. In particular, $\varnothing \subseteq E \subseteq S$, so

$$0 = n(\varnothing) \le n(E) \le n(S);$$

hence

$$\frac{0}{n(S)} \le \frac{n(E)}{n(S)} \le \frac{n(S)}{n(S)}$$

NCTM Standard
All students should understand that the measure of the likelihood of an event can be represented by a number from 0 to 1.

so that

$$0 \le P(E) \le 1.$$

The last inequality tells us that the probability of an event must be between 0 and 1, inclusive. If $P(E) = 0$, the event E contains no outcomes (hence E is an **impossible event**); if $P(E) = 1$, the event E equals the entire sample space S (hence E is a **certain event**).

For each of the examples considered thus far, we see that the probability is simply a ratio of the number of objects or outcomes of interest compared to the total number of objects or outcomes under consideration. The objects or outcomes of interest make up the event. Thus, a more general description of probability is

$$P(\text{event}) = \frac{\text{the number of objects or outcomes of interest}}{\text{the total number of objects or outcomes under consideration}}.$$

The primary use of a sample space is to make sure that you have accounted for all possible outcomes. The examples done thus far could likely be done without listing a sample space, but they prepare us for using a sample space to compute the probabilities in the next few examples.

Each of the experiments that we have investigated thus far involve doing an action with one object once: tossing a coin, rolling a die, spinning a spinner, drawing a card. Computing probabilities becomes more difficult when multiple actions or objects are involved. Examples of using multiple objects such as tossing three coins and rolling two dice follow.

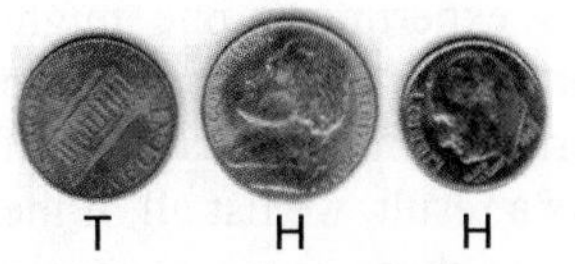

Figure 11.3

Example 11.4 When tossing three coins—a penny, a nickel, and a dime—what is the probability of getting exactly two heads (Figure 11.3)?

SOLUTION While it may seem that since there are three coins and two of them need to be heads, we might simply say that it is the probability of two out of three. This reasoning, however, does not take into consideration all of the possible outcomes. To do this, we will fall back on the idea of a sample space and event. The sample space for this experiment is

$$S = \{\overbrace{\text{HHH}}^{\text{3 heads}}, \overbrace{\text{HHT, HTH, THH}}^{\text{2 heads}}, \underbrace{\text{HTT, THT, TTH}}_{\text{1 head}}, \underbrace{\text{TTT}}_{\text{0 heads}}\}$$

where the first letter in each three-letter sequence represents the outcome of the penny, the second letter is the nickel, and the last letter is the dime. The event of getting exactly two heads is $A = \{\text{HHT, HTH, THH}\}$. Thus the probability of getting exactly two heads is

$$P(A) = \frac{n(A)}{n(S)} = \frac{3}{8}.$$ ■

Reflection from Research
Many mathematics educators recommend performing dozens of trials (e.g., rolling a die 100 times). However, many elementary children have not developed the attention span needed to sustain their interest for such lengths of time (Taylor & Biddulph, 1994).

This probability is based on *ideal* occurrences and is referred to as a **theoretical probability**. Another way to approach this problem is by actually tossing three coins many times and recording the results. Computing probability in this way by determining the ratio of the frequency of an event to the total number of repetitions is called **experimental probability**. Table 11.1 gives the observed results of tossing a penny, nickel, and dime 500 times.

TABLE 11.1

OUTCOME	FREQUENCY
HHH	71
HHT	67
HTH	56
THH	64
TTH	53
THT	61
HTT	66
TTT	62
Total	500

From Table 11.1, the outcomes of the event of getting exactly two heads occurred as follows: HHT, 67 times; HTH, 56 times; and THH, 64 times. Thus the experimental probability of getting exactly two heads is

$$\frac{67 + 56 + 64}{500} = \frac{187}{500} = .374,$$

which is comparable to the theoretical probability of

$$P(E) = \frac{n(E)}{n(S)} = \frac{3}{8} = .375.$$

Experimental probability has the advantage of being established via observations. The obvious disadvantage is that it depends on a particular set of repetitions of an experiment and may not generalize to other repetitions of the same type of experiment. In either case, however, the probability was found by determining a ratio. From this point on, all probabilities will be computed theoretically unless otherwise indicated.

Reflection from Research
A common error experienced by children considering probability with respect to sums of numbers from two dice is that they mistakenly believe that the sums are equally likely (Fischbein & Gazit, 1984).

Example 11.5 The experiment of tossing two fair, six-sided dice is performed and the sum of the dots on the two faces is recorded. Let A be the event of getting a total of 7 dots, B be the event of getting 8 dots, and C be the event of getting at least 4 dots. What is the probability of each of these events?

SOLUTION In determining the sample space for this experiment, one might consider listing only the sums of 2, 3, 4, and so forth. However, since these outcomes are not equally likely, the definition for determining the probability of an event with equally likely outcomes cannot be used. As a result, we list all of the outcomes of tossing two dice and then determine which of those outcomes yield sums of 2, 3, 4, and so forth. The sample space, S, for this experiment is shown in Figure 11.4(a).

(1,1) (1,2) (1,3) (1,4) (1,5) (1,6)	(1,1) (1,2) (1,3) (1,4) (1,5) (1,6)
(2,1) (2,2) (2,3) (2,4) (2,5) (2,6)	(2,1) (2,2) (2,3) (2,4) (2,5) (2,6)
(3,1) (3,2) (3,3) (3,4) (3,5) (3,6)	(3,1) (3,2) (3,3) (3,4) (3,5) (3,6)
(4,1) (4,2) (4,3) (4,4) (4,5) (4,6)	(4,1) (4,2) (4,3) (4,4) (4,5) (4,6)
(5,1) (5,2) (5,3) (5,4) (5,5) (5,6)	(5,1) (5,2) (5,3) (5,4) (5,5) (5,6)
(6,1) (6,2) (6,3) (6,4) (6,5) (6,6)	(6,1) (6,2) (6,3) (6,4) (6,5) (6,6)
(a)	**(b)**

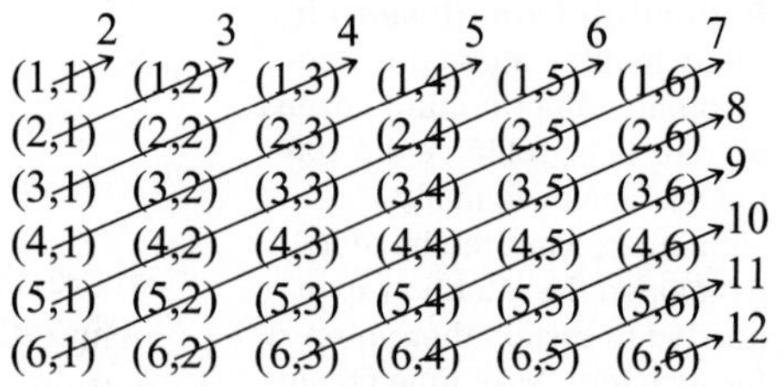

Figure 11.4

A question that often arises with this experiment is "why do you list both (1,2) and (2,1) when we are only interested in the sum of three?" To better understand this, imagine that the two dice are different colors, red and green. This would mean that 1 dot on the red die and 2 dots on the green die is a *different* outcome than 2 dots on the red die and 1 dot on the green die. Thus both outcomes are listed separately. By looking at the sample space in Figure 11.4(a) and the sums of dots (the numbers at the ends of the arrows) in Figure 11.4(b), the size of the sample space [$n(S) = 36$]

and the size of the various subsets representing events can be determined. Using this information, $P(A)$, $P(B)$, and $P(C)$ are shown in Table 11.2.

TABLE 11.2

EVENT E	$N(E)$	$P(E)$
A	$n(A) = 6$	$P(A) = \frac{6}{36} = \frac{1}{6}$
B	$n(B) = 5$	$P(B) = \frac{5}{36}$
C	$n(C) = 33$	$P(C) = \frac{33}{36} = \frac{11}{12}$

■

All of the examples discussed thus far have been experiments consisting of one action. In the case of tossing three coins or rolling two dice, it was still only one action, but performed on more than one object. We now want to consider experiments that consist of doing two or more actions in succession. For example, consider the experiment of tossing one coin three times. Would this experiment have a different sample space than the experiment of tossing three different coins once as in Example 11.4? No. In fact, it is often helpful in listing a sample space for experiments of this type to be aware of this connection. The next example is an illustration of an experiment of two actions done in succession.

Figure 11.5

Example 11.6   A jar contains four marbles: one red, one green, one yellow, and one white (Figure 11.5). If we draw two marbles from the jar, one after the other, without replacing the first one drawn, what is the probability of each of the following events?

A: One of the marbles is red.
B: The first marble is red or yellow.
C: The marbles are the same color.
D: The first marble is not white.
E: Neither marble is blue.

SOLUTION The sample space consists of the following outcomes. ("RG," for example, means that the first marble is red and the second marble is green.)

RG	GR	YR	WR
RY	GY	YG	WG
RW	GW	YW	WY

Thus $n(S) = 12$. Since there is exactly one marble of each color and all marbles are physically identical to the touch, we assume that all the outcomes are equally likely. Then

$A = \{RG, RY, RW, GR, YR, WR\}$, so $P(A) = \frac{6}{12} = \frac{1}{2}$.

$B = \{RG, RY, RW, YR, YG, YW\}$, so $P(B) = \frac{6}{12} = \frac{1}{2}$.

$C = \varnothing$, the empty event. That is, C is impossible, so $P(C) = \frac{0}{12} = 0$.

$D = \{RG, RY, RW, GR, GY, GW, YR, YG, YW\}$, so $P(D) = \frac{9}{12} = \frac{3}{4}$.

$E =$ the entire sample space, S. So $P(E) = \frac{12}{12} = 1$.   ■

In Examples 11.2 and 11.3, the experiments involved doing an action with one object once, but in Examples 11.4–11.6, the experiments involved either multiple objects (three coins, two dice) or doing an action multiple times (drawing two marbles). We will now tie the simpler experiments to the more complex ones.

Consider event B of Example 11.6, which is "The first marble is red or yellow." This event can be viewed as the union of two events: L = "The first marble is red" = {RG, RY, RW} and M = "The first marble is yellow" = {YR, YG, YW}. In other words, $B = L \cup M$ = {RG, RY, RW, YR, YG, YW}. Now consider the probabilities of events B, L, and M which are $P(B) = \frac{6}{12}$, $P(L) = \frac{3}{12}$, and $P(M) = \frac{3}{12}$. Thus in this case, where $B = L \cup M$, the equation $P(B) = P(L) + P(M)$ also holds.

To further investigate the relationship between the probability of the union of two events as the sum of the probabilities of the individual events, consider the following three events from the experiment in Example 11.6:

A = One of the marbles is red   = {RG, RY, RW, GR, YR, WR}
O = One of the marbles is yellow   = {YR, YG, YW, RY, GY, WY}
F = One of the marbles is red or yellow = {RG, RY, RW, GR, YR, WR,
                                            YG, YW, GY, WY}

Once again $F = A \cup B$. In this case, $P(A) = \frac{6}{12}$, $P(O) = \frac{6}{12}$, and $P(F) = P(A \cup O) = \frac{10}{12}$, but the sum of the probabilities of the individual events is *not* equal to the probability of the union; that is $P(A \cup O) \neq P(A) + P(O)$. Because the outcomes RY and YR are in both events A and O, they are counted twice when adding $P(A)$ and $P(O)$. Therefore, the intersection of A and O, $A \cap O$ = {RY, YR} needs to be considered. Since $P(A \cap O) = \frac{2}{12}$, the following equality holds:

$$P(A \cup O) = P(A) + P(O) - P(A \cap O) = \frac{6}{12} + \frac{6}{12} - \frac{2}{12} = \frac{10}{12}.$$

In the previous example, $L \cap M = \varnothing$ so $P(L \cap M) = 0$. Thus

$$P(L \cup M) = P(L) + P(M) - P(L \cap M) = \frac{3}{12} + \frac{3}{12} - 0 = \frac{6}{12}.$$

In Figure 11.6, observe how the region $A \cap B$ is shaded *twice*, once from A and once from B.

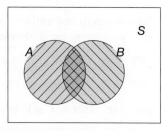

Figure 11.6

Thus, to find the number of elements in $A \cup B$, we calculate $n(A) + n(B)$. *But we have to subtract* $n(A \cap B)$ so that we do not count the elements of $A \cap B$ twice. Hence, $n(A \cup B) = n(A) + n(B) - n(A \cap B)$, for sets A and B. This property of sets generalizes to the following property of probability:

$$P(A \cup B) = P(A) + P(B) - P(A \cap B).$$

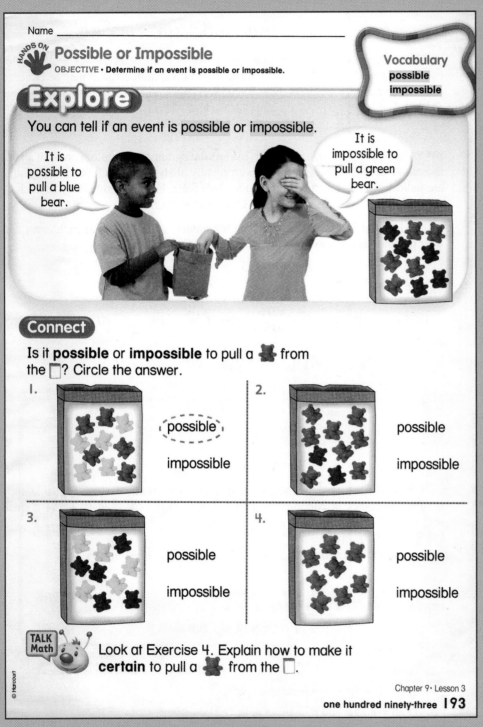

Name _____

Possible or Impossible
HANDS ON

OBJECTIVE · Determine if an event is possible or impossible.

Vocabulary
possible
impossible

Explore

You can tell if an event is possible or impossible.

It is possible to pull a blue bear.

It is impossible to pull a green bear.

Connect

Is it **possible** or **impossible** to pull a 🐻 from the ⬜? Circle the answer.

1.
possible
impossible

2.
possible
impossible

3.
possible
impossible

4.
possible
impossible

TALK Math
Look at Exercise 4. Explain how to make it **certain** to pull a 🐻 from the ⬜.

Chapter 9 · Lesson 3
one hundred ninety-three 193

© Harcourt

From Lesson 3 "Possible or Impossible" from HSP MATH, Student Edition (National), Grade 1 (2009 Edition), copyright ©2009 by Houghton Mifflin Harcourt Publishing Company.

In Example 11.6, event D is "The first marble is not white." This would mean that the complement of D, written $\overline{D}$ is "The first marble is white." Since event D and event $\overline{D}$ have no outcomes in common, $D \cap \overline{D} = \varnothing$. Because D and $\overline{D}$ are complements, $D \cup \overline{D} = S$. Hence,

$$1 = P(S) = P(D \cup \overline{D}) = P(D) + P(\overline{D}) - P(D \cap \overline{D}) = P(D) + P(\overline{D}).$$

This equation can be rewritten as $P(D) = 1 - P(\overline{D})$ or $P(\overline{D}) = 1 - P(D)$. Because the sample space for event D in Example 11.6 is quite large, it may be easier to find the probability of event $\overline{D} = \{WR, WG, WY\}$ and subtract it from 1. Thus $P(D) = 1 - \frac{3}{12} = \frac{9}{12}$.

Problem-Solving Strategy
Draw a Diagram

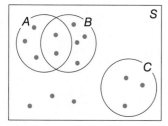

Figure 11.7

Example 11.7   Figure 11.7 shows a diagram of a sample space S of an experiment with equally likely outcomes. Events A, B, and C are indicated, their outcomes represented by points. Find the probability of each of the following events: $S, \varnothing, A, B, C, A \cup B, A \cap B, A \cup C, \overline{C}$.

SOLUTION   In Table 11.3, we tabulate the number of outcomes in each event and their probabilities. For example, $n(A) = 5$ and $n(S) = 15$, so $P(A) = \frac{5}{15} = \frac{1}{3}$.

TABLE 11.3

EVENT, E	$n(E)$	$P(E) = \dfrac{n(E)}{n(S)}$	EVENT, E	$n(E)$	$P(E) = \dfrac{n(E)}{n(S)}$
S	15	$\frac{15}{15} = 1$	$A \cup B$	9	$\frac{9}{15} = \frac{3}{5}$
$\varnothing$	0	$\frac{0}{15} = 0$	$A \cap B$	2	$\frac{2}{15}$
A	5	$\frac{5}{15} = \frac{1}{3}$	$A \cup C$	8	$\frac{8}{15}$
B	6	$\frac{6}{15} = \frac{2}{5}$	$\overline{C}$	12	$\frac{12}{15} = \frac{4}{5}$
C	3	$\frac{3}{15} = \frac{1}{5}$			

In Example 11.7, events A and C are disjoint, or **mutually exclusive**. That is, they have no outcomes in common. In such cases, $P(A \cup C) = P(A) + P(C)$, since $A \cap C = \varnothing$. Verify this in Example 11.7. Notice that $P(A \cup C) = \frac{8}{15} = \frac{5}{15} + \frac{3}{15} = \frac{1}{3} + \frac{1}{5} = P(A) + P(C)$.

We can summarize our observations about probabilities as follows.

PROPERTY

Properties of Probability

1. For any event A, $0 \le P(A) \le 1$.

2. $P(\varnothing) = 0$.

3. $P(S) = 1$, where S is the sample space.

4. For all events A and B, $P(A \cup B) = P(A) + P(B) - P(A \cap B)$.

5. If $\overline{A}$ denotes the complement of event A, then $P(\overline{A}) = 1 - P(A)$.

Observe in item 4, when $A \cap B = \varnothing$, that is, A and B are mutually exclusive, we have $P(A \cup B) = P(A) + P(B)$. The properties of probability apply to all experiments and sample spaces.

Finally, let's consider the case when the outcomes are *not* equally likely. For example, what if the regions on a spinner are not the same size?

| **Example 11.8** | For the spinner in Figure 11.8(a), what is the probability of pointing to the red region? |

SOLUTION Since the regions are not the same size, it cannot be said that the probability of pointing to the red region is one out of three. It is clear that the probability of pointing to the red is greater than half, but how much greater? Because each of the outcomes red, green, and blue are not equally likely, we cannot use the sample space $S = \{R, G, B\}$ to compute the probability. We can, however, determine some type of ratio for the probability. In this case, the spinner can be divided into eight equally shaped and sized regions [see Figure 11.8(b)]. Since five of the eight equally sized regions are red, we know that the probability of pointing to a red is the ratio of red regions to total regions or $\frac{5}{8}$.

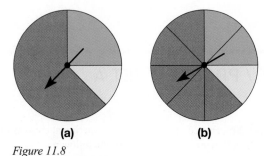

(a)   **(b)**

Figure 11.8

∎

| **Example 11.9** | A bag of candy contains 6 red gumballs, 3 green gumballs, and 2 blue gumballs. If one gumball is drawn from |

the bag, what is the probability that it will be red?

SOLUTION If we try to approach this problem using the sample space $S = \{R, G, B\}$, difficulties arise because there are a different number of each color of gumball. While we could write the sample space in a different way, it is simpler to view this probability as a ratio of gumballs of interest (red) to total gumballs. Since there are 6 red gumballs and a total of 11 gumballs altogether, the probability of getting a red gumball is $\frac{6}{11}$. ∎

In summary, probabilities are computed by determining a ratio of the number of objects of interest compared to total number of objects. In some cases this ratio can be determined directly. In other cases, we may list the sample space to ensure that we have accounted for all possible outcomes.

✓ **Check for Understanding:** Exercise/Problem Set A #7–21

MATHEMATICAL MORSEL

The following true story was reported in a newspaper article. A teacher was giving a standardized true/false achievement test when she noticed that Johnny was busily flipping a coin in the back of the room and then marking his answers. When asked what he was doing he replied, "I didn't have time to study, so instead I'm using a coin. If it comes up heads, I mark true, and if it comes up tails, I mark false." Half an hour later, when the rest of the students were done, the teacher saw Johnny still flipping away. She asked, "Johnny, what's taking you so long?" He replied, "It's like you always tell us. I'm just checking my answers."

Section 11.1   EXERCISE / PROBLEM SET A

EXERCISES

1. According to the weather report, there is a 20% chance of snow in the county tomorrow. Which of the following statements would be appropriate?
   a. Out of the next five days, it will snow one of those days.
   b. Of the 24 hours, snow will fall for 4.8 hours.
   c. Of past days when conditions were similar, one out of five had some snow.
   d. It will snow on 20% of the area of the county.

2. List the elements of the sample space for each of the following experiments.
   a. A quarter is tossed.
   b. A single die is rolled with faces labeled A, B, C, D, E, and F.
   c. A regular tetrahedron die (with four faces labeled 1, 2, 3, 4) is rolled and the number on the bottom face is recorded.
   d. The following "red-blue-yellow" spinner is spun once. (All sectors are equal in size and shape.)

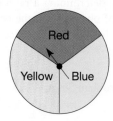

3. An experiment consists of tossing four coins. List each of the following.
   a. The sample space
   b. The event of a head on the first coin
   c. The event of three heads
   d. The event of a head or a tail on the fourth coin
   e. The event of a head on the second coin and a tail on the third coin

4. An experiment consists of tossing a regular dodecahedron die (with 12 congruent faces). List the following.
   a. The sample space
   b. The event of an even number
   c. The event of a number less than 8
   d. The event of a number divisible by 2 and 3
   e. The event of a number greater than 12

5. Identify which of the following events are certain (C), possible (P), or impossible (I).
   a. You throw a 2 on a die.
   b. A student in this class is less than 2 years old.
   c. Next week has only 5 days.

6. One way to find the sample space of an experiment involving two parts is to use the Cartesian product. For example, an experiment consists of tossing a dime and a quarter.

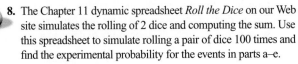

Sample space for dime $D = \{H, T\}$
Sample space for quarter $Q = \{H, T\}$

The sample space of the experiment is

$$D \times Q = \{(H, H), (H, T), (T, H), (T, T)\}.$$

Using this method, construct the sample space of the following experiment.

Toss a coin and roll a tetrahedron die (four faces).

7. A die is rolled 60 times with the following results recorded.

OUTCOME	1	2	3	4	5	6
FREQUENCY	10	9	10	12	8	11

Find the experimental probability of the following events.
a. Getting a 4
b. Getting an odd number
c. Getting a number greater than 3

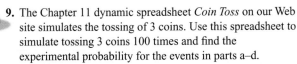

8. The Chapter 11 dynamic spreadsheet *Roll the Dice* on our Web site simulates the rolling of 2 dice and computing the sum. Use this spreadsheet to simulate rolling a pair of dice 100 times and find the experimental probability for the events in parts a–e.
a. The sum is even.
b. The sum is not 10.
c. The sum is a prime.
d. The sum is less than 9.
e. The sum is not less than 9.
f. Repeat parts a–e with 500 rolls.

9. The Chapter 11 dynamic spreadsheet *Coin Toss* on our Web site simulates the tossing of 3 coins. Use this spreadsheet to simulate tossing 3 coins 100 times and find the experimental probability for the events in parts a–d.
a. Getting no heads.
b. Getting at least 2 heads.
c. Getting at least one tail.
d. Getting exactly one tail.
e. Repeat parts a–d with 500 rolls.

10. Two dice are thrown. If each face is equally likely to turn up, find the following probabilities.
a. A 4 on the second die
b. An even number on each die
c. A total greater than 1

11. A card is drawn from a deck of 52 playing cards. What is the probability of drawing each of the following?
a. A black or a face card
b. An ace or a face card
c. Neither an ace nor a face card
d. Not an ace

12. A dropped thumbtack will land point up or point down.
a. Do you think one outcome will happen more often than the other? Which one?
b. The results for tossing a thumbtack 60 times are as follows.

Point up: 42 times
Point down: 18 times

What is the experimental probability that it lands point up? point down?
c. If the thumbtack was tossed 100 times, about how many times would you expect it to land point up? point down?

13. You have a key ring with five keys on it.
a. One of the keys is a car key. What is the probability of picking that one?
b. Two of the keys are for your apartment. What is the probability of selecting an apartment key?
c. What is the probability of selecting either the car key or an apartment key?
d. What is the probability of selecting neither the car key nor an apartment key?

14. An American roulette wheel has 38 slots around the rim. Two of them are numbered 0 and 00 and are green; the others are numbered from 1 to 36 and half are red, half are black. As the wheel is spun in one direction, a small ivory ball is rolled along the rim in the opposite direction. The ball has an equally likely chance of falling into any one of the 38 slots, assuming that the wheel is fair. Find the probability of each of the following.
a. The ball lands on 0 or 00.
b. The ball lands on 23.
c. The ball lands on a red number.
d. The ball does not land on 20–36.

15. What is the probability of getting yellow on each of the following spinners?

a.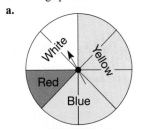

All eight sectors are equally sized and shaped.

b.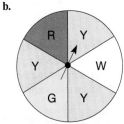

All six sectors are equally sized and shaped.

16. A die is made that has two faces marked with 2s, three faces marked with 3s, and one face marked with a 5. If this die is thrown once, find the following probabilities.
   a. Getting a 2
   b. Not getting a 2
   c. Getting an odd number
   d. Not getting an odd number

17. A card is drawn from a standard deck of cards. Find $P(A \cup B)$ in each part.
   a. $A = \{$getting a black card$\}$, $B = \{$getting a heart$\}$
   b. $A = \{$getting a diamond$\}$, $B = \{$getting an ace$\}$
   c. $A = \{$getting a face card$\}$, $B = \{$getting a spade$\}$
   d. $A = \{$getting a face card$\}$, $B = \{$getting a 7$\}$

18. With the spinner in Example 11.2(c), spin twice and record the color on each spin. For this experiment, consider the sample space and following events.

   A: getting a green on the first spin

   B: getting a yellow on the second spin

   $A \cup B$: getting a green on the first spin or a yellow on the second spin

	A	

	A	A	A	A
	RR	YR	GR	BR
B	RY	YY	GY	BY
	RG	YG	GG	BG
	RB	YB	GB	BB

Verify the following:

$$n(S) = 16, n(A) = 4, n(B) = 4$$
$$n(A \cup B) - 7, n(A \cap B) = 1$$
$$P(A) = \frac{4}{16}, P(B) = \frac{4}{16},$$
$$P(A \cup B) = \frac{7}{16}, \text{ and } P(A \cap B) = \frac{1}{16}.$$

Show that $P(A \cup B) = P(A) + P(B) - P(A \cap B)$. Apply this to find $P(A \cup B)$ in the following cases.
   a. A: getting a red on first spin
      B: getting same color on both spins
   b. A: getting a yellow or blue on first spin
      B: getting a red or green on second spin

19. For the experiment in Exercise 18 where a spinner is spun twice, consider the following events:

   A: getting a blue on the first spin

   B: getting a yellow on one spin

   C: getting the same color on both spins

Describe the following events and find their probabilities.
   a. $A \cup B$
   b. $B \cap C$
   c. $\overline{B}$

20. A student is selected at random. Let A be the event that the selected student is a sophomore and B be the event that the selected student is taking English. Write in words what is meant by each of the following probabilities.
   a. $P(A \cup B)$
   b. $P(A \cap B)$
   c. $1 - P(A)$

21. What is false about the following statements?
   a. The probability that it will rain today is 20% and the probability that it won't rain today is 60%.
   b. Since a deck of cards contains some face cards and some non-face cards, the probability of drawing a face card is $\frac{1}{2}$.
   c. The probability that I get an A in this course is 1.5.

PROBLEMS

22. Two fair six-sided dice are rolled and the sum of the dots on the top faces is recorded.
   a. Complete the table, showing the number of ways each sum can occur.

SUM	2	3	4	5	6	7	8	9	10	11	12
WAYS	1	2	3								

   b. Use the table to find the probability of the following events.

   A: The sum is prime.

   B: The sum is a divisor of 12.

   C: The sum is a power of 2.

   D: The sum is greater than 3.

23. The probability of a "geometric" event involving the concept of measure (length, area, volume) is determined as follows. Let $m(A)$ and $m(S)$ represent the measures of the event A and the sample space S, respectively. Then

$$P(A) = \frac{m(A)}{m(S)}.$$

For example, in the first figure, if the length of S is 12 cm and the length of A is 4 cm, then $P(A) = \frac{4}{12} = \frac{1}{3}$. Similarly, in the second figure, if the area of region B is 10 cm² and the area of region S is 60 cm², then $P(B) = \frac{10}{60} = \frac{1}{6}$.

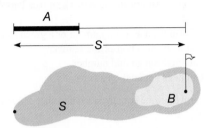

A bus travels between Albany and Binghamton, a distance of 100 miles. If the bus has broken down, we want to find the probability that it has broken down within 10 miles of either city.
  a. The road from Albany to Binghamton is the sample space. What is $m(S)$?
  b. Event A is that part of the road within 10 miles of either city. What is $m(A)$?
  c. Find $P(A)$.

24. The dartboard illustrated is made up of circles with radii of 1, 2, 3, and 4 units. A dart hits the target randomly. What is the probability that the dart hits the bull's-eye? (*Hint:* The area of a circle with radius r is πr^2.)

Section 11.1 **EXERCISE / PROBLEM SET B**

EXERCISES

1. For visiting a resort area you will receive a special gift.

CATEGORY I	CATEGORY II	CATEGORY III
A. New car	D. 25-inch color TV	G. Meat smoker
B. Food processor	E. AM/FM stereo	H. Toaster oven
C. $2500 cash	F. $1000 cash	I. $25 cash

The probabilities are as follows: A, 1 in 52,000; B, 25,736 in 52,000; C, 1 in 52,000; D, 3 in 52,000; E, 25,736 in 52,000; F, 3 in 52,000; G, 180 in 52,000; H, 180 in 52,000; I, 160 in 52,000.
  a. Which gifts are you most likely to receive?
  b. Which gifts are you least likely to receive?
  c. If 5000 people visit the resort, how many would be expected to receive a new car?

2. List the sample space for each experiment.
  a. Tossing a dime and a penny
  b. Tossing a nickel and rolling a die
  c. Drawing a marble from a bag containing one red and one blue marble and drawing a second marble from a bag containing one green and one white marble

3. A bag contains one each of red, green, blue, yellow, and white marbles. Give the sample space of the following experiments.
  a. One marble is drawn.
  b. One marble is drawn, then replaced, and a second one is then drawn.
  c. One marble is drawn, but not replaced, and a second one is drawn.

4. An experiment consists of tossing a coin and rolling a die. List each of the following.
  a. The sample space
  b. The event of getting a head
  c. The event of getting a 3
  d. The event of getting an even number
  e. The event of getting a head and a number greater than 4
  f. The event of getting a tail or a 5

5. Identify which of the following events are certain (C), possible (P), or impossible (I).
  a. There are at least four Sundays this month.
  b. It will rain today.
  c. You throw a head on a die.

6. Use the Cartesian product (see Part A, Exercise 6) to construct the sample space of the following experiment:

  Toss a coin, and draw a marble from a bag containing purple, green, and yellow marbles.

7. A loaded die (one in which outcomes are not equally likely) is tossed 1000 times with the following results.

OUTCOME	1	2	3	4	5	6
NUMBER OF TIMES	125	75	350	250	150	50

Find the experimental probability of the following events.
a. Getting a 2
b. Getting a 5
c. Getting a 1 or a 5
d. Getting an even number

8. Refer to Example 11.5, which gives the sample space for the experiment of rolling two dice, and give the theoretical probabilities of the events in parts a–e.
a. The sum is even.
b. The sum is not 10.
c. The sum is a prime.
d. The sum is less than 9.
e. The sum is not less than 9.
f. Compare your results with parts a–e to the results in Part A, Exercise 8. Which experimental probability is closer to the theoretical probability, 100 rolls or 500 rolls? Explain.

9. Refer to Example 11.4, in which three fair coins are tossed. Assign theoretical probabilities to the following events.
a. Getting a head on the first coin
b. Getting a head on the first coin and a tail on the second coin
c. Getting at least one tail
d. Getting exactly one tail
e. Compare your results in parts a–d to the results in Part A Exercise 9. Which experimental probability is closer to the theoretical probability, 100 tosses or 500 tosses? Explain.

10. Two dice are thrown. If each face is equally likely to turn up, find the following probabilities.
a. At least 7 dots in total
b. Total number of dots is greater than 1
c. An odd number on exactly one die.

11. A card is drawn at random from a deck of 52 playing cards. What is the probability of drawing each of the following?
a. A black card   **b.** A face card
c. Not a face card   **d.** A black face card

12. A weighted 6-sided die numbered 1–6 is tossed 75 times with the following results.

NUMBER	1	2	3	4	5	6
OCCURRENCES	24	12	15	8	10	6

a. What is the experimental probability of rolling a prime number?
b. If the die were rolled 200 times, how many times would you expect it to land on a 1?

13. A snack pack of colored candies contained the following:

COLOR	Brown	Tan	Yellow	Green	Orange
NUMBER	7	3	5	3	4

One candy is selected at random. Find the probability that it is of the following color.
a. Brown   **b.** Tan   **c.** Yellow
d. Green   **e.** Not brown   **f.** Yellow or orange

14. Find the probabilities of a ball landing on the following locations on an American roulette wheel (see Part A, Exercise 14).
a. The ball lands on an even number or a green slot.
b. The ball lands on a non-prime number.
c. The ball lands on an odd number.
d. The ball does not land on a zero.

15. A spinner with three equally sized and shaped sectors is spun once.

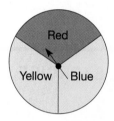

a. What is the probability of spinning red (R)?
b. What is the probability of spinning blue (B)?
c. What is the probability of spinning yellow (Y)?
d. Here the sample space is divided into three different events, R, B, and Y. Find the sum, $P(R) + P(B) + P(Y)$.
e. Repeat the preceding parts with the next spinner with eight sectors of equal size and shape. Do you get the same result as in part (d)?

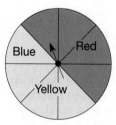

16. One die is thrown. If each face is equally likely to turn up, find the following probabilities.
a. Getting a 6
b. Not getting a 6
c. An even number turning up
d. An even number not turning up
e. The number dividing 6
f. The number not dividing 6

17. A card is drawn from a standard deck of cards. Find $P(A \cup B)$ in each part.

a. $A = \{$getting a heart$\}$, $B = \{$getting an even number$\}$
b. $A = \{$getting a club$\}$, $B = \{$getting a red card$\}$
c. $A = \{$getting an ace$\}$, $B = \{$getting a black card$\}$
d. $A = \{$getting a prime$\}$, $B = \{$getting a diamond$\}$

18. A bag contains six balls on which are the letters a, a, a, b, b, and c. One ball is drawn at random from the bag. Let A, B, and C be the events that balls a, b, or c are drawn, respectively.

a. What is $P(A)$?   **b.** What is $P(B)$?
c. What is $P(C)$?   **d.** Find $P(A) + P(B) + P(C)$.
e. An unknown number of balls, each lettered c, are added to the bag. It is known that now $P(A) = \frac{1}{4}$ and $P(B) = \frac{1}{6}$. What is $P(C)$?

19. Consider the experiment in Example 11.4 where three coins are tossed. Consider the following events:

A: The number of heads is 3.

B: The number of heads is 2.

C: The second coin lands heads.

Describe the following events and find their probabilities.
a. $A \cup B$ **b.** $\overline{B}$ **c.** $\overline{C}$ **d.** $B \cap C$

20. A card is drawn from a standard deck of cards. Let A be the event that the selected card is a spade and B be the event that the selected card is a face card. Write in words what is meant by each of the following probabilities.

a. $P(A \cup B)$
b. $P(A \cap B)$
c. $1 - P(B)$

21. What is false about the following statements?

a. Since there are 50 states, the probability of being born in Pennsylvania is $\frac{1}{50}$.
b. The probability that I am taking math is 0.80 and the probability that I am taking English is 0.50, so the probability that I am taking math and/or English is 1.30.
c. The probability that the basketball team wins its next game is $\frac{1}{3}$; the probability that it loses is $\frac{1}{2}$.

PROBLEMS

22. A bag contains 2 red balls, 3 blue balls, and 1 yellow ball.
a. What is the probability of drawing a red ball?
b. How many red balls must be added to the bag so that the probability of drawing a red ball is $\frac{1}{2}$?
c. How many blue balls must be added to the bag so that the probability of drawing a red ball is $\frac{1}{5}$?

23. A bag contains an unknown number of balls, some red, some blue, and some green. Find the smallest number of balls in the bag if the following probabilities are given. Give the P (green) for each situation.

a. $P(\text{red}) = \frac{1}{6}$, $P(\text{blue}) = \frac{1}{3}$

b. $P(\text{red}) = \frac{3}{5}$, $P(\text{blue}) = \frac{1}{6}$

c. $P(\text{red}) = \frac{1}{5}$, $P(\text{blue}) = \frac{3}{4}$

24. A paraglider wants to land in the unshaded region in the square field illustrated, since the shaded regions (four quarter circles) are briar patches. If he lost control and was going to hit the field randomly, what is the probability that he would miss a briar patch?

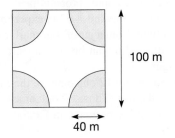

100 m

40 m

25. A microscopic worm is eating its way around the inside of a spherical apple of radius 6 cm. What is the probability that the worm is within 1 cm of the surface of the apple? (*Hint:* $V = \frac{4}{3}\pi r^3$, where r is the radius.)

26. Use the Chapter 11 eManipulative *Coin Toss* on our Web site to toss a single coin 100 times. From this experiment, determine an experimental probability of getting a head. Repeat the 100 toss experiment a few more times. Is the experimental probability the same for each experiment? Explain why or why not.

Analyzing Student Thinking

27. After working with some spinners, Jimmer concludes the following: If a spinner has 3 colors on it, then the probability of landing on one of those colors is $\frac{1}{3}$. Is he correct? Explain.

28. When rolling two dice (a red one and a blue one), Kyle claims that because the probability of rolling a 1 on the blue die is $\frac{1}{6}$ and the probability of rolling a 3 on the red die is $\frac{1}{6}$, then the probability of either of these events occurring is $\frac{2}{6}$. Is he correct? Explain.

29. Jaisha says that there are six outcomes when a die is tossed. Thus, there will be $2 \times 6 = 12$ outcomes when two dice are tossed. How should you respond?

30. James asserts that when tossing two coins, the probability of getting two heads is $\frac{1}{3}$ since there are three outcomes: 2 heads, a head and a tail, and 2 tails. How should you respond?

31. Melissa was tossing a quarter to try to determine the probability of getting heads after a certain number of tosses. She got five tails in a row! Jennifer said, "You are sure to get heads on the next toss!" Karen said, "No, she's definitely going to get tails!" Explain the reasoning of each of these students. Do you agree with either one? Explain.

32. Jessa was told that $P(\text{Event}) \leq 1$. She asks you what kind of event would give a probability of 1. How would you respond?

Problems Relating to the NCTM Standards and Curriculum Focal Points

1. The Focal Points for Grade 7 state "Students understand that when all outcomes of an experiment are equally likely, the theoretical probability of an event is the fraction of outcomes in which the event occurs." Provide an example of an experiment where the outcomes are not equally likely and one where the outcomes are equally likely.

2. The NCTM Standards state "All students should understand that the measure of the likelihood of an event can be represented by a number from 0 to 1." Explain why a probability cannot be greater than 1.

3. The NCTM Standards state "All students should understand and use appropriate terminology to describe complementary and mutually exclusive events." Explain what it means for two events to be mutually exclusive. How is knowing whether or not two events are mutually exclusive used when computing probabilities?

11.2   PROBABILITY AND COMPLEX EXPERIMENTS

STARTING POINT

Two red cubes, one white cube, and one blue cube are placed in a box. One cube is randomly drawn, its color is recorded, and it is returned to the box. A second cube is drawn and its color recorded. What is the probability of drawing a blue and a red cube? (*Hint*: Since order is not specified, this could be a BR or an RB.)

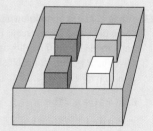

Tree Diagrams and Counting Techniques

In some experiments it is inefficient to list all the outcomes in the sample space. Therefore, we develop alternative procedures to compute probabilities.

A **tree diagram** can be used to represent the outcomes of an experiment. The experiment of drawing two marbles, one at a time, from a jar of four marbles without replacement, which was illustrated in Example 11.6, can be conveniently represented by the outcome tree diagram shown in Figure 11.9.

The diagram in Figure 11.9 shows that there are 12 outcomes in the sample space, since there are 12 right-hand endpoints on the tree. Those 12 outcomes are the same as those determined for the sample space of this experiment in Example 11.6. A tree diagram can also be used in the next example.

Problem-Solving Strategy
Draw a Diagram

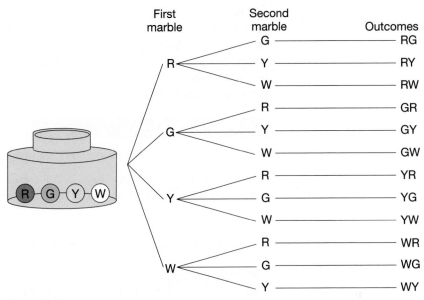

Figure 11.9

Example 11.10   Suppose that you can order a new sports car in a choice of five colors, [red, white, green, black, or silver (R, W, G, B, S)] and two types of transmissions, [manual or automatic (M, A)]. How many different types of cars can you order?

SOLUTION   Figure 11.10 shows that there are 10 types of cars corresponding to the 10 outcomes.

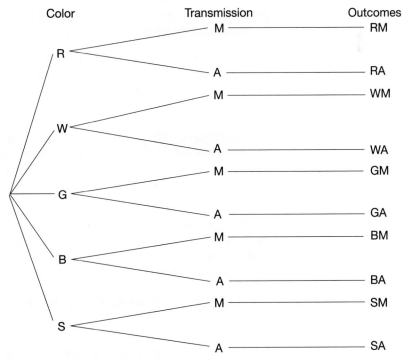

Figure 11.10

There are 10 different paths, or outcomes, for selecting cars in Example 11.10. Rather than count all the outcomes, we can actually compute the number of outcomes by making a simple observation about the tree diagram. Notice that there are five colors (five primary branches) and two transmission types (two secondary branches for each of the original five) or 10 (= 5 · 2) different combinations. This counting procedure suggests the following property.

PROPERTY

Fundamental Counting Property

If an event A can occur in r ways, and for each of these r ways, an event B can occur in s ways, then events A and B can occur, in succession, in $r \cdot s$ ways.

The fundamental counting property can be generalized to more than two events occurring in succession. This is illustrated in the next example.

Example 11.11 Suppose that pizzas can be ordered in 3 sizes (small, medium, large), 2 crust choices (thick or thin), 4 choices of meat toppings (sausage only, pepperoni only, both, or neither), and 2 cheese toppings (regular or double cheese). How many different ways can a pizza be ordered?

SOLUTION Since there are 3 size choices, 2 crust choices, 4 meat choices, and 2 cheese choices, by the fundamental counting property, there are $3 \cdot 2 \cdot 4 \cdot 2 = 48$ different types of pizzas altogether. ∎

Now let's apply the fundamental counting property to compute the probability of an event in a simple experiment.

Example 11.12 Find the probability of getting a sum of 11 when tossing a pair of fair dice.

SOLUTION Since each die has six faces and there are two dice, there are $6 \cdot 6 = 36$ possible outcomes according to the fundamental counting property. There are two ways of tossing an 11, namely (5, 6) and (6, 5). Therefore, the probability of tossing an eleven is $\frac{2}{36}$, or $\frac{1}{18}$. ∎

Example 11.13 A local hamburger outlet offers patrons a choice of four condiments: catsup, mustard, pickles, and onions. If the condiments are added or omitted in a random fashion, what is the probability that you will get one of the following types: catsup and onion, mustard and pickles, or one with everything?

SOLUTION Since we can view each condiment in two ways, namely as being either on or off a hamburger, there are $2^4 = 16$ various possible hamburgers (list them or draw a tree diagram to check this). Since there are three combinations you are interested in, the probability of getting one of the three combinations is $\frac{3}{16}$. ∎

 Check for Understanding: Exercise/Problem Set A #1–7

Probability Tree Diagrams

In addition to helping display and count outcomes, tree diagrams can be used to determine probabilities in complex experiments. By weighting the branches of a tree diagram with the appropriate probabilities, we can form a **probability tree diagram**,

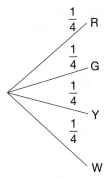

Figure 11.11

which in turn can be used to find probabilities of various events. For example, consider the jar containing four marbles—one red, one green, one yellow, and one white—that was used in Example 11.6 and at the beginning of this section. Suppose a single marble is drawn from the jar. What would the probability tree diagram corresponding to this experiment look like? Since each marble has an equally likely chance of being drawn, the probability of drawing any single marble is $\frac{1}{4}$, as is illustrated on each branch of the probability tree diagram in Figure 11.11. In the next example, two marbles are drawn without replacing the first marble before drawing a second time. This is referred to as **drawing without replacement**. If the marble *had* been replaced, it would be called **drawing with replacement**.

Example 11.14   If two marbles are drawn without replacement from the jar described above, what is the probability of getting a red marble and a white marble?

SOLUTION   This problem can be solved by extending the probability tree diagram in Figure 11.11, as shown in Figure 11.12. With only three marbles in the bag after the first marble is drawn, the probability on each branch of the second phase of the experiment is $\frac{1}{3}$. Since there are exactly 12 outcomes for this experiment, the probability of each outcome is represented at the end of each branch as $\frac{1}{12}$. To find the probability of getting a red and a white marble, we note that there are two possible ways of getting that outcome, RW and WR. Thus the probability of getting a red and white marble is

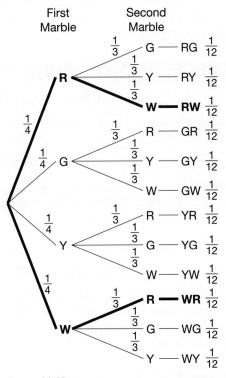

Figure 11.12

$$P(\text{RW}) + P(\text{WR}) = \frac{1}{12} + \frac{1}{12} = \frac{2}{12} = \frac{1}{6}.$$

It is important that some valuable connections be noted in the probability tree diagram shown in Figure 11.12. Consider the probabilities that lead to the outcome of RW, for example. The probability of getting a red on the first draw is $\frac{1}{4}$, the probability of getting a white on the second draw is $\frac{1}{3}$, and the probability of getting an RW as a final outcome is $\frac{1}{12}$. Each of these probabilities was determined based on the number of choices or outcomes. Notice, however, that the probability of the final outcome is equal to the product of the probabilities at the two stages leading to that outcome, namely $\frac{1}{4} \times \frac{1}{3} = \frac{1}{12}$. This observation gives rise to the following property, which is based on the fundamental counting property.

PROPERTY

Multiplicative Property of Probability

Suppose that an experiment consists of a sequence of simpler experiments. Then the probability of the final outcome is equal to the product of the probabilities of the simpler experiments that make up the sequence.

A second observation can be made about the probability tree diagram in Figure 11.12. The event of getting a red and a white has two possible outcomes $E = \{RW, WR\}$. This set has 2 elements and the sample space has 12 elements, so the probability could be determined by computing the ratio $\frac{2}{12}$. Since the two outcomes of getting a red and white in the event are mutually exclusive, the probability can be determined by adding up the probabilities in the individual outcomes, as was illustrated in the solution to Example 11.14. This method of adding the probabilities gives rise to the additive property of probability.

PROPERTY

Additive Property of Probability

Suppose that an event E is the union of pairwise mutually exclusive simpler events $E_1, E_2, \ldots, E_n$, where $E_1, E_2, \ldots, E_n$ are from a sample space S. Then

$$P(E) = P(E_1) + P(E_2) + \ldots + P(E_n).$$

The probabilities of the events $E_1, E_2, \ldots, E_n$ can be viewed as those associated with the ends of branches in a probability tree diagram.

Notice that this property is an extension of the property

$$P(A \cup B) = P(A) + P(B) - P(A \cap B)$$

where $A \cap B = \varnothing$, since we required that all the events be pairwise mutually exclusive (i.e., the intersection of all pairs of E's is the empty set).

The multiplicative and additive properties of probabilities are further illustrated and clarified in the following two examples.

Figure 11.13

Example 11.15 A jar contains three marbles, two black and one red (Figure 11.13). Two marbles are drawn *with replacement*. What is the probability that both marbles are black? Assume that the marbles are equally likely to be drawn.

SOLUTION 1 Figure 11.14(a) shows $3 \cdot 3 = 9$ equally likely branches in the tree, of which 4 correspond to the event "two black marbles are drawn." Thus the probability of drawing two black marbles with replacement is $\frac{4}{9}$. Instead of comparing the number of successful outcomes (4) with the total number of outcomes (9), we could have simply used the additive property of probability and added the individual probabilities at the ends of the branches in Figure 11.14(b). That is, the probability is $\frac{1}{9} + \frac{1}{9} + \frac{1}{9} + \frac{1}{9} = \frac{4}{9}$. Notice that the end of each branch in Figure 11.14(b) is weighted with a probability of $\frac{1}{9}$, since there are 9 equally likely outcomes. The probability of $\frac{1}{9}$ can also be determined by using the multiplicative property of probability and multiplying the probabilities on each of the branches that lead to the outcomes, $\frac{1}{3} \times \frac{1}{3} = \frac{1}{9}$.

NCTM Standard
All students should compute probabilities for simple compound events, using such methods as organized lists, tree diagrams, and area models.

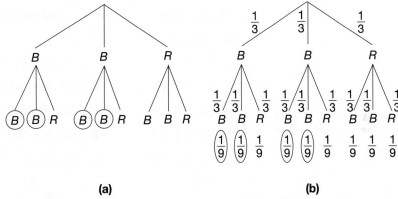

(a)   (b)

Figure 11.14

SOLUTION 2 The solution to this problem can be approached differently by labeling the probability tree diagram in a way that relies on the additive and multiplicative properties of probability. Figure 11.15 illustrates how the number of branches in part (a) can be reduced by collapsing similar branches and then weighting them accordingly, parts (b) and (c).

Problem-Solving Strategy
Draw a Diagram

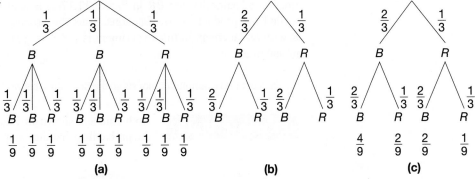

(a)   (b)   (c)

Figure 11.15

Next we must label the ends of the branches by relying on the multiplicative property of probability. Since the probability of drawing the first black marble is $\frac{2}{3}$, and the probability of drawing the second black marble is $\frac{2}{3}$, then the probability of drawing two black marbles in a row is $P(BB) = \frac{2}{3} \times \frac{2}{3} = \frac{4}{9}$, which is consistent with our first solution. The remainder of the diagram in Figure 11.15(c) can be filled out using $P(BR) = \frac{2}{3} \times \frac{1}{3} = \frac{2}{9}$, $P(RB) = \frac{1}{3} \times \frac{2}{3} = \frac{2}{9}$, and $P(RR) = \frac{1}{3} \times \frac{1}{3} = \frac{1}{9}$. ∎

While the additive property of probability follows quite naturally from properties of sets, the multiplicative property was based on an observation of patterns in the probability tree diagram in Figure 11.12 and on the fundamental counting property. The next example helps to illustrate why the multiplicative property works.

Figure 11.16

Example 11.16   Consider a jar with three black marbles and one red marble (Figure 11.16). For the experiment of drawing two marbles with replacement, what is the probability of drawing a black marble and then a red marble in that order?

SOLUTION   The entries in the 4×4 array in Figure 11.17(a) show all possible outcomes of drawing two marbles with replacement.

All possible draws

Second draw

	B	B	B	R
B	BB	BB	BB	BR
B	BB	BB	BB	BR
B	BB	BB	BB	BR
R	RB	RB	RB	RR

First draw

(a)

First draw B

	B	B	B	R
B	BB	BB	BB	BR
B	BB	BB	BB	BR
B	BB	BB	BB	BR
R	RB	RB	RB	RR

(b)

First draw B
Second draw R

	B	B	B	R
B	BB	BB	BB	BR
B	BB	BB	BB	BR
B	BB	BB	BB	BR
R	RB	RB	RB	RR

(c)

Figure 11.17

The outcomes in which B was drawn first, namely those with a B on the left, are surrounded by a rectangle in Figure 11.17(b). Notice that $\frac{3}{4}$ of the pairs are included in the rectangle, since 3 out of 4 marbles are black. In Figure 11.17(c), a dashed rectangle is drawn around those pairs where a B is drawn first and an R is drawn second. Observe that the portion surrounded by the dashed rectangle is $\frac{1}{4}$ of the pairs inside the rectangle, since $\frac{1}{4}$ of the marbles in the jar are red. The procedure used to find the fraction of pairs that are BR in Figure 11.17(c) is analogous to the model we used to find the product of two fractions. Thus the probability of drawing a B then an R with replacement in this experiment is $\frac{3}{4} \times \frac{1}{4} = \frac{3}{16}$, the *products* of the individual probabilities. ■

The next two examples demonstrate the flexibility that probability tree diagrams provide.

Example 11.17   Both spinners shown in Figure 11.18(a) are spun. Find the probability that they stop on the same color.

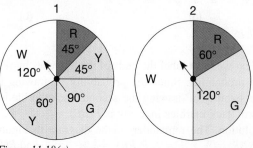

Figure 11.18(a)

SOLUTION In order to draw a probability tree diagram, we must first determine the probabilities of stopping on the various colors on each of the spinners. In Section 11.1, the spinners could be divided into equal regions to compute the appropriate probability. In this case, the degree measure can be used to describe the portion of the entire circle that each colored region occupies. On spinner 1, the red region occupies $45°$ of the total $360°$ around the center of the circle. Thus, the probability of spinner 1 stopping on a red is $P(R) = \frac{45}{360} = \frac{1}{8}$. Similarly the probabilities of spinner 1 stopping on a yellow, white, or green are $P(Y) = \frac{45 + 60}{360} = \frac{7}{24}$, $P(W) = \frac{120}{360} = \frac{1}{3}$, and $P(G) = \frac{90}{360}$, respectively. For spinner 2 the probabilities are $P(W) = \frac{180}{360} = \frac{1}{2}$, $P(R) = \frac{60}{360} = \frac{1}{6}$, and $P(G) = \frac{120}{360} = \frac{1}{3}$. These probabilities can now be used to label the appropriate branches of the tree diagram, as shown in Figure 11.18(b).

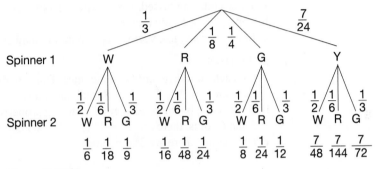

Figure 11.18(b)

The desired event is {WW, RR, GG}. By the multiplicative property of probability, $P(WW) = \frac{1}{3} \cdot \frac{1}{2} = \frac{1}{6}$, $P(RR) = \frac{1}{8} \cdot \frac{1}{6} = \frac{1}{48}$, and $P(GG) = \frac{1}{4} \cdot \frac{1}{3} = \frac{1}{12}$. By the additive property of probability, $P(\{WW, RR, GG\}) = \frac{1}{6} + \frac{1}{48} + \frac{1}{12} = \frac{13}{48}$. ∎

Problem-Solving Strategy
Draw a Diagram

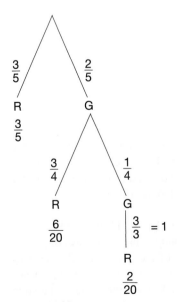

Figure 11.19

Example 11.18   A jar contains three red gumballs and two green gumballs. An experiment consists of drawing gumballs one at a time from the jar, without replacement, until a red one is obtained. Find the probability of the following events.

  A: Only one draw is needed.
  B: Exactly two draws are needed.
  C: Exactly three draws are needed.

SOLUTION In constructing the probability tree diagram, it is important to remember that this experiment involves drawing until a red gumball appears. As a result, the tree diagram (see Figure 11.19) terminates whenever a red is drawn. Since the gumballs are being drawn without replacement, the number of gumballs in the bag changes, as do the corresponding probabilities, after each gumball is drawn. Using the multiplicative property of probability, the probabilities at the end of each branch can easily be determined. Hence $P(A) = \frac{3}{5}$, $P(B) = \frac{2}{5} \cdot \frac{3}{4} = \frac{6}{20} = \frac{3}{10}$, and $P(C) = \frac{2}{5} \cdot \frac{1}{4} \cdot 1 = \frac{2}{20} = \frac{1}{10}$. ∎

In summary, the probability of a complex event can be found as follows:

1. Construct the appropriate probability tree diagram.
2. Assign probabilities to each branch.

3. Multiply the probabilities along individual branches to find the probability of the outcome at the end of each branch.

4. Add the probabilities of the relevant outcomes, depending on the event.

Finally we would like to examine a certain class of experiments whose outcomes can be counted using a more convenient procedure. Such experiments consist of a sequence of smaller identical experiments *each having two outcomes*. Coin-tossing experiments are in this general class since there are only two outcomes (heads/tails) on each toss.

Example 11.19

a. Three coins are tossed. How many outcomes are there?
b. Repeat for 4, 5, and 6 coins.
c. Repeat for n coins, where n is a counting number.

SOLUTION

a. For each coin there are two outcomes. Thus, by the fundamental counting property, there are $2 \times 2 \times 2 = 2^3 = 8$ total outcomes.
b. For 4 coins, by the fundamental counting property, there are $2^4 = 16$ outcomes. For 5 and 6 coins, there are $2^5 = 32$ and $2^6 = 64$ outcomes, respectively.
c. For n coins, there are 2^n outcomes. ■

Counting outcomes in experiments such as coin tosses can be done systematically. Figure 11.20 shows all the outcomes for the experiments in which 1, 2, or 3 coins are tossed.

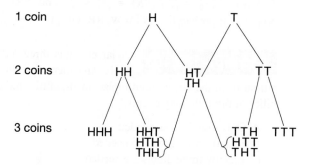

Outcomes in coin experiments
Figure 11.20

From the sample space for the experiment of tossing 1 coin we can determine the outcomes for an experiment of tossing 2 coins (Figure 11.20, second row). The two ways of getting exactly 1 head (middle two entries) are derived from the outcomes for tossing 1 coin. The outcome H for 1 coin yields the outcomes HT for two coins, while the outcome T for one coin yields TH for two coins.

In a similar way, the outcomes for tossing 3 coins (Figure 11.20, third row) are derived from the outcomes for tossing 2 coins. For example, the three ways of getting 2 heads when tossing 3 coins is the *sum* of the number of ways of getting 2 or 1 heads when tossing 2 coins. This can be seen by taking the 1 arrangement for getting 2 heads with 2 coins and making the third coin a tail. Similarly, take the arrangements of getting 1 head with 2 coins, and make the third coin a head. This gives all 3 possibilities.

We can abbreviate this counting procedure, as shown in Figure 11.21.

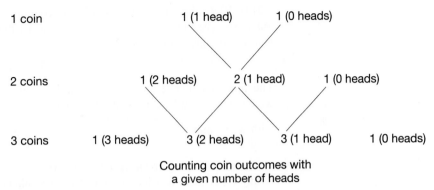

Counting coin outcomes with
a given number of heads

Figure 11.21

Problem-Solving Strategy
Look for a Pattern

Notice that the row of possible arrangements when tossing 3 coins begins with 1. Thereafter each entry is the sum of the two entries immediately above it until the final 1 on the right. This pattern generalizes to any whole number of coins. The number array that we obtain is **Pascal's triangle**. Figure 11.22 shows seven rows of Pascal's triangle.

								Sum
			1					2^0
1 coin		1		1				2^1
2 coins		1	2	1				$4 = 2^2$
3 coins		1	3	3	1			$8 = 2^3$
4 coins	1	4	6	4	1			$16 = 2^4$
5 coins	1	5	10	10	5	1		$32 = 2^5$
6 coins	1	6	15	20	15	6	1	$64 = 2^6$

Figure 11.22

Notice that the sum of the entries in the nth row is 2^n.

Example 11.20   Six fair coins are tossed. Find the probability of getting exactly 3 heads.

SOLUTION From Example 11.19 there are $2^6 = 64$ outcomes. Furthermore, the 6-coins row of Pascal's triangle (Figure 11.22) may be interpreted as follows:

1(6H) 6(5H) 15(4H) 20(3H) 15(2H) 6(1H) 1(0H).

Thus there are 20 ways of getting exactly 3 heads, and the probability of 3 heads is $\frac{20}{64} = \frac{5}{16}$. ∎

Notice in Example 11.20 that even though half the coins are heads, the probability is not $\frac{1}{2}$, as one might initially guess.

Example 11.21 Use Pascal's triangle to find the probability of getting at least four heads when tossing seven coins.

SOLUTION First, by the fundamental counting property, there are 2^7 possible outcomes when tossing 7 coins. Next, construct the row that begins 1, 7, 21, . . . in Pascal's triangle in Figure 11.22.

$$1 \quad 7 \quad 21 \quad 35 \quad 35 \quad 21 \quad 7 \quad 1$$

The first four numbers—1, 7, 21, and 35—represent the number of outcomes for which there are at least four heads. Thus the probability of tossing at least four heads with seven coins is $\dfrac{(1 + 7 + 21 + 35)}{2^7} = \dfrac{64}{128} = \dfrac{1}{2}$. ∎

Pascal's triangle provides a useful way of counting coin arrangements or outcomes in any experiment in which only two equally likely possibilities exist. For example, births (male/female), true/false exams, and target shooting (hit/miss) are sources of such experiments.

✔ **Check for Understanding:** Exercise/Problem Set A #8–13

MATHEMATICAL MORSEL

The University of Oregon football team has developed quite a wardrobe. Most football teams have two different uniforms: one for home games and one for away games. The University of Oregon team will have as many as 384 different uniform combinations from which to choose. Rather than the usual light and dark jerseys, they have 4 different colored jerseys: white, yellow, green, and black. Beyond that, however, they have 4 different colored pants, 4 different colored pairs of socks, 2 different colored pairs of shoes, and 2 different colored helmets with a 3rd one on the way. If all color combinations are allowed, the fundamental counting principle would suggest that they have $4 \times 4 \times 4 \times 2 \times 3 = 384$ possible uniform combinations. Whether a uniform consisting of a green helmet, black jersey, yellow pants, white socks, and black shoes would look stylish is debatable.

Section 11.2 EXERCISE / PROBLEM SET A

EXERCISES

1. The simplest tree diagrams have **one stage** (when the experiment involves just one action). For example, consider drawing one ball from a box containing a red, a white, and a blue ball. To draw the tree, follow these steps.

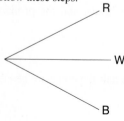

i. Draw a single dot.
ii. Draw one branch for each outcome.
iii. At the end of the branch, label it by listing the outcome.

Draw one-stage trees to represent each of the following experiments.

a. Tossing a dime
b. Drawing a marble from a bag containing one red, one green, one black, and one white marble
c. Choosing a TV program from among channels 2, 6, 9, 12, and 13

d. Spinning the following spinner, where all central angles are 120°

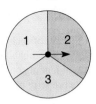

2. In each part, draw **two-stage** trees to represent the following experiments, which involve a sequence of two experiments.

   i. Draw the one-stage tree for the outcomes of the first experiment.
   ii. Starting at the end of *each branch* of the tree in step 1, draw the (one-stage) tree for the outcomes of the second experiment.

   a. Tossing a coin twice
   b. Drawing a marble from a box containing one yellow and one green marble, then drawing a marble from a box containing one yellow, one red, and one blue marble
   c. Having two children in the family

3. Trees may have more than two stages. Draw outcome trees to represent the following experiment: Tossing a coin three times

4. In some cases, what happens at the first stage of the tree affects what can happen at the next stage. For example, one ball is drawn from the box containing one red, one white, and one blue ball, but not replaced before the second ball is drawn.

   a. Draw the first stage of the tree.
   b. If the red ball was selected and not replaced, what possible outcomes are possible on the second draw? Starting at *R*, draw a branch to represent these outcomes.
   c. If the white was drawn first, what outcomes are possible on the second draw? Draw these branches.
   d. Do likewise for the case that blue was drawn first.
   e. How many total outcomes are possible?

5. A die is rolled. If it is greater than or equal to 3, a coin is tossed. If it is less than 3, a spinner with equal sections of purple, green, and black is spun. Draw a two-stage tree for this experiment.

6. For your vacation, you will travel from your home to New York City, then to London. You may travel to New York City by car, train, bus, or plane, and from New York to London by ship or plane.

   a. Draw a tree diagram to represent possible travel arrangements.
   b. How many different routes are possible?
   c. Apply the fundamental counting property to find the number of possible routes. Does your answer agree with part (b)?

7. Apricot Apparel sells 5 shirts in five different styles, six different sizes, and 10 different colors. How many different kinds of shirts do they sell?

8. Draw a probability tree diagram for drawing a ball from the following containers. An example for the first container is provided.

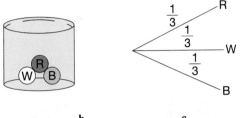

 a.   b.   c.

9. Another white ball is added to the container with one red, one white, and one blue ball. Since there are four balls, we could draw a tree with 4 branches, as illustrated. Each of these branches is equally likely, so we label them with probability $\frac{1}{4}$. However, we could combine the branches, as illustrated. Since two out of the four balls are white, $P(W) = \frac{2}{4} = \frac{1}{2}$, and the branch is so labeled.

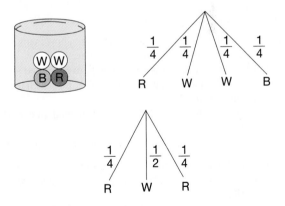

Draw a probability tree representing drawing one ball from the following containers. Combine branches where possible.

a. 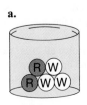   b.

10. The branches of a probability tree diagram may or may not represent equally likely outcomes. The given probability tree diagram represents the outcome for each of the following spinners. Write the appropriate probabilities along each branch in each case.

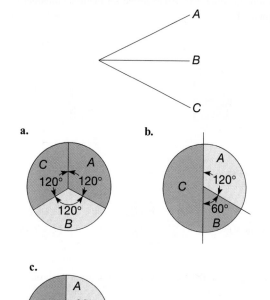

11. The spinner in part b of Exercise 10 is spun twice.
   a. Draw a two-stage outcome tree for this experiment.
   b. Turn the outcome tree into a probability tree diagram by labeling all of the branches with the appropriate probabilities.
   c. Determine the probability of each outcome by using the multiplicative property of probability.
   d. Find the probability of landing on the same color twice by using the additive property of probability.

12. A marble is drawn from a bag containing two white, one red, and one blue marble. Without replacing the first marble, a second marble is drawn.
   a. Draw a two-stage outcome tree for this experiment.
   b. Turn the outcome tree into a probability tree diagram by labeling all of the branches with the appropriate probabilities.
   c. Determine the probability of each outcome by using the multiplicative property of probability.
   d. Find the probability of getting a red and a white marble by using the additive property of probability.

13. The row of Pascal's triangle that starts 1, 4, . . . would be useful in finding probabilities for an experiment of tossing four coins.
   a. Interpret the meaning of each number in the row.
   b. Find the probability of exactly one head and three tails.
   c. Find the probability of at least one tail turning up.
   d. Should you bet in favor of getting exactly two heads or should you bet against it?

PROBLEMS

14. If each of the 10 digits is chosen at random, how many ways can you choose the following numbers?
   a. A two-digit code number, repeated digits permitted
   b. A three-digit identification card number, for which the first digit cannot be a 0
   c. A four-digit bicycle lock number, where no digit can be used twice
   d. A five-digit zip code number, with the first digit not zero

15. a. If eight horses are entered in a race and three finishing places are considered, how many finishing orders are possible?
   b. If the top three horses are Lucky One, Lucky Two, and Lucky Three, in how many possible orders can they finish?
   c. What is the probability that these three horses are the top finishers in the race?

16. Three children are born to a family.
   a. Draw a tree diagram to represent the possible order of boys (B) and girls (G).
   b. How many of the outcomes involve all girls? two girls, one boy? one girl, two boys? no girls?
   c. How do these results relate to Pascal's triangle?

17. In shooting at a target three times, on each shot you either hit or miss (and we assume these results are equally likely). The 1, 3, 3, 1 row of Pascal's triangle can be used to find the probabilities of hits and misses.

NUMBER OF HITS	3	2	1	0
NUMBER OF WAYS (8 TOTAL)	1	3	3	1
PROBABILITY	$\frac{1}{8}$	$\frac{3}{8}$	$\frac{3}{8}$	$\frac{1}{8}$

   a. Use Pascal's triangle to fill in the entries in the following table for shooting 4 times.

NUMBER OF HITS	4	3	2	1	0
NUMBER OF WAYS					
PROBABILITY					

   b. Which is more likely, that in three shots you will have three hits or that in four shots you will have three hits and one miss?

18. The Los Angeles Lakers and Portland Trailblazers are going to play a "best two out of three" series. The tree shows the possible outcomes.

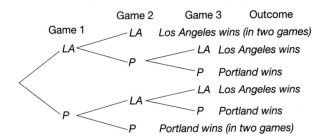

a. If the teams are evenly matched, each has a probability of $\frac{1}{2}$ of winning any game. Label each branch of the tree with the appropriate probability.
b. Find the probability that Los Angeles wins the series in two straight games and that Portland wins the series after losing the first game.
c. Find the following probabilities.
   i. Los Angeles wins when three games are played.
   ii. Portland wins the series.
   iii. The series requires three games to decide a winner.

19. Suppose that the Los Angeles Lakers and the Portland Trailblazers are not quite evenly matched in their "best two out of three" series. Let the probability that the Lakers win an individual game with Portland be $\frac{3}{5}$.
a. What is the probability that Portland wins an individual game?
b. Label the branches of the probability tree with the appropriate probability.
c. What is the probability that Portland wins in two straight games?
d. What is the probability that LA wins the series when losing the second game?
e. What is the probability that the series goes for three games?
f. What is the probability that LA wins the series?

20. Team A and team B are playing a "best three out of five" series to determine a champion. Team A is the stronger team with an estimated probability of $\frac{2}{3}$ of winning any game.
a. Team A can win the series by winning three straight games. That path of the tree would look like this:

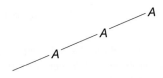

Label the branches with probabilities and find the probability that this occurs.

b. Team A can win the series in four games, losing one game and winning three games. This could occur as $BAAA$, $ABAA$, or $AABA$ (Why not $AAAB$?). Compare the probabilities of the following paths.
   i.
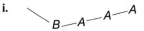
   ii.
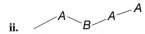
What do you observe? What is the probability that team A wins the series in four games?
c. The series could go to five games. Team A could win in this case by winning three games and losing two games (they must win the last game). List the ways in which this could be done. What is the probability of each of these ways? What is the probability of team A winning the series in five games?
d. What is the probability that team A will be the winner of the series? that team B will be the winner?

21. a. Complete the tree diagram to show the possible ways of answering a true/false test with three questions.

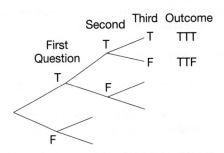

b. How many possible outcomes are there?
c. How many of these outcomes give the correct answers?
d. What is the probability of guessing all the correct answers?

22. Your drawer contains two blue socks, two brown socks, and two black socks. Without looking, you pull out two socks.
a. Draw a probability tree diagram (use E for blue, N for brown, K for black).
b. List the sample space.
c. List the event that you have a matched pair.
d. What is the probability of getting a matched pair?
e. What is the probability of getting a matched blue pair?

23. Your drawer contains two blue socks, two brown socks, and two black socks. What is the minimum number of socks that you would need to pull, at random, from the drawer to be sure that you have a matched pair?

24. A customer calls a pet store seeking a male puppy. An assistant looks and sees that they have three puppies but does not know the sex of any of them. What is the probability that the pet store has a male puppy?

25. A box contains four white and six black balls. A second box contains seven white and three black balls. A ball is picked at random from the first box and placed in the second box. A ball is then picked from the second box. What is the probability that it is white?

26. a. How many equilateral triangles of all sizes are in a $6 \times 6 \times 6$ equilateral triangle similar to the one in Problem 18 of Part B in Chapter 1, Section 1.2?
b. How many would be in an $8 \times 8 \times 8$ equilateral triangle?

| Section 11.2 | **EXERCISE / PROBLEM SET B** |

EXERCISES

1. Draw one-stage trees to represent each of the following situations.
  a. Having one child
  b. Choosing to go to Boston, Miami, or Los Angeles for vacation
  c. Hitting a free throw or missing
  d. Drawing a ball from a bag containing balls labeled A, B, C, D, and E

2. a. Draw a two-stage tree to represent the experiment of tossing one coin and rolling one die.
  b. How many possible outcomes are there?
  c. In how many ways can the first event (tossing one coin) occur?
  d. In how many ways can the second event (rolling one die) occur?
  e. According to the fundamental counting property, how many outcomes are possible for this experiment?

3. Draw a multiple-stage outcome tree diagram to represent having four children in a family (Use B for boy and G for girl.)

4. Outcome tree diagrams may not necessarily be symmetrical. For example, from the box containing one red, one white, and one blue ball, we will draw balls (without replacing) until the red ball is chosen. Draw the outcome tree.

5. A coin is tossed. If it lands heads up, a die will be tossed. If it lands tails up, a spinner with equal sections of blue, red, and yellow will be spun. Draw a two-stage tree for the experiment.

6. Bob has just left town A. There are five roads leading from town A to town B and four roads leading from town B to C. How many possible ways does he have to travel from A to C?

7. A computer company has the following options for their computers: three different size screens, two different kinds of disk drives, and six different amounts of memory. How many different kinds of computers do they offer?

8. The given tree represents the outcomes for each of the following experiments in which one ball is taken from the container. Write the appropriate probabilities along each branch for each case.

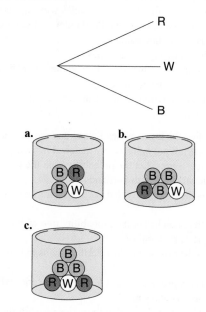

9. A container holds two yellow and three red balls. A ball will be drawn, its color noted, and then replaced. A second ball will be drawn and its color recorded. A tree diagram representing the outcomes is given.

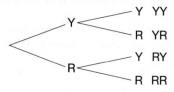

a. On the diagram, indicate the probability of each branch.
b. What is the probability of drawing YY? of drawing RY?
c. What is the probability of drawing at least one yellow?
d. Show a different way of computing part (c), using the complement event.

10. Draw probability tree diagrams for the following experiments.

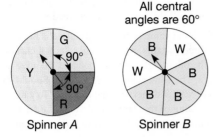

All central angles are 60°

Spinner *A*   Spinner *B*

a. Spinner *A* spun once
b. Spinner *B* spun once
c. Spinner *A* spun, then spinner *B* spun [*Hint:* Draw a two-stage tree combining results of parts (a) and (b).]

11. For an experiment, a die is rolled and then a coin is tossed.
a. Draw an outcome tree for this experiment.
b. Turn the outcome tree into a probability tree diagram by labeling all of the branches with the appropriate probabilities.

c. Determine the probability of each outcome by using the multiplicative property of probability.
d. Find the probability of getting an even number and a head by using the additive property of probability.

12. A marble is drawn from a bag containing four white, three red, and two blue marbles. Without replacing the first marble, a second marble is drawn.
a. Draw a two-stage outcome tree for this experiment.
b. Turn the outcome tree into a probability tree diagram by labeling all of the branches with the appropriate probabilities.
c. Determine the probability of each outcome by using the multiplicative property of probability.
d. Find the probability of getting a red and a white marble by using the additive property of probability.

13. Four coins are tossed.
a. Draw a tree diagram to represent the arrangements of heads (H) and tails (T).
b. How many outcomes involve all heads? three heads, one tail? two heads, two tails? one head, three tails? no heads?
c. How do these results relate to Pascal's triangle?

PROBLEMS

14. A given locality has the telephone prefix of 237.
a. How many seven-digit phone numbers are possible with this prefix?
b. How many of these possibilities have four ending numbers that are all equal?
c. What is the probability of having one of the numbers in part (b)?
d. What is the probability that the last four digits are consecutive (i.e., 1234)?

15. Many radio stations in the United States have call letters that begin with a W or a K and have four letters.
a. How many arrangements of four letters are possible as call letters?
b. What is the probability of having call letters KIDS?

16. A local menu offers choices from eight entrées, three varieties of potatoes, either salad or soup, and five beverages.
a. If you select an entrée with potatoes, salad or soup, and beverage, how many different meals are possible?
b. How many of these meals have soup?
c. What is the probability that a patron has a meal with soup?
d. What is the probability that a patron has a meal with french fries (one of the potato choices) and cola (one of the beverage choices)?

17. A family decides to have five children. Since there are just two outcomes, boy (B) and girl (G), for each birth and since

we will assume that each outcome is equally likely (this is not exactly true), Pascal's triangle can be applied.
a. Which row of Pascal's triangle would give the pertinent information?
b. In how many ways can the family have one boy and four girls?
c. In how many ways can the family have three boys and two girls?
d. What is the probability of having three boys? of having at least three boys?

18. The Houston Rockets and San Antonio Spurs will play a "best two out of three" series. Assume that Houston has a probability of $\frac{1}{3}$ of winning any game.
a. Draw a probability tree showing possible outcomes of the series. Label the branches with appropriate probabilities.
b. What is the probability that Houston wins in two straight games? that San Antonio wins in two straight games?
c. What is the probability that the series goes to three games?
d. What is the probability that Houston wins the series after losing the first game?
e. What is the probability that San Antonio wins the series?

19. a. Make a tree diagram to show all the ways that you can choose answers to a multiple-choice test with three questions. The first question has four possible answers, a, b, c, and d; the second has three possible answers, a, b, and c; the third has two possible answers, a and b.
 b. How many possible outcomes are there?
 c. Apply the fundamental counting property to find the number of possible ways. Does your answer agree with part (b)?
 d. If all the answer possibilities are equally likely, what is the probability of guessing the right set of answers?

20. Babe Ruth's lifetime batting average was .343. In three times at bat, what is the probability of the following? (*Hint:* Draw a probability tree diagram.)
 a. He gets three hits.
 b. He gets no hits.
 c. He gets at least one hit.
 d. He gets exactly one hit.

21. A coin will be thrown until it lands heads up or until the coin has been thrown five times.
 a. Draw a probability tree to represent this experiment.
 b. What is the probability that the coin is tossed just once? just twice? just three times? just four times?
 c. What is the probability of tossing the coin five times without getting a head?

22. You come home on a dark night and find the porchlight burned out. Since you cannot tell which key is which, you randomly try the five keys on your key ring until you find one that opens your apartment door. Two of the keys on your key ring unlock the door. Find the probability of opening the door on the first or second try.
 a. Draw the tree diagram for the experiment.
 b. Compute the probability of opening the door with the first or second key.

23. The ski lift at a ski resort takes skiers to the top of the mountain. As the skiers head down the trails, they have a variety of choices. Assume that at each intersection of trails, the skier is equally likely to go left or right. Find the percent (to the nearest whole percent) of the skiers who end up at each lettered location at the bottom of the hill.

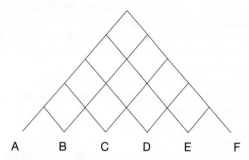

24. A prisoner is given 10 white balls, 10 black balls, and 2 boxes. He is told that his fate depends on drawing a ball from one of the two boxes. If it is white, the prisoner will go free; if it is black, he will remain in prison. Each box has an equally likely chance of being selected, but the prisoner can distribute the balls between the boxes to his advantage. How should he arrange the balls in the boxes to give himself the best chance for freedom?

25. In a television game show, a major prize is hidden behind one of three curtains. A contestant selects a curtain. Then one of the other curtains is opened and the prize is *not* there. The contestant can pick again. Should she switch or stay with her original choice? (To gain a better understanding of this problem, do the Chapter 11 eManipulative activity *Let's Make a Deal* on our Web site.)

26. A box contains four white and eight black balls. You pick out a ball with your left hand and don't look at it. Then you pick out a ball with your right hand and don't look at it.
 a. What is the probability the ball in your left hand is white?
 b. Next, you look at the ball in your right hand and it is black. Now what is the probability that the ball in your left hand is white?

27. Prove or disprove: In any set of four consecutive Fibonacci numbers, the difference of the squares of the middle pair equals the product of the end pair.

Analyzing Student Thinking

28. Maxwell knows how to find the probability of the king of hearts, which is represented by P(king and heart), but he is trying to figure out the probability of drawing a king or a heart at random from a deck of cards. He says, "*Or* means 'plus,' so the answer must be 17/52." Does *or* ever mean "plus"? How would you explain this problem to Maxwell?

29. Parker claims that if you draw a card, replace it, then draw a second card from a deck of 52 cards, there are 52 + 52 ways to do this. How should you respond?

30. Megan says that the probability of drawing two aces from a 52-card deck without replacing the first one is the same as if you draw an ace and a two without replacement. How should you respond?

31. Matthew asks you how to use Pascal's triangle to solve problems involving two dice. How should you respond?

32. Nancy says that the probability of choosing a king from a 52-card deck is 4/52 and the probability of drawing a heart is 13/52. Thus, the probability of drawing the king of hearts is (4 + 13)/52. Is she correct? Explain.

33. Using Pascal's triangle, Riley says that the probability of getting 3 or 4 heads when tossing five coins is $(10 + 10)/2^5$. Is he correct? Explain.

34. Herman's father was going on a business trip and wished to minimize his luggage. He brought two pairs of shoes, two shirts, two pairs of pants, and two sport coats. Assuming he would always wear one of each of these items, Herman says his dad will have eight different outfits, 2 + 2 + 2 + 2. Is he correct? Explain.

Problems Relating to the NCTM Standards and Curriculum Focal Points

1. The Focal Points for Grade 7 state "Students understand that when all outcomes of an experiment are equally likely, the theoretical probability of an event is the fraction of outcomes in which the event occurs." When drawing from a bag containing 2 red marbles and one white marble, there is a greater chance of getting a red marble. Explain how the idea of equally likely is used to determine that $P(\text{Red}) = \dfrac{2}{3}$.

2. The NCTM Standards state "All students should compute probabilities for simple compound events using such

methods as organized lists, tree diagrams, and area models." Explain how a tree diagram can be used to illustrate the Fundamental Counting Principle.

3. The NCTM Standards state "All students should describe events as likely or unlikely and discuss the degree of likelihood using such words as *certain*, *equally likely*, and *impossible*." Use the tools from this chapter to discuss the likelihood of having 4 boys in a family of 4 children.

11.3 ADDITIONAL COUNTING TECHNIQUES

STARTING POINT

Roberto and Rafael were having a contest to see who could make the most towers out of combinations of red and green blocks. Each tower must be exactly four blocks high and look different from all of the rest of the four-block towers. How many towers can you make? (Three example towers are shown.)

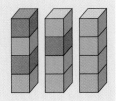

Children's Literature
www.wiley.com/college/musser
See "Anno's Mysterious Multiplying Jar" by Mitsumasa Anno.

Counting Techniques

Most of the examples and problems discussed thus far in this chapter have been solved by writing out the sample space or using a tree diagram. Suppose that the sample space is too large and a tree diagram too complex. For example, the question "What is the probability of having four of a kind in a random four-card hand dealt from a standard deck of cards?" has a sample space consisting of all four-card hands. Such a sample space would be unmanageable to list. This section introduces counting techniques that can be used to determine the size of a sample space or the number of elements in an event without having to list them.

The fundamental counting property in Section 11.2 can be used to count the number of ways that several events can occur in succession. It states that if an event A can occur in r ways and an event B can occur in s ways, then the two events can occur in succession in $r \times s$ ways. This property can be generalized to more than two events. For example, suppose that at a restaurant you have your choice of three appetizers, four soups, five main courses, and two desserts. Altogether, you have $3 \times 4 \times 5 \times 2$ or 120 complete meal choices. In this section we will apply the fundamental counting property to develop counting techniques for complicated arrangements of objects.

Permutations An ordered arrangement of objects is called a **permutation**. For example, for the three letters C, A, and T, there are six different three-letter permutations or "words" that we can make: ACT, ATC, CAT, CTA, TAC, and TCA. If we add a fourth letter to our list, say S, then there are exactly 24 different four-letter permutations, which are listed as follows:

ACST	CAST	SACT	TACS
ACTS	CATS	SATC	TASC
ASCT	CSAT	SCAT	TCAS
ASTC	CSTA	SCTA	TCSA
ATCS	CTAS	STAC	TSAC
ATSC	CTSA	STCA	TSCA

We used a systematic list to write down all the permutations by alphabetizing them in columns. Even so, this procedure is cumbersome and would get out of hand with more and more objects to consider. We need a general principle for counting permutations of several objects.

Let's go back to the case of three letters and imagine a three-letter permutation as a "word" that fills three blanks _ _ _ . We can count the number of permutations of the letters A, C, and T by counting the number of choices we have in filling each blank and applying the fundamental counting property. For example, in filling the first blank, we have three choices, since any of the three letters can be used: $\underline{3}$ - -. Then, in filling the second blank we have two choices *for each of the first three choices*, since either of the two remaining letters can be used: $\underline{3}\,\underline{2}$ -. Finally, to fill the third blank we have the one remaining letter: $\underline{3}\,\underline{2}\,\underline{1}$. Hence, by the fundamental counting property, there are 3 × 2 × 1 or 6 ways to fill all three blanks. This agrees with our list of the six permutations of A, C, and T.

We can apply this same technique to the problem of counting the four-letter permutations of A, C, S, and T. Again, imagine filling four blanks using each of the four letters. We have four choices for the first letter, three for the second, two for the third, and one for the fourth: $\underline{4}\,\underline{3}\,\underline{2}\,\underline{1}$. Hence, by the fundamental counting property, we have 4 × 3 × 2 × 1 or 24 permutations, just as we found in our list.

Our observations lead to the following generalization: Suppose that we have n objects from which to form permutations. There are n choices for the first object, $n - 1$ choices for the second object, $n - 2$ for the third, and so on, down to one choice for the last object. Hence, by the fundamental counting property, there are $n \times (n - 1) \times (n - 2) \times \ldots \times 3 \times 2 \times 1$ permutations of the n objects. For every whole number n, $n > 0$, the product $n \times (n - 1) \times (n - 2) \times \ldots \times 3 \times 2 \times 1$ is called **n factorial** and is written using an exclamation point as **$n!$**. (Zero factorial is defined to be 1.)

> **Example 11.22**   Evaluate the following expressions involving factorials.
>
> **a.** 5!   **b.** 10!   **c.** $\dfrac{10!}{7!}$

SOLUTION
a. $5! = 5 \times 4 \times 3 \times 2 \times 1 = 120$
b. $10! = 10 \times 9 \times 8 \times 7 \times 6 \times 5 \times 4 \times 3 \times 2 \times 1 = 3{,}628{,}800$
c. $\dfrac{10!}{7!} = \dfrac{10 \times 9 \times 8 \times 7 \times 6 \times 5 \times 4 \times 3 \times 2 \times 1}{7 \times 6 \times 5 \times 4 \times 3 \times 2 \times 1} = 10 \times 9 \times 8 = 720$
[NOTE: The fraction in part (c) was simplified first to simplify the calculation.]   ∎

Many calculators have a factorial key, such as $\boxed{n!}$ or $\boxed{x!}$. Entering a whole number and then pressing this key yields the factorial in the display.

Using factorials, we can count the number of permutations of n distinct objects.

THEOREM

The number of permutations of n distinct objects, taken all together, is $n!$.

Example 11.23

a. Miss Murphy wants to seat 12 of her students in a row for a class picture. How many different seating arrangements are there?
b. Seven of Miss Murphy's students are girls and 5 are boys. In how many different ways can she seat the 7 girls together on the left, then the 5 boys together on the right?

SOLUTION
a. There are $12! = 479,001,600$ different permutations, or seating arrangements, of the 12 students.
b. There are $7! = 5040$ permutations of the girls and $5! = 120$ permutations of the boys. Hence, by the fundamental counting property, there are $5040 \times 120 = 604,800$ arrangements with the girls seated on the left. ■

We will now consider permutations of a set of objects taken from a larger set. For example, suppose that in a certain lottery game, four different digits are chosen from the digits 0 through 9 to form a four-digit number. How many different numbers can be made? There are 10 choices for the first digit, 9 for the second, 8 for the third, and 7 for the fourth. By the fundamental counting property, then, there are $10 \times 9 \times 8 \times 7$, or 5040, different possible winning numbers. Notice that the number of permutations of 4 digits chosen from 10 digits is $10 \times 9 \times 8 \times 7 = 10!/6! = 10!/(10 - 4)!$.

We can generalize the preceding observation to permutations of r objects from n objects—in the example about 4-digit numbers, $n = 10$ and $r = 4$. Let $_nP_r$ denote the number of permutations of r objects chosen from n objects.

THEOREM

The number of permutations of r objects chosen from n objects, where $0 \le r \le n$, is

$$_nP_r = \frac{n!}{(n - r)!}.$$

To justify this result, imagine making a sequence of r of the objects. We have n choices for the first object, $n - 1$ choices for the second object, $n - 2$ choices for the third object, and so on down to $n - r + 1$ choices for the last object. Thus we have

$$_nP_r = n \times (n - 1) \times (n - 2) \times \ldots \times (n - r + 1)$$

$$= \frac{n!}{(n - r)!} \text{ total permutations.}$$

Many calculators have a special key for calculating $_nP_r$. To use this key, press the value of n, then the $\boxed{nPr}$ key, then the value of r, then $\boxed{=}$. The value of $_nP_r$ will be displayed. If such a key is not available, the following key strokes may be used: n $\boxed{x!}$ $\boxed{\div}$ $\boxed{(}$ n $\boxed{-}$ r $\boxed{)}$ $\boxed{x!}$ $\boxed{=}$.

Example 11.24	Using the digits 1, 3, 5, 7, and 9, with no repetitions of digits, how many

a. one-digit numbers can be made?
b. two-digit numbers can be made?
c. three-digit numbers can be made?
d. four-digit numbers can be made?
e. five-digit numbers can be made?

SOLUTION Each number corresponds to a permutation of the digits. In each case, $n = 5$.
a. With $r = 1$, there are $5!/(5 - 1)! = 5$ different one-digit numbers.
b. With $r = 2$, there are $5!/(5 - 2)! = 5!/3! = 20$ different two-digit numbers.
c. With $r = 3$, there are $5!/(5 - 3)! = 60$ different three-digit numbers.
d. With $r = 4$, there are $5!/(5 - 4)! = 120$ different four-digit numbers.
e. With $r = 5$, there are $5!/(5 - 5)! = 5!/0! = 120$ different five-digit numbers.
Recall that $0!$ is defined as 1.   ∎

Combinations   A collection of objects, *in no particular order*, is called a **combination**. Using the language of sets, we find that a combination is a subset of a given set of objects. For example, suppose that in a group of five students—Barry, Harry, Larry, Mary, and Teri—three students are to be selected to make a team. Each of the possible three-member teams is a combination. How many such combinations are there? We can answer this question by using our knowledge of permutations and the fundamental counting property.

If order did matter in the selection of the three students for this team, permutations would be used and would yield $_5P_3 = 5!/(5 - 3)! = 60$. Since order doesn't matter in this case, permutations would count more teams than there should be, so we need to divide out all of the extra teams. The permutations BHL, BLH, HBL, HLB, LBH, LHB are really just one combination, {B, H, L}. Figure 11.23 shows that for each three-person *combination*, there are six three-person *permutations*. This is consistent with the fact that three objects can be rearranged in $3! = 6$ different ways.

CORRESPONDING COMBINATIONS		ALL POSSIBLE 3-PERSON PERMUTATIONS
{B, H, L}	<—>	BHL, BLH, HBL, HLB, LBH, LHB
{B, H, M}	<—>	BHM, BMH, HBM, HMB, MBH, MHB
{B, H, T}	<—>	BHT, BTH, HBT HTB, TBH, THB
.		.
.		.
.		.
{L, M, T}	<—>	LMT, LTM, MLT, MTL, TLM, TML
Total number of combinations	=	Total number of permutations divided by 6 (= 3!), since there are six arrangements for each combination

Figure 11.23

To compute the number of possible combinations of three students chosen from a group of five, we can compute the number of permutations, $_5P_3 = 5!/(5 - 3)! = 60$, and divide out the repetition, $3! = 6$. This yields

$$_5C_3 = \frac{_5P_3}{3!} = \frac{60}{6} = 10,$$

which could also be written as

$$_5C_3 = \frac{_5P_3}{3!} = \frac{5!}{(5-3)! \, 3!} = 10.$$

In general, let $_nC_r$ denote the number of combinations of r objects chosen from a set of n objects. The total number of combinations, $_nC_r$, is equal to the number of permutations, $_nP_r$, divided by $r!$ (the repetition). Thus we have the following result.

Algebraic Reasoning
The idea of combinations also comes up when expanding expressions like $(x + 1)^5$ to be $x^5 + 5x^4 + 10x^3 + 10x^2 + 5x + 1$. The coefficient for each term can be found using combinations. For example, the coefficient for the x^2 term is $_5C_2$.

> ## THEOREM
>
> The number of combinations of r objects chosen from n objects, where $0 \le r \le n$, is
>
> $$_nC_r = \frac{_nP_r}{r!} = \frac{n!}{(n-r)! \times r!}.$$
>
> [NOTE: Occasionally, $_nC_r$ is denoted $\binom{n}{r}$ and read "n choose r."]

Many calculators have a key for calculating $_nC_r$. It is used like the $\boxed{nPr}$ key; press the value of n, then $\boxed{nCr}$, then the value of r, followed by $\boxed{=}$. The value of $_nC_r$ will be displayed.

Example 11.25

a. Evaluate $_6C_2$, $_{10}C_4$, $_{10}C_6$, and $_{10}C_{10}$.
b. How many 5-member committees can be chosen from a group of 30 people?
c. How many different 12-person juries can be chosen from a pool of 20 jurors?

SOLUTION

a. $_6C_2 = \dfrac{6!}{(6-2)! \times 2!} = \dfrac{6!}{4! \times 2!} = \dfrac{6 \times 5 \times 4 \times 3 \times 2 \times 1}{(4 \times 3 \times 2 \times 1) \times (2 \times 1)} = 15$

$_{10}C_4 = \dfrac{10!}{(10-4)! \times 4!} = \dfrac{10!}{6! \times 4!} = \dfrac{10 \times 9 \times 8 \times 7 \times 6!}{6! \times (4 \times 3 \times 2 \times 1)} = 210$

$_{10}C_6 = \dfrac{10!}{4! \times 6!} = 210$ from the previous calculations.

$_{10}C_{10} = \dfrac{10!}{0! \times 10!} = 1$

b. The number of committees is $_{30}C_5 = \dfrac{30!}{25! \times 5!} = 142{,}506.$

c. The number of juries is $_{20}C_{12} = \dfrac{20!}{8! \times 12!} = 125{,}970.$ ∎

✔ **Check for Understanding:** Exercise/Problem Set A #1–9

Pascal's Triangle and Combinations

Recall Pascal's triangle, the first six rows of which appear in Figure 11.24. It can be shown that the entries are simply values of $_nC_r$. For example, in the row beginning 1, 4, 6 the entries are the values $_4C_0 = 1$, $_4C_1 = 4$, $_4C_2 = 6$, $_4C_3 = 4$, $_4C_4 = 1$. In general, in the row beginning 1, n, the entries are the values of $_nC_r$, where $r = 0, 1, 2, 3, \ldots, n$.

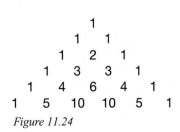

Figure 11.24

Example 11.26
A fair coin is tossed five times. Find the number of ways that two heads and three tails can appear.

SOLUTION An outcome can be represented as a five-letter sequence of H's and T's representing heads and tails. For example, THHTT represents a successful outcome. To count the successful outcomes, we imagine filling a sequence of five blanks, _ _ _ _ _, with two H's and three T's. If the two H's are placed first, then the three T's will just fill in the remaining spaces. From the five blanks, we will choose two of them to place our H's in. Since the H's are indistinguishable, the order in which they are placed doesn't matter. Therefore, there are $_5C_2 = 10$ ways of placing two H's in five blanks. The three T's go in the remaining three blanks. In the discussions in Section 11.2, it was determined that the number of ways of getting two heads when tossing five coins can be determined by examining the row that begins 1, 5, . . . in Pascal's triangle, which can be seen in Figure 11.24. ∎

The next example shows the power of using combinations rather than generating Pascal's triangle.

Example 11.27
On a 30-item true/false test, in how many ways can 27 or more answers be correct?

SOLUTION We can represent an outcome as a 30-letter sequence of C's and I's, for correct and incorrect. To count the number of ways that exactly 27 answers are correct, we count the number of ways that 27 of the 30 positions can have a C in them. There are $_{30}C_{27} = 4060$ such ways. Similarly, there are $_{30}C_{28} = 435$ ways that 28 answers are correct, $_{30}C_{29} = 30$ ways that 29 are correct, and $_{30}C_{30} = 1$ way that all 30 are correct. Thus there are $4060 + 435 + 30 + 1 = 4526$ ways to get 27 or more answers correct. (Using Pascal's triangle to solve this problem would involve generating 30 of its rows—a tedious procedure!) ∎

Example 11.28
At Frederico's Pizza they offer 10 different choices of toppings other than cheese. How many different combinations of toppings are available at Frederico's?

SOLUTION The solution to this problem can be viewed in two different ways. One way would be to count how many combinations there are with exactly 0 toppings, 1 topping, 2 toppings, 3 toppings, etc. and add them up. There are $_{10}C_0 = 1$ combinations with 0 toppings, $_{10}C_1 = 10$ combinations with 1 topping, $_{10}C_2 = 45$ combinations with 2 toppings, $_{10}C_3 = 120$ with 3 toppings, etc. Therefore, the total number of topping combinations is $1 + 10 + 45 + 120 + 210 + 252 + 210 + 120 + 45 + 10 + 1 = 1024$, which is the sum of all of the elements of the tenth row of Pascal's triangle.

The second way of looking at this problem is to think of having 10 blanks _ _ _ _ _ _ _ _ _ _, one for each topping. For each blank there are two choices; either put the topping on or leave it off. Thus there are $2 \cdot 2 \cdot 2 \cdot 2 \cdot 2 \cdot 2 \cdot 2 \cdot 2 \cdot 2 \cdot 2 = 2^{10} = 1024$ combinations of toppings. ∎

It is interesting to note that the sum of the elements in the row of Pascal's triangle beginning 1, 10, . . . is 2^{10}. Looking back at Figure 11.24, it can be seen that the same pattern holds for the first through fifth rows of Pascal's triangle as well. In general, the sum of all of the elements in the row of Pascal's triangle beginning 1, n, . . . is equal to 2^n.

✔ **Check for Understanding:** Exercise/Problem Set A #10–11

Probabilities Using Counting Techniques

We will now consider the problem posed at the beginning of the section, "What is the probability of having 4 of a kind in a random 4-card hand dealt from a standard deck of cards?" We know from previous sections that

$$P(\text{4 of a kind}) = \frac{\text{number of ways to have 4 of a kind}}{\text{number of 4-card hands}}.$$

In determining the number of 4-card hands, it must first be decided whether order matters. Because it only matters which cards you have and *not* the order in which they were dealt, order doesn't matter. There are 52 cards in a standard deck, so the number of 4-card hands is $_{52}C_4 = 270{,}725$. Since there is only one way to have 4 aces, one way to have 4 kings, one way to have 4 queens, and so forth, the number of ways to have 4 of a kind is 13. Thus,

$$P(\text{4 of a kind}) = \frac{13}{270{,}725} = \frac{1}{20{,}825}.$$

Example 11.29   Hideko and Salina are hoping to be selected from their class of 30 as the president and vice-president of the social committee. If the three-person committee (president, vice-president, and secretary) is selected at random, what is the probability that Hideko and Salina would be president and vice-president of the committee?

SOLUTION If this three-person committee didn't have offices within it, then the order in which the committee was selected wouldn't matter and combinations could be used. Since there are officers on the committee, we will assume that the first person selected is the president, the second person is the vice-president, and the secretary is the last one selected. This makes order important, and thus we will need to use permutations. In general, we want to find

$P(\text{Pres. \& VP are Salina and Hideko}) =$

$$\frac{\text{number of 3-person committees with Salina and Hideko as Pres. and VP}}{\text{total number of 3-person committees}}$$

The total number of possible committees is the number of permutations of 3 objects chosen from 30 objects, or $_{30}P_3 = 30 \cdot 29 \cdot 28 = 24{,}360$.

We now compute the number of committees that have the two friends as president and vice-president. Consider the three slots _ _ _ as the slots of president, vice-president, and secretary, respectively. In order to create the desired type of committee, the first slot would need to be filled by one of the two friends and the second slot by the other. Thus, there are only 2 choices for the first slot and 1 choice for the second slot. The third slot, however, could be filled by any one of the remaining 28 students in the class. The number of committees that would have had Hideko and Salina as the president and vice-president offices is $2 \cdot 1 \cdot 28 = 56$. Thus,

$$P(\text{Pres. \& VP are Salina and Hideko}) = \frac{56}{24{,}360} = \frac{1}{435}.$$ ∎

 Check for Understanding: Exercise/Problem Set A #12–14

MATHEMATICAL MORSEL

The following story of the $500,000 "sure thing" appeared in a national news magazine. A popular wagering device at several racetracks and jai alai frontons was called Pick Six. To win, one had to pick the winners of six races or games. The jackpot prize would continue to grow until someone won. At one fronton, the pot reached $551,331. Since there were eight possible winners in each of six games, the number of ways that six winners could occur was 8^6, or 262,144. To cover all of these combinations, a group of bettors bought a $2 ticket on every one of the combinations, betting $524,288 in total. Their risk was that someone else would do the same thing or be lucky enough to guess the correct combination, in which case they would have to split the pot. Neither event happened, so the betting group won $988,326.20, for a net pretax profit of $464,038.20. (The jai alai club kept part of the total amount of money bet.)

| Section 11.3 | EXERCISE / PROBLEM SET A

EXERCISES

1. Compute each of the following. Look for simplifications first.

   a. $\dfrac{10!}{8!}$

   b. $_9P_6$

   c. $\dfrac{102!}{99!}$

2. Find m and n so that

   a. $\dfrac{9!}{6!} = {}_mP_n$

   b. $19 \cdot 18 \cdot 17 \cdot 16 \cdot 15 = {}_mP_n$

3. Compute each of the following. Look for simplifications first.

   a. $\dfrac{12!}{8!\ 4!}$ **b.** $_6C_2$ **c.** $\dfrac{15!}{12!\ 3!}$

4. Find m and n so that

   a. $13 = {}_mC_n$ **b.** $\dfrac{10!}{3! \cdot 7!} = {}_mC_n$

5. Which is greater?

   a. $_{12}C_2$ or $_{12}P_2$ **b.** $_{12}C_9$ or $_{12}P_2$

6. Certain automobile license plates consist of a sequence of three letters followed by three digits.

   a. If no repetitions of letters are permitted, how many possible license plates are there?

   b. If no letters and no digits are repeated, how many license plates are possible?

7. A combination lock has 40 numbers on it.

   a. How many different three-number combinations can be made?

   b. How many different combinations are there if the numbers must all be different?

   c. How many different combinations are there if the second number must be different from the first and third?

   d. Why is the name *combination* lock inconsistent with the mathematical meaning of combination?

8. Mrs. Levanger's class of 28 students is seated in 4 rows of 7. In how many different ways can the first row of 7 be seated?

9. a. How many different 5-member teams can be made from a group of 12 people?

   b. How many different 5-card poker hands can be dealt from a standard deck of 52 cards?

10. How many different ways can five identical mathematics books and three identical English books be arranged on a shelf? (*Hint:* See Example 11.26.)

11. a. Verify that the entries in Pascal's triangle in the 1, 5, 10, 10, 5, 1 row are true values of $_5C_r$ for $r = 0, 1, 2, 3, 4, 5$.

   b. Verify that $_6C_3 = {}_5C_2 + {}_5C_3$.

12. Ten coins are tossed. Find the probability that the following number of heads appear.

   a. 9   **b.** 7   **c.** 5   **d.** 3   **e.** 1

13. Suppose a state's license plate contains 6 letters on it where the letters can be repeated. What is the probability that a license plate will contain the letters USA (in that order) somewhere in the 6 letters?

14. A school dance committee of 4 people is selected at random from a group of 6 ninth graders, 11 eighth graders, and 10 seventh graders.
    a. What is the probability that the committee has all seventh graders?
    b. What is the probability that the committee has no seventh graders?

PROBLEMS

15. a. Show that, in general, $_{n+1}C_r = {_n}C_{r-1} + {_n}C_r$.
    b. Explain how the result in part (a) shows that the entries in the "1, n, . . ." row of Pascal's triangle are the values of $_nC_r$ for $r = 0, 1, 2, . . . , n$.

16. In an effort to promote school spirit, Georgetown High School created ID numbers with just the letters G, H, and S. If each letter is used exactly three times,
    a. how many nine-letter ID numbers can be generated?
    b. what is the probability that a random ID number starts with GHS?

17. The license plates in the state of Utah consist of three letters followed by three single-digit numbers.
    a. If Edwardo's initials are EAM, what is the probability that his license plate will have his initials on it (in any order)?
    b. What is the probability that his license plate will have his initials in the correct order?

18. Kofi had forgotten the four-digit combination required to unlock his bike. He could still remember that the digits were 3, 4, 5, and 6 but couldn't remember their order. What is the greatest number of combinations that Kofi will have to try in order to unlock the lock?

19. Find the smallest values of m and n such that
    a. $_mP_n = {_{10}}C_7$.   b. $_mC_n = {_{15}}P_2$.

20. In a popular lottery game, five numbers are to be picked randomly from 1 to 36, with no repetitions.
    a. How many ways can these five winning numbers be picked without regard to order?
    b. Answer the same question for picking six numbers.

21. Suppose that there are 10 first-class seats on an airplane. How many ways can the following numbers of first-class passengers be seated?
    a. 10   b. 9   c. 8   d. 5
    e. r, where $0 \le r \le 10$

22. Ten chips, numbered 1 through 10, are in a hat. All of the chips are drawn in succession.
    a. In how many different sequences can the chips be drawn?
    b. How many of the sequences have chip 5 first?
    c. How many of the sequences have an odd-numbered chip first?
    d. How many of the sequences have an odd-numbered chip first and an even-numbered chip last?

23. How many five-letter "words" can be formed from the letters P-I-A-N-O if all the letters are different and the following restrictions exist?
    a. There are no other restrictions.
    b. The first letter is P.
    c. The first letter is a consonant.
    d. The first letter is a consonant and the last letter is a vowel (a, e, i, o, or u).

24. a. Show that $_{20}C_5 = {_{20}}C_{15}$ without computing $_{20}C_5$ or $_{20}C_{15}$.
    b. Show that, in general, $_nC_r = {_n}C_{n-r}$.
    c. Given that $_{50}C_7 = 99,884,400$, find $_{50}C_{43}$.

25. (Refer to the Initial Problem in Chapter 1.) The digits 1 through 9 are to be arranged in the array so that the sum of each side is 17.

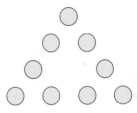

    a. How many possible arrangements are there?
    b. How many total arrangements are there with 1, 2, and 3 in the corners?
    c. Start with 1 at the top, 2 in the lower left corner, and 3 in the lower right corner. Note that the two digits in the 1 − 2 side must sum to 14. How many two-digit sums of 14 are there using 4, 5, 6, 7, 8, and 9?
    d. How many total solutions are there using 1, 2, and 3 as in part (c) and 5 and 9 in the 1 − 2 side?
    e. How many solutions are there for the puzzle, counting all possible arrangements?

    The following probability problems involve the use of combinations and permutations.

26. a. Four students are to be chosen at random from a group of 15. How many ways can this be done?
    b. If Glenn is one of the students, what is the probability that he is one of the four chosen? (Assume that all students are equally likely to be chosen.)
    c. What is the probability that Glenn and Mickey are chosen?

27. Five cards are dealt at random from a standard deck. Find the probability that the hand contains the following cards.
  a. 4 aces
  b. 3 kings and 2 queens
  c. 5 diamonds
  d. An ace, king, queen, jack, and ten

28. In a group of 20 people, 3 have been exposed to virus X and 17 have not. Five people are chosen at random and tested for exposure to virus X.
  a. In how many ways can the 5 people be chosen?
  b. What is the probability that *exactly* one of the people in the group has been exposed to the virus?
  c. What is the probability that 1 or 2 people in the group have been exposed to the virus?

| Section 11.3 | EXERCISE / PROBLEM SET B |

EXERCISES

1. Compute each of the following. Look for simplifications first.
  a. $_{20}P_{15}$
  b. $\dfrac{(n+1)!}{(n-2)!}$
  c. $_{57}P_{55}$

2. Find m and n so that
  a. $_mP_n = 23 \cdot 22 \cdot 21 \cdot 20$
  b. $_mP_n = \dfrac{11!}{9!}$

3. Compute each of the following. Look for simplifications first.
  a. $_{10}C_3$
  b. $\dfrac{23!}{13!10!}$
  c. $_{50}C_{45}$

4. Find m and n so that
  a. $\dfrac{16!}{12!\,4!} = {}_mC_n$
  b. $\dfrac{33 \cdot 32 \cdot 31 \cdot 30 \cdot 29}{5!} = {}_mC_n$

5. Which is greater?
  a. $_6P_2$ or $_6C_2$
  b. $_{12}P_2$ or $_6C_2$

6. If no repetitions are allowed, using the digits 0, 1, 2, 3, 4, 5, 6, 7, 8, 9,
  a. how many two-digit numbers can be formed?
  b. how many of these are odd?
  c. how many of these are even?
  d. how many are divisible by 3?
  e. how many are less than 40?

7. Suppose letters from the alphabet are randomly chosen to make up "words" (any arrangement of letters is considered a "word").
  a. How many different four-letter words are possible?
  b. How many different four-letter words are possible if no letter is repeated?
  c. How many four-letter words are possible if the first and last letter are the same?

8. In how many ways can eight chairs be arranged in a line?

9. A student must answer 7 out of 10 questions on a test.
  a. How many ways does she have to do this?
  b. How many ways does she have if she must answer the first two?

10. The distance from Lars's home to his school is 11 blocks: 7 blocks to the east and 4 blocks to the north. How many different paths are there from his house to his school? (NOTE: This is similar to counting the number of arrangements of 7 E's and 4 N's.)

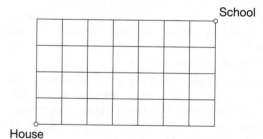

11. a. Use combinations to find the first 4 entries of the 20th row of Pascal's triangle.
  b. Use combinations to find the first 4 entries of the 21st row.
  c. Use the results of parts a and b to verify $_{21}C_2 = {}_{20}C_1 + {}_{20}C_2$ and $_{21}C_3 = {}_{20}C_2 + {}_{20}C_3$.

12. A young couple wants to have a family of 6 children. Assuming that having a boy or girl is equally likely, what is the probability of having the following number of girls in their family?
  a. 2   **b.** 3   **c.** 6

13. A class of 20 students is lined up in a random order each day to walk to lunch. What is the probability that Alex, Kobe, Maria, and Shantel would be lined up in that order somewhere in the line?

14. In the high school regional cross-country meet, Chino High, Don Lugo High, and Ontario High fielded six, five, and eight equally skilled runners, respectively. What is the probability that the Chino High team will finish in the top three places?

PROBLEMS

15. Ten children, four boys and six girls, are randomly placed in the bus line. What is the probability that all four boys are standing next to each other?

16. Solve for n.
   a. $_nP_2 = 72$ **b.** $_nC_2 = 66$

17. A jar contains three red, five green, and six blue marbles. If all of the marbles are drawn from the bag, what is the probability that the three red marbles are drawn in succession?

18. What is the probability of having two aces, two kings, and a queen in a five-card poker hand?

19. Yolanda's Yogurt House offers 3 different kinds of yogurt and 13 different kinds of toppings.
   a. How many different yogurt and topping combinations are possible?
   b. The weekly special is a yogurt with up to 3 toppings for $.99. How many different yogurt and topping combinations are available for the weekly special?

20. Social security numbers are of the form _ _ _-_ _-_ _ _ _, where the blanks are filled with the single digit numbers 0–9. If the blanks were filled with letters from the alphabet, instead of numbers, how many more social security numbers would be possible?

21. If a student must take six tests—T1, T2, T3, T4, T5, T6—in how many ways can the student take the tests if
   a. T2 must be taken immediately after T1?
   b. T1 and T2 can't be taken immediately after one another?

22. How many ways can the offices of president, vice-president, treasurer, secretary, parliamentarian, and representative be filled from a class of 30 students?

23. Using the word $MI_1S_1S_2I_2S_3S_4I_3P_1P_2I_4$, where each repeated letter is distinguishable, how many ways can the letters be arranged?

24. In any arrangement (list) of the 26 letters of the English alphabet, which has 21 consonants and 5 vowels, must there be some place where there are at least 3 consonants in a row? 4? 5?

25. If there are 10 chips in a box—4 red, 3 blue, 2 white, and 1 black—and 2 chips are drawn, what is the probability that
   a. the chips are the same color?
   b. exactly 1 is red?
   c. at least 1 is red?
   d. neither is red?

26. In how many ways can the numbers 1, 2, 3, 4, 5, 6, 7 be arranged so that
   a. 1 and 7 are adjacent?
   b. 1 and 7 are not adjacent?
   c. 1 and 7 are exactly three spaces apart?

27. There are 12 books on a shelf: 5 volumes of an encyclopedia, 4 of an almanac, and 3 of a dictionary. How many arrangements are there? How many arrangements are there with each set of titles together?

28. If a team of four players must be made from eight boys and six girls, how many teams can be made if
   a. there are no restrictions?
   b. there must be two boys and two girls?
   c. they must all be boys?
   d. they must all be girls?

Analyzing Student Thinking

29. Margaret claims that $\frac{8!}{16!} = \frac{8}{16} = \frac{1}{2}$. Is she correct? Explain.

30. Wayne claims that permutations should be used to count the number of different committees that could be selected from a group of people. Lowell thinks that combinations should be used. Who is correct? Explain.

31. The class president says she will use combinations to decide how many different ways the prom royalty of queen, first, and second assistant can be elected, but the class vice-president says she needs to use permutations. They ask you for advice. How should you respond?

32. Brielle asks if he can use Pascal's triangle to solve problems involving drawing a card from a deck since there are two outcomes of either drawing or not drawing. How should you answer this question?

33. Lily says that the middle number in every row of Pascal's triangle must be $_nC_{n/2}$. Is she correct? If not, what should she have said?

34. Julio, who works at a Subway shop, says that they have 64 different turkey subs since they have two types of bread, with or without lettuce, mayo, tomatoes, pickles, peppers, and onions. Is he correct? Explain.

35. The United States Supreme Court has 9 members. Jeff asserts that the probability of reaching a 5-to-4 majority is 5/9. How should you respond?

Problems Relating to the NCTM Standards and Curriculum Focal Points

1. The Focal Points for Grade 7 state "Students understand that when all outcomes of an experiment are equally likely, the theoretical probability of an event is the fraction of outcomes in which the event occurs." Explain how combinations and permutations help in determining the theoretical probability of an event.

2. The NCTM Standards state "All students should compute probabilities for simple compound events using such methods as organized lists, tree diagrams, and area models." Explain how combinations and permutations can be used to move beyond using "organized lists, tree diagrams, and area models."

11.4 SIMULATION, EXPECTED VALUE, ODDS, AND CONDITIONAL PROBABILITY

For Sterling's weekly lawn-mowing job, his parents have given him two choices for his method of payment.

Choice 1: He receives $10.
Choice 2: His parents place four $1 bills, one $5 bill, and two $10 bills in a bag and Sterling draws two bills from the bag.

In the long run, which is the better deal for Sterling? Justify your answer with mathematical reasoning.

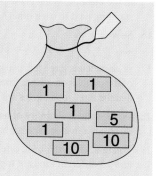

NCTM Standard
All students should use proportionality and a basic understanding of probability to make and test conjectures about the results of experiments and simulations.

Children's Literature
www.wiley.com/college/musser
See "Pigs at Odds" by Amy Axelrod.

Reflection from Research
Sixth grade students can begin to understand the relationship between the number of trials and the probability of an unlikely event. More trials model outcomes closer to the theoretical probability (Aspinwall & Tarr, 2001).

Simulation

In Section 11.1, the difference between theoretical and experimental probability was discussed and up to this point the majority of the examples have dealt with theoretical probability. For almost every example, experimental probability can also be computed by doing a simulation of the experiment. Simulations are used to model an experiment and provide the data to determine the experimental probability. In some cases, an experiment is difficult to analyze theoretically, so a simulation is done to estimate the theoretical probability.

A **simulation** is a representation of an experiment like using dice, coins, objects in a bag, or a random-number generator. There is a one-to-one correspondence between outcomes in the original experiment and outcomes in the simulated experiment. The probability that an outcome in the original experiment occurs is estimated to be the experimental probability of its corresponding outcome in the simulated experiment.

Example 11.30   When planning for a family, a husband and wife plan to stop having children after they have either two girls or four children. Since they want to begin saving for their childrens' college educations, they want to predict how many children they should expect to have. If the chances are equally likely of having a girl or a boy, what is the probability that they will have four children?

SOLUTION By assumption, since having a girl or a boy is equally likely, this situation can be simulated using a coin. We will let heads (H) represent a boy and tails (T) represent a girl. In simulating this experiment, we will toss the coin until there are two tails (two girls) or until the coin has been tossed four times (family of four). Below we have simulated the creation of 40 families by tossing coins. Since the question to be answered is to find the probability of having a family of four, all families of four are in boldface.

HTT	TT	**HHTT**	**HHHH**	HTHT	THT	**HTHT**	HTT
HHHT	**HHHH**	**THHH**	**HHHT**	**HTHT**	**HHHH**	**THHH**	**HTHT**
HHTH	**HTHH**	THT	THT	**HTHH**	**HHTH**	THT	THT
HTHT	TT	TT	TT	TT	**HHHT**	TT	TT
THHH	TT	TT	HTT	THT	**HHHT**	TT	**HHTT**

There are 40 families, of which 21 have four children. Thus the probability that the husband and wife have four children is $\frac{21}{40}$, or 52.5%.   ∎

This simulation could have been carried out using a spinner divided into two equal parts, drawing two pieces of paper (one marked B and the other G), or using a random-number table. In fact, the next example illustrates how a random-number table can be used to perform simulations.

Example 11.31 A cereal company has put six types of toy cars in its cereal boxes, one car per box. If the cars are distributed uniformly, what is the probability that you will get all six types of cars if you buy 10 boxes?

Problem-Solving Strategy
Do a Simulation

SOLUTION Simulate the experiment by using the whole numbers from 1 through 6 to represent the different cars. Use a table of random digits as the random-number generator (Figure 11.25). (Six numbered slips of paper or chips, drawn at random from a hat, or a six-sided die would also work. In this example we disregard 0, 7, 8, 9, since there are six types of toy cars.) Start anywhere in the table. (We started at the upper left.) Read until 10 numbers from 1 through 6 occur, ignoring 0, 7, 8, and 9. Record the sequence of numbers [Figure 11.25(b)]. Each such sequence of 10 numbers is a simulated outcome. (Simulated outcomes are separated by a vertical bar.) Six of these sequences appear in Figure 11.25(b). Successful outcomes contain 1, 2, 3, 4, 5, and 6 (corresponding to the six cars) and are marked "yes." Based on the simulation, our estimate of the probability is $\frac{2}{6} = 0.\overline{3}$. Using a computer to simulate the experiment yields an estimate of 0.257.

2	2	9	8	5	3	5	1	8	7	→	2	2	5	3	5	1	5	4	3	6	yes
7	5	0	4	3	9	6	3	6	4	→	3	6	4	6	1	5	3	3	5	6	no
7	7	7	6	1	9	5	9	3	3												
5	6	1	7	2	3	9	6	5	1	→	1	2	3	6	5	1	5	6	2	3	no
5	6	2	0	3	2	8	0	5	9	→	2	5	3	3	4	6	5	6	6	5	no
3	3	4	8	0	8	6	5	6	6												
9	5	6	7	9	1	3	6	8	3	→	6	1	3	6	3	4	4	4	2	5	yes
0	4	4	8	4	2	5	5	9	1	→	5	1	1	3	1	2	5	5	1	6	no
8	1	8	7	3	1	8	2	5	5												
1	9	7	6	0	3	2	5	2	3												

⋮

(a) Random digits   **(b)** Simulated outcomes

Figure 11.25   ∎

The previous example used a simulation to find the probability that you would get all six prizes if 10 boxes were purchased. For many collectors, a more useful question would be "How many boxes should I buy in order to get all six prizes?" This question is addressed in the following example.

| **Example 11.32** | A cereal company has put six types of toy cars in its cereal boxes, one car per box. If the cars are distributed uniformly, how many boxes should I buy in order to get all six types of cars? |

SOLUTION   To simulate this experiment, let the numbers on a die represent each of the six different types of cars. We will roll the die until all six numbers have turned up and then record how many rolls it took to obtain all six numbers. By repeating this 25 times, we will have the data necessary to determine a reasonable estimate of the number of boxes that should be purchased. The numbers below represent five of the 25 trials.

2, 2, 6, 5, 6, 4, 4, 2, 4, 4, 5, 1, 6, 2, 3 → 15 rolls (boxes)
5, 5, 4, 2, 3, 1, 1, 5, 1, 6 → 10 rolls (boxes)
2, 5, 5, 4, 4, 5, 6, 3, 2, 2, 6, 3, 4, 4, 2, 1 → 16 rolls (boxes)
4, 2, 2, 6, 3, 2, 3, 5, 6, 5, 6, 6, 3, 3, 6, 6, 3, 4, 4, 6, 1 → 21 rolls (boxes)
4, 5, 3, 6, 5, 2, 1 → 7 rolls (boxes)

After repeating this process 20 more times, we computed the average of the rolls needed to get all six toy cars. Based on this simulation, the average was 15.12 rolls. On average, a collector should buy 15 to 16 boxes of cereal to get all six types of cars.   ■

Another way to phrase the question in the previous example would be to say, "How many boxes would a collector *expect* to have to buy in order to get all six types of toy cars?" This idea of expected outcomes leads us to the next idea.

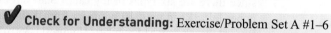 **Check for Understanding:** Exercise/Problem Set A #1–6

Expected Value

Probability can be used to determine values such as admission to games (with payoffs) and insurance premiums, using the idea of expected value.

| **Example 11.33** | A cube has three red faces, two green faces, and a blue face. A game consists of rolling the cube twice. You pay $2 to play. If both faces are the same color, you are paid $5 (you win $3). If not, you lose the $2 it costs to play. Will you win money in the long run? |

SOLUTION   Use a probability tree diagram (Figure 11.26). Let W be the event that you win. Then $W = \{RR, GG, BB\}$, and $P(W) = \frac{1}{2} \cdot \frac{1}{2} + \frac{1}{3} \cdot \frac{1}{3} + \frac{1}{6} \cdot \frac{1}{6} = \frac{7}{18}$. Hence $\frac{7}{18}$ (about 39%) of the time you will win, and $\frac{11}{18}$ (about 61%) of the time you will lose. If you play the game 18 times, you can expect to win 7 times and lose 11 times on average. Hence, your winnings, in dollars, will be $3 \times 7 + (-2) \times 11 = -1$. That is, you can expect to lose $1 if you play the game 18 times. On the average, you will lose $1/18 per game (about 6¢).

Problem-Solving Strategy
Draw a Diagram

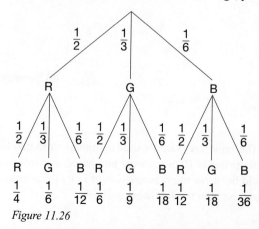

Figure 11.26

■

In Example 11.33, the amount in dollars that we expect to "win" on each play of the game is $3 \times \frac{7}{18} + (-2) \times \frac{11}{18} = -\frac{1}{18}$, called the expected value. Expected value is defined as follows.

DEFINITION

Expected Value

Suppose that the outcomes of an experiment are real numbers (values) called v_1, $v_2, \ldots, v_n$, and suppose that the outcomes have probabilities $p_1, p_2, \ldots, p_n$ respectively. The **expected value**, E, of the experiment is the sum

$$E = v_1 \cdot p_1 + v_2 \cdot p_2 + \cdots + v_n \cdot p_n.$$

The expected value of an experiment is the average value of the outcomes over many repetitions. The next example shows how insurance companies use expected values.

TABLE 11.4

AMOUNT OF CLAIM (NEAREST $2000)	PROBABILITY
0	0.80
$2,000	0.10
4,000	0.05
6,000	0.03
8,000	0.01
10,000	0.01

Example 11.34 Suppose that an insurance company has broken down yearly automobile claims for drivers from age 16 through 21, as shown in Table 11.4. How much should the company charge as its average premium in order to break even on its costs for claims?

SOLUTION Use the notation from the definition for expected value. Let $n = 6$ (the number of claim categories), and let the values $v_1, v_2, \ldots, v_n$ and the probabilities $p_1, p_2, \ldots, p_n$ be as listed in Table 11.5.

Thus the expected value, $E = 0(0.80) + 2000(0.10) + 4000(0.05) + 6000(0.03) + 8000(0.01) + 10,000(0.01) = 760$. Since the average claim value is $760, the average automobile insurance premium should be set at $760 per year for the insurance company to break even on its claims costs. ∎

TABLE 11.5

V	P
$v_1 = 0$	$p_1 = 0.80$
$v_2 = 2000$	$p_2 = 0.10$
$v_3 = 4000$	$p_3 = 0.05$
$v_4 = 6000$	$p_4 = 0.03$
$v_5 = 8000$	$p_5 = 0.01$
$v_6 = 10,000$	$p_6 = 0.01$

 Check for Understanding: Exercise/Problem Set A #7–10

Odds

The term *odds* is used often in the English language in situations ranging from horse racing to medical research. For example, hepatitis C is a disease of the liver. If a person is a chronic carrier of the virus, the odds of his developing cirrhosis of the liver are $1 : 4$. Under certain treatments for hepatitis C, the odds of achieving a substantial decrease in the presence of the virus are $2 : 3$. The use of the term *odds* may sound familiar, but what do these odds really mean and how are they related to probability?

When computing the probability of an event occurring, we examine the ratio of the favorable outcomes compared to the total number of possible outcomes. When people speak about odds in favor of an event, they are comparing the number of favorable outcomes of an event to the number of unfavorable outcomes of the event. This comparison assumes, as we will in this section, that outcomes are equally likely. According to this description, a person who is a chronic carrier of hepatitis C has one chance of developing cirrhosis and four chances of not developing it. Similarly, a person who undergoes a certain treatment has two chances of a substantial benefit and three chances of not having a substantial benefit.

In general, let E be an event in the sample space S and $\overline{E}$ be the event complementary to E. Then odds are defined formally as follows.

DEFINITION

Odds for Events with Equally Likely Outcomes

The **odds in favor** of event E are $n(E):n(\overline{E})$.

The **odds against** event E are $n(\overline{E}):n(E)$.

Example 11.35   If a six-sided die is tossed, what are the odds in favor of the following events?

a. Getting a 4   **b.** Getting a prime
c. Getting a number greater than 0   **d.** Getting a number greater than 6

SOLUTION

a. $1:5$, since there is one 4 and five other numbers
b. $3:3 = 1:1$, since there are three primes (2, 3, and 5) and three nonprimes
c. $6:0$ since all numbers are favorable to this event
d. $0:6$ since no numbers are favorable to this event   ∎

Notice that in Example 11.35(c) it is reasonable to allow the second number in the odds ratio to be zero.

Just like the sets E and $\overline{E}$ combine to make the entire sample space, the number of favorable outcomes combines with the number of unfavorable outcomes to yield the total number of possible outcomes. This connection allows a smooth transition between odds and probability.

It is possible to determine the odds in favor of an event E directly from its probability. For example, if $P(E) = \frac{5}{7}$, we would expect that, in the long run, E would occur five out of seven times and not occur two of the seven times. Thus the odds in favor of E would be $5:2$. When determining the odds in favor of E, we compare $n(E)$ and $n(\overline{E})$. Now consider $P(E) = \frac{5}{7}$ and $P(\overline{E}) = \frac{2}{7}$. If we compare these two probabilities in the same order, we have $P(E):P(\overline{E}) = \frac{5}{7}:\frac{2}{7} = \frac{5}{7} \div \frac{2}{7} = \frac{5}{2} = 5:2$, the odds in favor of E. The following discussion justifies the latter method of calculating odds. The odds in favor of E are

$$\frac{n(E)}{n(\overline{E})} = \frac{\dfrac{n(E)}{n(S)}}{\dfrac{n(\overline{E})}{n(S)}} = \frac{P(E)}{P(\overline{E})} = \frac{P(E)}{1 - P(E)}$$

Thus we can find the odds in favor of an event directly from the probability of an event.

THEOREM

The odds in favor of the event E are

$$P(E):1 - P(E) \quad \text{or} \quad P(E):P(\overline{E}).$$

The odds against E are

$$1 - P(E):P(E) \quad \text{or} \quad P(\overline{E}):P(E).$$

In fact, this result is used to define odds using probabilities in the case of unequally likely outcomes as well as equally likely outcomes.

Example 11.36   Find the odds in favor of event E, where E has the following probabilities.

a. $P(E) = \frac{1}{2}$ **b.** $P(E) = \frac{3}{4}$ **c.** $P(E) = \frac{5}{13}$

SOLUTION

a. Odds in favor of $E = \frac{1}{2} : (1 - \frac{1}{2}) = \frac{1}{2} : \frac{1}{2} = 1:1$

b. Odds in favor of $E = \frac{3}{4} : (1 - \frac{3}{4}) = \frac{3}{4} : \frac{1}{4} = 3:1$

c. Odds in favor of $E = \frac{5}{13} : (1 - \frac{5}{13}) = \frac{5}{13} : \frac{8}{13} = 5:8$ ■

Now suppose that you know the odds in favor of an event E. Can the probability of E be found? The answer is "yes!" For example, if the odds in favor of E are $2:3$, this means that the ratio of favorable outcomes to unfavorable outcomes is $2:3$. Thus in a sample space with five elements with two outcomes favorable to E and three unfavorable, $P(E) = \frac{2}{5} = \frac{2}{2+3}$. In general, we have the following.

THEOREM

If the odds in favor of E are $a : b$, then

$$P(E) = \frac{a}{a + b}.$$

Example 11.37   Find $P(E)$ given that the odds in favor of (or against) E are as follows.

a. Odds in favor of E are $3:4$.   **b.** Odds in favor of E are $9:2$.
c. Odds against E are $7:3$.   **d.** Odds against E are $2:13$.

SOLUTION

a. $P(E) = \dfrac{3}{3+4} = \dfrac{3}{7}$ **b.** $P(E) = \dfrac{9}{9+2} = \dfrac{9}{11}$

c. $P(E) = \dfrac{3}{7+3} = \dfrac{3}{10}$ **d.** $P(E) = \dfrac{13}{2+13} = \dfrac{13}{15}$ ■

 Check for Understanding: Exercise/Problem Set A #11–17

Conditional Probability

When drawing cards from a standard deck of 52 cards, we know that the probability of drawing an ace is $\frac{4}{52} = \frac{1}{13}$, since there are 4 aces in the deck. If a second draw is made, what is the probability of drawing an ace given that 1 ace has already been drawn? Our sample space is now 51 cards with 3 aces, so the probability is $\frac{3}{51}$. Even though both probabilities deal with drawing an ace, the results are different because the second example has an extra condition that reduces the size of the sample space. When such conditions are added that change the size of the sample space, it is referred to as *conditional* probability.

| Example 11.38 | When tossing three fair coins, what is the probability of getting two tails given that the first coin came up heads? |

SOLUTION When tossing three coins, there are eight outcomes: HHH, HHT, HTH, THH, HTT, THT, TTH, TTT. In this case, however, the condition of the first coin being a head has been added. This changes the possible outcomes to be {HHH, HHT, HTH, HTT}. There are only four possible outcomes in this reduced sample space. The only outcome fitting the description of having two tails in this sample space is HTT. Thus the conditional probability of getting two tails given that the first of the three coins is a head is $\frac{1}{4}$. ∎

Problem-Solving Strategy
Draw a Diagram

In Example 11.38 the original sample space is reduced to those outcomes having the given condition, namely H on the first coin. Let A be the event that exactly two tails appear among the three coins, and let B be the event the first coin comes up heads. Then $A = \{HTT, THT, TTH\}$ and $B = \{HHH, HHT, HTH, HTT\}$. We see that there is only one way for A to occur given that B occurs, namely HTT. (Note that $A \cap B = \{HTT\}$.) Thus the probability of A given B is $\frac{1}{4}$. The notation $P(A \mid B)$ means "the probability of A given B." So, $P(A \mid B) = \frac{1}{4}$. Notice that $P(A \mid B) = \frac{1}{4} = \frac{1/8}{4/8} = \frac{P(A \cap B)}{P(B)}$. That is, $P(A \mid B)$ is the relative frequency of event A *within* event B. This suggests the following.

DEFINITION

Conditional Probability

Let A and B be events in a sample space S where $P(B) \neq 0$. The **conditional probability** that event A occurs, given that event B occurs, denoted $P(A \mid B)$, is

$$P(A \mid B) = \frac{P(A \cap B)}{P(B)}.$$

A Venn diagram can be used to illustrate the definition of conditional probability. A sample space S of equally likely outcomes is shown in Figure 11.27(a). The reduced sample space, given that event B occurs, appears in Figure 11.27(b). From Figure 11.27(a) we see that $\frac{P(A \cap B)}{P(B)} = \frac{2/12}{7/12} = \frac{2}{7}$. From Figure 11.27(b) we see that $P(A \mid B) = \frac{2}{7}$. Thus $P(A \mid B) = \frac{P(A \cap B)}{P(B)}$.

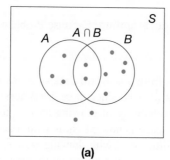

(a)

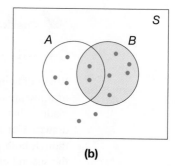

(b)

Figure 11.27

The next example illustrates conditional probability in the case of unequally likely outcomes.

| **Example 11.39** | Suppose a 20-sided die has the following numerals on its faces: 1, 1, 2, 2, 2, 3, 3, 4, 5, 6, 7, 8, 9, 10, 11, 12, 13, 14, |

15, 16. The die is rolled once and the number on the top face is recorded. Let A be the event the number is prime, and B be the event the number is odd. Find $P(A \mid B)$ and $P(B \mid A)$.

SOLUTION Assuming that the die is balanced, $P(A) = \frac{9}{20}$, since there are 9 ways that a prime can appear. Similarly, $P(B) = \frac{10}{20}$, since there are 10 ways that an odd number can occur. Also, $P(A \cap B) = P(B \cap A) = \frac{6}{20}$, since an odd prime can appear in 6 ways. Thus

$$P(A \mid B) = \frac{P(A \cap B)}{P(B)} = \frac{6/20}{10/20} = \frac{3}{5}$$

and

$$P(B \mid A) = \frac{P(B \cap A)}{P(A)} = \frac{6/20}{9/20} = \frac{2}{3}.$$

These results can be checked by reducing the sample space to reflect the given information, then assigning probabilities to the events as they occur as subsets of the *reduced sample space*. ∎

✔ **Check for Understanding:** Exercise/Problem Set A #18–21

MATHEMATICAL MORSEL

The French naturalist Buffon devised his famous needle problem from which π may be determined using probability methods. The method is as follows. Draw a number of parallel lines at a distance of 2 inches apart. Then drop a needle, whose length is one inch, at *random* onto the parallel lines. Buffon showed that the probability that the needle will touch one of the lines is $1/\pi$. Thus, π can be approximated by repeatedly tossing the needle onto the parallel lines and dividing the total number of times that a needle is tossed by the total number of times that it lands crossing one of the parallel lines.

| **Section 11.4** | **EXERCISE / PROBLEM SET A** |

EXERCISES

1. A penny gumball machine contains gumballs in eight different colors. Assume that there are a large number of gumballs equally divided among the eight colors.

  a. Estimate how many pennies you will have to use to get one of each color.

  b. Cut out eight identical pieces of paper and mark them with the digits 1–8. Put the pieces of paper in a container. Without looking, draw one piece and record its number. Replace the piece, mix the pieces up, and draw again. Repeat this process until all digits have appeared. Record how many draws it took. Repeat this experiment a total of 10 times and average the number of draws needed.

2. Use the Chapter 11 eManipulative activity *Simulation* on our Web site to simulate Problem 1 by doing the following.

   i. Click on one each of the numbers 1 through 8.

   ii. Press START and watch until all 8 numbers have drawn at least once.

   iii. Press PAUSE and record the number of draws.

   iv. Clear the draws and repeat. (Perform at least 20 repetitions.)

   v. Average the number of draws needed.

3. A cloakroom attendant receives five coats from five women and gets them mixed up. She returns the coats at random. Follow the following steps to find the probability that at least one woman receives her own coat.

   i. Cut out five pieces of paper, all the same size, and label them A, B, C, D, and E.

   ii. Put the pieces in a container and mix them up.

   iii. Draw the pieces out, one at a time, without replacing them, and record the order.

   iv. Repeat steps 2 and 3 a total of 25 times.

   v. Count the number of times at least one letter is in the appropriate place (A in first place, B in second place, etc.).

From this simulation, what is the approximate probability that at least one woman receives her own coat?

4. You are going to bake a batch of 100 oatmeal cookies. Because raisins are expensive, you will only put 150 raisins in the batter and mix the batter well. Follow the steps given to find out the probability that a cookie will end up without a raisin.

   i. Draw a 10 × 10 grid as illustrated. Each cell is represented by a two-digit number. The first digit is the horizontal scale and the second digit is the vertical scale. For example, 06 and 73 are shown.

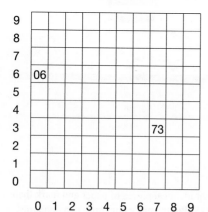

   ii. Given is a portion of a table of random digits. For each two-digit number in the table, place an × in the appropriate cell of your grid.

15	77	01	64	69	69	58	40	81	16
85	40	51	40	10	15	33	94	11	65
47	69	35	90	95	16	17	45	86	29
13	26	87	40	20	40	81	46	08	09
10	55	33	20	47	54	16	86	11	16
60	20	00	84	22	05	06	67	26	77
57	62	94	04	99	65	50	89	18	74
16	70	48	02	00	59	68	53	31	55
74	99	16	92	99	31	31	05	36	48
59	34	71	55	84	91	59	46	44	45
14	85	40	52	68	60	41	94	98	18
42	07	50	15	69	86	97	40	25	88
73	47	16	49	79	69	80	76	16	60
75	16	00	21	11	42	44	84	46	84
49	25	36	12	07	25	90	89	55	25

   a. Tally the number of squares that have no raisin indicated. What is the probability of selecting a cookie without a raisin?

   b. If your calculator can generate random numbers, generate another set of 150 numbers and repeat this experiment.

5. A young couple is planning their family and would like to have one child of each sex. On average, how many children should they plan for in order to have at least one boy and one girl.

   a. Describe a simulation that could be used to answer the above question.

   b. Perform at least 30 trials of the simulation and record your results.

   c. Repeat parts (a) and (b) using the Chapter 11 eManipulative activity *Simulation* on our Web site.

6. Explain how to simulate tossing two coins using the random number table in Exercise 4. Simulate tossing 2 coins 25 times and record your results.

7. From the data given, compute the expected value of the outcome.

OUTCOME	−2000	0	1000	3000
PROBABILITY	$\frac{1}{4}$	$\frac{1}{6}$	$\frac{1}{4}$	$\frac{1}{3}$

8. A study of attendance at a football game shows the following pattern. What is the expected value of the attendance?

WEATHER	ATTENDANCE	WEATHER PROBABILITY
Extremely cold	30,000	0.06
Cold	40,000	0.44
Moderate	52,000	0.35
Warm	65,000	0.15

9. A player rolls a fair die and receives a number of dollars equal to the number of dots showing on the face of the die.
   a. If the game costs $1 to play, how much should the player expect to win for each play?
   b. If the game costs $2 to play, how much should the player expect to win per play?
   c. What is the most the player should be willing to pay to play the game and not lose money in the long run?

10. For visiting a resort, you will receive one gift. The probabilities and manufacturer's suggested retail values of each gift are as follows: gift A, 1 in 52,000 ($9272.00); gift B, 25,736 in 52,000 ($44.95); gift C, 1 in 52,000 ($2500.00); gift D, 3 in 52,000 ($729.95); gift E, 25,736 in 52,000 ($26.99); gift F, 3 in 52,000 ($1000.00); gift G, 180 in 52,000 ($44.99); gift H, 180 in 52,000 ($63.98); gift I, 160 in 52,000 ($25.00). Find the expected value of your gift.

11. Which, if either, are more favorable odds, 50 : 50 or 100 : 100? Explain.

12. A die is thrown once.
    a. If each face is equally likely to turn up, what is the probability of getting a 5?
    b. What are the odds in favor of getting a 5?
    c. What are the odds against getting a 5?

13. A card is drawn at random from a standard 52-card deck. Find the following odds.
    a. In favor of drawing the ace of spades
    b. Against drawing a 2, 3, or 4

14. The spinner is spun once. Find the following odds.

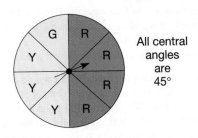

   All central angles are 45°

   a. In favor of getting a primary color (blue, red, or yellow)
   b. Against getting red or green

15. In each part, you are given the probability of event E. Find the odds in favor of event E and the odds against event E.
    a. $\frac{3}{5}$ b. $\frac{1}{4}$ c. $\frac{5}{6}$

16. In each part, you are given the following odds in favor of event E. Find $P(E)$.
    a. 9 : 1   b. 2 : 5   c. 12 : 5

17. Two fair dice are rolled, and the sum of the dots is recorded. In each part, give an example of an event having the given odds in its favor.
    a. 1 : 1   b. 1 : 5   c. 1 : 3

18. The diagram shows a sample space S of equally likely outcomes and events A and B. Find the following probabilities.
    a. $P(A)$ b. $P(B)$
    c. $P(A \mid B)$ d. $P(B \mid A)$

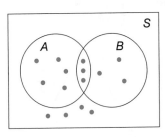

19. The spinner is spun once. (All central angles equal 60°.)

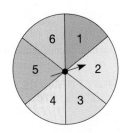

   a. What is the probability that it lands on 4?
   b. If you are told it has landed on an even number, what is the probability that it landed on 4?
   c. If you are told it has landed on an odd number, what is the probability that it landed on 4?

20. A container holds three red balls and five blue balls. One ball will be drawn and discarded. Then a second ball is drawn.
    a. What is the probability that the second ball drawn is red if you drew a red ball the first time?
    b. What is the probability of drawing a blue ball second if the first ball was red?
    c. What is the probability of drawing a blue ball second if the first ball was blue?

21. A six-sided die is tossed. What is the probability that it shows 2 if you know the following?
    a. It shows an even number.
    b. It shows a number less than 5.
    c. It does not show a 6.
    d. It shows 1 or 2.
    e. It shows an even number less than 4.
    f. It shows a number greater than 3.

PROBLEMS

22. Given is the probability tree diagram for an experiment. The sample space $S = \{a, b, c, d\}$. Also, event $A = \{a, b, c\}$ and event $B = \{b, c, d\}$. Find the following probabilities.

a. $P(A)$
b. $P(B)$
c. $P(A \cap B)$
d. $P(A \cup B)$
e. $P(A \mid B)$
f. $P(B \mid A)$

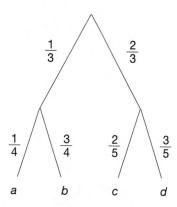

23. Given is a tabulation of academic award winners in a school.

	NUMBER OF STUDENTS RECEIVING AWARDS	NUMBER OF MATH AWARDS
Class 1	15	7
Class 2	16	8
Class 3	14	9
Class 4	20	11
Class 5	19	12
Class 6	21	14
Boys	52	29
Girls	53	32

A student is chosen at random from the award winners. Find the probabilities of the following events.

a. The student is in class 1.
b. The student is in class 4, 5, or 6.
c. The student won a math award.
d. The student is a girl.
e. The student is a boy who won a math award.
f. The student won a math award given that he or she is in class 1.
g. The student won a math award given that he or she is in class 1, 2, or 3.
h. The student is a girl, given that he or she won a math award.
i. The student won a math award, given that she is a girl.

24. In the World Series, the team that wins four out of seven games is the winner.
a. Would you agree or disagree with the following statement? The prospects for a long series decrease when the teams are closely matched.

b. If the probability that the American League team wins any game is p, what is the probability that it wins the series in four games?
c. If the probability that the National League team wins any game is q, what is the probability that it wins the series in four games? (NOTE: $q = 1 - p$.)
d. What is the probability that the series ends at four games?
e. Complete the following table for the given odds.

ODDS FAVORING AMERICAN LEAGUE	1 : 1	2 : 1	3 : 1	3 : 2
p				
q				
P(AMERICAN IN 4 GAMES)				
P(NATIONAL IN 4 GAMES)				
P(4-GAME SERIES)				

f. What conclusion can you state from this evidence about the statement in part (a)?

25. a. In a five-game World Series, there are four ways the American League could win ($NAAAA$, $ANAAA$, $AANAA$, and $AAANA$). Here, event A is an American League win, event N a National League victory. If $P(A) = p$ and $P(N) = q$, what is the probability of each sequence? What is the probability of the American League winning the series in five games?
b. Similarly, there are four ways the National League could win (verify this). What is the probability of the National League winning in five games?
c. What is the probability the series will end at five games?

26. a. There are ten ways the American League can win a six-game World Series. (There are 10 branches that contain four A's and two N's, where the last one is A.) If $P(A) = p$ and $P(N) = q$, what is the probability of the American League winning the World Series in six games? (NOTE: $q = 1 - p$.)
b. There are also ten ways the National League team can win a six-game series. What is the probability of that event?
c. What is the probability that the World Series will end at six games?

27. a. There are 20 ways each for the American League team or National League team to win a seven-game World Series. If $P(A) = p$ and $P(N) = q$, what is the probability of the American League winning? (NOTE: $q = 1 - p$.)
b. What is the probability of the National League winning?
c. What is the probability of the World Series going all seven games?

28. Summarize the results from Problems 24 to 27. Here
a. $P(A) = p$ and $P(N) = q$, where $p + q = 1$.

X = NUMBER OF GAMES	4	5	6	7
P(AMERICAN WINS)				
P(NATIONAL WINS)				
P(X GAMES IN SERIES)				

b. If the odds in favor of the American League are 1 : 1, complete the following table.

X = NUMBER OF GAMES	4	5	6	7
P(X)				

c. Find the expected value for the length of the series.

29. A snack company has put five different prizes in its snack boxes, one per box. Assuming that the same number of each toy has been used, follow the directions to conduct a simulation that will answer the question "How many boxes of snacks should you expect to buy in order to get all five toys?"
  a. Describe how to use the Chapter 11 eManipulative activity *Simulation* on our Web site to perform a simulation of this problem.
  b. Perform a simulation of at least 30 trials and record your results.

30. Eight points are evenly spaced around a circle. How many segments can be formed by joining these points?

Section 11.4 EXERCISE / PROBLEM SET B

EXERCISES

1. A candy bar company is having a contest. On the inside of each package, N, U, or T is printed in ratios 3 : 2 : 1. To determine how many packages you should buy to spell NUT, perform the following simulation.
  i. Using a die, let 1, 2, 3 represent N; let 4, 5 represent U; and let 6 represent T.
  ii. Roll the die and record the corresponding letter. Repeat rolling the die until each letter has been obtained.
  iii. Repeat step 2 a total of 20 times.

Average the number of packages purchased in each case.

2. Use the Chapter 11 eManipulative activity *Simulation* on our Web site to simulate Exercise 1 by doing the following.
  i. Click on one 1, two 2s, and three 3s.
  ii. Press START and watch until all three numbers 1, 2, and 3 appear at least once.
  iii. Press PAUSE and record the number of draws.
  iv. Clear the draws and repeat. (Perform at least 20 repetitions.)
  v. Average the number of candy bars purchased.

3. A family wants to have five children. To determine the probability that they will have at least four of the same sex, perform the following simulation.
  i. Use five coins, where H = girl and T = boy.
  ii. Toss the five coins and record how they land.
  iii. Repeat step 2 a total of 30 times.
  iv. Count the outcomes that have at least four of the same sex.

What is the approximate probability of having at least four of the same sex?

4. A bus company overbooks the 22 seats on its bus to the coast. It regularly sells 25 tickets. Assuming that there is a 0.1 chance of any passenger not showing up, complete the following steps to find the probability that at least one passenger will not have a seat.
  i. Let the digit 0 represent not showing up and the digits 1–9 represent showing up. Is $P(0) = 0.1$?
  ii. Given here is a portion of a random number table. Each row of 25 numbers represents the 25 tickets sold on a given day. In the first row, how many passengers did not show up (how many zeros appear)?

07018	31172	12572	23968	55216
52444	65625	97918	46794	62370
72161	57299	87521	44351	99981
17918	75071	91057	46829	47992
13623	76165	43195	50205	75736
27426	97534	89707	97453	90836
96039	21338	88169	69530	53300
68282	98888	25545	69406	29470
54262	21477	33097	48125	92982
66920	27544	72780	91384	47296
53348	39044	04072	62210	01209
34482	42758	40128	48136	30254
99268	98715	07545	27317	52459
95342	97178	10401	31615	95784
38556	60373	77935	64608	28949
39159	04795	51163	84475	60722
41786	18169	96649	92406	42733
95627	30768	30607	89023	60730
98738	15548	42263	79489	85118
75214	61575	27805	21930	94726
73904	89123	19271	15792	72675
33329	08896	94662	05781	59187
66364	94799	62211	37539	80172
68349	16984	86532	96186	53893
19193	99621	66899	12351	72438

This test can now be used to determine if the diagonals of various quadrilaterals are perpendicular as shown in Example 12.7.

Example 12.7   Determine if a parallelogram, a rhombus, a rectangle, and a square each have perpendicular diagonals.

SOLUTION   Using paper folding, it can be shown that the diagonals of a parallelogram are not always perpendicular (Figure 12.21), the diagonals of a rhombus are perpendicular (Figure 12.22), not all rectangles have perpendicular diagonals (Figure 12.23), and the diagonals of a square are perpendicular (Figure 12.24).

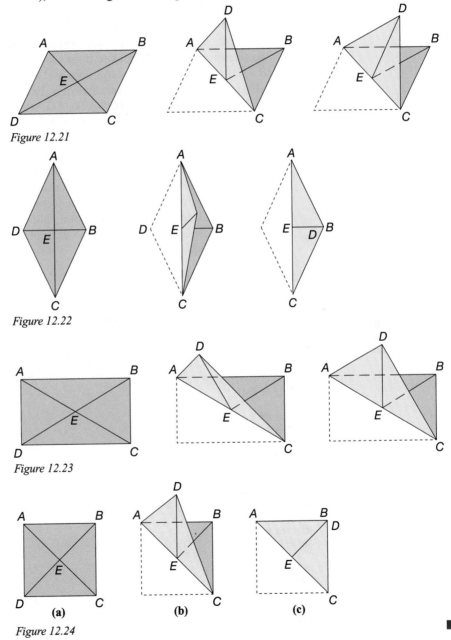

Figure 12.21

Figure 12.22

Figure 12.23

Figure 12.24

We have been using letters to label various shapes. We can also use the letters to name the various parts of these shapes. A line segment with endpoints A and B is represented by the symbol $\overline{AB}$. In Figure 12.24, $\overline{AB}$ represents the side with endpoints A and B.

Angles are represented in two ways, using the vertex of the angle, such as $\angle A$, or by using three letters where the middle letter is the vertex, such as $\angle ABC$. In Figure 12.24(c), we can name the angle at vertex A as $\angle A$ since there is only one angle there. However, we need to use three letters to name the angles in the square in Figure 12.24(a). For example, there are three angles at vertex A. They are $\angle DAB$, $\angle DAE$, and $\angle EAB$. Just as an angle is determined by three letters, a triangle is also determined by the letters naming its vertices. A triangle determined by vertices A, B, and C is represented by the $\triangle ABC$. $\triangle ABC$, $\triangle ABE$, and $\triangle DEC$ are three triangles in Figure 12.24(a).

In Figure 12.24(c), diagonal $\overline{DB}$ folds onto itself so that line segment $\overline{DE}$ and line segment $\overline{EB}$ match. In that case, E is called a **midpoint**. In the same figure, side $\overline{AD}$ matches exactly with side $\overline{AB}$, which indicates that they are the same length. In a quadrilateral, two sides are **adjacent** if they share a common vertex. Two sides are said to be **opposite** if they are not adjacent. In Figure 12.24(a), sides $\overline{AB}$ and $\overline{DC}$ are a pair of opposite sides and are the same length.

By using the type of analysis shown in Examples 12.6 and 12.7, several attributes of parallelograms, rhombi, rectangles, and squares can be determined. These attributes are summarized in Table 12.4. In addition, there are several other attributes listed in Table 12.4 that will be investigated in the Exercise/Problem Set. When an X is placed in the table, it means that *all* quadrilaterals of that type will have that attribute. If there is not an X, then none or only some of those types of quadrilaterals have that attribute. For example, some parallelograms can have diagonals that are perpendicular, but since not all parallelograms have that attribute, no X is placed in the parallelogram column next to "Diagonals are perpendicular." Deductive verifications of the attributes in Table 12.4 can be made when we get to Chapters 14, 15, or 16.

TABLE 12.4 Some Attributes of Quadrilaterals

ATTRIBUTE	PARALLELOGRAM	RHOMBUS	RECTANGLE	SQUARE
Adjacent sides are the same length		X		X
Both pairs of opposite sides are the same length	X	X	X	X
All angles are right angles			X	X
Both pairs of opposite sides are parallel	X	X	X	X
Adjacent sides are perpendicular			X	X
Diagonals are the same length			X	X
Diagonals intersect at the midpoint	X	X	X	X
Diagonals are perpendicular		X		X

✔ **Check for Understanding:** Exercise/Problem Set A #7–11

MATHEMATICAL MORSEL

The game of chess offers a myriad of changing patterns. To settle an old chess problem, a 25-year-old computer science student, Lewis Stiller, used a computer to perform one of the largest such computer searches. His search found that a king, a rook, and a bishop can defeat a king and two knights in 223 moves. Stiller's program ran for five hours and made 100 billion moves by working backward. Although this search, which was reported in *Scientific American*, was directed to solving a chess problem, the techniques Stiller developed can be used in solving other problems in mathematics.

Section 12.1   EXERCISE / PROBLEM SET A

EXERCISES

1. A group of students is shown the following shape and asked to identify it.

Is the student operating at level 0 or level 1 for each of the following?
a. "It is a triangle because it looks like a yield sign."
b. "It is not a triangle because it is upside down."
c. "It is a triangle because it has 3 straight sides."

2. Use the following shapes to answer each of the questions.

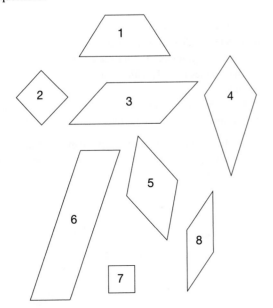

a. Which shapes are squares?
b. Which shapes are rectangles?
c. Which shapes are rhombi?
d. Suppose a student says shape 7 is a rectangle as well as a square "because both shapes have opposite sides that are the same length and both have right angles." At what Van Hiele level is the student thinking?

3. a. Sort the following triangles into two categories and describe each category.

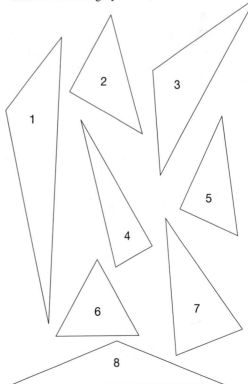

b. Repeat part a but sort into different categories.
c. If a student put shapes 2, 4, and 5 into a category because they all have "square corners," at what Van Hiele level is he thinking?
d. If another student put shapes 2, 4, and 5 together because "they all have a right angle," at what Van Hiele level is the student thinking?

4. How many triangles are in the following design?

5. How many squares are found in the following figure?

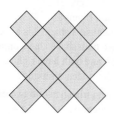

6. Trace the following figure and cut it into five pieces along the lines indicated. Rearrange the pieces to form a square. You must use all five pieces, have no gaps or overlaps, and not turn the pieces over.

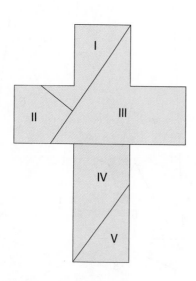

7. Given here are a variety of triangles. Sides with the same length are indicated. Right angles are indicated.

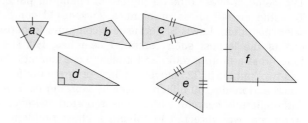

a. Name the triangles that are scalene.
b. Name the triangles that are isosceles.
c. Name the triangles that are equilateral.
d. Name the triangles that contain a right angle.

8. Find the following shapes in the figure.

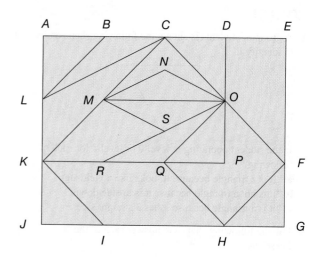

a. A square
b. A rectangle that is not a square
c. A parallelogram that is not a rectangle
d. An isosceles triangle with no right angles
e. A rhombus that is not a square
f. A scalene triangle with no right angles

9. Trace the following figure onto a piece of paper and use paper folding to determine if the lines are parallel. Explain your results.

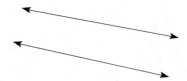

10. Trace the following figure onto a piece of paper and use paper folding to determine if the lines are perpendicular. Explain your results.

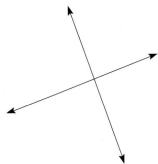

11. For the figures in parts a and b, use proper notation to name the following if possible:

   i. two diagonals

   ii. two pairs of opposite sides

   iii. three pairs of adjacent sides

   iv. a midpoint and the segment for which it is the midpoint

  a. Parallelogram

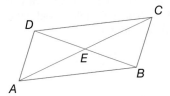

  b. Rectangle

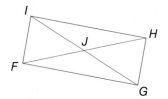

PROBLEMS

12. In the following table, if *A* belongs with *B*, then *X* belongs with *Y*. Which of (I), (II), or (III) is the best choice for *Y*?

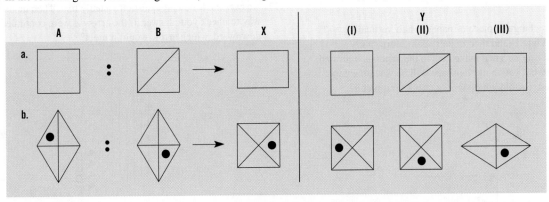

13. Fold a rectangular piece of paper on the dashed line as shown in each of the following figures. Then make cuts in the paper as indicated. Sketch what you think the shape will be when the paper is unfolded. Then unfold your paper to check your picture.

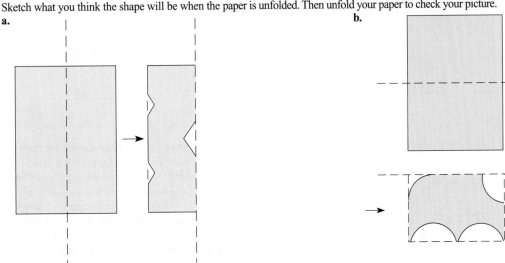

14. Each of the following shapes was obtained by folding a rectangular piece of paper in half vertically (lengthwise) and then making appropriate cuts in the paper. For each figure, draw the folded paper and show the cuts that must be made to make the figure. Try folding and cutting a piece of paper to check your answer.

a.   **b.**

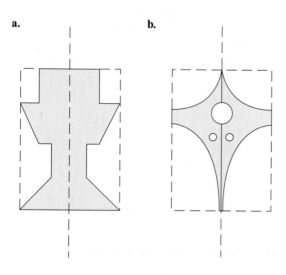

15. Fold a rectangular piece of paper in half vertically (dashed line 1) and then in half again horizontally (dashed line 2). Then make cuts in the paper as indicated. Sketch what you think the shape will be when the paper is unfolded. Unfold your paper to check your picture.

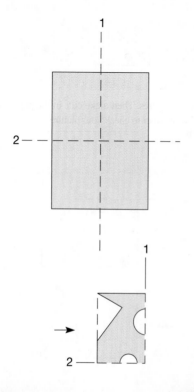

16. Fold the square first on line 1, then on line 2. Next, punch a hole, as indicated.

   a. Draw what you think the resulting shape will be. Unfold to check.

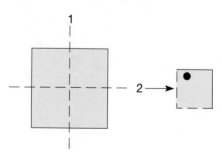

   b. To produce each figure, a square was folded twice, punched once, then unfolded. Find the fold lines and where the hole was punched.

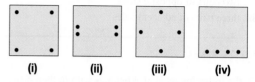

   (i)   **(ii)**   **(iii)**   **(iv)**

17. Answer the following question visually first. Then devise a way to check your answer. If the arrow A were continued downward, which arrow would it meet?

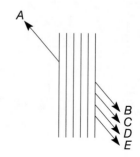

18. Which is longer, x or y?

   a.   **b.**

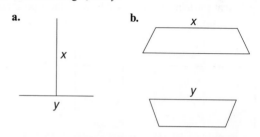

19. A problem that challenged mathematicians for many years concerns the coloring of maps. That is, what is the minimum number of colors necessary to color *any* map? Just recently it was finally proved with the aid of a computer that no map requires more than four colors. Some maps, however, can be colored with fewer than four colors. Determine the smallest number of colors necessary to color each map shown here. (NOTE: Two "countries" that share only one point can be colored the same color; however, if they have more than one point in common, they must be colored differently.)

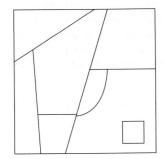

20. A portion of a triangular lattice is given. Which of the following can be drawn on it? You may find the Chapter 12 eManipulative *Geoboard—Triangular Lattice* on our Web site to be helpful in thinking about this problem.

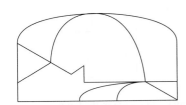

a. Parallel lines   **b.** Perpendicular lines

21. Which of the following quadrilaterals can be drawn on a triangular lattice?
a. Rhombus   **b.** Parallelogram
c. Square   **d.** Rectangle

22. Given the square lattice shown, draw quadrilaterals having $\overline{AB}$ as a side. You may find the Chapter 12 eManipulative *Geoboard* on our Web site to be helpful in thinking about this problem.

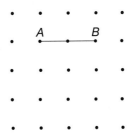

a. How many parallelograms are possible?
b. How many rectangles are possible?
c. How many rhombuses are possible?
d. How many squares are possible?

23. Use a tracing to show that the diagonals of a rectangle are congruent.

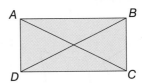

| Section 12.1 | **EXERCISE / PROBLEM SET B** |

EXERCISES

1. A group of students is shown the following shape and asked to identify it.

Is the student operating at level 0 or level 1 for each of the following?
a. "It is a square because it has 4 equal sides and 90 degree angles."

b. "It is a square because if you turn the paper it looks like a square."
c. "It is not a square. It is a diamond."

2. Use the following shapes to answer each of the questions.

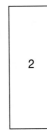

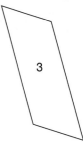

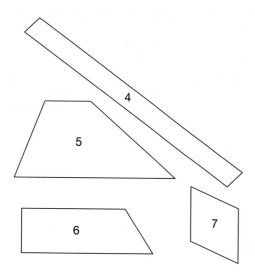

a. Which shapes are squares?
b. Which shapes are rhombi?
c. Which shapes are rectangles?
d. A student says that shapes 2, 3, 4, and 7 are all alike because they all have two pairs of opposite sides that are the same length. At what Van Hiele level is this student thinking?

3. a. Sort the following quadrilaterals into two categories and describe each category.

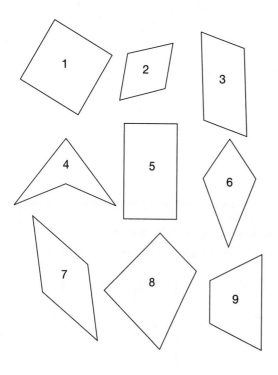

b. Repeat part a but sort into different categories.
c. If a student put shapes 1, 5, and 8 into a category because they all "have a right angle," at what Van Hiele level is the student thinking?
d. If another student put shapes 1, 2, 3, 5, 7, 8, and 9 together because "they are all related by the fact that they have at least one pair of parallel sides," at what Van Hiele level is the student thinking?

4. How many rectangles are found in the following design?

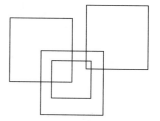

5. a. How many triangles are in the figure?
   b. How many parallelograms are in the figure?
   c. How many trapezoids are in the figure?

6. Trace the following figure and cut it into five pieces along the lines indicated. Rearrange the pieces to form a square. You must use all five pieces, have no gaps or overlaps, and not turn the pieces over.

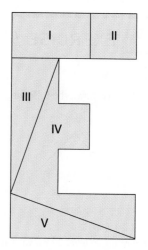

7. Several shapes are pictured here. Sides with the same length are indicated, as are right angles.

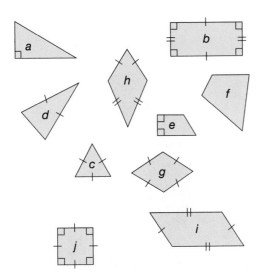

a. Which figures have a right angle?
b. Which figures have at least one pair of parallel sides?
c. Which figures have at least two sides with the same length?
d. Which figures have all sides the same length?

8. Find the following shapes in the figure.

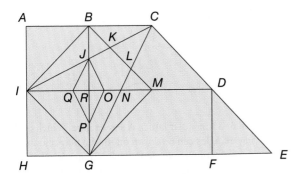

a. Three squares
b. A rectangle that is not a square
c. A parallelogram that is not a rectangle
d. An isosceles triangle with no right angles
e. A rhombus that is not a square
f. A scalene triangle with no right angles

9. Trace the following figure onto a piece of paper and use paper folding to determine if the lines are parallel. Explain your results.

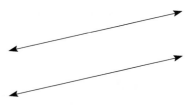

10. Trace the following figure onto a piece of paper and use paper folding to determine if the lines are perpendicular. Explain your results.

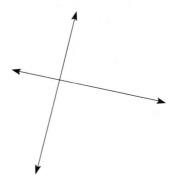

11. For the figures in parts a and b, use proper notation to name the following if possible:
  i. two diagonals
  ii. two pairs of opposite sides
  iii. three pairs of adjacent sides
  iv. a midpoint and the segment for which it is the midpoint

  a. Parallelogram

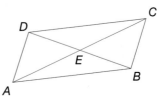

  b. Square

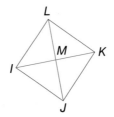

PROBLEMS

12. In the following table, if *A* belongs with *B*, then *X* belongs with *Y*. Which of (I), (II), or (III) is the best choice for *Y*?

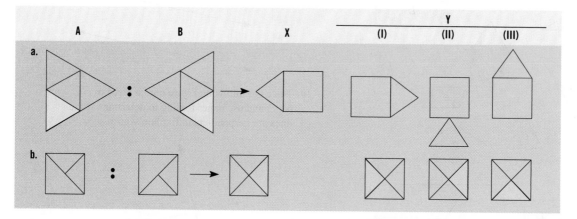

13. Are the lines labeled *l* and *m* parallel?

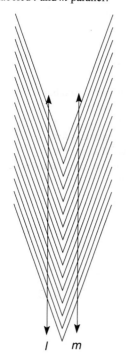

14. Which is longer, *x* or *y*?

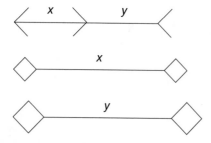

15. Determine the smallest number of colors necessary to color each map. (NOTE: Two "countries" that share only one point can be colored the same color; however, if they have more than one point in common, they must be colored differently.)

a.

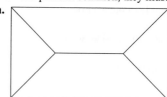

b.

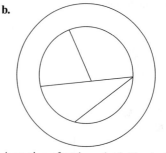

16. A portion of a triangular lattice is shown here. Which of the following triangles can be drawn on it? You may find the Chapter 12 eManipulative *Geoboard—Triangular Lattice* on our Web site to be helpful in thinking about this problem.

a. Equilateral triangle   **b.** Isosceles triangle
c. Scalene triangle

17. a. Make copies of the following large, uncut square. Find ways to cut the squares into each of the following numbers of smaller squares: 7, 8, 9, 10, 11, 12, 13, 14, 15, 16.

If you start with a large square

then you can cut it into 4 smaller squares like this

1	2
3	4

or into 6 smaller squares like this.

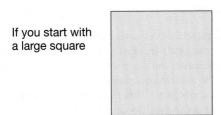

You can cut a square into 10 smaller squares this way

or this way.

b. Can you find more than one way to cut the squares for some numbers? Which numbers?

c. For which numbers can you cut the square into equal-sized smaller squares?

18. Use a tracing to show that the diagonals of a parallelogram bisect each other. That is, show that $\overline{AE}$ is congruent to $\overline{CE}$ and that $\overline{DE}$ is congruent to $\overline{BE}$.

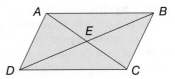

19. Use a tracing to show that the opposite sides of a rectangle are congruent.

20. Fold a rectangular piece of paper on the dashed line as shown in each of the following figures. Then make cuts in the paper as indicated. Sketch what you think the shape will be when the paper is unfolded. Then unfold your paper to check your picture.

a.

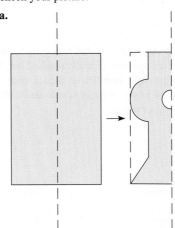

b.

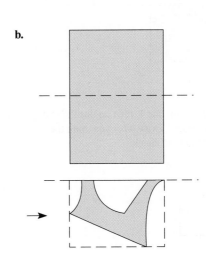

21. Each of the following shapes was obtained by folding a rectangular piece of paper in half horizontally and then making appropriate cuts in the paper. For each figure, draw the folded paper and show the cuts that must be made to make the figure. Try folding and cutting a piece of paper to check your answer.

a.

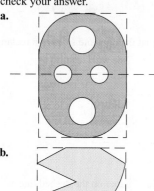

b.

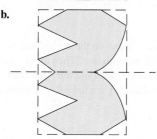

22. Fold a rectangular piece of paper in half vertically (dashed line 1) and then in half again horizontally (dashed line 2). Then make cuts in the paper as indicated. Sketch what you think the shape will be when the paper is unfolded. Unfold your paper to check your picture.

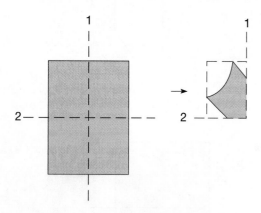

23. Fold the square first on line 1, then on line 2. Next, punch two holes, as indicated. Draw what you think the resulting shape will be. Unfold to check.

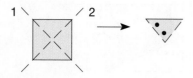

Analyzing Student Thinking

24. Bernie says that any three-sided figure is a triangle even if the sides are curved. Chandra says the sides have to make angles and the bottom has to be straight. Can you tell what van Hiele level would be indicated by answers such as these? Explain.

25. Naquetta made three categories of quadrilaterals: those whose diagonals are equal; those whose diagonals are perpendicular; and those whose diagonals bisect each other. Were there any quadrilaterals that fit into more than one category? Were there any quadrilaterals that did not fit into any category? Demonstrate for Naquetta how to correlate the results using a Venn diagram.

26. Daniel claims the triangle below is not isosceles because the sides attached to the top point are not the same length. At what van Hiele level is Daniel thinking and what could you do to help him see that it is an isosceles triangle?

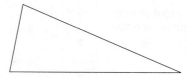

27. Janet wants to know how she can show that the opposite sides of a rectangle are the same length. What would you tell her?

28. Carla claims that the quadrilateral below is a rectangle but it is just "squished." At what van Hiele level is she thinking? What property of rectangles could you emphasize to help Carla see that this figure is not a rectangle?

29. Beth claims that since the diagonals of a rhombus are perpendicular, then she can build a rhombus around any two intersecting segments that are perpendicular by viewing these segments as diagonals and the endpoints of the segments as vertices of the rhombus. Is she correct? Explain.

30. Becky wants to know how to show that the diagonals of a parallelogram intersect at their midpoints. How would you respond?

1. The Focal Points for Prekindergarten state "Identifying shapes and describing spatial relationships." According to this Focal Point, at what Van Hiele level are prekindergarten students supposed to be thinking?

2. The Focal Points for Kindergarten state "Describing shapes and space." According to this Focal Point, at what Van Hiele level are kindergarten students supposed to be thinking?

3. The Focal Points for Grade 3 state "Describing and analyzing properties of two-dimensional shapes." According to this Focal Point, at what Van Hiele level should students be thinking in the third grade?

12.2   RELATIONSHIPS

STARTING POINT

In a group or with a partner, discuss the truth of the following statements and explain to each other why these statements are true or false.

- All squares are rectangles but not all rectangles are squares.
- Some rhombi are rectangles.
- The intersection of the set of scalene triangles and the set of equilateral triangles is the set of isosceles triangles.

Triangles and Quadrilaterals

The next level of geometric thinking as measured by the van Hiele theory is level 2, or relationships. As students do their analysis of shapes in level 1, they begin to notice properties that are common among various shapes. This leads to the identification of relationships between shapes. For example, our analysis of rhombi showed that the opposite sides of a rhombus are parallel. Since the definition of a parallelogram is a quadrilateral with two pairs of parallel sides, a rhombus is also a parallelogram. Our goal in this section is to investigate various relationships among triangles first and then among quadrilaterals.

Another aspect of thinking at van Hiele level 2 is forming more abstract definitions. In mathematics it is customary to state definitions using as few conditions as possible. Part of this skill is the ability to identify the necessary and extraneous parts of a definition. For example, we have defined a rectangle to be a quadrilateral with four right angles. In Table 12.4 in the previous section, it can be seen that the opposite sides of a rectangle are parallel and the same length. Must all of these properties be listed in the definition of a rectangle or is simply defining a rectangle as a quadrilateral with four right angles sufficient?

Triangles   When students think about triangles at van Hiele level 2, they begin to notice relationships among the various types of triangles. For example, they may think about questions such as, "Is it possible for an isosceles triangle to also be a right triangle?" This question is considered in the following example.

Example 12.8   In the Venn diagram in Figure 12.25, the left oval represents right triangles, the right oval represents triangles that are isosceles, and the intersection of the two ovals is represented by region III. Draw two examples of triangles in each of the three regions and describe characteristics of the triangles in each region.

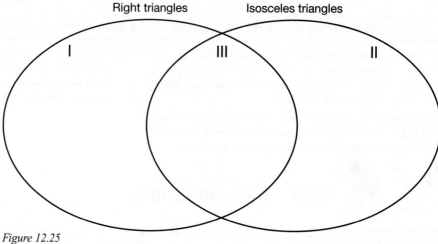

Figure 12.25

SOLUTION

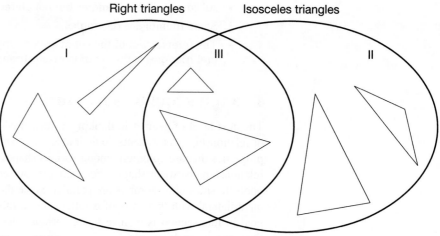

Figure 12.26

In Figure 12.26, the triangles in region I, but not in region II are right triangles that are not isosceles. The triangles in region III are isosceles right triangles. And the triangles in region II, but not in region I, are isosceles triangles that are not right triangles. ■

Example 12.8 looks at relationships of triangles classified by sides and classified by angles. Relationships among triangles can also be classified according to the lengths of the sides of the triangles. The diagram in Figure 12.27 illustrates such relationships.

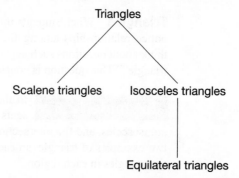

Figure 12.27

When a line is drawn between two types of triangles, the lower set of triangles is a subset of the upper one. This would mean that the set of all equilateral triangles is a subset of the set of isosceles triangles. In other words, every equilateral triangle is a special kind of isosceles triangle.

Quadrilaterals   As we move on to consider the relationships among the different types of quadrilaterals, we can begin by examining the properties that these various shapes have in common. It was established in Example 12.6 that both pairs of opposite sides of a rhombus, rectangle and a square are parallel. Since the description of a parallelogram is a quadrilateral with two pairs of parallel sides, rhombi, rectangles, and squares must also be parallelograms. Because a rhombus, rectangle, and square are all specific types of parallelograms, they have all of the properties of a parallelogram. The listing of the properties of these quadrilaterals shown in Table 12.4 illustrates this point. In the table, the properties of a parallelogram, other than opposite sides being parallel, are that the opposite sides are the same length and the diagonals intersect at their midpoints and therefore bisect each other. A rhombus, rectangle, and square have these same properties since they are parallelograms.

We have established how a rhombus, rectangle and square are all related to parallelograms but we have not discussed how they might be related to each other. The descriptions of these quadrilaterals in Table 12.3 can assist in answering this question. Since a square is a quadrilateral with four sides the same length, we know that it must also be a rhombus. A square is also a quadrilateral with four right angles. Thus, a square must also be a rectangle. A diagram for parallelograms, rhombi, rectangles, and squares, which is similar to Figure 12.27 for triangles, is displayed in Figure 12.28.

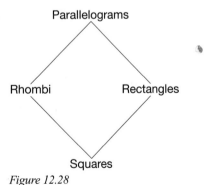

Figure 12.28

These relationships in Figure 12.28 can be further seen in Table 12.4 by noticing the common properties. The properties that the rhombus and rectangle have in common are the same properties that each has in common with a parallelogram. The square has all of the properties of a rhombus and all of the properties of a rectangle. It is clear that squares are special types of rectangles and special types of rhombi.

Table 12.3 introduced four common quadrilaterals. Table 12.5 introduces three more.

TABLE 12.5

MODEL	NAME	ABSTRACTION	DESCRIPTION
	Kite	**Kite**	Quadrilateral with two non-overlapping pairs of adjacent sides that are the same length.
	Bike frame	**Trapezoid**	Quadrilateral with exactly one pair of parallel sides.
	Drinking glass silhouette	**Isosceles trapezoid**	Quadrilateral with exactly one pair of parallel sides and the remaining sides are the same length.

Example 12.9   Figure 12.29 shows four quadrilaterals. Use foldings to verify that they are kites and trapezoids as labeled.

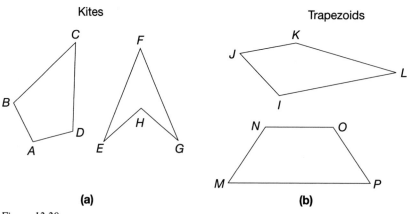

Figure 12.29

SOLUTION The top row in Figure 12.30 shows that *ABCD* in Figure 12.29(a) is a kite using a folding since $\overline{AB}$ folds onto $\overline{AD}$ and $\overline{CB}$ folds onto $\overline{CD}$. A similar folding shows that *EFGH* is a kite.

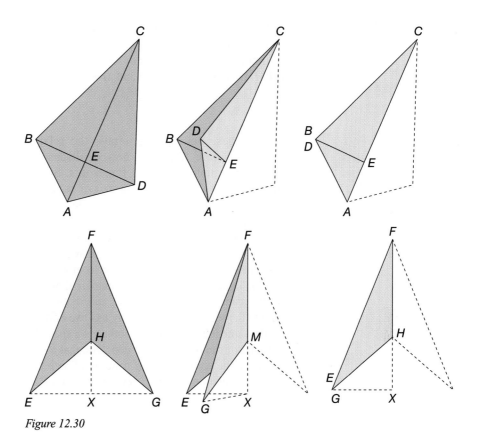

Figure 12.30

In both cases, there are two pairs of adjacent sides where each pair has the same length. It is important to note that these two pairs of adjacent sides are distinct and do not overlap. Another property that can be observed from the foldings is that the diagonals are perpendicular. The trapezoids in Figure 12.29(b) appear to have one pair of opposite sides parallel to each other. Again, this can be verified by foldings as shown in Figure 12.31.

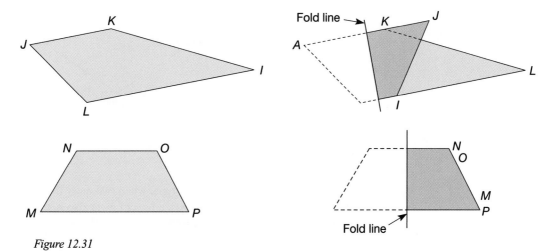

Figure 12.31

As can be seen in Figure 12.31, the foldings show that *IJKL* and *MNOP* both have a pair of parallel sides. Also, the other sides are not parallel. Thus, *IJKL* and *MNOP* are trapezoids. In the folding of *MNOP*, *N* folds onto *O* and *M* folds onto *P*. Thus, $\overline{MN}$ and $\overline{PO}$ have the same length and *MNOP* is an isosceles trapezoid.　■

With these new quadrilaterals, the relationships between them and those shown in Figure 12.28 can now be discussed. First consider the relationships between parallelograms and trapezoids. Since trapezoids have been defined as quadrilaterals with *exactly* one pair of parallel sides and a parallelogram has two pair of parallel sides, they are not related other than the fact that they are both quadrilaterals.

Now consider parallelograms and kites. Are parallelograms and kites related in any way? Since parallelograms are defined as quadrilaterals with 2 pairs of parallel sides, there is no restriction on the lengths of the sides. However, Table 12.4 shows that two kinds of parallelograms, namely rhombi and squares, have adjacent sides that are the same length. So are kites and rhombi related? Since a rhombus has 4 sides that are the same length, it clearly has two nonoverlapping pairs of adjacent sides that are the same length. Thus a rhombus is a special kind of kite. Since a square is a special kind of rhombus, we can conclude that a square is also a special kind of kite. In summary, the set of rhombi is a subset of both the set of parallelograms and the set of kites. The relationships between all of the quadrilaterals are shown in the diagram in Figure 12.32.

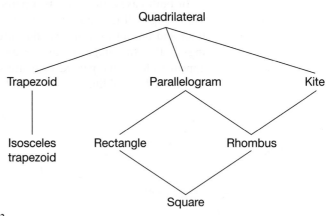

Figure 12.32

As in previous diagrams of this type, when two quadrilaterals are joined by a line segment or a series of line segments, a lower one is also in the set named by any one above it. The following example further illustrates these relationships.

Example 12.10	Place the shapes in Figure 12.33 into a two circle Venn diagram and label the circles appropriately.

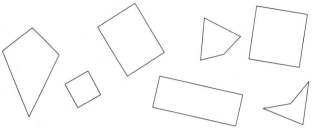

Figure 12.33

SOLUTION Figure 12.33 contains some rectangles, squares, and kites. It has been established that squares are rectangles with adjacent sides the same length, so squares could be placed in the same circle as rectangles. Similarly, it was just discussed that squares are kites, so squares could also be in the same circle as the kites. Thus, the shapes could be arranged as in the Venn diagram shown in Figure 12.34.

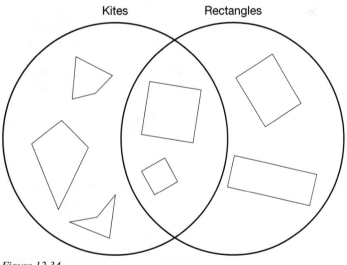

Figure 12.34

✔ **Check for Understanding:** Exercise/Problem Set A #1–6

NCTM Standard
All students should identify and describe line and rotational symmetry in two- and three-dimensional shapes and designs.

Symmetry

The concept of symmetry can be used in analyzing figures. Two-dimensional figures can have two distinct types of symmetry: reflection symmetry and rotation symmetry. Informally, a figure has **reflection symmetry** if there is a line that the figure can be "folded over" so that one-half of the figure matches the other half perfectly (Figure 12.35).

The "fold line" just described is called the figure's **line (axis) of symmetry**.

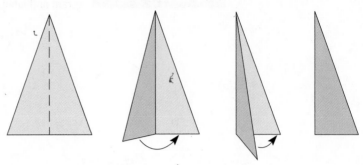

Figure 12.35

Children's Literature
www.wiley.com/college/musser
See "Shadows and Reflections"
by Tana Hoban.

Figure 12.36 shows several figures and their lines of reflection symmetry. The lines of symmetry are dashed. Many properties of figures, such as symmetry, can be demonstrated using tracings and paper folding.

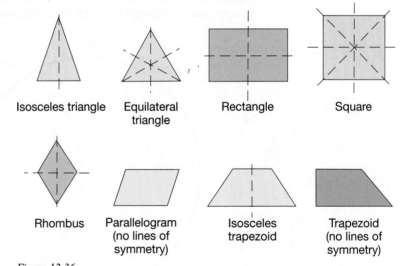

Isosceles triangle   Equilateral triangle   Rectangle   Square

Rhombus   Parallelogram (no lines of symmetry)   Isosceles trapezoid   Trapezoid (no lines of symmetry)

Figure 12.36

Example 12.11 uses symmetry to show a property of isosceles triangles.

Example 12.11   Suppose $\triangle ABC$ is isosceles where side $\overline{AB}$ and side $\overline{AC}$ are the same length (Figure 12.37). Show that $\angle ABC$ can be folded onto $\angle ACB$.

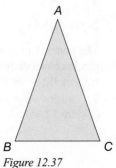

Figure 12.37

SOLUTION Fold the triangle so that vertex A remains fixed while vertex B folds onto vertex C. Semitransparent paper works well for this (Figure 12.38).

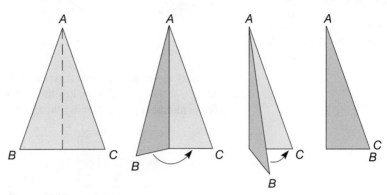

Figure 12.38

Observe that after folding, side $\overline{AB}$ coincides with side $\overline{AC}$. Since $\angle ABC$ exactly matches $\angle ACB$, they are said to be the same size. ∎

In an isosceles triangle, the angles that are the same size are opposite the sides that are the same length. These angles are called the **base angles** of an isosceles triangle (see $\angle B$ and $\angle C$ in Figure 12.38).

A useful device for finding lines of symmetry is a **Mira**, a Plexiglas "two-way" mirror. You can see reflections in it and also see through it. Hence, in the case of a reflection symmetry, the reflection image appears to be superimposed on the figure itself. Figure 12.39 shows how we could use a Mira to see that the base angles of an isosceles triangle are the same size.

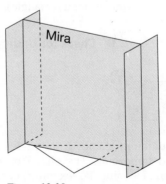

Figure 12.39

NCTM Standard
All students should examine the congruence, similarity, and line or rotational symmetry of objects using transformations.

The second type of symmetry of figures is rotation symmetry. A figure has **rotation symmetry** if there is a point, called the **center of rotation**, around which the figure can be rotated, *less than a full turn*, so that the image matches the original figure perfectly. (We will see more precise definitions of reflection and rotation symmetry in Chapter 16.) Figure 12.40 shows an investigation of rotation symmetry for an equilateral triangle. In Figure 12.40 the equilateral triangle is rotated counterclockwise $\frac{1}{3}$ of a turn. It could also be rotated $\frac{2}{3}$ of a turn and, of course, through a full turn to produce a matching image. Every figure can be rotated through a full turn using any point as the center of rotation to produce a matching image. Figures for which only a full turn produces an identical image do *not* have rotation symmetry.

Reflection from Research

Rotational symmetry is at least as easy to understand as line symmetry for primary children. Students benefit when the ideas are taught together (Morris, 1987).

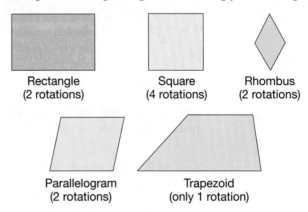

Figure 12.40

The next figure shows several types of figures and the number of turns up to and including one full turn that makes the image match the figure. See whether you can verify the numbers given. Tracing the figure and rotating your drawing may help you.

Rectangle
(2 rotations)

Square
(4 rotations)

Rhombus
(2 rotations)

Parallelogram
(2 rotations)

Trapezoid
(only 1 rotation)

Figure 12.41

In Figure 12.41, all figures except the trapezoid have rotation symmetry.

We see that shapes can have reflection symmetry without rotation symmetry (e.g., Figure 12.36 shows an isosceles triangle that is not equilateral) and rotation symmetry without reflection symmetry (e.g., Figure 12.41 shows a parallelogram that is not a rectangle).

 Check for Understanding: Exercise/Problem Set A #7–9

MATHEMATICAL MORSEL

Road signs come in all different shapes from circles and octagons to triangles and trapezoids. The shape of each sign has a particular use and meaning. For example, circular signs are used at railroad crossings and they represent the most potential danger to a driver. The next level of danger is the need to STOP at intersections, and thus the octagon is the shape used. Diamond- or rhombus-shaped signs are used for caution, while rectangles are used to provide direction and display regulations like the speed limit. The octagon and circle are used exclusively for stop signs and railroad crossings because of the need to be able to identify them at night as well as during the day. Rhombus- or rectangle-shaped signs, however, represent a lower level of danger and thus take on a variety of cautionary or directional meanings.

| Section 12.2 | EXERCISE / PROBLEM SET A

EXERCISES

1. In the Venn diagram below, draw two different triangles in each of the three regions where possible.

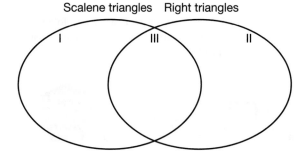

2. In the Venn diagram below, draw two different quadrilaterals in each of the three regions where possible.

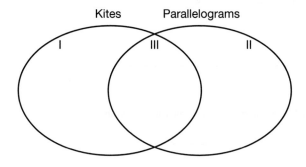

3. In the Venn diagram below, draw two different quadrilaterals in each of the three regions where possible.

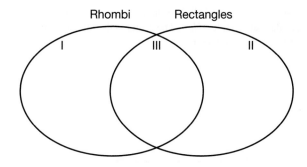

4. a. Which of the following pictures of sets best represents the relationship between isosceles triangles and scalene triangles? Label the sets and intersection (if it exists).

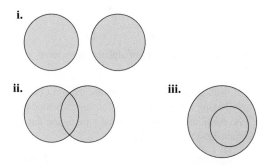

   b. Which represents the relationship between isosceles triangles and equilateral triangles?
   c. Which represents the relationship between isosceles triangles and right triangles?
   d. Which represents the relationship between equilateral triangles and right triangles?

5. Find the following shapes in the figure.

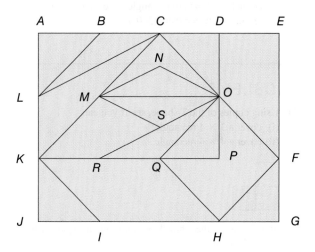

   a. An isosceles right triangle
   b. A kite that is not a rhombus
   c. A right scalene triangle
   d. A trapezoid that is not isosceles
   e. An isosceles trapezoid
   f. A parallelogram that is not a rectangle or a rhombus

6. Rectangles and parallelograms have some properties in common because a rectangle is a special kind of parallelogram. There are also properties that are only possessed by one shape. Identify two properties that rectangles and parallelograms have in common and one property that is possessed by one quadrilateral and not the other.

7. Determine the types of symmetry for each figure. Indicate the lines of symmetry and describe the turn symmetries.

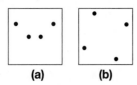

(a) **(b)**

8. Which capital letters of our alphabet have rotation symmetry?

9. **a.** How many lines of symmetry are there for each of the following national flags? Colors are indicated and should be considered. Assume the flags are laying flat and are rectangular, not square.

Argentina

Jamaica

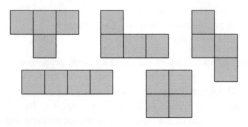

b. Which of the following national flags have rotation symmetry? What are the angles in each case (list measures between 0 and 360°)?

United Kingdom

Japan

10. Draw all of the lines of symmetry for each of the following traffic signs. Ignore the lettering or coloring of the sign and focus on the shape of the outer edge.

a. **b.** **c.**

d. **e.**

PROBLEMS

11. Using copies of the 3-shape, see if you can:
    (i) cover a 3 × 4 rectangle;
    (ii) cover a 4 × 4 rectangle.

In each case, either show how it is done or explain why it cannot be done.

12. A tetromino is formed by connecting four squares so that connecting squares share a complete side. In section 1.1, you found that there are 5 different tetrominoes.

Make two copies of each tetromino and use them to cover a 5 × 8 rectangle.

13. Use a tracing to find all the rotation symmetries of a square.

14. Use a tracing to find all the rotation symmetries of an equilateral triangle. (*Hint:* The center is the intersection of the reflection lines.)

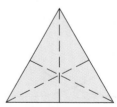

15. Isosceles trapezoids and rectangles are not related other than that they are both quadrilaterals. However, both have a property that is not common among most of the other quadrilaterals. Identify that property.

| Section 12.2 | EXERCISE / PROBLEM SET B

EXERCISES

1. In the Venn diagram below, draw two different triangles in each of the three regions where possible.

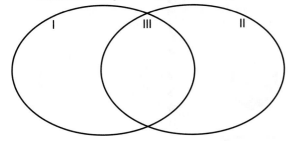

2. In the Venn diagram below, draw two different quadrilaterals in each of the three regions where possible.

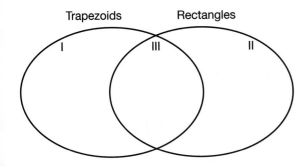

3. In the Venn diagram below, draw two different quadrilaterals in each of the three regions where possible.

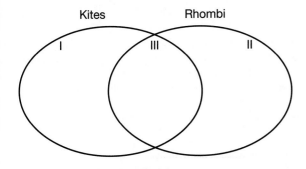

4. a. Which of the following pictures of sets best represents the relationship between rectangles and parallelograms? Label the sets and intersection (if it exists) appropriately.

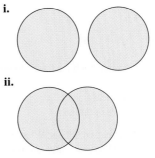

i.

ii.

iii.

b. Which represents the relationship between rectangles and rhombi?
c. Which represents the relationship between rectangles and squares?
d. Which represents the relationship between rectangles and isosceles triangles?

5. Find the following shapes in the figure.

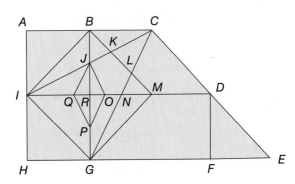

a. Seven right isosceles triangles that are congruent to each other
b. An isosceles triangle not congruent to any of those in part a
c. A kite that is not a rhombus
d. A right scalene triangle
e. A trapezoid that is not isosceles
f. An isosceles trapezoid

6. Rhombi and kites have some properties in common because a rhombus is a special kind of kite. There are also properties that are only possessed by one shape. Identify two properties that rhombi and kites have in common and one property that is possessed by one quadrilateral and not the other.

7. Determine the type(s) of symmetry for each figure. Indicate the lines of reflection symmetry and describe the turn symmetries.

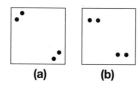

(a)   (b)

8. Which capital letters of our alphabet have the following symmetry?
a. Reflection symmetry in vertical line
b. Reflection symmetry in horizontal line

9. Given here are emblems from national flags. What types of symmetry do they have? Give lines or center and turn angle.
a. Korea   **b.** Burundi

c. Canada   **d.** Taiwan

10. Draw all of the lines of symmetry for each of the following traffic signs. Ignore the lettering or coloring of the sign and focus on the shape of the outer edge.

a.   b.   c.

d.   e.

PROBLEMS

11. a. Use paper folding to show that an isosceles trapezoid has reflection symmetry.

b. Are there any non-isosceles trapezoids that have a reflection symmetry?

12. Use a tracing to show that a rectangle has rotation symmetry.

13. The Chapter 12 Geometer's Sketchpad® activity *Name That Quadrilateral* on our Web site displays seven different quadrilaterals in the shape of a square. However, each quadrilateral is constructed with different properties. Some have right angles, some have congruent sides, and some have parallel sides. By dragging each of the points on each of the quadrilaterals, you can determine the most general name of each quadrilateral. Name all seven of the quadrilaterals.

14. A **pentomino** is made by five connected squares that touch only on a complete side.

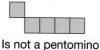

Is a pentomino   Is not a pentomino

Two pentominos are the same if they can be matched by turning or flipping, as shown.

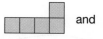

and

In the Initial Problem in Chapter 8, you found that there were 12 different pentomino shapes. (They are shown in the solution of the chapter's Initial Problem.)
a. Which of the pentominos have reflection symmetry? Indicate the line(s) of reflection.
b. Which of the pentominos have rotation symmetry? Indicate the center and angle(s).

15. Look at your set of pentominos.
a. Find three pentomino shapes that can fit together to form a 3 × 5 rectangle.
b. Using five of the pentominos, cover a 5 × 5 square.
c. Using each of the pentomino pieces once, make a 6 × 10 rectangle.

Analyzing Student Thinking

16. Gerald thinks that isosceles triangles and equilateral triangles are not related because isosceles triangles have two sides that are the same length and equilateral triangles have three sides that are the same length. Is he correct? Explain.

17. Keith used paper folding to show that a kite has one line of symmetry and asks if it is possible for a kite to have two lines of symmetry. How would you respond?

18. Steve notices that an isosceles trapezoid has a pair of parallel sides and a different pair of sides that are the same length. He also notices that a rectangle has a pair of sides that are parallel and a different pair of sides that are the same length. He wonders if a rectangle is a special kind of isosceles trapezoid. How would you respond?

19. Donyall was trying to follow the directions on an activity. It said to put all the rhombus shapes in one pile. Elyse told him to put the squares in there too, but Donyall said, "No, because the rhombi have to be slanty." What is your response?

20. Whitney says that a square is a kind of rectangle because it has all right angles and its opposite sides are parallel, but Bobby says that's not right because a square has all equal sides and a rectangle has a length and width that have to be different. How would you respond?

21. Willy says if a plane figure has reflection symmetry, it automatically has rotation symmetry. Is this true? Can you think of a counterexample? Explain.

22. Gail draws a horizontal line through a parallelogram and says, "If I cut along this line, the two pieces fit on top of each other. So this must be a line of symmetry." Do you agree? Explain.

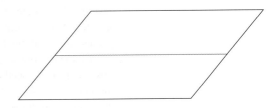

Problems Relating to the NCTM Standards and Curriculum Focal Points

1. The Focal Points for Kindergarten state "Describe shapes and space." List three attributes discussed in this section that could be used to "describe shapes."

2. The Focal Points for Grade 3 state "Describing and analyzing properties of two-dimensional shapes." Explain how the ideas presented in this section could be used to "analyze properties" of diagonals of quadrilaterals.

3. The NCTM Standards state "All students should examine the congruence, similarity, and line or rotational symmetry of objects using transformations." Discuss how you could have an elementary student examine line and rotational symmetry.

12.3   AN INTRODUCTION TO A FORMAL APPROACH TO GEOMETRY

STARTING POINT

Sketch or describe the following arrangements of three lines. If it is not possible, explain why not.
  Arrange three lines to create:

1. Zero points of intersection
2. Exactly one point of intersection
3. Exactly two points of intersection
4. Exactly three points of intersection
5. Exactly four points of intersection
6. Zero points of intersection with lines that are not parallel
7. Infinite number of points of intersection

Points and Lines in a Plane

In the first two sections of this chapter, geometry was studied at an informal level, the way that children first learn about geometric shapes. In section 12.1, the Van Hiele level 0 was introduced. It is at this level that students begin their understanding of geometry through recognition and naming shapes. Also in section 12.1, the Van Hiele level 1 was presented. At this level, students begin to see various parts or attributes of shapes. In section 12.2, the Van Hiele level 2 was covered. In that section, relationships among shapes became the focus. Namely, it was at that level that students could understand that a square is a rectangle because it has all of the attributes of a rectangle plus the fact that all sides are equal in length.

In this section we will look at the concepts covered in sections 12.1 and 12.2 from a more formal point of view. That is, the concepts of length and angle measure will have numbers attached to them and we will be able to talk about perpendicularity and parallelism using angle measure. This level of formality is usually used in the upper grades after students have developed an intuitive sense of geometric shapes.

Imagine that our square lattice is made with more and more points, so that the points are closer and closer together. Imagine also that a point takes up no space. Figure 12.42 gives a conceptual idea of this "ideal" collection of points. Finally, imagine that our lattice extends in every direction in two dimensions, without restriction. This infinitely large flat surface is called a **plane**. We can think of the **points** as locations in the plane. Points are represented using upper case letters. For example, we may call a point the letter A.

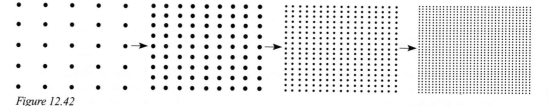

Figure 12.42

Figure 12.43(a) illustrates a **line**. Lines are considered to be straight and extend infinitely in opposite directions. The notation $\overleftrightarrow{AB}$ denotes the line containing the points A and B. The intuitive notions of point, line, and plane serve as the basis for the precise definitions that follow after Figure 12.43.

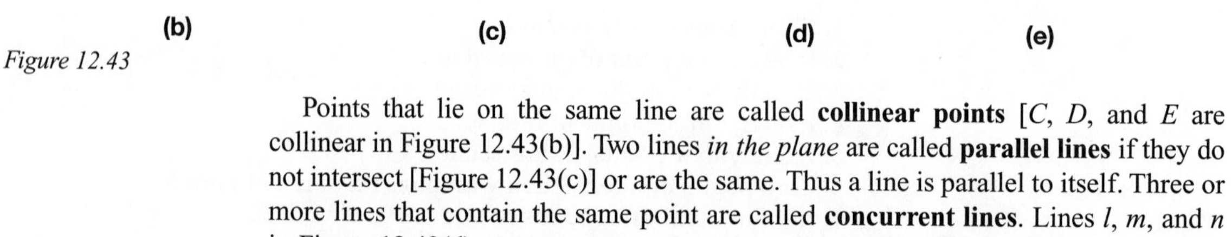

(a)

(b)

(c)

(d)

(e)

Figure 12.43

Points that lie on the same line are called **collinear points** [C, D, and E are collinear in Figure 12.43(b)]. Two lines *in the plane* are called **parallel lines** if they do not intersect [Figure 12.43(c)] or are the same. Thus a line is parallel to itself. Three or more lines that contain the same point are called **concurrent lines**. Lines l, m, and n in Figure 12.43(d) are concurrent, since they all contain point F. Lines r, s, and t in Figure 12.43(e) are not concurrent, since no point in the plane belongs to all three lines.

Because we cannot literally see the plane and its points, the geometric shapes that we will now study are abstractions. However, we can draw pictures and make models to help us imagine shapes, keeping in mind that the shapes exist only in our minds, just as numbers do. We will make certain assumptions about the plane and points in it. They have to do with lines in the plane and the distance between points.

> ## PROPERTY
>
> ### Points and Lines
>
> **1.** For each pair of points A, B ($A \neq B$) in the plane, there is a unique line $\overleftrightarrow{AB}$ containing them. 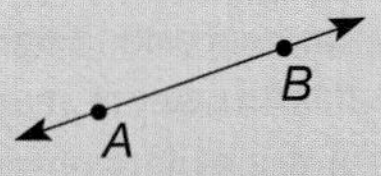
>
>
>
> **2.** Each line can be viewed as a copy of the real number line. The **distance** between two points A and B is the nonnegative difference of the real numbers a and b to which A and B correspond. The distance from A and B is written AB or BA. The numbers a and b are called the **coordinates** of A and B on $\overleftrightarrow{AB}$.
>
>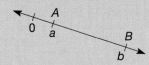
>
> **3.** If a point P is not on a line l, there is a unique line m, $m \neq l$, such that P is on m and m is parallel to l. We write $m \parallel l$ to mean m is parallel to l.
>
>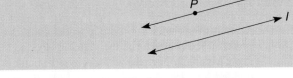

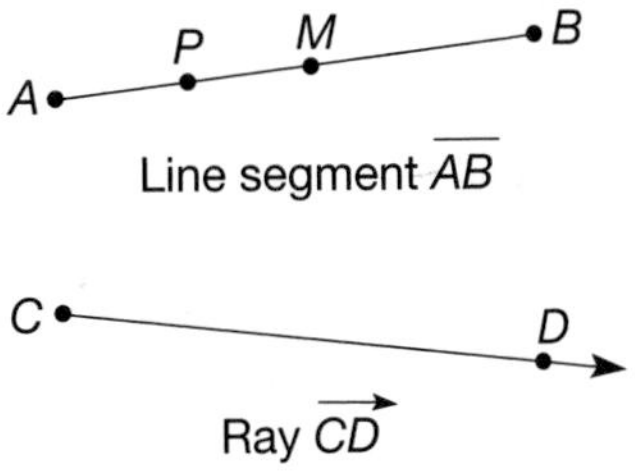

We can use our properties of lines to define line segments, rays, and angles. A point P is **between** A and B if the coordinate of P with reference to line $\overleftrightarrow{AB}$ is numerically between the coordinates of A and B. In Figure 12.44, M and P are between A and B. The **line segment**, $\overline{AB}$, consists of all the points between A and B on line $\overleftrightarrow{AB}$ together with points A and B. Points A and B are called the **endpoints** of $\overline{AB}$. The **length** of line segment $\overline{AB}$, written AB, is the distance between A and B. The **midpoint**, M, of a line segment $\overline{AB}$ is the point of $\overline{AB}$ that is **equidistant** from A and B, that is, $AM = MB$. The **ray** $\overrightarrow{CD}$ consists of all points of line $\overleftrightarrow{CD}$ on the same side of C as point D, together with the endpoint C (Figure 12.44).

✔️ **Check for Understanding:** Exercise/Problem Set A #1–2

Angles

An **angle** is the union of two line segments with a common endpoint *or* the union of two rays with a common endpoint (Figure 12.45). The common endpoint is called the **vertex** of the angle. The line segments or rays comprising the angle are called its **sides**. Angles

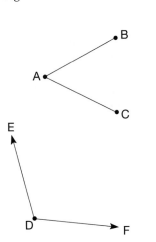

Line segment $\overline{AB}$

Ray $\overrightarrow{CD}$

Figure 12.44

Figure 12.45

can be denoted by naming a nonvertex point on one side, then the vertex, followed by a nonvertx point on the other side. For example, Figure 12.45 shows angle *BAC* and angle *EDF*. The symbol ∠*BAC* is used to denote angle *BAC*. (We could also call it ∠*CAB*.) As we know from our informal study, line segments and angles are used in studying various types of shapes in the plane, such as triangles and quadrilaterals.

Notice the blue region in Figure 12.46. It has the property that for *any* two points in this region, the line segment determined by the two points is also contained in the region. In this case, we say that the region is **convex**. This convex region is called the **interior** of the angle. The portion of the plane that is not the angle or the interior is called the **exterior** of the angle. In Figure 12.46, a portion of the exterior of the angle is shaded yellow. In it, we can find two points, *C* and *D* for example, that create a segment that is not completely contained in the yellow region. Thus, the yellow region is not convex and is called **concave**. An angle formed by two rays divides the plane into three regions: (1) the angle itself; (2) the interior of the angle; and (3) the exterior of the angle. Two angles that share a vertex, have a side in common, but whose interiors do not intersect are called **adjacent angles**. In Figure 12.47, ∠*ABC* and ∠*CBD* are adjacent angles.

Reflection from Research
Students are often misled by information included in the illustration of the angle; they may measure the "length" of the ray rather than the angle (Foxman & Ruddock, 1984).

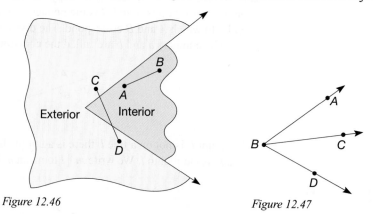

Figure 12.46   Figure 12.47

To measure angles, we use a semicircular device called a **protractor**. We place the center of the protractor at the vertex of the angle to be measured, with one side of the angle passing through the zero-degree (0°) mark (Figure 12.48). The protractor is evenly divided into 180 **degrees**, written 180°. Each degree can be further subdivided into 60 equal minutes, and each minute into 60 equal seconds, or we can use nonnegative real numbers to report degrees (such as 27.428°). The **measure of the angle** is equal to the real number on the protractor that the second side of the angle intersects. For example, the measure of ∠*BAC* in Figure 12.48 is 120°. The measure of ∠*BAC* will be denoted *m*(∠*BAC*). An angle measuring less than 90° is called an **acute angle**, an angle measuring 90° is called a **right angle**, and an angle measuring greater than 90° but less than 180° is an **obtuse angle**. An angle measuring 180° is called a **straight angle**. An angle whose measure is greater than 180°, but less than 360°, is called a **reflex angle**. In Figure 12.49, ∠*BAC* is acute, ∠*BAD* is a right angle, ∠*BAE* is obtuse, and ∠*BAF* is a straight angle.

NCTM Standard
All students should select and apply techniques and tools to accurately find length, area, volume, and angle measures to appropriate levels of precision.

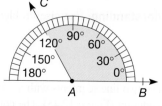

Figure 12.48

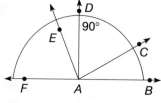

Figure 12.49

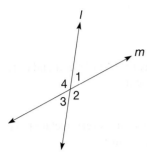

Figure 12.50

Algebraic Reasoning
The meaning of the "equals" sign is that the expressions on both sides represent the same numerical value. The proof at the right relies on the fact that since two different expressions are equal to 180°, they must be equal to each other. This is an example of the method of substitution that is commonly used in algebra.

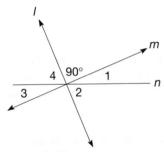

Figure 12.51

When two lines intersect, several angles are formed. In Figure 12.50, lines *l* and *m* form four angles, ∠1, ∠2, ∠3, and ∠4. We see that

$$m(\angle 1) + m(\angle 2) = 180° \qquad \text{and} \qquad m(\angle 3) + m(\angle 2) = 180°.$$

Hence

$$m(\angle 1) + m(\angle 2) = m(\angle 3) + m(\angle 2),$$

so that

$$m(\angle 1) = m(\angle 3).$$

Similarly, $m(\angle 2) = m(\angle 4)$. As shown in Figure 12.50, the two intersecting lines form four numbered angles. Any two of the angles that are not adjacent are called **vertical angles**. In Figure 12.50, ∠1 and ∠3 are vertical angles as are ∠2 and ∠4. In the discussion above, we have shown that $m(\angle 1) = m(\angle 3)$ and $m(\angle 2) = m(\angle 4)$. That is, vertical angles have the same measure. Angles having the same measure are called **congruent angles**. Based on the reasoning about Figure 12.50, we know that ∠1 is congruent to ∠3, written $\angle 1 \cong \angle 3$. Similarly line segments having the same length are called **congruent segments**. Informally, congruent objects are the same size and shape.

Two angles, the sum of whose measures is 180°, are called **supplementary angles**. In Figure 12.50 angles 1 and 2 are supplementary, as are angles 2 and 3. If two lines intersect to form a right angle, the lines are called **perpendicular**. Lines *l* and *m* in Figure 12.51 are perpendicular lines. We will write $l \perp m$ to denote that line *l* is perpendicular to line *m*. Two angles whose sum is 90° are called **complementary angles**. In Figure 12.51, angles 1 and 2 are complementary, as are angles 3 and 4.

> ✔ **Check for Understanding:** Exercise/Problem Set A #3–6

Angles Associated with Parallel Lines

If two lines *l* and *m* are intersected by a third line, *t*, we call line *t* a **transversal** (Figure 12.52). The three lines in Figure 12.53 form many angles.

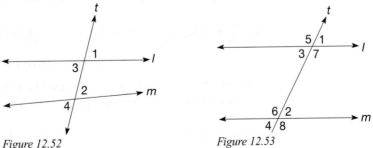

Figure 12.52   *Figure 12.53*

Angles 1 and 2 are called **corresponding angles**, since they are in the same locations relative to *l, m*, and *t*. Angles 3 and 4 are also corresponding angles. Our intuition tells us that if line *l* is parallel to line *m* (i.e., they point in the same direction), corresponding angles will have the same measure (Figure 12.53). Look at the various pairs of corresponding angles in Figure 12.53, where $l \parallel m$. Do they appear to have the same measure? Examples such as those in Figure 12.53 suggest the following property.

PROPERTY

Corresponding Angles

Suppose that lines l and m are intersected by a transversal t. Then $l \parallel m$ if and only if corresponding angles formed by l, m, and t are congruent.

Using the corresponding angles property, we can prove that every rectangle is a parallelogram. This is left for Part A Problem 18 in the Problem Set.

Example 12.12 In Figure 12.54, lines l and m are parallel. Show that $m(\angle 2) = m(\angle 3)$ using the corresponding angles property.

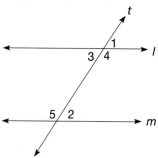

Figure 12.54

SOLUTION Since $l \parallel m$, by the corresponding angles property, $m(\angle 1) = m(\angle 2)$. But also, because $\angle 1$ and $\angle 3$ are vertical angles, we know that $m(\angle 1) = m(\angle 3)$. Hence $m(\angle 2) = m(\angle 3)$. ■

In the configuration in Figure 12.54, the pair $\angle 2$ and $\angle 3$ and the pair $\angle 4$ and $\angle 5$ are called **alternate interior angles**, since they are nonadjacent angles formed by l, m, and t, the union of whose interiors contains the region between l and m. Example 12.12 suggests another property of parallel lines and alternate interior angles.

THEOREM

Alternate Interior Angles

Suppose that lines l and m are intersected by a transversal t. Then $l \parallel m$ if and only if alternate interior angles formed by l, m, and t are congruent.

The complete verification of this result is left for Part A Problem 16 in the Problem Set.

We can use this result to prove a very important property of triangles. Suppose that we have a **triangle**, $\triangle ABC$. (The notation $\triangle ABC$ denotes the triangle that is the union of line segments $\overline{AB}$, $\overline{BC}$, and $\overline{CA}$.) Let line $l = \overleftrightarrow{AC}$ (Figure 12.55). By part three of the properties of points and lines, there is a line m parallel to l through point B in Figure 12.55. Then lines $\overleftrightarrow{AB}$ and $\overleftrightarrow{BC}$ are transversals for the parallel lines l and m.

Problem-Solving Strategy
Draw a Diagram

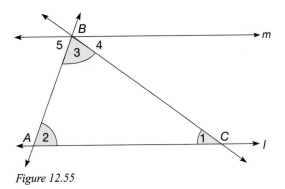

Figure 12.55

Algebraic Reasoning
The reasoning used in the proof at the right relies on an understanding of equality. This type of reasoning is also useful when solving systems of several equations in algebra.

Hence $\angle 1$ and $\angle 4$ are congruent alternate interior angles. Similarly $m(\angle 2) = m(\angle 5)$. Summarizing, we have the following results:

$$m(\angle 1) = m(\angle 4),$$
$$m(\angle 2) = m(\angle 5),$$
$$m(\angle 3) = m(\angle 3).$$

Notice also that $m(\angle 5) + m(\angle 3) + m(\angle 4) = 180°$, since $\angle 5$, $\angle 3$, and $\angle 4$ form a straight angle. But from the observations above, we see that

$$m(\angle 1) + m(\angle 2) + m(\angle 3) = m(\angle 4) + m(\angle 5) + m(\angle 3) = 180°.$$

This result is summarized next.

THEOREM

Angle Sum in a Triangle

The sum of the measures of the three vertex angles in a triangle is 180°.

As a consequence of this result, a triangle can have at most one right angle or at most one obtuse angle. A triangle that has a right angle is called a **right triangle**, a triangle with an obtuse angle is called an **obtuse triangle**, and a triangle in which *all* angles are acute is called an **acute triangle**. For right triangles, we note that two of the vertex angles must be acute and their sum is 90°. Hence they are complementary. In Figure 12.56, $\angle 1$ and $\angle 2$ are complementary, as are $\angle 3$ and $\angle 4$. Notice in Figure 12.56 that a small symbol " ⌐ " is used to indicate a right angle.

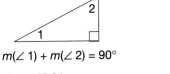

$m(\angle 1) + m(\angle 2) = 90°$

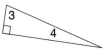

$m(\angle 3) + m(\angle 4) = 90°$

Figure 12.56

Since we were working at level 0 and level 1, the recognition and analysis levels, in Section 12.1, *descriptions* were provided for many geometric objects. Now that more terms have been formally introduced, formal definitions can be stated. Table 12.6 summarizes some of the definitions from this section.

TABLE 12.6

OBJECT	NAME	DEFINITION
	Line segment	Two points on a line, and all the points that lie between them.
	Parallel lines	Two lines distinct in the same plane that do not intersect.
	Angle	The union of two segments or rays with a common endpoint.
	Acute angle	An angle with a measure less than 90 degrees.
	Right angle	An angle that measures 90 degrees.
	Obtuse angle	An angle with a measure greater than 90 and less than 180 degrees.
	Straight angle	An angle that measures 180 degrees.
	Reflex angle	An angle with a measure greater than 180 degrees.
	Adjacent angles	Two angles that share a vertex and a side but no interior points.
	Vertical angles	Two nonadjacent angles formed by two intersecting lines.
	Supplementary angles	Two angles whose measures add to 180 degrees.
	Complementary angles	Two angles whose measures add to 90 degrees.
	Perpendicular lines	Two lines that intersect to form a right angle.
	Right triangle	A triangle with one right angle.
	Acute triangle	A triangle with three acute angles.
	Obtuse triangle	A triangle with one obtuse angle.

✔ **Check for Understanding:** Exercise/Problem Set A #7–9

Van Hiele Levels 1 and 2 Revisited

With all of these new terms and definitions, properties of shapes and relationships among them can be revisited. We will begin by looking at the relationships (van Hiele level 2) among triangles classified by angle measure (acute, right, obtuse) and triangles classified by side length (scalene, isosceles, equilateral).

Example 12.13   Sketch an example of an obtuse scalene triangle, an obtuse isosceles triangle, and an obtuse equilateral triangle. If it is not possible, explain why not.

SOLUTION

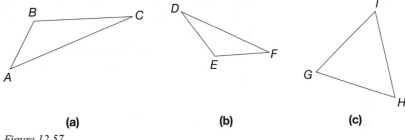

(a)   (b)   (c)

Figure 12.57

Figure 12.57(a) is an example of an obtuse scalene triangle since ∠B is obtuse and the sides are of different lengths. Figure 12.57(b) is an obtuse isosceles triangle since ∠E is obtuse and sides $\overline{ED}$ and $\overline{EF}$ are drawn to be congruent. Figure 12.57(c) is drawn to be an equilateral triangle. When two sides of a triangle are congruent, the angles opposite those sides are congruent. Since all three sides of an equilateral triangle are congruent, all three angles are congruent making them each 60°. Thus, it is not possible to have an obtuse equilateral triangle. ■

With angle measure and congruence formally defined, we can analyze some properties of angles in the various quadrilaterals. First, some angle pairs need to be defined. The two parallel sides of a trapezoid are called **bases**. Two angles whose common side is a base of a trapezoid are called **base angles**. There are two pairs of base angles in each trapezoid, one pair for each base. A pair of angles in a quadrilateral that have no sides in common are called **opposite angles**. A quadrilateral has two pairs of opposite angles. Figure 12.58(a) shows two pair of base angles and Figure 12.58(b) shows two pair of opposite angles in a trapezoid. In this trapezoid, ∠B and ∠C form one pair of base angles; ∠A and ∠D form the other. One pair of opposite angles is ∠B and ∠D; the other pair is ∠A and ∠C.

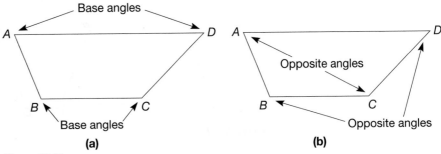

Figure 12.58

Example 12.14 Identify all pairs of angles that are congruent in the following shapes.

a. a kite **b.** a parallelogram
c. a rhombus **d.** a rectangle and a square
e. a trapezoid and an isosceles trapezoid

In order for a pair of angles to be considered congruent, they must be congruent for *all* possible shapes of quadrilaterals of that type. For example, a square is a type of kite and it has all 4 angles congruent, but there are many other shapes of kites for which all 4 angles are not congruent. Are there any pairs of angles that are congruent for all possible shapes of kites?

SOLUTION

a. Kite: Folding along a line of symmetry, it can be seen that kites have one pair of opposite angles that are congruent as shown in Figure 12.59(a). Here $\angle B$ and $\angle D$ are congruent.

b. Parallelogram: A parallelogram can be rotated onto itself as shown in Figure 12.59(b). Here $\angle A$ is congruent to $\angle C$ and $\angle B$ is congruent to $\angle D$. Thus, opposite angles are congruent.

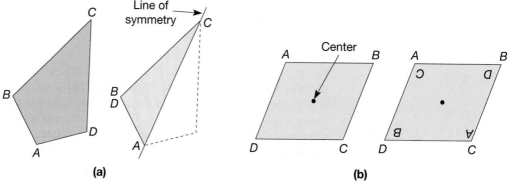

(a)   **(b)**

Figure 12.59

c. Rhombus: Since a rhombus is a special kind of parallelogram, it also has two pairs of congruent opposite angles.

d. Rectangle and square: By definition, rectangles and squares have four congruent angles so clearly any pair of angles will be congruent.

e. Trapezoid and isosceles trapezoid: In general, trapezoids do not have any pairs of congruent angles. However, the base angles of any isosceles trapezoid are congruent as can be seen by the folding in Figure 12.60. Here there are two pairs of congruent angles: $\angle A$ and $\angle B$ are congruent and $\angle C$ and $\angle D$ are congruent.

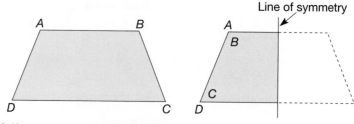

Figure 12.60

∎

A summary of these properties as well as others are shown in Table 12.7. When an X, 1 pair, 2 pairs, or all pairs is placed in the table, in means that *all* quadrilaterals of that type will have that attribute. If there is not an X, 1 pair, 2 pairs, or all pairs in the table, then none or only some of those types of quadrilaterals have that attribute.

TABLE 12.7

	QUADRILATERAL TYPE						
ATTRIBUTE	TRAPEZOID	ISOSCELES TRAPEZOID	KITE	PARALLELOGRAM	RHOMBUS	RECTANGLE	SQUARE
Adjacent sides are congruent			2 pairs		All pairs		All pairs
Opposite sides are congruent		1 pair		2 pairs	2 pairs	2 pairs	2 pairs
All angles are congruent						X	X
Opposite sides are parallel	1 pair	1 pair		2 pairs	2 pairs	2 pairs	2 pairs
Adjacent sides are perpendicular						X	X
Diagonals are congruent		X				X	X
Diagonals intersect at the midpoint				X	X	X	X
Diagonals are perpendicular			X		X		X
Opposite angles are congruent			1 pair	X	X	X	X
Base angles are congruent		X					
Opposite angles are bisected by diagonal			1 pair		2 pairs		2 pairs

 Check for Understanding: Exercise/Problem Set A #10–12

MATHEMATICAL MORSEL

An interesting result about surfaces is due to A. F. Moebius. Start with a rectangular strip ABCD. Twist the strip one-half turn to form the "twisted" strip ABCD. Then tape the two ends AB and CD to form a "twisted loop." Then draw a continuous line down the middle of one side of the loop. What did you find? Next, cut the loop on the line you drew. What did you find? Repeat, drawing a line down the middle of the new loop and cutting one more time. Surprise!

Section 12.3 | EXERCISE / PROBLEM SET A

EXERCISES

1. a. In the following figure, identify all sets of 3 or more collinear points.

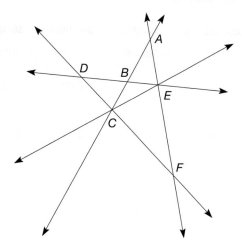

b. Identify all sets of concurrent lines.

2. Identify all of the different rays on the following line using the labeled points provided.

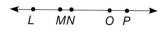

3. a. Identify all of the angles shown in the following figure.

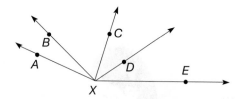

b. How many are obtuse?   **c.** How many are acute?

4. Determine which of the following angles represented on a square lattice are right angles. If one isn't, is it acute or obtuse?

a.

b.

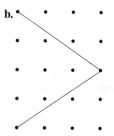

5. Use your protractor to measure ∠B and ∠C.

a.

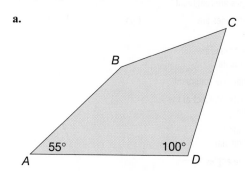

b.

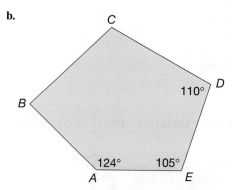

6. Using your knowledge of properties of parallelograms, name four pairs of congruent segments and eight pairs of congruent angles in the following figure. You may want to refer to Table 12.7.

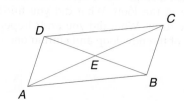

7. In the following figure

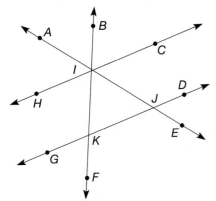

a. Identify 3 pairs of corresponding angles.
b. Identify 3 pairs of alternate interior angles.

8. Find the missing angle measure in the following triangles.

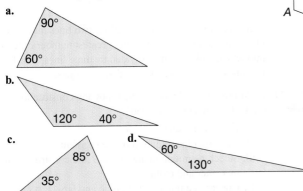

9. Consider the square lattice shown here.

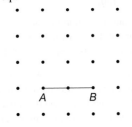

You may find the Chapter 12 eManipulative *Geoboard* on our Web site to be helpful in thinking about this problem.
a. How many triangles have $\overline{AB}$ as one side?
b. How many of these are isosceles?
c. How many are right triangles?
d. How many are acute?
e. How many are obtuse?

10. An angle is bisected when a segment is drawn from the vertex through the interior in such a way that the two new angles created have the same measure. Trace the kite, rhombus, and square below and use paper folding to determine in which cases the diagonal bisects the opposite angles.

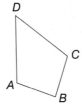 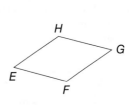 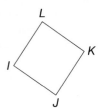

11. Consider the following sets.

T = all triangles A = acute triangles
S = scalene triangles R = right triangles
I = isosceles triangles O = obtuse triangles
E = equilateral triangles

   Draw an example of an element of the following sets, if possible.
   a. $S \cap A$ **b.** $I \cap O$ **c.** $O \cap E$

12. Consider the following sets.

K = kites B = rhombus
T = trapezoids R = rectangles
I = isosceles trapezoids S = squares
P = parallelograms

   Draw an example of an element of the following sets, if possible.
   a. $K \cap P$ **b.** $I \cap R$ **c.** $P - B$

PROBLEMS

13. In the figure, $m(\angle BFC) = 55°$, $m(\angle AFD) = 150°$, and $m(\angle BFE) = 120°$. Determine the measures of $\angle AFB$ and $\angle CFD$. (NOTE: Do not measure the angles with your protractor to determine these measures.)

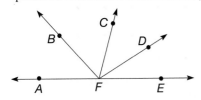

14. In the following figure, the measure of $\angle 1$ is 9° less than half the measure of $\angle 2$. Determine the measures of $\angle 1$ and $\angle 2$.

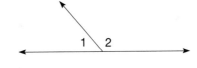

15. Determine the measures of the numbered angles if $m(\angle 1) = 80°$, $m(\angle 4) = 125°$, and l is parallel to m.

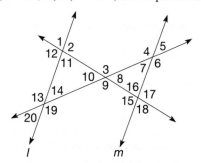

16. The first part of the alternate interior angles theorem was verified in Example 12.12. Verify the second part of the alternate interior angles theorem. In particular, assume that $m(\angle 1) = m(\angle 2)$ and show that $l \parallel m$.

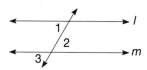

17. Angles 1 and 6 are called **alternate exterior angles**. (Can you see why?) Prove the following statements.

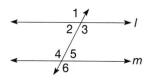

   a. If $m(\angle 1) = m(\angle 6)$, then $l \parallel m$.
   b. If $l \parallel m$, then $m(\angle 1) = m(\angle 6)$.
   c. State the results of parts (a) and (b) as a general property.

18. Using the corresponding angles property, prove that rectangle $ABCD$ is a parallelogram.

19. Use your protractor to measure angles with dots on their vertices in the following semicircle. Make a conjecture based on your findings.

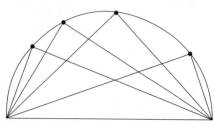

20. Two lines drawn in a plane separate the plane into three different regions if the lines are parallel.

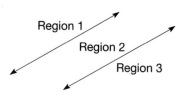

If the lines are intersecting, then they will divide the plane into four regions.

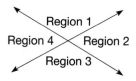

Thus, the greatest number of regions two lines may divide a plane into is four. Determine the greatest number of regions into which a plane can be divided by three lines, four lines, five lines, and ten lines. Generalize to n lines.

21. Redo Problem 19 by doing the following construction on the Geometer's Sketchpad®.

   i. Construct a segment $\overline{AB}$.
   ii. Construct the midpoint of the segment.
   iii. Select the midpoint and point B and construct a circle by center and radius.
   iv. Construct a point on the circle and label it point D.
   v. Construct segments to form the angle $\angle ADB$.
   vi. Measure $\angle ADB$.

After moving point D around the circle, what conclusions can you draw about the measure of $\angle ADB$? Is this consistent with the results from Problem 19?

22. A portion of a square lattice is shown here. Which of the following triangles can be drawn on it? You may find the Chapter 12 eManipulative *Geoboard-Square Lattice* on our Web site to be helpful in thinking about this problem.

   a. Acute triangle   **b.** Obtuse triangle
   c. Equiangular triangle

Section 12.3 | EXERCISE / PROBLEM SET B

EXERCISES

1. a. In the following figure, identify all sets of 3 or more collinear points.

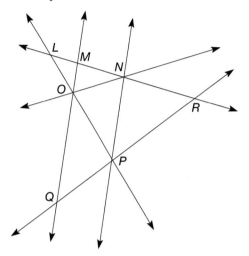

b. Identify all sets of concurrent lines.

2. Identify all of the segments contained in the following portion of a line.

3. a. Identify all of the acute angles in the following figure.

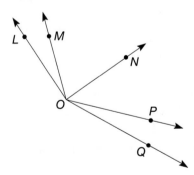

b. Identify all of the obtuse angles.
c. Identify all of the right angles.
d. Identify 2 pairs of adjacent angles.

4. Find the angle measure of the following angles drawn on triangular lattices. Use your protractor if necessary.

a.

b.

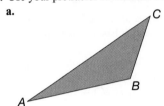

c.

5. Use your protractor to measure ∠A, ∠B, and ∠C.
a.

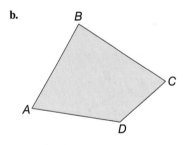

b.

6. Using your knowledge of the properties of kites, name three pairs of congruent segments and nine pairs of congruent angles in the following figure.

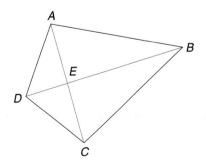

7. In the following figure

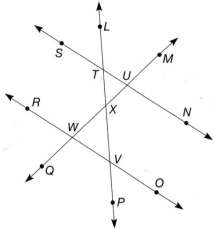

a. Identify 3 pairs of corresponding angles.
b. Identify 3 pairs of alternate interior angles.

8. Following are the measures of $\angle A$, $\angle B$, and $\angle C$. Can a triangle $\triangle ABC$ be made that has the given angles? Explain.
a. $m(\angle A) = 36$, $m(\angle B) = 78$, $m(\angle C) = 66$
b. $m(\angle A) = 124$, $m(\angle B) = 56$, $m(\angle C) = 20$
c. $m(\angle A) = 90$, $m(\angle B) = 74$, $m(\angle C) = 18$

9. Given the square lattice shown, answer the following questions.

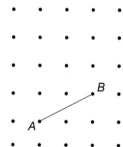

 You may find the Chapter 12 eManipulative *Geoboard* on our Web site to be helpful in thinking about this problem.
a. How many triangles have $\overline{AB}$ as one side?
b. How many of these are right triangles?
c. How many are acute triangles?
d. How many are obtuse triangles? [*Hint:* Use your answers to parts (a) to (c).]

10. Use a ruler to draw the diagonals of the following shapes. Now use a ruler to determine if the point where the diagonals meet is a midpoint of either diagonal.

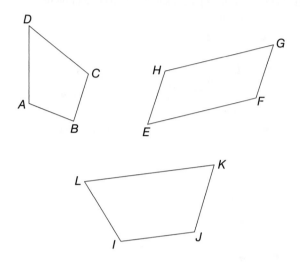

11. Consider the following sets.

T = all triangles A = acute triangles
S = scalene triangles R = right triangles
I = isosceles triangles O = obtuse triangles
E = equilateral triangles

Draw an example of an element of the following sets, if possible.
a. $S \cap R$ **b.** $T - (A \cup O)$ **c.** $T - (R \cup S)$

12. Consider the following sets.

K = kites B = rhombus
T = trapezoids R = rectangles
I = isosceles trapezoids S = squares
P = parallelograms

Draw an example of an element of the following sets, if possible.
a. $K - B$ **b.** $P - (B \cup R)$ **c.** $(B \cap P)$

PROBLEMS

13. In the following figure $\overline{AO}$ is perpendicular to $\overline{CO}$. If $m(\angle AOD) = 165°$ and $m(\angle BOD) = 82°$, determine the measures of $\angle AOB$ and $\angle BOC$. (NOTE: Do not measure the angles with your protractor to determine these measures.)

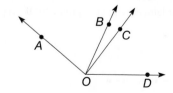

14. The measure of $\angle X$ is 9° more than twice the measure of $\angle Y$. If $\angle X$ and $\angle Y$ are supplementary angles, find the measure of $\angle X$.

15. Find the measures of $\angle 1$, $\angle 2$, $\angle 3$, and $\angle 4$ if some angles formed are related as shown and $l \parallel m \parallel n$.

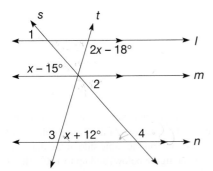

16. In this section we assumed that the corresponding angles property was true. Then we verified the alternate interior angles theorem. Some geometry books assume the alternate interior angles theorem to be true and build results from there. Assume that the only parallel line test we have is the alternate interior angles theorem and show the following to be true.

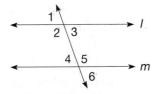

a. If $l \parallel m$, then corresponding angles have the same measure, namely, $m(\angle 1) = m(\angle 4)$.
b. If $m(\angle 3) = m(\angle 6)$, then $l \parallel m$.

17. Angles 1 and 3 are called **interior angles on the same side of the transversal**.

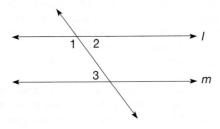

a. If $l \parallel m$, what is true about $m(\angle 1) + m(\angle 3)$?
b. Can you show the converse of the result in part (a): that if your conclusion about $m(\angle 1) + m(\angle 3)$ is satisfied, then $l \parallel m$?

18. In parallelogram $ABCD$, $\angle 1$ and $\angle 2$ are called **consecutive angles**, as are $\angle 2$ and $\angle 3$, $\angle 3$ and $\angle 4$, $\angle 4$ and $\angle 1$. Using the results of Problem 17, what can you conclude about any two consecutive angles of a parallelogram? What can you conclude about two opposite angles (e.g., $\angle 1$ and $\angle 3$)?

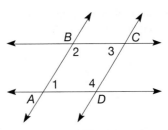

19. In the figure below, $l \parallel m \parallel n$ and three angle measures are indicated. Find the measures of the angles identified by a, b, c, d, and e.

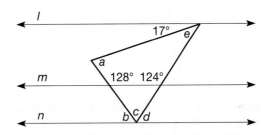

20. Draw a large copy of $\triangle ABC$ on scratch paper and cut it out.

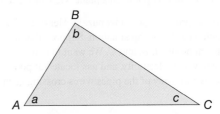

Fold down vertex B so that it lies on $\overline{AC}$ and so that the fold line is parallel to $\overline{AC}$.

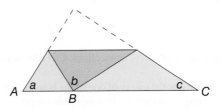

Now fold vertices A and C into point B.

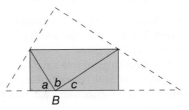

a. What does the resulting figure tell you about the measures of $\angle A$, $\angle B$, and $\angle C$? Explain.
b. What kind of polygon is the folded shape, and what is the length of its base?
c. Try this same procedure with two other types of triangles. Are the results the same?

21. Given three points, there is one line that can be drawn through them if the points are collinear.

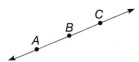

If the three points are noncollinear, there are three lines that can be drawn through pairs of points.

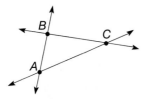

For three points, three is the greatest number of lines that can be drawn through pairs of points. Determine the greatest number of lines that can be drawn for four points, five points, and six points in a plane. Generalize to n points.

22. A famous problem, posed by puzzler Henry Dudenay, presented the following situation. Suppose that houses are located at points A, B, and C. We want to connect each house to water, electricity, and gas located at points W, G, and E, without any of the pipes/wires crossing each other.

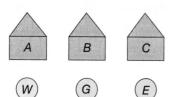

a. Try making all of the connections. Can it be done? If so, how?

b. Suppose that the owner of one of the houses, say B, is willing to let the pipe for one of his neighbors' connections pass through his house. Then can all of the connections be made? If so, how?

23. Consider the following statements as possible definitions of different quadrilaterals. Determine which of these definitions are correct. Explain.

a. Rectangle: A parallelogram with a right angle.

b. Kite: A quadrilateral with perpendicular diagonals.

c. Rhombus: A parallelogram with a pair of adjacent sides that are congruent.

Analyzing Student Thinking

24. Jonas used paper folding to show that a kite has one pair of congruent opposite angles and asks if it is possible for a kite to have two pairs of congruent opposite angles. How would you respond?

25. When Alora measured the angle below with her protractor, she read that it was 113°. Her brother measured it to be 67°. Who is correct? Explain the error that was likely made in reading the protractor.

26. Kent notices that when parallel lines are cut by a transversal, the measures of the angles outside of the parallel lines and on the same side of the transversal ($\angle 1$ and $\angle 2$ in the figure below) add up to 180°. He wonders if this is always true. How would you respond?

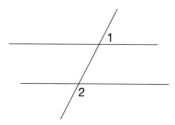

27. Troy says vertical angles have to be straight up and down like vertical lines; they can't be horizontal. Discuss.

28. Barrilee's sister in high school says that the definition of parallel lines in our book is wrong because a line *cannot* be parallel to itself. And the definition of trapezoid is wrong, too; it should be "a quadrilateral with *at least* one pair of parallel sides," not exactly one pair of parallel sides. That's what it says in her book, and she's taking geometry in high school. What is an explanation for these differences?

29. Tisha is trying to find how many rays are determined by three collinear points, R, S, and T. She thinks there are six: $\overrightarrow{RS}$, $\overrightarrow{ST}$, $\overrightarrow{RT}$, $\overrightarrow{TR}$, $\overrightarrow{TS}$, and $\overrightarrow{SR}$. Do you agree? Explain.

30. Rodney says if a triangle can be acute and isosceles at the same time, and another triangle can be equilateral and isosceles at the same time, then every triangle can be described by two of the triangle words. So there must be some triangle that is scalene and isosceles and another that is right and obtuse. What are the limits to Rodney's conjecture? What combinations are possible? Which are not?

1. The Focal Points for Grade 8 state "Analyzing two- and three-dimensional space and figures by using distance and angle." Discuss how distance and angle are used to analyze the various types of quadrilaterals.

2. The NCTM Standards state "All students should select and apply techniques and tools to accurately find length, area, volume, and angle measures to appropriate levels of

precision." Explain how to use a protractor to measure an angle (be specific with correct vocabulary).

3. The NCTM Standards state "All students should recognize geometric shapes and structures in the environment and specify their location." What are examples of concurrent lines, collinear points, and parallel lines in your environment?

12.4   REGULAR POLYGONS, TESSELLATIONS, AND CIRCLES

STARTING POINT

Two of the known facts about the sums of angles are:

1. The sum of the interior angles of a triangle is 180° degrees.
2. The sum of the angles around a single point is 360° degrees.

Using one or both of these facts, find $a + b + c + d + e$ where a, b, c, d, and e represent the marked interior angles of the pentagon at the right. Describe at least two methods that you can use for finding this sum.

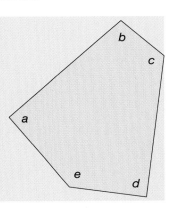

Regular Polygons

A **simple closed curve** in the plane is a curve that can be traced with the same starting and stopping points and without crossing or retracing any part of the curve (Figure 12.61). A simple closed "curve" made up of line segments is called a **polygon** (which means "many angles"). A polygon having all sides congruent is called **equilateral** and one having all angles congruent is called **equiangular**. A polygon that is both equilateral and equiangular is called a **regular polygon** or a **regular *n*-gon**. Figure 12.62

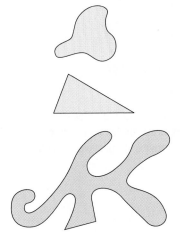

Figure 12.61

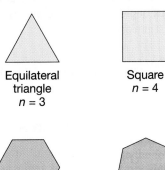

Equilateral triangle
$n = 3$

Square
$n = 4$

Regular pentagon
$n = 5$

Regular hexagon
$n = 6$

Regular heptagon
$n = 7$

Regular octagon
$n = 8$

Figure 12.62

shows several types of regular *n*-gons. Notice that *n* denotes the number of sides and the number of angles. Since the number of sides in the figure can be any whole number greater than 2, there are infinitely many regular polygons. The regular polygons in Figure 12.62 are all convex. In fact, all regular *n*-gons are convex.

The **center** of a polygon is the point that is equidistant from all vertices. In Figure 12.63, the segments from each of the vertices to the center are the same length.

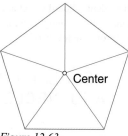

Figure 12.63

There are several angles of interest in regular *n*-gons. They are vertex angles, central angles, and exterior angles. A **vertex angle** (also called an **interior angle)** is formed by a vertex and the two sides that have the vertex as an endpoint (see Figure 12.64). A **central angle** is formed by the segments joining the center of a polygon with the two endpoints of one of the sides (see Figure 12.64). An **exterior angle** is formed by one side together with an extension of an adjacent side of the regular *n*-gon, as pictured in Figure 12.64.

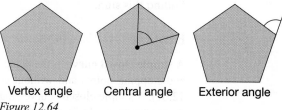

Vertex angle   Central angle   Exterior angle
Figure 12.64

Notice that the number of vertex angles, central angles, and the sides of a regular polygon are the same. But there are twice as many exterior angles as interior angles. Vertex angles and exterior angles are formed in all convex shapes whose sides are line segments.

✔ **Check for Understanding:** Exercise/Problem Set A #1–4

Angle Measures in Regular Polygons

To find the measure of the central angle of a regular *n*-gon, notice that the sum of the measures of *n* central angles is 360°. Figure 12.65 illustrates this when *n* = 5. Clearly these central angles are all congruent—the measure of any one of them is $\frac{360°}{5} = 72°$. In general, the measure of each central angle in a regular *n*-gon is $\frac{360°}{n}$.

We can find the measure of the vertex angles in a regular *n*-gon by using the angle sum in a triangle property. Consider a regular pentagon (*n* = 5; Figure 12.66). Let us

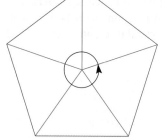

Figure 12.65

Figure 12.66

call the vertex angles $\angle v_1$, $\angle v_2$, $\angle v_3$, $\angle v_4$, and $\angle v_5$. Since all the vertex angles have the same measure, it suffices to find the vertex angle *sum* in the regular pentagon. The measure of each vertex angle, then, is one-fifth of this sum.

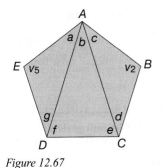

Figure 12.67

Problem-Solving Strategy
Draw a Picture

To find this sum, subdivide the pentagon into triangles using diagonals $\overline{AC}$ and $\overline{AD}$ (Figure 12.67). For example, A, B, and C are the vertices of a triangle, specifically $\triangle ABC$. Several new angles are formed, namely $\angle a$, $\angle b$, $\angle c$, $\angle d$, $\angle e$, $\angle f$, and $\angle g$. Notice that

$$m(\angle v_1) = m(\angle a) + m(\angle b) + m(\angle c),$$
$$m(\angle v_3) = m(\angle d) + m(\angle e),$$

and

$$m(\angle v_4) = m(\angle f) + m(\angle g).$$

Within each triangle ($\triangle ABC$, $\triangle ACD$, and $\triangle ADE$), we know that the angle sum is 180°. Hence

$$m(\angle v_1) + m(\angle v_2) + m(\angle v_3) + m(\angle v_4) + m(\angle v_5)$$
$$= m(\angle a) + m(\angle b) + m(\angle c) + m(\angle v_2) + m(\angle d)$$
$$\quad + m(\angle e) + m(\angle f) + m(\angle g) + m(\angle v_5)$$
$$= [m(\angle c) + m(\angle v_2) + m(\angle d)] + [m(\angle b) + m(\angle e) + m(\angle f)]$$
$$\quad + [m(\angle g) + m(\angle v_5) + m(\angle a)]$$
$$= 180° + 180° + 180°$$

since each bracketed sum is the angle sum in a triangle. Hence the angle sum in a regular pentagon is $3 \times 180° = 540°$. Finally, the measure of each vertex angle in the regular pentagon is $540° \div 5 = 108°$. The technique used here of forming triangles within the polygon can be used to find the sum of the vertex angles in any polygon.

Table 12.8 suggests a way of computing the measure of a vertex angle in a regular n-gon, for $n = 3, 4, 5, 6, 7, 8$. Verify the entries.

TABLE 12.8

	n	ANGLE SUM IN A REGULAR n-GON	MEASURE OF A VERTEX ANGLE
△	3	$1 \cdot 180°$	$180° \div 3 = 60°$
◻	4	$2 \cdot 180°$	$(2 \times 180°) \div 4 = 90°$
⬠	5	$3 \cdot 180°$	$(3 \times 180°) \div 5 = 108°$
⬡	6	$4 \cdot 180°$	$(4 \times 180°) \div 6 = 120°$
⬡	7	$5 \cdot 180°$	$(5 \times 180°) \div 7 = 128\tfrac{4}{7}°$
⯃	8	$6 \cdot 180°$	$(6 \times 180°) \div 8 = 135°$

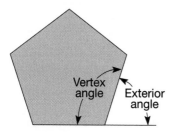

Figure 12.68

Algebraic Reasoning
Students often describe the computation of the measures of each of the angles in this theorem in words. This is a natural preliminary step to using variables.

The entries in Table 12.8 suggest a formula for the measure of the vertex angle in a regular *n*-gon. In particular, we can subdivide any *n*-gon into $(n - 2)$ triangles. Since each triangle has an angle sum of 180°, the angle sum in a regular *n*-gon is $(n - 2) \cdot 180°$. Thus each vertex angle will measure $\dfrac{(n - 2) \cdot 180°}{n}$. We can also express this as $\dfrac{180°n - 360°}{n} = 180° - \dfrac{360°}{n}$. Thus any vertex angle is supplementary to any central angle.

To measure the exterior angles in a regular *n*-gon, notice that the sum of a vertex angle and an exterior angle will be 180°, by the way the exterior angle is formed (Figure 12.68). Therefore, each exterior angle will have measure $180° - \left[180° - \dfrac{360°}{n}\right] = 180° - 180° + \dfrac{360°}{n} = \dfrac{360°}{n}$. Hence, the measure of any exterior angle is the same as the measure of a central angle!

We can summarize our results about angle measures in regular polygons as follows.

THEOREM		
Angle Measures in a Regular n-gon		
Vertex Angle	Central Angle	Exterior Angle
$\dfrac{(n - 2) \cdot 180°}{n}$	$\dfrac{360°}{n}$	$\dfrac{360°}{n}$

Remember that these results hold only for angles in *regular* polygons—not necessarily in arbitrary polygons. In the problem set, the central angle measure will be used when discussing rotation symmetry of polygons. We will use the vertex angle measure in the next section on tessellations.

✔ **Check for Understanding:** Exercise/Problem Set A #5–12

Tessellations

A **polygonal region** is a polygon together with its interior. An arrangement of polygonal regions having only sides in common that completely covers the plane is called a **tessellation**. We can form tessellations with arbitrary triangles, as Figure 12.69 shows. Pattern (a) shows a tessellation with a scalene right triangle, pattern (b) a tessellation with an acute isosceles triangle, and pattern (c) a tessellation with an obtuse scalene triangle.

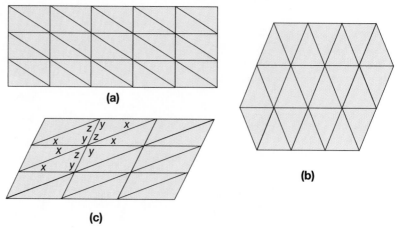

(a)

(b)

(c)

Figure 12.69

Note that angles measuring x, y, and z meet at each vertex to form a straight angle. As suggested by Figure 12.69, every triangle will tessellate the plane.

Every quadrilateral will form a tessellation also. Figure 12.70 shows several tessellations with quadrilaterals.

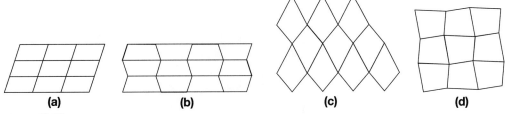

(a)   **(b)**   **(c)**   **(d)**

Figure 12.70

In pattern (a) we see a tessellation with a parallelogram; in pattern (b), a tessellation with a trapezoid; and in pattern (c), a tessellation with a kite. Pattern (d) shows a tessellation with an arbitrary quadrilateral of no special type. We can form a tessellation, starting with *any* quadrilateral, by using the following procedure (Figure 12.71).

1. Trace the quadrilateral [Figure 12.71(a)].
2. Rotate the quadrilateral 180° around the midpoint of any side. Trace the image [Figure 12.71(b)].
3. Continue rotating the image 180° around the midpoint of each of its sides, and trace the new image [Figures 12.71(c) and (d)].

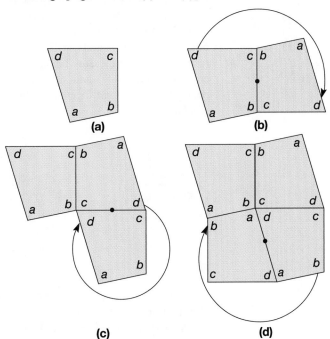

Figure 12.71

The rotation procedure described here can be applied to any triangle and to any quadrilateral, even nonconvex quadrilaterals.

Several results about triangles and quadrilaterals can be illustrated by tessellations. In Figure 12.69(c) we see that $x + y + z = 180°$, a straight angle. In Figure 12.71(d) we see that $a + b + c + d = 360°$ for the quadrilateral.

✔ **Check for Understanding:** Exercise/Problem Set A #13–15

Tessellations with Regular Polygons

Figure 12.72 shows some tessellations with equilateral triangles, squares, and regular hexagons. These are examples of tessellations each composed of copies of one regular polygon. Such tessellations are called **regular tessellations**.

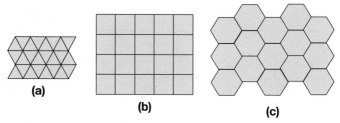

Figure 12.72

Notice that in pattern (a) six equilateral triangles meet at each vertex, in pattern (b) four squares meet at each vertex, and in pattern (c) three hexagons meet at each vertex. We say that the **vertex arrangement** in pattern (a)—that is, the configuration of regular polygons meeting at a vertex—is (3, 3, 3, 3, 3, 3). This sequence of six 3s indicates that six equilateral triangles meet at each vertex. Similarly, the vertex arrangement in pattern (b) is (4, 4, 4, 4), and in pattern (c) it is (6, 6, 6) for three hexagons.

Consider the measures of vertex angles in several regular polygons (Table 12.9). For a regular polygon to form a tessellation, its vertex angle measure must be a divisor of 360, since a whole number of copies of the polygon must meet at a vertex to form a 360° angle. Clearly, regular 3-gons (equilateral triangles), 4-gons (squares), and 6-gons (regular hexagons) will work. Their vertex angles measure 60°, 90°, and 120°, respectively, each measure being a divisor of 360°. For a regular pentagon, the vertex angle measures 108°, and since 108 is not a divisor of 360, we know that regular pentagons will not fit together without gaps or overlapping. Figure 12.73 illustrates this fact.

TABLE 12.9

n	MEASURE OF VERTEX ANGLE IN A REGULAR n-GON
3	60°
4	90°
5	108°
6	120°
7	$128\frac{4}{7}°$
8	135°
9	140°
10	144°
11	$147\frac{3}{11}°$
12	150°

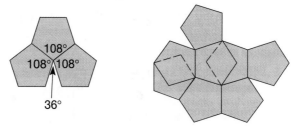

Figure 12.73

For regular polygons with more than six sides, the vertex angles are larger than 120° (and less than 180°). At least three regular polygons must meet at each vertex, yet the vertex angles in such polygons are too large to make exactly 360° with three or more of them fitting together. Hence we have the following result.

THEOREM

Tessellations Using Only One Type of Regular n-gon

Only regular 3-gons, 4-gons, or 6-gons form tessellations of the plane by themselves.

If we allow several different regular polygons with sides the same length to form a tessellation, many other possibilities result, as Figure 12.74 shows. Notice in Figure 12.74(d) that several different vertex arrangements are possible. Tessellations such as those in Figure 12.74 appear in patterns for floor and wall coverings and other symmetrical designs. Tessellations using two or more regular polygons are called **semiregular tessellations** if their vertex arrangements are identical. Thus, the tessellation in Figure 12.74(d) is *not* semiregular, but Figures 12.74(a), (b), and (c) are.

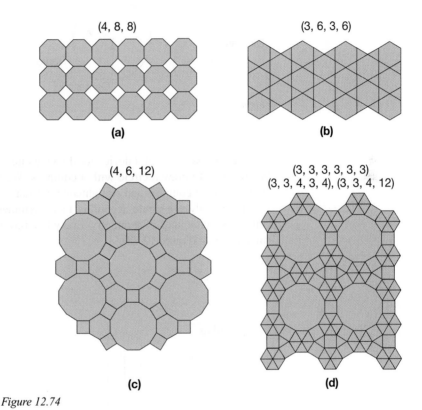

(4, 8, 8)

(3, 6, 3, 6)

(a)

(b)

(4, 6, 12)

(3, 3, 3, 3, 3, 3)
(3, 3, 4, 3, 4), (3, 3, 4, 12)

(c)

(d)

Figure 12.74

✔ **Check for Understanding:** Exercise/Problem Set A #16–19

Figure 12.75

Circles

If we consider regular *n*-gons in which *n* is very large, we can obtain figures with many vertices, all of which are the same distance from the center. Figure 12.75 shows a regular 24-gon, for example. Now imagine the figure that would result if you continually increased the number of sides. These figures would become more and more like a circle. A **circle** is the set of *all* points in the plane that are a fixed distance from a given point (called the **center**). The distance from the center to a point on the circle is called the **radius** of the circle. Any segment whose endpoints are the center and a point of the circle is also called a radius. The length of a line segment whose endpoints are on the circle and which contains the center is called a **diameter** of the circle. The line segment itself is also called a diameter. Figure 12.76 shows several circles and their centers.

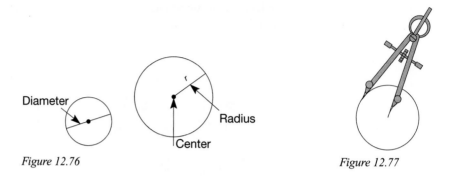

Figure 12.76   Figure 12.77

A **compass** is a useful device for drawing circles with different radii. Figure 12.77 shows how to draw a circle with a compass. We study techniques for constructing figures with a compass and straightedge in Chapter 14.

If we analyze a circle according to its symmetry properties, we find that it has infinitely many lines of symmetry. Every line through the center of the circle is a line of symmetry (Figure 12.78).

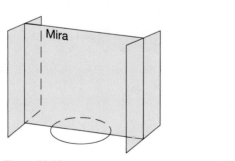

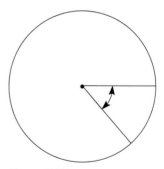

Figure 12.78   Figure 12.79

Also, a circle has infinitely many rotation symmetries, since every angle whose vertex is the center of the circle is an angle of rotation symmetry (Figure 12.79).

Many properties of a circle, including its area, are obtained by comparing the circle to regular *n*-gons with increasingly large values of *n*. We investigate several measurement properties of circles and other curved shapes in Chapter 13.

✔ **Check for Understanding:** Exercise/Problem Set A #20–21

MATHEMATICAL MORSEL

In 1994 the World Cup Soccer Championships were held in the United States. These games were held in various cities and in a variety of stadiums across the country. Unlike American football, soccer is played almost exclusively on natural grass. This presented a problem for the city of Detroit because its stadium, the Silverdome, is an indoor field with artificial turf. Growing grass in domed stadiums has yet to be done with much success, so the organizers turned to the soil scientists at Michigan State University. They decided to grow the grass outdoors on large pallets and then move these pallets indoors in time for the games. The most interesting fact of this endeavor is the shape of the pallets that they chose—hexagons! Since hexagons are one of the three regular polygons that form a regular tessellation, these pallets would fit together to cover the stadium floor but would be less likely to shift than squares or triangles.

Section 12.4   EXERCISE / PROBLEM SET A

EXERCISES

1. For each of the following shapes, determine which of the following descriptions apply.

   S: simple closed curve
   C: convex, simple closed curve
   N: *n*-gon

   a.

   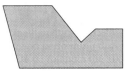

   b.

   c.

   d.

   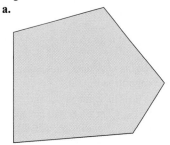

2. Use your protractor to measure each vertex angle in each of the following polygons. Extend the sides of the polygon, if necessary. Then find the sum of the measures of the vertex angles. What *should* the sum be in each case?

   a.

   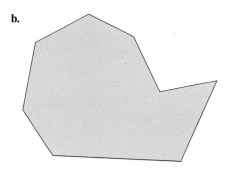

   b.

   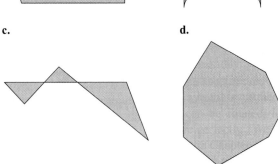

3. Using correct notation, identify three exterior angles and two vertex angles in pentagon *BDGJL*.

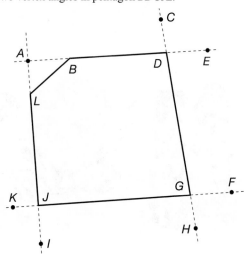

4. Draw the lines of symmetry in the following regular *n*-gons. How many does each have?

   a.   **b.**

   c.   **d.**

   e. This illustrates that a regular *n*-gon has how many lines of symmetry?
   f. If *n* is odd, each line of symmetry goes through a _____ and the _____ of the opposite side.
   g. If *n* is even, half of the lines of symmetry connect a _____ to the opposite _____. The other half connect the _____ of one side to the _____ of the opposite side.

5. Find the missing angle measures in each of the following quadrilaterals.
   a. 110° , 55°
   b. 72°
   c. *x* , *x* , *x* − 30° , $\frac{1}{2}x + 5°$

6. For the following regular *n*-gons, give the measure of a vertex angle, a central angle, and an exterior angle.
   a. 12-gon   **b.** 16-gon   **c.** 10-gon   **d.** 20-gon

7. The sum of the measures of the vertex angles of a certain polygon is 3420°. How many sides does the polygon have?

8. Given the following measures of a vertex angle of a regular polygon, determine how many sides each one has.
   a. 140°   **b.** 162°   **c.** 178°

9. Given are the measures of the central angles of regular polygons. How many sides does each one have?
   a. 30°   **b.** 72°   **c.** 5°

10. Given are the measures of the exterior angles of regular polygons. How many sides does each one have?
   a. 9°   **b.** 45°   **c.** 10°

11. Given are the measures of the vertex angles of regular polygons. What is the measure of the central angle of each one?
   a. 90°   **b.** 176°   **c.** 150°

12. Given are the measures of the exterior angles of regular polygons. What is the measure of the vertex angle of each one?
   a. 72°   **b.** 10°   **c.** 2°

13. On a square lattice, draw a tessellation with each of the following triangles. You may find the Chapter 12 eManipulative *Geoboard* on our Web site to be helpful in thinking about this problem.
   a.   **b.**

14. Given is a portion of a tessellation based on a scalene triangle. The angles are labeled from the basic tile.

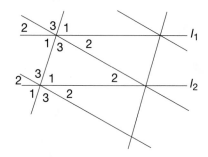

   a. Are lines l_1 and l_2 parallel?
   b. What does the tessellation illustrate about corresponding angles?

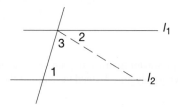

c. What is illustrated about alternate interior angles?

d. Angle 1 is an interior angle on the right of the transversal. Angles 2 and 3 together form the other interior angle on the right of the transversal. From the tessellation, what is true about $m(\angle 1) + [m(\angle 2) + m(\angle 3)]$? This result suggests that two lines are parallel if and only if the interior angles on the same side of a transversal are _____ angles.

15. Illustrated is a tessellation based on a scalene triangle with sides a, b, and c. The two shaded triangles are similar (have the same shape). For each of the corresponding three sides, find the ratio of the length of one side of the smaller triangle to the length of the corresponding side of the larger triangle. What do you observe about corresponding sides of similar triangles?

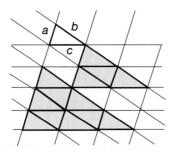

16. a. Given are portions of the (3, 3, 3, 3, 3, 3), (4, 4, 4, 4), and (6, 6, 6) tessellations. In the first, we have selected a vertex point and then connected the midpoints of the sides of polygons meeting at that vertex. The resulting figure is called the **vertex figure**. Draw the vertex figure for each of the other tessellations.

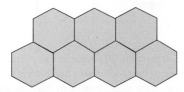

b. A tessellation is a regular tessellation if it is constructed of regular polygons and has vertex figures that are regular polygons. Which of the preceding tessellations are regular?

17. The **dual** of a tessellation is formed by connecting the centers of polygons that share a common side. The dual tessellation of the equilateral triangle tessellation is shown. Find the dual of the other tessellations.

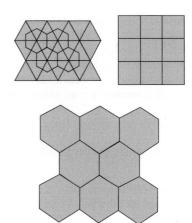

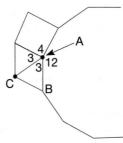

Complete the following statements.

a. The dual of the regular tessellation with triangles is a regular tessellation with _____.

b. The dual of the regular tessellation with squares is a regular tessellation with _____.

c. The dual of the regular tessellation with hexagons is a regular tessellation with _____.

18. A tessellation is a semiregular tessellation if it is made with regular polygons such that each vertex is surrounded by the same arrangement of polygons.

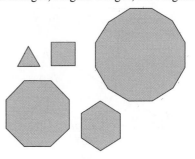

a. One of these arrangements was (3, 3, 4, 12), as shown. Can point B be surrounded by the same arrangement of polygons as point A? What happens to the arrangement at point C?

b. Can the arrangement (3, 3, 4, 12) be extended to form a semiregular tessellation? Explain.

c. Find another arrangement of regular polygons that fit around a single point but cannot be extended to a semiregular tessellation.

19. Shown are copies of an equilateral triangle, a square, a regular hexagon, a regular octagon, and a regular dodecagon.

a. Label the measure of one vertex angle for each polygon.

b. Use the Chapter 12 eManipulative activity *Tessellations* on our Web site to find the number of ways you can combine three of these figures (they may be repeated) to surround a point without gaps and overlaps.

c. By sketching, record each way you found.

20. Paper folding can be used to find the diameter and center of a circle.

Diameter: Fold the paper so one-half of the circle exactly lines up with the other half. This fold line will be the diameter.

Center: The center is found by using paper folding to find a second diameter. The center is the point where the two diameters intersect.

Trace the following circle onto a piece of paper and use paper folding to determine if the segment and point in the circle are the diameter and center.

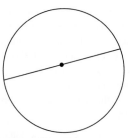

21. In the circle below, O is the center. What kind of triangle is $\triangle AOB$? Explain.

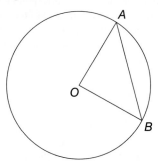

PROBLEMS

22. a. Given a square and a circle, draw an example where they intersect in exactly the number of points given.

   i. No points   **ii.** One point
  iii. Two points   **iv.** Three points

b. What is the greatest number of possible points of intersection?

23. Explain how the shaded portion of the tessellation illustrates the Pythagorean theorem for isosceles right triangles.

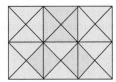

24. Calculate the measure of each lettered angle. Congruent angles and right angles are indicated.

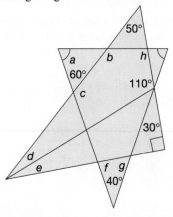

25. Complete the following table. Let V represent the number of vertices, D the number of diagonals from each vertex, and T the total number of diagonals.

POLYGON	V	D	T
Triangle			
Quadrilateral			
Pentagon			
Hexagon			
Heptagon			
Octagon			
.			
.			
.			
n-gon			

26. Suppose that there are 20 people in a meeting room. If every person in the room shakes hands once with every other person in the room, how many handshakes will there be?

27. In the five-pointed star that follows, what is the sum of the angle measures at A, B, C, D, and E? Assume that the pentagon is regular.

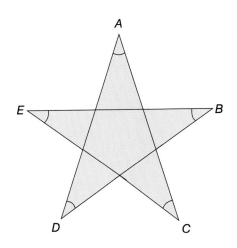

28. A man observed the semiregular floor tiling shown here and concluded after studying it that each angle of a *regular* octagon measures 135°. What was his possible reasoning?

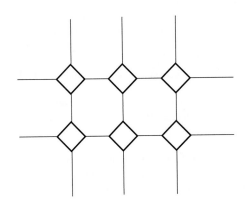

29. Find the maximum number of points of intersection for the following figures. Assume that no two sides coincide exactly.
    a. A triangle and a square
    b. A triangle and a hexagon
    c. A square and a pentagon
    d. An n-gon ($n > 2$) and a p-gon ($p > 2$)

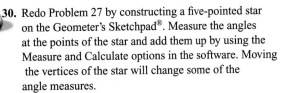

30. Redo Problem 27 by constructing a five-pointed star on the Geometer's Sketchpad®. Measure the angles at the points of the star and add them up by using the Measure and Calculate options in the software. Moving the vertices of the star will change some of the angle measures.
    a. What do you observe about the sum of the measured angles?
    b. Justify your observation from part (a).

31. Trace the following hexagon twice.

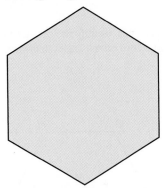

    a. Divide one hexagon into three identical parts so that each part is a rhombus.
    b. Divide the other hexagon into six identical kites.

Section 12.4 EXERCISE / PROBLEM SET B

EXERCISES

1. For each of the following shapes, determine which of the following descriptions apply.

    S: simple closed curve
    C: convex, simple closed curve
    N: n-gon

    a.

    b.
    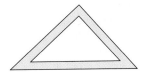

    c.
    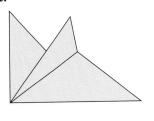

    d.

2. Use your protractor to measure each vertex angle in each polygon. Extend the sides of the polygon shown if necessary. Then find the sum of the measures of the vertex angles. What *should* the sum be in each case?

a.

b.

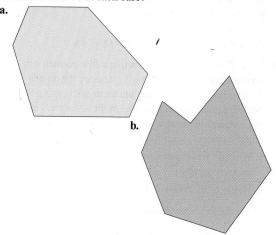

3. Using correct notation, identify two exterior angles, two vertex angles and two central angles in the hexagon *GHIJKL*.

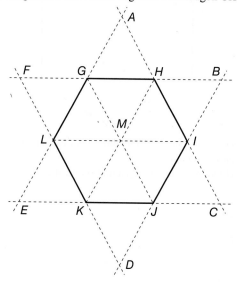

4. Describe angles of the rotation symmetries in the following regular *n*-gons.

a.

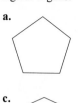

b.

c.

d.

e. Describe the angles of the rotation symmetries in a regular *n*-gon.

5. Find the missing angle measures in each of the following polygons.

a.

b.

c.

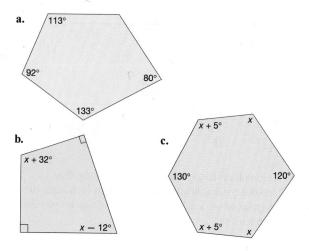

6. For each of the following regular *n*-gons, give the measure of a vertex angle, a central angle, and an exterior angle.
   a. 14-gon   **b.** 18-gon   **c.** 36-gon   **d.** 42-gon

7. The sum of the measures of the vertex angles of a certain polygon is 2880°. How many sides does the polygon have?

8. Given the following measures of a vertex angle of a regular polygon, determine how many sides it has.
   a. 150°   **b.** 156°   **c.** 174°

9. Given are the measures of the central angles of regular polygons. How many sides does each one have?
   a. 120°   **b.** 12°   **c.** 15°

10. Given are the measures of the exterior angles of regular polygons. How many sides does each one have?
   a. 18°   **b.** 36°   **c.** 3°

11. Given are the measures of the vertex angles of regular polygons. What is the measure of the central angle of each one?
   a. 140°   **b.** 156°   **c.** $x°$

12. Given are the measures of the exterior angles of regular polygons. What is the measure of the vertex angle of each one?
   a. 36°   **b.** 120°   **c.** $a°$

13. On a square lattice, draw a tessellation with each of the following quadrilaterals. You may find the Chapter 12 eManipulative *Geoboard* on our Web site to be helpful in thinking about this problem.

a.

b.

14. One theorem in geometry states the following: The line segment connecting the midpoints of two sides of a triangle is parallel to the third side and half its length. Explain how the figure in the given tessellation suggests this result.

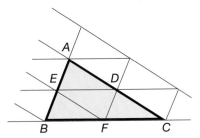

15. A theorem in geometry states the following: Parallel lines intersect proportional segments on all common transversals. In the portion of the tessellation given, lines l_1, l_2, and l_3 are parallel and t_1 and t_2 are transversals. Explain what this geometric result means, and use the portion of the tessellation to illustrate it.

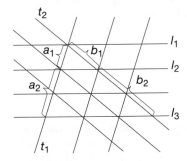

16. Given here are tessellations with equilateral triangles and squares.

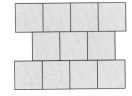

a. Draw the vertex figure for each tessellation.
b. Are these tessellations regular tessellations?

17. For each of the following tessellations, draw the dual and describe the type of polygon that makes up the dual.

a.
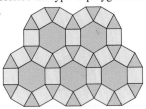

b.
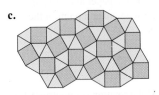

c.
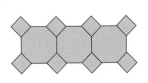

18. It will be shown later in this Exercise/Problem Set that there are only eight semiregular tessellations. They are pictured here. Identify each by giving its vertex arrangement.

a.
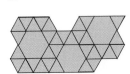

b.
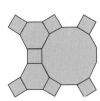

c.
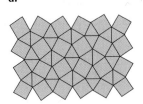

d.

e.

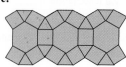

f.

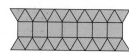

g.

h.

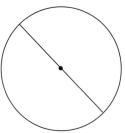

21. Trace the circles below onto a piece of paper and use paper folding to find the centers of each circle. Do the circles have the same center?

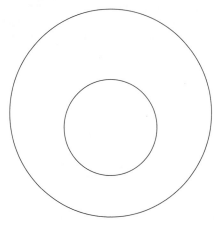

19. Using the polygons in Part A Exercise 19 and the Chapter 12 eManipulative activity *Tessellations* on our Web site, find the ways that you can combine the specified numbers of polygons to surround a point without gaps and overlaps. Record each way you found.
  a. Four polygons   **b.** Five polygons
  c. Six polygons   **d.** Seven polygons

20. Trace the following circle onto a paper and use paper folding to determine if the segment and point in the circle are the diameter and center.

PROBLEMS

22. a. Use a tracing to find all the rotation symmetries of the following regular *n*-gons.
  i. Regular pentagon

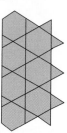

  ii. Regular hexagon

  b. How many rotation symmetries does each regular *n*-gon have?

23. Trace the hexagon twice.

  a. Divide one hexagon into four identical trapezoids.
  b. Divide the other hexagon into eight identical polygons.

24. The given scalene triangle is used as the basic tile for the illustrated tessellation.

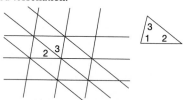

  a. Two of the angles have been labeled around the indicated point. Label the other angles (from basic tile).
  b. Which geometric results studied in this chapter are illustrated here?

25. Calculate the measure of each lettered angle. Congruent angles and right angles are indicated.

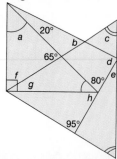

26. It was shown that a vertex angle of a regular n-gon measures $\dfrac{(n-2)\cdot 180}{n}$ degrees. If there are three regular polygons completely surrounding the vertex of a tessellation, then

$$\frac{(a-2)\cdot 180}{a} + \frac{(b-2)\cdot 180}{b} + \frac{(c-2)\cdot 180}{c} = 360,$$

where the three polygons have a, b, and c sides. Justify each step in the following simplification of the given equation.

$$\frac{a-2}{a} + \frac{b-2}{b} + \frac{c-2}{c} = 2$$

$$1 - \frac{2}{a} + 1 - \frac{2}{b} + 1 - \frac{2}{c} = 2$$

$$1 = \frac{2}{a} + \frac{2}{b} + \frac{2}{c}$$

$$\frac{1}{2} = \frac{1}{a} + \frac{1}{b} + \frac{1}{c}$$

27. Problem 26 gives an equation that whole numbers a, b, and c must satisfy if an a-gon, a b-gon, and a c-gon will completely surround a point.
 a. Let $a = 3$. Find all possible whole-number values of b and c that satisfy the equation.
 b. Repeat part (a) with $a = 4$.
 c. Repeat part (a) with $a = 5$.
 d. Repeat part (a) with $a = 6$.
 e. This gives all possible arrangements of three polygons that will completely surround a point. How many did you find?

28. The following data summarize the possible arrangements of three polygons surrounding a vertex point of a tessellation.

3, 7, 42	4, 5, 20	5, 5, 10	6, 6, 6
3, 8, 24	4, 6, 12		
3, 9, 18	4, 8, 8		
3, 10, 15			
3, 12, 12			

The (6, 6, 6) arrangement yields a regular tessellation. It has been shown that (3, 12, 12), (4, 6, 12), and (4, 8, 8) can be extended to form a semiregular tessellation. Consider the (5, 5, 10) arrangement.

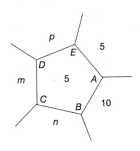

a. Point A is surrounded by (5, 5, 10). If point B is surrounded similarly, what is n?
 b. If point C is surrounded similarly, what is m?
 c. If point D is surrounded similarly, what is p?
 d. What is the arrangement around point E ? This shows that (5, 5, 10) cannot be extended to a semiregular tessellation.
 e. Show, in general, that this argument illustrates that the rest of the arrangements in the table cannot be extended to semiregular tessellations.

29. In a similar way, when four polygons—an a-gon, b-gon, c-gon, and d-gon—surround a point, it can be shown that the following equation is satisfied.

$$\frac{1}{a} + \frac{1}{b} + \frac{1}{c} + \frac{1}{d} = 1$$

a. Find the four combinations of whole numbers that satisfy this equation.
 b. One of these arrangements gives a regular tessellation. Which arrangement is it?
 c. The remaining three combinations can each surround a vertex in two different ways. Of those six arrangements, four cannot be extended to a semiregular tessellation. Which are they?
 d. The remaining two can be extended to a semiregular tessellation. Which are they?

30. a. When five polygons surround a point, they satisfy the following equation.

$$\frac{1}{a} + \frac{1}{b} + \frac{1}{c} + \frac{1}{d} + \frac{1}{e} = \frac{3}{2}$$

Find the two combinations of whole numbers that satisfy this equation.
 b. These solutions yield three different arrangements of polygons that can be extended to semiregular tessellations. Illustrate those patterns.
 c. When six polygons surround a point, they satisfy the following equation.

$$\frac{1}{a} + \frac{1}{b} + \frac{1}{c} + \frac{1}{d} + \frac{1}{e} + \frac{1}{f} = 2$$

Find the one combination that satisfies this equation. What type of tessellation is formed by this arrangement?
 d. Can more than six regular polygons surround a point? Why or why not?

31. a. Given a triangle and a circle, draw an example where they intersect in exactly the number of points given.
  i. No points **ii.** One point
  iii. Two points **iv.** Three points
 b. What is the greatest number of possible points of intersection?

Analyzing Student Thinking

32. Donna says she can tessellate the plane with any kind of triangle, but that's not true for quadrilaterals, because if you have a concave quadrilateral like the one shown, you can't do it. Is she correct? Discuss.

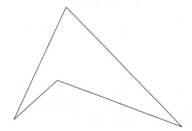

33. Tyrone says if you can tessellate the plane with a regular triangle and a regular quadrilateral, you must be able to tessellate the plane with a regular pentagon. In fact, he has made a rough sketch of the plane tessellated with regular pentagons, and you can see that they seem to fit together. What would be your response?

34. A student who was given a pentagon with four angle measures shown was asked to find the measure of the fifth angle. He said he would use the formula $\dfrac{(n-2) \cdot 180}{n}$ to find the missing angle. Will his method work? Discuss.

35. Two groups of students were arguing about the lines of symmetry in a regular octagon. One group said the lines of symmetry formed eight congruent triangles. The other group said no, they made eight congruent kites. Could both groups be right? Explain.

36. Clifton says that if you have enough sides for your polygon, it will be a circle. How would you respond?

37. Jackie says that if you add up all the exterior angles of a polygon, you get 720°, not 360°. Is she correct? Explain.

38. Marty says the sum of the angles in any plane figure is 180°. He uses a triangle as his example. Heather says, "No, the triangle is the exception." The sum of the angles in any plane figure *except the triangle* is 360°. How would you respond?

39. Jared wants to know if it is possible to draw a hexagon that has equal sides but not equal angles, or, on the other hand, equal angles but not equal sides. How would you respond?

Problems Relating to the NCTM Standards and Curriculum Focal Points

1. The Focal Points for Grade 8 state "Analyzing two- and three-dimensional space and figures by using distance and angle." Discuss the role that angle plays in constructing tessellations.

2. The NCTM Standards state "All students should select and apply techniques and tools to accurately find length, area, volume, and angle measures to appropriate levels of

precision." In order to find the sum of the interior angles of a polygon, do you need physical tools in order to have "appropriate levels of precision"? Explain.

3. The NCTM Standards state "All students should recognize geometric shapes and structures in the environment and specify their location." Describe three examples of tessellations in your environment.

12.5 DESCRIBING THREE-DIMENSIONAL SHAPES

STARTING POINT

The stack of blocks at the right would have the front view and side view as shown. Build two other block stacks that have the same front and side views. Sketch all four views (front, back, two sides) of the two stacks that you have constructed. How do the views for these two stacks compare to each other? How do they compare to the views of the original stack?

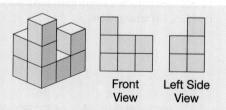

Front View   Left Side View

Planes, Skew Lines, and Dihedral Angles

Reflection from Research
According to research, spatial ability and problem-solving performance are strongly correlated. This suggests that skill in spatial visualization is a good predictor of mathematical problem solving (Tillotson, 1985).

We now consider three-dimensional space and investigate various three-dimensional shapes (i.e., shapes having length, width, *and* height). There are infinitely many planes in three-dimensional space. Figure 12.80 shows several possible relationships among planes in three-dimensional space. The shapes in Figure 12.80 are actually portions of planes, since planes extend infinitely in two dimensions. Notice in Figures 12.80(b) and (c) that two intersecting planes meet in a line. In three-dimensional space, two distinct planes are either parallel as in Figure 12.80(a) or intersect as in Figure 12.80(b).

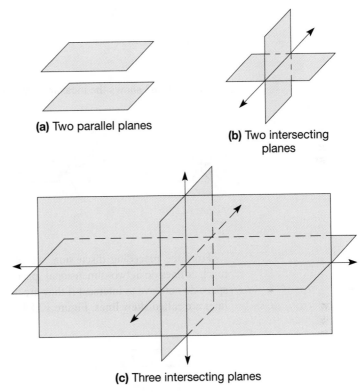

(a) Two parallel planes

(b) Two intersecting planes

(c) Three intersecting planes

Figure 12.80

We can define the angle formed by polygonal regions much as we defined angles in two dimensions. A **dihedral angle** is formed by the union of polygonal regions in space that share an edge. The polygonal regions forming the dihedral angle are called **faces** of the dihedral angle. Intuitively a dihedral angle is the angle created by two intersecting planes. Figure 12.81 shows several dihedral angles formed by intersecting rectangular regions. (Dihedral angles are also formed when planes intersect, but we will not investigate this situation.)

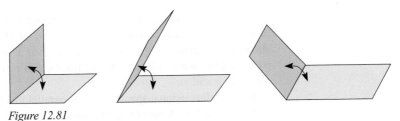

Figure 12.81

We can measure dihedral angles by measuring an angle between two line segments or rays contained in the faces (Figure 12.82). Notice that the line segments forming the sides of the angle in Figure 12.82 are *perpendicular* to the line segment that is the intersection of the faces of the dihedral angle.

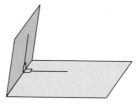

Figure 12.82

Figure 12.83 shows the measurements of several dihedral angles.

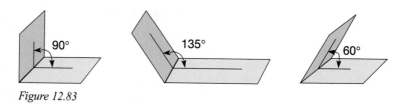

Figure 12.83

From the preceding discussion, we see that planes act in three-dimensional space much as lines do in two-dimensional space. On the other hand, lines in three-dimensional space do not have to intersect if they are not parallel. Such nonintersecting, nonparallel lines are called **skew lines**. Figure 12.84 shows a pair of skew lines, l and m.

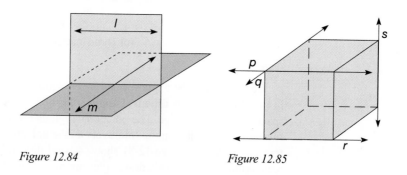

Figure 12.84   *Figure 12.85*

Thus in three-dimensional space, there are three possible relationships between two lines: They are parallel, they intersect, or they are skew lines. Figure 12.85 shows these relationships among the edges of a cube. Notice that lines p and r are parallel, lines p and q intersect, and lines q and s are skew lines (as are lines r and s, and lines p and s).

In three-dimensional space a line l is parallel to a plane $\mathcal{P}$ if l and $\mathcal{P}$ do not intersect [Figure 12.86(a)]. A line l is perpendicular to a plane $\mathcal{P}$ if l is perpendicular to every line in $\mathcal{P}$ that l intersects [Figure 12.86(b)].

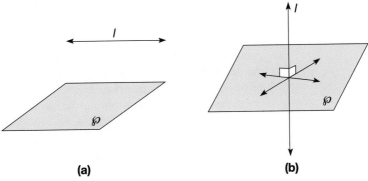

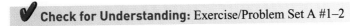

Figure 12.86

✔ **Check for Understanding:** Exercise/Problem Set A #1–2

Polyhedra

The cube shown in Figure 12.85 is an example of a general category of three-dimensional shapes called polyhedra. A polyhedron is the three-dimensional analog of a polygon. A **polyhedron** (plural: **polyhedra**) is the union of polygonal regions, any two of which have at most a side in common, such that a connected finite region in space is enclosed without holes. Figure 12.87(a) shows examples of polyhedra. Figure 12.87(b) contains shapes that are not polyhedra. In Figure 12.87(b), shape (i) is not a polyhedron, since it has a hole; shape (ii) is not a polyhedron, since it is curved; and shape (iii) is not a polyhedron, since it does not enclose a finite region in space.

Reflection from Research
Using paper and drinking straws to build 3-D shapes allows students the opportunity to construct their own knowledge about these shapes and their properties. Then, through talking about their models, the students are able to learn and use new vocabulary in a meaningful way (Koester, 2003).

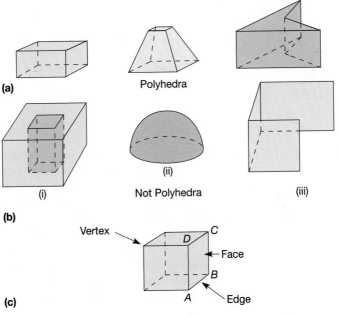

Figure 12.87

A polyhedron is **convex** if every line segment joining two of its points is contained inside the polyhedron or is on one of the polygonal regions. The first two polyhedra in Figure 12.87(a) are convex; the third is not. The polygonal regions of a polyhedron are called **faces**, the line segments common to a pair of faces are called **edges**, and the points of intersection of the edges are called **vertices**. In Figure 12.87(c), some of the vertices are A, B, C, and D. Some of the edges are $\overline{AB}$ and $\overline{CD}$, and one of the faces is $ABCD$.

Polyhedra can be classified into several general types. For example, **prisms** are polyhedra with two opposite faces that are identical polygons. These faces are called the **bases**. The vertices of the bases are joined to form **lateral faces** that must be parallelograms. If the lateral faces are rectangles, the prism is called a **right prism**, and the dihedral angle formed by a base and a lateral face is a right angle. Otherwise, the prism is called an **oblique prism**. Figure 12.88 shows a variety of prisms, named according to the types of polygons forming the bases and whether they are right or oblique.

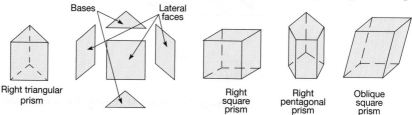

Figure 12.88

Since there are infinitely many types of polygons to use as the bases, there are infinitely many types of prisms.

Pyramids are polyhedra formed by using a polygon for the base and a point not in the plane of the base, called the **apex**, that is connected with line segments to each vertex of the base. Figure 12.89 shows several pyramids, named according to the type of polygon forming the base. Pyramids whose bases are regular polygons fall into two categories. Those whose lateral faces are isosceles triangles are called **right regular pyramids**. Otherwise, they are **oblique regular pyramids**.

Children's Literature
www.wiley.com/college/musser
See "Mummy Math: An Adventure in Geometry" by Cindy Neuschwander.

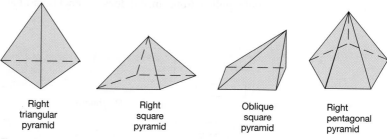

Figure 12.89

Polyhedra with regular polygons for faces have been studied since the time of the ancient Greeks. A **regular polyhedron** is one in which all faces are identical regular polygonal regions and all dihedral angles have the same measure. The ancient Greeks were able to show that there are exactly five regular convex polyhedra, called the **Platonic solids**. They are analyzed in Table 12.10, according to number of faces, vertices, and edges, and shown in Figure 12.90. An interesting pattern in Table 12.10 is that $F + V = E + 2$ for all five regular polyhedra. That is, the number of faces plus vertices equals the number of edges plus 2. This result, known as **Euler's formula**, holds for *all* convex polyhedra, not just regular polyhedra. For example, verify Euler's formula for each of the polyhedra in Figures 12.87, 12.88, and 12.89.

NCTM Standard
All students should describe attributes and parts of two- and three-dimensional shapes.

TABLE 12.10

POLYHEDRON	FACES, F	VERTICES, V	EDGES, E
Tetrahedron	4	4	6
Hexahedron	6	8	12
Octahedron	8	6	12
Dodecahedron	12	20	30
Icosahedron	20	12	30

NCTM Standard
All students should precisely describe, classify, and understand relationships among types of two- and three-dimensional objects using their defining properties.

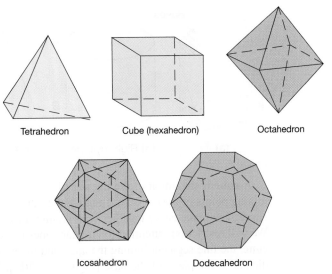

Tetrahedron   Cube (hexahedron)   Octahedron

Icosahedron   Dodecahedron

Figure 12.90

If we allow several different regular polygonal regions to serve as the faces, then we can investigate a new family of polyhedra, called semiregular polyhedra. A **semiregular polyhedron** is a polyhedron with several different regular polygonal regions for faces but with the same arrangement of polygons at each vertex. Prisms with square faces and regular polygons for bases are semiregular polyhedra. Figure 12.91 shows several types of semiregular polyhedra.

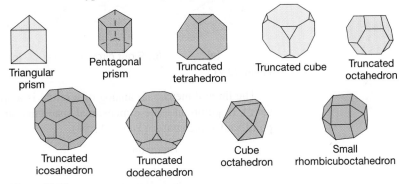

Triangular prism   Pentagonal prism   Truncated tetrahedron   Truncated cube   Truncated octahedron

Truncated icosahedron   Truncated dodecahedron   Cube octahedron   Small rhombicuboctahedron

Figure 12.91

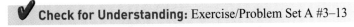

Check for Understanding: Exercise/Problem Set A #3–13

Curved Shapes in Three Dimensions

There are three-dimensional curved shapes analogous to prisms and pyramids, namely cylinders and cones. Consider two identical simple closed curves having the same orientation and contained in parallel planes. The union of the line segments joining corresponding points on the simple closed curves and the interiors of the simple closed curves is called a **cylinder** [Figure 12.92(a)]. Each simple closed curve together with its interior is called a **base of the cylinder**. In a **right circular cylinder**, a line segment $\overline{AB}$ connecting a point A on one circular base to its corresponding point B on the other circular base is perpendicular to the planes of the bases [Figure 12.92(b)]. In an **oblique cylinder**, the bases are parallel, yet line segments connecting corresponding points are not perpendicular to the planes of the bases [Figure 12.92(c)]. In this book we restrict our study to right circular cylinders.

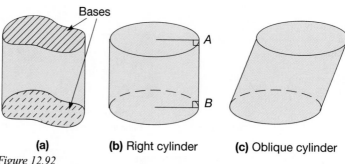

(a)   **(b)** Right cylinder   **(c)** Oblique cylinder

Figure 12.92

A **cone** is the union of the interior of a simple closed curve and all line segments joining points of the curve to a point, called the **apex**, which is not in the plane of the curve. The plane curve together with its interior is called the **base** [Figure 12.93(a)]. We will restrict our attention to circular cones (bases are circles). In a **right circular cone**, the line segment joining the apex and the center of the circular base is perpendicular to the plane of the base [Figure 12.93(b)]. In an **oblique circular cone**, this line segment is not perpendicular to the plane of the base [Figure 12.93(c)]. Cones and cylinders appear frequently in construction and design.

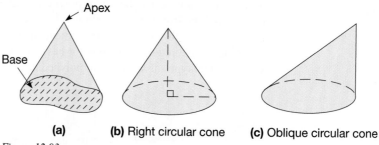

(a)   **(b)** Right circular cone   **(c)** Oblique circular cone

Figure 12.93

The three-dimensional analog of a circle is a sphere. A **sphere** is defined as the set of all points in three-dimensional space that are the same distance from a fixed point, called the **center** (Figure 12.94).

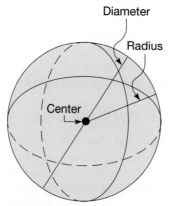

Figure 12.94

Any line segment joining the center to a point on the sphere is also called a **radius** of the sphere; its *length* is also called *the* radius of the sphere. A segment joining two points of the sphere and containing the center is called a **diameter** of the sphere; its *length* is also called *the* diameter of the sphere. Spherical shapes are important in many areas.

Planets, moons, and stars are essentially spherical. Thus measurement aspects of spheres are very important in science. We consider measurement aspects of cones, cylinders, spheres, and other shapes in Chapter 13.

A summary of the definitions and images of polyhedra, prisms, pyramids, cylinders, and cones follows (Table 12.11).

TABLE 12.11

NAME	IMAGE		DEFINITION
Polyhedron			The union of polygonal regions, any two of which have at most a side in common, such that a connected finite region in space is enclosed without holes.
Prism	Right	Oblique	A polyhedra with two identical polygons, called bases, as faces that are in parallel planes. The remaining faces that connect the bases are parallelograms.
Pyramid	Right	Oblique	A polyhedra formed by using a polygon for the base and a point not in the plane of the base, called the apex, which is connected with line segments to each vertex of the base.
Cylinder	Right	Oblique	The union of line segments that join corresponding points of identical simple closed curves in parallel planes. The simple closed curves are oriented the same way and their interiors are also included.
Cone	Right	Oblique	The union of the interior of a simple closed curve and all of the line segments joining points of the curve to a point, called the apex, which is not in the plane of the curve

✔ **Check for Understanding:** Exercise/Problem Set A #14–16

MATHEMATICAL MORSEL

The sphere is one of the most commonly occurring shapes in nature. Hail stones, frog eggs, tomatoes, oranges, soap bubbles, the Earth, and the moon are a very few examples of spherelike shapes. The regular occurrence of the spherical shape is not coincidental. One explanation for the frequency of the sphere's appearance is that for a given surface area, the sphere encloses the greatest volume. In other words, a sphere requires the least amount of natural material to surround a given volume. This may help explain why animals curl up in a ball when it is cold outside.

| Section 12.5 | **EXERCISE / PROBLEM SET A**

EXERCISES

1. a. In the following figure, identify a pair of planes that appears to be parallel.

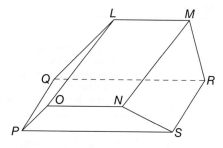

b. Identify nine pairs of lines that appear to be parallel.
c. Identify four pairs of skew lines.
d. Describe an acute dihedral angle by naming two faces of the angle with its edge.
e. Describe an obtuse dihedral angle.

2. Given is a prism with bases that are regular pentagons.

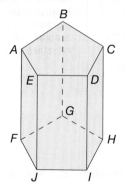

a. Is there a plane in the picture that appears to be parallel to the plane containing points A, B, C, D, and E? If so, name the points that it contains.
b. Is there a plane in the picture that appears to be parallel to the plane containing points C, D, I, and H? If so, name the points that it contains.
c. What is the measure of the dihedral angle between plane $AEJF$ and plane $ABGF$?

3. Which of the following figures are polyhedra and which are not? If it is not a polyhedra, explain why not. If it is a polyhedra, describe all of the faces (e.g., 3 triangles and two trapezoids).

a.

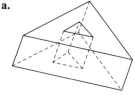

b.

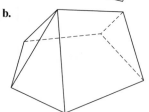

c.

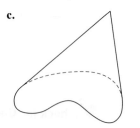

4. For each of the following prisms, (i) Name the bases of the prism. (ii) Name the lateral faces of the prism. (iii) Name the faces that are hidden from view. (iv) Name the prism by type.

a.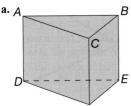

b.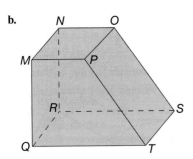

5. Name the following pyramids according to type.
   a. The base is a square.

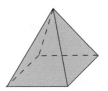

b. 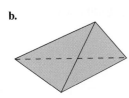   c.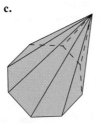

6. Shown are patterns or **nets** for several three-dimensional figures. Copy and cut each one out. Then fold each one up to form the figure. Name the three-dimensional figure you have made in each case.

a.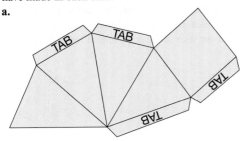

b.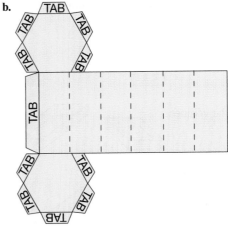

c.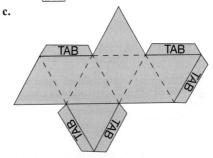

d. Most nets for three-dimensional shapes are not unique. Sketch another net for each shape you made in this exercise. Be sure to include tabs for folding. Try each one to check your answer.

7. Draw a net for each of the following polyhedra. Be sure to include tabs for folding. Cut out and fold your patterns to check your answers.

a.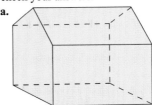

b. A right hexagonal pyramid

8. Which of the following patterns folds into a cube? If one does, what number will be opposite the X?

a.
1		
4	X	2	5
3		

b.
1	X	3	
		2	4	5

c.
	3	X	1
5	2	4	

d.
1			
3	5	2	4
			X

e.
1	3	X
		2	4
		5

f.
3	X	
	1	4
	2	5

9. Drawing a prism can be done by following these steps:

Draw the bases.

Connect the vertices.

Dot the hidden edges
or leave them out.

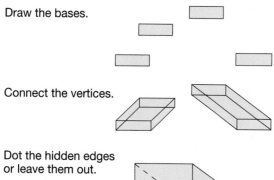

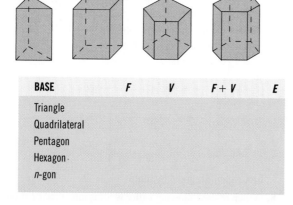

Top view   Bottom view

Draw the following prisms.
a. Square prism
b. Pentagonal prism (bottom view)

10. a. Given are samples of prisms. Use these prisms to complete
the following table. Let F represent the number of faces, V
the number of vertices, and E the number of edges.

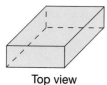

BASE	F	V	$F + V$	E
Triangle				
Quadrilateral				
Pentagon				
Hexagon				
n-gon				

b. Is Euler's formula satisfied for prisms?

11. a. Given are pictures of three-dimensional shapes. Use
them to complete the following table. Let F represent
the number of faces, V the number of vertices, and
E the number of edges.
i.

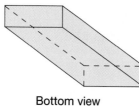

ii.

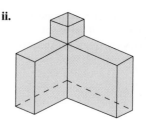

BASE	F	V	$F + V$	E
i.				
ii.				

b. Is Euler's formula satisfied for these figures?

12. A vertex arrangement of a polyhedron is a description of
the polygonal faces that meet at a vertex. For example the
vertex arrangement of the following triangular prism is
square-square-triangle, or 4-4-3.

Triangular
prism

Since it is a semiregular polyhedron, all vertex
arrangements are the same. Describe the vertex
arrangements of the following polyhedra and verify that
they are semiregular polyhedra.

Pentagonal
prism

Truncated
tetrahedron

Truncated cube

Truncated
octahedron

13. When a three-dimensional shape is cut by a plane, the figure that
results is a cross-section. Identify the cross-section formed in the
following cases. The Chapter 12 eManipulative activity *Slicing
Solids* on our Web site may be helpful for parts (a) and (b).

a.

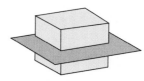

b.

14. The right cylinder is cut by a plane as indicated. Identify the resulting cross-section.

15. a. The picture illustrates the intersection between a sphere and a plane. What is true about all such intersections?

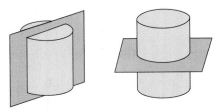

b. When the intersecting plane contains the center of the sphere, the cross-section is called a **great circle** of the sphere. How many great circles are there for a sphere?

16. Sketch an oblique cone with a base that looks like the following simple closed curve.

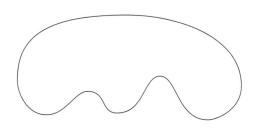

PROBLEMS

17. a. Describe what you see.

b. Which is the highest step?

18. How many 1 × 1 × 1 cubes are in the following stack?

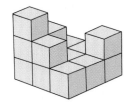

19. All faces of the following cube are different.

Which of these cubes could represent a different view of the preceding cube?

a.   **b.**   **c.**

20. Pictured is a stack of cubes. Also given are the top view, the front view, and the right-side view. (Assume that the only hidden cubes are ones that support a pictured cube.)

Top   Front   Right side

Give the three views of each of the following stacks of cubes.

a.   **b.**   **c.**

21. In the figure, the drawing on the left shows a shape. The drawing on the right tells you how many cubes are on each base square. The drawing on the right is called a **base design**.

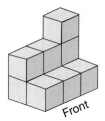

| 2 | 2 | 3 |
| 1 | 1 | 1 |

a. Which is the correct base design for this shape?

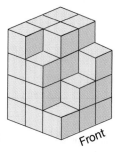

(i)
4	4	4
3	3	3
1	2	4

(ii)
4	4	4
3	4	4
1	2	3

(iii)
4	4	4
3	4	5
1	1	1

b. Make a base design for each shape.

i.

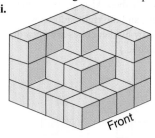

ii.

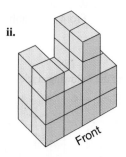

22. When folded, the figures on the left become one of the figures on the right. Which one? Make models to check.

a.

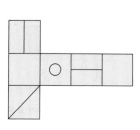

(i)

(ii)

(iii)

(iv)

(v)

(vi)

b.

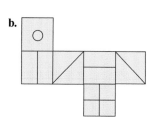

23. If the cube illustrated is cut by a plane midway between opposite faces and the front portion is placed against a mirror, the entire cube appears to be formed. The cutting plane is called a **plane of symmetry**, and the figure is said to have **reflection symmetry**.

a.

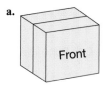

How many planes of symmetry of this type are there for a cube?

b.

A plane passing through pairs of opposite edges is also a plane of symmetry, as illustrated. How many planes of symmetry of this type are there in a cube?

c. How many planes of symmetry are there for a cube?

24. The line connecting centers of opposite faces of a cube is an **axis** (plural: **axes**) **of rotational symmetry**, since the cube can be turned about the axis and appears to be in the same position. In fact, the cube can be turned about that axis four times before returning to its original position, as shown.

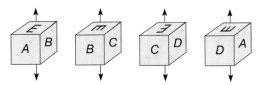

This axis of symmetry is said to have order 4. How many axes of symmetry of order 4 are there in a cube?

25. The line connecting opposite pairs of vertices of a cube is also an axis of symmetry.

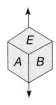

a. What is the order of this axis (how many turns are needed to return it to the original arrangement)?
b. How many axes of this order are there in a cube?

26. The line connecting midpoints of opposite edges is an axis of symmetry of a cube.

a. What is the order of this axis?
b. How many axes of this order are there in a cube?

27. What is the shape of a piece of cardboard that is made into a center tube for a paper towel roll?

28. Show how to slice a cube with four cuts to make a regular tetrahedron. (*Hint:* Slice a clay cube with a cheese cutter or draw lines on a paper or plastic cube.)

| Section 12.5 | **EXERCISE / PROBLEM SET B** |

EXERCISES

1. a. In the following figure, identify three pairs of lines that appear to be parallel.

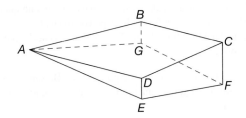

b. Identify four pairs of skew lines.
c. Describe an acute dihedral angle.
d. Describe an obtuse dihedral angle.

2. The dihedral angle, $\angle AED$, of the tetrahedron pictured can be found by the following procedure.

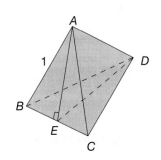

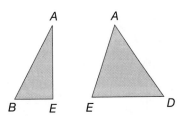

a. The face of the tetrahedron is an equilateral triangle, $\triangle ABC$. As one segment of the dihedral angle, $\overline{AE}$ is perpendicular to $\overline{BC}$. In an equilateral triangle, the perpendicular segment from a vertex to a side cuts the side in half. Find the length of $\overline{BE}$ and $\overline{AE}$, if we assume the edges of the tetrahedron have length 1.

b. Using similar reasoning, find the length of $\overline{DE}$.

c. Label the length of the sides of $\triangle AED$. Use a scale drawing and a protractor to approximate the measure of $\angle AED$.

3. Which of the following figures are polyhedra and which are not? If it is not a polyhedra, explain why not. If it is a polyhedra, describe all of the faces (e.g. 3 triangles and two trapezoids).

a. 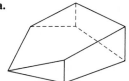   **b.**

c.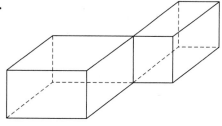

4. Name the following prisms by type.

a.   b.   c.
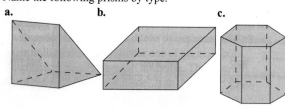

5. Which of the following figures are prisms? Which are pyramids?

a.

b.   **c.**

6. Following are patterns or nets for several three-dimensional figures. Copy and cut each one out. Then fold each one up to form the figure. Name the three-dimensional figure you have made in each case.

a.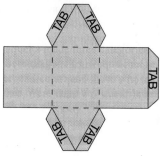

b.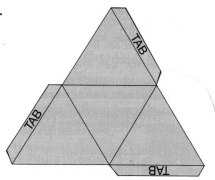

c.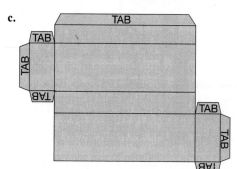

d. Most nets for three-dimensional shapes are not unique. Sketch another net for each shape you made. Be sure to include tabs for folding. Try each one to check your answer.

7. Draw a net for the following polyhedron. Be sure to include tabs for folding. Cut out and fold your pattern to check your answer.

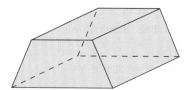

8. Which of the pentominos in Problem 14 of Set 12.2B will fold up to make a box with no lid? Mark the bottom of the box with an X.

9. Drawing a pyramid can be done by following these steps.

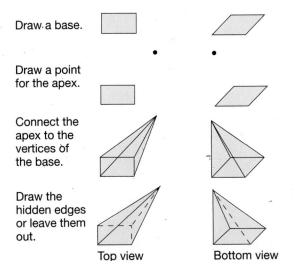

Draw a base.

Draw a point for the apex.

Connect the apex to the vertices of the base.

Draw the hidden edges or leave them out.

Top view   Bottom view

Draw the following pyramids.
a. A triangular pyramid
b. A hexagonal pyramid (bottom view)

10. a. Given are samples of pyramids. Use them to complete the following table. Let F represent the number of faces, V the number of vertices, and E the number of edges.

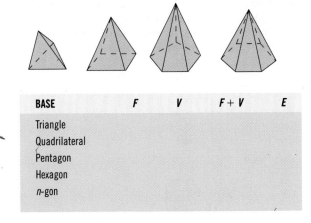

BASE	F	V	F + V	E
Triangle				
Quadrilateral				
Pentagon				
Hexagon				
n-gon				

b. Is Euler's formula satisfied for pyramids?

11. a. Given are pictures of three-dimensional shapes. Use them to complete the following table. Let F represent the number of faces, V the number of vertices, and E the number of edges.

i.   ii.

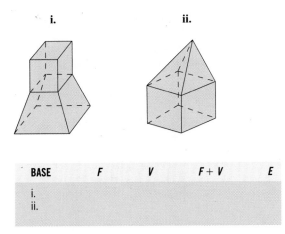

BASE	F	V	F + V	E
i.				
ii.				

b. Is Euler's formula satisfied for these figures?

12. Describe the vertex arrangements (see #12 in set A) of the following polyhedra and verify that they are semiregular polyhedra.

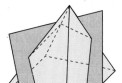

Truncated icosahedron   Truncated dodecahedron   Cube octahedron   Small rhombicuboctahedron

13. Identify the cross-section formed in the following cases. The Chapter 12 eManipulative activity *Slicing Solids* on our Web site may be helpful in visualizing the cross-sections.
    a.   b.

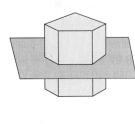

14. The following cone is cut by a plane as indicated. Identify the resulting cross-section in each case.
    a.   b.   c.

15. Imagine a cylinder containing three spheres that exactly touch the top and sides (like a can of three tennis balls). Suppose a plane cuts the cylinder and three spheres as shown. What would the cross section look line?

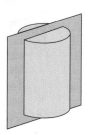

16. Sketch an oblique cylinder with bases in the shape of the following simple closed curve.

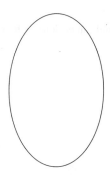

PROBLEMS

17. **a.** Which dark circle is behind the others in the figure? Look at the figure for one minute before answering.

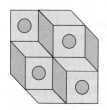

b. Is the small cube attached to the front or the back of the large cube?

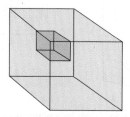

18. How many $1 \times 1 \times 1$ cubes are in the following stack?

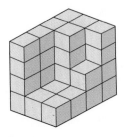

19. All the faces of the cube on the left have different figures on them. Which of the three other cubes could represent a different view? Explain.

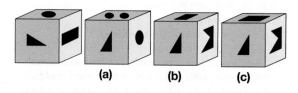

(a)   (b)   (c)

20. Following is pictured a stack of cubes. (Assume that the only hidden cubes are ones that support a pictured cube; see Problem 20 in Part A, for example.) Give three views of each of the following stacks of cubes.

a.

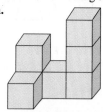

b.

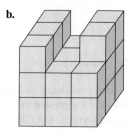

21. Following are shown three views of a stack of cubes. Determine the largest possible number of cubes in the stack. What is the smallest number of cubes that could be in the stack? Make a base design for each answer (see Problem 21 in Part A).

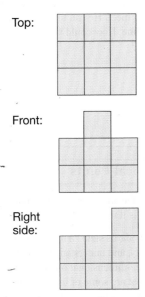

Top:

Front:

Right side:

22. Eight small cubes are put together to form one large cube as shown.

Suppose that all six sides of this larger cube are painted, the paint is allowed to dry, and the cube is taken apart.
   a. How many of the small cubes will have paint on just one side? on two sides? on three sides? on no sides?
   b. Answer the questions from part (a), this time assuming the large cube is formed from 27 small cubes.
   c. Answer the questions from part (a), this time assuming the large cube is formed from 64 small cubes.
   d. Answer the questions from part (a), but assume the large cube is formed from n^3 small cubes.

23. Use the Chapter 12 eManipulative activity *Slicing Solids* on our Web site to determine which of the following cross-sections are possible when a plane cuts a cube.
   a. A square
   b. A rectangle
   c. An isosceles triangle
   d. An equilateral triangle

   e. A trapezoid
   f. A parallelogram
   g. A pentagon
   h. A regular hexagon

24. Use the Chapter 12 eManipulative activity *Slicing Solids* on our Web site to determine which of the following cross-sections are possible when a plane cuts an octahedron.
   a. A square
   b. A rectangle
   c. An isosceles triangle
   d. An equilateral triangle
   e. A trapezoid
   f. A parallelogram
   g. A pentagon
   h. A regular hexagon

25. How many planes of symmetry do the following figures have? (Models may help.)
   a. A tetrahedron
   b. A square pyramid
   c. A pentagonal prism
   d. A right circular cylinder

26. Find the axes of symmetry for the following figures. Indicate the order of each axis. (Models may help.)
   a. A tetrahedron
   b. A pentagonal prism

27. How many axes of symmetry do the following figures have?
   a. A right square pyramid
   b. A right circular cone
   c. A sphere

28. A regular tetrahedron is attached to a face of a square pyramid with equilateral faces where the faces of the tetrahedron and the pyramid are identical triangles. What is the fewest number of faces possible for the resulting polyhedron? (Use a model—it will suggest a surprising answer. However, a complete mathematical solution is difficult.)

Analyzing Student Thinking

29. Rene says two distinct planes either intersect or they don't. If they don't, then they're parallel. It's the same thing with lines; either they intersect or they're parallel. How would you respond to Rene?

30. Mario says a polygon is a simple closed figure with straight-line sides, and a polyhedron is a simple closed figure with polygonal sides. How could you clarify Mario's thinking here?

31. Cheryl says she doesn't know if a right triangular pyramid should have a right triangle base. How can you help her?

32. Tatiana says that the circle and the sphere have the same definition: a set of points at an equal distance from the center. Do you agree? How could you explain the need for a difference in the two definitions? What would the difference be?

33. Alicia wonders if it is possible to draw a polygon that has no line of symmetry. She also questions whether it is possible to find a prism that has no plane of symmetry. How would you respond?

34. The Platonic solids have faces made of regular triangles, regular quadrilaterals, or regular pentagons. Koji asks why you couldn't have a Platonic solid with faces of regular hexagons. How would you respond?

35. Jesse said that he can see how three planes can intersect in a single point because it is like the place where two walls and the ceiling meet. He can't see how three planes could intersect in a line. How could you help Jesse see how this could be done?

Problems Relating to the NCTM Standards and Curriculum Focal Points

1. The Focal Points for Grade 5 state "Describing three-dimensional shapes and analyzing their properties, including volume and surface area." Describe some properties of polyhedra that distinguish them from three-dimensional shapes that are not polyhedra.

2. The Focal Points for Grade 8 state "Analyzing two- and three-dimensional space and figures by using distance and angle." What is the angle between two intersecting planes called and how is it measured?

3. The NCTM Standards state "All students should precisely describe, classify, and understand relationships among types of two- and three-dimensional objects using their defining properties." What are some of the defining properties of the three-dimensional shapes we have discussed in this section?

END OF CHAPTER MATERIAL

Solution of Initial Problem

Describe a solid shape that will fill each of the holes in this template as well as pass through each hole.

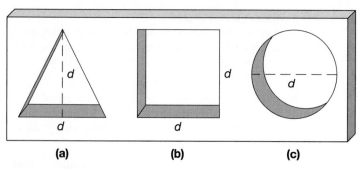

Figure 12.95

Strategy: Use a Model

The cylinder in Figure 12.96(a) whose base has diameter d and whose height is d, will pass through the square and circle exactly [Figure 12.95(b) and (c)]. We will modify a model of this cylinder to get a shape with a triangular cross-section. If we slice the cylinder along the heavy lines in Figure 12.96(b), the resulting model will pass through the triangular hole exactly. Figure 12.96(c) shows the resulting model that will pass through all three holes exactly in Figure 12.95.

(a)   **(b)**   **(c)**

Figure 12.96

Additional Problems Where the Strategy "Use a Model" Is Useful

1. Which of the following can be folded into a closed box?
   a.
   b.
   c.

2. If a penny is placed on a table, how many pennies can be placed around it, where each new penny touches the penny in the center and two other pennies?

3. Twenty-five cannonballs are stacked in a 5×5 square rack on the floor. What is the greatest number of cannonballs that can be stacked on these 25 to form a stable pyramid of cannonballs?

People in Mathematics

Cathleen Synge Morawetz (1923–   )
Cathleen Synge Morawetz said that she liked to construct "engines and levers" as a youngster, but wasn't good in arithmetic. "I used to get bad marks in mental arithmetic." Her father was the Irish mathematician J. L. Synge, and her mother studied mathematics at Trinity College. In college, she gravitated from engineering to mathematics and did her doctoral thesis on the analysis of shock waves. Her professional research has focused on the applications of differential equations. She became the first woman in the United States to head a mathematics institute, the Courant Institute of Mathematical Sciences in New York. "The burden of raising children still falls on the woman, at a time that's very important in her career. I'm about to institute a new plan of life, according to which women would have their children in their late teens and their mothers would bring them up. I don't mean the grandmother would give up her career, but she's already established, so she can afford to take time off to look after the children."

R. L. Moore (1882–1974)
A Texan to the core, R. L. Moore was a rugged individualist whose specialty was topology. His methods were highly original, both in research and teaching. As a professor at the University of Texas, he encouraged originality in his students by discouraging them from reading standard expositions and requiring them to work things out for themselves, in true pioneer spirit. His Socratic style became known as the "Moore method." One of his students, Mary Ellen Rudin, describes it this way: "He always looked for people who had not been influenced by other mathematical experiences. His technique was to feed all kinds of problems to us. He gave us lists of mathematical statements. Some were true, some were false, some were very easy to prove or disprove, others very hard. We worked on whatever we jolly well pleased." Moore taught at the University of Texas until he was 86 years old. Even though he wanted to continue teaching, the university made him retire. The Mathematics-Physics Hall at the University of Texas was named after him.

CHAPTER REVIEW

Review the following terms and exercises to determine which require learning or relearning—page numbers are provided for easy reference.

SECTION 12.1 Recognizing and Analyzing Geometric Shapes

VOCABULARY/NOTATION

van Hiele Levels
    Level 0—Recognition 578
    Level 1—Analysis 578
    Level 2—Relationships 579
    Level 3—Deduction 579
    Level 4—Axiomatics 579
Level 0
    Triangles 580
    Quadrilaterals 580
    Isosceles triangles 582
    Equilateral triangles 582
    Rectangles 582
    Squares 582
    Geoboard 582
    Square dot paper 582
    Square lattice 582
    Triangular geoboard 583
    Triangular dot paper 583
    Triangular lattice 583

Level 1
    Line segment 584
    Angle 584
    Right angle 584
    Perpendicular segments 584
    Parallel line segments 584
    Endpoints 584
    Sides 584
    Vertex 584
    Vertices 584
    Same length 586
    Triangle 586
    Sides of a triangle 586
    Angles of a triangle 586
    Vertex of a triangle 586
    Scalene triangle 587
    Isosceles triangle 587
    Equilateral triangle 587

Right triangle 587
Quadrilateral 588
Sides of the quadrilateral 588
Angles of the quadrilateral 588
Vertex of the quadrilateral 588
Parallelogram 588
Rhombus 588
Rhombi 588
Rectangle 588
Square 588
Diagonal 590
$\overline{AB}$ 591
$\angle A$ or $\angle ABC$ 592
$\triangle ABC$ 592
Midpoint 592
Adjacent sides 592
Opposite sides 592

EXERCISES

1. Briefly explain the following four van Hiele levels.
   a. Recognition **b.** Analysis
   c. Relationships **d.** Deduction

2. Give examples of how the following shapes are represented in the physical world.
   a. A line segment   **b.** A right angle
   c. A triangle   **d.** An angle
   e. Parallel lines   **f.** A square

    g. A rectangle   **h.** A parallelogram
    i. A rhombus   **j.** Perpendicular segments
    k. A scalene triangle   **l.** An isosceles triangle

3. Give paper-folding definitions of
   a. perpendicular lines.   **b.** parallel lines.

4. Identify characteristics of the sides and diagonals of the following shapes: parallelogram, rhombus, rectangle, square.

SECTION 12.2 Relationships

VOCABULARY/NOTATION

Kite 606
Trapezoid 606
Isosceles trapezoid 606

Reflection symmetry 609
Line (axis) of symmetry 609
Base angles 611

Mira 611
Rotation symmetry 611
Center of rotation 611

EXERCISES

1. Consider the following sets of triangles
   T = all triangles S = scalene triangles
   I = isosceles triangles E = equilateral triangles
   Identify all subset relations among these sets. For example scalene triangles are a subset of triangles and this is written as $S \subseteq T$.

2. Consider the following sets of quadrilaterals
   K = kites B = rhombi
   R = rectangles P = parallelograms
   S = squares
   Identify all subset relations among these sets.

3. Describe the lines of symmetry in the following shapes.
   a. An isosceles triangle   **b.** An equilateral triangle
   c. A rectangle   **d.** A square
   e. A rhombus   **f.** A parallelogram
   g. A trapezoid   **h.** An isosceles trapezoid

4. Describe the rotation symmetries in the following shapes (not counting one complete rotation as a symmetry).
   a. An isosceles triangle   **b.** An equilateral triangle
   c. A rectangle   **d.** A square
   e. A rhombus   **f.** A parallelogram
   g. A trapezoid   **h.** An isosceles trapezoid
   i. A regular n-gon

SECTION 12.3 An Introduction to a Formal Approach to Geometry

VOCABULARY/NOTATION

Plane 618
Point, A 618
Line, $\overleftrightarrow{AB}$ 618
Collinear points 618
Parallel lines, $l \parallel m$ 618
Concurrent lines 618
Distance, AB 619
Coordinates 619
Between 619
Line segment, $\overline{AB}$ 619
Endpoints 619
Length 619
Midpoint 619
Equidistant 619
Ray, $\overrightarrow{CD}$ 619
Angle 619

Vertex of an angle 619
Sides of an angle 619
Convex 620
Interior of an angle 620
Exterior of an angle 620
Concave 620
Adjacent angles 620
Protractor 620
Degrees 620
Measure of an angle, $m(\angle ABC)$ 620
Acute angle 620
Right angle 620
Obtuse angle 620
Straight angle 620
Reflex angle 620
Vertical angles 621

Congruent angles 621
Congruent segments 621
Supplementary angles 621
Perpendicular lines, $l \perp m$ 621
Complementary angles 621
Transversal 621
Corresponding angles 621
Alternate interior angles 622
Triangle, $\triangle ABC$ 622
Right triangle 622
Obtuse triangle 622
Acute triangle 622
Bases of a trapezoid 625
Base angles of a trapezoid 625
Opposite angles 625

EXERCISES

1. Distinguish between convex and concave shapes.

2. Describe physical objects that can be used to motivate abstract definitions of the following.
   a. Point   **b.** Ray
   c. Line   **d.** Plane
   e. Line segment   **f.** Angle

3. Show that any two vertical angles are congruent.

4. Using the result in Exercise 3, show how each of the following statements involving parallel lines infers the other.
   i. Corresponding angles are congruent.
   ii. Alternate interior angles are congruent.

5. Draw and cut out a triangular shape. Tear off the three angular regions and arrange them side to side with their vertices on the same point. How does this motivate the result that the sum of the angles in a triangle is 180°?

6. Which of the following shapes have pairs of opposite angles congruent? Explain how paper folding and tracing could be used to justify your conclusions.
   a. Trapezoid   **e.** Rectangle
   b. Isosceles trapezoid   **f.** Square
   c. Parallelogram   **g.** Kite
   d. Rhombus

SECTION 12.4 Regular Polygons, Tessellations, and Circles

VOCABULARY/NOTATION

Simple closed curve　635
Polygon　635
Equilateral polygon　635
Equiangular polygon　635
Regular polygon　635
Regular n-gon　635
Center of a polygon　636

Vertex angle　636
Interior angle　636
Central angle　636
Exterior angle　636
Polygonal region　638
Tessellation　638
Regular tessellation　640

Vertex arrangement　640
Semiregular tessellation　641
Circle　641
Center　641
Radius　641
Diameter　642
Compass　642

EXERCISES

1. Sketch a square with its center and label the following.
   a. All vertex angles　　**b.** All central angles
   c. All exterior angles

2. How is the measure of a central angle in a regular n-gon related to the number of its sides?

3. How is the measure of an exterior angle of a regular n-gon related to the measure of a central angle?

4. Use the results in Exercises 2 and 3 to derive the angle measure of a vertex angle in a regular n-gon.

5. Which regular n-gons tessellate the plane and why?

6. Determine the number of types of symmetries of a circle.
   a. Reflection　　**b.** Rotation

SECTION 12.5 Describing Three-Dimensional Shapes

VOCABULARY/NOTATION

Dihedral angle　653
Faces of a dihedral angle　653
Skew lines　654
Polyhedron (polyhedra)　655
Convex polyhedron　655
Faces　655
Edges　655
Vertices　655
Prisms　656
Bases　656
Lateral faces　656
Right prism　656

Oblique prism　656
Pyramid　656
Apex of a pyramid　656
Right regular pyramid　656
Oblique regular pyramid　656
Regular polyhedron　656
Platonic solids　656
Euler's formula　656
Semiregular polyhedron　657
Cylinder　657
Base of a cylinder　657
Right circular cylinder　657

Oblique cylinder　657
Cone　658
Apex of a cone　658
Base of a cone　658
Right circular cone　658
Oblique circular cone　658
Sphere　658
Center　658
Radius　658
Diameter　658

EXERCISES

1. Give examples of the following (or portion of the following if the item is infinite) in the physical world.
   a. Parallel planes　　　　**b.** Intersecting planes
   c. Three intersecting planes　**d.** A dihedral angle
   e. Skew lines　　　　　　**f.** A polyhedron

2. Describe the Platonic solids.

3. State Euler's formula, and illustrate it with one of the Platonic solids.

4. Give examples of how the following are represented in the physical world.
   a. A right cylinder　　**b.** A right cone
   c. A sphere

CHAPTER TEST
KNOWLEDGE
1. True or false?

   a. Every isosceles triangle is equilateral.
   b. Every rhombus is a kite.
   c. A circle is convex.
   d. Vertical angles have the same measure.
   e. A triangle has at most one right angle or one obtuse angle.
   f. A regular pentagon has five diagonals.
   g. A cube has 6 faces, 8 vertices, and 12 edges.
   h. There are exactly three different regular tessellations each using congruent regular n-gons, where $n = 3$, 4, or 6.
   i. A pyramid has a square base.
   j. Skew lines are the same as parallel lines.
   k. A regular hexagon has exactly three reflection symmetries.
   l. The vertex angle of any regular n-gon has the same measure as any exterior angle of the same n-gon.
   m. A circle has infinitely many rotation symmetries.
   n. It is possible to have a right scalene triangle.

2. In the following figure, identify
   a. a pair of corresponding angles.
   b. a pair of alternate interior angles.

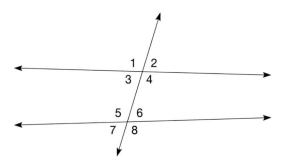

3. Write a precise mathematical definition of a circle.

4. What is the complete name of the following objects?

   (a)   **(b)**

5. Sketch the following. (Please label the sides and angles to emphasize the unique features of the object.)
   a. Obtuse scalene triangle
   b. A trapezoid that is not isosceles

SKILL
6. Explain how to use paper folding to show that the diagonals of a rhombus are perpendicular.

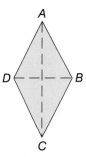

7. Determine the measures of all the dihedral angles of a right prism whose bases are regular octagons.

8. What is the measure of a vertex angle in a regular 10-gon?

9. Determine the number of reflection symmetries a regular 9-gon has. How many rotations less than 360° map a regular 13-gon onto itself?

10. In the following figure, $l \parallel m$. Given the angle measures indicated on the figure, find the measures of the angles identified by a, b, c, d, e, and f.

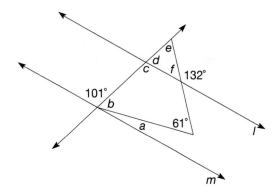

11. Determine the number of faces, vertices, and edges for the hexagonal pyramid shown. Verify Euler's formula for this pyramid.

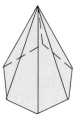

12. Select a letter of the alphabet that has the following properties. Sketch the lines of symmetry and/or describe the angles of rotation.
a. Rotational symmetry but not reflexive symmetry
b. Reflexive but not rotational symmetry
c. Neither reflexive nor rotational symmetry

UNDERSTANDING

13. The corresponding angles property states that $m(\angle 1) = m(\angle 2)$ in the figure. Angles $\angle 3$ and $\angle 4$ are called interior angles on the same side of the transversal. Prove that $m(\angle 3) + m(\angle 4) = 180°$.

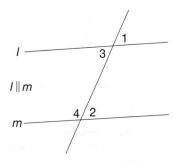

14. Using the result of Problem 13, show that if a parallelogram has one right angle, then the parallelogram must be a rectangle.

15. a. Let one circle represent the set of trapezoids and the other circle represent the set of parallelograms. Which of the following diagrams best represents the relationship between trapezoids and parallelograms?
b. Let one circle represent the set of kites and the other circle represent the set of rectangles. Which of the following diagrams best represents the relationship between kites and rectangles?

i   ii   iii

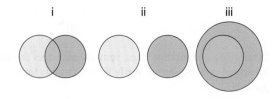

16. The equation for computing the measure of the vertex angle of a regular n-gon can be written as $\frac{(n-2)180}{n}$. Explain how it is derived.

17. Given the top view of a stack of blocks where the numbers indicate how high each stack of blocks is, which of the following pictures represents the same stack?

Top view

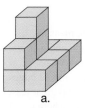

a.   b.

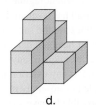

c.   d.

PROBLEM SOLVING/APPLICATION

18. A prism has 96 edges. How many vertices and faces does it have? Explain.

19. Use the figure to show that any convex 7-gon has the sum of its vertex angles equal to 900°.

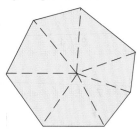

20. Determine whether it is possible to tessellate the plane using only a combination of regular 5-gons and regular 7-gons.

21. We know that squares alone will tessellate the plane. We also know that a combination of squares and regular octagons will tessellate the plane. Explain why these tessellations work but regular octagons alone will not.

22. In the following seven-pointed star, find the sum of the measures of the angles A, B, C, D, E, F, and G.

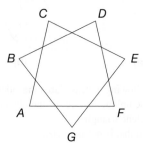

Measurement

CHAPTER

13

FOCUS ON

Archimedes—Mathematical Genius from Antiquity

rchimedes (287–212 B.C.E.) is considered to have been the greatest mathematician in antiquity.

In fact, he is ranked by many with Sir Isaac Newton and Carl Friedrich Gauss as one of the three greatest mathematicians of all time. Perhaps the most famous story about him is that of his discovery of the principle of buoyancy; namely, a body immersed in water is buoyed up by a force equal to the weight of the water displaced. Legend has it that he discovered the buoyancy principle while bathing and was so excited that he ran naked into the street shouting "Eureka!"

In mathematics, Archimedes discovered and verified formulas for the surface area and volume of a sphere.

His method for deriving the volume of a sphere, called the *Archimedean method*, involved a lever principle. He compared a sphere of radius r and a cone of radius $2r$ and height $2r$ to a cylinder also of radius $2r$ and height $2r$. Using cross-sections, Archimedes deduced that the cone and sphere as solids, placed two units from the fulcrum of the lever, would balance the solid cylinder placed one unit from the fulcrum.

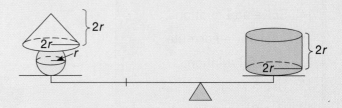

Hence, the volume of the cone plus the volume of the sphere equals $\frac{1}{2}$ the volume of the cylinder. However, the volume of the cone was known to be $\frac{1}{3}$ the volume of the cylinder, so that the volume of the sphere must be $\frac{1}{6}$ the volume of the cylinder. Thus the volume of the sphere is $\frac{1}{6}(8\pi r^3)$, which is $\frac{4}{3}\pi r^3$. The original description of the Archimedean method was thought to be permanently lost until its rediscovery in Constantinople, now Istanbul, in 1906.

Archimedes is credited with anticipating the development of some of the ideas of calculus, nearly 2000 years before its creation by Sir Isaac Newton (1642–1727) and Gottfried Wilhelm Leibniz (1646–1716).

STRATEGY 18

Use Dimensional Analysis

The strategy Use Dimensional Analysis is useful in applied problems that involve conversions among measurement units. For example, distance–rate–time problems or problems involving several rates (ratios) are sometimes easier to analyze via dimensional analysis. Additionally, dimensional analysis allows us to check whether we have reported our answer in the correct measurement units.

INITIAL PROBLEM

David was planning a motorcycle trip across Canada. He drew his route on a map and estimated the length of his route to be 115 centimeters. The scale on his map is 1 centimeter = 39 kilometers. His motorcycle's gasoline consumption averages 75 miles per gallon of gasoline. If gasoline costs $3 per gallon, how much should he plan to spend for gasoline? (Hint: 1 mile is approximately 1.61 kilometers.)

CLUES

The Use Dimensional Analysis strategy may be appropriate when

- Units of measure are involved.
- The problem involves physical quantities.
- Conversions are required.

A solution of this Initial Problem is on page 746.

INTRODUCTION

Figure 13.1

T he measurement process allows us to analyze geometric figures using real numbers. For example, suppose that we use a sphere to model the Earth (Figure 13.1). Then we can ask many questions about the sphere, such as "How far is it around the equator? How much surface area does it have? How much space does it take up?" Questions such as these can lead us to the study of the measurement of length, area, and volume of geometric figures, as well as other attributes. In the first section of this chapter we introduce **holistic measurement**, using natural or **nonstandard units** such as "hands" and "paces." We also study two systems of standard units, namely the English system or customary system of units, which we Americans use, and the metric system, or *Système International* (SI), which virtually all other countries use. In the other sections, we study abstract mathematical measurement of geometric shapes, exploring length, area, surface area, and volume.

> ### Key Concepts from NCTM Curriculum Focal Points

- **PREKINDERGARTEN:** Identifying measurable attributes and comparing objects by using these attributes.
- **GRADE 1:** Composing and decomposing geometric shapes.
- **GRADE 2:** Developing an understanding of linear measurement and facility in measuring lengths.
- **GRADE 4:** Developing an understanding of area and determining the areas of two-dimensional shapes.
- **GRADE 5:** Describing three-dimensional shapes and analyzing their properties, including volume and surface area.
- **GRADE 7:** Developing an understanding of and using formulas to determine surface areas and volumes of three-dimensional shapes.

13.1 MEASUREMENT WITH NONSTANDARD AND STANDARD UNITS

STARTING POINT

When carpet is purchased for a room, a salesman might ask, "How many *yards* do you need?" When ordering concrete to pour a sidewalk, the dispatcher will ask, "How many *yards* do you need?" Are *yards* in both of these situations the same? Explain.

NCTM Standard
All students should recognize the attributes of length, volume, weight, area, and time.

Nonstandard Units

The measurement process is defined as follows.

> ### DEFINITION
>
> #### *The Measurement Process*
>
> 1. Select an object and an attribute of the object to measure, such as its length, area, volume, weight, or temperature.
> 2. Select an appropriate unit with which to measure the attribute.
> 3. Determine the number of units needed to measure the attribute. (This may require a measurement device.)

Children's Literature
www.wiley.com/college/musser
See "How Big Is a Foot?" by
Rolf Myller.

For example, to measure the length of an object, we might see how many times our hand will span the object. Figure 13.2 shows a stick that is four "hand spans" long. "Hands" are still used as a unit to measure the height of horses.

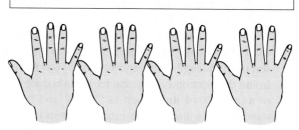

Figure 13.2

For measuring longer distances, we might use the length of our feet placed heel to toe or our pace as our unit of measurement. For shorter distances, we might use the width of a finger as our unit (Figure 13.3). Regardless, in every case, we can select some appropriate unit and determine how many units are needed to span the object. This is an *informal* measurement method of measuring length, since it involves naturally occurring units and is done in a relatively imprecise way.

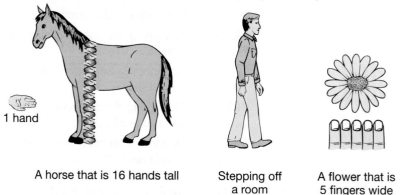

1 hand

A horse that is 16 hands tall   Stepping off a room   A flower that is 5 fingers wide

Figure 13.3

To measure the area of a region informally, we select a convenient two-dimensional shape as our unit and determine how many such units are needed to cover the region. Figure 13.4 shows how to measure the area of a rectangular rug, using square floor tiles as the unit of measure. By counting the number of squares inside the rectangular border, and estimating the fractional parts of the other squares that are partly inside the border, it appears that the area of the rug is between 15 and 16 square units (certainly, between 12 and 20).

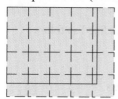

Figure 13.4

To measure the capacity of water that a vase will hold, we can select a convenient container, such as a water glass, to use as our unit and count how many glassfuls are required to fill the vase (see Figure 13.5). This is an informal method of measuring volume. (Strictly speaking, we are measuring the *capacity* of the vase, namely the amount that it will hold. The volume of the vase would be the amount of material

Figure 13.5

Name _____

Hands-On Activity

Nonstandard Units

> I will use nonstandard units, like cubes and paper clips, to measure the pencil.

Get Ready

Main Idea

I will select and use nonstandard units to describe length.

Vocabulary

nonstandard unit

measure

length

You can use different units to **measure length**.

Remember
Line up the end of the pencil with the end of your unit of measure.

The pencil measures

about __6__ cubes long or

about __8__ paper clips long.

✓ Check

Find the object. Select and draw your unit of measure.
Use your unit to measure the object.

1. Unit of measure: _____

   Measurement: about _____

2. **Glue Stick** Unit of measure: _____

   Measurement: about _____

3. **Talk About It** How would your measurement in Exercise 2 be different if you used a smaller unit of measure?

Chapter 12   Lesson 1   three hundred seventy-nine **379**

Copyright © Macmillan/McGraw-Hill, a division of The McGraw-Hill Companies, Inc.

comprising the vase itself.) Other holistic volume measures are found in recipes: a "dash" of hot sauce, a "pinch" of salt, or a "few shakes" of a spice, for example.

Measurement using nonstandard units is adequate for many needs, particularly when accuracy is not essential. However, there are many other circumstances when we need to determine measurements more precisely and communicate them to others. That is, we need standard measurement units as discussed next.

✔ **Check for Understanding:** Exercise/Problem Set A #1–2

Standard Units

The English System   The **English system** of units arose from natural, non-standard units. For example, the foot was literally the length of a human foot and the yard was the distance from the tip of the nose to the end of an outstretched arm (useful in measuring cloth or "yard goods"). The inch was the length of three barley corns, the fathom was the length of a full arm span (for measuring rope), and the acre was the amount of land that a horse could plow in one day (Figure 13.6).

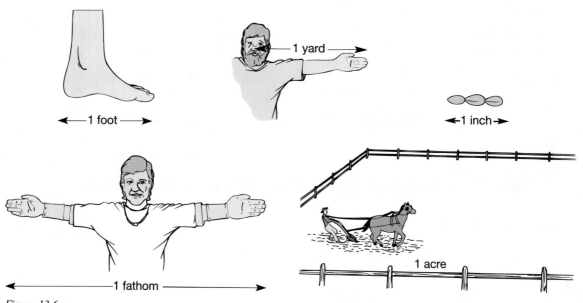

Figure 13.6

NCTM Standard
All students should develop common referents for measures to make comparisons and estimates.

Length   The natural English units were standardized so that the foot was defined by a prototype metal bar, and the inch defined as $\frac{1}{12}$ of a foot, the yard the length of 3 feet, and so on for other lengths (Table 13.1). A variety of ratios occur among the English units of length. For example, the ratio of inches to feet is $12:1$, of feet to yards is $3:1$,

TABLE 13.1

UNIT	FRACTION OR MULTIPLE OF 1 FOOT
Inch	$\frac{1}{12}$ ft
Foot	1 ft
Yard	3 ft
Rod	$16\frac{1}{2}$ ft
Furlong	660 ft
Mile	5280 ft

of yards to rods is $5\frac{1}{2}:1$, and of furlongs to miles is $8:1$. A considerable amount of memorization is needed in learning the English system of measurement.

Area   Area is measured in the English system using the square foot (written ft^2) as the fundamental unit. That is, to measure the area of a region, the number of squares, 1 foot on a side, that are needed to cover the region is determined. This is an application of tessellating the plane with squares (see Chapter 12). Other polygons could, in fact, be used as fundamental units of area. For example, a right triangle, an equilateral triangle, or a regular hexagon could also be used as a fundamental unit of area. For large regions, square yards are used to measure areas, and for very large regions, acres and square miles are used to measure areas. Table 13.2 gives the relationships among various English system units of area. Here again, the ratios between area units are not uniform.

TABLE 13.2

UNIT	MULTIPLE OF 1 SQUARE FOOT
Square inch	1/144 ft^2
Square foot	1 ft^2
Square yard	9 ft^2
Acre	43,560 ft^2
Square mile	27,878,400 ft^2

Example 13.1 shows how to determine some of the entries in Table 13.2. A more general strategy, called dimensional analysis, appears later in this section.

Example 13.1   Compute the ratios square feet : square yards and square feet : square miles.

SOLUTION   Since there are 3 feet in 1 yard and 1 square yard measures 1 yard by 1 yard, we see that there are 9 square feet in 1 square yard [Figure 13.7(a)]. Therefore, the ratio of square feet to square yards is $9:1$.

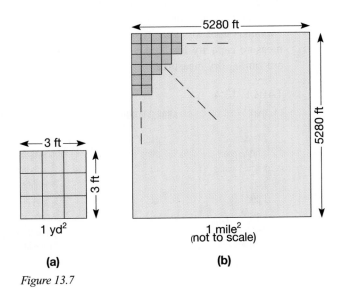

(a)   **(b)**

Figure 13.7

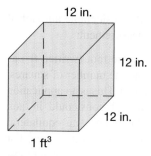

12 in.

12 in.

12 in.

1 ft^3

Figure 13.8

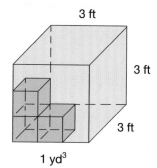

3 ft

3 ft

3 ft

1 yd^3

Figure 13.9

Next imagine covering a square, 1 mile on each side, with square tiles, each 1 foot on a side [Figure 13.7(b)]. It would take an array of square with 5280 rows, each row having 5280 tiles. Hence it would take $5280 \times 5280 = 27{,}878{,}400$ square feet to cover 1 square mile. So the ratio of square feet to square miles is $27{,}878{,}400:1$. ■

Volume In the English system, volume is measured using the cubic foot as the fundamental unit (Figure 13.8). To find the volume of a cubical box that is 3 feet on each side, imagine stacking as many cubic feet inside the box as possible (Figure 13.9). The box could be filled with $3 \times 3 \times 3 = 27$ cubes, each measuring 1 foot on an edge. Each of the smaller cubes has a volume of 1 cubic foot (written ft^3), so that the larger cube has a volume of 27 ft^3. The larger cube is, of course, 1 cubic yard (1 yd^3). It is common for topsoil and concrete to be sold by the cubic yard, for example. In the English system, we have several cubic units used for measuring volume. Table 13.3 shows some relationships among them. Note the variety of volume ratios in the English system.

TABLE 13.3

UNIT	FRACTION OR MULTIPLE OF A CUBIC FOOT
Cubic inch (1 in^3)	1/1728 ft^3
Cubic foot	1 ft^3
Cubic yard (1 yd^3)	27 ft^3

Example 13.2   Verify the ratio of in^3 : ft^3 given in Table 13.3.

SOLUTION Since there are 12 inches in each foot, we could fill a cubic foot with $12 \times 12 \times 12$ smaller cubes, each 1 inch on an edge. Hence there are $12^3 = 1728$ cubic inches in 1 cubic foot. Consequently, each cubic inch is $\frac{1}{1728}$ of a cubic foot. ■

Figure 13.9 shows cubes, one foot on each side, being stacked *inside* the cubic yard to show that the volume of the box is 27 ft^3. If the larger box were a solid, we would still say that its volume is 27 ft^3. Notice that 27 ft^3 of water can be poured into the open box but no water can be poured *into* a solid cube. To distinguish between these two physical situations, we use the words **capacity** (how much the box will hold) and *volume* (how much material makes up the box). Often, however, the word *volume* is used for capacity. The English system uses the units shown in Table 13.4 to measure capacity for liquids. In addition to these liquid measures of capacity, there are similar dry measures.

TABLE 13.4

UNIT	ABBREVIATION	RELATION TO PRECEDING UNIT
1 teaspoon	tsp	
1 tablespoon	tbsp	3 teaspoons
1 liquid ounce	oz	2 tablespoons
1 cup	c	8 liquid ounces
1 pint	pt	2 cups
1 quart	qt	2 pints
1 gallon	gal	4 quarts
1 barrel	bar	31.5 gallons

Weight In the English system, weight is measured in pounds and ounces. In fact, there are two types of measures of weight—troy ounces and pounds (mainly for precious metals), and avoirdupois ounces and pounds, the latter being more common. We will use the avoirdupois units. The weight of 2000 pounds is 1 English ton. Smaller weights are measured in drams and grains. Table 13.5 summarizes these English system units of weight. Notice how inconsistent the ratios are between consecutive units.

TABLE 13.5 English System Units of Weight (Avoirdupois)

UNIT	RELATION TO PRECEDING UNIT
1 grain	
1 dram	$27\frac{11}{32}$ grains
1 ounce	16 drams
1 pound	16 ounces
1 ton	2000 pounds

Technically, the concepts of weight and mass are different. Informally, mass is the measure of the amount of matter of an object and weight is a measure of the force with which gravity attracts the object. Thus, although your mass is the same on Earth and on the Moon, you weigh more on Earth because the attraction of gravity is greater on Earth. We will not make a distinction between weight and mass. We will use English units of weight and metric units of mass, both of which are used to weigh objects.

Temperature Temperature is measured in **degrees Fahrenheit** in the English system. The Fahrenheit temperature scale is named for Gabriel Fahrenheit, a German instrument maker, who invented the mercury thermometer in 1714. The freezing point and boiling point of water are used as reference temperatures. The freezing point is arbitrarily defined to be 32° Fahrenheit, and the boiling point 212° Fahrenheit. This gives an interval of exactly 180° from freezing to boiling (Figure 13.10).

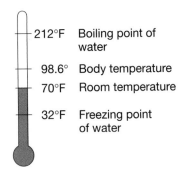

212°F Boiling point of water

98.6° Body temperature

70°F Room temperature

32°F Freezing point of water

Figure 13.10

The Metric System In contrast to the English system of measurement units, the **metric system** of units (or Système International d'Unités) incorporates all of the following features of an ideal system of units.

An Ideal System of Units

1. The fundamental unit can be accurately reproduced without reference to a prototype. (Portability)
2. There are simple (e.g., decimal) ratios among units of the same type. (Convertibility)
3. Different types of units (e.g., those for length, area, and volume) are defined in terms of each other, using simple relationships. (Interrelatedness)

Length In the metric system, the fundamental unit of length is the **meter** (about $39\frac{1}{2}$ inches). The meter was originally defined to be one ten-millionth of the distance from the equator to the North Pole along the Greenwich-through-Paris meridian. A prototype platinum-iridium bar representing a meter was maintained in the International Bureau of Weights and Measures in France. However, as science advanced, this definition was changed so that the meter could be reproduced anywhere in the world. Since 1960, the meter has been defined to be precisely 1,650,763.73 wavelengths of orange-red light in the spectrum of the element krypton 86. Although this definition may seem highly technical, it has the advantage of being reproducible in a laboratory anywhere. That is, no standard meter prototype need be kept. This is a clear advantage over older versions of the English system. We shall see that there are many more.

The metric system is a decimal system of measurement in which multiples and fractions of the fundamental unit correspond to powers of ten. For example, one thousand meters is a **kilometer**, one-tenth of a meter is a **decimeter**, one-hundredth of a meter is a **centimeter**, and one-thousandth of a meter is a **millimeter**. Table 13.6 shows some relationship among metric units of length. Notice the simple ratios among units of length in the metric system. (Compare Table 13.6 to Table 13.1 for the English system, for example.) From Table 13.6 we see that 1 **dekameter** is equivalent to 10 meters, 1 **hectometer** is equivalent to 100 meters, and so on. Also, 1 dekameter is equivalent to 100 decimeters, 1 kilometer is equivalent to 1,000,000 millimeters, and so on. (Check these.)

TABLE 13.6

UNIT	SYMBOL	FRACTION OR MULTIPLE OF 1 METER
1 millimeter	1 mm	0.001 m
1 centimeter	1 cm	0.01 m
1 decimeter	1 dm	0.1 m
1 meter	1 m	1 m
1 dekameter	1 dam	10 m
1 hectometer	1 hm	100 m
1 kilometer	1 km	1000 m

From the information in Table 13.6, we can make a metric "converter" diagram to simplify changing units of length. Locate consecutive metric abbreviations for units of length starting with the largest prefix on the left (Figure 13.11). To convert from, say, hectometers to centimeters, count spaces from "hm" to "cm" in the diagram, and move the decimal point in the same direction as many spaces as are indicated in the diagram (here, four to the right). For example, 13.23685 hm = 132,368.5 cm. Similarly, 4326.9 mm = 4.3269 m, since we move three spaces to the left in the diagram when going from "mm" to "m." It is good practice to use measurement sense as a check. For example, when converting from mm to hm, we have fewer "hm's" than "mm's," since 1 hm is longer than 1 mm.

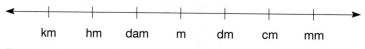

Figure 13.11

Figure 13.12 shows *relative* comparisons of lengths in English and metric systems. Lengths that are measured in feet or yards in the English system are commonly measured in meters in the metric system. Lengths measured in inches in the English system are measured in centimeters in the metric system. (By definition, 1 in. is exactly 2.54 cm.) For example, in metric countries, track and field events use meters instead of yards for the lengths of races. Snowfall is measured in centimeters in metric countries, not inches.

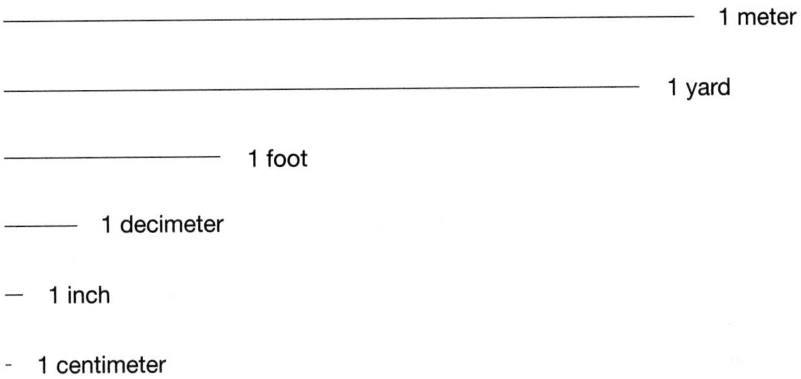

——————————————————————————————————————— 1 meter

——————————————————————————————— 1 yard

——————————————— 1 foot

——————— 1 decimeter

— 1 inch

- 1 centimeter

Figure 13.12

From Table 13.6 we see that certain prefixes are used in the metric system to indicate fractions or multiples of the fundamental unit. Table 13.7 gives the meanings of many of the metric prefixes. The three most commonly used prefixes are in italics. We will see that these prefixes are also used with measures of area, volume, and weight. Compare the descriptions of the prefixes in Table 13.7 with their uses in Table 13.6. Notice how the prefixes signify the ratios to the fundamental unit.

TABLE 13.7

PREFIX	MULTIPLE OR FRACTION	
atto-	10^{-18}	Science
femto-	10^{-15}	
pico-	10^{-12}	
nano-	10^{-9}	
micro-	10^{-6}	
milli-	$10^{-3} = \frac{1}{1000}$	Everyday life
centi-	$10^{-2} = \frac{1}{100}$	
deci-	$10^{-1} = \frac{1}{10}$	
deka-	10	
hecto-	$10^2 = 100$	
kilo-	$10^3 = 1000$	
mega-	10^6	Science
giga-	10^9	
tera-	10^{12}	
peta-	10^{15}	
exa-	10^{18}	

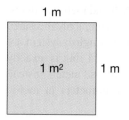

1 m

1 m²   1 m

Figure 13.13

Area In the metric system, the fundamental unit of area is the square meter. A square that is 1 meter long on each side has an area of **1 square meter**, written 1 m² (Figure 13.13). Areas measured in square feet or square yards in the English system are measured in square meters in the metric system. For example, carpeting would be measured in square meters.

Smaller areas are measured in square centimeters. A **square centimeter** is the area of a square that is 1 centimeter long on each side. For example, the area of a piece of notebook paper or a photograph would be measured in square centimeters (cm²). Example 13.3 shows the relationship between square centimeters and square meters.

Example 13.3   Determine the number of square centimeters in 1 square meter.

SOLUTION A square with area 1 square meter can be covered with an array of square centimeters. In Figure 13.14 we see part of the array.

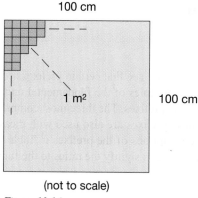

100 cm

1 m²   100 cm

(not to scale)

Figure 13.14

There are 100 rows, each row having 100 square centimeters. Hence there are 100 × 100 = 10 000 square centimeters needed to cover the square meter. Thus 1 m² = 10 000 cm². (NOTE: Spaces are used instead of commas to show groupings in large numbers.) ∎

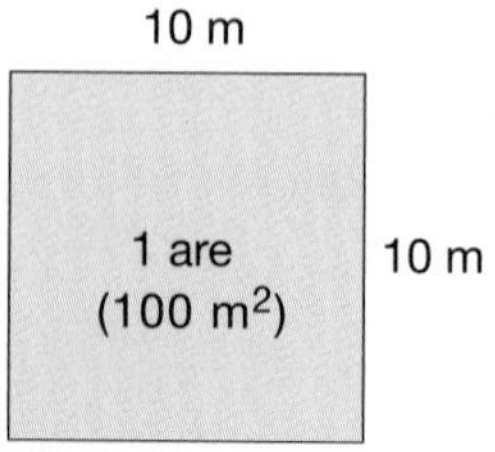

10 m

1 are
(100 m²)   10 m

Figure 13.15

Very small areas, such as on a microscope slide, are measured using square millimeters. A **square millimeter** is the area of a square whose sides are each 1 millimeter long.

In the metric system, the area of a square that is 10 m on each side is given the special name **are** (pronounced "air"). Figure 13.15 illustrates this definition. An are is approximately the area of the floor of a large two-car garage and is a convenient unit for measuring the area of building lots. There are 100 m² in 1 are.

An area equivalent to 100 ares is called a **hectare**, written 1 ha. Notice the use of the prefix "hect" (meaning 100). The hectare is useful for measuring areas of farms and ranches. We can show that 1 hectare is 1 square hectometer by converting each to square meters, as follows.

$$1 \text{ ha} = 100 \text{ ares} = 100 \times (100 \text{ m}^2) = 10\ 000 \text{ m}^2$$

NCTM Standard
All students should carry out simple unit conversions such as centimeters to meters, within a system of measurement.

Also,

$$1 \text{ hm}^2 = (100 \text{ m}) \times (100 \text{ m}) = 10\ 000 \text{ m}^2.$$

Thus 1 ha = 1 hm^2.

Finally, very large areas are measured in the metric system using square kilometers. One **square kilometer** is the area of a square that is 1 kilometer on each side. Areas of cities or states, for example, are reported in square kilometers. Table 13.8 gives the ratios among various units of area in the metric system. See if you can verify the entries in the table.

TABLE 13.8

UNIT	ABBREVIATION	FRACTION OR MULTIPLE OF 1 SQUARE METER
Square millimeter	mm^2	0.000001 m^2
Square centimeter	cm^2	0.0001 m^2
Square decimeter	dm^2	0.01 m^2
Square meter	m^2	1 m^2
Are (square dekameter)	a (dam^2)	100 m^2
Hectare (square hectometer)	ha (hm^2)	10 000 m^2
Square kilometer	km^2	1 000 000 m^2

From Table 13.8, we see that the metric prefixes for square units should *not* be interpreted in the abbreviated forms as having the same meanings as with linear units. For example, 1 dm^2 is not one-tenth of 1 m^2; rather, 1 dm^2 is one-hundredth of 1 m^2. Conversions among units of area can be done if we use the metric converter in Figure 13.16 but move the decimal point *twice* the number of spaces that we move between units. This is due to the fact that area involves *two* dimensions. For example, suppose that we wish to convert 3.7 m^2 to mm^2. From Figure 13.16, we move three spaces to the right from "m" to "mm," so we will move the decimal point $3 \cdot 2 = 6$ (the "2" is due to the *two* dimensions) places to the right. Thus 3.7 m^2 = 3 700 000 mm^2. Since 1 m^2 = $(1000 \text{ mm})^2$ = 1 000 000 mm^2, we have 3.7 m^2 = $3.7 \times (1\ 000\ 000)$ mm^2 = 3 700 000 mm^2, which is the same result that we obtained using the metric converter.

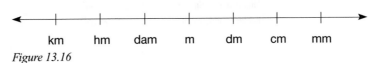

km   hm   dam   m   dm   cm   mm

Figure 13.16

Volume The fundamental unit of volume in the metric system is the liter. A **liter**, abbreviated L, is the volume of a cube that measures 10 cm on each edge (Figure 13.17). We can also say that a liter is 1 **cubic decimeter**, since the cube in Figure 13.17 measures 1 dm on each edge. Notice that the liter is defined with reference to the meter, which is the fundamental unit of length. The liter is slightly larger than a quart. Many soft-drink containers have capacities of 1 or 2 liters.

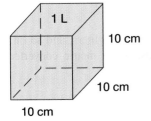

Figure 13.17

Imagine filling the liter cube in Figure 13.17 with smaller cubes, 1 centimeter on each edge. Figure 13.18 illustrates this. Each small cube has a volume of 1 **cubic centimeter** (1 cm³). It will take a 10 × 10 array (hence 100) of the centimeter cubes to cover the bottom of the liter cube. Finally, it takes 10 layers, each with 100 centimeter cubes, to fill the liter cube to the top. Thus 1 liter is equivalent to 1000 cm³. Recall that the prefix "milli-" in the metric system means one-thousandth. Thus we see that 1 **milliliter** is equivalent to 1 cubic centimeter, since there are 1000 cm³ in 1 liter. Small volumes in the metric system are measured in milliliters (cubic centimeters). Containers of liquid are frequently labeled in milliliters.

NCTM Standard

All students should understand such attributes as length, area, weight, volume, and size of angle and select the appropriate type of unit for measuring each attribute.

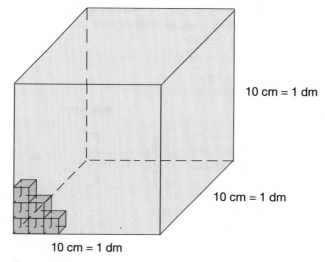

10 cm = 1 dm
10 cm = 1 dm
10 cm = 1 dm

Figure 13.18

Large volumes in the metric system are measured using cubic meters. A **cubic meter** is the volume of a cube that measures 1 meter on each edge (Figure 13.19). Capacities of large containers such as water tanks, reservoirs, or swimming pools are measured using cubic meters. A cubic meter is also called a **kiloliter**. Table 13.9 gives the relationships among commonly used volume units in the metric system.

1 m³
1 m
1 m
1 m

Figure 13.19

TABLE 13.9

UNIT	ABBREVIATION	FRACTION OR MULTIPLE OF 1 LITER
Milliliter (cubic centimeter)	mL (cm³)	0.001 L
Liter (cubic decimeter)	L (dm³)	1 L
Kiloliter (cubic meter)	kL (m³)	1000 L

In the metric system, capacity is usually recorded in liters, milliliters, and so on. We can make conversions among metric volume units using the metric converter (Figure 13.20).

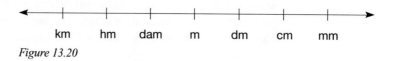

km   hm   dam   m   dm   cm   mm

Figure 13.20

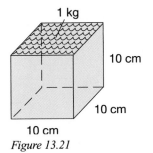

Figure 13.21

To convert among volume units, we count the number of spaces that we move left or right in going from one unit to another. Then we move the decimal point exactly *three* times that number of places, since volume involves three dimensions. For example, in converting 187.68 cm³ to m³, we count two spaces to the left in Figure 13.20 (from cm to m). Then we move the decimal point 2 · 3 = 6 (the "3" is due to *three* dimensions) places to the left, so that 187.68 cm³ = 0.00018768 m³.

Mass   In the metric system, a basic unit of mass is the kilogram. One **kilogram** is the mass of 1 liter of water in its densest state. (Water expands and contracts somewhat when heated or cooled.) A kilogram is about 2.2 pounds in the English system. Notice that the kilogram is defined with reference to the liter, which in turn was defined relative to the meter. Figure 13.21 shows a liter container filled with water, hence a mass of 1 kilogram (1 kg). This illustrates the interrelatedness of the metric units meter, liter, and kilogram.

From the information in Table 13.9, we can conclude that 1 milliliter of water weighs $\frac{1}{1000}$ of a kilogram. This weight is called a **gram**. Grams are used for small weights in the metric system, such as ingredients in recipes or nutritional contents of various foods. Many foods are packaged and labeled by grams. About 28 grams are equivalent to 1 ounce in the English system.

We can summarize the information in Table 13.9 with the definitions of the various metric weights in the following way. In the metric system, there are three basic cubes: the cubic centimeter, the cubic decimeter, and the cubic meter (Figure 13.22).

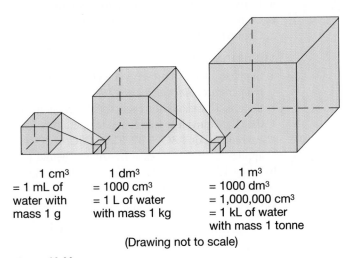

1 cm³	1 dm³	1 m³
= 1 mL of water with mass 1 g	= 1000 cm³ = 1 L of water with mass 1 kg	= 1000 dm³ = 1,000,000 cm³ = 1 kL of water with mass 1 tonne

(Drawing not to scale)

Figure 13.22

TABLE 13.10

CUBE	VOLUME	MASS (WATER)
1 m³	1 kL	1 tonne
1 dm³	1 L	1 kg
1 cm³	1 mL	1 g

The cubic centimeter is equivalent in volume to 1 milliliter, and, if water, it weighs 1 gram. Similarly, 1 cubic decimeter of volume is 1 liter and, if water, weighs 1 kilogram. Finally, 1 cubic meter of volume is 1 kiloliter and, if water, weighs 1000 kilograms, called a **metric ton** (tonne). Table 13.10 summarizes these relationships.

Temperature   In the metric system, temperature is measured in **degrees Celsius**. The Celsius scale is named after the Swedish astronomer Anders Celsius, who devised it in 1742. This scale was originally called "centigrade." Two reference temperatures are used, the freezing point of water and the boiling point of water. These are defined to be, respectively, zero degrees Celsius (0°C) and 100 degrees Celsius (100°C). A metric thermometer is made by dividing the interval from freezing to boiling into

100 degrees Celsius. Figure 13.23 shows a metric thermometer and some useful metric temperatures.

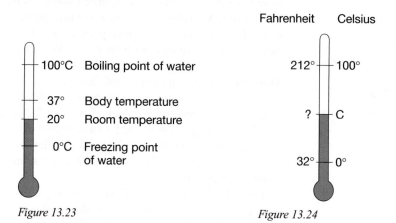

Figure 13.23   *Figure 13.24*

The relationship between degrees Celsius and degrees Fahrenheit (used in the English system) is derived next.

Example 13.4

a. Derive a conversion formula for degrees Celsius to degrees Fahrenheit.
b. Convert 37°C to degrees Fahrenheit.
c. Convert 68°F to degrees Celsius.

SOLUTION

a. Suppose that C represents a Celsius temperature and F the equivalent Fahrenheit temperature. *Since there are 100° Celsius for each 180° Fahrenheit* (Figure 13.24), there is 1° Celsius for each 1.8° Fahrenheit. If C is a temperature above freezing, then the equivalent Fahrenheit temperature, F, is 1.8C degrees Fahrenheit above 32° Fahrenheit, or 1.8C + 32. Thus 1.8C + 32 = F is the desired formula. (This also applies to temperatures at freezing or below, hence to all temperatures.)
b. Using 1.8C + 32 = F, we have 1.8(37) + 32 = 98.6° Fahrenheit, which is normal human body temperature.
c. Using 1.8C + 32 = F and solving C, we find $C = \dfrac{F - 32}{1.8}$. Hence room temperature of 68° Fahrenheit is equivalent to $C = \dfrac{68 - 32}{1.8} = 20°$ Celsius.   ∎

Water is densest at 4°C. Therefore, the precise definition of the kilogram is the mass of 1 liter of water at 4°C.

From the preceding discussion, we see that the metric system has all of the features of an ideal system of units: portability, convertibility, and interrelatedness. These features make learning the metric system simpler than learning the English system of units. The metric system is the preferred system in science and commerce throughout the world. Moreover, only a handful of countries use a system other than the metric system.

✔ **Check for Understanding:** Exercise/Problem Set A #3–18

Dimensional Analysis

When working with two (or more) systems of measurement, there are many circumstances requiring conversions among units. The procedure known as dimensional analysis can help simplify the conversion. In **dimensional analysis**, we use unit ratios that are equivalent to 1 and treat these ratios as fractions. For example, suppose that we wish to convert 17 feet to inches. We use the unit ratio 12 in./1 ft (which is 1) to perform the conversion.

$$17 \text{ ft} = 17 \cancel{\text{ ft}} \times \frac{12 \text{ in.}}{1 \cancel{\text{ ft}}}$$
$$= 17 \times 12 \text{ in.}$$
$$= 204 \text{ in.}$$

Hence, a length of 17 ft is the same as 204 inches. Dimensional analysis is especially useful if several conversions must be made. Example 13.5 provides an illustration.

| **Example 13.5** | A vase holds 4286 grams of water. What is its capacity in liters? |

Problem Solving Strategy
Use Dimensional Analysis

SOLUTION Since 1 mL of water weighs 1 g and 1 L = 1000 mL, we have

$$4286\text{g} = 4286\cancel{\text{g}} \times \frac{1\cancel{\text{mL}}}{1\cancel{\text{g}}} \times \frac{1 \text{ L}}{1000 \cancel{\text{mL}}}$$
$$= \frac{4286}{1000}\text{L} = 4.286 \text{ L}.$$

NCTM Standard
All students should compare and order objects by attributes of length, volume, weight, area, and time.

Consequently, the capacity of the vase is 4.286 liters.   ∎

In Example 13.6 we see a more complicated application of dimensional analysis. Notice that treating the ratios as fractions allows us to use multiplication of fractions. Thus we can be sure that our answer has the proper units.

| **Example 13.6** | The area of a rectangular lot is 25,375 ft². What is the area of the lot in acres? Use the fact that 640 acres = 1 |

square mile.

SOLUTION We wish to convert from square feet to acres. Since 1 mile = 5280 ft, we can convert from square feet to square miles. That is, 1 mile² = 5280 ft × 5280 ft = 27,878,400 ft². Hence

$$25,375 \text{ ft}^2 = 25,375 \cancel{\text{ ft}^2} \times \frac{1 \cancel{\text{mile}^2}}{27,878,400 \cancel{\text{ ft}^2}} \times \frac{640 \text{ acres}}{1 \cancel{\text{mile}^2}}$$
$$= \frac{25,375 \times 640}{27,878,400}\text{acres} = 0.58 \text{ acre (to two places).}   ∎$$

Example 13.7 shows how to make conversions between English and metric system units. We do not advocate memorizing such conversion ratios, since rough approximations serve in most circumstances. However, there are occasions when accuracy is needed. In fact, the English system units are now legally defined *in terms* of metric system units. Recall that the basic conversion ratio for lengths is 1 inch : 2.54 centimeters, exactly.

Example 13.7 A pole vaulter vaulted 19 ft $4\frac{1}{2}$ in. Find the height in meters.

SOLUTION Since 1 meter is a little longer than 1 yard and the vault is about 6 yards, we estimate the vault to be 6 meters. Actually,

$$19 \text{ ft } 4\frac{1}{2} \text{ in.} = 232.5 \text{ in.}$$

$$= 232.5 \text{ in.} \times \frac{2.54 \text{ cm}}{1 \text{ in.}} \times \frac{1 \text{ m}}{100 \text{ cm}}$$

$$= \frac{232.5 \times 2.54}{100} \text{m} = 5.9055 \text{ m.} \qquad \blacksquare$$

Algebraic Reasoning
The understanding of algebraic simplifications such as
$$\frac{3}{3} = \frac{x}{x} = \frac{ft.}{ft.} = 1 \text{ (when } x \neq 0 \text{) is}$$
critical to being able to effectively use dimensional analysis.

Our final example illustrates how we can make conversions involving different types of units, here distance and time.

Problem Solving Strategy
Use Dimensional Analysis

Example 13.8 Suppose that a bullet train is traveling 200 mph. How many feet per second is it traveling?

SOLUTION

$$200\frac{\text{mi}}{\text{hr}} \cdot \frac{5280 \text{ ft}}{1 \text{ mi}} \cdot \frac{1 \text{ hr}}{3600 \text{ sec}} = 293\frac{1}{3} \text{ ft/sec.} \qquad \blacksquare$$

 Check for Understanding: Exercise/Problem Set A #19–22

MATHEMATICAL MORSEL

In 1958, fraternity pledges at M.I.T. (where "Math Is Truth") were ordered to measure the length of Harvard Bridge—not in feet or meters, but in "Smoots," one Smoot being the height of their 5-foot 7-inch classmate, Oliver Smoot. Handling him like a ruler, the pledges found the bridge to be precisely 364.4 Smoots long. Thus began a tradition: The bridge has been faithfully. "re-Smooted" each year since, and its new sidewalk is permanently scored in 10-Smoot intervals. Oliver Smoot went on to become an executive with a trade group in Washington, D.C.

Section 13.1 EXERCISE / PROBLEM SET A

EXERCISES

1. Measure the length, width, and height of this textbook using the following items.
   a. Paper clip
   b. Stick of gum
   c. Will your results for parts a and b be the same as your classmates? Explain.

2. In your elementary classroom, you find the following objects. For each object, list attributes that could be measured and how you could measure them.
   a. A student's chair **b.** A wastebasket
   c. A bulletin board **d.** An aquarium

3. Calculate the following.
   a. How many inches in a mile?
   b. How many yards in a mile?
   c. How many square yards in 43,560 square feet?
   d. How many cubic inches in a cubic yard?
   e. How many ounces in 500 pounds?
   f. How many cups in a quart?
   g. How many cups in a gallon?
   h. How many tablespoons in a cup?

4. In the grid below fill in the empty cells so all of the values on the same row are equal.

Inches	Feet	Yards	Miles
12,672			
	66		
		3080	
			3.4

5. In the grid below fill in the empty cells so all of the values on the same row are equal.

Ounce	Pound	Ton
48		
	7	
		3

6. Choose the most realistic measures of the following objects.
   a. The length of a small paper clip: 28 mm, 28 cm, or 28 m?
   b. The height of a 12-year-old boy: 48 mm, 148 cm, or 48 m?
   c. The length of a shoe: 27 mm, 27 cm, or 27 m?

7. Choose the most realistic measures of the volume of the following objects.
   a. A juice container: 900 mL, 900 cL, or 900 L?
   b. A tablespoon: 15 mL, 15 cL, or 15 L?
   c. A pop bottle: 473 mL, 473 cL, or 473 L?

8. Choose the most realistic measures of the mass of the following objects.
   a. A 6-year-old boy: 23 mg, 23 g, or 23 kg?
   b. A pencil: 10 mg, 10 g, or 10 kg?
   c. An eyelash: 305 mg, 305 g, or 305 kg?

9. Choose the best estimate for the following temperatures.
   a. The water temperature for swimming: 22°C, 39°C, or 80°C?
   b. A glass of lemonade: 10°C, 5°C, or 40°C?

10. The metric prefixes are also used with measurement of time. If "second" is the fundamental unit of time, what multiple or fraction of a second are the following measurements?
    a. Megasecond   b. Millisecond
    c. Microsecond   d. Kilosecond
    e. Centisecond   f. Picosecond

11. Using the meanings of the metric prefixes, how do the following units compare to a meter? If it exists, give an equivalent name.
    a. "Kilomegameter"   b. "Hectodekameter"
    c. "Millimillimicrometer"   d. "Megananometer"

12. Use the metric converter to complete the following statements.

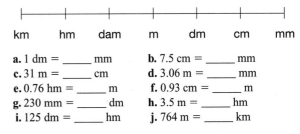

km   hm   dam   m   dm   cm   mm

   a. 1 dm = _____ mm   b. 7.5 cm = _____ mm
   c. 31 m = _____ cm   d. 3.06 m = _____ mm
   e. 0.76 hm = _____ m   f. 0.93 cm = _____ m
   g. 230 mm = _____ dm   h. 3.5 m = _____ hm
   i. 125 dm = _____ hm   j. 764 m = _____ km

13. Use the metric converter to complete the following statements.
    a. 1 cm^2 = _____ mm^2 b. 610 dam^2 = _____ hm^2
    c. 564 m^2 = _____ km^2 d. 821 dm^2 = _____ m^2
    e. 0.382 km^2 = _____ m^2 f. 9.5 dm^2 = _____ cm^2
    g. $6\,540\,000 \text{ m}^2$ = _____ km^2 h. 9610 mm^2 = _____ m^2

14. Use the metric converter to answer the following questions.
    a. One cubic meter contains how many cubic decimeters?
    b. Based on your answer in part (a), how do we move the decimal point for each step to the right on the metric converter?
    c. How should we move the decimal point for each step left?

15. Using a metric converter if necessary, convert the following measurements of mass.
    a. 95 mg = _____ cg
    b. 7 kg = _____ g
    c. 940 mg = _____ g

16. Convert the following measures of capacity.
    a. 5 L = _____ cL
    b. 53 L = _____ daL
    c. 4.6 L = _____ mL

17. A container holds water at its densest state. Give the missing numbers or missing units in the following table.

	VOLUME	CAPACITY	MASS
a.	$? \text{ cm}^3$	34 mL	34 g
b.	$? \text{ dm}^3$	? L	18 kg
c.	23 cm^3	23 ?	23 g

18. Convert the following (to the nearest degree).
    a. Moderate oven (350°F) to degrees Celsius
    b. A spring day (60°F) to degrees Celsius
    c. 20°C to degrees Fahrenheit
    d. Ice-skating weather (0°F) to degrees Celsius
    e. −5°C to degrees Fahrenheit

19. By using dimensional analysis, make the following conversions.
   a. 3.6 lb to oz
   b. 55 mi/hr to ft/min
   c. 35 mi/hr to in./sec
   d. $575 per day to dollars per minute

20. Prior to conversion to a decimal monetary system, the United Kingdom used the following coins.

   1 pound = 20 shillings   1 penny = 2 half-pennies
   1 shilling = 12 pence   1 penny = 4 farthings

   (Pence is the plural of penny.)

   a. How many pence were there in a pound?
   b. How many half-pennies in a pound?

21. One inch is defined to be exactly 2.54 cm. Using this ratio, convert the following measurements.
   a. 6-inch snowfall to cm
   b. 100-yard football field to m

22. In performing a dimensional analysis problem, a student does the following:

$$22 \text{ ft} = 22 \text{ ft} \times \frac{1 \text{ ft}}{12 \text{ in.}} = \frac{22}{12} \text{in.} = 1.83 \text{ in.}$$

   a. What has the student done wrong?
   b. How would you explain to the student a way of checking that units are correct?

PROBLEMS

23. A gallon of water weighs about 8.3 pounds. A cubic foot of water weighs about 62 pounds. How many gallons of water (to one decimal place) would fill a cubic foot container?

24. An adult male weighing about 70 kg has a red blood cell count of about 5.4×10^6 cells per microliter of blood and a blood volume of approximately 5 liters. Determine the approximate number of red blood cells in the body of an adult male.

25. The density of a substance is the ratio of its mass to its volume:

$$\text{Density} = \frac{\text{mass}}{\text{volume}}.$$

   Density is usually expressed in terms of grams per cubic centimeter (g/cm^3). For example, the density of copper is 8.94 g/cm^3.
   a. Express the density of copper in kg/dm^3.
   b. A chunk of oak firewood weighs about 2.85 kg and has a volume of 4100 cm^3. Determine the density of oak in g/cm^3, rounding to the nearest thousandth.
   c. A piece of iron weighs 45 ounces and has a volume of 10 in^3. Determine the density of iron in g/cm^3, rounding to the nearest tenth.

26. The features of portability, convertibility, and interrelatedness were described as features of an ideal measurement system. Through an example, explain why the English system has none of these features.

27. Light travels 186,282 miles per second.
   a. Based on a 365-day year, how far in miles will light travel in one year? This unit of *distance* is called a **light-year**.
   b. If a star in Andromeda is 76 light-years away from Earth, how many miles will light from the star travel on its way to Earth?

   c. The planet Jupiter is approximately 480,000,000 miles from the sun. How long does it take for light to travel from the sun to Jupiter?

28. A train moving 50 miles per hour meets and passes a train moving 50 miles per hour in the opposite direction. A passenger in the first train sees the second train pass in 5 seconds. How long is the second train?

29. a. If 1 inch of rainfall fell over 1 acre of ground, how many cubic inches of water would that be? How many cubic feet?
   b. If 1 cubic foot of water weighs approximately 62 pounds, what is the weight of a uniform coating of 1 inch of rain over 1 acre of ground?
   c. The weight of 1 gallon of water is about 8.3 pounds. A rainfall of 1 inch over 1 acre of ground means about how many gallons of water?

30. A ruler has marks placed at every unit. For example, an 8-unit ruler has a length of 8 and has seven marks on it to designate the unit lengths.

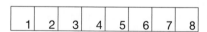

   This ruler provides three direct ways to measure a length of 6; from the left end to the 6 mark, from the 1 mark to the 7 mark, and from the 2 to the 8.
   a. Show how all lengths from 1 through 8 can be measured using only the marks at 1, 4, and 6.
   b. Using a blank ruler 9 units in length, what is the fewest number of marks necessary to be able to measure lengths from 1 to 10 units? How would marks be placed on the ruler?
   c. Repeat for a ruler 10 units in length.

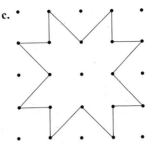

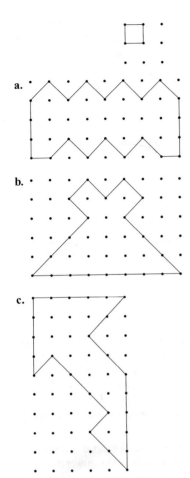

a.

b.

c.

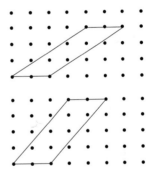

c.

13. How many pieces of square floor tile, 1 foot on a side, would you have to buy to tile a floor that is 11 feet 6 inches by 8 feet?

14. Use Hero's formula to find the area of the triangle whose sides are given (round to one decimal place).
   a. 4 km, 5 km, 8 km
   b. 8 m, 15 m, 17 m

15. Find the area of the triangle in Set B Exercise 7.

16. Find the area of the parallelogram in Set B Exercise 8.

17. Shown are corresponding parallelograms with sides the same length.

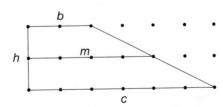

d. Verify your results from parts (a), (b), and (c) by using the Chapter 13 eManipulative activity *Geoboard* on our Web site. Which region has the largest area? by how much?

12. Using the triangular unit shown as the fundamental area unit, find the area of the following figures.

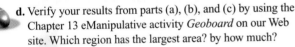

a. For each of the parallelograms shown, use the Chapter 13 eManipulative activity *Geoboard* on our Web site to determine the lengths of the sides and the area of the parallelograms.
b. Based on what you found in part (a), how would you respond to the statement "The area of a parallelogram is the product of the lengths of its sides"?

18. A trapezoid is pictured here.

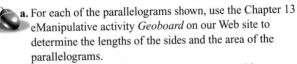

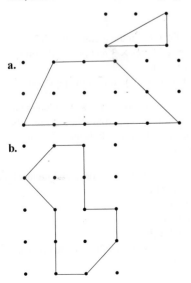

a. Part of the area formula for a trapezoid is $\frac{1}{2}(b + c)$, the average of the two parallel sides. Find $\frac{1}{2}(b + c)$ for this trapezoid.
b. The segment pictured with length m is called the **midsegment** of the trapezoid because it connects midpoints of the nonparallel sides. Find m.
c. How do the results of parts (a) and (b) compare?

19. a. A trapezoid is illustrated on a square lattice. What is its area?

b. If all dimensions of the trapezoid are tripled, what is the area of the resulting trapezoid?

c. If the ratio of lengths of sides of two trapezoids is $1:3$, what is the ratio of the areas of the trapezoids?

20. Information is given about a circle in Set B Exercise 9. Fill in the missing entries of the table. r = radius, d = diameter, A = area. Use a calculator and give answers to two decimal places.

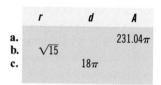

	r	d	A
a.			231.04π
b.	$\sqrt{15}$		
c.		18π	

21. Find the area of each rhombus.

a.

b.

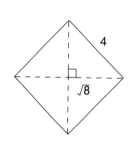

22. Represent the following lengths on a square lattice.

  a. $\sqrt{5}$ **b.** $\sqrt{17}$

  c. $\sqrt{18}$ **d.** $\sqrt{29}$

23. Find the length of the side not given.

  a.   **b.**

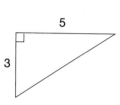 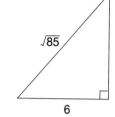

24. Use the triangle inequality to determine which of the following sets of lengths could be used to build a triangle.

  a. $x = \sqrt{50}, y = 3.47, z = 4.28$

  b. $x = 9, y = 9, z = 9$

  c. $x = 1, y = 7, z = 6$

 25. Use the Chapter 13 Geometer's Sketchpad® activity *Same Base, Same Height, Same Area* on our Web site to find an acute, obtuse, and right triangle with the same area.

  a. Sketch the triangles on your paper.

  b. Do they have the same perimeters?

  c. How do the areas and perimeters of these triangles appear to be related?

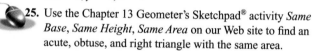 **26.** Use the Chapter 13 Geometer's Sketchpad® activity *Parallelogram Area* on our Web site to answer the question, "Does a larger perimeter always yield a larger area?" Explain your findings.

PROBLEMS

27. a. In building roofs, it is common for each 12 feet of horizontal distance to rise 5 feet in vertical distance. Why might this be more common than a roof that rises 6 feet for each 12 feet? (Consider distance measured along the roof.)

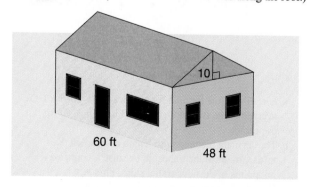

b. Find the area of the roof on the pictured building.

c. How many sheets of 4 feet × 3 feet plywood would be needed to cover the roof?

d. Into what dimensions would you cut the plywood?

28. There is an empty lot on a corner that is 80 m long and 30 m wide. When coming home from school, Gail cuts across the lot diagonally. How much distance (to the nearest meter) does she save?

29. A room is 8 meters long, 5 meters wide, and 3 meters high. Find the following lengths.

  a. Diagonal of the floor

  b. Diagonal of a side wall

  c. Diagonal of an end wall

  d. Diagonal from one corner of the floor to the opposite corner of the ceiling

30. Consecutive terms in a Fibonacci sequence can be used to generate Pythagorean triples, whole numbers that could represent the lengths of the three sides in a right triangle. The process works as follows:

   i. Choose any four consecutive terms of any Fibonacci sequence.
   ii. Let *a* be the product of the first and last of these four terms.
   iii. Let *b* be twice the product of the middle two terms.
   iv. Then *a* and *b* are the legs of a right triangle. To find the length of the hypotenuse, use $c = \sqrt{a^2 + b^2}$.

Use the Fibonacci sequence 1, 1, 2, 3, 5, 8, 13, 21, . . . to answer the following questions.

   a. Using the terms 2, 3, 5, and 8, find values of *a*, *b*, and *c*.
   b. Using the terms 5, 8, 13, and 21, find values of *a*, *b*, and *c*.
   c. Using the terms starting with 13, find values of *a*, *b*, and *c*.
   d. Write out more terms of the sequence. Is *c* one of the terms in this sequence in each of parts (a), (b), and (c)? Verify that *a*, *b*, and *c* in parts (a), (b), and (c) satisfy $a^2 + b^2 = c^2$.

31. A regular hexagon can be divided into six equilateral triangles.

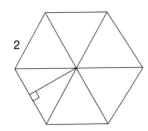

   a. The altitude of an equilateral triangle bisects the base. If each side has length 2, find the length of the altitude.
   b. What is the area of one triangle?
   c. What is the area of the regular hexagon?

32. An artist is drawing a scale model of the design plan for a new park. If she is using a scale of 1 inch = 12 feet, and the area of the park is 36,000 square feet, what area of the paper will the scale model cover?

33. There are only two rectangles whose sides are whole numbers and whose area and perimeter are the same numbers. What are they?

34. A baseball diamond is a square 90 feet on a side. To pick off a player stealing second base, how far must the catcher throw the ball?

35. A man has a garden 10 meters square to fence. How many fence posts are needed if each post is 1 meter from the adjacent posts?

36. Given are lengths of three sides. Will these sides form a right triangle?
   a. 48, 14, 56   **b.** 54, 12, 37   **c.** 21, 22, 23
   d. 15, 8, 16   **e.** 61, 11, 60   **f.** 84, 13, 100

37. The diagram here was used by President James Garfield to prove the Pythagorean theorem.

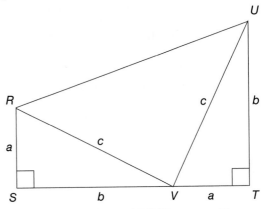

   a. Explain why quadrilateral *RSTU* is a trapezoid.
   b. What is the area of *RSTU*?
   c. Show that $\triangle RVU$ is a right triangle.
   d. Find the areas of the three triangles.
   e. Prove the Pythagorean theorem using parts (a)–(d).

38. a. Imagine the largest square plug that fits into a circular hole. How well does the plug fit? That is, what percentage of the circular hole does the square plug occupy?

   b. Now imagine the largest circular plug that fits into a square hole. How well does this plug fit? That is, what percentage of the square hole does the circular plug occupy?

   c. Which of the two plugs described in parts (a) and (b) fits the hole better?

39. Find *x*.

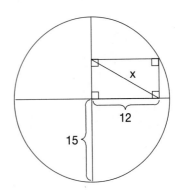

40. A spider and a fly are in a room that has length 8 m, width 4 m, and height 4 m. The spider is on one end wall 1 cm from the floor midway from the two side walls. The fly is caught in the spider's web on the other end wall 1 cm from the ceiling and also midway from the two side walls. What is the shortest distance the spider can walk to enjoy his meal? (*Hint:* Draw a two-dimensional picture.)

41. **a.** Trace the square, cut along the solid lines, and rearrange the four pieces into a rectangle (that is not a square). Find the areas of the square and the rectangle. Is your result surprising?

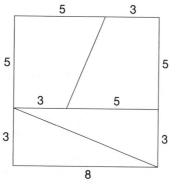

b. Change the dimensions 3, 5, 8 in the square in part (a) to 5, 8, 13, respectively. Now what is the area of the square? the rectangle? In connection with part (a), are these results even more surprising? Try again with 8, 13, 21, and so on.

42. Find the area of the shaded region.

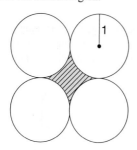

43. A **hexafoil** is inscribed in a circle of radius 1. Find its area. (The petals are formed by swinging a compass of radius 1 with the center at the endpoints of the petals.)

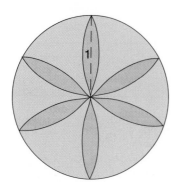

44. The circles in the figure have radii 6, 4, 4, and 2. Which is larger—the shaded area inside the big circle or the shaded area outside the big circle?

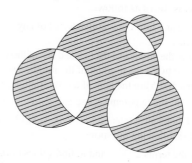

45. There are about 7 billion people on Earth. Suppose that they all lined up and held hands, each person taking about 2 yards of space.
   a. How long a line would the people form?
   b. The circumference of the Earth is about 25,000 miles at the equator. How many times would the line of people wrap around the Earth?

46. **a.** In the dart board shown, the radius of circle A is 1, of circle B is 2, and of circle C is 3. Hitting A is worth 20 points; region B, 10 points; and region C, 5 points. Is this a fair dart board? Discuss.
   b. What point structure would make it a fair board if region A is worth 30 points?

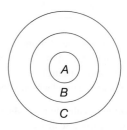

47. **a.** Find the area of an equilateral triangle whose sides have a length of 6 units.
   b. If an equilateral triangle has sides of length a, apply Hero's formula to derive a formula for the area of an equilateral triangle.

48. Use the Chapter 13 Geometer's Sketchpad® activity *Triangle Inequality* on our Web site to answer the question "When is the equation $PQ + QR = PR$ true?" Explain.

Analyzing Student Thinking

49. Jordan asks, "Isn't the perimeter of an n-gon simply n times the length of any side?" How should you respond?

50. Elise says that to calculate the area of a triangle, the triangle must have one side that is horizontal so you can have a height. How should you respond?

51. Ethan sees a right triangle whose hypotenuse has length a and whose sides have length b and c. When asked about the relationship among the three sides, he says "$a^2 + b^2 = c^2$." How should you respond?

52. To try to distinguish between the formulas of the circumference and area of a circle, Alayna says that the formula that contains the r^2 must be the area formula since the r^2 indicates two dimensions. Is she correct? Explain.

53. Dana says that if the length of a side of a square is doubled, then the area of the new square is four times as large as the original square. Also, if the side is tripled, the area of the new square is six times as large as the original square. How should you respond?

54. When Carol was finding the area of a rectangle that had a length of 13 cm and a width of 12 cm, she got an answer of 156 cm^2 so she squared 156 and got an answer of 24,336 square cm. Did she do something wrong? Explain.

55. Diana says she knows the formula for the area of a triangle is one half of the base times the height. She wonders if it makes a difference which side she uses for the base. For example, in the figure below, she knows AD is 5.5 and wonders if she could use 10 as the base. How would you respond?

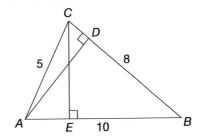

56. Ryan says that the area of a square becomes larger as the perimeter of a square increases, so that must be true for a rectangle as well. Do you agree with Ryan? Explain.

---

1. The Focal Points for Grade 4 state "Developing an understanding of area and determining the areas of two-dimensional shapes." Explain your understanding of area and how it differs from length.

2. The NCTM Standards state "All students should develop, understand, and use formulas to find the area of rectangles

and related triangles and parallelograms." Explain how the area of a parallelogram is developed in this section.

3. The NCTM Standards state "All students should develop and use formulas to determine the circumference of circles." Discuss how the formula for the circumference of a circle is developed in this section.

13.3   SURFACE AREA

STARTING POINT

At Bobbi's Baby Bargains, they make and sell baby blocks in sets of 24 blocks. Bobbi has asked you to design a box to package these blocks that will require the least amount of cardboard. What is your recommendation? Provide a justification as to why your design is the most efficient.

Prisms

Problem-Solving Strategy
Use a Model

The **surface area** of a three-dimensional figure is, literally, the total area of its exterior surfaces. For three-dimensional figures having bases, the **lateral surface area** is the surface area minus the areas of the bases. For polyhedra such as prisms and pyramids, the surface area is the sum of the areas of the polygonal faces.

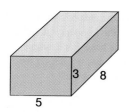

Figure 13.45

Example 13.14 shows how to find the surface area of a right rectangular prism.

Example 13.14   Find the surface area of a box in the shape of a right prism whose bases are rectangles with side lengths 5 and 8, and whose height is 3 (Figure 13.45).

SOLUTION We can "disassemble" this box into six rectangles (Figure 13.46).

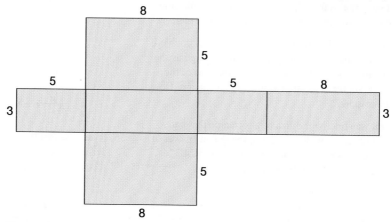

Figure 13.46

If we consider the 5 × 8 faces to be the bases, the lateral surface area of this box is 2[(3 × 5) + (3 × 8)] = 78 square units. Since each base has area 5 × 8 = 40 square units, the surface area is 78 + 80 = 158 square units. ∎

In the solution of Example 13.14, the "disassembled" box is sometimes referred to as a **net**. Nets of three-dimensional shapes like polyhedra, cylinders, and cones can help you visualize the components of the surface area. The following theorem depicts a prism and its net.

THEOREM

Surface Area of a Right Prism

The surface area S of a right prism with height h whose bases each have area A and perimeter P is

$$S = 2A + Ph.$$

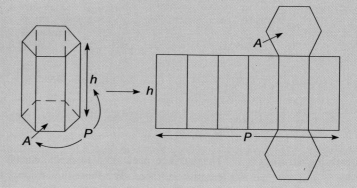

 Check for Understanding: Exercise/Problem Set A #1–3

Cylinders

The surface area of a right circular cylinder can be approximated using a sequence of right regular prisms with increasingly many faces (Figure 13.47).

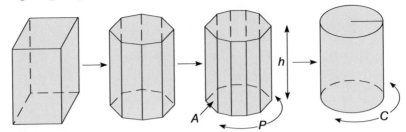

Figure 13.47

For each prism, the surface area is $2A + Ph$, where A and P are the area and perimeter, respectively, of the base, and h is the height of the prism. As the number of sides of the base increases, the perimeter P more and more closely approximates the circumference, C, of the base of the cylinder (Figure 13.47). Thus we have the following result.

Algebraic Reasoning
In the algebraic manipulation at the right, πr^2 is substituted for A and $2\pi r$ is substituted for C. This is possible because $A = \pi r^2$ and $C = 2\pi r$. Such substitutions highlight the importance of understanding that equality means everything on the left side of an equal sign represents the same thing as what is on the right.

THEOREM

Surface Area of a Right Circular Cylinder

The surface area S of a right circular cylinder whose base has area A, radius r, and circumference C, and whose height is h is

$$S = 2A + Ch$$
$$= 2(\pi r^2) + (2\pi r)h = 2\pi r(r + h).$$

NCTM Standard
All students should use two-dimensional representations of three-dimensional objects to visualize and solve problems such as those involving surface area and volume.

The figure in the preceding theorem box shows how to verify the formula for the surface area of a right circular cylinder by "slicing" the cylinder open and "unrolling" it to form a rectangle plus the two circular bases. The area of each circular base is πr^2. The area of the rectangle is $2\pi rh$, since the length of the rectangle is the circumference of the cylinder. Thus the total surface area is $2\pi r^2 + 2\pi rh$.

NOTE: Rather than attempt to memorize this formula, it is easier to imagine the cylinder sliced open to form a rectangle and two circles and then use area formulas for rectangles and circles, as we have just done.

 Check for Understanding: Exercise/Problem Set A #4–5

Pyramids

The surface area of a pyramid is obtained by summing the areas of the triangular faces and the base. Example 13.15 illustrates this for a square pyramid.

Example 13.15 Find the surface area of a right square pyramid whose base measures 20 units on each side and whose faces are isosceles triangles with edges of length 26 units [Figure 13.48(a)].

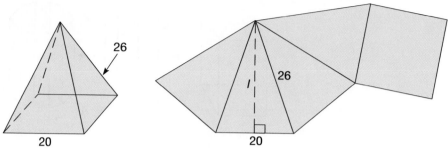

Figure 13.48   Figure 13.49

SOLUTION The area of the square base is $20^2 = 400$ square units. Each face is an isosceles triangle whose height, l, we must determine [Figure 13.49]. By the Pythagorean theorem, $l^2 + 10^2 = 26^2 = 676$, so $l^2 = 576$. Hence $l = \sqrt{576} = 24$. Thus the area of each face is $\frac{1}{2}(20 \cdot 24) = 240$ square units. Finally, the surface area of the prism is the area of the base plus the areas of the triangular faces, or $400 + 4(240) = 1360$ square units. ∎

The height, l, as in Figure 13.49, of each triangular face of a right regular pyramid is called the **slant height** of the pyramid. In general, the surface area of a right regular pyramid is determined by the slant height and the base. Recall that a right regular pyramid has a regular n-gon as its base.

The sum of the areas of the triangular faces of a right regular pyramid is $\frac{1}{2}Pl$. This follows from the fact that each face has height l and base of length P/n, where n is the number of sides in the base. So each face has area $\frac{1}{2}(P/n)l$. Since there are n of these faces, the sum of the areas is $n[\frac{1}{2}(P/n)l] = \frac{1}{2}Pl$. Thus we have the following result.

THEOREM

Surface Area of a Right Regular Pyramid

The surface area S of a right regular pyramid whose base has area A and perimeter P, and whose slant height is l is

$$S = A + \tfrac{1}{2}Pl.$$

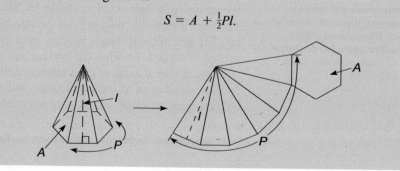

✓ **Check for Understanding:** Exercise/Problem Set A #6–7

Cones

The surface area of a right circular cone can be obtained by considering a sequence of right regular pyramids with increasing numbers of sides in the bases (Figure 13.50).

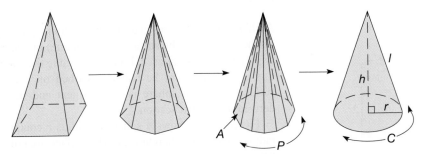

Figure 13.50

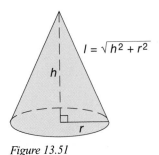

Figure 13.51

The surface area of each right pyramid is $A + \frac{1}{2}Pl$, where A is the area of the base of the pyramid, P is the perimeter of the base, and l is the slant height. As the number of sides in the bases of the pyramids increases, the perimeters of the bases approach the circumference of the base of the cone (Figure 13.50). For the right circular cone, the **slant height** is the distance from the apex of the cone to the base of the cone measured along the surface of the cone (Figure 13.51).

If the height of the cone is h and the radius of the base is r, then the slant height, l, is $\sqrt{h^2 + r^2}$. The lateral surface area of the cone is one-half the product of the circumference of the base ($2\pi r$) and the slant height. This is analogous to the sum of the areas of the triangular faces of the pyramids. Combining the area of the base and the lateral surface area, we obtain the formula for the surface area of a right circular cone.

THEOREM

Surface Area of a Right Circular Cone

The surface area S of a right circular cone whose base has area A and circumference C, and whose slant height is l is

$$S = A + \tfrac{1}{2}Cl.$$

If the radius of the base is r and the height of the cone is h, then

$$S = \pi r^2 + \tfrac{1}{2}(2\pi r)l = \pi r^2 + \pi r\sqrt{h^2 + r^2}.$$

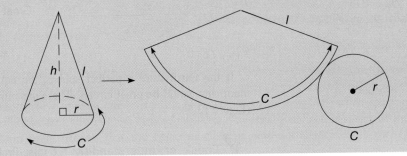

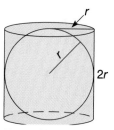

Figure 13.52

The lateral surface area of a cone is the surface area minus the area of the base. Thus the formula for the lateral surface area of a cone is $\pi r \sqrt{h^2 + r^2}$.

✔ **Check for Understanding:** Exercise/Problem Set A #8–9

Spheres

Archimedes made a fascinating observation regarding the surface area and volume of a sphere. Namely, the surface area (volume) of a sphere is two-thirds the surface area (volume) of the smallest cylinder containing the sphere. (Archimedes was so proud of this observation that he had it inscribed on his tombstone.) The formula for the surface area of a sphere is derived next and the formula for the volume will be derived in the next section.

Figure 13.52 shows a sphere of radius r contained in a cylinder whose base has radius r and whose height is $2r$. The surface area of the cylinder is $2\pi r^2 + 2\pi r(2r) = 6\pi r^2$. Thus, from Archimedes' observation, the formula for the surface area of a sphere of radius r is $\frac{2}{3}(6\pi r^2) = 4\pi r^2$.

Algebraic Reasoning
In the surface area equation, the variable r represents a number. But more specifically, it represents the length of a geometric object. Namely, r is the radius of a sphere.

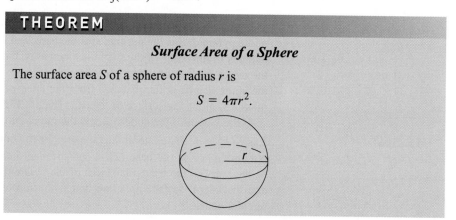

THEOREM

Surface Area of a Sphere

The surface area S of a sphere of radius r is

$$S = 4\pi r^2.$$

A **great circle** of a sphere is a circle on the sphere whose radius is equal to the radius of the sphere. It is interesting that the surface area of a sphere, $4\pi r^2$, is exactly *four* times the area of a great circle of the sphere, πr^2. A great circle is the intersection of the sphere with a plane through the center of the sphere (Figure 13.53).

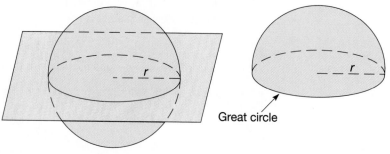

Great circle

Figure 13.53

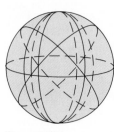

Figure 13.54

If the Earth were a perfect sphere, the equator and the circles formed by the meridians would be great circles. There are infinitely many great circles of a sphere (Figure 13.54).

✔ **Check for Understanding:** Exercise/Problem Set A #10–12

MATHEMATICAL MORSEL

One of the most famous problems in mathematics is the four-color problem. It states that at most four colors are required to color any two-dimensional map where no two neighboring countries have the same color. In 1976, Kenneth Appel and Wolfgang Haken of the University of Illinois solved this problem in a unique way. To check out the large number of cases, they wrote a program that took over 1200 hours to run on high-speed computers. Although there are mathematicians who prefer not to acknowledge this type of proof for fear that the computer may have erred, the problem is generally accepted as solved. For the purists, though, the famous Hungarian mathematician Paul Erdos is said to have mused that God has a thin little book that contains short, elegant proofs of all the significant theorems in mathematics. However, since the approach taken by Appel and Haken fills 460 pages in a journal, it may not be found in the thin little book.

Section 13.3 EXERCISE / PROBLEM SET A

EXERCISES

1. Find the surface area of the following prisms.

   a.

   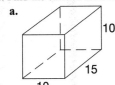

   b.

   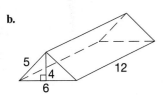

2. Find the surface area of each right prism with the given features.
   a. The bases are equilateral triangles with sides of length 8; height = 10.
   b. The bases are trapezoids with bases of lengths 7 and 9 perpendicular to one side of length 6; height = 12.

3. Refer to the following figure.

   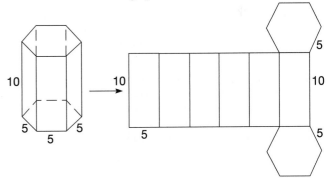

   a. Find the area of each hexagonal base.
   b. Find the total surface area of the prism.

4. Find the surface area of the following cylinders.

   a.   b.

   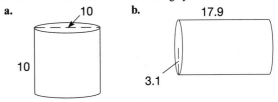

5. Find the surface area of the following cans to the nearest square centimeter.
  a. Coffee can $r = 7.6$ cm, $h = 16.3$ cm
  b. Soup can $r = 3.3$ cm, $h = 10$ cm

6. Find the surface area of the following square pyramids.
  a.   **b.**

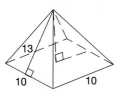   

7. Find the surface area of a right pyramid with the following features: The base is a regular hexagon with sides of length 12; height = 14.

8. Find the surface area of the following cones.
  a.   **b.**

9. Find the surface area.

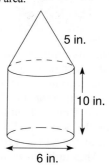

10. Find the surface area of the following spheres (to the nearest whole square unit).
  a. $r = 6$ **b.** $r = 2.3$
  c. $d = 24$ **d.** $d = 6.7$

11. Find the surface area of the following ball whose diameter is shown.

12. Which has the largest surface area—a right circular cone with diameter of base 1 and height 1 or a right circular cylinder with diameter of base 1 and height 1 or a sphere of radius 1?

PROBLEMS

13. A room measures 4 meters by 7 meters and the ceiling is 3 meters high. A liter of paint covers 20 square meters. How many liters of paint will it take to paint all but the floor of the room?

14. A scale model of a new engineering building is being built for display. A scale of 5 cm = 3 m is being used. It took 27,900 square centimeters of cardboard to construct the exposed surfaces of the model. What will be the area of the exposed surfaces of the building in square meters?

15. Suppose that you have 36 unit cubes like the one shown. Those cubes could be arranged to form right rectangular prisms of various sizes.

  a. Sketch an arrangement of the cubes in the shape of a right rectangular prism that has a surface area of exactly 96 square units.
  b. Sketch an arrangement of the cubes in the shape of a right rectangular prism that has a surface area of exactly 80 square units.

  c. What arrangement of the cubes gives a right rectangular prism with the smallest possible surface area? What is this minimum surface area?
  d. What arrangement of the cubes gives a right rectangular prism with the largest possible surface area? What is this maximum surface area?

16. A new jumbo-sized cereal box is to be produced. Each dimension of the regular-sized box will be doubled. How will the amount of cardboard required to make the new box compare to the amount of cardboard required to make the old box?

17. a. Assuming that the Earth is a sphere with an equatorial diameter of 12,760 kilometers, what is the radius of the Earth?
  b. What is the surface area of the Earth?
  c. If the land area is 135,781,867 square kilometers, what percent of the Earth's surface is land?

18. Suppose that the radius of a sphere is reduced by half. What happens to the surface area of the sphere?

19. A square 6 centimeters on a side is rolled up to form the lateral surface of a right circular cylinder. What is the surface area of the cylinder, including the top and the bottom?

20. Given a sphere with diameter 10, find the surface area of the smallest cylinder containing the sphere.

EXERCISES

1. Find the surface area of each prism.

a.

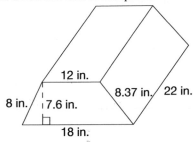

b.

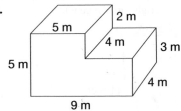

2. Find the surface area of each right prism with the given features.
   a. The base is a right triangle with legs of length 5 and 12; height = 20.
   b. The base is a rectangle with lengths 4 and 7; height = 9.

3. A right prism has a base in the shape of a regular hexagon with a 12-cm side and height to a side of $6\sqrt{3}$ cm as shown. If the sides of the prism are all squares, determine the total surface area of the prism.

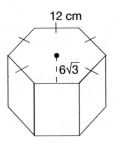

4. Find the surface area of the following cylinders.

a.   b.

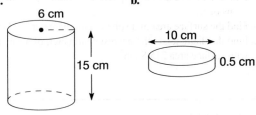

5. Find the surface area of the following cans to the nearest square centimeter.
   a. Juice can $r = 5.3$ cm, $h = 17.7$ cm
   b. Shortening can $r = 6.5$ cm, $h = 14.7$ cm

6. Find the surface area of the following pyramids.

a.   b.

7. Find the surface area of the right pyramid with the following features:

   The base is a 10-by-18 rectangle; height = 12.

8. Find the surface area of each cone (to the nearest whole square unit).

a.   b.

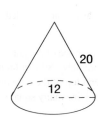
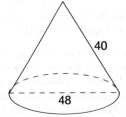

9. Find the surface area. Round your answers to the nearest square inch.

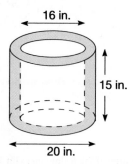

16 in.

15 in.

20 in.

10. a. Find the surface area of a sphere with radius 3 cm in terms of π.
b. Find the surface area of a sphere with diameter 24.7 cm.
c. Find the diameter, to the nearest centimeter, of a sphere with surface area 215.8 cm^2.

11. Find the surface area of the following ball whose circumference is as shown.

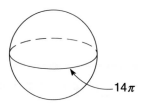

14π

12. Which has the larger surface area—a cube with edge length 1 or a sphere with diameter 1?

PROBLEMS

13. The top of a rectangular box has an area of 96 square inches. Its side has area 72 square inches, and its end has area 48 square inches. What are the dimensions of the box?

14. A right circular cylinder has a surface area of 112π. If the height of the cylinder is 10, find the diameter of the base.

15. Thirty unit cubes are stacked in square layers to form a tower. The bottom layer measures 4 cubes $\times$ 4 cubes, the next layer 3 cubes $\times$ 3 cubes, the next layer 2 cubes $\times$ 2 cubes, and the top layer a single cube.
a. Determine the total surface area of the tower of cubes.
b. Suppose that the number of cubes and the height of the tower were increased so that the bottom layer of cubes measured 8 cubes $\times$ 8 cubes. What would be the total surface area of this tower?
c. What would be the total surface area of the tower if the bottom layer measured 20 cubes $\times$ 20 cubes?

16. a. If the ratio of the sides of two squares is $2:5$, what is the ratio of their areas?
b. If the ratio of the edges of two cubes is $2:5$, what is the ratio of their surface areas?
c. If all the dimensions of a rectangular box are doubled, what happens to its surface area?

17. A tank for storing natural gas is in the shape of a right circular cylinder. The tank is approximately 380 feet high and 250 feet in diameter. The sides and top of the cylinder must be coated with a special primer. How many square feet of surface must be painted?

18. A paper cup has the shape shown in the following drawing (called a **frustum** of a right circular cone).

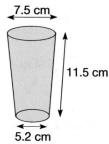

7.5 cm

11.5 cm

5.2 cm

If the cup is sliced open and flattened, the sides of the cup have the shape shown next.

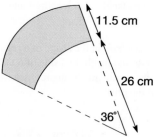

11.5 cm

26 cm

36°

Use the dimensions given to calculate the number of square meters of paper used in the construction of 10,000 of these cups.

19. Let a sphere with surface area 64π be given.
a. Find the surface area of the smallest cube containing the sphere.
b. Find the surface area of the largest cube contained in the sphere.

20. A barber pole consists of a cylinder of radius 10 cm on which one red, one white, and one blue helix, each of equal width, are painted. The cylinder is 1 meter high. If each stripe makes a constant angle of 60° with the vertical axis of the cylinder, how much surface area is covered by the red stripe?

Analyzing Student Thinking

21. Carter asserts that if the bases of a prism are hexagons, then the lateral surface area of the prism is six times the area of any face. Is he correct? Explain.

22. When using the formula $S = 2\pi r(r + h)$, Amberly claims that this is the formula for the volume since the r, r, and h suggest three dimensions. How should you respond?

23. A problem shows a right regular pyramid with the perimeter of the base and the height from the apex of the pyramid to the center of the base given. Tara, who is asked to find the surface area of the pyramid, says that she can't because she doesn't know the slant height. How should you respond?

24. Kennedy says that it is impossible for the lateral surface area of a right circular cylinder to be equal to the sum of the areas of the bases since the areas of the bases involve π. Is she correct? Explain.

25. Mason says that the area of a sphere doubles if you double the radius. How should you respond?

26. In making a (two-dimensional) net of a cylinder, Jalen was confused. He thought that since the bases were circles that two of the edges of the lateral surface would be round. He wondered how it could be a rectangle. How would you help Jalen visualize what the net should be?

27. Mark wants to make a tall skinny cone and a short fat cone (without their bases). He has two circles of the same size and wants to know if he can make both cones from these circles or if one circle needs to be larger than the other. How would you respond?

Problems Relating to the NCTM Standards and Curriculum Focal Points

1. The Focal Points for Grade 1 state "Composing and decomposing geometric shapes." Explain how the knowledge of composing and decomposing shapes is used to find surface areas.

2. The Focal Points for Grade 7 state "Developing an understanding of and using formulas to determine surface areas and volumes of three-dimensional shapes." Explain

your understanding of the formula used to determine the surface area of a cone.

3. The NCTM Standards state "All students should develop strategies to determine the surface area and volumes of selected prisms, pyramids, and cylinders." Explain the strategies you use to find the surface areas of these three-dimensional shapes.

13.4   VOLUME

STARTING POINT

The box has a volume of 12 cubic feet. If all three dimensions were doubled, how much would that affect the volume of the new box? Would the volume be doubled, tripled, . . . ?

A college student who was 4 ft, 6 in. tall and weighed 80 pounds wanted to play professional basketball. He read about some magic pills that would double his height to a dominant 9 ft tall. If his proportions were similar, what would he expect to weigh at his new height?

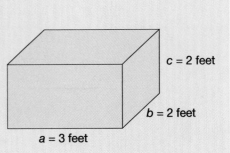

$c = 2$ feet

$b = 2$ feet

$a = 3$ feet

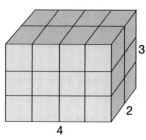

Figure 13.55

Figure 13.56

Prisms

The **volume** of a three-dimensional figure is a measure of the amount of space that it occupies. To determine the volume of a three-dimensional prism, we imagine the figure filled with unit cubes. A rectangular prism whose sides measure 2, 3, and 4 units, respectively, can be filled with $2 \cdot 3 \cdot 4 = 24$ unit cubes (Figure 13.55). The volume of a cube that is 1 unit on each edge is **1 cubic unit**. Hence the volume of the rectangular prism in Figure 13.55 is 24 cubic units.

As with units of area, we can subdivide 1 cubic unit into smaller cubes to determine volumes of rectangular prisms with dimensions that are terminating decimals. For example, we can subdivide our unit of length into 10 parts and make a tiny cube whose sides are $\frac{1}{10}$ of a unit on each side (Figure 13.56). It would take $10 \cdot 10 \cdot 10 = 1000$ of these tiny cubes to fill our unit cube. Hence the volume of our tiny cube is 0.001 cubic unit. This subdivision procedure can be used to motivate the following volume formula, which holds for any right rectangular prism whose sides have real number lengths.

DEFINITION

Volume of a Right Rectangular Prism

The volume V of a right rectangular prism whose dimensions are positive real numbers a, b, and c is

$$V = abc.$$

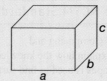

Reflection from Research
Learning how to visualize how many cubes are contained in a rectangular box can be complex for students. Having students make predictions of box contents based on pictures of boxes may be critical in helping them see these objects more abstractly (Battista, 1999).

From the formula for the volume of a right rectangular prism, we can immediately determine the volume of a cube, since every cube is a special right rectangular prism with all edges the same length. Volume is reported in cubic units.

THEOREM

Volume of a Cube

The volume V of a cube whose edges have length s is

$$V = s^3.$$

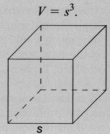

A useful interpretation of the volume of a right rectangular prism formula is that the volume is the product of the area of a base and the corresponding height. For example, the area of one base is $a \cdot b$ and the corresponding height is c. We could choose any face to serve as a base and measure the height perpendicularly from that base. Imagine a right prism as a deck of very thin cards that is transformed into an oblique prism (Figure 13.57).

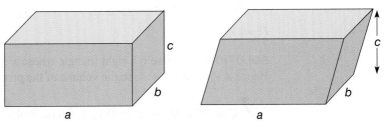

Figure 13.57

It is reasonable to assume that the oblique prism has the same volume as the original prism (thinking again of a deck of cards). Thus we can obtain the volume of the oblique prism by calculating the product of the area of a base and its corresponding height. The height is c, the distance between the planes containing its bases. This general result holds for all prisms.

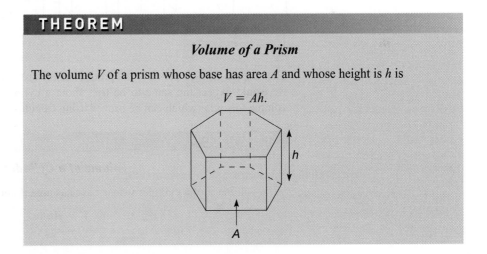

THEOREM

Volume of a Prism

The volume V of a prism whose base has area A and whose height is h is

$$V = Ah.$$

Example 13.16 gives an application of the volume of a prism formula.

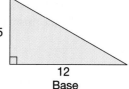

Find the volume of a right triangular prism whose height is 4 and whose base is a right triangle with legs of lengths 5 and 12 (Figure 13.58).

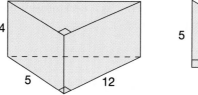

Figure 13.58

SOLUTION The base is a right triangle whose area is $(5 \times 12)/2 = 30$ square units. Hence $A = 30$ and $h = 4$, so the volume of the prism is $30 \times 4 = 120$ cubic units. ∎

✔ **Check for Understanding:** Exercise/Problem Set A #1–3

Cylinders

The volume of a cylinder can be approximated using prisms with increasing numbers of sides in their bases (Figure 13.59).

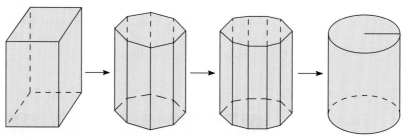

Figure 13.59

The volume of each prism is the product of the area of its base and its height. Hence we would expect the same to be true about a cylinder. This suggests the following volume formula (which can be proved using calculus).

THEOREM

Volume of a Cylinder

The volume V of a cylinder whose base has area A and whose height is h is

$$V = Ah.$$

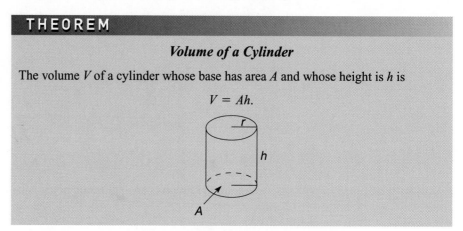

If the base of the cylinder is a circle of radius r, then $V = \pi r^2 h$.

Note that the volume of an arbitrary cylinder, such as those in Figure 13.60, is simply the product of the area of its base and its height.

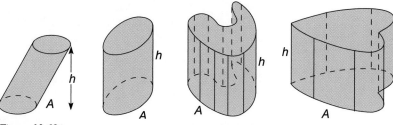

Figure 13.60

✔️ **Check for Understanding:** Exercise/Problem Set A #4–5

Pyramids

To determine the volume of a square pyramid, we start with a cube and consider the four diagonals from a particular vertex to the other vertices (Figure 13.61). Taking the diagonals three at a time, we can identify three pyramids inside the cube (Figure 13.62).

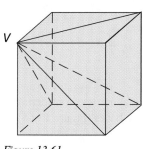

Figure 13.61

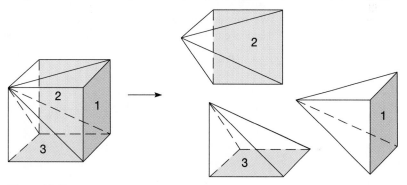

Figure 13.62

The pyramids are identical in size and shape and intersect only in faces or edges, so that each pyramid fills one-third of the cube. (Three copies of the pattern in Figure 13.63 can be folded into pyramids that can be arranged to form a cube.) Thus the volume of each pyramid is one-third of the volume of the cube. This result holds in general for pyramids with any base.

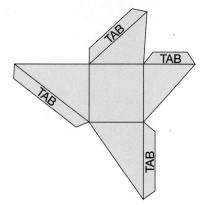

Figure 13.63

> ### THEOREM
>
> #### *Volume of a Pyramid*
>
> The volume V of a pyramid whose base has area A and whose height is h is
>
> $$V = \frac{1}{3}Ah.$$
>
>

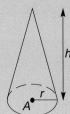 **Check for Understanding:** Exercise/Problem Set A #6–7

Cones

We can determine the volume of a cone in a similar manner by considering a sequence of pyramids with increasing numbers of sides in the bases (Figure 13.64).

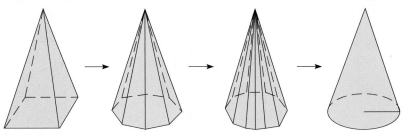

Figure 13.64

Since the volume of each pyramid is one-third of the volume of the smallest prism containing it, we would expect the volume of a cone to be one-third of the volume of the smallest cylinder containing it. This is, in fact, the case. That is, the volume of a cone is one-third of the product of the area of its base and its height. This property holds for right and oblique cones.

> ### THEOREM
>
> #### *Volume of a Cone*
>
> The volume V of a cone whose base has area A and whose height is h is
>
> $$V = \frac{1}{3}Ah.$$

Figure 13.65

For a cone with a circular base of radius r, the volume of the cone is $\frac{1}{3}\pi r^2 h$.

 Check for Understanding: Exercise/Problem Set A #8–9

Spheres

In Section 13.3 it was stated that Archimedes observed that the volume of a sphere is two-thirds the volume of the smallest cylinder containing the sphere. Figure 13.65 shows this situation. The volume of the cylinder is

$$V = (\pi r^2)2r = 2\pi r^3.$$

Hence the volume of the sphere is $\frac{2}{3}(2\pi r^3)$, or $\frac{4}{3}\pi r^3$. Thus we have derived a formula for the volume of a sphere.

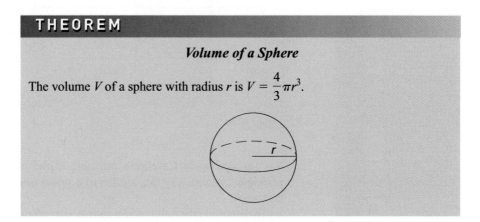

THEOREM

Volume of a Sphere

The volume V of a sphere with radius r is $V = \dfrac{4}{3}\pi r^3$.

As an aid to recall and distinguish between the formulas for the surface area and volume of a sphere, observe that the r in $4\pi r^2$ is *squared*, an area unit, whereas the r in $\frac{4}{3}\pi r^3$ is *cubed*, a volume unit.

Table 13.11 summarizes the volume and surface area formulas for right prisms, right circular cylinders, right regular pyramids, right circular cones, and spheres. The indicated dimensions are the area of the base, A; the height, h; the perimeter or circumference of the base, P or C; and the slant height, l. By observing similarities, one can minimize the amount of memorization.

TABLE 13.11

GEOMETRIC SHAPE	SURFACE AREA	VOLUME
Right prism	$S = 2A + Ph$	$V = Ah$
Right circular cylinder	$S = 2A + Ch$	$V = Ah$
Right regular pyramid	$S = A + \frac{1}{2}Pl$	$V = \frac{1}{3}Ah$
Right circular cone	$S = A + \frac{1}{2}Cl$	$V = \frac{1}{3}Ah$
Sphere	$S = 4\pi r^2$	$V = \frac{4}{3}\pi r^3$

The remainder of this section presents a more formal derivation of the volume and surface area of a sphere. First, to find the volume of a sphere, we use Cavalieri's principle, which compares solids where cross-sections have equal areas.

Cavalieri's Principle

Suppose that two three-dimensional solids are contained between two parallel planes such that every plane parallel to the two given planes cuts cross-sections of the solids with equal areas. Then the volumes of the solids are equal.

Figure 13.66 shows an illustration of Cavalieri's principle applied to cylinders. Notice that a plane cuts each cylinder, forming circular cross-sections of area πr^2. Hence, by Cavalieri's principle, the cylinders have equal volume.

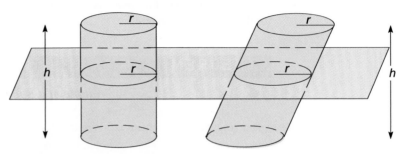

Figure 13.66

We can also apply Cavelieri's principle to the prisms in Figure 13.57. Cavalieri's principle explains why the volume of a prism or cylinder depends only on the base and height.

To determine the volume of a sphere, consider the solid shape obtained by starting with a cylinder of radius r and height $2r$, and removing two cones. We will call the resulting shape S (Figure 13.67).

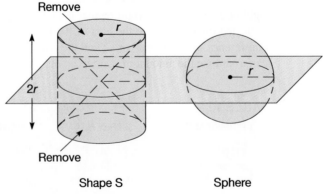

Figure 13.67

Imagine cutting shape S and the sphere with a plane that is a units above the center of the sphere. Figure 13.68 shows front and top views.

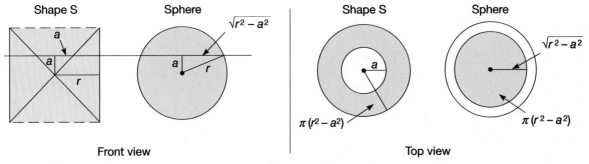

Front view   Top view

Figure 13.68

Using the top view, we show next that each cross-sectional area is $\pi(r^2 - a^2)$. First, for shape S, the cross-section is a "washer" shape with outside radius r and inside radius a. Therefore, its area is $\pi r^2 - \pi a^2 = \pi(r^2 - a^2)$. Second, for the sphere, the cross-section is a circle of radius $\sqrt{r^2 - a^2}$. (Refer to the right triangle in the front view and apply the Pythagorean theorem.) Hence, the cross-sectional area of the sphere is $\pi(\sqrt{r^2 - a^2})^2$, or $\pi(r^2 - a^2)$ also. Thus the plane cuts equal areas, so that by Cavalieri's principle, the sphere and shape S have the *same* volume. The volume of shape S is the volume of the cylinder minus the volume of two cones that were removed. Therefore,

$$\text{volume of shape } S = \pi r^2 \cdot (2r) - 2\left(\frac{1}{3}\pi r^2 \cdot r\right)$$
$$= 2\pi r^3 - \frac{2\pi}{3}r^3$$
$$= \frac{6\pi r^3}{3} - \frac{2\pi r^3}{3}$$
$$= \frac{4}{3}\pi r^3.$$

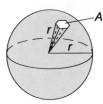

Figure 13.69

Since the sphere and shape S have the same volume, the volume of the sphere is $\frac{4}{3}\pi r^3$.

To determine the surface area of a sphere, we imagine the sphere comprised of many "pyramids" of base area A and height r, the radius of the sphere. In Figure 13.69, the "pyramid" has a base of area A and volume V. The ratio $\frac{A}{V}$ is

$$\frac{A}{V} = \frac{A}{\frac{1}{3}Ar} = \frac{3}{r}.$$

If we fill the sphere with a large number of such "pyramids," of arbitrarily small base area A, the ratio of $\frac{A}{V}$ should also give the ratio of the surface area of the sphere to the volume of the sphere. (The total volume of the "pyramids" is approximately the volume of the sphere, and the total area of the bases of the "pyramids" is approximately the surface area of the sphere.) Hence, for the sphere we expect

$$\frac{A}{V} = \frac{3}{r},$$

so

$$A = \frac{3}{r} \cdot V$$
$$= \frac{3}{r} \cdot \frac{4}{3}\pi r^3$$
$$= 4\pi r^2.$$

This is, in fact, the surface area of the sphere. Again, we would need calculus to verify the result rigorously.

Notice that the formulas obtained from Cavalieri's principle were the same as those obtained from Archimedes' observation.

✔ **Check for Understanding:** Exercise/Problem Set A #10–11

MATHEMATICAL MORSEL

On the TV quiz show *Who Wants to Be a Millionaire?*, contestants are asked more and more difficult questions and receive more money for each correct answer. They continue until they either answer a question incorrectly or have earned a million dollars. After answering the $32,000 question correctly, contestant David Honea moved on to the $64,000 question. The question was "Which of the five Great Lakes is the second largest in area after Lake Superior?" David answered Lake Huron, but the show said that the correct answer was Lake Michigan. After being encouraged by other contestants, he challenged the answer a short time later. When the show producers investigated the question, they found that Lake Michigan has the second largest volume but, as David indicated, Lake Huron has the second largest area. He was invited back to the show and eventually won $125,000.

Section 13.4 EXERCISE / PROBLEM SET A

EXERCISES

1. Find the volume of each prism.

a.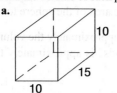

b.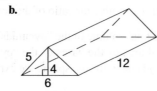

2. The Fruity O's cereal box is 2.5 inches by 7 inches by 10.25 inches and the Mini Toasties cereal box is 3 inches by 6 inches by 9.75 inches. Which box can hold the most cereal?

3. The hole for the foundation of a home is shaped like the following figure. If the hole is dug 4.5 feet deep, how many cubic feet of dirt is taken from the hole?

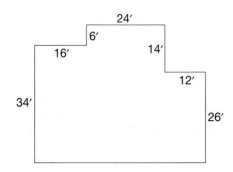

4. Find the volume of the following cylinders.

a.

b.

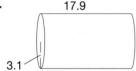

5. Find the volume of each can to the nearest centimeter.
   a. Coffee can $r = 7.6$ cm, $h = 16.3$ cm
   b. Soup can $r = 3.3$ cm, $h = 10$ cm

6. Find the volume of each square pyramid.

a.   **b.**

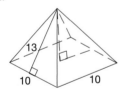 

7. Consider the pyramid in Exercise 6(a).
   a. Suppose one of the sides of the base is doubled to make the base a 10 by 20 rectangle but the height remains the same. What is the volume of the new pyramid?
   b. Suppose the slant height is doubled from 13 to 26 and the base remains a 10 by 10 square. What is the volume of this new pyramid?
   c. How do the volumes of (a) and (b) compare?

8. Find the volume of the following cones.

a.   **b.**

9. a. If the height is doubled in the two cones in Exercise 8 and the radius remains the same, what happens to the volume?
   b. If the radius is doubled in the two cones in Exercise 8 and the height remains the same, what happens to the volume?

10. Find the volume of the following spheres (to the nearest whole cubic unit).
   a. A sphere with $r = 6$
   b. A sphere with $d = 24$

11. Racquet balls are typically sold in cylindrical cans containing two balls. If a racquet ball has a diameter of 2.25 inches and the two balls fit exactly into the can so they touch the sides, top, and bottom of the can, how much space in the can is not occupied by the balls?

PROBLEMS

12. Following are shown base designs for stacks of unit cubes (see #21 in Exercise/Problem Set A, Section 12.5). For each one, determine the volume and total surface area (including the bottom) of the stack described.

a.

3	4	2
1	1	3

b.

1	4
2	

c.

3	3	3
1	2	3
1	2	3

13. Find the volume of each of the following solid figures, rounding to the nearest cubic inch.

a.

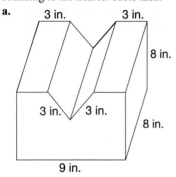

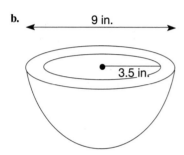

b.

14. A standard tennis ball can is a cylinder that holds three tennis balls.
   a. Which is greater, the circumference of the can or its height?
   b. If the radius of a tennis ball is 3.5 cm, what percent of the can is occupied by air, not including the air inside the balls?

15. Find the volume of each right prism with the given features.
   a. The bases are equilateral triangles with sides of length 8; height = 10.
   b. The bases are trapezoids with bases of lengths 7 and 9 perpendicular to one side of length 6; height = 12.
   c. The base is a right triangle with legs of length 5 and 12; height = 20.

16. A cylindrical aquarium has a circular base with diameter 2 feet and height 3 feet. How much water does the aquarium hold, in cubic feet?

17. The Great Wall of China is about 1500 miles long. The cross-section of the wall is a trapezoid 25 feet high, 25 feet wide at the bottom, and 15 feet wide at the top. How many cubic yards of material make up the wall?

18. The Pyramid Arena in Memphis, Tennessee, has a square base that measures approximately 548 feet on a side. The arena is 321 feet high.
   a. Calculate its volume.
   b. Calculate its lateral surface area.

19. a. A pipe 8 inches in diameter and 100 yards long is filled with water. Find the volume of the water in the pipe, in cubic yards.

   b. A pipe 8 centimeters in diameter and 100 meters long is filled with water. Find the volume of the water in the pipe, in cubic meters.
   c. Which is the easier computation, part (a) or part (b), or are they equivalent?

20. A scale model of a new engineering building is being built for display, using a scale of 5 cm = 3 m. The volume of the scale model is 396,000 cubic centimeters. What will be the volume of the finished structure in cubic meters?

21. Two designs for an oil storage tank are being considered: spherical and cylindrical. The two tanks would have the same capacity and would each have an inside diameter of 60 feet.
   a. What would be the height of the cylindrical tank?
   b. If 1 cubic foot holds 7.5 gallons of oil, what is the capacity of each tank in gallons?
   c. Which of the two designs has the smallest surface area and would thus require less material in its construction?

22. A sculpture made of iron has the shape of a right square prism topped by a sphere. The metal in each part of the sculpture is 2 mm thick. If the dimensions are as shown and the density of iron is 7.87 g/cm^3, calculate the approximate weight of the sculpture in kilograms.

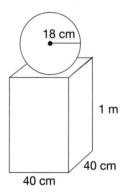

23. The volume of an object with an irregular shape can be determined by measuring the volume of water it displaces.
   a. A rock placed in an aquarium measuring $2\frac{1}{2}$ feet long by 1 foot wide causes the water level to rise $\frac{1}{4}$ inch. What is the volume of the rock?
   b. With the rock in place, the water level in the aquarium is $\frac{1}{2}$ inch from the top. The owner wants to add to the aquarium 200 solid marbles, each with a diameter of 1.5 cm. Will the addition of these marbles cause the water in the aquarium to overflow?

24. Suppose that all the dimensions of a square prism are doubled.
   a. How would the volume change?
   b. How would the surface area change?

25. a. How does the volume of a circular cylinder change if its radius is doubled?
   b. How does the volume of a circular cylinder change if its height is doubled?

26. In designing a pool, it could be filled with three pipes each 9 centimeters in diameter, two pipes each 12 centimeters in diameter, or one pipe 16 centimeters in diameter. Which design will fill the pool the fastest?

27. a. Find the volume of a cube with edges of length 2 meters.
  b. Find the length of the edges of a cube with volume twice that of the cube in part (a).

28. A do-it-yourselfer wants to dig some holes for fence posts. He has the option of renting posthole diggers with diameter 6 inches or 8 inches. The amount of dirt removed by the larger posthole digger is what percent greater than the amount removed by the smaller?

29. A water tank is in the shape of an inverted circular cone with diameter 10 feet and height 15 feet. Another conical tank is to be built with height 15 feet but with one-half the capacity of the larger tank. Find the diameter of the smaller tank.

30. The following sphere, right circular cylinder, and right circular cone have the same volume. Find the height of the cylinder and the slant height of the cone.

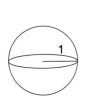

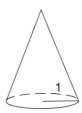

31. Lumber is measured in board feet. A **board foot** is the volume of a square piece of wood measuring 1 foot long, 1 foot wide, and 1 inch thick. A surfaced "two by four" actually measures $1\frac{1}{2}$ inches thick by $3\frac{1}{2}$ inches wide, a "two by six" measures $1\frac{1}{2}$ by $5\frac{1}{2}$, and so on ($\frac{1}{4}$ inch is planed off each rough surface). Plywood is sold in exact dimensions and is differentiated by thickness (e.g., $\frac{1}{2}$ inch, $\frac{5}{8}$ inch, etc.). Find the number of board feet in the following pieces of lumber.

a. A 6-foot long two by four
b. A 10-foot two by eight
c. A 4 foot-by-8 foot sheet of $\frac{3}{4}$-inch plywood
d. A 4 foot-by-6 foot sheet of $\frac{5}{8}$-inch plywood

32. Suppose that you have 10 separate unit cubes. Then the total volume is 10 cubic units and the total surface area is 60 square units. If you arrange the cubes as shown, the volume is still 10 cubic units, but now the surface area is only 36 square units (convince yourself this is true by counting faces). For each of the following problems, assume that all the cubes are stacked to form a single shape sharing complete faces (no loose cubes allowed).

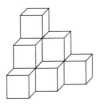

a. How can you arrange 10 cubes to get a surface area of 34 square units? Draw a sketch.
b. What is the greatest possible surface area you can get with 10 cubes? Sketch the arrangement.
c. How can you arrange the 10 cubes to get the least possible surface area? What is this area?
d. Answer the questions in parts (b) and (c) for 27 and 64 cubes.
e. What arrangement has the greatest surface area for a given number of cubes?
f. What arrangement seems to have the least surface area for a given number of cubes? (Consider cases with n^3 cubes for whole numbers n.)
g. Biologists have found that an animal's surface area is an important factor in its regulation of body temperature. Why do you think desert animals such as snakes are long and thin? Why do furry animals curl up in a ball to hibernate?

| Section 13.4 | EXERCISE / PROBLEM SET B |

EXERCISES

1. Find the volume of each prism.
  a.

  b.

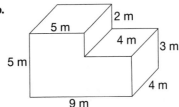

2. For greater strength, some shipping boxes are in the shape of a triangular prisms. What is the volume of a box with 8-inch sides on the equilateral base and a height of 20 inches?

3. How much water does the pool in the following figure hold?

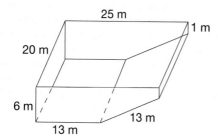

25 m

1 m

20 m

6 m

13 m

13 m

4. Find the volume of the following cylinders

a.

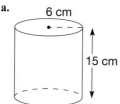

6 cm

15 cm

b.

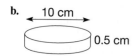

10 cm

0.5 cm

5. Find the volume of each can.
   a. Juice can $r = 5.3$ cm, $h = 17.7$ cm
   b. Shortening can $r = 6.5$ cm, $h = 14.7$ cm

6. Find the volume of each pyramid.

a.   **b.**

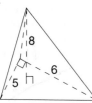   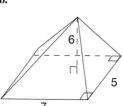

8

5   6

6

5

7

7. Consider the pyramid in Exercise 6(a).
   a. Suppose the length of the two legs on the base, 5 and 6, are cut in half, 2.5 and 3. What is the volume of the new pyramid?
   b. Suppose the length of the altitude is cut from 8 to 4. What is the volume of this new pyramid?
   c. Which of the two pyramids has a greater volume? Why?

8. Find the volume of the following cones.
   a.   **b.**

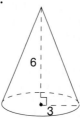   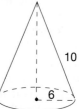

6   10

3   6

9. a. If the height is tripled in the two cones in Exercise 8 and the radius remains the same, what happens to the volume?
   b. If the radius is tripled in the two cones in Exercise 8 and the height remains the same, what happens to the volume?

10. Find the volume of the following spheres (to the nearest whole cubic unit).
   a. A sphere with $r = 2.3$
   b. A sphere with $d = 6.7$

11. Golf balls are often sold in boxes containing 12 balls arranged as shown. If a golf ball has a diameter of 1.68 inches and the 12 balls fit exactly into the box so they touch the sides, top, and bottom of the box, how much space in the box is not occupied by the balls?

PROBLEMS

12. Following are base designs for stacks of unit cubes (see #21 in Exercise/Problem Set A, Section 12.5). For each one, determine the volume and surface area (including the bottom) of the stack described.

a.

1	2	4	3

b.

2	3
1	5

c.

1	4	5	6
2	3		

13. a. Find the volume, to the nearest cubic centimeter, of a soft-drink can with a diameter of 5.6 centimeters and a height of 12 centimeters.
   b. If the can is filled with water, find the weight of the water in grams.

14. Given are three cardboard boxes.

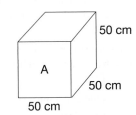

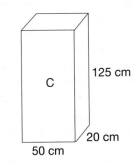

a. Find the volume of each box.
b. Find the surface area of each box.
c. Do boxes with the same volume always have the same surface area?
d. Which box used the least amount of cardboard?

15. The first three steps of a 10-step staircase are shown.
a. Find the amount of concrete needed to make the exposed portion of the 10-step staircase.
b. Find the amount of carpet needed to cover the fronts, tops, and sides of the concrete steps.

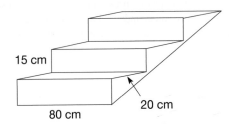

16. The Pyramid of Cheops has a square base 240 yards on a side. Its height is 160 yards.
a. What is its volume?
b. What is the surface area of the four exterior sides?

17. A vegetable garden measures 20 feet by 30 feet. The grower wants to cover the entire garden with a layer of mushroom compost 2 inches thick. She plans to haul the compost in a truck that will hold a maximum of 1 cubic yard. How many trips must she make with the truck to haul enough compost for the garden?

18. A soft-drink cup is in the shape of a right circular cone with capacity 250 milliliters. The radius of the circular base is 5 centimeters. How deep is the cup?

19. A 4-inch-thick concrete slab is being poured for a circular patio 10 feet in diameter. Concrete costs $50 per cubic yard. Find the cost of the concrete, to the nearest cent.

20. The circumference of a beach ball is 73 inches. How many cubic inches of air does the ball hold? Round your answer to the nearest cubic inch.

21. a. You want to make the smallest possible cubical box to hold a sphere. If the radius of the sphere is r, what percent of the volume of the box will be air (to the nearest percent)?
b. For a child's toy, you want to design a cube that fits inside a sphere such that the vertices of the cube just touch the sphere. If the radius of the sphere is r, what percent of the volume of the sphere is occupied by the cube?

22. An aquarium measures 25 inches long by 14 inches wide by 12 inches high. How much does the water filling the aquarium weigh? (One cubic foot of water weighs 62.4 pounds.)

23. a. How does the volume of a sphere change if its radius is doubled?
b. How does the surface area of a sphere change if its radius is doubled?

24. a. If the ratio of the sides of two squares is $2:5$, what is the ratio of their areas?
b. If the ratio of the edges of two cubes is $2:5$, what is the ratio of their volumes?
c. If all the dimensions of a rectangular box are doubled, what happens to its volume?

25. It is estimated that the average diameter of peeled logs coming into your sawmill is 16 inches.
a. What is the thickness of the largest square timber that can be cut from the average log?
b. If the rest of the log is made into mulch, what percent of the original log is the square timber?

26. The areas of the faces of a right rectangular prism are 24, 32, and 48 square centimeters. What is the volume of the prism?

27. While rummaging in his great aunt's attic, Bernard found a small figurine that he believed to be made out of silver. To test his guess, he looked up the density of silver in his chemistry book and found that it was 10.5 g/cm^3. He found that the figure weighed 149 g. To determine its volume, he dropped it into a cylindrical glass of water. If the diameter of the glass was 6 cm and the figurine was pure silver, by how much should the water level in the glass rise?

28. A baseball is composed of a spherical piece of cork with a 2-centimeter radius, which is then wrapped by string until a sphere with a diameter of 12 centimeters is obtained. If an arbitrary point is selected in the ball, what is the probability that the point is in the string?

29. An irrigation pump can pump 250 liters of water per minute. How many hours should the system work to water a rectangular field 75 m by 135 m to a depth of 3 cm?

30. If a tube of caulking lays a 40-foot cylindrical bead $\frac{1}{4}$ inch in diameter, how long will a $\frac{1}{8}$-inch bead be?

31. A rectangular piece of paper can be rolled into a cylinder in two different directions. If there is no overlapping, which cylinder has the greater volume, the one with the long side of the rectangle as its height, or the one with the short side of the rectangle as its height, or will the volumes be the same?

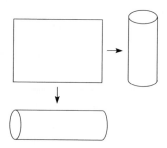

Analyzing Student Thinking

32. Jefferson claims that he found a cube where the number that represents the surface area is the same as the number that represents the volume. Is this possible? Explain.

33. Nedra wanted to find the volume of a square pyramid. She knew the area of the base and the slant height. Does she have enough information? Explain.

34. Carson says that the volume of a sphere triples when you triple its radius. How should you respond?

35. Pedro claims that if the radius of the base of a cone is doubled and the height of the cone is tripled, then the volume of the new cone is six times the volume of the original cone. Is he correct? Explain.

36. Hester Ann wants to build a big box in the shape of a cube to keep her blocks in. The blocks are all little cubes 3″ on a side, and she has 56 blocks. She needs to know what the inside dimensions of the box should be to make sure all the blocks will fit, yet have the big box be as small as possible. How would you help her figure out the problem? Would there be any space left over in the box for extra blocks later on?

37. Gloria says that the way she remembers the formula for the volume of a sphere is to simply multiply the surface area of the sphere by one-third. Does this work? Explain.

38. Austin wonders if it is possible to have a cylinder with a volume without π in it since the formula for the volume of a cylinder is $V = \pi r^2 h$. For example, he wants to know if there could be a cylinder with a volume of 500 cm^3. How would you respond?

Problems Relating to the NCTM Standards and Curriculum Focal Points

1. The Focal Points for Grade 5 state "Describing three-dimensional shapes and analyzing their properties, including volume and surface area." If a cylinder is described as having a volume of 24 cubic units, is it possible to describe the dimensions of the cylinder? Explain.

2. The Focal Points for Grade 7 state "Developing an understanding of and using formulas to determine surface areas and volumes of three-dimensional shapes." Explain your understanding of the relationship between the formulas for the volume of a cylinder and a cone.

3. The NCTM Standards state "All students should develop strategies to determine the surface area and volumes of selected prisms, pyramids, and cylinders." Explain the strategies you use to find the volumes of these three-dimensional shapes.

END OF CHAPTER MATERIAL

Solution of Initial Problem

David was planning a motorcycle trip across Canada. He drew his route on a map and estimated the length of his route to be 115 centimeters. The scale on his map is 1 centimeter = 39 kilometers. His motorcycle's gasoline consumption averages 75 miles per gallon of gasoline. If gasoline costs $3 per gallon, how much should he plan to spend for gasoline? (*Hint*: 1 mile is approximately 1.61 kilometers.)

Strategy: Use Dimensional Analysis

David set up the following ratios.

1 cm/39 km (map scale)

75 miles/1 gallon (gasoline consumption)

The length of his trip, then, is about

$$115 \text{ cm} \times \frac{39 \text{ km}}{1 \text{ cm}} = 115 \times 39 \text{ km} = 4485 \text{ km}.$$

Since 1 mile = 1.61 km (to two places), the length of his trip is

$$4485 \text{ km} \times \frac{1 \text{ mile}}{1.61 \text{ km}} = \frac{4485}{1.61} \text{ miles}$$
$$= 2785.7 \text{ miles (to one decimal place)}.$$

Hence David computed his gasoline expenses as follows.

$$2785.7 \text{ miles} \times \frac{1 \text{ gallon}}{75 \text{ miles}} \times \frac{3 \text{ dollars}}{\text{gallon}} =$$
$$\frac{2785.7 \times 3}{75} \text{ dollars} = \$111.43$$

To use the strategy Use Dimensional Analysis, set up the ratios of units (such as km/cm) so that when the units are simplified (or canceled) as fractions, the resulting unit is the one that was sought.

Notice how the various units cancel to produce the end result in dollars. Summarizing, David converted distance (the length of his trip) to dollars (gasoline expense) via the product of ratios.

$$115 \text{ cm} \times \frac{39 \text{ km}}{1 \text{ cm}} \times \frac{1 \text{ mile}}{1.61 \text{ km}} \times \frac{1 \text{ gallon}}{75 \text{ miles}} \times \frac{3 \text{ dollars}}{1 \text{ gallon}}$$
$$= \$111.43$$

Additional Problems Where the Strategy "Use Dimensional Analysis" Is Useful

1. Bamboo can grow as much as 35.4 inches per day. If the bamboo continues to grow at this rate, about how many meters tall, to the nearest tenth of a meter, would it be at the end of a week? (Use 1 in. = 2.54 cm.)
2. A foreign car's gas tank holds 50 L of gasoline. What will it cost to fill the tank if regular gas is selling for $1.09 a gallon? (1 L = 1.057 qt.)
3. We see lightning before we hear thunder because light travels faster than sound. If sound travels at about 1000 km/hr through air at sea level at 15°C and light travels at 186,282 mi/sec, how many times faster is the speed of light than the speed of sound?

People in Mathematics

Leonhard Euler (1707–1783)
Leonhard Euler was one of the most prolific of all mathematicians. He contributed to the areas of calculus, number theory, algebra, geometry, and trigonometry. He published 530 books and papers during his lifetime and left much unpublished work at the time of his death. From 1771 on, he was totally blind, yet his mathematical discoveries continued. He would work mentally, and then dictate to assistants, sometimes using a large chalkboard on which to write the formulas for them. He asserted that some of his most valuable discoveries were found while holding a baby in his arms. Much of our modern mathematical notation has been influenced by his writing style. For instance, the modern use of the symbol π *is* due to Euler. In geometry, he is best known for the Euler line of a triangle and the formula $V - E + F = 2$, which relates the number of vertices, edges, and faces of any simple closed polyhedron.

Maria Agnesi (1718–1799)
Maria Agnesi was famous for the highly regarded *Instituzioni Analitiche*, a 1020-page, two-volume presentation of algebra, analytic geometry, and calculus. Published in 1748, it brought order and clarity to the mathematics invented by Descartes, Newton, Leibniz, and others in the seventeenth century. Agnesi was the eldest of 21 children in a wealthy Italian family. She was a gifted child, with an extraordinary talent for languages. Her parents encouraged her to excel, and she received the best schooling available. Agnesi began work on *Instituzioni Analitiche* at age 20 and finished it 10 years later, supervising its printing on presses installed in her home. After its publication, she was appointed honorary professor at the University of Bologna. But instead, Agnesi decided to dedicate her life to charity and religious devotion, and she spent the last 45 years of her life caring for the sick, aged, and indigent.

CHAPTER REVIEW

Review the following terms and exercises to determine which require learning or relearning—page numbers are provided for easy reference.

SECTION 13.1 Measurement with Nonstandard and Standard Units

VOCABULARY/NOTATION

Holistic measurement   679
Nonstandard units: "hand," "pace,"
   "dash," "pinch," etc.   679
Standard units   682
English system of units for
   Length: inch (in.)   682
          foot (ft)   682
          yard (yd)   682
          mile (mi)   682
   Area: square inch (in^2)   683
         square foot (ft^2)   683
         square yard (yd^2)   683
         acre   683
         square mile (mi^2)   683
   Volume: cubic inch (in^3)   684
           cubic foot (ft^3)   684
           cubic yard (yd^3)   684
   Capacity: teaspoon (tsp)   684
             tablespoon (tbsp   684
             liquid ounce (oz)   684

cup (c)   684
pint (pt)   684
quart (qt)   684
gallon (gal)   684
barrel (bar)   684
Weight: grain   685
        dram   685
        ounce (oz)   685
        pound (lb)   685
        ton (t)   685
Temperature: degrees Fahrenheit
             (°F)   685
Metric system of units for
Length: meter (m)   686
        decimeter (dm)   686
        centimeter (cm)   686
        millimeter (mm)   686
        dekameter (dam)   686
        hectometer (hm)   686
        kilometer (km)   686

Area: square meter (m^2)   688
      square centimeter
      (cm^2)   688
      square millimeter
      (mm^2)   688
      are (a)   688
      hectare (ha)   688
      square kilometer (km^2)   689
Volume: liter (L)   689
        cubic decimeter (dm^3)   689
        cubic centimeter (cm^3)   690
        milliliter (mL)   690
        cubic meter (m^3)   690
        kiloliter (kL)   690
Mass: kilogram (kg)   691
      gram (g)   691
      metric ton (T)   691
Temperature: degrees Celsius (°C)   691
Dimensional analysis   693

EXERCISES

1. List the three steps in the measurement process.
2. What is meant by an informal measurement system?
3. Names three units of measurement used to measure the following in the English system.
   a. Length   b. Area
   c. Volume   d. Capacity
   e. Weight

4. List the three attributes of an ideal system of units.

5. Name three units of measurement used to measure the following in the metric system.
   a. Length   b. Area   c. Volume   d. Capacity   e. Mass

6. Name five common prefixes in the metric system.

7. Convert 54°C to °F.

8. A speed of 70 miles per hour is equivalent to how many kilometers per hour (use 1 in. = 2.54 cm)?

SECTION 13.2 Length and Area

VOCABULARY/NOTATION

Distance from point P to point Q,
   PQ,   700
Unit distance   700
Perimeter   701
Circumference   702

pi (π)   702
Area   703
Square unit   703
Base of a triangle   705
Height of a triangle   705

Height of a parallelogram   705
Height of a trapezoid   706
Hypotenuse of a right triangle   707
Legs of a right triangle   707

EXERCISES

1. Find perimeters of the following.

  a. A rectangle with side lengths 5 and 7

  b. A parallelogram with side lengths 11 and 14

  c. A rhombus whose sides have length 3.5

  d. A kite with side lengths 3 and 6.4

  e. A square whose sides have length 6

  f. A circle whose radius is 5

2. Find areas of the following.

  a. A right triangle whose legs have length 4.1 and 5.3

  b. A circle whose diameter is 10

  c. A parallelogram with sides of length 8 and 10, and height 6 to the shorter side

  d. A square whose sides have length 3.5

  e. A trapezoid whose bases have length 7 and 11 and whose height is 4.5

  f. A rhombus whose sides have length 9 and whose height to one side is 6

3. State the Pythagorean theorem in the following ways.

  a. Geometrically in terms of squares

  b. Algebraically in terms of squares

4. What does the triangle inequality have to say about a triangle two of whose sides are 7 and 9?

SECTION 13.3 Surface Area

VOCABULARY/NOTATION

Surface area 721	Net 722	Slant height of a cone 725
Lateral surface area 721	Slant height of a pyramid 724	Great circle 726

EXERCISES

1. Sketch a right rectangular prism, label lengths of its sides 4, 5, and 6, and find its surface area.

2. Find the surface area of a right cylinder whose base has radius 3 and whose height is 7.

3. Find the surface area of a right square pyramid whose base has side lengths of 6 and whose height (not slant height) is 4.

4. Find the surface area of a right circular cone whose base has radius 5 and whose height is 12.

5. Find the surface area of a sphere whose diameter is 12.

SECTION 13.4 Volume

VOCABULARY/NOTATION

Volume 732	Cubic unit 732

EXERCISES

1. Sketch a right rectangular prism, label lengths of its sides 4, 5, and 6, and find its volume.

2. Find the volume of a right cylinder whose base has radius 3 and whose height is 7.

3. Find the volume of a right square pyramid whose base has side lengths of 6 and whose height (not slant height) is 4.

4. Find the volume of a right circular cone whose base has radius 5 and whose height is 12.

5. Find the volume of a sphere whose diameter is 12.

CHAPTER TEST

KNOWLEDGE

1. True or false?

   a. The prefix *milli* means "one thousand times."

   b. The English system has all the properties of an ideal measurement system.

   c. The formula for the volume of a circular cylinder is $V = \pi r^2 h$, where r is the radius of the base and h is the height.

   d. The formula for the surface area of a sphere is $A = \frac{4}{3}\pi r^2$.

   e. If, in a right triangle, the length of the hypotenuse is a and the lengths of the other two sides are b and c, then $a^2 + b^2 = c^2$.

   f. The formula for converting degrees Celsius into degrees Fahrenheit is $F = \frac{9}{5}C + 32$.

   g. One milliliter of water in its densest state has a mass of 1 kilogram.

   h. The surface area of a right square pyramid whose base has sides of length s and whose triangular faces have height h is $2hs + s^2$.

2. The mass of 1 cm^3 of water is _____ gram(s).

3. What geometric shape is used to measure

   a. area?   **b.** volume?

SKILL

4. If 1 inch is exactly 2.54 cm, how many kilometers are in a mile?

5. Seven cubic hectometers are equal to how many cubic decimeters?

6. What is the area of a circle whose circumference is 2?

7. What is the volume of a prism whose base is a rectangle with dimensions 7.2 cm by 3.4 cm and whose height is 5.9 cm?

8. Find the volume of a pyramid whose base is a pentagon with perimeter 17 cm and area 13 cm^2 and whose height is 12 cm.

9. If all three dimensions of a box are tripled, the volume of the new box is _____ times bigger than the volume of the original box.

10. Find the perimeter of the following figure and leave the result in exact form.

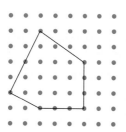

11. Perform each of the following conversions

a. 1 yd	= _____ in.	**b.** 1 gallon	= _____ pints
c. 8 yd^3	= _____ ft^3	**d.** 543 mm^2 =	_____ cm^2
e. 543 cm^3	= _____ m^3	**f.** 15 mm	= _____ m
g. 225 cm^3	= _____ mL	**h.** 3.78 g	= _____ mg

UNDERSTANDING

12. Show how one can use the formula for the area of a rectangle to derive the area of a parallelogram.

13. Explain why the interrelatedness attribute of an ideal system of measurement is useful in the metric system.

14. Describe one aspect of the metric system that should make it much easier to learn than the English system.

15. List the following from smallest to largest.

   i. The perimeter of a square with 6-cm sides.

   ii. The perimeter of a rectangle with one side 7 cm and the other side 6 cm.

   iii. The perimeter of a triangle with one side 6 cm and one side 6 cm, and the length of the third side not given.

16. Choose the most realistic measure for the following objects.

   a. The weight of a cinder block

      10 kg   100 kg   100 g

   b. The height of a two-story building

      60 cm   6 m   0.6 km

   c. The volume of a can of soda

      500 mL   50 L   50 mL

17. Given the area of a rectangle is bh and the area of a parallelogram is bh, explain why the area of the triangle with base b and height h, indicated in the following figure, can be found by using the equation $A = \frac{1}{2}b \cdot h$.

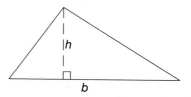

18. If a cylinder and a cone have congruent bases and congruent volumes, are the height of the cone and the height of the cylinder related? If so, how? If not, why not?

PROBLEM SOLVING/APPLICATION

19. The cube shown has edges of length *s*.

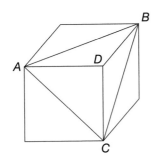

  a. Find the area of △*ABC*.
  b. Find the volume of pyramid *ABCD*.

20. Sound travels 1100 feet per second in air. Assume that the Earth is a sphere of diameter 7921 miles. How many hours would it take for a plane to fly around the equator at the speed of sound and at an altitude of 6 miles?

21. Find the surface area and volume of the following solids:

  a. Four faces are rectangles; the other two are trapezoids with two right angles.

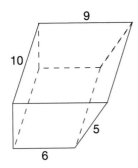

  b. Right circular cylinder

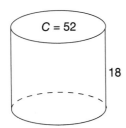

22. Find the area of the shaded region in the following figure. Note that the quadrilateral is a square and the arc is a portion of a circle with radius 2 ft and center on the lower left vertex of the square.

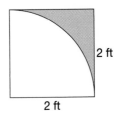

23. A sketch of the Surenkov home is shown in the following figure, with the recent sidewalk addition shaded. Using the measurements indicated on the figure and the fact that the sidewalk is 4 inches thick with right angles at all corners, determine how many yards of concrete it took to create the new sidewalk.

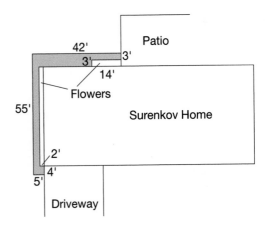

24. An airplane flying around the equator travels 24,936 miles in an entire orbit and the circumference of the Earth at the equator is 24,901 miles.

  a. What is the altitude of the airplane in miles (*exactly*)?
  b. *Approximately* what was the plane's altitude in feet (within 100 ft)?

Geometry Using Triangle Congruence and Similarity

CHAPTER 14

FOCUS ON *Euclid—Father of Geometry*

E uclid of Alexandria (circa 300 B.C.E.) has been called the "father of geometry."

Euclid authored many works, but he is most famous for *The Elements*, which consisted of thirteen books, five of which are concerned with plane geometry, three with solid geometry, and the rest with geometric explanations of mathematics now studied in algebra.

After Plato (circa 400 B.C.E.) developed the method of forming a proof, and Aristotle (circa 350 B.C.E.) distinguished between axioms and postulates, Euclid organized geometry into a single logical system. Although many of the results of Euclidean geometry were known, Euclid's unique contribution was the use of definitions, postulates, and axioms with statements to be proved, called propositions or theorems. The first such proposition was "Describe an equilateral triangle on a given finite straight line," which showed how to construct an equilateral triangle with a given side length using only a compass and straightedge. Other famous theorems included in *The Elements* are the Pons Asinorum Theorem (the angles at the base of an isosceles triangle are congruent), the proof of the infinitude of primes (which was covered in Chapter 5), and the Pythagorean Theorem, for which Euclid has his own original proof which is shown next (using appropriate pictured triangles, it can be shown that the areas of the two colored squares are equal to respectively colored rectangles).

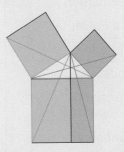

In modern geometry, some of Euclid's theorems are now taken as postulates because the "proofs" that he offered had logical shortcomings. Nevertheless, most of the theorems and much of the development contained in a typical high school geometry course today are taken from Euclid's *Elements*.

Euclid founded the first school of mathematics in Alexandria, Greece. As one story goes, a student who had learned the first theorem asked Euclid, "But what shall I get by learning these things?" Euclid called his slave and said, "Give him three pence, since he must make gain out of what he learns." As another story goes, a king asked Euclid if there were not an easier way to learn geometry than by studying *The Elements*. Euclid replied by saying, "There is no royal road to geometry."

STRATEGY 19
Identify Subgoals

Many complex problems can be broken down into *subgoals*—that is, intermediate results that lead to a final solution. Instead of seeking a solution to the entire problem directly, we can often obtain information that we can piece together to solve the problem. One way to employ the Identify Subgoals strategy is to think of other information that you wish the problem statement contained. For example, saying, "If I only knew such and such, I could solve it," suggests a subgoal, namely, the missing information.

INITIAL PROBLEM

An eastbound bicycle enters a tunnel at the same time that a westbound bicycle enters the other end of the tunnel. The eastbound bicycle travels at 10 kilometers per hour, the westbound bicycle at 8 kilometers per hour. A fly is flying back and forth between the two bicycles at 15 kilometers per hour, leaving the eastbound bicycle as it enters the tunnel. The tunnel is 9 kilometers long. How far has the fly traveled in the tunnel when the bicycles meet? (Hint: In determining the subgoal, it may be helpful to ask yourself the following types of questions:

a. Can I determine how far each bike travels?
b. Can I determine how long until the bikes meet?
c. Do I need to know how many times the fly turns around?)

CLUES

The Identify Subgoals strategy may be appropriate when

- A problem can be broken down into a series of simpler problems.
- The statement of the problem is very long and complex.
- You can say, "If I only knew . . . , then I could solve the problem."
- There is a simple, intermediate step that would be useful.

A solution of this Initial Problem is on page 815.

INTRODUCTION

NCTM Standard
All students should explore
congruence and similarity.

In Chapters 12 and 13, we studied a variety of two- and three-dimensional shapes and their properties. In this chapter, we study congruence and similarity of triangles and applications of these ideas. Applications of congruence will include the construction of two-dimensional geometric shapes using specific instruments or tools. The classical construction instruments are an unmarked straightedge, a compass, and a writing implement, such as a pencil. From the time of Plato, the ancient Greeks studied geometric constructions. Applications of similarity will include indirect measurement and several other constructions.

Key Concepts from NCTM Curriculum Focal Points

- **GRADE 1:** Children compose and decompose plane and solid figures (e.g., by putting two isosceles triangles together to make a rhombus), thus building an understanding of part-whole relationships as well as the properties of the original and composite shapes.

- **GRADE 3:** Through building, drawing, and analyzing two-dimensional shapes, students understand attributes and properties of two-dimensional space and the use of those attributes and properties in solving problems, including applications involving congruence and symmetry.

- **GRADE 7:** Students solve problems about similar objects (including figures) by using scale factors that relate corresponding lengths of the objects or by using the fact that relationships of lengths within an object are preserved in similar objects.

14.1   CONGRUENCE OF TRIANGLES

STARTING POINT

For the two triangles below, Corey said that triangle A was *congruent* to triangle B. Whitney claimed that triangle A was *equal* to triangle B. Who is correct, and what is the difference between equality and congruence?

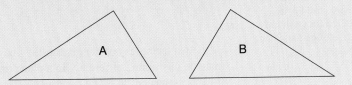

Triangle Congruence

In an informal way, we say that two geometric figures are congruent if they can be superimposed so as to coincide. We will make this idea precise for specific figures.

Recall that if two line segments $\overline{AB}$ and $\overline{CD}$ have the same length, we say that they are **congruent line segments**. Similarly, if two angles $\angle PQR$ and $\angle STU$ have the same measure, we call them **congruent angles**. We indicate congruent segments and angles using marks as shown in Figure 14.1.

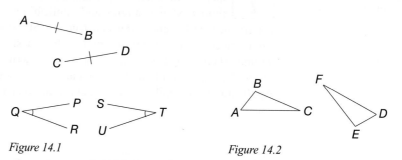

Figure 14.1   *Figure 14.2*

Suppose that we have two triangles, $\triangle ABC$ and $\triangle DEF$, and suppose that we pair up the vertices, $A \leftrightarrow D$, $B \leftrightarrow E$, $C \leftrightarrow F$ (Figure 14.2). This notation means that vertex A in $\triangle ABC$ is paired with vertex D in $\triangle DEF$, vertex B is paired with vertex E, and vertex C is paired with vertex F. Then we say that we have formed a **correspondence** between $\triangle ABC$ and $\triangle DEF$. Side $\overline{AB}$ in $\triangle ABC$ corresponds to side $\overline{DE}$, side $\overline{BC}$ corresponds to side $\overline{EF}$, and side $\overline{AC}$ corresponds to side $\overline{DF}$. Similarly, $\angle ABC$, $\angle BAC$, and $\angle ACB$ correspond to $\angle DEF$, $\angle EDF$, and $\angle DFE$, respectively. We are especially interested in correspondences between triangles such that all corresponding sides and angles are congruent. If such a correspondence exists, the triangles are called congruent triangles (Figure 14.3).

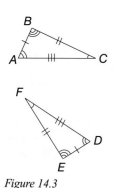

Figure 14.3

Children's Literature
www.wiley.com/college/musser
See "The Greedy Triangle" by Marilyn Burns.

Reflection from Research
The dominant strategy in young children for verifying congruence is edge matching (Beilin, 1982).

Algebraic Reasoning
The concept of congruence in geometry is closely related to the concept of equality in algebra. By studying the similarities and differences between equality and congruence, students will better understand both concepts.

DEFINITION

Congruent Triangles

Suppose that $\triangle ABC$ and $\triangle DEF$ are such that under the correspondence $A \leftrightarrow D$, $B \leftrightarrow E$, $C \leftrightarrow F$ all corresponding sides are congruent and all corresponding vertex angles are congruent. Then $\triangle ABC$ is **congruent** to $\triangle DEF$, and we write $\triangle ABC \cong \triangle DEF$.

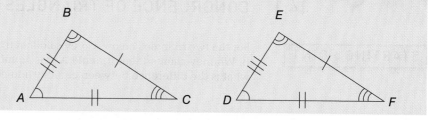

If two triangles are congruent, they have the same size and shape. However, they may be positioned differently in a plane or in space. Note that the symbol "$\cong$" stands for "is congruent to." The congruence symbol looks like the "equals" sign, but they have different meanings. The "equals" sign means *the same* so it is usually used with numbers like $2 = \frac{6}{3}$ or $m\angle A = m\angle B$ or $AB = DE$. Since congruence means the same size and shape, it is used with objects like triangles, angles, and segments ($\triangle ABC \cong \triangle DEF$, $\angle A \cong \angle B$, $\overline{AB} \cong \overline{DE}$). If we use the "equals" sign with something other than numbers like $\triangle ABC = \triangle DEF$, then the two triangles are not only the same size and shape but are actually the same triangle because they are the same set of points. Every triangle is equal and congruent to itself under the correspondence that pairs each vertex with itself. To demonstrate that two triangles are congruent, we need to give the explicit correspondence between vertices and verify that corresponding sides and angles are congruent. Example 14.1 gives an illustration.

NCTM Standard
Instructional programs should enable all students to recognize reasoning and proof as essential and powerful parts of mathematics.

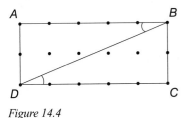

Figure 14.4

Example 14.1 Show that the diagonal $\overline{BD}$ of rectangle $ABCD$ on the square lattice in Figure 14.4 divides the rectangle into two congruent triangles $\triangle ABD$ and $\triangle CDB$.

SOLUTION We observe that $AB = CD = 5$, $AD = CB = 2$, and $BD = DB$. Since $\overline{AB} \parallel \overline{DC}$, we have that $m(\angle ABD) = m(\angle CDB)$ by the alternate interior angle theorem. Similarly, since $\overline{AD} \parallel \overline{BC}$, we have $m(\angle BDA) = m(\angle DBC)$. Also, $m(\angle A) = m(\angle C) = 90°$, since $ABCD$ is a rectangle. Consequently, under the correspondence $A \leftrightarrow C$, $B \leftrightarrow D$, $D \leftrightarrow B$, all corresponding sides and corresponding angles are congruent. Thus $\triangle ABD \cong \triangle CDB$. ∎

Example 14.1 shows that it is important to choose the correspondence between vertices in triangles *carefully*. For example, if we use the correspondence $A \leftrightarrow C$, $B \leftrightarrow B$, $D \leftrightarrow D$, it is *not* true that corresponding sides are congruent. For example, side $\overline{AB}$ corresponds to side $\overline{CB}$, yet $\overline{AB} \not\cong \overline{CB}$. Corresponding angles are not congruent under this correspondence either, since $\angle ABD$ is not congruent to $\angle CBD$.

✔ **Check for Understanding:** Exercise/Problem Set A #1–2

SAS Triangle Congruence

We can apply simpler conditions to verify the congruence of two triangles. Suppose that instead of having the three side lengths and three angle measures specified for a triangle, we are given only two of the side lengths and the measure of the angle formed by the two sides. Figure 14.5 shows an example.

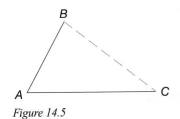

Figure 14.5

We can complete the triangle ($\triangle ABC$) in only one way, namely by connecting vertex B to vertex C. That is, the two given sides and the included angle determine a unique triangle. This observation is the basis of the side–angle–side congruence property.

PROPERTY

Side–Angle–Side (SAS) Congruence

If two sides and the included angle of a triangle are congruent, respectively, to two sides and the included angle of another triangle, then the triangles are congruent. Here, $\triangle ABC \cong \triangle DEF$.

The SAS congruence property tells us that it is sufficient to verify that two sides and an included angle of one triangle are congruent, respectively, to their corresponding parts of another triangle, to establish that the triangles are congruent. Example 14.2 gives an illustration.

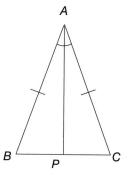

Figure 14.6

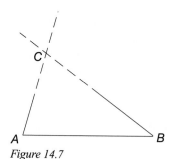

Figure 14.7

Example 14.2 In Figure 14.6, $\overline{AB} \cong \overline{AC}$ and $\angle BAP \cong \angle CAP$. Show that $\triangle BAP \cong \triangle CAP$.

SOLUTION Consider the correspondence $B \leftrightarrow C$, $A \leftrightarrow A$, $P \leftrightarrow P$. We have (i) $\overline{AP} \cong \overline{AP}$, (ii) $\angle BAP \cong \angle CAP$, and (iii) $\overline{AB} \cong \overline{AC}$. Hence, by (i), (ii), (iii), and the SAS congruence property, $\triangle BAP \cong \triangle CAP$. ∎

From the result of Example 14.2, we can conclude that $\angle ABP \cong \angle ACP$ in Figure 14.6, since these angles correspond in the congruent triangles. Thus the base angles of an isosceles triangle are congruent. In Section 14.3, Part A Problem 21, we investigate the converse result, namely, that if two angles of a triangle are congruent, the triangle is isosceles.

✔ **Check for Understanding:** Exercise/Problem Set A #3–4

ASA Triangle Congruence

A second congruence property for triangles involves two angles and their common side. Suppose that we are given two angles, the sum of whose measures is less than 180°. Also suppose that they share a common side. Figure 14.7 shows an example. The extensions of the noncommon sides of the angles intersect in a unique point C. That is, a unique triangle, $\triangle ABC$, is formed. This observation can be generalized as the angle–side–angle congruence property.

PROPERTY

Angle–Side–Angle (ASA) Congruence

If two angles and the included side of a triangle are congruent, respectively, to two angles and the included side of another triangle, then the two triangles are congruent. Here, $\triangle ABC \cong \triangle DEF$.

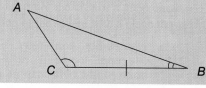 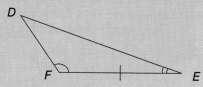

NOTE: Although we are assuming ASA congruence as a property, it actually can be shown to be a theorem that follows from the SAS congruence property.

Example 14.3 illustrates an application of the ASA congruence property.

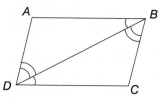

Figure 14.8

Example 14.3 Show that the diagonal in Figure 14.8 divides a parallelogram into two congruent triangles.

SOLUTION Line $\overleftrightarrow{DB}$ is a transversal for lines $\overleftrightarrow{AB}$ and $\overleftrightarrow{DC}$. Since $\overleftrightarrow{AB} \parallel \overleftrightarrow{DC}$, we know (i) $\angle ABD \cong \angle CDB$ by the alternate interior angle property. Similarly, $\angle ADB$ and $\angle CBD$ are alternate interior angles formed by the transversal $\overleftrightarrow{BD}$ and parallel lines $\overleftrightarrow{AD}$ and $\overleftrightarrow{BC}$. Hence (ii) $\angle ADB \cong \angle CBD$. Certainly, (iii) $\overline{BD} \cong \overline{DB}$. Thus by (i), (ii), (iii), and the ASA congruence property, we have established that $\triangle ABD \cong \triangle CDB$. ∎

Since $\triangle ABD \cong \triangle CDB$, the six corresponding parts of the two triangles are congruent. Thus we have the following theorem.

THEOREM

Opposite Sides and Angles of a Parallelogram

Opposite sides of a parallelogram are congruent.
Opposite angles of a parallelogram are congruent.

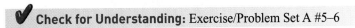

The complete verifications of these results about parallelograms are left for Part A Problem 18 in the Problem Set.

✔ **Check for Understanding:** Exercise/Problem Set A #5–6

SSS Triangle Congruence

The third and final congruence property for triangles that we will consider involves just the three sides. Suppose that we have three lengths x, y, and z units long, where the sum of any two lengths exceeds the third, with which we wish to form triangles as the lengths of the sides. If we lay out the longest side, we can pivot the shorter sides from the endpoints. Figure 14.9 illustrates this process.

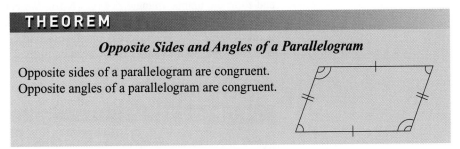

Lay off the longest side.

(a)

Pivot a shorter side from one endpoint.

(b)

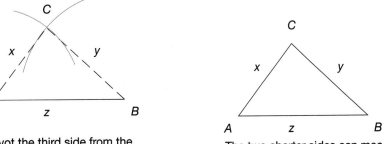

Pivot the third side from the other end.

(c)

The two shorter sides can meet in only one point, C, above $\overline{AB}$.

(d)

Figure 14.9

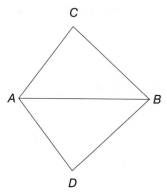

Figure 14.10

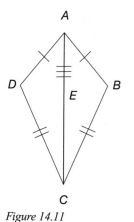

Figure 14.11

Problem-Solving Strategy
Draw a Picture

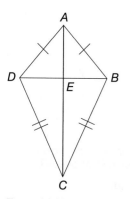

Figure 14.12

Notice that in pivoting the shorter sides [Figure 14.9(c)], we are drawing parts of two circles of radii x and y units, respectively. The two circles intersect at point C above $\overline{AB}$ and form the unique triangle $\triangle ABC$. [NOTE: We could also have extended our circles below $\overline{AB}$ so that they would intersect in another point, say D (Figure 14.10).] Once points A and B have been located and the position of point C has been found (above $\overline{AB}$ here) *only one* such triangle, $\triangle ABC$, can be formed. This observation is the basis of the side–side–side congruence property. (NOTE: This property can also be proved from the SAS congruence property.)

PROPERTY

Side–Side–Side (SSS) Congruence

If three sides of a triangle are congruent, respectively, to three sides of another triangle, then the two triangles are congruent. Here, $\triangle ABC \cong \triangle DEF$.

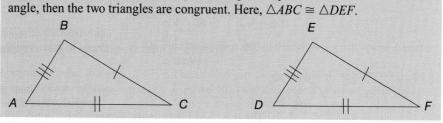

By the SSS congruence property it is sufficient to verify that corresponding sides in two triangles are congruent in order to establish that the triangles are congruent. Example 14.4 gives an application of the SSS congruence property.

Example 14.4 Suppose that $ABCD$ is a kite with $\overline{AB} \cong \overline{AD}$ and $\overline{BC} \cong \overline{DC}$. Show that the diagonal $\overline{AC}$ divides the kite into two congruent triangles (Figure 14.11).

SOLUTION We know (i) $\overline{AB} \cong \overline{AD}$ and (ii) $\overline{BC} \cong \overline{DC}$. Also, (iii) $\overline{AC} \cong \overline{AC}$. Using the correspondence $A \leftrightarrow A$, $B \leftrightarrow D$, and $C \leftrightarrow C$, we have that all three pairs of corresponding sides of $\triangle ABC$ and $\triangle ADC$ are congruent. Thus $\triangle ABC \cong \triangle ADC$ by (i), (ii), (iii), and the SSS congruence property. ∎

From the result of Example 14.4, we can make several observations about kites. In particular, $\angle BAC \cong \angle DAC$, since they are corresponding angles in the congruent triangles (Figure 14.11). That is, $\overleftrightarrow{AC}$ divides $\angle DAB$ into two congruent angles, and we say that line $\overleftrightarrow{AC}$ is the **angle bisector** of $\angle DAB$. Notice that $\overleftrightarrow{AC}$ is the angle bisector of $\angle BCD$ as well, since $\angle BCA \cong \angle DCA$. We also observe that $\angle ADC \cong \angle ABC$, since they are corresponding angles in the congruent triangles, namely $\triangle ADC$ and $\triangle ABC$. Thus two of the opposite angles in a kite are congruent.

The following example utilizes the SAS congruence property.

Example 14.5 Show that the diagonals of a kite are perpendicular to each other.

SOLUTION First, we draw kite $ABCD$ showing its pairs of diagonals and congruent sides (Figure 14.12).

Because $ABCD$ is a kite, we know that $\overline{AB} \cong \overline{AD}$. From the previous example, $\angle DAE \cong \angle BAE$. Also, $\overline{AE} \cong \overline{AE}$. Thus, $\triangle DAE \cong \triangle BAE$ by the SAS congruence property. Because the corresponding parts of congruent triangles are congruent, $\angle AEB \cong \angle AED$ and thus $m\angle AEB = m\angle AED$. Since $\angle AEB$ and $\angle AED$ are adjacent angles that form a straight angle, we know that $m\angle AEB + m\angle AED = 180°$. Since $\angle AEB \cong \angle AED$ and the sum of their measures is 180°, $\angle AEB$ is a right angle and so $\overline{AC} \perp \overline{DB}$. ■

We might wonder whether there are "angle–angle–angle," "angle–angle–side," or "side–side–angle" congruence properties. In the problem set of this section, we will see that only one of these properties is a congruence property.

✔ **Check for Understanding:** Exercise/Problem Set A #7–8

MATHEMATICAL MORSEL

In his *Elements*, Euclid showed that in four cases— SAS, ASA, AAS, and SSS—if three corresponding parts of two triangles are congruent, all six parts are congruent in pairs. Interestingly, it is possible to have *five* (of the six) parts of one triangle congruent to *five* parts of a second triangle *without* the two triangles being congruent (i.e., the sixth parts are not congruent). Although it seems impossible, there are infinitely many such pairs of "5-con" triangles, as they have been named by a mathematics teacher. These 5-con triangles have three angles and two sides congruent. However, the congruent sides are not corresponding sides. Two such triangles are pictured.

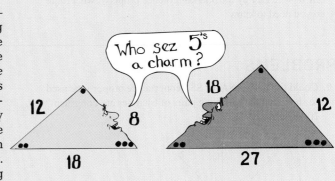

Section 14.1   EXERCISE / PROBLEM SET A

EXERCISES

1. Given that $\triangle RST \cong \triangle JLK$, complete the following statements.
   a. $\triangle TRS \cong \triangle$ _____   **b.** $\triangle TSR \cong \triangle$ _____
   c. $\triangle SRT \cong \triangle$ _____   **d.** $\triangle JKL \cong \triangle$ _____

2. In the given pairs of triangles, congruent sides and angles are marked. Write an appropriate congruence statement about the triangles:

   a.

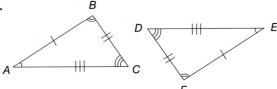

   b.

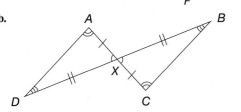

3. You are given $\triangle RST$ and $\triangle XYZ$ with $\angle S \cong \angle Y$. To show $\triangle RST \cong \triangle XYZ$ by the SAS congruence property, what more would you need to know?

4. $\triangle ABC$ and $\triangle WXY$ are shown.

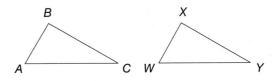

   a. To apply the SAS congruence property to prove $\triangle ABC \cong \triangle WXY$, you could show that $\overline{AB} \cong$?, that $\angle B \cong$?, and that $\overline{BC} \cong$?.
   b. Name two other sets of corresponding information that would allow you to apply the SAS congruence property.

5. You are given $\triangle RST$ and $\triangle XYZ$ with $\angle S \cong \angle Y$. To show $\triangle RST \cong \triangle XYZ$ by the ASA congruence property, what more would you need to know? Give two different answers.

| Section 14.3 | **EXERCISE / PROBLEM SET A**

EXERCISES

1. Given a line segment $\overline{AB}$, construct a line segment, $\overline{DE}$, on line l that is congruent to $\overline{AB}$.

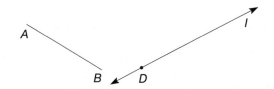

2. Given are an angle and a ray. Copy the angle such that the ray is one side of the copied angle.

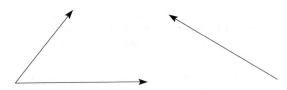

3. Construct the perpendicular bisector for each of the following segments.

a.

b.

4. Construct the angle bisector for each of the following angles.

a.   **b.**

5. Construct a line perpendicular to the given line through point P.

6. Construct a line perpendicular to the given line through point P.

• P

7. Construct a line through point P parallel to the given line.

• P

8. Draw a quadrilateral like the one shown.

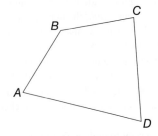

a. Construct a line through B, parallel to $\overline{AD}$.
b. Construct a line through C, parallel to $\overline{AD}$.
c. Through B, construct a line perpendicular to $\overline{CD}$.
d. Through A, construct a line perpendicular to $\overline{CD}$.

9. Draw a figure similar to the one shown.

• P

a. Construct the line perpendicular to line l through point P. Call this line m.
b. Construct a line through point P that is perpendicular to line m. Call this line k.
c. What is the relationship between line k and line l? Explain why.

PROBLEMS

10. Using only a compass and straightedge, construct angles with the following measures.
a. 90°   **b.** 45°
c. 135°   **d.** 67.5°

11. A **median** of a triangle is a segment joining a vertex and the midpoint of the opposite side. Construct the three

medians of the given triangle. What do you notice about how the three medians intersect?

12. An **altitude** of a triangle is a segment from one vertex perpendicular to the line containing the opposite side. Construct the three altitudes of the given triangle. What do you notice about how the three altitudes intersect?

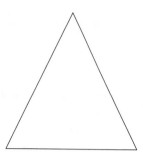

13. Use your compass and straightedge and a unit segment to construct the figures described.

a. Construct a right triangle with legs 3 units and 4 units in length. How long *should* the hypotenuse of your right triangle be? Use your compass to mark off units along the hypotenuse to check your answer.

b. Construct a right triangle with legs 5 units and 12 units in length. How long *should* the hypotenuse of your right triangle be? Use your compass to mark off units along the hypotenuse to check your answer.

c. Construct a right triangle with a leg 8 units and hypotenuse 17 units in length. How long *should* the other leg be? Use your compass to mark off units along the leg to check your answer.

14. Use △*ABC* to perform the following construction.

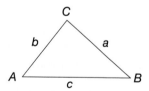

a. Use your compass and straightedge to construct △*PQR* such that *PQ* = 3*c*, *PR* = 3*b*, and *QR* = 3*a*.

b. How do the measures of ∠*A*, ∠*B*, and ∠*C* compare to the measures of ∠*P*, ∠*Q*, and ∠*R*? (Use your protractor to check.)

c. What can you conclude about the relationship between △*ABC* and △*PQR*? Justify your answer.

d. Which of the three similarity properties of triangles does this construction verify?

15. Use △*ABC* to perform the following construction: Use your compass and straightedge to construct △*PQR* such that ∠*P* ≅ ∠*A* and ∠*Q* ≅ ∠*B*.

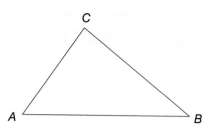

a. What is the ratio of the lengths of corresponding sides of the triangles? That is, find $\dfrac{PQ}{AB}$, $\dfrac{PR}{AC}$, and $\dfrac{QR}{BC}$. (Use your ruler here.) How do the ratios compare?

b. What can you conclude about the relationship between △*ABC* and △*PQR*? Justify your answer.

c. Which of the three similarity properties of triangles does this construction verify?

16. Both the medians and the angle bisectors of a triangle contain the vertices of the triangle. Under what circumstances will a median and an angle bisector coincide?

17. Use the Geometer's Sketchpad® to construct a triangle, △*ABC*, with all three angle bisectors and all three medians. By moving the vertices *A*, *B*, and/or *C*, determine what type(s) of triangles have exactly one median that coincides with an angle bisector.

18. Both the perpendicular bisectors and medians of a triangle pass through the midpoints of the sides of the triangles. Under what circumstances will a perpendicular bisector and median coincide?

19. Use the Geometer's Sketchpad® to construct a triangle, △*ABC*, with all three perpendicular bisectors and all three medians. By moving the vertices *A*, *B*, and/or *C*, determine what type(s) of triangles have exactly one median that coincides with a perpendicular bisector.

20. Complete the justification of construction 3, that is, that $\overleftrightarrow{PQ}$ is the perpendicular bisector of $\overline{AB}$.

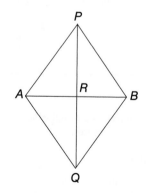

a. To show that $\triangle APQ \cong \triangle BPQ$ by the SSS congruence property, identify the three pairs of corresponding congruent sides.

b. To show that $\triangle APR \cong \triangle BPR$ by the SAS congruence property, identify the three pairs of corresponding congruent parts.

c. Explain why $\overline{PQ} \perp \overline{AB}$.

d. Explain why $\overline{PQ}$ bisects $\overline{AB}$.

21. Show the following result: If two angles of a triangle are congruent, the triangle is isosceles. (*Hint:* Bisect the third angle and apply AAS.)

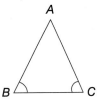

Section 14.3 EXERCISE / PROBLEM SET B

EXERCISES

1. Given a line segment $\overline{AB}$, construct a line segment, $\overline{DE}$, on line l.

2. Given $\angle ABC$ and ray $\overrightarrow{OP}$, construct $\angle MOP$ congruent to $\angle ABC$.

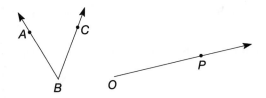

3. Construct the perpendicular bisector of $\overline{PQ}$ using a compass and straightedge.

   a. P ─────────── Q

   b.

4. Construct the bisector of $\angle R$ using a compass and straightedge.

   a.

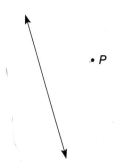

   b.

7. Construct a line through point P parallel to the given line.

5. Construct the line perpendicular to l through P using a compass and straightedge.

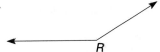

6. Construct the line perpendicular to l through P using a compass and straightedge.

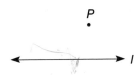

8. Draw an angle like the one shown, but with longer sides. Construct the following lines using a compass and straightedge.

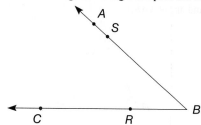

a. The line perpendicular to $\overline{AB}$ at point S
b. The line perpendicular to $\overline{BC}$ through point S
c. The line parallel to $\overline{AB}$ through point R
d. The line parallel to $\overline{BC}$ through point A

9. Draw a figure similar to the one shown.

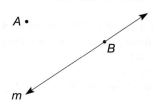

a. Construct a line through B perpendicular to m. Call this line n.
b. Construct a line through A parallel to m. Call this line p.
c. What is the relationship between n and p? Explain.

PROBLEMS

10. Given are two acute angles with measures a and b. Using a compass and straightedge, construct the following.

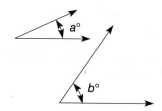

a. An angle with measure $a + b$
b. An angle with measure $2a$
c. An angle with measure $b - a$
d. An angle with measure $(a + b)/2$

11. Construct the three medians of the following triangle.

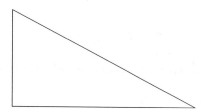

12. Construct the three altitudes of the given triangle. What do you notice about the location of the point where these altitudes intersect?

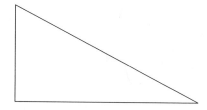

13. Given are $\overline{AB}$, $\angle C$, and $\angle D$. Using construction techniques with a compass and straightedge, construct the following.

a. A triangle with angles congruent to $\angle C$ and $\angle D$ and the included side congruent to $\overline{AB}$
b. An isosceles triangle with two sides of length AB and the included angle congruent to $\angle D$

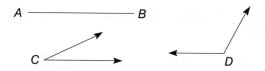

14. a. Given is a construction procedure for copying a triangle. Follow it to copy $\triangle RST$.

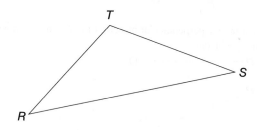

i. Draw a ray and copy segment $\overline{RS}$ of the triangle. Call the copy $\overline{DE}$.
ii. Draw an arc with center D and radius RT.
iii. Draw an arc with center E and radius ST. This arc should intersect the arc drawn in step 2. Call the intersection point F.
iv. With a straightedge, connect points D and F and points E and F.

b. Write a justification of the construction procedure.

15. A method sometimes employed by drafters to bisect a line segment $\overline{AB}$ follows. Explain why this method works.

A •————————————• B

Angles of 45° are drawn at points A and B, and the point of intersection of their sides is labeled C. A perpendicular is drawn from point C to $\overline{AB}$. Point D bisects $\overline{AB}$.

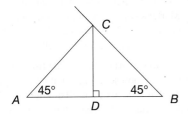

16. Use $\triangle ABC$ and your compass and straightedge to perform the following construction: Construct $\triangle PQR$ where $PQ = 2c$, $PR = 2b$, and $\angle P \cong \angle A$.

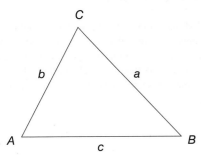

a. How does the length of $\overline{RQ}$ compare to the length of $\overline{CB}$? (Use your compass to check your answer.) How do the measures of $\angle B$ and $\angle C$ compare to the measures of $\angle Q$ and $\angle R$? (Use your compass or a protractor to compare the angles.)
b. What can you conclude about the relationship between $\triangle ABC$ and $\triangle PQR$? Justify your answer.
c. Which of the three similarity properties of triangles does this construction verify?

17. Both the perpendicular bisectors and altitudes of a triangle are perpendicular to the line containing the sides. Under what circumstances will a perpendicular bisector and altitude coincide?

18. Use the Geometer's Sketchpad® to construct a triangle, $\triangle ABC$, with all three perpendicular bisectors and all three altitudes. By moving the vertices A, B, and/or C, determine what type(s) of triangles have exactly one altitude that coincides with a perpendicular bisector.

19. Using AB as unit length, construct segments of the given length with a compass and straightedge.

A ————————— B

a. $\sqrt{10}$ **b.** $\sqrt{6}$ **c.** $\sqrt{12}$ **d.** $\sqrt{15}$

20. A rectangle similar to rectangle $ABCD$ can be constructed as follows.

1. Draw diagonal $\overline{AC}$ in rectangle $ABCD$. Extend the diagonal through point C if you want a rectangle larger than $ABCD$.
2. Pick any point on $\overleftrightarrow{AC}$ and call it P.
3. Construct perpendiculars from point P to $\overleftrightarrow{AB}$ and to $\overleftrightarrow{AD}$.
4. Label the points of intersection Q and R. $ABCD \sim AQPR$. Explain why this is true.

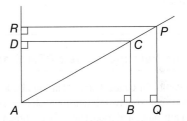

21. Prove the following result: If a point is equidistant from the endpoints of a segment, it is on the perpendicular bisector of the segment. (*Hint:* Connect C with the midpoint D of segment $\overline{AB}$ and show that $\overline{CD}$ is perpendicular to $\overline{AB}$.)

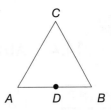

22. Two neighbors at points A and B will share the cost of extending electric service from a road to their houses. A line will be laid that is equidistant from their two houses. How can they determine where the line should run?

Analyzing Student Thinking
23. Gwennette is looking at an isosceles triangle. She says, "I thought in an isosceles triangle, the altitude, the median, and the angle bisector were all supposed to be the same line segment. Mine are all different." How should you respond?

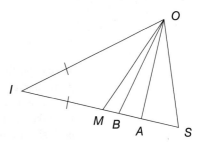

24. Tammy is constructing a perpendicular bisector of a segment. She wonders if it would make any difference if, after she draws the arcs from one end of the segment, she changes the compass before she draws the arcs from the other end. The line still looks perpendicular. How would you respond?

25. Ty is studying the construction to bisect an angle similar to the one shown in Figure 14.30. He says, "Shouldn't point R be selected so that $BP = PR$?" How should you respond?

26. When constructing a perpendicular line through a point on a line using the construction shown in Figure 14.27, Bo asked if PA must be equal to PB. How should you respond? He also asked if PA and QA have to be equal. How would you respond?

27. When copying an angle, an arc is drawn to intersect both sides of the angle. Madison notices that both of the points where the arc intersects the sides are the same distance from the vertex. She asks if that has to be the case or if the constructions could be altered to use points that are different distances from the vertex. How would you respond?

28. When constructing triangles with three line segments of different lengths, Latisha says you have to draw the longest side first. Marlena says it doesn't matter; you can even start with the shortest side. Latisha says, "Then the triangles won't match." Which student is correct?

29. Glen is trying to construct the altitude from one of the acute angles in an obtuse triangle, but he can't get it to stay inside the triangle. He asks you, "Isn't the altitude supposed to be inside the triangle?" What should you say?

Problems Relating to the NCTM Standards and Curriculum Focal Points

1. The Focal Points for Grade 3 state "Through building, drawing, and analyzing two-dimensional shapes, students understand attributes and properties of two-dimensional space and the use of those attributes and properties in solving problems, including applications involving congruence and symmetry." Discuss how this Focal Point is addressed by doing the constructions in this section.

2. The NCTM Standards state "All students should create and critique inductive and deductive arguments concerning geometric ideas and relationships, such as congruence, similarity, and the Pythagorean relationship." Describe an example from this section where a deductive argument was used.

14.4 ADDITIONAL EUCLIDEAN CONSTRUCTIONS

STARTING POINT

The three neighboring cities of Logan, Mendon, and Clarkston decided to combine resources to build an airport. Each city, however, wanted an assurance that their residents would not have to drive any farther than the residents from any other city to get to the new airport. Based on the map of the cities shown here, sketch your proposed location of the new airport. Explain how you located it and why it satisfies each city's criterion.

Mendon
○

Logan
○

Clarkston
○

Constructing Circumscribed and Inscribed Circles

We can perform several interesting constructions that involve triangles and circles. In particular, every triangle can have a circle circumscribed around it, and every triangle can have a circle inscribed within it (Figure 14.38). The **circumscribed circle** contains the vertices of the triangle as points on the circle. The **inscribed circle** touches each side of the triangle at exactly one point.

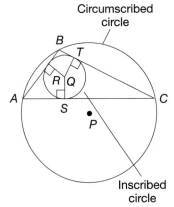

Circumscribed circle

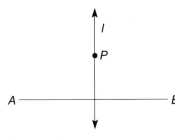

Inscribed circle

Figure 14.38

In Figure 14.38, line $\overleftrightarrow{AB}$ is said to be **tangent** to the inscribed circle, since the line and circle intersect at exactly one point, and all other points of the circle lie entirely on one side of the line. Similarly, lines $\overleftrightarrow{BC}$ and $\overleftrightarrow{AC}$ are tangent to the inscribed circle.

In Figure 14.38, point P is the center of the circumscribed circle, so $PA = PB = PC$. Thus P is equidistant from the vertices of $\triangle ABC$. Point P is called the **circumcenter** of $\triangle ABC$. Point Q is the center of the inscribed circle and is called the **incenter** of $\triangle ABC$. The inscribed circle intersects each of the three sides of $\triangle ABC$ at R, S, and T. Notice that $QR = QS = QT$, since each length is the radius of the inscribed circle. To construct the circumscribed and inscribed circles for a triangle, we need to construct the circumcenter and the incenter of the triangle. Example 14.8 provides the basis for constructing the circumcenter.

Example 14.8   Suppose that $\overline{AB}$ is a line segment with perpendicular bisector l. Show that point P is on l if and only if P is equidistant from A and B; that is, $AP = BP$ (Figure 14.39).

SOLUTION Suppose that P is on l, the perpendicular bisector of $\overline{AB}$. Let M be the midpoint of $\overline{AB}$ (Figure 14.40). Then $\triangle PMA \cong \triangle PMB$ by the SAS congruence property (verify this). Hence $PA = PB$, so P is equidistant from A and B. This shows that the points on the perpendicular bisector of $\overline{AB}$ are equidistant from A and B. To complete the argument, we would have to show that if a point is equidistant from A and B, then it must be on l. This is left for Part B Problem 14 in the Problem Set. ∎

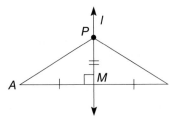

Figure 14.39

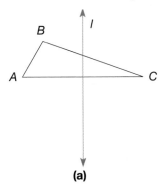

Figure 14.40

Example 14.8 shows that the circumcenter of a triangle must be a point on each of the perpendicular bisectors of the sides. Thus to find the circumcenter of a triangle, we find the perpendicular bisectors of the sides of the triangle. (Actually, any two of the perpendicular bisectors will suffice.)

8 Circumscribed Circle of a Triangle Since all of the points on the perpendicular bisector of a segment are equidistant from the endpoints of the segment, we will use perpendicular bisectors to construct the circumscribed circle.

Procedure (Figure 14.41): Given $\triangle ABC$, construct point P that is equidistant from A, B, and C.

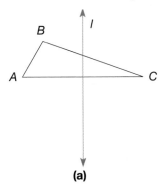

(a)

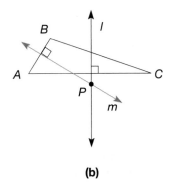

(b)

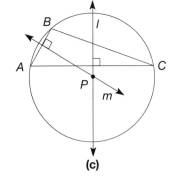

(c)

Figure 14.41

1. Using the perpendicular bisector construction, construct line l, the perpendicular bisector of side $\overline{AC}$ [Figure 14.41(a)].

2. Similarly, construct line m, the perpendicular bisector of side $\overline{AB}$. The intersection of lines l and m is point P, the circumcenter of $\triangle ABC$ [Figure 14.41(b)]. The circle with center P and radius PA is the circumscribed circle of $\triangle ABC$ [Figure 14.41(c)].

Justification (Figure 14.41): Since P is on line l, P is equidistant from A and C, by Example 14.8. Hence $PA = PC$. Also, P is on line m, so P is equidistant from A and B. Thus $PA = PB$. Combining results, we have $PA = PB = PC$. Thus the circle whose center is P and whose radius is PA will contain points A, B, and C.

To find the incenter of a triangle, we need to define what is meant by the distance from a point P to a line l [Figure 14.42(a)]. Suppose that $\overleftrightarrow{PQ}$ is the line through P that is perpendicular to l. Let R be the intersection of line $\overleftrightarrow{PQ}$ and line l [Figure 14.42(b)]. Then we define the **distance from P to l** to be the distance PR. That is, we measure the distance from a point to a line by measuring along a line that is *perpendicular* to the given line, here l, through the given point, here P. Point R is the point on line l closest to point P.

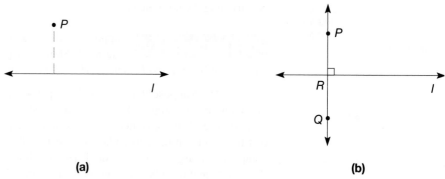

(a)   **(b)**

Figure 14.42

To find the incenter of a triangle, we must locate a point that is equidistant from the sides of the triangle as shown next.

9 Inscribed Circle of a Triangle
Since all of the points on an angle bisector are equidistant from the sides of the angle, we will use angle bisectors to construct the inscribed circle.

Procedure (Figure 14.43):

1. Using the angle bisector construction, construct line l, the bisector of $\angle CAB$ [Figure 14.43(a)].

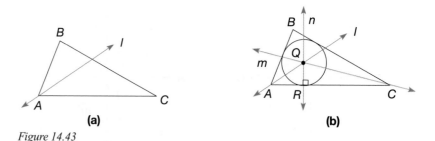

(a)   **(b)**

Figure 14.43

2. Similarly, construct line m, the bisector of $\angle BCA$. Let Q be the point of intersection of lines l and m. Then Q is the incenter of $\triangle ABC$ [Figure 14.43(b)]. To construct the inscribed circle, first construct the line n containing Q such that n is perpendicular to $\overline{AC}$. Let R be the intersection of line n and $\overline{AC}$. Then construct the circle, center at Q, whose radius is QR. This is the inscribed circle of $\triangle ABC$ [Figure 14.43(b)].

Justification: The justification for this construction is developed in the problem set.

Two other centers are commonly associated with triangles, the orthocenter and the centroid. The **orthocenter** is the intersection of the altitudes, and the **centroid** is the intersection of the medians of a triangle. The centroid has the property that it is the

Figure 14.44

center of mass of a triangular region. That is, if a triangular shape is cut out of some material of uniform density, the triangle will balance at the centroid (Figure 14.44).

✔ **Check for Understanding:** Exercise/Problem Set A #1–4

Constructing Regular Polygons

There are infinitely many values of n for which a regular n-gon can be constructed with compass and straightedge, *but* not for every n. In this subsection we will see how to construct several infinite families of regular n-gons. We will also learn a condition on the prime factorization of n that determines which regular n-gons can be constructed.

10 Equilateral Triangle

Procedure [Figure 14.45(a)]:

1. Choose points A and B arbitrarily.

2. Place the compass point at A and open the compass to the distance AB.

3. With the compass point at A, construct arc 1 of radius AB. Do the same thing with the compass point at B to construct arc 2. Label the intersection of the arcs point C. Then $\triangle ABC$ is equilateral.

Reflection from Research

Individual steps in a construction should be placed on separate transparencies. Overlaying these transparencies in the appropriate sequence helps students follow the sequence and allows teachers to refer back to any step at any time (Sobel & Maletsky, 1988).

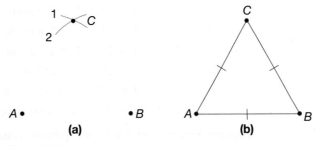

Figure 14.45

Justification [Figure 14.45(b)]: From steps 2 and 3, we find that $AB = AC = BC$. Hence $\triangle ABC$ is equilateral.

Constructing $3 \cdot 2^n$-gons We can use the construction of an equilateral triangle as the basis for constructing an infinite family of regular n-gons. For example, suppose that we find the circumscribed circle of an equilateral triangle [Figure 14.46(a)]. Let P be the circumcenter. Bisect the central angles, $\angle V_1PV_2$, $\angle V_2PV_3$, and $\angle V_3PV_1$, to locate points V_4, V_5, and V_6 on the circle [Figure 14.46(b)]. These six

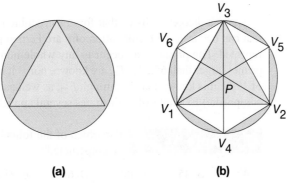

(a)   **(b)**

Figure 14.46

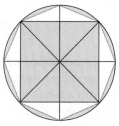

Figure 14.47

points are the vertices of a regular 6-gon (hexagon). Next bisect the central angles in the regular 6-gon, inscribed in a circle, to construct a regular 12-gon, then a 24-gon, and so on. Theoretically, then, we can construct an infinite family of regular n-gons, namely the family for $n = 3, 6, 12, 24, 48, \ldots, 3 \cdot 2^k, \ldots$, where k is any whole number.

Because we know how to construct right angles, we can construct a square. Then if a square is inscribed in a circle, we can bisect the central angles to locate the vertices of a regular 8-gon, then a 16-gon, and so on (Figure 14.47). Thus we could theoretically construct a regular n-gon for $n = 2^k$, where k is any whole number greater than 1.

In general, once we have constructed a regular n-gon, we can construct an infinite family of regular polygons, namely those with $n \cdot 2^k$ sides, where k is any whole number. In the Problem Set, we will investigate this family with $n = 5$. We will show that it is possible to construct a regular pentagon, and hence to construct regular n-gons for $n = 5, 10, 20, 40, 80, \ldots, 5 \cdot 2^k, \ldots$, where k is a whole number.

Gauss's Theorem for Constructible Regular n-gons   A remarkable result about the construction of regular n-gons tells us precisely the values of n for which a regular n-gon can be constructed. To understand the result, we need a certain type of prime number, called a Fermat prime. A **Fermat prime** is a prime number of the form $F_k = 2^{(2^k)} + 1$, where k is a whole number.

For the first few whole-number values of k, we obtain the following results.

$$F_0 = 2^{(2^0)} + 1 = 2^1 + 1 = 3, \text{ a prime;}$$
$$F_1 = 2^{(2^1)} + 1 = 2^2 + 1 = 5, \text{ a prime;}$$
$$F_2 = 2^{(2^2)} + 1 = 2^4 + 1 = 17, \text{ a prime;}$$
$$F_3 = 2^{(2^3)} + 1 = 2^8 + 1 = 257, \text{ a prime;}$$
$$F_4 = 2^{(2^4)} + 1 = 2^{16} + 1 = 65{,}537, \text{ a prime;}$$
$$F_5 = 2^{(2^5)} + 1 = 2^{32} + 1 = (641) \cdot (6{,}700{,}417), \textit{ not a prime.}$$

Thus there are at least five Fermat primes, namely 3, 5, 17, 257, and 65,537, but not every number of the form $2^{(2^k)} + 1$ is a prime. [Also, not every prime is of the form $2^{(2^k)} + 1$. For example, 7 is a prime, but not a Fermat prime.] A result, due to the famous mathematician Gauss, gives the conditions that n must satisfy in order for a regular n-gon to be constructible.

THEOREM

Gauss's Theorem for Constructible Regular n-gons

A regular n-gon can be constructed with straightedge and compass if and only if the only odd prime factors of n are distinct Fermat primes.

Gauss's theorem tells us that for constructible regular n-gons, the only odd primes that can occur in the factorization of n are Fermat primes with no Fermat prime factor repeated. The prime 2 can occur to any whole-number power. At this time, no Fermat primes larger than 65,537, F_4, are known, nor is it known whether any others *exist*. (As of 1999, it is known that F_5 through F_{23}, as well as over 100 other Fermat numbers, are composite.) Example 14.9 illustrates several applications of Gauss's theorem.

Example 14.9   For which of the following values of n can a regular n-gon be constructed?

a. 40   **b.** 45   **c.** 60   **d.** 64   **e.** 21

SOLUTION

a. $n = 40 = 2^3 \cdot 5$. Since the only odd prime factor of 40 is 5, a Fermat prime, a regular 40-gon can be constructed.

b. $n = 45 = 3^2 \cdot 5$. Since the (Fermat) prime 3 occurs more than once in the factorization of n, the odd prime factors are not *distinct* Fermat primes. Hence a regular 45-gon cannot be constructed.

c. $n = 60 = 2^2 \cdot 3 \cdot 5$. The odd prime factors of n are the distinct Fermat primes 3 and 5. Therefore, a regular 60-gon can be constructed.

d. $n = 64 = 2^6$. There are no odd factors to consider. Hence a regular 64-gon can be constructed.

e. $n = 21 = 3 \cdot 7$. Since 7 is not a Fermat prime, a regular 21-gon cannot be constructed.   ■

The proof of Gauss's theorem is very difficult. The theorem is a remarkable result in the history of mathematics and helped make Gauss one of the most respected mathematicians of all time.

✔ **Check for Understanding:** Exercise/Problem Set A #5–9

Constructing Segment Lengths

The use of similar triangles allows us to construct products and quotients of real-number lengths. Example 14.10 gives the construction for the product of two real numbers.

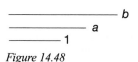

Figure 14.48

Example 14.10   Suppose that a and b are positive real numbers representing the lengths of line segments (Figure 14.48) and we have a segment of length 1. Show how to construct a line segment whose length is $a \cdot b$.

SOLUTION Let $\overline{PQ}$ be a line segment of length a [Figure 14.49(a)]. Let R be any point not on line $\overleftrightarrow{PQ}$ such that $PR = 1$ [Figure 14.49(b)]. Let S be a point on ray $\overrightarrow{PR}$ such that $PS = b$ [Figure 14.49(b)]. Construct segment $\overline{QR}$, and construct a line l through point S such that $l \parallel \overleftrightarrow{QR}$ [Figure 14.49(c)].

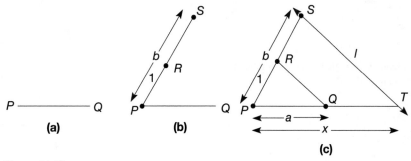

Figure 14.49

Let T be the intersection of lines l and $\overrightarrow{PQ}$. Then $\angle PQR \cong \angle PTS$ by the corresponding angles property. Since $\angle RPQ \cong \angle SPT$, we know that $\triangle PRQ \sim \triangle PST$ by the AA similarity property. Let $x = PT$. Then, using similar triangles,

$$\frac{a}{1} = \frac{x}{b},$$

so that $a \cdot b = x$. Thus we have constructed the product of the real numbers a and b.   ■

✔ **Check for Understanding:** Exercise/Problem Set A #10–11

MATHEMATICAL MORSEL

In writing his book on geometry, called *The Elements*, Euclid produced a new proof of the Pythagorean theorem. In 1907, when Elisha Loomis was preparing the manuscript for the book *The Pythagorean Proposition* (which eventually had over 370 *different* proofs of the Pythagorean theorem), he noted that there were two or three American textbooks on geometry in which Euclid's proof does not appear. He mused that the authors must have been seeking to show their originality or independence. However, he said, "The leaving out of Euclid's proof is like the play of *Hamlet* with Hamlet left out."

| Section 14.4 | **EXERCISE / PROBLEM SET A** |

EXERCISES

1. Copy the given triangle and construct the circle circumscribed about the triangle.

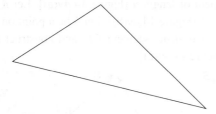

2. Copy the given triangle and construct the circle inscribed inside the triangle.

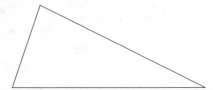

3. Use the Geometer's Sketchpad® to construct a triangle and a circle inscribed in the triangle.
  a. Submit a printout of the construction.
  b. Move the vertices of the triangle to create a wide range of different types of triangles (acute, obtuse, right) and fill in the blank of the following statement.

    The center of the inscribed circle always lies _____ the triangle.

4. The lines containing the altitudes of a triangle meet at a single point, called the orthocenter. The position of the orthocenter is determined by the measures of the angles. Construct the three altitudes for each of the following triangles. Then complete the statements in parts (a)–(c).

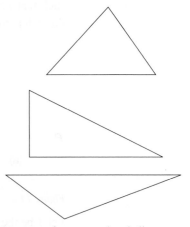

  a. The orthocenter of an acute triangle lies _____ the triangle.
  b. The orthocenter of a right triangle is the _____.
  c. The orthocenter of an obtuse triangle lies _____ the triangle.
  d. Use the Chapter 14 Geometer's Sketchpad® activity *Orthocenter* on our Web site to investigate a wide range of acute, obtuse, and right triangles. Do your conclusions for parts (a), (b), and (c) still hold?

5. Construct an equilateral triangle with sides congruent to the given segment.

_____

6. Construct a circle using any compass setting. Without changing the compass setting, mark off arcs of the radius around the circle (each mark serving as center for the next arc). Join consecutive marks to form a polygon. Is the polygon a regular polygon? If so, which one?

7. a. Follow steps i to vi to inscribe a particular regular n-gon in a circle.

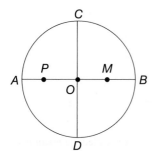

  i. Draw a circle with center O.
  ii. In this circle, draw a diameter $\overline{AB}$.
  iii. Construct another diameter, $\overline{CD}$, that is perpendicular to $\overline{AB}$.
  iv. Bisect $\overline{OB}$. Let M be its midpoint.
  v. Using M as the center and CM as the radius, draw an arc intersecting $\overline{AO}$. Call the intersection point P.
  vi. Mark off arcs of radius CP around the circle and connect consecutive points.
  b. What regular n-gon have you constructed?

8. Which of the following regular n-gons can be constructed with compass and straightedge?
  a. 120-gon   **b.** 85-gon   **c.** 36-gon
  d. 80-gon   **e.** 63-gon   **f.** 75-gon
  g. 105-gon   **h.** 255-gon   **i.** 340-gon

9. It has been shown that a regular n-gon can be constructed using a Mira if and only if n is of the form $2^r \cdot 3^s \cdot p_1 \ldots p_k$ where the $p_1, \ldots, p_k$ are primes of the form $2^u \cdot 3^v + 1$. (Note: $r, s, u, v,$ are all whole numbers and $u \neq 0$.) Which of the following regular n-gons can be constructed using a Mira?
  a. 7-gon   **b.** 11-gon   **c.** 78-gon

10. The following construction procedure can be used to divide a segment into any given number of congruent segments. Draw a segment and follow the steps listed.

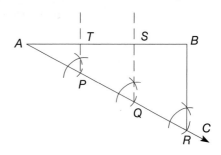

  i. Construct any ray $\overrightarrow{AC}$ not collinear with $\overline{AB}$.
  ii. With any arbitrary compass setting, mark off three congruent segments on $\overrightarrow{AC}$ (here, $\overline{AP}$, $\overline{PQ}$, and $\overline{QR}$).
  iii. Construct $\overline{BR}$.
  iv. Construct lines parallel to $\overline{BR}$ through P and Q.

  Into how many congruent pieces has $\overline{AB}$ been divided? (NOTE: To divide $\overline{AB}$ into k congruent segments, where k is a whole number, mark off k congruent segments on $\overline{AC}$ in step 2.)
  v. We can simplify the procedure described in the preceding exercise by constructing only $\overline{SQ}$ parallel to $\overline{BR}$. Then use the compass opening as $\overline{SB}$ and mark off congruent segments along $\overline{AB}$. Use this technique to divide $\overline{AB}$ into six congruent pieces.

11. Copy the segments of lengths 1, 3, and $\sqrt{2}$ as shown onto your paper. Use the method shown in Example 14.10 to construct a segment of length $3\sqrt{2}$.

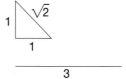

PROBLEMS

12. Using only a compass and straightedge, construct angles with the following measures.
  a. 15°   **b.** 75°   **c.** 105°

13. Construct a triangle with angles of 30°, 60°, and 90°. With your ruler, measure the lengths in centimeters of the hypotenuse and the shortest leg. Next, construct two more triangles of different sizes but with angles of 30°, 60°, and 90°. Again measure the lengths of the hypotenuse and the shortest leg. What is the relationship between the length of the hypotenuse and the length of the shorter leg in a 30°–60°–90° triangle?

14. A golden rectangle, as described in Chapter 7, can be constructed using a compass and straightedge as follows.

   i. Construct any square $ABCD$.

   ii. Bisect side $\overline{AB}$ and call the midpoint M.

   iii. Set the radius of your compass as MC. Using point M as the center of your arc, make an arc that intersects $\overleftrightarrow{AB}$ at P.

   iv. Construct $\overline{PQ} \parallel \overline{AD}$ and $\overline{DQ} \parallel \overline{AB}$.

   v. Now $APQD$ is a golden rectangle.

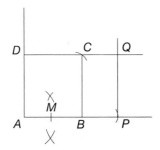

Construct a golden rectangle starting with a square that has sides of some length you choose. Using a ruler, measure the length and width of your rectangle in centimeters. Calculate the ratio of length : width for your rectangle. How does your ratio compare to the golden ratio?

15. a. Draw an acute triangle and find its circumcenter.

   b. Repeat part (a) with a different acute triangle.

   c. What do you notice about the location of the circumcenter of an acute triangle?

16. a. Construct an obtuse triangle and find its circumcenter.

   b. Repeat part (a) with a different obtuse triangle.

   c. What do you notice about the location of the circumcenter of an obtuse triangle?

17. An interesting result attributed to Napoleon Bonaparte can be observed in the following construction.

   i. Draw any triangle $\triangle PQR$.

   ii. Using a compass and straightedge, construct an equilateral triangle on each side of $\triangle PQR$.

   iii. Use your compass and straightedge to locate the centroid of each equilateral triangle: C_1, C_2, C_3.

   iv. Connect C_1, C_2, and C_3 to form a triangle.

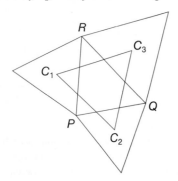

a. Draw a triangle and perform the steps 1–4. What kind of triangle is $\triangle C_1C_2C_3$? Use your ruler and protractor to check.

b. Repeat the construction for two different types of triangles $\triangle PQR$. What kind of triangle is $\triangle C_1C_2C_3$?

c. Can you summarize your observations?

18. In this section a construction was given to find the product of any two lengths. Use that construction to find the length $1/a$ for any given length a. The case $a > 1$ is shown in the following figure.

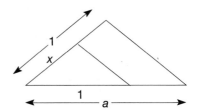

19. a. If $\dfrac{a}{x} = \dfrac{x}{b}$ then x is called the **mean proportional** or **geometric mean** between a and b. One method of constructing the geometric mean is pictured. Assuming $a \ge b$, mark off AC of length a, and find point B such that BC has length b, where B is between A and C. Then mark off BD of length a, and draw two large arcs with centers A and D and radius a. If the arcs intersect at E, then $x = EB$. Following this method, construct the geometric mean between 1 and 2 where the length 1 is any given length. What length have you constructed?

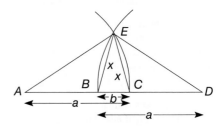

b. Prove that the x in the diagram is, in fact, the geometric mean between the a and b given.

20. A woman wants to divide a short strip of plastic into five congruent pieces but has no ruler available. If she has a pencil and a sheet of lined paper, how can she use them to mark off five congruent segments?

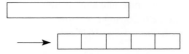

Section 14.4 | **EXERCISE / PROBLEM SET B**

EXERCISES

1. Copy the given triangle and use a compass and straightedge to find its circumcenter.

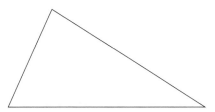

2. Copy the given triangle and construct the circle inscribed inside the triangle.

3. The location of the circumcenter changes depending on the type of triangle. Construct the circumcenter for the following acute, right, and obtuse triangles and complete the statements in parts (a)–(c).

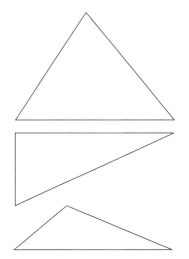

    a. The circumcenter of an acute triangle lies _____ the triangle.
    b. The circumcenter of a right triangle lies _____ the triangle.
    c. The circumcenter of an obtuse triangle lies _____ the triangle.
    d. Use the Chapter 14 Geometer's Sketchpad® activity *Circumcenter* on our Web site to investigate a wide range of acute, right and obtuse triangles. Do your conclusions for parts (a), (b), and (c) still hold?

4. The three medians of a triangle are concurrent at a point called the centroid. This point is the center of gravity or balance point of a triangle. Construct the three medians of the following triangles and complete the statement in part (a).

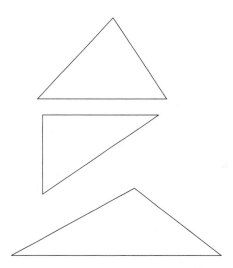

    a. The centroid always lies _____ the triangle.
    b. Use the Chapter 14 Geometer's Sketchpad® activity *Centroid* on our Web site to investigate a wider range of triangles. Do your conclusions for part (a) still hold?

5. Use the Geometer's Sketchpad® to construct an equilateral triangle. Submit a printout of the construction and describe the similarities between the compass and straightedge construction in Part A, Exercise 5 and the construction done on the computer.

6. a. If you bisected the central angles of the regular polygon constructed in Part A, Exercise 6 and connected consecutive points along the circle, what regular *n*-gon would be constructed?
    b. List two other regular polygons of this family that can be constructed.

7. a. If you bisected the central angles of the regular *n*-gon constructed in Part A, Exercise 7 and connected the consecutive points along the circle, what regular *n*-gon would be constructed?
    b. Repeating the bisecting process to this new regular *n*-gon, what regular *n*-gon would be constructed?
    c. List two other regular polygons of this family that can be constructed.

8. List all regular polygons with fewer than 100 sides that can be constructed with compass and straightedge. (*Hint:* Apply Gauss's theorem.)

9. Find the first 10 regular *n*-gons that can be constructed using a Mira (see Part A, Exercise 10).

10. **a.** Use the procedure in Part A, Exercise 11 to divide $\overline{AB}$ into four congruent pieces.

A ——————————— B

b. Find another procedure that can be used to divide $\overline{AB}$ into four congruent parts (using construction techniques from Section 14.3).

11. Copy the segments of lengths 1, 2 and $\sqrt{5}$ as shown onto your paper. Use the method shown in Example 14.10 to construct a segment of length $2\sqrt{5}$.

PROBLEMS

12. Explain how to construct angles with the following measures.
    a. 135°   **b.** 75°   **c.** 72°   **d.** 108°

13. Follow the given steps to construct a regular decagon. (A justification of this construction follows in Problem 13 of Exercise/Problem Set 14.5B.)
    a. Taking AB as a unit length, construct a segment $\overline{CD}$ of length $\sqrt{5}$. (*Hint:* Apply the Pythagorean theorem.)
    b. Using $\overline{AB}$ and $\overline{CD}$, construct a segment $\overline{EF}$ of length $\sqrt{5} - 1$.
    c. Bisect segment $\overline{EF}$ forming segment $\overline{EG}$. What is the length of $\overline{EG}$?
    d. Construct a circle with radius AB.
    e. With a compass open a distance EG, make marks around the circle. Connecting adjacent points will yield a decagon.

A ——————————— B

14. Complete the Solution for Example 14.8.

15. **a.** Construct a right triangle and find its circumcenter.
    b. Repeat part (a) with a different right triangle.
    c. What do you notice about the location of the circumcenter of a right triangle?

16. By constructing a variety of acute, right, and obtuse triangles and finding their incenters, determine whether the incenter is always inside the triangle.

17. An interesting result called Aubel's theorem can be observed in the following construction.

    Step 1. Draw any quadrilateral *ABCD*.
    Step 2. Using a compass and straightedge, construct a square on each side of quadrilateral *ABCD*.
    Step 3. Locate the midpoint of each square: M_1, M_2, M_3, M_4. Connect the midpoints of opposite squares with line segments.

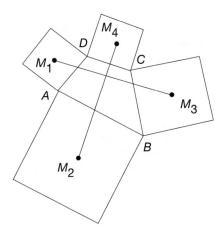

a. Draw a convex quadrilateral and perform the preceding steps. Use your ruler to measure the lengths of segments $\overline{M_1M_3}$ and $\overline{M_2M_4}$. Use your protractor to measure the angles formed where $\overline{M_1M_3}$ and $\overline{M_2M_4}$ intersect.

b. Repeat the construction for two more quadrilaterals. Let one quadrilateral be concave, in which case the squares will overlap. Measure the segments and angles described in part (a).

c. What conclusion can you draw?

18. By Gauss's theorem we know that it is not possible to construct a regular heptagon (7-gon) using only straightedge and compass. It is possible, however, to make an angle measuring $\dfrac{180°}{7}$, or approximately 25.7°, with toothpicks using a technique attributed to C. Johnson, *Mathematical Gazette*, No. 407, 1975. Seven congruent toothpicks can be arranged as shown in the following figure, where points *A*, *B*, *C*, and *D* are collinear. When the toothpicks are arranged in this way, the angle at *A* will measure $\dfrac{180°}{7}$.

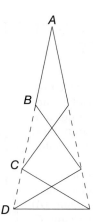

d. Explain why Q is therefore equidistant from $\overleftrightarrow{AB}$ and $\overleftrightarrow{AC}$.

e. Use these results to justify construction 9, the procedure for constructing the incenter of a triangle.

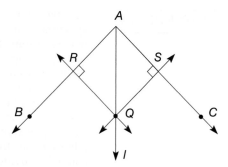

a. Arrange seven toothpicks as shown and then use your protractor to measure the angle at A.

b. What is the measure of the central angle of a regular heptagon?

c. If you can construct an angle of $\dfrac{180°}{7}$, how can you construct a regular heptagon?

19. To locate the incenter of a triangle, we need to locate a point that is equidistant from the sides of the triangle. Suppose that point A is equidistant from $\overleftrightarrow{YX}$ and $\overleftrightarrow{YZ}$. Show that $\overrightarrow{YA}$ is the angle bisector of $\angle XYZ$.

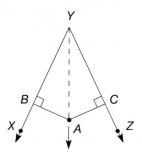

20. If line l is the bisector of $\angle BAC$ and point Q is on l, verify that Q is equidistant from the sides $\overline{AB}$ and $\overline{AC}$ of $\angle BAC$ by completing the following.

a. Let line $\overleftrightarrow{QR}$ be perpendicular to $\overleftrightarrow{AB}$, where R is on $\overleftrightarrow{AB}$. What is the distance from Q to $\overleftrightarrow{AB}$?

b. Let line $\overleftrightarrow{QS}$ be perpendicular to $\overleftrightarrow{AC}$, where S is on $\overleftrightarrow{AC}$. What is the distance from Q to $\overleftrightarrow{AC}$?

c. Is $\triangle ARQ \cong \triangle ASQ$? Justify your answer.

 Analyzing Student Thinking

21. Roseanne was trying to find the circumcenter of a triangle. She constructed the perpendicular bisectors of two of the sides, but she was wondering if she needed to construct all three. How should you respond?

22. Mallory says that the circumcenter is always inside of its triangle. Is she correct? Explain.

23. Craig said he had a new way to construct a regular hexagon. He said a regular hexagon is just six equilateral triangles stuck together, so he could just construct one equilateral triangle, and then construct matching triangles on two of its sides, and just keep going that way until he had six of them. Will Craig end up with a regular hexagon? How can you be sure?

24. Samantha says that the centroid may be on its triangle as opposed to being in the interior. Is she correct? Explain.

25. Chase claims that the incenter and circumcenter are the same in an equilateral triangle. Is he correct? Explain.

26. Spencer says that the orthocenter is always inside of its triangle. Is he correct? Explain.

27. Joan wanted to construct a segment that would be $\sqrt{5}$ inches long, but she didn't know how. Roberto said, "You can make it the diagonal of a certain rectangle." Joan tells you she doesn't understand that. Is Roberto correct? Discuss.

Problems Relating to the NCTM Standards and Curriculum Focal Points

1. The Focal Points for Grade 3 state "Through building, drawing, and analyzing two-dimensional shapes, students understand attributes and properties of two-dimensional space and the use of those attributes and properties in solving problems, including applications involving congruence and symmetry." What are some of the attributes of triangles that you have come to understand as a result of doing some of the constructions in this section?

2. The NCTM Standards state "Instructional programs should enable all students to recognize reasoning and proof as essential and powerful parts of mathematics." Describe an example from this section where reasoning and proof were used.

14.5   GEOMETRIC PROBLEM SOLVING USING TRIANGLE CONGRUENCE AND SIMILARITY

STARTING POINT

The two parallelograms below have congruent corresponding sides, but the parallelograms themselves are not congruent. The two triangles below have congruent corresponding sides and, by the SSS triangle congruence, the triangles are congruent. These two ideas are related to some principles of fence building.

When building a gate for a fence, a crosspiece (A), like the one shown, is added to ensure a stronger more stable gate that won't sag. Why does the diagonal (A) add so much strength that the 2 parallel pieces (B and C) couldn't provide? How is this strengthening crosspiece related to the SSS triangle congruence?

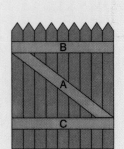

Applications of Triangle Congruence

Problem-Solving Strategy
Draw a Picture

In this section we apply triangle congruence and similarity properties to prove properties of geometric shapes. Many of these results were observed informally in Chapter 12. Our first result is an application of the SAS congruence property that establishes a property of the diagonals of a rectangle.

Example 14.11   Show that the diagonals of a rectangle are congruent.

SOLUTION   Suppose that $ABCD$ is a rectangle [Figure 14.50(a)].

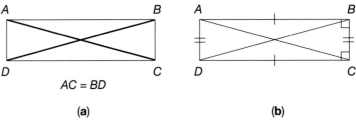

(a)   (b)

Figure 14.50

Then $ABCD$ is a parallelogram (from Chapter 12). By a theorem in Section 14.1, the opposite sides of $ABCD$ are congruent [Figure 14.50(b)]. In particular, $\overline{AB} \cong \overline{DC}$. Consider $\triangle ABC$ and $\triangle DCB$; $\angle ABC \cong \angle DCB$, since they are both right angles. Also, $\overline{CB} \cong \overline{BC}$. Hence, $\triangle ABC \cong \triangle DCB$ by the SAS congruence property. Consequently, $\overline{AC} \cong \overline{BD}$, as desired.   ∎

The next result is a form of a converse of the theorem in Example 14.11.

Example 14.12   In parallelogram *ABCD*, if the diagonals are congruent, it is a rectangle.

SOLUTION   Suppose that *ABCD* is a parallelogram with $\overline{AC} \cong \overline{BD}$ [Figure 14.51(a)].

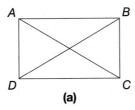

(a)   **(b)**

Figure 14.51

Since *ABCD* is a parallelogram, $\overline{AD} \cong \overline{BC}$. Therefore, since $\overline{DC} \cong \overline{DC}$, $ADC \cong \triangle BCD$ by SSS [Figure 14.51(b)]. By corresponding parts, $\angle ADC \cong \angle BCD$. But $\angle ADC$ and $\angle BCD$ are also supplementary because $\overline{AD} \parallel \overline{BC}$. Consequently, $m \angle ADC = m \angle BCD = 90°$ and *ABCD* is a rectangle. ■

Next we verify that every rhombus is a parallelogram using the ASA congruence property and the alternate interior angles theorem.

Example 14.13   Show that every rhombus is a parallelogram [Figure 14.52(a)].

Problem-Solving Strategy
Draw a Picture

SOLUTION   Let *ABCD* be a rhombus. Thus $\overline{AB} \cong \overline{BC} \cong \overline{CD} \cong \overline{DA}$. Construct diagonal $\overline{BD}$ and consider $\triangle ABD$ and $\triangle CDB$ [Figure 14.52(b)].

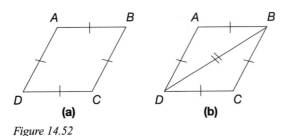

(a)   **(b)**

Figure 14.52

Since $\overline{BD} \cong \overline{DB}$, it follows that $\triangle ABD \cong \triangle CDB$ by the SSS congruence property. Hence $\angle ABD \cong \angle CDB$, since they are corresponding angles in the congruent triangles. By the alternate interior angles theorem, $\overline{AB} \parallel \overline{DC}$. Also $\angle ADB \cong \angle CBD$, so that $\overline{AD} \parallel \overline{BC}$. Therefore, *ABCD* is a parallelogram, since the opposite sides are parallel. ■

Next we prove a result about quadrilaterals that is applied in the Epilogue, following Chapter 16.

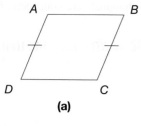

(a)

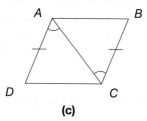

(b)

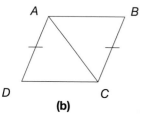

(c)

Figure 14.53

Example 14.14 If two sides of a quadrilateral are parallel and congruent, then the quadrilateral is a parallelogram.

SOLUTION Let $ABCD$ be a quadrilateral with $\overline{AD} \parallel \overline{BC}$ and $\overline{AD} \cong \overline{BC}$ [Figure 14.53(a)]. Draw in diagonal $\overline{AC}$ [Figure 14.53(b)]. Since $\overline{AD} \parallel \overline{BC}$, $\overline{AC}$ is a transversal and $\angle DAC \cong \angle BCA$ [Figure 14.53(c)].

Thus $\triangle DAC \cong \triangle BCA$ by SAS, since $\overline{AC}$ is common to both triangles. By corresponding parts, $\angle ACD \cong \angle CAB$. Therefore, $\overline{AB} \parallel \overline{DC}$, since $\angle ACD$ and $\angle CAB$ are congruent alternate interior angles. Finally, $ABCD$ is a parallelogram, since $\overline{AD} \parallel \overline{BC}$ and $\overline{AB} \parallel \overline{DC}$. ∎

Converse of the Pythagorean Theorem

Using several geometric constructions and the SSS congruence property, we can prove an important result about right triangles, namely the converse of the Pythagorean theorem.

Example 14.15 Suppose that the lengths of the sides of $\triangle ABC$ are a, b, and c with $a^2 + b^2 = c^2$ (Figure 14.54). Show that $\triangle ABC$ is a right triangle.

SOLUTION Construct a segment $\overline{DE}$ of length b using construction 1 [Figure 14.55(a)]. Next, using construction 5, construct line $\overleftrightarrow{EF}$ such that $\overleftrightarrow{EF} \perp \overline{DE}$ at point E [Figure 14.55(b)]. Next, locate point G on line $\overleftrightarrow{EF}$ so that $EG = a$, using construction 1 [Figure 14.55(c)].

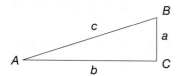

Figure 14.54

Problem-Solving Strategy
Draw a Picture

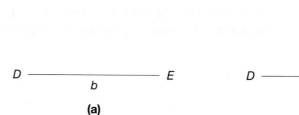

(a) **(b)**

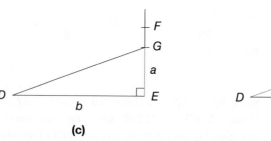

(c) **(d)**

Figure 14.55

Then $\triangle DEG$ is a right triangle. By the Pythagorean theorem, $DG^2 = DE^2 + EG^2 = a^2 + b^2$. Hence $DG^2 = c^2$, since $a^2 + b^2 = c^2$ by assumption. Thus $DG = c$ [Figure 14.55(d)]. But then $\triangle ACB \cong \triangle DEG$ by the SSS congruence property. Therefore, $\angle ACB \cong \angle DEG$, a right angle, so that $\triangle ACB$ is a right triangle. ∎

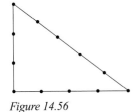

Figure 14.56

Converse of the Pythagorean Theorem

A triangle having sides of lengths a, b, and c, where $a^2 + b^2 = c^2$, is a right triangle.

The converse of the Pythagorean theorem has an interesting application. When carpenters erect the walls of a house, usually they need to make the walls perpendicular to each other. A common way to do this is to use a 12-foot string loop with knots at 1-foot intervals (Figure 14.56). If this loop is stretched into a 3–4–5 triangle, the angle between the "3" and "4" sides must be a right angle by the converse of the Pythagorean theorem, since $3^2 + 4^2 = 5^2$.

Application of Triangle Similarity

The next example presents an interesting result about the midpoints of the sides of a triangle using the SAS similarity property, the SSS similarity property, and the SAS congruence property.

Example 14.16 Given $\triangle ABC$, where P, Q, R are the midpoints of the sides $\overline{AB}$, $\overline{BC}$, and $\overline{AC}$, respectively [Figure 14.57(a)], show that $\triangle APR$, $\triangle PBQ$, $\triangle RQC$, and $\triangle QRP$ are all congruent and that each triangle is similar to $\triangle ABC$.

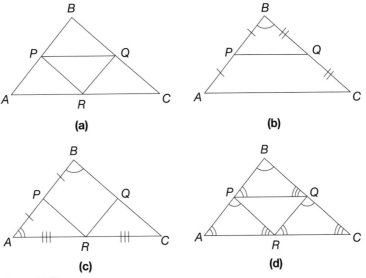

Figure 14.57

SOLUTION Consider $\triangle ABC$ and $\triangle PBQ$ [Figure 14.57(b)]. We will first show that these triangles are similar using the SAS similarity property. Since P and Q are the midpoints of their respective sides, we know that $PB = \frac{1}{2}AB$ and that $BQ = \frac{1}{2}BC$. Certainly, $\angle ABC \cong \angle PBQ$, so that $\triangle ABC \sim \triangle PBQ$ by the SAS similarity property. Using a similar argument, we can show that $\triangle APR \sim \triangle ABC$ [Figure 14.57(c)] and that $\triangle RQC \sim \triangle ABC$ [Figure 14.57(d)]. Also, $\triangle QRP \sim \triangle ABC$ by the SSS similarity property (verify). Since $AP = PB$, $\triangle APR \cong \triangle PBQ$ by the ASA congruence property (verify). In similar fashion, we have $\triangle PBQ \cong \triangle RQC$. Combining our results, we can show that $\triangle RQC \cong \triangle QRP$ using the SSS congruence property. Thus we have that all four smaller triangles are congruent. ■

The Midquad Theorem   The next result is related to Example 14.16.

> **Example 14.17**   Refer to Figure 14.58(a). Suppose that $\triangle ABC$ is a triangle and points P and Q are on $\overline{AB}$ and $\overline{BC}$, respectively, such that $\dfrac{BP}{BA} = \dfrac{BQ}{BC}$; that is, P and Q divide $\overline{BA}$ and $\overline{BC}$ proportionally. Show that $\overline{PQ} \parallel \overline{AC}$ and $\dfrac{PQ}{AC} = \dfrac{BP}{BA}$.

SOLUTION   Consider $\triangle BPQ$ [Figure 14.58(b)]. Since $\dfrac{BP}{BA} = \dfrac{BQ}{BC}$ and $\angle PBQ \cong \angle ABC$, we have that $\triangle ABC \sim \triangle PBQ$ by the SAS similarity property. Hence $\angle BPQ \cong \angle BAC$, since they are corresponding angles in the similar triangles [Figure 14.58(c)].

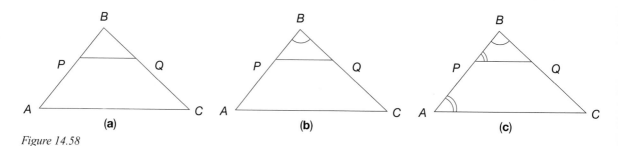

Figure 14.58

Thus $\overline{PQ} \parallel \overline{AC}$. Also, $\dfrac{PQ}{AC} = \dfrac{BP}{BA}$, since corresponding sides are proportional in the similar triangles (verify this).   ∎

From Example 14.17 we see that a line segment that divides two sides of a triangle proportionally is parallel to the third side and proportional to it in the same ratio. In particular, if points P and Q in Example 14.17 were midpoints of the sides, then $\overline{PQ} \parallel \overline{AC}$ and $PQ = \frac{1}{2}AC$. The segment, such as $\overline{PQ}$, that joins the midpoints of two sides of a triangle is called a **midsegment** of the triangle.

Using the result of Example 14.17 regarding the midsegment of a triangle, we can deduce a surprising result about quadrilaterals. Suppose that $ABCD$ is any quadrilateral in the plane (Figure 14.59).

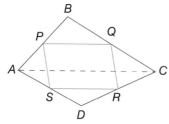

Figure 14.59

Let P, Q, R, and S be the midpoints of the sides. We call $PQRS$ the **midquad** of $ABCD$, since it is a quadrilateral that is formed by joining midpoints of the sides of $ABCD$. By Example 14.17, $\overline{PQ} \parallel \overline{AC}$ and $\overline{SR} \parallel \overline{AC}$. Thus $\overline{PQ} \parallel \overline{SR}$. Similarly, $\overline{PS} \parallel \overline{QR}$. Therefore, $PQRS$ is a parallelogram.

THEOREM

Midquad Theorem

The midquad of any quadrilateral is a parallelogram.

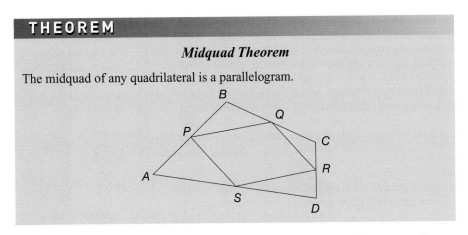

NCTM Standard

Instructional programs should enable all students to make and investigate mathematical conjectures.

The preceding proof shows that *PQRS* is a parallelogram. But could it be a square? a rectangle? a rhombus? Part A Problem 10 in the Problem Set contains some problems that will lead you to decide precisely under what conditions these special quadrilaterals are possible.

MATHEMATICAL MORSEL

Although the name of the Greek mathematician Pythagoras (circa 500 B.C.E.) is associated with the famous Pythagorean theorem, there is no doubt that this result was known prior to the time of Pythagoras. In fact, the discovery of a Babylonian method for finding the diagonal of a square, given the length of the side of the square, suggests that the theorem was known more than 1000 years before Pythagoras. Although Pythagoras is credited with this theorem that he may not have originated, he has another significant achievement that is attributed to Euclid. Pythagoras' greatest achievement was that he was the first European who insisted that postulates must be set down first when developing geometry. Euclid, however, is often given credit for this significant development in mathematics.

Section 14.5   PROBLEM SET A

PROBLEMS

1. Answer the questions to prove the following property: If a line bisects the vertex angle of an isosceles triangle, it is the perpendicular bisector of the base.

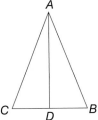

a. You are given that △*ABC* is isosceles with base $\overline{BC}$ and that $\overline{AD}$ bisects ∠*CAB*. What pairs of angles or segments are congruent because of the given information?

b. What other pair of corresponding angles of △*ABD* and △*ACD* are congruent? Why?

c. What congruence property can be used to prove △*ABD* ≅ △*ACD*?

d. Why is ∠*ADC* ≅ ∠*ADB* and $\overline{DC}$ ≅ $\overline{DB}$?

e. Why is $\overline{AD}$ ⊥ $\overline{BC}$?

f. Why is $\overline{AD}$ the perpendicular bisector of $\overline{BC}$?

2. Given rhombus *ABCD* with diagonals meeting at point *E*, prove that the diagonals of a rhombus are perpendicular to each other. (*Hint:* Show that $\triangle ABE \cong \triangle CBE$.)

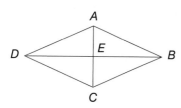

3. Quadrilateral *STUV* is a rhombus and $\angle S$ is a right angle. Show that *STUV* is a square.

4. Prove that the diagonals of a parallelogram bisect each other.

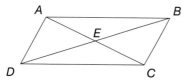

5. Construct a parallelogram with adjacent sides and one diagonal congruent to the given segments.

a		b
one side		second
	d	side
	diagonal	

6. Quadrilateral *STUV* is a rhombus and diagonals $\overline{SU}$ and $\overline{TV}$ are congruent. Show that *STUV* is a square.

7. Construct a rhombus with sides and one diagonal congruent to the given segment.

a

8. Construct an isosceles trapezoid with bases and legs congruent to the given segments.

a		b
base		base
	c	
	leg	

9. If $\overline{CD} \perp \overline{AB}$ in $\triangle ABC$ and *AC* is the geometric mean of *AD* and *AB*, prove that $\triangle ABC$ is a right triangle. (*Hint:* Show that $\triangle ADC \sim \triangle ACB$.)

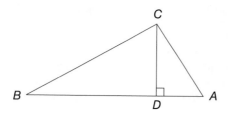

10. The midquad theorem in this section states that the midquad of any quadrilateral *PQRS* is a parallelogram.

a. Use the fact that each side of the midquad is parallel to and one-half the length of a diagonal of the quadrilateral to determine under what conditions the midquad $M_1M_2M_3M_4$ will be a rectangle.

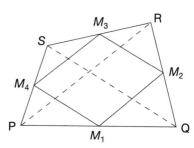

b. Under what conditions will the midquad $M_1M_2M_3M_4$ be a rhombus?

c. Under what conditions will the midquad $M_1M_2M_3M_4$ be a square?

11. Complete the following argument, which uses similarity to prove the Pythagorean theorem. Let $\triangle ABC$ have $\angle C$ as a right angle. Let $\overline{CD}$ be perpendicular to $\overline{AB}$.

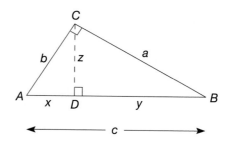

a. Then $\triangle ADC \sim \triangle ACB$. Why?

b. Also, $\triangle BDC \sim \triangle BCA$. Why? Thus $\dfrac{b}{x} = \dfrac{x+y}{b}$, or $b^2 = x^2 + xy$. Also $\dfrac{a}{y} = \dfrac{x+y}{a}$, or $a^2 = xy + y^2$.

c. Show that $a^2 + b^2 = c^2$.

12. a. Show that the diagonals of kite *ABCD* are perpendicular. (*Hint:* Show that $\triangle AEB \cong \triangle AED$.)

b. Find a formula for the area of a kite in terms of the lengths of its diagonals.

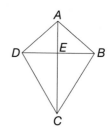

13. Show that the SSS congruence property follows from the SAS congruence property. (*Hint:* Referring to the following figure, assume the SAS congruence property and suppose that the respective sides of $\triangle ABC$ and $\triangle A'B'C'$ are congruent as marked. Assume that $\angle A$ is acute and then construct $\triangle ABD$ as illustrated so that $\angle BAD \cong \angle B'A'C'$ and $AD = A'C'$. Without using the SSS congruence property, show $\triangle BAD \cong \triangle B'A'C'$, $\triangle BAD \cong \triangle BAC$, etc.)

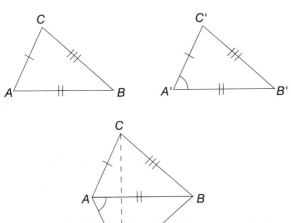

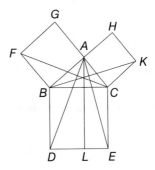

14. Show that the AA similarity property follows from the SAS similarity property. Referring to the following figure, suppose that $\angle A \cong \angle A'$ and $\angle B \cong \angle B'$. Show that $\triangle ABC \sim \triangle A'B'C'$ without using the AA similarity property. (*Hint:* If $\dfrac{AC}{AB} = \dfrac{A'C'}{A'B'}$, then $\triangle ABC \sim \triangle A'B'C'$ by the SAS similarity property. If $\dfrac{AC}{AB} \neq \dfrac{A'C'}{A'B'}$, a D' can be found on $\overline{A'C'}$ such that $\dfrac{AC}{AB} = \dfrac{A'D'}{A'B'}$. Use the SAS similarity property to reach a contradiction.)

15. Euclid's proof of the Pythagorean theorem is as follows. Refer to the figure and justify each part.

a. Show that $\triangle ABD \cong \triangle FBC$ and $\triangle ACE \cong \triangle KCB$.
b. Show that the area of $\triangle ABD$ plus the area of $\triangle ACE$ is one-half the area of square $BCED$.
c. Show that the area of $\triangle FBC$ is one-half the area of square $ABFG$, and that the area of $\triangle KCB$ is one-half the area of square $ACKH$.
d. Show that the area of square $ABFG$ plus the area of square $ACKH$ is the area of square $BCED$.
e. How does this prove the Pythagorean theorem?

16. In addition to the midquad of any quadrilateral being a parallelogram, there is an interesting property that relates the area of the midquad to the area of the original quadrilateral. Use the Chapter 14 Geometer's Sketchpad® activity *Midquad* on our Web site to investigate this relationship. What relationship do you observe?

Section 14.5 **PROBLEM SET B**

PROBLEMS

1. Answer the following questions to prove that the diagonals of a rhombus bisect the vertex angles of the rhombus.

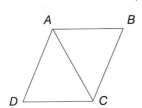

a. Given the rhombus $ABCD$ and diagonal $\overline{AC}$, what pairs of corresponding sides of $\triangle ABC$ and $\triangle ADC$ are congruent?
b. What other pair of corresponding sides are congruent? Why?
c. What congruence property can be used to show that $\triangle ABC \cong \triangle ADC$?
d. Why is $\angle BAC \cong \angle DAC$ and $\angle BCA \cong \angle DCA$?
e. Why does $\overline{AC}$ bisect $\angle DAB$ and $\angle DCB$?

2. Another justification that the diagonal of a rhombus bisects the vertex angles follows from the following questions.
   a. Since a rhombus is a parallelogram, $\overline{AB} \parallel \overline{CD}$ and $\overline{AD} \parallel \overline{BC}$. What pairs of angles are thereby congruent?
   b. $\angle 1 \cong \angle 2$ and $\angle 3 \cong \angle 4$. Why?
   c. Can we say $\angle 1 \cong \angle 4$ and $\angle 2 \cong \angle 3$? Why?

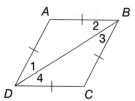

3. Given that $\triangle PQR$ is an equilateral triangle, show that it is also equiangular.

4. Prove: If a trapezoid is isosceles, its opposite angles are supplementary.

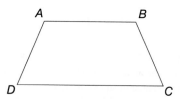

5. A rhombus is sometimes defined as a parallelogram with two adjacent congruent sides. If parallelogram $DEFG$ has congruent sides $\overline{DE}$ and $\overline{EF}$, verify that it has four congruent sides (thus satisfying our definition of a rhombus).

6. Prove that every rectangle is a parallelogram.

7. Quadrilateral $HIJK$ is a rectangle, and adjacent sides $\overline{HI}$ and $\overline{IJ}$ are congruent. Prove that $HIJK$ is a square.

8. Construct a rectangle with a side and a diagonal congruent to the given segments.

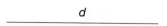

   side   diagonal

9. Construct a square with diagonals congruent to the given segment.

d

10. a. Prove: If diagonals of a quadrilateral are perpendicular bisectors of each other, the quadrilateral is a rhombus.
   b. Construct a rhombus with diagonals congruent to the two segments given.

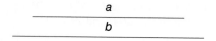

a

b

11. Prove: Two isosceles triangles, $\triangle DEF$ and $\triangle RST$, are similar if a base angle of one is congruent to a base angle of the other. (Let $\angle D$ and $\angle R$ be the congruent base angles and $\angle E$ and $\angle S$ be the nonbase angles.)

12. In $\triangle ABC$, $\overline{CD} \perp \overline{AB}$ and CD is the geometric mean of AD and DB. Prove that $\triangle ABC$ is a right triangle.

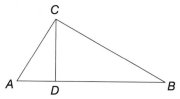

13. Refer to the next figure. To inscribe a regular decagon in a circle of radius 1, it must be possible to construct the length x.

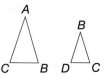

   a. What are $m(\angle BAC)$, $m(\angle ABC)$, and $m(\angle ACB)$?
   b. An arc of length x is constructed with center B, meeting $\overline{AC}$ at point D. What are $m(\angle BCD)$ and $m(\angle CBD)$?
   c. What is $m(\angle ABD)$? What special kind of triangle is $\triangle ABD$?
   d. What are the lengths of $\overline{AD}$ and $\overline{DC}$?
   e. Consider the following triangles copied from the preceding drawing. Label angle and side measures that are known. Are these triangles similar?

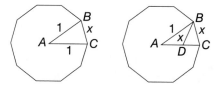

   f. Complete the proportions: $\dfrac{AC}{?} = \dfrac{BC}{?}$ or $\dfrac{1}{?} = \dfrac{x}{?}$.
   g. Solve this proportion for x. [*Hint:* You may need to recall the quadratic formula. To solve the equation $ax^2 + bx + c = 0$, use $x = (-b \pm \sqrt{b^2 - 4ac})/2a$.]
   h. Can we construct a segment of length x?

14. Show that the ASA congruence property follows from the SAS congruence property. (*Hint:* Referring to the following figure, if $AC = A'C'$, then $\triangle ABC \cong \triangle A'B'C'$ by the SAS congruence property. If not, find a D' on $\overline{A'C'}$ such that $AC = A'D'$, show that $\triangle ABC \cong \triangle A'B'D'$, and use the SAS congruence property to reach a contradiction.)

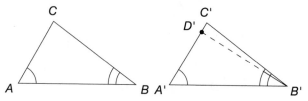

15. Show that the SSS similarity property follows from the SAS similarity property. (*Hint:* Referring to the figure, assume the SAS similarity property and suppose that the sides in $\triangle ABC$ and $\triangle A'B'C'$ are proportional, as marked. Assume that $\angle A$ is acute and construct $\triangle ABD$ as illustrated so that $\angle BAD \cong \angle B'A'C$, and $\dfrac{AD}{AB} = \dfrac{A'C'}{A'B'}$. Show that $\triangle BAD \sim \triangle B'A'C'$ and $\triangle BAD \cong \triangle BAC$; use the SAS congruence property.)

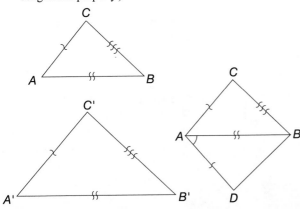

Analyzing Student Thinking

16. Willard asks, "Why do I have to prove that a rhombus is a parallelogram when it is obvious when looking at a rhombus that the opposite sides are parallel?" How should you respond?

17. Victoria wants to prove that the angle bisector of the angle opposite of the base of an isosceles triangle is also a median. She says that she can use SSS to do this. Do you agree? Explain.

18. Charlotte says she gets confused about what she can use or not use when proving properties of a parallelogram. For example, she says that she doesn't know if she can use the fact that the diagonals bisect each other to prove that the opposite sides are congruent. How would you respond?

19. Camden claims that the midquad of an isosceles trapezoid is a rhombus. Do you agree? Explain.

20. Braymen claims that if a parallelogram has congruent diagonals, then it is a rectangle. Weston disagrees because he thinks you would have to know that there is a right angle somewhere in order to know it is a rectangle. Who is correct? Explain.

21. Falisha claims that the midquad of a rectangle is a square. Do you agree? Explain.

22. Caesar says, "I know a rhombus is a parallelogram because having two pairs of parallel sides is one of the properties of a rhombus." Does this constitute a proof? You may want to refer back to what you know about van Hiele levels.

Problems Relating to the NCTM Standards and Curriculum Focal Points

1. The Focal Points for Grade 3 state "Through building, drawing, and analyzing two-dimensional shapes, students understand attributes and properties of two-dimensional space and the use of those attributes and properties in solving problems, including applications involving congruence and symmetry." Discuss how triangle congruence was used in this section to establish properties of other two-dimensional shapes.

2. The NCTM Standards state "Instructional programs should enable all students to make and investigate mathematical conjectures." What is a mathematical conjecture?

END OF CHAPTER MATERIAL

Solution of Initial Problem

An eastbound bicycle enters a tunnel at the same time that a westbound bicycle enters the other end of the tunnel. The eastbound bicycle travels at 10 kilometers per hour, the westbound bicycle at 8 kilometers per hour. A fly is flying back and forth between the two bicycles at 15 kilometers per hour, leaving the eastbound bicycle as it enters the tunnel. The tunnel is 9 kilometers long. How far has the fly traveled in the tunnel when the bicycles meet?

Strategy: Identify Subgoals

We know the rate at which the fly is flying (15 km/h). If we can determine the time that the fly is traveling, we can determine the distance the fly travels, since distance = rate $\times$ time. Therefore, our subgoal is to find the time that the fly travels. But this is the length of time that it takes the two bicycles to meet.

Let t be the time in hours that it takes for the bicycles to meet. The eastbound bicycle travels $10 \cdot t$ kilometers and the westbound bicycle travels $8 \cdot t$ kilometers. This yields

$$10t + 8t = 9,$$

so that

$$18t = 9,$$

or

$$t = \frac{1}{2}.$$

Therefore, the time that it takes for the bicycles to meet is $\frac{1}{2}$ hour. (This reaches our subgoal.) Consequently, the fly travels for $\frac{1}{2}$ hour, so that the fly travels $15 \times \frac{1}{2} = 7\frac{1}{2}$ km.

Additional Problems Where the Strategy "Identify Subgoals" Is Useful

1. Find the smallest square that has a factor of 360.
2. The areas of the sides of a rectangular box are 24 cm^2, 32 cm^2, and 48 cm^2. What is the volume of the box?
3. Thirty-two percent of n is 128. Find n mentally.

People in Mathematics

Hypatia (370?–415)
Hypatia is the first woman mathematician to be mentioned in the history of mathematics. She was the daughter of the mathematician Theon of Alexandria, who is chiefly known for his editions of Euclid's *Elements*. At the university in Alexandria, she was a famous lecturer in philosophy and mathematics, but we do not know if she had an official teaching position. It is said that she followed the practice of philosophers of her time, dressing in a tattered cloak and holding public discussions in the center of the city. Hypatia became a victim of the prejudice of her time. Christians in Alexandria were hostile toward the university and the pagan Greek culture it represented. There were periodic outbreaks of violence, and during one of these incidents Hypatia was killed by a mob of Christian fanatics.

Benoit Mandelbrot (1924–)
Benoit Mandelbrot once said, "Clouds are not spheres, mountains are not cones, coastlines are not circles, and bark is not smooth, nor does lightning travel in a straight line." This is how he describes the inspiration for fractal geometry, a new field of mathematics that finds order in chaotic, irregular shapes and processes. Mandelbrot was largely responsible for developing the mathematics of fractal geometry while at IBM's Watson Research Center. "The question I raised in 1967 is, 'How long is the coast of Britain?' and the correct answer is 'It all depends.' It depends on the size of the instrument used to measure length. As the measurement becomes increasingly refined, the measured length will increase. Thus the coastline is of infinite length in some sense."

CHAPTER REVIEW

Review the following terms and exercises to determine which require learning or relearning—page numbers are provided for easy reference.

SECTION 14.1 Congruence of Triangles

VOCABULARY/NOTATION

Congruent line segments, $\overline{AB} \cong \overline{DE}$
756

Congruent angles, $\angle ABC \cong \angle DEF$
756

Correspondence between $\triangle ABC$ and
$\triangle DEF$, $A \leftrightarrow D, B \leftrightarrow E, C \leftrightarrow F$
756

Congruent triangles, $\triangle ABC \cong \triangle DEF$
756

Angle bisector   760

EXERCISES

1. State the definition of congruent triangles.

2. State the following congruence properties.

    a. SAS   **b.** ASA   **c.** SSS

3. Decide whether $\triangle ABC \cong \triangle DEF$ under the following conditions. Which of the properties in Exercise 2 justify the

congruences? If the triangles are not congruent, sketch a figure to show why not.

    a. $\overline{AB} \cong \overline{DE}, \overline{BC} \cong \overline{EF}, \overline{CA} \cong \overline{FD}$

    b. $\overline{AB} \cong \overline{DE}, \angle C \cong \angle F, \overline{BC} \cong \overline{EF}$

    c. $\angle A \cong \angle D, \angle B \cong \angle E, \overline{AB} \cong \overline{DE}$

    d. $\angle B \cong \angle E, \overline{BC} \cong \overline{EF}, \overline{AB} \cong \overline{DE}$

SECTION 14.2 Similarity of Triangles

VOCABULARY/NOTATION

Similar triangles, $\triangle ABC \sim$ Fractals   770   Self-similar   771
  $\triangle DEF$ 767   Koch curve   771   Sierpinski triangle or gasket   771
Indirect measurement   769

EXERCISES

1. State the definition of similar triangles.

2. State the following similarity properties.

    a. SAS   **b.** AA   **c.** SSS

3. Decide whether $\triangle ABC \sim \triangle DEF$ under the following conditions. Which of the properties in Exercise 2 justify the similarity? If the triangles are not similar, sketch a figure to show why not.

    a. $\dfrac{AB}{DE} = \dfrac{BC}{EF}, \angle A \cong \angle D$

    b. $\dfrac{AB}{DE} = \dfrac{BC}{EF} = \dfrac{AC}{DF}$

    c. $\angle B \cong \angle E, \angle C \cong \angle F$

4. Describe three ways to calculate the height of a tree using similarity.

SECTION 14.3 Basic Euclidean Constructions

VOCABULARY/NOTATION

Arc   781

EXERCISES

1. Draw a line segment and copy it.

2. Draw an angle and copy it.

3. Draw a line segment and construct its perpendicular bisector.

4. Draw an angle and bisect it.

5. Draw a line and mark point P on it. Construct a line through P perpendicular to the line.

6. Draw a line and a point P not on the line. Construct a line through P perpendicular to the line.

7. Draw a line and a point P not on the line. Construct a line through P parallel to the line.

SECTION 14.4 Additional Euclidean Constructions

VOCABULARY/NOTATION

Circumscribed circle   794   Circumcenter   795   Orthocenter   796
Inscribed circle   794   Incenter   795   Centroid   796
Tangent line to a circle   795   Distance from a point to a line   796   Fermat prime   798

EXERCISES

1. List the steps required to construct the circumscribed circle of a triangle.

2. List the steps required to construct the inscribed circle of a triangle.

3. Draw a line segment and construct an equilateral triangle having the line segment as one of its sides.

4. Describe how to construct the following regular n-gons.
  a. A square
  b. A hexagon
  c. An octagon

5. Draw a line segment $\overline{AB}$ and construct a second line segment whose length is $AB\sqrt{3}$.

SECTION 14.5 Geometric Problem Solving Using Triangle Congruence and Similarity

VOCABULARY/NOTATION

Midsegment of a triangle   810   Midquad   810

EXERCISES

1. State and prove the converse of the Pythagorean theorem.

2. Show how the midsegment theorem is used to prove the midquad theorem.

CHAPTER TEST

KNOWLEDGE

1. True or false?
  a. Two triangles are congruent if two sides and the included angle of one triangle are congruent, respectively, to two sides and the included angle of the other triangle.
  b. Two triangles are similar if two sides of one triangle are proportional to two sides of the other triangle.
  c. The opposite sides of a parallelogram are congruent.
  d. The diagonals of a kite are perpendicular.
  e. Every rhombus is a kite.
  f. The diagonals of a parallelogram bisect each other.
  g. The circumcenter of a triangle is the intersection of the altitudes.
  h. The incenter of a triangle is equidistant from the vertices.

2. Which of the following are congruence properties for triangles?

SAS, ASA, SSA, SSS, AAA

SKILL

3. For which of the following values of n can a regular n-gon be constructed with a compass and straightedge?

  a. 36   **b.** 85   **c.** 144   **d.** 4369

4. Construct a regular 12-gon with a compass and straightedge.

5. Construct the circumcenter and incenter for the same equilateral triangle. What conclusion can you draw?

6. Determine which of the following pairs of triangles are congruent. Justify your conclusion.

a.

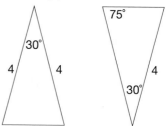

b.

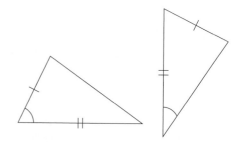

7. In the following figure, $AC = 20$, $CE = 5$, $DE = 3$, and $BE = 9$. Determine if $\triangle ABE \sim \triangle CDE$. Justify your answer.

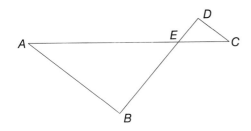

8. Construct the line parallel to line l through point P using a compass and straightedge.

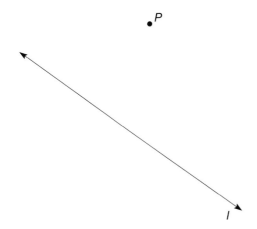

UNDERSTANDING

9. Given segment $\overline{AB}$ as the unit segment, construct a segment $\overline{AC}$ where the length of $\overline{AC}$ is $\sqrt{5}$. Then construct a square with area 5.

10. Prove or disprove: If $\triangle ABC \cong \triangle CBA$, then $\triangle ABC$ is isosceles.

11. Prove or disprove: If $\triangle ABC \cong \triangle BCA$, then $\triangle ABC$ is equilateral.

12. If possible, construct two noncongruent triangles that have corresponding sides of length 1.5 inches and corresponding angles with measure $75°$. If this is not possible, explain why not.

13. Explain how similar triangles can be used to determine the height of a tree.

14. Explain, in detail, what it means for two triangles to be congruent by the SAS congruence property.

15. In the following figure, line l and point P are given. The rest of the marks on the figure indicate the construction of a line through P that is perpendicular to l. The following steps describe the construction.

  a. Draw an arc with center P to intersect l in two places. Label these points of intersection A and B.

  b. Draw an arc with center A on the side of l that is opposite of P.

  c. Keeping the same measure on the compass as in part (b), draw an arc with center B to intersect the arc drawn in part (b), Label this point of intersection C.

  d. Draw line $\overleftrightarrow{PC}$. This is the desired perpendicular.

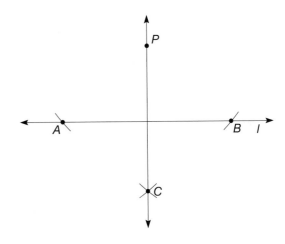

Explain why this series of steps yields the desired result of "a line through P that is perpendicular to l."

16. a. State the mathematical definition of *similar*.

  b. Determine whether the following statements are true or false according to the definition.

    i. Notebook paper (8.5 in. by 11 in.) is similar to an index card (3 in. by 5 in.).

    ii. A right triangle is similar to an equilateral triangle.

    iii. A circle of radius 1 inch is similar to a circle of radius 5 meters.

PROBLEM SOLVING/APPLICATION

17. Given: trapezoid $ABCD$.

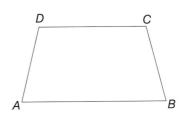

  a. Prove: If $\angle A \cong \angle B$, then $\overline{AD} \cong \overline{BC}$.

  b. Prove: If $\overline{AD} \cong \overline{BC}$, then $\angle A \cong \angle B$.

18. a. According to Gauss's theorem, a regular 9-gon cannot be constructed with a compass and straightedge. Why?

   b. What is the measure of a central angle in a regular 9-gon?

   c. Suppose that one wanted to trisect a 60° angle (i.e., divide it into three congruent angles) with a compass and straightedge. What angle would be constructed?

   d. What conclusion can you draw from parts (a), (b), and (c) regarding the possibility of trisecting a 60° angle?

19. In $\triangle ABC$, segment $\overline{PQ} \parallel \overline{BC}$ and $\angle AQP$ is a right angle.

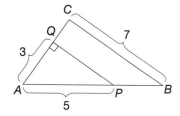

   a. Find the length of $\overline{PQ}$.

   b. Find the area of $\triangle ABC$.

20. On her early morning walk, Jinhee noticed that when she walked under a streetlight, her shadow would get longer the farther she was away from the light. She decided to use her shadow to find out how tall the light was. When she was 12 feet from the base of the light, her shadow was 4 feet long. She is 5 feet 6 inches tall. How tall is the light?

Geometry Using Coordinates

FOCUS ON

René Descartes and Coordinate Geometry

The subjects of algebra and geometry had evolved on parallel tracks until René Descartes (1596–1650) developed a method of joining them.

them via equations. These equations were obtained by picturing the curves in the plane. Each point, P, in the plane was labeled using pairs of numbers, or "coordinates," determined by two perpendicular reference lines.

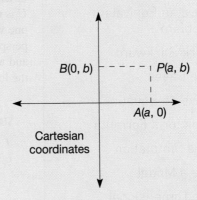

Cartesian
coordinates

This important contribution made possible the development of the calculus. Because of this contribution, Descartes has been called the "father of modern mathematics." The coordinate system used in analytic geometry is called the Cartesian coordinate system in his honor.

Descartes' analytic geometry was designed to study the mathematical attributes of lines and curves by representing

What is impressive about the coordinate approach is that geometric problems can be represented using algebraic equations. Then algebra can be applied to these equations without regard to their geometric representations. Finally, the result of the algebra can be reinterpreted to produce a solution to the original geometric problem.

Brief Timeline for Geometry

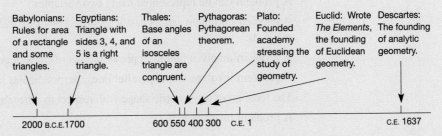

Babylonians: Rules for area of a rectangle and some triangles.

Egyptians: Triangle with sides 3, 4, and 5 is a right triangle.

Thales: Base angles of an isosceles triangle are congruent.

Pythagoras: Pythagorean theorem.

Plato: Founded academy stressing the study of geometry.

Euclid: Wrote *The Elements*, the founding of Euclidean geometry.

Descartes: The founding of analytic geometry.

2000 B.C.E. 1700   600 550 400 300   C.E. 1   C.E. 1637

Problem-Solving Strategies

1. Guess and Test
2. Draw a Picture
3. Use a Variable
4. Look for a Pattern
5. Make a List
6. Solve a Simpler Problem
7. Draw a Diagram
8. Use Direct Reasoning
9. Use Indirect Reasoning
10. Use Properties of Numbers
11. Solve an Equivalent Problem
12. Work Backward
13. Use Cases
14. Solve an Equation
15. Look for a Formula
16. Do a Simulation
17. Use a Model
18. Use Dimensional Analysis
19. Identify Subgoals
20. **Use Coordinates**

STRATEGY 20

Use Coordinates

In many two-dimensional geometry problems, we can use a "grid" of squares overlaid on the plane, called a coordinate system, to gain additional information. This numerical information can then be used to solve problems about two-dimensional figures. Coordinate systems also can be used in three-dimensional space and on curved surfaces such as a sphere (e.g., the Earth).

INITIAL PROBLEM

A surveyor plotted a triangular building lot shown in the figure below. He described the locations of stakes T and U relative to stake S. For example, U is recorded as East 207′, North 35′. This would mean that to find stake U, one would walk due east 207 feet and then due north for 35 feet. From the perspective of the diagram shown, one would go right from point S 207 feet and up 35 feet to get to U. Use the information provided to find the area of the lot in square feet.

STAKE	POSITION RELATIVE TO S
U	East 207′, North 35′
T	East 40′, North 185′

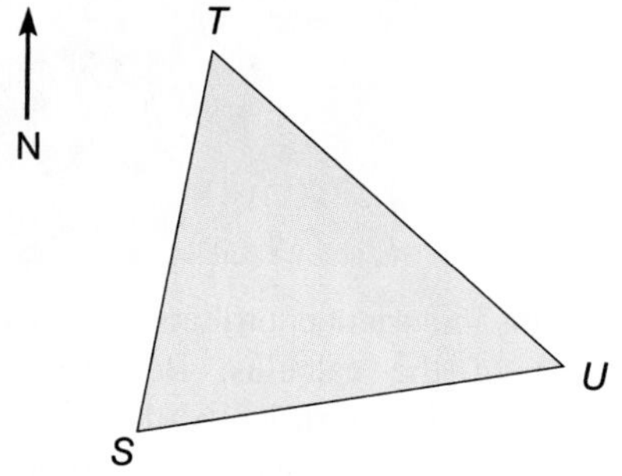

CLUES

The Use Coordinates strategy may be appropriate when

- A problem can be represented using two variables.
- A geometry problem cannot easily be solved by using traditional Euclidean methods.
- A problem involves finding representations of lines or conic sections.
- A problem involves slope, parallel lines, perpendicular lines, and so on.
- The location of a geometric shape with respect to other shapes is important.
- A problem involves maps.

A solution of this Initial Problem is on page 858.

INTRODUCTION

I n this chapter we study geometry using the coordinate plane. Using a coordinate system on the plane, which was introduced in Section 9.3, we are able to derive many elegant geometrical results about lines, polygons, circles, and so on. In Section 15.1 we introduce the basic ideas needed to study geometry in the coordinate plane. Then in Section 15.2 we prove properties of geometric shapes using these concepts. Finally, Section 15.3 contains many interesting problems that can be solved using coordinate geometry.

> **Key Concepts from NCTM Curriculum Focal Points**
>
> - **GRADE 3:** Describing and analyzing properties of two-dimensional shapes.
> - **GRADE 6:** Writing, interpreting, and using mathematical expressions and equations.
> - **GRADE 8:** Analyzing two- and three-dimensional space and figures by using distance and angle.

15.1   DISTANCE AND SLOPE IN THE COORDINATE PLANE

STARTING POINT

The points $A = (0, 0)$, $B = (2, 3)$, and $C = (5, -1)$ are plotted on the axes at the right. Locate a fourth point D such that A, B, C, and D are the vertices of a parallelogram. Justify your selection. Are there other points that will work? If so, how many?

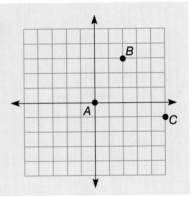

Children's Literature
www.wiley.com/college/musser
See "The Fly on the Ceiling" by
Julie Glass.

Distance

The use of coordinates as developed in Section 9.4 allows us to analyze many properties of geometric figures. For example, we can find distances between points in the plane using coordinates. Consider points $P(x_1, y_1)$ and $Q(x_2, y_2)$ (Figure 15.1). We can use point $R(x_2, y_1)$ to form a right triangle, $\triangle PQR$. Notice that the length of the horizontal segment $\overline{PR}$ is $x_2 - x_1$ and that the length of the vertical segment $\overline{QR}$ is $y_2 - y_1$. We wish to find the length of $\overline{PQ}$. By the Pythagorean theorem,

$$PQ^2 = PR^2 + QR^2,$$

so

$$PQ = \sqrt{PR^2 + QR^2}.$$

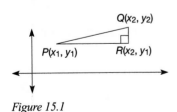

Figure 15.1

But

$$PR^2 = (x_2 - x_1)^2 \text{ and } QR^2 = (y_2 - y_1)^2.$$

Hence $PQ = \sqrt{(x_2 - x_1)^2 + (y_2 - y_1)^2}$. This yields the following distance formula.

NCTM Standard
All students should find the distance between points along horizontal and vertical lines of a coordinate system.

Algebraic Reasoning
The distance formula is an example of using variables to *efficiently* describe a method of computation.

THEOREM

Coordinate Distance Formula

If P is the point (x_1, y_1) and Q is the point (x_2, y_2), the distance from P to Q is

$$PQ = \sqrt{(x_2 - x_1)^2 + (y_2 - y_1)^2}.$$

$Q(x_2, y_2)$

$P(x_1, y_1)$

We have verified the coordinate distance formula in the case that $x_2 \ge x_1$ and $y_2 \ge y_1$. However, this formula holds for *all* pairs of points in the plane. For example, if $x_1 \ge x_2$, we would use $(x_1 - x_2)^2$ in the formula. But $(x_1 - x_2)^2 = (x_2 - x_1)^2$, so that the formula will yield the same result.

Collinearity Test   We can use the coordinate distance formula to determine whether three points are collinear. Recall that points P, Q, and R are collinear with Q between P and R if and only if $PQ + QR = PR$; that is, the distance from P to R is the sum of the distances from P to Q and Q to R (Figure 15.2).

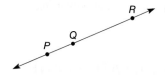

Figure 15.2

| **Example 15.1** | Use the coordinate distance formula to show that the points $P = (-5, -4)$, $Q = (-2, -2)$, and $R = (4, 2)$ are collinear. |

SOLUTION

$$PQ = \sqrt{[(-5) - (-2)]^2 + [(-4) - (-2)]^2} = \sqrt{9 + 4} = \sqrt{13}$$

$$QR = \sqrt{[(-2) - 4]^2 + [(-2) - 2]^2} = \sqrt{36 + 16} = 2\sqrt{13}$$

$$PR = \sqrt{[(-5) - 4]^2 + [(-4) - 2]^2} = \sqrt{81 + 36} = 3\sqrt{13}$$

Thus $PQ + QR = \sqrt{13} + 2\sqrt{13} = 3\sqrt{13} = PR$, so P, Q, and R are collinear.   ■

Example 15.1 is a special case of the following theorem.

THEOREM

Collinearity Test

Points $P(x_1, y_1)$, $Q(x_2, y_2)$, and $R(x_3, y_3)$ are collinear with Q between P and R if and only if $PQ + QR = PR$, or, equivalently,

$$\sqrt{(x_2 - x_1)^2 + (y_2 - y_1)^2} + \sqrt{(x_3 - x_2)^2 + (y_3 - y_2)^2}$$
$$= \sqrt{(x_3 - x_1)^2 + (y_3 - y_1)^2}.$$

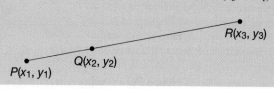

Midpoint Formula   Next we determine the midpoint of a line segment.

Consider $P(x_1, y_1)$ and $Q(x_2, y_2)$. Let $R(x_2, y_1)$ be the vertex of a right triangle that has $\overline{PQ}$ as the hypotenuse [see Figure 15.3(a)]. Then $\left(\dfrac{x_1 + x_2}{2}, y_1\right)$ and $\left(x_2, \dfrac{y_1 + y_2}{2}\right)$ are midpoints of $\overline{PR}$ and $\overline{QR}$, respectively [see Figure 15.3(a)]. Now let M be the intersection of the vertical line through midpoint $\left(\dfrac{x_1 + x_2}{2}, y_1\right)$ and the horizontal line through midpoint $\left(x_2, \dfrac{y_1 + y_2}{2}\right)$ [see Figure 15.3(b)]. Hence the coordinates of the midpoint M are $\left(\dfrac{x_1 + x_2}{2}, \dfrac{y_1 + y_2}{2}\right)$. We can verify that M is the midpoint of segment $\overline{PQ}$ by showing that $PM = MQ$ and that P, M, and Q are collinear [see Figure 15.3(b)]. This is left for the Problem Set.

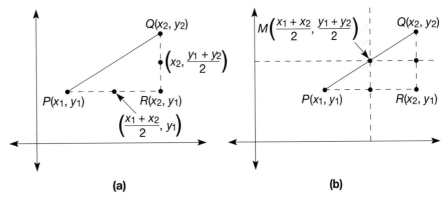

(a)   (b)

Figure 15.3

Algebraic Reasoning
The midpoint formula is something that could be memorized, but would be better remembered if understood. Algebraic reasoning helps one better understand the statement at the bottom of the theorem box, which clarifies the meaning of the formula. Namely, the equation for the x-coordinate of the midpoint is simply the average of the x-coordinates of the endpoints. A similar statement is true for the y-coordinates.

THEOREM

Midpoint Formula

If P is the point (x_1, y_1) and Q is the point (x_2, y_2), the midpoint, M, of $\overline{PQ}$ is the point

$$\left(\frac{x_1 + x_2}{2}, \frac{y_1 + y_2}{2}\right).$$

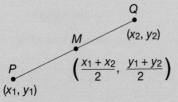

In words, the coordinates of the midpoint of a segment are the averages of the x-coordinates and y-coordinates of the endpoints, respectively.

Example 15.2   Find the coordinates of the midpoints of the three sides of $\triangle ABC$, where $A = (-6, 0)$, $B = (0, 8)$, $C = (10, 0)$ [Figure 15.4(a)].

SOLUTION

$$\text{midpoint of } \overline{AB} = \left(\frac{-6 + 0}{2}, \frac{0 + 8}{2} \right) = (-3, 4)$$

$$\text{midpoint of } \overline{BC} = \left(\frac{0 + 10}{2}, \frac{8 + 0}{2} \right) = (5, 4)$$

$$\text{midpoint of } \overline{AC} = \left(\frac{-6 + 10}{2}, \frac{0 + 0}{2} \right) = (2, 0) \, [\text{Figure 15.4(b)}]$$

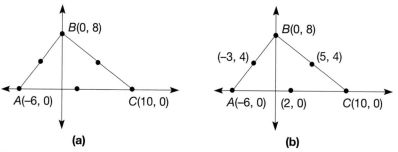

Figure 15.4

✔ **Check for Understanding:** Exercise/Problem Set A #1–5

Slope

The slope of a line is a measure of its inclination from the horizontal.

NCTM Standard
All students should explore relationships between symbolic expressions and graphs of lines, paying particular attention to the meaning of intercept and slope.

DEFINITION

Slope of a Line

Suppose that P is the point (x_1, y_1) and Q is the point (x_2, y_2).

The **slope of line** $\overleftrightarrow{PQ}$ is the ratio $\dfrac{y_2 - y_1}{x_2 - x_1}$, provided $x_1 \neq x_2$. If $x_1 = x_2$, that is, $\overleftrightarrow{PQ}$ is vertical, then the slope of $\overleftrightarrow{PQ}$ is undefined.

Note that $\dfrac{y_2 - y_1}{x_2 - x_1} = \dfrac{y_1 - y_2}{x_1 - x_2}$, so that it does not matter which endpoint we use first in computing the slope of a line. However, we must be consistent in the numerator and denominator; that is, we subtract the coordinates of Q from the coordinates of P, or vice versa. The slope of a line is often defined informally as "rise over the run." The **slope of a line segment** is the slope of the line containing it.

Example 15.3   Find the slope of these lines: (a) line l containing $P(-8, -6)$ and $Q(10, 5)$, (b) line m containing $R(2, 1)$ and $S(20, 12)$, and (c) line n containing $T(-3, 11)$ and $U(4, 11)$ (Figure 15.5).

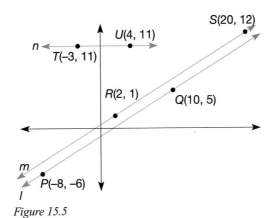

Figure 15.5

Algebraic Reasoning
Arithmetic is the foundation for algebra. This can be seen in the computation of the slope. If addition and subtraction of integers are not well understood, computing the slope of a line would be very difficult.

SOLUTION

a. Using the coordinates of P and Q, the slope of $l = \dfrac{5 - (-6)}{10 - (-8)} = \dfrac{11}{18}$.

b. Using the coordinates of R and S, the slope of $m = \dfrac{12 - 1}{20 - 2} = \dfrac{11}{18}$. Hence lines l and m have equal slopes.

c. Using points T and U, the slope of line $n = \dfrac{11 - 11}{4 - (-3)} = 0$. Note that line n is horizontal. ∎

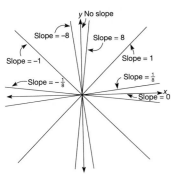

Figure 15.6

Figure 15.6 shows examples of lines with various slopes. A horizontal line, such as line n in Example 15.3, has slope 0. As the slope increases, the line "rises" to the right. A line that rises steeply from left to right has a large positive slope. A vertical line has no slope. On the other hand, a line that declines steeply from left to right has a *small* negative slope. For example, in Figure 15.6, the line with slope -8 is steeper than the line with slope -1. A line with a negative slope near zero, such as the line in Figure 15.6 having slope $-\frac{1}{8}$, declines gradually from left to right.

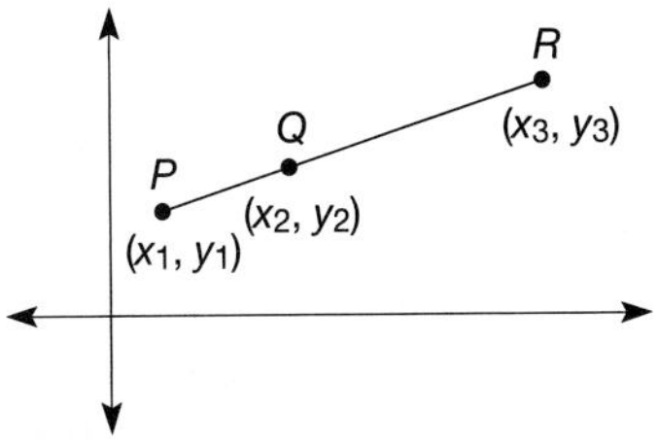

Slope and Collinearity   Using slopes, we can determine whether several points are collinear. For example, if points P, Q, and R are collinear, then the slope of segment $\overline{PQ}$ is equal to the slope of segment $\overline{PR}$ (Figure 15.7). That is, if P, Q, and R are collinear, then $\dfrac{y_2 - y_1}{x_2 - x_1} = \dfrac{y_3 - y_1}{x_3 - x_1}$ provided that the slopes exist. If P, Q, and R are collinear and lie on a vertical line, then segments $\overline{PQ}$ and $\overline{PR}$ have no slope.

On the other hand, suppose that P, Q, and R are such that the slope of segment $\overline{PQ}$ is equal to the slope of segment $\overline{QR}$. It can be shown that the points P, Q, and R are collinear.

Figure 15.7

> ### THEOREM
>
> #### *Slope and Collinearity*
>
> Points P, Q, and R are collinear if and only if
>
> **1.** the slopes of $\overline{PQ}$ and $\overline{QR}$ are equal, or
> **2.** the slopes of $\overline{PQ}$ and $\overline{QR}$ are undefined (i.e., P, Q, and R are on the same vertical line).

NCTM Standard
All students should use coordinate geometry to represent and examine the properties of geometric shapes.

Slopes of Parallel Lines   In Figure 15.5 it appears that lines l and m, which have the same slope, are parallel. We can determine whether two lines are parallel by computing their slopes.

> ### THEOREM
>
> #### *Slopes of Parallel Lines*
>
> Two lines in the coordinate plane are parallel if and only if
>
> **1.** their slopes are equal, or
> **2.** their slopes are undefined.

In Example 15.3, lines l and m each have slope $\frac{11}{18}$ and thus are parallel by the slopes of parallel lines theorem.

Slopes of Perpendicular Lines   Just as we are able to identify the relationship of the slopes of parallel lines, we can identify the relationship of the slopes of perpendicular lines. Consider two perpendicular lines l_1 and l_2 with slopes m_1 and m_2 respectively [see Figure 15.8(a)]. If these lines intersect in the origin, then the equation of l_1 is $y = m_1 x$ and the equation of l_2 is $y = m_2 x$. To find a relationship between the slopes, we will identify one point on each line. If $x = 1$, then the point $(1, m_1)$ is on l_1 and the point $(1, m_2)$ is on l_2 as shown in Figure 15.8(b).

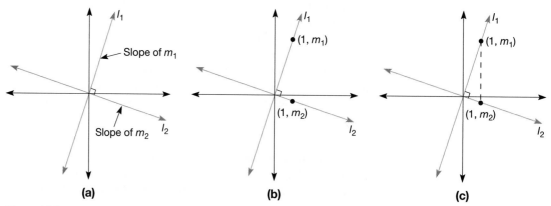

Figure 15.8

Since the two lines are perpendicular, they intersect to form a right angle at the origin. Thus, the points $(1, m_1)$, $(1, m_2)$, and the origin are the vertices of a right triangle as show in Figure 15.8(c). The Pythagorean theorem will be applied to this right

1.2 **Parallels and Perpendiculars**

The design at the right is made from a circle and two overlapping rectangles. One way to make a crop circle with this design is to place stakes at key points and connect the stakes with string outlining the regions. However, you first need to find the location of these points. You can use what you know about coordinate geometry to analyze the design's key points and features.

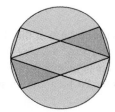

Problem **1.2** **Parallels and Perpendiculars**

This diagram shows some of the key points in the design. The design has reflection symmetry in both the x-axis and the y-axis. The radius is 5 units.

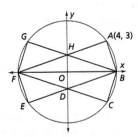

A. Find the coordinates of points B, C, E, F, and G.

B. List all pairs of parallel lines. How do the slopes of the lines in each pair compare? Explain why this makes sense.

C. List all pairs of perpendicular lines. How do the slopes of the lines in each pair compare? Explain why this makes sense.

D. Locate a new point $K(2, y)$ on the circle. Draw a line segment from point K to the point $(5, 0)$. Can you draw a rectangle with this segment as one side and all its vertices on the circle? If so, give the coordinates of the vertices.

8 The Shapes of Algebra

triangle to find a relationship between m_1 and m_2. The length of one leg is the distance from the origin to the point $(1, m_1)$ or $\sqrt{1 + m_1^2}$. The length of the other leg is the distance from the origin to the point $(1, m_2)$ or $\sqrt{1 + m_2^2}$. The length of the hypotenuse is $m_1 - m_2$. By the Pythagorean theorem, we have

$$\left(\sqrt{1 + m_1^2}\right)^2 + \left(\sqrt{1 + m_2^2}\right)^2 = (m_1 - m_2)^2$$
$$1 + m_1^2 + 1 + m_2^2 = m_1^2 - 2m_1m_2 + m_2^2$$
$$2 = -2m_1m_2$$
$$-1 = m_1m_2$$

Thus the produce of the slopes of l_1 and l_2 is -1.

Conversely, to show that *if* the product of the slopes of two lines is 21, *then* the lines are perpendicular, we can use a similar argument. This is left for Part B Problem 22 in the Problem Set. In summary, we have the following result.

NCTM Standard
All students should use coordinate geometry to examine special geometric shapes such as regular polygons or those with pairs of parallel or perpendicular sides.

THEOREM

Slopes of Perpendicular Lines

Two lines in the coordinate plane are perpendicular if and only if

1. the product of their slopes is -1, or

2. one line is horizontal and the other is vertical.

Example 15.4 shows how slopes can be used to analyze the diagonals of a rhombus.

Example 15.4 Show that the diagonals of *PQRS* in Figure 15.9 form right angles at their intersection.

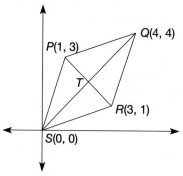

Figure 15.9

SOLUTION The slope of diagonal $\overline{PR}$ is $\dfrac{2}{-2} = -1$, and the slope of diagonal $\overline{QS}$ is $\dfrac{4}{4} = 1$.

Since the product of their slopes is -1, the diagonals form right angles at T by the slopes of perpendicular lines theorem. Each side of *PQRS* has length $\sqrt{10}$. Thus it is a rhombus. In fact, the result in Example 15.4 holds for *any* rhombus. This result is presented as a problem in Section 15.3. ∎

Check for Understanding: Exercise/Problem Set A #6–14

MATHEMATICAL MORSEL

Descartes was creative in many fields: philosophy, physics, cosmology, chemistry, physiology, and psychology. But he is best known for his contributions to mathematics. He was a frail child of a noble family. As one story goes, due to his frailty, Descartes had a habit of lying in bed, thinking for extended periods. One day, while watching a fly crawling on the ceiling, he set about trying to describe the path of the fly in mathematical language. Thus was born analytic geometry—the study of mathematical attributes of lines and curves.

Section 15.1   EXERCISE / PROBLEM SET A

EXERCISES

1. Find the distance between the following pairs of points.
   a. $(0, 0), (3, -2)$ **b.** $(-4, 2), (-2, 3)$

2. Use the distance formula to determine whether points $P, Q,$ and R are collinear.
   a. $P(-1, 4), Q(-2, 3),$ and $R(-4, 1)$
   b. $P(-2, 1), Q(3, 4),$ and $R(12, 10)$

3. The endpoints of a segment are given. Find the coordinates of the midpoint of the segment.
   a. $(0, 2)$ and $(-3, 2)$ **b.** $(-5, -1)$ and $(3, 5)$
   c. $(-2, 3)$ and $(-3, 6)$ **d.** $(3, -5)$ and $(3, -7)$

4. Given are the coordinates of the vertices of a triangle. Use the coordinate distance formula to determine whether the triangle is a right triangle.
   a. $A(-2, 5), B(0, -1), C(12, 3)$
   b. $D(2, 3), E(-2, -3), F(-6, 1)$

5. Draw the quadrilateral $ABCD$ whose vertices are $A(3, 0),$ $B(6, 6), C(6, 9),$ and $D(0, 6).$ Divide each of the coordinates by 3 and graph the new quadrilateral $A'\,B'\,C'\,D'.$ For example, A' has coordinates $(1, 0).$ How do the lengths of corresponding sides compare?

6. Find the slopes of the lines containing the following pairs of points.
   a. $(3, 2)$ and $(5, 3)$ **b.** $(-2, 1)$ and $(-5, -3)$

7. Use the ratio $\dfrac{y_2 - y_1}{x_2 - x_1}$ and the ratio $\dfrac{y_1 - y_2}{x_1 - x_2}$ to compute the slopes of the lines containing the following points. Do both ratios give the same result?
   a. $(1, 4)$ and $(5, 2)$ **b.** $(-2, -3)$ and $(3, 2)$

8. To gain a sense of how the numerical values of the slope are related to the visual appearance, use the Chapter 15 Geometer's Sketchpad® activity *Slope* on our Web site. Move the line to see the slope change dynamically. Describe what lines with the following slopes look like.
   a. 5   **b.** $-\dfrac{1}{3}$ **c.** -7 **d.** $\dfrac{8}{9}$

9. Use slopes to determine whether the points $A(3, -2),$ $B(1, 2),$ and $C(-3, 10)$ are collinear.

10. Use slopes to determine whether $\overline{AB} \parallel \overline{PQ}.$
    a. $A(-1, 0), B(4, 5), P(3, 9), Q(-2, 4)$
    b. $A(0, 4), B(6, 8), P(-4, -6), Q(2, -2)$
    c.

    $A(-55, 37)$ $B(47, 87)$
    $P(-45, 18)$ $Q(55, 66)$

11. Determine whether the quadrilaterals with the given vertices are parallelograms.
    a. $(1, 4), (4, 4), (5, 1),$ and $(2, 1)$
    b. $(1, -1), (6, -1), (6, -4),$ and $(1, -4)$

12. Give the slope of a line perpendicular to $\overleftrightarrow{AB}$.
    a. $A(1, 6), B(2, 5)$ **b.** $A(0, 4), B(-6, -5)$
    c. $A(4, 2), B(-5, 2)$ **d.** $A(-1, 5), B(-1, 3)$

13. In each part, use the Chapter 15 eManipulative activity *Coordinate Geoboard* on our Web site to determine whether any of the line segments joining the given points are perpendicular.
    a. $(2, 2), (2, 4),$ and $(5, 4)$
    b. $(-3, 4), (0, -1),$ and $(5, 2)$
    c. $(-5, -4), (3, 2),$ and $(5, 2)$
    d. $(-2, -2), (1, 4),$ and $(5, -4)$

14. Determine which of the quadrilaterals, with the given vertices, is a rectangle.
    a. $(-10, -5), (-6, 15), (14, 11),$ and $(10, -9)$
    b. $(-2, 1), (2, 9), (6, 7), (2, -2)$

PROBLEMS

15. Consider the following quadrilateral.

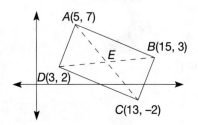

A(5, 7)

B(15, 3)

E

D(3, 2)

C(13, –2)

a. Verify that *ABCD* is a rectangle.

b. What do you observe about the lengths *BD* and *AC*?

c. What do you observe about $\overline{AE}$ and $\overline{CE}$ and about $\overline{BE}$ and $\overline{DE}$?

d. Are $\overline{AC}$ and $\overline{BD}$ perpendicular? Explain.

e. Summarize the properties you have observed about rectangle *ABCD*.

16. Using *only* the array of points and points *A*(2, 4) and *B*(4, 4) as the endpoints of one side of a quadrilateral, answer the following questions. The Chapter 15 eManipulative *Coordinate Geoboard* on our Web site will help in solving this problem.

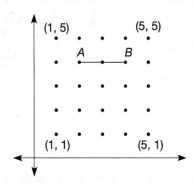

(1, 5)   (5, 5)

A   B

(1, 1)   (5, 1)

a. Use coordinates to list all possible parallelograms that can be constructed on the above array.

b. Use coordinates to list all possible rectangles.

c. Use coordinates to list all possible rhombi.

d. Use coordinates to list all possible squares.

17. On the Chapter 15 eManipulative activity *Coordinate Geoboard* on our Web site construct triangles that have vertices with the given coordinates. Describe the triangles as scalene, isosceles, equilateral, acute, right, or obtuse. Explain.

a. (0, 0), (0, −4), (4, −4)

b. (−3, −1), (1, 2), (5, −1)

18. Generating many examples of perpendicular lines where the product of their slopes is −1 is easily done on the Chapter 15 Geometer's Sketchpad® activity *Perpendicular Lines* on our Web site. Use this activity to find the slopes of lines that are perpendicular to the lines with the given slopes below.

a. 0.941   **b.** −0.355   **c.** 9.625

19. A pole is supported by two sets of guy wires fastened to the ground 15 meters from the pole. The shorter set of wires has slope $\pm\frac{4}{3}$. The wires in the longer set are each 50 meters long.

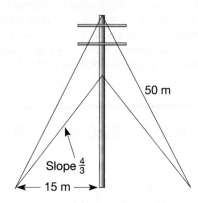

50 m

Slope $\frac{4}{3}$

15 m

a. How high above the ground is the shorter set of wires attached?

b. What is the length of the shorter set of wires?

c. How tall is the pole to the nearest centimeter?

d. What is the slope of the longer set of wires to two decimal places?

20. A freeway ramp connects a highway to an overpass 10 meters above the ground. The ramp, which starts 150 meters from the overpass, is 150.33 meters long and 9 meters wide. What is the **percent grade** (rise/run expressed as a percent) of the ramp to three decimal places?

21. Let *P*, *Q*, *R*, and *S* be any points on line *l* as shown. By drawing horizontal and vertical segments, draw right triangles $\triangle PQO$ and $\triangle RST$. Follow the given steps to verify that the slope of line *l* is independent of the pairs of points selected.

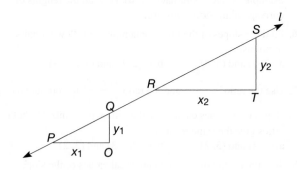

l

S

y_2

R

x_2

T

Q

y_1

P

x_1 O

a. Show that $\triangle PQO \sim \triangle RST$.

b. Show that $\dfrac{y_1}{x_1} = \dfrac{y_2}{x_2}$.

c. Is the slope of $\overline{PQ}$ equal to the slope of $\overline{RS}$? Explain.

22. In the development of the midpoint formula, points P and Q have coordinates (x_1, y_1) and (x_2, y_2), respectively, and M is the point $\left(\dfrac{x_1 + x_2}{2}, \dfrac{y_1 + y_2}{2}\right)$. Use the coordinate distance formula to verify that P, M, and Q are collinear and that $PM = MQ$.

23. Cartesian coordinates may be generalized to three-dimensional space. A point in space is determined by giving its location relative to three axes as shown. Point P with coordinates (x_1, y_1, z_1) is plotted by going x_1 along the x-axis, y_1 along the y-direction, and z_1 in the z-direction. Plot the following points in three-dimensional space.

a. $(2, 1, 3)$ **b.** $(-2, 1, 0)$ **c.** $(3, -1, -2)$

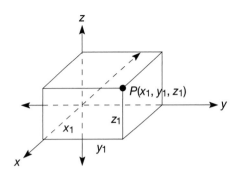

Section 15.1 EXERCISE / PROBLEM SET B

EXERCISES

1. Find the distance between the following pairs of points.
  a. $(2, 3), (-1, -5)$ **b.** $(-3, 5), (-3, -2)$

2. Use the distance formula to determine whether points P, Q, and R are collinear.
  a. $P(-2, -3), Q(2, -1)$, and $R(10, 3)$
  b. $P(2, 7), Q(-2, -7)$, and $R(3, 10.5)$

3. The point M is the midpoint of $\overline{AB}$. Given the coordinates of the following points, find the coordinates of the third point.
  a. $A(-3, -1), M(-1, 3)$
  b. $B(-5, 3), M(-7, 3)$
  c. $A(1, -3), M(4, 1)$
  d. $M(0, 0), B(-2, 5)$

4. Given are the coordinates of the vertices of a triangle. Use the coordinate distance formula to determine whether the triangle is a right triangle.
  a. $G(-3, -2), H(5, -2), I(1, 2)$ **b.** $L(1, 4), M(5, 2), N(4, 0)$

5. Draw a triangle ABC whose vertices are $A(8, 4), B(4, 4)$, $C(8, 1)$. Multiply each of the coordinates by 2 and graph the new triangle $A'B'C'$. For example A' has coordinates $(16, 8)$.
  a. How do the lengths of the corresponding sides compare?
  b. How do the slopes of the corresponding sides compare?

6. Find the slope of each line containing the following pairs of points.
  a. $(-1, 2)$ and $(6, -3)$ **b.** $(6, 5)$ and $(6, -2)$

7. Use the ratio $\dfrac{y_2 - y_1}{x_2 - x_1}$ and the ratio $\dfrac{y_1 - y_2}{x_1 - x_2}$ to compute the slopes of the lines containing the following points. Do both ratios give the same result?
  a. $(-4, 5)$ and $(6, -3)$ **b.** $(1, -3)$ and $(-2, -5)$

8. Given are the slopes of several lines. Indicate whether each line is horizontal, vertical, rises to the right, or rises to the left.
  a. $\frac{3}{4}$ **b.** no slope   **c.** 0   **d.** $-\frac{5}{6}$

9. Use slopes to determine if the points $A(0, 7), B(2, 11)$, and $C(-2, 1)$ are collinear.

10. Determine which pairs of segments are parallel.
  a. The segment from $(3, 5)$ to $(8, 3)$ and the segment from $(0, 8)$ to $(8, 5)$.
  b. The segment from $(-4, 5)$ to $(4, 2)$ and the segment from $(-3, -2)$ to $(5, -5)$.
  c.

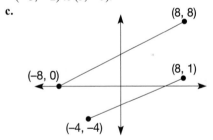

(8, 8)
(-8, 0)
(8, 1)
(-4, -4)

11. Determine whether the quadrilaterals with the given vertices are parallelograms.
  a. $(1, -2), (4, 2), (6, 2)$, and $(3, -2)$
  b. $(-10, 5), (-5, 10), (10, -5)$, and $(5, -10)$

12. Use slopes to show that $\overline{AB} \perp \overline{PQ}$.
  a. $A(0, 4), B(-6, 3), P(-2, -2), Q(-3, 4)$
  b. $A(-2, -1), B(2, 3), P(4, 1), Q(0, 5)$

13. In each part, use the Chapter 15 eManipulative activity *Coordinate Geoboard* on our Web site to determine which, if any, of the triangles with the given vertices is a right triangle.
  a. $(-5, -4), (-1, 4)$, and $(1, 2)$
  b. $(4, -4), (0, 2)$, and $(-3, 0)$
  c. $(2, -3), (4, 4)$, and $(-1, -2)$

14. Determine which of the quadrilaterals, with the given vertices, is a rectangle.
  a. $(0, 0), (12, 12), (16, 8)$, and $(4, -4)$
  b. $(-3, 8), (0, 12), (12, 3)$, and $(9, -1)$

PROBLEMS

15. Which of the following properties are true of the given kites? Explain.

a. The diagonals are congruent.

b. The diagonals are perpendicular to each other.

c. The diagonals bisect each other.

d. The kite has two right angles.

i.

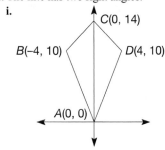

ii.

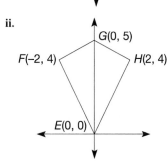

16. Using only the 5 × 5 array of points, how many segments can be drawn making a right angle at an endpoint of the given segment? The Chapter 15 eManipulative *Coordinate Geoboard* on our Web site will help in solving this problem.

a.

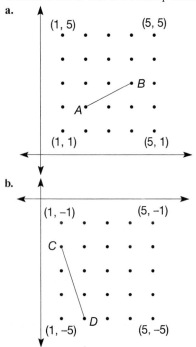

b.

17. On the Chapter 15 eManipulative activity *Coordinate Geoboard* on our Web site construct triangles that have vertices with the given coordinates. Describe the triangles as scalene, isosceles, equilateral, acute, right, or obtuse. Explain.

a. $(-3, 1), (1, 3), (5, -4)$ **b.** $(-4, -2), (-1, 3), (4, -2)$

18. What general type of quadrilateral is $ABCD$, where $A = (0, 0), B = (-4, 3), C = (-1, 7),$ and $D = (6, 8)$? Describe it as completely as you can.

19. Three of the vertices of a parallelogram have coordinates $P(2, 3), Q(5, 7),$ and $R(10, -5)$.

a. Find the coordinates of the fourth vertex of the parallelogram. (*Hint:* There is more than one answer.)

b. Determine the area of each parallelogram.

20. a. Draw quadrilateral $ABCD$ where $A(4, -2), B(4, 2), C(-2, 2),$ and $D(-2, -2)$.

b. Multiply each coordinate by 3 and graph quadrilateral $A'B'C'D'$. For example, A' has coordinates $(12, -6)$.

c. How do the perimeters of $ABCD$ and $A'B'C'D'$ compare?

d. How do the areas of $ABCD$ and $A'B'C'D'$ compare?

e. Repeat parts (b) to (d), but divide each coordinate by 2.

21. The percent grade of a highway is the amount that the highway rises (or falls) in a given horizontal distance. For example, a highway with a 4% grade rises 0.04 mile for every 1 mile of horizontal distance.

a. How many feet does a highway with a 6% grade rise in 2.5 miles?

b. How many feet would a highway with a 6% grade rise in 90 miles if the grade remained constant?

c. How is percent grade related to slope?

22. Prove the following statement: If the product of the slopes of l and m is -1, lines l and m are perpendicular. (*Hint:* Show that $\triangle OPQ$ is a right triangle.)

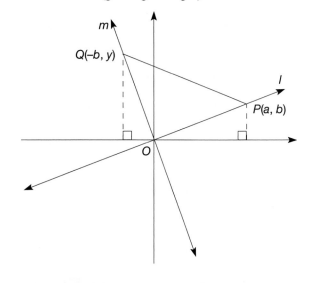

23. Locations on the Earth's surface are measured by two sets of circles. **Parallels of latitude** are circles at constant distances from the equator used to identify locations north or south, called **latitude**. The latitude of the North Pole, for example, is 90°N, that of the equator is 0°, and that of the South Pole is 90°S. Great circles through the North and South poles, called **meridians**, are used to identify locations east or west, called **longitude**. The half of the great circle through the poles and Greenwich, England, is called the **prime meridian**. Points on the prime meridian have longitude 0°E. Points east of Greenwich and less than halfway around the world from it have longitudes between 0 and 180°E. Points west of Greenwich and less than halfway around the world from it have longitudes between 0 and 180°W. Here are the latitudes and longitudes of several cities, to the nearest degree.

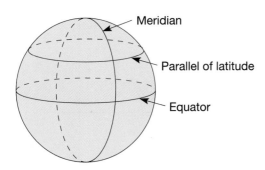

CITY	LATITUDE	LONGITUDE
London	52°N	0°E
New York	41°N	74°W
Moscow	56°N	38°E
Nome, Alaska	64°N	165°W
Beijing	40°N	116°E
Rio de Janeiro	23°S	43°W
Sydney	34°S	151°E

a. Which cities are above the equator? Which are below?
b. Which city is farthest from the equator?
c. Are there points in the United States, excluding Alaska and Hawaii, with east longitudes? Explain.
d. What is the latitude of all points south of the equator and the same distance from the equator as London?
e. What is the longitude of a point exactly halfway around the world (north of the equator) from New York?
f. What are the latitude and longitude of a point diametrically opposite Sydney? That is, the point in question and Sydney are the endpoints of a diameter of the Earth.

24. The coordinate distance formula can also be generalized to three-dimensional space. Let P have coordinates (a, b, c) and Q have coordinates (x, y, z). The faces of the prism are parallel to the coordinate planes.

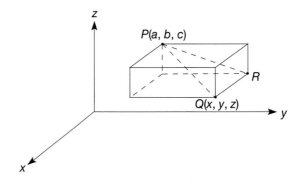

a. What are the coordinates of point R?
b. What is the distance PR? (*Hint:* Pythagorean theorem.)
c. What is the distance QR?
d. What is the distance PQ? (*Hint:* Pythagorean theorem.)

Analyzing Student Thinking
25. Brayden believes that lines that have no slope are the same as lines that have slope zero. How can you help him understand the difference?

26. Shirdena found the slope of the segment with end points $(-2, 7)$ and $(-5, -8)$ as follows: $[7 - (-8)]/[-2 - (-5)] = 15/3$. Her friend found the slope as follows: $[(-8) - 7]/[(-5) - (-2)] = -15/-3$. They wondered how a segment could have different slopes. How would you respond?

27. Tenille and Jana were asked to determine if a triangle on a coordinate plane is a right triangle. Tenille said that she was going to check the slopes of the two shorter sides to see if they were perpendicular. Jana said that she was going to use the distance formula and use the converse of the Pythagorean Theorem. Which student is correct? Explain.

28. Kimberly says she knows that the slopes of two parallel lines are equal. But what if they are opposites, like 4 and -4, does this mean anything special? What would you say to Kimberly?

29. Markelle and Bobbi were asked to determine if three points on a coordinate plane were collinear. Markelle said that she was going to check the slopes of two pairs of points. Bobbi said that she was going to use the distance formula on three pairs of points. Which student is correct? Explain.

30. Janelle was trying to find the distance between $(3, 7)$ and $(9, 6)$ in the coordinate plane. She knew the formula was $D = \sqrt{(9 - 3)^2 + (6 - 7)^2}$. So she took the square root and got $(9 - 3) + (6 - 7) = 5$. Did she get the correct answer? Explain.

31. Edmund was working on the same problem, but his numbers under the radical looked different: $D = \sqrt{(9 - 3)^2 + (7 - 6)^2}$. Janelle told him he couldn't subtract the numbers that way. He had to subtract the coordinates in the same order. So he had to put $6 - 7$, not $7 - 6$. Who is correct? Are they both correct? Explain.

Problems Relating to the NCTM Standards and Curriculum Focal Points

1. The Focal Points for Grade 3 state "Describing and analyzing properties of two-dimensional shapes." If you were given the coordinates of the vertices of a two-dimensional shape, explain how coordinate geometry could be used to analyze properties of that shape.

2. The NCTM Standards state "All students should explore relationships between symbolic expressions and graphs of lines, paying particular attention to the meaning of intercept and slope." What is the meaning of slope?

3. The NCTM Standards state "All students should use coordinate geometry to examine special geometric shapes such as regular polygons or those with pairs of parallel or perpendicular sides." If you were given the coordinates of 4 points, explain how you could use coordinate geometry to determine if those 4 points could be the vertices of a square.

15.2 EQUATIONS AND COORDINATES

STARTING POINT

In the graph at the right, line l contains the point $P = (-1, 4)$ and has a slope of $m = -\dfrac{2}{3}$. Identify three other points on line l and justify how you know each lies on the line.

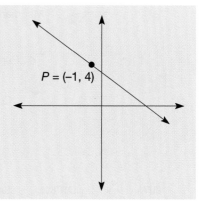

$P = (-1, 4)$

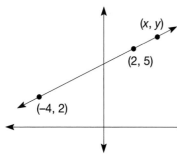

Figure 15.10

Equations of Lines

We can determine equations that are satisfied by the points on a particular line. For example, consider the line l containing points $(-4, 2)$ and $(2, 5)$ (Figure 15.10). Suppose that (x, y) is an arbitrary point on line l. We wish to find an equation in x and y that is satisfied by the coordinates of the point (x, y). We will use the slope of l to do this. Using the points $(-4, 2)$ and $(2, 5)$, the slope of l is $\dfrac{5 - 2}{2 - (-4)} = \dfrac{1}{2}$. Using the points $(-4, 2)$ and (x, y), the slope of l is $\dfrac{y - 2}{x - (-4)} = \dfrac{y - 2}{x + 4}$. Since the slope of l is $\dfrac{1}{2}$ and $\dfrac{y - 2}{x + 4}$, we have

$$\frac{y - 2}{x + 4} = \frac{1}{2}.$$

Algebraic Reasoning
Reasoning about graphs is more than just plotting a few points and drawing a line through them. Reasoning about graphs allows one to see that the coordinates of each point on the graph satisfy the equation. In other words, the graph is a picture of all of the solutions of the equations.

Continuing,

$$y - 2 = \frac{1}{2}(x + 4),$$

$$y - 2 = \frac{1}{2}x + 2,$$

or finally,

$$y = \frac{1}{2}x + 4.$$

That is, we have shown that every point (x, y) on line l satisfies the equation $y = \frac{1}{2}x + 4$. [NOTE: We could also have used the points $(2, 5)$ and (x, y), and solved $\frac{y - 5}{x - 2} = \frac{1}{2}$ to obtain $y = \frac{1}{2}x + 4$.]

In our equation for line l, the "x" term is multiplied by the slope of l, namely $\frac{1}{2}$. Also, the constant term, 4, is the y-coordinate of the point at which l intersects the y-axis.

Slope-Intercept Equation of a Line   We can show that every line in the plane that is not vertical has an equation of the form $y = mx + b$, where m is the slope of the line and b, called the **y-intercept**, is the y-coordinate of the point at which the line intersects the y-axis (Figure 15.11).

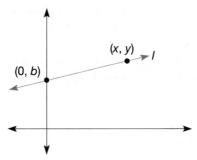

Figure 15.11

Generalizing from the preceding argument, suppose that l is a line containing the point $(0, b)$ such that the slope of l is m and that (x, y) is an arbitrary point on l (Figure 15.11). Then, since the slope of l is m, we have

$$\frac{y - b}{x - 0} = m,$$

so that

$$y - b = mx,$$
$$y = mx + b.$$

Thus every point (x, y) on l satisfies the equation $y = mx + b$.

It is also true that if (x, y) is a point on the plane such that $y = mx + b$, then (x, y) is on line l. Thus the equation $y = mx + b$ describes all points (x, y) that are on line l.

If a line l is vertical and hence has no slope, it must intersect the horizontal axis at a point, say $(a, 0)$. Then all of the points on l will satisfy the equation $x = a$ (Figure 15.12). That is, the x-coordinate of each point on l is a, and the y-coordinate is an arbitrary real number.

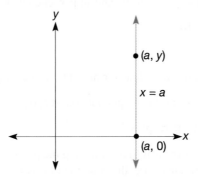

Figure 15.12

We can summarize our results about equations of lines in the coordinate plane as follows:

THEOREM

Slope-Intercept Equation of a Line

Every line in the plane has an equation of the form (1) $y = mx + b$ where m is the slope of the line and b is the y-intercept, or (2) $x = a$ if the slope of the line is undefined (i.e., the line is vertical).

The equation $y = mx + b$ is called the **slope-intercept equation of a line**, since m is the slope and b is the y-intercept of the line.

Example 15.5 Find the equations for the lines l_1, l_2, l_3, and l_4 satisfying the following conditions (Figure 15.13).

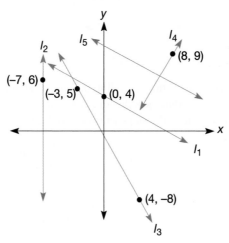

Figure 15.13

a. l_1 has slope $\dfrac{-3}{5}$ and y-intercept 4.

b. l_2 is a vertical line containing the point $(-7, 6)$.
c. l_3 contains the points $(-3, 5)$ and $(4, -8)$.
d. l_4 contains the point $(8, 9)$ and is perpendicular to the line l_5, whose equation is
$$y = \frac{-4}{7}x + 10.$$

SOLUTION
a. By the equation of a line formula (1) in the Slope-Intercept Equation of a Line Theorem the slope-intercept equation of l_1 is $y = \dfrac{-3}{5}x + 4$, since the slope of l_1 is $\dfrac{-3}{5}$ and the y-intercept is 4.

b. The line l_2 is a vertical line containing the point $(-7, 6)$, so that l_2 also contains the point $(-7, 0)$. Therefore, the equation of l_2 is $x = -7$.

c. The slope of l_3 is $\dfrac{5 - (-8)}{-3 - 4} = \dfrac{13}{-7} = \dfrac{-13}{7}$, so l_3 has an equation of the form

$y = \dfrac{-13}{7}x + b$. We can find b by using the fact that the point $(-3, 5)$ is on l_3.

We substitute -3 and 5 for x and y, respectively, in the equation of l_3, as follows:

$$5 = \frac{-13}{7}(-3) + b,$$

$$5 = \frac{39}{7} + b,$$

so

$$5 - \frac{39}{7} = b,$$

$$\frac{-4}{7} = b.$$

Therefore, the equation of l_3 is

$$y = \frac{-13}{7}x - \frac{4}{7}.$$

We could also have used the fact that $(4, -8)$ is on l_3 to find b.

d. Since l_4 is perpendicular to the line $y = \dfrac{-4}{7}x + 10$, we know that the slope of l_4

is $\dfrac{7}{4}$, by the Slopes of Perpendicular Lines Theorem. Hence l_4 has an equation of

the form $y = \dfrac{7}{4}x + b$. Since the point $(8, 9)$ is on l_4, we can substitute 8 for x and 9

for y in the equation $y = \dfrac{7}{4}x + b$. Thus we have

$$9 = \frac{7}{4} \cdot 8 + b,$$
$$9 = 14 + b,$$
$$-5 = b.$$

Consequently, the equation of l_4 is

$$y = \frac{7}{4}x - 5.$$ ■

Point-Slope Equation of a Line   In Example 15.5(d) the coordinates of a

point, $(8, 9)$, and the slope of the line, $\dfrac{7}{4}$, were known. Even though we did not know

both the slope and the y-intercept, we were able to find the equation of the line. Generalizing, suppose that (x_1, y_1) is a point on a line l having slope m. If (x, y) is any other point on l, then

$$\frac{y - y_1}{x - x_1} = m \quad \text{or} \quad y - y_1 = m(x - x_1).$$

This is summarized next.

> ## THEOREM
>
> ### *Point-Slope Equation of a Line*
>
> If a line contains the point (x_1, y_1) and has slope m, then the point-slope equation of the line is
>
> $$y - y_1 = m(x - x_1).$$

 Check for Understanding: Exercise/Problem Set A #1–13

Solutions of Simultaneous Equations

Consider the equations $y = 4x + 2$ and $y = -3x + 5$. The first line has slope 4, and the second line has slope -3, so that the lines must intersect (Figure 15.14).

Algebraic Reasoning
Algebraic reasoning is more than just solving equations by manipulating them. It helps one see the connection between graphs and equations. For example, since the graph of an equation is the set of all points that satisfy it, the point where the graphs of two equations intersect has coordinates that satisfy both equations. Thus, the point of intersection is the solution to the system of two equations.

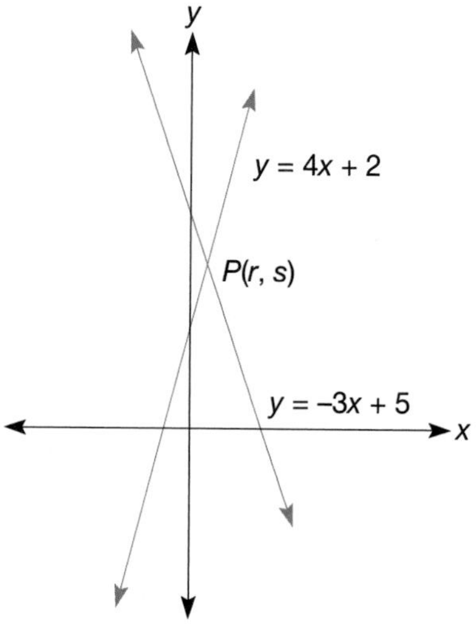

Figure 15.14

We can find the point P where the two lines intersect by using the fact that P lies on *both* lines. That is, the coordinates of P must satisfy both equations. Hence if r and s are the coordinates of P, we must have $s = 4r + 2$ and $s = -3r + 5$, so that

$$4r + 2 = -3r + 5.$$

Therefore,

$$7r = 3 \qquad \text{or} \qquad r = \frac{3}{7}.$$

Thus the x-coordinate of P is $\frac{3}{7}$. Using the first of the two equations, we find

$$s = 4\left(\frac{3}{7}\right) + 2,$$

or

$$s = \frac{26}{7}.$$

Consequently, $P = (\frac{3}{7}, \frac{26}{7})$ is the point of intersection of the two lines. (We could have used either equation to find s, since r and s must satisfy both equations.) We say that the point $P = (\frac{3}{7}, \frac{26}{7})$ is a **simultaneous solution** of the equations, since it satisfies both of them. The equations whose simultaneous solution we seek are called **simultaneous equations** or a system of equations.

The algebraic process of solving simultaneous equations has an interesting geometric interpretation. When we solve a pair of simultaneous equations such as

$$(1)\ ax + by = c$$

and

$$(2)\ dx + ey = f,$$

where a, b, c, d, e, and f represent constant coefficients and x and y are variables, we are finding the point of intersection of two lines in the coordinate plane. Note that x and y appear to the first power only. In the case that $b \neq 0$ in equation (1), and $e \neq 0$ in equation (2), we can rewrite these equations as follows. (Verify this.)

$$(1)'\ y = -\frac{a}{b}x + \frac{c}{b}$$

and

$$(2)'\ y = -\frac{d}{e}x + \frac{f}{e}.$$

We recognize these equations of *lines* in the plane. Suppose that line l has equation $(1)'$ as its equation and line m has equation $(2)'$ as its equation. Then there are three possible geometric relationships between lines l and m.

a. $l = m$ [Figure 15.15(a)].
b. $l \parallel m$ and $l \neq m$ [Figure 15.15(b)].
c. l intersects m in exactly one point (x, y) [Figure 15.15(c)].

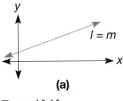
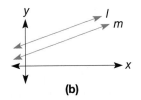
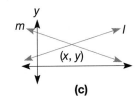

| (a) | (b) | (c) |

Figure 15.15

If $l = m$ as in case (a), then *all* the points (x, y) that satisfy the equation of l will also satisfy the equation of m. Thus, for this case, equations (1) and (2) will have infinitely many simultaneous solutions. For case (b), in which the lines l and m are different parallel lines, there will be no points in common for the two lines. Hence equations (1) and (2) will have no simultaneous solutions in this case. Finally, for case (c), in which the lines intersect in a unique point $P = (x, y)$, we will have only one simultaneous solution to the equations (1) and (2), namely, the x- and y-coordinates of point P.

Now let us consider this situation starting with the equations of the lines. If they have infinitely many solutions, the lines that they represent are coincident. If they have no solutions, their lines are different parallel lines. Finally, if they have a unique solution, their lines intersect at only one point. We can find conditions on the numbers a, b, c, d, e, and f in equations (1) and (2) in order to determine how many simultaneous solutions there are for the equations. This is left for Part A Problem 27 in the Problem Set.

THEOREM

Solutions of Simultaneous Equations

Let a, b, c, d, e, and f be real-number constants and x and y be variables. Then the equations

$$ax + by = c$$

and

$$dx + ey = f$$

have zero, one, or infinitely many solutions if and only if the lines they represent are parallel, intersect in exactly one point, or are coincident, respectively.

The following example illustrates the preceding geometric interpretation of simultaneous equations.

Example 15.6   Graph the following pairs of equations, and find their simultaneous solutions.

a. $x + y = 7$ **b.** $2x + y = 5$ **c.** $x + y = 7$
    $-28 = -4x - 4y$ $-12 + 3y = -6x$ $2x + y = 5$

SOLUTION

a. We can rewrite the equations as follows:

$$(1)\, x + y = 7$$

and

$$(2)\, 4x + 4y = 28$$

or, multiplying both sides of the second equation by $\frac{1}{4}$,

$$(1)'\, x + y = 7$$

and

$$(2)'\, x + y = 7$$

Hence the equations represent the *same* line, namely the line $y = -x + 7$ [Figure 15.16(a)]. Every point on this line is a simultaneous solution of the pair of equations.

b. Rewrite the equations in slope-intercept form.

$$y = -2x + 5$$
$$y = -2x + 4$$

Here the equations represent lines with the same slope (i.e., parallel lines) but different y-intercepts. Therefore the equations have no simultaneous solution [Figure 15.16(b)].

c. Rewrite the equations in slope-intercept form.

$$y = -x + 7$$
$$y = -2x + 5$$

Here the equations represent lines with different slopes, namely -1 and -2. The lines are intersecting lines [Figure 15.16(c)], so the equations will have a unique simultaneous solution. Equating the expressions for y, we obtain

$$-x + 7 = -2x + 5$$
$$x + 7 = 5$$
$$x = -2.$$

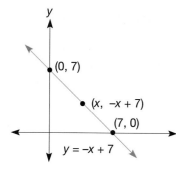

(a)

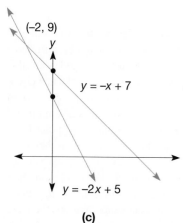

(b)

(c)

Figure 15.16

Substituting -2 for x in the first equation, we have $y = -(-2) + 7 = 9$. Thus the point $(-2, 9)$ is the only simultaneous solution of the two equations. [Check to see that $(-2, 9)$ is a simultaneous solution.] ∎

✔ **Check for Understanding:** Exercise/Problem Set A #14–18

Equations of Circles

Circles also have equations that can be determined using the distance formula. Recall that a circle is the set of points that are a fixed distance (i.e., the radius) from the center of the circle (Figure 15.17). Let the point $C = (a, b)$ be the center of the circle

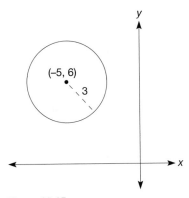

Figure 15.17

and r be the radius. Suppose that the point $P = (x, y)$ is on the circle. Then, by the definition of the circle, $PC = r$, so that $PC^2 = r^2$. But by the distance formula,

$$PC^2 = (x - a)^2 + (y - b)^2.$$

Therefore, $(x - a)^2 + (y - b)^2 = r^2$ is the equation of the circle.

Children's Literature
www.wiley.com/college/musser
See "The Librarian Who
Measured the Earth" by
Kathryn Lasky.

THEOREM

Equation of a Circle
The circle with center (a, b) and radius r has the equation
$$(x - a)^2 + (y - b)^2 = r^2.$$

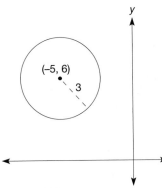

Figure 15.18

Example 15.7 Find the equation of the circle whose center is $(-5, 6)$ and whose radius is 3.

SOLUTION In the equation of a circle formula, $(a, b) = (-5, 6)$ and $r = 3$. Consequently, the equation of the circle (shown in Figure 15.18) is

$$[x - (-5)]^2 + (y - 6)^2 = 3^2 \quad \text{or} \quad (x + 5)^2 + (y - 6)^2 = 9. \quad ∎$$

✔ **Check for Understanding:** Exercise/Problem Set A #19–21

MATHEMATICAL MORSEL

Many words in mathematics have their origins in Hindu and Arabic words. The earliest Arabic arithmetic is that of al-Khowarizmi (circa C.E. 800). In referring to his book on Hindu numerals, a Latin translation begins "Spoken has Algoritmi." Thus we obtain the word *algorithm*, which is a procedure for calculating. The mathematics book *Hisab-al-jabr-w'almugabalsh*, also written by al-Khowarizmi, became known as "al-jabr," our modern-day "algebra."

Section 15.2 | EXERCISE / PROBLEM SET A

EXERCISES

1. Show that point P lies on the line with the given equation.
   a. $y = 7x - 2; P(1, 5)$
   b. $y = -\frac{2}{3}x + 5; P(-6, 9)$

2. For each of the following equations, find three points whose coordinates satisfy the equation.
   a. $2x - 3y = 6$
   b. $x + 4y = 0$

3. Identify the slope and the y-intercept for each line.
   a. $y = \frac{3}{2}x - 5$ **b.** $2x - 7y = 8$

4. Write each equation in the form $y = mx + b$. Identify the slope and y-intercept.
   a. $2y = 6x + 12$ **b.** $4y - 3x = 0$

5. Write the equation of the line, given its slope m and y-intercept b.
   a. $m = 3, b = 7$
   b. $m = -1, b = -3$
   c. $m = \frac{2}{3}, b = 5$

6. Point P has coordinates $(-2, 3)$. Give the coordinates of three other points on a horizontal line containing P.

7. **a.** Graph the following lines on the same coordinate system.
      i. $y = 2x + 3$
      ii. $y = -3x + 3$
      iii. $y = \frac{1}{2}x + 3$
   b. What is the relationship between these lines?
   c. Describe the lines of the form $y = cx + d$, where d is a fixed real number and c can be any real number.

8. Write the equation of each line that satisfies the following.
   a. Vertical through $(1, 3)$
   b. Vertical through $(-5, -2)$
   c. Horizontal through $(-3, 6)$
   d. Horizontal through $(3, -3)$

9. Write an equation in point-slope form using the following points and slopes.
   a. $(2, -3); m = -2$
   b. $(-1, -4); m = \dfrac{3}{2}$

10. Write the equation of a line in slope-intercept form that passes through the given point and is parallel to the line whose equation is given.
    a. $(5, -1); y = 2x - 3$
    b. $(-1, 0); 3x + 2y = 6$

11. Write the equation of the line that passes through the given point and is perpendicular to the line whose equation is given.
    a. $(6, 0); y = \frac{2}{3}x - 1$
    b. $(1, -3); 2x + 4y = 6$

12. Write the equation in (i) point-slope form and (ii) slope-intercept form for $\overleftrightarrow{AB}$.
    a. $A(6, 3), B(0, 2)$
    b. $A(-4, 8), B(3, -6)$

13. Graph the line described by each equation.
    a. $y = 2x - 1$ **b.** $y = -3x + 2$
    c. $y = \frac{1}{2}x + 1$ **d.** $x = -2$
    e. $y = 3$ **f.** $2x = -6y$

14. One method of solving simultaneous linear equations is the **graphical method**. The two lines are graphed and, if they intersect, the coordinates of the intersection point are determined. Graph the following pairs of lines to determine their simultaneous solutions, if any exist.
    a. $y = 2x + 1$ $y = \frac{1}{2}x + 4$
    b. $x + 2y = 4$ $x + 2y = -2$
    c. $-2x + 3y = 9$ $x + y = -2$
    d. $-2x + 3y = 9$ $4x - 6y = -18$

15. One algebraic method for solving a system of equations is the **substitution method**. Solve the pair of equations

$$2x + y = 3$$
$$x - 2y = 5$$

using the following steps:

  i. Express y in terms of x in the first equation.
  ii. Since the y-value of the point of intersection satisfies both equations, we can substitute this new name for y in place of y in the second equation. Do this.
  iii. The resulting equation has only the variable x. Solve for x.
  iv. By substituting the x-value into either original equation, the value of y is found. Solve for y.

Solve using the substitution method.
  a. $y = -2x + 3$ **b.** $2x - y = 6$
      $y = 3x - 5$ $5x - y = 5$

16. Another algebraic method of solving systems of equations, the **elimination method**, involves eliminating one variable by adding or subtracting equivalent expressions. Consider the system

$$2x + y = 7$$
$$3x - y = 3.$$

  i. Add the left-hand sides of the equations and the right-hand sides. Since the original terms were equal, the resulting sums are also equal. Notice that the variable y is eliminated.
  ii. Solve the equation you obtained in step 1.
  iii. Substitute this value of the variable into one of the original equations to find the value of the other variable.
  Sometimes another operation is necessary before adding the equations of a system in order to eliminate one variable.
  a. What equation results when adding the given equations? Is one variable eliminated?

$$2x - 3y = 6$$
$$4x + 5y = 1$$

  b. Now multiply the first equation by -2. Is one variable eliminated when the two equations are added?
  c. What is the solution of the system of equations?

17. Solve the following systems of equations, using any method.
  a. $y = 6x + 2$
      $y = 3x - 7$
  b. $2x + y = -8$
      $x - y = -4$
  c. $3x - y = 4$
      $6x + 3y = -12$
  d. $3x + 5y = 9$
      $4x - 8y = 17$

18. Identify whether the following systems have a unique solution, no solution, or infinitely many solutions.
  a. $y = 2x + 5$
      $y = 2x - 3$
  b. $3x - 2 = y$
      $3x - y = 2$
  c. $y = -x + 3$
      $y = 2x - 1$
  d. $2x - 3y = 5$
      $3x - 2y = 5$
  e. $4x - y = 6$
      $8x - 2y = 6$
  f. $3x - y = 5$
      $-6x + 2y = -10$

19. Show that point P lies on the circle with the given equation.
  a. $P(3, 4); x^2 + y^2 = 25$
  b. $P(-3, 5); x^2 + y^2 = 34$

20. Identify the center and radius of each circle whose equation is given.
  a. $(x - 3)^2 + (y - 2)^2 = 25$
  b. $(x + 1)^2 + (y - 3)^2 = 49$

21. **a.** Write the equation of a circle with center $C(-2, 3)$ and radius of length 2.
  b. Write the equation of the circle with center $C(3, -4)$ that passes through $P(2, -6)$.
  c. Write the equation of the circle that has center $C(-3, -5)$ and passes through the origin.
  d. Write the equation of the circle for which $A(-2, -1)$ and $B(6, -3)$ are the endpoints of a diameter.

PROBLEMS

22. Find the equation of the circumscribed circle for the triangle whose vertices are A(-1, 2), B(-1, 8), and C(-5, 4).

23. The vertices of a triangle have coordinates (0, 0), (1, 5), and (-4, 3). Find the equations of the lines containing the sides of the triangle.

24. Find the equation of the line containing the median $\overline{AD}$ of $\triangle ABC$ with vertices $A(3, 7)$, $B(1, 4)$, and $C(11, 2)$.

25. Find the equation of the line containing altitude $\overline{PT}$ of $\triangle PRS$ with vertices $P(3, 5)$, $R(-1, 1)$, and $S(7, -3)$.

26. A catering company will cater a reception for $4.50 per person plus fixed costs of $200.
  a. Complete the following chart.

NUMBER OF PEOPLE	30	50	75	100	n
TOTAL COST, y					

  b. Write a linear equation representing the relationship between number of people (x) and total costs (y).
  c. What is the slope of this line? What does it represent?
  d. What is the y-intercept of this line? What does it represent?

27. For the system of equations

$$ax + by = c$$
$$dx + ey = f,$$

find the conditions on a, b, c, d, e, and f, where b and e are nonzero, such that the equations have
a. infinitely many solutions.
b. no solution.
c. a unique solution.

28. Another coordinate system in the plane, called the **polar coordinate system**, identifies a point with an angle θ and a real number r. For example, $(3, 60°)$ gives the coordinates of point P shown. The positive x-axis serves as the initial side of the angle. Angles may be measured positively (counterclockwise) or negatively (clockwise). Plot the following points, and indicate which quadrant they are in or which axis they are on.

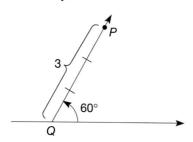

a. $(5, 45°)$
b. $(3, 125°)$
c. $(1, -170°)$
d. $(2, 240°)$
e. $(1.5, 300°)$
f. $(4, -270°)$

29. Rectangle $ABCD$ is given. Point P is a point within the rectangle such that the distance from P to A is 3 units, from P to B is 4 units, and from P to C is 5 units. How far is P from D?

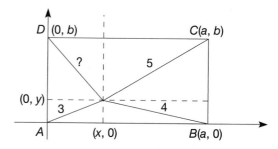

30. The junior class is planning a dance. The band will cost $400, and advertising costs will be $100. Food will be supplied at $2 per person.
a. How many people must attend the dance in order for the class to break even if tickets are sold at $7 each?
b. How many people must attend the dance in order for the class to break even if tickets are sold at $6 each?
c. How many people must attend the dance if the class wants to earn a $400 profit and sells tickets for $6 each?

31. a. Use the graphical method to predict solutions to the simultaneous equations

$$x^2 + y^2 = 1$$
$$y = \frac{x}{2} + 1.$$

How many solutions do you expect?
b. Use the substitution method to solve the simultaneous equations.

Section 15.2 **EXERCISE / PROBLEM SET B**

EXERCISES

1. Show that point P lies on the line with the given equation.
a. $-2x = 6y + 3$; $P(7.5, -3)$
b. $3y = 4x + 2$; $P(4, 6)$

2. For each of the following equations, find three points whose coordinates satisfy the equation.
a. $x - y = 4$ **b.** $x = 3$

3. Identify the slope and the y-intercept for each line.
a. $y = -3x + 2$
b. $2y = 5x - 6$

4. Write each equation in the form $y = mx + b$. Identify the slope and y-intercept.
a. $8y - 2 = 0$
b. $3x - 4y = 12$

5. Write the equation of each line, given its slope m and y-intercept b.
a. $m = -2, b = 5$ **b.** $m = \frac{7}{3}, b = -2$
c. $m = -3, b = -\frac{1}{4}$

6. Point P has coordinates $(-2, 3)$. Give the coordinates of two other points on a vertical line containing P.

7. a. Graph the following lines on the same coordinate system.
    i. $y = 2x$ **ii.** $y = 2x + 3$ **iii.** $y = 2x - 5$
b. What is the relationship among these lines?
c. Describe the lines of the form $y = cx + d$, where c is a fixed real number and d can be any real number.

8. Find the equation of the lines described.
a. Slope is -3 and y-intercept is -5
b. Vertical line through $(-2, 3)$
c. Contains $(6, -1)$ and $(3, 2)$

9. Write an equation in point-slope form using the following points and slopes.
   a. $(-5, 1)$; $m = 4$ **b.** $(2, 6)$; $m = -\dfrac{2}{5}$

10. Write the equation of a line in slope-intercept form that passes through the given point and is parallel to the line whose equation is given.
    a. $(1, -2)$; $y = -x - 2$ **b.** $(2, -5)$; $3x + 5y = 1$

11. Write the equation of the line that passes through the given point and is perpendicular to the line whose equation is given.
    a. $(-2, 5)$; $y = -2x + 1$ **b.** $(-5, -4)$; $3x - 2y = 8$

12. Write the equation in (i) point-slope form and (ii) slope-intercept form for $\overleftrightarrow{AB}$.
    a. $A(-5, 2), B(-3, 1)$ **b.** $A(4, 7), B(10, 7)$

13. Graph the line described by each equation.
    a. $y = 2x + 5$ **b.** $y = \frac{1}{3}x - 2$
    c. $y = 3$ **d.** $x = -4$

14. Solve the following simultaneous equations using the graphical method. (See Exercise 14, Part 15.2A.)
    a. $y = x$ $y = -x + 4$
    b. $y = 2x$ $y = \frac{1}{2}x + 6$
    c. $x + y = 5$ $y = -x - 5$
    d. $3y = 5x + 1$ $-10x + 6y = 2$

15. Use the substitution method to find the solution of the following systems of linear equations, if a solution exists. If no solution exists, explain. (See Exercise 15, Part 15.2A.)
    a. $y = 2x - 4$ $y = -5x + 17$
    b. $4x + y = 8$ $5x + 3y = 3$
    c. $x - 2y = 1$ $x = 2y + 3$
    d. $x - y = 5$ $2x - 4y = 7$

16. Use the elimination method to solve the following systems of equations. (See Exercise 16, Part 15.2A.)
    a. $5x + 3y = 17$
    $2x - 3y = -10$
    b. $4x - 4y = -3$
    $7x + 2y = 6$

17. Solve the following systems of equations, using any method.
    a. $y = 3x - 15$ $y = -2x + 10$
    b. $x + y = 5$ $2x + y = 6$
    c. $2x - 5y = 1$ $x - 2y = 1$

18. Determine whether the following systems have a unique solution, no solution, or infinitely many solutions.
    a. $2x - 3y = 6$ $4x - 6y = -7$
    b. $3x = 2y$ $4x - y = 2$
    c. $3y = 2x - 6$ $4x - 6y = 12$

19. Show that point P lies on the circle with the given equation.
    a. $P(-3, 7)$; $(x + 1)^2 + (y - 2)^2 = 29$
    b. $P(\sqrt{5}, -3)$; $x^2 + (y + 5)^2 = 9$

20. Identify the center and radius of each circle identified by the following equations.
    a. $(x - 2)^2 + (y + 5)^2 = 64$
    b. $(x + 3)^2 + (y - 4)^2 = 20$

21. Write the equation for each circle described as follows.
    a. Center $(-1, -2)$ and radius $\sqrt{5}$
    b. Center $(2, -4)$ and passing through $(-2, 1)$
    c. Endpoints of a diameter at $(-1, 6)$ and $(3, 2)$

PROBLEMS

22. **a.** Use the graphical method to predict solutions to the simultaneous equations

    $$x^2 + y^2 = 1$$
    $$x^2 + (y - 3)^2 = 1.$$

    How many solutions do you expect?
    b. Use the substitution method to solve the simultaneous equations.

23. Find the equation of the perpendicular bisector of the segment whose endpoints are $(-3, -1)$ and $(6, 2)$.

24. Find the equations of the diagonals of the rectangle $PQRS$ with vertices $P(-2, -1)$, $Q(-2, 4)$, $R(8, 4)$, and $S(8, -1)$.

25. Find the equation of the perpendicular bisector of side $\overline{AB}$ of $\triangle ABC$, where $A = (0, 0)$, $B = (2, 5)$, and $C = (10, 5)$.

26. A cab company charges a fixed fee of $0.60 plus $0.50 per mile.
    a. Find the cost of traveling 10 miles; of traveling 25 miles.
    b. Write an expression for the cost, y, of a trip of x miles.

27. **a.** A manufacturer can produce items at a cost of $0.65 per item with an operational overhead of $350. Let y represent the total production costs and x represent the number of items produced. Write an equation representing costs.
    b. The manufacturer sells the items for $1 per item. Let y represent the revenue and x represent the number of items sold. Write an equation representing revenue.
    c. How many items does the manufacturer need to sell to break even?

28. **a.** Sketch the graph of the equation $xy = 1$. Choose a variety of values for x. For example, use $x = -10, -5, -1, -0.5, -0.1, 0.1, 0.5, 1, 5, 10$, and other values. The graph is called a **hyperbola**.
    b. Why can't x or y equal 0?
    c. What happens to the graph when x is near 0? Be sure to include cases when $x > 0$ and when $x < 0$.

29. **a.** Sketch the graph of the equation $y = x^2$. Choose a variety of values for x. For example, use $x = -5, -2, -1, 0, 1, 2, 5$, and other values. The graph is called a **parabola**.
    b. Sketch a graph of the equation $y = -x^2$. How is its graph related to the graph in part (a)?

30. a. Sketch the graph of the equation $\dfrac{x^2}{4} + \dfrac{y^2}{9} = 1$.

(*Hint:* Choose values of x between -2 and 2, and note that each value of x produces two values of y.) The graph is called an **ellipse**.

b. Sketch the graph of the equation $\dfrac{x^2}{9} + \dfrac{y^2}{4} = 1$. Choose values of x between -3 and 3. How is the graph related to the graph in part (a)?

31. Find the equation of the circumscribed circle for the triangle whose vertices are $J(4, 5)$, $K(8, -3)$, and $L(-4, 3)$.

Analyzing Student Thinking

32. Stuart wanted to express a horizontal line through $(3, 4)$ in slope-intercept form. However, he did not know what to use for m because he only had one point to figure out the slope. How can you help?

33. Bethany wanted to express a vertical line through $(3, 4)$ in slope-intercept form but could not determine its y-intercept. How can you help?

34. Jimmie was trying to figure out the equation of the line containing the points $(3, 7)$ and $(-5, 9)$. He thought the slope was $-1/4$, so he could put that number in place of the m in the slope-intercept form of a linear equation, $y = mx + b$. But he was very worried about which of the two points to use to substitute for the x and y in the equation. Should he use $(3, 7)$ or $(-5, 9)$? Discuss.

35. Sondra was working on solving simultaneous linear equations. She had the equations $y = 4x - 5$ and $3x + 2y = 7$, and after substituting the value of y from the first equation into the second, she got the answer $x = 17/11$. She said that she was done. Do you agree? Explain.

36. Hakim was trying to solve a problem about circles that asked whether $(-5, 4)$ was on the circle $(x + 5)^2 + (y - 4)^2 = 9$. He suddenly realized that $(-5, 4)$ was the center of the circle. Therefore, he said, "Yes, $(-5, 4)$ is on the circle." Do you agree? Explain.

37. Cole was asked to find the equation of a circle that contains point $(3, 4)$ and has a center at $(0, 0)$. However, he says that he needs to know the radius to be able to use the formula. How can you help?

38. When Marla was sketching the graph of a linear equation, $y = -2x + 5$, without graph paper, she found that her line seemed to bend, as shown in the figure. What went wrong?

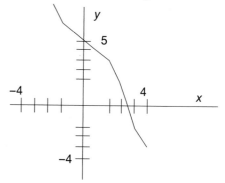

Problems Relating to the NCTM Standards and Curriculum Focal Points

1. The Focal Points for Grade 6 state "Writing, interpreting, and using mathematical expressions and equations." What does it mean "to solve an equation"?

2. The NCTM Standards state "All students should explore relationships between symbolic expressions and graphs of lines, paying particular attention to the meaning of intercept and slope." What is the meaning of y-intercept?

15.3   GEOMETRIC PROBLEM SOLVING USING COORDINATES

STARTING POINT

The figure at the right is a rhombus. The diagonals of a rhombus have a variety of properties such as being perpendicular to each other. Select one of these properties and use the coordinates provided to justify that property.

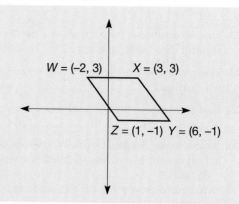

Using Coordinates to Solve Problems

We can use coordinates to solve a variety of geometric problems. The following property of triangles provides an example.

Example 15.8   Suppose that two medians of a triangle are congruent [Figure 15.19(a)]. Show that the triangle is isosceles. (Recall that a median is a line segment joining a vertex to the midpoint of the opposite side.)

Problem-Solving Strategy
Draw a Picture

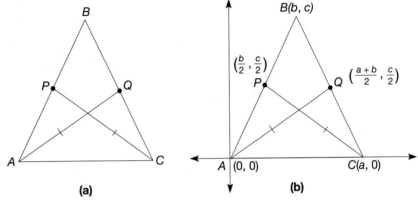

(a)

(b)

Figure 15.19

SOLUTION Choose a coordinate system so that $A = (0, 0)$, $C = (a, 0)$, and $B = (b, c)$ [Figure 15.19(b)]. Let P and Q be the midpoints of sides $\overline{AB}$ and $\overline{BC}$, respectively.

Then $P = \left(\dfrac{b}{2}, \dfrac{c}{2}\right)$ and $Q = \left(\dfrac{a + b}{2}, \dfrac{c}{2}\right)$. We wish to show that $AB = BC$, that is,

that $\sqrt{b^2 + c^2} = \sqrt{(b - a)^2 + c^2}$. Squaring both sides, we must show $b^2 + c^2 = b^2 - 2ab + a^2 + c^2$ or, simplifying, that $2ab = a^2$. We know that $AQ = CP$, so that

$$\left(\frac{a + b}{2}\right)^2 + \left(\frac{c}{2}\right)^2 = \left(\frac{b}{2} - a\right)^2 + \left(\frac{c}{2}\right)^2 = \left(\frac{b - 2a}{2}\right)^2 + \left(\frac{c}{2}\right)^2.$$

Expanding, we have

Algebraic Reasoning
By using variables for this solution, we have shown that the results hold for any values that we substitute in for the variables. Thus, the geometric relationship always holds.

$$\frac{a^2 + 2ab + b^2}{4} + \frac{c^2}{4} = \frac{b^2 - 4ab + 4a^2}{4} + \frac{c^2}{4}$$
$$a^2 + 2ab + b^2 + c^2 = 4a^2 - 4ab + b^2 + c^2$$
$$6ab = 3a^2,$$
$$2ab = a^2,$$

as desired. Thus $\overline{AB} \cong \overline{BC}$, so that $\triangle ABC$ is isosceles.   ■

Centroid of a Triangle

We can use coordinates to verify an interesting result about the three medians of any triangle.

THEOREM

Centroid of a Triangle

The medians of $\triangle PQR$ are concurrent at a point G that divides each median in a ratio of $2:1$.

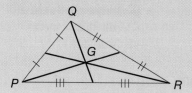

The point G is called the **centroid** of $\triangle PQR$.

PROOF Choose a coordinate system having $P(0, 0)$, $R(c, 0)$, and $Q(a, b)$ (Figure 15.20).

Problem-Solving Strategy
Draw a Picture

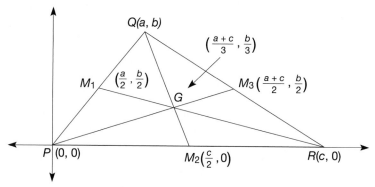

Figure 15.20

Let M_1, M_2, and M_3 be the midpoints of sides $\overline{PQ}$, $\overline{PR}$, and $\overline{QR}$.

Then, $M_1 = \left(\dfrac{a}{2}, \dfrac{b}{2}\right)$, $M_2 = \left(\dfrac{c}{2}, 0\right)$, and $M_3 = \left(\dfrac{a+c}{2}, \dfrac{b}{2}\right)$. Consider the point

$G = \left(\dfrac{a+c}{3}, \dfrac{b}{3}\right)$. Using slopes, we will show that P, G, and M_3 are collinear.

$$\text{slope of } \overline{PG} = \frac{\dfrac{b}{3} - 0}{\dfrac{a+c}{3} - 0} = \frac{b}{a+c}$$

$$\text{slope of } \overline{PM_3} = \frac{\dfrac{b}{2} - 0}{\dfrac{a+c}{2} - 0} = \frac{b}{a+c}$$

Therefore, P, G, and M_3 are collinear.

In a similar way, we can show that Q, G, and M_2 are collinear, as are R, G, and M_1. This is left for Part B Problem 13 in the Problem Set. Hence point G is on all three medians, so that the medians intersect at G.

Finally, we will show that G divides the median $\overline{PM_3}$ in a ratio of $2:1$. The similar verification for the other two medians is left for Part B Problem 14 in the Problem Set.

$$PG = \sqrt{\left(\frac{a+c}{3}\right)^2 + \left(\frac{b}{3}\right)^2}$$

$$= \frac{\sqrt{(a+c)^2 + b^2}}{3}$$

$$GM_3 = \sqrt{\left(\frac{a+c}{2} - \frac{a+c}{3}\right)^2 + \left(\frac{b}{2} - \frac{b}{3}\right)^2}$$

$$= \sqrt{\left(\frac{a+c}{6}\right)^2 + \left(\frac{b}{6}\right)^2}$$

$$= \frac{\sqrt{(a+c)^2 + b^2}}{6}$$

$$= \frac{1}{2}PG$$

Thus, the ratio $PG:GM_3 = 2:1$.   ■

Orthocenter of a Triangle

The next result shows how equations of lines can be used to verify properties of triangles.

THEOREM

Orthocenter of a Triangle

The altitudes of $\triangle PQR$ are concurrent at a point O called the **orthocenter** of the triangle.

PROOF   Consider $\triangle PQR$ with altitudes l, m, and n from P, Q, and R, respectively [Figure 15.21(a)]. Choose a coordinate system having $P(0, 0)$, $Q(a, b)$, and $R(c, 0)$ [Figure 15.21(b)]. Since $l \perp \overleftrightarrow{QR}$ the slope of l is $\dfrac{c-a}{b}$. (Verify.)

Problem-Solving Strategy
Draw a Picture

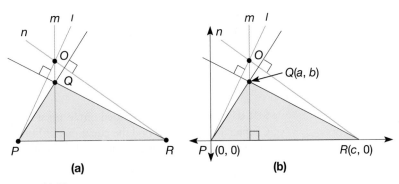

(a)   **(b)**

Figure 15.21

Hence, the equation of l is $y = \dfrac{c - a}{b}x$, since l contains $(0, 0)$. The equation of m is $x = a$, since m is a vertical line through $Q(a, b)$. Thus l and m intersect at point $O = \left(a, \dfrac{(c - a)a}{b}\right)$. (Verify.) To find the equation of n, we first find its slope. Since $n \perp \overleftrightarrow{PQ}$ the slope of n is $\dfrac{-a}{b}$. (Verify.) Hence the equation of n is of the form $y = -\dfrac{a}{b}x + d$ for some d. Using the fact that $R = (c, 0)$ is on n, we have

Problem-Solving Strategy
Solve an Equation

$$0 = \frac{-a}{b}c + d, \quad \text{so} \quad d = \frac{ac}{b}.$$

Thus the equation of n is $y = \dfrac{-a}{b}x + \dfrac{ac}{b}$. To show that l, m, and n meet at one point, all we need to show is that point $O = \left(a, \dfrac{(c - a)a}{b}\right)$ is on line n. Substituting a for x in the equation of n, we obtain

$$\begin{aligned} y &= \frac{-a}{b}a + \frac{ac}{b} \\ &= \frac{ac}{b} - \frac{aa}{b} \\ &= \frac{(c - a)a}{b}, \end{aligned}$$

the y-coordinate of O! Hence the three altitudes—l, m, and n—intersect at point O. ∎

Circumcenter of a Triangle

The next example illustrates a geometric construction in the coordinate plane using equations of lines and circles.

Example 15.9 Find the equation of the circumscribed circle for the triangle whose vertices are $O = (0, 0)$, $P = (2, 4)$, and $Q = (6, 0)$ (Figure 15.22).

Problem-Solving Strategy
Draw a Picture

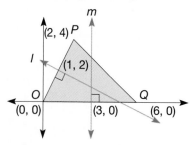

Figure 15.22

SOLUTION The circumscribed circle for a triangle contains all three vertices (see Chapter 14). First, we find the equations of lines l and m, the perpendicular bisectors of $\overline{OP}$ and $\overline{OQ}$. The intersection of lines l and m is the circumcenter of $\triangle OPQ$. To find the equation of line l, we need its slope. The slope of $\overline{OP}$ is $\dfrac{4 - 0}{2 - 0} = 2$, so that the slope of l is $-\frac{1}{2}$ by the slopes of perpendicular lines theorem. Hence the equation of line l is $y = -\frac{1}{2}x + b$, for some b. The midpoint of $\overline{OP}$ is $(1, 2)$, by the midpoint formula, so the point $(1, 2)$ satisfies the equation of line l. Thus $2 = (-\frac{1}{2})(1) + b$, so $b = \frac{5}{2}$. Therefore, the equation of line l is $y = -\frac{1}{2}x + \frac{5}{2}$.

Line m is vertical and contains $(3, 0)$, the midpoint of $\overline{OQ}$. Hence the equation of line m is $x = 3$. To find the circumcenter of $\triangle OPQ$, then, we need to find the point (x, y) satisfying the following simultaneous equations:

Problem-Solving Strategy
Solve an Equation

$$y = -\frac{1}{2}x + \frac{5}{2} \quad \text{and} \quad x = 3.$$

Using $x = 3$, we have

$$y = -\frac{1}{2}(3) + \frac{5}{2}, \quad \text{or} \quad y = 1.$$

Thus the point $C = (3, 1)$ is the circumcenter of $\triangle OPQ$.

To find the radius of the circumscribed circle, we use the distance formula. Since $(0, 0)$ is on the circle (we can use any vertex), the radius is $\sqrt{(3 - 0)^2 + (1 - 0)^2} = \sqrt{10}$. Thus, by the equation of a circle formula, the equation of the circumscribed circle is

$$(x - 3)^2 + (y - 1)^2 = 10.$$

As a check, verify that all the vertices of the triangle—namely $(0, 0)$, $(6, 0)$, and $(2, 4)$—satisfy this equation. Hence all are on the circle. Figure 15.23 shows the circumscribed circle. ∎

Figure 15.23

In this chapter we have restricted our attention to equations of circles and lines. However, using coordinates, it is possible to write equations for other sets of points in the plane and thus to investigate many other geometric problems, such as properties of curves other than lines and circles.

MATHEMATICAL MORSEL

Any three noncollinear points are contained on a circle. However, a remarkable result concerning nine points in a triangle, known as the nine-point circle theorem, states that all the following nine points lie on a single circle determined by $\triangle PQR$.

  A, B, C: the midpoints of the sides
  D, E, F: the "feet" of the altitudes
  G, H, I: the midpoints of the segments joining the vertices (P, Q, R) to the orthocenter, O

This circle is called the "Feuerbach circle" after a German mathematician, Karl Feuerbach, who proved several results about it.

Section 15.3   PROBLEM SET A

PROBLEMS

1. The coordinates of three vertices of a parallelogram are given. Find the coordinates of the fourth vertex. (There are three correct answers for each part.)
   a. (0, 0), (0, 5), (3, 0)   **b.** (−2, −2), (2, 3), (5, 3)

2. The coordinates of three vertices of a square are given. Find the coordinates of the fourth vertex.
   a. (−2, −1), (3, −1), (3, 4)   **b.** (−3, 0), (0, −2), (2, 1)

3. When using coordinate methods to verify results about polygons, it is often important how you choose the axes of the coordinate system. For example, it is often advantageous to put one vertex at the origin. Label the missing coordinates in the following diagrams.
   a. Square *ABCD*

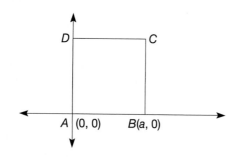

   b. Rectangle *EFGH*

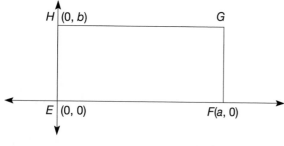

4. Right triangle *QRS* is placed in a coordinate system as shown.

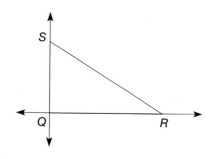

a. If $QR = 6$ and $QS = 4$, find the coordinates of the vertices of $\triangle QRS$.
b. If $QR = a$ and $QS = b$, find the coordinates of the vertices of $\triangle QRS$.

5. Given is isosceles triangle *XYZ* with $XY = YZ$, $XZ = 8$, and the altitude from *Y* having length 5. Find the coordinates of the vertices in each of the coordinate systems described.
   a. *X* is at the origin, $\overleftrightarrow{XZ}$ is the *x*-axis, and *Y* is in the first quadrant.
   b. $\overleftrightarrow{XZ}$ is the *x*-axis, the *y*-axis is a line of symmetry, and the *y*-coordinate of *Y* is positive.

6. Given $R(5, −2)$, $S(3, 0)$, $T(−4, −1)$, and $U(−2, −3)$, show that *RSTU* is a parallelogram.

7. Given the coordinates of $A(4, 1)$, $B(0, 7)$, $C(3, 9)$, and $D(7, 3)$, show that *ABCD* is a rectangle.

8. Given is $\triangle ABC$ with $A(−3, 6)$, $B(5, 8)$, and $C(3, 2)$.
   a. Let *M* be the midpoint of $\overline{AC}$. What are its coordinates?
   b. Let *N* be the midpoint of $\overline{BC}$. What are its coordinates?
   c. Find the slope of $\overline{MN}$ and the slope of $\overline{AB}$. What do you observe?
   d. Find the lengths of $\overline{MN}$ and $\overline{AB}$. What do you observe?

9. Use coordinates to prove that the diagonals of a rectangle are congruent.

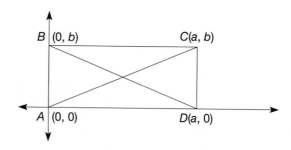

10. Given is $\triangle ABC$ with vertices $A(0, 0)$, $B(24, 0)$, and $C(18, 12)$.
    a. Find the equation of the line containing the median from vertex *A*.
    b. Find the equation of the line containing the median from vertex *B*.

c. Find the equation of the line containing the median from vertex C.

d. Find the intersection of the lines in parts (a) and (b). Does this point lie on the line in part (c)?

e. What result about the medians is illustrated?

f. What is the name of the point where the medians intersect?

11. Given $P(a, b)$, $Q(a + c, b + c)$, $R(a + d, b - d)$, and $S(a + c + d, b + c - d)$, determine whether the diagonals of $PQRS$ are congruent.

12. Given in the following figure is $\triangle ABC$ with vertices $A(0, 0)$, $B(a, b)$, and $C(c, 0)$. If $\triangle ABC$ is an isosceles triangle with $AB = BC$, show the following results.

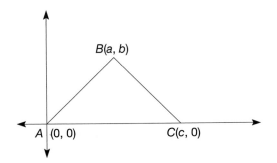

a. $c = 2a$.

b. The median from B is perpendicular to $\overline{AC}$.

13. Given is $\triangle RST$ with vertices $R(0, 0)$, $S(8, 6)$, and $T(11, 0)$.

a. Find the equation of the line containing the altitude from vertex R.

b. Find the equation of the line containing the altitude from vertex S.

c. Find the equation of the line containing the altitude from vertex T.

d. Find the intersection point of the lines in parts (a) and (b). Does this point lie on the line in part (c)?

e. What is the name of the point where the altitudes intersect?

14. Use coordinates to show that the diagonals of a parallelogram bisect each other.

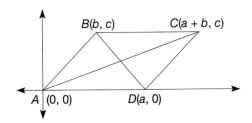

15. In the proof in this section concerning the orthocenter of a triangle, verify the following statements.

a. The slope of l is $\dfrac{c - a}{b}$.

b. The lines l and m intersect at the point $\left(a, \dfrac{(c - a)a}{b}\right)$.

c. The slope of n is $-\dfrac{a}{b}$.

16. Can an equilateral triangle with a horizontal side be formed on a square lattice? If so, show one. If not, explain why not.

17. The other day, I was taking care of two girls whose parents are mathematicians. The girls are both whizzes at math. When I asked their ages, one girl replied, "The sum of our ages is 18." The other stated, "The difference of our ages is 4." What are the girls' ages?

18. Seven cycle riders and nineteen cycle wheels go past. How many bicycles and how many tricycles passed by the house?

19. Mike and Joan invest $11,000 together. If Mike triples his money and Joan doubles hers, they will have $29,000. How much did each invest?

20. Marge went to a bookstore and paid $16.25 for a used math book, using only quarters and dimes. How many quarters and dimes did she have if she spent all of her 110 coins?

21. a. How many paths of length 7 are there from A to C? (*Hint:* At each vertex, write the number of ways to get there directly from A. Look for a pattern.)

b. How many of these paths go through B? (*Hint:* Apply the fundamental counting property.)

c. What is the probability that the path will go through B?

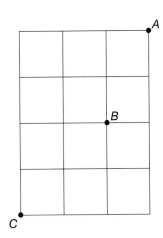

PROBLEMS

1. The coordinates of three vertices of a rectangle are given. Find the coordinates of the fourth vertex.
  a. $(4, 2), (4, 5), (-1, 2)$ **b.** $(-2, 1), (0, -1), (3, 2)$

2. Two vertices of a figure are $(-4, 0)$ and $(2, 0)$.
  a. Name the coordinates of the third vertex above the x-axis if the figure is an equilateral triangle. (*Hint:* One of the coordinates is irrational.)
  b. Name the coordinates of the other two vertices above the x-axis if the figure is a square.

3. Parallelogram *IJKL* is placed in a coordinate system such that I is at the origin and $\overline{IJ}$ is along the x-axis. The coordinates of $I, J,$ and L are shown. Give the coordinates of point K in terms of $a, b,$ and c.

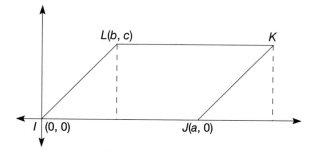

4. Rhombus *MNOP* is placed in a coordinate system such that M is at the origin and $\overline{MN}$ is along the x-axis. The coordinates for points $M, N,$ and P are given.

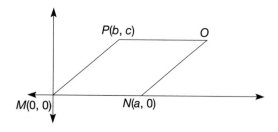

  a. Find the coordinates of point O in terms of $a, b,$ and c.
  b. What special relationship exists among $a, b,$ and c because *MNOP* is a rhombus?

5. The coordinate axes may be established in different ways. Suppose that rectangle *ABCD* is a rectangle with $AB = 10$ and $AD = 8$. Find the coordinates of the vertices in each of the coordinate systems described.

  a. $\overleftrightarrow{AB}$ is the x-axis, and the y-axis is a line of symmetry.
  b. The x-axis is a horizontal line of symmetry (let $\overleftrightarrow{AB}$ also be horizontal), and the y-axis is a vertical line of symmetry.

6. Given the points $A(-4, -1), B(1, -1), C(4, 3),$ and $D(-1, 3),$ show that *ABCD* is a rhombus.

7. Given the points $A(-3, -2), B(1, -3), C(2, 1),$ and $D(-2, 2),$ show that *ABCD* is a square.

8. Determine whether the diagonals of *EFGH* bisect each other, where $E(-1, -7), F(-3, -5), G(-2, 2),$ and $H(0, 0)$.

9. Given $\triangle ABC$ with vertices $A(0, 0), B(12, 6),$ and $C(18, 0),$
  a. Find the equation of the perpendicular bisector of $\overline{AB}$.
  b. Find the equation of the perpendicular bisector of $\overline{BC}$.
  c. Find the equation of the perpendicular bisector of $\overline{AC}$.
  d. Find the intersection of the lines in parts (a) and (b) and call it D. Does point D lie on the line in part (c)?
  e. Find the distance from D to each of the points $A, B,$ and C. What do you notice about these distances?
  f. What is the name of point D?

10. Use coordinates to show that the midpoint of the hypotenuse of a right triangle is equidistant from all three vertices.

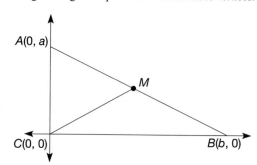

11. In Problem 10, Part 15.3A, let M be the centroid of the triangle (i.e., the point where the three medians are concurrent).
  a. Find the length of the median from A, the length AM, and the ratio of AM to the length of the median from A.
  b. Find the length of the median from B, the length BM, and the ratio of BM to the length of the median from B.
  c. Find the length of the median from C, the length CM, and the ratio of CM to the length of the median from C.
  d. Describe the location of the centroid.

12. Use coordinates to verify that the diagonals of a rhombus are perpendicular. (*Hint:* $a^2 = b^2 + c^2$.)

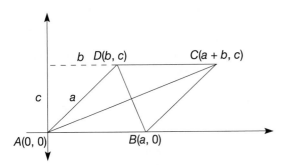

13. In the proof in this section concerning the centroid of a triangle, verify the following statements.
a. Points Q, G, and M_2 are collinear.
b. Points R, G, and M_1 are collinear.

14. In the proof in this section concerning the centroid of a triangle, verify the following statements.
a. The point G divides the median QM_2 in a ratio $2:1$.
b. The point G divides the median RM_1 in a ratio $2:1$.

15. Given is an equilateral triangle on a coordinate system.

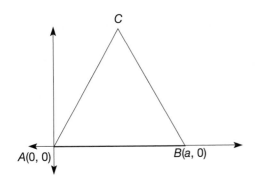

a. Find the coordinates of point C.
b. Find the perpendicular bisector of $\overline{AB}$, the median from point C, and the altitude from point C. Do these share points?
c. Do the perpendicular bisector of $\overline{BC}$, the median, and the altitude from point A share points?
d. Do the perpendicular bisector of $\overline{AC}$, the median, and the altitude from point B share points?
e. What general conclusion about equilateral triangles have you shown?

16. a. Given that $ABCD$ is an arbitrary quadrilateral, and points M and N are the midpoints of the diagonals $\overline{AC}$ and $\overline{BD}$, respectively, show that

$$AB^2 + BC^2 + CD^2 + DA^2 = BD^2 + AC^2 + 4(MN)^2.$$

b. What does the result in part (a) imply about a parallelogram?

17. Arrange the numbers 1, 2, 3, 4, 5, 6, 8, 9, 10, 11, 12, 13 around the cube shown so that the sum of the four edges that determine a face is always 28 and the sum of the three edges that lead into any vertex is 21.

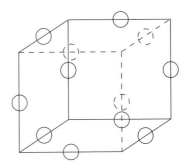

18. A quiz had some 3-point and some 4-point questions. A perfect score was 100 points. Find out how many questions were of each type if there were a total of 31 questions on the quiz.

19. A laboratory produces an alloy of gold, silver, and copper having a weight of 44 grams. If the gold weighs 3 grams more than the silver and the silver weighs 2 grams less than the copper, how much of each element is in the alloy?

20. The sum of two numbers is 148 and their difference is 16. What are the two numbers?

21. Six years ago, in a state park, the deer outnumbered the foxes by 80. Since then, the number of deer has doubled and the number of foxes has increased by 20. If there is now a total of 240 deer and foxes in the park, how many foxes were there six years ago?

22. My son gave me a set of table mats he bought in Mexico. They were rectangular and made of straw circles joined together in this way: All the circles on the edges of each mat were white and the inner circles black. I noted that there were 20 white circles and 15 black circles. Is it possible to make such a rectangular mat where the number of black circles is the same as the number of white circles?

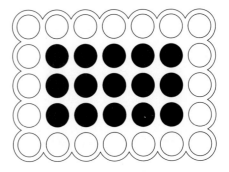

Analyzing Student Thinking

23. Holly wants to prove that the midpoints of the sides of any quadrilateral form a parallelogram. For her quadrilateral, she plans to use the coordinates $(-a, 0)$, $(0, c)$, (d, e), and $(b, 0)$ where a, b, c, and d are positive real numbers. She wants to know if she can use fewer letters to name her vertices. How would you respond?

24. Once she has the coordinates of a quadrilateral determined (see #23), Holly asks how she would go about proving that the midpoints of the sides of any quadrilateral form a parallelogram. What general proof outline would you suggest to her?

25. To prove the medians of a triangle are concurrent, Molly wants to know if she could use $(-a, 0)$, $(c, 0)$ and $(0, b)$, where a, b, and c are positive real numbers, as the vertices of the triangle. Her textbook typically uses the vertices $(0, 0)$, (a, b), and $(c, 0)$ for proofs like this. Molly wants to know if her vertices will work. How should you respond?

26. Jolene wanted to do a coordinate proof involving a right triangle. She wanted to place the vertices at point $(0, 0)$, $(a, 0)$, and (b, c) where the right angle was at the point

$(a, 0)$ and where a, b, and c are positive real numbers. Is this a good choice of vertices? Explain.

27. Herbert wants to find the equation of the perpendicular bisector of the hypotenuse of the right triangle with vertices at $(0, 0)$, $(a, 0)$, and $(0, b)$ where a and b are positive real numbers. He reasons that the perpendicular bisector goes through the midpoint of the hypotenuse and the vertex of the right angle. Is he correct? Discuss.

28. Shelley was placing a rhombus on coordinate axes with vertices at $(0, 0)$, (a, b), $(-a, b)$, and $(0, 2b)$ where a and b are positive real numbers. She wanted to name the vertices using the fewest number of letters. Assuming that the $(0, 0)$ and (a, b) are correct, is she assuming too much to think that the other two vertices could be labeled $(-a, b)$ and $(0, 2b)$? If so, what would Shelley have to explain in order to justify her labeling?

Problems Relating to the NCTM Standards and Curriculum Focal Points

1. The Focal Points for Grade 6 state "Writing, interpreting, and using mathematical expressions and equations." Explain how equations could be used to show that the diagonals of a parallelogram bisect each other.

2. The Focal Points for Grade 8 state "Analyzing two- and three-dimensional space and figures by using distance and angle." Give an example of how coordinate geometry is used

to analyze properties of a two-dimensional shape using distance.

3. The NCTM Standards state "All students should use coordinate geometry to represent and examine the properties of geometric shapes." Identify three different properties of shapes in this section that are examined using coordinate geometry.

END OF CHAPTER MATERIAL

Solution of Initial Problem

A surveyor plotted a triangular building lot shown in the figure below. He described the locations of stakes T and U relative to

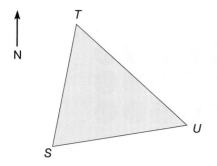

stake S. For example, U is recorded as East 207′, North 35′. This would mean that to find stake U, one would walk due east 207 feet and then due north for 35 feet. From the perspective of the diagram shown, one would go right from point S 207 feet and up 35 feet to get to U. Use the information provided to find the area of the lot in square feet.

STAKE	POSITION RELATIVE TO S
U	East 207′, North 35′
T	East 40′, North 185′

Strategy: Use Coordinates

First, place the triangle on a coordinate system and then surround it with a rectangle (Figure 15.24). Each triangle, A, B, and C, is

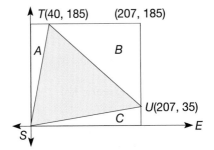

Figure 15.24

a right triangle. We can compute the area of each triangle, then subtract their total areas from the area of the rectangle:

$$\text{Area of triangle } A = \frac{40 \times 185}{2} = 3700 \text{ ft}^2$$

$$\text{Area of triangle } B = \frac{167 \times 150}{2} = 12{,}525 \text{ ft}^2$$

$$\text{Area of triangle } C = \frac{207 \times 35}{2} = 3622.5 \text{ ft}^2$$

$$\text{Area of rectangle} = 207 \times 185 = 38{,}295 \text{ ft}^2$$

Hence the area of a surveyed triangle $= 38{,}295 \text{ ft}^2 - (3700 + 12{,}525 + 3622.5) \text{ ft}^2 = 18{,}447.5 \text{ ft}^2$.

Additional Problems Where the Strategy "Use Coordinates" Is Useful

1. Prove that the diagonals of a kite are perpendicular. [*Hint:* Consider the kite with coordinates $(0, 0)$, (a, b), $(-a, b)$, and $(0, c)$, where $c > b$.]
2. An explorer leaves base camp and travels 4 km north, 3 km west, and 2 km south. How far is he from the base camp?
3. Prove that $\overline{BC}$ is parallel to $\overline{DE}$, where D and E are the centers of the squares (Figure 15.25). (*Hint:* Use slopes.)

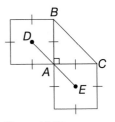

Figure 15.25

People in Mathematics

Shiing-Shen Chern (1911–2004) Shiing-Shen Chern is noted for his pioneering work in differential geometry, a branch of mathematics that has been used to extend Einstein's theory of general relativity. Born and educated in China, Chern did advanced study in Germany and France during the 1930s. He returned to China to organize a mathematics institute in Shanghai. The largest part of his working life has been spent in the United States, at the Institute of Advanced Study, the University of Chicago, and the University of California at Berkeley. In 1982, Chern was chosen to become the first director of the Mathematical Sciences Research Institute; the acronym MSRI is commonly pronounced "misery" by the researchers at the institute, perhaps in recognition of the frustrations they have experienced when attacking difficult problems.

H. S. M. Coxeter (1907–2003) H. S. M. Coxeter is known for his research and expositions of geometry. He is the author of 11 books, including *Introduction to Geometry, Projective Geometry, Non-Euclidean Geometry, The Fifty-Nine Icosahedra*, and *Mathematical Recreations and Essays*. He contends that Russia, Germany, and Austria are the countries that do the best job of teaching geometry in the schools, because they still regard it as a subject worth studying. "In English-speaking countries, there was a long tradition of dull teaching of geometry. People thought that the only thing to do in geometry was to build a system of axioms and see how you would go from there. So children got bogged down in this formal stuff and didn't get a lively feel for the subject. That did a lot of harm."

CHAPTER REVIEW

Review the following terms and exercises to determine which require learning or relearning—page numbers are provided for easy reference.

SECTION 15.1 Distance and Slope in the Coordinate Plane

VOCABULARY/NOTATION

Coordinate distance formula   824   Midpoint formula   825   Slope of a line segment   826
Collinearity test   824   Slope of a line   826

EXERCISES

The points $P(3, 4)$, $Q(5, -2)$, $R(6, 8)$, $S(10, -4)$, and $T(7, 3)$ are used in the following.

1. Find the distance PQ.

2. Find the midpoint M of $\overline{PQ}$.

3. Determine whether P, Q, and M are collinear.

4. Find the slopes of $\overline{PM}$ and $\overline{MQ}$. What does your answer prove?

5. Determine whether $\overleftrightarrow{PQ} \parallel \overleftrightarrow{RS}$.

6. Determine whether $\overline{TM} \perp \overline{PQ}$.

SECTION 15.2 Equations and Coordinates

VOCABULARY/NOTATION

y-intercept   837   Point-slope equation of a line   839   Simultaneous equations   841
Slope-intercept equation of a line   838   Simultaneous solutions   841

EXERCISES

The points $P(4, -7)$, $Q(0, 3)$, $R(3, 2)$, $S(5, -1)$, and $T(-2, 5)$ are used in the following.

1. Write the slope-intercept form of $\overleftrightarrow{PQ}$.

2. Write the point-slope form of $\overleftrightarrow{RS}$.

3. Describe the three types of outcomes possible when solving two linear equations simultaneously.

4. Write the equation of the circle with center at T and diameter 10.

SECTION 15.3 Geometric Problem Solving Using Coordinates

VOCABULARY/NOTATION

Centroid   850   Orthocenter   851

EXERCISES

The points $P(0, 0)$, $Q(0, 5)$, and $R(12, 0)$ are used in the following.

1. Find the centroid of $\triangle PQR$.

2. Find the orthocenter of $\triangle PQR$.

3. Find the center of the circumscribed circle of $\triangle PQR$.

CHAPTER TEST

KNOWLEDGE

1. True or false?
  a. A point $(a, 0)$ is on the x-axis.
  b. The quadrants are labeled I-IV clockwise beginning with the upper left quadrant.
  c. The midpoint of the segment with endpoints $(a, 0)$ and $(b, 0)$ is $((a + b)/2, 0)$.
  d. The y-intercept of a line is always positive.
  e. A pair of simultaneous equations of the form $ax + by = c$ may have *exactly* 0, 1, or 2 simultaneous solutions.
  f. The orthocenter of a triangle is the intersection of the altitudes.
  g. The equation $x^2 + y^2 = r^2$ represents a circle whose center is the origin and whose radius is $\sqrt{r^2}$.
  h. If two lines are perpendicular and neither line is vertical, the slope of each line is the multiplicative inverse of the slope of the other.

2. Name and write the equations for two different forms of linear equations.

SKILL

3. Find the length, midpoint, and slope of the line segment with endpoints $(1, 2)$ and $(5, 7)$.

4. Find the equations of the following lines.
  a. The vertical line containing $(-1, 7)$
  b. The horizontal line containing $(-1, 7)$
  c. The line containing $(-1, 7)$ with slope 3
  d. The line containing $(-1, 7)$ and perpendicular to the line $2x + 3y = 5$

5. Find the equation of the circle with center $(-3, 4)$ and radius 5.

6. Without finding the solutions, determine whether the following pairs of equations have zero, one, or infinitely many simultaneous solutions.
  a. $3x + 4y = 5$ **b.** $3x - 2y = -9$
  $\quad\ \ 6x + 8y = 11$ $\quad\ \ x + y = -1$
  c. $x - y = -1$ **d.** $x + 5 = 0$
  $\quad\ \ y - x = 1$ $\quad\ \ 2x + 7y = 10$

7. Write the equation $3x - 4y = 8$ in slope-intercept form.

8. Find the equation of the perpendicular bisector of the segment described in Exercise 3.

UNDERSTANDING

9. Determine how many simultaneous solutions the equations $x^2 + y^2 = r^2$ and $ax + by = c$ *may* have. Explain.

10. Explain why the following four equations could not contain the four sides of a rectangle, but *do* contain the four sides of a parallelogram.
$$2x - 4y = 7$$
$$2x - 4y = 13$$
$$3x + 5y = 8$$
$$3x + 5y = -2$$

11. Find 3 points on the circle described in Exercise 5.

12. Explain how the Pythagorean theorem is related to the distance formula.

13. Plot the points $L(2, 2)$, $M(5, 1)$, $N(6, 4)$, and $O(3, 5)$ on a set of axes and determine exactly what type of quadrilateral $LMNO$ is. Justify your conclusion.

14. If the midpoint of a segment is $(3, 5)$ and one endpoint is $(-1, 7)$, what are the coordinates of the other endpoint?

15. If line l has a slope of 2 and contains the point $(-1, -2)$, what are three other points that lie on l?

16. Let $A = (2, 3)$, $B = (3, 6)$, and $C = (6, 5)$.
  a. Sketch $\triangle ABC$ on a set of axes.
  b. Determine if $\triangle ABC$ is equilateral, isosceles, or scalene. Explain your reasoning.
  c. Determine if $\triangle ABC$ is acute, obtuse, or right. Explain your reasoning.

PROBLEM SOLVING/APPLICATION

17. Give the most complete description of the figure $ABCD$, where A, B, C, and D are the midpoints of the square determined by the points $(0, 0)$, $(a, 0)$, (a, a), and $(0, a)$, and where a is positive. Prove your assertion.

18. For the triangle pictured, prove the following relationships.

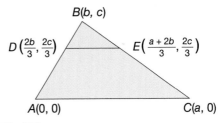

  a. $\overline{DE} \parallel \overline{AC}$
  b. $DE = \frac{1}{3}AC$

State the new theorem that you have proved.

19. The quadrilateral $LMNO$ in the following figure is a parallelogram.

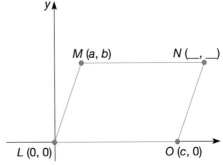

  a. Find the coordinates of vertex N based on the coordinates of the other vertices already listed in the figure.
  b. Using the given information and the results of part (a), show that the diagonals of a parallelogram bisect each other.

Geometry Using Transformations

The Geometric Art of M. C. Escher

Maurits Escher was born in the Netherlands in 1898.

Although his school experience was largely a negative one, he looked forward with enthusiasm to his two hours of art each week. His father urged him into architecture to take advantage of his artistic ability. However, that endeavor did not last long. It became apparent that Escher's talent lay more in the area of decorative arts than in architecture, so Escher began the formal study of art when he was in his twenties. His work includes sketches, woodcuts, mezzotints, lithographs, and water-colors.

Escher's links with mathematics and mathematical form are apparent. The following works illustrate various themes related to mathematics.

Approaches to Infinity

Circle Limit III illustrates one of three Circle Limit designs based on a hyperbolic tessellation. Notice how the fish seem to swim to infinity. This work gave rise to a paper by H. S. M. Coxeter entitled "The Non-Euclidean Symmetry of Escher's Picture *Circle Limit III*."

Symmetries

Shells and Starfish, which was developed from a pattern of stars and diamond shapes on a square grid, possesses several rotation symmetries.

Metamorphosis

Escher is perhaps most famous for his ever-changing pictures. *Fish* shows arched fish evolving, appearing, and disappearing across the drawing.

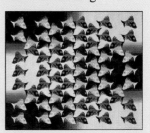

Methods that lead to constructions such as the above are discussed in this chapter.

STRATEGY 21
Use Symmetry

Several types of geometric and numerical symmetry can occur in mathematical problems. Geometric symmetry involves a correspondence between points that preserves shape and size. For example, the actions of sliding, turning, and flipping lead to types of symmetry. Numerical symmetry occurs, for example, when numerical values can be interchanged and yet the results are equivalent. As an illustration, suppose that 5 coins are tossed. Knowing that 3 heads and 2 tails can occur in 10 ways, we can determine the number of ways that 2 heads and 3 tails can occur. We simply replace each "head" by "tail," and vice versa, using the fact that each arrangement of n heads and m tails ($n + m = 5$) corresponds to exactly one arrangement of m heads and n tails. Hence there are also 10 ways that 2 heads and 3 tails can occur.

INITIAL PROBLEM

Houses A and B are to be connected to a television cable line l, at a transformer point P. Where should P be located so that the sum of the distances, $AP + PB$, is as small as possible?

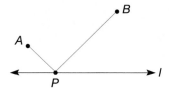

CLUES

The Use Symmetry strategy may be appropriate when

- Geometry problems involve transformations.
- Interchanging values does not change the representation of the problem.
- Symmetry limits the number of cases that need to be considered.
- Pictures or algebraic expressions are symmetric.

A solution of this Initial Problem is on page 916.

INTRODUCTION

NCTM Standard
All students should recognize
and apply slides, flips, and
turns.

Children's Literature
www.wiley.com/college/musser
See "A Cloak for the Dreamer"
by Aileen Friedman.

I n Chapter 12 we observed informally that many geometric figures have symmetry properties, such as rotation or reflection symmetry. In this chapter we give a precise description of symmetry in the plane in terms of functions or mappings between points. Mappings of points in the plane will be called transformations. Using transformations, we give precise meanings to the ideas of congruence of figures and similarity of figures. Finally, by studying congruence and similarity via transformations, we can derive many important geometric properties that can be used to solve geometry problems.

Key Concepts from NCTM Curriculum Focal Points

- **KINDERGARTEN:** Describing shapes and space.
- **GRADE 3:** Through building, drawing, and analyzing two-dimensional shapes, students understand attributes and properties of two-dimensional space and the use of those attributes and properties in solving problems, including applications involving congruence and symmetry.
- **GRADE 4:** By using transformations to design and analyze simple tilings and tessellations, students deepen their understanding of two-dimensional space.
- **GRADE 7:** Students solve problems about similar objects (including figures) by using scale factors that relate corresponding lengths of the objects or by using the fact that relationships of lengths within an object are preserved in similar objects.

16.1   TRANSFORMATIONS

STARTING POINT

Each of the following pairs of triangles are congruent, which means they are the same shape and size. Since they are congruent, one triangle in each pair could be moved to lie exactly on top of the other. Trace $\triangle ABC$ onto another piece of paper. Lay your tracing on $\triangle ABC$ and move it to $\triangle A'B'C'$. Describe the movement in terms of a slide, flip, or turn. Repeat for $\triangle DEF$.

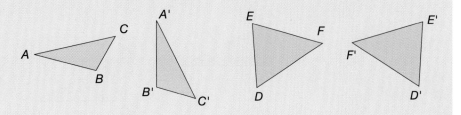

Isometries

In Chapter 12 we investigated symmetry properties of geometric figures by means of motions that make a figure coincide with itself. For example, the kite in Figure 16.1 has reflection symmetry, since there is a line, $\overleftrightarrow{BD}$, over which the kite can be folded to make the two halves match.

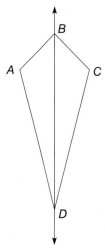

Figure 16.1

Notice that when we fold the kite over $\overleftrightarrow{BD}$, we are actually forming a one-to-one correspondence between the points of the kite. For example, points A and C correspond to each other, points along segments $\overline{AB}$ and $\overline{CB}$ correspond, and points along segments $\overline{AD}$ and $\overline{CD}$ correspond. In this chapter we will investigate correspondences between points of the plane. A **transformation** is a one-to-one correspondence between points in the plane such that each point P is associated with a unique point P', called the **image** of P.

Transformations that preserve the size and shape of geometric figures are called **isometries** (*iso* means "same" and *metry* means "measure") or **rigid motions**. In the remainder of this subsection, we'll study the various types of isometries.

Translations   Consider the following transformation that acts like a "slide."

Example 16.1   Describe a transformation that will move $\triangle ABC$ of Figure 16.2 to coincide with $\triangle A'B'C'$.

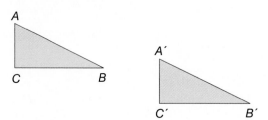

Figure 16.2

SOLUTION Slide the triangle so that A moves to A' (Figure 16.3).

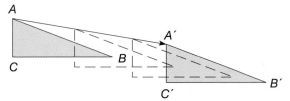

Figure 16.3

Since B' and C' are the same distance and direction from B and C, respectively, as A' is from A, point B' is the image of B and point C' is the image of C. Thus $\triangle ABC$ moves to $\triangle A'B'C'$. Trace $\triangle ABC$ and slide it using the arrow from A to A'. ∎

The sliding motion of Example 16.1 can be described by specifying the distance and direction of the slide. The arrow from A to A' in Figure 16.3 conveys this information. A transformation that "slides" each point in the plane in the same direction and for the same distance is called a translation. For the transformations considered in this section, we will assume that we can obtain the image of a polygon by connecting the images of the vertices of the original polygon, as we did in Example 16.1.

To give a precise definition to a translation or "sliding" transformation, we need the concept of directed line segment. Informally, a line segment $\overline{AB}$ can be directed in two ways: (1) pointing from A to B or (2) pointing from B to A (Figure 16.4). We denote the **directed line segment** from A to B as $\overrightarrow{AB}$ Two directed line segments are called **equivalent** if they are parallel, have the same length, and point in the same direction.

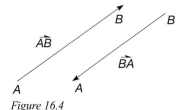

Figure 16.4

Reflection from Research
Translations are the easiest transformations for students to visualize when compared to reflections and rotations (Schultz & Austin, 1983).

DEFINITION

Translation

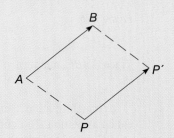

Suppose that A and B are points in the plane. The **translation** associated with directed line segment $\overrightarrow{AB}$, denoted $\textbf{\textit{T}}_{AB}$, is the transformation that maps each point P to the point P' such that $\overrightarrow{PP'}$ is equivalent to $\overrightarrow{AB}$.

Directed line segment $\overrightarrow{PP'}$ is equivalent to $\overrightarrow{AB}$ so that $\overrightarrow{PP'} \parallel \overrightarrow{AB}$ and $PP' = AB$. Thus quadrilateral $PP'BA$ is a parallelogram, since it has a pair of opposite sides that are parallel and congruent. We can imagine that P is "slid" by the translation T_{AB} in the direction from A to B for a distance equal to AB.

Rotations   An isometry that corresponds to turning the plane around a fixed point is described next.

Example 16.2   Describe a transformation that will move $\triangle ABC$ of Figure 16.5 to coincide with $\triangle A'B'C'$.

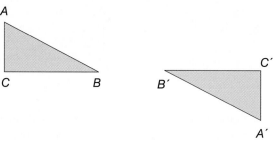

Figure 16.5

Reflection from Research
Young children were more successful performing rotations after being taught about them using a dynamic (or motion) approach rather than a static approach (Moyer, 1978).

SOLUTION   We can turn $\triangle ABC$ 180° around point P, the midpoint of segment $\overline{BB'}$, to coincide with $\triangle A'B'C$ (Figure 16.6).

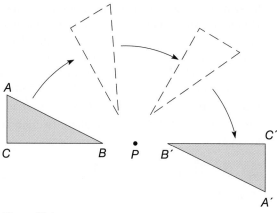

Figure 16.6

Trace $\triangle ABC$, and turn your tracing around point P to verify this.   ◼

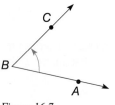

Figure 16.7

A transformation that corresponds to a turning motion as in Example 16.2 is called a rotation. To define a rotation, we need the concept of directed angle. Angle $\angle ABC$ is said to be a **directed angle** if it satisfies the following properties:

1. If $m(\angle ABC) = 0$, then the measure of the directed angle is 0°.

2. If $\angle ABC$ is a straight angle, then the measure of the directed angle is 180°.

3. See Figure 16.7.
   a. Let ray $\overrightarrow{BA}$ be turned around point B through the smallest possible angle so that the image of ray $\overrightarrow{BA}$ coincides with ray $\overrightarrow{BC}$.
   b. If the direction of the turn is *counterclockwise*, the **measure of the directed angle** is the *positive* number $m(\angle ABC)$. If the direction is *clockwise*, the measure is the *negative* number $-m(\angle ABC)$. We denote the directed angle $\angle ABC$ by $\measuredangle ABC$.

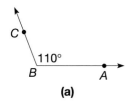

(a)

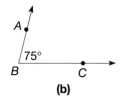

(b)

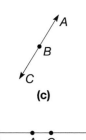

(c)

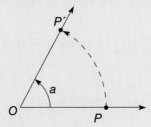

(d)

Figure 16.8

Algebraic Reasoning
In algebra, we talk about functions like $f(x) = 3x - 2$ where numbers are the input and output. Transformations are also functions with geometric objects as inputs and outputs. For example, a rotation, $R_{O,a}$ maps a segment $\overline{AB}$ to the segment $\overline{A'B'}$ and is written in function notation as $R_{O,a}(\overline{AB}) = \overline{A'B'}$.

For directed angle $\sphericalangle ABC$, ray $\overrightarrow{BA}$ is called the **initial side** and ray $\overrightarrow{BC}$ is called the **terminal side**. In directed angle $\sphericalangle ABC$, the initial side is given by the ray whose vertex is the vertex of the angle, here B, and that contains the point listed first in the name of the angle, here A. For example, in directed angle $\sphericalangle CBA$ the initial side is $\overrightarrow{BC}$. Notice that the measure of directed angle $\sphericalangle CBA$ is the *opposite* of the measure of directed angle $\sphericalangle ABC$, since the initial side of directed angle $\sphericalangle CBA$ is ray $\overrightarrow{BC}$, while the initial side of directed angle $\sphericalangle ABC$ is $\overrightarrow{BA}$. Example 16.3 gives several examples of directed angles.

| **Example 16.3** | Find the measure of each of the directed angles $\sphericalangle ABC$ in Figure 16.8. |

SOLUTION
a. The measure of directed angle $\sphericalangle ABC$ is $110°$, since initial side $\overrightarrow{BA}$ can be turned counterclockwise through $110°$ around point B to coincide with terminal side $\overrightarrow{BC}$.
b. The measure of directed angle $\sphericalangle ABC$ is $-75°$, since initial side $\overrightarrow{BA}$ can be turned clockwise through $75°$ to coincide with terminal side $\overrightarrow{BC}$.
c. The measure of directed angle $\sphericalangle ABC$ is $180°$, since $\angle ABC$ is a straight angle.
d. The measure of directed angle $\sphericalangle ABC$ is $0°$, since $m(\angle ABC) = 0°$. ∎

We can now define a rotation. In Section 16.2 we prove that rotations are isometries.

DEFINITION

Rotation

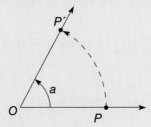

The **rotation** with center O and angle with measure a, denoted $\boldsymbol{R_{O,a}}$, is the transformation that maps each point P other than O to the point P' such that

1. the measure of directed angle $\sphericalangle POP'$ is a, and
2. $OP' = OP$.

Point O is mapped to itself by $R_{O,a}$.

NOTE: If a is positive, $R_{O,a}$ is counterclockwise, and if a is negative, $R_{O,a}$ is clockwise. Intuitively, point P is "turned" by $R_{O,a}$ around the center, O, through a directed angle of measure a to point P'.

Reflections Another isometry corresponds to flipping the plane over a fixed line.

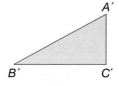

Describe a transformation that will move $\triangle ABC$ of Figure 16.9 to coincide with $\triangle A'B'C'$.

NCTM Standard
All students should describe a motion or series of motions that will show that two shapes are congruent.

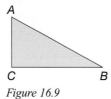

Figure 16.9

SOLUTION Flip $\triangle ABC$ over the perpendicular bisector of segment $\overline{AA'}$ (Figure 16.10).

Reflection from Research
Reflections having vertical or horizontal mirror lines tend to be easier for students to visualize than reflections having diagonal mirror lines (Dixon, 1995).

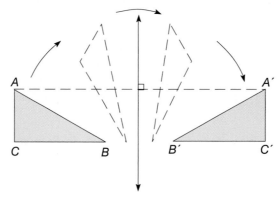

Figure 16.10

Then point A moves to point A', point B to B', and C to C'. Hence $\triangle ABC$ moves to $\triangle A'B'C'$. Trace Figure 16.9, and fold your tracing to verify this. ∎

A transformation that "flips" the plane over a fixed line is called a reflection.

DEFINITION

Reflection

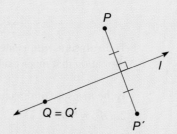

Suppose that l is a line in the plane. The **reflection** in line l, denoted M_l, is the transformation that maps points as follows:

1. Each point P not on line l is mapped to the point P' such that l is the perpendicular bisector of segment $\overline{PP'}$.

2. Each point Q on line l is mapped to itself.

STUDENT PAGE SNAPSHOT

LESSON
3 Transformations

OBJECTIVE: Identify, predict, and describe the results of transformations.

Learn

PROBLEM The space shuttle turns 180 degrees after liftoff and looks as if it is flying upside down. Before entering orbit, the space shuttle turns again to a right-side-up position. How can you describe this movement?

A **transformation** is the movement of a figure by a translation, reflection, or rotation.

TERM	DEFINITION	EXAMPLE
Translation	A translation, or a slide, moves a figure to a new position along a straight line.	
Rotation	A rotation, or a turn, moves a figure around a point.	
Reflection	A reflection, or a flip, flips a figure over a line.	

So, the space shuttle rotates 180 degrees when it moves from upside-down to right-side-up.

Quick Review

Do the figures appear congruent? Write *yes* or *no*.

1.
2.
3.
4.
5.

Vocabulary

transformation   rotation
translation   reflection

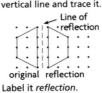

▲ The space shuttle rotates shortly after liftoff.

Activity 1 Draw examples of transformations.
Materials ■ pattern block ■ dot paper

Step 1	Step 2	Step 3	Step 4
Trace the pattern block.	Slide the block in any direction and trace it.	Trace another pattern block. Turn the block clockwise 90° and trace it.	Flip the block over a vertical line and trace it.

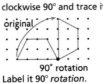

original	original	original / 90° rotation	original reflection
Label it *original*.	Label it *translation*.	Label it *90° rotation*.	Label it *reflection*.

• How is a counterclockwise rotation different from a clockwise rotation?

• Predict how the rotated figure would look if the point of rotation were in the center of the original figure.

550

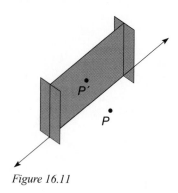

Figure 16.11

One can envision the effect of the reflection in line *l* by imagining a mirror in line *l* perpendicular to the plane. Then points on either side of *l* are mapped to the other side of *l*, and points on *l* remain fixed. A Mira can be used to find reflection images easily (Figure 16.11). We prove that reflections are isometries in the next section.

Glide Reflections   Next we define a transformation that is a combination of a translation and a reflection, called a glide reflection.

Example 16.5   Is there a translation that will move △*ABC* of Figure 16.12 to coincide with △*A'B'C'*? What about a rotation? a reflection?

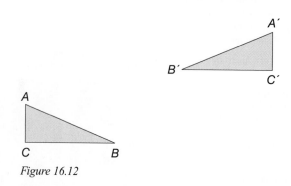

Figure 16.12

SOLUTION   No single transformation that we have studied thus far will suffice. Use tracings to convince yourself. However, with a combination of a translation and a reflection, we can move △*ABC* to △*A'B'C'* (Figure 16.13).

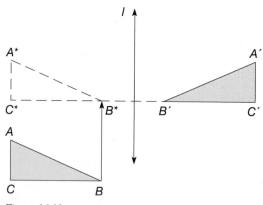

Figure 16.13

First, apply the translation T_{BB*} to move △*ABC* to △*A*B*C**, a triangle that can be reflected onto △*A'B'C'*. Then reflect △*A*B*C** in line *l* onto △*A'B'C'*. Notice that directed line segment $\overrightarrow{BB^*}$ is parallel to the reflection line *l*.   ∎

A transformation formed by combining a translation and a reflection over a line parallel to the directed line segment of the translation, as in Example 16.5, is called a glide reflection.

DEFINITION

Glide Reflection

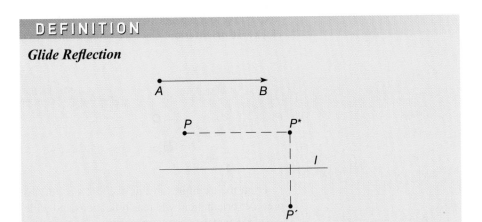

Suppose that A and B are different points in the plane and that line l is parallel to directed line segment $\overrightarrow{AB}$. The combination of the translation T_{AB} followed by the reflection M_l is called the **glide reflection** determined by $\overrightarrow{AB}$ and **glide axis** l. That is, P is first mapped to $P*$ by T_{AB}. Then $P*$ is mapped to P' by M_l. The combination of T_{AB} followed by M_l maps P to P'.

It can be shown that as long as $l \parallel \overrightarrow{AB}$, the glide reflection image can be found by translating first, then reflecting, or vice versa. Example 16.6 shows the effect of a glide reflection on a triangle.

Example 16.6	In Figure 16.14(a), find the image of $\triangle PQR$ under the glide reflection T_{AB} followed by M_l.

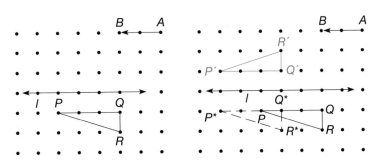

Figure 16.14

SOLUTION We observe that the translation T_{AB} maps each point two units to the left [Figure 16.14(b)]. That is, T_{AB} maps $\triangle PQR$ to $\triangle P*Q*R*$. The reflection M_l reflects $\triangle P*Q*R*$ across line l to $\triangle P'Q'R'$. Equivalently, we can reflect $\triangle PQR$ across line l, then slide its image to the left. In each case, the image of $\triangle PQR$ is $\triangle P'Q'R'$. Since glide reflections are combinations of two isometries, a translation and a reflection, they, too, are isometries. ∎

In Example 16.6 observe that $\triangle PQR$ was translated, then reflected across line l to $\triangle P'Q'R'$. Thus the "orientation" of $\triangle P'Q'R'$ is opposite that of $\triangle PQR$. In Figure 16.15, $\triangle PQR$ is said to have **clockwise orientation**, since tracing the triangle from P to Q to R is a clockwise tracing. Similarly, $\triangle P'Q'R'$ in Figure 16.15 has **counter-clockwise orientation**, since a tracing from P' to Q' to R' is counterclockwise.

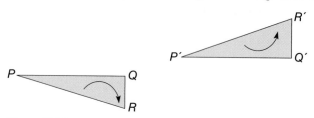

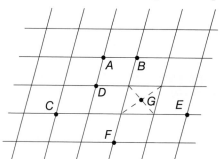

Figure 16.15

From the examples in this section, we can observe that translations and rotations preserve orientation, whereas reflections and glide reflections reverse orientation.

In elementary school, translations, rotations, reflections, and glide reflections are frequently called "slides," "turns," "flips," and "slide flips," respectively. Next, we will see how to apply these transformations to analyze symmetry patterns in the plane.

✔ **Check for Understanding:** Exercise/Problem Set A #1–22

NCTM Standard
All students should recognize and create shapes that have symmetry.

Symmetry

Consider a tessellation of the plane with parallelograms (Figure 16.16).

Figure 16.16

Reflection from Research
Car hubcaps or toys such as the Spirograph can be used to help students investigate rotational symmetry (Flores, 1992).

We can identify several translations that map the tessellation onto itself. For example, the translations T_{AB}, T_{CD}, and T_{EF} all map the tessellation onto itself. To see that T_{AB} maps the tessellation onto itself, make a tracing of the tessellation, place the tracing on top of the tessellation, and move the tracing according to the translation T_{AB}. The tracing will match up with the original tessellation. (Remember that the tessellation fills the plane.) A figure has **translation symmetry** if there is a translation that maps the figure onto itself. Every tessellation of the plane with parallelograms like the one in Figure 16.16 has translation symmetry.

For the tessellation in Figure 16.16, there are several rotations, through less than 360°, that map the tessellation onto itself. For example, the rotations $R_{A,180}$ and $R_{G,180}$ map the tessellation onto itself. Note that G is the intersection of the diagonals of a parallelogram. (Use your tracing paper to see that these rotations map the tessellation onto itself.) A figure has **rotation symmetry** if there is a rotation through an angle greater than 0° and less than 360° that maps the figure onto itself.

In Figure 16.17, a tessellation with isosceles triangles and trapezoids is pictured. Again, imagine that the tessellation fills the plane. In Figure 16.17, reflection M_l maps the tessellation onto itself, as does M_m. A figure has **reflection symmetry** if there is a reflection that maps the figure onto itself. The tessellation in Figure 16.17 has translation symmetry and reflection symmetry, but not rotation symmetry.

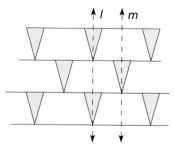

Figure 16.17

Figure 16.18 illustrates part of a tessellation of the plane that has translation, rotation, and reflection symmetry.

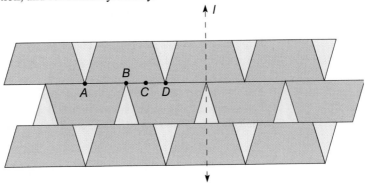

Figure 16.18

For example, $R_{C,180}$ is a rotation that maps the tessellation onto itself, where point C is the midpoint of segment $\overline{BD}$. (You can use a tracing of the tessellation to check this.) The translation T_{AD} can be used to show that the tessellation has translation symmetry, while the reflection M_l can be used to show reflection symmetry. This tessellation also has glide reflection symmetry. For example, consider the glide reflection formed by T_{AB} followed by M_{AB}. (M_{AB} is the reflection in the line containing $\overline{AB}$.) This glide reflection maps the tessellation onto itself. A figure has **glide reflection symmetry** if there is a glide reflection that maps the figure onto itself. (Notice that, in this case, neither the translation T_{AB}, nor the reflection M_{AB} alone, maps the tessellation to itself.)

Symmetrical figures appear in nature, art, and design. Interestingly, all symmetrical patterns in the plane can be analyzed using translations, rotations, reflections, and glide reflections.

NCTM Standard
All students should recognize and apply geometric ideas and relationships in areas outside the mathematics classroom, such as art, science, and everyday life.

Children's Literature
www.wiley.com/college/musser
See "Sweet Clara and the Freedom Quilt" by Deborah Hopkinson.

✔ **Check for Understanding:** Exercise/Problem Set A #23–24

Making Escher-Type Patterns

The artist M. C. Escher used tessellations and transformations to make intriguing patterns that fill the plane. Figure 16.19 shows how to produce such a pattern. Side $\overline{AB}$ of the square $ABDC$ [Figure 16.19(a)] is altered to form the outline of a cat's head [Figure 16.19(b)]. Then the curved side from A' to B' is translated so that A' is mapped to C' and B' is mapped to D'. Thus the curve connecting C' to D' is the same size and shape as the curve connecting A' to B'. All other points remain fixed. The resulting shape will tessellate the plane [Figure 16.19(c)]. Using translations, tessellations of the plane with parallelograms can be altered to make Escher-type patterns.

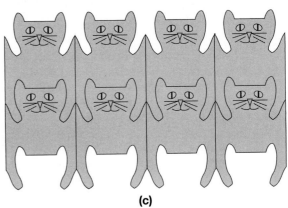

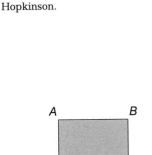

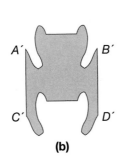

(a)   **(b)**   **(c)**

Figure 16.19

Rotations can also be used to make Escher-type drawings. Figure 16.20 shows a triangle that has been altered by rotation to produce an Escher-type pattern. Side $\overline{AC}$ of $\triangle ABC$ [Figure 16.20(a)] is altered arbitrarily, provided that points A and C are not moved [Figure 16.20(b)]. Then, using point C as the center of a rotation, altered side $\overline{AC}$ is rotated so that A is rotated to B [Figure 16.20(c)]. The result is an alteration of side $\overline{BC}$. The shape in Figure 16.20(c) will tessellate the plane as shown in Figure 16.20(d). Other techniques for making Escher-type patterns appear in the Exercise/Problem Sets. Many Escher-type patterns are tessellations of the plane having a variety of types of symmetry. For example, the tessellation in Figure 16.19(c) has translation and reflection symmetry, while the tessellation in Figure 16.20(d) has translation and rotation symmetry.

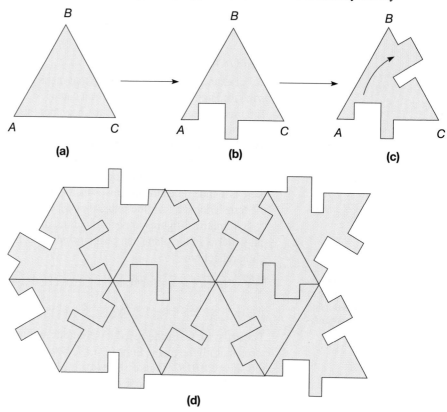

Figure 16.20

✔ **Check for Understanding:** Exercise/Problem Set A #25–26

Similitudes

Thus far we have investigated transformations that preserve size and shape, namely isometries. Next we investigate transformations that preserve shape but not necessarily size.

Size Transformations   First we consider transformations that can change size.

Example 16.7   In Figure 16.21, find the image of $\triangle ABC$ under each of the following transformations.

a. Each point P is mapped to the point P' on the ray $\overrightarrow{OP}$ such that $OP' = 2 \cdot OP$. That is, OP' is twice the distance OP.

b. Each point P is mapped to the point P'' on the ray $\overrightarrow{OP}$ such that $OP'' = \frac{1}{2} \cdot OP$.

NCTM Standard
All students should describe sizes, positions, and orientations of shapes under informal transformations such as flips, turns, slides, and scaling.

Figure 16.21

SOLUTION

a. To locate A', imagine ray $\overrightarrow{OA}$ [Figure 16.22(a)]. Then A' is the point on $\overrightarrow{OA}$ so that $OA' = 2 \cdot OA$. Locate B' and C' similarly. The image of $\triangle ABC$ is $\triangle A'B'C'$.

b. To locate A'', imagine ray $\overrightarrow{OA}$ [Figure 16.22(b)]. Locate A'' on $\overrightarrow{OA}$ so that $OA'' = \frac{1}{2} OA$. Locate B'' and C'' similarly. The image of $\triangle ABC$ is $\triangle A''B''C''$.

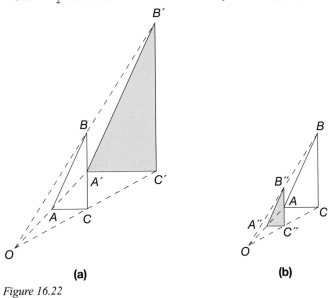

(a)   (b)

Figure 16.22   ∎

Transformations such as those in Example 16.7 that uniformly stretch or shrink geometric shapes are called size transformations.

DEFINITION

Size Transformations

The **size transformation** $S_{O,k}$, with **center** O and **scale factor** k (where k is a positive real number), is the transformation that maps each point P to the point P' such that P' is on ray $\overrightarrow{OP}$, and $OP' = k \cdot OP$ where

a. if $k > 1$,
   then P is between O and P', or

b. if $k < 1$,
   then P' is between O and P.

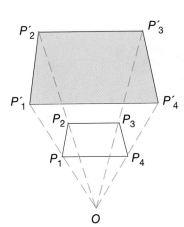

Figure 16.23

(NOTE: Size transformations are also called **magnifications**, **dilations**, and **dilitations**.)

Notice that points O, P, and P' are collinear. If $k > 1$, a size transformation enlarges shapes and if $k < 1$, a size transformation shrinks shapes. If $k = 1$, then $P' = P$ (i.e., each point is mapped to itself). Figure 16.23 illustrates the effect of a size transformation on a quadrilateral, with $k > 1$. A size transformation maps a polygon $\mathscr{P}$ to a polygon $\mathscr{P}'$ having the same shape, as illustrated in Figure 16.23. Also, we can show that a size transformation maps a triangle to a similar triangle.

Similitudes Next we consider the combination of a size transformation followed by an isometry. Figure 16.24 illustrates this is a special case.

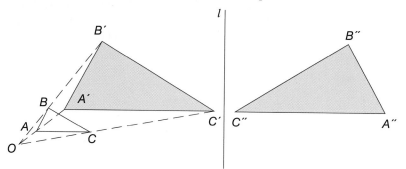

Figure 16.24

The size transformation $S_{O,k}$ maps $\triangle ABC$ to $\triangle A'B'C'$. By properties of size transformations, corresponding angles of $\triangle A'B'C'$ and $\triangle ABC$ are congruent, and corresponding sides of the two triangles are proportional. Thus $\triangle A'B'C' \sim \triangle ABC$. The reflection, M_l, maps $\triangle A'B'C'$ to $\triangle A''B''C''$. Since M_l is an isometry, we know that $\triangle A'B'C' \cong \triangle A''B''C''$. Therefore, corresponding angles of $\triangle A'B'C'$ and $\triangle A''B''C''$ are congruent, as are corresponding sides. Combining our results, we see that corresponding angles of $\triangle ABC$ and $\triangle A''B''C''$ are congruent and that corresponding sides are proportional. Hence $S_{O,k}$ followed by M_l maps $\triangle ABC$ to a triangle similar to it, namely $\triangle A''B''C''$.

Generalizing the foregoing discussion, it can be shown that given similar triangles $\triangle ABC$ and $\triangle A''B''C''$, there exists a combination of a size transformation followed by an isometry that maps $\triangle ABC$ to $\triangle A''B''C''$.

DEFINITION

Similitude

A **similitude** is a combination of a size transformation followed by an isometry.

In Figure 16.24 we also could have first flipped $\triangle ABC$ across l and then magnified it to $\triangle A''B''C''$. In general, it can be shown that any similitude also can be expressed as the combination of an isometry followed by a size transformation.

✔ **Check for Understanding:** Exercise/Problem Set A #27–28

MATHEMATICAL MORSEL

Two symmetrical patterns are considered to be equivalent if they have exactly the same types of symmetry. As recently as 1891, it was finally proved that there are only 17 inequivalent symmetry patterns in the plane. However, the Moors, who lived in Spain from the eighth to the fifteenth centuries, were aware of all 17 types of symmetry patterns. Examples of the patterns, such as the one shown here, were used to decorate the Alhambra, a Moorish fortress in Granada.

Section 16.1 EXERCISE / PROBLEM SET A

EXERCISES

1. In each part, draw the image of the quadrilateral under the translation T_{AB}. It may be helpful to use the Chapter 13 eManipulative activity *Geoboard* on our Web site to determine the images.

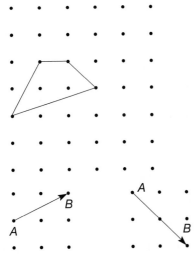

2. Draw $\overline{PQ}$ and $\overrightarrow{AB}$. With tracing paper on top, trace segment $\overline{PQ}$ and point A. Slide the tracing paper (without turning) so that the traced point A moves to point B. Make impressions of points P and Q by pushing your pencil tip down. Label these impressions P' and Q'. Draw segment $\overline{P'Q'}$, the translation image of segment $\overline{PQ}$.

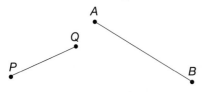

3. Use the following graph to answer the questions in parts (a), (b), and (c).

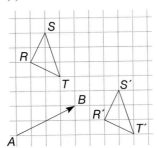

a. On graph paper, draw three other directed line segments that describe T_{AB}. (*Hint:* The directed line segments must have the same length and direction.)

b. Draw three directed line segments that describe a translation that moves points down 3 units and right 4 units.
c. Draw two directed line segments that describe the translation that maps $\triangle RST$ to $\triangle R'S'T'$.

4. According to the definition of a translation, the quadrilateral $PP'BA$ is a parallelogram where P' is the image of P under T_{AB}. Use this to construct the image, P', with a compass and straightedge. (*Hint:* Construct the line parallel to $\overrightarrow{AB}$ through P.)

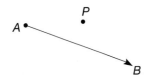

5. Find the measure of each of the following directed angles $\angle ABC$.

a.
b.

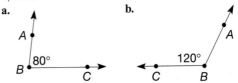

6. A protractor and tracing paper may be used to find rotation images. For example, find the image of point A under a rotation of $-50°$ about center O by following these four steps.

1. Draw ray $\overrightarrow{OA}$.
2. With ray $\overrightarrow{OA}$ as the initial side, use your protractor to draw a directed angle $\angle AOB$ of $-50°$.
3. Place tracing paper on top and trace point A.
4. Keep point O fixed and turn the tracing paper until point A is on ray $\overrightarrow{OB}$. Make an imprint with your pencil for A'.

Using a protractor and tracing paper, find the rotation image of point A about point O for the following directed angles.
a. $75°$ b. $-90°$ c. $-130°$ d. $180°$

7. Use a protractor and a ruler to find the $60°$ counterclockwise rotation of $\triangle ABC$ around point O.

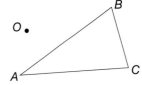

8. Find the rotation image of $\overline{AB}$ about point O for each of the following directed angles.

a. $-90°$

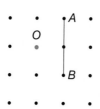

b. $90°$

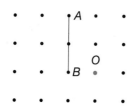

9. Find the 90° clockwise rotation about the point O for each of the following quadrilaterals. It may be helpful to use the Chapter 13 eManipulative *Geoboard* on our Web site to determine the images.

a.

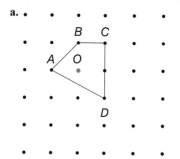

b.

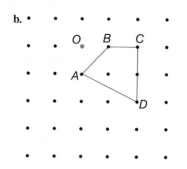

10. Give the coordinates of P', the point that is the image of P under $R_{O,90°}$. (*Hint:* Think of rotating $\triangle OPQ$.)

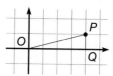

11. Give the coordinates of the images of the following points under $R_{O,90°}$.

a. $(2, 3)$ **b.** $(-1, 3)$ **c.** $(-1, -4)$
d. $(-4, -2)$ **e.** $(2, -4)$ **f.** (x, y)

12. Give the coordinates of the images of the following points under $R_{O,180°}$ where O is the origin.

a. $(3, -1)$ **b.** $(-6, -3)$ **c.** $(-4, 2)$

13. We could express the results of $R_{O,90°}$ applied to $(4, 2)$ in the following way:

$$(4, 2) \xrightarrow{R_{O,\,90°}} (-2, 4)$$

Complete the following statements.

a. $(x, y) \xrightarrow{R_{O,\,90°}} (?, ?)$

b. $(x, y) \xrightarrow{R_{O,-180°}} (?, ?)$

14. The rotation image of a point or figure may be found using a compass and straightedge. The procedure is similar to that with a protractor except that the directed angle is constructed rather than measured with a protractor. Also recall that $OA = OA'$. Construct the rotation image of A about point O for the following directed angles.

$A \cdot$

$O \cdot$

a. $-90°$ **b.** $-45°$ **c.** $180°$

15. The reflection image of point P can be found using tracing paper as follows.

1. Choose a point C on line l.
2. Trace line l and points P and C on your tracing paper.
3. Flip your tracing paper over, matching line l and point C.
4. Make an impression for P'.

Using this procedure, find P'.

16. Find the reflection of point *A* in each of the given lines.

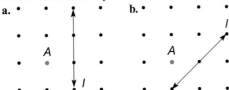

a.   **b.**

c.

17. a. Let M_x be the reflection in the *x*-axis. Graph the triangle with vertices $A(1, 2)$, $B(3, 5)$, and $C(6, 1)$ and its image under the reflection M_x.

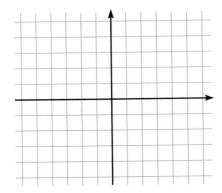

b. What are the coordinates of the images of points *A*, *B*, and *C* under the reflection M_x?

c. If point *P* has coordinates (a, b), what are the coordinates of its image under M_x?

18. The reflection image of point *A* in line *l* can be constructed with a compass and straightedge. Recall that line *l* is the perpendicular bisector of $\overline{AA'}$. If point *P* is the intersection of $\overline{AA'}$ and *l*, then $\overline{AA'} \perp l$ and $AP = PA'$. Using a compass and straightedge, find A'.

19. a. Graph $\triangle ABC$ with $A(-2, 1)$, $B(0, 3)$, and $C(3, 2)$ and its image under this glide reflection: T_{PQ} followed by M_x.

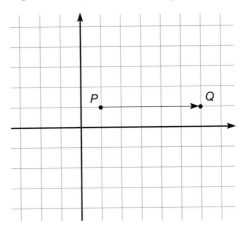

b. What are the coordinates of the images of points *A*, *B*, and *C* under this glide reflection: T_{PQ} followed by M_x?

c. If point *R* has coordinates (a, b), what are the coordinates of its image under this glide reflection: T_{PQ} followed by M_x?

20. Using a compass and straightedge, construct the glide reflection image of $\overline{AB}$ under the glide reflection: T_{XY} followed by M_l.

21. Which of the following triangles have the same orientation as the given triangle? Explain.

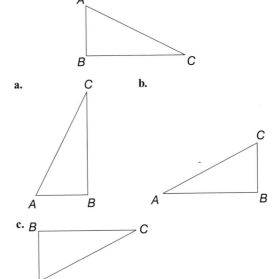

a.   **b.**

c.

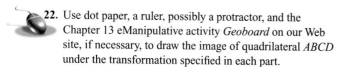

22. Use dot paper, a ruler, possibly a protractor, and the Chapter 13 eManipulative activity *Geoboard* on our Web site, if necessary, to draw the image of quadrilateral *ABCD* under the transformation specified in each part.

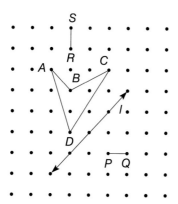

   a. T_{RS}
   b. $R_{B,90°}$
   c. M_l
   d. M_l followed by T_{PQ}

23. Identify the types of symmetry present in the following patterns. Assume that they are infinite patterns.

   a.

   b.

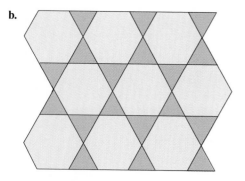

c.

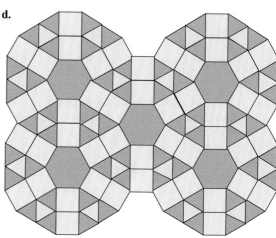

d.

24. Starting with the arrow at the left, an image can be created that has rotation symmetry as shown on the right.

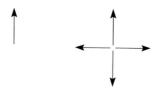

   Start with the arrow on the left and create an image that has
   a. Reflection symmetry, but not rotation symmetry
   b. Translation Symmetry (*Hint:* you may have to describe an infinite pattern)
   c. Reflection symmetry, but not translation symmetry

25. Trace a translation of the curve to the opposite side of the parallelogram. Verify that the resulting shape will tessellate the plane.

   a.   **b.**

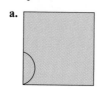   

   c.   **d.**

   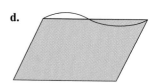

26. Trace the rotation of the curve (a curve could be made up of line segments) to an adjacent side of the square or triangle. Verify that the resulting shape will tessellate the plane.

a.

b.

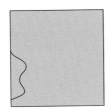

27. On the square lattice portions here, find $S_{O,2}(P)$.

a.

b.

c.

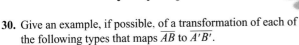

28. Use tracing paper and a ruler to draw the image of each figure under the given size transformation.

a. $S_{P,3}$

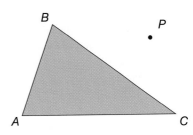

b. $S_{P,2/3}$

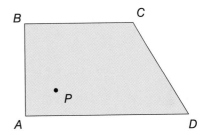

PROBLEMS

29. Give an example of a transformation of each of the following types that maps A to A'.
  a. Translation   **b.** Rotation
  c. Reflection   **d.** Glide reflection

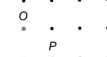

30. Give an example, if possible, of a transformation of each of the following types that maps $\overline{AB}$ to $\overline{A'B'}$.
  a. Translation   **b.** Rotation
  c. Reflection   **d.** Glide reflection

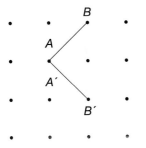

31. For each given transformation, plot $\triangle ABC$, with $A(2, 3)$, $B(-1, 4)$, and $C(-2, 1)$, and its image. Decide whether the transformation is a translation, rotation, reflection, glide reflection, or none of these. The notation $F(x, y)$ denotes the image of the point (x, y) under transformation F.
  a. $F(x, y) = (y, x)$
  b. $F(x, y) = (y, -x)$
  c. $F(x, y) = (x + 2, y - 3)$

32. Using the Chapter 16 eManipulative activity *Rotation Transformation* on our Web site perform a rotation on any combination of pattern blocks that you would like. By manipulating the center and angle of rotation, answer the following question: When constructing rotations, how does the location of the center of rotation affect the distance the image moves?

33. Being able to visualize how the location of the point O affects the image in a size transformation can be difficult. Use the Chapter 16 Geometer's Sketchpad® activity *Size Transformation* on our Web site to see the effects of moving point O and answer the question: Does moving the center of a size transformation closer to the original figure make the image smaller, larger, or have no effect on the size of the image? Explain.

| Section 16.1 | **EXERCISE / PROBLEM SET B** |

EXERCISES

1. In each part, draw the image of the polygon under the translation T_{AB}. It may be helpful to use the Chapter 13 eManipulative activity *Geoboard* on our Web site to determine the images.

a.

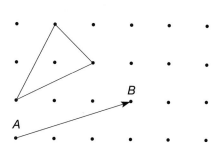

b.

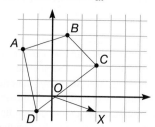

2. Draw $\triangle EFG$ and $\overline{XY}$. Using tracing paper, draw the image of $\triangle EFG$ under translation T_{XY} (see Part A Exercise 2).

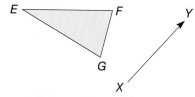

3. a. Find the coordinates of the images of the vertices of quadrilateral *ABCD* under T_{OX}.

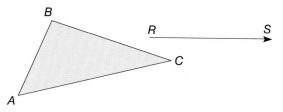

b. Given a point (x, y), what are the coordinates of its image under T_{OX}?

4. Using a compass and straightedge, construct the image of $\triangle ABC$ under the translation that maps *R* to *S* (see part A Exercise 4).

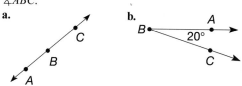

5. Find the measure of each of the following directed angles $\measuredangle ABC$.

6. Given $\overline{AB}$ and point *O*, use a protractor and tracing paper to find the image $\overline{AB}$ of under $R_{O,a}$ for each of the following values of *a* (see Part A Exercise 6).

$$A \text{———} B$$

$$O$$

a. 60°　　**b.** −90°　　**c.** 180°

7. Use a protractor and ruler to find the 90° clockwise rotation of $\triangle ABC$ about point *O*.

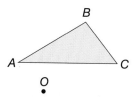

8. Find the rotation of $\overline{AB}$ about the point *O* for each of the following directed angles.

a. 180°　　　　**b.** 90°

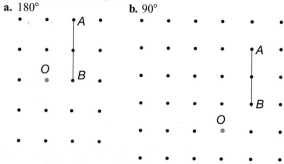

9. Find the 90° clockwise rotation about the point O for each of the following quadrilaterals. It may be helpful to use the Chapter 13 eManipulative activity *Geoboard* on our Web site to determine the images.

a.
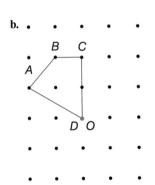

b.
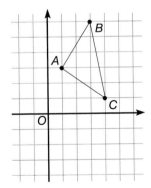

10. Draw the image of $\triangle ABC$ under $R_{O,-90°}$. What are the coordinates of A', B', and C'?

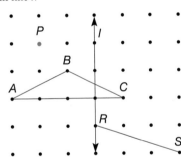

11. Give the coordinates of the images of the following points under $R_{O,-90°}$.
    a. $(1, 5)$ b. $(-1, 3)$ c. $(-2, -4)$
    d. $(-3, -1)$ e. $(5, -2)$ f. (x, y)

12. Give the coordinates of the images of the following points under $R_{O,-90°}$ where O is the origin.
    a. $(2, 3)$ b. $(-3, 1)$ c. $(-5, -4)$

13. Complete the following statements.
    a. $(x, y) \xrightarrow{R_{O,-90°}} (?, ?)$ b. $(x, y) \xrightarrow{R_{O,180°}} (?,?)$

14. Using a compass and straightedge, construct the 90° clockwise rotation of $\triangle ABC$ about point O.

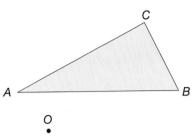

15. Using tracing paper, find the image of $\overline{AB}$ under M_l for the following segments.
    a.   b.

16. Find the reflection images of point P, segment $\overline{RS}$, and $\triangle ABC$ in line l.

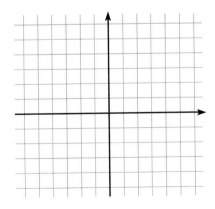

17. a. Graph $\triangle ABC$ with $A(2, 1)$, $B(3, -5)$, and $C(6, 3)$ and its image under M_y, the reflection in the y-axis.

b. What are the coordinates of the points A, B, and C under M_y?

c. If point P has coordinates (a, b), what are the coordinates of its image under M_y?

18. Using a compass and straightedge, construct the reflection of the following figures in line *l*.

a.

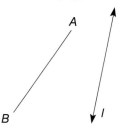

b.

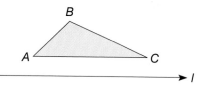

19. a. Graph △*ABC*, with *A*(1, 1), *B*(3, 1), and *C*(4, 6), and its image under this glide reflection: T_{XY} followed by M_l where *l* is the line *y* = *x*

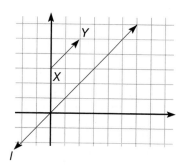

b. What are the coordinates of the images of *A*, *B*, and *C*?

c. If the point *P* has coordinates (*x*, *y*), what are the coordinates of its image under this glide reflection: T_{XY} followed by M_l?

20. Using a compass and straightedge, construct the glide reflection image of $\overline{AB}$ under the glide reflection: T_{YX} followed by M_l.

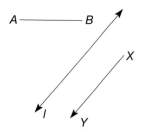

21. Which of the following polygons has the same orientation as the given polygon? Explain.

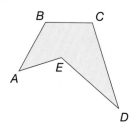

a.

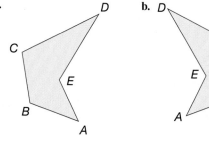

b.

c.

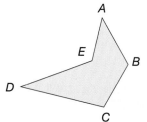

22. Use dot paper, a ruler, possibly a protractor, and the Chapter 13 eManipulative activity *Coordinate Geoboard* on our Web site, if necessary, to draw the image of quadrilateral *ABCD* under the transformation specified in each part.

a. T_{QP} **b.** $R_{Q,180°}$ **c.** M_l **d.** M_l followed by T_{SR}

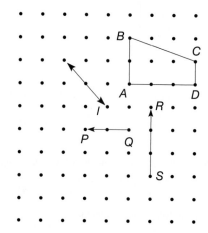

23. Identify the types of symmetry present in the following patterns. Assume that they are infinite patterns.
a. *Summer Stars*

b. *Seesaw*

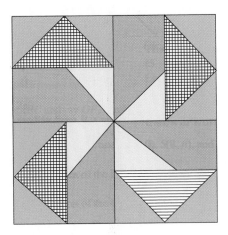

c. *Road to California*

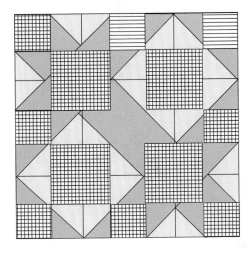

d. *Log Cabin*

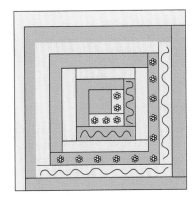

24. The letter B could be used to create an image that has reflection symmetry as shown.

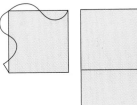

Use the letter B to create an image that has
a. Rotation symmetry
b. Translation symmetry (*Hint:* you may have to describe an infinite pattern)
c. Glide reflection symmetry

25. Trace the translation of the curves to the opposite sides to create a shape that tessellates. Use the grid to show that the shape will tessellate the plane.
a.

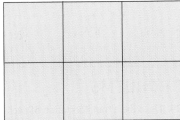

b.

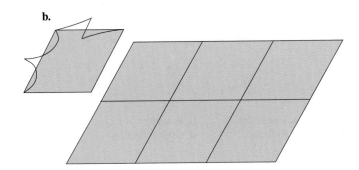

26. An Escher pattern can also be created by rotating a curve on one half of a side 180° around the midpoint, M, of the side as shown.

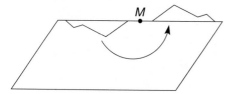

Trace a rotation of the curve from one half of a side to the other half of the side in the square or triangle. Verify that the resulting shape will tessellate the plane.

a.

b.

27. Find the image of $\overline{AB}$ under each of the transformations shown.

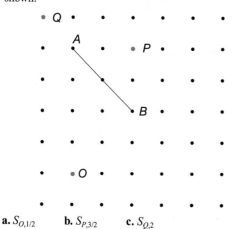

a. $S_{O,1/2}$ b. $S_{P,3/2}$ c. $S_{Q,2}$

28. Use tracing paper and a ruler to draw the image of each figure under the given size transformation.

a. $S_{P,1/2}$

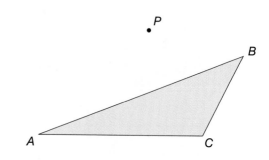

b. $S_{P,3}$

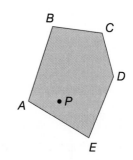

PROBLEMS

29. Describe a transformation of each of the following types (if possible) that maps $\overline{AB}$ to $\overline{A'B'}$.

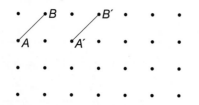

a. Translation   b. Rotation
c. Reflection   d. Glide reflection

30. Describe a transformation of each of the following types (if possible) that maps $\overline{AB}$ to $\overline{A'B'}$.

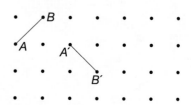

a. Translation   b. Rotation
c. Reflection   d. Glide reflection

31. For each given transformation, plot △*ABC*—with *A*(2, 3), *B*(−1, 4), and *C*(−2, 1)—and its image. Decide whether the transformation is a translation, rotation, reflection, glide reflection, or none of these. The notation *F*(*x*, *y*) denotes the image of the point (*x*, *y*) under transformation *F*. The Chapter 15 eManipulative activity *Coordinate Geoboard* on our Web site may help in the process.
   a. $F(x, y) = (2x, -y)$
   b. $F(x, y) = (-x + 4, -y + 2)$
   c. $F(x, y) = (-x, y + 2)$

32. **a.** Draw the image of the circle C_1 under $S_{O,2}$.
    b. Draw the image of the circle C_2 under $S_{P,1/2}$.

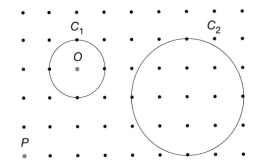

33. Using the Chapter 16 eManipulative activity *Reflection Transformation* on our Web site, perform a reflection of any combination of pattern blocks that you would like. Move the line of reflection and describe how the image moves. Does the location of the line affect the size or shape of the image? Explain.

Analyzing Student Thinking

34. Kwan Lee says if you have to slide a figure four units down and four units to the right, you have to count that as two separate slides. Maureen says, "No, you can do it all at once. It's sort of like going southeast on a map." Do you agree? Explain.

35. Owen says a 180° turn is the same thing as flipping a figure over a line. Is this ever true? Discuss.

36. Armando claims that, on a coordinate plane, a reflection in the *x*-axis followed by a reflection in the line through (0, 0) and (1, 1) is the same as a reflection in the *y*-axis. Do you agree? Explain.

37. Taten claims that a glide reflection followed by a glide reflection is a glide reflection. Do you agree? Explain.

38. Kalil claims that if an isometry that reverses orientation is followed by one that reverses orientation, the result will be one that reverses orientation. Do you agree? Explain.

39. Rosario claims that $S_{O,k}$ followed by $S_{O,m}$ will be $S_{O,km}$. Do you agree? Explain.

40. Marco claims that if $S_{O,k}$ is followed by $S_{O,-k}$, the result will be no transformation. Do you agree? Explain.

41. Bernadette claims that a similitude follow by a similitude is a similitude. Do you agree? Explain.

Problems Relating to the NCTM Standards and Curriculum Focal Points

1. The Focal Points for Grade 3 state "Through building, drawing, and analyzing two-dimensional shapes, students understand attributes and properties of two-dimensional space and the use of those attributes and properties in solving problems, including applications involving congruence and symmetry." For which of the transformations discussed in this section are the original figure and its image congruent?

2. The Focal Points for Grade 4 state "By using transformations to design and analyze simple tilings and tessellations, students deepen their understanding of two-dimensional space." How can transformations be used to make different kinds of tessellations?

3. The NCTM Standards state "All students should describe sizes, position, and orientations of shapes under informal transformations such as flips, turns, slides, and scaling." Which of the informal transformations change the orientation of a figure and which maintain the orientation?

13. a. Suppose that r and s are lines such that $r \parallel s$. Show that the combination of M_r followed by M_s is equivalent to a translation. [*Hint:* Let A be any point that is x units from r. Let $A' = M_r(A)$ be y units from s. Consider the distance from A to A'.]

b. How are the distance and direction of the translation related to lines r and s?

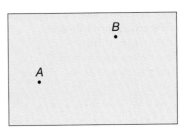

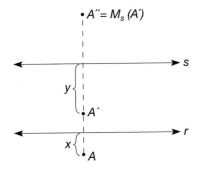

14. On the billiard table, ball A is to carom off two of the rails (sides) and strike ball B.

a. Draw the path for a successful shot.

b. Using a reflection and congruent triangles, give an argument justifying your drawing in part (a).

15. $ABCD$ is a square with side length a, while $EFGH$ is a square with side length b. Describe a similarity transformation that will map $ABCD$ to $EFGH$.

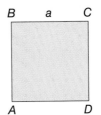

PROBLEM SET B

PROBLEMS

1. Triangle ABC is equilateral. Point G is the circumcenter (also the incenter). Which of the following transformations will map $\triangle ABC$ onto itself?

a. $R_{G,120°}$ **b.** $R_{G,60°}$ **c.** M_{AF} **d.** $S_{C,1}$

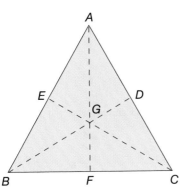

2. For equilateral triangle ABC in Exercise 1, list three different rotations and three different reflections that map $\triangle ABC$ onto itself.

3. $ABCDE$ is a regular pentagon with center O. Points F, G, H, I, J are the midpoints of the sides. List all the

reflections and all the rotations that map the pentagon onto itself.

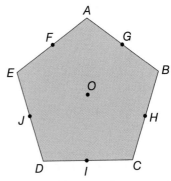

4. $ABCD$ is a parallelogram. List all the isometries that map $ABCD$ onto itself.

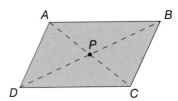

5. a. Using the triangle ABC, find the image of point P under the following sequence of half-turns:
$H_C(H_B(H_A(H_C(H_B(H_A(P))))))$
b. Apply the same sequence to point Q.
c. Write a conjecture based on your observations.

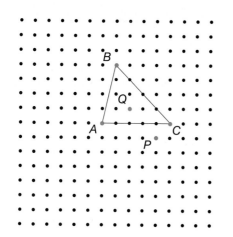

6. Find a combination of isometries that will map $\triangle ABC$ to $\triangle A'B'C'$, or explain why this is impossible.

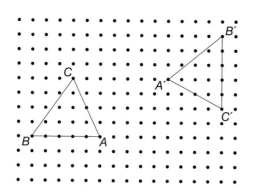

7. Show how the combination of M_r, followed by $S_{O,1/2}$ will map $\triangle ABC$ onto $\triangle A'B'C'$.

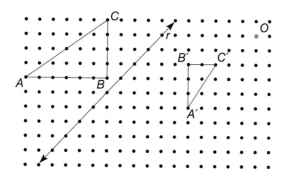

8. Points P, Q, and R are the midpoints of the sides of $\triangle ABC$.

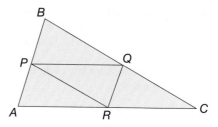

a. Show $S_{A,2} (\triangle APR) = \triangle ABC$, $S_{B,2} (\triangle PBQ) = \triangle ABC$, and $S_{C,2} (\triangle QCR) = \triangle BCA$.
b. How does part (a) show that $PBQR$ is a parallelogram?

9. Suppose that $ABCD$ is a parallelogram. Show that the diagonals $\overline{AC}$ and $\overline{BD}$ bisect each other.

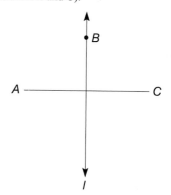

[*Hint:* Let P be the midpoint of $\overline{AC}$ and show that $H_P(B) = D$.]

10. Suppose that point B is on the perpendicular bisector l of $\overline{AC}$. Use M_l to show that $AB = BC$ (i.e., that B is equidistant from A and C).

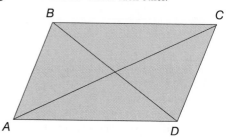

11. Suppose that lines r and s intersect at point P.

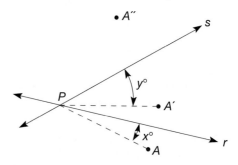

a. Show that M_r followed by M_s is a rotation.

b. How are the center and angle of the rotation related to r and s? [*Hint:* Let $A' = M_r(A)$ and suppose that the angle formed by $\overrightarrow{PA}$ and r measures x. Let $A'' = M_s(A')$ and suppose that the angle formed by $\overrightarrow{PA}$ and s measures y.]

12. On the billiard table, ball A is to carom off three rails, then strike ball B.

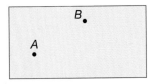

a. Draw the path for a successful shot.

b. Using three reflections, give an argument justifying your drawing in part (a).

13. Suppose that $ABCD$ is a rhombus. Use reflections M_{AC} and M_{BD} to show that $ABCD$ is a parallelogram.

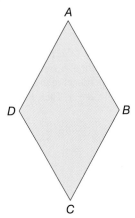

14. Euclid's proof of the Pythagorean theorem involves the following diagram. In the proof, Euclid states that $\triangle ABD \cong \triangle FBC$ and that $\triangle ACE \cong \triangle KCB$. Find two rotations that demonstrate these congruences.

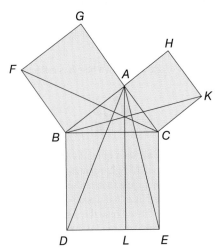

15. A **Reuleaux triangle** is a curved three-sided shape (see the figure). Each curved side is a part of a circle whose radius is the length of the side of the equilateral triangle. Find the area of a Reuleaux triangle if the length of the side of the triangle is 1.

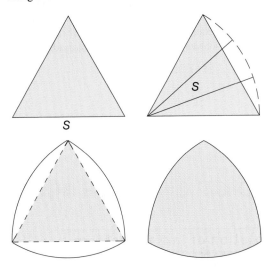

Analyzing Student Thinking

16. Annie reflected an isosceles triangle in the line containing the "unequal" side. She claims that the image of the triangle together with the original triangle forms a rhombus with the "unequal side" being one of its diagonals. Is she correct? Explain.

17. Chris says that he can move any figure to a congruent figure using only reflections. Is he correct? Explain.

18. Reuben claims that he can express a half-turn using two reflections. Is he correct? Explain.

19. Eva says that there are only two isometries that map a rhombus onto itself—namely, the reflections in the two diagonals. Is she correct? Explain.

20. Lee says a parallelogram has a line of symmetry in between two of the parallel sides. What properties of reflection could you use to explain that this is not a line of symmetry?

21. Jaime drew this picture of one hole at a miniature golf course. He says he can hit the ball from point A and have it follow the path he showed and end up in the hole at point B. How accurate is his thinking on this problem? Discuss.

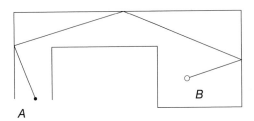

1. The Focal Points for Grade 4 state "By using transformations to design and analyze simple tilings and tessellations, students deepen their understanding of two-dimensional space." Describe an example from this section where transformations are used to analyze and prove properties of quadrilaterals.

2. The NCTM Standards state "All students should describe a motion or series of motions that will show that two shapes are congruent." Find an example from this section where a series of motions is used to show two shapes are congruent.

END OF CHAPTER MATERIAL

Solution of Initial Problem

Houses A and B are to be connected to a television cable line l, at a transformer point P. Where should P be located so that the sum $AP + PB$ is as small as possible?

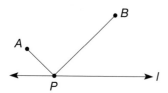

Strategy: Use Symmetry

Reflect point B across line l to point B'. Then $\triangle BPB'$ is isosceles, and line l is a line of reflection symmetry for $\triangle BPB'$. Hence $BP = B'P$, so the problem is equivalent to locating P so that the sum $AP + PB'$ is as small as possible. By the triangle inequality, we must have A, P, and B' collinear.

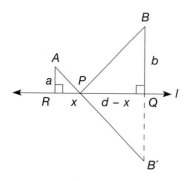

Let point Q be the intersection of $\overline{BB'}$ and l. Let R be the point on l such that $AR \perp l$. Since points A, P, and B' are collinear and

$\triangle BPB'$ is isosceles, we have $\angle APR \cong \angle B'PQ \cong \angle BPQ$. But then, $\triangle APR \sim \triangle BPQ$ by the AA similarity property. Thus corresponding sides are proportional in these triangles. Let $RP = x$ and $RQ = d$, so that $PQ = d - x$. Then, by similar triangles,

$$\frac{x}{d - x} = \frac{a}{b},$$

so that

$$bx = ad - ax$$
$$ax + bx = ad$$
$$x(a + b) = ad$$
$$x = \frac{ad}{a + b},$$

Hence, locate point P along $\overline{RQ}$ so that $RP = \dfrac{ad}{a + b}$.

Additional Problems Where the Strategy "Use Symmetry" Is Useful

1. The 4×4 quilt of squares shown here has reflective symmetry.

Explain how to find all such quilts having reflective symmetry that are made up of 12 light squares and 4 dark squares.

2. Find all three-digit numbers that can serve as house numbers when the numbers are installed upside-down or right-side-up. Assume that the 1 and 8 are read the same both ways.

3. The 4th number in the 41st row of Pascal's triangle is 9880. What is the 38th number of the 41st row?

People in Mathematics

Edward G. Begle (1914–1978)

Edward G. Begle could be called the father of the "New Math." Influenced by the success of *Sputnik* in 1957, the U.S. government, through its National Science Foundation, embarked on a systematic revision of the K–12 curriculum in the late 1950s. Although Begle was well on his way to becoming a first-rate research mathematician, he was asked to lead this effort, called the School Mathematics Study Group (SMSG), due to his unique talent for administration. He moved to Stanford, where he coordinated the SMSG for many years. In addition to this project, he initiated the National Longitudinal Study of Mathematical Abilities (NLSMA), which set a standard for subsequent such studies. Begle, whose respect for mathematics education grew as he worked with SMSG, stated that "Mathematics education is more complicated than you expected even though you expected it to be more complicated than you expected."

Jaime Escalante (1930–2010)

Jaime Escalante began teaching at Garfield High in East Los Angeles as a seasoned mathematics teacher, having taught for 11 years in Bolivia. But he was not prepared for this run-down inner-city school, where gang violence abounded and neither parents nor students were interested in education. After the discouraging first day on the job, he vowed, "First I'm going to teach them responsibility, and I'm going to teach them respect, and then I'm going to quit." He succeeded but stayed on to build, year after year, a team of mathematics students with the Advanced Placement calculus exam as their Olympic competition. He built their self-confidence and trained, coached, and prodded them as a coach might train athletes. Students would go to the Advanced Placement exam wearing their school jackets, yelling "Defense, Defense!" The movie *Stand and Deliver* was about Escalante's successes as a teacher at Garfield.

CHAPTER REVIEW

Review the following terms and exercises to determine which require learning or relearning—page numbers are provided for easy reference.

SECTION 16.1 Transformations

VOCABULARY/NOTATION

Transformation, T 866
Image of a point, P' 866
Isometry 866
Rigid motion 866
Directed line segment, $\overrightarrow{AB}$ 867
Equivalent directed line segments 867
Translation, T_{AB} 867
Directed angle, $\angle ABC$ 868
Measure of a directed angle 868
Initial side 869

Terminal side 869
Rotation with center O and angle with measure a, $R_{O,a}$ 869
Reflection in line l, M_l (or M_{AB} if $l = \overleftrightarrow{AB}$) 870
Glide reflection determined by directed line segment $\overrightarrow{AB}$ and glide axis l (or T_{AB} followed by M_{AB}) 873
Clockwise orientation 873
Counterclockwise orientation 874
Translation symmetry 874

Rotation symmetry 874
Reflection symmetry 874
Glide reflection symmetry 875
Escher-type patterns 875
Size transformation $S_{O,k}$ with center O and scale factor k 877
Magnification 877
Dilation 877
Dilitation 877
Similitude 878

EXERCISES

1. Draw directed line segment $\overrightarrow{AB}$ and P anywhere. Show how to find the image of P determined by T_{AB}.

2. Draw a directed angle of measure a and vertex O and P anywhere. Show how to find the image of P determined by $R_{O,a}$.

3. Draw a line l, Q on l, and P anywhere. Show how to find the images of Q and P determined by M_l.

4. Draw a line l, a directed line segment $\overrightarrow{AB}$ parallel to l, and P anywhere. Show how to find the image of P determined by the glide reflection l and $\overrightarrow{AB}$.

5. Sketch a pattern that has translation symmetry. What must be true about such patterns?

6. Sketch a pattern that has a rotation symmetry of less than 180°.

7. Sketch a pattern that has reflection symmetry.

8. Sketch a pattern that has glide reflection symmetry. What must be true about such patterns?

9. Draw $\triangle ABC$ and point O anywhere. Show how to find the image of $\triangle ABC$ determined by $S_{O,2}$.

10. Using the idea of a similitude, show that any two equilateral triangles are similar.

SECTION 16.2 Congruence and Similarity Using Transformations

VOCABULARY/NOTATION

Image of a point P under a translation, $T_{AB}(P)$ 890
Image of a point P under a rotation, $R_{O,a}(P)$ 890
Image of a point P under a reflection, $M_l(P)$ 890

Image of a point P under a glide reflection: T_{AB} followed by M_l, $M_l(T_{AB}(P))$ 890
Isometry   892
Congruent polygons, $\mathcal{P} \cong \mathcal{P}'$ 895
Congruent shapes $\mathcal{S} \cong \mathcal{S}'$ 895

Similar shapes, $\mathcal{S} \sim \mathcal{S}'$ 898
Similar polygons, $\mathcal{P} \sim \mathcal{P}'$ 898
Transformation geometry   898

EXERCISES

1. Name the four types of isometries.

2. Given that an isometry maps line segments to line segments and preserves angle measure, show that the isometry maps any triangle to a congruent triangle.

3. Given that an isometry maps lines to lines and preserves angle measure, show that the isometry maps parallel lines to parallel lines.

4. Describe how isometries are used to prove that two triangles are congruent.

5. Given that size transformations map line segments to line segments and preserve angle measure, show that size transformations map any triangle to a similar triangle.

6. Explain why size transformations preserve parallelism.

7. Describe how similarity is used to prove that two triangles are similar.

SECTION 16.3 Geometric Problem Solving Using Transformations

VOCABULARY/NOTATION

Half-turn with center O, H_O 908

EXERCISE

1. Given a triangle and any point O, find the half-turn image of the triangle determined by the point O.

CHAPTER TEST

KNOWLEDGE

1. True or false?

   a. A translation maps a line *l* to a line parallel to *l*.
   b. If the direction of a turn is clockwise, the measure of the directed angle associated with the turn is positive.
   c. A reflection reverses orientation.
   d. A regular tessellation of square tiles has translation, rotation, reflection, and glide reflection symmetry.
   e. An isometry preserves distance and angle measure.
   f. An isometry preserves orientation.
   g. A size transformation preserves angle measure and ratios of length.
   h. A similarity transformation is a size transformation followed by an isometry.

2. List the properties that are preserved by isometries but not size transformations.

3. Which of the transformations leaves exactly one point fixed when performed on the entire plane?

4. Which of the following transformations map the segment $\overline{AB}$ to $\overline{A'B'}$ in such a way that $\overline{AB} \parallel \overline{A'B'}$? (There may be more than one correct answer.)

   a. Translation
   b. Rotation
   c. Reflection
   d. Glide reflection
   e. Size transformation

5. Which of the following transformations map the segment $\overline{AB}$ to $\overline{A'B'}$ in such a way that $\overline{AA'} \parallel \overline{BB'}$? (There may be more than one correct answer.)

   a. Translation
   b. Rotation
   c. Reflection
   d. Glide reflection
   e. Size transformation

6. Each of the following notations describes a specific transformation. Identify the general type of transformation corresponding to each notational description.

   a. $S_{M,3}(Q)$
   b. $R_{N,b}(Q)$
   c. $M_n(Q)$
   d. $M_n(T_{xy}(Q))$
   e. $T_{xy}(Q)$

SKILL

7. For each of the following, trace the figure onto a piece of paper and perform the indicated transformation on the quadrilateral.

   a. Reflect about line *m*.

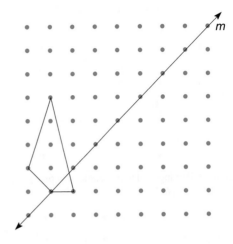

   b. Rotate 90° about point *O*.

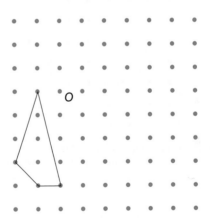

   c. Translate parallel to the directed line segment $\overset{1}{M}N$.

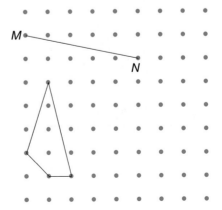

8. Find the following points on the square lattice.
  a. $T_{AB}(P)$ **b.** $R_{C,90°}(P)$
  c. $M_{OC}(P)$ **d.** $T_{PB}(M_{OC}(P))$

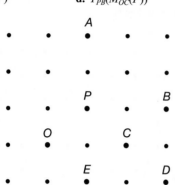

9. Trace the following grid and triangle on a piece of paper and find $S_{O,3}(\triangle ABC)$.

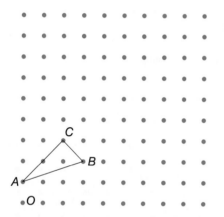

10. Determine which of the following types of symmetry apply to the tessellation shown here: translation, rotation, reflection, glide reflection (assume that the tessellation fills the plane).

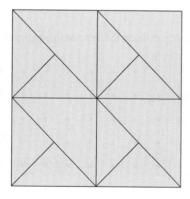

11. Describe the following isometries as they relate to the triangles shown.

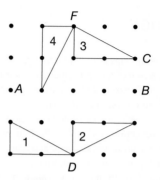

a. The reflection that maps 3 to 2
b. The rotation that maps 3 to 4
c. The translation that maps 3 to 1

UNDERSTANDING

12. Explain how to prove that the square $ABCD$ is similar to the square $EFGH$

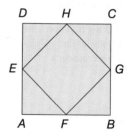

13. Explain why performing two glide reflections, one after the other, yields either a translation or a rotation.

14. Given that l, m, and n are perpendicular bisectors of sides $\overline{AB}$, $\overline{BC}$, and $\overline{AC}$, respectively, find the image of B after applying successively M_l followed by M_n, followed by M_m.

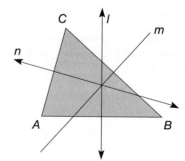

15. In each of the following cases $\triangle XYZ \cong \triangle X'Y'Z'$. Identify the type of isometry that maps $\triangle XYZ$ to $\triangle X'Y'Z'$ as either rotation, translation, reflection, glide reflection, or none.

a.

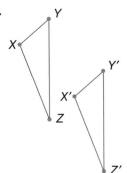

b.

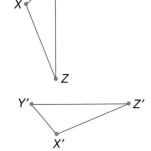

c.

16. Trace the following figure onto a piece of paper. Sketch the approximate location of the image of $\triangle XYZ$ under the rotation $R_{O,60°}$.

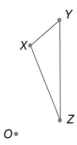

17. Let $M = (-1, 5)$ and $N = (3, -1)$. Give the coordinates of the images of the points $A = (1, 1)$, $B = (-2, -4)$, and $C = (x, y)$ under the transformation T_{MN}.

PROBLEM SOLVING/APPLICATION

18. Find AB, AC, and CE for the figure shown.

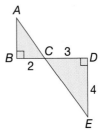

19. Given isosceles $\triangle ABC$, where M is the midpoint of $\overline{AB}$, prove that $\overleftrightarrow{CM}$ is a symmetry line for $\triangle ABC$.

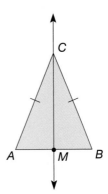

20. In the following figure, $\triangle ABC \cong \triangle A'B'C'$. Completely describe a transformation that maps $\triangle ABC$ to $\triangle A'B'C'$ (i.e., if the transformation is a reflection, then construct the line of reflection; if the transformation is a translation, then construct the directed line segment, etc.).

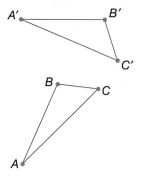

21. In the following figure, is $\triangle ABC$ the image of $\triangle XYZ$ under a size transformation? Justify your conclusion.

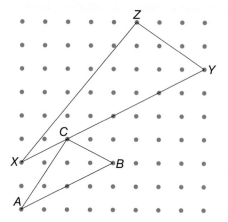

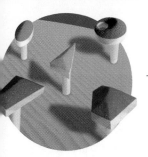

Epilogue

AN ECLECTIC APPROACH TO GEOMETRY

Introduction

NCTM Standard
Instructional programs should
enable all students to select and
use various types of reasoning
and methods of proof.

Three approaches to geometry were presented in Chapters 14–16:

1. The traditional Euclidean approach using congruence and similarity

2. The coordinate approach

3. The transformation approach

A fourth common approach is the vector approach. The value of multiple approaches to problem solving is that a theorem may be proved using *any* of several methods, one of which may lead to an *easy* proof. Facility using these various approaches gives one "mathematical power" when making proofs in geometry. This section gives a proof of the midsegment theorem using each of the three approaches. The problem set contains problems where you may choose the approach that you feel will lead to an easy solution.

The Midsegment Theorem

In Section 14.5 it was shown that the midsegment of a triangle is parallel and equal to one-half the length of the third side. Following are three different proofs, the first using congruence, the second using coordinates, and the third using transformations.

CONGRUENCE PROOF Let $\overline{PQ}$ be a midsegment of $\triangle ABC$ as shown in Figure E.1(a). Extend $\overline{PQ}$ through Q to R so that $PQ = QR$, and draw $\overline{CR}$ [Figure E.1(b)].

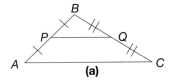
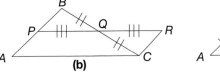
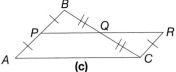

Figure E.1

By SAS, $\triangle PBQ \cong \triangle RCQ$, since $\angle PQB$ and $\angle RQC$ are vertical angles. Consequently, $\angle PBQ \cong \angle RCQ$ by corresponding parts. Viewing these parts as a pair of congruent alternate interior angles, we have $\overline{AP} \parallel \overline{CR}$. Again, by corresponding parts, $\overline{PB} \cong \overline{CR}$. Also, since $\overline{AP} \cong \overline{PB}$, we have $\overline{AP} \cong \overline{CR}$ [Figure E.1(c)]. Thus, by Example 14.13, *APRC* is a parallelogram, since $\overline{AP} \parallel \overline{CR}$ and $\overline{A} \cong \overline{CR}$. It follows that $\overline{PQ} \parallel \overline{AC}$ and $PQ = \frac{1}{2}AC$. ∎

COORDINATE PROOF Let $\overline{PQ}$ be a midsegment of $\triangle ABC$ with coordinates as shown in Figure E.2. By the midpoint formula, the coordinates of P are $(\frac{a}{2}, \frac{b}{2})$ and of Q are $(\frac{a+c}{2}, \frac{b}{2})$. Since P and Q have the same y-coordinate, namely $\frac{b}{2}$, $\overline{PQ}$ is horizontal; hence it is parallel to the x-axis and thus to $\overline{AC}$. Also, $PQ = \frac{a+c}{2} - \frac{a}{2} = \frac{c}{2}$ and $AC = c$. Thus $PQ = \frac{1}{2}AC$.

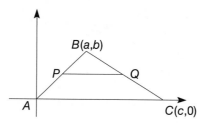

Figure E.2 ■

TRANSFORMATION PROOF Let $\overline{PQ}$ be a midsegment of $\triangle ABC$ as shown in Figure E.3. Consider the size transformation $S_{B,2}$. Under $S_{B,2}$, the image of P is A and the image of Q is C. Thus, according to the properties of size transformations, $\overline{PQ} \parallel \overline{AC}$ and $PQ = \frac{1}{2}AC$, since the scale factor is 2.

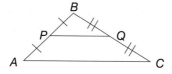

Figure E.3 ■

If the coordinate and transformation proofs seem to be much easier, it is because much work went into developing concepts *before* we applied them in these proofs. For example, we applied the midpoint formula in the coordinate proof and properties of size transformations in the transformation proof.

The following Problem Set will provide practice in proving geometric relationships using the three approaches. Your choice of approach is a personal one. You may find one approach to be preferable (easier?) to a friend's. You will find that comparing the various proofs and discussing the merits of the various approaches is worthwhile.

E EXERCISE / PROBLEM SET A

1. Prove: Consecutive angles of a parallelogram $ABCD$ are supplementary. (Use congruence geometry.)

2. The sides of $DEFG$ have midpoints M, N, O, and P, as shown. Verify that $MNOP$ is a parallelogram.

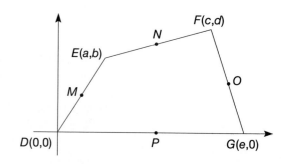

3. Suppose that $\triangle ABC$ is isosceles with $AB = AC$. Let P be the point on $\overline{BC}$ so that $\overline{AP}$ bisects $\angle BAC$. Use the

transformation M_{AP} to show that $\angle ABC \cong \angle ACB$.

4. In quadrilateral $ABCD$, both pairs of opposite sides are congruent. Prove that $ABCD$ is a parallelogram. (*Hint:* Draw diagonal $\overline{BD}$.) (Do two proofs, one congruence and one coordinate.)

5. Prove: In an isosceles triangle, the medians to the congruent sides are congruent. (Do two proofs, one congruence and one

Prove Problems 6–8 using any approach.

6. A rectangle is sometimes defined as a parallelogram with at least one right angle. If parallelogram $PQRS$ has a right angle at P, verify that $PQRS$ has four right angles.

7. Prove: The diagonals of a square are perpendicular.

8. In quadrilateral $PQRS$, both pairs of opposite angles are congruent. Prove that $PQRS$ is a parallelogram.

E | EXERCISE / PROBLEM SET B

1. If a pair of opposite sides of $ABCD$ are parallel and congruent, then it is a parallelogram. (*Hint:* Let $\overline{AB} \parallel \overline{DC}$, $\overline{AB} \cong \overline{DC}$ and draw $\overline{BD}$.) (Use congruence geometry.)

2. Given is trapezoid $ABCD$ with $AB \parallel CD$. M is the midpoint of $\overline{AD}$ and N is the midpoint of $\overline{BC}$. Show that $MN = \frac{1}{2}(AB + DC)$ and $\overline{MN} \parallel \overline{AB}$. (Use coordinates.)

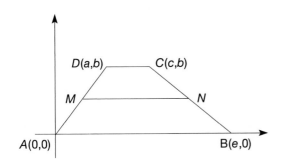

3. Suppose that $ABCD$ is a parallelogram and P is the intersection of the diagonals.
  a. Show that $H_P(A) = C$ and $H_P(B) = D$.
  b. How does part (a) show that a parallelogram has rotation symmetry?

4. In $ABCD$, the diagonals bisect each other at E. Prove that $ABCD$ is a parallelogram. (Use coordinates.)

5. Verify that the diagonals of a rhombus are perpendicular. (Do two proofs, one congruence and one coordinate.)

Prove Problems 6–8 using any approach.

6. Given parallelogram $LMNO$ with perpendicular diagonals $\overline{LN}$ and $\overline{MO}$ intersecting at P, prove that $LMNO$ is a rhombus.

7. Show that the diagonals of an isosceles trapezoid are congruent.

8. Quadrilateral $HIJK$ is a rectangle where HJ and IK intersect at L and are perpendicular. Prove that $HIJK$ is a square.

Topic 1

ELEMENTARY LOGIC

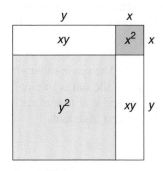

Figure T1.1

Logic allows us to determine the validity of arguments, in and out of mathematics. The validity of an argument depends on its logical form, not on the particular meaning of the terms it contains. For example, the argument, "All X's are Y's; all Y's are Z's; therefore all X's are Z's" is valid no matter what X, Y, and Z are. In this topic section we will study how logic can be used to represent arguments symbolically and to analyze arguments using tables and diagrams.

Statements

Often, ideas in mathematics can be made clearer through the use of variables and diagrams. For example, the equation $2m + 2n = 2(m + n)$, where the variables m and n are whole numbers, can be used to show that the sum of any two arbitrary even numbers, $2m$ and $2n$ here, is the even number $2(m + n)$. Figure T1.1 shows that $(x + y)^2 = x^2 + 2xy + y^2$, where each term in the expanded product is the area of the rectangular region so designated.

In a similar fashion, symbols and diagrams can be used to clarify logic. Statements are the building blocks on which logic is built. A **statement** is a declarative sentence that is true or false but not both. Examples of statements include the following:

1. Alaska is geographically the largest state of the United States. (True)

2. Texas is the largest state of the United States in population. (False)

3. $2 + 3 = 5$. (True)

4. $3 < 0$. (False)

The following are not statements.

1. Oregon is the best state. (Subjective)

2. Help! (An exclamation)

3. Where were you? (A question)

4. The rain in Spain. (Not a sentence)

5. This sentence is false. (Neither true nor false!)

Statements are usually represented symbolically by lowercase letters (e.g., p, q, r, and s).

New statements can be created from existing statements in several ways. For example, if p represents the statement "The sun is shining," then the **negation** of p, written $\sim p$ and read "not p," is the statement "The sun is not shining." When a statement is true, its negation is false and when a statement is false, its negation is true; that is, a statement and its negation have opposite truth values. This relationship between a statement and its negation is summarized using a **truth table**:

p	$\sim p$
T	F
F	T

This table shows that when the statement p is T, then $\sim p$ is F and when p is F, $\sim p$ is T.

Logical Connectives

Two or more statements can be joined, or connected, to form **compound statements**. The four commonly used **logical connectives** "and," "or," "if–then," and "if and only if" are studied next.

AND   If p is the statement "It is raining" and q is the statement "The sun is shining," then the **conjunction** of p and q is the statement "It is raining and the sun is shining" or, symbolically, "$p \land q$." The conjunction of two statements p and q is true exactly when both p and q are true. This relationship is displayed in the next truth table.

p	q	$p \land q$
T	T	T
T	F	F
F	T	F
F	F	F

Notice that the two statements p and q each have two possible truth values, T and F. Hence there are four possible combinations of T and F to consider.

OR   The **disjunction** of statements p and q is the statement "p or q," symbolically, "$p \lor q$." In practice, there are two common uses of "or": the exclusive "or" and the inclusive "or." The statement "I will go or I will not go" is an example of the use of the **exclusive "or,"** since either "I will go" is true or "I will not go" is true, but both cannot be true at the same time. The **inclusive "or"** (called "and/or" in everyday language) allows for the situation in which both parts are true. For example, the statement "It will rain or the sun will shine" uses the inclusive "or"; it is true if (1) it rains, (2) the sun shines, or (3) it rains and the sun shines. That is, the inclusive "or" in $p \lor q$ allows for both p and q to be true. In mathematics, we agree to use the inclusive "or," whose truth values are summarized in the next truth table.

p	q	$p \lor q$
T	T	T
T	F	T
F	T	T
F	F	F

Example T1.1 Determine whether the following statements are true or false, where p represents "Rain is wet" and q represents "Black is white."

a. $\sim p$ **b.** $p \wedge q$ **c.** $(\sim p) \vee q$

d. $p \wedge (\sim q)$ **e.** $\sim(p \wedge q)$ **f.** $\sim[p \vee (\sim q)]$

SOLUTION

a. p is T, so $\sim p$ is F.   **b.** p is T and q is F, so $p \wedge q$ is F.

c. $\sim p$ is F and q is F, so $(\sim p) \vee q$ is F.   **d.** p is T and $\sim q$ is T, so $p \wedge (\sim q)$ is T.

e. p is T and q is F, so $p \wedge q$ is F and $\sim(p \wedge q)$ is T.

f. p is T and $\sim q$ is T, so $p \vee (\sim q)$ is T and $\sim[p \vee (\sim q)]$ is F.   ■

IF-THEN   One of the most important compound statements is the implication. The statement "If p, then q, " denoted by "$p \rightarrow q$," is called an **implication** or **conditional** statement; p is called the **hypothesis**, and q is called the **conclusion**. To determine the truth table for $p \rightarrow q$, consider the following conditional promise given to a math class: "If you average at least 90% on all tests, then you will earn an A." Let p represent "Your average is at least 90% on all tests" and q represent "You earn an A." Then there are four possibilities:

AVERAGE AT LEAST 90%	EARN AN A	PROMISE KEPT
Yes	Yes	Yes
Yes	No	No
No	Yes	Yes
No	No	Yes

Notice that the only way the promise can be broken is in line 2. In lines 3 and 4, the promise is not broken, since an average of at least 90% was not attained. (In these cases, a student may still earn an A—it does not affect the promise either way.) This example suggests the following truth table for the conditional.

p	q	$p \rightarrow q$
T	T	T
T	F	F
F	T	T
F	F	T

One can observe that the truth values for $p \wedge q$ and $q \wedge p$ are always the same. Also, the truth tables for $p \vee q$ and $q \vee p$ are identical. However, it is not the case that the truth tables of $p \rightarrow q$ and $q \rightarrow p$ are identical. Consider this example: Let p be "You live in New York City" and q be "You live in New York State." Then $p \rightarrow q$ is true, whereas $q \rightarrow p$ is not true, since you may live in Albany, for example. The conditional $q \rightarrow p$ is called the converse of $p \rightarrow q$. As the example shows, a conditional may be true, whereas its converse may be false. On the other hand, a conditional and its converse may both be true. Two other variants of a conditional occur in mathematics, the contrapositive and the inverse.

Given conditional: $p \rightarrow q$

The **converse** of $p \rightarrow q$ is $q \rightarrow p$.

The **inverse** of $p \rightarrow q$ is $(\sim p) \rightarrow (\sim q)$.

The **contrapositive** of $p \rightarrow q$ is $(\sim q) \rightarrow (\sim p)$.

The following truth table displays the various truth values for these four conditionals.

p	q	$\sim p$	$\sim q$	CONDITIONAL $p \rightarrow q$	CONTRAPOSITIVE $\sim q \rightarrow \sim p$	CONVERSE $q \rightarrow p$	INVERSE $\sim p \rightarrow \sim q$
T	T	F	F	T	T	T	T
T	F	F	T	F	F	T	T
F	T	T	F	T	T	F	F
F	F	T	T	T	T	T	T

Notice that the columns of truth values under the conditional $p \rightarrow q$ and its contrapositive are the same. When this is the case, we say that the two statements are logically equivalent. In general, two statements are **logically equivalent** when they have the same truth tables. Similarly, the converse of $p \rightarrow q$ and the inverse of $p \rightarrow q$ have the same truth table; hence, they, too, are logically equivalent. In mathematics, replacing a conditional with a logically equivalent conditional often facilitates the solution of a problem.

Example T1.2   Prove that if x^2 is odd, then x is odd.

SOLUTION   Rather than trying to prove that the given conditional is true, consider its logically equivalent contrapositive: If x is not odd (i.e., x is even), then x^2 is not odd (i.e., x^2 is even). Even numbers are of the form $2m$, where m is a whole number. Thus the square of $2m$, $(2m)^2 = 4m^2 = 2(2m^2)$, is also an even number since it is of the form $2n$, where $n = 2m^2$. Thus if x is even, then x^2 is even. Therefore, the contrapositive of this conditional, our original problem, is also true.   ■

IF AND ONLY IF   The connective "p if and only if q," called a **biconditional** and written $p \leftrightarrow q$, is the conjunction of $p \rightarrow q$ and its converse $q \rightarrow p$. That is, $p \leftrightarrow q$ is logically equivalent to $(p \rightarrow q) \wedge (q \rightarrow p)$. The truth table of $p \leftrightarrow q$ follows.

p	q	$p \rightarrow q$	$q \rightarrow p$	$(p \rightarrow q) \wedge (q \rightarrow p)$	$p \leftrightarrow q$
T	T	T	T	T	T
T	F	F	T	F	F
F	T	T	F	F	F
F	F	T	T	T	T

Notice that the biconditional $p \leftrightarrow q$ is true when p and q have the same truth values and false otherwise.

Often in mathematics the words *necessary* and *sufficient* are used to describe conditionals and biconditionals. For example, the statement "Water is necessary for the formation of ice" means "If there is ice, then there is water." Similarly, the statement "A rectangle with two adjacent sides the same length is a sufficient condition to determine a square" means "If a rectangle has two adjacent sides the same length, then it is a square." Symbolically we have the following:

$p \rightarrow q$ means **q is necessary for p**
$p \rightarrow q$ means **p is sufficient for q**
$p \leftrightarrow q$ means **p is necessary and sufficient for q**

Arguments

Deductive or **direct reasoning** is a process of reaching a conclusion from one (or more) statements, called the hypothesis (or hypotheses). This somewhat informal definition can be rephrased using the language and symbolism in the preceding section. An **argument** is a set of statements in which one of the statements is called the conclusion and the rest comprise the hypothesis. A **valid argument** is an argument in which the conclusion must be true whenever the hypothesis is true. In the case of a valid argument, we say that the conclusion *follows from* the hypothesis. For example, consider the following argument: "If it is snowing, then it is cold. It is snowing. Therefore, it is cold." In this argument, when the two statements in the hypothesis— namely "If it is snowing, then it is cold" and "It is snowing"—are both true, then one can conclude that "It is cold." That is, this argument is valid since the conclusion follows from the hypothesis.

An argument is said to be an **invalid argument** if its conclusion can be false when its hypothesis is true. An example of an invalid argument is the following: "If it is raining, then the streets are wet. The streets are wet. Therefore, it is raining." For convenience, we will represent this argument symbolically as $[(p \rightarrow q) \land q] \rightarrow p$. This is an invalid argument, since the streets could be wet from a variety of causes (e.g., a street cleaner, an open fire hydrant, etc.) without having had any rain. In this example, $p \rightarrow q$ is true and q may be true, while p is false. The next truth table also shows that this argument is invalid, since it is possible to have the hypothesis $[(p \rightarrow q) \land q]$ true with the conclusion p false.

p	q	$p \rightarrow q$	$(p \rightarrow q) \land q$
T	T	T	T
T	F	F	F
F	T	T	T
F	F	T	F

The argument with hypothesis $[(p \rightarrow q) \land \sim p]$ and conclusion $\sim q$ is another example of a common invalid argument form, since when p is F and q is T, $[(p \rightarrow q) \land \sim p]$ is T and $\sim q$ is F.

Three important valid argument forms, used repeatedly in logic, are discussed next.

Modus Ponens: $[(p \rightarrow q) \land p] \rightarrow q$ In words **modus ponens**, which is also called the **law of detachment**, says that whenever a conditional statement and its hypothesis are true, the conclusion is also true. That is, the conclusion can be "detached" from the conditional. An example of the use of this law follows.

> If a number ends in zero, then it is a multiple of 10.
> Forty is a number that ends in zero.
> Therefore, 40 is a multiple of 10.

(NOTE: Strictly speaking, the sentence "a number ends in zero" is an "open" sentence, since no particular number is specified; hence the sentence is neither true nor false as given. The sentence "Forty is a number that ends in zero" is a true statement. Since the use of open sentences is prevalent throughout mathematics, we will permit such "open" sentences in conditional statements without pursuing an in-depth study of such sentences.)

The following truth table verifies that the law of detachment is a valid argument form.

p	q	$p \to q$	$(p \to q) \wedge p$
T	T	T	T
T	F	F	F
F	T	T	F
F	F	T	F

Notice that in line 1 in the preceding truth table, when the hypothesis $(p \to q) \wedge p$ is true, the conclusion, q, is also true. This law of detachment is used in everyday language and thought.

Diagrams can also be used to determine the validity of arguments. Consider the following argument.

All mathematicians are logical.
Pólya is a mathematician.
Therefore, Pólya is logical.

This argument can be pictured using an **Euler diagram** (Figure T1.2). The "mathematician" circle within the "logical people" circle represents the statement "All mathematicians are logical." The point labeled "Pólya" in the "mathematician" circle represents "Pólya is a mathematician." Since the "Pólya" point is within the "logical people" circle, we conclude that "Pólya is logical."

The second common valid argument form follows.

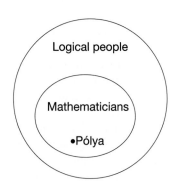

Figure T1.2

Hypothetical Syllogism: $[(p \to q) \wedge (q \to r)] \to (p \to r)$

The following argument is an application of this law:

If a number is a multiple of 8, then it is a multiple of 4.
If a number is a multiple of 4, then it is a multiple of 2.
Therefore, if a number is a multiple of 8, it is a multiple of 2.

Hypothetical syllogism, also called the **chain rule**, can be verified using an Euler diagram (Figure T1.3). The circle within the "multiples of 4" circle represents the "multiples of 8" circle. Then the "multiples of 4" circle is within the "multiples of 2" circle. Thus, from the diagram, it must follow that "If a number is a multiple of 8, then it is a multiple of 2," since all the multiples of 8 are within the "multiples of 2" circle.

The following truth table also proves the validity of hypothetical syllogism.

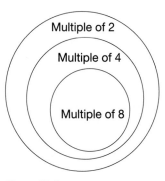

Figure T1.3

p	q	r	$p \to q$	$q \to r$	$p \to r$	$(p \to q) \wedge (q \to r)$
T	T	T	T	T	T	T
T	T	F	T	F	F	F
T	F	T	F	T	T	F
T	F	F	F	T	F	F
F	T	T	T	T	T	T
F	T	F	T	F	T	F
F	F	T	T	T	T	T
F	F	F	T	T	T	T

Observe that in rows 1, 5, 7, and 8 the hypothesis $(p \to q) \wedge (q \to r)$ is true. In both of these cases, the conclusion, $p \to r$, is also true; thus the argument is valid.

The final valid argument we study here is used often in mathematical reasoning.

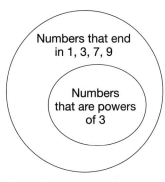

Figure T1.4

Modus Tollens: $[(p \rightarrow q) \wedge \sim q] \rightarrow \sim p$ Consider the following argument:

If a number is a power of 3, then it ends in a 9, 7, 1, or 3.
The number 3124 does not end in a 9, 7, 1, or 3.
Therefore, 3124 is not a power of 3.

This argument is an application of **modus tollens**. Figure T1.4 illustrates this argument. All points outside the larger circle represent numbers not ending in 1, 3, 7, or 9. Clearly, any point outside the larger circle must be outside the smaller circle. Thus, since 3124 is outside the "powers of 3" circle, it is not a power of 3. In words, modus tollens says that whenever a conditional is true and its conclusion is false, the hypothesis is also false.

The next truth table provides a verification of the validity of this argument form.

p	q	$p \rightarrow q$	$(p \rightarrow q) \wedge \sim q$	$\sim p$
T	T	T	F	F
T	F	F	F	F
F	T	T	F	T
F	F	T	T	T

Notice that row 4 is the only instance when the hypothesis $(p \rightarrow q) \wedge \sim q$ is true. In this case, the conclusion of $[(p \rightarrow q) \wedge \sim q] \rightarrow \sim p$, namely $\sim p$, is also true. Hence the argument is valid. Notice how the validity of modus tollens also can be shown using modus ponens with a contrapositive:

$$[(p \rightarrow q) \wedge \sim q] \leftrightarrow [(\sim q \rightarrow \sim p) \wedge \sim q] \text{ and } [(\sim q \rightarrow \sim p) \wedge \sim q] \rightarrow \sim p.$$

All three of these valid argument forms are used repeatedly when reasoning, especially in mathematics. The first two should seem quite natural, since we are schooled in them informally from the time we are young children. For example, a parent might say to a child: "If you are a good child, then you will receive presents." Needless to say, every little child who wants presents learns to be good. This, of course, is an application of the law of detachment.

Similarly, consider the following statements:

If you are a good child, then you will get a new bicycle.
If you get a new bicycle, then you will have fun.

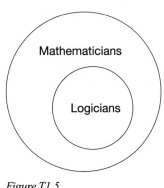

Figure T1.5

The conclusion children arrive at is "If I am good, then I will have fun," an application of the law of syllogism.

The three argument forms we have been studying can also be applied to statements that are modified by "quantifiers," that is, words such as *all, some, every*, or their equivalents. Here, again, Euler diagrams can be used to determine the validity or invalidity of various arguments. Consider the following argument:

All logicians are mathematicians.
Some philosophers are not mathematicians.
Therefore, some philosophers are not logicians.

Figure T1.6

The first line of this argument is represented by the Euler diagram in Figure T1.5. However, since the second line guarantees that there are "some" philosophers outside the "mathematician" circle, a dot is used to represent at least one philosopher who is *not* a mathematician (Figure T1.6). Observe that, due to the dot, there is always a philosopher who is not a logician; hence the argument is valid. (Note that the word *some* means "at least one.")

Next consider the argument:

All rock stars have green hair.
No presidents of banks are rock stars.
Therefore, no presidents of banks have green hair.

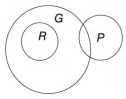

Figure T1.7

An Euler diagram that represents this argument is shown in Figure T1.7, where *G* represents all people with green hair, *R* represents all rock stars, and *P* represents all bank presidents. Note that Figure T1.7 allows for presidents of banks to have green hair, since the circles *G* and *P* may have an element in common. Thus the argument, as stated, is invalid since the hypothesis can be true while the conclusion is false. The validity or invalidity of the arguments given in the Exercise/Problem Set can be determined in this way using Euler diagrams. Be sure to consider *all* possible relationships among the sets before drawing any conclusions.

T1 EXERCISE / PROBLEM SET A

EXERCISES

1. Determine which of the following are statements.
   a. What's your name?
   b. The rain in Spain falls mainly in the plain.
   c. Happy New Year!
   d. Five is an odd number.

2. Write the following in symbolic form using $p, q, r, \sim, \wedge,$ $\vee, \rightarrow, \leftrightarrow$, where p, q, and r represent the following statements:

   p: The sun is shining.
   q: It is raining.
   r: The grass is green.

   a. If it is raining, then the sun is not shining.
   b. It is raining and the grass is green.
   c. The grass is green if and only if it is raining and the sun is shining.
   d. Either the sun is shining or it is raining.

3. If p is T, q is F, and r is T, find the truth values for the following:
   a. $p \wedge \sim q$ **b.** $\sim(p \vee q)$
   c. $(\sim p) \rightarrow r$ **d.** $(\sim p \wedge r) \leftrightarrow q$
   e. $(\sim q \wedge p) \vee r$ **f.** $p \vee (q \leftrightarrow r)$
   g. $(r \wedge \sim p) \vee (r \wedge \sim q)$ **h.** $(p \wedge q) \rightarrow (q \vee \sim r)$

4. Write the converse, inverse, and contrapositive for each of the following statements.
   a. If I teach third grade, then I am an elementary school teacher.
   b. If a number has a factor of 4, then it has a factor of 2.

5. Construct one truth table that contains truth values for all of the following statements and determine which are logically equivalent.
   a. $(\sim p) \vee (\sim q)$ **b.** $(\sim p) \vee q$ **c.** $(\sim p) \wedge (\sim q)$
   d. $p \rightarrow q$ **e.** $\sim(p \wedge q)$ **f.** $\sim(p \vee q)$

PROBLEMS

6. Determine the validity of the following arguments.
   a. All professors are handsome.
       Some professors are tall.
       Therefore, some handsome people are tall.
   b. If I can't go to the movie, then I'll go to the park.
       I can go to the movie.
       Therefore, I will not go to the park.

   c. If you score at least 90%, then you'll earn an A.
       If you earn an A, then your parents will be proud.
       You have proud parents.
       Therefore, you scored at least 90%.
   d. Some arps are bomps.
       All bomps are cirts.
       Therefore, some arps are cirts.

e. All equilateral triangles are equiangular.
All equiangular triangles are isosceles.
Therefore, all isosceles triangles are equilateral.

f. If you work hard, then you will succeed.
You do not work hard.
Therefore, you will not succeed.

g. Some girls are teachers.
All teachers are college graduates.
Therefore, all girls are college graduates.

h. If it doesn't rain, then the street won't be wet.
The street is wet.
Therefore, it rained.

7. Determine a valid conclusion that follows from each of the following statements and explain your reasoning.
a. If you study hard, then you will be popular.
You will study hard.

b. If Scott is quick, then he is a basketball star.
Scott is not a basketball star.

c. All friends are respectful.
All respectful people are trustworthy.

d. Every square is a rectangle.
Some parallelograms are rhombi.
Every rectangle is a parallelogram.

8. Which of the laws (modus ponens, hypothetical syllogism, or modus tollens) is being used in each of the following arguments?

a. If Joe is a professor, then he is learned. If you are learned, then you went to college. Joe is a professor, so he went to college.

b. All women are smart. Helen of Troy was a woman. So Helen of Troy was smart.

c. If you have children, then you are an adult. Bob is not an adult, so he has no children.

d. If today is Tuesday, then tomorrow is Wednesday. Tomorrow is Saturday, so today is not Tuesday.

e. If I am broke, I will ride the bus. When I ride the bus, I am always late. I'm broke, so I am going to be late.

9. Decide the truth value of each of the following.
a. Alexander Hamilton was once president of the United States.
b. The world is flat.
c. If dogs are cats, then the sky is blue.
d. If Tuesday follows Monday, then the sun is hot.
e. If Christmas day is December 25, then Texas is the largest state in the United States.

10. Draw an Euler diagram to represent the following argument and decide whether it is valid.

All timid creatures (T) are bunnies (B).
All timid creatures are furry (F).
Some cows (C) are furry.
Therefore, all cows are timid creatures.

T1 EXERCISE / PROBLEM SET B

EXERCISES

1. Let r, s, and t be the following statements:

r: Roses are red.

s: The sky is blue.

t: Turtles are green.

Translate the following statements into English.
a. $r \wedge s$ b. $r \wedge (s \vee t)$
c. $s \rightarrow (r \wedge t)$ d. $(\sim t \wedge t) \rightarrow \sim r$

2. Fill in the headings of the following table using p, q, $\wedge$, $\vee$, $\sim$, and $\rightarrow$.

p	q				
T	T	T	F	T	T
T	F	F	T	F	T
F	T	T	T	F	F
F	F	T	T	F	T

3. Suppose that $p \rightarrow q$ is known to be false. Give the truth values for the following:
a. $p \vee q$ b. $p \wedge q$
c. $q \rightarrow p$ d. $\sim q \rightarrow p$

4. Prove that the conditional $p \rightarrow q$ is logically equivalent to $\sim p \vee q$.

5. State the hypothesis (or hypotheses) and conclusion for each of the following arguments.
a. All football players are introverts. Tony is a football player, so Tony is an introvert.
b. Bob is taller than Jim, and Jim is taller than Sue. So Bob is taller than Sue.
c. Penguins are elegant swimmers. No elegant swimmers fly, so penguins don't fly.

6. Use a truth table to determine which of the following are always true.
a. $(p \rightarrow q) \rightarrow (q \rightarrow p)$ b. $\sim p \rightarrow p$
c. $[p \wedge (p \rightarrow q)] \rightarrow q$ d. $(p \vee q) \rightarrow (p \wedge q)$
e. $(p \wedge q) \rightarrow p$

7. Using each pair of statements, determine whether (i) p is necessary for q; (ii) p is sufficient for q; (iii) p is necessary and sufficient for q.
a. p: Bob has some water.
q: Bob has some ice, composed of water.
b. p: It is snowing.
q: It is cold.
c. p: It is December.
q: 31 days from today it is January.

PROBLEMS

8. If possible, determine the truth value of each statement. Assume that a and b are true, p and q are false, and x and y have unknown truth values. If a value can't be determined, write "unknown."

a. $p \to (a \lor b)$ **b.** $b \to (p \lor a)$

c. $x \to p$ **d.** $a \lor p$

e. $b \land q$ **f.** $b \to x$

g. $a \land (b \lor x)$ **h.** $(y \lor x) \to a$

i. $(y \land b) \to p$ **j.** $a \lor x) \to (b \land q)$

k. $x \to a$ **l.** $x \lor p$

m. $\sim x \to x$ **n.** $x \lor (\sim x)$

o. $\sim[y \land (\sim y)]$

9. Rewrite each argument in symbolic form, then check the validity of the argument.

a. If today is Wednesday (w), then yesterday was Tuesday (t). Yesterday was Tuesday, so today is Wednesday.

b. The plane is late (l) if it snows (s). It is not snowing. Therefore, the plane is not late.

c. If I do not study (s), then I will eat (e). I will not eat if I am worried (w). Hence, if I am worried, I will study.

d. Meg is married (m) and Sarah is single (s). If Bob has a job (j), then Meg is married. Hence Bob has a job.

10. Use the following Euler diagram to determine which of the following statements are true. (Assume that there is at least one person in every region within the circles.)

a. All women are mathematicians.

b. Euclid was a woman.

c. All mathematicians are men.

d. All professors are humans.

e. Some professors are mathematicians.

f. Euclid was a mathematician and human.

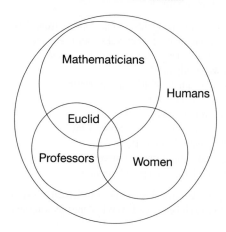

TOPIC REVIEW

VOCABULARY/NOTATION

Statement, p 927
Negation, $\sim p$ 927
Truth table   928
Compound statements   928
Logical connectives   928
Conjunction (and), $p \land q$ 928
Disjunction (or), $p \lor q$ 928
Exclusive "or"   928
Inclusive "or"   928
Implication/conditional (if . . . then), $p \to q$ 929

Hypothesis   929
Conclusion   929
Converse   929
Inverse   929
Contrapositive   929
Logically equivalent statements   930
Biconditional (if and only if), $p \leftrightarrow q$ 930
Is necessary for   930
Is sufficient for   930
Is necessary and sufficient for   930

Deductive/direct reasoning   931
Argument   931
Valid argument   931
Invalid argument   931
Modus ponens (law of detachment)   931
Euler diagram   932
Hypothetical syllogism (chain rule)   932
Modus tollens   933

ELEMENTARY LOGIC TEST

KNOWLEDGE

1. True or false?

a. The disjunction of p and q is true whenever p is true and q is false.

b. If $p \to q$ is true, then $\sim p \to \sim q$ is true.

c. In the implication $q \to p$, the hypothesis is p.

d. $[(p \to q) \land (q \to r)] \to (p \to r)$ is the modus tollens.

e. "I am older than 20 or younger than 30" is an example of an exclusive "or."

f. A statement is a sentence that is true or false, but not both.

g. The converse of $p \to q$ is $\sim p \to \sim q$.

h. $p \to q$ means p is necessary for q.

SKILL

2. Find the converse, inverse, and contrapositive of each.

   a. $p \to \sim q$ **b.** $\sim p \to q$ **c.** $\sim q \to \sim p$

3. Decide the truth value of each statement.

   a. $4 + 7 = 11$ and $1 + 5 = 6$.
   b. $2 + 5 = 7 \leftrightarrow 4 + 2 = 8$.
   c. $3 \cdot 5 = 12$ or $2 \cdot 6 = 11$.
   d. If $2 + 3 = 5$, then $1 + 2 = 4$.
   e. If $3 + 4 = 6$, then $8 \cdot 4 = 31$.
   f. If 7 is even, then 8 is even.

4. Use Euler diagrams to check the validity of each argument.

   a. Some men are teachers. Sam Jones is a teacher. Therefore, Sam Jones is a man.
   b. Gold is heavy. Nothing but gold will satisfy Amy. Hence nothing that is light will satisfy Amy.
   c. No cats are dogs. All poodles are dogs. So some poodles are not cats.
   d. Some cows eat hay. All horses eat hay. Only cows and horses eat hay. Frank eats hay, so Frank is a horse.
   e. All chimpanzees are monkeys. All monkeys are animals. Some animals have two legs. So some chimpanzees have two legs.

5. Complete the following truth table.

p	q	$p \wedge q$	$p \vee q$	$p \to q$	$\sim p$	$\sim q$	$\sim q \leftrightarrow p$	$\sim q \to \sim p$
T			F		T			
	T	F						
F			F	F				T
			T					

UNDERSTANDING

6. Using an Euler diagram, display an invalid argument. Explain.

7. Is it ever the case that the conjunction, disjunction, and implication of two statements are all true at the same time? all false? If so, what are the truth values of each statement? If not, explain why not.

PROBLEM SOLVING/APPLICATION

8. In a certain land, every resident either always lies or always tells the truth. You happen to run into two residents, Bob and Sam. Bob says, "If I am a truth teller, then Sam is a truth teller." Is Bob a truth teller? What about Sam?

9. The binary connective $\updownarrow$ is defined by the following truth table:

p	q	$p \updownarrow q$
T	T	F
T	F	T
F	T	T
F	F	T

Compose a statement using only the connective $\updownarrow$ that is logically equivalent to

   a. $\sim p$
   b. $p \wedge q$
   c. $p \vee q$

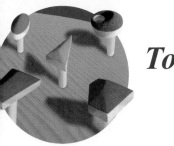

Topic 2

CLOCK ARITHMETIC: A MATHEMATICAL SYSTEM

The mathematical systems that we studied in Chapters 1 through 8 consisted of the infinite sets of whole numbers, fractions, and integers, together with their usual operations and properties. However, there are also mathematical systems involving finite sets.

Clock Arithmetic

The hours of a 12-clock are represented by the finite set {1, 2, 3, 4, 5, 6, 7, 8, 9, 10, 11, 12}. The problem "If it is 7 o'clock, what time will it be in 8 hours?" can be represented as the addition problem $7 \oplus 8$ (we use a circle around the "plus" sign here to distinguish this clock addition from the usual addition). Since 8 hours after 7 o'clock is 3 o'clock, we write $7 \oplus 8 = 3$. Notice that $7 \oplus 8$ can also be found simply by adding 7 and 8, then subtracting 12, the clock number, from the sum, 15. Instead of continuing to study 12-clock arithmetic, we will simplify our discussion about clock arithmetic by considering the 5-clock next (Figure T2.1).

In the 5-clock, the sum of two numbers is found by adding the two numbers as whole numbers, except that when this sum is greater than 5, 5 is subtracted. Thus, in the 5-clock, $1 \oplus 2 = 3$, $3 \oplus 4 = 2$ (i.e., $3 + 4 - 5$), and $3 \oplus 3 = 1$. Since $1 \oplus 5 = 1$, $2 \oplus 5 = 2$, $3 \oplus 5 = 3$, $4 \oplus 5 = 4$, and $5 \oplus 5 = 5$, the clock number 5 acts like the additive identity. For this reason, it is common to replace the clock number with a zero. Henceforth, 0 will be used to designate the clock number. Addition in the 5-clock is summarized in the table in Figure T2.2.

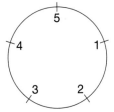

$\oplus$	0	1	2	3	4
0	0	1	2	3	4
1	1	2	3	4	0
2	2	3	4	0	1
3	3	4	0	1	2
4	4	0	1	2	3

Figure T2.1   *Figure T2.2*

It can be shown that 5-clock **addition** is a commutative, associative, and closed binary operation. Also, 0 is the additive identity, since $a \oplus 0 = a$ for all numbers a in the 5-clock. Finally, every 5-clock number has an opposite or additive inverse: $1 \oplus 4 = 0$ (the identity), so 4 and 1 are opposites of each other; $2 \oplus 3 = 0$, so 2 and 3 are opposites of each other; and $0 \oplus 0 = 0$, so 0 is its own opposite.

Subtraction in the 5-clock can be defined in three equivalent ways. First, similar to the take-away approach for whole numbers, a number can be subtracted by counting backward. For example, $2 \ominus 4 = 3$ on the 5-clock, since counting backward 4 from 2 yields 1, 0, 4, 3. One can also use the missing-addend approach, namely $2 \ominus 4 = x$ if and only if $2 = 4 \oplus x$. Since $4 \oplus 3 = 2$, it follows that $x = 3$. Finally, $2 \ominus 4$ can be found by the adding-the-opposite method; that is, $2 \ominus 4 = 2 \oplus 1 = 3$, since 1 is the opposite of 4.

Example T2.1   Calculate in the indicated clock arithmetic.

a. $6 \oplus 8$ (12-clock)   **b.** $4 \oplus 4$ (5-clock)   **c.** $7 \oplus 4$ (9-clock)
d. $8 \ominus 2$ (12-clock)   **e.** $1 \ominus 4$ (5-clock)   **f.** $2 \ominus 5$ (7-clock)

SOLUTION
a. In the 12-clock, $6 \oplus 8 = 6 + 8 - 12 = 2$.
b. In the 5-clock, $4 \oplus 4 = 4 + 4 - 5 = 3$.
c. In the 9-clock, $7 \oplus 4 = 7 + 4 - 9 = 2$.
d. In the 12-clock, $8 \ominus 2 = 6$ since $8 = 2 \oplus 6$.
e. In the 5-clock, $1 \ominus 4 = 1 + 1 = 2$ by adding the opposite.
f. In the 7-clock, $2 \ominus 5 = 2 + 2 = 4$. ∎

$\otimes$	0	1	2	3	4
0	0	0	0	0	0
1	0	1	2	3	4
2	0	2	4	1	3
3	0	3	1	4	2
4	0	4	3	2	1

Figure T2.3

Multiplication in clock arithmetic is viewed as repeated addition. In the 5-clock, $3 \otimes 4 = 4 \oplus 4 \oplus 4 = 2$. The 5-clock multiplication table is shown in Figure T2.3.

As with addition, there is a shortcut for finding products. For example, to find $3 \otimes 4$ in the 5-clock, first multiply 3 and 4 as whole numbers. This result, 12, exceeds 5, the number of the clock. In the 5-clock, imagine counting 12 starting with 1, namely, 1, 2, 3, 4, 5, 1, 2, 3, 4, 5, 1, 2. Here you must go around the circle twice ($2 \times 5 = 10$) plus two more clock numbers. Thus $3 \otimes 4 = 2$. Also, notice that 2 is the remainder when 12 is divided by 5. In general, to multiply in any clock, first take the whole-number product of the two clock numbers. If this product exceeds the clock number, divide by the clock number—the remainder will be the clock product. Thus $7 \otimes 9$ in the 12-clock is 3, since 63 leaves a remainder of 3 when divided by 12.

As with clock addition, clock multiplication is a commutative and associative closed binary operation. Also, $1 \otimes n = n \otimes 1 = n$, for all n, so 1 is the multiplicative identity. Since $1 \otimes 1 = 1$, $2 \otimes 3 = 1$, and $4 \otimes 4 = 1$, every nonzero element of the 5-clock has a reciprocal or multiplicative inverse. Notice that $0 \otimes n = 0$ for all n, since 0 is the additive identity (zero); this is consistent with all of our previous number systems, namely zero times any clock number is zero.

Division in the 5-clock can be viewed using either of the following two equivalent approaches: (1) missing factor or (2) multiplying by the reciprocal of the divisor. For example, using (1), $2 \oslash 3 = n$ if and only if $2 = 3 \otimes n$. Since $3 \otimes 4 = 2$, it follows that $n = 4$. Alternatively, using (2), $2 \oslash 3 = 2 \otimes 2 = 4$, since 2 is the reciprocal of 3 in the 5-clock.

$\otimes$	0	1	2	3	4	5
0	0	0	0	0	0	0
1	0	1	2	3	4	5
2	0	2	4	0	2	4
3	0	3	0	3	0	3
4	0	4	2	0	4	2
5	0	5	4	3	2	1

Figure T2.4

Although every nonzero number in the 5-clock has a reciprocal, this property does not hold in every clock. For example, consider the multiplication table for the 6-clock (Figure T2.4). Notice that the number 1 does not appear in the "2" row. This means that there is no number n in the 6-clock such that $2 \otimes n = 1$. Also consider 2 in the 12-clock and the various multiples of 2. Observe that they are always even; hence 1 is never a multiple of 2. Thus 2 has no reciprocal in the 12-clock. This lack of reciprocals applies to every n-clock, where n is a composite number. For example, in the 9-clock, the number 3 (as well as 6) does not have a reciprocal. Thus, in composite number clocks, some divisions are impossible.

Example T2.2   Calculate in the indicated clock arithmetic (if possible).

a. $5 \otimes 7$ (12-clock)   **b.** $4 \otimes 2$ (5-clock)
c. $6 \otimes 5$ (8-clock)   **d.** $1 \oslash 3$ (5-clock)
e. $2 \oslash 5$ (7-clock)   **f.** $2 \oslash 6$ (12-clock)

SOLUTION

a. $5 \otimes 7 = 11$ in the 12-clock, since $5 \times 7 = 35$ and 35 divided by 12 has a remainder of 11.

b. $4 \otimes 2 = 3$ in the 5-clock, since $4 \times 2 = 8$ and 8 divided by 5 has a remainder of 3.

c. $6 \otimes 5 = 6$ in the 8-clock, since 30 divided by 8 has a remainder of 6.

d. $1 \oslash 3 = 1 \otimes 2 = 2$ in the 5-clock, since 2 is the reciprocal of 3.

e. $2 \oslash 5 = 2 \otimes 3 = 6$ in the 7-clock, since 3 is the reciprocal of 5.

f. $2 \oslash 6$ in the 12-clock is not possible, because 6 has no reciprocal. ∎

Other aspects of various clock arithmetics that can be studied, such as ordering, fractions, and equations, are covered in the Exercise/Problem Set.

Congruence Modulo *m*

Clock arithmetics are examples of finite mathematical systems. Interestingly, some of the ideas found in clock arithmetics can be extended to the (infinite) set of integers. In clock arithmetic, the clock number is the additive identity (or the zero). Thus a natural association of the integers with the 5-clock, say, can be obtained by wrapping the integer number line around the 5-clock, where 0 corresponds to 5 on the 5-clock, 1 with 1 on the clock, -1 with 4 on the clock, and so on (Figure T2.5).

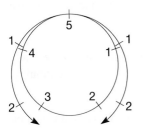

Figure T2.5

In this way, there are infinitely many integers associated with each clock number. For example, in the 5-clock in Figure T2.5, the set of integers associated with 1 is $\{\ldots, -14, -9, -4, 1, 6, 11, \ldots\}$. It is interesting to note that the difference of any two of the integers in this set is a multiple of 5. In general, this fact is expressed symbolically as follows:

DEFINITION

Congruence Mod m

Let a, b, and m be integers, $m \geq 2$. Then $a \equiv b \bmod m$ if and only if $m \mid (a - b)$.

In this definition, we need to use an extended definition of divides to the system of integers. We say that $a \mid b$, for integers a ($\neq 0$) and b, if there is an integer x such that $ax = b$. The expression $a \equiv b \bmod m$ is read **a is congruent to b mod m.** The term "mod m" is an abbreviation for "modulo m."

Example T2.3 Using the definition, determine which are true. Justify your conclusion.

a. $13 \equiv 7 \bmod 2$ **b.** $5 \equiv 11 \bmod 6$ **c.** $-5 \equiv 14 \bmod 6$ **d.** $-7 \equiv -22 \bmod 5$

SOLUTION

a. $13 \equiv 7 \bmod 2$ is true, since $13 - 7 = 6$ and $2 \mid 6$.

b. $5 \equiv 11 \bmod 6$ is true, since $5 - 11 = -6$ and $6 \mid -6$.

c. $-5 \equiv 14 \bmod 6$ is false, since $-5 - 14 = -19$ and $6 \nmid -19$.

d. $-7 \equiv -22 \bmod 5$ is true, since $-7 - (-22) = 15$ and $5 \mid 15$. ∎

If the "mod m" is omitted from the congruence relation $a \equiv b \bmod m$, the resulting expression, $a \equiv b$, looks much like the equation $a = b$. In fact, congruences and equations have many similarities, as can be seen in the following seven results. (For simplicity, we will omit the "mod m" henceforth unless a particular m needs to be specified. As before, $m \geq 2$.)

1. $a \equiv a$ for all clock numbers a.
This is true for any m, since $a - a = 0$ and $m \mid 0$.

2. If $a \equiv b$, then $b \equiv a$.
This is true since if $m \mid (a - b)$, then $m \mid -(a - b)$ or $m \mid (b - a)$.

3. If $a \equiv b$ and $b \equiv c$, then $a \equiv c$.
The justification of this is left for the Problem Set, Part A, 10.

4. If $a \equiv b$, then $a + c \equiv b + c$.
If $m \mid (a - b)$, then $m \mid (a - b + c - c)$, or $m \mid [(a + c) - (b + c)]$; that is, $a + c \equiv b + c$.

5. If $a \equiv b$, then $ac \equiv bc$.
The justification of this is left for the Problem Set, Part B, 12.

6. If $a \equiv b$ and $c \equiv d$, then $ac \equiv bd$.
Results 5 and 3 can be used to justify this as follows: If $a \equiv b$, then $ac \equiv bc$ by result 5. Also, if $c \equiv d$, then $bc \equiv bd$ by result 5. Since $ac \equiv bc$ and $bc \equiv bd$, we have $ac \equiv bd$ by result 3.

7. If $a \equiv b$ and n is a whole number, then $a^n \equiv b^n$.
This can be justified by using result 6 repeatedly. For example, since $a \equiv b$ and $a \equiv b$ (using $a \equiv b$ and $c \equiv d$ in result 6), we have $aa \equiv bb$ or $a^2 \equiv b^2$. Continuing, we obtain $a^3 \equiv b^3$, $a^4 \equiv b^4$, and so on.

Congruence mod m can be used to solve a variety of problems. We close this section with one such problem.

> **Example T2.4**   What are the last two digits of 3^{30}?

SOLUTION The number 3^{30} is a large number, and its standard form will not fit on calculator displays. However, suppose that we could find a smaller number, say n, that did fit on a calculator display so that n and 3^{30} have the same last two digits. If n and 3^{30} have the same last two digits, then $3^{30} - n$ has zeros in its last two digits, and vice versa. Thus we have that $100 \mid (3^{30} - n)$, or $3^{30} \equiv n \bmod 100$. We now proceed to find such an n. Since 3^{30} can be written as $(3^6)^5$, let's first consider $3^6 = 729$. Because the last two digits of 729 are 29, we can write $3^6 \equiv 29 \bmod 100$. Then, from result 7, $(3^6)^5 \equiv 29^5 \bmod 100$. Since $29^5 = 20{,}511{,}149$ and $20{,}511{,}149 \equiv 49 \bmod 100$, by result 3 we can conclude that $(3^6)^5 \equiv 49 \bmod 100$. Thus, 3^{30} ends in 49. ■

T2   EXERCISE / PROBLEM SET A

EXERCISES

1. Calculate in the clock arithmetics indicated.
   a. $8 \oplus 11$ (12-clock)   **b.** $1 \ominus 5$ (7-clock)
   c. $3 \otimes 4$ (6-clock)   **d.** $3 \oslash 2$ (5-clock)
   e. $7 \oplus 6$ (10-clock)   **f.** $5 \ominus 7$ (9-clock)
   g. $4 \otimes 7$ (11-clock)   **h.** $2 \oslash 9$ (13-clock)

2. Find the opposite and reciprocal (if it exists) for each of the following.
   a. 3 (7-clock)   **b.** 5 (12-clock)
   c. 7 (8-clock)   **d.** 4 (8-clock)

3. In clock arithmetics, a^n means $a \times a \times \ldots \times a$ (n factors of a). Calculate in the clocks indicated.
   a. 7^3 (8-clock)   **b.** 4^5 (5-clock)
   c. 2^6 (7-clock)   **d.** 9^4 (12-clock)

4. Determine whether these congruences are true or are false.
   a. $14 \equiv 3 \bmod 3$ **b.** $-3 \equiv 7 \bmod 4$
   c. $43 \equiv -13 \bmod 14$ **d.** $7 \equiv -13 \bmod 2$
   e. $23 \equiv -19 \bmod 7$ **f.** $-11 \equiv -7 \bmod 8$

5. Explain how to use the 5-clock addition table to find $1 \ominus 4$ in the 5-clock.

6. Using the 5-clock table, explain why 5-clock addition is commutative.

7. In the 5-clock, $\frac{1}{3}$ is defined to be $1 \oslash 3$, which equals $1 \otimes 2 = 2$. Using this definition of a clock fraction, calculate

$\frac{1}{3} \oplus \frac{1}{2}$. Then add $\frac{1}{3}$ and $\frac{1}{2}$ as you would fractions, except do it in 5-clock arithmetic. Are your answers the same in both cases? Try adding, subtracting, multiplying, and dividing $\frac{3}{4}$ and $\frac{2}{3}$ in 5-clock in this way.

PROBLEMS

8. Suppose that "less than" is defined in the 5-clock as follows: $a < b$ if and only if $a \oplus c = b$ for some nonzero number c. Then $1 < 3$ since $1 \oplus 2 = 3$. However, $3 < 1$ also since $3 \oplus 3 = 1$. Thus, although this definition is consistent with our usual definition, it produces a result very different from what happens in the system of whole numbers. For each of the following, find an example that is inconsistent with what one would expect to find for whole numbers.
  a. If $a < b$, then $a \oplus c < b \oplus c$.
  b. If $a < b$ and $c \neq 0$, then $a \otimes c < b \otimes c$.

9. Find all possible replacements for x to make the following true.
  a. $3 \otimes x = 2$ in the 7-clock
  b. $2 \otimes x = 0$ in the 12-clock
  c. $5 \otimes x = 0$ in the 10-clock
  d. $4 \otimes x = 5$ in the 8-clock

10. Prove: If $a + c \equiv b + c$, then $a \equiv b$.

11. Prove: If $a \equiv b$ and $b \equiv c$, then $a \equiv c$.

12. Find the last two digits of 3^{48} and 3^{49}.

13. Find the last three digits of 4^{101}.

T2   EXERCISE / PROBLEM SET B

EXERCISES

1. Calculate in the clock arithmetics indicated.
  a. $3 \otimes (4 \oplus 5)$ and $(3 \otimes 4) \oplus (3 \otimes 5)$ in the 7-clock
  b. $2 \otimes (3 \oplus 6)$ and $(2 \otimes 3) \oplus (2 \otimes 6)$ in the 12-clock
  c. $5 \otimes (7 \ominus 3)$ and $(5 \otimes 7) \ominus (5 \otimes 3)$ in the 9-clock
  d. $4 \otimes (3 \ominus 5)$ and $(4 \otimes 3) \ominus (4 \otimes 5)$ in the 6-clock
  e. What do parts (a) to (d) suggest?

2. Calculate as indicated [i.e., in $2^4 \otimes 3^4$, calculate 2^4, then 3^4, then multiply your results, and in $(2 \otimes 3)^4$, calculate $2 \otimes 3$, then find the fourth power of your product].
  a. $3^2 \otimes 5^2$ and $(3 \otimes 5)^2$ in the 7-clock
  b. $2^3 \otimes 3^3$ and $(2 \otimes 3)^3$ in the 6-clock
  c. $5^4 \otimes 6^4$ and $(5 \otimes 6)^4$ in the 10-clock
  d. What do parts (a) to (c) suggest?

3. Make a 7-clock multiplication table and use it to find the reciprocals of 1, 2, 3, 4, 5, and 6.

4. Find the following in the 6-clock.
  a. -2 **b.** -5 **c.** $(-2) \otimes (-5)$ **d.** $2 \otimes 5$
  e. -3 **f.** -4 **g.** $(-3) \otimes (-4)$ **h.** $3 \otimes 4$
  What general result similar to one in the integers is suggested by parts (c), (d), (g), and (h)?

5. In each part, describe all integers n, where $-20 \leq n \leq 20$, which make these congruences true.
  a. $n \equiv 3 \bmod 5$ **b.** $4 \equiv n \bmod 7$
  c. $12 \equiv 4 \bmod n$ **d.** $7 \equiv 7 \bmod n$

6. Show, by using an example in the 12-clock, that the product of two nonzero numbers may be zero.

7. List all of the numbers that do not have reciprocals in the clock given.
  a. 8-clock   **b.** 10-clock   **c.** 12-clock
  d. Based on your findings, predict the numbers in the 36-clock that don't have reciprocals. Check your prediction.

PROBLEMS

8. Find reciprocals of the following:
  a. 7 in the 8-clock   **b.** 4 in the 5-clock
  c. 11 in the 12-clock   **d.** 9 in the 10-clock
  e. What general idea is suggested by parts (a) to (d)?

9. State a definition of "square root" for clock arithmetic that is consistent with our usual definition. Then find all square roots of the following if they exist.

  a. 4 in the 5-clock   **b.** 1 in the 8-clock
  c. 3 in the 6-clock   **d.** 7 in the 12-clock
  e. What do you notice that is different or similar about square roots in clock arithmetics?

10. The system of rational numbers was divided into the three disjoint sets: (i) negatives, (ii) zero, and (iii) positives. The set of positives was closed under both addition and multiplication. Show that it is impossible to find two disjoint nonempty sets to serve as positives and negatives in the 5-clock. (*Hint:* Let 1 be positive and another number be negative, say $-1 \equiv 4$. Then show that if the set of positive 5-clock numbers is closed under addition, this situation is impossible. Observe that this holds in all clock arithmetics.)

11. Explain why multiplication is closed in any clock.

12. Prove: If $a \equiv b$, then $ac \equiv bc$.

13. Prove or disprove: If $ac \equiv bc \bmod 6$ and $c \not\equiv 0 \bmod 6$, then $a \equiv b \bmod 6$.

14. Suppose that you want to know the remainder when 3^{100} is divided by 7. If r is the remainder and q is the quotient, then $3^{100} = 7q + r$ or $3^{100} - r = 7q$. Thus $7 \mid (3^{100} - r)$ or $3^{100} \equiv r \bmod 7$. (Recall that for the remainder r, we have $0 \le r < 7$.) Now $3^5 = 243 \equiv 5 \bmod 7$. So $(3^5)^2 \equiv 5^2 \bmod 7$ or $3^{10} \equiv 25 \equiv 4 \bmod 7$. Thus $3^{100} = (3^{10})^{10} \equiv 4^{10} \bmod 7$. But $4^{10} = 16^5 \equiv 2^5 \equiv 4 \bmod 7$. Thus the remainder is 4. Find the remainder when 7^{101} is divided by 8. (*Hint:* $7^{101} = 7^{100} \cdot 7$.)

TOPIC REVIEW

VOCABULARY/NOTATION

Clock arithmetic   939
  Addition, $a \oplus b$ 939
  Subtraction, $a \ominus b$ 939

Multiplication, $a \otimes b$ 940
Division, $a \oslash b$ 940

Congruence modulo, m, $a \equiv b$, mod m 941

CLOCK ARITHMETIC TEST

KNOWLEDGE

1. True or false?
   a. The 12-clock is comprised of the numbers 0, 1, 2, 3, 4, 5, 6, 7, 8, 9, 10, 11, 12.
   b. Addition in the 5-clock is associative.
   c. The number 1 is the additive identity in the 7-clock.
   d. The number 4 is its own multiplicative inverse in the 5-clock.
   e. Every clock has an additive inverse for each of its elements.
   f. Every number is congruent to itself mod m.
   g. If $a \equiv b \bmod 7$, then either $a - b = 7$ or $b - a = 7$.
   h. If $a \equiv b$ and $c \equiv b$, then $a \equiv c$.

SKILL

2. Calculate.
   a. $5 \oplus 9$ in the 11-clock
   b. $8 \otimes 8$ in the 9-clock
   c. $3 \ominus 7$ in the 10-clock
   d. $4 \oslash 9$ in the 13-clock
   e. 2^4 in the 5-clock
   f. $(2 \ominus 5)^3 \otimes 6$ in the 7-clock

3. Show how to do the following calculations easily mentally by applying the commutative, associative, identity, inverse, or distributive properties.
   a. $3 \oplus (9 \oplus 7)$ in the 10-clock
   b. $(8 \otimes 3) \otimes 4$ in the 11-clock

   c. $(5 \otimes 4) \oplus (5 \otimes 11)$ in the 15-clock
   d. $(6 \otimes 3) \oplus (3 \otimes 4) \oplus (3 \otimes 3)$ in the 13-clock

4. Find the opposite and the reciprocal (if they exist) of the following numbers in the indicated clocks. Explain.
   a. 4 in the 7-clock
   b. 4 in the 8-clock
   c. 0 in the 5-clock
   d. 5 in the 12-clock

5. In each part, describe the set of all numbers n that make the congruence true.
   a. $n \equiv 4 \bmod 9$ where $-15 \le n \le 15$
   b. $15 \equiv 3 \bmod n$ where $1 < n < 20$
   c. $8 \equiv n \bmod 7$

UNDERSTANDING

6. Using a clock as a model, explain why 4 does not have a reciprocal in the 12-clock.

7. Explain (a) why 0 cannot be used for m and (b) why 1 is not used for m in the definition of $a \equiv b \bmod m$.

8. Explain why $a \equiv a \bmod m$.

PROBLEM SOLVING/APPLICATION

9. If January 1 of a non-leap year falls on a Monday, show how congruence mod 7 can be used to determine the day of the week for January 1 of the next year.

Answers To

EXERCISE/PROBLEM SETS—PART A, CHAPTER REVIEWS, CHAPTER TESTS, AND TOPICS SECTION

Section 1.1A

1. a. 8

  b. 1. Understand: Triangles have 3 sides and are formed by the sides and parts of the diagonals.

    2. Devise a plan: Sketch various triangles.

    3. Carry out the plan: Make sure that all possible triangles are sketched.

    4. Look back: Check by sketching the triangles on another piece of paper. Compare with your original sketches. Do you have the same triangles in both cases?

2. 52

3. 36 ft × 78 ft

4. 88

5. $9 = 4 + 5$. If n is odd, then both $n - 1$ and $n + 1$ are even and $n = \dfrac{n-1}{2} + \dfrac{n+1}{2}$.

6. $6 \div 6 + 6 + 6 = 13$

7.

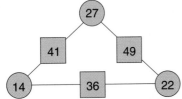

8.

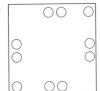

9. No; $0 + 1 + 2 + 3 + 4 + 5 + 6 + 7 + 8 + 9 = 45$, which is too large.

10. For example, beginning at corner: 2, 10, 5, 4, 8, 6, 3, 7, 9

11. a. 2: None   3: 27, 28, 29

    4: None   5: None   6: None

  b. 2: 106, 107   3: 70, 71, 72   4: None

    5: None   6: 33, 34, 35, 36, 37, 38

  c. 2: None   3: None

    4: 37, 38, 39, 40

    5: None

    6: None

12. Row 1: 9, 3, 4; row 2: 8, 2, 5; row 3: 7, 6, 1

13. Run three consecutive 5-minute timers concurrently with two consecutive 8-minute timers. There will be 1 minute left on the 8-minute timer.

14. a. 1839

  b. 47

15. For example, row 1: 3, 5; row 2: 7, 1, 8, 2; row 3: 4, 6

16. U = 9, S = 3, R = 8, A = 2, P = 1, E = 0, C = 7

17. 3

18. Top pair: 8, 5; second pair from the top: 4, 1; third pair from the top: 6, 3; bottom pair: 2, 7. There are other correct answers.

19. $\dfrac{4(n + 10) + 200}{4} - n = (n + 10) + 50 - n$
$$= n + 60 - n = 60$$

20. For example, $98 - 7 + 6 + 5 - 4 + 3 - 2 + 1 = 100$, and $9 - 8 + 76 - 5 + 4 + 3 + 21 = 100$.

21. 1 and 12, 9 and 10

22.

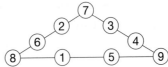

23.

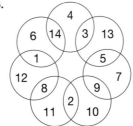

24. 22

Section 1.2A

1. a. 9, 16, 25   The Answer column is comprised of perfect squares.
   b. 9   **c.** 13
   d. 23 $[1 + 3 + 5 + \cdots + (2n - 1) = n^2]$

2. a. 32   **b.** $\dfrac{1}{27}$ **c.** 21   **d.** 1287

3. a.

D	D	D
D	D	
	□	

   b.

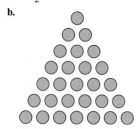

4. a. $5556^2 - 4445^2 = 11{,}111{,}111$
   b. $55{,}555{,}556^2 - 44{,}444{,}445^2 = 1{,}111{,}111{,}111{,}111{,}111.$

5.

60	6	10
30	6	5
2	1	2

6. a.

TRIANGLE NUMBER	NUMBER OF DOTS IN SHAPE
1	1
2	3
3	6
4	10
5	15
6	21

The numbers in the "Number of Dots" column satisfy the formula $\dfrac{n(n + 1)}{2}$ where n is the number in the first column.

   b.

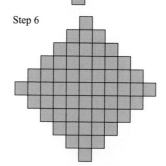

   c. 55 dots
   d. Yes, the 13th number.
   e. No, the 16th number has 136 and the 17th number has 153.
   f. $\dfrac{n(n + 1)}{2}$ **g.** $\dfrac{100(101)}{2} = 5050$

7. 3 weighings

8. $19 + 18 + \cdots + 2 + 1 = \dfrac{19 \cdot 20}{2} = 190$

9. a. 46, 69, 99   **b.** 43, 57, 73

10. a. $3 + 6 = 9$ **b.** $10 + 15 = 25$
   c. $45 + 55 = 100$, $190 + 210 = 400$, $(n - 1)$st + nth
   d. 36 is the 8th triangular number and is the 6th square number.
   e. Some possible answers: $4 - 1 = 3$, $49 - 4 = 45$, $64 - 49 = 15$, $64 - 36 = 28$, $64 - 9 = 55$, $169 - 64 = 105$.

11. $10,737,418.23 if paid the second way

12. For n triangles, perimeter $= n + 2$

NUMBER OF TRIANGLES	1	2	3	4	5	6	10	38	n
PERIMETER	3	4	5	6	7	8	12	40	$n + 2$

13. a. In the 4, 6, 12, 14, . . . column   **b.** In the 2, 8, 10, 16, . . . column
   c. In the 3, 7, 11, 15, . . . column   **d.** In the 5, 13, . . . column

14. $100^3 = 1{,}000{,}000$

15. 34, 55, 89, 144, 233, 377; $144 \times 233 = 33{,}552$

16. 987

17. a. Sums are 1, 1, 2, 3, 5, 8, 13. Each sum is a Fibonacci number.
   b. Next three sums: 21, 34, 55

18. a. Sum is 20.
   b. Sum of numbers inside the circle is always twice the number directly below the center of the circle.

19. a. Step 5

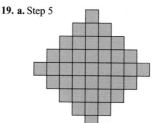

Step 6

   b.

STEP	NUMBER OF SQUARES
1	1
2	5
3	13
4	25
5	41
6	61

   c. 85   **d.** 10th, 181; 20th, 761; 50th, 4901

20. 23

21. a. 18   **b.** 66

22. a. Lt Blue, Lt Blue, Blue, Lt Blue
 b. Green, Blue, Green, Yellow
 c. Red, Blue, Blue, Purple

23. There are many answers possible. For example $1, \frac{3}{2}, \frac{5}{4}, \frac{7}{8}, \ldots$.
 The numerators are odd numbers—they increase by twos. The denominators of the fractions are powers of 2: $2^0 = 1$, $2^1 = 2$, $2^2 = 4$, etc.

CHAPTER REVIEW
Section 1.1
1. Try Guess and Test

2. Use a Variable or Guess and Test

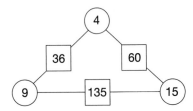

3. Draw a Picture—289 tiles

Section 1.2
1. Look for a Pattern
$$1234321 \times (1 + 2 + 3 + 4 + 3 + 2 + 1) = 4444^2$$

2. Solve a Simpler Problem
a. 9   **b.** 1296

3. Make a List
a. 3: 1, 3, 9
b. 4: 1, 3, 9, 27
c. 364 grams

Chapter 1 Test
1. Understand the problem; devise a plan; carry out the plan; look back

2. Guess and Test; Use a Variable; Look for a Pattern; Make a List; Solve a Simpler Problem; Draw a Picture

3. \$5 allowance.

4. Answers may vary.

5. Amanda had 31 hard-boiled eggs to sell.

6. Exercises are routine applications of known procedures, whereas problems require the solver to take an original mental step.

7. Any of the 6 clues under Guess and Test.

8. Any of the 8 clues under Use a Variable.

9. 4×4: 1, 2, 3, 4; 3, 4, 1, 2; 4, 3, 2, 1; 2, 1, 4, 3. The 2×2 is impossible. 3×3: 1, 3, 2; 3, 2, 1; 2, 1, 3.

10. 6

11. 30

12. Head and tail are 4 inches long and the body is 22 inches long.

13. 256

14.

15.

X	X	X	X	X
X	X	X	X	
X	X	X		X
X	X	X		X

16. 2 nickels & 10 dimes; 5 nickels, 6 dimes, & 1 quarter; 8 nickels, 2 dimes, & 2 quarters.

17. Let x, $x + 1$, and $x + 2$ be any three consecutive numbers. Their sum is $(x) + (x + 1) + (x + 2) = 3x + 3 = 3(x + 1)$.

18. 4 different triangles. 2, 6, 6; 3, 5, 6; 4, 5, 5; 4, 4, 6

19. Baseball is 0.5 pounds, football is 0.75 pounds, soccer ball is 0.85 pounds.

20. By using a simpler problem and looking for a pattern.
 1 table $\Rightarrow$ 3 chairs
 2 tables $\Rightarrow$ 4 chairs
 3 tables $\Rightarrow$ 5 chairs
 31 tables $\Rightarrow$ 31 + 2 chairs

21. a. 39¢, 55¢, 74¢   **b.** 86¢, 131¢   **c.** 44¢, 64¢, 88¢

Section 2.1A
1. a. {6, 7, 8}   **b.** {2, 4, 6, 8, 10, 12, 14}   **c.** {2, 4, 6, ..., 150}

2. a. No   **b.** Yes   **c.** No
 d. No   **e.** No   **f.** No   **g.** No

3. a. T   **b.** T   **c.** T
 d. F   **e.** F

4.

$$x \longleftrightarrow a \qquad x \searrow a \qquad x \searrow a \qquad x \searrow a$$
$$y \searrow b \qquad y \searrow b \qquad y \searrow b \qquad y \searrow b$$
$$z \searrow c \qquad z \longleftrightarrow c \qquad z \searrow c \qquad z \searrow c$$

5. b, c, and e

6. a. Yes   **b.** No   **c.** No   **d.** Yes

7. $\varnothing$, $\{a\}$, $\{b\}$, $\{c\}$, $\{a, b\}$, $\{a, c\}$, $\{b, c\}$, $\{a, b, c\}$

8. $\varnothing$, $\{\triangle\}$, $\{\bigcirc\}$

9. a. $\notin$ **b.** $\subset, \subseteq$ **c.** $\subset, \subseteq$ **d.** $\not\subset, \sim$ **e.** $\in$ **f.** $\subseteq, =, \sim$

10. a. 2   **b.** 99   **c.** 201   **d.** infinite set   **e.** infinite set

11. $\{6, 9, 12, 15, 18, \ldots\}$ where $6 \leftrightarrow 3, 9 \leftrightarrow 6, 12 \leftrightarrow 9, a \leftrightarrow a - 3$.
 $\{9, 12, 15, 18, 21, \ldots\}$ where $9 \leftrightarrow 3, 12 \leftrightarrow 6, 15 \leftrightarrow 9, a \leftrightarrow a - 6$.
 There are other correct answers

12. a. $\{2, 4, 6, 8, 10, \ldots\} = A$
 b. $\{4, 8, 12, 16, 20, \ldots\} = B$
 c. Yes. Since all of the numbers in set B are even, they are also in set A.
 d. Yes. $x \in A$ maps to $2x \in B$ so $2 \leftrightarrow 4, 4 \leftrightarrow 8, 6 \leftrightarrow 12$, etc.
 e. No. $2 \in A$ but $2 \notin B$.
 f. Yes. $B \subseteq A$ and $2 \in A$ but $2 \notin B$.

13. a. F   **b.** F   **c.** T

14. a.

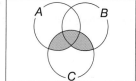

b.

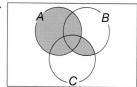

c. Parentheses placement is important.

15. a.

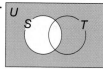

b.

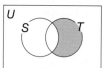

c.

16. a.

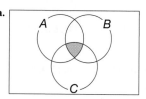

b.

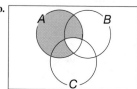

c.

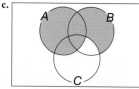

17. a. $(B \cap C) - A$ **b.** $C - (A \cup B)$
c. $[A \cup (B \cap C)] - (A \cap B \cap C)$. Note: There are many other correct answers.

18. a.

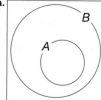

b.

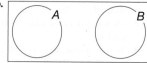

19. a.

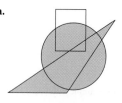

b.

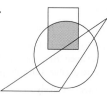

c.

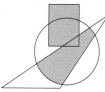

d.

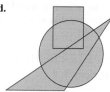

e.

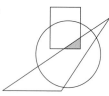

f.

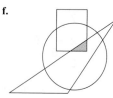

20. a. Women *or* Americans who have won Nobel Prizes
b. Nobel Prize winners who are American women
c. American winners of the Nobel Prize in chemistry

21. a. $\{b, c\}$ **b.** $\{b, c, e\}$ **c.** $\{a\}$

22. a. $\{\bigcirc, /\}$
b. $\{0, 1, 2, \cdots, 11\}$
c. All single people
d. $\{a, b, c, d\}$

23. a. $\{2, 6, 10, 14, \ldots\}$
b. $\varnothing$
c. $A - B = \varnothing$ if $A \subseteq B$

24. a. $\{0, 1, 2, 3, 4, 5, 6, 8, 10\}$ **b.** $\{0, 2, 4, 6, 8, 10\}$
c. $\{0, 2, 4\}$ **d.** $\{0, 4, 8\}$
e. $\{2, 6, 10\}$ **f.** $\{1, 2, 3, 5, 6, 10\}$
g. $\varnothing$

25. a. {January, June, July, August}   **b.** {January}
c. $\varnothing$
d. {January, June, July}
e. {March, April, May, September, October, November}
f. {January}

26. a. Yes   **b.** $\{3, 6, 9, 12, 15, 18, 21, 24, \ldots\}$
c. $\{6, 12, 18, 24, \ldots\}$ **d.** $A \cup B = A, A \cap B = B$

27. a. $\overline{A \cup B} = \overline{A} \cap \overline{B} = \{6\}$. Yes, the sets are the same.
b. $\overline{A \cup B}$ and $\overline{A} \cap \overline{B}$ are both represented by

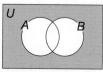

Yes, the diagrams are the same.

28. a. $\{(a, b), (a, c)\}$
b. $\{(5, a), (5, b), (5, c)\}$
c. $\{(a, 1), (a, 2), (a, 3), (b, 1), (b, 2), (b, 3)\}$
d. $\{(2, 1), (2, 4), (3, 1), (3, 4)\}$
e. $\{(a, 5), (b, 5), (c, 5)\}$
f. $\{(1, a), (2, a), (3, a), (1, b), (2, b), (3, b)\}$

29. a. 8   **b.** 12

30. a. 2   **b.** 4   **c.** Not possible
  d. 25   **e.** 0   **f.** Not possible

31. a. $A = \{a\}, B = \{2, 4, 6\}$
  b. $A = B = \{a, b\}$

32. a. T   **b.** F   **c.** F   **d.** F

33. a. Three elements; eight elements
  b. y elements; $x + y$ elements

34. 24

35. a. 1   **b.** 2   **c.** 4   **d.** 8   **e.** 32
  f. $2 \cdot 2 \cdot 2 \cdots 2$ (2 appears n times)

36. a. Possible   **b.** Not possible

37. a. When $D \subseteq E$ **b.** When $E \subseteq D$ **c.** When $E = D$

38. The Cartesian product of the set of skirts with the set of blouses will determine how many outfits can be formed—56 in this case.

39. 31 matches

40. Yes. Use lines perpendicular to the base.

41. Yes. Use lines perpendicular to the chord.

42. a. 7   **b.** 19   **c.** 49

43. Twenty-five were butchers, bakers, *and* candlestick makers.

44. Analogies between set operations and arithmetic operations are not direct. One could say that $A - B$ means you take all the elements of B away from A. However, $A \times B$ is a set of ordered pairs such that the first elements come from A and the second elements come from B. So all the elements of A are "paired" with all the elements of B, but not multiplied.

Section 2.2A

1. 314-781-9804, identification: 13905, identification; 6, cardinal; 7814, identification; 28, ordinal; $10, cardinal; 20, ordinal

2. a. Attribute common to all sets that match or are equivalent to the set $\{a, b, c, d, e, f, g\}$
  b. Attribute common to all sets that match or are equivalent to $\{a\}$
  c. Impossible
  d. How many elements are in the empty set?

3. Put in one-to-one correspondence with the set $\{1, 2, 3, 4, 5, 6\}$.

4. 8; 5

5. A set containing 3 elements, such as $\{a, b, c\}$, can be matched with a proper subset of a set with 7 elements, such as $\{t, u, v, w, x, y, z\}$.

6. a. $<$ **b.** $>$ **c.** $>$
  All solutions can be found by plotting the numbers on a number line.

7. a. |||||||||

  b. ∩∩|||

  c. 𝟫𝟫𝟫∩∩∩|||

  d. 𝟤𝟫𝟫∩∩∩|

8. a. LXXVI
  b. XLIX
  c. CXCII
  d. MDCCXLI

9. a.

10. a.

11. a. 12   **b.** 4270   **c.** 3614   **d.** 1991
  e. 976   **f.** 3245   **g.** 42   **h.** 404
  i. 3010   **j.** 14   **k.** 52   **l.** 333

12. a.

b. CXXXI   **c.**

13. a. Egyptian
  b. Mayan
  c. No. For example, to represent 10 requires two symbols in the Mayan system, but only one in either the Egyptian or Babylonian systems.

14. 1967

15. IV and VI, IX and XI, and so on; the Egyptian system was not positional, so there should not be a problem with reversals.

16. a. (i) 30, (ii) 24, (iii) 47, (iv) 57
  b. Add the digits of the addends (or subtrahend and minuend).

17. MCMXCIX. It was introduced in the fall of 1998.

18. 18 pages

19. $1993 \times (1 + 2 + 3 + 4 + \cdots + 1994)$

20. Do a three-coin version first. For five coins, start by comparing two coins. If they balance, use a three-coin test on the remaining coins. If they do not balance, add in one of the good coins and use a three-coin test.

21. a. (i) 42, (ii) 625, (iii) 3533, (iv) 89,801
  b. (i) $\pi\epsilon$, (ii) $\psi\mu\delta$, (iii) $'\beta\rho\upsilon\gamma$, (iv) $'\kappa'\alpha\phi\lambda\delta$
  c. No.

Section 2.3A

1. a. $7(10) + 0(1)$
  b. $3(100) + 0(10) + 0(1)$
  c. $9(100) + 8(10) + 4(1)$
  d. $6(10^7) + 6(10^3) + 6(10)$

2. a. 1207   **b.** 500,300   **c.** 8,070,605   **d.** 2,000,033,040

3. a. 100   **b.** 1   **c.** 1000

4. a. 12   **b.** 4   **c.** quintillion
  d. septillion   **e.** 24   **f.** 9
  g. 30   **h.** decillion

5. a. Two billion
   b. Eighty-seven trillion
   c. Fifty-two trillion six hundred seventy-two billion four hundred five million one hundred twenty-three thousand one hundred thirty-nine

6. a. 7,603,059
   b. 206,000,453,000

7. Any three of the following five attributes: digits: 0, 1, 2, 3, 4, 5, 6, 7, 8, 9; grouping by tens; place value; additive; multiplicative

8. 3223_{four}

9. a.

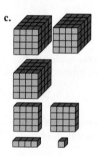

   b.

   c.

10. 2, 1, 2, 0

11. a.

10	1
• •	• • • •

   b.

5^2	5^1	1
• •	• •	•

c.

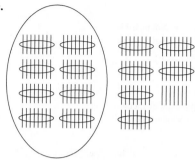

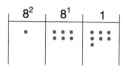

8^2	8^1	1
•	• • •	• • •

12. a. 222_{five}
   b. 333_{five}; 32143_{five}

13. 23

14. Improper digit symbols for the given bases—can't have an 8 in base eight or a 4 in base three

15. a. T   **b.** F   **c.** F

16. a. In base five, 1, 2, 3, 4, 10, 11, 12, 13, 14, 20, 21, 22, 23, 24, 30, 31, 32, 33, 34, 40, 41, 42, 43, 44, 100
   b. In base two, 1, 10, 11, 100, 101, 110, 111, 1000, 1001, 1010, 1011, 1100, 1101, 1110, 1111, 10000
   c. In base three, 1, 2, 10, 11, 12, 20, 21, 22, 100, 101, 102, 110, 111, 112, 120, 121, 122, 200, 201, 202, 210, 211, 212, 220, 221, 222, 1000
   d. 255, 300, 301, 302 (in base six)
   e. 310_{four}

17. a. $15_{\text{seven}} = 1(7) + 5(1)$
   b. $123_{\text{seven}} = 1(7^2) + 2(7) + 3(1)$
   c. $5046_{\text{seven}} = 5(7^3) + 0(7^2) + 4(7) + 6(1)$

18. a. 333_{four}
   b. 1000_{four}, 1001_{four}, 1002_{four}, 1003_{four}, 1010_{four}

19. $2400 = 6666_{\text{seven}}$
   $2402 = 10001_{\text{seven}}$
   10001_{seven} has more digits because it is greater than 7^4.

20. a. 613_{eight} **b.** 23230_{four} **c.** 110110_{two}

21. a. 194   **b.** 328
   c. 723   **d.** 129
   e. 1451   **f.** 20,590

22. a. 531   **b.** 7211

23. a. 177_{sixteen}
   b. $B7D_{\text{sixteen}}$
   c. 2530_{sixteen}
   d. $5ED2_{\text{sixteen}}$

24. a. 202_{six}; 62_{twelve}
   b. 332_{six}; $T8_{\text{twelve}}$
   c. 550_{six}; 156_{twelve}
   d. 15142_{six}; $14E2_{\text{twelve}}$

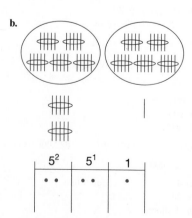

25. a. five   **b.** nine   **c.** eleven

26. a. Seven   **b.** Forty-seven
   c. Twelve   **d.** $x \geq 7$, $x = 3y - 5$

27. a. It must be 0, 2, 4, 6, or 8.
   b. It must be 0 or 2.
   c. It must be a 0.
   d. It may be any digit in base 5.

28. 1024 pages

29. 57

30. a. If final answer is *abcdef*, then the first two digits (*ab*) give the month of birth, the second two (*cd*) give the date of birth, and the last two (*ef*) give the year of birth.
   b. If birthday is *ab/cd/ef*, then the result will be $100{,}000a + 10{,}000b + 1{,}000c + 100d + 10e + f$. For example, begin by calculating $4(10a + b) + 13$.

PROBLEMS WHERE THE STRATEGY "DRAW A DIAGRAM" IS USEFUL

1. Draw a tree diagram. There are $3 \cdot 2 \cdot 2 = 12$ combinations.

2. Draw a diagram tracing out the taxi's path: 5 blocks north and 2 blocks east.

3. Draw a diagram showing the four cities: 15,000 arrive at Canton.

CHAPTER REVIEW
Section 2.1
1. Verbal description, listing, set-builder notation

2. a. T   **b.** T   **c.** T   **d.** T   **e.** T   **f.** T
   g. F   **h.** F   **i.** F   **j.** F   **k.** T   **l.** F

3. $\{1, 2, 3, 4, 5, 6, 7\}$

4. An infinite set can be matched with a proper subset of itself.

5. 7

Section 2.2
1. No—it should be house *numeral*.

2. a. How much money is in your bank account?
   b. Which place did you finish in the relay race?
   c. What is your telephone number?

3. a. T   **b.** T   **c.** F   **d.** T   **e.** T   **f.** T   **g.** F   **h.** F

4. a. 111   **b.** 114   **c.** 168

5. a. ∩∩∩|||||||| **b.** XXXVII   **c.**

6. IV ≠ VI shows that the Roman system is positional. However, this system does not have place value. Every place value system is positional.

Section 2.3
1. a. Digits tell how many of each place value is required.
   b. Grouping by ten establishes the place values.
   c. Place values allow for large numbers with few numerals.
   d. Digits are *multiplied* by the place values and then all resulting values are *added*.

2. The names of 11 and 12 are unique; the names of 13–19 read the ones digits first, then say "teen." The numerals 21–29 are read from left to right, where twenty means 2 tens and the second digit is the number of ones.

3. a. F   **b.** T   **c.** F   **d.** T

4. It gives you insight into base 10.

Chapter 2 Test

1. a. F   **b.** T   **c.** T   **d.** T   **e.** F
   f. F   **g.** T   **h.** F   **i.** F   **j.** F

2. 19

3. The intersection is an empty set.

4. a. $\{a, b, c, d, e\}$ **b.** { } or ∅   **c.** $\{b, c\}$
   d. $\{(a, e), (a, f), (a, g), (b, e), (b, f), (b, g), (c, e), (c, f), (c, g)\}$
   e. $\{d\}$ **f.** $\{e\}$

5. a. 32   **b.** 944   **c.** 381   **d.** 106   **e.** 21   **f.** 142

6. a. $7 \times 100 + 5 \times 10 + 9$
   b. $7 \times 1000 + 2$ **c.** $1 \times 2^6 + 1 \times 2^3 + 1$

7.

8.
   Babylonian:

   Roman: CLVII

   Egyptian:

   Mayan:

9. 4034_{five}

10. $[A - (B \cup C)] \cup (B \cap C)$ There are other correct answers.

11. IV ≠ VI; thus position is important, but there is no place value as in $31 \neq 13$, where the first 3 means "3 tens" and the second three means "3 ones."

12. a. True for all A and B
   b. True for all A and B
   c. True whenever $A = B$
   d. True whenever $A = B$ or where A or B is empty

13. $(b, a), (b, c), (d, a), (d, c)$

14. Zero, based on groups of 20, $18 \cdot 20$, etc.

15.

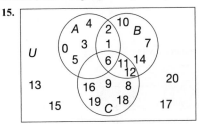

16. No. There are 26 letters and 41 numbers.

17.

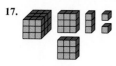

$$\begin{array}{c|c|c|c} 3^3 & 3^2 & 3^1 & 3^0 \\ \bullet & \bullet & \bullet & \bullet \\ & \bullet & \bullet & \bullet \\ & & & \bullet \end{array}$$

18. 97

19. $a = 6, b = 8$

20. 8

21. 37,905 Four "fine" bars spaced apart—one for each place value.

22. a. None   **b.** 4   **c.** 5

23. Mayan
Babylonian needs 21
Mayan needs 23
Roman needs 15

Section 3.1A

1. a. 4   3

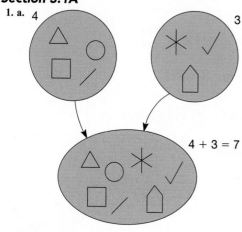

$4 + 3 = 7$

b.

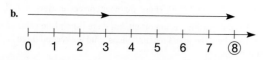

$$\begin{array}{ccccccccc} 0 & 1 & 2 & 3 & 4 & 5 & 6 & 7 & ⑧ \end{array}$$

2. Only a. and b. are true. c. is false because $D \cap E \neq \varnothing$.

3. a. Closed   **b.** Closed
c. Not closed, $1 + 2 = 3$ **d.** Not closed, $1 + 2 = 3$
e. Closed

4. a. Closure
b. Commutativity
c. Associativity
d. Identity
e. Commutativity
f. Associativity and commutativity

5.

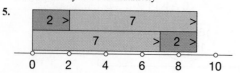

They differ in the order of the bars, but are the same because the total length in both cases is 9.

6. Associative property and commutative property for whole-number addition

7. a. 67, 107   **b.** 51, 81   **c.** 20, 70

8. a.

+	0	1	2	3	4
0	0	1	2	3	4
1	1	2	3	4	10
2	2	3	4	10	11
3	3	4	10	11	12
4	4	10	11	12	13

b. (i) $4_{\text{five}} + ? = 13_{\text{five}}, ? = 4_{\text{five}}$ (ii) $3_{\text{five}} + ? = 11_{\text{five}}, ? = 3_{\text{five}}$
(iii) $4_{\text{five}} + ? = 12_{\text{five}}, ? = 3_{\text{five}}$ (iv) $2_{\text{five}} + ? = 10_{\text{five}}, ? = 3_{\text{five}}$

9. a. $4_{\text{five}} + 3_{\text{five}} = 12_{\text{five}}, 12_{\text{five}} - 4_{\text{five}} = 3_{\text{five}}, 12_{\text{five}} - 3_{\text{five}} = 4_{\text{five}}$
b. $1_{\text{five}} + 4_{\text{five}} = 10_{\text{five}}, 10_{\text{five}} - 1_{\text{five}} = 4_{\text{five}}, 10_{\text{five}} - 4_{\text{five}} = 1_{\text{five}}$
c. $2_{\text{five}} + 4_{\text{five}} = 11_{\text{five}}, 4_{\text{five}} + 2_{\text{five}} = 11_{\text{five}}, 11_{\text{five}} - 2_{\text{five}} = 4_{\text{five}}$

10. $11 - 3 = 8$ and $11 - 8 = 3$. Measurement take-away or missing addend

11. a. $7 - 2 = 5$, set model, take-away
b. $7 - 3 = 4$, measurement model, missing addend
c. $6 - 4 = 2$, set model, comparison approach

12. a. No; that is, $3 - 5$ is not a whole number.
b. No; that is, $3 - 5 \neq 5 - 3$.
c. No; that is, $(6 - 3) - 1 \neq 6 - (3 - 1)$.
d. No, $5 - 0 = 5$ but $0 - 5 \neq 5$.

13. a. Measurement, take-away model; no comparison since $120 has been removed from the original amount of $200:

$$200 - 120 = x$$

b. Set, missing addend, comparison, since two different sets of tomato plants are being compared:

$$24 - 18 = x$$

c. Measurement, missing-addend model; no comparison since we need to know what additional amount will make savings equal $1795

$$1240 + x = 1795$$

14. a. Kofi has 3 dollars and needs 8 dollars to go to the movie. How much more money does he need?
b. Tabitha and Salina both had 8 yards of fabric and Tabitha used 3 yards to make a skirt. How much does she have left?
c.

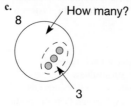

How many?

d.

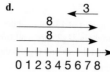

15. The rest of the counting numbers

16. $123 - 45 - 67 + 89 = 100$

17.

25	11	12	22
14	20	19	17
18	16	15	21
13	23	24	10

18. Sums of numbers on all six sides are the same as are sums on the "half-diagonals," lines from center to edge.

19. a. (i) 363, (ii) 4884, (iii) 55
b. 69, 78, 79, or 89

20. 4, 8, 12, 16, 20

21. One arrangement has these sides: 9, 3, 4, 7; 7, 2, 6, 8; 8, 1, 5, 9.

Section 3.2A

1. a. 2×4 **b.** 4×2 **c.** 3×7

2. a.

	d	e
a	(a, d)	(a, e)
b	(b, d)	(b, e)
c	(c, d)	(c, e)

b.

c.

d.

3. a. Rectangular array approach, since there are rows and columns of tiles.

$$n = 15 \cdot 12$$

b. Cartesian product approach, since we are looking at a set of 3 pairs of shorts, each of which is paired with one of a set of eight tee shirts.

$$x = 3 \cdot 8$$

c. Repeated addition, since the number of pencils could be found by adding $3 + 3 + \cdots + 3$ where the sum has 36 terms.

$$p = 36 \cdot 3$$

4. a. 36   **b.** 68   **c.** 651   **d.** 858

5. a. No. $2 \times 4 = 8$ **b.** Yes
c. No. $3 \times 3 = 9$ **d.** Yes
e. Yes   **f.** Yes   **g.** Yes
h. Yes   **i.** Yes   **j.** Yes

6. a. Commutative
b. Commutative
c. Distributive property of multiplication over addition
d. Identity

7. a. $4 \cdot 60 + 4 \cdot 37$
b. $21 \cdot 6 + 35 \cdot 6$
c. $37 \cdot 60 - 37 \cdot 22$
d. $(5 + 2)x$
e. $(5 - 3)(a + 1)$

8. a. $45(11) = 45(10 + 1)$ **b.** $39(102) = 39(100 + 2)$
c. $23(21) = 23(20 + 1)$ **d.** $97(101) = 97(100 + 1)$

9. a. $(372 + 2) \times 12 = 4488$
There are other possible ways.
b. $374 \times (11 + 1) = 4488$
There are other possible ways.

10. a. $5(23 \times 4) = 23(5 \times 4) = 23 \times 20 = 460$, There are other possible ways.
b. $12 \times 25 = 3(4 \times 25) = 300$, There are other possible ways.

11. a. (In base five)

×	0	1	2	3	4
0	0	0	0	0	0
1	0	1	2	3	4
2	0	2	4	11	13
3	0	3	11	14	22
4	0	4	13	22	31

b. (i) $3_{\text{five}} \times 2_{\text{five}} = 11_{\text{five}}$, $11_{\text{five}} \div 3_{\text{five}} = 2_{\text{five}}$, $11_{\text{five}} \div 2_{\text{five}} = 3_{\text{five}}$
(ii) $3_{\text{five}} \times 4_{\text{five}} = 22_{\text{five}}$, $4_{\text{five}} \times 3_{\text{five}} = 22_{\text{five}}$, $22_{\text{five}} \div 4_{\text{five}} = 3_{\text{five}}$
(iii) $2_{\text{five}} \times 4_{\text{five}} = 13_{\text{five}}$, $4_{\text{five}} \times 2_{\text{five}} = 13_{\text{five}}$, $13_{\text{five}} \div 4_{\text{five}} = 2_{\text{five}}$

12. a. Measurement—How many 3 pints can be measured out?
b. Sharing—How many tarts can be partitioned to each of 4 members?
c. Measurement—How many groups of 3 straws each can be formed?

13. a. Fifteen students are to be divided into 3 teams. How many on each team? Answers may vary.
b. Fifteen students are put into teams of 3 each. How many teams? Answers may vary.

14. a. $48 = 8 \times 6$ **b.** $51 = 3 \cdot x$ **c.** $x = 5 \cdot 13$

15. a. 0   **b.** 2   **c.** 12   **d.** 8   **e.** 32   **f.** 13

16. If the remainder were larger than the divisor, then the remainder column would be taller than the rest of the rectangle and the extra portion above the top could be taken off to create a new remainder column. In other words, the divisor could divide into the dividend more times until the remainder is smaller than the divisor.

17. a. $3 \div 2 \neq$ whole number   **b.** $4 \div 2 \neq 2 \div 4$
c. $(12 \div 3) \div 2 \neq 12 \div (3 \div 2)$
d. $5 \div 1 = 5$, but $1 \div 5 \neq 5$
e. $12 \div (4 + 2) \neq 12 \div 4 + 12 \div 2$

18. 1704

19. $3.84

20. Approximately $2.48.

21. $90,000

22. Push 1; multiplicative identity

23. Yes, because multiplication is repeated addition

24. a. Row 1: 4, 3, 8; row 2: 9, 5, 1; row 3: 2, 7, 6
   b. Row 1: 2^4, 2^3, 2^8; row 2: 2^9, 2^5, 2^1; row 3: 2^2, 2^7, 2^6

25. $31 + 33 + 35 + 37 + 39 + 41 = 216$;
   $43 + 45 + 47 + 49 + 51 + 53 + 55 = 343$;
   $57 + 59 + 61 + 63 + 65 + 67 + 69 + 71 = 512$

26. 9, 5, 4, 6, 3, 2, 1, 7, 8

27. $\dfrac{2(n + 10) + 100}{2} - n = 60$

28. 1st place: Pounce, Michelle
   2nd place: Hippy, Kevin
   2nd place: Hoppy, Jason
   3rd place: Bounce, Wendy

29. 3 cups of tea, 2 cakes, and 7 people

30. 3^{29}

31. Put three on each pan. If they balance, the lighter one of the other two will be found in the next weighing. If three of the coins are lighter, then weigh one of these three against another of these three. If they balance, the third coin is the lighter one. If they do not balance, choose the lighter one.

32. Yes, providing $c \neq 0$.

Section 3.3A

1. a. 19   **b.** 16

2. $2 < 10, 8 < 10, 10 > 2, 10 > 8$

3. Yes

4. a. Yes   **b.** No. $2 \neq 3$ and $3 \neq 2$, but $2 = 2$.

5. a. 3^4 **b.** $2^4 \cdot 3^2$ **c.** $6^3 \cdot 7^2$
   d. $x^2 y^4$ **e.** $a^2 b^2$ or $(ab)^2$ **f.** $5^3 6^3$ or $(5 \cdot 6)^3$

6. $3^4 > 4^3 > 2^5 > 5^2$

7. a. $3 \cdot x \cdot x \cdot y \cdot y \cdot y \cdot y \cdot y \cdot z$
   b. $7 \cdot 5 \cdot 5 \cdot 5$
   c. $7 \cdot 5 \cdot 7 \cdot 5 \cdot 7 \cdot 5$

8. a. 5^7 **b.** 3^{10} **c.** 10^7 **d.** 2^8 **e.** 5^4 **f.** 6^7

9. $5^{2 \cdot 7}, (5^2)^7, (5^7)^2, 5^{7+7}, 5^7 \cdot 5^7$. There are other possible answers.

10. Always true when $n = 1$. If $n > 1$, true only when $a = 0$ or $b = 0$.

11. a. $x = 6$ **b.** $x = 5$
   c. x can be any whole number.

12. a. 1,679,616   **b.** 50,625   **c.** 1875

13. a. $15 - 3 \cdot 5 = 0$ **b.** $2 \cdot 25 = 50$
   c. $9 \cdot 4 - 2 \cdot 8 = 36 - 16 = 20$
   d. $\dfrac{6 + 2(27 - 16)^2 + 16}{6(27 - 16)} = \dfrac{6 + 2 \cdot 121 + 16}{66} = 4$

14. a. $2 \cdot 3^2 - 4 = 2 \cdot 9 - 4 = 14$; $2(3^2 - 4) = 10$
   b. $4^2 - 3 \cdot 4 \div 2 = 16 - 6 = 10$; $(4^2 - 3) \cdot (4 \div 2) = 26$

15. $(a^m)^n = \underbrace{a^m \cdot a^m \cdots a^m}_{\substack{n \text{ factors} \\ n \text{ addends}}}$
   $= a^{\overbrace{m + m + \cdots + m}}$
   $= a^{mn}$

16. a. $6^{10} = (2 \cdot 3)^{10} = 2^{10} \cdot 3^{10} < 3^{10} \cdot 3^{10} = 3^{20}$
   b. $9^9 = (3^2)^9 = 3^{18} < 3^{20}$
   c. $12^{10} = (4 \cdot 3)^{10} = 4^{10} \cdot 3^{10} > 3^{10} \cdot 3^{10} = 3^{20}$

17. a. 200¢ or \$2.00   **b.** 6400¢ or \$64.00   **c.** Price $= 25 \cdot 2^n$ cents

18. When $a = n(A)$ and $b = n(B)$, $a < b$ means A can be matched to a proper subset of B. Also, $b < c$ when $c = n(C)$ means the B can be matched to a proper subset of C. In that matching, the proper subset of B that matches A is matched to a proper subset of a proper subset of C. Thus, since A can be matched to a proper subset of C, $a < c$.

19. a. $17 + 18 + 19 + \cdots + 25 = 4^3 + 5^3$;
   $26 + 27 + 28 + \cdots + 36 = 5^3 + 6^3$
   b. $9^3 + 10^3 = 82 + 83 + \cdots + 100$
   c. $12^3 + 13^3 = 145 + \cdots + 169$
   d. $n^3 + (n + 1)^3 = (n^2 + 1) + (n^2 + 2) + \cdots + (n + 1)^2$

20. $4(2^4) = 64$

21. a. The only one-digit squares are 1, 4, and 9. The only combination of these that is a perfect square is 49.
   b. 169, 361
   c. 1600, 1936, 2500, 3600, 4900, 6400, 8100, 9025
   d. 1225, 1444, 4225, 4900
   e. 1681   **f.** 1444, 4900, 9409

22. The second one

23. a. If $a < b$, then $a + n = b$ for some nonzero n.
   Then $(a + c) + n = b + c$, or $a + c < b + c$.
   b. If $a < b$, then $a - c < b - c$ for all c, where $c \leq a, c \leq b$.
   Proof: If $a < b$, then $a + n = b$ for some nonzero n.
   Hence $(a - c) + n = b - c$, or $a - c < b - c$.

PROBLEMS WHERE THE STRATEGY "USE DIRECT REASONING" IS USEFUL

1. Since the first and last digits are the same, their sum is even. Since the sum of the three digits is odd, the middle digit must be odd.

2. Michael, Clyde, Jose, Andre, Ralph

3. The following triples represent the amount in the 8-, 3-, and 5-liter jugs, respectively, after various pourings:
   (8, 0, 0), (5, 3, 0), (5, 0, 3), (2, 3, 3), (2, 1, 5), (7, 1, 0), (7, 0, 1), (4, 3, 1), (4, 0, 4).

CHAPTER REVIEW
Section 3.1

1. a. $5 + 4 = n(\{a, b, c, d, e\}) + n(\{f, g, h, i\}) = n(\{a, b, c, d, e\} \cup \{f, g, h, i\}) = 9$
   b.

   $$0 \quad 1 \quad 2 \quad 3 \quad 4 \quad 5 \quad 6 \quad 7 \quad 8 \quad 9$$

2. a. Associative   **b.** Identity   **c.** Commutative   **d.** Closure

3. a. $5 + 6 = 5 + (5 + 1) = (5 + 5) + 1 = 10 + 1 = 11$;
   associativity for addition, doubles, adding ten
   b. $7 + 9 = (6 + 1) + 9 = 6 + (1 + 9) = 6 + 10 = 16$;
   associativity, combinations to ten, adding ten

4. a. $7 - 3 = n(\{a, b, c, d, e, f, g\} - \{e, f, g\}) = n(\{a, b, c, d\}) = 4$.
   b. $7 - 3 = n$ if and only if $7 = 3 + n$. Thus, $n = 4$.

5. To find $7 - 2$, find 7 in the "2" column. The answer is in the row containing 7, namely 5.

6. None

Section 3.2

1. a. 15 altogether:

b. 15 altogether:

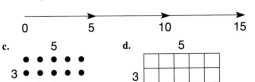

c.

d.

2. a. Identity   **b.** Commutative   **c.** Associative   **d.** Closure

3. a. $7 \times 27 + 7 \times 13 = 7(27 + 13) = 7(40) = 280$
   b. $8 \times 17 - 8 \times 7 = 8(17 - 7) = 8(10) = 80$

4. a. $6 \times 7 = 6(6 + 1) = 6 \times 6 + 6 \times 1 = 36 + 6 = 42$;
   distributivity
   b. $9 \times 7 = (10 - 1)7 = 10 \times 7 - 7 = 70 - 7 = 63$; distributivity

5. a. $17 \div 3 = 5$ remainder 2:

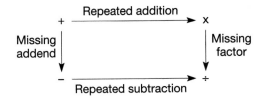

b. $17 \div 3 = 5$ remainder 2:

6. To find $63 \div 7$, look for 63 in the "7" column. The answer is the row containing 63, namely 9.

7. a. $7 \div 0 = n$ if and only if $7 = 0 \times n$. Since $0 \times n = 0$ for all n, there is no answer for $7 \div 0$.
   b. $0 \div 7 = n$ if and only if $0 = 7 \times n$. Therefore, $n = 0$.
   c. $0 \div 0 = n$ if and only if $0 = 0 \times n$. Since any number will work for n, there is no unique answer for $0 \div 0$.

8. $39 \div 7:39 = 7 \times 5 + 4$ where 5 is the quotient and 4 is the remainder

9. None

10. This diagram shows how subtraction, multiplication, and division are all connected to addition.

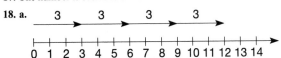

Section 3.3

1. $a < b\ (b > a)$ if there is nonzero whole number n such that $a + n = b$.

2. a. $a + c < b + c$ **b.** $a \times c < b \times c$

3. $5^4 = 5 \times 5 \times 5 \times 5$

4. a. $7^{3 \times 4} = 7^{12}$ **b.** $(3 \times 7)^5 = 21^5$
   c. $5^{(7-3)} = 5^4$ **d.** $4^{12+13} = 4^{25}$

5. Use a pattern: $5^3 = 125$, $5^2 = 25$, $5^1 = 5$, $5^0 = 1$, since we divided by 5 each time.

Chapter 3 Test

1. a. F   **b.** T   **c.** T   **d.** F   **e.** F
   f. F   **g.** F   **h.** T   **i.** F   **j.** T

2.

	ADD	SUBTRACT	MULTIPLY	DIVIDE
Closure	T	F	T	F
Commutative	T	F	T	F
Associative	T	F	T	F
Identity	T	F	T	F

3. a. Commutative for multiplication (CM)
   b. IM   **c.** AA   **d.** AM   **e.** D   **f.** CA

4. a. $30 + 10 + 9 + 2$ **b.** $40 + 80 + 7 + 7$
   c. $(5 \cdot 2)73$
   d. $10 \times 33 + 2 \times 33$

5. 64 R1

6. a. 3^{19} **b.** 5^{24} **c.** 7^{15} **d.** 2^2 **e.** 14^{15} **f.** 36^{12}

7. a. $13(97 + 3)$; distributivity
   b. $(194 + 6) + 86$; associativity and commutativity
   c. $23(7 + 3)$; commutativity and distributivity
   d. $(25 \cdot 8)123$; commutativity and associativity

8. a. sharing   **b.** measurement   **c.** measurement

9. a. Since there are two sets, comparison can be used with either missing-addend, $137 + x = 163$, or take-away, $163 - 137 = 26$.
   b. missing-addend, $973 + x = 1500$
   c. take-away, $\$5 - \$1.43 = \$3.57$

10. A

11. a. $(7^3)^4 = (7 \cdot 7 \cdot 7)^4 = (7 \cdot 7 \cdot 7)(7 \cdot 7 \cdot 7)(7 \cdot 7 \cdot 7)(7 \cdot 7 \cdot 7) = 7^{12}$
   b. $(7^3)^4 = 7^3 \cdot 7^3 \cdot 7^3 \cdot 7^3 = 7^{3+3+3+3} = 7^{12}$

12. $3 \div 0 = n$ if and only if $n \cdot 0 = 3$. But $n \cdot 0 = 0$.

13. $a^m \cdot b^m = \underbrace{a \cdot a \cdots a}_{m} \cdot \underbrace{b \cdot b \cdots b}_{m} =$
$\underbrace{ab \cdot ab \cdots ab}_{m} = (a \cdot b)^m$

14. $(2 \cdot 3)^2 = 36$ but $2 \cdot 3^2 = 2 \cdot 9 = 18$

15. Not commutative. For example, $B \Omega C = D$ and $C \Omega B = A$.

16. $\{2, 3, 4, 5, \ldots\}$

17. One number is even and one number is odd.

18. a.

Three added together 4 times is 12.

b.   Four rows of three
        make 12 squares.

19.

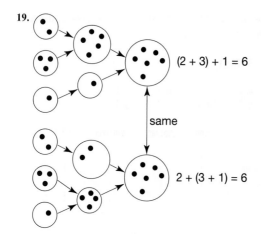

$(2 + 3) + 1 = 6$

same

$2 + (3 + 1) = 6$

20. a.

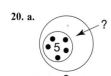

How many more need to be added to the set of 5 to make it a set of 8?

8

b.

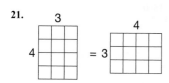

8

5   ?

0 1 2 3 4 5 6 7 8 9 10

21.

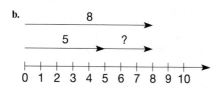

22. $64 = 8^2 = 4^3$

23. $2 \cdot 2 = 2 + 2$ and $0 \cdot 0 = 0 + 0$

Section 4.1A

1. a. 105
b. 4700
c. 1300
d. 120

2. a. $43 - 17 = 46 - 20 = 26$
b. $62 - 39 = 63 - 40 = 23$
c. $132 - 96 = 136 - 100 = 36$
d. $250 - 167 = 283 - 200 = 83$

3. a. 579   **b.** 903
c. 215   **d.** 333

4. a. $198 + 387 = 200 + 385 = 585$
b. $84 \times 5 = 42 \times 10 = 420$
c. $99 \times 53 = 5300 - 53 = 5247$
d. $4125 \div 25 = 4125 \times \frac{4}{100} = 165$

5. a. 290,000,000,000
b. 14,700,000,000
c. 91,000,000,000
d. 84×10^{14}
e. 140×10^{15}
f. 102×10^{15}

6. a. $32 + 20 = 52, 52 + 9 = 61, 61 + 50 = 111, 111 + 6 = 117$
b. $54 + 20 = 74, 74 + 8 = 82, 82 + 60 = 142, 142 + 7 = 149$
c. $19 + 60 = 79, 79 + 6 = 85, 85 + 40 = 125, 125 + 9 = 134$
d. $62 + 80 = 142, 142 + 4 = 146, 146 + 20 = 166, 166 + 7 = 173, 173 + 80 = 253, 253 + 1 = 254$

7. a. $84 \div 14 = 42 \div 7 = 6$
b. $234 \div 26 = 117 \div 13 = 9$
c. $120 \div 15 = 240 \div 30 = 8$
d. $168 \div 14 = 84 \div 7 = 12$

8. Underestimate so that fewer than the designated amount of pollutants will be discharged.

9. a. (i) 4000 to 6000, (ii) 4000, (iii) 4900, (iv) about 5000
b. (i) 1000 to 5000, (ii) 1000, (iii) 2400, (iv) about 2700
c. (i) 7000 to 11,000, (ii) 7000, (iii) 8100, (iv) about 8400

10. a. 600 to 1200
b. 20,000 to 60,000
c. 3200 to 4000

11. a. $63 \times 97 \approx 63 \times 100 = 6300$
b. $51 \times 212 \approx 50 \times 200 = 10,000$
c. $3112 \div 62 \approx 3000 \div 60 = 50$
d. $103 \times 87 \approx 100 \times 87 = 8700$
e. $62 \times 58 \approx 60 \times 60 = 3600$
f. $4254 \div 68 \approx 4200 \div 70 = 60$

12. a. 370   **b.** 700   **c.** 1130
d. 460   **e.** 3000

13. a. $4 \times 350 = 1400$
b. 60^3
c. 500^4
d. $5 \times 800 = 4000$

14. a. $30 \times 20 = 600, 31 \times 20 = 620$
$30 \times 23 = 690, 30 \times 25 = 750$
b. $35 \times 40 = 1400,$
$40 \times 40 = 1600$
$30 \times 40 = 1200, 30 \times 45 = 1350$
c. $50 \times 27 = 1350, 50 \times 25 = 1250$
$50 \times 30 = 1500, 45 \times 30 = 1350$
d. $75 \times 10 = 750, 70 \times 12 = 840$
$75 \times 12 = 900, 80 \times 10 = 800$

15. There are many acceptable estimates. One reasonable one is listed for each part.
a. 42 and 56
b. 12 and 20
c. 1 and 4

16. a. 4   **b.** 13

17. a. 4^5 **b.** 3^7 **c.** 4^7 **d.** 3^6

18. a. $17 \times 817 \times 100 = 1,388,900$
b. $10 \times 98 \times 673 = 659,540$
c. $50 \times 4 \times 674 \times 899 = 2 \times 100 \times 674 \times 899 = 119,837,200$
d. $8 \times 125 \times 783 \times 79 = 1000 \times 783 \times 79 = 61,857,000$

19. a. 12, 7   **b.** 31, 16
    c. 6, 111   **d.** 119, 828

20. $10^2 + 100^2 = 10,100$; $588^2 + 2353^2 = 5,882,353$

21. Yes, yes, no

22. a. Yes   **b.** Yes   **c.** Yes

23. Yes, yes, yes

24. a. 30   **b.** 83,232
    c. 4210   **d.** 32

25. 7782

26. True

27. a. 1357×90
    b. 6666×66
    c. $78 \times 93 \times 456$
    d. $123 \times 45 \times 67$

28. One possible method to find a range for $742 - 281$ is $700 - 200 = 500$ and $700 - 300 = 400$. The answer is between 400 and 500.

29. 177,777,768,888,889

30. 5643, 6237

31. a. 4225, 5625, 9025
    b. $(10a + 5)^2 = 100a^2 + 100a + 25 = 100a(a + 1) + 25$

32. Yes

33. The first factor probably ends in 9 rather than 8.

34. a. $54 \times 46 = 50^2 - 4^2 = 2484$
    b. $81 \times 79 = 80^2 - 1 = 6399$
    c. $122 \times 118 = 120^2 - 2^2 = 14,396$
    d. $1210 \times 1190 = 1200^2 - 10^2 = 1,439,900$

35. True, Express the product as $(898,000 + 423) \times (112,000 + 303)$. Use distributivity twice, then add.

36. $(439 \times 6852) \times 1000 + 268 \times 6852 = 3,009,864,336$

37. a. $76 \times (54 + 97)$
    b. $(4 \times 13)^2$
    c. $13 + (59^2 \times 47)$
    d. $(79 - 43) \div 2 + 17^2$

38. a. $57 \times 53 = 3021$
    b. $(10a + b)(10a + 10 - b) = 100a^2 + 100a + 10b - b^2 = 100a(a + 1) + b(10 - b)$.
    c. Problem 32 is the special case when $b = 5$.

39. (i) Identify the digit in the place to which you are rounding. (ii) If the digit in the place to its right is a 5, 6, 7, 8, or 9, add one to the digit to which you are rounding. Otherwise, leave the digit as it is. (iii) Put zeros in all the places to the right of the digit to which you are rounding.

40. $3 \cdot 5 \cdot 7 \cdot 9 \cdot 11 \cdot 13 \cdot 15 \cdot 17 = 34,459,425$

41. Fill the 3-liter pail and pour it into the 5-liter pail. Refill the 3-liter pail and pour as much as possible into the partially filled 5-liter pail. There will be 1 liter left in the 3-liter pail.

Section 4.2A

1. a.

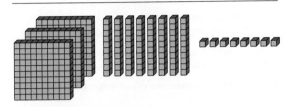

b.

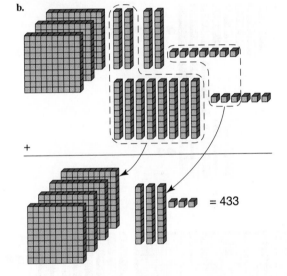

$= 433$

2. a.

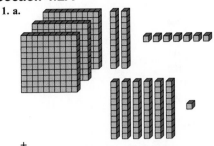

b.

15   //////
             // $= 47$
+ 32

3. Expanded form; commutative and associative properties of addition; distributive property of multiplication over addition; single-digit addition facts; place value.

4. a. 986   **b.** 909

5. a. 598   **b.**   322
+396   799
14   +572
180   13
800   180
994   1500
               1693

6. a. 1229   **b.** 13,434

7. a. 751   **b.** 1332

8. a. Simple; requires more writing
    b. Simple; requires more space; requires drawing lattice

9. The sum is 5074 both ways! This works because the numerals 1, 8 stay as 1 and 8 while 6 and 9 trade places.

10. Left-hand sum; compare sum of each column, from left to right.

11. a. ABC   **b.** CBA

12. a.

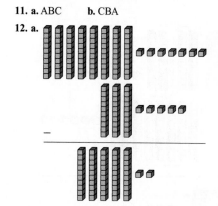

b.

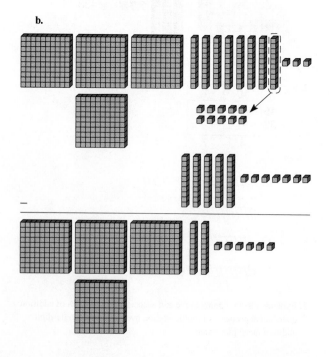

13. a.

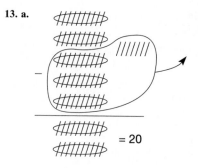

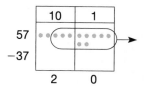

b.

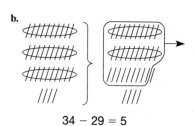

$$34 - 29 = 5$$

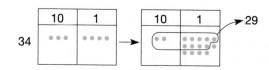

14 8, 12, 13, 12

15. (b), (a), (c)

16. a. 477   **b.** 776   **c.** 1818

17. 62, 63, 64, 65, 70, 80, 100; $38
Other answers are possible.

18. a. 358   **b.** 47,365

19. a. 135   **b.** 17,476

20. a.

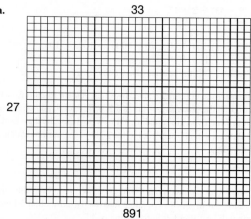

b.
$$\begin{array}{r} 33 \\ \times\, 27 \\ \hline 21 \\ 210 \\ 60 \\ +600 \\ \hline 891 \end{array}$$

c. The 21 is the 21 unit squares in the lower right. The 210 is the 21 longs at the bottom. The 60 is the 6 longs in the upper right. The 600 is the 6 flats.

21.

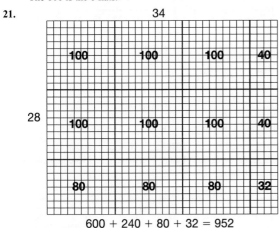

$$600 + 240 + 80 + 32 = 952$$

22. a.

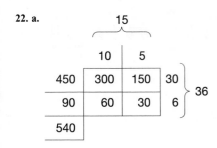

b.

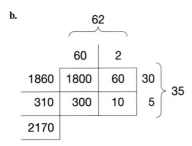

23. Expanded form; distributivity; expanded form; associativity for $\times$; place value; place value; addition

24. a. 1426 **b.** 765

25. a. 3525
   b. 153,244

26. a. 2380 **b.** 2356

27. a. 56 **b.** 42 **c.** 60

28. a. 1550 **b.** 2030 **c.** 7592

29. a.
$$\begin{array}{r} 13\,\overline{)899} \\ -650 \quad 50(13) \\ \hline 249 \\ -130 \quad 10(13) \\ \hline 119 \\ -91 \quad 7(13) \\ \hline 28 \\ -26 \quad 2(13) \\ \hline 2 \end{array}$$
$$2 + 69(13) = 899$$

b.
$$\begin{array}{r} 23\,\overline{)5697} \quad 200(23) \\ -4600 \\ \hline 1097 \quad 30(23) \\ -690 \\ \hline 407 \quad 10(23) \\ -230 \\ \hline 177 \quad 7(23) \\ -161 \\ \hline 16 \end{array}$$
$$16 + 247(23) = 5697$$

30. Subtract 6 seven times to reach 0.

31. a. 6: $24 - 4 - 4 - 4 - 4 - 4 - 4 = 0$
   b. 8: $56 - 7 - 7 - 7 - 7 - 7 - 7 - 7 - 7 = 0$
   c. Subtract the divisor from the dividend until the difference is 0. The total number of subtractions is the quotient.

32. a. (i) q: 15 r: 74   (ii) q: 499 r: 70   (iii) q: 3336 r: 223
   b. This method finds the decimal value of the remainder that will yield the remainder when multiplied by the divisor.

33.

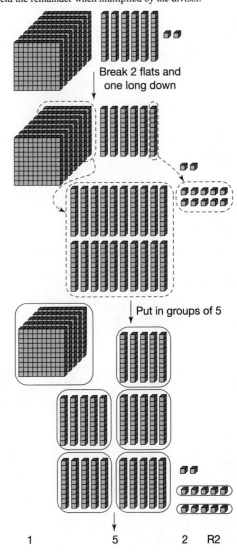

34. Bringing down the 3 is modeled by exchanging the 7 leftover flats for 70 longs, making a total of 73 longs.

35. Larry is not carrying properly; Curly carries the wrong digit; Moe forgets to carry.

36. One answer is $359 + 127 = 486$.

37. a. For example, $863 + 742 = 1605$
b. For example, $347 + 268 = 615$

38. $1 + 2 + 34 + 56 + 7 = 100$; also, $1 + 23 + 4 + 5 + 67 = 100$

39. a. $990 + 077 + 000 + 033 + 011$
b. (i) $990 + 007 + 000 + 003 + 111$;
(ii) $000 + 770 + 000 + 330 + 011$
(iii) $000 + 700 + 000 + 300 + 111$

40. a. Equal
b. Differ by 2
c. Yes
d. Difference of products is 10 times the vertical 10s-place difference.

41. a.

X	X	X	X	X
X	X	X	X	X
X	X	X	X	X
X	X	X	X	X

b. $1 + 2 + 3 + 4 = \frac{1}{2}(4 \times 5)$
c. $\frac{1}{2}(50 \times 51) = 1275$; $\frac{1}{2}(75 \times 76) = 2850$

42. $888 + 777 + 444 = 2109$; $888 + 666 + 555 = 2109$

43. Bob: 184; Jennifer: 120; Suzie: 206; Tom: 2081

44.
$$5314 \times 79$$
$$28$$
$$736$$
$$2109$$
$$3527$$
$$45$$
$$419806$$

45. All eventually arrive at 6174, then these digits are repeated.

Section 4.3A

1. a.
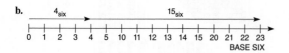
b.

2. a. 3_{four}
b. 100_{four}
c. 331_{four}
d. 12013_{four}

3. a. 114_{six}
b. 654_{seven}
c. 10012_{four}

4. a. 55_{six} **b.** 123_{six}
c. 1130_{six} **d.** 1010_{six}

5. a. 62_{seven} **b.** 102_{four}

6. a. 1201_{five}
b. 1575_{eight}

7. a.
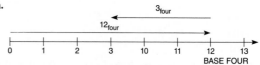
b.
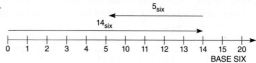

8. a. 13_{four}
b. 31_{four}
c. 103_{four}

9. a. 4_{six} **b.** 456_{seven}
c. 2322_{four}

10. a. 17_{eight} **b.** 101_{two} **c.** 13_{four}

11. $10201_{three} - 2122_{three} = 10201_{three} + 100_{three} - 10000_{three} + 1_{three} = 1002_{three}$; the sums, in columns, of a number and its complement must be all twos.

12. a.
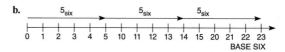
b.

13. a.
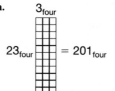
$23_{four} = 201_{four}$
b.
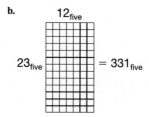
$23_{five} = 331_{five}$

14. a. 122_{four}
b. 234_{five}
c. 132_{four}

15. a.
b.
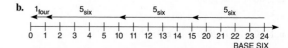

16. a. 11_{six} **b.** 54_{seven} **c.** 132_{four}

17. a. 3_{four} **b.** 5_{six} **c.** 4_{eight}

18. Thought One

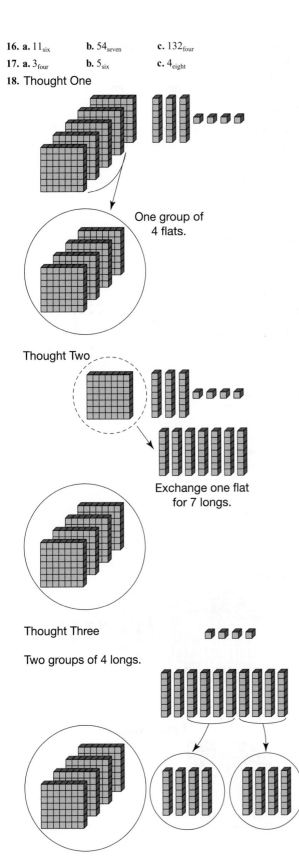

Thought Four

Exchange two longs for 14 ones.

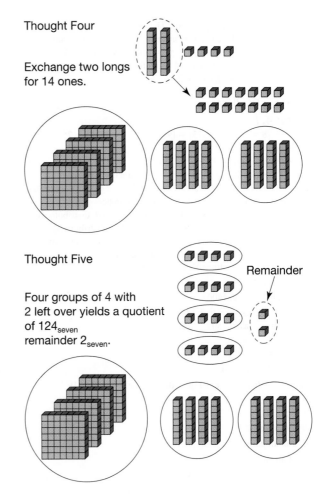

Thought Five

Four groups of 4 with 2 left over yields a quotient of 124_{seven} remainder 2_{seven}.

Remainder

19. Six

20. Steve has $2, Tricia has $23, Bill has $40, Jane has $50.

21. 39,037,066,084

22. 125

23. The only digits in base four are 0, 1, 2, 3. In any number base, the number of digits possible is equal to the number used as the base. Since 0 is always the first digit, the last digit that can be used for any number base is one less than the number. For example, in base ten (our number base) there are ten different digits and the greatest is 9, which is one less than ten.

24. To subtract 4 from 1, you need to regroup from the fives place. That makes the 1 an 11_6, and when you subtract 4, the answer is 2. To subtract the 3 from the 1 (which was previously a 2) in the fives place, you need to regroup from the twenty-fives place. That makes the 1 an 11_6, and when you subtract 3 the answer is 3. In the twenty-fives place you subtract 2 from 3 (which was previously a 4) and the answer is 1. So the final answer is 132_{five}.

PROBLEMS WHERE THE STRATEGY "USE INDIRECT REASONING" IS USEFUL

1. Assume that x can be even. Then $x^2 + 2x + 1$ is odd. Therefore, x cannot be even.

2. Suppose that n is odd. Then n^4 is odd; therefore, n cannot be odd.

3. Assume that both x and y are odd. Then $x = 2m + 1$ and $y = 2n + 1$ for whole numbers m and n. Thus $x^2 = 4m^2 + 4m + 1$ and $y^2 = 4n^2 + 4n + 1$, or $x^2 + y^2 = 4(m^2 + n^2 + m + n) + 2$, which has a factor of 2 but not 4. Therefore, it cannot be a square, since it only has one factor of 2.

CHAPTER REVIEW
Section 4.1
1. **a.** $97 + 78 = 97 + (3 + 75) = (97 + 3) + 75 = 100 + 75 = 175$; associativity
   b. $267 \div 3 = (270 - 3) \div 3 = (270 \div 3) - (3 \div 3) = 90 - 1 = 89$; right distributivitity of division over subtraction
   c. $(16 \times 7) \times 25 = 25 \times (16 \times 7) = (25 \times 16) \times 7 = 400 \times 7 = 2800$; commutativity, associativity, compatible numbers
   d. $16 \times 9 - 6 \times 9 = (16 - 6) \times 9 = 10 \times 9 = 90$; distributivity
   e. $92 \times 15 = 92(10 + 5) = 920 + 460 = 1380$; distributivity
   f. $17 \times 99 = 17(100 - 1) = 1700 - 17 = 1683$; distributivity
   g. $720 \div 5 = 1440 \div 10 = 144$; compensaton
   h. $81 - 39 = 82 - 40 = 42$; compensation
2. **a.** $400 < 157 + 371 < 600$
   b. 720,000   **c.** 1400
   d. $25 \times 56 = 5600 \div 4 = 1400$
3. **a.** 47,900   **b.** 4750   **c.** 570
4. **a.** Not necessary
   b. $7 \times (5 - 2) + 3$
   c. $15 + 48 \div (3 \times 4)$
5. **a.** 11   **b.** 6   **c.** 10   **d.** 8   **e.** 10   **f.** 19

Section 4.2
1. 982 in all parts
2. 172 in all parts
3. 3096 in all parts
4. 9 R 10 in all parts

Section 4.3
1. 1111_{six} in all parts
2. 136_{seven} in all parts
3. 1332_{four} in all parts
4. 2_{five} R 31_{five} in all parts

Chapter 4 Test
1. **a.** F   **b.** F   **c.** F   **d.** F
2. **a.** One possibility is
```
   376
 +594
   10
  160
  800
  970
```
   b. One possibility is
```
   56
  ×73
   18
  150
  420
 3500
 4088
```
3. **a.**

```
   5   6   8
   4   9   3
  0/1 1/ 1/
  /9 /5 /1
 1   0   6   1
```

b.

```
     1   9   6
  0/2 1/ 
  /3 7/ 8/ 3
 7 0/6 4/ 
  /7 3/ 2/ 7
   2   5   2
```

4. **a.** $54 + 93 + 16 + 47 = 54 + 16 + 93 + 47 = 70 + 140 = 210$
   b. $9225 - 2000 = 7225$
   c. $3497 - 1362 = 2135$
   d. $25 \times 52 = \frac{100}{4} \times 52 = 100 \times \frac{52}{4} = 1300$
5. 234 R 8
6. **a.** (i) 2500, (ii) 2500 to 2900, (iii) 2660, (iv) 2600
   b. (i) 350,000, (ii) 350,000 to 480,000, (iii) 420,000, (iv) 420,000
7. $32 \times 21 = (30 + 2)(20 + 1)$
   $= (30 + 2)20 + (30 + 2)1$
   $= 30 \cdot 20 + 2 \cdot 20 + 30 \cdot 1 + 2 \cdot 1$
   $= 600 + 40 + 30 + 2$
   $= 672$
8. Since we are finding 321×20, not simply 321×2
9. Commutativity and associativity
10.

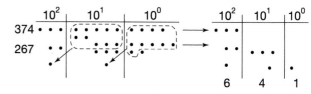

11. Answers may vary
```
       168 R 37
         8
        60
       100
    43)7261
      -4300
       2961
      -2580
        381
       -344
         37
```
12. Thought One

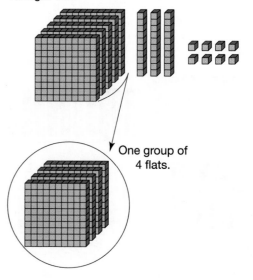

One group of 4 flats.

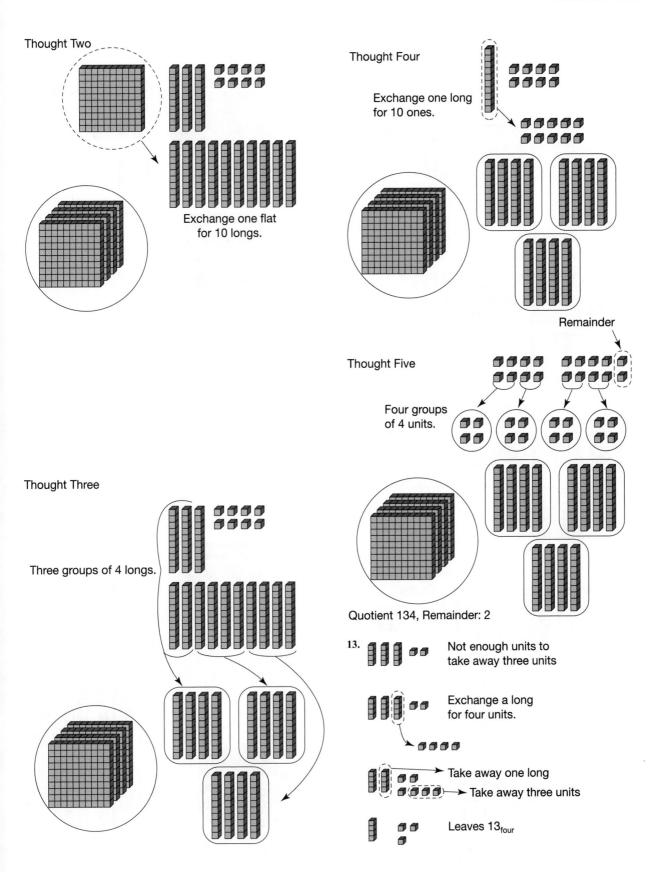

Thought Two

Exchange one flat for 10 longs.

Thought Three

Three groups of 4 longs.

Thought Four

Exchange one long for 10 ones.

Remainder

Thought Five

Four groups of 4 units.

Quotient 134, Remainder: 2

13. Not enough units to take away three units

Exchange a long for four units.

Take away one long
Take away three units

Leaves 13_{four}

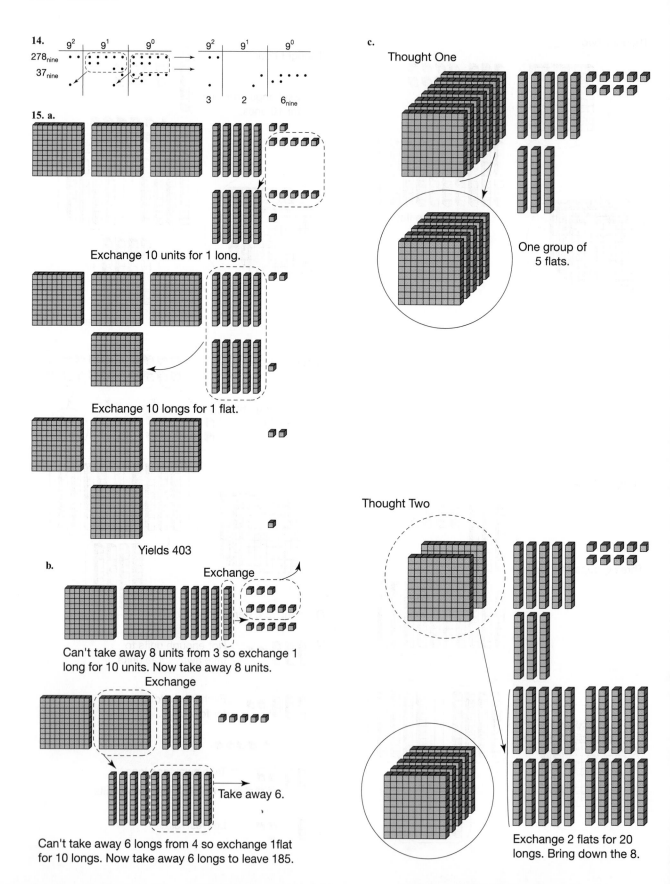

14.

278_{nine}
37_{nine}
3 2 6_{nine}

15. a.

Exchange 10 units for 1 long.

Exchange 10 longs for 1 flat.

Yields 403

b.

Exchange

Can't take away 8 units from 3 so exchange 1 long for 10 units. Now take away 8 units.

Exchange

Take away 6.

Can't take away 6 longs from 4 so exchange 1 flat for 10 longs. Now take away 6 longs to leave 185.

c.

Thought One

One group of 5 flats.

Thought Two

Exchange 2 flats for 20 longs. Bring down the 8.

Thought Three

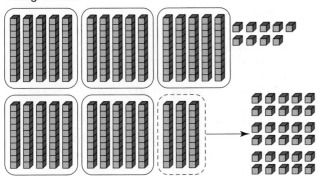

Five groups of 5 longs.

Exchange 3 longs for 30 units. Bring down the 9.

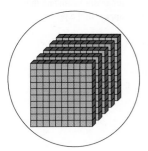

Thought Four

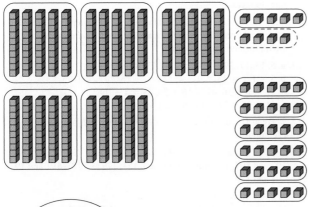

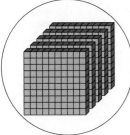

Seven groups of 5 units with 4 remaining yields a quotient of 157 and remainder of 4.

16.

Intermediate	Standard
492	2
× 37	6 1
14	492
630	× 37
2800	3444
60	14760
2700	18204
12000	
18204	

In both cases the ones (7) in the number 37 is multiplied by each of the ones, tens, and hundreds of 492. Similarly the tens (3) of 37 is multiplied by each of the ones, tens, and hundreds of 492.

17. The advantage of the standard algorithm is that it is short. The disadvantage is that because of its brevity, it loses some meaning. The advantage of the lattice is that all of the multiplication is done first and then all of the addition, which eliminates some confusion. The disadvantage is its length.

18. The subtract-from-the base algorithm appears to be more natural for young students. The only disadvantage is its lack of use because of the tradition of the standard algorithm.

19.

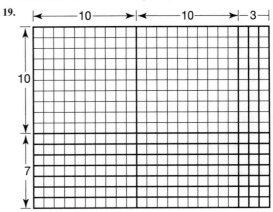

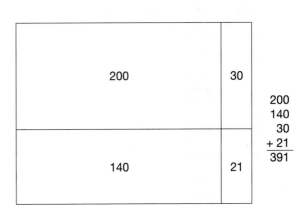

20. H = 2, E = 5, S = 6

21. $a = 7$, $b = 5$, $c = 9$; 62,015

22. A = 5, B = 6; A = 4, B = 7; A = 3, B = 8; A = 2, B = 9. The roles of A and B can be reversed. In all cases C = 1, D = 2.

Section 5.1A

1. 2, 3, 5, 7, 11, 13, 17, 19, 23, 29, 31, 37, 41, 43, 47, 53, 59, 61, 67, 71, 73, 79, 83, 89, 97

2. a.
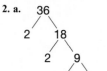
b.

c.

d.
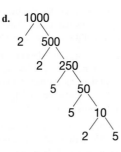

3. a. $2^3 \times 3^3$
  b. $2^2 \times 3 \times 5 \times 7^2$
  c. $3 \times 5^2 \times 11$
  d. $2 \times 3^2 \times 7 \times 11^2 \times 13$

4. a. T, ● ● ●
            ● ● ●
            ● ● ●
  b. F, There is no whole number x such that $12x = 6$.
  c. T, ● ● ● ● ● ● ●
            ● ● ● ● ● ● ●
            ● ● ● ● ● ● ●
  d. F, There is no whole number x such that $6x = 3$.
  e. T, ● ● ● ●
            ● ● ● ●
            ● ● ● ●
            ● ● ● ●
  f. F, There is no whole number x such that $0x = 5$.
  g. T, ●
            ●
            ●
            ●
            ●
            ●
            ●
            ●
            ●   **h.** T, ● ● ●
                        ● ● ●
                        ● ● ●
                        ● ● ●
                        ● ● ●
                        ● ● ●
                        ● ● ●
                        ● ● ●
                        ● ● ●
                        ● ● ●
                        ● ● ●
                        ● ● ●
                        ● ● ●

5. 1, 3, and 7

6. a. $4 \nmid 5$ and $4 \nmid 3$, but $4 \mid (5 + 3)$ **b.** T

7. a. $8 \mid 152$, since $8 \times 19 = 152$
  b. $x = 15{,}394$ by long division
  c. Yes. $15{,}394 \times 8 = 123{,}152$

8. a. 4 only   **b.** 3, 4

9. a. and c.

10. a. Yes   **b.** No   **c.** Yes

11. a. T, 3 is a factor of 9
  b. T, 3 and 11 are different prime factors of 33

12. a. F; $3 \nmid 80$ **b.** F; $3 \nmid 10{,}000$
  c. T; $4 \mid 00$ **d.** T; $4 \mid 32{,}304$ and $3 \mid 32{,}304$

13. a. $2 \mid 12$ **b.** $3 \mid 123$
  c. $2 \mid 1234$ **d.** $5 \mid 12{,}345$

14. 2, 3, 5, 7, 11, 13, 17, 19. No others need to be checked.

15. a. $2^2 \times 3^2$ **b.** 1, 2, 3, 4, 6, 9, 12, 18, 36
  c. $4 = 2^2, 6 = 2 \times 3, 9 = 3^2, 12 = 2^2 \times 3, 18 = 2 \times 3^2,$
        $36 = 2^2 \times 3^2$
  d. The divisors of 36 have the same prime factors as 36, and they appear at most as many times as they appear in the prime factorization of 36.
  e. It has at most two 13s and five 29s and has no other prime factors.

16. For 5, $5 \mid 10(a \cdot 10 + b)$ or $5 \mid (a \cdot 10^2 + b \cdot 10)$; therefore, if $5 \mid c$, then $5 \mid (a \cdot 10^2 + b \cdot 10 + c)$. Similar for 10.

17. (a), (b), (d), and (e)

18. a. Yes   **b.** No
  c. Composite numbers greater than 4

19. 333,333,331 has a factor of 17.

20. $p(0) = 17, p(1) = 19, p(2) = 23, p(3) = 29$:
    $p(16) = 16^2 + 16 + 17 = 16(17) + 17$ is not prime.

21. a. They are all primes.
  b. The diagonal is made up of the numbers from the formula $n^2 + n + 41$.

22. The numbers with an even number of ones have 11 as a factor. Also, numbers that have a multiple-of-three number of ones (e.g., 111) have 3 as a factor. That leaves the numbers with 5, 7, 11, 13, and 17 ones to factor.

23. Only $7(= 5 + 2)$. For the rest, since one of the two primes would have to be even, 2 is the only candidate, but the other summand would then be a multiple of 5.

24. a. 5, 13, 17, 29, 37, 41, 53, 61, 73, 89, and 97.
  b. $5 = 1 + 4, 13 = 9 + 4, 17 = 1 + 16, 29 = 4 + 25,$
        $37 = 1 + 36, 41 = 16 + 25, 53 = 4 + 49,$
        $61 = 25 + 36, 73 = 9 + 64, 89 = 25 + 64, 97 = 16 + 81$

25. There are no other pairs, since every even number besides 2 is composite.

26. 3 and 5, 17 and 19, 41 and 43, 59 and 61, 71 and 73, 101 and 103, 107 and 109, 137 and 139, 149 and 151, 179 and 181, 191 and 193, 197 and 199

27. a. Many correct answers are possible.
  b. Let n be an odd whole number greater than 6. Take prime p (not 2) less then n. $n - p$ is an even number that is a sum of primes a and b. Then $n = a + b + p$.

28. Yes

29. 34,227 and 36,070

30. a. 6, Each has a factor of 2 and 3.
  b. 3, The only common factor is 3.

31. 2520

32. $2^2 \times 3 \times 5 = 60$

33. 3. Proof: $n + (n + 1) + (n + 2) = 3n + 3 = 3(n + 1)$

34. Use a variable; the numbers $a, b, a + b, a + 2b, 2a + 3b, 3a + 5b,$ $5a + 8b, 8a + 13b, 13a + 21b, 21a + 34b$ have a sum of $55a + 88b$, which is $11(5a + 8b)$, or 11 times the seventh number.

35. **a.** Use distributivity.
    b. $1001! + 2, 1001! + 3, \ldots, 1001! + 1001$

36. $\$3.52 - \$2.91 = \$.61 = 61¢$ is not a multiple of 3.

37. 504. Since the number is a multiple of 7, 8, and 9, the only three-digit multiple is $7 \cdot 8 \cdot 9$.

38. 61

39. $abcabc = abc(1001) = abc(7 \cdot 11 \cdot 13)$, 7 and 11

40. **a.** Apply the test for divisibility by 11 to any four-digit palindrome.
    b. A similar proof applies to every palindrome with an even number of digits.

41. 151 and 251

42. Conjecture: If $7 \mid abcd$, then $7 \mid bcd,00a$.
    Proof: Using expanded form, we know:
    $$bcd,00a + abcd = (100,000b + 10,000c + 1000d + a) +$$
    $$(1000a + 100b + 10c + d)$$
    $$= 100,100b + 10,010c + 1001d + 1001a$$
    $$= 7(14,300b + 1430c + 143d + 143a)$$
    Thus, $7 \mid (bcd,00a + abcd)$. Since $7 \mid abcd$, we know $7 \mid bcd,00a$.

43. $289 = 17^2$ is the first non-prime.

44. $11 \mid [a(1001) + b(99) + c(11) - a + b - c + d]$ if and only if $11 \mid (-a + b - c + d)$. Therefore, we only need to check the $-a + b - c + d$ part.

45. $11 \times 101,010,101 = 1,111,111,111$
    $13 \times 8,547,008,547 = 111,111,111,111$
    $17 \times 65,359,477,124,183 = 1,111,111,111,111,111,111$

46. **a.** $n = 10$ **b.** $n = 15$ **c.** $n = 10$

47. $n = 16; p(17) = 323 = 17 \cdot 19$, composite, $p(18) = 359$, prime

Section 5.2A

1. **a.** 6 **b.** 12 **c.** 60

2. **a.** $2 \cdot 2 \cdot 3 \cdot 3$
   b. $1, 2, 3, 4 = 2 \cdot 2, 6 = 2 \cdot 3, 9 = 3 \cdot 3, 12 = 2 \cdot 2 \cdot 3,$ $18 = 2 \cdot 3 \cdot 3, 36 = 2 \cdot 2 \cdot 3 \cdot 3$
   c. Every prime factor of a divisor of 36 is a prime factor of 36.
   d. It contains only factors of 7^4 or 17^2.
   e. 15; $1, 7, 7^2, 7^3, 7^4, 17, 7 \cdot 17, 7^2 \cdot 17, 7^3 \cdot 17, 7^4 \cdot 17, 17^2, 7 \cdot 17^2,$ $7^2 \cdot 17^2, 7^3 \cdot 17^2, 7^4 \cdot 17^2$

3. **a.** 6 **b.** 14 **c.** 12

4. **a.** 2 **b.** 6 **c.** 6

5. **a.** 6 **b.** 121 **c.** 3 **d.** 2

6. **a.** 6 **b.** 13 **c.** 8 **d.** 37

7. **a.** 17 **b.** 15 **c.** 7 **d.** 39

8. **a.**

9. **a.** 120 **b.** 84 **c.** 84

10. **a.** 24 **b.** 20 **c.** 63 **d.** 40

11. **a.** 360 **b.** 770 **c.** 135

12. **a.** 6 **b.** 5 **c.** 13 **d.** 1
    e. $3^3 \cdot 5^3 \cdot 11^5$ **f.** $2^2 \cdot 3^4 \cdot 13$

13. **a.** $2 \cdot 3 \cdot 5$ **b.** $2^3 \cdot 3^2$ **c.** $2^4 \cdot 3^{11} \cdot 5^6 \cdot 11^9 \cdot 13$
    d. $2^3 \cdot 3^7 \cdot 7 \cdot 11^7 \cdot 13^2$

14. **a.**
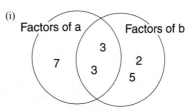
```
2 | 21  24  63  70
2 | 21  12  63  35
2 | 21   6  63  35
3 | 21   3  63  35
3 |  7   1  21  35
5 |  7   1   7  35
7 |  7   1   7   7
     1   1   1   1
   2³·3²·5·7
```
b.
```
 2 | 20  36  42  33
 2 | 10  18  21  33
 3 |  5   9  21  33
 3 |  5   3   7  11
 5 |  5   1   7  11
 7 |  1   1   7  11
11 |  1   1   1  11
      1   1   1   1
   2²·3²·5·7·11
```
c.
```
2 | 15  35  42  80
2 | 15  35  21  40
2 | 15  35  21  20
2 | 15  35  21  10
3 | 15  35  21   5
5 |  5  35   7   5
7 |  1   7   7   1
     1   1   1   1
   2⁴·3·5·7
```

15. **a.** 13, 354, 273 **b.** $2^3 \cdot 3^6 \cdot 7^5 \cdot 11^5 \cdot 2^3 \cdot 3^{10} \cdot 7^8 \cdot 11^5, 3^4 \cdot 7^3$

16. **a.**
(i)
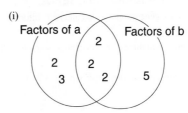
Factors of a: 7, 3; (intersection) 3; Factors of b: 2, 5
(ii) GCF (63, 90) = $3 \cdot 3$
LCM (63, 90) = $2 \cdot 3 \cdot 3 \cdot 5 \cdot 7$

b.
(i)
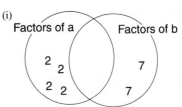
Factors of a: 2, 2, 3; (intersection) 2, 2; Factors of b: 5
(ii) GCF (48, 40) = $2 \cdot 2 \cdot 2$
LCM (48, 40) = $2 \cdot 2 \cdot 2 \cdot 2 \cdot 3 \cdot 5$

c.
(i)
Factors of a: 2, 2, 2, 2; Factors of b: 7, 7
(ii) GCF (16, 49) = 1
LCM (16, 49) = $2 \cdot 2 \cdot 2 \cdot 2 \cdot 7 \cdot 7$

17. LCM, (12, 18)

18. **a.** All except 6, 12, 18, 20, 24 **b.** 12, 18, 20, 24 **c.** 6

19. **a.** amicable **b.** not amicable **c.** amicable

20. All

21. **a.** $a = 2 \times 3^3$ **b.** $a = 2^2 \times 7^3 \times 11^2$

22. **a.** 1 **b.** $2^1 = 2$ **c.** $2^2 = 4$
    d. $2^1 \times 3^1 = 6$ **e.** $2^4 = 16$ **f.** $2^2 \times 3 = 12$
    g. $2^6 = 64$ **h.** $2^3 \times 3 = 24$

23. **a.** 2, 3, 5, 7, 11, 13; primes
    b. 4, 9, 25, 49, 121, 169; primes squared
    c. 6, 10, 14, 15, 21, 22; the product of two primes, or 8, 27, 125 or any prime to the third power
    d. $2^4, 3^4, 5^4, 7^4, 11^4, 13^4$; a prime to the fourth power

24. 6, 28, 496, 8128

25. 1, 5, 7, 11, 13, 17, 19, 23

26. 16 candy bars

27. Chickens, \$2; ducks, \$4; and geese, \$5

28. None, since each has only one factor of 5

29. 773

30. a. 11, 101, 1111　　**b.** 1111

31. 41, 7, 11, 73, 67, 17, 13

32. 31

33. $343 = 7 \cdot 49$. Let $a + b = 7$. Then $7 \mid (10a + 10b)$. But $7 \mid 91$, so $7 \mid 91a$. Then $7 \mid (10a + 10b + 91a)$ or $7 \mid (100a + 10b + a)$.

34. GCF(54, 27) = 27, LCM(54, 27) = LCM(54, 18) = LCM(18, 27) = 54

35. a. Fill 8, pour 8 into 12, fill 8, pour 8 into 12, leaves 4 ounces in the 8 ounce container.
　　b. Fill 11, pour 11 into 7, empty 7, pour 4 into 7, fill 11, pour 11 into 7, leaves 8 ounces in 11 ounce container, empty 7, pour 8 into 7, leave 1 ounce in 11 ounce container.

PROBLEMS WHERE THE STRATEGY "USE PROPERTIES OF NUMBERS" IS USEFUL

1. Mary is 71 unless each generation married and had children very young.

2. Four folding machines and three stamp machines, since the LCM of 45 and 60 is 180

3. Let p and q be any two primes. Then $p^6 q^{12}$ will have $7 \cdot 13 = 91$ factors.

CHAPTER REVIEW
Section 5.1
1. $17 \times 13 \times 11 \times 7$

2. 90, 91, 92, 93, 94, 95, 96, 98, 99, 100

3. a. F　　**b.** F　　**c.** T　　**d.** F　　**e.** T　　**f.** T
　　g. T　　**h.** T

4. All are factors.

5. Check to see whether the last two digits are 00, 25, 50, or 75.

Section 5.2
1. 24

2. 36

3. 27

4. 432

5. Multiply each prime by 2.

6. $81 \times 135 = $ GCF(81, 135) $\times$ LCM(81, 135)

Chapter 5 Test
1. a. F　　**b.** T　　**c.** T　　**d.** F　　**e.** T　　**f.** T
　　g. T　　**h.** F　　**i.** F　　**j.** T

2. a. Three can be divided into 6 evenly.
　　b. Six divided by 3 is 2.
　　c. The statement 3 divides 6 is true. (Answers may vary)

3. a. $2^3 \cdot 5 \cdot 3$　　**b.** $2^4 \cdot 5^2 \cdot 3^3$　　**c.** $3^2 \cdot 7 \cdot 13$

4. a. 2, 4, 8, 11　　**b.** 2, 3, 5, 6, 10　　**c.** 2, 3, 4, 5, 6, 8, 9, 10

5. a. 24　　**b.** 16　　**c.** 27

6. a. $2^3 \cdot 3$; $2^4 \cdot 3^2 \cdot 5$　　**b.** 7; $2 \cdot 3 \cdot 5 \cdot 7^2$　　**c.** $2^3 \cdot 3^4 \cdot 5^3$; $2^7 \cdot 3^5 \cdot 5^7$
　　d. 41; 128,207　　**e.** 1; 6300

7.

$$\begin{array}{r} 6 \text{ R } 123 \\ 1025 \overline{)6273} \end{array}$$

$$\begin{array}{r} 8 \text{ R } 41 \\ 123 \overline{)1025} \end{array}$$

$$\begin{array}{r} 3 \text{ R } 0 \\ 41 \overline{)123} \end{array}$$

GCF(1025, 6273) = 41

8. LCM(18, 24) = 72

9. All the crossed-out numbers greater than 1 are composite.

10. No, because if two numbers are equal, they must have the same prime factorization.

11. $x + (x + 1) + (x + 2) + (x + 3) = 4x + 6 = 2(2x + 3)$

12. a. $4 \mid 36$ and $6 \mid 36$ but $24 \nmid 36$.
　　b. If $2 \mid m$ and $9 \mid m$ then $18 \mid m$.

13. LCM$(a, b) = (a \cdot b)/$GCD$(a, b) = 270/3 = 90$.

14.

　　$4 \mid 8$　　$3 \nmid 8$

15. $n = m$ because they have the same prime factorization; Fundamental Theorem of Arithmetic

16. $2^3 \cdot 3^2 \cdot 5 \cdot 7 = 2520$

17. If two other prime numbers differ by 3, one is odd and one is even. The even one must have a factor of 2.

18. a. $2^3 \cdot 5$　　**b.** $2^3 \cdot 3^3 \cdot 5$

19. 24, 25, 26, 27, 28; or 32, 33, 34, 35, 36

20. 1, 4, 9, 16; They are perfect squares.

21. $n = 11$

22. $a = 15, b = 180$; and $a = 45, b = 60$

23. 36

Section 6.1A
1. a. $\frac{1}{3}$　　**b.** $\frac{3}{7}$　　**c.** $\frac{7}{10}$　　**d.** $\frac{4}{6}$ or $\frac{2}{3}$

2. a. (i)　　　　　　(ii)

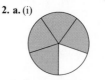

　　b. (i)　　　　　　(ii)

　　c. (i)　　　　　　(ii)

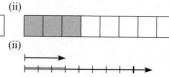

　　d. (i)　　　　　　(ii)

3. a. 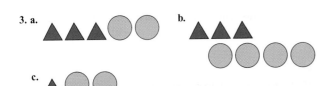   **b.**

c.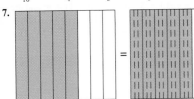

4. No. The regions are not the same size.

5. a. $\frac{15}{45}$ or $\frac{1}{3}$ **b.** $\frac{26}{45}$ **c.** $\frac{41}{45}$

6. a. $\frac{1}{10}$ **b.** $\frac{1}{4}$ **c.** $\frac{1}{3}$ **d.** $\frac{1}{3}$

7.

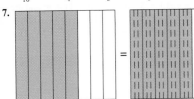

The computer allows you to change the number of dividing lines of the area. Do this until the new dividing lines match up with the old ones so that either each original piece is cut into more pieces or the same number of original pieces are combined into newer equal-sized larger pieces.

8. (a), (b), and (d)

9 a. Not equal   **b.** Not equal   **c.** Equal   **d.** Equal

10. a. $\frac{3}{4}$ **b.** $\frac{7}{8}$ **c.** $\frac{9}{13}$ **d.** $\frac{11}{5}$

11. a. $5\frac{15}{32}$ **b.** $2\frac{185}{216}$

12. a.(i) $\frac{11}{17} < \frac{12}{17} < \frac{13}{17}$ (ii) $\frac{1}{7} < \frac{1}{6} < \frac{1}{5}$
   b. Increasing numerators, decreasing denominators

13. a. $\frac{3}{7} < \frac{9}{20} < \frac{14}{27}$ **b.** $\frac{17}{39} < \frac{6}{13} < \frac{25}{51}$

14. Based on a few examples, it appears as if $\frac{a+c}{b+d}$ is always between $\frac{a}{b}$ and $\frac{c}{d}$.

15. a. $\frac{17}{23} < \frac{51}{68}, \frac{68}{91}$ **b.** $\frac{50}{687} < \frac{43}{567}, \frac{93}{1254}$
   c. $\frac{597}{2511} < \frac{214}{897}, \frac{811}{3408}$ **d.** $\frac{93}{2811} < \frac{3}{87}, \frac{96}{2898}$

16. a. $\frac{58}{113}, \frac{51}{100}$ **b.** $\frac{30}{113}, \frac{27}{100}$ **c.** $\frac{14}{113}, \frac{12}{100}$

17. a. The fractions are decreasing.
   b. The fraction may be more than 1.

18. 2003

19. a.   **b.**

c.   **d.**

e.   **f.**

20. Yes, since $\frac{288 \cdots 86}{588 \cdots 83} = \frac{26 \cdot 11 \cdots 1}{53 \cdot 11 \cdots 1} = \frac{26}{53}$.

21. $\frac{1}{8}$

22. a. False. Explanations will vary.
   b. False. Explanations will vary.
   c. True. Explanations will vary.
   d. True. Explanations will vary.

23. Both $12 \div 2$ and $18 \div 3$ are the GCF(12, 18)
   a. 24   **b.** 26

24. Only (c) is correct. Explanations will vary.

25. 15

26. 562,389

27. 41

28. 2200

29. 15

30. a. 50, 500, etc.
   b. 25, 250, etc.
   c. 4, 40, 400, etc.
   d. 75, 750, etc.

31. There are infinitely many such fractions. Two are $\frac{15}{28}$ and $\frac{31}{56}$.

Section 6.2A

1. a.

$\frac{2}{5}$ $\frac{1}{3}$ $\frac{11}{15}$

b.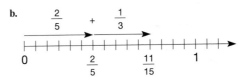

2. $\frac{5}{9} + \frac{7}{12} = \frac{20}{36} + \frac{21}{36} = \frac{41}{36}$

$\frac{5}{9} + \frac{7}{12} = \frac{40}{72} + \frac{42}{72} = \frac{82}{72}$

$\frac{5}{9} + \frac{7}{12} = \frac{60}{108} + \frac{63}{108} = \frac{123}{108}$

$\frac{5}{9} + \frac{7}{12} = \frac{80}{144} + \frac{84}{144} = \frac{164}{144}$

Other correct answers are possible.

3. a. + = $= \frac{5}{6}$

b.  + = $= \frac{5}{8}$

c. + = + $= 1\frac{5}{12}$

4. a. 3/4
 b. 3/4
 c. 16/21
 d. 167/144
 e. 460/663
 f. 277/242
 g. 617/1000
 h. 9/10
 i. 15,059/100,000

5. a. $\frac{23}{6}$ **b.** $\frac{23}{8}$ **c.** $\frac{26}{5}$ **d.** $\frac{64}{9}$

6. a. $3\frac{11}{12}, 1\frac{5}{12}$ **b.** $13\frac{8}{21}, 2\frac{1}{21}$ **c.** $38\frac{1}{12}, 6\frac{1}{4}$

7. a. $\frac{59}{56} = 1\frac{3}{56}$ **b.** $\frac{47}{40} = 1\frac{7}{40}$

8. a. 29/20 or $1\frac{9}{20}$ **b.** $\frac{70}{48} = 1\frac{11}{24}$

9. a.

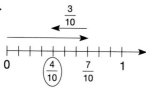

b.

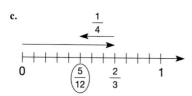

c.

$\frac{1}{4}$

0   $\left(\frac{5}{12}\right)$ $\frac{2}{3}$ 1

10. a. 4/11 **b.** 13/63 **c.** 1/20
 d. 23/54 **e.** 154/663 **f.** 11/1000

11. a. $1\frac{5}{12}$ **b.** $2\frac{1}{21}$ **c.** $6\frac{1}{4}$

12. a. $\frac{93}{40} = 2\frac{13}{40}$ **b.** $\frac{1}{35}$

13. a. $\frac{27}{90} = \frac{3}{10}$ **b.** $\frac{8}{45}$

14. a. $\frac{3}{7} + \frac{2}{7} = \frac{5}{7}$ **b.** $\frac{1}{3} + \frac{1}{6} = \frac{1}{2}$

15. a. $1\frac{1}{9}$ **b.** $2\frac{5}{6}$ **c.** $10\frac{1}{5}$

16. a. $8\frac{3}{7} - 3 = 5\frac{3}{7}$ **b.** $9\frac{4}{8} - 3 = 6\frac{1}{2}$
 c. $11\frac{5}{7} - 7 = 4\frac{5}{7}$ **d.** $8\frac{2}{6} - 4 = 4\frac{1}{3}$

17. a. (i) 13 to 15, (ii) 14 **b.** (i) 2 to 4, (ii) 2
 c. (i) 15 to 18, (ii) 16

18. a. $10 + 3\frac{1}{2} = 13\frac{1}{2}$ **b.** $9\frac{1}{2} - 5\frac{1}{2} = 4$
 c. $7 + 5 + 2\frac{1}{2} = 14\frac{1}{2}$

19. 15 **20.** $\frac{5}{12}$

21. Let t = years of lifetime, t = 72 years

22. $\frac{7}{12}$

23. $\frac{13}{30}$

24. $\frac{1}{36}$

25. When borrowing 1, he does not think of it as $\frac{5}{5}$. Have him use blocks (i.e., base five pieces could be used with long = 1).

26. a. 1 **b.** 1 **c.** Yes; only perfect numbers

27. Yes. $\dfrac{1 + 3 + 5 + 7 + 9}{11 + 13 + 15 + 17 + 19}$, $\dfrac{1 + 3 + 5 + 7 + 9 + 11}{13 + 15 + 17 + 19 + 21 + 23}$.
In general, the numerator is $1 + 3 + \cdots + (2n - 1) = n^2$ and the denominator is $[1 + 3 + \cdots + (2m - 1)] - [1 + 3 + \cdots + (2n - 1)]$, where $m = 2n$. This difference is $m^2 - n^2 = 4n^2 - n^2 = 3n^2$. Thus the fraction is always $n^2/3n^2 = \frac{1}{3}$.

28. $1 - \dfrac{1}{2^{100}} = \dfrac{2^{100} - 1}{2^{100}}$

29. a. $\frac{3}{6}$ **b.** 18 **c.** 56 **d.** $\frac{18}{56}$
 e. No, $\frac{3}{10} \oplus \frac{1}{2} = \frac{4}{12} = \frac{1}{3} \neq \frac{9}{26} = \frac{6}{20} \oplus \frac{3}{6}$

30. The sum is 1.

31. a. $\frac{1}{5} = \frac{1}{6} + \frac{1}{30}$ **b.** $\frac{1}{7} = \frac{1}{8} + \frac{1}{56}$ **c.** $\frac{1}{17} = \frac{1}{18} + \frac{1}{306}$

32. 28 matches

33. 1299 0s are necessary. 300 9s are necessary.

Section 6.3A

1. $\frac{1}{3} \times 5$:

$5 \times \frac{1}{3}$:

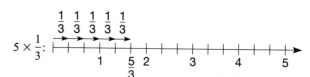

2. a. $\frac{2}{5}$ **b.** $\frac{5}{6}$

c. $\frac{3}{10}$

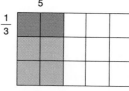

3. a. $\frac{3}{5} \times \frac{3}{4} = \frac{9}{20}$ **b.** $\frac{4}{7} \times \frac{1}{6} = \frac{4}{42} = \frac{2}{21}$

4. a. $\frac{21}{11}$ **b.** $\frac{1}{3}$ **c.** $\frac{9}{121}$ **d.** $\frac{1}{108}$

5. a. $<$ **b.** $\frac{4}{3} > \frac{2}{3}$ **c.** Order is reversed

6. a. Associativity and commutativity for fraction multiplication
   b. Distributivity for multiplication over addition
   c. Associativity for fraction multiplication

7. a. $\frac{3}{14}$ **b.** $\frac{1}{5}$ **c.** $\frac{2}{5}$ **d.** $\frac{15}{26}$ **e.** $\frac{6}{49}$
   f. $\frac{40}{189}$ **g.** $\frac{49}{50}$ **h.** $\frac{5}{18}$

8. a. $\frac{14}{15}$ **b.** $\frac{14}{5}$ or $2\frac{4}{5}$

9. a. $11\frac{5}{9}$ **b.** $\frac{341}{32} = 10\frac{21}{32}$ **c.** 9

10. a. No   **b.** No

11. a. $4 \div \frac{1}{3} = 12.$

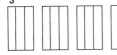

b. $2\frac{1}{2} \div \frac{1}{4} = 10.$

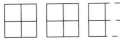

c. $3 \div \frac{3}{4} = 4.$

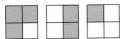

12. a.

 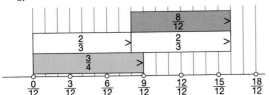

b.

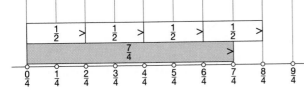

c.

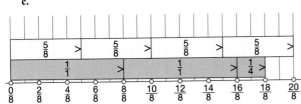

13. a. 5   **b.** $\frac{4}{3}$ **c.** $\frac{33}{39}$ or $\frac{11}{13}$

14. a. $\frac{5}{4}$ **b.** 1   **c.** $\frac{13}{7}$ **d.** $\frac{1}{2}$

15. a. $\frac{21}{10}$ **b.** $\frac{91}{18}$ **c.** $\frac{10}{13}$

16. a. $1\frac{17}{28}$ **b.** $1\frac{1}{2}$ **c.** $1\frac{2}{3}$ **d.** $\frac{3}{4}$

17. a. $\frac{49}{121}$ **b.** $\frac{17}{24}$ **c.** $\frac{1}{6}$

18. a. $\frac{9}{20}$ **b.** $\frac{14}{5} = 2\frac{4}{5}$

19. a. $\frac{250}{63} = 3\frac{61}{63}$ **b.** $\frac{15}{4} = 3\frac{3}{4}$ **c.** 6

20. a. $\frac{98}{117}$ **b.** $\frac{4}{9}$

21. a. $21 \times \frac{3}{7} = 9$ **b.** $35 \times \frac{3}{7} = 15$ **c.** $1 \times \frac{3}{8} = \frac{3}{8}$
   d. $3 \times 54 + \frac{5}{9} \times 54 = 162 + 30 = 192$

22. a. $30 \times 5 = 150$ **b.** $56 \div 8 = 7$
   c. $72 \div 9 = 8$ **d.** $31 \times 6 = 186$

23. a. $12 \times 12 = 144$
   b. $5^3 = 125$

24. a. 1100   **b.** 3000
   c. 12,200   **d.** 31,200

25. a. $\frac{15}{31}$ **b.** $\frac{56}{67}$ **c.** $\frac{231}{102}$ or $\frac{77}{34}$

26. a. $\frac{127}{144}$ **b.** $\frac{61}{96}$

27. 32 loads

28. Approximately 16,787,000 barrels per day

29. 432

30. a. $12\frac{4}{5}$ gallons, or nearly 13 gallons
   b. About $5\frac{1}{2}$ gallons more

31. 60 employees

32. 8:00

33. a. $2\frac{1}{2}$ cups   **b.** $\frac{5}{8}$ cup   **c.** $\frac{25}{12}$ or $2\frac{2}{12}$ cups

34. Gale, 9 games; Ruth, 5 games; Sandy, 10 games

35. a. $54,150   **b.** After 8 years

36. 1

37. a. $\frac{11}{16 * 5}$ **b.** Yes   **c.** $4\frac{11}{8} \div 2 = 2\frac{11}{16}$; $10\frac{9}{16} \div 2 = 5\frac{9}{32}$

38. Sam: $\frac{18}{12} = 1\frac{1}{2}$, addition (getting common denominator);
   Sandy: $\frac{20}{9} = 2\frac{2}{9}$, division (using reciprocal).

39. 60 apples

40. 21 years old

41. Even though the remaining part of a group is two-fifths of the whole, it is only two out of three parts needed to make another three-fifths. Thus, we have two-thirds of a group of three-fifths.

PROBLEMS WHERE THE STRATEGY "SOLVE AN EQUIVALENT PROBLEM" IS USEFUL

1. Solve by finding how many numbers are in $\{7, 14, 21, \ldots, 392\}$ or in $\{1, 2, 3, \ldots, 56\}$.

2. Rewrite 2^{30} as 8^{10} and 3^{20} as 9^{10}. Since $8 < 9$, we have $8^{10} < 9^{10}$.

3. First find eight such fractions between 0 and 1, namely $\frac{1}{9}, \frac{2}{9}, \frac{3}{9}, \ldots, \frac{8}{9}$. Then divide each of these fractions by 3: $\frac{1}{27}, \frac{2}{27}, \frac{3}{27}, \ldots, \frac{8}{27}$.

CHAPTER REVIEW
Section 6.1

1. Because $4 > 2$

2.

3. The numerator of the improper fraction is greater than the denominator. A mixed number is the sum of a whole number and a proper fraction.

4. a. $\dfrac{8}{19} < \dfrac{24}{56}$ b. Equal

5. $\dfrac{24}{56} = \dfrac{3}{7}, \dfrac{8}{19}, \dfrac{12}{28} = \dfrac{15}{35} = \dfrac{3}{7}$

6. $\dfrac{2}{5} < \dfrac{2+5}{5+12} < \dfrac{5}{12}$

Section 6.2

1. a.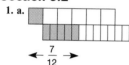

$\xleftarrow{\hspace{0.8cm}} \dfrac{7}{12} \xrightarrow{\hspace{0.8cm}}$

$\dfrac{1}{8} \nearrow$

2. a. $1\frac{14}{45}$ b. $\frac{16}{75}$

3. a. Commutative   b. Identity   c. Associative   d. Closure

4. None

5. a. $5\frac{2}{8} + \frac{1}{8} + 3\frac{7}{8} = 9\frac{1}{4}$. Compensation, associativity

   b. $31\frac{1}{8} - 5 = 26\frac{1}{8}$. Equal additions

   c. $1\frac{3}{5}$. Commutativity, associativity

6. a. 12 to 14   b. $17 + 24\frac{1}{2} = 41\frac{1}{2}$ c. 23

Section 6.3

1.

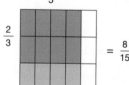

$= \dfrac{8}{15}$

2. a. $\frac{4}{15}$ b. $\frac{3}{2}$

3. a. Inverse   b. Associative   c. Identity
   d. Closure   e. Associative

4. $\dfrac{a}{b}\left(\dfrac{c}{d} + \dfrac{e}{f}\right) = \dfrac{a}{b} \times \dfrac{c}{d} + \dfrac{a}{b} \times \dfrac{e}{f};$

   $\dfrac{3}{17} \times \dfrac{4}{9} + \dfrac{14}{17} \times \dfrac{4}{9} = \left(\dfrac{3}{17} + \dfrac{14}{17}\right) \times \dfrac{4}{9} = \dfrac{4}{9}$

5. $\dfrac{12}{25} \div \dfrac{1}{5} = \dfrac{12}{25} \div \dfrac{5}{25} = \dfrac{12}{5}$

   $\dfrac{12}{25} \div \dfrac{1}{5} = \dfrac{12}{25} \times \dfrac{25}{5} = \dfrac{12}{5}$

6. None

7. a. $\left(\frac{2}{3} \times 9\right) \times 5 = 6 \times 5 = 30$. Commutativity and associativity

   b. $(25 \times 2) + \left(25 \times \frac{2}{5}\right) = 50 + 10 = 60$. Distributivity

8. a. 35 to 48   b. $3\frac{1}{2} \times 4 = 14$

Chapter 6 Test

1. a. T   b. F   c. F   d. T
   e. T   f. F   g. T   h. F

2. Number: relative amount represented
   Numeral: representing a part-to-whole relationship

3. Closure for division of nonzero elements or multiplicative inverse of nonzero elements

4. a. $\frac{2}{3}$ b. $\frac{17}{18}$ c. $\frac{2}{5}$ d. $\frac{41}{189}$

5. a. $\frac{38}{11}$ b. $5\frac{11}{16}$ c. $\frac{37}{7}$ d. $11\frac{2}{11}$

6. a. $\frac{3}{4}$ b. $\frac{7}{3}$ c. $\frac{16}{92}$

7. a. $\frac{31}{36}$ b. $\frac{11}{75}$ c. $\frac{3}{4}$ d. $\frac{64}{49}$

8. a. $\frac{5}{2} \cdot \left(\frac{3}{4} \cdot \frac{2}{5}\right) = \left(\frac{5}{2} \cdot \frac{2}{5}\right) \cdot \frac{3}{4} = \frac{3}{4}$

   b. $\frac{4}{7} \cdot \frac{3}{5} + \frac{4}{5} \cdot \frac{3}{5} = \left(\frac{4}{7} + \frac{4}{5}\right)\frac{3}{5} = \frac{48}{35} \cdot \frac{3}{5} = \frac{144}{175}$

   c. $\left(\frac{13}{17} + \frac{5}{11}\right) + \frac{4}{17} = \left(\frac{13}{17} + \frac{4}{17}\right) + \frac{5}{11} = 1\frac{5}{11}$

   d. $\frac{3}{8} \cdot \frac{5}{7} - \frac{4}{9} \cdot \frac{3}{8} = \frac{3}{8}\left(\frac{5}{7} - \frac{4}{9}\right) = \frac{3}{8} \cdot \frac{17}{63} = \frac{51}{504} = \frac{17}{168}$

9. a. $35\frac{4}{5} \div 9\frac{2}{7} \approx 36 \div 9 = 4$

   b. $3\frac{5}{8} \times 14\frac{2}{3} \approx 4 \times 15 = 60$

   c. $3\frac{4}{9} + 13\frac{1}{5} + \frac{3}{13} = (3 + 13) + \left(\frac{4}{9} + \frac{1}{5} + \frac{3}{13}\right) \approx 16 + 1 = 17$
   Answers may vary.

10. The fraction $\frac{6}{12}$ represents 6 of 12 equivalent parts (or 6 eggs), whereas $\frac{12}{24}$ represents 12 of 24 equivalent parts (or 12 halves of eggs). NOTE: This works best when the eggs are hard-boiled.

11. $\dfrac{a}{b} < \dfrac{c}{d}$ if and only if $\dfrac{ad}{bd} < \dfrac{bc}{bd}$ if and only if $ad < bc$

12. NOTE: For simplicity we will express our fractions using a common denominator.

$$\dfrac{a}{c}\left(\dfrac{b}{c} - \dfrac{d}{c}\right) = \dfrac{a}{c}\left(\dfrac{b-d}{c}\right) = \dfrac{a(b-d)}{c^2} = \dfrac{ab - ab}{c^2}$$

$$= \dfrac{ab}{c^2} - \dfrac{ad}{c^2} = \dfrac{a}{c} \cdot \dfrac{b}{c} - \dfrac{a}{c} \cdot \dfrac{d}{c}.$$

13.

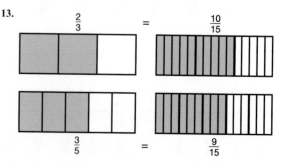

14.

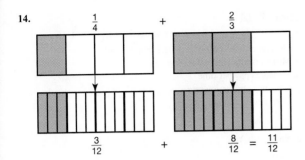

$$\frac{1}{4} + \frac{2}{3}$$

$$\frac{3}{12} + \frac{8}{12} = \frac{11}{12}$$

15.

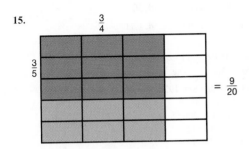

$$\frac{3}{4}$$

$$\frac{3}{5}$$

$$= \frac{9}{20}$$

16. a. Problem should include 2 groups of size $\frac{3}{4}$. How much all together?
b. Problem should include 2 wholes being broken into groups of size $\frac{1}{3}$. How may groups?
c. Problem should include $\frac{2}{5}$ of a whole being broken into 3 groups. How big is each group?

17. a.

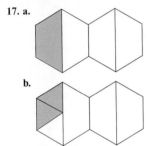

b.

18. $\dfrac{n}{n+1} < \dfrac{n+1}{n+2}$ if and only if $n(n+2) < (n+1)^2$.
However, since $n^2 + 2n < n^2 + 2n + 1$, the latter inequality is always true when $n \geq 0$.

19. 90

20. $240,000

21. $\frac{2}{5} = \frac{56}{140} < \frac{57}{140}, \frac{58}{140}, \frac{59}{140} < \frac{60}{140} = \frac{3}{7}$

22. $4 \div \frac{2}{3} = 6$

Section 7.1A

1. a. 75.603   **b.** 0.063   **c.** 306.042

2. a. (i) $4(\frac{1}{10}) + 5(\frac{1}{100})$; (ii) $\frac{45}{100}$
b. (i) $3 + 1(\frac{1}{10}) + 8(\frac{1}{100}) + 3(\frac{1}{1000})$; (ii) $\frac{3183}{1000}$
c. $2(10) + 4 + 2(\frac{1}{10}) + 5(\frac{1}{10,000})$; (ii) $\frac{242,005}{10,000}$

3. a. 746,000   **b.** 0.746   **c.** 746,000,000

4. a. Thirteen thousandths
b. Sixty-eight thousand four hundred eighty-five and five hundred thirty-two thousandths
c. Eighty-two ten thousandths
d. Eight hundred fifty-nine and eighty thousand five hundred nine millionths

5. There should be no "and." The word "and" is reserved for indicating the location of the decimal point.

6. (b), (c), (d), and (e)

7. a. R   **b.** T, 3 places   **c.** R   **d.** T, 4 places
Explanation: Highest power of 2 and/or 5

8. a. 0.085, 0.58, 0.85
b. 780.9999, 781.345, 781.354
c. 4.09, 4.099, 4.9, 4.99

9. a. $\frac{5}{9} < \frac{19}{34}$ **b.** $\frac{18}{25} < \frac{38}{52}$

10. a. $\frac{4}{5} < \frac{7}{8} < \frac{9}{10}$ **b.** $\frac{43}{40} < \frac{539}{500} < \frac{27}{25}$ **c.** $\frac{3}{5} < \frac{5}{8} < \frac{7}{9}$

11. Lucas and Amy were arrested and Juan was let go.

12. a. $18.47 - 10 = 8.47$; equal additions
b. $1.3 \times 70 = 91$; commutativity and distributivity
c. $7 + 5.8 = 12.8$; commutativity and associativity
d. $17 \times 2 = 34$; associativity and commutativity
e. 0.05124; powers of ten   **f.** 39.07, left to right
g. $72 + 4 = 76$; distributivity
h. 15,000; powers of ten

13. a. $\frac{1}{4} \times 44 = 11$ **b.** $\frac{3}{4} \times 80 = 60$
c. $35 \times \frac{2}{5} = 14$ **d.** $\frac{1}{5} \times 65 = 13$
e. $65 \times \frac{4}{5} = 52$ **f.** $380 \times \frac{1}{20} = 19$

14. a. 6,750,000   **b.** 0.00019514
c. 296 followed by 26 zeros   **d.** 29,600

15. a. 16 to 19; $5 + 6 + 7 = 18$
b. 420 to 560; $75 \times 6 = 450$
c. 10   **d.** 40

16. a. $48 \div 3 = 16$ **b.** $\frac{1}{4} \times 88 = 22$
c. $125 \times \frac{1}{5} = 25$ **d.** $56,000 \times \frac{1}{4} = 14,000$
e. $15,000 \div 750 = 20$ **f.** $\frac{3}{5} \times 500 = 300$

17. a. 97.3   **b.** 350   **c.** 350   **d.** 0.018
e. 0.0183   **f.** 0.5   **g.** 0.50

18. One possible answer:

26.2	20.96	47.16
52.4	31.44	10.48
15.72	41.92	36.68

19. At least 90 cents per hour

20. $\dfrac{6}{10} + \dfrac{783}{1000} + \dfrac{29}{100} = \dfrac{600}{1000} + \dfrac{783}{1000} + \dfrac{290}{1000} = \dfrac{1673}{1000} = 1.673$.
Because the least common multiple of all the denominators (in this case, 1000) is always present; one only has to multiply the numerator and denominator of the other fractions by an appropriate power of 10. With the other problem, finding the LCM or LCD is more complicated.

Section 7.2A

1. a. (i) 47.771, (ii) 485.84
  b. Same as in part (a)

2. a. (i) 0.17782, (ii) 4.7
  b. Same as in part (a)

3. a. 2562.274   **b.** 6908.3

4. None

5. a. 5.9×10^1 **b.** 4.326×10^3
  c. 9.7×10^4 **d.** 1.0×10^6
  e. 6.402×10^7 **f.** 7.1×10^{10}

6. a. 4.16×10^{16}m   **b.** 3.5×10^9m

7. a. 3.658×10^6 **b.** 5.893×10^9

8. a. 5.2×10^2 **b.** 8.1×10^3 **c.** 4.1×10^2

9. a. 1.0066×10^{15} **b.** 1.28×10^{14}

10. a. 1.286×10^9, 3.5×10^7
  b. About 36.7 times greater

11. a. Approximately 4.5×10^6 hours
  b. Approximately 517 years
  c. Approximately 4.6×10^4 km/hr.

12. a. $0.\overline{7}$ **b.** $0.47\overline{12}$ **c.** $0.\overline{18}$

13. a. 0.317417417417   **b.** 0.317474747474   **c.** 0.317444444444

14. a. $\frac{16}{99}$ **b.** $\frac{43}{111}$ **c.** $\frac{359}{495}$

15. Approximately 1600 light-years

16. Nonterminating; denominator is not divisible by only 2 or 5 after simplification.

17. a. $\frac{1}{8}$ **b.** $\frac{1}{16}$ **c.** $1/5^8$ **d.** $1/2^{17}$

18. a. $\frac{3}{9} = \frac{1}{3}$ **b.** $\frac{5}{9}$ **c.** $\frac{7}{9}$ **d.** $2\frac{8}{9}$ **e.** 6

19. a. $\frac{3}{99} = \frac{1}{33}$ **b.** $\frac{5}{99}$ **c.** $\frac{7}{99}$ **d.** $\frac{37}{99}$ **e.** $\frac{64}{99}$ **f.** $5\frac{97}{99}$

20. a. $\frac{3}{999} = \frac{1}{333}$ **b.** $\frac{5}{999}$ **c.** $\frac{7}{999}$ **d.** $\frac{19}{999}$ **e.** $\frac{827}{999}$ **f.** $3\frac{217}{999}$

21. a. (i) $\frac{23}{99}$, (ii) $\frac{10}{999}$, (iii) $\frac{769}{999}$, (iv) $\frac{9}{9} = 1$, (v) $\frac{57}{99} = \frac{19}{33}$, (vi) $\frac{1827}{9999} = \frac{203}{1111}$

22. a. $1/99999 = 0.\overline{00001}$
  b. $x/99999$ where $1 \le x \le 99998$, where digits in x are not all the same

23. a. 2   **b.** 6   **c.** 0   **d.** 7

24. Disregarding the first two digits to the right of the decimal point in the decimal expansion of $\frac{1}{71}$, they are the same.

25. $0.94376 \approx 364 \div 365 \times 363 \div 365$ and so on

26. $7.93

27. $31,250

28. $8.91

29. 32

30. $82.64

31. 20.32 cm by 25.4 cm

32. Approximately $125

33. 2.4-liter 4-cylinder is 0.6 liter per cylinder.
  3.5-liter V-6 is $0.58\overline{3}$ liter per cylinder.
  4.9-liter V-8 is 0.6125 liter per cylinder.
  6.8 liter V-10 is 0.68 liter per cylinder.

34. 14 moves

Section 7.3A

1. a. $5:6$ **b.** $\frac{5}{11}$ **c.** Cannot be determined   **d.** 15

2. Each is an ordered pair of numbers. For example,
  a. Measures efficiency of an engine
  b. Measures pay per time
  c. Currency conversion rate
  d. Currency conversion rate

3. a. $\frac{1}{4}$ **b.** $\frac{2}{5}$ **c.** $\frac{5}{1}$ or 5

4. a. No   **b.** Yes

5. 3.8, yes

6. a. 20   **b.** 18   **c.** 8   **d.** 30

7. a. 0.64   **b.** 8.4   **c.** 0.93   **d.** 1.71
  e. 2.17   **f.** 0.11

8. $\dfrac{36¢}{42¢} = \dfrac{18\text{ oz}}{21\text{ oz}}$, $\dfrac{18\text{ oz}}{36¢} = \dfrac{21\text{ oz}}{42¢}$, $\dfrac{42¢}{36¢} = \dfrac{21\text{ oz}}{18\text{ oz}}$

9. a. $24:2 = 48:4 = 96:8 = 192:16$
  b. $13.50:1 = 27:2 = 81:6$
  c. $300:12 = 100:4 = 200:8$
  d. $20:15 = 4:3 = 16:12$
  e. $32:8 = 16:4 = 48:12$

10. 62.5 mph

11. a. 17 cents for 15 ounces
  b. 29 ounces for 13 cents
  c. 73 ounces for 96 cents

12. 40 ounces

13. $16\frac{1}{2}$ days

14. 15 peaches

15. 1024 ounces

16. About $30\frac{2}{3}$ years

17. 4.8 pounds

18. 24,530 miles

19. About 1613 feet

20. About 29″

21. a. 30 teachers   **b.** $942.86   **c.** $1650

22. a. 2.48 AU
  b. 93,000,000 miles or 9.3×10^7 miles
  c. 2.31×10^8 miles

23. a. Approximately 416,666,667
  b. Approximately 6,944,444
  c. Approximately 115,741
  d. About 12 noon
  e. About 22.5 seconds before midnight
  f. Less than $\frac{1}{10}$ of a second before midnight (0.0864 second before midnight)

24. 120 miles away

25. 1, 2, 4, 8, 16, 32, 2816 cents

26. Eric: .333 Morgan: .333

27. 81 dimes

28. $17.50

29. 119¢ (50, 25, 10, 10, 10, 10, 1, 1, 1, 1); 219¢ if a silver dollar is used.

30. Yes; the first player always wins by going to a number with ones digit one.

31. Start both timers at the same time. Start cooking the object when the 7-minute timer runs out—there will be 4 minutes left on the 11-minute timer. When the 11-minute timer runs out, turn it over to complete the 15 minutes.

32. $\frac{8}{7} \times 11 = 12\frac{4}{7}$ seconds

33. If you scale down the 180 miles in 4 hours to 45 miles in 1 hour, then scale up, that would mean 450 miles in 10 hours. But that would be the total amount; Melvina shouldn't add that to the 180 miles she had initially.

Section 7.4A

1. a. 22%, 0.22, $\frac{11}{50}$ **b.** 85%, 0.85, $\frac{17}{20}$ **c.** 57%, 0.57, $\frac{57}{100}$

2. 1/2, 0.5; 7/20, 35%; 0.25, 25%; 0.125, 12.5%; 1/80, 1.25%; 5/4, 1.25; 3/4, 75%

3. a. (i) 5, (ii) 6.87, (iii) 0.458, (iv) 3290
  b. (i) 12, (ii) 0.93, (iii) 600, (iv) 3.128
  c. (i) 13.5, (ii) 7560, (iii) 1.08, (iv) 0.0099

4. a. 252 **b.** 144 **c.** 231 **d.** 195 **e.** 40 **f.** 80

5. a. 56 **b.** 76 **c.** 68 **d.** 37.5 **e.** 150 **f.** $133\frac{1}{3}$

6. a. 32 **b.** 37 **c.** 183 **d.** 70 **e.** 122 **f.** 270

7. a. 40% $\times$ 70 = 28 **b.** 60% $\times$ 30 = 18
  c. 125% $\times$ 60 = $\frac{5}{4}$ $\times$ 60 = 75 **d.** 50% $\times$ 200 = 100
  e. 20% $\times$ 70 = 14 **f.** 10% $\times$ 300 = 30
  g. 1% $\times$ 60 = 0.6 **h.** 400% $\times$ 180 = 4 $\times$ 180 = 720

8. a. $4.70 **b.** $2.60 **c.** $13.50 **d.** $6.50

9. a. 56%
  (i)

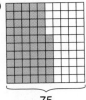

How many squares are equal to 42?

  (ii) $\dfrac{42}{75} = \dfrac{x}{100}$ (iii) 42 = x $\cdot$ 75

  b. 163.88
  (i)

How many squares are equal to 42?

  (ii) $\dfrac{17}{100} = \dfrac{x}{964}$ (iii) 0.17 $\cdot$ 964 = x

  c. $423\frac{9}{37}$
  (i)

  (ii) $\dfrac{156.67}{x} = \dfrac{37}{100}$
  (iii) 0.37 $\cdot$ x = 156.6

d. approximately 71%
  (i)

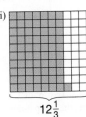

How many squares are equal to $8\frac{3}{4}$?

  (ii) $\dfrac{8\frac{3}{4}}{12\frac{1}{3}} = \dfrac{x}{100}$ (iii) $8\frac{3}{4} = x \cdot 12\frac{1}{3}$

  e. $5\frac{13}{27}$
  (i)

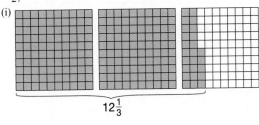

  (ii) $\dfrac{225}{100} = \dfrac{12\frac{1}{3}}{x}$ (iii) $2.25 \cdot x = 12\frac{1}{3}$

10. a. 33.6 **b.** 2.7 **c.** 82.4 **d.** 48.7% **e.** 55.5%
  f. 123.5 **g.** 33.3% **h.** 213.3 **i.** 0.5 **j.** 0.1

11. a. 56.7 **b.** 115.5 **c.** 375.6
  d. 350 **e.** 2850 **f.** 15,680

12. a. 129 **b.** 30.87 **c.** 187.5
  d. 62.5% **e.** $5.55 **f.** $14

13. a. $20.90 **b.** $7.76 **c.** $494.92 **d.** $249.91

14. 8.5%

15. 1946 students

16. a. $5120.76 **b.** About $53.05 more

17. $(100)(1.0004839)^{15}$ = 100.73, about 73 cents

18. 5.7%; 94.3%

19. a. About 5.72×10^{10}
  b. 55.3%

20. a. 72.5 quadrillion BTU
  b. Nuclear, 10.6%; crude oil, 17.2%; natural gas, 30.1%; renewables 9.9%; coal, 32.1%. Percentages don't add up to 100% due to rounding.

21. The discount is 13% or the sales price should be $97.75.

22. $5000

23. a. 250 **b.** 480 **c.** 15

24. $4875

25. a. About 16.3% **b.** About 34.8%
  c. 3.64×10^{14} square meters **d.** 0.44% or about $\frac{11}{25}$ of 1%

26. No; 3 grams is 4% of 75 grams, but 7 grams is 15% of 46.6 grams, giving different U.S. RDA of protein.

27. 31.68 inches

28. The result is the same

29. 32%

30. 119 to 136

31. If the competition had x outputs, then $x + 0.4x = 6$, or $1.4x = 6$. There is no whole number for x, therefore, the competition couldn't have had x outputs.

32. $10\% + 5\% = 15\%$ off, whereas 10% off, then 5% off is equivalent to finding $90\% \times 95\% = 85.5\%$, or 14.5% off. Conclusion: Add the percents.

33. An increase of about 4.9%

34. The player who is faced with 3 petals loses. Reasoning backward, so is the one faced with 6, since whatever she takes, the opponent can force her to 3. The same for 9. Thus the first player will lose. The key to this game is to leave the opponent on a multiple of 3.

35. Let P be the price. Option (i) is $P \times 80\% \times 106\%$, whereas (ii) is $P \times 106\% \times 80\%$. By commutativity, they are equal.

36. $14,751.06

37. $59,000

38. $9052.13

39. $\dfrac{4.7}{172.8} \approx 2.72\%$

40. $50,000. If you make a table, you can see that you will keep more of your money up to $50,000, namely 50% of $50,000, or $25,000. However, at $51,000 you keep only 49% of $51,000, or $24,990, and it goes down from there until you keep $0 at $100,000! Observe that there is symmetry around $50,000.

41. $9.25

42. 35 or 64 years old.

43. 34, 36, 44, 54, 76, 146

44. Pilot should fly when there is no wind.

PROBLEMS WHERE THE STRATEGY "WORK BACKWARD" IS USEFUL

1. Working backward, we have $87 - 59 + 18 = 46$. So they must have gone 46 floors the first time.

2. If she ended up with 473 cards, she brought $473 - 9 + 2 - 4 - 2 + 7 - 5 + 3 = 465$.

3. Working backward, $\{[(13 \cdot 4 + 6)3 \div 2] - 9\} \div 6 = 13$ is the original number.

CHAPTER REVIEW
Section 7.1

1. $3 \times 10 + 7 + 1 \times (1/10) + 4 \times (1/100) + 9 \times (1/1000)$

2. Two and three thousand seven hundred ninety-eight ten thousandths

3. (a) and (c)

4. a. Shade 24 small squares and 3 strips of ten squares. Thus, $0.24 < 0.3$.
  b. 0.24 is to the left of 0.3.
  c. $\dfrac{24}{100} < \dfrac{30}{100}(= \dfrac{3}{10})$
  d. Since $2 < 3$, $0.24 < 0.3$.

5. a. 24.6. Use commutativity and associativity to find $0.25 \times 8 = 2$.
  b. 9.6. Use commutativity and distributivity to find $2.4(1.3 + 2.7)$.
  c. 18.72. Use compensation to find $15.72 + 3.00$.
  d. 7.53. Use equal additions to find $27.53 - 20.00$.

6. a. Between 48 and 108   **b.** 14
  c. $8.5 - 2.4 = 6.1$ **d.** $400 \div 50 = 8$

Section 7.2

1. a. 21.009   **b.** 36.489   **c.** 153.55   **d.** 36.9
2. a. $0.\overline{384615}$ **b.** $0.\overline{396}$ **c.** $\frac{1}{2}$
3. a. $\frac{3671}{999}$ **b.** $\frac{23{,}891}{990}$

Section 7.3

1. A ratio is an ordered pair, and a proportion is a statement saying that two ratios are equal.

2. a. No, since $\frac{7}{13} \neq \frac{3}{5}$.   **b.** Yes, since $12 \times 25 = 15 \times 20$.

3. $\frac{a}{b} = \frac{c}{d}$ if and only if (i) $ad = bc$ or (ii) $\frac{a}{b}$ and $\frac{c}{d}$ are equivalent to the same fraction.

4. a. $\frac{58}{24} < \frac{47}{16}$, so 58¢ for 24 oz is the better buy.
  b. $\frac{3.45}{7} > \frac{5.11}{11}$, so $5.11 for 11 pounds is the better buy.

5. $4\frac{1}{3}$ cups

Section 7.4

1. a. $56\% = 0.56 = \frac{56}{100}(= \frac{14}{25})$
  b. $0.48 = 48\% = \frac{48}{100}(= \frac{12}{25})$
  c. $\frac{1}{8} = 0.125 = 12.5\%$

2. a. $48 \times \frac{1}{4} = 12$ **b.** $\frac{1}{3} \times 72 = 24$
  c. $\frac{3}{4} \times 72 = 54$ **d.** $\frac{1}{5} \times 55 = 11$

3. a. $25\% \times 80 = 20$ **b.** $50\% \times 200 = 100$
  c. $33\frac{1}{3}\% \times 60 = 20$ **d.** $66\frac{2}{3}\% \times 300 = 200$

4. a. $16,000   **b.** 59%

Chapter 7 Test

1. a. F   **b.** T   **c.** T   **d.** F   **e.** F   **f.** T   **g.** T   **h.** T

2. a. $3 \cdot 10^1 + 2 \cdot 1 + 1 \cdot \left(\dfrac{1}{10^1}\right) + 9\left(\dfrac{1}{10^2}\right) + 8\left(\dfrac{1}{10^3}\right)$

  b. $3 \cdot \left(\dfrac{1}{10^4}\right) + 4 \cdot \left(\dfrac{1}{10^5}\right) + 2 \cdot \left(\dfrac{1}{10^6}\right)$

3. Hundred

4. a. The ratio of red to green is 9:14, or the ratio of green to red is 14:9.
  b. 9:23 or 14:23

5. a. 17.519   **b.** 6.339   **c.** 83.293   **d.** 500

6. a. $\frac{103}{1000} < \frac{400}{1000}$ and $0.1 < 0.4$; therefore, $0.103 < 0.4$
  b. $\frac{997}{10{,}000} < \frac{1000}{10{,}000}$ and $0.09 < 0.10$; therefore, $0.0997 < 0.1$

7. a. $0.\overline{285714}$ **b.** 0.625   **c.** 0.14583 **d.** $0.\overline{4}$

8. a. Terminating
  b. Nonterminating
  c. Terminating

9. a. $\frac{4}{11}$ **b.** $\frac{11}{30}$ **c.** $\frac{909}{2500}$

10. a. $0.52, \frac{52}{100}$ **b.** $125\%, \frac{125}{100}$ **c.** $0.68, 68\%$

11. 18

12. a. $53 \times 0.48 \approx 52 \times 0.5 = 52 \div 2 = 26$
   b. $1469.2 \div 26.57 = 14.692 \div 0.2657 \approx 16 \div 0.25 =$
   $16 \div \frac{1}{4} = 16 \times 4 = 64$
   c. $33 \div 0.76 \approx 33 \div 0.75 = 33 \times \frac{4}{3} = 44$
   d. $442.78 \times 18.7 \approx 450 \times 20 = 9000$

13. $3\%, \frac{2}{7}, 0.3, \frac{1}{3}$

14. 123,456,789 has prime factors other than 2 or 5.

15. 37 $\boxed{\div}$ 100 $\boxed{\times}$ 58 is 37% of 58.

16. a. Bernard got 80% of the questions correct on his math test. If he got 48 correct, how many questions were on the test?
   b. Of his 140 times at bat for the season, Jose got a hit 35 times. What percent of the time did he get a hit? (Answers may vary.)

17. If we convert 1.3 and 0.2 to fractions before adding, the denominator of the sum is 10 and thus the sum has one digit to the right of the decimal. $\left(\frac{13}{10} + \frac{2}{10} = \frac{15}{10} = 1.5\right)$. When multiplying, the denominators are multiplied, giving a denominator of 10^2 (two digits to the right of the decimal) in the product $\left(\frac{13}{10} \times \frac{2}{10} = \frac{26}{10^2} = 0.26\right)$.

18. 7

19. $2520

20. $522

21. 9.6 inches

22. 5.37501, 5.37502, 5.37503 (Answers may vary.)

23. 28

24. If the competition has 4 new styles, then 6 new styles is 50% more. If the competition has 5 new styles, then 6 new styles is 20% more. In other words, 6 styles is 40% more than 4.28 styles and 0.28 of a style makes no sense.

25. $870

Section 8.1A

1. All are integers
   a. Positive   **b.** Negative   **c.** Neither

2. a. *RRRRB*   **b.** *BRRBBBBB*
   c. 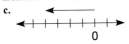   **d.**

3. a. *BBB*   **b.** *RRRRR*
   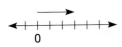

   c. *BR*

4. a. -3 **b.** 4   **c.** 0
   d. 168   **e.** -56 **f.** 1235

5. a. *I*   **b.** $\{\ldots, -4, -3, -2, -1, 1, 2, 3, 4, \ldots\}$ **c.** $\varnothing$

6. a.
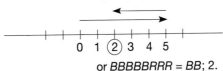
or *BBBBBRRR = BB*; 2.

b.

or *RRR RR* = -5.

7. a. $-14 + 6 = [-8 + (-6)] + 6 = -8 + (-6 + 6) = -8 + 0 = -8$
   b. $17 + (-3) = (14 + 3) + (-3) = 14 + (3 + (-3)) = 14 + 0 = 14$

8. Top: 5; second: $-1, 6$; third: $-2, 1$

9. a. T   **b.** F   **c.** F   **d.** T

10. a. Commutative property of addition
   b. Additive inverse property

11. a. 635   **b.** -17

12. a. -5 **b.** 12   **c.** -78 **d.** -11

13. a. 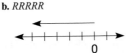   **b.** *BBBB BBBBB* $= 9$
   RRRRR

14. a. -4 **b.** 12   **c.** 1   **d.** 1

15. a. 26   **b.** -5 **c.** 370   **d.** -128

16. a. Five minus two
   b. Negative six or opposite of six (both equivalent)
   c. Negative three or opposite of three

17. a. 5   **b.** 17   **c.** 2
   d. -2 **e.** -2 **f.** 2

18. $64

19. a. Yes; $-3 - 7$ is an integer
   b. No; $3 - 2 \neq 2 - 3$
   c. No; $5 - (4 - 1) \neq (5 - 4) - 1$
   d. No; $5 - 0 \neq 0 - 5$

20. If $a - b = c$, then $a + (-b) = c$. Then $a + (-b) + b = c + b$, or $a = b + c$.

21. a. (i) When a and b have the same sign or when one or both are 0, (ii) when a and b are nonzero and have opposite signs, (iii) never, (iv) all integers will work.
   b. Only condition (iv)

22. First row: $7, -14, 1$; second row: $-8, -2, 4$; third row: $-5, 10, -11$

23. a. (i) $9 - 4$, (ii) $4 - 9$, (iii) $4 - 4$,
   (iv) $9 - [(4 - 4) - 4]$, (v) $(9 - 4) - 4$,
   (vi) $[(9 - 4) - 4] - 4$
   b. All integers
   c. Any integer that is a multiple of 4
   d. If GCF$(a, b) = 1$, then all integers; otherwise, just multiples of GCF

24. Second: $2, -24$; third: $4, -2, -22$; bottom: -7

25. As long as we have integers, this algorithm is correct. Justification:
   $72 - 38 = (70 + 2) - (30 + 8) = (70 - 30) + (2 - 8) = 40 + (-6) = 34$.

26.

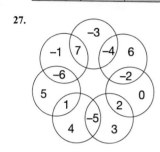

14	18	
	4	
10	7	
		15
9	8	

27.

-3, -1, 7, -4, 6, -6, -2, 5, 1, 2, 0, -5, 4, 3

28. If you have 3 black chips in the circle and you need to subtract 8, there aren't enough black chips there. You are always allowed to add a "neutral" set of chips (zero) to the circle, that is, a pair consisting of one black and one red. By adding 5 black and 5 red you can subtract 8 black chips, leaving 5 red chips, or -5.

Section 8.2A

1. a. $2 + 2 + 2 + 2 = 8$ or $4 \times 2 = 8$
b. $(-3) + (-3) + (-3) = -9$ or $3 \times (-3) = -9$
c. $(-1) + (-1) + (-1) + (-1) + (-1) + (-1) = -6$ or $6 \times (-1) = -6$

2. a. (i) $6 \times (-1) = -6, 6 \times (-2) = -12, 6 \times (-3) = -18$;
(ii) $9 \times (-1) = -9, 9 \times (-2) = -18, 9 \times (-3) = -27$
b. Positive times negative equals negative.

3. a. -30 **b.** 32 **c.** -15 **d.** 39

4. a. $RR\ RR\ RR = -6$
b. $BBBBBBBBBBBB = 12$
$RRRRRRRRRRRR$

5. Distributivity of multiplication over addition; additive inverse; multiplication by 0

6. Adding the opposite approach to subtraction; distributivity of multiplication over addition; $(-a)b = -(ab)$; adding opposite approach; distributivity of multiplication over subtraction.

7. a. -2592 **b.** 1938 **c.** $97,920$

8. a. 3 **b.** -86

9. a. -6 **b.** 5 **c.** -15

10. a. -47 **b.** -156 **c.** 1489

11. Yes to all parts

12. a. 16 **b.** -27 **c.** 16 **d.** 25 **e.** -243 **f.** 64

13. Positive: (c), (d); negative: (e)

14. a. $\frac{1}{100}$ **b.** $\frac{1}{64}$ **c.** $\frac{1}{64}$ **d.** $\frac{1}{125}$

15. a. $\frac{1}{4^2} \cdot 4^6 = 4^4$ **b.** $4^{-2+6} = 4^4$ **c.** $\frac{1}{5^4} \cdot \frac{1}{5^2} = \frac{1}{5^6} = 5^{-6}$ **d.** Yes

16. a. $\frac{1/3^2}{3^5} = \frac{1}{3^7}$ **b.** $3^{-2-5} = 3^{-7} = \frac{1}{3^7}$ **c.** $6^{10}, 6^{10}$ **d.** Yes

17. a. $3^3 = 27$ **b.** 6 **c.** $3^8 = 6561$

18. a. 0.000037 **b.** 0.0000000245

19. a. 4×10^{-4} **b.** 1.6×10^{-6} **c.** 4.95×10^{-10}

20. a. 7.22×10^{-25} **b.** 8.28×10^{-26} **c.** 2.5×10^{-10}
d. 4×10^{-37} **e.** 8×10^{14} **f.** 2.05×10^{-7}

21. a. -3 is left of 2. **b.** -6 is left of -2. **c.** -12 is the left of -3.

22. a. $-5, -2, 0, 2, 5$ **b.** $-8, -6, -5, 3, 12$
c. $-11, -8, -5, -3, -2$ **d.** $108, -72, -36, 23, 45$

23. a. $<$ **b.** $>$

24. a. $43{,}200, -240, -180, 12, -5, 3$

25. a. -10 and -8 **b.** -8 **c.** No

26. a. ?$-$
b. (i) ?$+$ (ii) $+$ $-$ (iii) $+$ $-$
$-$? $-$ $+$ $-$ $+$

27. a. (i) When x is negative, (ii) when x is nonnegative (zero or positive), (iii) never, (iv) all integers
b. Only (iv)

28. This is correct, by $a(-1) = -a$.

29. Put the amounts on a number line, where positive numbers represent assets and negative numbers represent liabilities. Clearly, $-10 < -5$.

30. First row: $-2, -9, 12$; second row: $-36, 6, -1$; third row: $3, -4, -18$

31. $x < y$ means $y = x + p$ for some $p > 0$, $y^2 = (x + p)^2 = x^2 + 2xp + p^2$. Since $x > 0$ and $p > 0$, $2xp + p^2 > 0$. Therefore, $x^2 < y^2$.

32. 1.99×10^{-23} grams per atom of carbon

33. a. 1.11×10^{-2}
b. About 2.33×10^8 seconds, or 7.4 years

34. 100 sheep, 0 cows, and 0 rabbits or 1 sheep, 19 cows, and 80 rabbits

35. True. Every whole number can be expressed in the form $3n$, $3n + 1$, or $3n + 2$. If these three forms are squared, the squares will be of the form $3m$ or $3m + 1$.

36. 30 cents

37. Assume $ab = 0$ and $b \neq 0$. Then $ab = 0 \cdot b$. Since $ac = bc$ and $c \neq 0$ implies that $a = b$, we can cancel the b's in $ab = 0 \cdot b$. Hence $a = 0$. Similarly, if we assume $a \neq 0$.

PROBLEMS WHERE THE STRATEGY "USE CASES" IS USEFUL

1. Case 1: odd + even + odd = even.
Case 2: even + odd + even = odd.
Since only Case 1 has an even sum, two of the numbers must be odd.

2. $m^2 - n^2$ is positive when $m^2 > n^2$.
Case 1: $m > 0, n > 0$. Here m must be greater than n.
Case 2: $m > 0, n < 0$. Here $m > -n$.
Case 3: $m < 0, n > 0$. Here $-m > n$.
Case 4: $m < 0, n < 0$. Here $m < n$.

3. Case 1: If $n = 5m$, then $n^2 = 25m^2$ and hence is a multiple of 5.
Case 2: If $n = 5m + 1$, then $n^2 = 25m^2 + 10m + 1$, which is one
more than a multiple of 5.
Case 3: If $n = 5m + 2$, then $n^2 = 25m^2 + 20m + 4$, which is 4
more than (hence one less than) a multiple of 5.
Case 4: If $n = 5m + 3$, then $n^2 = 25m^2 + 30m + 9$, which is one
less than a multiple of 5.
Case 5: If $n = 5m + 4$, then $n^2 = 25m^2 + 40m + 16$, which is one
more than a multiple of 5.

CHAPTER REVIEW
Section 8.1
1. a. Use black chips for positive integers and red chips for negative
integers.
  b. Arrows representing positive integers point to the right, and
  arrows representing negative integers point to the left.

2. a. $BBBBBBBRRRR = BBB$
  b.

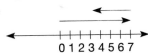
$$0\ 1\ 2\ 3\ 4\ 5\ 6\ 7$$

3. a. Identity   **b.** Inverse   **c.** Commutativity
  d. Associativity   **e.** Closure

4. a.

$BBBBB$ RR $3 - (-2) = 5$

  b. $3 - (-2) = 3 + 2 = 5$
  c. $3 - (-2) = n$ if and only if $3 = (-2) + n$; therefore, $n = 5$.

5. (a) only

Section 8.2
1. a. $(-2) + (-2) + (-2) + (-2) + (-2) = -10$
  b. $(-5)2 = -10, (-5)1 = -5, (-5)0 = 0, (-5)(-1) = 5,$
  $(-5)(-2) = 10$

2. a. Commutativity   **b.** Associativity   **c.** Closure
  d. Identity   **e.** Cancellation

3. Let $a = 3$ and $b = 4$.

4. $n = 0$; zero divisors

5. $a \div b = c$ if and only if $a = bc$.

6. None

7. a. Positive—even number of negative numbers
  b. Negative—odd number of negative numbers
  c. 0—zero is a factor

8. $7^3 = 7 \times 7 \times 7, 7^2 = 7 \times 7, 7^1 = 7, 7^0 = 1, 7^{-1} = \frac{1}{7}$, etc.

9. a. 7.9×10^{-5} **b.** 0.0003   **c.** 4.58127×10^2
  d. 23,900,000

10. a. -21 is to the left of -17 **b.** $-21 + 4 = -17$

11. a. $>$: Property of less than and multiplication by a negative
  b. $<$: Transitivity
  c. $<$: Property of less than and multiplication by a positive
  d. $<$: Property of less than and addition

Chapter 8 Test
1. a. T   **b.** F   **c.** F   **d.** T
  e. F   **f.** F   **g.** F   **h.** T

2. $a^{-n} = \dfrac{1}{a^n}$

3. (b) and (c)

4. Take-away, missing-addend, add-the-opposite

5. a. -6 **b.** 42   **c.** 48   **d.** -8
  e. -30 **f.** 3   **g.** -52 **h.** -12

6. a. $3(-4 + 2) = 3(-2) = -6, 3(-4) + 3(2) = -12 + 6 = -6$
  b. $-3[-5 + (-2)] = -3(-7) = 21, (-3)(-5) + (-3)(-2) = 15 + 6 = 21$

7. a. 8.2×10^{12} **b.** 6×10^{-6}

8. $n = -4$

9. a. Associativity   **b.** Associativity and commutativity
  c. Distributivity   **d.** Commutativity and distributivity

10. a.   (i) $BBBBBBBBBBBBBRRRRR = 13$
  (ii) $8 - (-5) = 8 + 5 = 13$
  (iii) $8 - (-5) = c$ if and only if $8 = c + (-5)$; $c = 13$.
  b.   (i) $RR \rightarrow BBBBBRRRRRRR = 5$
  (ii) $(-2) - (-7) = -2 + 7 = 5$
  (iii) $(-2) - (-7) = c$ if and only if $-2 = c + (-7)$; $c = 5$.

11. a. Negative   **b.** Negative   **c.** Positive   **d.** Positive

12. a.

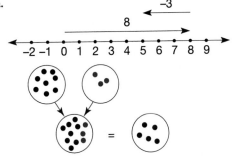

  b.

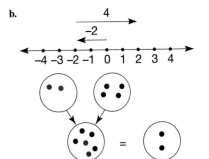

  c.

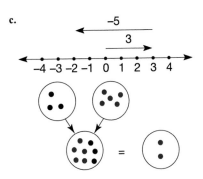

13. (i) take-away

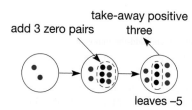

add 3 zero pairs   take-away positive three

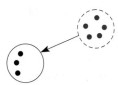

leaves −5

(ii) missing-addend
What needs to be
added to a set of 3 to
get −2?

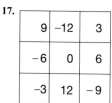

14. a. $3 \times 4 = 12$ **b.** $-2 \times 4 = -8$
$\quad\quad 2 \times 4 = 8$ $-2 \times 3 = -6$
$\quad\quad 1 \times 4 = 4$ $-2 \times 2 = -4$
$\quad\quad 0 \times 4 = 0$ $-2 \times 1 = -2$
$\quad\quad -1 \times 4 = -4$ $-2 \times 0 = 0$
$\quad\quad -2 \times 4 = -8$ $-2 \times -1 = 2$
$\quad\quad\quad\quad\quad\quad\quad\quad\quad\quad\quad\quad -2 \times -2 = 4$
$\quad\quad\quad\quad\quad\quad\quad\quad\quad\quad\quad\quad -2 \times -3 = 6$
$\quad\quad\quad\quad\quad\quad\quad\quad\quad\quad\quad\quad -2 \times -4 = 8$

15. No; let $a = 2, b = 3, c = 4$, then $a(b \cdot c) = 24$,
but $a \cdot b \times a \cdot c = 48$.

16. a. $30, -30$ **b.** $120, 60$ **c.** $-900, -3600$ **d.** $-1, -2$

17.

9	−12	3
−6	0	6
−3	12	−9

18.

−256	2	−64
8	32	128
−16	512	−4

19. $a - b = b - a$ is the same as $a - b = -(a - b)$. The only number that is equal to its opposite is 0, so $a - b = 0$ which means $a = b$.

20. a. 20   **b.** 18   **c.** 6

Section 9.1A

1. a. $\frac{-2}{3}$ where $-2, 3$ are integers
   b. $\frac{-31}{6}$ where $-31, 6$ are integers
   c. $\frac{10}{1}$ where $10, 1$ are integers

2. a. I, N, Q   **b.** Q

3. $\frac{-3}{1}, \frac{3}{-1}, -\frac{3}{1}, -\frac{-3}{-1}$

4. (a) and (b)

5. a. $\frac{-5}{7}$ **b.** $\frac{-3}{5}$ **c.** $\frac{2}{5}$ **d.** $\frac{-4}{5}$

6. a. $\frac{-1}{9}$ **b.** $\frac{-4}{3}$ **c.** $\frac{1}{4}$ **d.** $\frac{-1}{8}$

7. a. $2\frac{5}{8}$ **b.** $1\frac{3}{5}$

8. a. 2   **b.** $-\frac{5}{3}$

9. a. $\frac{24}{143}$ **b.** $-\frac{9}{154}$

10. a. W, F, I, N, Q   **b.** I, Q

11. a. Associative property for addition
   b. Commutative property for addition

12. a. $\frac{2}{3}$ **b.** 2   **c.** $\frac{5}{7}$ **d.** $\frac{-31}{36}$

13. a. $1\frac{121}{1368}$ **b.** $-1\frac{17}{78}$

14. a. I, Q   **b.** None

15. a. $\frac{14}{27}$ **b.** $\frac{-35}{18}$ **c.** $\frac{5}{18}$ **d.** $\frac{1}{4}$

16. a. $\frac{-11}{17}$ **b.** $\frac{-3}{14}$ **c.** $\frac{31}{21}$ **d.** $\frac{2}{7}$

17. a. $-\frac{455}{3456}$ **b.** $-\frac{6}{25}$

18. a. I, Q   **b.** F, I, Q

19. a. Commutative property for multiplication
   b. Distributive property of multiplication over addition

20. a. $-90,687$ **b.** -1

21. a. $\frac{4}{3}$ **b.** $\frac{-1}{6}$ **c.** $\frac{-9}{20}$ **d.** $\frac{-7}{5}$

22. a. $1\frac{329}{703}$ **b.** $\frac{24}{35}$

23. a. -77 **b.** $\frac{4}{75}$

24. a. $\frac{-9}{11} < \frac{-3}{11}$ **b.** $\frac{-1}{3} < \frac{2}{5}$
   c. $\frac{-9}{10} < \frac{-5}{6}$ **d.** $\frac{-9}{8} < \frac{-10}{9}$

25. a. $\frac{-152}{201} < \frac{-231}{356}$ **b.** $\frac{-500}{345} < \frac{-761}{532}$

26. a. Property of less than and addition
   b. Property of less than and multiplication by a negative

27. a. $x < \dfrac{-4}{3}$ **b.** $x < \dfrac{-1}{12}$

28. a. $x < \dfrac{3}{2}$ **b.** $x < \dfrac{-3}{4}$

29. a. $x > \dfrac{5}{4}$ **b.** $x > -\dfrac{3}{2}$

30. a. $\frac{-43}{88} < \frac{-37}{76}, \frac{-80}{164} = \frac{-20}{41}$
   b. $\frac{-59}{97} < \frac{-68}{113}, \frac{-127}{210}$

31. There are many correct answers.
   a. For example, $\frac{-2}{3}, \frac{-5}{7}$, and $\frac{-3}{5}$
   b. For example, $\frac{-6}{7}, \frac{-11}{13}$, and $\frac{-13}{15}$

32. $a/b = an/bn$ if and only if $a(bn) = b(an)$. The last equation is true due to associativity and commutativity of integer multiplication.

33. a. $\dfrac{a}{b}, \dfrac{c}{d}$ are rational numbers so b and d are not zero (definition of rational numbers), $\dfrac{a}{b} \cdot \dfrac{c}{d} = \dfrac{ac}{bd}$ (definition of multiplication), ac and bd are integers (closure of integer multiplication), $bd \neq 0$ (zero divisors property); therefore, $\dfrac{ac}{bd}$ is a rational number. Similar types of arguments hold for parts (b) to (e).

34. a. $a/b = c/d + e/f$
   b. If $a/b - c/d = e/f$, then $a/b + (-c/d) = e/f$. Add c/d to both sides. Then $a/b = c/d + e/f$. Also, if $a/b = c/d + e/f$, add $-c/d$ to both sides. Then $a/b + (-c/d) = e/f$ or $a/b - c/d = e/f$.
   c. If $a/b - c/d = e/f$, then $a/b = c/d + e/f$. Adding $-c/d$ to both sides will yield $a/b + (-c/d) = e/f$. Hence, $a/b - c/d = a/b + (-c/d)$.

35. $\dfrac{a}{b}\left(\dfrac{c}{d}+\dfrac{e}{f}\right)=\dfrac{a}{b}\left(\dfrac{cf+de}{df}\right)=\dfrac{a\,(cf+de)}{bdf}=$

$\dfrac{acf+ade}{bdf}=\dfrac{acf}{bdf}+\dfrac{ade}{bdf}=\dfrac{ac}{bd}+\dfrac{ae}{bf}=$

$\dfrac{a}{b}\cdot\dfrac{c}{d}+\dfrac{a}{b}\cdot\dfrac{e}{f}$, using addition and multiplication of rational numbers and distributivity of integers

36. If $a/b < c/d$, then $a/b + p/q = c/d$ for some positive p/q. Therefore, $a/b + p/q + e/f = c/d + e/f$, or $a/b + e/f + p/q = c/d + e/f$ for positive p/q. Thus $a/b + e/f < c/d + e/f$.

37. $\left(-\dfrac{a}{b}\right)+\left[-\left(-\dfrac{a}{b}\right)\right]=\left(-\dfrac{a}{b}\right)+\dfrac{a}{b}$. Therefore, by additive cancellation, $-\left(-\dfrac{a}{b}\right)=\dfrac{a}{b}$.

38. Start both timers. When the 5-minute timer expires, start it again. When the 8-minute timer expires, start it again; the 5-minute timer will have 2 minutes left on it. When the 5-minute timer expires, start measuring, since the 8-minute timer will have 6 minutes left.

Section 9.2A

1. a. Irrational
   b. Rational
   c. Irrational
   d. Rational
   e. Irrational
   f. Irrational
   g. Rational
   h. Rational

2. No; if it did, π would be a rational number. This is an approximation to π.

3. a. $\sqrt{5}$
   b. $\sqrt{8}=2\sqrt{2}$
   c. $\sqrt{20}=2\sqrt{5}$

4. a. $\sqrt{2}$ **b.** $\sqrt{3}$
   c.

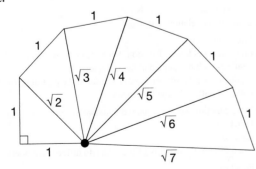

5. a. $\sqrt{34}$ **b.** $\sqrt{20}=2\sqrt{5}$ **c.** 6
6. a. $4\sqrt{3}$ **b.** $3\sqrt{7}$ **c.** $9\sqrt{2}$

7. a. 19   **b.** 27

8. a. Distributive property of multiplication over addition
   b. Yes; 8π
   c. No, the numbers under the radical are not the same.

9. a. 2×3, 6
   b. 2×5, 10
   c. 3×4, 12
   d. 3×5, 15
   e. $\sqrt{a}\times\sqrt{b}=\sqrt{a\times b}$

10. a. $\dfrac{4}{2}$, 2   **b.** $\dfrac{6}{2}$, 3   **c.** $\dfrac{16}{8}$, 2   **d.** $\dfrac{21}{7}$, 3   **e.** $\dfrac{\sqrt{a}}{\sqrt{b}}=\sqrt{\dfrac{a}{b}}$

11. 0.56, $0.565565556\ldots$, $0.565566555666\ldots$, $0.\overline{56}$, $0.5\overline{66}$, $0.56656665\ldots$, $0.\overline{566}$

12. There are many correct answers. One is $0.37414243\ldots$

13. For example, $\sqrt{10}$, $\sqrt{11}$, $\sqrt{12}$, $3.060060006\ldots$

14. a. 2.65   **b.** 3.95   **c.** 0.19

15. For example, if $r_1 = 3.5$, then $r_3 = 3.6055516$ and $s_3 = 3.6055509$. Therefore $\sqrt{13}\approx 3.60555$.

16. The numbers decrease in size, 1.

17. a. $0.3 < 0.5477225$
   b. $0.5 < 0.7071067$
   Square root is larger than number.

18. a. 5   **b.** 2   **c.** 243   **d.** 81   **e.** 8   **f.** $\frac{1}{125}$

19. a. -3 **b.** Not real   **c.** 2

20. a. 25
   b. 3.804 (rounded)
   c. 7,547,104.282 (rounded)
   d. 9,018,968.484 (rounded)

21. a. $\sqrt[4]{64}$ **b.** $\sqrt[3]{37}$

22. a.

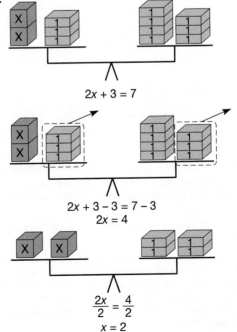

b.

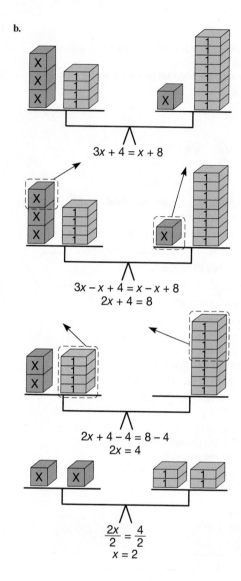

$$3x + 4 = x + 8$$

$$3x - x + 4 = x - x + 8$$
$$2x + 4 = 8$$

$$2x + 4 - 4 = 8 - 4$$
$$2x = 4$$

$$\frac{2x}{2} = \frac{4}{2}$$
$$x = 2$$

23. a. -8 **b.** 5 **c.** $\dfrac{-5}{9}$ **d.** $3\sqrt{2}$

24. a. 9 **b.** 5 **c.** 5 **d.** $\dfrac{1}{2}$ **e.** $\dfrac{-7}{6}$ **f.** 2π

25. a. $x > \dfrac{-11}{3}$ **b.** $x \le 4$ **c.** $x > \dfrac{9}{5}$ **d.** $x \le \dfrac{22}{27}$

26. Let $\sqrt{3} = a/b$. Then $3 = a^2/b^2$ or $a^2 = 3b^2$. Count prime factors.

27. When you get to the step $a^2 = 9 \cdot b^2$, this can be written as $a^2 = 3^2 \cdot b^2$. Thus both sides have an even number of prime factors and no contradiction arises.

28. Assume not. Then $(a/b)^3 = 2$ for some rational a/b. Count prime factors.

29. a. By closure of real-number multiplication, $5\sqrt{3}$ is a real number, and thus a rational or an irrational number. Assume that it is rational, say $m = 5\sqrt{3}$. Since $m/5$ is rational and $\sqrt{3}$ is irrational, we have a contradiction. Therefore, $5\sqrt{3}$ must be irrational.
b. Argue as in part (a); replace 5 with any nonzero rational and $\sqrt{3}$ with any irrational.

30. a. $1 + \sqrt{3} = a/b$ so $\sqrt{3} = (a - b)/b$, which is a rational number, and this is a contradiction because $\sqrt{3}$ is an irrational number.
b. Argue as in part (a); assume that the number is rational and solve for $\sqrt{3}$.

31. a. Apply 29(b).   **b.** Apply 30(b).   **c.** Apply 30(b).

32. $\sqrt{a} + \sqrt{b} \ne \sqrt{a + b}$ except when $a = 0$ or $b = 0$. There is no consistent analogy between multiplication and addition.

33. $\sqrt{a} \cdot \sqrt{b} = \sqrt{ab}$ is true for all a and b, where $a \ge 0$ and $b \ge 0$.

34. $\{(3n, 4n, 5n) \mid$ is a nonzero whole number$\}$ is an infinite set of Pythagorean triples.

35. For example, if $u = 2$, $v = 1$, then $a = 4$, $b = 3$, $c = 5$.
If $u = 3$, $v = 2$, then $a = 12$, $b = 5$, $c = 13$.
$u = 8$, $v = 3$, $(48, 55, 73)$
$u = 8$, $v = 5$, $(39, 80, 89)$
$u = 8$, $v = 7$, $(15, 112, 113)$

36. $3, 4, 5$; $1, 2, 3$; $2, 3, 4$; $-1, 0, 1$

37. Yes; 1 or -1

38. Cut from the longer wire a piece that is $\frac{1}{3}$ the sum of the lengths of the original pieces.

39. Mr. Milne

40. 20 and 64

Section 9.3A

1. a. $\{(a, a), (a, b), (b, c), (c, b)\}$
b. $\{(1, x), (2, y), (3, y), (4, z)\}$
c. $\{(1, 1), (2, 2), (3, 3), (4, 4), (5, 5), (6, 6), (2, 3), (3, 2), (2, 5),$
$(5, 2), (3, 5), (5, 3)\}$
d. $\{(2, 2), (4, 4), (6, 6), (8, 8), (10, 10), (12, 12), (4, 2), (6, 2), (8, 2),$
$(10, 2), (12, 2), (8, 4), (12, 4), (12, 6)\}$

2. a.

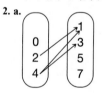

b.

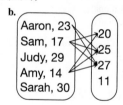

3. a. "was president number"
b. "is the capital of"

4. a. R, T   **b.** S   **c.** T

5. a. Reflexive only   **b.** None
c. Equivalence relation   **d.** None

6. a. Transitive only
b. Equivalence relation. Partition: Each set in the partition will have numbers with the same number of factors.
c. Equivalence relation. Partition: Each set in the partition will have numbers with the same tens digits.

7. a. Not a function, since b is paired with two different numbers
b. Function
c. Function
d. Not a function, since 3 is paired with two different numbers

8. a. Function
b. Function
c. Not a function, since some college graduates have more than one degree
d. Function

9. a. Yes   **b.** Yes
   c. No, since the number 1 is paired with two different numbers.
   d. Yes
   e. No, since the letter b is paired with both b and c (and the letter d is paired with both e and f).

10. a. $(0, 0)$, $(2, 10)$, $(4, 116)$. Range: $\{0, 10, 116\}$
   b. $(1, 3)$, $(2, 4)$, $(9, 11)$. Range: $\{3, 4, 11\}$
   c. $(1, 2)$, $\left(2, \dfrac{9}{4}\right)$, $\left(3, \dfrac{64}{27}\right)$. Range: $\left\{2, \dfrac{9}{4}, \dfrac{64}{27}\right\}$

11. a. 100   **b.** 81   **c.** 3   **d.** 2

12. a. $\{(0, 0), (1, 0), (4, 60)\}$, $\begin{array}{l}0 \to\ 0\\ 1 \to\ 0\\ 4 \to 60\end{array}$

x	f(x)
0	0
1	0
4	60

   b. $f(x) = \sqrt{x}$ for $x \in \{1, 4, 9\}$, $\begin{array}{l}1 \to 1\\ 4 \to 2\\ 9 \to 3\end{array}$

x	f(x)
1	1
4	2
9	3

   c. $f(x) = 2x$ for $x \in \{1, 2, 10\}$, $\{(1, 2), (2, 4), (10, 20)\}$

x	f(x)
1	2
2	4
10	20

   d. $f(x) = 11x$ for $x \in \{5, 6, 7\}$, $\{(5, 55), (6, 66), (7, 77)\}$, $\begin{array}{l}5 \to 55\\ 6 \to 66\\ 7 \to 77\end{array}$

13. a. 29, 18, 17   **b.** 7, 10, 4   **c.** $\dfrac{7}{9}, \dfrac{6}{9}, \dfrac{5}{6}$ **d.** 5, 3, 4

14. a. $240, $89.75, $2240.50, $100
   b. $4321.30, $181.34   **c.** $22,780

15. a. 0.44   **b.** 0.56   **c.** 0.67   **d.** 4.61

16. Fraction equality is an equivalence relation. The equivalence class containing $\frac{1}{2}$ is $\{\frac{1}{2}, \frac{2}{4}, \frac{3}{6}, \frac{4}{8}, \frac{5}{10}, \ldots\}$.

17. a. 32; 212; 122; -40
   b. 0; 100; 40; -40
   c. Yes; -40

18. 3677

19. a. $C(x) = 85 + 35x$
   b. $C(18) = 715$. The total amount spent by a member after 18 months is $715.
   c. After 27 months

20. a. $r = \dfrac{1}{2}$
   b. 2400, 1200, 600, 300, 150, 75

21. a.

n	T(n)
1	4
2	12
3	20
4	28
5	36
6	44
7	52
8	60

   b. Arithmetic sequence with $a = 4$ and $d = 8$
   c. $T(n) = 4 + (n - 1)8$ or $T(n) = 8n - 4$
   d. $T(20) = 156$; $T(150) = 1196$
   e. Domain: $\{1, 2, 3, 4, \ldots\}$
   Range: $\{4, 12, 20, 28, \ldots\}$

22. a.

n	T(n)
1	3
2	9
3	18
4	30
5	45
6	63
7	81
8	108

   b. Neither
   c. $T(n) = \dfrac{3n(n + 1)}{2}$
   d. $T(15) = 360$. $T(100) = 15,150$
   e. Domain: $\{1, 2, 3, 4, \ldots\}$
   Range: $\{3, 9, 18, 30, \ldots\}$

23. a.

n = NUMBER OF YEARS	ANNUAL INTEREST EARNED	VALUE OF ACCOUNT
0	0	100
1	5	105
2	5	110
3	5	115
4	5	120
5	5	125
6	5	130
7	5	135
8	5	140
9	5	145
10	5	150

   b. Arithmetic sequence with $a = 100$ and $d = 5$.
   $A(n) = 100 + 5n$

24. a.

n = NUMBER OF YEARS	ANNUAL INTEREST EARNED	VALUE OF ACCOUNT
0	0	100
1	5	105
2	5.25	110.25
3	5.51	115.76
4	5.79	121.55
5	6.08	127.63
6	6.38	134.01
7	6.70	140.71
8	7.04	147.75
9	7.39	155.13
10	7.76	162.89

b. Geometric sequence with $a = 100$ and $r = 1.05$. $A(n) = 100(1.05)^n$
c. $12.89

25. $h(1) = 48$, $h(2) = 64$, $h(3) = 48$; 4 seconds

26. Convert the number to base two. Since the largest possible telephone number, 999-9999, is between $2^{23} = 8388608$ and $2^{24} = 16777216$, the base two numeral will have at most 24 digits. Ask, in order, whether each digit is 1. This process takes 24 questions. Then convert back to base ten.

27. a. Arithmetic, 5, 1002   **b.** Geometric, 2, 14×2^{199}
c. Arithmetic, 10, 1994   **d.** Neither

28. 228

29. Answers will vary.

Section 9.4A

1.

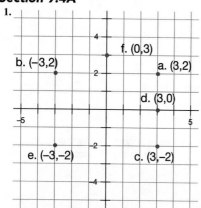

a. 1st quadrant   **b.** 2nd quadrant   **c.** 4th quadrant
d. x-axis   **e.** 3rd quadrant   **f.** y-axis

2. a. III and IV   **b.** IV   **c.** III

3.

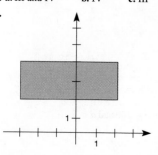

4. a.

x	f(x)
−2	−1
−1	1
0	3
1	5
2	7

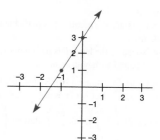

b.

x	m(x)
−2	50
−1	45
0	40
1	35
2	30

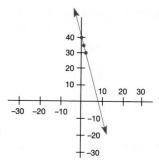

c.

x	g(x)
−2	−18.9
−1	−11.7
0	−4.5
1	2.7
2	9.9

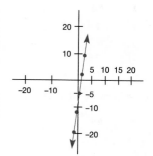

5. a.   (i)

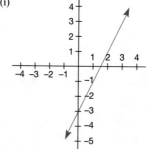

(ii)

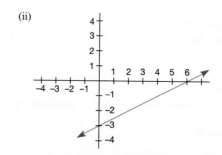

(iii)

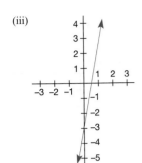

(iv)

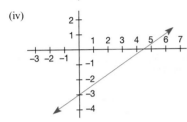

b. The larger the coefficient of x, the greater the slope or steeper the slant.

c. It changes the slant from lower left to upper right to a slant from upper left to lower right.

(i)

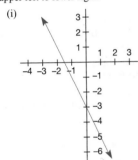

(ii)

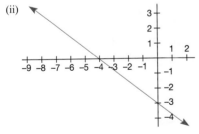

6. a. The line gets closer to being vertical.
  b. The line is horizontal.
  c. The line slants from upper left to lower right.

7. a. (i)

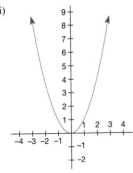

(ii)

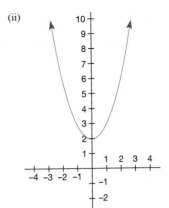

(iii)

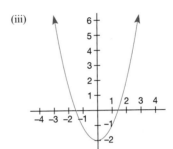

(iv)

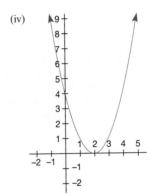

(v)

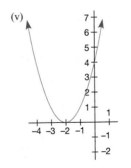

b. (ii) shifts the graph of (i) two units up, (iii) shifts the graph of (i) two units down, (iv) shifts the graph of (i) two units to the right, (v) shifts the graph of (i) two units to the left.
c. The graph of $f(x) = x^2 + 4$ should be the same as the graph in (i) except it is shifted up 4 units. The graph of $f(x) = (x-3)^2$ should be the same as the graph in (i) except it is shifted 3 units to the right.

8. a. Changing *b* has the effect of moving the parabola to the left or right.
b. Changing *c* has the effect of moving the parabola up or down.

9. a. (i)

(ii)

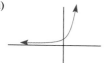

(iii)

(iv)

b. When the base is greater than 1, the larger the base, the steeper the rise of its graph from left to right, especially in the first quadrant. When the base is between 0 and 1, the closer to zero, the steeper the fall of its graph from left to right, especially in the second quadrant.

c.

$f(x) = 10^x$ $f(x) = (0.95)^x$

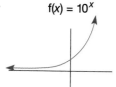 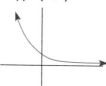

10. a. The right part comes closer to the *y*-axis and the left part gets closer to the *x*-axis
b. It is a horizontal line.
c. The graph is decreasing from left to right instead of increasing.

11. a.

x	h(x)
−2	−20
−1	−4
0	0
1	−2
2	−4
3	0

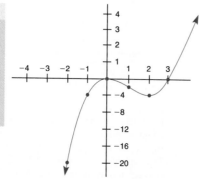

b.

x	s(x)
−2	10
−1	3
0	2
1	1
2	−6

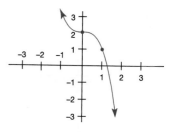

12. a. (i) P(0.5) = $0.39
(ii) P(5.5) = $1.59
(iii) P(11.9) = $3.03
(iv) P(12.1) = $3.27
b. Domain: 0 oz. < *w* ≤ 13 oz
Range = {39¢, 63¢, 87¢, $1.11, $1.35, $1.59, $1.83, $2.07, $2.31, $2.55, $2.79, $3.03, $3.27}

c.

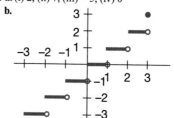

Ounces
Graph for first class
mail up to 6 oz.

d. 20 × 39 cents = $7.80 for 20 pieces or 20 × $\frac{3}{4}$ = 15 oz is $3.75.

13. a. (i) 2, (ii) 7, (iii) −5, (iv) 0
b.

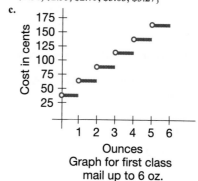

14. a.

b.

c.

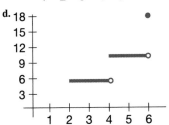

d.

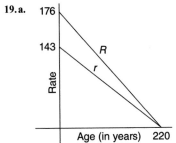

15. a. Exponential   **b.** Quadratic   **c.** Cubic

16. a. Domain = $\{x \mid -2 \leq x \leq 3\}$
Range = $\{y \mid -1 \leq y \leq 3\}$
b. Not a function   **c.** Not a function
d. Domain is the set of all real numbers. Range is the set of all positive real numbers.

17. a. (i) 3, (ii) −4, (iii) 0
b. Domain = $\{x \mid -3 \leq x \leq 6\}$
Range = $\{y \mid -4 \leq y \leq 3\}$
c. 0, 2, 5

18. a. $d(4) = 2.4$ miles, $d(5.5) \approx 2.81$ miles
b. Approximately 2.16 miles
c. Domain is the set of all nonnegative real numbers.
Range is the set of all nonnegative real numbers up to the farthest number of miles one can see.

19. a.

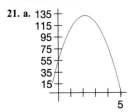

b. Between 123.5 and 152
c. Heart rates go down. The graph shows this information by falling from left to right.

20. a. The length of the shadow varies as time passes. Exponential.
b. $L(5) = 150$, $L(8) = 1100$, $L(2.5) = 50$ **c.** 4.5, 6
d. It is too dark to cast a shadow.

21. a.

b. Approximately 0.58 second and 3.8 seconds
c. In approximately 5.1 seconds   **d.** Approximately 131 feet

22. a.

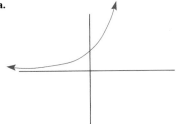

b. 6.6 billion
c. Approximately 29.8 years
d. Approximately 50 years

23. (a)
24. 130 drops 160 off on the top floor and returns. 210 takes the elevator to the top while 130 stays behind. 160 returns and comes up to the top with 130.
25. As b gets larger in a positive direction, the graph near the y-axis looks more like a parabola opening up. Similarly b is negative but as $|b|$ gets larger, the graph near the y-axis looks more like a parabola opening down.

PROBLEMS WHERE THE STRATEGY "SOLVE AN EQUATION" IS USEFUL

1. $27,000
2. 840
3. 4

CHAPTER REVIEW
Section 9.1

1. Every fraction and every integer is a rational number and the operations on fractions and integers are the same as the corresponding operations on rational numbers.
2. The a and b in $\dfrac{a}{b}$ are nonzero integers for rationals but are whole numbers for fractions.
3. The restriction that denominators are positive must be stated when dealing with rational numbers.
4. The number $-\frac{3}{4}$ is the additive inverse of $\frac{3}{4}$, and $\frac{-3}{4}$ is read "negative three over four"; however, they are equal.
5. a. T   **b.** T   **c.** F   **d.** T
   e. T   **f.** T   **g.** T   **h.** F
   i. F   **j.** T   **k.** T   **l.** T
6. a. Commutativity for addition
   b. Associativity for multiplication
   c. Multiplicative identity
   d. Distributivity
   e. Associativity for addition
   f. Multiplicative inverse
   g. Closure for addition
   h. Additive inverse
   i. Additive identity
   j. Closure for multiplication
   k. Commutativity for multiplication
   l. Additive cancellation

7. a. No, since $\frac{-5}{11}$ is to the left of $\frac{-3}{7}$.

  b. $\frac{-33}{77} < \frac{-35}{77}$ is false.

  c. $\frac{-3}{7} = \frac{-5}{11} + \frac{2}{77}$

  d. $-33 < -35$ is false.

8. a. $\frac{-2}{3} < \frac{7}{5}$; transitivity

  b. $<$; property of less than and multiplication by a positive

  c. $\frac{5}{8}$; property of less than and addition

  d. $<$; property of less than and multiplication by a negative

  e. Between; density property

Section 9.2

1. Every rational number is a real number, and operations on rational numbers as real numbers are the same as rational-number operations.

2. Rational numbers can be expressed in the form $\frac{a}{b}$, where a and b are integers, $b \neq 0$; irrational numbers cannot.

  Also rational numbers have repeating decimal representations, whereas irrational numbers do not.

3. None

4. Completeness. Real numbers fill the entire number line, whereas the rational-number line has "holes" where the irrationals are.

5. a. T   **b.** T   **c.** T
  d. T   **e.** T   **f.** F
  g. T   **h.** F

6. (i) $a^m a^n = a^{m+n}$
   (ii) $a^m b^m = (ab)^m$
   (iii) $(a^m)^n = a^{mn}$
   (iv) $a^m \div a^n = a^{m-n}$

7. $x = -\frac{13}{3}$ in all four cases.

8. a. $\frac{3}{7}$

  b. $x < \frac{17}{10}$

Section 9.3

1. a. Yes.
  b. Neither symmetric nor transitive
  c. Not transitive

2. a. $\{(1, 10), (2, 9), (3, 8), (4, 7), (5, 6), (6, 5), (7, 4), (8, 3), (9, 2), (10, 1)\}$, symmetric
  b. $\{(12, 8), (11, 7), (10, 6), (9, 5), (8, 4), (7, 3), (6, 2), (5, 1)\}$
  c. $\{(1, 12), (12, 1), (2, 6), (6, 2), (3, 4), (4, 3)\}$, symmetric
  d. $\{(12, 6), (10, 5), (8, 4), (6, 3), (4, 2), (2, 1)\}$

3. a. (i) 1, 7, 13, 19, 25; (ii) 2, 8, 32, 128, 512
  b. (i) 6; (ii) 4

4. a. T   **b.** F   **c.** F   **d.** F

5. a. Dawn → Jones, Jose → Ortiz, Amad → Rasheed
  b.

FIRST NAME	SURNAME
Dawn	Jones
Jose	Ortiz
Amad	Rasheed

  c. (Dawn, Jones), (Jose, Ortiz), (Amad, Rasheed)

6.

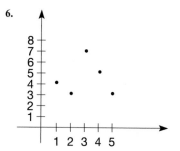

Range = $\{3, 4, 5, 7\}$

7. For example, the area of a circle with radius r is πr^2, the circumference of a circle with radius r is $2\pi r$, and the volume of a cube having side length s is s^3.

Section 9.4

1. a. Cubic

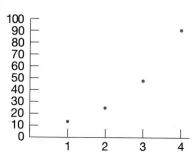

  b. Exponential

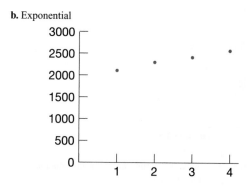

  c. Quadratic

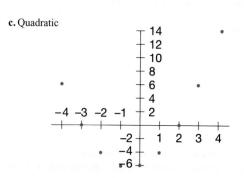

d. Linear

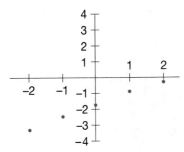

2.

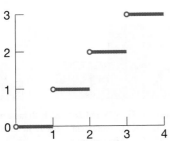

3.

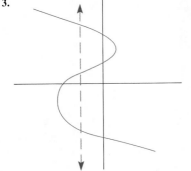

Chapter 9 Test

1. a. F **b.** T **c.** F **d.** F **e.** T
f. F **g.** T **h.** F **i.** T **j.** F

2. a. i, ii, iii **b.** i, ii, iii **c.** i, iii **d.** i, iii **e.** i, ii, iii

3. Arrow Diagrams, Tables, Machines, Ordered Pairs, Graphs, Formulas, Geometric Transformations (any 6 is sufficient)

4. a. $\frac{-23}{21}$ **b.** $\frac{-6}{55}$ **c.** $\frac{-1}{28}$

5. a. Commutativity and associativity
b. Commutativity, distributivity, and identity for multiplication

6. a. $\left\{ x \mid x > \frac{-12}{7} \right\}$ **b.** $\frac{177}{98}$

7. a. 729 **b.** 128 **c.** $\frac{1}{243}$

8. a. **b.** **c.**

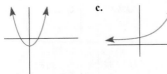

9. $14.1\%, \frac{7}{5}, \underline{1.41411411}\ldots, 1.\overline{41}, \sqrt{2}, 1.41\overline{42}$

10. a. 16 **b.** $6\sqrt{3}$ **c.** $7\sqrt{5}$ **d.** -1

11. a. $\{(a, c), (b, c), (c, a), (c, d), (d, a), (d, e), (e, b)\}$
b. $\{(a, a), (a, b), (b, a), (c, e), (d, d), (e, c), (e, e)\}$, symmetric
c. $\{(1, 2), (2, 1), (-2, 3), (-1, -1), (-3, -2), (-2, -3), (3, -2)\}$, symmetric

12. $\frac{-3}{7} = \frac{-3}{7} \cdot \frac{-1}{-1} = \frac{(-3)(-1)}{7(-1)} = \frac{3}{-7}$

13. No. For example, $\frac{1}{-2} < \frac{-1}{3}$; however, $3 > 2$.

14. $\frac{1}{5^{-7}} = \frac{1}{(1/5^7)} = 5^7$

15.

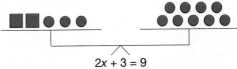

$2x + 3 = 9$

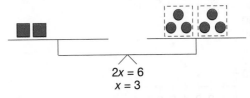

$2x + 3 - 3 = 9 - 3$

$2x = 6$
$x = 3$

16. Since $\sqrt{17}$ is irrational, it has a nonrepeating, nonterminating decimal representation. But $4.1231\overline{0562}$ is repeating, so it is rational. Thus, the two numbers cannot be equal.

17. 2, 6, 10, 14, . . . is an arithmetic sequence, and 2, 6, 18, 54, . . . is geometric.

18. First one is a function. Second one is not, 3 has no image. Third one is not, 2 has two images.

19. a. $\{(1, 1), (2, 2), (3, 3), (4, 4)\}$
b. None
c. $\{(1, 1), (2, 2), (3, 3), (4, 4), (1, 4), (4, 1), (3, 2), (2, 3)\}$
d. Same as part (c)

20. a. Exponential
b. Quadratic
c. Cubic

21. Suppose $\sqrt{8} = \frac{a}{b}$, where $\frac{a}{b}$ is a rational number. Then $8b^2 = a^2$. But this is impossible, since $8b^2 = 2^3b^2$ has an odd number of prime factors, whereas a^2 has an even number.

22. 105

23. 3

24. Only when $x = 0$ or when $a = b$

25. a. \$241 **b.** $C(n) = 4(n-1)^2 + 3(2n-1)$

26. $t = 3$

27. $0.45455455545555\ldots, 0.45616116111\ldots, 0.46363663666\ldots$
(Answers may vary.)

28. $187, 3 + (n-1)\cdot 4$

29. a.

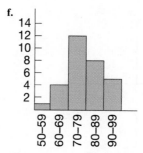

b.

n	2^n
1	2
2	4
3	8
4	16
5	32
6	64

c.

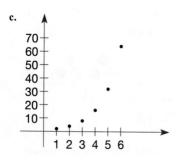

d. $f(n) = 2^n$

30. Any a and b where both a and b are not zero.

31. $F(C) = 1.8C + 32$

32. $f(x) = 0.75(220 - x)$

Section 10.1A

1. a. 58, 63, 65, 67, 69, 70, 72, 72, 72, 74, 74, 76, 76, 76, 76, 78, 78, 80, 80, 80, 82, 85, 85, 86, 88, 92, 92, 93, 95, 98

b. 58, 98

c. 76

d.

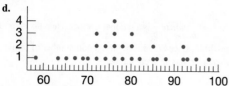

e.

50 − 59	1
60 − 69	4
70 − 79	12
80 − 89	8
90 − 99	5

f.

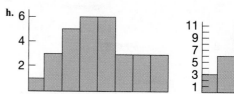

g. 70–79

h.

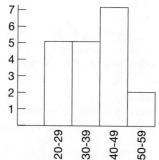

i. For increment 5, 73 to 78 and 78 to 83 both have 6. For increment 8, 74 to 82 has 11. For increment 5, the 12 in 73–83 is close to the 11 in 74 to 82 for increment 8.

2.

15.	8 9
16.	1 3 4
17.	0 5
18.	1 2 5 5 5
19.	2 4
20.	2 3 6 9 9
21.	1 4 8
22.	0 0 1

3. a.

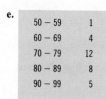

4. a.

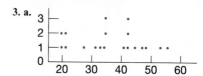

CLASS 2		CLASS 1
	5	7 8 9
8 7 6	6	0 2
9 7 7 5	7	2 5 6 6 9
7 7 5 5 4 3 2	8	0 0 1 6 6 6 7
5 2 2 2 0 0	9	3 3 3

b. Class 2

5. a. Portland   **b.** 4 months; 0 month
   c. December (6.0 inches); July (0.5 inch)
   d. August (4.0 inches); January (2.7 inches)
   e. New York City (40.3 inches) (Portland's total = 37.6 inches)

6. a.

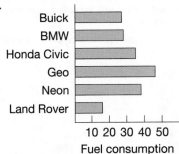

   b. Land Rover; Geo   **c.** Geo; Land Rover
   d. Buick, $8266.67
      BMW, $7971.43
      Honda Civic, $6377.14
      Geo, $4852.17
      Neon, $5873.68
      Land Rover, $13,950
   e. A histogram could not be used because the categories on the horizontal axis are not numbers that can be broken into different intervals.

7. a.

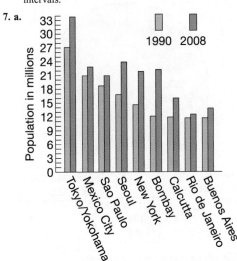

World's Largest Urban Areas
(*Source: World Almanac*)

   b. Bombay   **c.** Rio de Janeiro

8. a.

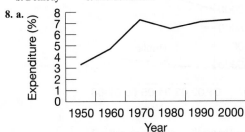

b.

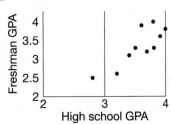

   c. The first; the second

9. a. Taxes   **b.** 20.3%
   c. 64°   **d.** Natural resources
   e. Social assistance, transportation, health and rehabilitation, and natural resources
   f. 23°, 26°

10. Grants to local governments, $1,269,000,000; salaries and fringe benefits, $1,161,000,000; grants to organizations and individuals, $873,000,000; operating, $621,000,000; other, $576,000,000

11. a. $15,000,000   **b.** $5,000,000   **c.** $85,000,000

12. a.

Students

1910	🚶🚶🚶🚶	🚶 = 5,000,000
1920	🚶🚶🚶🚶	
1930	🚶🚶🚶🚶🚶	
1940	🚶🚶🚶🚶🚶	
1950	🚶🚶🚶🚶🚶	
1960	🚶🚶🚶🚶🚶🚶🚶	
1970	🚶🚶🚶🚶🚶🚶🚶🚶	
1980	🚶🚶🚶🚶🚶🚶🚶	
1990	🚶🚶🚶🚶🚶🚶🚶	
2000	🚶🚶🚶🚶🚶🚶🚶🚶🚶	

Each stick figure represents 5,000,000 students
   b. 1910s, 1920s, 1950s, 1960s, 1980s, 1990s
   c. Bar or line graph

13. a.

   b. No outliers

c.

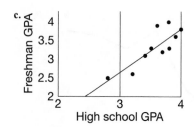

14. a.

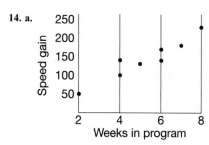

b. No outliers

c.

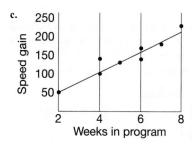

15. a. and **b.**

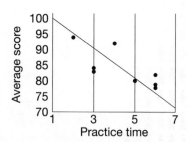

c. They should look similar.

16. a. and **b.**

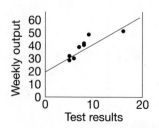

c. They should look similar.

17. a. 84   **b.** ~89

18. a. The number of bars increases because the range is still the same but divided into smaller intervals.
  b. Because of the gaps in the data such as from 7 to 12 and from 14 to 22, when the cell width gets small, the cells in those intervals will have no values in them.

19. a. Double bar graph or pictograph for comparing two sets of data.

b.

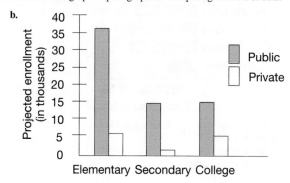

20. a. Circle graph—compare parts of a whole

b.

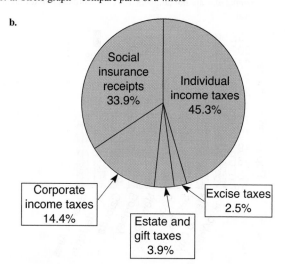

21. a. Double line graph or bar graph to show trends.

b.

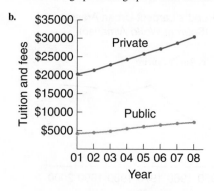

c. Private—The graph is generally steeper.

22. a. Multiple bar graph to allow comparison.

b.

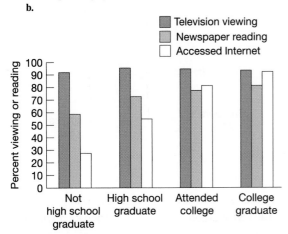

23. a. Bar graph or line graph to show a trend.

b.

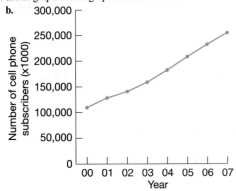

24. a. Multiple bar graph or line graph to show a trend.

b.

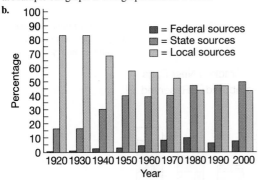

c. Federal funds increased steadily until sometime during the 1980s, then decreased. State funds increased steadily. Local funds decreased steadily until the 1980s and provide less than half of school funds.

25. a–b.

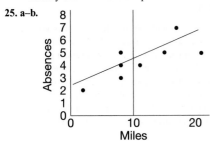

c. 6

26.

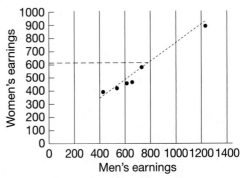

The corresponding weekly salary for a woman is about $600.

Section 10.2A

1. a.

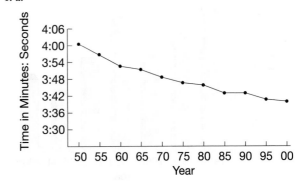

b. It makes the downward trend more apparent.

2. a.

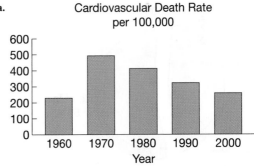

b.

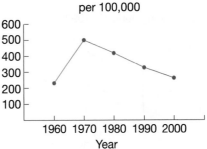

c. Answers will vary

3. a. Yes **b.** Different vertical scale **c. i.** **d. ii.**

4.

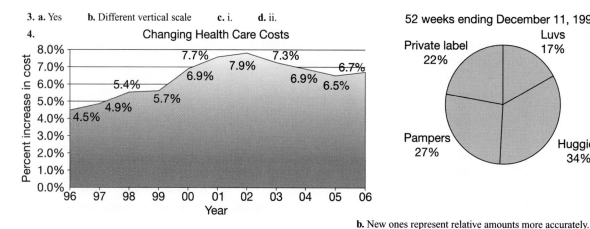

5.

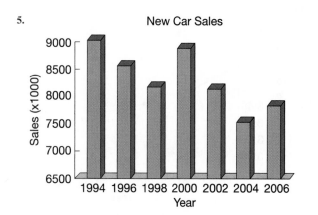

6.

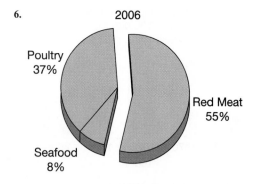

7. a.

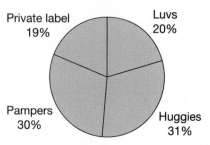

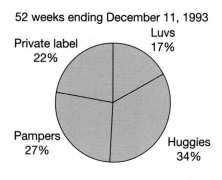

b. New ones represent relative amounts more accurately. **c.** No

8.

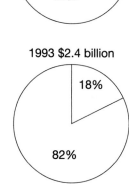

It gives the impression that every graph represents the same amount of money.

9.

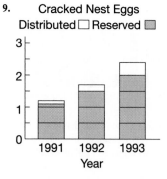

10. The height of "Dad's" sack should be close to three times as tall as the "other" sack and it is not even twice as tall. The height of "The Kid's" sack should be close to twice as tall (200%) and it is only about 30% taller. Finally, the height of "Mom's" sack should be more than 3 times (300%) as tall as "The Kid's" sack and it is only about 50% taller. The graph could be more mathematically correct if the sack heights were all proportional to the percent that they represented while keeping the width and depth of all of the sacks constant.

11. a. (ii), (iii) and (iv).
  b. In (i), the volume represented on the right is actually 8 times as large.

12. Cropped vertical axis, horizontal instead of vertical bars, reverse the order of the categories.

13. Population = set of lightbulbs manufactured.
  Sample = package of 8 chosen.

14. Population = set of full-time students enrolled at the university.
  Sample = set of 100 students chosen to be interviewed.

15. a. $\sqrt{2}$ or about 1.4 in. Because the graphs are two-dimensional, their revenues vary as the square of their radii and $1^2 : \sqrt{2}^2 = 1 : 2 = 5,000,000 : 10,000,000$.
  b. $\sqrt[3]{2}$ or about 1.3 in. Because the graphs are three-dimensional, their revenues vary as the cube of their radii and $1^3 : \sqrt[3]{2}^3 = 1 : 2 = 5,000,000 : 10,000,000$.

16.

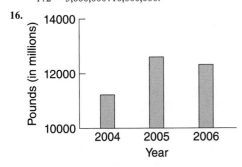

17.

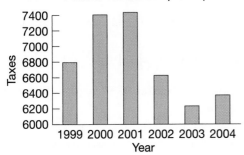

18.

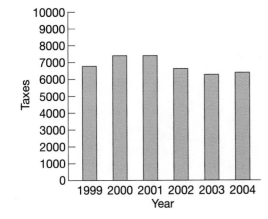

19. Indices of Products for Which a U.S. Farmer would have received $100 in 1992.

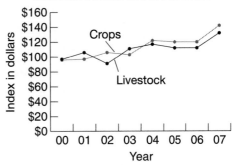

20. Population = the set of fish in the lake. Sample = the 500 fish that are caught and are examined for tags. Bias results from the fact that some of the tagged fish may be caught or die before the sample is taken and the fish might not redistribute throughout the lake.

21. Population = set of all doctors. Sample = the set of 20 doctors chosen. Bias results from the fact that they will commission studies until they get the result they want.

Section 10.3A

1. a. $9.8\overline{3}$; 9.5; 9   **b.** $14.1\overline{6}$; 13.5; no mode
  c. $0.48\overline{3}$; 1.9; no mode   **d.** $-4.\overline{2}$; 0; 0

2. a. Median: $\frac{3}{2} + \sqrt{7}$
    Mode: $3 + \sqrt{7}$
    Mean: $\frac{5}{6} + \sqrt{7}$
  b. Median: 4π
    Mode: 4π
    Mean: $\frac{11}{3}\pi$
  c. Median: 6.37
    Mode: 5.37
    Mean: $\frac{37}{6} + .37 \approx 6.54$

3. No student is average overall. On the math test, Doug is closest to the mean; on the reading test, Rob is closest.

4. 584 students

5. Yes but the remaining 6 students must all have perfect scores and all 18 students must score 59.

6. a. {1}, Answers may vary   **b.** {1, 7, 7}, Answers may vary

7.

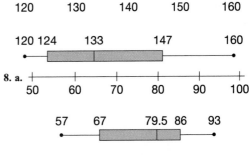

8. a.

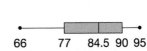

  b. Class 2; all five statistics are higher than their counterparts for Class 1.

9. a. The upper quartile: 86
  b. The median: 84.5
  c. The lower quartile: 67

10.

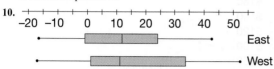

A trend toward greater growth west of the Mississippi

11. a.

```
7 | 14 55 62
6 | 09 30 60
5 | 04 09 11 12 12 21 21 21 34 36 46 48 63 64 69 73 83 83 86
4 | 52 62 65 75 75 93
```

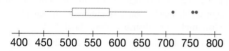

b. Aaron's, Bond's, and Ruth's totals are mild outliers.

12. a. 0; 0
  b. 6.6̄; 2.58 (to two places)
  c. 371.61; 19.28 (to two places)

13. a. 2; $\sqrt{2}$ **b.** 18; $3\sqrt{2}$ **c.** 50; $5\sqrt{2}$
  d. 72; $6\sqrt{2}$. If the variance is v and the standard deviation is s, and if all data are multiplied by r, the new variance is r^2v and the new standard deviation is $\sqrt{r^2} \cdot s$.
  e. Their standard deviations are all the same and all three sets of data are arithmetic sequences with a difference of 5.

14. 18, 18.5, 19, 2.6, 1.61

15. −0.55, −1.76, 0.36, 1.71, −0.32, −0.10, 0.66

16. a. 84%, z-score = 1
  b. 97.5%, z-score = 2

17. A: test score > 95
  B: 90 < test score ≤ 95
  C: 80 < test score ≤ 90
  D: 75 < test score ≤ 80
  F: test score ≤ 75

18. a. 87th percentile
  b. 87%

19. Approximately 38.3

20. 24.128 or 24

21. Set 1: 1, 3, 3, 5   SD = $\sqrt{2}$
  Set 2: 1, 5, 5, 9   SD = $2\sqrt{2}$
  Answers may vary

22. 293

23. 76.81 to two places

24. 1456

25. Test 1: her z-score (0.65) is slightly higher than on test 2 (0.63).

26. Mode, since this represents the most frequently sold size.

27. a. The distribution with the smaller variance

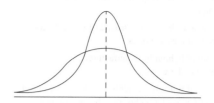

b. The distribution with the larger mean

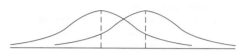

28. a. 1.14 (to two places)
  b. 1.99 (to two places)
  c. 97.5%

PROBLEMS WHERE THE STRATEGY "LOOK FOR A FORMULA" IS USEFUL

1. The first allowance yields $7 + 21 + 35 + \cdots + 7(2 \cdot 30 - 1)$, which equals $7(1 + 3 + 5 + \cdots + 59)$. Since $1 + 3 + 5 + \cdots + (2n - 1) = n^2$ and 59 is $2 \cdot 30 - 1$, the total is $7 \cdot 30^2 = \$63$. The other way, the total is $30 \cdot 2 = \$60$. He should choose the first way.

2. Let x be its original height. Its height after several days would be given by $x\left(\dfrac{3}{2}\right)\left(\dfrac{4}{3}\right)\left(\dfrac{5}{4}\right)\cdots$. One can see that the product of these fractions leads to this formula: $x\left(\dfrac{3}{2}\right)\left(\dfrac{4}{3}\right)\left(\dfrac{5}{4}\right)\cdots\left(\dfrac{n + 1}{n}\right) = \dfrac{n + 1}{2}$.
Therefore, since $\dfrac{n + 1}{2} > 100$ when $n + 1 > 200$, or when $n > 199$, it would take 199 days.

3. Pairing the first ray on the right with the remaining rays would produce 99 angles. Pairing the second ray on the right with the remaining ones would produce 98 angles. Continuing in this way, we obtain $99 + 98 + 97 + \cdots + 1$ such angles. But this sum is $(100 \cdot 99)/2$ or 4950. Thus 4950 different angles are formed.

CHAPTER REVIEW
Section 10.1

1.

CLASS 1		CLASS 2
	1	7
3 3	2	5 9
9 7	3	9
1	4	0 0 0 0 9
	5	1 2 2
	6	
9 8 6 4 4 2	7	
2 1 0	8	0 5 9
6 4 4 4 0	9	2 5 7 7 9

2.

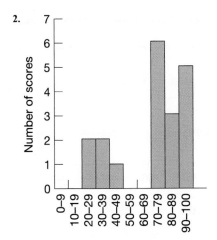

3.

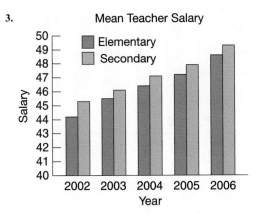

4.

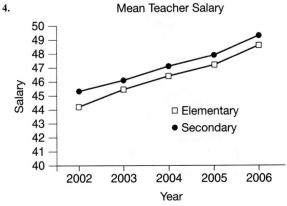

5.

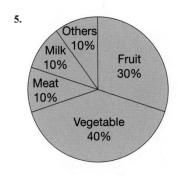

6.

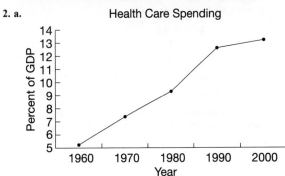

The point (18, 340) is an outlier.
Fifteen inches of rain should correspond to $245,000 in sales.
For sales of $260,000, the rain should be around 13.5 inches.

Section 10.2

1.

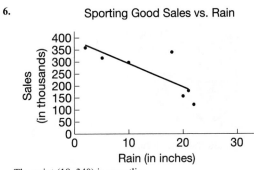

2. a.

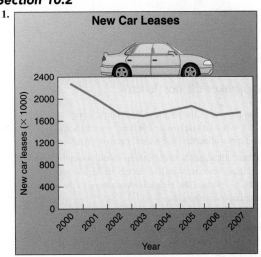

b.

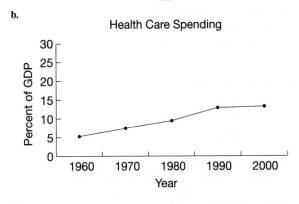

28. a. I   **b.** II   **c.** III   **d.** III   **e.** IV   **f.** y-axis

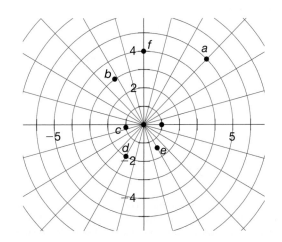

29. AP: $x^2 + y^2 = 9$ ①
  BP: $(a - x)^2 + y^2 = 16$ ②
  CP: $(a - x)^2 + (b - y)^2 = 25$ ③
  DP: Want to find $x^2 + (b - y)^2 = DP^2$
  ③ − ② $(b - y)^2 - y^2 = 9$
  + ① $x^2 + y^2 = 9$
  ─────────────────────
  $(b - y)^2 + x^2 = 18$, so $DP = \sqrt{18}$

30. a. 100 people
  b. 125 people
  c. 225 people

31. a. 2
  b. $(0, 1)$ and $\left(-\frac{4}{5}, \frac{3}{5}\right)$

Section 15.3A

1. a. $(3, 5), (-3, 5)$, or $(3, -5)$
  b. $(1, -2), (-5, -2)$, or $(9, 8)$

2. a. $(-2, 4)$ **b.** $(-1, 3)$

3. a. $C(a, a), D(0, a)$ **b.** $G(a, b)$

4. a. $Q(0, 0), R(6, 0), S(0, 4)$
  b. $Q(0, 0), R(a, 0), S(0, b)$

5. a. $X = (0, 0), Y = (8, 0), Z = (4, 5)$
  b. $X = (-4, 0), Y = (4, 0), Z = (0, 5)$

6. Slope of $\overline{RS} = \dfrac{-2 - 0}{5 - 3} = -1$;

  slope of $\overline{TU} = \dfrac{-1 + 3}{-4 + 2} = -1$; $\overline{RS} \parallel \overline{TU}$;

  slope of $\overline{ST} = \dfrac{0 + 1}{3 + 4} = \dfrac{1}{7}$;

  slope of $\overline{RU} = \dfrac{-2 + 3}{5 + 2} = \dfrac{1}{7}$; $\overline{ST} \parallel \overline{RU}$. Since both pairs of opposite sides are parallel, $RSTU$ is a parallelogram.

7. Slope of $\overline{AB} = -\frac{3}{2}$ and slope of $\overline{CD} = -\frac{3}{2}$, so $\overline{AB} \parallel \overline{CD}$. Slope of $\overline{BC} = \frac{2}{3}$ and slope of $\overline{AD} = \frac{2}{3}$, so $\overline{BC} \parallel \overline{AD}$. Since $\left(-\frac{3}{2}\right)\left(\frac{2}{3}\right) = -1$, $\overline{AB} \perp \overline{BC}$. Thus $ABCD$ is a parallelogram (opposite sides parallel) with a right angle, and thus a rectangle.

8. a. $(0, 4)$ **b.** $(4, 5)$
  c. Both equal 1/4, $\overline{MN} \parallel \overline{AB}$
  d. $MN = \sqrt{17}$, $AB = \sqrt{68} = 2\sqrt{17}$, $MN = (1/2)AB$

9. $AC = \sqrt{a^2 + b^2}$; $BD = \sqrt{(0 - a)^2 + (b - 0)^3} = \sqrt{a^2 + b^2}$

10. a. $y = \frac{2}{7}x$
  b. $y = -\frac{2}{5}x + \frac{48}{5}$
  c. $y = 2x - 24$
  d. $(14, 4)$; yes
  e. The medians are concurrent (meet at a single point).
  f. centroid

11. Yes

12. a. If $AB = BC$, then $\sqrt{a^2 + b^2} = \sqrt{(a - c)^2 + b^2}$ or $a^2 = (a - c)^2$, $a^2 = a^2 - 2ac + c^2$, $c^2 = 2ac$, and then $c = 2a$.
  b. The midpoint of $\overline{AC}$ has coordinates $(a, 0)$, and thus the median from B is vertical and thereby perpendicular to horizontal $\overline{AC}$

13. a. $y = \frac{1}{2}x$ **b.** $x = 8$
  c. $y = -\frac{4}{3}x + \frac{44}{3}$ **d.** $(8, 4)$, yes
  e. orthocenter

14. The midpoint of $\overline{AC}$ is $\left(\dfrac{a + b}{2}, \dfrac{c}{2}\right)$. The midpoint of $\overline{BD}$ is $\left(\dfrac{b + a}{2}, \dfrac{c}{2}\right)$. The diagonals meet at the midpoint of each, thus bisecting each other.

15. a. The slope of $\overline{QR}$ is $\dfrac{b}{a - c}$, so the slope of l (perpendicular to $\overline{QR}$) is $-\left(\dfrac{a - c}{b}\right)$ or $\dfrac{c - a}{b}$.
  b. Since the point has an x-coordinate of a, it is on line m. Substituting into $y = \dfrac{c - a}{b}x$ yields $\dfrac{(c - a)a}{b} = \left(\dfrac{c - a}{b}\right)a$. which is satisfied, so the point lies on line l also.
  c. The slope of $\overline{PQ}$ is $\dfrac{b}{a}$, so the slope of n (perpendicular to $\overline{PQ}$) is $\dfrac{-a}{b}$.

16. Impossible. The length of the horizontal side is $2a$. The height is b, a whole number. Also, $\sqrt{a^2 + b^2} = 2a$, so $a^2 + b^2 = 4a^2$, $b^2 = 3a^2$, $\dfrac{b}{a} = \sqrt{3}$, which is irrational.

17. 7 and 11 years old

18. 5 tricycles and 2 bicycles

19. Mike, $7000; Joan, $4000

20. 75 dimes and 35 quarters

21. a. 35 paths   **b.** 18 paths   **c.** $\frac{18}{35}$

ADDITIONAL PROBLEMS WHERE THE STRATEGY "USE COORDINATES" IS USEFUL

1. One of the diagonals of the kite is on the y-axis and the other is parallel to the x-axis. Thus they are perpendicular.

2. On a coordinate map, starting at $(0, 0)$, where north is up, he goes to $(0, 4)$, then to $(-3, 4)$, then to $(-3, 2)$. Thus his distance from base camp is $\sqrt{3^2 + 2^2} = \sqrt{13}$ km.

3. Place the figure on a coordinate system with A at the origin, $B = (0, 2m)$, and $C = (2m, 0)$. Then $E = (m, -m)$ and $D = (-m, m)$. The slope of $\overline{BC} = -1$, as does the slope of $\overline{DE}$. Thus they are parallel.

CHAPTER REVIEW
Section 15.1
1. $\sqrt{40} = 2\sqrt{10}$

2. $(4, 1)$

3. Yes

4. P, Q, and M are collinear.

5. Yes

6. No

Section 15.2
1. $y = -\frac{5}{2}x + 3$

2. $y = 2 - (-\frac{3}{2})(x - 3)$

3. There are one, none, or infinitely many solutions.

4. $(x + 2)^2 + (y - 5)^2 = 25$

Section 15.3
1. $(4, \frac{5}{3})$

2. $(0, 0)$

3. $(6, 2\frac{1}{2})$

Chapter 15 Test
1. a. T
b. F
c. T
d. F
e. F
f. T
g. T
h. F

2. Slope-intercept: $y = mx + b$
Point-slope: $(y - y_0) = m(x - x_0)$

3. Length is $\sqrt{41}$; midpoint is $(3, 4.5)$; slope is $\frac{5}{4}$.

4. a. $x = -1$
b. $y = 7$
c. $y = 3x + 10$
d. $2y - 3x = 17$

5. $(x + 3)^2 + (y - 4)^2 = 5^2$, or $x^2 + 6x + y^2 - 8y = 0$

6. a. 0
b. 1
c. Infinitely many
d. 1

7. $y = \frac{3}{4}x - 2$

8. $(y - 4\frac{1}{2}) = -\frac{4}{5}(x - 3)$

9. 0, 1, or 2, since a circle and a line may meet in 0, 1, or 2 points

10. The first pair of lines is parallel, the last pair is parallel, but no two of the lines are perpendicular.

11. $(-3, -1)$, $(-3, 9)$, $(-8, 4)$, $(2, 4)$, any values of x and y that satisfy the equation.

12. As seen in the following figure,

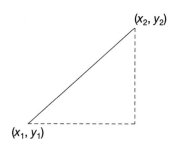

a right triangle can be constructed between the pair of points and the legs of the triangle have lengths $|x_2 - x_1|$ and $|y_2 - y_1|$. Using the Pythagorean theorem, we can find the length of the hypotenuse as $\sqrt{(x_2 - x_1)^2 + (y_2 - y_1)^2}$, which is the distance formula.

13. All sides have length $\sqrt{10}$. The slope of $\overline{LM}$ is $-\frac{1}{3}$ and the slope of $\overline{MN}$ is 3, so $\angle LMN$ is a right angle. Thus, $LMNO$ is a square.

14. $(7, 3)$

15. Any point on the line $y = 2x$ [e.g., $(0, 0)$, $(1, 2)$, $(2, 4)$]

16. a.

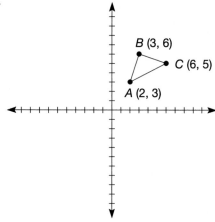

b. Isosceles triangle: $AB = \sqrt{10}$, $BC = \sqrt{10}$, $AC = \sqrt{20}$
c. Right triangle: $AB^2 + BC^2 = AC^2$

17. $ABCD$ is a square, since it is a parallelogram whose diagonals are perpendicular and congruent (verify).

18. a. The slopes of $\overline{DE}$ and $\overline{AC}$ are both zero.
b. $DE = \frac{a + 2b}{3} - \frac{2b}{3} = \frac{a}{3}$. Therefore, $DE = \frac{1}{3}AC$.

In $\triangle ABC$, if $DB = \frac{1}{3}AB$ and $EB = \frac{1}{3}CB$, then $DE = \frac{1}{3}AC$ and $\overline{DE} \parallel \overline{AC}$.

19. a. $N = (a + c, b)$
b. The midpoint of $\overline{LN}$ is $\left(\frac{a + c}{2}, \frac{b}{2}\right)$ and the midpoint of $\overline{MO}$ is $\left(\frac{a + c}{2}, \frac{b}{2}\right)$. Since the midpoints coincide, the diagonals bisect each other.

Section 16.1A

1. a. 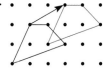 **b.**

2.

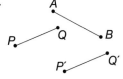

3. a. Any directed line segment that goes right 4, up 2

b.

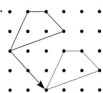

c. Down 4, right 5

4. Construct a line through P parallel to $\overline{AB}$. Then with a compass, mark off $\overline{PP'}$ having the length of AB.

NOTE: P' should be to the right and above B.

5. a. $-80°$ **b.** $120°$

6. a.

b.

c. **d.**

7.

8. a. **b.**

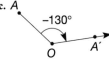

9. a.

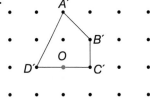

b.

10. $(-1, 4)$

11. a. $(-3, 2)$ **b.** $(-3, -1)$
 c. $(4, -1)$ **d.** $(2, -4)$
 e. $(4, 2)$ **f.** $(-y, x)$

12. a. $(-3, 1)$ **b.** $(6, 3)$
 c. $(4, -2)$ **d.** $(-x, -y)$

13. a. $(-y, x)$ **b.** $(-x, -y)$

14. a. **b.**

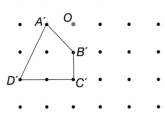

c.

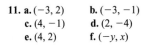

15.

16. a. 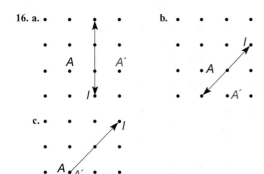   **b.**

c.

17. a.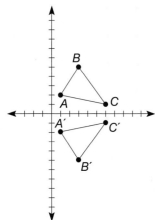

b. $A' = (1, -2)$, $B' = (3, -5)$, $C' = (6, -1)$ **c.** $(a, -b)$

18. Construct a line through A perpendicular to l (to point P on l), extend beyond l, and mark off A' such that $PA' = AP$.

19. a.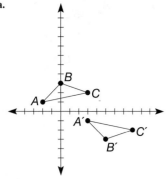

b. $A' = (3, -1)$, $B' = (5, -3)$, $C' = (8, -2)$
c. $(a + 5, -b)$

20. Construct lines, through A and B, parallel to $\overleftrightarrow{XY}$ and mark off the translation. Then construct perpendiculars to l through A' and B' to find the reflection of the translated image.

21. a. Same; A to B to C is counterclockwise in each case.
 b. Same
 c. Opposite

22. a.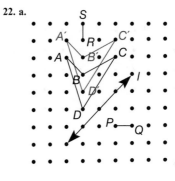

b.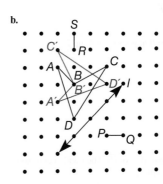

c.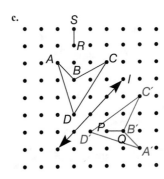

d.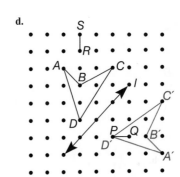

23. a. Translation, rotation, reflection, glide reflection
 b. Translation, rotation, reflection, glide reflection
 c. Translation, rotation, reflection, glide reflection
 d. Translation, rotation, reflection, glide reflection

24. a.

b.
... ...

c. Others are possible.

25. a. 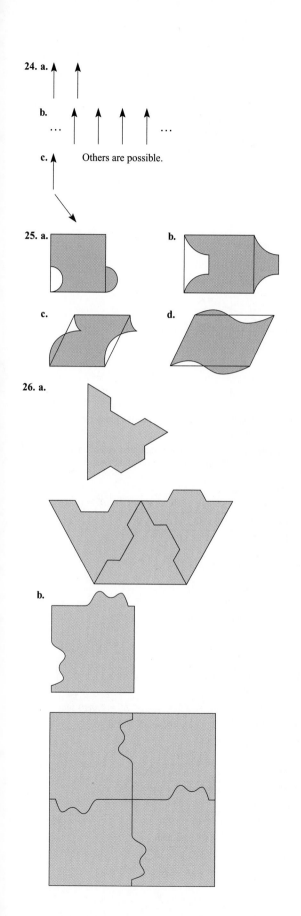 **b.**

c. **d.**

26. a.

b.

27. a.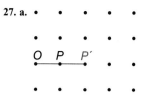

b.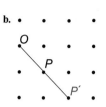

c.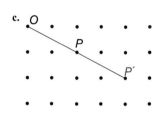

28. a.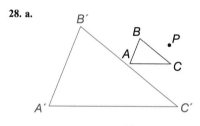

b.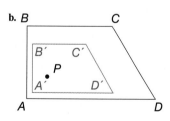

29. a. $T_{AA'}$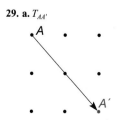

b. $R_{0,-90}$ is one possibility.

c. M_l

d. T_{XY} followed by M_l is one possibility.

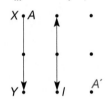

30. a. Not possible
b. $R_{A,-90}$

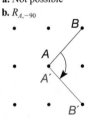

c. M_l

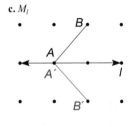

d. Not possible

31. a. Reflection

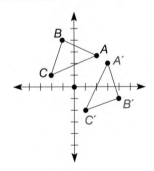

b. Rotation

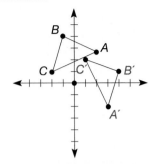

c. Translation

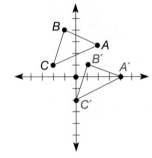

32. The farther the center is from the object, the greater the image is from the original.

33. Moving the center of a size transformation does not effect the size of the image. It only effects the location of the image.

Section 16.2A

1. a. $A = (1, 3); B = (2, 1)$ **b.** $A' = (-1, 4); B' = (0, 2)$
  c. $AB = \sqrt{(1-2)^2 + (3-1)^2} = \sqrt{5};$
    $A'B' = \sqrt{(-1-0)^2 + (4-2)^2} = \sqrt{5}$

2. a. Yes, both have slope $\dfrac{q}{p}$.
  b. Yes, both have length $\sqrt{p^2 + q^2}$.
  c. Yes, by definition.

3. a. $\overline{OX} \perp \overline{OY}$ since (slope of $\overline{OX}$)(slope of $\overline{OY}$) =
    $\left(\dfrac{y}{x}\right) \cdot \left(\dfrac{x}{-y}\right) = -1.$
  b. $OX = \sqrt{x^2 + y^2}, OY = \sqrt{(-y)^2 + x^2} = \sqrt{y^2 + x^2}$
  c. Yes, by definition.

4. $A' = (-2, 5), B' = (4, 3); AB = \sqrt{2^2 + 6^2} = 2\sqrt{10}$ and
  $A'B' = \sqrt{(-6)^2 + 2^2} = 2\sqrt{10}$, so $AB = A'B'$.

5. a. $A = (1, 2), B = (2, 0)$
  b. $A' = (-1, 2), B' = (-2, 0)$
  c. $AB = \sqrt{(1-2)^2 + (2-0)^2} = \sqrt{5}$
  d. $A'B' = \sqrt{(-1+2)^2 + (2-0)^2} = \sqrt{5}$

6. a. $(a, -b)$
  b. $AB = \sqrt{(a-c)^2 + (b-d)^2};$
    $A' = (a, -b), B' = (c, -d)$, and
    $A'B' = \sqrt{(a-c)^2 + (-b+d)^2}$
          $= \sqrt{(a-c)^2 + (b-d)^2}$

7. a. The midpoint of $\overline{XY} = \left(\dfrac{x+y}{2}, \dfrac{y+x}{2}\right)$. Since its x- and y-coordinates are equal, it lies on line l.

b. The slope of $\overline{XY} = \dfrac{x-y}{y-x} = -1$, and the slope of line l is 1.

Since $(-1)(1) = -1$, $\overline{XY} \perp l$.

c. Yes, line l is the perpendicular bisector of $\overline{XY}$.

8. a. $A = (2, 1)$, $B = (-2, 3)$
b. $A' = (4, -1)$, $B' = (0, -3)$
c. $AB = \sqrt{(2+2)^2 + (1-3)^2} = 2\sqrt{5}$;
$A'B' = \sqrt{(4-0)^2 + (-1+3)^2} = 2\sqrt{5}$

9. a. Rotation   **b.** Translation   **c.** Glide reflection

10. a. Translation   **b.** Reflection   **c.** Glide reflection   **d.** Rotation

11. a.

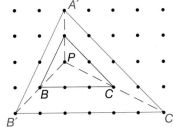

b. $\sqrt{5}, 2\sqrt{5}; 2$ **c.** 3, 6; 2   **d.** $2\sqrt{2}, 4\sqrt{2}; 2$
e. They are parallel.

12. a.

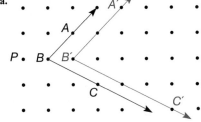

b. They are equal.

13. No; the lines $\overleftrightarrow{SS}$, $\overleftrightarrow{RRS}$ and $\overleftrightarrow{TT'}$ do not meet at a common point. (If it were a size transformation, they would meet at the center.) Also $RS/R'S' = 2$ but $RT/R'T' = \frac{5}{3} \neq 2$, so the ratios of sides are not equal.

14. a. A size transformation of scale factor $\frac{3}{2}$ followed by a rotation.

b. A size transformation of scale factor $\frac{1}{3}$ followed by a reflection or glide reflection.

15. a. Since $\overrightarrow{PQ}$, $\overrightarrow{BB}$, $\overrightarrow{XX}$, and $\overrightarrow{AA}$ are equivalent directed line segments by the definition of T_{PQ}, $\overline{PQ} \parallel \overline{BB'} \parallel \overline{XX'} \parallel \overline{AA'}$ and $\overline{PQ} \cong \overline{BB'} \cong \overline{XX'} \cong \overline{AA'}$. In each case, one pair of opposite sides is congruent and parallel, so $BB'X'X$ and $BB'A'A$ are both parallelograms.

b. $\overleftrightarrow{B'X'} \parallel \overleftrightarrow{BA}$ and $\overleftrightarrow{B'A'} \parallel \overleftrightarrow{BA}$, since they contain opposite sides of parallelograms. However, since through B' there can only be one line parallel to $\overleftrightarrow{BA}$, $\overleftrightarrow{B'X'}$ and $\overleftrightarrow{B'A'}$ must be the same line. Therefore, A', X', and B' are collinear.

16. Since translations preserve distances, $PQ = P'Q'$, $QR = Q'R'$, and $RP = R'P'$. Thus $\triangle PQR \cong \triangle P'Q'R'$. Therefore, $\angle PQR \cong \angle P'Q'R'$, since they are corresponding parts of congruent triangles.

17. $p \parallel q$ implies that $\angle 1 \cong \angle 2$. Since rotations preserve angle measures, $\angle 1 \cong \angle 3$ and $\angle 2 \cong \angle 4$. Thus $\angle 3 \cong \angle 4$ and $p' \parallel q'$ by the corresponding angles property.

18. Since reflections preserve distances, $AB = A'B'$, $BC = B'C'$, and $AC = A'C'$. Since A, B, and C are collinear, $AB + BC = AC$. Therefore, $A'B' + B'C' = AB + BC = AC = A'C'$ and A', B', and C' are collinear.

19. $q \parallel p$ implies that $\angle 1 \cong \angle 2$. Since reflections preserve angle measures, $\angle 1 \cong \angle 1'$ and $\angle 2 \cong \angle 2'$, where $\angle 1'$ and $\angle 2'$ are the images, respectively, of $\angle 1$ and $\angle 2$. Thus $\angle 2' \cong \angle 1'$ and $p' \parallel q'$ by the corresponding angles property.

20. Since isometries map segments to segments and preserve distances, $\overline{AB} \cong \overline{A'B'}$, $\overline{BC} \cong \overline{B'C'}$, and $\overline{CA} \cong \overline{C'A'}$. Thus, by the SSS congruence property, $\triangle ABC \cong \triangle A'B'C'$.

21. a. One, just T_{PQ}
b. Infinitely many; the center C may be any point on the perpendicular bisector of $\overline{PQ}$, and $\angle PCQ$ is the rotation angle.

22. a. The point where $\overleftrightarrow{PP'}$ and $\overleftrightarrow{QQ'}$ intersect
b. Greater than 1
c. Where $\overleftrightarrow{PP'}$ and $\overleftrightarrow{QQ'}$ intersect, less than 1

23. Construct line through Q' parallel to $\overline{QR}$. The intersection of that line and l is R'.

24. Let point R be the intersection of line l and segment $\overline{PP'}$ and let S be the intersection of l and $\overline{QQ'}$. Then $\triangle QRS \cong \triangle Q'RS$ by SAS congruence. Hence $RQ = RQ'$ and $\angle QRS \cong \angle Q'RS$. Thus $\triangle PRQ \cong \triangle P'RQ'$. We can see this by subtracting $m(\angle QRS)$ from $90°$, which is the measure of $\angle PRS$, and subtracting $m(\angle Q'RS)$ from $90°$, which is the measure of $\angle P'RS$. Thus $\triangle PRQ \cong \triangle P'RQ'$ by the SAS congruence property. Consequently, $\overline{PQ} \cong \overline{P'Q'}$, since these sides correspond in $\triangle PRQ$ and $\triangle P'RQ'$. Thus $PQ = P'Q'$, as desired.

25. Yes, a translation

Section 16.3A
1. a. $H_D(H_C(H_B(H_A(P)))) = P$
b. $H_D(H_C(H_B(H_A(Q)))) = Q$
c. This combination of four half-turns around the vertices of a parallelogram maps each point to itself.

2. Impossible. Even though corresponding sides have the same length, corresponding diagonals do not. Yet isometries preserve distance.

3. a.

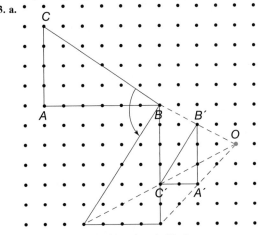

b. Yes; $R_{B,90°}$ followed of $S_{O,1/2}$ is a similitude.

4. (d), since $A \to A$, $B \to D$, $C \to C$, $D \to B$

5. M_{EG}, M_{FH}, H_P, $R_{P,360°}$

6. a. For example, M_{AD}, M_{BE}, M_{CF}, $R_{O,60°}$, $R_{O,120°}$, and $R_{O,180°}$, $R_{O,240°}$, $R_{O,300°}$, $R_{O,360°}$
  b. 12 (6 reflections and 6 rotations)

7. Yes. Let E and F be the midpoints of sides $\overline{AB}$ and $\overline{CD}$. Then M_{EF} and $R_{A,360°}$ will work.

8. a. The sum of the areas of the two red rectangles equals the areas of the two red parallelograms.
  b. The red figure has been translated which preserves areas.
  c. The areas of the two red parallelograms in (3) are equal to the areas of the two respective red parallelograms in (4) and then the ones in (5)
  d. The area of the red square region in (1) equals the sum of the areas of the two red square regions in (5).

9. Let M be the midpoint of $\overline{AC}$. Hence $H_M(A) = C$, $H_M(C) = A$. We know that $H_M(B)$ is on $\overleftrightarrow{CD}$, since $H_B(\overleftrightarrow{AB}) \parallel \overleftrightarrow{AB}$ and C is on $H_M(\overleftrightarrow{AB})$. Similarly, $H_M(B)$ is on $\overleftrightarrow{AD}$, so that $H_M(B)$ is on $\overleftrightarrow{CD}, \cap \overleftrightarrow{AD}$. That is, $H_M(B) = D$. Hence $(\triangle ABC) = \triangle CDA$ so that $\triangle ABC \cong \triangle CDA$.

10. a. $H_M(\angle ADC) = \angle CBA$, so that $\angle ADC \cong \angle CBA$ Similarly, $\angle BAD \cong \angle DCB$.
  b. $H_M(\overline{AB}) = (\overline{DC})$, so $\overline{AB} \cong \overline{DC}$, and so on.

11. Let $l = \overleftrightarrow{BP}$. Then $M_l(A)$ is on $\overleftrightarrow{BC}$, but since $AB = BC$, we must have $M_l(A) = C$. Thus $M_l(\triangle ABP) = \triangle CBP$, so $\triangle ABP \cong \triangle CBP$. Hence $\angle BPA \cong \angle BPC$, but since these angles are supplementary, each is a right angle. Since $AP = CP$, $\overleftrightarrow{BP}$ is the perpendicular bisector of $\overline{AC}$.

12. a. From Problem 11, points A and C are on the perpendicular bisector of $\overline{BD}$, so $\overline{AC} \perp \overline{BD}$.
  b. Since $\overline{AC}$ is the perpendicular bisector of $\overline{BD}$, $M_{AC}(B) = D$, $M_{AC}(D) = B$, $M_{AC}(A) = A$, and $M_{AC}(C) = C$. Hence $M_{AC}(ABCD) = ADCB$, so the kite has reflection symmetry.

13. a. $AA' = 2x$ and $A'A'' = 2y$, so that $AA'' = 2(x + y)$. Also, A, A', and A'' are collinear since $\overline{AA'} \perp r$, $r \parallel s$ and $\overline{A'A''} \perp s$. Hence, M_r, followed by M_s is equivalent to the translation $T_{AA''}$. Since A was arbitrary, M_r followed by M_s is $T_{AA''}$ since orientation is preserved.
  b. The direction of the translation is perpendicular to r and s, from r toward s, and the distance is twice the distance between r and s.

14. a. (Any two intersecting rails can be used.)
  Let $B' = M_l(B)$, and $B'' = M_m(B')$.
  Let $P = \overleftrightarrow{AB''} \cap m$. Shoot ball A toward point P.
  b. Let $Q = \overleftrightarrow{PB'} \cap l$. Then use an argument as in Example 16.13.

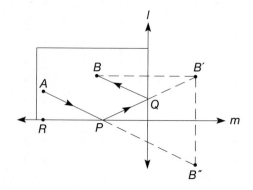

15. Consider $S_{A,bla}$. This size transformation will map $ABCD$ to a square $A'B'C'D'$ congruent to $EFGH$. Then from Section 16.2, we know that there is an isometry J that maps $A'B'C'D'$ to $EFGH$. Hence the combination of $S_{A,bla}$ and J is the desired similarity transformation.

ADDITIONAL PROBLEMS WHERE THE STRATEGY "USE SYMMETRY" IS USEFUL

1. Place any two squares on a 4×4 square grid. Reflect those two squares across a diagonal and across a vertical line through the center as shown. If two more squares are produced in either of these cases, that pattern will have reflective symmetry with four dark squares.

2. There are three digits that read the same upside down: 0, 1, and 8. Since house numbers do not begin with zero, there are $2 \cdot 3 \cdot 3 = 18$ different such house numbers.

3. Pascal's triangle has reflective symmetry along a vertical line through its middle. In the 41st row, the 1st and 41st numbers are equal, as are the 2nd and 40th, the 3rd and 39th, and 4th and 38th. Thus the 38th number is 9880.

CHAPTER REVIEW
Section 16.1

1. $A \longrightarrow B$
$P \longrightarrow P'$

2.
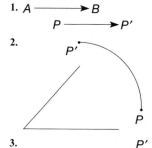

3.

4.
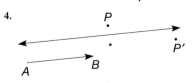

5. · · · ● ● ● ● ● ● ● · · ·

They must be infinite in one direction.

6.
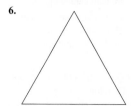

7.

8. . . . • • • • . . .

They must be infinite in one direction.

9.

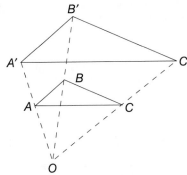

10. Apply a size transformation to get the triangles congruent, then use an isometry to map one to the other.

Section 16.2

1. Translations, rotations, reflections, and glide reflections

2. The image of a triangle will be a triangle with sides and angles congruent to the original triangle, hence congruent to it.

3. The corresponding alternate interior angles formed by the transversals will be congruent, hence the image of parallel lines will be parallel.

4. One triangle is mapped to the other using a combination of a translation, rotation, or reflection.

5. A triangle will map to a triangle with corresponding angles congruent. Thus, the triangles are similar by AA.

6. Similitudes preserve angle measure. Congruent alternate interior angles formed by a translation will map to congruent alternate interior angles.

7. Using a size transformation, the triangles can be made to be congruent. Then an isometry can be used to map one triangle to the other. The combination of the size transformation and the isometry is a similarity that takes one triangle to the other.

Section 16.3

1.

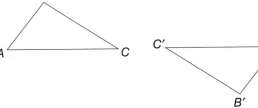

Chapter 16 Test

1. **a.** T **b.** F **c.** T **d.** T **e.** T **f.** F
   g. T **h.** T

2. Distance

3. Rotation

4. (a) and (e)

5. (a) and (c)

6. **a.** Size transformation
   b. Rotation
   c. Reflection
   d. Glide reflection
   e. Translation

7. a.

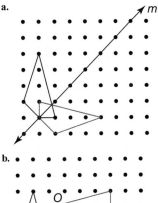

b.

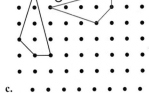

c.

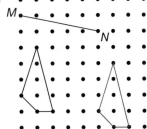

8. a. *D* **b.** *E* **c.** *E* **d.** *D*

9.

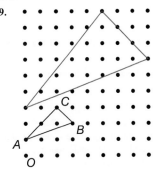

10. Translation, reflection, and glide reflection

11. a. M_{AB} **b.** $R_{F,-90°}$ **c.** T_{CD}

12. Let P be the intersection of $\overline{EG}$ and $\overline{FH}$. Then $R_{P,45°}$ $(S_{P,\sqrt{2}}(EFGH)) = ABCD$; thus $ABCD$ is similar to $EFGH$.

13. The result of two glide reflections is an isometry that preserves orientation. Therefore, the isometry must be a translation or a rotation.

14. B

15. a. Reflection   **b.** Translation   **c.** Rotation

16.

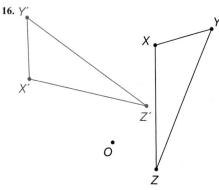

17. $A' = (5, -5)$
$B' = (2, -10)$
$C' = (x + 4, y - 6)$

18. $AB = \frac{8}{3}$; $AC = \frac{10}{3}$; $CE = 5$

19. $\triangle AMC \cong \triangle BMC$ by SSS. Therefore, $\angle AMC \cong \angle BMC$, or $m(\angle AMC) = m(\angle BMC) = 90°$.
Since $M_{CM}(A) = B$ and $M_{CM}(C) = C$, we have $M_{CM}(\triangle ABC) = \triangle BAC$. This means that $\overleftrightarrow{CM}$ is a symmetry line for $\triangle ABC$.

20.

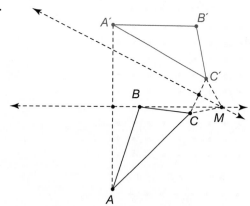

The transformation is a rotation with the center labeled M and $\angle CMC'$ is the angle of rotation.

21. No, because the lines $\overleftrightarrow{XA}$, $\overleftrightarrow{ZC}$, and $\overleftrightarrow{BY}$ are not concurrent.

Section E-A

1. $\overline{AB} \parallel \overline{DC}$ by definition of a parallelogram; $\angle A$ and $\angle D$ are supplementary, since they are interior angles on the same side of a transversal. Since $\overline{AD} \parallel \overline{BC}$, $\angle A$ and $\angle B$ are supplementary. Similarly, $\angle C$ is supplementary to $\angle B$ and $\angle D$.

2. Slope of $\overline{MN}$ = slope of $\overline{OP} = \dfrac{d}{c}$, so $\overline{MN} \parallel \overline{OP}$. slope of $\overline{MN}$ = slope of $\overline{ON} = \dfrac{b}{a-e}$, so $\overline{MP} \parallel \overline{ON}$. Therefore $MNOP$ is a parallelogram.

3. Let $l = \overleftrightarrow{AP}$. Then $M_l(B)$ is on $\overrightarrow{AC}$, since $\angle BAP \cong \angle CAP$. Because $AB = AC$, however, we must have $M_l(B) = C$. Thus $M_l(C) = B$, so that $M_l(\triangle ABP) = \triangle ACP$. Hence $\angle ABP \cong \angle ACP$.

4. *Congruence proof:* $AB = CD$, $AD = CB$, and $BD = DB$. Therefore $\triangle ABD \cong \triangle CDB$ by SSS. By corresponding parts, $\angle ADB \cong \angle CBD$, so $\overline{AD} \parallel \overline{CB}$. Since $\overline{AD}$ and $\overline{CB}$ are parallel and congruent, $ABCD$ is a parallelogram.
Coordinate proof: If A, B, and D have coordinates $(0, 0)$, (a, b), and $(c, 0)$, respectively, then C must have coordinates $(a + c, b)$, since both pairs of opposite sides are congruent.

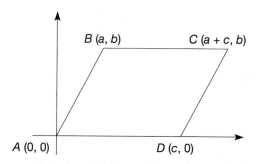

Using slopes, we have $\overline{AB} \parallel \overline{DC}$ and $\overline{AD} \parallel \overline{BC}$.

5. Consider the following isosceles triangle with the appropriate coordinates.

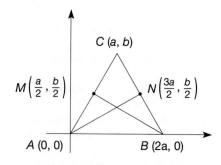

Congruence proof: $AM = BN$, $\angle A \cong \angle B$, and $AB = BA$. Thus $\triangle ABN \cong \triangle BAM$ by SAS. By corresponding parts, $AN = BM$.
Coordinate proof:

$$AN = \sqrt{\left(2a - \frac{a}{2}\right)^2 + \left(-\frac{b}{2}\right)^2} = \sqrt{\left(\frac{3a}{2}\right)^2 + \left(\frac{b}{2}\right)^2};$$

$$BM = \sqrt{\left(2a - \frac{a}{2}\right)^2 + \left(-\frac{b}{2}\right)^2} = \sqrt{\left(\frac{3a}{2}\right)^2 + \left(\frac{b}{2}\right)^2};$$

6. Because $\overline{PQ} \parallel \overline{SR}$ and $\overline{PS} \parallel \overline{QR}$ and interior angles on the same side of the transversal are supplementary, $\angle Q$ and $\angle S$ must also be right angles since they are supplementary to $\angle P$. Further, since opposite angles of a parallelogram are congruent, $\angle R$ must also be a right angle.

7. Slope of $\overline{AC} = \dfrac{a - 0}{a - 0} = 1;$

slope of $\overline{BD} = \dfrac{a - 0}{0 - a} = -1;$

since $1(-1) = -1, \overline{AC} \perp \overline{BD}.$

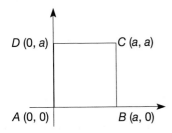

8. $m(\angle P) = m(\angle R)$ and $m(\angle Q) = m(\angle S)$ (opposite angles are congruent); $m(\angle P) + m(\angle Q) + m(\angle R) + m(\angle S) = 360°$ (vertex angles of quadrilateral total 360°); $m(\angle P) + m(\angle Q) + m(\angle P) + m(\angle Q) = 360°$, so $m(\angle P) + m(\angle Q) = 180°$; thus $\angle P$ and $\angle Q$ are supplementary and $\overline{PS} \parallel \overline{QR}$ (interior angles on same side of transversal are supplementary). Similarly, $m(\angle P) + m(\angle S) + m(\angle P) + m(\angle S) = 360°$, $m(\angle P) + m(\angle S) = 180°$, P and S are supplementary, and $\overline{PQ} \parallel \overline{SR}$. Since both pairs of opposite sides are parallel, $PQRS$ is a parallelogram.

Section T1A

1. (b) and (d)

2. a. $q \rightarrow \sim p$
  b. $q \wedge r$
  c. $r \leftrightarrow (q \wedge q)$
  d. $p \vee q$

3. a. T   **b.** F   **c.** T
  d. T   **e.** T   **f.** T
  g. T   **h.** T

4. a. If I am an elementary school teacher, then I teach third grade. If I do not teach third grade, then I am not an elementary school teacher. If I am not an elementary school teacher, then I do not teach third grade.
  b. If a number has a factor of 2, then it has a factor of 4. If a number does not have a factor of 4, then it does not have a factor of 2. If a number does not have a factor of 2, then it does not have a factor of 4.

5.

p	q	$\sim p$	$\sim q$	$(\sim p) \vee (\sim q)$	$(\sim p) \vee q$	$(\sim p) \wedge (\sim q)$	$p \rightarrow q$	$\sim (p \wedge q)$	$\sim (p \vee q)$
T	T	F	F	F	T	F	T	F	F
T	F	F	T	T	F	F	F	T	F
F	T	T	F	T	T	F	T	T	F
F	F	T	T	T	T	T	T	T	T

$(\sim p) \vee (\sim q)$ is logically equivalent to $\sim (p \wedge q)$.
$(\sim p) \vee q$ is logically equivalent to $p \rightarrow q$
$(\sim p) \wedge (\sim q)$ is logically equivalent to $\sim (p \vee q)$.

6. a. Valid   **b.** Invalid   **c.** Invalid   **d.** Valid
  e. Invalid   **f.** Invalid   **g.** Invalid   **h.** Valid

7. a. You will be popular.
  b. Scott is not quick.
  c. All friends are trustworthy.
  d. Every square is a parallelogram.

8. a. Hypothetical syllogism
  b. Modus ponens
  c. Modus tollens
  d. Modus tollens
  e. Hypothetical syllogism

9. a. F   **b.** F   **c.** T
  d. T   **e.** F

10. Invalid

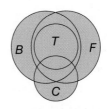

ELEMENTARY LOGIC TEST

1. a. T   **b.** F
  c. F   **d.** F
  e. F   **f.** T
  g. F   **h.** F

2. a. $\sim q \rightarrow p, \sim p \rightarrow q, q \rightarrow \sim p$
  b. $q \rightarrow \sim p, p \rightarrow \sim q, \sim q \rightarrow p$
  c. $\sim p \rightarrow \sim q, q \rightarrow p, p \rightarrow q$

3. a. T   **b.** F   **c.** F
  d. F   **e.** T   **f.** T

4. a. Invalid   **b.** Valid   **c.** Valid
  d. Invalid   **e.** Invalid

5.

p	q	$p \wedge q$	$p \vee q$	$p \rightarrow q$	$\sim p$	$\sim q$	$\sim q \leftrightarrow p$	$\sim q \rightarrow \sim p$
T	T	T	T	T	F	F	F	T
F	T	F	T	T	T	F	T	T
F	F	F	F	T	T	T	F	T
T	F	F	T	F	F	T	T	F

6. For example: Some B's are A's. All C's are B's. Therefore, all C's are A's.

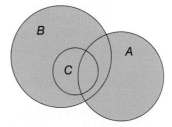

7. All are true when both the hypothesis and conclusion are true. The only time an implication is false, the disjunction is true. Therefore, they are not all false at the same time.

8. Both Bob and Sam are truth tellers.

9. a. $p \updownarrow p$ **b.** $(p \updownarrow q) \updownarrow (p \updownarrow q)$ **c.** $(p \updownarrow p) \updownarrow (q \updownarrow q)$

Section T2A

1. a. 7   **b.** 3
 c. 0   **d.** 4
 e. 3   **f.** 7
 g. 6   **h.** 6

2. a. 4, 5
 b. 7, 5
 c. 1, 7
 d. 4, does not exist

3. a. 7   **b.** 4
 c. 1   **d.** 9

4. a. F   **b.** F   **c.** T
 d. T   **e.** T   **f.** F

5. $1 - 4 = n$ if and only if $1 = 4 + n$. Look for a "1" in the "4" row; the number heading the column that the "1" is in represents n, namely 2.

6. The table is symmetric across the upper left/lower right diagonal.

7. $\frac{1}{3} \oplus \frac{1}{2} = 2 \oplus 3 = 5, \frac{1}{3} \oplus \frac{1}{2} = \frac{2}{1} \oplus \frac{3}{1} = 5$ (NOTE: Normally $\frac{1}{3} = \frac{2}{6}$, but $6 = 1$ in the 5-clock.) Yes. For example, $\frac{3}{4} \oplus \frac{2}{3} = 2 \oplus 4 = 1$. On the other hand, $\frac{3}{4} \oplus \frac{2}{3} = \frac{17}{12}$, and $\frac{17}{12} = \frac{2}{2} = 1$ in 5-clock arithmetic.

8. a. If $1 < 2$, then $1 + 3 < 2 + 3$. But $4 \not< 0$ in the whole numbers.
 b. If $2 < 3$ and $2 \neq 0$, then $2 \cdot 2 < 2 \cdot 3$. But $4 \not< 1$ in the whole numbers.

9. a. $\{3\}$ **b.** $\{0, 6\}$ **c.** $\{0, 2, 4, 6, 8\}$ **d.** $\{\ \}$

10. If $a + c \equiv b + c$, then $a + c + (-c) \equiv b + c + (-c)$, or $a \equiv b$.

11. If $a \equiv b$ and $b \equiv c$, then $m \mid (a - b)$ and $m \mid (b - c)$. Therefore, $m \mid [(a - b) + (b - c)]$ or $m \mid (a - c)$. Thus $a \equiv c$.

12. 61, 83

13. 504

CLOCK ARITHMETIC TEST

1. a. F   **b.** T
 c. F   **d.** T
 e. F   **f.** T
 g. F   **h.** T

2. a. 3   **b.** 1
 c. 6   **d.** 12
 e. 1   **f.** 6

3. a. $3 \oplus (9 \oplus 7) = 10 \oplus 9 = 9$
 b. $(8 \otimes 3) \otimes 4 = 8 \otimes 1 = 8$
 c. $(5 \otimes 4) \oplus (5 \otimes 11) = 5 \otimes 0 = 0$
 d. $(6 \otimes 3) \oplus (3 \otimes 4) \oplus (3 \otimes 3) = 3 \otimes 0 = 0$

4. a. 3, 2
 b. 4; the reciprocal doesn't exist since all multiples of 4 are either 4 or 8 in the 8-clock.
 c. 0; the reciprocal doesn't exist since all multiples of 0 are 0 in the 5-clock.
 d. 7, 5

5. a. $\{-14, -5, 4, 13\}$
 b. $\{2, 3, 4, 6, 12\}$
 c. $\{7k + 1; k$ is any integer$\}$

6. All multiples of 4 land on 4, 8, or 12, never on 1.

7. a. 0 cannot be a divisor.
 b. 1 divides everything, thus all numbers would be congruent.

8. Because m divides $a - a$.

9. There are 365 days in a nonleap year and $365 = 1$ mod 7. Thus January 1 will fall one day later, or on a Tuesday.

Photo Credits

Chapter 1
Page 1: ©AP/Wide World Photos. Page 40 (left and right): The Granger Collection, New York.

Chapter 2
Page 83 (left): Courtesy of the Bryn Mawr College Library. Page 83 (right): Courtesy of Professor G. L. Alexanderson.

Chapter 3
Page 87: J-L Charmet/Science Photo Library/Photo Researchers. Page 129 (left): ©UPPA/Photoshot. Page 129 (right): Courtesy of George M. Bergman, University of California, Berkeley.

Chapter 4
Page 133 (left column, first): Photo Researchers; (left column, second and third): The National Museum American History ©2010 Smithsonian Institution; (left column, fourth): NMPFT/Science & Society Picture Library. Page 133 (right column, first): NMPFT/Science & Society Picture Library; (right column, second): Corbis Images; (right column, third): ThinkStock LLC/Index Stock. Page 141: Texas Instruments images used with permission. Page 177 (left): ACME/UPI/The Bettmann/©Corbis. Page 177 (right): Courtesy of Dartmouth College Library, Hanover, New Hampshire.

Chapter 5
Page 181: Granger Collection. Page 211 (left): Reproduced by permission of the Masters and Fellows of Trinity College Cambridge. Page 211 (right): Courtesy of Constance Reid.

Chapter 6
Page 215: The Art Archive/British Museum/The Kobal Collection, Ltd. Page 259 (left): Courtesy of Evelyn Granville. Page 259 (right): Courtesy of Professor G. L. Alexanderson.

Chapter 7
Page 263: Eberhard Otto. Page 314 (left): George M. Bergman, University of California, Berkeley. Page 314 (right): The Mittag-Leffler Institute, Djursholm, Sweden.

Chapter 8
Page 319: The Needham Research Institute, Cambridge, England. Page 352 (left): Courtesy of Sylvia Wiegand. Page 352 (right): Courtesy Kadon Enterprises, Inc., www.gamepuzzles.com.

Chapter 9
Page 355: Newberry Library, Chicago/Superstock. Page 428 (left): Courtesy of Paul Cohen. Page 428 (right): Courtesy of Leon Harkleroad and Bela Andrasfai.

Chapter 10
Page 503 (left): UPI/Bettmann/©Corbis. Page 503 (right): Laura Wulf/Harvard University News Office.

Chapter 11
Page 509 (left): Granger Collection. Page 509 (top right and top left): PhotoDisc, Inc./Getty Images. Page 509 (bottom left and bottom right): Bettmann/©Corbis. Page 571 (left): Photo by Joe Munroe/Ohio Historical Society/ Courtesy Caltech Archives. Page 571 (right): UPI/ Bettmann/©Corbis.

Chapter 12
Page 575 (left and right): Courtesy of Dr. Pierre van Hiele. Page 671 (left): Courtesy of Cathleen Synge Morawetz. Photo by James Hamilton. Page 671 (right): Prints and Photographs Collection, CN00509, The Dolph Briscoe Center for American History, The University of Texas at Austin.

Chapter 13
Page 677: Granger Collection. Page 747 (left): Bettmann/ ©Corbis. Page 747 (right): Culver Pictures, Inc.

Chapter 14
Page 753: Granger Collection. Page 816 (left): Bettmann/ ©Corbis. Page 816 (right): Hank Morgan/Photo Researchers.

Chapter 15
Page 821: Sheila Terry/Science Photo Library/Photo Researchers, Inc. Page 859 (left): Courtesy of George

Index

List of Symbols

Symbol	Meaning	Page	Symbol	Meaning	Page
$\{\ldots\}$	set braces	45	$a^{m/n}$	mth power of the nth root of a	381
$\{x\vert\ldots\}$	set builder notation	45	$f(a)$	image of a under the function f	399
$\in$	is an element of	46	$\bar{x}$	mean	483
$\notin$	is not an element of	46	$P(E)$	probability of event E	513
$\{\}$ or $\varnothing$	empty set	46	$_nP_r$	number of permutations	547
$=$	equal to	46	$_nC_r$	number of combinations	549
$\neq$	is not equal to	46	$P(A\vert B)$	probability of A given B	562
$\sim$	is equivalent to (sets)	46	$\overline{AB}$	line segment AB	591, 619
$\subseteq$	is a subset of	46	$\angle ABC$	angle ABC	592, 620
$\nsubseteq$	is not a subset of	46	$\triangle ABC$	triangle ABC	592, 622
$\subset$	is a proper subset of	47	$\overleftrightarrow{AB}$	line AB	618
U	universal set	47	AB	the length of segment $\overline{AB}$	619
$\cup$	union of sets	48	$m\Vert l$	m is parallel to l	619
$\cap$	intersection of sets	49	$\overrightarrow{AB}$	ray AB	619
$\overline{A}$	complement of a set	50	$m(\angle ABC)$	measure of angle ABC	620
$-$	difference of sets	50	$l\perp m$	l is perpendicular to m	621
(a, b)	ordered pair	51	$\leftrightarrow$	correspondence	756
$\times$	Cartesian product of sets	51	$\cong$	is congruent to	756
$n(\ldots)$	number of elements in a set	60	$\sim$	is similar to	767
$<$	is less than	61	$\overrightarrow{AB}$	directed line segment from A to B	867
$>$	is greater than	61	T_{AB}	translation determined by $\overrightarrow{AB}$	867
$\leq$	less than or equal to	61	$\measuredangle ABC$	directed angle ABC	868
$\geq$	greater than or equal to	61	$R_{O,a}$	rotation around O with directed angle of measure a	869
$3_{\text{five}}\ (3_5)$	three base five	75			
a^m	exponent (m)	77, 122	M_l	reflection in line l	870
$\approx$	is approximately	140	M_{AB}	reflection in line containing AB	875
$\vert$	divides	186	$S_{O,k}$	size transformation with center O and scale factor k	877
$\nmid$	does not divide	186			
$n!$	n factorial	192	$T_{AB}(P)$	image of P under T_{AB}	890
GCF	greatest common factor	198	$R_{O,a}(P)$	image of P under $R_{O,a}$	890
LCM	least common multiple	202	$M_l(P)$	image of P under M_l	890
$.\overline{abcd}$	repeating decimal	281	$M_l(T_{AB}(P))$	image of P under T_{AB} followed by M_l	890
$a:b$	ratio	288			
$\%$	percent	299	H_O	half-turn with center O	908
-3	negative number	321	$\sim$	negation (logic)	927
$-a$	opposite of a number	322	$\wedge$	conjunction (and)	928
$\vert a\vert$	absolute value	332	$\vee$	disjunction (or)	928
a^{-n}	negative integer exponent	342	$\rightarrow$	implication (if-then)	929
$\sqrt{}$	square root	379	$\leftrightarrow$	biconditional (if and only if)	930
π	pi $(3.14159\ldots)$	379	$\oplus, \ominus, \otimes, \oslash$	clock arithmetic operations	939–40
$\sqrt[n]{}$	nth root	380	$a\equiv b\bmod m$	a is congruent to b modulo m	941
$a^{1/n}$	nth root of a	381			